1908
Ex Parte Sharpe defines more clearly the role of the juvenile court to include *parens patriae.*

Legislation establishes juvenile justice in Canada (Juvenile Delinquents Act) and in England (Children Act).

1890
Children's Aid Society of Pennsylvania, a foster home for the juvenile delinquent used as an alternative to reform schools, is established.

1891
Supreme Court of Minnesota establishes the doctrine of parental immunity.

1870
Illinois Supreme Court reverses Dan O'Connell's vagrancy sentence to the Chicago Reform School due to lack of due process procedures in *People v. Turner.*

1897
Ex Parte Becknell, a California decision that reverses the sentence of a juvenile who has not been given a jury trial.

1910
Compulsory school acts.

1875–1900
Case Law begins to deal with protective statutes.

1899
Illinois Juvenile Court Act.

1870　　**1880**　　**1890**　　**1900**　　**1910**

1868
Passage of the Fourteenth Amendment to the U.S. Constitution.

1889
Board of children's guardians is established in Indiana and given jurisdiction over neglected and dependent children.

1866
Massachusetts establishes that the state has power over children under 16 whose parents are "unfit."

1886
First neglect case is heard in Massachusetts.

1884
The state assumes the authority to take neglected children and place them in an institution. See *Reynolds v. Howe*, 51 Conn. 472, 478 (1884).

1881
Michigan begins child protection with the Michigan Public Acts of 1881.

1903–1905
Many other states pass juvenile court acts.

1905
Commonwealth v. Fisher—Pennsylvania Court upholds the constitutionality of the Juvenile Court Act.

1906
Massachusetts passes an act to provide for the treatment of children not as criminals but as children in need of guidance and aid.

1959
Standard Family Court Act
of National Council on
Crime and Delinquency
establishes that juvenile
hearings are to be informal.

1918
Chicago area studies are
conducted by Shaw and
McKay.

1930
Children's Charter.

1920

1930

1940

1950

1960

1924
Federal Probation Act.

1954
Brown v. Board of Education,
a major school desegregation
decision.

continued on back endsheets…

www.wadsworth.com

www.wadsworth.com is the World Wide Web site for Thomson Wadsworth and is your direct source to dozens of online resources.

At *www.wadsworth.com* you can find out about supplements, demonstration software, and student resources. You can also send email to many of our authors and preview new publications and exciting new technologies.

www.wadsworth.com
Changing the way the world learns®

JUVENILE DELINQUENCY

9th edition

THEORY, PRACTICE, AND LAW

LARRY J. SIEGEL
University of Massachusetts—Lowell

BRANDON C. WELSH
University of Massachusetts—Lowell

JOSEPH J. SENNA
Northeastern University

THOMSON
★
WADSWORTH

Australia | Canada | Mexico | Singapore | Spain
United Kingdom | United States

THOMSON
WADSWORTH

Juvenile Delinquency: Theory, Practice, and Law, Ninth Edition
Larry J. Siegel/Brandon C. Welsh/Joseph J. Senna

V.P., Editor in Chief: **Eve Howard**
Development Editor: **Shelley Murphy**
Assistant Editor: **Jana Davis**
Editorial Assistant: **Elise Smith**
Technology Project Manager: **Susan DeVanna**
Marketing Manager: **Terra Schultz**
Marketing Assistant: **Annabelle Yang**
Advertising Project Manager: **Stacey Purviance**
Project Manager, Editorial Production: **Jennie Redwitz**
Art Director: **Vernon Boes**
Print Buyer: **Doreen Suruki**
Permissions Editor: **Sarah Harkrader**

Production Service: **Linda Jupiter, Jupiter Productions**
Text Designer: **John Walker**
Photo Researcher: **Don Murie, Meyers Photo-Art**
Copy Editor: **Lunaea Weatherstone**
Illustrator: **Scientific Illustrators**
Cover Designer: **Yvo Riezebos**
Cover Image: © **Farhan Baig/Getty**
Compositor: **R&S Book Composition**
Proofreader: **Debra Gates**
Indexer: **Medea Minnich**
Text and Cover Printer: **CTPS**

For more information about our products, contact us at:
Thomson Learning Academic Resource Center
1-800-423-0563
For permission to use material from this text or product, submit a request online at **http://www.thomsonrights.com.**
Any additional questions about permissions can be submitted by email to **thomsonrights@thomson.com.**

Library of Congress Control Number: 2004111579

Student Edition: ISBN-13: 978-0-534-64566-3
ISBN-10: 0-534-64566-6

Instructor's Edition: ISBN-13: 978-0-495-00087-7
ISBN-10: 0-495-00087-6

Thomson Higher Education
10 Davis Drive
Belmont, CA 94002-3098
USA

Asia (including India)
Thomson Learning
5 Shenton Way
#01-01 UIC Building
Singapore 068808

Australia/New Zealand
Thomson Learning Australia
102 Dodds Street
Southbank, Victoria 3006
Australia

Canada
Thomson Nelson
1120 Birchmount Road
Toronto, Ontario M1K 5G4
Canada

UK/Europe/Middle East/Africa
Thomson Learning
High Holborn House
50–51 Bedford Row
London WC1R 4LR
United Kingdom

Latin America
Thomson Learning
Seneca, 53
Colonia Polanco
11560 Mexico
D.F. Mexico

Spain (including Portugal)
Thomson Paraninfo
Calle Magallanes, 25
28015 Madrid, Spain

DEDICATIONS

*To my wife, Therese J. Libby, and my children,
Julie, Andrew, Eric, and Rachel*
        —L.J.S.

To my wife, Jennifer, and our son, Ryan
        —B.C.W.

About the Authors

LARRY J. SIEGEL

Larry J. Siegel was born in the Bronx in 1947. While attending City College of New York in the 1960s he was introduced to the study of crime and justice in courses taught by sociologist Charles Winick. After graduation he attended the newly opened program in criminal justice at the State University of New York at Albany, where he earned both his M.A. and Ph.D. After completing his graduate work, Dr. Siegel began his teaching career at Northeastern University, where he worked closely with colleague Joseph Senna on a number of texts and research projects. After leaving Northeastern, he held teaching positions at the University of Nebraska–Omaha and Saint Anselm College in New Hampshire. He is currently a professor at the University of Massachusetts–Lowell.

Dr. Siegel has written extensively in the area of crime and justice, including books on juvenile law, delinquency, criminology, and criminal procedure. He is a court-certified expert on police conduct and has testified in numerous legal cases. He resides in Bedford, New Hampshire, with his wife Therese J. Libby, Esq., and their children.

BRANDON C. WELSH

Brandon C. Welsh was born in Canada. He received his undergraduate and M.A. degrees at the University of Ottawa and his Ph.D. from Cambridge University in England. He is currently an associate professor in the Department of Criminal Justice at the University of Massachusetts–Lowell. He teaches graduate and undergraduate courses on crime prevention, juvenile delinquency, policing, and international criminology.

His research interests focus on the prevention of crime and delinquency and the economic analysis of crime prevention programs. Dr. Welsh has published extensively in these areas and is the author or editor of five books.

JOSEPH J. SENNA

Joseph J. Senna was born in Brooklyn, New York. He graduated from Brooklyn College, Fordham University Graduate School of Social Service, and Suffolk University Law School. Mr. Senna has spent over fourteen years teaching law and justice courses at Northeastern University. In addition, he has served as an Assistant District Attorney, Director of Harvard Law School Prosecutorial Program, and consultant to numerous criminal justice organizations.

His academic specialities include the areas of Criminal Law, Constitutional Due Process, Criminal Justice, and Juvenile Law. Mr. Senna lives with his wife and sons outside of Boston.

Brief Contents

PART ONE: THE CONCEPT OF DELINQUENCY   1

1   CHILDHOOD AND DELINQUENCY   2

2   THE NATURE AND EXTENT OF DELINQUENCY   32

PART TWO: THEORIES OF DELINQUENCY   63

3   INDIVIDUAL VIEWS OF DELINQUENCY   64

4   SOCIOLOGICAL VIEWS OF DELINQUENCY   106

5   DEVELOPMENTAL VIEWS OF DELINQUENCY   142

PART THREE: SOCIAL, COMMUNITY, AND ENVIRONMENTAL
INFLUENCES ON DELINQUENCY   171

6   GENDER AND DELINQUENCY   172

7   THE FAMILY AND DELINQUENCY   200

8   PEERS AND DELINQUENCY: JUVENILE GANGS AND GROUPS   232

9   SCHOOLS AND DELINQUENCY   272

10   DRUG USE AND DELINQUENCY   304

11   DELINQUENCY PREVENTION: SOCIAL AND DEVELOPMENTAL PERSPECTIVES   334

PART FOUR: THE JUVENILE JUSTICE SYSTEM   363

12   JUVENILE JUSTICE: THEN AND NOW   364

13   POLICE WORK WITH JUVENILES   392

14   JUVENILE COURT PROCESS: PRETRIAL, TRIAL, AND SENTENCING   420

15   JUVENILE CORRECTIONS: PROBATION, COMMUNITY TREATMENT,
AND INSTITUTIONALIZATION   456

16   DELINQUENCY AND JUVENILE JUSTICE ABROAD   496

17   THE FUTURE OF DELINQUENCY AND JUVENILE JUSTICE   524

Contents

Preface   xxvii

PART ONE: THE CONCEPT OF DELINQUENCY   1

1   CHILDHOOD AND DELINQUENCY   2

The Adolescent Dilemma   4
Adolescent Stress   4
Youth in Crisis   5
Are There Reasons for Hope?   8

FOCUS ON DELINQUENCY: ADOLESCENT RISK TAKING   9

The Study of Juvenile Delinquency   10

The Development of Childhood   12
Childhood in the Middle Ages   12
Development of Concern for Children   14
Childhood in America   16

The Concept of Delinquency   18
Delinquency and *Parens Patriae*   18
The Legal Status of Delinquency   18
Legal Responsibility of Youth   19

Status Offenders   20
The History of Status Offenses   20
The Status Offender in the Juvenile Justice System   23

POLICY AND PRACTICE: KEEPING TRUANTS IN SCHOOL   24
Reforming Status Offense Laws   24

POLICY AND PRACTICE: INCREASING SOCIAL CONTROL OVER JUVENILES AND THEIR PARENTS   26
Increasing Social Control   27

SUMMARY   28

KEY TERMS   29

QUESTIONS FOR DISCUSSION   29

VIEWPOINT   29

DOING RESEARCH ON THE WEB   30

NOTES   30

2   THE NATURE AND EXTENT OF DELINQUENCY   32

Official Statistics   34
     Crime Trends in the United States   34
     Measuring Official Delinquency   35
     What the Future Holds   36
     Are the UCR Data Valid?   37
FOCUS ON DELINQUENCY: FACTORS AFFECTING JUVENILE CRIME RATES   38
Self-Reported Delinquency   40
     Self-Report Data   41
Correlates of Delinquency   42
     Gender and Delinquency   42
     Racial Patterns in Delinquency   44
     Social Class and Delinquency   47
     Age and Delinquency   47
Chronic Offending: Careers in Delinquency   49
     Landmark Study: *Delinquency in a Birth Cohort*   49
     Who Becomes a Chronic Delinquent?   50
     Stability in Crime: From Delinquent to Criminal   51
     Policy Implications   52
Juvenile Victimization   52
     Victimization in the United States   52
     Victim/Offender Association   54
     Victimization Risk   54
FOCUS ON DELINQUENCY: ADOLESCENT VICTIMS OF VIOLENCE   55
     The Youngest Victims   56
FOCUS ON DELINQUENCY: DELINQUENT AND VICTIM: ONE AND THE SAME?   57
SUMMARY   58
KEY TERMS   58
QUESTIONS FOR DISCUSSION   59
VIEWPOINT   59
DOING RESEARCH ON THE WEB   59
NOTES   59

PART TWO: THEORIES OF DELINQUENCY   63

3   INDIVIDUAL VIEWS OF DELINQUENCY   64

Choice Theory and Classical Criminology   66
     The Rational Delinquent   67
FOCUS ON DELINQUENCY: THE BENEFITS OF DELINQUENCY   68
     Shaping Delinquent Choices   68
     Choosing Delinquent Acts   70

Preventing Delinquency 72

General Deterrence 72

Specific Deterrence 73

Situational Crime Prevention 74

Why Do Delinquents Choose Crime? 75

Trait Theories: Biosocial and Psychological Views 75

Origins of Trait Theory 76

Contemporary Biosocial Theory 77

Biochemical Factors 77

Neurological Dysfunction 78

FOCUS ON DELINQUENCY: DIET AND DELINQUENCY 79

FOCUS ON DELINQUENCY: ATTENTION DEFICIT/HYPERACTIVITY DISORDER 81

Genetic Influences 82

Evolutionary Theory 85

Psychological Theories of Delinquency 86

Psychodynamic Theory 86

FOCUS ON DELINQUENCY: DISRUPTIVE BEHAVIOR DISORDER 88

Behavioral Theory 89

Cognitive Theory 92

Psychological Characteristics and Delinquency 94

Personality and Delinquency 94

Intelligence and Delinquency 96

Critiquing Individual-Level Theories 98

Trait Theory and Delinquency Prevention 98

SUMMARY 99

KEY TERMS 100

QUESTIONS FOR DISCUSSION 100

VIEWPOINT 101

DOING RESEARCH ON THE WEB 101

NOTES 101

4   SOCIOLOGICAL VIEWS OF DELINQUENCY 106

Social Structure Theories 108

Social Structure/Social Problems 108

Structure, Culture, and Delinquency 111

Social Disorganization Theory 112

Anomie/Strain 116

Cultural Deviance Theory 120

Social Process Theories 121

Socialization and Crime 121

FOCUS ON DELINQUENCY: RANDOM FAMILY 123

POLICY AND PRACTICE: DARE TO BE YOU 125

Theories of Socialization   126
Learning Theories   126
Control Theories   127

Social Reaction Theories   129
The Labeling Process   129
The Effect of Labeling   130
The Juvenile Justice Process and Labeling   131
Evaluating Labeling Theory   131

Social Conflict Theory   132
Law and Justice   132
The Conflict Concept of Delinquency   133

Sociological Theories and Social Policy   133
Social Structure Theories and Social Policy   134
Social Process and Social Policy   134
Social Reaction and Social Policy   134
Social Conflict and Social Policy   135

SUMMARY   136

KEY TERMS   137

QUESTIONS FOR DISCUSSION   137

VIEWPOINT   137

DOING RESEARCH ON THE WEB   137

NOTES   138

5   **DEVELOPMENTAL VIEWS OF DELINQUENCY   142**

Life-Course View   144
The Glueck Research   145

Contemporary Life Course Concepts   146
Age of Onset   146
Adolescent Limited vs. Life-Course Persisters   147
Problem Behavior Syndrome   147

POLICY AND PRACTICE: THE FAST TRACK PROJECT   148
Multiple Pathways   148
Continuity of Crime and Delinquency   150

Life-Course Theories   151
The Social Development Model   151

FOCUS ON DELINQUENCY: THE PATH TO DELINQUENCY   152
Interactional Theory   154
Sampson and Laub: Age-Graded Theory   156

FOCUS ON DELINQUENCY: SHARED BEGINNINGS, DIVERGENT LIVES   158

Latent Trait Theories   160
General Theory of Crime   160
Analyzing the GTC   162

Evaluating the Developmental View   165

SUMMARY 166

KEY TERMS 166

QUESTIONS FOR DISCUSSION 166

VIEWPOINT 166

DOING RESEARCH ON THE WEB 167

NOTES 167

PART THREE: SOCIAL, COMMUNITY, AND ENVIRONMENTAL INFLUENCES ON DELINQUENCY 171

6   GENDER AND DELINQUENCY 172

Gender Differences in Development 174

    Socialization Differences 174

    Cognitive Differences 175

    Personality Differences 175

    What Causes Gender Differences? 176

Gender Differences and Delinquency 177

    Gender Patterns in Delinquency 178

    Violent Behavior 178

Trait Views: Are Female Delinquents Born that Way? 178

    Early Psychological Explanations 180

    Contemporary Trait Views 180

FOCUS ON DELINQUENCY: THE BIOSOCIAL STUDY OF FEMALE DELINQUENCY 182

Socialization Views 184

    Socialization and Delinquency 184

    Contemporary Socialization Views 186

POLICY AND PRACTICE: PREVENTING TEEN PREGNANCY 187

FOCUS ON DELINQUENCY: DESISTING FROM DELINQUENCY: LIFE TRANSFORMATIONS 188

Liberal Feminist Views 190

    Support for Liberal Feminism 190

    Critiques of Liberal Feminism 190

Critical Feminist Views 191

    Crime and Patriarchy 191

FOCUS ON DELINQUENCY: POWER, GENDER, AND ADOLESCENT DATING VIOLENCE 192

    Power-Control Theory 193

Gender and the Juvenile Justice System 194

SUMMARY 195

KEY TERMS 196

QUESTIONS FOR DISCUSSION 196

VIEWPOINT 196

DOING RESEARCH ON THE WEB 196

NOTES 197

7 THE FAMILY AND DELINQUENCY 200

The Changing American Family 202
Family Makeup 202
Childcare 203
Economic Stress 203

The Family's Influence on Delinquency 203
Family Breakup 204
Family Conflict 206

FOCUS ON DELINQUENCY: FOR BETTER OR FOR WORSE: DOES DIVORCE MATTER? 207
Family Efficacy 208
Family Deviance 210
Do Families Matter? 211

Child Abuse and Neglect 211
A Historical Perspective 212
Defining Abuse and Neglect 213

FOCUS ON DELINQUENCY: THE SEXUAL EXPLOITATION OF CHILDREN 214
The Extent of Child Abuse 214
Causes of Child Abuse and Neglect 216
The Child Protection System: Philosophy and Practice 217
The Abused Child in Court 220
Disposition of Abuse and Neglect Cases 222

Abuse, Neglect, and Delinquency 222
Case Studies of the Effects of Child Abuse 223
Cohort Studies of the Effects of Child Abuse 223
The Abuse–Delinquency Link 224

The Family and Delinquency Control Policy 225

SUMMARY 225

POLICY AND PRACTICE: FATHERING AFTER VIOLENCE PROJECT 226

KEY TERMS 227

QUESTIONS FOR DISCUSSION 227

VIEWPOINT 227

DOING RESEARCH ON THE WEB 228

NOTES 228

8 PEERS AND DELINQUENCY: JUVENILE GANGS AND GROUPS 232

Adolescent Peer Relations 234
Peer Relations and Delinquency 235
The Structure of Peer Relations 235

Youth Gangs 237

    What Are Gangs? 238

    The Study of Juvenile Gangs and Groups 238

    What Factors Explain Changes in Gang Activity? 242

Contemporary Gangs 243

    Gang Names 243

    Gang Types 243

FOCUS ON DELINQUENCY: "GETTING HIGH AND GETTING BY":
DRUG DEALING GANGS AND GANG BOYS IN SOUTHWEST TEXAS 244

    Location 246

    Age 248

    Gender 248

    Formation 250

    Leadership 251

    Communications 251

    Criminality 252

    Ethnic and Racial Composition 255

Why Do Youths Join Gangs? 259

    Anthropological View 259

    Social Disorganization/Sociocultural View 260

    Anomie View 260

    Psychological View 261

    Rational Choice View 262

Controlling Gang Activity 263

    Law Enforcement Efforts 263

POLICY AND PRACTICE: BOSTON'S YOUTH VIOLENCE STRIKE FORCE (YVSF) 265

    Community Control Efforts 265

    Why Gang Control Is Difficult 266

SUMMARY 267

KEY TERMS 268

QUESTIONS FOR DISCUSSION 268

VIEWPOINT 268

DOING RESEARCH ON THE WEB 268

NOTES 268

9 SCHOOLS AND DELINQUENCY 272

The School in Modern American Society 274

    Socialization and Status 274

    Education in Crisis 275

Academic Performance and Delinquency 277

    School Failure and Delinquency 278

    The Causes of School Failure 278

    School Climate 280

Delinquency within the School 281

FOCUS ON DELINQUENCY: DROPPING OUT 282

School Shootings 284

FOCUS ON DELINQUENCY: BULLYING IN SCHOOL 285

The Community and School Crime 287

Reducing School Crime 287

Improving School Climate 289

POLICY AND PRACTICE: SAFE HARBOR: A SCHOOL-BASED VICTIM
ASSISTANCE AND VIOLENCE PREVENTION PROGRAM 291

Legal Rights within the School 292

Compulsory School Attendance 292

Free Speech 292

School Prayer 294

School Discipline 295

Privacy 296

JUVENILE LAW IN REVIEW: *BOARD OF EDUCATION OF INDEPENDENT SCHOOL
DISTRICT NO. 92 OF POTTAWATOMIE COUNTY ET AL., v. EARLS ET AL.* 297

Academic Privacy 298

The Role of the School in Delinquency Control Policy 298

SUMMARY 299

KEY TERMS 300

QUESTIONS FOR DISCUSSION 300

VIEWPOINT 300

DOING RESEARCH ON THE WEB 301

NOTES 301

10   **DRUG USE AND DELINQUENCY 304**

Frequently Abused Drugs 306

Marijuana and Hashish 306

Cocaine 306

Heroin 307

Alcohol 307

Other Drug Categories 308

Trends in Teenage Drug Use 310

The Monitoring the Future (MTF) Survey 310

The PRIDE Survey 311

The National Survey on Drug Use and Health 311

Are the Survey Results Accurate? 311

Why Do Youths Take Drugs? 312

Social Disorganization 312

Peer Pressure 313

Family Factors 313

Genetic Factors 314

Emotional Problems 314

Problem Behavior Syndrome   315

Rational Choice   315

Pathways to Drug Abuse   315

Adolescents Who Distribute Small Amounts of Drugs   315

FOCUS ON DELINQUENCY: PROBLEM BEHAVIORS AND SUBSTANCE ABUSE   316

Adolescents Who Frequently Sell Drugs   317

Teenage Drug Dealers Who Commit Other Delinquent Acts   318

Losers and Burnouts   319

Persistent Offenders   319

Drug Use and Delinquency   320

Drugs and Chronic Offending   320

Explaining Drug Use and Delinquency   321

Drug Control Strategies   321

Law Enforcement Efforts   322

Education Strategies   324

Community Strategies   324

POLICY AND PRACTICE: DRUG ABUSE RESISTANCE EDUCATION (D.A.R.E.)   325

Treatment Strategies   326

Harm Reduction   327

What Does the Future Hold?   328

SUMMARY   329

KEY TERMS   329

QUESTIONS FOR DISCUSSION   330

VIEWPOINT   330

DOING RESEARCH ON THE WEB   330

NOTES   331

11   DELINQUENCY PREVENTION: SOCIAL AND DEVELOPMENTAL PERSPECTIVES   334

The Many Faces of Delinquency Prevention   336

Costs of Delinquency: A Justification for Prevention   336

A Brief History of Delinquency Prevention   338

Classifying Delinquency Prevention   340

POLICY AND PRACTICE: HEAD START   341

Early Prevention of Delinquency   342

Home-Based Programs   343

Improving Parenting Skills   344

Daycare Programs   345

Preschool   346

School Programs in the Primary Grades   347

Prevention of Delinquency in the Teenage Years   349

Mentoring   349

School Programs for Teens   351

After-School Programs 352

Job Training 354

Comprehensive Community-Based Programs 355

Future of Delinquency Prevention 356

POLICY AND PRACTICE: BLUEPRINTS FOR VIOLENCE PREVENTION 357

SUMMARY 358

KEY TERMS 358

QUESTIONS FOR DISCUSSION 358

VIEWPOINT 359

DOING RESEARCH ON THE WEB 359

NOTES 359

PART FOUR: THE JUVENILE JUSTICE SYSTEM 363

12 | **JUVENILE JUSTICE: THEN AND NOW 364**

Juvenile Justice in the Nineteenth Century 366

Urbanization 366

The Child-Saving Movement 367

House of Refuge 367

Were They Really Child Savers? 368

Development of Juvenile Institutions 369

Children's Aid Society 369

Society for the Prevention of Cruelty to Children 370

A Century of Juvenile Justice 371

The Illinois Juvenile Court Act and Its Legacy 371

Reforming the System 373

Juvenile Justice Today 375

The Juvenile Justice Process 376

Conflicting Values in Juvenile Justice 380

Criminal Justice vs. Juvenile Justice 380

FOCUS ON DELINQUENCY: SIMILARITIES AND DIFFERENCES BETWEEN JUVENILE AND ADULT JUSTICE SYSTEMS 381

A Comprehensive Juvenile Justice Strategy 382

Prevention 382

Intervention 382

Graduated Sanctions 383

Institutional Programs 383

Alternative Courts 383

POLICY AND PRACTICE: TEEN COURTS 384

Future of Juvenile Justice 385

POLICY AND PRACTICE: ABOLISH THE JUVENILE COURT? 387

SUMMARY 388

KEY TERMS 389

QUESTIONS FOR DISCUSSION 389

VIEWPOINT 389

DOING RESEARCH ON THE WEB 390

NOTES 390

13   POLICE WORK WITH JUVENILES 392

History of Juvenile Policing 394

Community Policing in the New Millennium 394

The Community Policing Model 396

The Police and Juvenile Offenders 397

Police Services 398

Police Roles 398

Police and Violent Juvenile Crime 399

Police and the Rule of Law 400

The Arrest Procedure 400

Search and Seizure 401

Custodial Interrogation 402

Discretionary Justice 403

Environmental Factors 405

Police Policy 405

Situational Factors 406

Bias and Police Discretion 406

FOCUS ON DELINQUENCY: JUVENILE RACE, GENDER, AND ETHNICITY IN POLICE DECISION MAKING 408

Limiting Police Discretion 409

Police Work and Delinquency Prevention 410

Aggressive Law Enforcement 410

Police in Schools 410

Community-Based Policing Services 412

Problem-Oriented Policing 413

POLICY AND PRACTICE: BOSTON'S OPERATION CEASEFIRE 414

SUMMARY 415

KEY TERMS 415

QUESTIONS FOR DISCUSSION 416

VIEWPOINT 416

DOING RESEARCH ON THE WEB 416

NOTES 417

14   JUVENILE COURT PROCESS: PRETRIAL, TRIAL, AND SENTENCING 420

The Juvenile Court and Its Jurisdiction 422

Court Case Flow 422

The Actors in the Juvenile Courtroom   422

Juvenile Court Process   426

Release or Detain?   427

POLICY AND PRACTICE: THE DETENTION DIVERSION ADVOCACY PROGRAM   430

Bail for Children   431

The Intake Process   431

JUVENILE LAW IN REVIEW: _SCHALL v. MARTIN_   432

Diversion   433

The Petition   434

The Plea and Plea Bargaining   435

Transfer to the Adult Court   436

Waiver Procedures   436

Due Process in the Juvenile Waiver Procedure   437

Should Youths Be Transferred to Adult Court?   437

JUVENILE LAW IN REVIEW: _KENT v. UNITED STATES_ and _BREED v. JONES_   438

Juvenile Court Trial   440

Constitutional Rights at Trial   441

Disposition   442

JUVENILE LAW IN REVIEW: _IN RE GAULT_   443

Juvenile Sentencing Structures   445

Sentencing Reform   446

The Death Penalty for Juveniles   447

The Child's Right to Appeal   449

Confidentiality in Juvenile Proceedings   449

SUMMARY   451

KEY TERMS   452

QUESTIONS FOR DISCUSSION   452

VIEWPOINT   452

DOING RESEARCH ON THE WEB   453

NOTES   453

15   JUVENILE CORRECTIONS: PROBATION, COMMUNITY TREATMENT, AND INSTITUTIONALIZATION   456

Juvenile Probation   458

Historical Development   458

Expanding Community Treatment   459

Contemporary Juvenile Probation   460

Organization and Administration   462

Duties of Juvenile Probation Officers   462

Probation Innovations   464

Intensive Supervision   465

Electronic Monitoring   465

Restorative Justice   466

Balanced Probation   467

Restitution   468

Residential Community Treatment   470

Nonresidential Community Treatment   471

POLICY AND PRACTICE: THREE MODEL NONRESIDENTIAL PROGRAMS   472

Secure Corrections   473

History of Juvenile Institutions   473

Juvenile Institutions Today: Public and Private   475

Population Trends   475

Physical Conditions   476

The Institutionalized Juvenile   477

Male Inmates   479

Female Inmates   479

Correctional Treatment for Juveniles   480

Individual Treatment Techniques: Past and Present   481

Group Treatment Techniques   481

Educational, Vocational, and Recreational Programs   482

Wilderness Programs   483

Juvenile Boot Camps   483

The Legal Right to Treatment   485

The Struggle for Basic Civil Rights   486

Juvenile Aftercare and Reentry   487

Supervision   488

POLICY AND PRACTICE: USING THE INTENSIVE
AFTERCARE PROGRAM (IAP) MODEL   482

Aftercare Revocation Procedures   490

SUMMARY   490

KEY TERMS   491

QUESTIONS FOR DISCUSSION   491

VIEWPOINT   491

DOING RESEARCH ON THE WEB   492

NOTES   492

16   DELINQUENCY AND JUVENILE JUSTICE ABROAD   496

Delinquency around the World   498

Europe   498

The Americas   499

Australia and New Zealand   499

Asia   500

Africa   500

FOCUS ON DELINQUENCY: YOUTH VIOLENCE ON THE RISE IN JAPAN   501

International Comparisons   502

Problems of Cross-National Research   502

Benefits of Cross-National Research   503

Juvenile Violence   504

Juvenile Property Crime   505

Juvenile Drug Use   505

Conclusion: What Do the Trends Tell Us?   506

Juvenile Justice Systems across Countries   508

Juvenile Policing   508

Age of Criminal Responsibility: Minimum and Maximum   510

Presence of Juvenile Court   510

Transfers to Adult Court   510

Sentencing Policies   511

POLICY AND PRACTICE: PRECOURT DIVERSION
PROGRAMS AROUND THE WORLD   512

Incarcerated Juveniles   513

POLICY AND PRACTICE: THE CHANGING NATURE
OF YOUTH JUSTICE IN CANADA   514

Aftercare   515

A Profile of Juvenile Justice in England   515

Apprehension and Charge   517

Bail   517

Precourt Diversion   517

Prosecution   518

Youth Court   518

Sentencing   519

SUMMARY   520

KEY TERMS   520

QUESTIONS FOR DISCUSSION   521

VIEWPOINT   521

DOING RESEARCH ON THE WEB   522

NOTES   522

17   **THE FUTURE OF DELINQUENCY AND JUVENILE JUSTICE   524**

The Concept of Delinquency   526

Theories of Delinquency   528

Social, Community, and Environmental Influences on Delinquency   528

The Juvenile Justice System   531

POLICY AND PRACTICE: THE TARGETED COMMUNITY
ACTION PLANNING (TCAP)   532

Crisis in the U.S. Juvenile Justice System   537

Juvenile Justice Abroad   538

SUMMARY   538

KEY TERMS   539

QUESTIONS FOR DISCUSSION   539

VIEWPOINT 539

DOING RESEARCH ON THE WEB 539

NOTES 539

Appendix: Excerpts from the U.S Constitution 541

Glossary 543

Case Index 555

Name Index 557

Subject Index 571

Photograph Credits 587

Preface

On June 2, 2004, an 11-year-old girl at Okubo Elementary School in Sasebo, 650 miles southwest of Tokyo, led a fellow sixth grader to an empty classroom during their school lunch hour and then stabbed her to death with a box cutter. A teacher found the victim, Satomi Mitarai, 12, lying in a pool of blood. Her father, Kyoji Mitarai, a journalist with a Japanese newspaper, rushed to the school only to find his daughter had already died. He later told reporters, "When I arrived, Satomi was already lying there collapsed. I couldn't believe what I was seeing. I can't put in words what I'm feeling right now. I can't understand it at all. I don't have a clue." Satomi's slayer confessed to police, "I have done a bad thing." The motive for this horrendous crime: Police were told that the killer believed Satomi had posted insulting messages on the Internet, "[She] wrote messages I didn't like... I asked her to stop but we fell into an argument. I got tired of it."

Satomi's murder is not unique, even in Japan, a nation known for its very low crime rate. In July of 2003, a 12-year-old Nagasaki boy was accused of kidnapping and molesting a 4-year-old boy and killing him by shoving him off a roof. The same month, a 14-year-old boy was arrested in the fatal beating of a 13-year-old classmate in Okinawa. In 1997 a 14-year-old cut the head off a 10-year-old boy. Outraged Japanese citizens have demanded action and lawmakers have responded by lowering the age of criminal responsibility from 16 to 14. Nonetheless, the Japanese juvenile justice system emphasizes rehabilitation over punishment for minors. The boy who killed the 10-year-old in 1997 was freed from custody in March at age 21.*

Cases such as the Satomi Mitarai murder have sparked interest in the study of juvenile delinquency not only in the United States but also around the world. Inexplicable incidents of violence occur all too frequently in schools, homes, and public places. Teen gangs can be found in most major cities. About one million youth are the victims of serious neglect and sexual and physical abuse each year. Considering the concern over the problems of youth, it is not surprising that courses on juvenile delinquency have become popular offerings on the nation's college campuses. We have written *Juvenile Delinquency: Theory, Practice, and Law* to help students understand the nature of juvenile delinquency and its causes and correlates, as well as the current strategies being used to control or eliminate its occurrence. Our text also reviews the legal rules that have been set down to either protect innocent minors or control adolescent misconduct, and explores questions such as: Can children be required to submit to drug testing in school? Can teachers search suspicious students or use corporal punishment as a method of discipline? Should children be allowed to testify on closed circuit TV in child abuse cases? Should a minor be given a death penalty sentence?

Because the study of juvenile delinquency is a dynamic, ever-changing field of scientific inquiry and because the theories, concepts, and processes of this area of study are constantly evolving, we have updated *Juvenile Delinquency* to reflect the changes that have taken place in the study of delinquent behavior during the past few years.

Like its predecessors, the ninth edition includes a review of recent legal cases, research studies, and policy initiatives. It aims at providing groundwork for the study of juvenile delinquency by analyzing and describing the nature and extent of delinquency,

---

*The Associated Press, "Japanese Girl Fatally Stabs a Classmate," *New York Times,* June 2, 2004, p. A12.

the suspected causes of delinquent behavior, and the environmental influences on youthful misbehavior. It also covers what most experts believe are the critical issues in juvenile delinquency and analyzes crucial policy issues, including the use of pretrial detention, waiver to adult court, and restorative justice programs.

GOALS AND OBJECTIVES

Our primary goals in writing this edition remain the same as in the previous editions:

1. To be as objective as possible, presenting the many diverse views and perspectives that characterize the study of juvenile delinquency and reflect its interdisciplinary nature. We take no single position nor do we espouse a particular viewpoint or philosophy.

2. To maintain a balance of research, theory, law, policy, and practice. It is essential that a text on delinquency not be solely a theory book, without presenting the juvenile justice system, or contain sections on current policies without examining legal issues and cases.

3. To be as thorough and up to date as possible. We have attempted to include the most current data and information available.

4. To make the study of delinquency interesting as well as informative. We want to encourage readers' interest in the study of delinquency so that they will pursue it at an undergraduate or graduate level.

We have tried to provide a text that is both scholarly and informative, comprehensive yet interesting, well organized and objective, as well as provocative and thought provoking.

ORGANIZATION OF THE TEXT

The ninth edition of *Juvenile Delinquency* has 17 chapters:

I Chapter 1 contains extensive material on the history of childhood and the legal concept of delinquency and status offending. This material enables the reader to understand how the concept of adolescence evolved over time and how that evolution influenced the development of the juvenile court and the special status of delinquency.

I Chapter 2 covers the measurement of delinquent behavior, trends and patterns in teen crime, and also discusses the correlates of delinquency, including race, gender, class, age, and chronic offending.

I Chapter 3 covers individual-level views of the causes of delinquency, which include choice, biological, and psychological theories.

I Chapter 4 looks at theories that hold that economic, cultural, and environmental influences control delinquent behavior. These include structure, process, reaction, and conflict theories.

I Chapter 5 covers the newly emerging developmental theories of delinquency, including the onset, continuity, paths, and termination of a delinquent career.

I Chapter 6, "Gender and Delinquency," explores the sex-based differences that are thought to account for the gender patterns in the delinquency rate.

I Chapter 7 covers the influence of families on children and delinquency. The concept of child abuse is covered in detail and the steps in the child protection system are reviewed.

I Chapter 8 reviews the effects peers have on delinquency and the topic of teen gangs.

I Chapter 9 looks at the influence of schools and the education process as well as delinquency within the school setting.

- Chapter 10 reviews the influence drugs and substance abuse have on delinquent behavior and what is being done to reduce teenage drug use.

- Chapter 11 covers delinquency prevention and the efforts being made to help kids desist from criminal activities.

- Chapter 12 gives extensive coverage to the emergence of state control over children in need and the development of the juvenile justice system. It also covers the contemporary juvenile justice system, the major stages in the justice process, the role of the federal government in the juvenile justice system, an analysis of the differences between the adult and juvenile justice systems, and the legal rights of children.

- Chapter 13 discusses the role of police in delinquency prevention. It covers legal issues such as major court decisions on searches and *Miranda* rights of juveniles. It also contains material on race and gender effects on police discretion as well as efforts by police departments to control delinquent behavior.

- Chapter 14 covers the juvenile court process, including information on plea bargaining in juvenile court as well as the use of detention and transfer to adult jails. It contains an analysis of the critical factors that influence the waiver decision, the juvenile trial, and sentencing.

- Chapter 15 on juvenile corrections covers material on probation and other community dispositions, including restorative justice programs. It also covers secure juvenile corrections with emphasis on legal issues such as right to treatment and programs such as boot camps.

- Chapter 16 looks at delinquency around the world and examines efforts to control antisocial youth in other nations.

- Chapter 17 is a new chapter for this edition. It looks at the future of delinquent behavior and juvenile justice.

WHAT'S NEW IN THIS EDITION

- Chapter 1 covers changes in the treatment of status offenders, parental responsibility laws, and curfews. It has the most recent data on child well-being, housing, health care, and education.

- Chapter 2 updates recent trends and patterns in delinquency and juvenile victimization. It contains new information on the victim/offender relationship.

- Chapter 3 contains new research findings on mental illness and delinquency, conduct disorders, disruptive behavior disorder, diet and delinquency, and the genetic basis of delinquency.

- Chapter 4 covers the most recent developments in social theory. It has a review of the important book *Random Family* and new research on collective efficacy. It also reviews the Dare to Be You (DTBY) program.

- Chapter 5 has a new box on the Fast Track program. There is a new section on the paths to delinquency and a review of the important book *Shared Beginnings, Divergent Lives*, by John Laub and Robert Sampson.

- Chapter 6 has data from a recent research project showing that boys rather than girls are more likely to be arrested for sexually related offenses such as prostitution. It contains reviews of programs to combat teen pregnancy. There is a new box that explains why girls desist from delinquency.

- Chapter 7 has updated material on the legacy of divorce. The newest data on child abuse and sexual abuse are presented as well as a review of the Fathering After Violence Project.

- Chapter 8 contains a new box entitled "Getting High and Getting By," which looks at drug dealing gangs and gang boys in southwest Texas. There is the latest data on gang membership and new material on rural gangs. A new box looks at Boston's Youth Violence Strike Force (YVSF).

I Chapter 9 now covers the "No Child Left Behind" program and new measures designed to reduce school crime, including the Safe Harbor program.

I Chapter 10 now includes coverage of harm reduction approaches to illicit drug use and updated findings on racial discrimination associated with the War on Drugs.

I Chapter 11 has updated material on what works in delinquency prevention, including national programs on mentoring and job training.

I Chapter 12 has updated material on teen courts and expanded coverage of drug courts.

I Chapter 13 has a new box on Boston's Operation Ceasefire program and expanded coverage of police work and delinquency prevention.

I Chapter 14 has added new research on public defender services for indigent juveniles and the death penalty for juveniles.

I Chapter 15 has expanded coverage of restorative justice and added tables on state comparisons of juvenile offenders in custody.

I Chapter 16 contains a new box on youth justice in Canada.

I Chapter 17, a new chapter, looks at the future of delinquency and juvenile justice.

LEARNING TOOLS

The text contains the following features designed to help students learn and comprehend the material:

Chapter Outline and Objectives Each chapter begins with an outline and a list of chapter objectives.

CNN Chapter Opener Each chapter now opens with a new vignette from a CNN feature story, accompanied by a CNN video clip on the student CD-ROM.

Concept Summary This new feature is used throughout the text to help students review material in an organized fashion.

Focus on Delinquency As in previous editions, these boxed inserts focus attention on topics of special importance and concern. For example, in Chapter 3 a box called "Diet and Delinquency" discusses whether children's food intake can affect their behavior.

Juvenile Law in Review Some chapters include boxes focusing on major Supreme Court cases that influence and control the juvenile justice system. For example, *In re Gault*, which defines the concept of due process for youthful offenders, is discussed in a box in Chapter 14.

Policy and Practice These boxes discuss major initiatives and programs. For example, in Chapter 16, a box entitled "Precourt Diversion Programs around the World" tells how keeping youths who have become involved in minor delinquent acts from being formally processed through the juvenile justice system has become a top priority of many countries.

Weblinks In the margins of every chapter are links to websites that can be used to help students enrich their understanding of important issues and concepts found within the text.

Chapter Summary Each chapter ends with a summary list of key concepts from the chapter. These correlate with the chapter objectives.

Viewpoint and **Doing Research on the Web** Each chapter ends with a feature called Viewpoint that presents a hypothetical case for the student to analyze, followed by a new Doing Research on the Web feature, which presents material related to the case that can be found in articles on InfoTrac® College Edition and the World Wide Web.

Key Terms Key terms are defined throughout the text when they appear in a chapter.

Questions for Discussion Each chapter ends with thought-provoking discussion questions.

Running Glossary Definitions appear in the text margin where the key terms are introduced, as well as in the comprehensive glossary at the end of the book.

SUPPLEMENTS

A number of supplements are provided by Thomson Wadsworth to help instructors use *Juvenile Delinquency,* Ninth Edition in their courses and to aid students in preparing for exams. (Available to qualified adopters. Please consult your local sales representative for details.)

For Students

Student CD-ROM (packaged free with text)—NEW to this edition Included on the CD-ROM are chapter-based CNN video clips with critical thinking questions relating to key points from the text. Student responses can be saved and e-mailed to instructors.

Study Guide An extensive *Study Guide* has been developed for this edition. Because students learn in different ways, a variety of pedagogical aids are included. The guide outlines each chapter, includes major terms and learning objectives, and provides extensive practice tests, including multiple choice, true/false, fill-in-the-blank, short answer, and essay questions.

Companion Website The Student Companion Website provides chapter outlines and summaries, tutorial quizzing, a final exam, the text's glossary, flashcards, a crossword puzzle, Concentration game, InfoTrac College Edition exercises, web links, a link to the Opposing Viewpoints Resource Center (OVRC), and the multi-step Concept Builder, which includes review, application, and exercise questions on chapter-based key concepts.

InfoTrac® College Edition Students receive four months of real-time access to Info-Trac College Edition's online database of continuously updated, full-length articles from hundreds of journals and periodicals. By doing a simple keyword search, students can quickly generate a list of related articles, then select relevant articles to explore and print out for reference or further study.

Crime Scenes 2.0: An Interactive Criminal Justice CD-ROM This highly visual and interactive program casts students as the decision makers as they explore all aspects of the criminal justice system. Exciting videos and supporting documents put students in the midst of a juvenile murder trial, a prostitution case that turns into manslaughter, and several other scenarios. This product received the gold medal in higher education and silver medal for video interface from *NewMedia Magazine's Invision Awards.*

Crime and Evidence in Action CD-ROM This engaging resource will take students on an interactive exploration of three criminal investigations. Students will explore each case beginning with crime scene investigation and procedures. They will then delve into the various aspects of trial proceedings, incarceration, and parole. Through each step of the process, students are encouraged to apply what they have learned in the text—they even receive detailed feedback that allows them to pinpoint areas and topics that need further exploration. The related website also includes Post-Scenario and Forensics Quizzing, an online Resource Library, Background Information on Suspects, and much more.

Mind of a Killer CD-ROM Based on Eric Hickey's book *Serial Murderers and Their Victims*, this award-winning CD-ROM offers viewers a look at the psyches of the world's most notorious killers. Students can view confessions of and interviews with serial killers, and they can examine famous cases through original video documentaries and news footage. Included are 3-D profiling simulations, extensive mapping systems that seek to find out what motivates these killers.

Careers in Criminal Justice Interactive CD-ROM 3.0 This engaging self-exploration CD-ROM provides an interactive discovery of the wide range of careers in criminal justice. Students can gather information on various careers from the job descriptions, salaries, employment requirements, sample tests, and video profiles of criminal justice professionals presented on this valuable tool.

Careers in Criminal Justice: Your Guide to Internships and Jobs in the Criminal Justice System, Fifth Edition Written by J. Scott Harr and Kären Hess, this practical book helps students develop a search strategy to find employment in criminal justice and related fields. Each chapter includes "insider's views," written by individuals in the field and addressing promotions and career planning.

Guide to Careers in Criminal Justice This concise 60-page booklet provides a brief introduction to the exciting and diverse field of criminal justice. Students can learn about opportunities in law enforcement, courts, and corrections and how they can go about getting these jobs.

Criminal Justice Internet Investigator III This handy brochure lists the most useful criminal justice links on the World Wide Web. It includes the most popular criminal justice and criminology sites featuring online newsletters, grants and funding information, statistics, and more.

Internet Guide for Criminal Justice Developed by Daniel Kurland and Christina Polsenberg, this easy reference text helps newcomers as well as experienced Web surfers use the Internet for criminal justice research.

Internet Activities for Criminal Justice This 60-page booklet shows how to best utilize the Internet for research via searches and activities.

For Instructors

Instructor's Manual The manual includes expanded lecture outlines, learning objectives, discussion topics, key terms, classroom activities, relevant websites, media resources, and a test bank that will not only help time-pressed teachers communicate more effectively with their students but will also strengthen the coverage of course material. Each chapter has multiple choice, true/false, fill-in-the-blank, short answer, and essay questions.

WebTutor™ Toolbox Preloaded with content and available free via pincode when packaged with this text, WebTutor ToolBox for WebCT pairs all the content of this text's rich Book Companion Website with all the sophisticated course management functionality of a WebCT product. Instructors may assign materials (including online quizzes) and have the results flow *automatically* to their gradebook. ToolBox is ready to use as soon as an instructor logs on; or, the preloaded content can be customized by uploading images and other resources, adding weblinks, or creating unique practice materials. Students only have access to student resources on the website. Instructors can enter a pincode for access to password-protected Instructor Resources. Contact your Thomson representative for information on packaging WebTutor ToolBox with this text.

WebTutor™ Advantage on WebCT With WebTutor Advantage's text-specific, preformatted content and total flexibility, instructors can easily create and manage their own custom course websites! WebTutor Advantage's course management tool gives instructors the ability to provide virtual office hours, post syllabi, set up threaded discussions, track student progress with the quizzing material, and much more. For students, WebTutor Advantage offers real-time access to a full array of study tools, plus chapter outlines, summaries, learning objectives, glossary flashcards (with audio), practice quizzes, weblinks, and InfoTrac College Edition exercises. Instructors can access password-protected Instructor Resources for lectures and class preparation. WebTutor Advantage also provides robust communication tools, such as a course calendar, asynchronous discussion, real-time chat, a whiteboard, and an integrated e-mail system. And WebTutor Advantage now comes with a daily news feed from NewsEdge, an authoritative source for late-breaking news of interest to instructors and their students.

ExamView® This computerized testing software helps instructors create and customize exams in minutes. The software comes preloaded with a thorough test bank. Instructors can easily edit and import their own questions and graphics, change test layouts, and reorganize questions. This software also offers the ability to test and grade online. It is available for both Windows and Macintosh.

Multimedia Manager for Juvenile Delinquency 2006: A Microsoft® PowerPoint® Tool This valuable resource contains all of the art from the book as well as interactive learning tools that will enhance classroom lectures. In addition, instructors can choose from ready-made dynamic slides or customize their own with the art files provided from the text.

CNN® Today Videos Exclusively from Thomson Wadsworth, the CNN Today Video series offers compelling videos that feature current news footage from the Cable News Network's comprehensive archives. Juvenile Delinquency Volumes I through VI each provide a collection of two- to eight-minute clips on hot topics in juvenile delinquency. Available to qualified adopters, these videotapes are great lecture launchers as well as classroom discussion pieces.

Wadsworth Criminal Justice Video Library The Wadsworth Criminal Justice Video Library offers an exciting collection of videos to enrich lectures. Qualified adopters may select from a wide variety of professionally prepared videos covering various aspects of policing, corrections, and other areas of the criminal justice system. The selections include videos from *Films for the Humanities & Sciences, A&E American Justice Series* videos, and *CourtTV* videos that feature provocative one-hour court cases to illustrate seminal high-profile cases in depth. For 2005, 15 new *CourtTV* titles have been added to our video options for adopters.

Opposing Viewpoints Resource Center This online center allows instructors to expose their students to all sides of today's most compelling issues, including gun control, media violence, genetic engineering, environmental policy, prejudice, abortion, health care reform, and dozens more. The Opposing Viewpoints Resource Center draws on Greenhaven Press's acclaimed social issues series, as well as core reference content from other Gale and Macmillan Reference USA sources. The result is a dynamic online library of current event topics—the facts as well as the arguments of each topic's proponents and detractors. Special sections focus on critical thinking (and walk students through how to critically evaluate point-counterpoint arguments) and researching and writing papers. To take a quick tour of the OVRC, visit www.gale.com/OpposingViewpoints/index.htm.

ACKNOWLEDGMENTS

We would like to give special thanks to our terrific and supportive production manager, Jennie Redwitz, and production editor Linda Jupiter, without whom this volume would have never been published, and Shelley Murphy, the world's most wonderful development editor. We also appreciate the efforts of our fabulous editors, Eve Howard and Sabra Horne; Jana Davis, assistant editor; Susan DeVanna, technology project manager; and Terra Schultz, marketing manager. Copy editor Lunaea Weatherstone did a terrific job and it was a pleasure to work with her. Our thanks to Debra Gates for her meticulous proofreading, and kudos to Medea Minnich for such thorough indexes.

The preparation of this text would not have been possible without the aid of our colleagues who helped by reviewing the previous editions and giving us important suggestions for improvement. Reviewers for the Ninth Edition are

James Foster, University of Louisville

Tim Hart, College of the Sequoias

Robert Hoff, Schenectady Community College

Kathy Hughes, Henderson Community College

Eric Jensen, University of Idaho

Jill Miller, Missouri Western State College

Jerry Neapolitan, Tennessee Tech University

Gary O'Bireck, Elmira College

Reviewers of the previous editions include: Robert Agnew, Fred Andes, Richard Ball, Sarah Boggs, Thomas Calhoun, Steve Christiansen, Scott Decker, Steven Frazier, Fred Hawley, Tonya Hilligoss, Vincent Hoffman, David Horton, Fred Jones, Irwin Kantor, James Larson, Richard Lawrence, Elizabeth McConnell, Clayton Mosher, Harold Osborne, Barbara Owen, Ray Paternoster, Joseph Rankin, Studipto Roy, Jeff Rush, Thomas Segady, Theresa A. Severance, Richard Siebert, Paul Steele, Leslie Sue, Stanley Swart, Pam Tontodonato, Paul Tracy, William Waegel, Bill Wagner, Kim Weaver, Mervin White, Michael Wiatrowski, and Robert W. Winslow.

Many thanks to all!

Larry Siegel
Brandon Welsh

The Concept of Delinquency

The field of juvenile delinquency has been an important area of study since the turn of the twentieth century. Academicians, practitioners, policy makers, and legal scholars have devoted their attention to basic questions about the nature of youth crime: How should the concept of juvenile delinquency be defined? Who commits delinquent acts? How much delinquency occurs each year? Is the rate of delinquent activity increasing or decreasing? What can we do to prevent delinquency?

Part One reviews these basic questions in detail. Chapter 1 discusses the current state of American youth and the challenges they face. It covers the origins of society's concern for children and the development of the concept of delinquency. It shows how the definition of delinquency was developed and how the legal definition has evolved. While society has chosen to treat adult and juvenile law violators separately, it has also expanded the definition of youthful misbehaviors eligible for social control; these are referred to as *status offenses.* Status offenses include such behaviors as truancy, running away, and incorrigibility. Critics suggest that juveniles' noncriminal behavior is probably not a proper area of concern for law enforcement agencies.

Chapter 2 examines the nature and extent of delinquent behavior. It discusses how social scientists gather information on juvenile delinquency and provides an overview of some of the major trends in juvenile crime. Chapter 2 also discusses some of the critical factors related to delinquency, such as race, gender, class, and age. It covers the concept of the chronic delinquent, those who continually commit delinquent acts in their youth and continue to offend as adults.

Chapter 1 Childhood and Delinquency

Chapter 2 The Nature and Extent of Delinquency

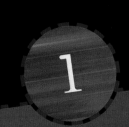

Childhood and Delinquency

1

Chapter Outline

The Adolescent Dilemma

Adolescent Stress

Youth in Crisis

Are There Reasons for Hope?

FOCUS ON DELINQUENCY: Adolescent Risk Taking

The Study of Juvenile Delinquency

The Development of Childhood

Childhood in the Middle Ages

Development of Concern for Children

Childhood in America

The Concept of Delinquency

Delinquency and *Parens Patriae*

The Legal Status of Delinquency

Legal Responsibility of Youth

Status Offenders

The History of Status Offenses

The Status Offender in the Juvenile Justice System

POLICY AND PRACTICE: Keeping Truants in School

Reforming Status Offense Laws

POLICY AND PRACTICE: Increasing Social Control over Juveniles and their Parents

Increasing Social Control

Chapter Objectives

1. Become familiar with the problems of youth in American culture

2. Understand the concepts of adolescent risk taking

3. Develop an understanding of the history of childhood

4. Become familiar with the concept of *parens patriae*

5. Be able to discuss development of a special legal status for minor offenders

6. Know what is meant by the terms "juvenile delinquent" and "status offender"

7. Understand the differences between delinquency and status offending

8. Know what is meant by parental responsibility laws

9. Become familiar with juvenile curfew laws

10. Identify the efforts being made to reform status offense laws

CNN. View the CNN video clip of this story and answer related Critical Thinking questions on your Juvenile Delinquency 9e CD-ROM.

It is difficult to be a teen today. Some kids are being raised in areas with poor housing, underfunded schools, and law-violating youth gangs. Others are being socialized in dysfunctional families and consequently may suffer from child abuse and neglect. Some have been labeled as "losers" from the day they were born. No one is more at risk than kids whose parents are convicted criminals and serving prison sentences. They often face a multitude of social problems with little help or social support. To help them, No More Victims (NMV), an organization founded in 1993 by Marilyn K. Gambrell, an author and former Texas parole officer, works with children and their parents to help them cope with the roadblocks in their lives. NMV teaches kids to understand their personal pain and in so doing learn to stop hurting themselves and others. The NMV program makes use of the skills and understanding of successful former clients and human service personnel to offer education, emotional support, and empowerment to children whose parents have been incarcerated. NMV addresses such issues as parent-child relationships, addictions, and victimization, and also helps families transition from incarceration into the community. It seeks to deter the violent, abusive, and victimizing behavior by using creative and innovative programming. For example, NMV helps parents understand how failure to pay child support is not only a financial issue, but also an emotional issue for the child.

What can be done to help troubled youth? While programs such as No More Victims can be beneficial, there are millions of youth who are at risk for drug use and other forms of anti-social behavior. Some children live in environments that hinder their development. They may become habitually aggressive; their violence may then persist into their adulthood.[1] It is not surprising that this latest generation of adolescents has been described as cynical and preoccupied with material acquisitions.[2] By age 18, American youth have spent more time in front of a television set than in the classroom; each year they may see up to 1,000 rapes, murders, and assaults on TV. Can such prolonged exposure to violence have an impact on child development?

TABLE 1.1

Key Indicators of Children's Well-Being

	Total	White	African American	Asian and Pacific Islander	American Indian	Latino
Percent low-birthweight babies	7.8	6.9	13.4	7.8	7.2	6.5
Infant mortality rate (deaths per 1,000 live births)	6.8	5.7	13.5	4.7	9.7	5.4
Child death rate (deaths per 100,000 children aged 1–14)	22	20	31	15	29	19
Rate of teen deaths by accident, homicide and suicide (deaths per 100,000 teens aged 15–19)	50	48	63	28	92	47
Teen birth rate (births per 1,000 females aged 15–17)	23	13	41	9	31	51
Percent of teens who are high school dropouts (aged 16–19)	8	6	10	5	10	17
Percent of teens not attending school and not working (aged 16–19)	9	7	14	6	18	13
Percent of children living in families where no parent has full time year round employment	25	19	42	19	43	31
Percent of children in poverty	17	9	32	12	35	29
Percent of families with children headed by a single parent	28	22	59	13	49	30

SOURCE: Anna Casey Foundation, Kids Count, 2004, www.aecf.org/kidscount/databook/indicators.htm. (Accessed on August 27, 2004.)

THE ADOLESCENT DILEMMA

Why does America, considered the richest country on Earth, come up short in many areas of child welfare? As Table 1.1 shows, problems still exist in important areas of child care beginning at birth and continuing through adolescence. Minority children often face more problems than more well-off Caucasian youth. Though teen birth rates have been in a decade-long decline, teenage mothers account for more than 10 percent of all births. One-third of all mothers are unmarried women, and more than 20 percent of new mothers have less than a high school education. Many children enter the world with deficits ranging from low birthweight to living with a single teenage mother.

Adolescent Stress

The problems of American society and the daily stress of modern life have had a significant effect on our nation's youth as they go through their tumultuous teenage years. Adolescence is unquestionably a time of transition. During this period, the self, or basic personality, is still undergoing a metamorphosis and is vulnerable to a host of external determinants as well as internal physiological changes.[3]

Adolescence is a time of trial and uncertainty for many youths. They may become extremely vulnerable to emotional turmoil and experience anxiety, humiliation, and mood swings. Adolescents also undergo a period of biological development that proceeds at a far faster pace than at any other time in their lives except infancy. Over a period of a few years, their height, weight, and sexual characteristics change dramatically. The average age at which girls reach puberty today is 12.5 years; 150 years ago, girls matured sexually at age 16. But although they may become biologically mature and capable of having children as early as 14, many youngsters remain emotionally and intellectually immature. By the time they reach 15, a significant number of teenagers are approaching adulthood unable to adequately meet the requirements and responsibilities of the workplace, family, and neighborhood. Many suffer from health problems, are educational underachievers, and are already skeptical about their ability to enter the American mainstream.

In later adolescence (ages 16 to 18), youths may experience a life crisis that famed psychologist Erik Erikson labeled the struggle between **ego identity** and **role diffusion.**

ego identity
According to Erik Erikson, ego identity is formed when a person develops a firm sense of who he is and what he stands for.

role diffusion
According to Erik Erikson, role diffusion occurs when youths spread themselves too thin, experience personal uncertainty, and place themselves at the mercy of leaders who promise to give them a sense of identity they cannot develop for themselves.

According to Erik Erikson, the teenage years are often quite tumultuous. Many youth experience role diffusion and are looking for a sense of identity. Some, like these girls watching Britney Spears perform during the start of her Onyx Hotel Tour in San Diego, March 2, 2004, wear look-alike outfits and model their behavior after rock stars and entertainers.

AP/Wide World Photos

Ego identity is formed when youths develop a firm sense of who they are and what they stand for. Role diffusion occurs when they experience personal uncertainty, spread themselves too thin, and place themselves at the mercy of leaders who promise to give them a sense of identity they cannot mold for themselves.[4] Psychologists also find that late adolescence is a period dominated by the yearning for independence from parental domination.[5] Given this explosive mixture of biological change and desire for autonomy, it isn't surprising that the teenage years are a time of rebelliousness and conflict with authority at home, at school, and in the community.

Youth in Crisis

There are approximately 70 million children in the United States, a number that is projected to increase to about 78 million by 2020.[6] During the "baby boom" (1946 to 1964), the number of children grew rapidly; then, after declining in the 1970s and 1980s, the number of children began to increase again in 1990. Children are projected to remain a fairly stable percentage of the total population, making up about 24 percent of the population by the year 2020.

Problems in the home, the school, and the neighborhood, coupled with health and developmental hazards, have placed a significant portion of American youth "**at risk.**" Youths considered at risk are those dabbling in various forms of dangerous conduct such as drug abuse, alcohol use, and precocious sexuality. They are living in families that, because of economic, health, or social problems, are unable to provide adequate care and discipline. Though it is impossible to determine precisely the number of at-risk youth, the Children's Defense Fund, a Washington, D.C.–based advocacy group reports that:

▌ An estimated three million children are reported to state child protective service agencies each year.

▌ An estimated 40 percent to 80 percent of the families whose kids become child protective service cases have problems with alcohol or drugs.

at-risk youths
Young people who are extremely vulnerable to the negative consequences of school failure, substance abuse, and early sexuality.

The mission of the **Children's Defense Fund** is to "Leave No Child Behind"; to ensure every child a Healthy Start, a Head Start, a Fair Start, a Safe Start, and a Moral Start in life; and a successful passage to adulthood with the help of caring families and communities. The CDF tries to provide a strong, effective voice for kids who cannot vote, lobby, or speak for themselves. Visit their website at www.childrensdefense.org. For an up-to-date list of web links, go to http://cj.wadsworth.com/siegel_jd9e.

More than a half million kids are now in foster care, a 35 percent increase since 1990.

More than 5 million children live in households headed by a relative other than a parent; 39 percent of these children—2.13 million—live in these households with no parent.[7]

These data indicate that millions of youth are at risk for social problems, including delinquency and drug abuse.

Data on population characteristics such as this can be found at the website of the U.S. Census Bureau at www.census.gov. For an up-to-date list of web links, go to http://cj.wadsworth.com/siegel_jd9e.

Adolescent Poverty According to the U.S. Census Bureau, though the poverty rate has been declining, more than 10 percent of all Americans are now considered poor.[8] More than 30 million Americans still live in poverty, earning an income below $13,700 a year for a family of three. Included in this group of poor Americans are almost 12 million indigent children. About 18 percent of children are living in impoverished families today (see Figure 1.1). The likelihood of a child under 18 years old living in poverty is greater than that of any other age group.

Health Problems Many children are now suffering from chronic health problems and receive inadequate health care. One reason is that so many are living in poverty: Children living below the poverty line are less likely (71 percent) to be in very good or excellent health compared to children in higher-income families (86 percent).[9]

The number of U.S. children covered by health insurance is declining and will continue to do so for the foreseeable future. A 2003 national survey found that at least 10 percent of children have no health insurance; the percentage of children without health coverage ranged from more than 20 percent in Texas to 5 percent in Vermont, Rhode Island and Wisconsin.[10] Without health benefits or the means to afford medical care, these children are likely to have health problems that impede their long-term development.

Family Problems Divorce strikes about half of all new marriages, and many families sacrifice time with each other to afford more affluent lifestyles. Today, about 70 per-

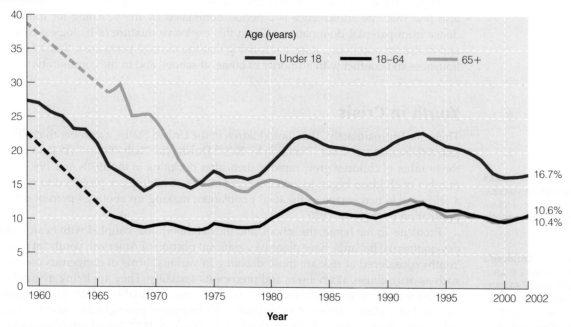

NOTES: Data points represent the midpoints of the respective years.
Data for people 18–64 and 65 and older are not available from 1960–1965.

FIGURE 1.1
Poverty Rates by Age: 1960–2002

SOURCE: *Current Population Survey, 1960–2003 Annual Social and Economic Supplements* (Washington, DC: U.S. Census Bureau).

Percent

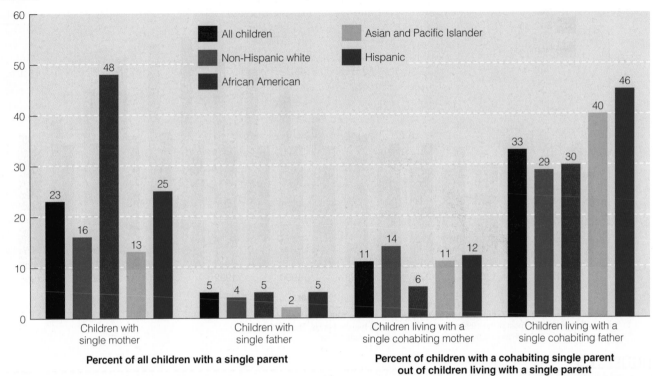

NOTES: The parent is the householder or partner, in an unmarried-partner household. Single means the parent has no spouse in the household. People of Hispanic origin may be of any race.

FIGURE 1.2

Living Arrangements of Children by Race and Ethnicity, 2000

SOURCE: U.S. Census Bureau, Annual Demographic Supplement to the March 2002 Current Population Survey, 2004.

cent of children under age 18 live with two married parents, down from 77 percent in 1980. About one-fifth of children live with only their mothers, 5 percent live with only their fathers, and 4 percent live with neither of their parents.[11] The statistics on living arrangements are skewed by race. As Figure 1.2 shows, more African American and Hispanic children are living with only one parent than white children.

Because of family problems, children are being polarized into two distinct economic groups: those in affluent, two-earner, married-couple households and those in poor, single-parent households.[12]

 Formed in 1985, the **Children's Rights Council (CRC)** is a national nonprofit organization based in Washington, D.C., that works to assure children meaningful and continuing contact with both their parents and extended family regardless of the parents' marital status. More information can be found at their website: www.gocrc.com. For an up-to-date list of web links, go to http://cj.wadsworth.com/siegel_jd9e.

Substandard Living Conditions Many children live in substandard housing— high-rise, multiple-family dwellings—which can have a negative influence on their long-term psychological health.[13] Adolescents living in deteriorated urban areas are prevented from having productive and happy lives. Many die from random bullets and drive-by shootings. Some are homeless and living on the street, where they are at risk of drug addiction and sexually transmitted diseases (STDs), including AIDS. Today about one-third of U.S. households with children have one or more of the following three housing problems: physically inadequate housing, crowded housing, or housing that costs more than 30 percent of the household income.[14]

Inadequate Educational Opportunity Although all young people face stress in the education system, the risks are greatest for the poor, members of racial and ethnic minorities, and recent immigrants. These children usually attend the most under-funded schools, receive inadequate educational opportunities, and have the fewest opportunities to achieve conventional success. For example, by the time they reach the

Victims aged 7–17

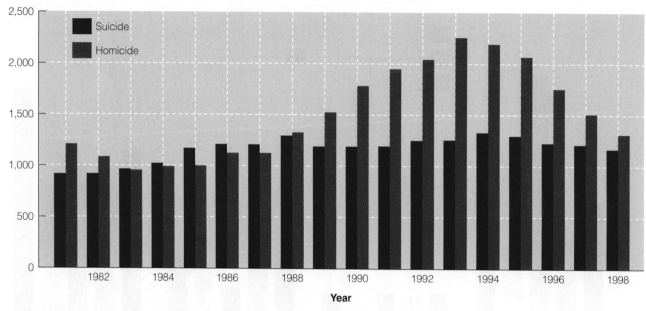

NOTE: Suicides of juveniles aged 7–17 increased from the early to the late 1980s and then remained relatively constant for most of the 1990s, in contrast to juvenile murder trends. The number of suicides peaked in 1994 and the number of murders peaked a year earlier.

FIGURE 1.3
Teen Suicide

SOURCE: Howard N. Snyder and Monica H. Swahn, *Juvenile Suicides, 1981–1998* (Washington, DC: Office of Juvenile Justice and Delinquency Prevention, 2004).

fourth grade, students in poorer public schools have lower achievement scores in mathematics than those in more affluent districts.[15]

The rate of *retention*—being forced to repeat a grade—is far higher than it should be in most communities. Retention rates are associated with another major educational problem—dropping out.[16] In 2000–01, for example, not a single large city school district in the United States had four-year high school completion rates of 80 percent or better. (Dropping out will be discussed further in Chapter 9.)[17]

Teen Suicide Considering these stressful life circumstances, it may come as no surprise that teens have a high suicide rate. A total of 20,775 youths aged 7 to 17 committed suicide in the U.S. between 1981 and 1998, making it the fourth leading cause of death for people in this age group. In those years, 4 percent of all individuals who committed suicide were younger than age 18.[18] Figure 1.3 shows the recent trend in juvenile suicide and homicide victimization. Between 1983 and 1987, more teens died from suicide than from homicide; in recent years, the proportion of teen deaths from homicides seems to be increasing.

Considering that youth are at risk during the most tumultuous time of their lives, it comes as no surprise that they are willing to engage in risky, destructive behavior, as the Focus on Delinquency box entitled "Adolescent Risk Taking" suggests.

Are There Reasons for Hope?

Despite the many hazards faced by teens, there are some bright spots on the horizon. Teenage birthrates nationwide have declined substantially during the past decade.[19] Since 1991, the U.S. birthrate for teenagers aged 15 to 19 declined 30 percent to about 43 births per 1,000 teen girls (from 61.8 births per 1,000 in 1991). Birthrates for teenagers aged 15 to 17 and African American girls have shown the greatest decline (see

Adolescent Risk Taking

The Centers for Disease Control and Prevention (CDC) reports that, in the United States, 70 percent of all deaths among youth and young adults from 10 to 24 years of age result from only four causes: motor vehicle crashes, unintentional injuries, homicide, and suicide. The reason may be that many high school students engage in risky behaviors that increase their likelihood of death from violence, accident, or self-destruction. A survey conducted by the Center found that about 20 percent of youths rarely or never wore a seat belt, 37 percent had ridden with a driver who had been drinking alcohol, and 18 percent had carried a weapon. Adolescents frequently engage in risky substance abuse: 51 percent of those surveyed had drunk alcohol, 26 percent had used marijuana, and about 36 percent of high school students had smoked cigarettes during the month prior to the survey. Nor did kids refrain from risky sexual activities: about half of all high school students surveyed had engaged in sexual relations; 43 percent of sexually active students had not used birth control.

Why do youths take such chances? Some research suggests that risk taking is actually normative among teens. For example, motor vehicle crashes are a leading cause of death among young people, making problem driving behavior a significant public concern. Recent research by Raymond Bingham and Jean Shope found that kids who are involved in auto accidents are actually among the best students in their class. Although they drank more than average, they smoked less. Their findings suggest that risky driving patterns may be found among any teen group.

Criminologist Nanette Davis suggests that merely trying to survive the adolescent experience in America makes kids prone to take risks. Risk behaviors are emotionally edgy, dangerous, exciting, hazardous, challenging, and volatile. Youths are forced into risky behavior as they try to negotiate the hurdles of adolescent life—learning to drive, date, drink, work, relate, and live. Davis finds that social developments in the United States have increased the risks of growing up for all children. It is a society that is prone to suffer severe economic upswings and downturns. Planning a future is problematic when job elimination and corporate downsizing are accepted business practices and divorce and family restructuring are epidemic. It is a culture that overemphasizes consumerism with often troubling results. In high schools, peer respect is "bought" through the accumulation of material goods; the right clothes, electronic gear, and car are required for popularity. Underprivileged youths are driven to illegal behavior in an effort to gain the material goods they can't afford. Drug deals and theft may be a shortcut to acquiring coveted name-brand clothes and athletic shoes. Kids learn to be part of the "cult of individualism," which makes them self-involved and self-centered. Children are taught to put their own interests above those of others. People occupy their own private worlds without caring for the rights of others. In an effort to fit into this fast-paced environment, some kids become risk takers who engage in chancy behaviors.

Some adolescents may not choose to take risks, but are forced into them in order to survive in a hostile environment. For example, though joining gangs may put kids at risk for drug use and violence, in some neighborhoods choosing not to join may put them in even greater peril. Some kids living in high crime areas may join with the toughest kids in the neighborhood as a method of coping with a hostile environment; some choose to carry weapons for protection. They believe that the benefits of protection and respect outweigh the dangers of arrest and punishment. Research shows that such confrontive coping measures expose these youth to violence and danger.

Adulthood may not bring a respite from risk taking. The uncertainties of modern society may prolong risk-taking behavior. Jobs have become unpredictable, and many undereducated and undertrained youths find themselves competing with hundreds of other applicants for the same low-paying job; they are a "surplus product." Under these circumstances, continued risk taking may be a plausible alternative for fitting into our consumer-oriented society.

Critical Thinking

1. Do kids engage in risky behavior because they feel there is nothing to lose as an adolescent? Would a campaign to inform them of the danger of taking risks, such as early sex, help reduce risky behaviors?

2. What are the benefits of risk taking? Millions of people take risks every day and get involved in risky activities ranging from mountain climbing to diving in shark-filled waters. Why do people take such risks?

InfoTrac College Edition Research

Why do kids take risks? Could it be that they believe their parents will never find out? To read more, go to N. R. Saltmarsh, "Adolescent Risk Taking Tied to Perceived Parental Monitoring," *TB & Outbreaks Week* (June 26, 2001).

To find out more, use "teenage risk taking" as keywords on InfoTrac College Edition.

For more on the repercussions of adolescent drinking and driving, read Jennifer C. Sabel, Lillian S. Bensley, and Juliet Van Eenwyk, "Associations between adolescent drinking and driving involvement and self-reported risk and protective factors in students in public schools in Washington State," *Journal of Studies on Alcohol* 65:213–217 (2004).

SOURCES: Andrew Rasmussen, Mark S. Aber, and Arvinkumar Bhana, "Adolescent coping and neighborhood violence: perceptions, exposure, and urban youths' efforts to deal with danger," *American Journal of Community Psychology* 33:61–75 (2004); Raymond Bingham and Jean Shope, "Adolescent Problem Behavior and Problem Driving in Young Adulthood," *Journal of Adolescent Research* 19:205–223 (2004); Jo Anne Grunbaum et al., *Youth Risk Behavior Surveillance: United States, 2001* (Centers for Disease Control, *Morbidity and Mortality Weekly Report*, June, 28, 2002); Laura Kann et al., *Youth Risk Behavior Surveillance—United States, 1997* (Centers for Disease Control, August 14, 1998); Nanette Davis, *Youth Crisis: Growing Up in the High-Risk Society* (New York: Praeger, Greenwood Publishing, 1998).

FIGURE 1.4
Teen Birth Rates

SOURCE: *Births: Final Data for 2002,*
National Vital Statistics Reports,
Dec. 17, 2003.

Birth rate per 1,000 women aged 15–19 years in specified group

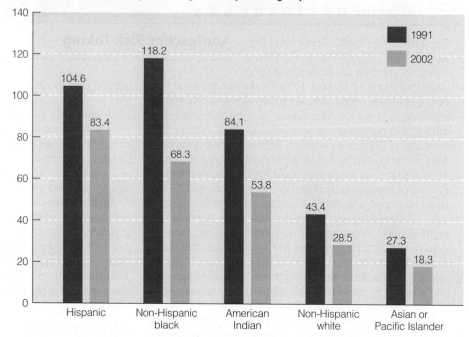

Figure 1.4).[20] The data indicate that more young girls are using birth control and practicing safe sex.

There are other signs of improvement in adolescent health care. Fewer children with health risks are being born today than in 1990. This probably means that fewer women are drinking alcohol during pregnancy, smoking cigarettes, or receiving late or no prenatal care. Since 1990 the number of children immunized against disease has also increased.[21] Due in large part to improvements in medical technology, the infant mortality rate—the number of children who die before their first birthday—has declined about 30 percent during the past decade (from 10.6 per 1,000 births in 1991 to 7 per 1,000 births today).[22] Although education is still a problem area, more parents are reading to their young children, and math achievement is rising in grades 4 through 12. And while the dropout problem still exists, the most recent Census Department data indicates 85 percent of U.S. adults aged 25 and over had completed at least high school in 2003, an all-time high; 27 percent of adults aged 25 and over had a college degree, another record.[23]

TO QUIZ YOURSELF ON THIS MATERIAL, go to the Juvenile Delinquency 9e website.

THE STUDY OF JUVENILE DELINQUENCY

juvenile delinquency
Participation in illegal behavior by a minor who falls under a statutory age limit.

chronic delinquent offender (also known as chronic juvenile offenders, chronic delinquents, or chronic recidivists)
Youths who have been arrested four or more times during their minority and perpetuate a striking majority of serious criminal acts. This small group, known as the "chronic 6 percent," is believed to engage in a significant portion of all delinquent behavior; these youths do not age out of crime but continue their criminal behavior into adulthood.

The problems of youth in modern society are both a major national concern and an important subject for academic study. This text focuses on one area of particular concern: **juvenile delinquency,** or criminal behavior committed by minors. The study of juvenile delinquency is important both because of the damage suffered by its victims and the problems faced by its perpetrators.

More than 2 million youths are now arrested each year for crimes ranging in seriousness from loitering to murder.[24] Though most juvenile law violations are minor, some young offenders are extremely dangerous and violent. More than 700,000 youths belong to more than 20,000 gangs in the United States. Violent street gangs and groups can put fear into an entire city (see Chapter 8 for more on gangs). Youths involved in multiple serious criminal acts—referred to as lifestyle, repeat, or **chronic delinquent offenders**—are now recognized as a serious social problem. State juvenile authorities must deal with these offenders, along with responding to a range of other social

In 1999 Julie Ann Barnes, a homeless teen, was living with her 37-year-old boyfriend in a cold-storage warehouse in Worcester, Massachusetts, when they started a fire by knocking over a candle during an argument. They left the building without reporting the fire and went to a nearby mall to hang out. Six firefighters died while fighting the blaze. Ms. Barnes was initially vilified for having caused one of the most devastating fires in state history, but public sentiment changed when it became known that she was developmentally disabled, neglected by her parents, left to wander the streets, and most likely the victim of sexual abuse. Rather than face manslaughter charges, she was placed in the custody of a foster family. Should adolescents with such troubled pasts be held accountable for their actions?

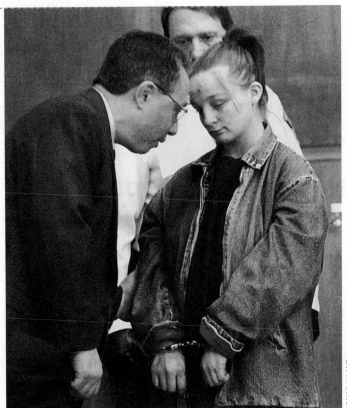

AP/Wide World Photos

problems, including child abuse and neglect, school crime and vandalism, family crises, and drug abuse.

Given the diversity and gravity of these problems, there is an urgent need for strategies to combat such a complex social phenomenon as juvenile delinquency. But formulating effective strategies demands a solid understanding of delinquency's causes and prevention. Is delinquency a function of psychological abnormality? A collective reaction by youths against destructive social conditions? The product of a disturbed home life and disrupted socialization? Does serious delinquent behavior occur only in large urban areas among lower-class youths? Or is it spread throughout the entire social structure? What impact do family life, substance abuse, school experiences, and peer relations have on youth and their law-violating behaviors? We know that most youthful law violators do not go on to become adult criminals (what is known as the **aging-out process**). Yet we do not know why some youths become chronic delinquents whose careers begin early and persist into their adulthood. Why does the onset of delinquency begin so early in some children? Why does the severity of their offenses escalate? What factors predict the **persistence,** or continuation, of delinquency, and conversely, what are the factors associated with its desistance, or termination? Unless the factors that control the onset and termination of a delinquent career are studied in an orderly and scientific manner, developing effective prevention and control efforts will be difficult.

The study of delinquency also involves analysis of the law enforcement, court, and correctional agencies designed to treat youthful offenders who fall into the arms of the law—known collectively as the **juvenile justice system.** How should police deal with minors who violate the law? What are the legal rights of children? For example, should minors who commit murder receive the death penalty? What kind of correctional programs are most effective with delinquent youths? How useful are educational, community, counseling, and vocational development programs? Is it true, as some critics claim, that most efforts to rehabilitate young offenders are doomed to failure?[25] Should we adopt a punishment or a treatment orientation to combat delinquency, or something in between?

aging-out process (also known as desistance or spontaneous remission)
The tendency for youths to reduce the frequency of their offending behavior as they age; aging-out is thought to occur among all groups of offenders.

persistence
The process by which juvenile offenders persist in their delinquent careers rather than aging out of crime.

juvenile justice system
The segment of the justice system, including law enforcement officers, the courts, and correctional agencies, designed to treat youthful offenders.

In sum, the scientific study of delinquency requires understanding the nature, extent, and cause of youthful law violations and the methods devised for their control. We also need to study important environmental and social issues associated with delinquent behavior, including substance abuse, child abuse and neglect, education, and peer relations. This text investigates these aspects of juvenile delinquency along with the efforts being made to treat problem youths and prevent the spread of delinquent behavior. Our study begins with a look back to the development of the concept of childhood and how children were first identified as a unique group with its own special needs and behaviors.

TO QUIZ YOURSELF ON THIS MATERIAL, go to the Juvenile Delinquency 9e website.

THE DEVELOPMENT OF CHILDHOOD

The treatment of children as a distinct social group with special needs and behavior is, in historical terms, a relatively new concept. It is only for the past 350 years or so that any mechanism existed to care for even the most needy children, including those left orphaned and destitute. How did this concept of concern for children develop?

Childhood in the Middle Ages

paternalistic family
A family style wherein the father is the final authority on all family matters and exercises complete control over his wife and children.

In Europe, during the Middle Ages (1500 A.D. to 700 A.D.), the concept of childhood as we know it today did not exist. In the **paternalistic family** of the time, the father was the final authority on all family matters and exercised complete control over the social, economic, and physical well being of his wife and children.[26] Children who did not obey were subject to severe physical punishment, even death.

The Lower Classes For peasant children, the passage into adulthood was abrupt. As soon as they were physically capable, children of all classes were expected to engage in adult roles. Among the working classes, males engaged in farming and/or learning a skilled trade, such as masonry or metalworking; females aided in food preparation or household maintenance.[27] Some peasant youths went into domestic or agricultural service on the estate of a powerful landowner or into trades or crafts, perhaps as a blacksmith or farrier (horseshoe maker).

This view of medieval childhood was shaped by Philippe Aries, whose influential book *Centuries of Childhood* is considered a classic of historical scholarship. Aries argued that most young people were apprenticed, became agricultural or factory workers, and generally entered adult society at a very early age.[28] According to Aries, high infant mortality rates kept parents emotionally detached from their children. Paintings of the time depict children as mini-adults who were sent off to work as soon as they were capable. Western culture did not have a sense of childhood as a distinct period of life until the very late nineteenth and early twentieth centuries.

Though Aries's view that children in the Middle Ages were treated as "miniature adults" has become the standard view, in a recent book, historian Nicholas Orme puts forth evidence that medieval children may have been valued by their parents and did experience a prolonged period of childhood. In his *Medieval Children*, Orme finds that the medieval mother began to care for her children even before their delivery. Royal ladies borrowed relics of the Virgin Mary from the church to protect their unborn children, while poorer women used jasper stones or drawings of the cross, which were placed across their stomachs to ensure a healthy and uneventful birth. Parents associated their children's birthdays with a saint's feast day. Medieval children devised songs, rhymes, and games. Some simple games made use of cherry pits or hazelnuts, but children also had toys, which included dolls and even mechanical toys made for royalty.[29]

Children of the Nobility Though their lives were quite different, children of the affluent, landholding classes also assumed adult roles at an early age. Girls born into

As soon as they were physically capable, children of the Middle Ages were expected to engage in adult roles. Among the working classes, males engaged in peasant farming or learned a skilled trade, such as masonry or metalworking; females aided in food preparation or household maintenance. Some peasant youth went into domestic or agricultural service on the estate of a powerful landowner or into trades or crafts, such as blacksmith or farrier (horseshoer).

The Pierpont Morgan Library/Art Resource, NY

aristocratic families were educated at home and married in their early teens. A few were taught to read, write, and do sufficient mathematics to handle household accounts in addition to typical female duties such as supervising servants and ensuring the food supply of the manor.

At age 7 or 8, boys born to landholding families were either sent to a monastery or cathedral school to be trained for lives in the church or selected to be a member of the warrior class and sent to serve a term as a squire—an apprentice and assistant to an experienced knight. At age 21, young men of the knightly classes completed their term as squire, received their own knighthood, and returned home to live with their parents. Most remained single because it was widely believed there should only be one married couple residing in a manor or castle. To pass the time and maintain their fighting edge, many entered the tournament circuit, engaging in melees and jousts to win fame and fortune. Upon the death of their fathers, young nobles assumed their inherited titles, married, and began their own families.

The customs and practices of the time helped shape the lives of children and, in some instances, greatly amplified their hardships and suffering. **Primogeniture** required that the oldest surviving male child inherit family lands and titles. He could then distribute them as he saw fit to younger siblings. There was no absolute requirement, however, that portions of the estate be distributed equally; so many youths who received no lands were forced to enter religious orders, become soldiers, or seek wealthy patrons. Primogeniture often caused intense family rivalry that led to blood feuds and tragedy.

primogeniture
During the Middle Ages, the right of first-born sons to inherit lands and titles, leaving their brothers the option of a military or religious career.

Dower The *dower system* mandated that a woman's family bestow money, land, or other wealth (called a *dowry*) on a potential husband or his family in exchange for his marriage to her. In return, the young woman received a promise of financial assistance, called a *jointure,* from the groom's family. Jointure provided a lifetime income if a wife outlived her mate. The dower system had a significant impact on the role of women in medieval society and consequently on the role of children. Within this system, a father or male guardian had the final say in his daughter's choice of marital partner as he could threaten to withhold her dowry. Some women were denied access to marriage simply because of their position in the family.

A father with many daughters and few sons might find himself financially unable to obtain suitable marriages for them. Consequently, the youngest girls in many families were forced either to enter convents or stay at home, with few prospects for marriage and family.

The dower system had far-reaching effects on the position of women in society, forcing them into the role of second-class citizens dependent upon their fathers, brothers, and guardians. It established a pattern in which females who did not conform to what males considered to be acceptable standards of feminine behavior could receive harsh sanctions; it established a sexual double standard that in part still exists today.

Childrearing The harshness of medieval life influenced childrearing practices during the fifteenth and sixteenth centuries. For instance, newborns were almost immediately handed over to *wet nurses,* who fed and cared for them during the first two years of their life. These women often lived away from the family so that parents had little contact with their children. Even the wealthiest families employed wet nurses, because it was considered demeaning for a noblewoman to nurse. Wrapping a newborn entirely in bandages, or **swaddling,** was a common practice. The bandages prevented any movement and enabled the wet nurse to manage the child easily. This practice was thought to protect the child, but it most likely contributed to high infant mortality rates because the child could not be kept clean.

Discipline was severe during this period. Young children of all classes, both peasant and wealthy, were subjected to stringent rules and regulations. They were beaten severely for any sign of disobedience or ill temper. Many children of this time would be considered abused by today's standards. The relationship between parent and child was remote. Children were expected to enter the world of adults and to undertake responsibilities early in their lives, sharing in the work of siblings and parents. Children thought to be suffering from disease or retardation were often abandoned to churches, orphanages, or foundling homes.[30]

The roots of the impersonal relationship between parent and child can be traced to high mortality rates, which made sentimental and affectionate relationships risky. Parents were reluctant to invest emotional effort in relationships that could so easily be terminated by violence, accidents, or disease. Many believed that children must be toughened to ensure their survival in a hostile world. Close family relationships were viewed as detrimental to this process. Also, because the oldest male child was viewed as the essential player in a family's well-being, younger male and female siblings were considered economic and social liabilities.

Development of Concern for Children

Throughout the seventeenth and eighteenth centuries, a number of developments in England heralded the march toward the recognition of children's rights. Some of these events eventually affected the juvenile legal system as it emerged in America. They include (1) changes in family style and childcare, (2) the English Poor Laws, (3) the apprenticeship movement, and (4) the role of the chancery court.[31]

Changes in Family Structure Family structure and the role of children began to change after the Middle Ages. Extended families, which were created over centuries, gave way to the nuclear family structure with which we are familiar today. It became more common for marriage to be based on love and mutual attraction between men

---

swaddling
The practice during the Middle Ages of completely wrapping newborns in long bandage-like clothes in order to restrict their movements and make them easier to manage.

and women rather than on parental consent and paternal dominance. The changing concept of marriage—from an economic arrangement to an emotional commitment—also began to influence the way children were treated within the family structure. Though parents still rigidly disciplined their children, they formed closer parental ties and developed greater concern for their offspring's well-being.

To provide more control over children, grammar and boarding schools were established and began to flourish in many large cities during this time.[32] Children studied grammar, Latin, law, and logic, often beginning at a young age. Teachers in these institutions regularly ruled by fear, and flogging was their main method of discipline. Students were beaten for academic mistakes as well as moral lapses. Such brutal treatment fell on both the rich and the poor throughout all levels of educational life, including boarding schools and universities. This treatment abated in Europe with the rise of the Enlightenment, but it remained in full force in Great Britain until late in the nineteenth century. Although this brutal approach to children may be difficult to understand now, the child in that society was a second-class citizen.

Toward the close of the eighteenth century, the work of such philosophers as Voltaire, Rousseau, and Locke launched a new age for childhood and the family.[33] Their vision produced a period known as the Enlightenment, which stressed a humanistic view of life, freedom, family, reason, and law. The ideal person was sympathetic to others and receptive to new ideas. These new beliefs influenced both the structure and lifestyle of the family. The father's authority was tempered, discipline in the home became more relaxed, and the expression of love and affection became more commonplace among family members. Upper- and middle-class families began to devote attention to childrearing, and the status of children was advanced.

As a result of these changes, in the nineteenth century children began to emerge as a readily distinguishable group with independent needs and interests. Parents often took greater interest in their upbringing. In addition, serious questions arose over the treatment of children in school. Public outcries led to a decrease in excessive physical discipline. Restrictions were placed on the use of the whip, and in some schools, the imposition of academic assignments or the loss of privileges replaced corporal punishment. Despite such reforms, many children still led harsh lives. Girls were still undereducated, punishment was still primarily physical, and schools continued to mistreat children.

Poor Laws Government action to care for needy children can be traced to the **Poor Laws** of Britain. As early as 1535, the English passed statutes allowing for the appointment of overseers to place destitute or neglected children as servants in the homes of the affluent.[34] The Poor Laws forced children to serve during their minority in the care of families who trained them in agricultural, trade, or domestic services. The Elizabethan Poor Laws of 1601 were a model for dealing with poor children for more than 200 years. These laws created a system of church wardens and overseers who, with the consent of justices of the peace, identified vagrant, delinquent, and neglected children and took measures to put them to work. Often this meant placing them in poorhouses or workhouses, or apprenticing them to masters.

The Apprenticeship Movement Under the apprenticeship concept, children were placed in the care of adults who trained them to discharge various duties and obtain different skills. Voluntary apprentices were bound out by parents or guardians who wished to secure training for their children. Involuntary apprentices were compelled by the authorities to serve until they were 21 or older. The master-apprentice relationship was similar to the parent-child relationship in that the master had complete responsibility for and authority over the apprentice. If an apprentice was unruly, a complaint could be made and the apprentice could be punished. Incarcerated apprentices were often placed in rooms or workshops apart from other prisoners and were generally treated differently from those charged with a criminal offense. Even at this early stage, the conviction was growing that the criminal law and its enforcement should be applied differently to children.

Poor Laws
English statutes that allowed the courts to appoint overseers over destitute and neglected children, allowing placement of these children as servants in the homes of the affluent.

chancery courts
Court proceedings created in fifteenth-
century England to oversee the lives of high-
born minors who were orphaned or
otherwise could not care for themselves.

Chancery Court After the fifteenth century, a system of **chancery courts** became a significant arm of the British legal system. They were originally established as "courts of equity" to handle matters falling outside traditional legal actions. These early courts were based on the traditional English system in which a chancellor acted as the "King's conscience" and had the ability to modify the application of legal rules and provide relief considering the circumstances of individual cases. The courts were not concerned with technical legal issues; rather, they focused on rendering decisions or orders that were fair or equitable. With respect to children, the chancery courts dealt with issues of guardianship of children who were orphaned, their property and inheritance rights, and the appointment of guardians to protect them until they reached the age of majority and could care for themselves. For example, if a wealthy father died prior to his heir's majority, or if there were some dispute as to the identity (or legitimacy) of his heir, the crown might ask the case to be decided by the chancery court in an effort to ensure that inheritance rights were protected (and taxes collected!).

parens patriae
Power of the state to act on behalf of the
child and provide care and protection equivalent to that of a parent.

Chancery court decision-making rested on the proposition that children and other incompetents were under the protective control of the king; thus, the Latin phrase *parens patriae* was used, referring to the role of the king as the father of his country. The concept was first used by English kings to establish their right to intervene in the lives of the children of their vassals—children whose position and property were of direct concern to the monarch.[35] The concept of *parens patriae* became the theoretical basis for the protective jurisdiction of the chancery courts acting as part of the crown's power. As time passed, the monarchy used *parens patriae* more and more to justify its intervention in the lives of families and children by its interest in their general welfare.[36]

The chancery courts dealt with the property and custody problems of the wealthier classes. They did not have jurisdiction over children charged with criminal conduct. Juveniles who violated the law were handled within the framework of the regular criminal court system. Nonetheless, the concept of *parens patriae* grew to refer primarily to the responsibility of the courts and the state to act in the best interests of the child.

Childhood in America

While England was using its chancery courts and Poor Laws to care for children in need, the American colonies were developing similar concepts. The colonies were a haven for poor and unfortunate people looking for religious and economic opportunities denied them in England and Europe. Along with early settlers, many children came not as citizens but as indentured servants, apprentices, or agricultural workers. They were recruited from the various English workhouses, orphanages, prisons, and asylums that housed vagrant and delinquent youths during the sixteenth and seventeenth centuries.[37]

At the same time, the colonies themselves produced illegitimate, neglected, abandoned, and delinquent children. The colonies' initial response to caring for such unfortunate children was to adopt court and Poor Laws systems similar to those in England. Involuntary apprenticeship, indenture, and binding out of children became integral parts of colonization in America. For example, Poor Law legislation requiring poor and dependent children to serve apprenticeships was passed in Virginia in 1646 and in Massachusetts and Connecticut in 1673.[38]

The master in colonial America acted as a surrogate parent, and in certain instances, apprentices would actually become part of the nuclear family structure. If they disobeyed their masters, apprentices were punished by local tribunals. If masters abused apprentices, courts would make them pay damages, return the children to the parents, or find new guardians. Maryland and Virginia developed an orphan's court that supervised the treatment of youths placed with guardians and ensured that they were not mistreated or taken advantage of by their masters. These courts did not supervise children living with their natural parents, leaving intact the parents' right to care for their children.[39]

© Christie's Images/Corbis

By the beginning of the nineteenth century, as the agrarian economy began to be replaced by industry, the apprenticeship system gave way to the factory system. Yet the problems of how to deal effectively with growing numbers of dependent youths increased. Early American settlers believed that hard work, strict discipline, and rigorous education were the only reliable means to salvation. A child's life was marked by work alongside parents, some schooling, prayer, more work, and further study. Work in the factories, however, often taxed young laborers by placing demands on them that they were too young to endure. To alleviate a rapidly developing problem, the Factory Act of the early nineteenth century limited the hours children were permitted to work and the age at which they could begin to work. It also prescribed a minimum amount of schooling to be provided by factory owners.[40] This and related statutes were often violated, and conditions of work and school remained troublesome issues well into the twentieth century. Nevertheless, the statutes were a step in the direction of reform.

Controlling Children In America, as in England, moral discipline was rigidly enforced. "Stubborn child" laws were passed that required children to obey their parents.[41] It was not uncommon in the colonies for children who were disobedient or disrespectful to their families to be whipped or otherwise physically chastised. Children were often required to attend public whippings and executions because these events were thought to be important forms of moral instruction. Parents often referred their children to published works and writings on behavior and discipline and expected them to follow their precepts carefully. The early colonists, however, viewed family violence as a sin, and child protection laws were passed as early as 1639 (in New Haven, Connecticut). These laws were generally symbolic and rarely enforced. They expressed the community's commitment to God to oppose sin; offenders usually received lenient sentences.[42]

While most colonies adopted a protectionist stance, few cases of child abuse were actually brought before the courts. There are several explanations for this neglect. The absence of child abuse cases may reflect the nature of life in what were extremely religious households. Children were productive laborers and respected as such by their parents. In addition, large families provided many siblings and kinfolk who could care for children and relieve stress-producing burdens on parents.[43] Another view is that though many children were harshly punished in Early American families, the acceptable limits of discipline were so high that few parents were charged with assault. Any punishment that fell short of maiming or permanently harming a child was considered within the sphere of parental rights.[44]

TO QUIZ YOURSELF ON THIS MATERIAL, go to the Juvenile Delinquency 9e website.

THE CONCEPT OF DELINQUENCY

Considering the rough treatment handed out to children who misbehaved at home or at school, it should come as no surprise that children who actually broke the law and committed serious criminal acts were dealt with harshly. Before the twentieth century, little distinction was made between adult and juvenile offenders. Although judges considered the age of an offender when deciding punishments, both adults and children were often eligible for the same forms of punishment—prison, corporal punishment, and even the death penalty. In fact, children were treated with extreme cruelty at home, at school, and by the law.[45]

Over the years, this treatment changed, as society became sensitive to the special needs of children. Beginning in the mid-nineteenth century, as immigrant youth poured into America, there was official recognition that children formed a separate group with its own separate needs. Around the nation, in cities such as New York, Boston, and Chicago, groups known as **child savers** were being formed to assist children in need. They created community programs to serve needy children, and lobbied for a separate legal status for children, which ultimately led to the development of a formal juvenile justice system. The child saving movement will be discussed more fully in Chapter 12.

child savers
Nineteenth-century reformers who developed programs for troubled youth and influenced legislation creating the juvenile justice system; today some critics view them as being more concerned with control of the poor than with their welfare.

Delinquency and *Parens Patriae*

The current treatment of juvenile delinquents is a byproduct of this developing national consciousness. The designation *delinquent* became popular at the onset of the twentieth century when the first separate juvenile courts were instituted. The child savers believed that treating minors and adults equivalently violated the humanitarian ideals of American society. Consequently, the newly emerging juvenile justice system operated under the *parens patriae* philosophy. Minors who engaged in illegal behavior were viewed as victims of improper care, custody, and treatment at home. Dishonest behavior was a sign that the state should step in and take control of the youths before they committed more serious crimes. The state, through its juvenile authorities, should act in the **best interests of the child.** This means that children should not be punished for their misdeeds but instead should be given the care and custody necessary to remedy and control wayward behavior. It makes no sense to find children guilty of specific crimes, such as burglary or petty larceny, because that stigmatizes them and labels them as thieves or burglars. Instead, the catchall term *juvenile delinquency* should be used, as it indicates that the child needs the care, custody, and treatment of the state.

best interests of the child
A philosophical viewpoint that encourages the state to take control of wayward children and provide care, custody, and treatment to remedy delinquent behavior.

The Legal Status of Delinquency

Though the child savers fought hard for a separate legal status of "juvenile delinquent" early in the twentieth century, the concept that children could be treated differently before the law can actually be traced back much farther to its roots in the British legal tradition. Early English jurisprudence held that children under the age of 7 were legally incapable of committing crimes. Children between the ages of 7 and 14 were responsible for their actions, but their age might be used to excuse or lighten their punishment. Our legal system still recognizes that many young people are incapable of making mature judgments and that responsibility for their acts should be limited. Children can intentionally steal cars and know full well that the act is illegal, but they may be incapable of fully understanding the consequences of their behavior and the harm it may cause. Therefore, the law does not punish a youth as it would an adult, and it sees youthful misconduct as evidence of unreasoned or impaired judgment.

Today, the legal status of "juvenile delinquent" refers to a minor child who has been found to have violated the penal code. Most states define "minor child" as an individual who falls under a statutory age limit, most commonly 17 or 18 years of age.

Because of their minority status, juveniles are usually kept separate from adults and receive different consideration and treatment under the law. For example, most large police departments employ officers whose sole responsibility is youth crime and delinquency. Every state has some form of separate juvenile court with its own judges, probation department, and other facilities. Terminology is also different: Adults are tried in court; children are adjudicated. Adults can be punished; children are treated. If treatment is mandated, children can be sent to secure detention facilities; they cannot normally be committed to adult prisons.

Children also have their own unique legal status. Minors apprehended for a criminal act are usually charged with being a "juvenile delinquent" regardless of the crime they commit. These charges are usually confidential, trial records are kept secret, and the name, behavior, and background of delinquent offenders are sealed. Eliminating specific crime categories and maintaining secrecy are efforts to shield children from the stigma of a criminal conviction and to prevent youthful misdeeds from becoming a lifelong burden.

Legal Responsibility of Youth

In our society, the actions of adults are controlled by two types of law: criminal and civil. Criminal laws prohibit activities that are injurious to the well-being of society and threaten the social order, for example, drug use, theft, and rape; they are legal actions brought by state authorities against private citizens. Civil laws, on the other hand, control interpersonal or private activities and are usually initiated by individual citizens. The ownership and transfer of property, contractual relationships, and personal conflicts (torts) are the subject of the civil law. Also covered under the civil law are provisions for the care and custody of those people who cannot care for themselves—the mentally ill, incompetent, or infirm.

Today, the juvenile delinquency concept occupies a legal status falling somewhere between criminal and civil law. Under *parens patriae*, delinquent acts are not considered criminal violations, nor are delinquents considered "criminals." Children cannot be found "guilty" of a crime and punished like adult criminals. The legal action against them is considered more similar (though not identical) to a civil action that determines their "need for treatment." This legal theory recognizes that children who violate the law are in need of the same care and treatment as law-abiding citizens who cannot care for themselves and require state intervention into their lives.

Delinquent behavior is sanctioned less heavily than criminality because the law considers juveniles as being less responsible for their behavior than adults. As a class, adolescents are believed to (1) have a stronger preference for risk and novelty, (2) assess the potentially negative consequences of risky conduct less unfavorably than adults, (3) have a tendency to be impulsive and more concerned with short-term than long-term consequences, (4) have a different appreciation of time and self-control, and (5) be more susceptible to peer pressure.[46] Although many adolescents may be more responsible and calculating than adults, under normal circumstances the law is willing to recognize age as a barrier to having full responsibility over one's actions.

Although youths share a lesser degree of legal responsibility than adults, they are subject to arrest, trial, and incarceration. Their legal predicament has prompted the courts to grant them many of the same legal protections granted to adults accused of criminal offenses. These legal protections include the right to consult an attorney, to be free from self-incrimination, and to be protected from illegal searches and seizures. In addition, state legislatures are toughening legal codes and making them more punitive in an effort to "get tough" on dangerous youth.

Although appreciation of the criminal nature of the delinquency concept has helped increase the legal rights of minors, it has also allowed state authorities to declare that some offenders are "beyond control" and cannot be treated as children. This recognition has prompted the policy of **waiver,** or transferring legal jurisdiction over the most serious and experienced juvenile offenders to the adult court for criminal prosecution. To the dismay of reformers, waived youth may find themselves

waiver (also known as bindover or removal)
Transferring legal jurisdiction over the most serious and experienced juvenile offenders to the adult court for criminal prosecution.

TO QUIZ YOURSELF ON THIS MATERIAL, go to the Juvenile Delinquency 9e website.

serving time in adult prisons.[47] So though the *parens patriae* concept is still applied to children whose law violations are not considered serious, the more serious juvenile offenders can be declared "legal adults" and placed outside the jurisdiction of the juvenile court.

STATUS OFFENDERS

status offense
Conduct that is illegal only because the child is under age.

A child also becomes subject to state authority for committing **status offenses**—actions that would not be considered illegal if perpetrated by an adult; such conduct is illegal only because the child is under age. For example, 44 of the 50 states have some form of law prohibiting minors from purchasing, using, or possessing tobacco products. These statutes impose a variety of sanctions, including a monetary fine, suspension from school, and denial of a driver's license. In Florida, repeat offenders may lose their license or be prohibited from obtaining one. For example, in Plantain, Florida, teens must appear before the judge with their parent or guardian, must view an anti-smoking video, and experience a lecture from a throat cancer survivor.[48] Exhibit 1.1 illustrates some typical status offense statutes.

Figure 1.5 illustrates some typical status offenses. It is extremely difficult to evaluate the annual number of status offenses as most cases escape police detection, and those that do not are more often than not handled informally. Yet, according to data compiled by the Federal Bureau of Investigation, more than 300,000 juveniles are arrested each year for such status type offenses as running away from home, breaking curfew, and violating liquor laws.[49]

The History of Status Offenses

A historical basis exists for status offense statutes. It was common practice early in the nation's history to place disobedient or runaway youths in orphan asylums, residen-

FIGURE 1.5
Status Offenses

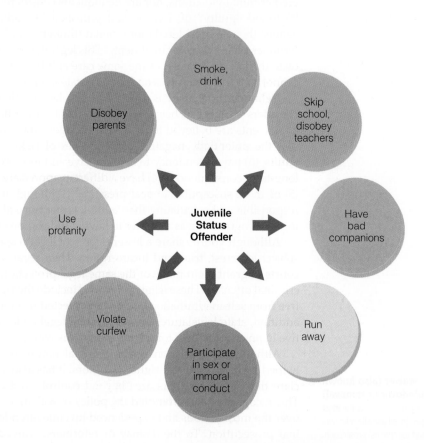

EXHIBIT **1.1**

Status Offense Laws: Maryland, Louisiana, and Wisconsin

Maryland

"Child" means an individual under the age of 18 years. "Child in need of supervision" is a child who requires guidance, treatment, or rehabilitation and:

1. Is required by law to attend school and is habitually truant;
2. Is habitually disobedient, ungovernable, and beyond the control of the person having custody of him;
3. Deports himself so as to injure or endanger himself or others; or
4. Has committed an offense applicable only to children.

Louisiana

"Child in need of supervision" means a child who needs care or rehabilitation because:

1. Being subject to compulsory school attendance, he is habitually truant from school or willfully violates the rules of the school;
2. He habitually disobeys the reasonable and lawful demands of his parents, and is ungovernable and beyond their control;
3. He absents himself from his home or usual place of abode without the consent of his parent;
4. He purposefully, intentionally and willfully deceives, or misrepresents the true facts to any person holding a retail dealer's permit, or his agent, associate, employee or representative, for the purposes of buying or receiving alcoholic beverages or beer, or visiting or loitering in or about any place where such beverages are the principal commodities sold or handled;
5. His occupation, conduct, environment or associations are injurious to his welfare; or
6. He has committed an offense applicable only to children.

Wisconsin

The court has exclusive original jurisdiction over a child alleged to be in need of protection or services which can be ordered by the court, and:

1. Who is without a parent or guardian;
2. Who has been abandoned;
3. Who has been the victim of sexual or physical abuse including injury which is self-inflicted or inflicted by another by other than accidental means;
4. Whose parent or guardian signs the petition requesting jurisdiction and states that he or she is unable to care for, control or provide necessary special care or special treatment for the child;
5. Who has been placed for care or adoption in violation of law;
6. Who is habitually truant from school, after evidence is provided by the school attendance officer that the activities under s. 118.16(5) have been completed;
7. Who is habitually truant from home and either the child or a parent, guardian or a relative in whose home the child resides signs the petition requesting jurisdiction and attests in court that reconciliation efforts have been attempted and have failed;
8. Who is receiving inadequate care during the period of time a parent is missing, incarcerated, hospitalized, or institutionalized;
9. Who is at least age 12, signs the petition requesting jurisdiction, and attests in court that he or she is in need of special care and treatment which the parent, guardian, or legal custodian is unwilling to provide;
10. Whose parent, guardian, or legal custodian neglects, refuses, or is unable for reasons other than poverty to provide necessary care, food, clothing, medical or dental care, or shelter so as to seriously endanger the physical health of the child;
11. Who is suffering emotional damage for which the parent or guardian is unwilling to provide treatment, which is evidenced by one or more of the following characteristics, exhibited to a severe degree: anxiety, depression, withdrawal, or outward aggressive behavior;
12. Who, being under 12 years of age, has committed a delinquent act as defined in s. 48.12;
13. Who has not been immunized as required by s. 140.05(16) and not exempted under s. 140.05(16)(c); or
14. Who has been determined, under s. 48.30(5)(c), to be not responsible for a delinquent act by reason of mental disease or defect.

SOURCES: MD Courts and Judicial Proceedings Code Ann. § 3-8A-01 (2002); LA Code Juv. Proc. Ann. art. 13 § 12 (West 1979, amended 1987) and WI Stat. Ann. § 48.13 (West 1979, amended 1987).

tial homes, or houses of refuge.[50] In 1646, the Massachusetts Stubborn Child Law was enacted, which provided that "If any man have a stubborne and rebellious sonne of sufficient years and understanding, which will not obey the voice of his father or the voice of his mother, and that when they have chastened him will not harken unto them . . ." they could bring him before the court and testify that he would not obey. If the magistrate then found the child to be unrepentant and incapable of control, such a child could be put to death.[51]

When the first juvenile courts were established in Illinois, the Chicago Bar Association described part of their purpose as follows:

> The whole trend and spirit of the [1899 Juvenile Court Act] is that the State, acting through the Juvenile Court, exercises that tender solicitude and care over its neglected, dependent wards that a wise and loving parent would exercise with reference to his own children under similar circumstances.[52]

State control over a child's noncriminal behavior is believed to support and extend the *parens patriae* philosophy because it is assumed to be in the best interests of the child. Typically, status offenders are petitioned to the juvenile court when it is determined that their parents are unable or unwilling to care for or control them and that the

It is illegal for a minor to engage in what are called status offenses—actions that would not be considered illegal if perpetrated by an adult; such conduct is illegal only because the child is underage. The two young girls shown here are status offenders because underage smoking is prohibited by law.

© Stone/Getty Images

offender's behavior is self-destructive or harmful to society. For example, research shows that young teenage girls are much more likely to engage in precocious sex while under the influence of alcohol if they are involved with older teens. Parents may petition their underage daughter to juvenile court if they feel their sexual behavior is getting out of control and they are powerless to stop its occurrence.[53] The case now falls within the jurisdiction of state legal authorities and failure to heed a judicial command might result in detention in the juvenile correctional system.

At first, juvenile codes referred to status offenders as **wayward minors,** sometimes failing to distinguish them in any significant way from juvenile delinquents. Both classes of children could be detained in the same detention centers and placed in the same youth correctional facilities. A trend begun in the 1960s has resulted in the creation of separate status offense categories—children, minors, persons, youths, or juveniles in need of supervision (CHINS, MINS, PINS, YINS, or JINS)—which vary from state to state. The purpose of creating separate status offender categories was to shield noncriminal youths from the stigma attached to the label "juvenile delinquent" and to signify that they were troubled youths who had special needs and problems.

Most states now have separate categories for juvenile conduct that would not be considered criminal if committed by an adult; these sometimes pertain to neglected or dependent children as well.[54] Of these, more than 10 states use the term "child in need of supervision," while the remainder use such terms as "unruly child," "incorrigible child," and "minor in need of supervision."[55]

Even where there are separate legal categories for delinquents and status offenders, the distinction between them has become blurred. Some noncriminal conduct may be included in the definition of delinquency, and some less serious criminal offenses occasionally may be included within the status offender definition.[56]

In some states, the juvenile court judge is granted discretion to substitute a status offense for a delinquency charge.[57] Replacing a juvenile delinquency charge with a status offense charge can be used as a bargaining chip to encourage youths to admit to the charges against them in return for a promise of being treated as a (less stigmatized) status offender receiving less punitive treatment. Concept Summary 1.1 summarizes the differences among delinquents, adult criminals, and status offenders.

wayward minors
Early legal designation of youths who violate the law because of their minority status; now referred to as status offenders.

Concept Summary 1.1

Treatment Differences among Juvenile Delinquents, Status Offenders, and Adults

	Juvenile Delinquent	Status Offender	Adult
Act	Delinquent	Behavior forbidden to minors	Criminal
Enforcement	Police	Police	Police
Detention	Secure detention	Nonsecure shelter care	Jail
Adjudication	Juvenile court	Juvenile court	Criminal court
Correctional Alternative	State training school	Community treatment facility	Prison

The Status Offender in the Juvenile Justice System

Separate status offense categories may avoid some of the stigma associated with the delinquency label, but they can have relatively little practical effect on the child's treatment. Youths in either category can be picked up by the police and brought to a police station. They can be petitioned to the same juvenile court, where they have a hearing before the same judge and come under the supervision of the probation department, the court clinic, and the treatment staff. At a hearing, status offenders may see little difference between the treatment they receive and the treatment of the delinquent offenders sitting across the room. Although status offenders are usually not detained or incarcerated with delinquents, they can be transferred to secure facilities if they are repeatedly unruly and considered uncontrollable. Some states are more likely to prosecute status offenses formally in the juvenile court, while others handle most cases informally. Within individual states, some courts make a habit of prosecuting status offenders, and others will divert most cases to treatment institutions.[58]

Efforts have been ongoing to reduce the penalties and stigma borne by status offenders and help kids avoid becoming status offenders. The Policy and Practice box entitled "Keeping Truants in School" illustrates how government agencies are focusing on one type of status offense: school **truancy.**

The federal government's **Office of Juvenile Justice and Delinquency Prevention (OJJDP),** an agency created to identify the needs of youths and fund policy initiatives in the juvenile justice system, made it a top priority to encourage the removal of status offenders from secure lockups, detention centers, and post-disposition treatment facilities that also house delinquent offenders.[59] States in violation of the initiative are ineligible to receive part of the millions in direct grants for local juvenile justice annually awarded by the federal government.[60] This initiative has been responsible for significantly lowering the number of status offenders kept in secure confinement.

Despite this mandate, juvenile court judges in many states can still detain status offenders in secure lockups if the youths are found in "contempt of court." The act that created the OJJDP was amended in 1987 to allow status offenders to be detained and incarcerated for violations of "valid court orders."[61] Children have been detained for such behavior as wearing shorts to court, throwing paper on the floor, and, in one Florida case involving a pregnant teenager, for not keeping a doctor's appointment.[62] Several studies have found that as a result of deinstitutionalization, children who can no longer be detained are being recycled or "relabeled" as delinquent offenders so they can be housed in secure facilities. Even more troubling is the charge that some minors no longer subject to detention as status offenders are being committed involuntarily and inappropriately to in-patient drug treatment facilities and psychiatric hospitals.[63]

Change in the treatment of status offenders reflects the current attitude toward children who violate the law. On the one hand, there appears to be a national movement to severely sanction youths who commit serious, violent offenses. On the other hand, a great effort has been made to remove nonserious cases, such as those involving status offenders, from the official agencies of justice and place these youths in informal, community-based treatment programs.

truancy
Staying out of school without permission.

Office of Juvenile Justice and Delinquency Prevention (OJJDP)
Branch of the U.S. Justice Department charged with shaping national juvenile justice policy through disbursement of federal aid and research funds.

To learn more about the efforts to remove status offenders from secure lockups, go to Gwen A. Holden and Robert A. Kapler, **"Deinstitutionalizing Status Offenders: A Record of Progress"** at www.ncjrs.org/pdffiles/jjjf95.pdf. For an up-to-date list of web links, go to http://cj.wadsworth.com/siegel_jd9e.

Keeping Truants in School

Every day, hundreds of thousands of youth are absent from school; many are absent without an excuse and deemed truant. Some large cities report that unexcused absences can number in the thousands on certain days.

In general, the proportion of truancy cases handled in juvenile court is relatively small. However, the juvenile justice system increasingly serves as the final stop for truants and as a mechanism for intervening with chronic truants. Recent statistics available on the extent of truancy cases in juvenile court clearly demonstrate how important it is for schools and communities to confront this issue. Truancy accounts for 26 percent of all formally handled status offense cases, representing an 85 percent increase in truancy cases in juvenile court since 1989. What causes truancy? Among the factors identified are the following:

I *Family factors.* These include lack of guidance or parental supervision, domestic violence, poverty, drug or alcohol abuse in the home, lack of awareness of attendance laws, and differing attitudes toward education.

I *School factors.* These include school climate issues—such as school size and attitudes of teachers, other students, and administrators —and inflexibility in meeting the diverse cultural and learning styles of the students.

I *Economic influences.* These include employed students, single-parent homes, high mobility rates, parents who hold multiple jobs, and a lack of affordable transportation and childcare.

I *Student variables.* These include drug and alcohol abuse, lack of understanding of attendance laws, lack of social competence, mental health difficulties, and poor physical health.

THE COSTS OF TRUANCY

Truancy places significant social burdens on society. Students with the highest truancy rates have the lowest academic achievement rates and have high dropout rates as well. Truancy can also be linked to juvenile delinquency in several ways. Kids who are chronically truant seem at high risk for future criminality and drug abuse. There is also evidence that high rates of truancy can be linked to high rates of daytime burglary and vandalism. In some jurisdictions, a significant portion of all burglaries and aggravated assaults occurring between 8:00 A.M. and 1:00 P.M. on weekdays are committed by juveniles.

COMBATING TRUANCY

Because of the social cost of truancy, local jurisdictions, with the aid of the federal government, are sponsoring truancy control efforts. A few significant efforts are described below:

1. The State Attorney's Office in Jacksonville, Florida, provides a precourt diversion program for truant youths and their families. The school district refers families to the program when chronic truancy has not been solved by school-based intervention. Following the referral, a hearing is conducted with the parent, youth, school attendance social worker, and volunteer hearing officer. A contract is negotiated that includes plans for reducing truancy and accessing services and community supports. A case manager makes home visits and monitors the family's compliance with the plan. In the fall of 2000, a school-based component was added to address prevention and early intervention at two elementary schools, where an onsite case manager monitors attendance and provides early outreach.

2. The University of Hawaii in Honolulu is building on a previous program to prevent truancy in the Wai'anae area. Attendance officers in two elementary schools work to provide early outreach to young students and their families when absences become chronic. Community resources are used to address the issues that may prevent youths from attending school regularly. In addition, the schools work with the Honolulu police department to provide Saturday truancy workshops for youths with chronic truancy problems and their families.

Reforming Status Offense Laws

For the past two decades, national commissions have called for reform of status offense laws. More than 20 years ago, the National Council on Crime and Delinquency, an influential privately funded think tank, recommended removing status offenders from the juvenile court.[64] In 1976, the federal government's National Advisory Commission on Criminal Justice Standards and Goals, a task force created to develop a national crime policy, opted for the nonjudicial treatment of status offenders: "The only conduct that should warrant family court intervention is conduct that is clearly self-destructive or otherwise harmful to the child." To meet this standard, the commission suggested that the nation's juvenile courts confine themselves to controlling five status offenses: habitual truancy, repeated disregard for parental authority, repeated running away, repeated use of intoxicating beverages, and delinquent acts by youths

3. The Suffolk County Probation Department's (Yaphank, New York) South County Truancy Reduction Program builds on community policing efforts, targeting elementary and middle school students who have illegal absences. A probation officer monitors attendance in collaboration with school personnel, facilitates access to school- and community-based services needed by the student and family to establish regular school attendance, and observes attendance and other school-based indicators to ensure that the student's attendance and engagement at school are improving. A similar model is in existence at the local high school.

4. The mayor's Anti-Gang Office in Houston, Texas, placed an experienced case manager in one high school to identify students with chronic truancy patterns. Through home visits and school-based supports, students and their families are provided with services, support, and resources to address truancy. The program also works with community police officers, who provide a "knock and talk" service for youths and their families when truancy continues to be an issue. The officers assess family functioning and deliver information about the law and truancy outcomes; they also issue the official summons to court for a truancy petition.

5. King County Superior Court in Seattle, Washington, offers families three options after a truancy petition is filed: attending an evening workshop, participating in a community truancy board hearing, or proceeding to court on the charges. The workshop includes education about truancy law and outcomes and facilitates planning between the parent and youth for addressing the cause of truancy. Community truancy boards composed of local community members hear the case, develop a plan for use with the youth and family, and monitor compliance with the stipulated agreement. In the fall of 2000, a school-based component was added to address prevention and early intervention.

6. Children and families attending Philadelphia schools who are subpoenaed by Philadelphia Family Court for non-attendance are required to appear in the Regional Truancy Court. There is a comprehensive individual/family develop-

ment assessment on each client. Home visits occur every two weeks and are designed to strengthen the partnership between provider and family. They also give providers an opportunity to identify the assets and resources available to the individual and family, allow the family to interact in the comfort and familiarity of their own environment, and reduce the potential for artificial barriers and challenges that may occur. Case managers link the family to support systems determined by the family's development plan, ensuring that required services are available and appropriate for the family.

Critical Thinking

Some kids are persistently truant and do not wish to attend school. Should the educational system provide support for these children or simply let them skip classes and then formally drop out once they are of legal age? Is there any purpose to devoting limited resources to kids who simply do not want to learn?

InfoTrac College Edition Research

For some children, school attendance is so distressing that they have difficulty attending school, a problem that often results in prolonged absence and truancy. To find out why this phenomenon occurs, read Neville J. King and Gail A. Bernstein, "School Refusal in Children and Adolescents: A Review of the Past 10 Years," *Journal of the American Academy of Child and Adolescent Psychiatry* 40(2):197 (February 2001).

SOURCES: Myriam Baker, Jane Nady Sigmon, and M. Elaine Nugent, *Truancy Reduction: Keeping Students in School* (Washington, DC: Office of Juvenile Justice and Delinquency Prevention, 2001); Philadelphia Department of Human Services, Court Based Programs, http://dhs.phila.gov/intranet/PGintrahome_pub.nsf/Content/Prevention+-+Court+Based+Programs. (Accessed on August 4, 2004.)

under the age of 10.[65] The American Bar Association's National Juvenile Justice Standards Project, designed to promote significant improvements in the way children are treated by the police and the courts, called for the end of juvenile court jurisdiction over status offenders: "A juvenile's acts of misbehavior, ungovernability, or unruliness which do not violate the criminal law should not constitute a ground for asserting juvenile court jurisdiction over the juvenile committing them."[66]

These calls for reform prompted a number of states, including New York, to experiment with replacing juvenile court jurisdiction over most status offenders with community-based treatment programs.[67] Kentucky, for example, has amended its status offense law to eliminate vague terms and language. Instead of labeling a child who is "beyond control of school" as a status offender, the state is now required to show that a student has repeatedly violated "lawful regulations for the government of the school," with the petition describing the behaviors "and all intervention strategies

Those in favor of retaining the status offense category point to society's responsibility to care for troubled youths. Others maintain that the status offense should remain a legal category so that juvenile courts can force a youth to receive treatment. Although it is recognized that a court appearance can produce a stigma, the taint may be less important than the need for treatment. Many state jurisdictions, prompted by concern over serious delinquency, have enacted laws that actually expand social control over juveniles.

CURFEW LAWS

From the 1880s through the 1920s, American cities created curfew laws designed to limit the presence of children on city streets after dark. Today, about two-thirds of large U.S. cities have curfew laws.

As a general rule, the courts have upheld the use of juvenile curfew laws as long as (1) the language of the statute shows a compelling government interest for use of the curfew and (2) the language of the curfew law is consistent with this narrowly defined interest. Curfew ordinances must also allow youth to be out during curfew hours under certain circumstances (for example, in the company of their parents, coming or going to work or school, and in the event of an emergency).

Evaluations of the benefits of curfews yield mixed results. Andra Bannister and her associates surveyed more than 400 police agencies and found that most had curfew ordinances in effect for several years. In the majority of cases, police felt that curfew was an effective tool to control vandalism, graffiti, night-time burglary, and auto theft. Those jurisdictions that did not have curfew laws reported that their absence was a result of political objections rather than perceived ineffectiveness. In an important analysis of the effectiveness of curfews on gang crime, Eric Fritsch, Troy Caeti, and Robert Taylor found that passage of a curfew law in Dallas, coupled with police use of ag-

Increasing Social Control over Juveniles and their Parents

gressive curfew and truancy enforcement, appeared to reduce violent gang crimes. Though gang crimes did increase somewhat in areas of the city with less aggressive policing, the *displacement effect* was not significant.

Although these findings are persuasive, other research efforts failed to find such dramatic effects. For example, one study conducted by Mike Males and Dan Macallair, which focused on curfew laws in California, found that youth curfews do not reduce youth crime and if anything may actually increase delinquent activities For the entire state of California there was no category of crime (misdemeanors, violent crime, property crime, etc.) that significantly declined in association with youth curfews. In a comprehensive systematic review of the existing literature on curfews, criminologist Ken Adams found little evidence that juvenile crime and victimization were influenced in any way by the implementation of curfew laws.

These results indicate that juvenile curfews are not the panacea some people believe. It is possible that after curfews are implemented, victimization levels increased significantly during non-curfew hours, an indication that rather than suppressing delinquency, curfews merely shift the time of occurrence of the offenses.

PARENTAL RESPONSIBILITY LAWS

Since the early twentieth century, there have been laws aimed at disciplining parents for contributing to the delinquency of a minor. The first of these was enacted in Colorado in 1903, and today 42 states and the District of Columbia maintain similar laws. Such laws allow parents to be sanctioned in juvenile courts for behaviors associated with their child's misbehavior. Some states (Florida, Idaho, Virginia) require parents to reim-

attempted by the school."[68] A few states, such as Maine, Delaware, Idaho, and Washington, have attempted to eliminate status offense laws and treat these youths as neglected or dependent children, giving child protective services the primary responsibility for their care. However, juvenile court judges strongly resist removal of status jurisdiction. They believe that reducing their authority over children leads to limiting juvenile court jurisdiction to only the most hard-core juvenile offenders and interferes with their ability to help youths before they commit serious antisocial acts.[69] Their concerns are fueled by research that shows that many status offenders, especially runaways living on the street, have serious emotional problems and engage in self-destructive behaviors ranging from substance abuse to self-mutilation.[70]

Legislative changes may be cosmetic because when efforts to remedy the child's problems through a social welfare approach fail, the case may be referred to the juvenile court for more formal processing.[71]

Those who favor removing status offenders from juvenile court authority charge that their experience with the legal system further stigmatizes these already troubled youths, exposes them to the influence of "true" delinquents, and enmeshes them in a system that cannot really afford to help them.[72] Reformer Ira Schwartz, for one, argues that status offenders "should be removed from the jurisdiction of the courts alto-

burse the government for the costs of detention or care of their children. Others (Maryland, Missouri, Oklahoma) demand that parents make restitution payments, such as paying for damage caused by their children who vandalized a school. All states except New Hampshire have incorporated parental liability laws within their statutes, though most recent legislation places limits on recovery somewhere between $250 (Vermont) and $15,000 (Texas); the average is $2,500. Other states (Colorado, Texas, Louisiana) require parents as well as children to participate in counseling and community service activities.

Parents may also be held civilly liable, under the concept of vicarious liability, for the damages caused by a child. In some states, parents are responsible for up to $300,000 in damages; in others the liability cap is $3,500 (sometimes home-owner's insurance covers at least some of the liability). Parents can also be charged with civil negligence if they should have known of the damage a child was about to inflict but did nothing to stop the child—for example, when they give a weapon to an emotionally unstable youth. Juries have levied awards of up to $500,000 in such cases.

An extreme form of discipline for parents makes them criminally liable for the illegal acts of their children. Since 1990 there have been more than 18 cases in which parents have been ordered to serve time in jail because their children have been truant from school. Civil libertarians charge that these laws violate the constitutional right to due process and seem to be used only against lower-class parents. They find little evidence that punishing parents can deter delinquency. State laws of this kind have been successfully challenged in the lower courts.

Critical Thinking

1. Is it fair to punish parents for the misdeeds of their children? What happens if parents tried to control their teenager and failed? Should they be held liable?

2. Why should all youths be forced to meet a curfew simply because a few are rowdy and get in trouble with the law? Is it fair to punish the innocent for the acts of the guilty?

InfoTrac College Edition Research

To learn more about the legal and social effects of curfews, use "curfews" as a keyword on InfoTrac College Edition.

SOURCES: Kenneth Adams, "The Effectiveness of Juvenile Curfews at Crime Prevention," *The Annals of the American Academy of Political and Social Science* 587:136–159 (May 2003); Mike Males and Dan Macallair, *The Impact of Juvenile Curfew Laws in California* (San Francisco: Justice Policy Institute, 1998); Jerry Tyler, Thomas Segady, and Stephen Austin, "Parental Liability Laws: Rationale, Theory, and Effectiveness," *Social Science Journal* 37:79–97 (2000); Andra Bannister, David Carter, and Joseph Schafer, "A National Police Survey on the Use of Juvenile Curfews," *Journal of Criminal Justice* 29:233–240 (2001); Mike Reynolds, Ruth Seydlitz, and Pamela Jenkins, "Do Juvenile Curfew Laws Work? A Time-Series Analysis of the New Orleans Law," *Justice Quarterly* (2000); Mike Males and Dan Macallair, "An Analysis of Curfew Enforcement and Juvenile Crime in California," *Western Criminology Review* (September 1999); Joannie M. Schrof, "Who's Guilty?" *U.S. News & World Report* 126:60 (May 17, 1999); William Ruefle and Kenneth Mike Reynolds, "Curfews and Delinquency in Major American Cities," *Crime and Delinquency* 41:347–363 (1995); *Juvenile Justice Reform Initiatives in the States* (Washington, DC: Office of Juvenile Justice and Delinquency Prevention, 1997); Gilbert Geis and Arnold Binder, "Sins of Their Children: Parental Responsibility for Juvenile Delinquency," *Notre Dame Journal of Law, Ethics, and Public Policy* 5:303–322 (1991); David McDowall and Colin Loftin, "The Impact of Youth Curfew Laws on Juvenile Crime Rates," *Crime and Delinquency* 46:76–92 (2000); Eric Fritsch, Tory Caeti, and Robert Taylor, "Gang suppression through saturation patrol, aggressive curfew, and truancy enforcement: A quasi-experimental test of the Dallas anti-gang initiative," *Crime and Delinquency* 45:122–139 (1999).

gether."[73] Schwartz maintains that status offenders would best be served not by juvenile courts but by dispute resolution and mediation programs designed to strengthen family ties, as "status offense cases are often rooted in family problems."[74]

Increasing Social Control

Those in favor of retaining the status offense category point to society's responsibility to care for troubled youths. Some have suggested that the failure of the courts to extend social control over wayward youths neglects the rights of concerned parents who are not able to care for and correct their children.[75] Others maintain that the status offense should remain a legal category so that juvenile courts can "force" a youth into receiving treatment.[76] Although it is recognized that a court appearance can produce negative stigma, the taint may be less important than the need for treatment.[77] Many state jurisdictions, prompted by concern over serious delinquency, have enacted laws that actually expand social control over juveniles.[78] The Policy and Practice box entitled "Increasing Social Control over Juveniles and their Parents" discusses this issue in greater detail.

Do **curfew laws** work in reducing the rate of youth crime? To find out, visit the following site at the Center for Juvenile and Criminal Justice: www.cjcj.org/pubs/curfew/curfew.html. For an up-to-date list of web links, go to http://cj.wadsworth.com/siegel_jd9e.

Research shows that a majority of youth routinely engage in some form of status offenses and that those who refrain form an atypical minority.[79] "Illegal" acts such as teen sex and substance abuse have become normative and commonplace. It makes little sense to have the juvenile court intervene with kids who are caught in what has become routine teenage behavior. In contrast, juvenile court jurisdiction over status offenders may be defended if in fact the youths' offending patterns are similar to those of delinquents. Is their current offense only the tip of an antisocial iceberg, or are they actually noncriminal youths who need only the loving hand of a substitute parent-figure interested in their welfare? Some find that status offenders are quite different from delinquents, but others note that many status offenders also had prior arrests for delinquent acts and that many delinquents exhibited behaviors that would define them as status offenders.[80]

These disparate findings may be explained in part by the fact that there may be different types of status offenders, some similar to delinquents and others who are quite different.[81] It might be more realistic to divide status offenders into three groups: first-time status offenders, chronic status offenders, and those with both a delinquent record and a status offense record.[82] The fact that many young offenders have mixed delinquent–status offender records indicates that these legal categories are not entirely independent. It is also recognized that some "pure" first-time status offenders are quite different from delinquents and that a juvenile court experience can be harmful to them and escalate the frequency and seriousness of their law-violating behaviors.[83]

The removal of these status offenders from the juvenile court is an issue that continues to be debated. The predominant view today is that many status offenders and delinquents share similar social and developmental problems and that consequently both categories should fall under the jurisdiction of the juvenile court. Not surprisingly, research does show that the legal processing of delinquents and status offenders remains quite similar.[84]

Summary

- The study of delinquency is concerned with the nature and extent of the antisocial behavior of youths, the causes of youthful law violations, the legal rights of juveniles, and prevention and treatment.

- The problems of American youths have become an important subject of academic study. Many children live in poverty, have inadequate health care, and suffer family problems.

- Adolescence is a time of taking risks, which can get kids into trouble.

- Our modern concept of a separate social status for children differs significantly from the past.

- In earlier times relationships between children and parents were remote. Punishment was severe, and children were expected to take on adult roles early in their lives.

- With the start of the seventeenth century came greater recognition of the needs of children. In Great Britain, the chancery court movement, the Poor Laws, and apprenticeship programs helped reinforce the idea of children as a distinct social group. In colonial America, many of the characteristics of English family living were adopted.

- In the nineteenth century, delinquent and runaway children were treated no differently from criminal defendants.

- During this time, however, increased support for the concept of *parens patriae* resulted in steps to reduce the responsibility of children under the criminal law.

- The concept of delinquency was developed in the early twentieth century. Before that time, criminal youths and adults were treated in almost the same fashion. A group of reformers, referred to as child savers, helped create a separate delinquency category to insulate juvenile offenders from the influence of adult criminals.

- The status of juvenile delinquency is still based on the *parens patriae* philosophy, which holds that children have the right to care and custody and that if parents are not capable of providing that care the state must step in to take control.

- Delinquents are given greater legal protection than adult criminals and are shielded from stigma and labels.

- More serious juvenile cases may be transferred or waived to the adult court. Juvenile courts also have jurisdiction over noncriminal status offenders, whose offenses (truancy, running away, sexual misconduct) are illegal only because of their minority status.

I Some experts have called for an end to juvenile court control over status offenders, charging that it further stigmatizes already troubled youths. Some research indicates that status offenders are harmed by juvenile court processing. Other research indicates that status offenders and delinquents are quite similar.

I There has been a successful effort to separate status offenders from delinquents and maintain separate facilities for those who need to be placed in a shelter care program.

I Ongoing efforts have been made to exert greater control over youthful misbehavior. Curfew laws and parental responsibility laws are examples of this type of social control. Their success seems problematic.

I The treatment of juveniles is an ongoing dilemma. Still uncertain is whether young law violators respond better to harsh punishments or to benevolent treatment.

Key Terms

ego identity, p. 4
role diffusion, p. 4
at-risk youth, p. 5
juvenile delinquency, p. 10
chronic delinquent offenders, p. 10
aging-out process, p. 11
persistence, p. 11
juvenile justice system, p. 11

paternalistic family, p. 12
primogeniture, p. 13
swaddling, p. 14
Poor Laws, p. 15
chancery courts, p. 16
parens patriae, p. 16
child savers, p. 18
best interests of the child, p. 18

waiver, p. 19
status offenses, p. 20
wayward minors, p. 22
truancy, p. 23
Office of Juvenile Justice and
  Delinquency Prevention (OJJDP),
  p. 23

Questions for Discussion

1. Is it fair to have a separate legal category for youths? Considering how dangerous young people can be, does it make more sense to group offenders on the basis of what they have done and not their age?

2. At what age are juveniles truly capable of understanding the seriousness of their actions?

3. Is it fair to institutionalize a minor simply for being truant or running away from home? Should the jurisdiction of status offenders be removed from juvenile

court and placed with the state department of social services or some other welfare organization?

4. Should delinquency proceedings be secretive? Does the public have the right to know who juvenile criminals are?

5. Can a "get tough" policy help control juvenile misbehavior, or should *parens patriae* remain the standard?

6. Should juveniles who commit felonies such as rape or robbery be treated as adults?

Viewpoint

As the governor of a large southern state, you have been asked to grant a pardon to a young man by his family and friends. Nathaniel B. was convicted of second-degree murder in 1995 and received a sentence of 28 years in the state penal system. Tried as an adult, he was found guilty of murder for intentionally killing Mr. Barry G., his English teacher, because he was angry over receiving a failing grade and being suspended for throwing water balloons. During trial, Nathaniel's attorney claimed that the gun Nathaniel brought to school had gone off accidentally after he pointed it at Mr. G. in an attempt to force him to let him talk to two girls in the classroom.

"As he's holding the gun up, he's overwhelmed with tears," Nathaniel's lawyer told the jury. "His hand begins to shake, and the gun discharges. The gun discharged in

the hands of an inexperienced 13-year-old with a junk gun." The prosecutor countered that Nathaniel's act was premeditated. He was frustrated because he was receiving an F in the class, and he was angry because he was being barred from talking to the girls. His victim "had no idea of the rage, hate, the anger, the frustration" filling the young man. There was also damaging information from police, who reported that Nathaniel told a classmate he was going to return to school and shoot the teacher; he said he'd be "all over the news."

At his sentencing hearing, Nathaniel read a statement: "Words cannot really explain how sorry I am, but they're all I have." His mother, Polly, blamed herself for her son's actions, claiming that he was surrounded by domestic abuse and alcoholism at home.

Now that he has served seven years in prison, Nathaniel's case has come to your attention. As governor, you recognize that his conviction and punishment raise a number of important issues. His mother claims that his actions were a product of abuse and violence in the home. You have read research showing that many habitually aggressive children have been raised in homes in which they are physically brutalized by their parents; this violence then persists into adulthood.[85] Even though he was only 13 at the time of the crime, he has been sentenced to more than 20 years in an adult prison.

▌ Should children who are subject to brutal treatment, such as Nathaniel, be punished again by the justice system?

▌ Should Nathaniel be held personally responsible for actions that may in fact have been caused by a home life beyond his control?

▌ Even though he was only 13 years old when he committed his crime, Nathaniel's case was heard in an adult court, and he received a long sentence to an adult prison. Should minor children who commit serious crimes, as Nathaniel did, be treated as an adult, or should they be tried within an independent juvenile justice system oriented to treatment and rehabilitation?

▌ Would you pardon Nathaniel now that he has served more than seven years in prison?

Doing Research on the Web

Before you make your decision in Nathaniel's case, you might want to look at the following websites:

Bibliography of Children's Rights, at University of North Carolina (accessed on July 26, 2004):

http://library.law.unc.edu/research/research_guides/ bibliography_childrens_rights.html.

The Coalition for Juvenile Justice (CJJ) has championed children and promoted community safety. The coalition's website provides information on judicial waiver (accessed on July 26, 2004):

www.juvjustice.org/resources/waiver.html.

Notes

1. Robin Malinosky-Rummell and David Hansen, "Long-Term Consequences of Childhood Physical Abuse," *Psychological Bulletin* 114:68–79 (1993).
2. Nanette Davis, *Youth Crisis: Growing Up in the High-Risk Society* (New York: Praeger, Greenwood Publishing, 1998).
3. Susan Crimmins and Michael Foley, "The Threshold of Violence in Urban Adolescents." Paper presented at the annual meeting of the American Society of Criminology, Reno, Nevada, November 1989.
4. Erik Erikson, *Childhood and Society* (New York: W. H. Norton, 1963).
5. Roger Gould, "Adult Life Stages: Growth toward Self-Tolerance," *Psychology Today* 8:74–78 (1975).
6. U.S. Bureau of the Census, *Population Estimates and Projections* (Washington, DC: U.S. Census Bureau, 2004).
7. Children's Defense Fund, "Key Facts About Children and Families in Crisis," www.childrensdefense.org/data/keyfacts_families.asp. (Accessed on July 26, 2004.)
8. U.S. Bureau of the Census, *Poverty in the United States, 2000* (Washington, DC: U.S. Census Bureau, 2004).
9. Interagency Forum on Child and Family Statistics, "America's Children: Key National Indicators of Well-Being, 2003."
10. Children's Defense Fund press release, "Children's Defense Fund Analysis Shows Percentage of Uninsured Children Varies by State," October 24, 2003, www.childrensdefense.org/pressreleases/2003/031024.asp. (Accessed on July 26, 2004.)
11. Interagency Forum on Child and Family Statistics, "America's Children."
12. David Eggebeen and Daniel Lichter, "Race, Family Structure, and Changing Poverty among American Children," *American Sociological Review* 56:801–817 (1991).
13. Gary Evans, Nancy Wells, and Annie Moch, "Housing and Mental Health: A Review of the Evidence and a Methodological and Conceptual Critique," *Journal of Social Issues*, 59:475–501 (2003).
14. Interagency Forum on Child and Family Statistics, "America's Children."
15. National Center for Education Statistics, "Poverty and Student Mathematics Achievement," 2003, http://nces.ed.gov/programs/coe/2003/section2/indicator12.asp. (Accessed on July 26, 2004.)
16. National Center for Education Statistics, *Fast Facts* (Washington, DC: U.S. Department of Education, 2001).
17. National Center for Education Statistics, "Public High School Dropouts and Completers from the Common Core of Data," http://nces.ed.gov/pubs2004/dropout00-01/#6. (Accessed on July 26, 2004.)
18. Howard N. Snyder and Monica H. Swahn, *Juvenile Suicides, 1981–1998* (Washington, DC: Office of Juvenile Justice and Delinquency Prevention, 2004).
19. Centers for Disease Control news release, "New CDC Report Shows Teen Birth Rate Hits Record Low: U.S. Births Top 4 Million in 2000" (Atlanta: Centers for Disease Control, July 24, 2001).
20. J.A. Martin, B.E. Hamilton, P.D. Sutton, S. J. Ventura, F. Mnacker, and M.L. Munson, "Births: Final Data for 2002," *National Vital Statistics Reports*, 52:10 (2003), www.cdc.gov/nchs/data/nvsr52/nvsr52_10.pdf. (Accessed on July 26, 2004.)
21. National Education Goals Panel, *The National Education Goals Report, Building a Nation of Learners* (Washington, DC: U.S. Government Printing Office, 1997), pp.111–124.
22. Kenneth Kochanek and Joyce Martin, *Supplemental Analyses of Recent Trends in Infant Mortality* (Washington, D.C.: National Center for Health Statistics, 2004), www.cdc.gov/nchs/products/pubs/pubd/hestats/infantmort/infantmort.htm. (Accessed on July 26, 2004.)
23. Bureau of the Census, *Educational Attainment in the United States, 2003* (Washington, DC: Bureau of the Census, 2004).
24. Federal Bureau of Investigation, *Crime in the United States, 2002* (Washington, DC: Government Printing Office, 2003), p. 228.
25. John Whitehead and Steven Lab, "A Meta-Analysis of Juvenile Correctional Treatment," *Journal of Research in Crime and Delinquency* 26:276–295 (1989).

26. See Lawrence Stone, *The Family, Sex, and Marriage in England: 1500–1800* (New York: Harper & Row, 1977).

27. This section relies on Jackson Spielvogel, *Western Civilization* (St. Paul: West, 1991), pp. 279–86.

28. Philippe Aries, *Centuries of Childhood: A Social History of Family Life* (New York: Knopf, 1962).

29. Nicholas Orme, *Medieval Children* (New Haven: Yale University Press, 2003).

30. Aries, *Centuries of Childhood.*

31. See Douglas R. Rendleman, "Parens Patriae: From Chancery to the Juvenile Court," *South Carolina Law Review* 23:205 (1971).

32. See Stone, *The Family, Sex, and Marriage in England,* and Lawrence Stone, ed., *Schooling and Society: Studies in the History of Education* (Baltimore: Johns Hopkins University Press, 1970).

33. Ibid.

34. See Wiley B. Sanders, "Some Early Beginnings of the Children's Court Movement in England," *National Probation Association Yearbook* (New York: National Council on Crime and Delinquency, 1945).

35. Douglas Besharov, *Juvenile Justice Advocacy—Practice in a Unique Court* (New York: Practicing Law Institute, 1974), p. 2.

36. Rendleman, "Parens Patriae," p. 209.

37. See Anthony Platt, "The Rise of the Child Saving Movement: A Study in Social Policy and Correctional Reform," *Annals of the American Academy of Political and Social Science* 381:21–38 (1969).

38. Robert H. Bremner, ed., and John Barnard, Tamara K. Hareven, and Robert M. Mennel, asst. eds., *Children and Youth in America* (Cambridge: Harvard University Press, 1970), p. 64.

39. Elizabeth Pleck, "Criminal Approaches to Family Violence, 1640–1980," in Lloyd Ohlin and Michael Tonry, eds., *Family Violence* (Chicago: University of Chicago Press, 1989), pp. 19–58.

40. Ibid.

41. John R. Sutton, *Stubborn Children: Controlling Delinquency in the United States, 1640–1981* (Berkeley: University of California Press, 1988).

42. Pleck, "Criminal Approaches to Family Violence," p. 29.

43. John Demos, *Past, Present and Personal* (New York: Oxford University Press, 1986), pp. 80–88.

44. Elizabeth Pleck, *Domestic Tyranny: The Making of Social Policy against Family Violence from Colonial Times to the Present* (New York: Oxford University Press, 1987), pp. 28–30.

45. Graeme Newman, *The Punishment Response* (Philadelphia: J. B. Lippincott, 1978), pp. 53–79; Aries, *Centuries of Childhood.* The history of childhood juvenile justice is discussed in detail in Chapter 13.

46. Stephen J. Morse, "Immaturity and Irresponsibility," *Journal of Criminal Law and Criminology* 88:15–67 (1997).

47. Shay Bilchik "Sentencing Juveniles to Adult Facilities Fails Youths and Society," *Corrections Today* 65:21 (2003).

48. M. Wakefield and G. Giovino, "Teen Penalties for Tobacco Possession, Use, and Purchase: Evidence and Issues," *Tobacco Control,* 12:6–13 (2003).

49. Federal Bureau of Investigation, *Crime in the United States, 1999* (Washington, DC: U.S. Government Printing Office, 2000), p. 222.

50. See David Rothman, *The Discovery of the Asylum* (Boston: Little, Brown, 1971).

51. Quote from Jerry Tyler, Thomas Segady, and Stephen Austin, "Parental Liability Laws: Rationale, Theory, and Effectiveness" *Social Science Journal,* 37:79–97 (2000).

52. Reports of the Chicago Bar Association Committee, 1899, cited in Anthony Platt, *The Child Savers* (Chicago: University of Chicago Press, 1969), p. 119.

53. L. Kris Gowen, S. Shirley Feldman, Rafael Diaz, and Donnovan Somera Yisrael, "A Comparison of the Sexual Behaviors and Attitudes of Adolescent Girls with Older vs. Similar-Aged Boyfriends," *Journal of Youth and Adolescence,* 33:167–176 (2004).

54. John L. Hutzler, *Juvenile Court Jurisdiction over Children's Conduct: 1982 Comparative Analysis of Juvenile and Family Codes and National Standards* (Pittsburgh: National Center for Juvenile Justice, 1982), p. 2.

55. Ibid.

56. Susan Datesman and Mikel Aickin, "Offense Specialization and Escalation among Status Offenders," *Journal of Criminal Law and Criminology* 75:1246–1275 (1985).

57. Ibid.

58. David J. Steinharthe, *Status Offenses: The Future of Children* 6(3) (The David and Lucile Packard Foundation, Winter 1996).

59. See Solomon Kobrin and Malcolm Klein, *National Evaluation of the Deinstitutionalization of Status Offender Programs—Executive Summary* (Los Angeles: Social Science Research Institute, University of Southern California, 1982).

60. OJJDP Annual Report 2000 (June 2001).

61. 42 U.S.C.A. 5601–5751 (1983 and Supp. 1987).

62. Claudia Wright, "Contempt No Excuse for Locking Up Status Offenders, Says Florida Supreme Court," *Youth Law News* 13:1–3 (1992).

63. Steinharthe, *Status Offenses,* p. 5.

64. National Council on Crime and Delinquency, "Juvenile Curfews—A Policy Statement," *Crime and Delinquency* 18:132–133 (1972).

65. National Advisory Commission on Criminal Justice Standards and Goals, *Juvenile Justice and Delinquency Prevention* (Washington, DC: Government Printing Office, 1977), p. 311.

66. American Bar Association Joint Commission on Juvenile Justice Standards, *Summary and Analysis* (Cambridge: Ballinger, 1977), sect. 1.1.

67. Martin Rouse, "The Diversion of Status Offenders, Criminalization, and the New York Family Court," rev. version. Paper presented at the American Society of Criminology, Reno, NV, November 1989), p. 12.

68. Gail Robinson and Tim Arnold, "Changes in Laws Impacting Juveniles—An Overview," *The Advocate* 22:4, 14–15 (2000), http://dpa.state.ky.us/library/advocate/july00/Juvenile.htm. (Accessed on July 26, 2004.)

69. Barry Feld, "Criminalizing the American Juvenile Court," in Michael Tonry, ed., *Crime and Justice, A Review of Research* (Chicago: University of Chicago Press, 1993), p. 232.

70. Kimberly Tyler et al., "Self-Mutilation and Homeless Youth: The Role of Family Abuse, Street Experiences, and Mental Disorders," *Journal of Research on Adolescence,* 13:457–474 (2003).

71. Marc Miller, "Changing Legal Paradigms in Juvenile Justice," in Peter Greenwood, ed., *The Juvenile Rehabilitation Reader* (Santa Monica, CA: Rand Corporation, 1985) p. 44.

72. Thomas Kelley, "Status Offenders Can Be Different: A Comparative Study of Delinquent Careers," *Crime and Delinquency* 29:365–380 (1983).

73. Ira Schwartz, *(In)justice for Juveniles: Rethinking the Best Interests of the Child* (Lexington, MA: Lexington Books, 1989), p. 171.

74. Ibid.

75. Lawrence Martin and Phyllis Snyder, "Jurisdiction over Status Offenses Should Not Be Removed from the Juvenile Court," *Crime and Delinquency* 22:44–47 (1976).

76. Lindsay Arthur, "Status Offenders Need a Court of Last Resort," *Boston University Law Review* 57:631–644 (1977).

77. Martin and Snyder, "Jurisdiction over Status Offenses Should Not Be Removed from the Juvenile Court," p. 47.

78. David McDowall and Colin Loftin, "The Impact of Youth Curfew Laws on Juvenile Crime Rates," *Crime and Delinquency* 46:76–92 (2000).

79. Carolyn Smith, "Factors Associated with Early Sexual Activity among Urban Adolescents," *Social Work* 42:334–346 (1997).

80. Charles Thomas, "Are Status Offenders Really So Different?" *Crime and Delinquency* 22:438–455 (1976); Howard Snyder, *Court Careers of Juvenile Offenders* (Washington, DC: Office of Juvenile Justice and Delinquency Prevention, 1988), p. 65.

81. Randall Shelden, John Horvath, and Sharon Tracy, "Do Status Offenders Get Worse? Some Clarifications on the Question of Escalation," *Crime and Delinquency* 35:202–216 (1989).

82. Solomon Kobrin, Frank Hellum, and John Peterson, "Offense Patterns of Status Offenders," in D. Shichor and D. Kelly, eds., *Critical Issues in Juvenile Delinquency* (Lexington, MA: Lexington Books, 1980), pp. 203–35.

83. Schwartz, *(In)justice for Juveniles,* pp. 378–79.

84. Chris Marshall, Ineke Marshall, and Charles Thomas, "The Implementation of Formal Procedures in Juvenile Court Processing of Status Offenders," *Journal of Criminal Justice* 11:195–211 (1983).

85. For a thorough review, see Malinosky-Rummell and Hansen, "Long-Term Consequences of Childhood Physical Abuse."

2 The Nature and Extent of Delinquency

Chapter Outline

Official Statistics

Crime Trends in the United States

Measuring Official Delinquency

What the Future Holds

Are the UCR Data Valid?

FOCUS ON DELINQUENCY: Factors Affecting Juvenile
Crime Rates

Self-Reported Delinquency

Self-Report Data

Correlates of Delinquency

Gender and Delinquency

Racial Patterns in Delinquency

Social Class and Delinquency

Age and Delinquency

Chronic Offending: Careers in Delinquency

Landmark Study: *Delinquency in a Birth Cohort*

Who Becomes a Chronic Delinquent?

Stability in Crime: From Delinquent to Criminal

Policy Implications

Juvenile Victimization

Victimization in the United States

Victim/Offender Association

Victimization Risk

FOCUS ON DELINQUENCY: Adolescent Victims of Violence

FOCUS ON DELINQUENCY: Delinquent and Victim:
One and the Same?

The Youngest Victims

Chapter Objectives

1. Know what is meant by the term "official delinquency"
2. Understand how the FBI's *Uniform Crime Report* (UCR) is collected
3. Be familiar with the recent trends in juvenile delinquency
4. Understand how self-report data are collected and what they say about juvenile crime
5. Recognize the factors that affect the juvenile crime rate
6. Be aware of the gender patterns in delinquency
7. Appreciate the factors that cause racial differences in delinquency
8. Be able to debate the issue of class position and delinquency
9. Be aware of the debate over the role age plays in delinquency
10. Understand the concept of the chronic persistent offender
11. Be familiar with the relationship between childhood and victimization

CNN. View the CNN video clip of this story and answer related Critical Thinking questions on your Juvenile Delinquency 9e CD-ROM.

In late August 2003, varsity and junior varsity football players from W. C. Mepham High School in Bellmore, New York, went to a four-day training camp in Pennsylvania. While there, three varsity players aged 16 to 17 began hazing several junior varsity players aged 13 to 14. The hazing soon began to resemble a bizarre sexual ritual. The younger boys were sodomized with a broomstick, pine cones, and golf balls. When one of the boys told his parents what had happened, they complained to school authorities. The parents were told it was their responsibility to call the police. It was not, they found out, school policy to notify authorities about incidents that happen off campus. The press soon got hold of the story and it made headlines around the nation. The Bellmore-Merrick school board decided to cancel all of Mepham High School's football games. Later, the district charged the senior boys with offenses, including involuntary deviate sexual intercourse, kidnapping, aggravated assault, unlawful restraint, and false imprisonment. On November 13, 2003, a Pennsylvania juvenile court judge granted defense counsels request to try the case in juvenile court rather than transfer it to an adult court, which would dispense punishment rather than treatment. One of the teens was ordered to spend time in a detention center, another was sent to a military-style boot camp, and the third received probation. All three were barred from returning to school once their sentence was completed; they were to be home schooled for the remainder of their high school careers.

The Mepham hazing incident is but one of millions of serious illegal acts committed by young people each year. Just how common *are* serious acts of juvenile delinquency? Who commits delinquent acts, and where are these acts most likely to occur? Is the juvenile crime rate increasing or decreasing? Are juveniles more likely than adults to become the victims of crime? To understand the causes of delinquent behavior and to devise effective means to reduce their occurrence, we must seek answers to these questions.

Delinquency experts have devised a variety of methods to measure the nature and extent of delinquency (see Exhibit 2.1). We begin with a description of the most widely used sources of data on crime and delinquency. We also examine the information these resources furnish on juvenile crime rates and trends. These data sources will then be used to provide information on the characteristics of adolescent law violators.

EXHIBIT **2.1**

Sources of Delinquency Data

Official Data	Official data are based on the criminal incidents reported to the nation's police departments. This information is collected and disseminated on an annual basis by the Federal Bureau of Investigation (FBI) in their Uniform Crime Report (UCR) program. The UCR records both the total number of crimes reported to the police for major offense categories such as murder and rape, and the total number of arrests made for *any crime* that is cleared or solved. Because the age of arrestees is recorded, official data can be used to study trends and patterns in the delinquency rate. Youths with an arrest record are referred to as "official delinquents." Their actions are considered recorded or **official delinquency,** and their behavior becomes part of the "official statistics."
Self-Report Data	Self-report data are obtained from anonymous surveys or interviews, often conducted in schools, which query adolescents about their participation in illegal acts such as drug abuse and vandalism. Self-report data are aimed at assessing criminal acts that have gone undetected by the police either because victims fail to report crime or because the crime is victimless, for example, drug abuse. They measure the extent of unrecorded juvenile delinquency, the so-called **dark figures of crime.** These data can also be used to compare the personal characteristics, such as race and gender, of official delinquents with those youths whose criminal activity remains undetected.
Victim Data	Victim surveys ask those who have experienced crime firsthand to tell about the episode. Victim data include crimes reported to the police as well as crimes that the victim failed to report. They provide important information on where victimization takes place, the likelihood of victimization, and the kinds of personal behaviors and lifestyles that increase the chances of becoming a crime victim. The most widely used of these is the federally sponsored National Crime Victimization Survey (NCVS), an annual survey of thousands of citizens selected in communities across the nation.

OFFICIAL STATISTICS

official delinquency
Delinquent acts that result in arrest by local police. These are included in the FBI's arrest data.

dark figures of crime
Incidents of crime and delinquency that go undetected by police.

Federal Bureau of Investigation (FBI)
Arm of the U.S. Department of Justice that investigates violations of federal law, gathers crime statistics, runs a comprehensive crime laboratory, and helps train local law enforcement officers.

Uniform Crime Report (UCR)
Compiled by the FBI, the UCR is the most widely used source of national crime and delinquency statistics.

Part I offenses (also known as index crimes)
Offenses including homicide and non-negligent manslaughter, forcible rape, robbery, aggravated assault, burglary, larceny, arson, and motor vehicle theft; recorded by local law enforcement officers, these crimes are tallied quarterly and sent to the FBI for inclusion in the UCR.

Part II offenses
All crimes other than Part I offenses; recorded by local law enforcement officers, arrests for these crimes are tallied quarterly and sent to the FBI for inclusion in the UCR.

Each year the U.S. Justice Department's **Federal Bureau of Investigation (FBI)** compiles information gathered by police departments on the number of criminal acts reported by citizens and the number of persons arrested. This information is published in the *Uniform Crime Report* **(UCR),** the most widely used source of national crime and delinquency statistics.

The UCR is compiled from statistics sent to the FBI from more than 16,000 police departments. It groups offenses into two categories. **Part I offenses,** also known as **index crimes,** include homicide and non-negligent manslaughter, forcible rape, robbery, aggravated assault, burglary, larceny, arson, and motor vehicle theft. Police record every reported incident of these offenses and report them on a quarterly basis to the FBI. Data are broken down by city, county, metropolitan area, and geographical divisions. In addition, the UCR provides information on individuals who have been arrested for these and all other criminal offenses, including vandalism, liquor law violations, and drug trafficking. These are known as **Part II offenses.** The arrest data are presented by age, sex, and race.

The UCR uses three methods to express crime data. First, the number of crimes reported to the police and arrests made are expressed as raw figures (for example, more than 16,500 murders occurred in 2003). Second, crime rates per 100,000 people are computed. That is, when the UCR indicates that the murder rate was 5.7 in 2003, it means that about 6 people in every 100,000 were murdered between January 1 and December 31 of 2003. Third, the FBI computes changes in the number and rate of crimes over time. For example, murder rates declined 6.3 percent between 1999 and 2003.

Crime Trends in the United States

The U.S. crime rate skyrocketed between 1960, when 3.3 million crimes were reported to police agencies, and 1981, when more than 13 million crimes were recorded. The crime rate began to decline in the 1990s. In 2003 about 11.7 million crimes were reported to the police, a small drop from the year before. Nonetheless, though the rate of decline may be stabilizing, the number of reported crimes has declined by about

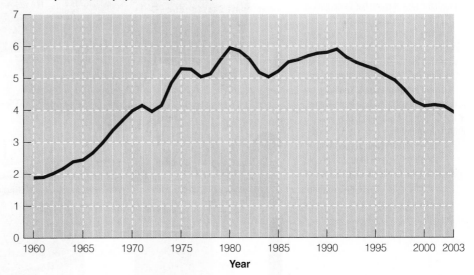

Crime rate per 100,000 population (in 1000s)

3 million from the 1991 peak (see Figure 2.1).[1] The decade-long crime drop has been encouraging. However, although the number and rate of crime has undergone a dramatic decline, millions of serious criminal incidents still occur each year.

Measuring Official Delinquency

Because the UCR arrest statistics are **disaggregated** (broken down) by age of suspects, they can be used to estimate adolescent crime. Juvenile arrest data must be interpreted with caution, however. First, the number of teenagers arrested does not represent the actual number of youths who have committed delinquent acts. Some offenders are never counted because they are never caught. Others are counted more than once because multiple arrests of the same individual for different crimes are counted separately in the UCR. Consequently, the total number of arrests does not equal the number of people who have been arrested. Put another way, if 2 million arrests of youths under 18 years of age were made in a given year, we could not be sure if 2 million individuals had been arrested once or if 500,000 chronic offenders had been arrested four times each. In addition, when an arrested offender commits multiple crimes, only the most serious one is recorded. Therefore, if 2 million juveniles are arrested, the number of crimes committed is at least 2 million, but it may be much higher.

Despite these limitations, the nature of arrest data remains constant over time. Consequently, arrest data can provide some indication of the nature and trends in juvenile crime. What does the UCR tell us about delinquency?

disaggregated
Analyzing the relationship between two or more independent variables (such as murder convictions and death sentence) while controlling for the influence of a dependent variable (such as race).

To get the **UCR online,** as well as to access other important information, go to www.fbi.gov. For an up-to-date list of web links, go to http://cj.wadsworth.com/siegel_jd9e.

Official Delinquency In 2003 (the latest data available), 13.6 million arrests were made, or about 4,700 per 100,000 population. Of these, about 2.2 million were for serious Part I crimes and 11.4 million for less serious Part II crimes. Juveniles under 18, who make up about 26 percent of the population, were responsible for about 22 percent of all arrests for index crimes, including 16 percent of the violent crime arrests and 29 percent of the property crime arrests (see Table 2.1).

About 1.2 million juvenile arrests were made in 2003 for Part II offenses. Included in this total were 87,000 arrests for running away from home, 137,000 for disorderly conduct, 138,000 for drug abuse violations, and 95,000 for curfew violations.

Juvenile Crime Trends Juvenile crime continues to have a significant influence on the nation's overall crime statistics. As Figure 2.2 shows, the juvenile arrest rate began to climb in the 1960s, peaked in the mid-1990s, and then began to fall; it has since been in decline. Even the teen murder rate, which had remained stubbornly high, has

Though the rate of crime has undergone a dramatic decline, millions of serious criminal incidents still occur each year, leaving devastated families and shattered victims in their wake. Here, Yvette Tucker Griffin (left) of Hampton, Virginia, and Carolyn Peters of Powell, Kentucky, cry during the second "Million Mom March" at the Capitol in Washington, May 9, 2004. Both women lost their sons (James Tucker, III, and David Allan, respectively) in shootings. Several thousand people gathered at the Capitol to urge renewal of a federal ban on assault weapons.

IN MEMORY OF
JAMES E. TUCKER III
(HAMPTON, VA)

MAR 31, 1984 - JAN 4, 2003

AP/Wide World Photos

undergone a decline during the past few years.[2] For example, 1,700 youths were arrested for murder in 1997, a number that by 2003 had declined by more than half (783). Similarly, 3,800 juveniles were arrested for rape in 1997, and 2,966 in 2003. This decline in juvenile violence is especially welcome considering that its rate was approaching epidemic proportions.

Though juvenile crime rates have been in decline for the past decade, they tend to ebb and flow over long periods of time. What factors account for change in the crime and delinquency rate? This is the topic of the Focus on Delinquency box entitled "Factors Affecting Juvenile Crime Rates."

What the Future Holds

Some experts, such as criminologist James A. Fox, predict a significant increase in teen violence if current population trends persist. The nation's teenage population will increase by 15 percent, or more than 9 million, between now and 2010; the number in the

TABLE 2.1

Persons Arrested, by Age

	Under 15	Under 18*	Over 18
Index violent crime	5%	15%	85%
Index property crime	11%	29%	71%
Index total	9%	26%	74%
Total all crimes	5%	16%	84%

Because of rounding, the percentages may not add up to 100%.

*Under 18 includes ages under 15.

SOURCE: FBI, *Crime in the United States, 2003*, p. 280.

FIGURE 2.2
Juvenile Arrest Trends

SOURCE: Howard Snyder, *Juvenile Arrests 2001* (Washington, DC: Office of Juvenile Justice and Delinquency Prevention, 2003, updated); FBI, *Crime in the United States, 2003* (Washington, DC: FBI, 2004).

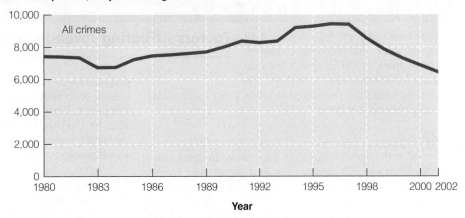

Arrest rate per 100,000 juveniles aged 10–17

NOTE: Rates are people arrested aged 10–17 per 100,000 people aged 10–17 in the resident population.

high-risk ages between 15 and 17 will increase by more than 3 million, or 31 percent. There are approximately 50 million school-age children in the United States, many under age 10—more than we have had for decades. Though many come from stable homes, others lack stable families and adequate supervision; these are some of the children who will soon enter their prime crime years. As a result, Fox predicts a wave of youth violence even greater than that of the past 10 years.[3]

In contrast, economist Steven Levitt believes that even though teen crime rates may eventually rise, their influence on the nation's total crime rate may be offset by the growing number of crime-free senior citizens.[4] Also Levitt believes that punitive policies such as putting more kids behind bars and adding police may help control delinquency. One problem on the horizon: the maturation of "crack babies" who spent their early childhood years in families and neighborhoods ravaged by crack cocaine. Coupled with a difficult home environment, these children may turn out to be extremely prone to delinquency activity, producing the increase in the delinquency predicted by James A. Fox.[5]

Are the UCR Data Valid?

Questions have been raised about the validity and accuracy of UCR's "official" crime data. Victim surveys show that fewer than half of all victims report the crime to police. Because official data are derived entirely from police records, we can assume that a significant number of crimes are not accounted for in the UCR. There are also concerns that police departments make systematic errors in recording crime data or manipulate crime data to give the public the impression that they are highly effective crime fighters.[6]

Using official arrest data to measure delinquency rates is particularly problematic. Arrest records only count adolescents who have been *caught,* and these youths may be different from those who evade capture. In addition, victimless crimes such as drug and alcohol use are significantly undercounted using this measure.

The National Incident-Based Reporting System (NIBRS) The FBI is currently instituting a new program that collects data on each reported crime incident. Instead of submitting statements about the kinds of crime that individual citizens report to the police and summary statements of resulting arrests, the new program will require local police agencies to provide at least a brief account of each incident and arrest, including the incident, victim, and offender information. Under NIBRS, law enforcement authorities will provide information to the FBI on each criminal incident involving 46 specific offenses that occur in their jurisdiction, including the 8 Part I

Factors Affecting Juvenile Crime Rates

Crime rates climb and fall, reflecting a variety of social and economic conditions. Though there is still disagreement over what causes crime rate fluctuations, the following factors are considered to play a major role in determining patterns and trends.

AGE

Change in the age distribution of the population deeply influences crime and delinquency rates. As a general rule, juvenile males commit more crime than any other population segment. Consequently, the crime rate follows the proportion of young males in the population. The post–World War II baby-boom generation reached their teenage years in the 1960s, creating an extremely large pool of teenagers. Not surprisingly, the crime rate began to increase sharply between 1960 and 1980 when these youth were in their prime crime years. With the "graying" of society and a decline in the birthrate, the overall crime rate began to decline in the mid-1990s. Some criminologists fear crime rates will begin to climb when the number of juveniles in the population begins to increase.

ECONOMY

In the short term, a poor economy may actually help lower crime rates. Unemployed parents are at home to supervise children and guard their homes. Because there is less to spend, a poor economy means that there are actually fewer valuables worth stealing. For example, 2002 research conducted by Gary Kleck and Ted Chiricos discovered that there was no relationship between unemployment rates and the rate of most crimes that desperate kids might commit, including robbery, shoplifting, residential burglary, theft of motor vehicle parts, and automobile theft.

Despite the weak association, it is possible that long-term periods of economic weakness and unemployment eventually lift crime rates. Chronic teenage unemployment rates may produce a perception of hopelessness that leads to crime and delinquency. Violence may be a function of urban problems and the economic deterioration in the nation's inner cities. Our nation's economy is now fueled by the service and technology industries. Youths who at one time might have obtained low-skill jobs in factories and shops find these legitimate economic opportunities no longer exist. Low-skill manufacturing jobs have been dispersed to overseas plants; most new jobs that don't require specialized skills are in the low-paying service area. Lack of real economic opportunity may encourage drug dealing, theft, and violence. Experts fear that a long-term economic downturn coupled with a relatively large number of teens in the population will produce the high delinquency rates of the late eighties and early nineties.

DRUGS

Drug use has been linked to fluctuations in the crime and delinquency rate. Abusers are particularly crime-prone, so as drug use levels increase, so too do crime rates. When teen violence skyrocketed in the 1980s, it was no coincidence that this period also witnessed increases in drug trafficking and arrests for drug crimes. Teenage substance abusers commit a significant portion of all serious crimes and inner city drug abuse problems may account in part for the persistently high violent-crime rate. Groups and gangs that are involved in the urban drug trade recruit juveniles because they work cheaply, are immune from heavy criminal penalties, and are daring and willing to take risks. Arming themselves for protection, these youthful dealers pose a threat to neighborhood adolescents, who in turn arm themselves for self-protection. The result is an "arms race" that produces an increasing spiral of violence.

Drug abuse may also have a more direct influence on teen crime patterns—for example, when alcohol-abusing kids engage in acts of senseless violence. Users may turn to theft and violence for money to purchase drugs and support drug habits. Increases in teenage drug use may be a precursor to higher violence rates in the future.

MEDIA

Some experts argue that violent media can influence youth crime. As the availability of media with a violent theme skyrocketed with the introduction of home video players, DVDs, cable TV, computer and video games, and so on, so too did teen violence rates. According to a recent analysis of all available scientific data, conducted by Brad Bushman and Craig Anderson, watching violence on TV is correlated to aggressive behaviors, especially for kids with a preexisting tendency toward crime and violence.

ONGOING SOCIAL PROBLEMS

As the level of social problems increases—divorce, school dropout, teen pregnancy, and racial inequality—so do crime and delinquency rates. For example, cross-national research indicates that child homicide rates are greatest in those nations, including the United States, that have the highest rates of teenage mothers and of children born out of wedlock. Children living in single-parent homes are twice as likely to be impoverished than those in two-parent homes, and are consequently at greater risk for juvenile delinquency. For example, recent research by Greg Pogarsky, Alan Lizotte, and Terence Thornberry found that children born to the youngest teen mothers are most at risk for delinquency, especially if they are raised in single-parent homes. Currently, the number of teen pregnancies is on the decline and so too are teen crime rates.

Racial inequality has also been linked to crime rates. Violence rates may be high among African Americans because they lack the resources afforded to whites. Black communities lack the cohesiveness that is required to exert social control over residents. As a result a neighborhood argument may spiral out of control into a lethal homicide.

ABORTION

In a controversial work, John J. Donohue III and Steven Levitt found empirical evidence that the recent drop in the crime rate can be attributable to the availability of legalized abortion. In 1973, *Roe v. Wade* legalized abortion nationwide. Within a few years of *Roe v. Wade,* more than 1 million abortions were being performed annually, or roughly one abortion for every three live births. Donohue and Levitt suggest that the decrease in the crime rate that began approximately eighteen years later, in 1991, can be related to the fact that the first group of potential offenders affected by the abortion decision began reaching the peak age of criminal activity. It is possible that the link between crime rates and abortion is the result of two mechanisms: (1) selective abortion on the part of women most at risk for having children who would engage in delinquent activity, and (2) improved childrearing or environmental circumstances caused by better maternal, familial, or fetal circumstances because women are having fewer children. If abortion were illegal, they find, crime rates might be 10 to 20 percent higher than they currently are with legal abortion.

GUNS

Another important influence on violence rates is the number of weapons in the hands of teens. In 2003, 27,000 kids were arrested on weapons-related charges. More than 60 percent of the homicides committed by juveniles involve firearms. Guns can turn a schoolyard fight into a homicide. Their presence creates a climate in which kids who would otherwise shun firearms begin to carry them to "protect" themselves. As the number of guns in the hands of children increases, so do juvenile violence rates. Guns are related to violence rates: the higher the violence rates in a neighborhood, the more likely kids are to carry guns, most likely for self-protection.

GANGS

The explosive growth in teenage gangs has also contributed to teen violence rates. Surveys indicate that there are more than 750,000 gang members in the United States. A large and growing number of juveniles who kill do so in groups of two or more; multiple-offender killings have doubled since the mid-1980s. Gang-related violence is frequently compounded by the use of firearms. Research indicates that in major cities about one-third of kids who are gang members carry a gun all or most of the time.

JUVENILE JUSTICE POLICY

Some law enforcement experts have suggested that a reduction in crime rates may be attributed to a recent "get tough" attitude toward delinquency and drug abuse. Police have become more aggressive. New laws call for mandatory incarceration for juvenile offenders. Juveniles may even be eligible for the death penalty. Putting potentially high-rate offenders behind bars may help to stabilize crime rates.

Critical Thinking

1. Considering the changes happening in society today, do you predict that teen crime rates will increase or decrease?

2. What factors do you suppose increase the likelihood that children born to teen mothers will eventually become involved in antisocial behaviors?

3. Does the finding that abortion helps reduce teen crime rates affect your attitude, either pro or con, for maintaining the legality of abortion?

InfoTrac College Edition Research

To read the original paper on the association between legalized abortion and juvenile crime rates, go to John J. Donohue III and Steven Levitt, "The Impact of Legalized Abortion on Crime," *Quarterly Journal of Economics* 116:379–420 (2001).

SOURCES: Greg Pogarsky, Alan Lizotte, and Terence Thornberry, "The Delinquency of Children Born to Young Mothers: Results from the Rochester Youth Development Study," *Criminology* 41:1249–1286 (2003); Philip Cook and Jens Ludwig, "Does Gun Prevalence Affect Teen Gun Carrying After All?" *Criminology* 42:27–54 (2004); Maria Velez, Lauren Krivo, and Ruth Peterson, "Structural Inequality and Homicide: An Assessment of the Black-White Gap in Killings," *Criminology* 41:645–672 (2003); William Wells and Julie Horney, "Weapon Effects and Individual Intent to Do Harm: Influences on the Escalation of Violence," *Criminology* 40:265–296 (2002); Jeffrey Johnson et al., "Television Viewing and Aggressive Behavior During Adolescence and Adulthood," *Science* 295:2468–2471 (2002); Brad Bushman and Craig Anderson, "Media Violence and the American Public," *American Psychologist* 56:477–489 (2001); Gary Kleck and Ted Chiricos, "Unemployment and Property Crime: A Target-Specific Assessment of Opportunity and Motivation as Mediating Factors," *Criminology* 40:649–680 (2002); John J. Donohue III and Steven D. Levitt, "Legalized Abortion and Crime" (June 24, 1999, unpublished paper, University of Chicago); Donald Green, Dara Strolovitch, and Janelle Wong, "Defended Neighborhoods, Integration, and Racially Motivated Crime," *American Journal of Sociology* 104:372–403 (1998); Robert O'Brien, Jean Stockard, and Lynne Isaacson, "The Enduring Effects of Cohort Characteristics on Age-Specific Homicide Rates, 1960–1995," *American Journal of Sociology* 104:1061–1095(1999); Scott Decker and Susan Pennell, *Arrestees and Guns: Monitoring the Illegal Firearms Market* (Washington, DC: National Institute of Justice, 1995); G. David Curry, Richard Ball, and Scott Decker, "Estimating the National Scope of Gang Crime from Law Enforcement Data," in C. Ronald Huff, ed., *Gangs in America*, 2nd ed. (Newbury Park, CA: Sage Publications, 1996).

crimes. Arrest information on the 46 offenses plus 11 lesser offenses is also provided in NIBRS. These expanded crime categories would include numerous additional crimes, such as blackmail, embezzlement, drug offenses, and bribery. This would allow a national database on the nature of crime, victims, and criminals to be developed. So far 22 states have implemented their NIBRS program and 12 others are in the process of finalizing their data collections. When this new UCR program is fully implemented and adopted across the nation, it should provide significantly better data on juvenile crime than exists today.

TO QUIZ YOURSELF ON THIS MATERIAL, go to the Juvenile Delinquency 9e website.

SELF-REPORTED DELINQUENCY

Official statistics are useful for examining general trends, but they cannot tell us how many youths commit crimes but are never arrested. Nor do they reveal much about the personality, attitudes, and behavior of individual delinquents. To get information at this level, criminologists have developed alternative sources of delinquency statistics, the most commonly used source being **self-reports** of delinquent behavior.

self-reports
Questionnaire or survey technique that asks subjects to reveal their own participation in delinquent or criminal acts.

Self-report studies are designed to obtain information from youthful subjects about their violations of the law. Youths arrested by police may be interviewed at the station house; an anonymous survey can be distributed to every student in a high school; boys in a detention center may be asked to respond to a survey; or youths randomly selected from the population of teenagers can be questioned in their homes. Self-report information can be collected in one-to-one interviews or through a self-administered questionnaire, but more commonly this information is gathered through a mass distribution of anonymous questionnaires.

Self-report surveys can include all segments of the population. They provide information on offenders who have never been arrested and are therefore not part of the official data. They also measure behavior that is rarely detected by police, such as drug abuse, because their anonymity allows youths to freely describe their illegal activities. Surveys can also include items measuring personality characteristics, behavior, and attitudes.

Exhibit 2.2 shows one format for asking self-report questions. Youths are asked to indicate how many times they have participated in illegal or deviant behavior. Other formats allow subjects to record the precise number of times they engaged in each delinquent activity. Note that the reporting period is limited to the previous 12 months; some surveys question lifetime activity.

Questions not directly related to delinquent activity are often included on self-report surveys. Information on self-image, intelligence, personality, leisure activities, school activities, attitudes toward family, friends, and school may be collected. Self-report surveys also gather information on family background, social status, race, and sex. Reports of delinquent acts can be correlated with this information to create a much more complete picture of delinquent offenders than official statistics can provide.

EXHIBIT 2.2

Self-Report Survey Questions

Please indicate how often in the past 12 months you did each act. (Check the best answer.)

	Never Did Act	One Time	2–5 Times	6–9 Times	10+ Times
Stole something worth less than $50	_____	_____	_____	_____	_____
Stole something worth more than $50	_____	_____	_____	_____	_____
Used cocaine	_____	_____	_____	_____	_____
Been in a fistfight	_____	_____	_____	_____	_____
Carried a weapon such as a gun or knife	_____	_____	_____	_____	_____
Fought someone using a weapon	_____	_____	_____	_____	_____

TABLE 2.2

Self-Reported Delinquent Activity, High School Seniors, 2003, during Past 12 Months

Type of Crime	Total %	Committed Only Once (%)	Committed More than Once (%)
Set fire on purpose	4	2	2
Damaged school property	13	6	7
Damaged work property	7	3	4
Auto theft	5	2	3
Auto part theft	6	3	3
Breaking and entering	23	10	13
Theft of less than $50	27	13	14
Theft of more than $50	9	4	5
Shoplifting	28	12	15
Gang fight	19	10	9
Hurt someone badly enough so that they needed medical care	13	6	7
Used force to steal	4	2	2
Hit teacher or supervisor	3	1	2
Got into serious fight	14	7	7

SOURCE: *Monitoring the Future, 2003* (Ann Arbor, MI: Institute for Social Research, 2004).

Criminologists have used self-report studies of delinquency for more than 40 years.[7] Though there are always questions about the validity of answers, studies designed to test the accuracy of self-reports indicate that they may be a valuable source of information on the activities of youths who have had contact with the juvenile justice system as well as on the dark figures of crime—that is, those who have escaped official notice.[8]

Self-Report Data

To find out more about **Institute of Social Research's Monitoring the Future program,** check out the **NAACP** website at www.naacp.org/. For an up-to-date list of web links, go to http://cj.wadsworth.com/siegel_jd9e.

Researchers at the University of Michigan's Institute for Social Research (ISR)[9] conduct an annual national self-report survey, called Monitoring the Future (MTF), which involves a sample of about 3,000 youths. Table 2.2 contains some of the data from the 2003 MTF survey.

A surprising number of these *typical* teenagers reported involvement in serious criminal behavior. About 13 percent reported hurting someone badly enough that the victim needed medical care (7 percent said they did it more than once). About 27 percent reported stealing something worth less than $50, and another 9 percent stole something worth more than $50; 28 percent reported shoplifting; 13 percent had damaged school property.

If the ISR data are accurate, the juvenile crime problem is much greater than official statistics would lead us to believe. There are approximately 40 million youths between the ages of 10 and 18. Extrapolating from the MTF findings, this group accounts for more than 100 percent of all theft offenses reported in the UCR. More than 3 percent of the students said they used a knife or a gun in a robbery. At this rate, high school students commit 1.2 million armed robberies per year. In comparison, the UCR tallies about 235,000 armed robberies for all age groups in 2003. Over the past decade, the MTF surveys indicate that with a few exceptions, self-reported teenage participation in theft, violence, and damage-related crimes seems to be more stable than the trends reported in the UCR arrest data.

There is also some question about the accuracy of self-report data. There is evidence that reporting accuracy differs among racial, ethnic, and gender groups. For example, one recent study found that although girls were more willing than boys to disclose drug use, Hispanic girls are significantly more likely than Hispanic boys to

TO QUIZ YOURSELF ON THIS MATERIAL, go to the Juvenile Delinquency 9e website.

underreport their use of cocaine. Such gender/cultural differences might provide a skewed and inaccurate portrait of criminal and or delinquent activity—in other words, girls' drug use seems to be increasing, but it is only because they are more willing to admit use than boys.[10] (See Concept Summary below on reporting ways to measure crime.)

Concept Summary 2.1
Measuring Crime

	Uniform Crime Report	National Crime Victimization Survey	ISR Self-Report
Source	Police records	Victim surveys	Student survey
Frequency	Annual	Annual	Annual
Number	17,000 police departments	40,000 households	2,300 students
Reporting Strengths	Consistent measure	Consistent measure	Consistent measure
	Records homicides	Records unreported crimes	Includes adolescents
	Includes arrest data	Includes victim and offender information	Includes drug use
Weaknesses	Only measures crimes reported to police	Relies on victims' memories	Relies on adolescent drug abusers' memories
	Police department recording errors	Does not include substance abuse or homicide	Omits kids who are out of school or refuse participation

CORRELATES OF DELINQUENCY

An important aspect of delinquency research is measurement of the personal traits and social characteristics associated with adolescent misbehavior. If, for example, a strong association exists between delinquent behavior and family income, then poverty and economic deprivation must be considered in any explanation of the onset of adolescent criminality. If the delinquency-income association is not present, other forces may be responsible for producing antisocial behavior. It would be fruitless to concentrate delinquency control efforts in areas such as job creation and vocational training if social status were found to be unrelated to delinquent behavior. Similarly, if only a handful of delinquents are responsible for most serious crimes, crime control policies might be made more effective by identifying and treating these offenders. The next sections discuss the relationship between delinquency and the characteristics of gender, race, social class, and age.

Gender and Delinquency

Males are significantly more delinquent than females. The teenage gender ratio for serious violent crime is approximately 4 to 1, and for property crime approximately 2 to 1, male to female.

One relationship reverses this general pattern: Girls are more likely than boys to be arrested as runaways. There are two possible explanations for this. Girls could be more likely than boys to run away from home, or police may view the female runaway as the more serious problem and therefore be more likely to process females through official justice channels. This may reflect paternalistic attitudes toward girls, who are viewed as likely to "get in trouble" if they are on the street.

In recent years arrests of female delinquents have been increasing faster than those for males. Between 1994 and 2004, the number of arrests of male delinquents decreased about 22 percent, whereas the number of female delinquents arrested increased about 12 percent (though as Figure 2.3 shows they are down from their peak).

FIGURE 2.3

Arrest Trends by Gender

SOURCE: Howard Snyder, *Juvenile Arrests 2001* (Washington, DC: Office of Juvenile Justice and Delinquency Prevention, 2003, updated); FBI, *Crime in the United States, 2003* (Washington, DC: FBI, 2004).

Arrest rate per 100,000 males/females aged 10–17

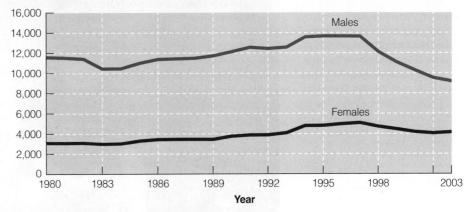

Arrest rate per 100,000 females aged 10–17

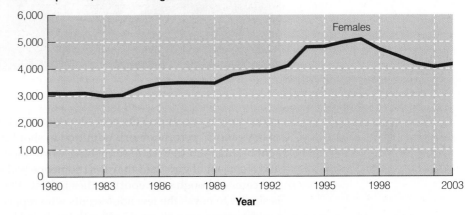

NOTE: Rates are people arrested aged 10–17 per 100,000 people aged 10–17 in the resident population.

TABLE 2.3

Percentage of High School Seniors Admitting to at Least One Offense during the Past 12 Months, by Gender

Crime Category	Males	Females
Serious fight	19	9
Gang fight	25	15
Hurt someone badly	19	5
Used a weapon to steal	6	1
Stole less than $50	34	21
Stole more than $50	14	5
Shoplift	31	23
Breaking and entering	29	17
Arson	7	1
Damaged school property	20	6

SOURCE: *Monitoring the Future, 2003* (Ann Arbor, MI: Institute for Social Research, 2004).

The change in serious violent crime arrests was even more striking: Males decreased 33 percent, whereas females' violent-crime arrests remained stable during this period of declining crime rates, decreasing only 2 percent.

Self-report data also seem to show that the incidence of female delinquency is much higher than believed earlier, and that the most common crimes committed by males are also the ones most female offenders commit.[11] Table 2.3 shows the percentages of males and females who admitted in the latest MTF survey to engaging

Girls are increasing their involvement in violence at a faster pace than boys. It is no longer surprising when young women commit armed robberies and murders. Police say 15-year-old Holly Harvey (right), and 16-year-old Sandy Ketchum of Fayetteville, Georgia, were involved in a romantic relationship and that Harvey's family had tried to keep them apart. The two are accused of stabbing to death Harvey's grandparents. Harvey had a list inked on her arm that read, "kill, keys, money, jewelry."

in delinquent acts during the past 12 months. As the table indicates, about 31 percent of boys and 23 percent of girls admitted to shoplifting, 14 percent of boys and 5 percent of girls said they stole something worth more than $50, and 19 percent of boys and 5 percent of girls said they hurt someone badly enough that they required medical care. Although self-report studies indicate that the content of girls' delinquency is similar to boys', the few adolescents who reported engaging frequently in serious violent crime are still predominantly male.[12] However, like the official arrest data show, over the past decade girls have increased their self-reported delinquency whereas boys report somewhat less involvement. Because the relationship between gender and delinquency rate is so important, this topic will be discussed further in Chapter 6.

Racial Patterns in Delinquency

There are approximately 40 million white and 9 million African American youths aged 5 to 17, a ratio of about 4.5 to 1. Yet racial minorities are disproportionately represented in the arrest statistics (see Figure 2.4). African American youths are arrested for a disproportionate number of murders, rapes, robberies, and assaults, whereas white youths are arrested for a disproportionate share of arsons. Among Part II crimes, white youths are disproportionately arrested for alcohol-related violations.

Self-Report Differences Official statistics show that minority youths are much more likely than white youths to be arrested for serious criminal behavior. To many delinquency experts, this pattern reflects discrimination in the juvenile justice system. In other words, African American youths are more likely to be formally arrested by the police, who, in contrast, will treat white youths informally. One way to examine this issue is to compare the racial differences in self-report data with those found in the official delinquency records. Given the disproportionate numbers of African Americans arrested, charges of racial discrimination would be supported if we found little difference between the number of self-reported minority and white crimes.

Early researchers found that the relationship between race and self-reported delinquency was virtually nonexistent.[13] This suggests that racial differences in the official crime data may reflect the fact that African American youths have a much greater

FIGURE 2.4

Juvenile Arrest Rates for All
Crimes by Race, 1980–2003

SOURCE: FBI, *Uniform Crime Report,
2003* (Washington, DC: FBI, 2004).

Arrest rate per 100,000 people aged 10–17

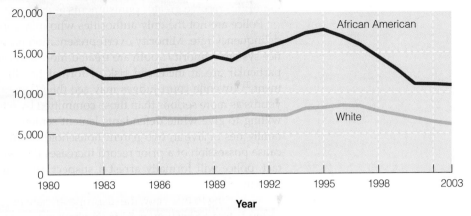

Arrest rate per 100,000 people aged 10–17

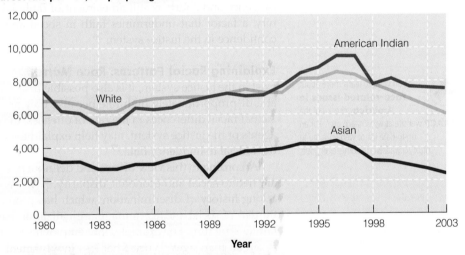

NOTES: Rates are people arrested aged 10–17 per 100,000 people aged 10–17 in the resident population.
People of Hispanic ethnicity may be of any race, i.e., white, African American, American Indian, or Asian.
Arrests of Hispanics are not reported separately.

chance of being arrested and officially processed.[14] Self-report studies also suggest
that the delinquent behavior rates of African American and white teenagers are generally similar and that differences in arrest statistics may indicate discrimination by
police.[15] The MTF survey, for example, generally shows that offending differences between African American and white youths are marginal.[16] However, some experts
warn that African American youths may underreport more serious crimes, limiting
the ability of self-reports to be a valid indicator of racial differences in the crime rate.[17]

Are the Data Valid? The view that the disproportionate amount of African American official delinquency is a result of bias has found some support in research studies.
For example, recent research shows that poor, male juvenile suspects belonging to
ethnic minorities are more likely to be formally arrested than suspects who are white,
female, and affluent.[18] Police routinely search, question, and detain all African American males in an area if a violent criminal has been described as "looking or sounding
black"; this is called "racial profiling." Findings from a recent national survey of driving practices show that young black and Hispanic males are more likely to be stopped
by police and suffer citations, searches, and arrests, as well as being the target of force
even though they are no more likely to be in the possession of illegal contraband than
white drivers.[19]

African American youth who develop a police record are more likely to be severely
punished if they are picked up again and sent back to juvenile court.[20] Consequently,

the racial discrimination present at the early stages of the justice system ensures that minorities receive greater punishments at its conclusion.

Police are not the only authorities who may contribute to racial differences in the delinquency rate. Minority overrepresentation occurs at all stages of the juvenile justice system. Minority youth are treated more severely, and minority drug offenders in particular are at increased risk of formal handling, detention, and custody placement.[21] Juvenile court judges may see the offenses committed by African American youths as more serious than those committed by white offenders.[22] Judges seem more willing to give white defendants lenient sentences if, for example, they show strong family ties or live in two-parent households.[23] Any form of racial bias is crucial because possession of a prior record increases the likelihood that upon subsequent contact, police will formally arrest a suspect rather than release the individual with a warning.[24]

According to this view, the disproportionate number of minority youth who are arrested is less a function of their involvement in serious crime and more the result of race-based decision making found in the juvenile justice system.[25] Institutional racism by police and courts is still an element of daily life in the African American community, a factor that undermines faith in social and political institutions and weakens confidence in the justice system.[26]

 If you want to learn more about **race-related issues in America,** check out the **NAACP** website at www.naacp.org/. For an up-to-date list of web links, go to http://cj.wadsworth.com/siegel_jd9e.

Explaining Racial Patterns: Race Matters Although evidence of racial bias does exist in the justice system, it is also possible that African American youths are arrested at a disproportionately high rate because they are currently committing more crime. Actual racial differences in the rate of offenses, rather than bias and discrimination by agents of the justice system, may help explain the persistent racial disparities found in the official delinquency data.[27]

According to this view of race and delinquency, racial differentials in the crime rate are tied to social and economic disparity.[28] African Americans have suffered through a long history of discrimination, which has produced lasting emotional scars.[29] The burden of social and economic marginalization has weakened the African American family structure. For example, low employment rates among minority males place a strain on marriages. When families are weakened or disrupted, their ability to act as social control agents is compromised. Divorce and separation rates are significantly associated with crime and violence rates in the African American community.[30]

Even during times of economic growth, lower-class African Americans are left out of the economic mainstream, a fact that is met with a growing sense of frustration and failure.[31] As a result of being shut out of educational and economic opportunities enjoyed by the rest of society, minority youth may be exposed to the lure of illegitimate gain and criminality. In addition to these social deficits, there is evidence that, in at least some jurisdictions, young African American males are treated more harshly by the justice system than members of any other group.[32] African Americans, especially those who are indigent or unemployed, receive longer sentences than whites who commit the same types of crimes. It is possible that some judges view poor blacks as antisocial, considering them more dangerous and likely to recidivate than white offenders.[33] Yet when African Americans are the victims of crime, their predicament receives less public concern and media attention than that afforded white victims.[34]

Racial differentials in the crime rate may also be tied to frustrations over perceived racism, discrimination, and economic disparity. Even during times of economic growth, many economically disadvantaged African Americans believe they are being left out of the mainstream and feel a growing sense of frustration.[35] Such frustration may be magnified by frequent exposure to violence. African Americans who live in poor areas with high crime rates may be disproportionately violent because they are exposed to more violence in their daily lives than other racial and economic groups. Research has shown that such exposure is a significant risk factor for violent behavior.[36]

However, even among at-risk African American kids growing up in communities categorized by poverty, high unemployment levels, and single-parent households, those who manage to live in stable families with reasonable income and educational achievement are much less likely to engage in violent behaviors than those lacking family support.[37] Consequently, racial differences in the delinquency rate would evaporate if the social and economic characteristics of racial minorities were improved to levels currently enjoyed by whites.[38]

In summary, official data indicate that African American youths are arrested for more serious crimes than whites. However, self-report studies show that the differences in the rate of delinquency between the races are insignificant. Therefore some experts believe that official differences in the delinquency rate are an artifact of bias in the justice system: Police are more likely to arrest and courts are more likely to convict young African Americans.[39] To those who believe that the official data has validity, the participation of African American youths in serious criminal behavior is generally viewed as a function of their socioeconomic position and the racism they face.

Social Class and Delinquency

Defining the relationship between economic status and delinquent behavior is a key element in the study of delinquency. If youth crime is purely a lower-class phenomenon, its cause must be rooted in the social forces that are found solely in lower-class areas: poverty, unemployment, social disorganization, culture conflict, and alienation.[40] However, if delinquent behavior is spread throughout the social structure, its cause must be related to some noneconomic factor: intelligence, personality, socialization, family dysfunction, educational failure, or peer influence. According to this line of reasoning, providing jobs or economic incentives would have little effect on the crime rate.

At first glance, the relationship between class and crime seems clear. Youths who lack wealth or social standing are the most likely to use criminal means to achieve their goals. Communities that lack economic and social opportunities produce high levels of frustration. Kids who live in these areas believe that they can never compete socially or economically with adolescents being raised in more affluent areas. They may turn to criminal behavior for monetary gain and psychological satisfaction.[41] Family life is disrupted in these low-income areas, and law-violating youth groups thrive in a climate that undermines and neutralizes adult supervision.[42]

Research on Social Class and Delinquency The social class–delinquency relationship was challenged by pioneering self-report studies, specifically those that revealed no direct relationship between social class and the commission of delinquent acts.[43] Instead, socioeconomic class was related to the manner of official processing by police, court, and correctional agencies.[44] In other words, though both poor and affluent kids get into fights, shoplift, and take drugs, only the indigent are likely to be arrested and sent to juvenile court.[45]

Those who fault self-report studies point to the inclusion of trivial offenses (for example, using a false ID) in most self-report instruments. Although middle- and upper-class youths may appear to be as delinquent as those in the lower class, it is because they engage in significant amounts of status offenses and not serious delinquent acts.[46]

In sum, there are those experts who believe that antisocial behavior occurs at all levels of the social strata. Other experts argue that although some middle- and upper-class youths engage in some forms of minor illegal activity and theft offenses, it is members of the underclass who are responsible for the majority of serious delinquent acts such as gang violence.[47]

Age and Delinquency

Age is inversely related to criminality: As youthful offenders mature, their offending rates decline.[48] Official statistics tell us that young people are arrested at a disproportionate rate to their numbers in the population, and this finding is supported by victim

To get information on the **economic status of America's children,** go to the federal government's website on children at www.childstats.gov. For an up-to-date list of web links, go to http://cj.wadsworth.com/siegel_jd9e.

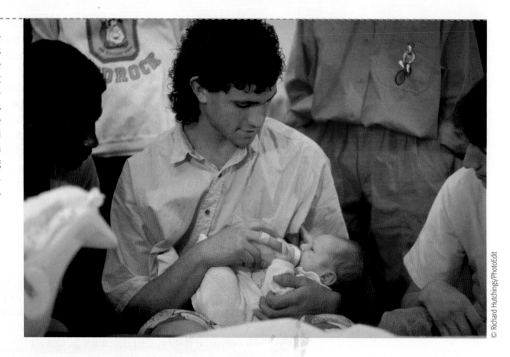

© Richard Hutchings/PhotoEdit

Why does crime decline with age? One reason may be that with maturity comes an increased level of responsibility. Crime may be an exciting social activity that provides adventure, but such risky behavior is inconsistent with the responsibilities of young people who marry, enlist in the armed services, or enroll in vocational training courses. It is unlikely that the teen father shown here would risk committing a foolish crime.

surveys. Youths 17 and under make up about 10 percent of the total U.S. population, but they account for 27 percent of the index crime arrests and 17 percent of the arrests for all crimes. In contrast, adults 50 and older, who make up 32 percent of the population, account for only about 10 percent of arrests. Self-report studies also indicate that rates for crimes such as assault, robbery, and trespass decline substantially between the ages of 17 and 23; the incidence of some illegal acts, such as substance abuse, may increase.[49]

Why Does Crime Decline with Age? Why do people commit less crime as they age? One view is that the relationship is constant: Regardless of race, sex, social class, intelligence, or any other social variable, people commit less crime as they age; this is referred to as the aging-out process.[50] According to this view, even the most chronic juvenile offenders will commit less crime as they age.[51]

Delinquency experts have developed a number of reasons for the aging-out process:

I Growing older means having to face the future. Young people, especially the indigent and antisocial, tend to "discount the future."[52] Why should they delay gratification when faced with an uncertain future?

I With maturity comes the ability to resist the "quick fix" to problems.[53] Research shows that some kids may turn to crime as a way to solve the problems of adolescence, loneliness, frustration, and fear of peer rejection. As they mature, conventional means of problem solving become available. Life experience helps former delinquents seek nondestructive solutions to their personal problems.[54]

I Maturation coincides with increased levels of responsibility. Petty crimes are a risky and exciting social activity that provides adventure in an otherwise boring world. As youths grow older, they take on new responsibilities that are inconsistent with criminality.[55] For example, young people who marry, enlist in the armed services, or enroll in vocational training courses are less likely to pursue criminal activities.[56]

I Personalities can change with age. As youths mature, rebellious youngsters may develop increased self-control and be able to resist antisocial behavior.[57]

I Young adults become more aware of the risks that accompany crime. As adults, they are no longer protected by the kindly arms of the juvenile justice system.[58]

Age of Onset Age may influence delinquent behavior in other ways. For example, evidence exists that people who demonstrate antisocial tendencies at a very early age are more likely to commit more crime for a longer duration; this is referred to as the **age of onset.** According to this view, there are two classes of offenders. The first begin committing crime in late adolescence, typically with their peers, and then cease offending as they enter young adulthood. These youngsters begin to desist from illegal or deviant activities as they mature and begin to realize that crime is too dangerous, physically taxing, and unrewarding, and punishments too harsh and long lasting, to become a way of life.[59]

The second group of delinquents are those who begin their offending careers early in life and maintain a high rate of offending throughout their lifespan. Early onset of crime is a marker for their chronic offending patterns. Research supports this by showing that children who will later become delinquents begin their deviant careers at a very early (preschool) age and that the earlier the onset of delinquency the more frequent, varied, and sustained the criminal career.[60] Early onset delinquents typically have a history of disruptive behavior beginning in early childhood with truancy, cruelty to animals, lying, and theft.[61] Early onset has been linked with careers in delinquency, a subject that is discussed in detail below.

age of onset
Age at which youths begin their delinquent careers; early onset is believed to be linked with chronic offending patterns.

TO QUIZ YOURSELF ON THIS MATERIAL, go to the Juvenile Delinquency 9e website.

CHRONIC OFFENDING: CAREERS IN DELINQUENCY

Although most adolescents age out of crime, a relatively small number of youths begin to violate the law early in their lives and continue at a high rate well into adulthood (persistence).[62] The association between early onset and high-rate persistent offending has been demonstrated in samples drawn from a variety of cultures, time periods, and offender types.[63] These offenders are resistant to change and seem immune to the effects of punishment. Arrest, prosecution, and conviction do little to slow down their offending careers. These so-called chronic offenders are responsible for a significant amount of all delinquent and criminal activity.

Current interest in the delinquent life cycle was also prompted by the "discovery" in the 1970s of the chronic delinquent offender. According to this view, a relatively small number of youthful offenders commit a significant percentage of all serious crimes, and many of these same offenders grow up to become chronic adult criminals.

Chronic offenders can be distinguished from other delinquent youths. Many youthful law violators are apprehended for a single instance of criminal behavior such as shoplifting or joyriding. **Chronic offenders** begin their delinquent careers at a young age (under 10 years old, referred to as early onset), have serious and persistent brushes with the law, and may be excessively violent and destructive. They do not age out of crime but continue their law-violating behavior into adulthood.[64] Most research shows that early and repeated delinquent activity is the best predictor of future adult criminality.

A number of research efforts have set out to chronicle the careers of serious delinquent offenders. The next sections describe these initiatives.

chronic offender
A delinquent with five or more juvenile arrests.

Landmark Study: *Delinquency in a Birth Cohort*

The concept of the chronic career offender is most closely associated with the research efforts of Marvin Wolfgang.[65] In 1972, Wolfgang, Robert Figlio, and Thorsten Sellin published a landmark study, *Delinquency in a Birth Cohort.* They followed the delinquent careers of a cohort of 9,945 boys born in Philadelphia from birth until they reached age 18. Data were obtained from police files and school records. Socioeconomic status was determined by locating the residence of each member of the cohort and assigning him the median family income for that area. About one-third of the boys (3,475) had some police contact. The remaining two-thirds (6,470) had none.

Those boys who had at least one contact with the police committed a total of 10,214 offenses.

The most significant discovery of Wolfgang and his associates was that of the so-called chronic offender. The data indicated that 54 percent (1,862) of the sample's delinquent youths were repeat offenders. The repeaters could be further categorized as nonchronic recidivists and chronic recidivists. Nonchronic recidivists had been arrested more than once but fewer than five times. The 627 boys labeled chronic recidivists had been arrested five times or more. Although these offenders accounted for only 18 percent of the delinquent population (6 percent of the total sample), they were responsible for 52 percent of all offenses. Known today as the "chronic 6 percent," this group perpetrated 71 percent of the homicides, 82 percent of the robberies, and 64 percent of the aggravated assaults.

Arrest and juvenile court experience did little to deter chronic offenders. In fact, the greater the punishment, the more likely they were to engage in repeat delinquent behavior. Strict punishment also increased the probability that further court action would be taken. Two factors stood out as encouraging recidivism: the seriousness of the original offense and the severity of the punishment. The researchers concluded that efforts of the juvenile justice system to eliminate delinquent behavior may be futile.

Wolfgang and his colleagues conducted a second cohort study with children born in 1958 and substantiated the finding that a relatively few chronic offenders are responsible for a significant portion of all delinquent acts.[66] Wolfgang's results have been duplicated in a number of research studies conducted in locales across the United States and also in Great Britain.[67]

Who Becomes a Chronic Delinquent?

Who is at risk of becoming a chronic offender? As might be expected, kids who have been exposed to a variety of personal and social problems at an early age are the most at risk for repeat offending. One important study of delinquent offenders in Orange County, California, conducted by Michael Schumacher and Gwen Kurz, found that specific personal factors (see Exhibit 2.3) could predict chronic offending and that those youths who manifested these problems in the home and at school were at high risk for repeat offending.[68]

Other research studies have found that early involvement in criminal activity (for example, getting arrested before age 15), relatively low intellectual development, and parental drug involvement were the key predictive factors for chronicity.[69] Some of the most important findings are illustrated in Exhibit 2.4.

EXHIBIT 2.3

Characteristics that Predict Chronic Offending

School Behavior/ Performance Factor	▌ Attendance problems (truancy or a pattern of "skipping" school)
	▌ Behavior problems (recent suspensions or expulsion)
	▌ Poor grades (failing two or more classes)
Family Problem Factor	▌ Poor parental supervision and control
	▌ Significant family problems (illness, substance abuse, discord)
	▌ Criminal family members
	▌ Documented child abuse, neglect, or family violence
Substance Abuse Factor	▌ Alcohol or drugs by minors in any way but experimentation
Delinquency Factor	▌ Stealing pattern of behavior
	▌ Runaway pattern of behavior
	▌ Gang member or associate

SOURCE: Michael Schumacher and Gwen Kurz, *The 8% Solution: Preventing Serious Repeat Juvenile Crime* (Thousand Oaks, CA: Sage Publications, 1999).

EXHIBIT **2.4**

Childhood Risk Factors for Persistent Delinquency

Individual Factors	I Early antisocial behavior
	I Emotional factors such as high behavioral activation and low behavioral inhibition
	I Poor cognitive development
	I Low intelligence
	I Hyperactivity
Family Factors	I Parenting
	I Maltreatment
	I Family violence
	I Divorce
	I Parental psychopathology
	I Familial antisocial behaviors
	I Teenage parenthood
Family Structure	I Large family size
Peer Factors	I Association with deviant peers
	I Peer rejection
School and Community Factors	I Failure to bond to school
	I Poor academic performance
	I Low academic aspirations
	I Living in a poor family
	I Neighborhood disadvantage
	I Disorganized neighborhoods
	I Concentration of delinquent peer groups
	I Access to weapons

SOURCE: Gail Wasserman et al., "Risk and Protective Factors of Child Delinquency," *Child Delinquency Bulletin Series* (Washington, DC: Office of Juvenile Justice and Delinquency Prevention, 2003).

Stability in Crime: From Delinquent to Criminal

Do chronic juvenile offenders grow up to become chronic adult criminals? One study that followed a sample (approximately 10%) of the original Philadelphia cohort (974 subjects) to age 30 found that 70 percent of the "persistent" adult offenders had also been chronic juvenile offenders. Chronic juvenile offenders had an 80 percent chance of becoming adult offenders and a 50 percent chance of being arrested four or more times as adults.[70] Paul Tracy and Kimberly Kempf-Leonard conducted a follow-up study of all subjects in the second 1958 cohort study by Wolfgang and his associates. By age 26, Cohort II subjects were displaying the same behavior patterns as their older peers. Kids who started their delinquent careers early, committed a violent crime, and continued offending throughout adolescence were most likely to persist in criminal behavior as adults. Delinquents who began their offending careers with serious offenses or who quickly increased the severity of their offending early in life were most likely to persist in their criminal behavior into adulthood. Severity of offending rather than frequency of criminal behavior had the greatest impact on later adult criminality.[71] Using data from the second birth cohort, Kempf-Leonard and her associates found that delinquents can be divided into different subgroups based on the seriousness of their offending, and that those falling into the most serious category (chronic delinquents who commit violent acts) have a much greater chance of becoming an adult offender than other delinquent youths.[72]

Children who are found to be disruptive and antisocial as early as age 5 or 6 are the most likely to exhibit stable, long-term patterns of disruptive behavior through adolescence.[73] They have measurable behavior problems in areas such as learning and motor skills, cognitive abilities, family relations, and other areas of social, psychological, and physical functioning.[74] Youthful offenders who persist are more likely to abuse alcohol, get into trouble while in military service, become economically dependent, have lower aspirations, get divorced or separated, and have a weak employment record.[75] They do not specialize in one type of crime; rather, they engage in a variety of criminal acts, including theft, drugs, and violent offenses. Apprehension and punishment seem to have little effect on their offending behavior. A recent study that followed the offending careers of nearly 2,000 serious, chronic youthful offenders for 10 years after their release from the California Youth Authority found they were arrested on 24,615 occasions over the following decade—an average of 22 arrests each. More than 90 percent had been rearrested during the following decade, and their arrests were for an average of nine property crimes, four violent offenses, three drug crimes, and six other type crimes.[76] This recent research suggests the axiom, "The best predictor of future behavior is past behavior."

Policy Implications

Efforts to chart the life cycle of crime and delinquency will have a major influence on both theory and policy. Rather than simply asking why youths become delinquent or commit antisocial acts, theorists are charting the onset, escalation, frequency, and cessation of delinquent behavior. Research on delinquent careers has also influenced policy. If a relatively few offenders commit a great proportion of all delinquent acts and then persist as adult criminals, it follows that steps should be taken to limit their criminal opportunities.[77] One approach is to identify persistent offenders at the beginning of their offending careers and provide early treatment.[78] This might be facilitated by research aimed at identifying traits (for example, impulsive personalities) that can be used to classify high-risk offenders.[79] Because many of these youths suffer from a variety of problems, treatment must be aimed at a broad range of educational, family, vocational, and psychological problems. Focusing on a single problem, such as a lack of employment, may be ineffective.[80]

TO QUIZ YOURSELF ON THIS MATERIAL, go to the Juvenile Delinquency 9e website.

JUVENILE VICTIMIZATION

Juveniles are also victims of crime, and data from victim surveys can help us understand the nature of juvenile victimization. One source of juvenile victimization data is the National Crime Victimization Survey (NCVS), an ongoing cooperative effort of the Bureau of Justice Statistics of the U. S. Department of Justice and the U. S. Census Bureau.[81] The NCVS is a household survey of victims of criminal behavior that measures the nature of the crime and the characteristics of victims.

The total annual sample size of the NCVS has been about 40,000 households containing about 75,000 individuals. The sample is broken down into subsamples of 10,000 households, and each group is interviewed twice a year. The NCVS has been conducted annually for more than 30 years.

Victimization in the United States

The NCVS provides estimates of the total number of personal contact crimes (assault, rape, robbery) and household victimizations (burglary, larceny, vehicle theft). The survey indicates that currently about 23 million criminal incidents occur each year. Being the target or victim of rape, robbery, or assault is a terrible burden and one that can have considerable long-term consequences. If we translate the value of pain, emotional trauma, disability, and risk of death into dollar terms, the cost is $450 billion, or $1,800 for every person in the United States.[82] At first glance these figures seem overwhelming, but victimization rates are stable or declining for most crime categories.

Juveniles are much more likely to become crime victims than adults. They have a more dangerous lifestyle, which places them at risk for crime. They spend a great deal of time in one of the most dangerous areas in the community, the local school, and hang out with the most dangerous people, fellow teenagers!

Many of the differences between NCVS data and official statistics can be attributed to the fact that victimizations are frequently not reported. Only about half of all violent victimizations and 40 percent of all property crimes are reported to the police each year.

Young Victims NCVS data indicate that young people are much more likely to be the victims of crime than adults (see Figure 2.5).[83]

The chance of victimization declines with age. The difference is particularly striking when we compare teens under age 19 with people over age 65. Teens are more than 20 times as likely to become victims of violent crimes than their grandparents. The data also show that male teenagers have a significantly higher chance than females of becoming victims of violent crime, and that African American youth have a greater chance of becoming victims of violent crimes than white teenagers of the same age.[84]

FIGURE 2.5

Violent Crime Rates by Age of Victim

SOURCE: Bureau of Justice Statistics, www.ojp.usdoj.gov/bjs/glance/vage.htm.

Age (years)

| 12–15 | 20–24 | 35–49 | 65 + |
| 16–19 | 25–34 | 50–64 | |

Adjusted victimization rate per 1,000 people in age group

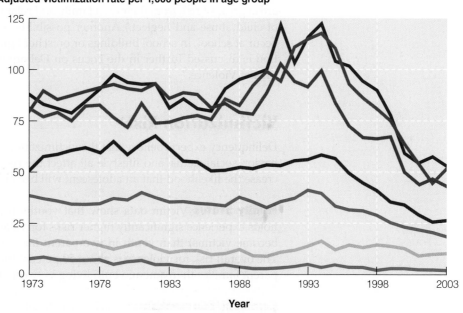

TABLE 2.4

Juvenile Self-Reported Victimization, Class of 2003

	Once	More than Once
Something stolen < $50	27%	17%
Something stolen > $50	18%	7%
Damaged your property	20%	11%
Injured you with a weapon	3%	2%
Threatened you with a weapon	9%	7%

SOURCE: *Monitoring the Future, 2003* (Ann Arbor, MI: Institute for Social Research, 2004).

As part of their Monitoring the Future program, the Institute for Social Research also collects data on teen victimization. The most recent data available (2003) indicate that each year a significant number of adolescents become crime victims (see Table 2.4). This and other self-report surveys reveal that, if anything, the NCVS seriously *underreports* juvenile victimization, and that the true rate of juvenile victimization may actually be several times higher.[85]

Victim/Offender Association

NCVS data can also tell us something about the relationship between victims and offenders. This information is available because victims of violent personal crimes, such as assault and robbery, can identify the age, sex, and race of their attackers.

In general, teens tend to be victimized by their peers. A majority of teens were shown to have been victimized by other teens, whereas victims age 20 and over identified their attackers as being 21 or older. However, people in almost all age groups who were victimized by *groups* of offenders identified their attackers as teenagers. Violent crime victims report that a disproportionate number of their attackers are young, ranging in age from 16 to 25.

The data also tell us that victimization is intraracial (within race). White teenagers tend to be victimized by white teens, and African American teenagers tend to be victimized by African American teens.

Most teens are victimized by people with whom they are acquainted, and their victimization is more likely to occur during the day. In contrast, adults are more often victimized by strangers and at night. One explanation for this pattern is that youths are at greatest risk from their own family and relatives. (Chapter 8 deals with the issue of child abuse and neglect.) Another possibility is that many teenage victimizations occur at school, in school buildings or on school grounds. The issue of teen victimization is discussed further in the Focus on Delinquency box entitled "Adolescent Victims of Violence."

Victimization Risk

Delinquency experts believe that the victimization is not a random event. Personal behavior, social status, and lifestyle all affect the risk of victimization. These factors increase the likelihood that an adolescent will become a victim of violent crime.

Family Status Victim data show that youths being raised in single-parent households experience significantly higher risks for violence (60 out of every 1,000 children become victims) than youth in two-parent families (40 out of every 1,000 children). The overall risk for violence is about 50 percent higher among youth living in single-parent families than among youth living in two-parent families.[86]

Community Composition Kids living in highly disadvantaged communities will have the greatest chance of becoming crime victims. These areas lack the social cohesion to

Adolescent Victims of Violence

How many adolescents experience extreme physical and sexual violence, and what effect does the experience have on their lives? To answer these critical questions, Dean Kilpatrick, Benjamin Saunders, and Daniel Smith conducted interviews with 4,023 adolescents aged 12 to 17 to obtain information on their substance use, abuse, delinquency, and post-traumatic stress disorder (PTSD), as well as their experiences with sexual assault, physical assault, physically abusive punishment, and witnessing acts of violence.

Kilpatrick and his colleagues found that rates of interpersonal violence and victimization among adolescents in the United States are extremely high. Approximately 1.8 million adolescents aged 12 to 17 have been sexually assaulted, and 3.9 million have been severely physically assaulted. Another 2.1 million have been punished by physical abuse. The most common form of youth victimization is witnessing violence, with approximately 8.8 million youths indicating that they have seen someone else being shot, stabbed, sexually assaulted, physically assaulted, or threatened with a weapon.

The study shows distinct racial and ethnic patterns in youth victimization. There is a much higher incidence of all types of victimization among black and Native American adolescents; more than half of black, Hispanic, and Native American adolescents surveyed have witnessed violence in their lifetimes. Native American adolescents had the largest rate for sexual assault victimizations; whites and Asians reported the lowest. Native Americans, African Americans, and Hispanics also reported the highest rate of physical assault victimization; 20 to 25 percent of each group reported experiencing at least one physical assault.

Gender also plays a role in increasing the exposure to violence. Girls are at greater risk of sexual assault than boys (13.0 percent versus 3.4 percent). Boys are at significantly greater risk of physical assault than girls (21.3 percent versus 13.4 percent). A substantial number of all adolescents (43.6 percent of boys and 35 percent of girls) reported having witnessed violence. Physically abusive punishment was similar for boys (8.5 percent) and girls (10.2 percent).

WHAT ARE THE OUTCOMES OF ABUSE AND VIOLENCE?

The research discovered a clear relationship exists between youth victimization and mental health problems and delinquent behavior. For example:

▐ Negative outcomes in victims of sexual assault were three to five times the rates observed in nonvictims.

▐ The lifetime prevalence of post-traumatic stress disorder (PTSD) is 8.1 percent, indicating that approximately 1.8 million adolescents have met the criteria for PTSD at some point during their lifetime.

▐ Girls were significantly more likely than boys to have lifetime PTSD (10.1 percent versus 6.2 percent).

▐ Among boys who had experienced sexual assault, 28.2 percent had PTSD at some point in their lives. The rate of lifetime PTSD among boys who had not been sexually assaulted was 5.4 percent.

▐ Sexually assaulted girls had a lifetime PTSD rate of 29.8 percent, compared with only 7.1 percent of girls with no sexual assault history.

Experiencing either a physical assault or physically abusive punishment was associated with a lifetime PTSD rate of 15.2 percent for boys. The rate of lifetime PTSD in boys who had not been physically assaulted or abusively punished was 3.1 percent. Approximately 25 percent of physically assaulted or abused adolescents reported lifetime substance abuse or dependence. Rates of substance problems among adolescents who had not been physically assaulted or abused were roughly 6 percent. The percentage of boys who were physically assaulted and had committed an index offense was 46.7 percent, compared with 9.8 percent of boys who were not assaulted. Similarly, 29.4 percent of physically assaulted girls reported having engaged in serious delinquent acts at some point in their lives, compared with 3.2 percent of girls who had not been assaulted.

The Kilpatrick research shows that youths aged 12 to 17 are at great risk from violent acts and that those who experience violent victimizations suffer significant social problems. Protecting adolescents must become a significant national priority.

Critical Thinking

1. Should people who abuse or harm adolescent children be punished more severely than those who harm adults?
2. Would you advocate the death penalty for someone who rapes an adolescent female?

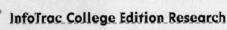 InfoTrac College Edition Research

To read more about this topic, go to InfoTrac College Edition and read the following article: Arthur H. Green, "Child Sexual Abuse: Immediate and Long-Term Effects and Intervention," *Journal of the American Academy of Child and Adolescent Psychiatry* 32:890–902 (1993).

SOURCE: Dean Kilpatrick, Benjamin Saunders, and Daniel Smith, *Youth Victimization: Prevalence and Implications* (Washington, DC: National Institute of Justice, 2003).

---

protect youth, especially those living in single-parent families. As the number of single-parent households increases, neighborhoods lose the resources to protect kids because fewer adults are available to monitor youth activities. Those adults who are available are more economically distressed and have less time and motivation to work with community leaders to control youth.[87]

High-Risk Lifestyle Children who have high-risk lifestyles—drinking, taking drugs, getting involved in crime—maintain a much greater chance of victimization.[88] For example, young runaways are at high risk for victimization; the longer they are exposed to street life, the greater their risk of becoming crime victims.[89] Teenage males have an extremely high victimization risk because their lifestyle places them at risk both at school and once they leave school grounds. They spend a great deal of time hanging out with their friends and in recreational pursuits. They may obtain a false ID to go drinking in the neighborhood bar or hang out in taverns at night, which places them at risk because many fights and assaults occur in places that serve liquor. Those who have histories of engaging in serious delinquency, getting involved in gangs, carrying guns, and selling drugs have an increased chance of being shot and killed themselves.[90]

As they mature, kids with high-risk lifestyles continue to have a high victimization risk, which continues into young adulthood. College students who spend several nights each week partying and who take recreational drugs are much more likely to suffer violent crime than those who avoid such risky lifestyles.[91] The association between lifestyle and juvenile victimization may be explained in part by the fact that kids who bear a number of risk factors for crime (such as carrying guns), and engage in delinquent and other antisocial activity, may be at the highest risk for victimization. The relationship between risk taking and victimization is explored further in the Focus on Delinquency box entitled "Delinquent and Victim: One and the Same?"

The Youngest Victims

Children under age 6 are often the target of criminal and sexual assaults. In the majority of instances, parents and other family members are the perpetrators (parents in about 36 percent of all instances, and nonparental family offenders in another 17 percent).[92] A recent study finds that babysitters make up a relatively small portion of

Despite some sensational cases, the number of children abducted or murdered by strangers is less than commonly thought. However, when a young child is victimized the impact can devastate an entire community. Here, kidnap victim Carlie Brucia, 11, is shown being led away by an unidentified man February 1, 2004. This image was taken by an exterior motion-sensor surveillance camera at a car wash. Carlie's body was found five days after she was abducted. This tragic case sadly shows the vulnerability of children to predatory criminals.

© Getty Images

Delinquent and Victim: One and the Same?

Are adolescents with a high-risk lifestyle who commit delinquent acts themselves at great risk of becoming crime victims? This question intrigued researchers who have been conducting longitudinal studies in Denver and Pittsburgh.

To address this question, they used data gathered in the Denver Youth Survey and the Pittsburgh Youth Study. The Denver Youth Survey began in 1987 and is based on a sample of 1,527 girls and boys aged 7, 9, 11, 13, and 15, randomly selected from more than 20,000 households and repeatedly measured over time. The Pittsburgh Youth Study consisted of a random sample of 1,517 boys in the first, fourth, and seventh grades in inner city public schools in 1987 and also subject to repeated contact by the research team. The study employed a sample of nonvictims for means of comparison.

The researchers attempted to show whether kids who had a variety of personal and social risk factors were more likely to become crime victims than those who were risk free. They looked at a number of potential risk factors. Family risk factors included having a low socioeconomic status, being raised by parents who committed crimes, living in a single-parent household, and receiving poor parental supervision. Individual risk factors included receiving poor school grades; being involved in gang or group fights; carrying weapons; participating in serious assault, drug usage, and sales; associating with delinquent peers; and having a personality that could be labeled oppositional, hyperactive, or impulsive.

DELINQUENCY AND VICTIMIZATION

The research team found that a striking percentage of youths in the two samples were crime victims and had suffered serious injury as a result of assaults or robberies. Among males, 11 percent in Pittsburgh and 20 percent in Denver reported having been a victim, as did 10 percent of the females in Denver.

Several risk factors were significantly related to victimization at both sites and for both genders. Kids who became victims of serious crime were more likely than nonvictims to have participated in gang/group fights, carried a weapon, committed a serious assault, sold drugs, and associated with delinquent peers. Youths characterized by any one of these risk factors were generally two to four times more likely to become a crime victim than a youth who did not have the risk factor. For example, between 24 and 40 percent of males involved in gang/group fights had themselves been seriously injured; among females, 27 percent of those involved in gang/group fights had been seriously injured.

Carrying a weapon was another surefire way to become a crime victim. Males who carried weapons were approximately three times more likely to be victimized than those who did not carry weapons—27 percent to 33 percent of the weapons carriers became victims, as opposed to only 10 percent who did not carry weapons. To a somewhat lesser extent, family and other risk factors were associated with elevated levels of victimization. These included coming from a single-parent household, having an oppositional and hyperactive personality, and using drugs. Among males only, risk factors also included having poor school grades, being impulsive, and having parents involved in criminal activities.

There was a direct correlation between the number of risk factors youths had and their victimization potential. For example, only 6 to 8 percent of males with no risk factors were victimized compared with 50 to 70 percent who had four or more risk factors. Among females, those with no risk factors had a 5 percent chance of becoming victims; among those with two or more risk factors, 42 percent became victims. One of the most striking findings was that kids who carried a weapon and engaged in fights were the ones most prone to becoming victims themselves. Among males, 40 to 46 percent of those individuals who carried weapons and were assaultive were themselves victims; among females who carried weapons and were assaultive, 30 percent were victims.

Critical Thinking

Analysis of the data drawn from the Denver and Pittsburgh cohort studies shows that maintaining a high-risk lifestyle is a key factor in juvenile victimization. Is it possible to conclude, therefore, that successful delinquency prevention programs are likely to reduce juvenile victimization because most victims are themselves involved in delinquency?

InfoTrac College Edition Research

Though the present research shows a clear link between engaging in risky behaviors and victimization, not all studies have reached the same result or conclusion. To read a study conducted in Canada with dissimilar findings, go to Info-Trac College Edition and look up Wendy C. Regoeczi, "Adolescent Violent Victimization and Offending: Assessing the Extent of the Link," *Canadian Journal of Criminology* 42(4):493 (October 2000).

SOURCE: Rolf Loeber, Larry Kalb, and David Huizinga, *Juvenile Delinquency and Serious Injury Victimization* (Washington, DC: Office of Juvenile Justice and Delinquency Prevention, 2001).

offenders (0.5%) who commit violent crimes against all children, but somewhat more (about 4%) of those who committed crimes against young children (those under age 6).

Complete strangers accounted for 11 percent of those arrested for offenses against juveniles and 5.6 percent against young children. Despite some sensational cases, the number of children seriously harmed (abducted or murdered) by strangers is less than commonly thought.[93] Each year there are about 50 cases in which it can be verified that a child was abducted and killed by a stranger; in another 100 cases the circumstances remain unknown, except that a child was killed by a stranger. Although stranger victimizations may be less common than once thought, the fact that as many as three children are abducted and killed by strangers every week is extremely disturbing.

Summary

- Official delinquency refers to youths who are arrested.

- Arrest data comes from the FBI's *Uniform Crime Report* (UCR), an annual tally of crimes reported to police by citizens.

- The FBI gathers arrest statistics from local police departments. From these, it is possible to determine the number of youths who are arrested each year, along with their age, race, and gender.

- About 2 million youths are arrested annually.

- After a long increase in juvenile crime, there has been a decade of decrease in the number of juveniles arrested for violent and property crimes.

- Dissatisfaction with the UCR prompted criminologists to develop other means of measuring delinquent behavior. Self-reports are surveys in which subjects are asked to describe their misbehavior. Although self-reports indicate that many more crimes are committed than are known to the police, they also show that the delinquency rate is rather stable.

- The factors that are believed to shape and control teen delinquency rates include gang activity, drug abuse, teen gun ownership, abortion rates, economy status, punishment, and social conditions.

- Delinquents are disproportionately male, although female delinquency rates are rising faster.

- Minority youth are overrepresented in the delinquency rate, especially for violent crime. Experts are split on the cause of racial differences. Some criminologists suggest that institutional racism, such as police profiling, accounts for the racial differences in the crime rate. Others believe that high African American crime rates are a function of living in a racially segregated society.

- Disagreement also exists over the relationship between class position and delinquency. Some hold that adolescent crime is a lower-class phenomenon, whereas others see it throughout the social structure. Problems in methodology have obscured the true class–crime relationship. However, official statistics indicate that lower-class youths are responsible for the most serious criminal acts.

- There is general agreement that delinquency rates decline with age. Some experts believe this phenomenon is universal, whereas others believe a small group of offenders persists in crime at a high rate. The age–crime relationship has spurred research on the nature of delinquency over the course of a lifetime.

- Delinquency data show that a chronic persistent offender begins his or her offending career early in life and persists as an adult. Wolfgang and his colleagues identified chronic offenders in a series of cohort studies conducted in Philadelphia.

- Ongoing research has identified the characteristics of persistent offenders as they mature, and both personality and social factors help predict long-term offending patterns.

- The National Crime Victimization Survey (NCVS) is an annual survey conducted by agencies of the federal government that measures the nature of crime and the characteristics of victims.

- Teenagers are much more likely to become victims of crime than are people in other age groups.

Key Terms

official delinquency, p. 34
dark figures of crime, p. 34
Federal Bureau of Investigation (FBI), p. 34
Uniform Crime Report (UCR), p. 34
Part I offenses, index crimes, p. 34
Part II offenses, p. 34
disaggregated, p. 35
self-reports, p. 40
age of onset, p. 49
chronic offender, p. 49

Questions for Discussion

1. What factors contribute to the aging-out process?
2. Why are males more delinquent than females? Is it a matter of lifestyle, culture, or physical properties?
3. Discuss the racial differences found in the crime rate. What factors account for differences in the African American and white crime rates?
4. Should kids who have been arrested more than three times be given mandatory incarceration sentences?
5. Do you believe that self-reports are an accurate method of gauging the nature and extent of delinquent behavior?

Viewpoint

As a juvenile court judge, you are forced to make a tough decision during a hearing to decide whether a juvenile should be waived to the adult court. It seems that gang activity has become a way of life for residents living in local public housing projects. The Bloods sell crack, and the Wolfpack controls the drug market. When the rivalry between the two gangs explodes, 16-year-old Shatiek Johnson, a Wolfpack member, shoots and kills a member of the Bloods; in retaliation the Bloods put out a contract on his life. While in hiding, Shatiek is confronted by two undercover detectives who recognize the young fugitive. Fearing for his life, Shatiek pulls a pistol and begins firing, fatally wounding one of the officers. During the hearing you learn that Shatiek's story is not dissimilar from that of many other children raised in housing projects. With an absent father and a single mother who could not control her five sons, Shatiek lived in a world of drugs, gangs, and shootouts long before he was old enough to vote. By age 13, Shatiek had been involved in the gang beating death of a homeless man in a dispute over $10, for which he was given a one-year sentence at a youth detention center and released after six months. Now charged with a crime that could be considered first-degree murder if committed by

an adult, Shatiek could—if waived to the adult court—be sentenced to life in prison or even face the death penalty.

At the hearing, Shatiek seems like a lost soul. He claims he thought the police officers were killers out to collect the bounty put on his life by the Bloods. He says that killing the rival gang boy was an act of self-defense. The DA confirms that the victim was in fact a known gang assassin with numerous criminal convictions. Shatiek's mother begs you to consider the fact that her son is only 16 years old, that he has had a difficult childhood, and that he is a victim of society's indifference to the poor.

▌ Would you treat Shatiek as a juvenile and see if a prolonged stay in a youth facility could help this troubled young man?

▌ Would you bind him over to the adult system?

▌ Does a 16-year-old like Shatiek deserve a second chance?

▌ Is Shatiek's behavior common among adolescent boys?

▌ Is this case just the tip of a rising tide of juvenile violence?

Doing Research on the Web

Before you answer, you may want to do research on juvenile violence by using it as a subject guide on InfoTrac College Edition.

What factors influence the offending behavior of chronic offenders such as Shatiek Johnson? One suspected cause is dysfunctional family life. To find out more, go to

InfoTrac College Edition and read Deborah Gorman-Smith, Patrick H. Tolan, Rolf Loeber, and David B. Henry, "Relation of Family Problems to Patterns of Delinquent Involvement among Urban Youth," *Journal of Abnormal Child Psychology* 26(5):319 (October 1998).

Notes

1. Federal Bureau of Investigation, *Crime in the United States, 2002* (Washington, DC: United State Government Printing Office, 2003).
2. Thomas Bernard, "Juvenile Crime and the Transformation of Juvenile Justice: Is There a Juvenile Crime Wave?" *Justice Quarterly* 16:336–356 (1999).
3. James A. Fox, *Trends in Juvenile Violence: A Report to the United States Attorney General on Current and Future Rates of Juvenile Offending* (Boston: Northeastern University, 1996).
4. Steven Levitt, "The Limited Role of Changing Age Structure in Explaining Aggregate Crime Rates," *Criminology* 37:581–599 (1999).

5. Steven Levitt, "Understanding Why Crime Fell in the 1990s: Four Factors that Explain the Decline and Six that Do Not," *Journal of Economic Perspectives* (in press, 2004).

6. "Fox Butterfield Possible Manipulation of Crime Data Worries Top Police," *New York Times,* August 3, 1998, p. 1.

7. A pioneering effort of self-report research is A. L. Porterfield's *Youth in Trouble* (Fort Worth, TX: Leo Potishman Foundation, 1946); for a review, see Robert Hardt and George Bodine, *Development of Self-Report Instruments in Delinquency Research: A Conference Report* (Syracuse, NY: Syracuse University Youth Development Center, 1965); see also Fred Murphy, Mary Shirley, and Helen Witmer, "The Incidence of Hidden Delinquency," *American Journal of Orthopsychiatry* 16:686–696 (1946).

8. Mallie Paschall, Miriam Ornstein, and Robert Flewelling, "African-American Male Adolescents' Involvement in the Criminal Justice System: The Criterion Validity of Self-Report Measures in a Prospective Study," *Journal of Research in Crime and Delinquency* 38:174–187 (2001).

9. Jerald Bachman, Lloyd Johnston, and Patrick O'Malley, *Monitoring the Future: Questionnaire Responses from the Nation's High School Seniors, 2002* (Ann Arbor, MI: Institute for Social Research, 2003).

10. Julia Yun Soo Kim, Michael Fendrich, and Joseph S. Wislar, "The Validity of Juvenile Arrestees' Drug Use Reporting: A Gender Comparison," *Journal of Research in Crime and Delinquency* 37:419–432 (2000).

11. Michael Hindelang, Travis Hirschi, and Joseph Weis, *Measuring Delinquency* (Beverly Hills, CA: Sage Publications, 1981); Gary Jensen and Raymond Eve, "Sex Differences in Delinquency: An Examination of Popular Sociological Explanation," *Criminology* 13:427–448 (1976); Michael Hindelang, "Age, Sex, and the Versatility of Delinquent Involvements," *Social Problems* 18:522–535 (1979); James Short and F. Ivan Nye, "Extent of Unrecorded Juvenile Delinquency, Tentative Conclusions," *Journal of Criminal Law, Criminology, and Police Science* 49:296–302 (1958).

12. For a review, see Meda Chesney-Lind and Randall Shelden, *Girls, Delinquency and Juvenile Justice* (Pacific Grove, CA: Brooks/Cole, 1992), pp. 7–14.

13. Leroy Gould, "Who Defines Delinquency? A Comparison of Self-Report and Officially Reported Indices of Delinquency for Three Racial Groups," *Social Problems* 16:325–336 (1969); Harwin Voss, "Ethnic Differentials in Delinquency in Honolulu," *Journal of Criminal Law, Criminology, and Police Science* 54:322–327 (1963); Ronald Akers et al., "Social Characteristics and Self-Reported Delinquency," in Gary Jensen, ed., *Sociology of Delinquency* (Beverly Hills, CA: Sage Publications, 1981), pp. 48–62.

14. David Huizinga and Delbert Elliott, "Juvenile Offenders: Prevalence, Offender Incidence, and Arrest Rates by Race," *Crime and Delinquency* 33:206–223 (1987); see also Dale Dannefer and Russell Schutt, "Race and Juvenile Justice Processing in Court and Police Agencies," *American Journal of Sociology* 87:1113–1132 (1982).

15. Paul Tracy, "Race and Class Differences in Official and Self-Reported Delinquency," in Marvin Wolfgang, Terrence Thornberry, and Robert Figlio, eds., *From Boy to Man, from Delinquency to Crime* (Chicago: University of Chicago Press, 1987), p. 120.

16. Bachman, Johnston, and O'Malley, *Monitoring the Future,* pp. 102–104.

17. Samuel Walker, Cassia Spohn, and Miriam DeLone, *The Color of Justice: Race, Ethnicity and Crime in America* (Belmont, CA: Brooks/Cole, 1992), pp. 46–47.

18. Miriam Sealock and Sally Simpson, "Unraveling Bias in Arrest Decisions: The Role of Juvenile Offender Typescripts," *Justice Quarterly* 15:427–457 (1998).

19. Robin Shepard Engel and Jennifer Calnon, "Examining the Influence of Drivers' Characteristics during Traffic Stops with Police: Results from a National Survey," *Justice Quarterly* 21:49–90 (2004).

20. Rodney Engen, Sara Steen, and George Bridges, "Racial Disparities in the Punishment of Youth: A Theoretical and Empirical Assessment of the Literature," *Social Problems* 49:194–221 (2002).

21. Steven Belenko, Jane Sprott, and Courtney Petersen, "Drug and Alcohol Involvement among Minority and Female Juvenile Offenders: Treatment and Policy Issues," *Criminal Justice Policy Review* 15:3–36 (2004).

22. Christina Polsenberg and Kenneth Jackson, "Putting Race into Context: Race, Juvenile Justice Processing and Urbanization," paper presented at the American Society of Criminology meeting, Boston, November 1995 (updated version, 1996); for a general review, see Carl Pope and William Feyerherm, "Minority Status and Juvenile Justice Processing (Part I)," *Criminal Justice Abstracts* 22:327–335 (1990); see also Douglas Smith and Jody Klein, "Police Control of Interpersonal Disputes," *Social Problems* 31:468–481 (1984).

23. Christina DeJong and Kenneth Jackson, "Putting Race into Context: Race, Juvenile Justice Processing, and Urbanization," *Justice Quarterly* 15:487–504 (1998).

24. Donna Bishop and Charles Frazier, "The Influence of Race in Juvenile Justice Processing," *Journal of Research in Crime and Delinquency* 25:242–263 (1989).

25. Engen, Steen, and Bridges, "Racial Disparities in the Punishment of Youth," pp. 194–221.

26. David Eitle, Stewart D'Alessio, and Lisa Stolzenberg, "Racial Threat and Social Control: A Test of the Political, Economic, and Threat of Black Crime Hypotheses" *Social Forces* 81:557–576 (2002); Michael Leiber and Jayne Stairs, "Race, Contexts and the Use of Intake Diversion," *Journal of Research in Crime and Delinquency* 36:56–86 (1999); Darrell Steffensmeier, Jeffery Ulmer, and John Kramer, "The Interaction of Race, Gender, and Age in Criminal Sentencing: The Punishment Cost of Being Young, Black, and Male," *Criminology* 36:763–798 (1998).

27. Walker, Spohn, and DeLone, *The Color of Justice,* pp. 46–48.

28. Mallie Paschall, Robert Flewelling, and Susan Ennett, "Racial Differences in Violent Behavior among Young Adults: Moderating and Confounding Effects," *Journal of Research in Crime and Delinquency* 35:148–165 (1998).

29. Fox Butterfield, *All God's Children: The Bosket Family and the American Tradition of Violence* (New York: Avon, 1996).

30. Julie Phillips, "Variation in African-American Homicide Rates: An Assessment of Potential Explanations," *Criminology* 35:527–559 (1997).

31. Melvin Thomas, "Race, Class and Personal Income: An Empirical Test of the Declining Significance of Race Thesis, 1968–1988," *Social Problems* 40:328–339 (1993).

32. Michael Leiber and Jayne Stairs, "Race, Contexts and the Use of Intake Diversion," *Journal of Research in Crime and Delinquency* 36:56–86 (1999); Steffensmeier, Ulmer, and Kramer, "The Interaction of Race, Gender, and Age in Criminal Sentencing."

33. Tracy Nobiling, Cassia Spohn, and Miriam DeLone, "A Tale of Two Counties: Unemployment and Sentence Severity," *Justice Quarterly* 15:459–486(1998).

34. Alexander Weiss and Steven Chermak, "The News Value of African-American Victims: An Examination of the Media's Presentation of Homicide," *Journal of Crime and Justice* 21:71–84 (1998).

35. Thomas, "Race, Class and Personal Income."

36. Paschall, Flewelling, and Ennett, "Racial Differences in Violent Behavior among Young Adults."

37. Thomas McNulty and Paul Bellair, "Explaining Racial and Ethnic Differences in Adolescent Violence: Structural Disadvantage, Family Well-Being, and Social Capital," *Justice Quarterly* 20:1–32 (2003).

38. Julie Phillips, "White, Black, and Latino Homicide Rates: Why the Difference?" *Social Problems* 49:349–374 (2002).

39. Carl Pope and William Feyerherm, "Minority Status and Juvenile Processing: An Assessment of the Research Literature," paper presented at the American Society of Criminology meeting, Reno, Nevada, November 1989.

40. Jeffrey Fagan, Elizabeth Piper, and Melinda Moore, "Violent Delinquents and Urban Youths," *Criminology* 24:439–471 (1986).

41. Robert Agnew, "A General Strain Theory of Community Differences in Crime Rates," *Journal of Research in Crime and Delinquency* 36:123–155 (1999).

42. Bonita Veysey and Steven Messner, "Further Testing of Social Disorganization Theory: An Elaboration of Sampson and Groves's 'Community Structure and Crime'," *Journal of Research in Crime and Delinquency* 36:156–174 (1999).

43. James Short and Ivan Nye, "Reported Behavior as a Criterion of Deviant Behavior," *Social Problems* 5:207–213 (1958).

44. Classic studies include Ivan Nye, James Short, and Virgil Olsen, "Socioeconomic Status and Delinquent Behavior," *American Journal of Sociology* 63:381–389 (1958); Robert Dentler and Lawrence Monroe, "Social Correlates of Early Adolescent Theft," *American Sociological Review* 26:733–743 (1961); Charles Tittle, Wayne Villemez, and Douglas Smith, "The Myth of Social Class and Criminality: An Empirical Assessment of the Empirical Evidence," *American Sociological Review* 43:643–656 (1978).

45. R. Gregory Dunaway et al., "The Myth of Social Class and Crime Revisited: An Examination of Class and Adult Criminality," *Criminology* 38:589–632 (2000).

46. Delbert Eliott and Suzanne Ageton, "Reconciling Race and Class Differences in Self-Reported and Official Estimates of Delinquency," *American Sociological Review* 45:95–110 (1980); for a similar view, see John Braithwaite, "The Myth of Social Class and Criminality Reconsidered," *American Sociological Review* 46:35–58 (1981); Margaret Farnworth et al., *Measurement in the Study of Class and Delinquency: Integrating Theory and Research,* working paper no. 4, rev. (Albany, NY: Rochester Youth Development Survey, 1992), p. 19.

47. G. Roger Jarjoura and Ruth Triplett, "Delinquency and Class: A Test of the Proximity Principle," *Justice Quarterly* 14:765–792 (1997).

48. See David Farrington, "Age and Crime," in Michael Tonry and Norval Morris, eds., *Crime and Justice, An Annual Review*, vol. 7 (Chicago: University of Chicago Press, 1986), pp. 189–250.

49. Patrick O'Malley, Jerald Bachman, and Lloyd Johnston, "Period, Age and Cohort Effects on Substance Abuse among Young Americans: A Decade of Change, 1976–1986," *American Journal of Public Health* 78:1315–1321 (1989); Darrell Steffensmeier et al., "Age and the Distribution of Crime," *American Journal of Sociology* 94:803–831 (1989); Alfred Blumstein and Jacqueline Cohen, "Characterizing Criminal Careers," *Science* 237:985–991 (1987).

50. Travis Hirschi and Michael Gottfredson, "Age and the Explanation of Crime," *American Journal of Sociology* 89:552–584 (1983).

51. Michael Gottfredson and Travis Hirschi, "The True Value of Lambda Would Appear to Be Zero: An Essay on Career Criminals, Criminal Careers, Selective Incapacitation, Cohort Studies, and Related Topics," *Criminology* 24:213–234 (1986); further support for their position can be found in Lawrence Cohen and Kenneth Land, "Age Structure and Crime," *American Sociological Review* 52:170–183 (1987).

52. Edward Mulvey and John LaRosa, "Delinquency Cessation and Adolescent Development: Preliminary Data," *American Journal of Orthopsychiatry* 56:212–224 (1986).

53. Margo Wilson and Martin Daly, "Life Expectancy, Economic Inequality, Homicide, and Reproductive Timing in Chicago Neighbourhoods," *British Journal of Medicine* 31:1271–1274 (1997).

54. Timothy Brezina, "Delinquent Problem-Solving: An Interpretive Framework for Criminological Theory and Research," *Journal of Research in Crime and Delinquency* 37:3–30 (2000).

55. Gordon Trasler, "Cautions for a Biological Approach to Crime," in Sarnoff Mednick, Terrie Moffitt, and Susan Stack, eds., *The Causes of Crime, New Biological Approaches* (Cambridge: Cambridge University Press, 1987), pp. 7–25.

56. Alicia Rand, "Transitional Life Events and Desistance from Delinquency and Crime," in Wolfgang, Thornberry, and Figlio, eds., *From Boy to Man, from Delinquency to Crime*, pp. 134–163.

57. Marc Le Blanc, "Late Adolescence Deceleration of Criminal Activity and Development of Self- and Social-Control," *Studies on Crime and Crime Prevention* 2:51–68 (1993).

58. Barry Glassner et al., "Note on the Deterrent Effect of Juvenile vs. Adult Jurisdiction," *Social Problems* 31:219–221 (1983).

59. Neal Shover and Carol Thompson, "Age, Differential Expectations, and Crime Desistance," *Criminology* 30:89–104 (1992).

60. David Nurco, Timothy Kinlock, and Mitchell Balter, "The Severity of Preaddiction Criminal Behavior among Urban, Male Narcotic Addicts and Two Nonaddicted Control Groups," *Journal of Research in Crime and Delinquency* 30:293–316 (1993).

61. Rolf Loeber and David Farrington, "Young Children Who Commit Crime: Epidemiology, Developmental Origins, Risk Factors, Early Interventions, and Policy Implications," *Development and Psychopathology* 12:737–762 (2000).

62. D. Wayne Osgood, "The Covariation among Adolescent Problem Behaviors," paper presented at the American Society of Criminology meeting, Baltimore, November 1990.

63. Stephen Tibbetts, "Low Birth Weight, Disadvantaged Environment and Early Onset: A Test of Moffitt's Interactional Hypothesis," paper presented at the American Society of Criminology meeting, Boston, November 1995.

64. Arnold Barnett, Alfred Blumstein, and David Farrington, "A Prospective Test of a Criminal Career Model," *Criminology* 27:373–388 (1989).

65. Marvin Wolfgang, Robert Figlio, and Thorsten Sellin, *Delinquency in a Birth Cohort* (Chicago: University of Chicago Press, 1972).

66. Paul Tracy, Marvin Wolfgang, and Robert Figlio, *Delinquency in Two Birth Cohorts, Executive Summary* (Washington, DC: U.S. Department of Justice, 1985).

67. Lyle Shannon, *Assessing the Relationship of Adult Criminal Careers to Juvenile Careers: A Summary* (Washington, DC: U.S. Office of Juvenile Justice and Delinquency Prevention, 1982); Howard Snyder, *Court Careers of Juvenile Offenders* (Washington, DC: Office of Juvenile Justice and Delinquency

Prevention, 1988); D. J. West and David P. Farrington, *The Delinquent Way of Life* (London: Heinemann, 1977); Donna Hamparian et al., *The Violent Few* (Lexington, MA: Lexington Books, 1978).

68. Michael Schumacher and Gwen Kurz, *The 8% Solution: Preventing Serious Repeat Juvenile Crime* (Thousand Oaks, CA, Sage Publications, 1999).

69. Peter Jones et al., "Identifying Chronic Juvenile Offenders," *Justice Quarterly* 18:478–507 (2001).

70. See Wolfgang, Thornberry, and Figlio, eds., *From Boy to Man, from Delinquency to Crime*.

71. Paul Tracy and Kimberly Kempf-Leonard, *Continuity and Discontinuity in Criminal Careers* (New York: Plenum Press, 1996).

72. Kimberly Kempf-Leonard, Paul Tracy, and James Howell, "Serious, Violent, and Chronic Juvenile Offenders: The Relationship of Delinquency Career Types to Adult Criminality," *Justice Quarterly* 18:449–478 (2001).

73. R. Tremblay et al., "Disruptive Boys with Stable and Unstable High Fighting Behavior Patterns during Junior Elementary School," *Journal of Abnormal Child Psychology* 19:285–300 (1991).

74. Jennifer White et al., "How Early Can We Tell? Predictors of Childhood Conduct Disorder and Adolescent Delinquency," *Criminology* 28:507–535 (1990).

75. John Laub and Robert Sampson, "Unemployment, Marital Discord, and Deviant Behavior: The Long-Term Correlates of Childhood Misbehavior," paper presented at the annual meeting of the American Society of Criminology, Baltimore, November 1990; rev. version.

76. Michael Ezell and Amy D'Unger, "Offense Specialization among Serious Youthful Offenders: A Longitudinal Analysis of a California Youth Authority Sample" (unpublished report, Durham, NC: Duke University, 1998).

77. Kimberly Kempf, "Crime Severity and Criminal Career Progression," *Journal of Criminal Law and Criminology* 79:524–540 (1988).

78. Jeffrey Fagan, "Social and Legal Policy Dimensions of Violent Juvenile Crime," *Criminal Justice and Behavior* 17:93–133 (1990).

79. Peter Greenwood, *Selective Incapacitation* (Santa Monica, CA: Rand, 1982).

80. Terence Thornberry, David Huizinga, and Rolf Loeber, "The Prevention of Serious Delinquency and Violence," in James Howell et al., eds., *Sourcebook on Serious, Violent, and Chronic Juvenile Offenders* (Thousand Oaks, CA: Sage Publications, 1995).

81. Callie Marie Rennison and Michael Rand, *Criminal Victimization, 2002* (Washington, DC: Bureau of Justice Statistics, 2003).

82. Ted Miller, Mark Cohen, and Brian Wiersema, *The Extent and Costs of Crime Victimization: A New Look* (Washington, DC: National Institute of Justice, 1995).

83. Rennison and Rand, *Criminal Victimization, 2002*.

84. Craig A. Perkins, *Age Patterns of Victims of Serious Violent Crime* (Washington, DC: Bureau of Justice Statistics, 1997).

85. L. Edward Wells and Joseph Rankin, "Juvenile Victimization: Convergent Validation of Alternative Measurements," *Journal of Research in Crime and Delinquency* 32:301–304 (1995).

86. Janet L. Lauritsen, "How Families and Communities Influence Youth Victimization," *Juvenile Justice Bulletin* (Washington, DC, November 2003).

87. Ibid.

88. Lening Zhang, John W. Welte, and William F. Wieczorek, "Deviant Lifestyle and Crime Victimization," *Journal of Criminal Justice* 29:133–143 (2001).

89. Dan Hoyt, Kimberly Ryan, and Mari Cauce, "Personal Victimization in a High-Risk Environment: Homeless and Runaway Adolescents," *Journal of Research in Crime and Delinquency* 36:371–392 (1999).

90. Rolf Loeber et al., "Gun Injury and Mortality: The Delinquent Backgrounds of Juvenile Offenders," *Violence and Victims* 14:339–351 (1999).

91. Bonnie Fisher et al., "Crime in the Ivory Tower: The Level and Sources of Student Victimization," *Criminology* 36:671–710 (1998).

92. David Finkelhor and Richard Ormrod, "Crimes against Children by Babysitters," *Juvenile Justice Bulletin* (Office of Juvenile Justice and Delinquency Prevention, U.S. Department of Justice, September 2001).

93. Gerald Hotaling and David Finkelhor, "Estimating the Number of Stranger Abduction Homicides of Children: A Review of Available Evidence," *Journal of Criminal Justice* 18:385–399 (1990).

Theories of Delinquency

What causes delinquent behavior? Why do some youths enter a life of crime that persists into their adulthood? Are people products of their environment, or is the likelihood of their becoming a delinquent determined at birth?

Social scientists have speculated on the cause of delinquency for 200 years. They have observed facts about delinquent behavior and organized them into complex theoretical models. A *theory* is a statement that explains the relationship between abstract concepts in a meaningful way. For example, if scientists observe that delinquency rates are usually higher in neighborhoods with high unemployment rates, poor housing, and inadequate schools, they might theorize that environmental conditions influence delinquent behavior. This theory suggests that social conditions can exert a powerful influence on human behavior.

Since the study of delinquency is essentially interdisciplinary, it is not surprising that a variety of theoretical models have been formulated to explain juvenile misbehavior. Each reflects the training and orientation of its creator. Consequently, theories of delinquency reflect many different avenues of inquiry, including biology, psychology, sociology, political science, and economics. Chapter 3 reviews theories that hold that delinquency is essentially caused by individual-level factors, such as personal choices and decision making or by psychological and biological factors. Chapter 4 reviews social theories of delinquency that hold that youthful misbehavior is either caused by children's place in the social structure, their relationships with social institutions and processes, or their reaction to the effects of social conflict. Chapter 5 discusses those theories of delinquency that regard it as a developmental process, reflecting the changes that occur in young people's lives as they evolve during their life course.

Logic dictates that the competing theoretical models presented here cannot all be correct and that some of these may be barking up the wrong tree! Yet every branch of social science—sociology, psychology, political science, economics—contains competing theoretical models. Why people behave the way they do and how society functions are issues that are far from settled. So do not lose patience! Explaining delinquency is a highly complex phenomenon with many points of view.

Chapter 3 Individual Views of Delinquency

Chapter 4 Sociological Views of Delinquency

Chapter 5 Developmental Views of Delinquency

3

Individual Views of Delinquency

Chapter Outline

Choice Theory and Classical Criminology

The Rational Delinquent

FOCUS ON DELINQUENCY: The Benefits of Delinquency

Shaping Delinquent Choices

Choosing Delinquent Acts

Preventing Delinquency

General Deterrence

Specific Deterrence

Situational Crime Prevention

Why Do Delinquents Choose Crime?

Trait Theories: Biosocial and Psychological Views

Origins of Trait Theory

Contemporary Biosocial Theory

Biochemical Factors

Neurological Dysfunction

FOCUS ON DELINQUENCY: Diet and Delinquency

FOCUS ON DELINQUENCY: Attention Deficit
   Hyperactivity Disorder

Genetic Influences

Evolutionary Theory

Psychological Theories of Delinquency

Psychodynamic Theory

FOCUS ON DELINQUENCY: Disruptive Behavior Disorders

Behavioral Theory

Cognitive Theory

Psychological Characteristics and Delinquency

Personality and Delinquency

Intelligence and Delinquency

Critiquing Individual-Level Theories

Trait Theory and Delinquency Prevention

Chapter Objectives

1. Know the difference between choice theories and trait theories

2. Understand the concept of criminal choice

3. Be familiar with the concept of routine activities

4. Be able to discuss the pros and cons of general deterrence

5. Recognize what is meant by the term "specific deterrence" and how it differs from general deterrence

6. Understand the concept of situational crime prevention and be able to list the strategies now being used

7. Be familiar with Cesare Lombroso, the founder of biological criminology

8. Know the biochemical, neurological, and genetic factors linked to delinquency

9. Understand how the psychodynamic model of delinquency links antisocial behaviors to unconscious emotions and feelings

10. Understand why (according to the behavioral perspective) watching violent media causes violent behaviors

11. Know why some psychologists view delinquency as a function of improper information processing

12. Be familiar with the term "psychopath"

13. Recognize the issues linking intelligence to delinquency

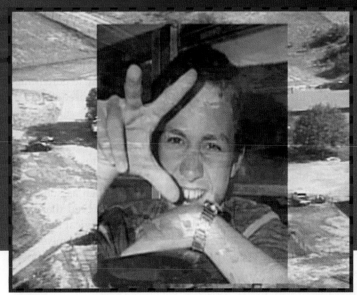

CNN. View the CNN video clip of this story and answer related Critical Thinking questions on your Juvenile Delinquency 9e CD-ROM.

On July 6, 2004, law enforcement authorities were summoned to the New Mexico ranch of ABC newsman Sam Donaldson. There they discovered the bodies of foreman Delbert Paul Posey, his wife, Tryone Posey, and her daughter, Mary Lee Schmid, 14. A day later, Posey's 14-year-old son, Cody, was arrested on charges of killing his father, stepmother, and stepsister.

The Posey family seemed to be happy and well-adjusted. They had been running one of Donaldson's southern New Mexico ranches for more than two years. Yet Donaldson and neighbors knew that Posey was a tough father who did not shy away from discipline. Cody Posey had seemed withdrawn and moody. Later, law enforcement officials learned that Cody may have been the victim of abuse and that he often showed up at school bruised and battered. He told police that his father had beaten him once too often and that after the last time, he took a gun from the barn and shot his family.

The Cody Posey case illustrates the fact that many delinquent acts are not caused by some environmental factor such as poverty or hopelessness but by individual behaviors and emotions. The Posey family did not live in an inner-city area but on the ranch of a wealthy TV personality. Cody's behavior was motivated not by his environment but by his own experiences and decision making.

Some delinquency experts believe that the decision to commit an illegal act is a product of an individual decision-making process that may be shaped by the personal characteristics of the decision maker. They reject the notion that delinquents are a product of their environment and instead search for an individual trait—selfish temperament, impulsive personality, abnormal hormones—to explain why some people may choose antisocial over conventional behaviors. If social and economic factors alone determine behavior, how is it that many youths residing in the most dangerous and deteriorated neighborhoods live law-abiding lives? According to the U.S. Census Bureau, more than 30 million Americans live in poverty, yet the vast majority of people do not become delinquents and criminals.[1] Research indicates that relatively few youths in any population, even the most economically disadvantaged, actually become hard-core, chronic delinquents.[2] The quality of neighborhood and family life may have little impact on the choices individuals make.[3]

If social factors are not responsible for the onset of delinquency, what is? To some theorists, the locus of delinquency is rooted in the *individual:* how the individual makes decisions, the quality of his or her biological makeup, and the personality and psychological profile.

choice theory
Holds that youths will engage in delinquent and criminal behavior after weighing the consequences and benefits of their actions; delinquent behavior is a rational choice made by a motivated offender who perceives that the chances of gain outweigh any possible punishment or loss.

There is more than one explanation for why individuals become crime prone. One position, referred to as **choice theory,** suggests that young offenders choose to engage in antisocial activity because they believe their actions will be beneficial and profitable. Whether they join a gang, steal cars, or sell drugs, their delinquent acts are motivated by the reasoned belief that crime can be a relatively risk-free way to better their personal situation. They have little fear of getting caught or of the consequences of punishment. Some are motivated by fantasies of riches, whereas others may simply enjoy the excitement and short-term gratification produced by criminal acts such as beating up an opponent or stealing a car.

All youthful misbehavior, however, cannot be traced to rational choice, profit motive, or criminal entrepreneurship. Some delinquent acts, especially violent ones, seem irrational, selfish, and/or hedonistic. Many forms of delinquency, such as substance abuse and vandalism, appear more impulsive than rational. It is believed that these antisocial behaviors may be inspired by aberrant physical or psychological traits that govern behavioral choices. Though some youths may choose to commit crime simply because they desire conventional luxuries and power, others may be driven by constitutional abnormalities, such as hyperactivity, low intelligence, biochemical imbalance, or genetic defects. This view of delinquency is referred to here generally as **trait theory** because it links delinquency to biological and psychological traits that control human development.

trait theory
Holds that youths engage in delinquent or criminal behavior due to aberrant physical or psychological traits that govern behavioral choices; delinquent actions are impulsive or instinctual rather than rational choices.

Choice and trait theories share common ground because they focus on the individual's mental and behavioral processes. All people are different, so that each person reacts to the same set of environmental and social conditions in a unique way. Faced with extreme stress and economic hardship, one person will seek employment, borrow money, save for the future, and live a law-abiding life; another will use antisocial or violent behavior to satisfy his or her needs.

This chapter first covers those theoretical models that focus on individual choice. Then it discusses the view that biological and psychological development controls youngsters' ability to make choices, rendering some of them violent, aggressive, and antisocial.

CHOICE THEORY AND CLASSICAL CRIMINOLOGY

free will
View that youths are in charge of their own destinies and are free to make personal behavior choices unencumbered by environmental factors.

The first formal explanations of crime and delinquency held that human behavior was a matter of choice. Because it was assumed that people had **free will** to choose their behavior, those who violated the law were motivated by personal needs such as greed, revenge, survival, and hedonism. Over 200 years ago, **utilitarian** philosophers Cesare Beccaria and Jeremy Bentham argued that people weigh the benefits and consequences of their future actions before deciding on a course of behavior.[4] Their writings formed the core of what is referred to today as **classical criminology.**

utilitarians
Those who believe that people weigh the benefits and consequences of their future actions before deciding on a course of behavior.

The classical view of crime and delinquency holds that the decision to violate the law comes after a careful weighing of the benefits and costs of criminal behaviors. Most potential law violators would cease their actions if the potential pain associated with a behavior outweighed its anticipated gain; conversely, law-violating behavior seems attractive if the future rewards seem far greater than the potential punishment.[5]

classical criminology
Holds that decisions to violate the law are weighed against possible punishments, and to deter crime the pain of punishment must outweigh the benefit of illegal gain; led to graduated punishments based on seriousness of the crime (let the punishment fit the crime).

According to the classical view, before youths decide to commit crime, they compare the possible benefits or profits, such as cash to buy cars, clothes, and other luxury items, with the potential costs or penalties, such as arrest followed by a long stay in a juvenile facility. If they believe that drug dealers are rarely caught and even then usually avoid severe punishments, the youths will more likely choose to become dealers than if they believe that dealers are almost always caught and punished by lengthy prison terms. They may know or hear about criminals who make a significant income

© Phil McCartey/PhotoEdit

Choice theorists would have us believe that delinquents are rational and calculating. But some delinquent acts such as vandalism seem more impulsive than cunning. Are the graffiti artists shown here cunning criminals or impetuous youth who are more spontaneous than devious?

-www- To read more about **Cesare Beccaria,** go to www.utm.edu/research/iep/b/ beccaria.htm. For an up-to-date list of web links, go to http://cj.wadsworth.com/ siegel_jd9e.

from their illegal activities and want to follow in their footsteps.[6] Put simply, in order to deter or prevent crime, the pain of punishment must outweigh the benefit of illegal gain.[7]

Classical criminologists argued that punishment should be only severe enough to deter a particular offense and that punishments should be graded according to the seriousness of particular crimes: "Let the punishment fit the crime." For example, Beccaria argued that it would be foolish to punish pickpockets and murderers in a similar fashion because this would encourage thieves to kill the victims or witnesses to their crimes.[8]

The popularity of the classical approach was in part responsible for the development of the prison as an alternative to physical punishment and the eventual creation of criminal sentences geared to the seriousness of crimes.[9] The choice approach dominated the policy of the U.S. justice system for about 150 years.

The Rational Delinquent

The view that delinquents are rational decision makers who *choose* to violate the law remains a popular theoretical approach to the study and control of delinquency. Its current popularity is in part due to the disappointing results of rehabilitative categories. Past efforts to treat known delinquents by treatment, counseling, and other rehabilitation techniques have been regarded by some experts as noble failures.[10] This failure, they argue, is a signal that delinquency is not merely a function of social ills, such as a lack of economic opportunity or family dysfunction. If it were, then educational enrichment, family counseling, job training programs, and the like should be more effective alternatives to crime. In reality, many affluent youths from "good" families choose to break the law, whereas most indigent adolescents are law abiding. The reasoning follows that, rich or poor, some youths are greedy and selfish and choose to break the law to satisfy their needs, urges, and desires. Their delinquent tendencies can only be controlled by threatening them with punishments severe enough to convince them that (1) "crime does not pay" and (2) they are better off choosing conventional rather than criminal solutions to satisfy their needs.[11] Those who subscribe to the rational choice model believe that the decision to commit a specific type of crime and the subsequent entry into a criminal lifestyle are a matter of personal decision making based on a weighing of available information; hence, the term *rational choice.*

According to this view, law-violating behavior occurs when a reasoning offender decides to take the chance of violating the law after considering his or her personal situation (need for money, learning experiences, opportunities for conventional success), values (conscience, moral values, need for peer approval), and situational factors (how well the target is protected, whether people are at home, how wealthy the neighborhood is, the likelihood of getting caught, the punishment if apprehended). Conversely, the decision to forgo law-violating behavior may be based on the growing perception that the economic benefits are no longer there or the probability of successfully completing a crime is less than the chances of being caught and punished. In this sense, delinquent behavior may be viewed as a form of problem-solving behavior that helps kids deal with the difficulties of negotiating their environment. The Focus on Delinquency box entitled "The Benefits of Delinquency" looks at this issue in more depth.

The Benefits of Delinquency

If delinquents are rational decision makers, it stands to reason that their behavior may be designed to overcome problems they face in their daily lives. In this sense, delinquency can be viewed as problem-solving behavior that can provide benefits that cannot be gained through legitimate behaviors.

Sociologist Timothy Brezina has identified some problems that delinquent behavior may address or improve.

▎ *Perceived control.* Brezina finds that a fundamental need of humans is to maintain a sense of mastery over their environment. Kids may turn to delinquent behaviors to restore control over their lives when conventional alternatives are unavailable. Adolescents may find themselves feeling "out of control" because society limits their opportunities and resources. They may also find themselves in the ironic situation of being forced to obey parents, teachers, and other authority figures while being socialized to be independent and self-regulating. Delinquency may allow some adolescents to exert control over their own lives and destinies, by helping them to avoid situations they find uncomfortable or repellant (for example, by cutting school or running away from an abusive home) or to obtain resources for desired activities and commodities (for example, by stealing or selling drugs to buy stylish outfits).

▎ *Positive self-evaluation.* According to Brezina, some delinquents are motivated to improve their self-evaluations. Adolescence is a time when peer evaluations are critical for feelings of self-worth. Kids who are not in the right clique or are socially isolated may suffer acute psychological distress. Delinquency may provide a means of countering negative evaluations, to attack symbolically or otherwise the source of the youths' self-rejecting attitudes. Delinquency may also provide a path for enhancing self-feelings, for example, by becoming part of a close-knit gang.

▎ *Negative affect.* Kids may sometimes feel they have been the target of undue punishment, sanctions, negative evaluations, and other hurtful experiences that cause them severe emotional distress. Drinking and drug taking may allow some kids to ward off depression and compensate for a lack of positive experiences: a form of self-medication. Some, angry at their mistreatment, may turn to violence to satisfy a desire for revenge or retaliation.

Brezina finds that there is a great deal of evidence that kids engage in antisocial acts in order to solve problems. The literature on drug and alcohol abuse is replete with examples of research showing that kids turn to substance abuse to increase their sense of personal power, to become more assertive, and to reduce tension and anxiety. Others may embrace deviant lifestyles such as the punk culture to offend conventional society and overcome their own ordinariness. Engaging in risky behavior helps some kids to feel alive and competent. There is also evidence that antisocial acts can provide positive solutions to problems. Violent kids, for example, may have learned that being aggressive with others is a good means to control the situation and get what they want; counterattacks may be one means of controlling people who are treating them poorly.

Just because an adolescent faces social problems does not necessarily mean he or she will turn to antisocial behavior to solve them. Most kids are faced with adverse situations while growing up, and relatively few deal with them by turning to violence or drug abuse. Why do some kids turn to antisocial acts to solve their life's problems?

▎ *Lack of conventional problem-solving alternatives.* Problem-solving techniques normally available to adults are generally denied adolescents, such as borrowing

Shaping Delinquent Choices

Lifestyle and opportunity help shape a youngster's decision to choose delinquency. What are some of the most important social developments that produce delinquent decision making?

Personal Freedom Adolescents whose parents are poor supervisors and allow them the freedom to socialize with peers are more likely to engage in deviant behaviors.[12] Teenage boys may have the highest crime rates because they, rather than girls, have the freedom to engage in unsupervised socialization.[13] Though girls are more closely supervised than boys, those who are physically mature seem to have more freedom. Physically mature girls have a lifestyle more similar to boys, and without parental supervision they are the ones most likely to have the opportunity to engage in antisocial acts.[14]

Getting a Job If lifestyle influences choice, can providing kids with "character building" activities—such as a part-time job after school—reduce their delinquent

money from a bank. Some youths may feel there is no escape from their problems and that there are few options open to them. When they have conflict with adults, they may turn to vandalism rather than to an attorney. They may engage in antisocial acts because they simply could not think of anything else to do. Some may lack self-control and act on impulse rather than reasoned thought.

I *Positive outcome expectancies.* Kids are more likely to commit delinquent acts to solve their problems if they perceive a positive outcome from their actions. They may have a here-and-now orientation and fail to realize that what may work in the short run, such as quitting school, will have long-term negative consequences.

I *The efficacy of delinquent adaptations.* Prior experiences with delinquent problem solving will enhance the likelihood of future experiences. Some kids have been successful at using antisocial methods to solve problems; they will turn to these successful strategies when similar situations arise. Once committed to delinquent strategies, kids may feel they have little to lose by using them again and again. Their commitment to conformity becomes weak and attenuated.

Brezina argues that viewing delinquency as a problem-solving device can help explain the aging-out phenomenon. As people mature, the level and intensity of the problems they face may diminish. The Sturm und Drang (storm and stress) of adolescence gives way to the relative tranquility of adulthood, without the worries of school and peer group approval. Family conflict is diminished as young adults find their own place in the world. Young adults have more power to control their own destiny and have acquired the skills through experience to become better problem solvers. At the same time, short-term solutions, appealing as they are to adolescents, may be far less so to adults who have reached a more mature life view. Going

to a drunken frat party may sound appealing to sophomores, but the risks involved make them off-limits to grads. As people mature, their thinking extends farther into the future, and risky behavior is a threat to long-range plans. Not all delinquents develop the capacity to apply mature evaluations. Some remain impulsive and lack self-control. Those who have experienced overwhelming social problems may find it difficult to develop long-range thinking, but the majority can and will choose not to commit crimes.

Critical Thinking

1. Brezina claims that, for a small group of offenders, the value associated with developing delinquent coping techniques remains compelling and contributes to their long-term involvement in crime. What can be done to convince such youth that they have chosen an inappropriate strategy?

2. Have you changed your problem-solving methods during your lifetime? Have your life experiences shaped your coping techniques?

InfoTrac College Edition Research

How do kids solve problems? To find out more about this topic, go to InfoTrac College Edition and use *problem solving* as a subject guide; then click on the subcategory of Problem Solving in Children.

SOURCES: Timothy Brezina, "Delinquent Problem-Solving: An Interpretive Framework for Criminological Theory and Research," *Journal of Research in Crime and Delinquency* 37:3–30 (2000); Andy Hochstetler; "Opportunities and Decisions: Interactional Dynamics in Robbery and Burglary Groups," *Criminology* 39:737–763 (2001).

involvement? Some but not all research efforts show that adolescent work experience actually increases delinquency rather than limits its occurrence. Rather than saving for college as their parents hope, kids who get jobs may be looking for an easy opportunity to acquire cash to buy drugs and alcohol; after-school jobs may attract teens who are more impulsive than ambitious.[15] At work, they will have the opportunity to socialize with deviant peers. This influence, combined with lack of parental supervision, increases criminal motivation.[16] Though some adults may think that providing teens with a job will reduce criminal activity—under the theory that idle hands are the devil's workshop—some aspects of the work experience, such as autonomy, increased social status among peers, and increased income, may neutralize the positive effects of working. If providing jobs is to have any positive influence on kids, the employment opportunity must also be able to provide a learning experience and support academic achievement.[17]

Joining a Gang Another social choice that kids make in an effort to improve their lifestyle—joining a gang—may also increase the likelihood of their delinquent activities. Gang members have been found to act like employers, providing their associates with security and the know-how to conduct "business deals." When Steven Levitt and Sudhir Alladi Venkatesh studied the financial rewards of being in a drug gang, they found that despite enormous risks to their health, life, and freedom, the average gang members earned slightly more than what they could in the legitimate labor market (about six to eleven dollars per hour).[18] Why did they stay in the gang? They believed that there was a strong potential for future riches if they stayed in the drug business and earned a "management" position (gang leaders earned a lot more than the rank and file members). Being in a teenage drug gang was based on perception of the potential for future criminal gain versus the reality of conventional alternatives and opportunities.[19] Teen gangs will be discussed further in Chapter 8.

Choosing Delinquent Acts

How are crimes planned? What makes one target inviting and another forbidding? The rational choice theory views the concepts of crime and criminality as two separate issues. Criminality is the propensity to engage in criminal or delinquent acts; crimes are events that are in violation of the criminal law.[20] There will always be a population of criminally motivated adolescents; unless they have criminal opportunities they will not be able to act upon their inclinations. Similarly, given an open opportunity for illegal gain, even the least criminally inclined youth may be motivated to act. The explanation for why a child eventually becomes a delinquent then is distinct from the reasons an individual delinquent decides to break into a particular house one day or sell narcotics the next. The decision to "choose" crime occurs when an offender decides to take the chance of violating the law after considering his or her situation (need for money, opportunities for conventional success), values (conscience, need for peer approval), and situational factors (the likelihood of getting caught, the punishment if apprehended). Conversely, the decision to forgo law-violating behavior may be based on the perception that the benefits are no longer worthwhile, or the probability of successfully completing a crime is less than the chance of being caught. For example, aging out may occur because as delinquents mature they begin to realize that the risks of crime are greater than the potential profits. The solution to crime, therefore, may be formulating policies that will cause the potential criminal to choose conventional behaviors.[21]

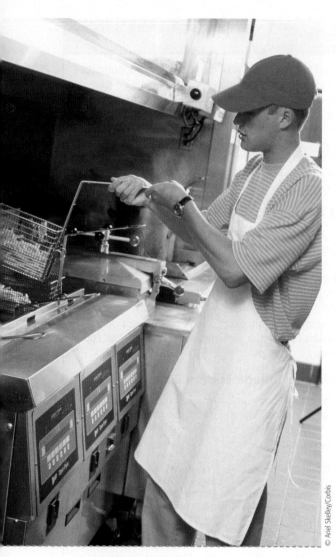

© Ariel Skelley/Corbis

Though some parents think that an after-school job will keep their kids out of trouble ("idle hands are the devil's workshop"), many delinquency experts believe that aspects of the work experience such as autonomy, increased social status among peers, and increased income, may neutralize the positive effects of working.

The Seduction of Crime Are there personal factors that influence delinquent decision making? Sociologist Jack Katz makes the provocative argument that kids choose delinquency because it can provide the excitement some kids crave; violating the law can be exciting and even seductive for those willing to take the risk.[22]

Katz argues that kids become involved in provocative situations that influence their behavior choices. Someone challenges their authority, heritage, or reputation, and they vanquish this opponent with a beating: "He called me a punk, so I beat his ass." Some want to maximize their pleasure by doing something exciting or risky: They break into a school and vandalize the building. Some crimes provide "sneaky thrills": Youths may shoplift merely to see if they can get away with it. Crime may be thrilling because it is a demonstration of personal competence.

FIGURE 3.1
Routine Activities Theory Posits the Interaction of Three Factors Help Explain Fluctuations in the Delinquency Rate

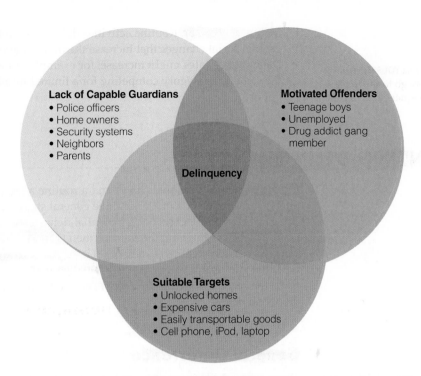

Lack of Capable Guardians
- Police officers
- Home owners
- Security systems
- Neighbors
- Parents

Motivated Offenders
- Teenage boys
- Unemployed
- Drug addict gang member

Delinquency

Suitable Targets
- Unlocked homes
- Expensive cars
- Easily transportable goods
- Cell phone, iPod, laptop

According to Katz, kids choose crime because it is seductive, a pleasurable exercise that can relieve tension, increase self-esteem, and provide pleasurable physical sensations.

Routine Activities Are there structural factors that influence delinquent decision making? According to **routine activities theory,** developed by Lawrence Cohen and Marcus Felson, the volume and distribution of **predatory crime** (violent crimes against the person and crimes in which an offender attempts to steal an object directly from its holder) are influenced by the interaction of three variables that reflect the routine activities found in everyday American life: the *lack of capable guardians* (such as home owners and their neighbors, friends, and relatives); the availability of *suitable targets* (such as homes containing easily salable goods); and the presence of *motivated offenders* (such as unemployed teenagers). If each of these components is present, there is greater likelihood that a predatory crime will take place. (See Figure 3.1.)[23]

routine activities theory
View that crime is a "normal" function of the routine activities of modern living; offenses can be expected if there is a motivated offender and a suitable target that is not protected by capable guardians.

predatory crime
Violent crimes against people, and crimes in which an offender attempts to steal an object directly from its holder.

I   *Lack of capable guardians.* According to the routine activities approach, general social change can filter down to influence delinquency rates and patterns. For example, one reason the delinquency rate may have trended upward between 1970 and 1990 is because the number of adult caretakers at home during the day (guardians) decreased as more women entered the workforce. Because mothers are at work and children are in daycare, homes are left unguarded and become more suitable targets. Similarly, with the growth of suburbia and the decline of the traditional neighborhood, the number of such familiar guardians as family, neighbors, and friends has diminished.[24] Research shows that crime levels are relatively low in neighborhoods where residents keep a watchful eye on their neighbors' property.[25]

I   *Suitable targets.* Routine activities theory suggests that the availability of suitable targets such as easily transportable commodities will increase delinquency rates.[26] Research has generally supported the fact that the more wealth a home contains, the more likely it will become a target.[27] As laptop computers, cell phones, and digital cameras become more commonplace, burglary rates should rise, simply because the more these high-priced and easily sold goods are available, the more offenders will be motivated to steal.[28]

To read an article on **how routine activities can be applied to delinquency through civil remedies such as curfews,** go to http://wcr.sonoma.edu/v4n1/Manuscripts/brunetarticle.pdf. For an up-to-date list of web links, go to http://cj.wadsworth.com/siegel_jd9e.

TO QUIZ YOURSELF ON THIS
MATERIAL, go to the Juvenile
Delinquency 9e website.

I *Motivated offenders.* Routine activities theory also links the delinquency rates to general social changes that increase the number and motivation of offenders. Delinquency rates might increase, for example, if there is a surplus of youths of the same age category competing for a limited number of jobs and educational opportunities.

PREVENTING DELINQUENCY

If delinquency is a rational choice and a routine activity, as some believe, then delinquency prevention is a matter of three general strategies: (1) It stands to reason that it can be prevented by convincing potential delinquents that they will be severely punished for committing delinquent acts; then (2) they must be punished so severely that they never again commit crimes; or (3) it must be so difficult to commit crimes that the potential gain is not worth the risk. The first of these strategies is called *general deterrence,* the second is *specific deterrence,* and the third, *situational crime prevention.* Each is discussed below.

General Deterrence

general deterrence
Crime control policies that depend on the fear of criminal penalties, such as long prison sentences for violent crimes; the aim is to convince law violators that the pain outweighs the benefit of criminal activity.

The **general deterrence** concept holds that the choice to commit delinquent acts is structured by the threat of punishment. If kids believe they will get away with illegal behavior, they may choose to commit crime.[29] If, on the other hand, kids believed that their illegal behavior would result in apprehension and severe punishment, then only the truly irrational would commit crime; they would be *deterred.*[30]

One of the guiding principles of deterrence theory is that *the more severe, certain, and swift the punishment, the greater its deterrent effect will be.*[31] Even if a particular crime carries a severe punishment, there will be relatively little deterrent effect if most people do not believe they will be caught.[32] Conversely, even a mild sanction may deter crime if people believe punishment is certain.[33] So if the justice system can convince would-be delinquents that they will be caught—for example, by putting more police officers on the street—they may decide that delinquency simply does not pay.[34]

Deterrence and Delinquency One might argue that kids are not deterred by the fear of punishment because, traditionally, juvenile justice is based on the *parens patriae* philosophy, which mandates that children be treated and not punished. This limits the power of the law to deter juvenile crime. Yet, in recent years, the increase in teenage violence, gang activity, and drug abuse has prompted a reevaluation of deterrence strategies. Police began to focus on particular problems in their jurisdiction rather than merely reacting after a crime occurred.[35] They began to use aggressive tactics to deter membership in drug-trafficking gangs.[36] Police are now more willing to use aggressive tactics, such as gang-busting units, to deter membership in drug-trafficking gangs. Youthful-looking officers have been sent undercover into high schools in order to identify, contact, and arrest student drug dealers.[37]

Juvenile courts have also attempted to initiate a deterrence strategy. Juvenile court judges have been willing to waive youths to adult courts; prior record may outweigh an offender's need for services in making this decision.[38] Legislators seem willing to pass more restrictive juvenile codes featuring mandatory incarceration sentences in juvenile facilities, and the number of incarcerated juveniles continues to increase. Adolescents are not even spared capital punishment: the U.S. Supreme Court has upheld the use of the death penalty for youths over 16.[39] The trend toward a more punitive, deterrence-based juvenile process will be discussed further in Chapters 12–15.

Can delinquency and drug abuse be deterred when so many teens consider it fun and socially acceptable? High school student Cathy (left) parties with other rave fans at an abandoned warehouse in Portland, Oregon. Oregon's rave scene is an escape for teens, a worry for parents, and a worrisome challenge for law enforcement officials.

Do General Deterrence Strategies Work?

The effectiveness of deterrence strategies is a topic of considerable debate. A number of studies have contributed data supporting deterrence concepts. Evidence indicates that the threat of police arrest can deter property crimes.[40] Areas of the country in which punishment is more certain seem to have lower delinquency rates; the more likely people are to anticipate punishment, the less likely they are to commit crimes.[41]

Though these findings are persuasive, there is actually little conclusive evidence that the threat of apprehension and punishment alone can deter crime.[42] More evidence exists that fear of social disapproval and informal penalties, criticisms, and punishments from parents and friends may actually be a greater deterrent to crime than legal punishments.[43]

Because deterrence strategies are based on the idea of a rational, calculating offender, they may not be effective when applied to immature young people. Minors tend to be less capable of making mature judgments about their behavior choices. For example, many younger offenders are unaware of the content of juvenile legal codes, so that imposition of a deterrence policy, such as mandatory waiver to the adult court for violent crimes, will have little effect on delinquency rates.[44] It seems futile, therefore, to try to deter delinquency through fear of legal punishment. Teens seem more fearful of being punished by their parents or of being the target of disapproval from their friends than they are of the police.[45]

It is also possible that for the highest-risk group of young offenders—teens living in economically depressed neighborhoods—the deterrent threat of formal sanctions may be irrelevant. Inner-city youngsters may not have internalized the norms of society, which hold that getting arrested is wrong. (See Chapter 4 for more on inner-city norms and values.) Young people in these areas have less to lose if arrested; they have a limited stake in society and are not worried about their future. They also may not make connections between their illegal behavior and punishment because they see many people in their neighborhood commit crimes and not get caught or punished.[46]

In sum, deterring delinquency through the fear of punishment may be of limited value because children may neither fully comprehend the seriousness of their acts nor the consequences they may face.[47] Though on the surface deterrence appears to have benefit as a delinquency control device, there is also reason to believe that it has limited demonstrable effectiveness.

Specific Deterrence

specific deterrence
Sending convicted offenders to secure incarceration facilities so that punishment is severe enough to convince offenders not to repeat their criminal activity.

The theory of **specific deterrence** holds that if offenders are punished severely, the experience will convince them not to repeat their illegal acts. Although general deterrence focuses on potential offenders, specific deterrence targets offenders who have already been convicted. Juveniles are sent to secure incarceration facilities with the understanding that their ordeal will deter future misbehavior.

Specific deterrence is a popular approach to crime control today. Unfortunately, relying on punitive measures may expand rather than reduce future delinquency.

Institutions quickly become overcrowded, and chronic violent offenders are packed into swollen facilities with juveniles who have committed non-serious and nonviolent crimes. The use of mandatory sentences for some crimes (usually violent crimes or drug dealing) means that all kids who are found to have committed those crimes must be institutionalized; first-time offenders may be treated the same as chronic recidivists. Some research studies show that arrest and conviction may under some circumstances lower the frequency of re-offending, a finding which supports specific deterrence.[48] However, other studies indicate that punishment has little real effect on reoffending and in some instances may in fact increase the likelihood that first-time offenders will commit new crimes (recidivate).[49] Kids who are placed in a juvenile justice facility are just as likely to become adult criminals as those treated with greater leniency.[50] In fact, a history of prior arrests, convictions, and punishments has proven to be the best predictor of rearrest among young offenders released from correctional institutions. Rather than deterring future offending, punishment may in fact encourage reoffending.[51]

Why does punishment encourage rather than reduce delinquency? According to some experts, institutionalization cuts youth off from prosocial supports in the community, making them more reliant on deviant peers. Incarceration may also diminish chances for successful future employment, reducing access to legitimate opportunities. Punishment strategies may stigmatize kids and help lock offenders into a delinquent career. Kids who are punished may also believe that the likelihood of getting caught twice for the same type of crime is remote: "Lightning never strikes twice in the same spot," they may reason; no one is that unlucky.[52] So although some researchers have found that punishment may reduce the frequency of future offending, the weight of the evidence suggests that time served has little impact on recidivism.

Situational Crime Prevention

situational crime prevention
Crime prevention method that relies on reducing the opportunity to commit criminal acts by (1) making them more difficult to perform, (2) reducing their reward, and (3) increasing their risks.

target-hardening technique
Crime prevention technique that makes it more difficult for a would-be delinquent to carry out the illegal act, for example, by installing a security device in a home.

To find **situational crime prevention resources,** go to this website maintained by Rutgers University: http://crimeprevention.rutgers.edu/resources/resources.htm. For an up-to-date list of web links, go to http://cj.wadsworth.com/siegel_jd9e.

TO QUIZ YOURSELF ON THIS MATERIAL, go to the Juvenile Delinquency 9e website.

Rather than deterring or punishing individuals in order to reduce delinquency rates, **situational crime prevention** strategies aim to reduce the opportunities people have to commit particular crimes. The idea is to make it so difficult to commit specific criminal acts that would-be delinquent offenders will be convinced that the risks of crime are greater than the rewards.[53] Controlling the situation of crime can be accomplished by increasing the effort, increasing the risks, and/or reducing the rewards attached to delinquent acts.

Increasing the effort to commit crime can involve **target-hardening techniques** such as placing steering locks on cars and putting unbreakable glass on storefronts. Some successful target-hardening efforts include installing a locking device on cars that prevents drunken drivers from starting the vehicle (breath-analyzed ignition interlock device).[54] *Access control* can be maintained by locking gates and fencing yards.[55] The *facilitators of crime* can be controlled by such measures as banning the sale of spray paint to adolescents in an effort to cut down on graffiti, or having photos put on credit cards to reduce their value if stolen.

Increasing the risks of crime might involve such measures as improving surveillance lighting, creating neighborhood watch programs, controlling building entrances and exits, installing burglar alarms and security systems, and increasing the number of private security officers and police patrols. The installation of street lights may convince would be burglars that their entries will be seen and reported.[56] Closed-circuit TV cameras have been shown to reduce the amount of car theft from parking lots while reducing the need for higher-cost security personnel.[57]

Reducing the rewards of crime could include strategies such as making car radios removable so they can be kept at home at night, marking property so that it is more difficult to sell when stolen, and having gender-neutral phone listings to discourage obscene phone calls. Tracking systems, such as those made by the LoJack Corporation, help police locate and return stolen vehicles. (See Concept Summary 3.1 for a summary of the different delinquency prevention strategies.)

Concept Summary 3.1

Overview of Choice-Based Delinquency Control Strategies

General Deterrence	Premise	People will commit crime and delinquency if they perceive that the benefits outweigh the risks. Crime is a function of the severity, certainty, and speed of punishment.
	Strengths	Suggests a practical solution to crime: Increase the certainty and severity of punishment. Punishment can be made proportionate to the seriousness of the crime. Increasing the severity of punishment will reduce delinquency.
Specific Deterrence	Premise	Punishing people severely will prevent future law violations. People learn from punishment that "crime does not pay." Punishment has practical applications and is therefore justified.
	Strengths	Provides a simple solution to the delinquency problem. Punishing more delinquents will reduce their involvement in criminal activity.
Situational Crime Prevention	Premise	Crime can be controlled by increasing the effort, increasing the risks, and reducing the rewards attached to committing offenses.
	Strengths	Shows the importance of situational factors in the delinquent act. Can be aimed at reducing or eliminating a specific type of delinquency, i.e., shoplifting in a mall, rather than eliminating all delinquency through social change.

Why Do Delinquents Choose Crime?

All the delinquency control methods based on choice theory assume the delinquent to be a motivated offender who breaks the law because he or she perceives an abundance of benefits and an absence of threat. Increase the threat and reduce the benefits, and the delinquency rate should decline.

This logic is hard to refute. After all, by definition, a person who commits an illegal act but is not rational cannot be considered a criminal or delinquent but instead is "not guilty by reason of insanity." To say that delinquents choose their crimes is for the most part entirely logical. Yet several questions remain unanswered by choice theorists. First, why do some people continually choose to break the law, even after suffering its consequences? Why are some kids law abiding even though they are indigent and have little chance of gaining economic success? Conversely, why do some affluent youths break the law when they have everything to lose and little more to gain?

Choice theorists also have problems explaining seemingly irrational crimes, such as vandalism, arson, and even drug abuse. To say a teenager who painted swastikas on a synagogue or attacked a gay couple was making a "rational choice" seems inadequate to explain such a destructive, purposeless act.

The relationships observed by rational choice theorists can also be explained in other ways. For example, though the high victimization rates in lower-class neighborhoods can be explained by an oversupply of motivated offenders, they may also be due to other factors, such as social conflict and disorganization.[58]

In sum, although choice theories can contribute to understanding criminal events and victim patterns, they leave a major question unanswered: Why do some people choose crime over legal activities?

TRAIT THEORIES: BIOSOCIAL AND PSYCHOLOGICAL VIEWS

Why, then, do delinquents choose crime over law-abiding behavior? A faithful and loyal choice theorist believes that selecting crime is usually part of an economic strategy, a function of carefully weighing the benefits of criminal over legal behavior. For example, youths decide to commit a robbery if they believe they will make a good profit, have a good chance of getting away with it, and, even if caught, stand little chance of being severely punished.

A number of delinquency experts believe that this model is incomplete. They believe it is wrong to infer that all youths choose crime simply because they believe its advantages outweigh its risks. If that were the case, how could senseless and profitless crimes such as vandalism and random violence be explained? These experts argue that human behavioral choices are a function of an individual's mental and/or physical makeup. Most law-abiding youths have personal traits that keep them within the mainstream of conventional society. In contrast, youths who choose to engage in repeated aggressive, antisocial, or conflict-oriented behavior manifest abnormal traits that influence their behavior choices.[59] Uncontrollable, impulsive behavior patterns place some youths at odds with society, and they soon find themselves in trouble with the law. Although delinquents may choose their actions, the decision is a product of all but uncontrollable mental and physical properties and traits.

The view that delinquents are somehow "abnormal" is not a new one. Some of the earliest theories of criminal and delinquent behavior stressed that crime was a product of personal traits and that measurable physical and mental conditions, such as IQ and body build, determined behavior. This view is generally referred to today as *positivism*. Positivists believe that the scientific method can be used to measure the causes of human behavior and that behavior is a function of often uncontrollable factors, such as mental illness.

The source of behavioral control is one significant difference between trait and choice theories. Whereas the former reasons that behavior is controlled by personal traits, the latter views behavior as purely a product of human reasoning. To a choice theorist, reducing the benefits of crime by increasing the likelihood and severity of punishment will eventually lower the crime rate. Biosocial, or trait, theory focuses less on the effects of punishment and more on the treatment of abnormal mental and physical conditions as a crime-reduction method. In the following section, the primary components of trait theory are reviewed.

Origins of Trait Theory

The first attempts to discover why criminal tendencies develop focused on the physical makeup of offenders. Biological traits present at birth were thought to predetermine whether people would live a life of crime.

The origin of this school of thought is generally credited to the Italian physician Cesare Lombroso (1835–1909).[60] Known as the father of criminology, Lombroso put his many years of medical research to use in his theory of **criminal atavism**.[61] Lombroso found that delinquents manifest physical anomalies that make them biologically and physiologically similar to our primitive ancestors. These atavistic individuals are savage throwbacks to an earlier stage of human evolution. Because of this link, the "born criminal" has such physical traits as enormous jaws, strong canines, a flattened nose, and supernumerary teeth (double rows, as in snakes). Lombroso made such statements as "It was easy to understand why the span of the arms in criminals so often exceeds the height, for this is a characteristic of apes, whose forelimbs are used in walking and climbing."[62]

Contemporaries of Lombroso refined the notion of a physical basis of crime. Rafaele Garofalo (1851–1934) shared Lombroso's belief that certain physical characteristics indicate a criminal or delinquent nature.[63] Enrico Ferri (1856–1929), a student of Lombroso, believed that a number of biological, social, and organic factors caused delinquency and crime.[64]

These early views portrayed delinquent behavior as a function of a single factor or trait, such as body build or defective intelligence. They had a significant impact on early American criminology, which relied heavily on developing a science of "criminal anthropology."[65] Eventually, these views evoked criticism for their unsound methodology and lack of proper scientific controls. Some researchers used captive offender populations and failed to compare experimental subjects with control groups of nondelinquents or undetected delinquents. These methodological flaws made it impossible to determine whether biological traits produce delinquency. It is equally

criminal atavism
The idea that delinquents manifest physical anomalies that make them biologically and physiologically similar to our primitive ancestors, savage throwbacks to an earlier stage of human evolution.

A complete list of the **crime-producing physical traits** identified by Lombroso is available online at www.d.umn.edu/~jhamlin1/lombroso.html. For an up-to-date list of web links, go to http://cj.wadsworth.com/siegel_jd9e.

TO QUIZ YOURSELF ON THIS MATERIAL, go to the Juvenile Delinquency 9e website.

plausible that police are more likely to arrest, and courts convict, the mentally and physically abnormal. By the middle of the twentieth century, biological theories had fallen out of favor as an explanation of delinquency.

CONTEMPORARY BIOSOCIAL THEORY

For most of the twentieth century, delinquency experts scoffed at the notion that a youth's behavior was controlled by physical conditions present at birth. During this period, the majority of delinquency research focused on social factors, such as poverty and family life, which were believed to be responsible for law-violating behavior. However, a small group of criminologists and penologists kept alive the biological approach.[66] Some embraced sociobiology, a perspective that suggests behavior will adapt to the environment in which it evolved.[67] Creatures of all species are influenced by their genetic inheritance and their innate need to survive and dominate others. Sociobiology had a tremendous effect on reviving interest in a biological basis for crime and delinquency, because if biological (genetic) makeup controls all human behavior, it follows that a person's genes should also be responsible for determining whether he or she chooses law-violating or conventional behavior.[68]

Today, those who embrace trait theory reject the traditional assumptions that all humans are born with equal potential to learn and achieve (**equipotentiality**) and that thereafter their behavior is controlled by external or social forces.[69] Traditional criminologists suggest (either explicitly or implicitly) that all people are born equal and that parents, schools, neighborhoods, and friends control subsequent development. Trait theorists argue that no two people (with rare exceptions, such as identical twins) are alike, and therefore each will react to environmental stimuli in a distinct way. They assume that a combination of personal traits and the environment produces individual behavior patterns. People with pathological traits such as brain damage, an abnormal personality, or a low IQ may have a heightened risk for crime. This risk is elevated by environmental stresses such as poor family life, educational failure, substance abuse, and exposure to delinquent peers. For example, low-birthweight babies have been found to suffer poor educational achievement later in life; academic deficiency has been linked to delinquency and drug abuse.[70] A mother's dietary intake during pregnancy can influence a child's IQ level later in life, and intelligence levels have been linked to delinquency.[71] The reverse may also apply: A supportive environment may be strong enough to counteract adverse biological and psychological traits.[72]

Biosocial theorists believe that it is the interaction between predisposition and environment that produces delinquency. Children born into a disadvantaged environment often do not get the social and familial support they need to overcome their handicaps. Lack of family support can have long-term physical consequences. For example, a child's neural pathways may be damaged by repeated child neglect or abuse. Once experiences are ingrained, the brain "remembers," and a pattern of electrochemical activation is established, which remains present across the lifespan.[73] The relatively small number of youths who suffer both physical and social handicaps, and who also lack social supports, are the ones who become early onset offenders and persist in a life of crime.[74]

Contemporary biosocial theorists seek to explain the onset of antisocial behaviors, such as aggression and violence, by focusing on the physical qualities of the offenders.[75] The majority of major research efforts appear to be concentrated in three distinct areas of study: biochemical factors, neurological dysfunction, and genetic influences. These three views are discussed in some detail below.

equipotentiality
View that all people are equal at birth and are thereafter influenced by their environment.

biosocial theory
The view that both thought and behavior have biological and social bases.

Biochemical Factors

There is a suspected relationship between antisocial behavior and biochemical makeup.[76] One view is that body chemistry can govern behavior and personality, including levels of aggression and depression.[77] For example, exposure to lead in the environment and subsequent lead ingestion has been linked to antisocial behaviors.[78]

When criminologists Paul Stretesky and Michael Lynch examined lead concentrations in air across counties in the United States, they found that areas with the highest concentrations of lead also reported the highest level of homicide.[79] Lead is not the only contaminant related to antisocial behavior. Exposure to the now banned PCB (polychlorinated biphenyls), a chemical once used in insulation materials, has been shown to influence brain functioning and intelligence levels.[80]

There is also evidence that diet may influence behavior through its impact on body chemistry. Of particular concern is an unusually high intake of such items as artificial food coloring, milk, and sweets. Some scientists believe that chronic under- or oversupply of vitamins, such as C, B3, and B6, may be related to restlessness and antisocial behavior in youths. Evidence also exists that allergies to foods can influence mood and behavior, resulting in personality swings between hyperactivity and depression.[81] This relationship is further explored in the Focus on Delinquency box entitled "Diet and Delinquency."

Hormonal Levels Hormonal levels are another area of biochemical research. Antisocial behavior allegedly peaks in the teenage years because hormonal activity is at its highest level during this period. Research suggests that increased levels of the male androgen testosterone are responsible for excessive levels of violence among teenage boys.[82]

Adolescents who experience more intense moods, mood swings, anxiety, and restlessness than people at other points in development also have the highest crime rates.[83] These mood and behavior changes have been associated with family conflict and antisocial behavior.

An association between hormonal activity and antisocial behavior is suggested because rates of both factors peak in adolescence.[84] Hormonal sensitivity may begin at the very early stages of life when the fetus can be exposed to abnormally high levels of testosterone while in the uterus. This may trigger a heightened response to the release of testosterone when an adolescent male reaches puberty. Although testosterone levels appear normal, the young male is at risk for overaggressive behavior responses.[85]

Hormonal activity as an explanation of gender differences in the delinquency crime rate will be discussed further in Chapter 6.

Neurological Dysfunction

neurological
Pertaining to the brain and nervous system structure.

Another focus of biosocial theory is the **neurological,** or brain and nervous system, structure of offenders. Studies measure indicators of system functioning, such as brain waves, heart rate, arousal levels, skin conductance and attention span, cognitive ability, and spatial learning, and then compare them to measures of antisocial behavior.

One view is that the neuroendocrine system, which controls brain chemistry, is the key to understanding violence and aggression. Imbalance in the central nervous system's chemical and hormonal activity has been linked to antisocial behavior and drug abuse. Research shows that persistent abnormality in the way the brain metabolizes glucose can be linked to substance abuse.[86]

Another view is that neurological dysfunction, commonly measured with an electroencephalogram (EEG), a CAT scan, or performance indicators (gross motor functions, visual processing, auditory-language functioning), is the key factor in causing aggression and violence. Children who manifest behavior disturbances may have identifiable neurological deficits, such as damage to the hemispheres of the brain.[87] This is sometimes referred to as **minimal brain dysfunction** (MBD), defined as an abnormality in the cerebral or brain structure that causes behavior injurious to a person's lifestyle and social adjustment. Impairment is produced by such factors as low birthweight, brain injury, birth complications, and inherited abnormality.[88] Research indicates that children exhibiting neurological impairment also have an increased risk for a variety of developmental problems, such as low IQ scores and cognitive impairment, which have been associated with delinquency.[89]

minimal brain dysfunction (MBD)
Damage to the brain itself that causes antisocial behavior injurious to the individual's lifestyle and social adjustment.

A number of research efforts have attempted to substantiate a link between neurological impairment and crime. There is evidence that this relationship can be detected

Diet and Delinquency

There is evidence that substances contained in common food products—for example, calcium propionate, a food preservative found in processed breads—can be linked to aggressive and antisocial behaviors. Stephen Schoenthaler has conducted a number of studies that indicate a significant association between diet and aggressive behavior patterns. In some cases, the relationship is direct; in others, a poor diet may compromise individual functioning, which in turn produces aggressive behavior responses. For example, a poor diet may inhibit school performance, and children who fail at school are at risk for delinquent behavior and criminality.

In one study of 803 New York City public schools, Schoenthaler found that the academic performance of 1.1 million schoolchildren rose 16 percent after their diets were modified. The number of "learning disabled" children fell from 125,000 to 74,000 in one year. No other changes in school programs for the learning disabled were initiated that year. In a similar experiment conducted in a correctional institution, violent and nonviolent antisocial behavior fell an average of 48 percent among 8,047 offenders after dietary changes were implemented. In both these studies, the improvements in behavior and academic performance were attributed to diets containing more vitamins and minerals as compared with the old diets. The greater amounts of these essential nutrients in the new diets were believed to have corrected impaired brain function caused by poor nutrition.

Schoenthaler also conducted three randomized controlled studies in which 66 elementary school children, 62 confined teenage delinquents, and 402 confined adult felons received dietary supplements—the equivalent of a diet providing more fruits, vegetables, and whole grains. In order to remove experimental bias, neither subjects nor researchers knew who received the supplement and who received a placebo. In each study, the subjects receiving the dietary supplement demonstrated significantly less violent and nonviolent antisocial behavior when compared to the control subjects who received placebos. The carefully collected data verified that a good diet, as defined by the World Health Organization, has significant behavioral benefits beyond its health effects.

In Phoenix, Arizona, Schoenthaler (along with Ian Bier) experimented with 468 students aged 6 to 12 years by giving one group a daily vitamin-mineral supplement at 50 percent of the U.S. recommended daily allowance (RDA) for four months and giving another group a placebo. He found that those receiving the vitamin supplement were involved in significantly less antisocial behavior, a finding that convinced him that poor nutritional habits in children that lead to low concentrations of vitamins in the blood impair brain function and subsequently cause violence and other serious antisocial behavior. Correction of nutrient intake, either through a well-balanced diet or low-dose vitamin-mineral supplementation, corrects the low concentrations of vitamins in blood, improves brain function, and subsequently lowers institutional violence and antisocial behavior by almost half.

Though more research is needed before the scientific community reaches a consensus on the influence of diet on crime, other research findings have backed up Schoenthaler's claims. It is possible that vitamins, minerals, chemicals, and other nutrients from a diet rich in fruits, vegetables, and whole grains can improve brain function, basic intelligence, and academic performance, all variables that have been linked to antisocial behavior.

Although this research is persuasive, the relationship between biochemical intake and abnormal behavior is far from settled. A number of controlled experiments have failed to substantiate any link between the two variables. Some research by Marcel Kinsbourne, for example, has found that sugar may actually have a calming effect on children rather than increase their aggressive behaviors. Further research is needed to fully understand the relationship between diet and delinquency.

Critical Thinking

1. If Schoenthaler is correct in his assumptions, should schools be required to provide a proper lunch for all children?

2. How would Schoenthaler explain the aging out process? Hint: Do people eat better as they mature? What about after they get married?

InfoTrac College Edition Research

To read more about the relationship between nutrition and behavior, use "nutrition" and "behavior" as key terms on InfoTrac College Edition. Read the following article: Willow Lawson, "Fighting Crime One Bite at a Time: Diet Supplements Cut Violence in Prisons," *Psychology Today* 36:22 (March–April 2003).

SOURCES: S. Dengate and A. Ruben, "Controlled Trial of Cumulative Behavioural Effects of a Common Bread Preservative," *Journal of Paediatrics and Child Health* 38:373–376 (2002); Stephen Schoenthaler, *Intelligence, Academic Performance, and Brain Function* (California State University, Stanislaus, 2000). See also Stephen Schoenthaler and Ian Bier, "The Effect of Vitamin-Mineral Supplementation on Juvenile Delinquency among American Schoolchildren: A Randomized Double-Blind Placebo-Controlled Trial," *Journal of Alternative and Complementary Medicine: Research on Paradigm, Practice, and Policy* 6:7–18 (2000); C. Bernard Gesch, Sean Hammond, Sarah Hampson, Anita Eves, and Martin Crowder, "Influence of Supplementary Vitamins, Minerals and Essential Fatty Acids on the Antisocial Behaviour of Young Adult Prisoners: Randomized, Placebo-Controlled Trial," *British Journal of Psychiatry* 181:22–28 (2002); Marcel Kinsbourne, "Sugar and the Hyperactive Child," *The New England Journal of Medicine* 330:355–356 (1994).

quite early and that children who suffer from measurable neurological deficits at birth are more likely to become criminals later in life.[90] For example, low-birthweight children are also likely to be early onset delinquents; low birthweight is highly correlated with neurological impairment.[91] Clinical analysis of death row inmates found that a significant number had suffered head injuries as children, resulting in damage to their central nervous system and neurological impairment.[92] Measurement of the brain activity of antisocial youths has revealed impairments that might cause them to experience otherwise unexplainable outbursts of anger, hostility, and aggression.[93] Evidence has been found linking the brain damage to mental disorders such as schizophrenia and depression.[94] Cross-national studies also support a link between neurological dysfunction and antisocial behavior.[95]

A number of research studies have used an electroencephalogram to measure the brain waves and activity of delinquents and then compared them with those of law-abiding adolescents. In what is considered the most significant investigation of EEG abnormality and delinquency, 335 violent delinquents were classified on the basis of their antisocial activities and measured on an EEG.[96] While youths who committed a single violent act had a 12 percent abnormality rate—the same as the general population—the habitually aggressive youths tested at a 57 percent abnormality rate, almost five times normal. Behaviors believed to be highly correlated with abnormal EEG functions include poor impulse control, inadequate social ability, hostility, temper tantrums, destructiveness, and hyperactivity.[97] The Focus on Delinquency box entitled "Attention Deficit/Hyperactivity Disorder" discusses this neurological condition associated with antisocial behavior in some detail.

Learning Disabilities One specific type of MBD that has generated considerable interest is **learning disability (LD),** a term that has been defined by the National Advisory Committee on Handicapped Children:

> *Children with special learning disabilities exhibit a disorder in one or more of the basic psychological processes involved in understanding or using spoken or written languages. They may be manifested in disorders of listening, thinking, talking, reading, writing or arithmetic. They include conditions which have been referred to as perceptual handicaps, brain injury, minimal brain dysfunction, dyslexia, developmental aphasia, etc. They do not include learning problems which are due to visual, hearing or motor handicaps, to mental retardation, emotional disturbance, or to environmental disadvantages.[98]*

Learning disabled kids usually exhibit poor motor coordination (for example, problems with poor hand-eye coordination, trouble climbing stairs, clumsiness), have behavior problems (lack of emotional control, hostility, cannot stay on task), and have improper auditory and vocal responses (do not seem to hear, cannot differentiate sounds and noises).

The relationship between learning disabilities and delinquency has been highlighted by studies showing that arrested and incarcerated children have a far higher LD rate than do children in the general population.[99] Though learning disabilities are quite common (approximately 10% of all youths have some form of learning disorders), estimates of LD among adjudicated delinquents range from 26 percent to 73 percent.[100] Do these statistics necessarily mean that learning disabilities somehow cause delinquent behavior?

Typically, there are two possible explanations of the link between learning disabilities and delinquency.[101] One view, known as the *susceptibility rationale,* argues that the link is caused by certain side effects of learning disabilities, such as impulsiveness, poor ability to learn from experience, and inability to take social cues. In contrast, the *school failure rationale* assumes that the frustration caused by the LD child's poor school performance will lead to a negative self-image and acting-out behavior.

A number of recent research efforts have found that the LD child may not be any more susceptible to delinquent behavior than the non-LD child and that the proposed link between learning disabilities and delinquency may be an artifact of bias in the way the juvenile justice system treats LD youths.[102] Because of social bias, LD kids are more likely to get arrested, and if petitioned to juvenile court, their poor school record can influence the outcome of the case. LD youths bring with them to court a record of school problems and low grades and a history of frustrating efforts by agents of the educational system to help them. When information is gleaned from the school personnel at juvenile trials, LD children's poor performance may work against them in the court. Consequently, the view that learning disabilities cause delinquency has

learning disability (LD)
Neurological dysfunction that prevents an individual from learning to his or her potential.

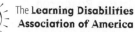
The **Learning Disabilities Association of America** aims to advance the education and general welfare of children and adults of normal or potentially normal intelligence who manifest disabilities of a perceptual, conceptual, or coordinative nature. To learn more about them, go to www.ldanatl.org. For an up-to-date list of web links, go to http://cj.wadsworth.com/siegel_jd9e.

Attention Deficit/Hyperactivity Disorder

Many parents have noticed that their children do not pay attention to them—they run around and do things in their own way. Sometimes this inattention is a function of age; in other instances it is a symptom of a common learning disability referred to as attention deficit/hyperactivity disorder (ADHD), a condition in which a child shows a developmentally inappropriate lack of attention, distractibility, impulsivity, and hyperactivity. The various symptoms of ADHD are listed below.

SYMPTOMS OF ADHD

Lack of Attention

I Frequently fails to finish projects
I Does not seem to pay attention
I Does not sustain interest in play activities
I Cannot sustain concentration on schoolwork or related tasks
I Is easily distracted

Impulsivity

I Frequently acts without thinking
I Often "calls out" in class
I Does not want to wait his or her turn
I Shifts from activity to activity
I Cannot organize tasks or work
I Requires constant supervision in line or games

Hyperactivity

I Constantly runs around and climbs on things
I Shows excessive motor activity while asleep
I Cannot sit still; is constantly fidgeting
I Does not remain in his or her seat in class
I Is constantly on the go like a "motor"
I Has difficulty regulating emotions
I Has difficulty getting started
I Has difficulty staying on track
I Has difficulty adjusting to social demands

No one is really sure how ADHD develops, but some psychologists believe it is tied to dysfunction in a section of the lower portion of the brain known as the reticular activating system. This area keeps the higher brain centers alert and ready for input. There is some evidence that this area is not working properly in ADHD kids and that their behavior is really the brain's attempt to generate new stimulation to maintain alertness. Other suspected origins are neurological damage to the frontal lobes of the brain, prenatal stress, and even food additives and chemical allergies. Some experts suggest that the condition might be traced to the neurological effects of abnormal levels of the chemicals dopamine and norepinephrine.

Children from any background can develop ADHD, but it is five to seven times more common in boys than girls. It does not affect intelligence, and ADHD children often show considerable ability with artistic endeavors. More common in the United States than elsewhere, ADHD tends to run in families, and there is some suggestion of an association with a family history of alcoholism or depression.

Estimates of ADHD in the general population range from 3 to 12 percent, but it is much more prevalent in adolescents, where some estimates reach as high as one-third of the population. ADHD children are most often treated by giving them doses of stimulants, most commonly Ritalin and Dexedrine (or dextroamphetamine), which, ironically, help these children control their emotional and behavioral outbursts. The antimanic, anticonvulsant drug Tegretol has also been used effectively.

ADHD usually results in poor school performance, including a high dropout rate, bullying, stubbornness, mental disorder, and a lack of response to discipline; these conditions are highly correlated with delinquent behavior. A series of research studies now link ADHD to the onset and continuance of a delinquent career and increased risk for antisocial behavior and substance abuse in adulthood. Children with ADHD are more likely to use illicit drugs, alcohol, and cigarettes in adolescence, are more likely to be arrested, to be charged with a felony, and to have multiple arrests than non-ADHD youths. There is also evidence that ADHD youths who also exhibit early signs of MBD and conduct disorder (for example, fighting) are the most at risk for persistent antisocial behaviors continuing into adulthood. Of course many, if not most, children who are diagnosed with ADHD do not engage in delinquent behavior, and new treatment techniques featuring behavior modification and drug therapies are constantly being developed to help children who have attention or hyperactivity problems.

Critical Thinking

Even if it could be proven that kids suffering from ADHD were more likely to engage in antisocial behaviors than non-ADHD kids:

1. Should those diagnosed with the condition be closely monitored by the school system?
2. Would that be fair to the majority of ADHD kids who never violate the law?
3. Would paying special attention to the ADHD population stigmatize them and actually encourage their law-violating behaviors?

InfoTrac College Edition Research

Use "attention deficit/hyperactive disorder" as a keyword search on InfoTrac College Edition.

SOURCES: Russell Barkley, Mariellen Fischer, Lori Smallish, and Kenneth Fletcher, "Young Adult Follow-up of Hyperactive Children: Antisocial Activities and Drug Use," *Journal of Child Psychology and Psychiatry* 45:195–211 (2004); Molina Pelham, Jr., "Childhood Predictors of Adolescent Substance Use in a Longitudinal Study of Children with ADHD" *Journal of Abnormal Psychology* 112:497–507 (2003); Peter Muris and Cor Meesters, "The Validity of Attention Deficit Hyperactivity and Hyperkinetic Disorder Symptom Domains in Nonclinical Dutch Children," *Journal of Clinical Child & Adolescent Psychology* 32:460–466 (2003); D. R. Blachman and S. P. Hinshaw, "Patterns of Friendship among Girls with and without Attention Deficit/Hyperactivity Disorder," *Journal of Abnormal Child Psychology* 30:625–640 (2002); Terrie Moffitt and Phil Silva, "Self-Reported Delinquency, Neuropsychological Deficit, and History of Attention Deficit Disorder," *Journal of Abnormal Child Psychology* 16:553–569 (1988); Karen Harding, Richard Judah, and Charles Gant, "Outcome-Based Comparison of Ritalin[R] versus Food-Supplement Treated Children with AD/HD," *Alternative Medicine Review* 8:319–330 (2003).

© Frank Siteman/Stock, Boston

Arousal theorists believe that, for a variety of genetic and environmental reasons, some people's brains function differently in response to environmental stimuli. All of us seek to maintain a preferred or optimal level of arousal. Too much stimulation may leave us anxious and stressed out; too little may make us bored and weary. Some kids may need the rush that comes from getting into scrapes and conflicts in order to feel relaxed and at ease.

The **National Center for Learning Disabilities (NCLD)** provides national leadership in support of children and adults with learning disabilities. Find out about their work at www.ld.org. For an up-to-date list of web links, go to http://cj.wadsworth.com/ siegel_jd9e.

arousal theorists
Delinquency experts who believe that aggression is a function of the level of an individual's need for stimulation or arousal from the environment. Those who require more stimulation may act in an aggressive manner to meet their needs.

been questioned, and the view that LD children are more likely to be arrested and officially labeled delinquent demands further inquiry. Self-reports show little differences between the behavior of LD and non-LD youth, a finding that supports the social bias view.[103]

Arousal Theory It has long been suspected that obtaining "thrills" is a motivator of crime. Adolescents may engage in such crimes as shoplifting and vandalism simply because they offer the attraction of getting away with it; delinquency is a thrilling demonstration of personal competence.[104] Is it possible that thrill seekers are people who have some form of abnormal brain functioning that directs their behavior?

Arousal theorists believe that, for a variety of genetic and environmental reasons, some people's brains function differently in response to environmental stimuli. All of us seek to maintain a preferred or optimal level of arousal: Too much stimulation leaves us anxious and stressed out; too little makes us feel bored and weary. There is, however, variation in the way children's brains process sensory input. Some nearly always feel comfortable with little stimulation, while others require a high degree of environmental input to feel comfortable. The latter group become "sensation seekers," who seek out stimulating activities that may include aggressive, violent behavior patterns.[105]

The factors that determine a person's level of arousal have not been fully determined. Suspected sources include brain chemistry (for example, serotonin levels) and brain structure. The number of nerve cells with receptor sites for neurotransmitters in the brain differs among people; some have many more than others. Another view is that adolescents with low heart rates are more likely to commit crimes because they seek stimulation to increase their arousal levels to normal levels.[106]

Genetic Influences

Individuals who share genes are alike in personality regardless of how they are reared, whereas rearing environment induces little or no personality resemblance.[107]

Biosocial theorists also study the genetic makeup of delinquents.[108] It has been hypothesized that some youths inherit a genetic configuration that predisposes them to violence and aggression.[109] Biosocial theorists believe that in the same way that people inherit genes for height and eye color, antisocial behavior characteristics and mental disorders may be passed down from one generation to the next. To test this assumption, parent-child and sibling behavior has been studied.

Parent-Child Similarities If antisocial tendencies are inherited, then the children of criminal parents should be more likely to become law violators than the offspring of conventional parents. A number of studies have found that parental criminality and deviance do, in fact, powerfully influence delinquent behavior.[110] For example, there is a significant relationship between parent and child suicide attempts.[111] Some of the most important data on parental deviance were gathered by Donald J. West and David P. Farrington as part of the long-term Cambridge Youth Survey. These cohort data indicate that a significant number of delinquent youths have criminal fathers.[112] Whereas 8 percent of the sons of noncriminal fathers eventually became chronic offenders, about 37 percent of youths with criminal fathers were multiple offenders.[113] In another important analysis, Farrington found that one type of parental deviance, schoolyard aggression or bullying, may be both inter- and intragenerational. Bullies have children who bully others, and these second-generation bullies grow up to father children who are also bullies, in a never-ending cycle.[114]

Farrington's findings are supported by some recent research data from the Rochester Youth Development Study (RYDS), a longitudinal analysis that has been monitoring the behavior of 1,000 area youths since 1988. RYDS researchers have also found an intergenerational continuity in antisocial behavior: Criminal fathers produce delinquent sons who grow up to have delinquent children themselves.[115] It is possible that at least part of the association is genetic.[116]

Sibling and Twin Similarities It stands to reason that if the cause of delinquency is in part genetic, the behavior of siblings should be similar because they share genetic material. Research does show that if one sibling engages in antisocial behavior, so does his/her brothers and sisters. The effect is greatest among same-sex sibs.[117]

Because siblings are usually brought up in the same household and share common life experiences, however, any similarity in their delinquent behavior might be a function of comparable environmental influences and not genetics at all. To guard against this, biosocial theorists have compared the behavior of twins and non-twin siblings and found that the twins, who share more genetic material, are also more similar in their behavior. This indicates that it is heredity and not environment that controls behavior.[118]

However, an even more rigorous test of genetic theory involves comparison of the behavior of identical monozygotic (MZ) twins with same-sex fraternal dizygotic (DZ) twins; although the former have an identical genetic makeup, the latter share only about 50 percent of their genetic combinations. Research has shown that MZ twins are significantly closer in their personal characteristics, such as intelligence, than are DZ twins.[119] Reviews of twin studies found that in almost all cases, MZ twins have delinquent and antisocial behavior patterns more similar than that of DZ twins.[120] For example, studies have consistently demonstrated a significantly higher risk for suicidal behavior among monozygotic twin pairs than dizygotic twin pairs.[121] Differences between MZ and DZ twins have been found in tests measuring psychological dysfunctions such as conduct disorders, impulsivity/antisocial behavior, and emotionality.[122] Ginette Dionne and colleagues found that differences between MZ and DZ twins in such delinquency-relevant measures as level of aggression and verbal skills could be detected as early as 19 months old, a finding which suggests that not only is there a genetic basis of crime but that poor verbal ability may be both inherited and a cause of aggressive behavior.

Though this seems to support a connection between genetic makeup and delinquency, little conclusive evidence exists of such an actual link. MZ twins are more likely to look alike and to share physical traits than DZ twins, and they are more likely to be treated similarly. Similarities in their shared behavior patterns may therefore be a function of socialization and environment and not heredity.[124] Critics have also

EXHIBIT 3.1

Findings from the Minnesota Study of Twins Reared Apart

▌ If you are a DZ twin and your co-twin is divorced, your risk of divorce is 30%; If you are an MZ (identical) twin and your co-twin is divorced, your risk of divorce to 45%, which is 25% above the rates for the Minnesota population. Since this was not true for DZ (fraternal) twins, we can conclude that genes do influence the likelihood of divorce.

▌ MZ twins become *more* similar with respect to abilities such as vocabularies and arithmetic scores as they age. As DZ twins get older they become less similar with respect to vocabularies and arithmetic scores.

▌ A P300 is a tiny electrical response (a few millionths of a volt) that occurs in the brain when a person detects something that is unusual or interesting. For example, if a person were shown nine circles and one square, a P300 brain response would appear after seeing the square because it's different. Identical (MZ) twin children have very similar looking P300s. By comparison, children who are fraternal (DZ) twins do not show as much similarity in their P300s. These results indicate that the way the brain processes information may be greatly influenced by genes.

▌ An EEG is a measure of brain activity or brain waves that can be used to monitor a person's state of arousal. MZ twins tend to produce strikingly similar EEG spectra, DZ twins show far less similarity.

SOURCE: Minnesota Study of Twins Reared Apart, www.psych.umn.edu/psylabs/mtfs/special.htm. Accessed on May 5, 2004.

challenged the methodology of these studies and suggest that those that show a conclusive genetic link to behavior use faulty data.[125]

Against this interpretation is research evidence that identical twins reared apart are quite as similar in many traits, including personality, intelligence, and attitudes, as twins who live in the same household.[126] One famous study of twin behavior still underway is the Minnesota Study of Twins Reared Apart. This research compares the behavior of MZ and DZ twin pairs who were raised together with that of others who were separated at birth and in some cases did not even know of each others' existence. The study shows some striking similarities in behavior and ability for twin pairs raised apart. An MZ twin reared away from a co-twin has about as good a chance of being similar to the co-twin in terms of personality, interests, and attitudes as one who has been reared with his or her co-twin. The conclusion: similarities between twins are due to genes, not the environment. (See Exhibit 3.1.)[127]

To learn more about **twin research,** go to University of Minnesota–Twin Cities Department of Psychology, Minnesota Twin Family Study, "What's Special about Twins to Science?" www.psych.umn.edu/psylabs/mtfs/special.htm. For an up-to-date list of web links, go to http://cj.wadsworth.com/siegel_jd9e.

Adoption Studies Another way to determine whether delinquency is an inherited trait is to compare the behavior of adopted children with that of their biological parents. If the criminal behavior of children is more like that of their biological parents (whom they have never met) than that of their adopted parents (who brought them up), it would indicate that the tendency toward delinquency is inherited, rather than shaped by the environment.

Studies of this kind have generally supported the hypothesis that there is a link between genetics and behavior.[128] Adoptees share many of the behavioral and intellectual characteristics of their biological parents despite the social and environmental conditions found in their adoptive homes. Genetic makeup is sufficient to counteract and/or negate even the most extreme environmental conditions, such as malnutrition and abuse.[129]

Some of the most influential research in this area has been conducted by Sarnoff Mednick. In one study, Mednick and Bernard Hutchings found that although only 13 percent of the adoptive fathers of a sample of adjudicated delinquent youths had criminal records, 31 percent of their biological fathers had criminal records.[130] Analysis of a control group's background indicated that about 11 percent of all fathers will have criminal records. Hutchings and Mednick were forced to conclude that genetics played at least some role in creating delinquent tendencies, because the biological fathers of delinquents were much more likely than the fathers of noncriminal youths to be criminals.[131]

In addition to a direct link between heredity and delinquency, the literature also shows that behavior traits indirectly linked to delinquency may be at least in part inherited. Biological parents of adopted hyperactive children are more likely to show symptoms of hyperactivity than are the adoptive parents.[132] Several studies have reported a higher incidence of psychological problems in parents of hyperactive children when compared to control groups. Although all hyperactive children do not become delinquent, the link between this neurological condition and delinquency has long been suspected.

Similarly, there is evidence (disputed) that intelligence is related to heredity and that low intelligence is a cause of impulsive delinquent acts that are easier to detect and more likely to result in arrest.[133] This connection can create the appearance of a relationship between heredity and delinquency. (See later in this chapter for more on IQ and delinquency.)

Connecting delinquent behavior to heredity is quite controversial because it implies that the cause of delinquency is (1) present at birth, and (2) "transmitted" from one generation to the next and immune to treatment efforts (because genes cannot be altered). Recent evaluations of the gene-crime relationship find that though a relationship can be detected, the better-designed research efforts provide less support than earlier and weaker studies.[134] If there is a genetic basis of delinquency, it is likely that genetic factors contribute to certain individual differences that interact with specific social and environmental conditions to bring about antisocial behavior.[135]

Evolutionary Theory

Some theorists have speculated that the human traits producing violence and aggression have been nurtured and produced through the long process of human evolution.[136] According to this **evolutionary theory,** the competition for scarce resources has influenced and shaped the human species.[137] Over the course of human existence, people have been shaped to engage in actions that promote their well-being and ensure the survival and reproduction of their genetic line. Males who are impulsive risk takers may be able to father more children; impulsive behavior is inherited and becomes intergenerational. It is not surprising that human history has been marked by war, violence, and aggression.

Crime rate differences between the genders then are less a matter of socialization than inherent differences in the mating patterns that have developed between the sexes over time.[138] Among young men, reckless, life-threatening "risk-proneness" is especially likely to evolve in societies where choosing not to compete means the inability to find suitable mates and to reproduce.[139] Aggressive males have had the greatest impact on the gene pool. The descendants of these aggressive males now account for the disproportionate amount of male aggression and violence.[140]

This evolutionary model suggests that a subpopulation of men has evolved with genes that incline them toward extremely low parental involvement. Sexually aggressive, they use their cunning to gain sexual conquests with as many females as possible. Because females would not willingly choose them as mates, they use stealth to gain sexual access—cheating—including such tactics as mimicking the behavior of more stable males.[141] Psychologist Byron Roth notes that these flamboyant, sexually aggressive males are especially attractive to younger, less intelligent women who begin having children at a very early age.[142] Their fleeting courtship process produces children with low IQs, aggressive personalities, and little chance of proper socialization in father-absent families. Because the criminal justice system treats them leniently, argues Roth, sexually irresponsible men are free to prey upon young girls. Over time, their offspring will yield an ever-expanding supply of offspring who are both antisocial and sexually aggressive.

Concept Summary 3.2 offers a summary of the major biosocial theories of delinquency.

evolutionary theory
Explaining the existence of aggression and violent behavior as positive adaptive behaviors in human evolution; these traits allowed their bearers to reproduce disproportionately, which has had an effect on the human gene pool.

TO QUIZ YOURSELF ON THIS MATERIAL, go to the Juvenile Delinquency 9e website.

Biosocial Theories

Biochemical	Premise	Crime, especially violence, is a function of diet, vitamin intake, hormonal imbalance, and/or food allergies.
	Strengths	Explains irrational violence. Shows how the environment interacts with personal traits to influence behavior.
Neurological	Premise	Criminals and delinquents often suffer brain impairment, as measured by the EEG. Learning disabilities such as attention deficit/hyperactive disorder and minimum brain dysfunction are related to antisocial behavior.
	Strengths	Helps explain relationship between child abuse and crime, and why there is a relationship between victimization and violence (i.e., people who suffer head trauma may become violent).
Genetic	Premise	Delinquent traits and predispositions are inherited. Criminality of parents can predict the delinquency of children.
	Strengths	Explains why only a small percentage of youths in a high-crime area become chronic offenders.
Evolutionary	Premise	Behavior patterns and reproductive traits, developed over the millennia, control behavior.
	Strengths	Explains male aggressiveness. Helps us understand why violence is so common.

PSYCHOLOGICAL THEORIES OF DELINQUENCY

Some experts view the cause of delinquency as essentially psychological.[143] After all, most behaviors labeled delinquent—for example, violence, theft, sexual misconduct—seem to be symptomatic of some underlying psychological problem. Psychologists point out that many delinquent youths have poor home lives, destructive relationships with neighbors, friends, and teachers, and conflicts with authority figures in general. These relationships seem to indicate a disturbed personality structure. Furthermore, numerous studies of incarcerated youths indicate that the youths' personalities are marked by negative, antisocial behavior characteristics. And because delinquent behavior occurs among youths in every racial, ethnic, and socioeconomic group, psychologists view it as a function of emotional and mental disturbance, rather than purely a result of social factors, such as racism, poverty, and class conflict. Although many delinquents do not manifest significant psychological problems, enough do to give clinicians a powerful influence on delinquency theory.

Because psychology is a complex and diversified discipline, more than one psychological perspective on crime exists. Three prominent psychological perspectives on delinquency are the psychodynamic, the behavioral, and the cognitive.[144] (See Figure 3.2.)

Psychodynamic Theory

According to **psychodynamic theory,** whose basis is the pioneering work of the Austrian physician Sigmund Freud (1856–1939), law violations are a product of an abnormal personality structure formed early in life and which thereafter controls human behavior choices.[145] In extreme cases, mental torment drives people into violence and aggression. The basis of psychodynamic theory is the assumption that human behavior is controlled by unconscious mental processes developed early in childhood.

Theory

Psychodynamic (Psychoanalytic)

Behavioral

Cognitive

Cause

Intrapsychic Processes
- Unconscious conflicts
- Childhood traumas
- Family abuse
- Neurosis
- Psychosis

Learning Processes
- Past experiences
- Stimulus
- Rewards and punishments

Information Processing
- Thinking
- Problem solving
- Script
- Moral development

FIGURE 3.2
Psychological Theories of Delinquency

Psychodynamic theory argues that the human personality contains three major components. The *id* is the unrestrained, primitive, pleasure-seeking component with which each child is born. The *ego* develops through the reality of living in the world and helps manage and restrain the id's need for immediate gratification. The *superego* develops through interactions with parents and other significant people and represents the development of conscience and the moral rules shared by most adults.

Psychodynamic theory suggests that unconscious motivations for behavior come from the id's action in response to two primal needs—sex and aggression. Human behavior is often marked by symbolic actions that reflect hidden feelings about these needs. For example, stealing a car may reflect a person's unconscious need for shelter and mobility to escape from hostile enemies (aggression) or perhaps an urge to enter a closed, dark, womblike structure that reflects the earliest memories (sex).

All three segments of the personality operate simultaneously. The id dictates needs and desires, the superego counteracts the id by fostering feelings of morality and righteousness, and the ego evaluates the reality of a position between these two extremes. If these components are properly balanced, the individual can lead a normal life. If one aspect of the personality becomes dominant at the expense of the others, the individual exhibits abnormal personality traits. (See Figure 3.3.)

Furthermore, the theory suggests that an imbalance in personality traits caused by a traumatic early childhood can result in long-term psychological difficulties. For example, if neglectful parents fail to develop a child's superego adequately, the child's id may become the predominant personality force; the absence of a strong superego results in an inability to distinguish clearly between right and wrong. Later, the youth may demand immediate gratification, lack compassion and sensitivity for the needs of others, disassociate feelings, act aggressively and impulsively, and demonstrate other psychotic symptoms. Antisocial behavior then may be the result of conflict or trauma occurring early in a child's development, and delinquent activity may become an outlet for violent and antisocial feelings.

Disorders and Delinquency According to Freud's version of psychodynamic theory, people who experience feelings of anxiety and are afraid that they are losing control of their personalities are said to be suffering from a form of *neuroses* and are referred to as *neurotics*. People who have lost total control and who are dominated by their primitive id are known as *psychotics*. Their behavior may be marked by bizarre episodes, hallucinations, and inappropriate responses. *Psychosis* takes many forms, the most common being labeled *schizophrenia*, a condition marked by illogical thought processes, distorted perceptions, and abnormal emotional expression. According to the classical psychoanalytic view, the most serious types of youthful antisocial behavior, such as murder, might be motivated by psychosis, whereas neurotic feelings would be responsible for less serious delinquent acts and status offenses, such as petty theft and truancy.[146]

Contemporary psychologists generally no longer use the term neuroses to describe all forms of unconscious conflict. It is now more common to characterize people with more specific types of conduct and mood *disorders*, including anxiety disorder, mood disorder, sleep disorder, and so on. The Focus on Delinquency entitled "Disruptive Behavior Disorder" describes one such disorder that has been linked to delinquent activities.

The Psychodynamic Tradition and Delinquency A number of psychologists and psychiatrists have expanded upon Freud's original model to explain the onset of antisocial behaviors. Erik Erikson speculated that many adolescents experience a life crisis in which they feel emotional, impulsive, and uncertain of their role and purpose.[147] He coined the

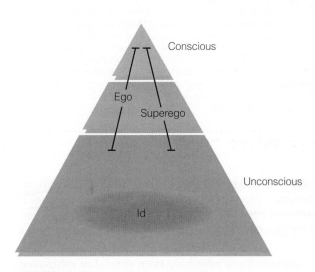

Conscious

Ego

Superego

Unconscious

Id

FIGURE 3.3
The Structure of the Id, Ego, and Superego

Disruptive Behavior Disorder

Most kids act out, especially when they are under stress. Younger children may become difficult when they are tired or hungry. They may defy parents and talk back to teachers. It would be unusual for a child not to go through the "terrible twos" or be reasonable and mature when they are three years old! However, kids who are frequently uncooperative and hostile and who seem to be much more difficult than other children the same age may be suffering from a psychological condition known as disruptive behavior disorder (DBD). If left untreated, this condition can have long-term effects on the child's social, family, and academic life.

DBD has two components. The first and more mild condition is referred to oppositional defiant disorder (ODD). Children suffering from ODD experience an ongoing pattern of uncooperative, defiant, and hostile behavior toward authority figures that seriously interferes with the youngster's day-to-day functioning. Symptoms of ODD may include frequent loss of temper; constant arguing with adults; defying adults or refusing adult requests or rules; deliberately annoying others; blaming others for mistakes or misbehavior; being angry and resentful; being spiteful or vindictive; or swearing or using obscene language. The person with ODD is moody and easily frustrated, has a low opinion of him- or herself, and may abuse drugs as a form of self-medication.

Kids with ODD act out in multiple settings, but their behavior is more noticeable at home or at school. It is estimated that five to fifteen percent of all school-age children have ODD. Though the causes of ODD are unknown, both biosocial and psychological sources are suspected.

The second element of DBD is conduct disorder (CD), which comprises a more serious group of behavioral and emotional problems in youngsters. Children and adolescents with CD have great difficulty following rules and behaving in a socially acceptable way. They are often viewed by other children, adults, and social agencies, as severely antisocial. Research shows that they are frequently involved in such activities as bullying, fighting, and cruelty to animals. Kids suffering from CD are more likely to carry weapons than other kids. Sexual assault and arson are common activities. Children with CD have trouble being truthful and think nothing of lying to cover up their activities. When they defy their parents, their activities are more serious than the ODD child: they cut school, stay out all night, or run away from home.

What causes CD? Numerous biosocial and psychological factors are suspected. There is evidence, for example, that interconnections between the frontal lobes and other brain regions may influence CD. There is also research showing that levels of serotonin can influence the onset of CD. CD has been shown to aggregate in families, suggesting a genetic basis of the disorder.

It is generally assumed that ODD is more treatable than CD. Treatment might include parent training programs to help manage the child's behavior, individual psychotherapy, anger management, family psychotherapy, and cognitive-behavioral therapy to assist problem solving.

Critical Thinking

1. Is it possible that kids who are routinely aggressive and seemingly "out of control" are suffering from some form of chemical deficiency? Or do you believe that such behavior is a result of significant psychological deficits?

2. Could kids who are routinely hostile and defiant toward authority figures be controlled by the threat of physical punishment? Which works better: fear or love?

InfoTrac College Edition Research

To read about the treatment of disruptive behavior disorder, go to InfoTrac College Edition and find: Nicolle M.H. van de Wiel, Stephanie H.M. van Goozen, Walter Matthys, Heddeke Snoek, and Herman van Engeland, "Cortisol and Treatment Effect in Children with Disruptive Behavior Disorders: a Preliminary Study," *Journal of the American Academy of Child and Adolescent Psychiatry* 43:1011–1018 (2004).

SOURCES: Paul Rohde, Gregory N. Clarke, David E. Mace, Jenel S. Jorgensen, John R. Seeley, "An Efficacy/Effectiveness Study of Cognitive-Behavioral Treatment for Adolescents with Comorbid Major Depression and Conduct Disorder." *Journal of the American Academy of Child and Adolescent Psychiatry* 43:660–669 (2004); Ellen Kjelsberg, "Gender and Disorder Specific Criminal Career Profiles in Former Adolescent Psychiatric In-Patients," *Journal of Youth & Adolescence* 33:261–270 (2004); Barbara Maughan, Richard Rowe, Julie Messer, Robert Goodman, Howard Meltzer, "Conduct Disorder and Oppositional Defiant Disorder in a National Sample: Developmental Epidemiology," *Journal of Child Psychology & Psychiatry & Allied Disciplines* 45:609–621 (2004); the American Academy of Child and Adolescent Psychiatry (AACAP), www.aacap.org (accessed on August 11, 2004); Jeffrey Burke, Rolf Loeber, and Boris Birmaher, "Oppositional Defiant Disorder and Conduct Disorder: A Review of the Past 10 Years, Part II," *Journal of the American Academy of Child & Adolescent Psychiatry* 41:1275–1294 (2002).

identity crisis
Psychological state, identified by Erikson, in which youth face inner turmoil and uncertainty about life roles.

phrase **identity crisis** to denote this period of inner turmoil and confusion. Erikson's approach might characterize the behavior of youthful drug abusers as an expression of confusion over their place in society, their inability to direct behavior toward useful outlets, and perhaps their dependency on others to offer them solutions to their problems.

It is also possible that youth crime is a result of unresolved mental anguish and internal conflict. Some children, especially those who have been abused or mistreated, may experience unconscious feelings associated with resentment, fear, and hatred. If this conflict cannot be reconciled, the children may regress to a state in which they become id dominated. This regression may be considered responsible for a great number of mental diseases, from neuroses to psychoses, and in many cases it may be related to criminal behavior.[148]

Another psychoanalytic view is that delinquents are id-dominated people who suffer from the inability to control impulsive drives. Perhaps because they suffered unhappy experiences in childhood or had families who could not provide proper love and care, delinquents suffer from weak or damaged egos that make them unable to cope with conventional society.[149]

In its most extreme form, delinquency may be viewed as a form of psychosis that prevents delinquent youths from appreciating the feelings of their victims or controlling their own impulsive needs for gratification. For example, in his classic work, psychoanalyst August Aichorn found that social stress alone could not produce such an emotional state. He identifies **latent delinquents** —youths whose troubled family life leads them to seek immediate gratification without consideration of right and wrong or the feelings of others.[150]

Others have viewed adolescent antisocial behavior as a consequence of feeling unable to cope with feelings of oppression. Criminality actually allows youths to strive by producing positive psychic results: helping them to feel free and independent; giving them the possibility of excitement and the chance to use their skills and imagination; providing the promise of positive gain; allowing them to blame others for their predicament (for example, the police); and giving them a chance to rationalize their own sense of failure ("If I hadn't gotten into trouble, I could have been a success").[151]

Is There a Psychodynamic Link to Delinquency? The psychodynamic view is supported by research that shows that a number of violent juvenile offenders suffer from some sort of personality disturbance. Violent youths have been clinically diagnosed as "overtly hostile," "explosive or volatile," "anxious," and "depressed."[152] Many delinquents exhibit indications of such psychological abnormalities as schizophrenia, paranoia, and obsessive behaviors; female offenders seem to have more serious mental health symptoms and psychological disturbances than male offenders.[153] Antisocial youths frequently come from families in which parents are unable to give love, set consistent limits, and provide the controls that allow children to develop the necessary personal tools to cope with the world in which they live.[154] The exploitive, destructive behavior of a youth may actually be a symbolic call for help. In fact, some psychoanalysts view delinquents' behavior as being motivated by an unconscious urge to be punished. These children who feel unloved at home assume the reason must be their own inadequacy—hence, they deserve punishment.

Though this evidence is persuasive, the association between mental disturbance and delinquency is unresolved. It is possible that any link is caused by some intervening variable or factor: troubled youth do poorly in school and school failure leads to delinquency; troubled youth have conflict-ridden social relationships, which make them prone to commit delinquent acts. It is also possible that the factors that cause mental turmoil also cause delinquency: kids who suffer child abuse are more likely to have mental anguish and commit violent acts; child abuse is the actual cause of both problems.[155] Further research is needed to clarify this important relationship.

Behavioral Theory

Not all psychologists agree that behavior is controlled by unconscious mental processes determined by parental relationships developed early in childhood. Behavioral psychologists argue that a person's personality is learned throughout life during interaction with others. Based primarily on the works of the American psychologist John B. Watson (1878–1958) and popularized by Harvard professor B. F. Skinner (1904–1990), **behaviorism** concerns itself solely with measurable events and not the unobservable psychic phenomena described by psychoanalysts.

Behaviorists suggest that individuals learn by observing how people react to their behavior. Behavior is triggered initially by a stimulus or change in the environment. If a particular behavior is reinforced by some positive reaction or event, that behavior will

latent delinquents
Youths whose troubled family life leads them to seek immediate gratification without consideration of right and wrong or the feelings of others.

behaviorism
Branch of psychology concerned with the study of observable behavior rather than unconscious processes; focuses on particular stimuli and responses to them.

be continued and eventually learned. However, behaviors that are not reinforced or are punished will be extinguished or become extinct. For example, if children are given a reward (ice cream for dessert) for eating their entire dinner, eventually they will learn to eat properly as a matter of habit. Conversely, if children are punished for some misbehavior, they will eventually learn to associate disapproval with that act and avoid it.

Social Learning Theory Not all behaviorists strictly follow the teachings of Watson and Skinner. Some hold that a person's learning and social experiences, coupled with his or her values and expectations, determine behavior. This is known as the **social learning** approach. The most widely read social learning theorists are Albert Bandura, Walter Mischel, and Richard Walters.[156] In general, they hold that children will model their behavior according to the reactions they receive from others, either positive or negative; the behavior of those adults they are in close contact with, especially parents; and the behavior they view on television and in movies. If children observe aggression and see that the aggressive behavior, such as an adult slapping or punching someone during an argument, is approved or rewarded, they will likely react violently during a similar incident. Eventually, the children will master the techniques of aggression and become more confident that their behavior will bring tangible rewards.[157]

By implication, social learning suggests that children who grow up in a home where violence is a way of life may learn to believe that such behavior is acceptable and rewarding. Even if parents tell children not to be violent and punish them if they are, the children will still model their behavior on the observed parental violence.

Thus, children are more likely to heed what parents *do* than what they *say.* By midchildhood, some children have already acquired an association between their use of aggression against others and the physical punishment they receive at home. Often their aggressive responses are directed at other family members and siblings. The family may serve as a training ground for violence because the child perceives physical punishment as the norm during conflict situations with others.[158]

Adolescent aggression is a result of disrupted dependency relations with parents. This refers to the frustration and anger a child feels when parents provide poor role models and hold back affection and nurturing. Children who lack close dependent ties to their parents may have little opportunity or desire to model themselves after them or to internalize their standards of behavior. In the absence of such internalized controls, the child's aggression is likely to be expressed in an immediate, direct, and socially unacceptable fashion such as violence and aggression.[159]

The Media and Delinquency One aspect of social learning theory that has received a great deal of attention is the belief that children will model their behavior after characters they observe on TV or see in movies. This phenomenon is especially critical considering the findings of the recent Henry J. Kaiser Family Foundation study, *Zero to Six: Electronic Media in the Lives of Infants, Toddlers, and Preschoolers* (2003).[160] This research found that children aged 6 and under spend an average of two hours a day using screen media such as TV and computers, about the same amount of time they spend playing outside, and significantly more than the amount they spend reading or being read to (about 39 minutes per day).

Nearly half of all children aged 6 and under have used a computer and just under a third have played video games. Even the youngest children—those under 2—are exposed to electronic media for more than two hours per day; more than 40 percent of those under 2 watch TV every day. But what do they watch? Marketing research indicates that adolescents aged 11 to 14 rent violent horror movies at a higher rate than any other age group; kids this age use older peers and siblings and apathetic parents to gain access to R-rated films. More than 40 percent of U.S. households now have cable TV, which features violent films and shows. Even children's programming is saturated with violence. Violent video games are also a problem. Americans now spend twice as much money on video games as they spend going to the movies. The core gaming audience is 8- to 14-year-old males. Eighty percent of the games produced are violent, with realistic graphics that include blood, decapitation, guns, knives, mutilation, and death. Video games may have a greater impact on their audience than TV and movies

social learning theory
The view that behavior is modeled through observation, either directly through intimate contact with others, or indirectly through media; interactions that are rewarded are copied, whereas those that are punished are avoided.

Does the media, including films, TV, and violent video games, influence violent behavior? The jury is still out on this controversial issue. While lab-based studies seem to show an association between violence and the media, millions of kids watch violent TV shows each day, go to see violent films, and play violent videos without suffering negative consequences or changes in their behavior.

©Alamy Images

because they immerse the player visually, auditorily, and physically rather than have them remain passive observers.[161]

A well-publicized study conducted by researchers at UCLA found that at least 10 network shows made heavy use of violence. Of the 161 television movies monitored (every one that aired that season), 23 raised concerns from viewers about their use of violence, violent theme, violent title, or inappropriate graphicness of a scene. Of the 118 theatrical films monitored, 50 raised concerns about their use of violence. Some television series may contain limited depictions of violence, each of which may be appropriate in its context.

However, it was found that commercials for these programs emphasized only the violent scenes with little in the way of context. Even some children's television programs were found to feature "sinister combat" as the theme of the show. The characters were portrayed as happy to fight with little provocation.[162] It is estimated that the average child views 8,000 TV murders before finishing elementary school.

TV and Violence Children are particularly susceptible to TV imagery. It is believed that many children consider television images to be real, especially when the images are authoritatively presented by adults (as in commercials). Some children, especially those who are considered "emotionally disturbed," may be unable to distinguish between fantasy and reality when watching TV shows.[163]

A number of research methods have been used to measure the effect of TV viewing on violent behavior. One method is to expose groups of subjects to violent TV shows in a laboratory setting and then compare their behavior to control groups who viewed nonviolent programming; observations have also been made in playgrounds, athletic fields, and residences. Other experiments require subjects to answer attitude surveys after watching violent TV shows. Still another approach is to use aggregate measures of TV viewing; for example, the number of violent TV shows on the air during a given time period is compared to crime rates during the same period.

Most evaluations of experimental data gathered using these techniques indicate that watching violence on TV is correlated to aggressive behaviors.[164] Such august bodies as the American Psychological Association and the National Institute of Mental Health support the TV-violence link.[165] Subjects who view violent TV shows are likely to commence aggressive behavior almost immediately. This phenomenon is demonstrated by numerous reports of copycat behavior after a particularly violent film or TV show is aired.

According to a recent analysis of all scientific data since 1975, Brad Bushman and Craig Anderson found that the weight of the evidence is that watching violence on

TV is correlated to aggressive behaviors and that the newest, most methodologically sophisticated work shows the greatest amount of association. Put another way, the weight of the experimental results indicates that violent media have an immediate impact on people with a preexisting tendency toward crime and violence. A study conducted by researchers at Columbia University found that kids who watched more than an hour of TV each day showed an increase in assaults, fights, robberies, and other acts of aggression later in life. About 6 percent of 14-year-olds who watched less than an hour of television a day became involved in aggressive acts between the ages of 16 and 22. The rate of aggressive acts skyrocketed to 22.5 percent when kids watched between one to three hours of TV. For kids who viewed more than three hours of TV per day, 28.8 percent were later involved in aggressive acts as adults. This association remained significant after previous aggressive behavior, childhood neglect, family income, neighborhood violence, parental education, and psychiatric disorders were controlled statistically. This research provides a direct link between TV viewing in adolescence and later aggressive behavior in adulthood.[166]

Though this evidence is persuasive, the relationship between TV viewing and violence is still uncertain. A number of critics claim that the evidence simply does not support the claim that TV viewing is related to antisocial behavior.[167] Some critics assert that experimental results are inconclusive and short-lived. Kids may have an immediate reaction to viewing violence on TV, but aggression is quickly extinguished once the viewing ends.[168] Experiments showing that kids act aggressively after watching violent TV shows fail to link aggression to actual criminal behaviors, such as rape or assault. Aggregate data are also inconclusive. Little evidence exists that areas with the highest levels of violent TV viewing also have rates of violent crime that are above the norm.[169] Millions of children watch violence every night yet fail to become violent criminals. And even if a violent behavior–TV link could be established, it would be difficult to show that antisocial people develop aggressive traits merely from watching TV. Aggressive youths may simply enjoy watching TV shows that conform to and support their behavioral orientation. On the other hand, it is possible that TV viewing may not have an immediate impact on behavior or one that is readily observable. Watching television may create changes in personality and cognition, which in the long term may produce behavioral changes. For example, recent research by Dimitri Christakis and his associates found that for every hour of television watched daily between the ages of 1 and 3, the risk of developing attention problems increased by 9 percent over the life course; attention problems have been linked to antisocial behaviors.[170] Further research is needed to clarify this important issue.

Cognitive Theory

cognitive theory
The branch of psychology that studies the perception of reality and the mental processes required to understand the world we live in.

A third area of psychology that has received increasing recognition in recent years has been **cognitive theory.** Psychologists with a cognitive perspective focus on mental processes—the way people perceive and mentally represent the world around them, and how they solve problems. The pioneers of this school were Wilhelm Wundt (1832–1920), Edward Titchener (1867–1927), and William James (1842–1920). The cognitive perspective contains several subgroups. Perhaps the most important for criminological theory is the moral and intellectual development branch, which is concerned with how people morally represent and reason about the world.

Jean Piaget (1896–1980), the founder of this approach, hypothesized that a child's reasoning processes develop in an orderly fashion, beginning at birth and continuing until age 12 and older.[171] At first, during the *sensorimotor stage*, children respond to the environment in a simple manner, seeking interesting objects and developing their reflexes. By the fourth and final stage, the *formal operational stage*, they have developed into mature adults who can use logic and abstract thought.

Lawrence Kohlberg applied the concept of developmental stages to issues in criminology.[172] He suggested that people travel through stages of moral development, during which the basis for moral and ethical decision making changes. It is possible that serious offenders have a moral orientation that differs from that of law-abiding citizens. Kohlberg's stages of development are as follows:

Stage 1. Right is obedience to power and avoidance of punishment.

Stage 2. Right is taking responsibility for oneself, meeting one's own needs, and leaving to others the responsibility for themselves.

Stage 3. Right is being good in the sense of having good motives, having concern for others, and "putting yourself in the other person's shoes."

Stage 4. Right is maintaining the rules of a society and serving the welfare of the group or society.

Stage 5. Right is based on recognized individual rights within a society with agreed-upon rules—a social contract.

Stage 6. Right is an assumed obligation to principles applying to all humankind—principles of justice, equality, and respect for human personality.

Kohlberg classified people according to the stage on this continuum at which their moral development has ceased to grow. In studies conducted by Kohlberg and his associates, criminals were found to be significantly lower in their moral judgment development than noncriminals of the same social background.[173] The majority of noncriminals were classified in stages three and four, whereas a majority of criminals were in stages one and two. Moral development theory, then, suggests that people who obey the law simply to avoid punishment or who have outlooks mainly characterized by self-interest are more likely to commit crimes than those who view the law as something that benefits all of society and who honor the rights of others. Subsequent research with delinquent youths has found that a significant number were in the first two moral development categories, whereas nondelinquents were ranked higher.[174] In addition, higher stages of moral reasoning are associated with such behaviors as honesty, generosity, and nonviolence, which are considered incompatible with delinquency.[175]

Information Processing Cognitive theorists who study information processing try to explain antisocial behavior in terms of perception and analysis of data. When people make decisions, they engage in a sequence of cognitive thought processes. They first *encode* information so that it can be interpreted. They then search for a proper response and decide upon the most appropriate action; finally, they act on their decision.[176]

According to this approach, adolescents who use information properly, who are better conditioned to make reasoned judgments, and who can make quick and reasoned decisions when facing emotion-laden events are the ones best able to avoid antisocial behavior choices.[177] In contrast, delinquency-prone adolescents may have cognitive deficits and use information incorrectly when they make decisions.[178] They have difficulty making the "right decision" while under stress. One reason is that they may be relying on mental "scripts" learned in their early childhood that tell them how to interpret events, what to expect, how they should react, and what the outcome of the interaction should be.[179] Hostile children may have learned improper scripts by observing how others react to events; their own parents' aggressive and inappropriate behavior would have considerable impact. Some children may have had early and prolonged exposure to violence, such as child abuse, which increases their sensitivity to teasing and maltreatment. They may misperceive behavioral cues because their decision making was shaped by traumatic life events.[180]

Oversensitivity to rejection by their peers is a continuation of sensitivity to rejection by parents.[181] Violence becomes a stable behavior because the scripts that emphasize aggressive responses are repeatedly rehearsed as the child matures. They view crime as an appropriate means to satisfy their immediate personal needs, which take precedent over more distant social needs such as obedience to the law.[182]

Violence-prone kids see the world around them as filled with aggressive people. They are overly sensitive and tend to over-react to provocation. As these children mature, they use fewer cues than most people to process information. Some use violence in a calculating fashion as a means of getting what they want; others react in an overly volatile fashion to the slightest provocation. When they attack victims, they may believe they are defending themselves, even though they are misreading the situation.[183] Adolescents who use violence as a coping technique with others are also more likely to exhibit other social problems, such as drug and alcohol abuse.[184]

There is also evidence that delinquent boys who engage in theft are more likely to exhibit cognitive deficits than nondelinquent youth. For example, they have a poor sense of time, leaving them incapable of dealing with or solving social problems in an effective manner.[185]

TO QUIZ YOURSELF ON THIS MATERIAL, go to the Juvenile Delinquency 9e website.

PSYCHOLOGICAL CHARACTERISTICS AND DELINQUENCY

Personality and Delinquency

Personality can be defined as the reasonably stable patterns of behavior, including thoughts and emotions, that distinguish one person from another.[186] An individual's personality reflects characteristic ways of adapting to life's demands and problems. The way we behave is a function of how our personality enables us to interpret life events and make appropriate behavioral choices.

Can the cause of delinquency be linked to personality? There has been a great deal of research on this subject and an equal amount of controversy and debate over the findings.[187] In their early work, Sheldon Glueck and Eleanor Glueck identified a number of personality traits that characterize delinquents:

self-assertiveness	suspicion
extroversion	poor personal skills
defiance	destructiveness
ambivalence	mental instability
impulsiveness	sadism
feeling unappreciated	hostility
narcissism	lack of concern for others
distrust of authority	resentment[188]

The Gluecks' research is representative of the view that delinquents maintain a distinct personality whose characteristics increase the probability that (1) they will be aggressive and antisocial and (2) their actions will involve them with agents of social control, ranging from teachers to police.

Personality and Antisocial Behaviors Since the Gluecks' findings were published, other research efforts have attempted to identify personality traits that would increase the chances for a delinquent career.[189] A common theme is that delinquents are hyperactive, impulsive individuals with short attention spans (attention deficit disorder), who frequently manifest conduct disorders, anxiety disorders, and depression.[190] These traits make them prone to problems ranging from psychopathology to drug abuse, sexual promiscuity, and violence.[191] Suspected traits include impulsivity, hostility, and aggressiveness.[192] The psychologist Hans Eysenck identified two important personality traits that he associated with antisocial behavior: extraversion and neuroticism. Eysenck defines **extraverts** as impulsive individuals who lack the ability to examine their own motives and behaviors; **neuroticism** produces anxiety, tension, and emotional instability.[193] Youths who lack self-insight and are impulsive and emotionally unstable are likely to interpret events differently than youths who are able to give reasoned judgments to life events. Though the former may act destructively, for

extravert
A person who behaves impulsively and doesn't have the ability to examine motives and behavior.

neuroticism
A personality trait marked by unfounded anxiety, tension, and emotional instability.

example, by using drugs, the latter will be able to reason that such behavior is ultimately self-defeating and life threatening. Youths who are both neurotic and extraverted often lack insight and are highly impulsive. They act self-destructively, for example, by abusing drugs, and are the type of offender who will repeat their criminal activity over and over.[194]

In a recent study evaluating the most widely used measures of personality, Joshua Miller and Donald Lynam found that variance within two dimensions—agreeableness and conscientiousness—seems most closely related to antisocial behaviors. Agreeableness involves the ability to use appropriate interpersonal strategies when dealing with others. Conscientiousness involves the ability to control impulses, carry out plans and tasks, maintain organizational skills, and follow one's internal moral code.[195] Miller and Lynam found that personality researchers now link antisocial behaviors to such traits as hostility, self-centeredness, spitefulness, jealousy, and indifference to others. Law violators tend to lack ambition, motivation, and perseverance, have difficulty controlling their impulses, and hold unconventional values and beliefs. Though Miller and Lynam show that these personal attributes are linked to crime, there is still some question about the direction of the linkage. On the one hand, it is possible that kids with these personality traits are programmed to commit crimes. On the other hand, it is possible that personality traits interact with environmental factors to alter behavior. For example, kids who are low in conscientiousness will most likely have poor educational and occupational histories, which limit their opportunity for advancement; this blocked opportunity renders them crime-prone.[196]

The Antisocial Personality It has also been suggested that chronic delinquency may result from a personality pattern or syndrome commonly referred to as the **psychopathic** or **sociopathic personality** (the terms are used interchangeably). Though no more than 3 percent of the male offending population may be classified as sociopathic, it is possible that a large segment of the persistent chronic offenders share this trait.[197]

Psychopathic (sociopathic) youths exhibit a low level of guilt and anxiety and persistently violate the rights of others. Although they may exhibit superficial charm and above-average intelligence, these often mask a disturbed personality that makes them incapable of forming enduring relationships with others. Frequently involved in such deviant behaviors as truancy, running away, lying, substance abuse, and impulsivity, psychopaths lack the ability to empathize with others. From an early age, the psychopath's home life was filled with frustrations, bitterness, and quarreling.

Consequently, throughout life, the sociopath is unreliable, unstable, demanding, and egocentric. Hervey Cleckley, a leading authority on psychopathy, uses this definition:

> [Psychopaths are] chronically antisocial individuals who are always in trouble, profiting neither from experience nor punishment, and maintaining no real loyalties to any person, group, or code. They are frequently callous and hedonistic, showing marked emotional immaturity, with lack of responsibility, lack of judgment, and an ability to rationalize their behavior so that it appears warranted, reasonable, and justified.[198]

Youths diagnosed as psychopaths are believed to be thrill seekers who engage in violent, destructive behavior. Some become gang members and engage in violent and destructive sexual escapades to compensate for a fear of responsibility and an inability to maintain interpersonal relationships.[199] Delinquents have been described as sensation seekers who desire a hedonistic pursuit of pleasure, an extraverted lifestyle, partying, drinking, and a variety of sexual partners.[200]

A number of factors have been found to contribute to the development of psychopathic/sociopathic personalities. They include having an emotionally disturbed parent, a lack of love, parental rejection during childhood, and inconsistent discipline.[201] Another view is that psychopathy has its basis in a measurable physical condition—psychopaths suffer from levels of arousal that are lower than those of the general population. Consequently, psychopathic youths may need greater-than-average stimulation to bring them up to comfortable levels. The road to psychopathy may be entered by people with abnormal brain structures.[202] Psychologists have attempted to treat patients diagnosed as psychopaths by giving them adrenaline, which increases their arousal levels.

Intelligence and Delinquency

Psychologists have long been concerned with the development of intelligence and its subsequent relationship to behavior. It has been charged that children with low IQs are responsible for a disproportionate share of delinquency.

Early criminologists believed that low intelligence was a major cause of delinquency. They thought that if it could be determined which individuals were less intelligent, it might be possible to identify potential delinquents before they committed socially harmful acts.[203] Because social scientists had a captive group of subjects in training schools and penal institutions, studies began to appear that measured the correlation between IQ and crime by testing adjudicated juvenile delinquents. Delinquent juveniles were believed to be inherently substandard in intelligence and naturally inclined to commit more crimes than more intelligent people. Thus, juvenile delinquents were used as a test group around which numerous theories about intelligence were built.

Nature Theory When the newly developed IQ tests were administered to inmates of prisons and juvenile training schools in the first decades of the twentieth century, a large proportion of the inmates scored low on the tests. Henry Goddard found in his studies in 1920 that many institutionalized people were what he considered "feebleminded" and thus concluded that at least half of all juvenile delinquents were mental defectives.[204]

Similarly, in 1926, William Healy and Augusta Bronner tested a group of delinquents in Chicago and Boston and found that 37 percent were subnormal in intelligence.[205] They concluded that delinquents were 5 to 10 times more likely to be mentally deficient than nondelinquent boys.

These and other early studies were embraced as proof that low IQ scores indicated potentially delinquent children and that a correlation existed between innate low intelligence and deviant behavior. IQ tests were believed to measure the inborn genetic makeup of individuals, and many criminologists accepted the predisposition of substandard individuals toward delinquency. This view is referred to as **nature theory** of intelligence.

nature theory
Holds that low intelligence is genetically determined and inherited.

nurture theory
Holds that intelligence is partly biological but mostly sociological; negative environmental factors encourage delinquent behavior and depress intelligence scores for many youths.

Nurture Theory Development of culturally sensitive explanations of human behavior in the 1930s led to the **nurture theory** of intelligence. This school of thought holds that intelligence must be viewed as partly biological but primarily sociological. Nurture theory argues that intelligence is not inherited and that low-IQ parents do not necessarily produce low-IQ children.[206] It discredits the notion that people commit crimes because they have low IQ scores. Instead, it holds that environmental stimulation from parents, relatives, schools, peer groups, and innumerable others creates a child's IQ level and that low IQs result from an environment that also encourages delinquent and criminal behavior.[207] For example, if educational environments could be improved, the result might be both an elevation in IQ scores and a decrease in delinquency.[208] Studies challenging the assumption that people automatically committed delinquent acts because they had below-average IQs began to appear as early as the 1920s. John Slawson's study of 1,543 delinquent boys in New York institutions found that although 80 percent of the delinquents achieved lower scores in abstract verbal intelligence than the general population, delinquents were about normal in mechanical aptitude and nonverbal intelligence. Slawson found no relationship between the number of arrests, the types of offenses, and IQ.[209] In 1931, Edwin Sutherland also evaluated IQ studies of criminals and delinquents and found evidence disputing the association between intelligence and criminality.[210] These findings did much to discredit the notion that a strong relationship existed between IQ and criminality, and for many years the IQ-delinquency link was ignored.

IQ and Delinquency Today A study published in the 1970s by Travis Hirschi and Michael Hindelang revived interest in the association between IQ and delinquency.[211] After conducting a thorough statistical analysis of IQ and delinquency data sets, Hirschi and Hindelang concluded both that IQ tests are a valid predictor of intelligence and that "the weight of evidence is that IQ is more important than race and social class" for predicting delinquent involvement. They argued that a low IQ increases the likelihood of delinquent behavior through its effect on school performance: Youths with low IQs do poorly in school, and school failure and academic incompetence are highly related to delinquency.

The Hirschi-Hindelang findings have been supported by a number of research efforts.[212] In their widely read *Crime and Human Nature*, James Q. Wilson and Richard Herrnstein concluded

> ...there appears to be a clear and consistent link between criminality and low intelligence. That is, taking all offenders as a group, and ignoring differences among kinds of crime, criminals seem, on the average, to be a bit less bright and to have a different set of intellectual strengths and weaknesses than do noncriminals as a group.[213]

Contemporary research efforts have continued to uncover an association between low IQ scores and antisocial behavior. Scores on intelligence tests have been used to predict violent behavior and to distinguish between groups of violent and nonviolent offenders.[214] However, among those social scientists who believe that IQ scores predict criminality, there is still disagreement on the direction of the association. Some believe that IQ has an *indirect* influence on delinquency. Children with a low IQ are more likely to engage in delinquent behavior because their poor verbal ability creates a frustrating school experience. According to this view, low IQ leads to school failure, and academic deficiency has consistently been associated with delinquency.[215] In contrast, some experts believe that IQ may have a *direct* influence on the onset of delinquent involvement. The key linkage between IQ and delinquency is the ability to manipulate abstract concepts. Low intelligence limits adolescents' ability to "foresee the consequences of their offending and to appreciate the feelings of victims."[216] Therefore, youths with limited intelligence are more likely to misinterpret events and gestures, act foolishly, take risks, and engage in harmful behavior.

IQ and Delinquency Controversy The relationship between IQ and delinquency is extremely controversial. It implies there is a condition present at birth that accounts for a child's delinquent behavior throughout the life cycle and that this condition is not easily changed or improved.[217] By implication, if delinquency is not spread evenly through the social structure, neither is intelligence.

The controversy has been fueled by charges that tests are culturally biased and invalid, which makes any existing evidence at best inconclusive. There is also research indicating that IQ level has negligible influence on delinquent behavior.[218] If, as some believe, the linkage between IQ and crime is indirect, then delinquency may be a reflection of poor school performance and educational failure.[219] As Wilson and Herrnstein put it, "A child who chronically loses standing in the competition of the classroom may feel justified in settling the score outside, by violence, theft, and other forms of defiant illegality."[220] Because the relationship runs from low IQ to poor school performance to frustration to delinquency, school officials need to recognize the problem and plan programs to help underachievers perform better in school. As the hypothesized relationship between IQ and delinquency, even if proved to be valid, is an indirect one, educational enrichment programs can help counteract any influence intellectual impairment has on the predilection of young people to commit crime.

Critiquing Individual-Level Theories

Individual-level studies have been criticized on a number of grounds. One view is that the research methodologies they employ are weak and invalid. Most research efforts use adjudicated or incarcerated offenders. It is often difficult to determine whether findings represent the delinquent population or merely those most likely to be arrested and adjudicated by officials of the justice system. For example, some critics have described the methods used in heredity studies as "poorly designed, ambiguously reported and exceedingly inadequate in addressing the relevant issues."[221]

Some critics also fear that individual-level research can be socially and politically damaging. If an above-average number of indigent youth become delinquent offenders, can it be assumed that the less affluent are impulsive, greedy, have low IQs, or are genetically inferior? To many social scientists, the implications of this conclusion are unacceptable in light of what is known about race, gender, and class bias.

Critics also suggest that individual-level theory is limited as a generalized explanation of delinquent behavior because it fails to account for the known patterns of criminal behavior. Delinquent behavior trends seem to conform to certain patterns linked to social-ecological rather than individual factors—social class, seasonality, population density, and gender roles. Social forces that appear to be influencing the onset and maintenance of delinquent behavior are not accounted for by explanations of delinquency that focus on the individual. If, as is often the case, the delinquent rate is higher in one neighborhood than another, are we to conclude that youths in the high-crime area are more likely to be watching violent TV shows or eating more sugar-coated cereals than those in low-crime neighborhoods? How can individual traits explain the fact that crime rates vary between cities and between regions?

Defending Individual-Level Theory The legitimization of social-psychological, psychiatric, and biosocial approaches to explaining deviant behavior may prove to be an important and productive paradigm shift in the decades ahead.[222]

Theorists who focus on individual behavior contend that critics overlook the fact that their research often gives equal weight to environmental and social as well as mental and physical factors.[223] For example, some people may have particular developmental problems that place them at a disadvantage in society, limit their chances of conventional success, and heighten their feelings of anger, frustration, and rage. Though the incidence of these personal traits may be spread evenly across the social structure, families in one segment of the population have the financial wherewithal to help treat the problem, whereas families in another segment may lack the economic means and the institutional support needed to help their children. Delinquency rate differences may be a result of differential access to opportunities either to commit crime or receive the care and treatment needed to correct and compensate for developmental problems.

In addition, individual-level theorists believe that, like it or not, youths are in fact different and may have differing potentials for antisocial acts. For example, gender differences in the violence rate may be explained by the fact that after centuries of aggressive mating behavior, males have become naturally more violent than females.[224] Male aggression may be more a matter of genetic transfer than socialization or cultural patterns.

Trait Theory and Delinquency Prevention

Because many individual-oriented theorists are also practitioners and clinicians, it is not surprising that a great deal of delinquency prevention efforts are based in psychological and biosocial theory.

As a group, individual perspectives on delinquency suggest that prevention efforts should be directed at strengthening a youth's home life and personal relationships. Almost all of these theoretical efforts point to the child's home life as a key factor in delinquent behavior. If parents cannot supply proper nurturing, love, care, discipline, nutrition, and so on, the child cannot develop properly. Whether one believes that delinquency has a biosocial basis, a psychological basis, or a combination of both, it is evident that delinquency prevention efforts should be oriented to reach children early in their development.

It is, therefore, not surprising that county welfare agencies and privately funded treatment centers have offered counseling and other mental health services to families referred by schools, welfare agents, and juvenile court authorities. In some instances, intervention is focused on a particular family problem that has the potential for producing delinquent behavior, such as alcohol and drug problems, child abuse, and sexual abuse. In other situations, intervention is more generalized and oriented toward developing the self-image of parents and children or improving discipline in the family. These programs are covered in Chapter 11.

In addition, individual approaches have been used to prevent court-adjudicated youths from engaging in further criminal activities. It has become almost universal practice for incarcerated and court-adjudicated youths to be given some form of mental and physical evaluation before they begin their term of correctional treatment. Such rehabilitation methods as psychological counseling and psychotropic medication (involving such drugs as Valium or Ritalin) are often prescribed. In some instances, rehabilitation programs are provided through drop-in centers that service youths who are able to remain in their homes, while more intensive programs require residential care and treatment. The creation of such programs illustrates how agents of the juvenile justice system believe that many delinquent youths and status offenders have psychological or physical problems and that their successful treatment can help reduce repeat criminal behavior. Faith in this treatment approach suggests widespread agreement among juvenile justice system professionals that the cause of delinquency can be traced to individual pathology; if not, why bother treating them?

Some questions remain about the effectiveness of individual treatment as a delinquency prevention technique. Little hard evidence exists that clinical treatment alone can prevent delinquency or rehabilitate known delinquents. It is possible that programs designed to help youths may actually stigmatize and label them, hindering their efforts to live conventional lives.[225] Because this issue is so critical, it will be discussed further in Chapter 4.

Summary

- Criminological theories that focus on the individual can be classified in two groups: choice theories and trait theories.

- Choice theory holds that people have free will to control their actions. Delinquency is a product of weighing the risks of crime against its benefits. If the risk is greater than the gain, people will choose not to commit crimes.

- One way of creating a greater risk is to make sure that the punishments associated with delinquency are severe, certain, and fast.

- Environment and opportunity shape delinquent decision making.

- Delinquency can be seductive and attractive, providing thrills and excitement.

- Routine activities theory maintains that a pool of motivated offenders exists and that they will take advantage of suitable targets unless they are heavily guarded.

- General deterrence theory holds that if delinquents are rational, an inverse relationship should exist between punishment and crime. The harsher, more certain, and swift the punishment, the more likely it will deter delinquency.

- General deterrence assumes that delinquents make a rational choice before committing delinquent acts.

- Research has not indicated that deterrent measures actually reduce the delinquency rate.

- Specific deterrence theory holds that the delinquency rate can be reduced if offenders are punished so severely that they never commit crimes again.

- There is little evidence that harsh punishments reduce the delinquency rate, perhaps because most delinquents are not severely punished.

- Choice theorists agree that if the punishment for delinquency could be increased the delinquency rate may fall. One method is to transfer youths to the criminal courts or to grant the adult justice system jurisdiction over serious juvenile cases. Similarly, some experts advocate incapacitation for serious juvenile offenders—for example, long-term sentences for chronic delinquents.

▌ Situational crime prevention strategies aim to reduce opportunities for crime to take place. By imposing obstacles that make it difficult to offend, such strategies strive to dissuade would-be offenders.

▌ Trait theories hold that delinquents do not choose to commit crimes freely but are influenced by forces beyond their control.

▌ Two types of trait theory are biological and psychological.

▌ One of the earliest branches of biological theory was formulated by Cesare Lombroso, who linked delinquency to inborn traits. Following his lead were theories based on genetic inheritance and body build. Although biological theory was in disrepute for many years, it has recently reemerged.

▌ Biochemical factors linked to delinquency include diet, hormones, and blood chemistry.

▌ Neurological factors include brain damage and ADHD.

▌ Some experts believe that delinquent tendencies may be inherited. Studies use twins and adoptees to test this theory.

▌ Psychological theories include the psychodynamic model, which links antisocial behaviors to unconscious emotions and feelings developed early in childhood.

▌ Kids suffering from disorders are more likely to engage in antisocial behaviors.

▌ The behavioral perspective emphasizes that children imitate the behavior they observe personally or view on television or movies. Children who are exposed to violence and see it rewarded may become violent as adults.

▌ Cognitive psychology is concerned with how people perceive the world. Criminality is viewed as a function of improper information processing or lack of moral development.

▌ Psychopaths are people with a total lack of concern for others. They may commit the most serious violent crimes.

▌ Intelligence has also been related to delinquency. Some studies claim to show that delinquents have lower IQs than nondelinquents.

▌ Many delinquency prevention efforts are based on psychological theory. Judges commonly order delinquent youths to receive counseling. Recently, some delinquent offenders have been given biochemical therapy.

Key Terms

choice theory, p. 66
trait theory, p. 66
free will, p. 66
utilitarians, p. 66
classical criminology, p. 66
routine activities theory, p. 71
predatory crime, p. 71
general deterrence, p. 72
specific deterrence, p. 73
situational crime prevention, p. 74
target-hardening technique, p. 74

criminal atavism, p. 76
equipotentiality, p. 77
biosocial theory, p. 77
neurological, p. 78
minimal brain dysfunction (MBD), p. 78
learning disability (LD), p. 80
arousal theorists, p. 82
evolutionary theory, p. 85
psychodynamic theory, p. 87
identity crisis, p. 88

latent delinquents, p. 89
behaviorism, p. 89
social learning theory, p. 90
cognitive theory, p. 92
extravert, p. 94
neuroticism, p. 94
psychopathic or sociopathic personality, p. 95
nature theory, p. 96
nurture theory, p. 96

Questions for Discussion

1. Is there such a thing as the "born criminal"? Are some people programmed at birth to commit crimes?

2. Is crime psychologically abnormal? Can there be "normal" crimes?

3. Apply psychodynamic theory to such delinquent acts as shoplifting and breaking and entering a house.

4. Can delinquent behavior be deterred by the threat of punishment? If not, how can it be controlled?

5. Should we incapacitate violent juvenile offenders for long periods of time—10 years or more?

6. Does watching violent TV and films encourage youth to be aggressive and antisocial? Do advertisements for beer featuring attractive, provocatively dressed young men and women encourage drinking and precocious sex? If not, why bother advertising?

7. Discuss the characteristics of psychopaths. Do you know anyone who fits the description?

Viewpoint

You are a state legislator who is a member of the subcommittee on juvenile justice. Your committee has been asked to redesign the state's juvenile code because of public outrage over serious juvenile crime. At an open hearing, a professor from the local university testifies that she has devised a surefire test to predict violence-prone delinquents. The procedure involves brain scans, DNA testing, and blood analysis. Used with samples of incarcerated adolescents, her procedure has been able to distinguish with 90 percent accuracy between youths with a history of violence and those who are exclusively property offenders. The professor testifies that if each juvenile offender were tested with her techniques, the violence-prone career offender could easily be identified and given special treatment.

Opponents argue that this type of testing is unconstitutional because it violates the Fifth Amendment protection against self-incrimination and can unjustly label nonviolent offenders. Any attempt to base policy on biosocial makeup seems inherently wrong and unfair.

Those who favor the professor's approach maintain that it is not uncommon to single out the insane or mentally incompetent for special treatment and that these conditions often have a biological basis. It is better that a few delinquents be unfairly labeled than seriously violent offenders be ignored until it is too late.

- Is it possible that some kids are born to be delinquents? Or do kids "choose" crime?
- Is it fair to test kids to see if they have biological traits related to crime, even if they have never committed a single offense?
- Should special laws be created to deal with the potentially dangerous offender?
- Should offenders be typed on the basis of their biological characteristics?

Doing Research on the Web

Before you address this issue, you may want to visit InfoTrac College Edition and use *psychological testing* in a keyword search. You may also want to research the law by using the keyword *self-incrimination*. Search the web for information on *criminal profiling*. You might want to read this article (accessed on August 11, 2004):

www.criminalprofiling.com/article.php?sid=264.

Notes

1. U.S. Census Bureau, *Current Population Survey (CPS), 2003 Annual Social & Economic Supplement (ASEC)*, www.census.gov/hhes/poverty/poverty02/pov02hi.html. (Accessed on August 11, 2004.)
2. Marvin Wolfgang, Robert Figlio, and Thorsten Sellin, *Delinquency in a Birth Cohort* (Chicago: University of Chicago Press, 1972).
3. Alan Lizotte, Terence Thornberry, Marvin Krohn, Deborah Chard-Wierschem, and David McDowall, "Neighborhood Context and Delinquency: A Longitudinal Analysis," in H. J. Kerner and E. Weitekamp, eds., *Cross-National Longitudinal Research on Human Development and Criminal Behavior* (Dordrecht, The Netherlands: Kluwer Academic Publishers, 1993), pp. 11–15.
4. Jeremy Bentham, *A Fragment on Government and an Introduction to the Principles of Morals and Legislation,* ed. Wilfred Harrison (Oxford: Basic Blackwell, 1967).
5. See Ernest Van den Haag, *Punishing Criminals* (New York: Basic Books, 1975).
6. Pierre Tremblay and Carlo Morselli, "Patterns in Criminal Achievement: Wilson and Abrahamsen Revisited," *Criminology* 38:633–660 (2000).
7. See James Q. Wilson, *Thinking about Crime* (New York: Basic Books, 1975).
8. Cesare Beccaria, *On Crimes and Punishments,* 6th ed., Henry Paolucci, trans. (Indianapolis: Bobbs-Merrill, 1977), p. 43.
9. F. E. Devine, "Cesare Beccaria and the Theoretical Foundations of Modern Penal Jurisprudence," *New England Journal on Prison Law* 7:8–21 (1982).
10. See Morgan Reynolds, *Crime and Punishment in America* (Washington, DC: National Center for Policy Analysis, 1995).
11. James Q. Wilson and Richard Herrnstein, *Crime and Human Nature* (New York: Simon and Schuster, 1985), p. 396.
12. D. Wayne Osgood, Janet Wilson, Patrick O'Malley, Jerald Bachman, and Lloyd Johnston, "Routine Activities and Individual Deviant Behavior," *American Sociological Review* 61:635–655 (1996).
13. Brenda Sims Blackwell, "Perceived Sanction Threats, Gender, and Crime: A Test and Elaboration of Power-Control Theory," *Criminology* 38:439–488 (2000).
14. Dana Haynie "Contexts of Risk: Explaining the Link between Girls' Pubertal Development and Their Delinquency Involvement," *Social Forces* 82:355–397 (2003).
15. Raymond Paternoster, Shawn Bushway, Robert Brame, and Robert Apel, "The Effect of Teenage Employment on Delinquency and Problem Behaviors," *Social Forces* 82:297–336 (2003).
16. Matthew Ploeger, "Youth Employment and Delinquency: Reconsidering a Problematic Relationship," *Criminology* 35:659–675 (1997).
17. Jeremy Staff and Christopher Uggen, "The Fruits of Good Work: Early Work Experiences and Adolescent Deviance," *Journal of Research in Crime and Delinquency* 40:263–290 (2003).
18. Steven Levitt and Sudhir Alladi Venkatesh, "An Economic Analysis of a Drug-Selling Gang's Finances," NBER Working Papers 6592, National Bureau of Economic Research, Inc., Cambridge, MA (1998).
19. Bill McCarthy, "New Economics of Sociological Criminology," *Annual Review of Sociology* 28:417–442 (2002).
20. Travis Hirschi, "Rational Choice and Social Control Theories of Crime," in D. Cornish and R. Clarke, eds., *The Reasoning Criminal* (New York: Springer-Verlag, 1986), p. 114.
21. See Derek Cornish and Ronald Clarke, eds., *The Reasoning Criminal* (New York: Springer-Verlag, 1986); see also Philip Cook, "The Demand and Supply of Criminal Opportunities," in Michael Tonry and Norval Morris, eds., *Crime and Justice,* vol. 7 (Chicago: University of Chicago Press, 1986), pp. 1–28; Ronald Clarke and Derek Cornish, "Modeling Offenders' Decisions: A Framework for Research and Policy," in Michael Tonry and Norval Morris, eds., *Crime and Justice,* vol. 6 (Chicago: University of Chicago

Press, 1985), pp. 147–187; Morgan Reynolds, *Crime by Choice: An Economic Analysis* (Dallas: Fisher Institute, 1985).

22. Jack Katz, *Seductions of Crime* (New York: Basic Books, 1988); see also Peter Wood, Walter Gove, James Wilson, and John Cochran, "Nonsocial Reinforcement and Habitual Criminal Conduct: An Extension of Learning," *Criminology* 35:335–366 (1997); Bill McCarthy, "Not Just 'For the Thrill of It': An Instrumentalist Elaboration of Katz's Explanation of Sneaky Thrill Property Crime," *Criminology* 33:519–539 (1995); Bill McCarthy and John Hagan, "Mean Streets: The Theoretical Significance of Situational Delinquency among Homeless Youths," *American Journal of Sociology* 3:597–627 (1992).

23. Lawrence Cohen and Marcus Felson, "Social Change and Crime Rate Trends: A Routine Activities Approach," *American Sociological Review* 44:588–608 (1979).

24. Denise Osborn, Alan Trickett, and Rob Elder, "Area Characteristics and Regional Variates as Determinants of Area Property Crime Levels," *Journal of Quantitative Criminology* 8:265–282 (1992).

25. Paul Bellair, "Informal Surveillance and Street Crime: A Complex Relationship," *Criminology* 38:137–167 (2000).

26. William Smith, Sharon Glave Frazee, and Elizabeth Davison, "Furthering the Integration of Routine Activity and Social Disorganization Theories: Small Units of Analysis and the Study of Street Robbery as a Diffusion Process," *Criminology* 38:489–521 (2000).

27. James Massey, Marvin Krohn, and Lisa Bonati, "Property Crime and Routine Activities of Individuals," *Journal of Research in Crime and Delinquency* 26:397 (1989).

28. Lawrence Cohen, Marcus Felson, and Kenneth Land, "Property Crime Rates in the United States: A Macrodynamic Analysis, 1947–1977, with Ex-Ante Forecasts for the Mid-1980's," *American Journal of Sociology* 86:90–118 (1980).

29. Daniel Nagin and Greg Pogarsky, "Integrating Celerity, Impulsivity, and Extralegal Sanction Threats into a Model of General Deterrence: Theory and Evidence," *Criminology* 39:865–892 (2001); R. Steven Daniels, Lorin Baumhover, William Formby, and Carolyn Clark-Daniels, "Police Discretion and Elder Mistreatment: A Nested Model of Observation, Reporting, and Satisfaction," *Journal of Criminal Justice* 27:209–225 (1999).

30. Nagin and Pogarsky, "Integrating Celerity, Impulsivity, and Extralegal Sanction Threats into a Model of General Deterrence: Theory and Evidence."

31. Beccaria, *On Crimes and Punishments*.

32. For the classic analysis on the subject, see Johannes Andenaes, *Punishment and Deterrence* (Ann Arbor: University of Michigan Press, 1974).

33. Daniel Nagin and Greg Pogarsky, "An Experimental Investigation of Deterrence: Cheating, Self-Serving Bias and Impulsivity," *Criminology* 41:167–195 (2003).

34. Tomislav V. Kovandzic and John J. Sloan, "Police Levels and Crime Rates Revisited: A County-Level Analysis from Florida (1980–1998)," *Journal of Criminal Justice* 30:65–76 (2002).

35. Michael White, James Fyfe, Suzanne Campbell, and John Goldkamp, "The Police Role in Preventing Homicide: Considering the Impact of Problem-Oriented Policing on the Prevalence of Murder," *Journal of Research in Crime and Delinquency* 40:194–226 (2003).

36. Eric Fritsch, Tory Caeti, and Robert Taylor, "Gang Suppression through Saturation Patrol, Aggressive Curfew, and Truancy Enforcement: A Quasi-Experimental Test of the Dallas Anti-Gang Initiative," *Crime and Delinquency* 45:122–139 (1999).

37. Bruce Jacobs, "Anticipatory Undercover Targeting in High Schools," *Journal of Criminal Justice* 22:445–457 (1994).

38. Leona Lee, "Factors Determining Waiver in a Juvenile Court," *Journal of Criminal Justice* 22:329–339 (1994).

39. *Wilkins v. Missouri; Stanford v. Kentucky*, 109 S.Ct. 2969 (1989).

40. Carol Kohfeld and John Sprague, "Demography, Police Behavior, and Deterrence," *Criminology* 28:111–136 (1990).

41. Steven Klepper and Daniel Nagin, "The Deterrent Effect of Perceived Certainty and Severity of Punishment Revisited," *Criminology* 27:721–746 (1989).

42. See Raymond Paternoster, "The Deterrent Effect of Perceived Certainty and Severity of Punishment: A Review of the Evidence and Issues," *Justice Quarterly* 42:173–217 (1987); idem, "Absolute and Restrictive Deterrence in a Panel of Youth: Explaining the Onset, Persistence/Desistance, and Frequency of Delinquent Offending," *Social Problems* 36:289–307 (1989).

43. Wanda Foglia, "Perceptual Deterrence and the Mediating Effect of Internalized Norms among Inner-City Teenagers," *Journal of Research in Crime and Delinquency* 34:414–442 (1997); Donald Green, "Measures of Illegal Behavior in Individual-Level Deterrence Research," *Journal of Research in Crime and Delinquency* 26:253–275 (1989); Charles Tittle, *Sanctions and Social Deviance: The Question of Deterrence* (New York: Praeger, 1980).

44. Eric Jensen and Linda Metsger, "A Test of the Deterrent Effect of Legislative Waiver on Violent Juvenile Crime," *Crime and Delinquency* 40:96–104 (1994).

45. Foglia, "Perceptual Deterrence and the Mediating Effect of Internalized Norms among Inner-City Teenagers."

46. Ibid.

47. Maynard Erickson and Jack Gibbs, "Punishment, Deterrence, and Juvenile Justice," in D. Shichor and D. Kelly, eds., *Critical Issues in Juvenile Justice* (Lexington, MA: Lexington Books, 1980), pp. 183–202.

48. Doris Layton MacKenzie and Spencer De Li, "The Impact of Formal and Informal Social Controls on the Criminal Activities of Probationers," *Journal of Research in Crime and Delinquency* 39:243–276 (2002).

49. Christina DeJong, "Survival Analysis and Specific Deterrence: Integrating Theoretical and Empirical Models of Recidivism," *Criminology* 35:561–576 (1997).

50. Paul Tracy and Kimberly Kempf-Leonard, *Continuity and Discontinuity in Criminal Careers* (New York: Plenum, 1996).

51. Pamela Lattimore, Christy Visher, and Richard Linster, "Predicting Re-arrest for Violence among Serious Youthful Offenders," *Journal of Research in Crime and Delinquency* 32:54–83 (1995).

52. Greg Pogarsky and Alex R. Piquero "Can Punishment Encourage Offending? Investigating the 'Resetting' Effect," *Journal of Research in Crime and Delinquency* 40:92–117 (2003).

53. Marcus Felson, "Routine Activities and Crime Prevention," in National Council for Crime Prevention, *Studies on Crime and Crime Prevention, Annual Review*, vol. 1 (Stockholm: Scandinavian University Press, 1992), pp. 30–34.

54. Andrew Fulkerson, "Blow and Go: The Breath-Analyzed Ignition Interlock Device as a Technological Response to DWI," *American Journal of Drug and Alcohol Abuse* 29:219–235 (2003)

55. Barry Webb, "Steering Column Locks and Motor Vehicle Theft: Evaluations for Three Countries," in Ronald Clarke, ed., *Crime Prevention Studies* (Monsey, NY: Criminal Justice Press, 1994), pp. 71–89.

56. David Farrington and Brandon Welsh, "Improved Street Lighting and Crime Prevention," *Justice Quarterly* 19:313–343 (2002).

57. Brandon Welsh and David Farrington, "Effects of Closed-Circuit Television on Crime," *Annals of the American Academy of Political and Social Science* 587:110–136 (2003).

58. Massey, Krohn, and Bonati, "Property Crime and the Routine Activities of Individuals."

59. David Shantz, "Conflict, Aggression, and Peer Status: An Observational Study," *Child Development* 57:1322–1332 (1986).

60. For an excellent review of Lombroso's work, as well as that of other well-known theorists, see Randy Martin, Robert Mutchnick, and W. Timothy Austin, *Criminological Thought, Pioneers Past and Present* (New York: Macmillan, 1990).

61. Marvin Wolfgang, "Cesare Lombroso," in Herman Mannheim, ed., *Pioneers in Criminology* (Montclair, NJ: Patterson Smith, 1970), pp. 232–271.

62. Gina Lombroso-Ferrero, *Criminal Man According to the Classification of Cesare Lombroso* (1911; reprint, Montclair, NJ: Patterson Smith, 1972), p. 7.

63. Rafaele Garofalo, *Criminology* [1914], reprint edition (Glenridge, NJ: Patterson Smith, 1968).

64. See Thorsten Sellin, "Enrico Ferri," in Mannheim, ed., *Pioneers in Criminology*, pp. 361–384.

65. Nicole Hahn Rafter, "Criminal Anthropology in the United States," *Criminology* 30:525–547 (1992).

66. Edmond O. Wilson, *Sociobiology: The New Synthesis* (Cambridge: Harvard University Press, 1975).

67. For a general review, see John Archer, "Human Sociobiology: Basic Concepts and Limitations," *Journal of Social Issues* 47:11–26 (1991).

68. Arthur Caplan, *The Sociobiology Debate: Readings on Ethical and Scientific Issues* (New York: Harper & Row, 1978).

69. See C. Ray Jeffrey, "Criminology as an Interdisciplinary Behavioral Science," *Criminology* 16:149–167 (1978).

70. Dalton Conley and Neil Bennett, "Is Biology Destiny? Birth Weight and Life Chances," *American Sociological Review* 654:458–467 (2000).

71. Ingrid Helland, Lars Smith, Kristin Saarem, Ola Saugstad, and Christian Drevon, "Maternal Supplementation with Very-Long-Chain n-3 Fatty Acids During Pregnancy and Lactation Augments Children's IQ at 4 Years of Age," *Pediatrics* 111:39–44 (2003).

72. Diana Fishbein, "Selected Studies on the Biology of Antisocial Behavior," in John Conklin, ed., *New Perspectives in Criminology* (Needham Heights, MA: Allyn & Bacon, 1996), pp. 26–38.

73. Anthony Walsh and Lee Ellis, "Shoring Up the Big Three: Improving Criminological Theories with Biosocial Concepts," paper presented at the annual Society of Criminology Meeting, San Diego, November 1997.

74. Terrie Moffitt, "Adolescence-Limited and Life-Course Persistent Anti-social Behavior: A Developmental Taxonomy," *Psychological Review* 100:674–701 (1993).

75. For a thorough review of the biosocial perspective, see Diana Fishbein, "Biological Perspectives in Criminology," *Criminology* 28:27–72 (1990); idem, "Selected Studies on the Biology of Antisocial Behavior," in Conklin, ed., *New Perspectives in Criminology,* pp. 26–38.

76. See Adrian Raine, *The Psychopathology of Crime* (San Diego: Academic Press, 1993); see also Leonard Hippchen, *The Ecologic-Biochemical Approaches to Treatment of Delinquents and Criminals* (New York: Van Nostrand Reinhold, 1978).

77. Paul Marshall, "Allergy and Depression: A Neurochemical Threshold Model of the Relation between the Illnesses," *Psychological Bulletin* 113:23–43 (1993); Elizabeth McNeal and Peter Cimbolic, "Antidepressants and Biochemical Theories of Depression," *Psychological Bulletin* 99:361–374 (1986); for an opposing view, see "Adverse Reactions to Food in Young Children," *Nutrition Reviews* 46:120–121 (1988).

78. David Bellinger, "Lead," *Pediatrics* 113:1016–1022 (2004); Jeff Evans, "Asymptomatic, High Lead Levels Tied to Delinquency," *Pediatric News* 37:13 (2003); Herbert Needleman, Christine McFarland, Roberta Ness, Stephen Fienberg, and Michael Tobin, "Bone Lead Levels in Adjudicated Delinquents: A Case Control Study," *Neurotoxicology and Teratology* 24:711–717 (2002).

79. Paul Stretesky and Michael Lynch, "The Relationship between Lead Exposure and Homicide," *Archives of Pediatric Adolescent Medicine* 155:579–582 (2001).

80. Jens Walkowiak, Jörg-A. Wiener, Annemarie Fastabend, Birger Heinzow, Ursula Krämer, Eberhard Schmidt, Hans-J. Steingürber, Sabine Wundram, and Gerhard Winneke "Environmental Exposure to Polychlorinated Biphenyls and Quality of the Home Environment: Effects on Psychodevelopment in Early Childhood," *The Lancet* 358:92–93 (2001).

81. Marshall, "Allergy and Depression: A Neurochemical Threshold Model of the Relation between the Illnesses," pp. 23–29.

82. A. Maras, M. Laucht, D. Gerdes, C. Wilhelm, S. Lewicka, D. Haack, L. Malisova, and M. H. Schmidt, "Association of Testosterone and Dihydrotestosterone with Externalizing Behavior in Adolescent Boys and Girls," *Psychoneuroendocrinology* 28:932–940 (2003).

83. Christy Miller Buchanan, Jacquelynne Eccles, and Jill Becker, "Are Adolescents the Victims of Raging Hormones? Evidence for Activational Effects of Hormones on Moods and Behavior at Adolescence," *Psychological Bulletin* 111:62–107 (1992).

84. Alex Piquero and Timothy Brezina, "Testing Moffitt's Account of Adolescent-Limited Delinquency," *Criminology* 39:353–370 (2001).

85. Fishbein, "Selected Studies on the Biology of Antisocial Behavior."

86. Diana Fishbein, "Neuropsychological Function, Drug Abuse, and Violence, a Conceptual Framework," *Criminal Justice and Behavior* 27:139–159 (2000).

87. Kytja Voeller, "Right-Hemisphere Deficit Syndrome in Children," *American Journal of Psychiatry* 143:1004–1009 (1986).

88. Moffitt, "Adolescence-Limited and Life-Course Persistent Antisocial Behavior."

89. Leila Beckwith and Arthur Parmelee, "EEG Patterns of Preterm Infants, Home Environment, and Later IQ," *Child Development* 57:777–789 (1986).

90. Adrian Raine, Patricia Brennan, Brigitte Mednick, and Sarnoff Mednick, "High Rates of Violence, Crime, Academic Problems, and Behavioral Problems in Males with Both Early Neuromotor Deficits and Unstable Family Environments," *Archives of General Psychiatry* 53:544–549 (1966).

91. Stephen Tibbetts, "Low Birth Weight, Disadvantaged Environment and Early Onset: A Test of Moffitt's Interactional Hypothesis," paper presented at the American Society of Criminology meeting, Boston, November 1995.

92. Dorothy Otnow Lewis, Jonathan Pincus, Marilyn Feldman, Lori Jackson, and Barbara Bard, "Psychiatric, Neurological, and Psychoeducational Characteristics of 15 Death Row Inmates in the United States," *American Journal of Psychiatry* 143:838–845 (1986).

93. See R. R. Monroe, *Brain Dysfunction in Aggressive Criminals* (Lexington, MA: D.C. Heath, 1978).

94. Adrian Raine et al., "Interhemispheric Transfer in Schizophrenics, Depressives and Normals with Schizoid Tendencies," *Journal of Abnormal Psychology* 98:35–41 (1989).

95. Jean Seguin, Robert Pihl, Philip Harden, Richard Tremblay, and Bernard Boulerice, "Cognitive and Neuropsychological Characteristics of Physically Aggressive Boys," *Journal of Abnormal Psychology* 104:614–624 (1995).

96. D. Williams, "Neural Factors Related to Habitual Aggression—Consideration of Differences between Habitual Aggressives and Others Who Have Committed Crimes of Violence," *Brain* 92:503–520 (1969).

97. Charlotte Johnson and William Pelham, "Teacher Ratings Predict Peer Ratings of Aggression at 3-Year Follow-Up in Boys with Attention Deficit Disorder with Hyperactivity," *Journal of Consulting and Clinical Psychology* 54:571–572 (1987).

98. Cited in Charles Post, "The Link between Learning Disabilities and Juvenile Delinquency: Cause, Effect, and 'Present Solutions,'" *Juvenile and Family Court Journal* 31:59 (1981).

99. For a general review, see Concetta Culliver, "Juvenile Delinquency and Learning Disability: Any Link?" Paper presented at the Academy of Criminal Justice Sciences, San Francisco, April 1988.

100. Joel Zimmerman, William Rich, Ingo Keilitz, and Paul Broder, "Some Observations on the Link between Learning Disabilities and Juvenile Delinquency," *Journal of Criminal Justice* 9:9–17 (1981); J. W. Podboy and W. A. Mallory, "The Diagnosis of Specific Learning Disabilities in a Juvenile Delinquent Population," *Juvenile and Family Court Journal* 30:11–13 (1978).

101. Charles Murray, *The Link between Learning Disabilities and Juvenile Delinquency: A Current Theory and Knowledge* (Washington, DC: Government Printing Office, 1976).

102. Robert Pasternak and Reid Lyon, "Clinical and Empirical Identification of Learning Disabled Juvenile Delinquents," *Journal of Correctional Education* 33:7–13 (1982).

103. Zimmerman et al., "Some Observations on the Link between Learning Disabilities and Juvenile Delinquency."

104. Katz, *Seductions of Crime*, pp. 12–15.

105. Lee Ellis, "Arousal Theory and the Religiosity-Criminality Relationship," in Peter Cordella and Larry Siegel, eds., *Contemporary Criminological Theory* (Boston: Northeastern University, 1996), pp. 65–84.

106. Adrian Raine, Peter Venables, and Sarnoff Mednick, "Low Resting Heart Rate at Age 3 Years Predisposes to Aggression at Age 11 Years: Evidence from the Mauritius Child Health Project," *Journal of the American Academy of Adolescent Psychiatry* 36:1457–1464 (1997).

107. David Rowe, *The Limits of Family Influence: Genes, Experiences and Behavior* (New York: Guilford Press, 1995), p. 64.

108. For a review, see Lisabeth Fisher DiLalla and Irving Gottesman, "Biological and Genetic Contributors to Violence—Widom's Untold Tale," *Psychological Bulletin* 109:125–129 (1991).

109. Ibid.

110. For an early review, see Barbara Wooton, *Social Science and Social Pathology* (London: Allen and Unwin, 1959); John Laub and Robert Sampson, "Unraveling Families and Delinquency: A Reanalysis of the Gluecks' Data," *Criminology* 26:355–380 (1988).

111. Ping Qin, "The Relationship of Suicide Risk to Family History of Suicide and Psychiatric Disorders," *Psychiatric Times* 20 (2003), www.psychiatrictimes.com/p031262.html. (Accessed August 11, 2004.)

112. D. J. West and D. P. Farrington, "Who Becomes Delinquent?" in D. J. West and D. P. Farrington, eds., *The Delinquent Way of Life* (London: Heinemann, 1977), pp. 1–28; D. J. West, *Delinquency: Its Roots, Careers, and Prospects* (Cambridge, MA: Harvard University Press, 1982).

113. West, *Delinquency*, p. 114.

114. David Farrington, "Understanding and Preventing Bullying," in Michael Tonry, ed., *Crime and Justice*, vol. 17, (Chicago: University of Chicago Press, 1993), pp. 381–457.

115. Terence Thornberry, Adrienne Freeman-Gallant, Alan Lizotte, Marvin Krohn, and Carolyn Smith. "Linked Lives: The Intergenerational Transmission of Antisocial Behavior," *Journal of Abnormal Child Psychology* 31:171–185 (2003).

116. David Rowe and David Farrington, "The Familial Transmission of Criminal Convictions," *Criminology* 35:177–201 (1997).

117. Abigail Fagan and Jake Najman, "Sibling Influences on Adolescent Delinquent Behaviour: An Australian Longitudinal Study," *Journal of Adolescence* 26:547–559 (2003).

118. Louise Arseneault, Terrie Moffitt, Avshalom Caspi, Alan Taylor, Fruhling Rijsdijk, Sara Jaffee, Jennifer Ablow, and Jeffrey Measelle, "Strong Genetic Effects on Cross-situational Antisocial Behaviour among 5-year-old Children According to Mothers, Teachers, Examiner-Observers, and Twins' Self-Reports," *Journal of Child Psychology and Psychiatry* 44:832–848 (2003).

119. For a general review, see Nancy Segal, *Entwined Lives: Twins and What They Tell Us about Human Behavior* (New York: Dutton, 2000); David Rowe, "Sibling Interaction and Self-Reported Delinquent Behavior: A Study of 265 Twin Pairs," *Criminology* 23:223–240 (1985); Nancy Segal, "Monozygotic and Dizygotic Twins: A Comparative Analysis of Mental Ability Profiles," *Child Development* 56:1051–1058 (1985).

120. Sarnoff Mednick and Jan Volavka, "Biology and Crime," in Norval Morris and Michael Tonry, eds., *Crime and Justice*, vol. 1 (Chicago: University of Chicago Press, 1980), pp. 85–159; Lee Ellis, "Genetics and Criminal Behavior," *Criminology* 10:43–66 (1982); Karl O. Christiansen, "A Preliminary

Study of Criminality among Twins," in S. A. Mednick and Karl O. Christiansen, eds., *The Biosocial Bases of Criminal Behavior* (New York: Gardner Press, 1977).

121. Qin, "The Relationship of Suicide Risk to Family History of Suicide and Psychiatric Disorders."

122. Jane Scourfield, Marianne Van den Bree, Neilson Martin, Peter McGuffin, "Conduct Problems in Children and Adolescents: A Twin Study," *Archives of General Psychiatry* 61:489–496 (2004); Jeanette Taylor, Bryan Loney, Leonardo Bobadilla, William Iacono, and Matt McGue, "Genetic and Environmental Influences on Psychopathy Trait Dimensions in a Community Sample of Male Twins," *Journal of Abnormal Child Psychology* 31:633–645 (2003).

123. Ginette Dionne, Richard Tremblay, Michel Boivin, David Laplante, and Daniel Perusse, "Physical Aggression and Expressive Vocabulary in 19-Month-Old Twins," *Developmental Psychology* 39:261–273 (2003).

124. Alice Gregory, Thalia Eley, and Robert Plomin. "Exploring the Association between Anxiety and Conduct Problems in a Large Sample of Twins Aged 2–4," *Journal of Abnormal Child Psychology* 32:111–123 (2004).

125. Glenn Walters, "A Meta-Analysis of the Gene-Crime Relationship," *Criminology* 30:595–613 (1992).

126. T. J. Bouchard, D. T. Lykken, D. T. McGue, N. L. Segal, and A. Tellegen, "Sources of Human Psychological Differences: The Minnesota Study of Twins Reared Apart," *Science* 250:223–228 (1990).

127. Thomas Bouchard, "Genetic and Environmental Influences on Intelligence and Special Mental Abilities," *American Journal of Human Biology* 70:253–275 (1998); Some findings from the Minnesota study can be accessed from their website at www.psych.umn.edu/psylabs/mtfs/special.htm.

128. Remi Cadoret, Colleen Cain, and Raymond Crowe, "Evidence for a Gene-Environment Interaction in the Development of Adolescent Antisocial Behavior," *Behavior Genetics* 13:301–310 (1983).

129. Rowe, *The Limits of Family Influence*, p. 110.

130. Bernard Hutchings and Sarnoff Mednick, "Criminality in Adoptees and Their Adoptive and Biological Parents: A Pilot Study," in Mednick and Christiansen, eds., *Biosocial Bases of Criminal Behavior.*

131. For similar findings, see William Gabrielli and Sarnoff Mednick, "Urban Environment, Genetics, and Crime," *Criminology* 22:645–653 (1984).

132. Jody Alberts-Corush, Philip Firestone, and John Goodman, "Attention and Impulsivity Characteristics of the Biological and Adoptive Parents of Hyperactive and Normal Control Children," *American Journal of Orthopsychiatry* 56:413–423 (1986).

133. Wilson and Herrnstein, *Crime and Human Nature*, p. 131.

134. Walters, "A Meta-Analysis of the Gene-Crime Relationship."

135. Wilson and Herrnstein, *Crime and Human Nature*, p. 108.

136. Lawrence Cohen and Richard Machalek, "A General Theory of Expropriative Crime: An Evolutionary Ecological Approach," *American Journal of Sociology* 94:465–501 (1988).

137. For a general review, see Martin Daly and Margo Wilson, "Crime and Conflict: Homicide in Evolutionary Psychological Theory," in Michael Tonry, ed., *Crime and Justice, An Annual Edition* (Chicago: University of Chicago Press, 1997), pp. 51–100.

138. David Rowe, Alexander Vazsonyi, and Aurelio Jose Figuerodo, "Mating-Effort in Adolescence: A Conditional of Alternative Strategy," *Personal Individual Differences* 23:105–115 (1997).

139. Ibid.

140. Lee Ellis, "The Evolution of Violent Criminal Behavior and Its Nonlegal Equivalent," in Harry Hoffman, ed., *Crime in Biological, Social, and Moral Contexts* (New York: Praeger, 1990), pp. 61–81.

141. Ellis and Walsh, "Gene-Based Evolutionary Theories of Criminology."

142. Byron Roth, "Crime and Child Rearing," *Society* 34:39–45 (1996).

143. For a thorough review of this issue, see David Brandt and S. Jack Zlotnick, *The Psychology and Treatment of the Youthful Offender* (Springfield, IL: Charles C. Thomas, 1988).

144. Spencer Rathus, *Psychology* (New York: Holt, Rinehart and Winston, 1996), pp. 11–21.

145. See Sigmund Freud, *An Outline of Psychoanalysis*, James Strachey, trans. (New York: Norton, 1963).

146. Seymour Halleck, *Psychiatry and the Dilemmas of Crime* (Berkeley: University of California Press, 1971).

147. See Erik Erikson, *Identity, Youth, and Crisis* (New York: Norton, 1968).

148. David Abrahamsen, *Crime and Human Mind* (New York: Columbia University Press, 1944), p. 137.

149. See Fritz Redl and Hans Toch, "The Psychoanalytic Perspective," in Hans Toch, ed., *Psychology of Crime and Criminal Justice* (New York: Holt, Rinehart and Winston, 1979), pp. 193–195.

150. August Aichorn, *Wayward Youth* (New York: Viking Press, 1935).

151. Halleck, *Psychiatry and the Dilemmas of Crime.*

152. Jennifer Beyers and Rolf Loeber, "Untangling Developmental Relations between Depressed Mood and Delinquency in Male Adolescents," *Journal of Abnormal Child Psychology* 31:247–267 (2003).

153. Dorothy Espelage, Elizabeth Cauffman, Lisa Broidy, Alex Piquero, Paul Mazerolle, and Hans Steiner, "A Cluster-Analytic Investigation of MMPI Profiles of Serious Male and Female Juvenile Offenders," *Journal of the American Academy of Child & Adolescent Psychiatry* 42:770–777 (2003).

154. Brandt and Zlotnick, *The Psychology and Treatment of the Youthful Offender*, pp. 72–73.

155. Eric Silver, "Mental Disorder and Violent Victimization: The Mediating Role of Involvement in Conflicted Social Relationships," *Criminology* 40:191–212 (2002).

156. See Albert Bandura and Frances Menlove, "Factors Determining Vicarious Extinction of Avoidance Behavior through Symbolic Modeling," *Journal of Personality and Social Psychology* 8:99–108 (1965); Albert Bandura and Richard Walters, *Social Learning and Personality Development* (New York: Holt, Rinehart and Winston, 1963).

157. David Perry, Louise Perry, and Paul Rasmussen, "Cognitive Social Learning Mediators of Aggression," *Child Development* 57:700–711 (1986)

158. Bonnie Carlson, "Children's Beliefs about Punishment," *American Journal of Orthopsychiatry* 56:308–312 (1986).

159. Albert Bandura and Richard Walters, *Adolescent Aggression* (New York: Ronald Press, 1959), p. 32.

160. Victoria Rideout, Elizabeth Vandewater, and Ellen Wartella, *Zero to Six: Electronic Media in the Lives of Infants, Toddlers and Preschoolers.* (Menlo Park, CA.: Kaiser Family Foundation, 2003).

161. Michael Brody, "Playing with Death," *The Brown University Child and Adolescent Behavior Letter* 16:8 (2000).

162. UCLA Center for Communication Policy, Television Violence Monitoring Project (Los Angeles, 1995); Associated Press, "Hollywood Is Blamed in Token Booth Attack," *Boston Globe*, November 28, 1995, p. 30.

163. Joyce Sprafkin, Kenneth Gadow, and Monique Dussault, "Reality Perceptions of Television: A Preliminary Comparison of Emotionally Disturbed and Nonhandicapped Children," *American Journal of Orthopsychiatry* 56:147–152 (1986).

164. Wendy Wood, Frank Wong, and J. Gregory Chachere, "Effects of Media Violence on Viewers' Aggression in Unconstrained Social Interaction," *Psychological Bulletin* 109:371–383 (1991); Lynette Friedrich-Cofer and Aletha Huston, "Television Violence and Aggression: The Debate Continues," *Psychological Bulletin* 100:364–371 (1986).

165. American Psychological Association, *Violence on TV*, a social issue release from the Board of Social and Ethical Responsibility for Psychology (Washington, DC: APA, 1985).

166. Brad Bushman and Craig Anderson, "Media Violence and the American Public Revisited," *American Psychologist* 56:448-450 (2002); Jeffrey Johnson, Patricia Cohen, Elizabeth Smailes, Stephanie Kasen, and Judith Brook, "Television Viewing and Aggressive Behavior During Adolescence and Adulthood," *Science* 295:2468–2471 (2002).

167. Jonathon Freedman, "Television Violence and Aggression: What the Evidence Shows," in S. Oskamp, ed., *Applied Social Psychology Annual: Television as a Social Issue* (Newbury Park, CA: Sage Publications, 1988), pp. 144–162.

168. Jonathon Freedman, "Effect of Television Violence on Aggressiveness," *Psychological Bulletin* 96:227–246 (1984); idem, "Television Violence and Aggression: A Rejoinder," *Psychological Bulletin* 100:372–378 (1986).

169. Steven Messner, "Television Violence and Violent Crime: An Aggregate Analysis," *Social Problems* 33:218–235 (1986).

170. Dimitri Christakis, Frederick Zimmerman, David DiGiuseppe, and Carolyn McCarty, "Early Television Exposure and Subsequent Attentional Problems in Children," *Pediatrics* 113:708–713 (2004).

171. See Jean Piaget, *The Moral Judgement of the Child* (London: Keagan Paul, 1932).

172. Lawrence Kohlberg, *Stages in the Development of Moral Thought and Action* (New York: Holt, Rinehart and Winston, 1969).

173. L. Kohlberg, K. Kauffman, P. Scharf, and J. Hickey, *The Just Community Approach in Corrections: A Manual* (Niantic, CT: Connecticut Department of Corrections, 1973).

174. Scott Henggeler, *Delinquency in Adolescence* (Newbury Park, CA: Sage Publications, 1989), p. 26.

175. Ibid.

176. K. A. Dodge, "A Social Information Processing Model of Social Competence in Children," in M. Perlmutter, ed., *Minnesota Symposium in Child Psychology*, vol. 18 (Hillsdale, NJ: Erlbaum, 1986), pp. 77–125.

177. Adrian Raine, Peter Venables, and Mark Williams, "Better Autonomic Conditioning and Faster Electrodermal Half-Recovery Time at Age 15 Years as Possible Protective Factors against Crime at Age 29 Years," *Developmental Psychology* 32:624–630 (1996).

178. Jean Marie McGloin and Travis Pratt, "Cognitive Ability and Delinquent Behavior among Inner-City Youth: A Life-Course Analysis of Main, Mediating, and Interaction Effects," *International Journal of Offender Therapy & Comparative Criminology* 47:253–271 (2003).

179. L. Huesman and L. Eron, "Individual Differences and the Trait of Aggression," *European Journal of Personality* 3:95–106 (1989).

180. Judith Baer and Tina Maschi, "Random Acts of Delinquency: Trauma and Self-Destructiveness in Juvenile Offenders," *Child & Adolescent Social Work Journal* 20:85–99 (2003).

181. Rolf Loeber and Dale Hay, "Key Issues in the Development of Aggression and Violence from Childhood to Early Adulthood," *Annual Review of Psychology* 48:371–410 (1997).

182. Tony Ward and Claire Stewart, "The Relationship Between Human Needs and Criminogenic Needs," *Crime & Law* 9:219–225 (2003).

183. J. E. Lochman, "Self and Peer Perceptions and Attributional Biases of Aggressive and Nonaggressive Boys in Dyadic Interactions," *Journal of Consulting and Clinical Psychology* 55:404–410 (1987).

184. Kathleen Cirillo et al., "School Violence: Prevalence and Intervention Strategies for At-Risk Adolescents," *Adolescence* 33:319–331 (1998).

185. Leilani Greening, "Adolescent Stealers' and Nonstealers' Social Problem-Solving Skills," *Adolescence* 32:51–56 (1997).

186. See Walter Mischel, *Introduction to Personality*, 4th ed. (New York: Holt, Rinehart and Winston, 1986).

187. D. A. Andrews and J. Stephen Wormith, "Personality and Crime: Knowledge and Construction in Criminology," *Justice Quarterly* 6:289–310 (1989); Donald Gibbons, "Comment—Personality and Crime: Non-Issues, Real Issues, and a Theory and Research Agenda," *Justice Quarterly* 6:311–324 (1989).

188. Sheldon Glueck and Eleanor Glueck, *Unraveling Juvenile Delinquency* (Cambridge: Harvard University Press, 1950).

189. See Hans Eysenck, *Personality and Crime* (London: Routledge and Kegan Paul, 1977).

190. David Farrington, "Psychobiological Factors in the Explanation and Reduction of Delinquency," *Today's Delinquent* 7:37–51 (1988).

191. Laurie Frost, Terrie Moffitt, and Rob McGee, "Neuropsychological Correlates of Psychopathology in an Unselected Cohort of Young Adolescents," *Journal of Abnormal Psychology* 98:307–313 (1989).

192. Edelyn Verona and Joyce Carbonell, "Female Violence and Personality," *Criminal Justice and Behavior* 27:176–195 (2000).

193. Hans Eysenck and M. W. Eysenck, *Personality and Individual Differences* (New York: Plenum, 1985).

194. Catrien Bijleveld and Jan Hendriks, "Juvenile Sex Offenders: Differences Between Group and Solo Offenders," *Psychology, Crime & Law* 9:237–246 (2003).

195. Joshua Miller and Donald Lynam, "Personality and Antisocial Behavior," *Criminology* 39:765–799 (2001).

196. Ibid., pp. 781–782.

197. Linda Mealey, "The Sociobiology of Sociopathy: An Integrated Evolutionary Model," *Behavioral and Brain Sciences* 18:523–540 (1995).

198. Hervey Cleckley, "Psychopathic States," in S. Aneti, ed., *American Handbook of Psychiatry* (New York: Basic Books, 1959), pp. 567–569.

199. Lewis Yablonsky, *The Violent Gang* (Baltimore: Penguin, 1971), pp. 195–205.

200. Helen Raskin White, Erich Labouvie, and Marsha Bates, "The Relationship between Sensation Seeking and Delinquency: A Longitudinal Analysis," *Journal of Research in Crime and Delinquency* 22:197–211 (1985).

201. Rathus, *Psychology*, p. 452.

202. A. Raine, T. Lencz, K. Taylor, J. B. Hellige, S. Bihrle, L. Lacasse, M. Lee, S. Ishikawa, and P. Colletti, "Corpus Callosum Abnormalities in Psychopathic Antisocial Individuals," *Archives of General Psychiatry* 60:1134–1142 (2003).

203. L. M. Terman, "Research on the Diagnosis of Predelinquent Tendencies," *Journal of Delinquency* 9:124–130 (1925); idem, *Measurement of Intelligence* (Boston: Houghton Mifflin, 1916). For example, see M. G. Caldwell, "The Intelligence of Delinquent Boys Committed to Wisconsin Industrial School," *Journal of Criminal Law and Criminology* 20:421–428 (1929); and C. Murcheson, *Criminal Intelligence* (Worcester, MA: Clark University, 1926), pp. 41–44.

204. Henry Goddard, *Efficiency and Levels of Intelligence* (Princeton, NJ: Princeton University Press, 1920).

205. William Healy and Augusta Bronner, *Delinquency and Criminals: Their Making and Unmaking* (New York: Macmillan, 1926).

206. Joseph Lee Rogers, H. Harrington Cleveland, Edwin van den Oord, and David Rowe, "Resolving the Debate over Birth Order, Family Size, and Intelligence," *American Psychologist* 55:599–612 (2000).

207. Kenneth Eels, *Intelligence and Cultural Differences* (Chicago: University of Chicago Press, 1951), p. 181.

208. Sorel Cahahn and Nora Cohen, "Age versus Schooling Effects on Intelligence Development," *Child Development* 60:1239–1249 (1989).

209. John Slawson, *The Delinquent Boys* (Boston: Budget Press, 1926).

210. Edwin Sutherland, "Mental Deficiency and Crime," in Kimball Young, ed., *Social Attitudes* (New York: Henry Holt, 1973).

211. Travis Hirschi and Michael Hindelang, "Intelligence and Delinquency: A Revisionist Review," *American Sociological Review* 42:471–586 (1977).

212. Terrie Moffitt and Phil Silva, "IQ and Delinquency: A Direct Test of the Differential Detection Hypothesis," *Journal of Abnormal Psychology* 97:1–4 (1988); E. Kandel et al., "IQ as a Protective Factor for Subjects at a High Risk for Antisocial Behavior," *Journal of Consulting and Clinical Psychology* 56:224–226 (1988); Christine Ward and Richard McFall, "Further Validation of the Problem Inventory for Adolescent Girls: Comparing Caucasian and Black Delinquents and Nondelinquents," *Journal of Consulting and Clinical Psychology* 54:732–733 (1986).

213. Wilson and Herrnstein, *Crime and Human Nature*, p. 148.

214. Alex Piquero, "Frequency, Specialization, and Violence in Offending Careers," *Journal of Research in Crime and Delinquency* 37:392–418 (2000).

215. Terrie Moffitt, William Gabrielli, Sarnoff Mednick, and Fini Schulsinger, "Socioeconomic Status, IQ, and Delinquency," *Journal of Abnormal Psychology* 90:152–156 (1981); for a similar finding, see L. Hubble and M. Groff, "Magnitude and Direction of WISC-R Verbal Performance IQ Discrepancies among Adjudicated Male Delinquents," *Journal of Youth and Adolescence* 10:179–183 (1981).

216. David Farrington, "Juvenile Delinquency," in John C. Coleman, ed., *The School Years* (London: Routledge, 1992), p. 137.

217. Robert McCall and Michael Carriger, "A Meta-Analysis of Infant Habituation and Recognition Memory Performance as Predictors of Later IQ," *Child Development* 64:57–79 (1993).

218. H. D. Day, J. M. Franklin, and D. D. Marshall, "Predictors of Aggression in Hospitalized Adolescents," *Journal of Psychology* 132:427–435 (1998).

219. Deborah Denno, "Sociological and Human Developmental Explanations of Crime: Conflict or Consensus," *Criminology* 23:141–174 (1985).

220. Ibid., p. 171.

221. Glenn Walters and Thomas White, "Heredity and Crime: Bad Genes or Bad Research," *Justice Quarterly* 27:455–485 (1989), at p. 478.

222. John Cochran, Peter Wood, and Bruce Arneklev, "Is the Religiosity-Delinquency Relationship Spurious? A Test of Arousal and Social Control Theories," *Journal of Research in Crime and Delinquency* 31:92–113 (1994).

223. Lee Ellis, "Genetics and Criminal Behavior," *Criminology* 10:43–66 (1982), at p. 58.

224. Lee Ellis, "The Evolution of the Nonlegal Equivalent of Aggressive Criminal Behavior," *Aggressive Behavior* 12:57–71 (1986).

225. Edwin Schur, *Radical Nonintervention: Rethinking the Delinquency Problem* (Englewood Cliffs, NJ: Prentice-Hall, 1973).

4 Sociological Views of Delinquency

Chapter Outline

Social Structure Theories
Social Structure/Social Problems
Structure, Culture, and Delinquency
Social Disorganization Theory
Anomie/Strain
Cultural Deviance Theory

Social Process Theories
Socialization and Crime
FOCUS ON DELINQUENCY: Random Family
POLICY AND PRACTICE: Dare to Be You
Theories of Socialization
Learning Theories
Control Theories

Social Reaction Theories
The Labeling Process
The Effect of Labeling
The Juvenile Justice Process and Labeling
Evaluating Labeling Theory

Social Conflict Theory
Law and Justice
The Conflict Concept of Delinquency

Sociological Theories and Social Policy
Social Structure Theories and Social Policy
Social Process and Social Policy
Social Reaction and Social Policy
Social Conflict and Social Policy

Chapter Objectives

1. Know what is meant by the term "social disorganization"
2. Understand the relationships among neighborhood fear, unemployment, change, and lack of cohesion, and their influence on delinquent behavior patterns
3. Be familiar with the concepts of strain and anomie
4. Comprehend the elements of General Strain Theory and the concept of negative affective states
5. Understand how cultural deviance creates a breeding ground for gangs and law-violating groups
6. Know the social processes that have been linked to delinquency
7. Be able to differentiate between learning and control theories
8. Identify the elements of labeling and stigma that reinforce delinquency
9. Recognize the role social conflict plays in creating an environment that breeds antisocial behaviors
10. Be familiar with the social programs that have been designed to improve neighborhood conditions, help children be properly socialized, and reduce conflict

CNN. View the CNN video clip of this story and answer related Critical Thinking questions on your Juvenile Delinquency 9e CD-ROM.

Public officials in Washington, D.C., are concerned because a number of high-profile juvenile crimes have made headlines on the local news. In one recent incident, a Washington bus driver was hit by a stray bullet during a gun battle between rival youth gangs on a busy street in a residential area in broad daylight. Soon after, a 16-year-old bystander was shot fatally as he was leaving a high school dance. The shooter was a 15-year-old assailant who was actually aiming at members of a rival gang or "crew." These incidents are alarming to Washington officials, but they are by no means unique. Though juvenile murder rates have trended downward nationwide, there are disturbing reports of increased gang activity and violent killings in some of the nation's biggest cities. Are there social forces now brewing in urban areas which may regenerate juvenile violence, the scourge of the inner cities during the 1980s and early 1990s?

Many delinquency experts believe it is a mistake to ignore social and environmental factors in trying to understand the cause of adolescent misbehavior.[1] According to this view, most delinquents are indigent and desperate, not calculating or evil. They grew up in deteriorated parts of town and lacked the social support and economic resources familiar to more affluent members of society. Understanding delinquent behavior, then, requires us to account for the destructive influence these social forces have on human behavior

Social theorists believe that explanations of delinquency as an individual-level phenomenon fail to account for the consistent social patterns found in the crime rate. We know that youths are more likely to commit crimes if they live in the poorest neighborhoods within large urban areas; the South and/or West have higher delinquency rates than the Northeast and/or Midwest. It seems unlikely that a majority of kids who "choose" crime all live in a particular neighborhood or that kids in one state are more likely to choose crime, while those in another choose conventional activities. It seems equally unlikely that most kids with physical or mental problems live in a particular section of town and/or that some regions of the nation produce children with higher rates of biological and/or psychological abnormality than others. As you have learned, some experts believe that watching violent TV shows and films contributes to adolescent aggression. If this were so, how can regional/community/neighborhood differences in the delinquency rate be explained? Adolescents watch similar TV shows

You can visit the **No More Victims** website at www.nmvi.org. For an up-to-date list of web links, go to http://cj.wadsworth.com/siegel_jd9e.

107

and films in all regions of the country and all parts of the city. If violence has a biological or psychological origin, should it not be distributed more evenly throughout the social structure? The fact that crime rates are highest in the poorest neighborhoods seems more than a coincidence.

To some delinquency experts, these facts can only mean one thing: The cause of delinquency rests within the dynamics of the social world. They point to cultural norms, social processes, and social institutions as the key elements that shape human behavior. When these elements are strained, crime rates increase. Political unrest and mistrust, economic stress, and family disintegration are social changes that have been found to precede sharp increases in crime rates. When traditional social institutions and values predominate, the crime rate declines.[2]

Another important social change has been the rapid advance in technology and its influence on the social system. People who lack the requisite social and educational training have found that the road to success is almost impassable. The lack of opportunity for upward mobility may make drug dealing and other crimes an attractive solution to socially deprived but economically enterprising people.[3]

The shape of intergroup and interpersonal relationships may also be a source of delinquent behavior. The dynamics of interactions between individuals and important social institutions—families, peers, schools, jobs, criminal justice agencies, and the like—shape human behavior.[4] The relationship of one social class or group to another, or to the power structure that controls the nation's legal and economic system, may also be closely related to delinquency. It seems logical that people on the lowest rung of the economic ladder will have the greatest incentive to commit crimes. They may be either enraged and frustrated by their lack of economic success, or simply financially desperate and disillusioned. In either instance, crime may appear to be an attractive means to financial success.

This chapter reviews the most prominent social theories of delinquency. They are divided into four groups: (1) social structure theories, which hold that delinquency is a function of a person's place in the economic structure; (2) social process theories, which view delinquency as a result of poor socialization or upbringing; (3) social reaction theories, which view delinquent careers as a function of stigma and labeling; and (4) social conflict theories, which consider delinquent behavior to be a product of economic inequality.

SOCIAL STRUCTURE THEORIES

The United States, the world's richest country, still has more than 34 million people living in poverty, about 12 percent of the total population. As you may recall, living below the poverty level today means that a family of three must have an income below $13,700 a year. Included within this group of poor Americans are almost 12 million indigent children.[5]

culture of poverty
View that lower-class people form a separate culture with their own values and norms, which are sometimes in conflict with conventional society.

In 1966, sociologist Oscar Lewis coined the phrase "**culture of poverty**" to describe the crushing burden faced by the urban poor.[6] According to Lewis, the culture of poverty is marked by apathy, cynicism, helplessness, and mistrust of institutions such as police and government. Mistrust of authority prevents the impoverished from taking advantage of the few conventional opportunities available to them. The result is a permanent underclass whose members have little chance of upward mobility or improvement. This extreme level of economic and social hardship has been related to psychological adjustment: People who live in poverty are more likely to suffer low self-esteem, depression, and loneliness.[7]

Social Structure/Social Problems

Nowhere are social problems more pressing than in the inner-city neighborhoods that experience constant population turnover as their more affluent residents move to stable communities or suburbs. While the American economy has been generally

A mother and her young children at home in their room at the Lydia E. Hoffman Family Residence, Bronx, New York. The charity was founded as a temporary shelter for homeless families in 1996. The United States, the world's richest country, still contains more than 34 million people living in poverty, about 12 percent of the total population. Some delinquency experts associate harsh and deprived living conditions with the onset of antisocial behavior.

robust, social conditions have worsened in many blighted urban areas during the past decade, and their residents have suffered.[8] As a city becomes *hollowed out*, with a deteriorated inner core surrounded by less devastated communities, delinquency rates spiral upward.[9] Those remaining are forced to live in communities with poorly organized social networks, alienated populations, and high crime.[10] The impoverished are deprived of a standard of living enjoyed by most other citizens, and their children suffer from much more than financial hardship. They attend poor schools, live in substandard housing, and lack good health care. More than half of families in poverty are fatherless and husbandless; many are supported entirely by government aid despite a concerted national effort to limit eligibility for public assistance.

Chronic Unemployment Neighborhoods that provide few employment opportunities are the most vulnerable to predatory crime. Unemployment destabilizes households, and unstable families are more likely to produce children who choose aggression as a means of dealing with limited opportunity.[11] Lack of employment opportunity also limits the authority of parents, reducing their ability to influence children. Because adults cannot serve as role models, gangs whose members are both feared and respected dominate local culture. Predatory crime increases to levels that cannot easily be controlled by police.

Child Poverty Children are hit especially hard by poverty. Hundreds of studies have documented the association among family poverty and children's health, achievement, and behavior impairments.[12] Besides their increased chance of physical illness, poor children are much more likely than wealthy children to suffer various social and physical ills, ranging from low birthweight to a limited chance of earning a college degree. Many live in substandard housing—high-rise, multiple-family dwellings—which can

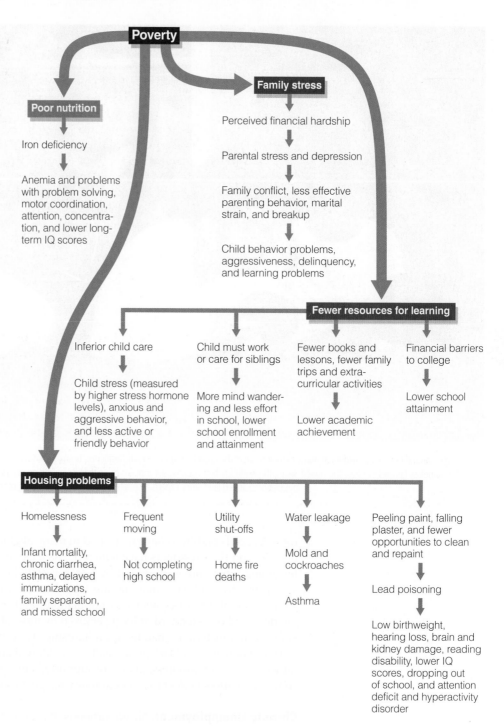

FIGURE 4.1

Examples of Documented Pathways from Poverty to Adverse Child Outcomes

SOURCE: Arloc Sherman, *Poverty Matters* (Washington, DC: Children's Defense Fund, 1997), p. 23.

Poverty

Poor nutrition

Iron deficiency

Anemia and problems with problem solving, motor coordination, attention, concentration, and lower long-term IQ scores

Family stress

Perceived financial hardship

Parental stress and depression

Family conflict, less effective parenting behavior, marital strain, and breakup

Child behavior problems, aggressiveness, delinquency, and learning problems

Fewer resources for learning

Inferior child care

Child stress (measured by higher stress hormone levels), anxious and aggressive behavior, and less active or friendly behavior

Child must work or care for siblings

More mind wandering and less effort in school, lower school enrollment and attainment

Fewer books and lessons, fewer family trips and extracurricular activities

Lower academic achievement

Financial barriers to college

Lower school attainment

Housing problems

Homelessness

Infant mortality, chronic diarrhea, asthma, delayed immunizations, family separation, and missed school

Frequent moving

Not completing high school

Utility shut-offs

Home fire deaths

Water leakage

Mold and cockroaches

Asthma

Peeling paint, falling plaster, and fewer opportunities to clean and repaint

Lead poisoning

Low birthweight, hearing loss, brain and kidney damage, reading disability, lower IQ scores, dropping out of school, and attention deficit and hyperactivity disorder

have a negative influence on their long-term psychological health.[13] For poor children, the cycle of poverty can lead to a variety of adverse outcomes, including life- and health-endangering conditions (see Figure 4.1). Providing adequate care to children under these circumstances can be an immense undertaking.

underclass
Group of urban poor whose members have little chance of upward mobility or improvement.

truly disadvantaged
According to William Julius Wilson, those people who are left out of the economic mainstream and reduced to living in the most deteriorated inner-city areas.

Racial Disparity Members of the urban **underclass**, typically minority group members, are referred to as the **truly disadvantaged**.[14] Race-based economic disparity haunts these members of the underclass and their children over the course of their lifespan. Even if they value education and other middle-class norms, their desperate life circumstances (for example, high unemployment and nontraditional family structures) may prevent them from developing the skills, habits, and styles that lead first to educational success and later to success in the workplace.

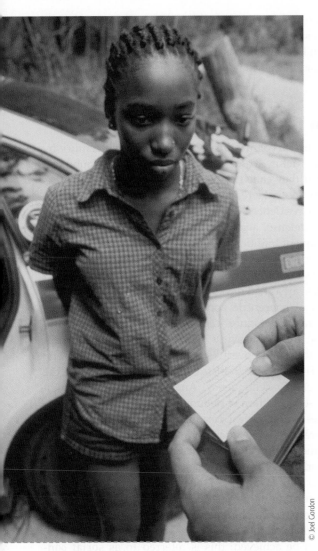

A young African American girl is arrested in Florida. Racial disparity has been linked to the onset of delinquency and drug abuse. As a result, minority group members are often over-represented in arrest statistics. What can be done to break the cycle of poverty, racism, and despair, that still haunts the United States?

© Joel Gordon

Racial disparity has been linked to the onset of delinquency and drug abuse. While some whites use their economic, social, and political advantages to live in sheltered, gated communities protected by security guards and police, many minorities are denied similar protections and privileges.[15] Because they are forced to live in impoverished, crime-ridden communities, minority males are often over-represented in the arrest statistics, and in some jurisdictions, a significant portion of all minority males are under criminal justice system control.[16] Research shows that states with a substantial minority population have a much higher imprisonment rate than those with predominantly Caucasian populations.[17] The collateral costs of this injustice, such as paying for lawyers and court costs, perpetuate poverty by absorbing what money there is and depriving families and children of the support it could otherwise bring.[18] Racial disparity in the justice system has been linked to the fear some Caucasians have of young black men, which in most instances is disproportionate to the amount of crime African Americans actually commit.[19]

Race and Economic Disparity William Julius Wilson is one of the nation's most prominent experts on race and its effect on poverty. In his most recent book, *The Bridge over the Racial Divide: Rising Inequality and Coalition Politics,* Wilson argues that despite economic gains, there is a growing inequality in American society, and ordinary families, of all races and ethnic origins, are suffering. Whites, Latinos, African Americans, Asians, and Native Americans must therefore begin to put aside their differences and concentrate more on what they have in common—their aspirations, problems, and hopes. There needs to be mutual cooperation across racial lines.[20] Despite its continuing presence, Wilson finds that racism is becoming more subtle and hard to detect. Whites believe that African Americans are responsible for their own inferior economic status because of their cultural traits. Because even affluent whites fear corporate downsizing, they are unwilling to vote for governmental assistance to the poor. Whites are continuing to be suburban dwellers, further isolating poor minorities in central cities and making their problems distant and unimportant. Wilson believes that the changing marketplace, with its reliance on sophisticated computer technologies, is continually decreasing demand for low-skilled workers, which impacts African Americans more negatively than other better-educated and affluent groups.

Economic disparity will continually haunt members of the underclass and their children over the course of their lifespan. If interracial economic disparity would end, so too might differences in the crime and delinquency rate.[21]

Structure, Culture, and Delinquency

Some delinquency experts tie delinquency rates to socioeconomic conditions and cultural values. According to this view, neighborhoods that experience high levels of poverty will also have high delinquency rates. Long-term, unremitting poverty undermines a community and its residents, instilling within them a sense of hopelessness that makes antisocial forms of behavior seem attractive.

This structural theory finds delinquency to be a consequence of the inequalities built into the social structure. Kids growing up in disadvantaged areas are at risk for delinquency because they find little hope that they can be successful in the conventional world. Areas that experience high levels of poverty, in which the basic stabilizing

To read **an interview with William Julius Wilson,** leading scholar of urban poverty, go to www.pbs.org/fmc/interviews/wilson.htm. For an up-to-date list of web links, go to http://cj.wadsworth.com/siegel_jd9e.

forces of society—the family, school, and neighborhood—have become ineffective, also have high delinquency rates. Residents of such areas are frustrated by their inability to become part of the "American Dream." There are actually a number of different structural theories of delinquency and these will now be discussed in some detail.

Social Disorganization Theory

Social disorganization theory was first recognized early in the twentieth century by sociologists Clifford Shaw and Henry McKay. These Chicago-based scholars found that delinquency rates were high in what they called **transitional neighborhoods**—areas that had changed from affluence to decay. Here, factories and commercial establishments were interspersed with private residences. In such environments, teenage gangs developed as a means of survival, defense, and friendship. Gang leaders recruited younger members, passing on delinquent traditions and ensuring survival of the gang from one generation to the next, a process referred to as **cultural transmission.**

While mapping delinquency rates in Chicago, Shaw and McKay noted that distinct ecological areas had developed that could be visualized as a series of concentric zones, each with a stable delinquency rate (see Figure 4.2).[22]

The areas of heaviest delinquency concentration appeared to be the poverty-stricken, transitional, inner-city zones. The zones farthest from the city's center were the least prone to delinquency. Analysis of these data indicated a stable pattern of delinquent activity in the ecological zones over a 65-year period.[23] These patterns persisted as different ethnic or racial groups moved into the zone. Shaw and McKay found that delinquency was tied to neighborhood characteristics rather than the personal characteristics or culture of the residents.

According to their social disorganization view, a healthy, organized community has the ability to regulate itself so that common goals (such as living in a crime-free area) can be achieved; this is referred to as **social control.**[24] Those neighborhoods that become disorganized are incapable of social control because they are wracked by deterioration and economic failure.[25] Though the evidence that crime rates soar during periods of high unemployment is inconclusive, Shaw and McKay claimed that areas continually hurt by poverty and long-term unemployment also experience social disorganization.[26] (See Figure 4.3.) While cultural and social conditions have changed—for example, we live in a much more heterogeneous, mobile society than they did—the most important of Shaw and McKay's findings, that crime rates correspond to neighborhood structure, still holds up.[27]

Consequences of Disorganization Social disorganization is related to a long list of collateral social problems, residential instability, family disruption, and ethnic/racial conflict.[28] Social institutions such as schools and churches cannot work effectively in the climate of alienation and mistrust that characterizes disorganized areas. Typically, the absence of political power limits access to external funding and protection; without outside resources and financial aid, the neighborhood cannot get back on its feet.[29] Children who reside in these disorganized neigh-

social disorganization theory
Posits that delinquency is a product of the social forces existing in inner-city, low-income areas.

transitional neighborhood
Area undergoing a shift in population and structure, usually from middle-class residential to lower-class mixed use.

cultural transmission
Cultural norms and values that are passed down from one generation to the next.

social control
Ability of social institutions to influence human behavior; the justice system is the primary agency of formal social control.

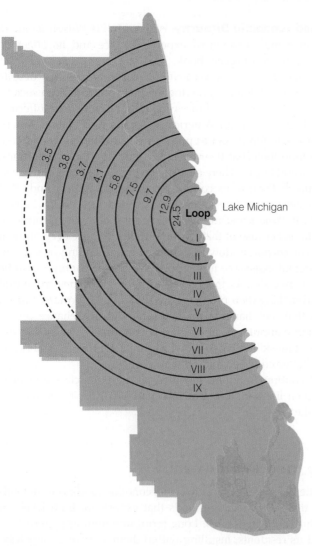

FIGURE 4.2

Concentric Zones Map of Chicago

Note: Arabic numbers represent the rate of male delinquency.

SOURCE: Clifford R. Shaw et al., *Delinquency Areas* (Chicago: University of Chicago Press, 1929), p. 99. Used by permission of the publisher.

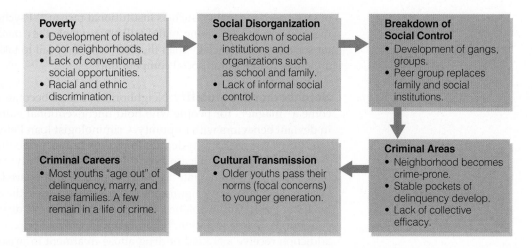

FIGURE 4.3
Social Disorganization
Theory

Poverty
- Development of isolated poor neighborhoods.
- Lack of conventional social opportunities.
- Racial and ethnic discrimination.

Social Disorganization
- Breakdown of social institutions and organizations such as school and family.
- Lack of informal social control.

Breakdown of Social Control
- Development of gangs, groups.
- Peer group replaces family and social institutions.

Criminal Areas
- Neighborhood becomes crime-prone.
- Stable pockets of delinquency develop.
- Lack of collective efficacy.

Cultural Transmission
- Older youths pass their norms (focal concerns) to younger generation.

Criminal Careers
- Most youths "age out" of delinquency, marry, and raise families. A few remain in a life of crime.

To find out more about **the work of Shaw and McKay,** read the article at www.csiss.org/classics/content/66. For an up-to-date list of web links, go to http://cj.wadsworth.com/siegel_jd9e.

gentrified
The process of transforming a lower-class area into a middle-class enclave through property rehabilitation.

poverty concentration effect
According to sociologist William Julius Wilson, the consolidation of poor minority group members in urban areas.

borhoods find that involvement with conventional social institutions, such as schools and after-school programs, is either absent or blocked, which puts them at risk for recruitment into gangs.[30] These problems are stubborn and difficult to overcome. Even when an attempt is made to revitalize a disorganized neighborhood by creating institutional support programs such as community centers and better schools, the effort may be countered by the ongoing drain of deep-rooted economic and social deprivation.[31] Some of the factors that create and maintain social disorganization are discussed next.

Community Change Urban areas have a life cycle during which they undergo significant change: from affluent to impoverished, from impoverished to rehabilitated or **gentrified,** from residential to commercial, from stable to transient. As communities go through these changes, levels of delinquency also change.[32] Neighborhood change precedes increasing rates of delinquency.[33]

Communities on the downswing are likely to experience increases in the number of single-parent families, changes in housing from owner- to renter-occupied units, a loss of semiskilled and unskilled jobs, and a growth in numbers of discouraged, unemployed workers who are no longer seeking jobs.[34] These communities also tend to develop mixed-use areas in which commercial and residential properties stand side by side. Areas in which retail establishments are abandoned have the highest crime rates.[35]

The changing racial makeup of communities may also influence delinquency rates. Areas undergoing change in their racial composition will experience increases in delinquency rates.[36] This may reflect fear of racial conflict. Adults may encourage teens to terrorize the newcomers; the result is conflict, violence, and disorder.

Poverty Concentration It is not surprising to find that the most economically disadvantaged neighborhoods also have the highest rates of serious crimes such as homicide.[37] Sociologist William Julius Wilson has described why this phenomenon occurs. White working and middle-class families flee inner-city poverty areas, resulting in a **poverty concentration effect,** in which elements of the most disadvantaged population are consolidated in urban ghettos. As the working and middle classes move out, they take with them their financial and institutional resources and support. Businesses are disinclined to locate in poverty areas; banks become reluctant to lend money for new housing or businesses.[38] Urban areas marked by concentrated poverty become isolated and insulated from the social mainstream and more prone to delinquency and gang activity.[39]

Poverty concentration may motivate young African American males to enter the drug trade, an enterprise that increases the likelihood they will become involved in violent crimes.[40] Minority group members living in these areas also suffer other forms of race-based inequality, such as institutional racism.[41] Psychologists warn that under these circumstances, young males will envy people they perceive as doing much better socially and financially than themselves. If they fail to take aggressive tactics, they are going to lose out in social competition.[42]

Neighborhood Instability Neighborhoods may become unstable when they become a "magnet" for people who hold unconventional values and desire to engage in deviant behaviors with impunity. Criminologist Joan Petersilia has warned that as a result of America's two-decade-long imprisonment boom, more than 500,000 inmates are now being released back into the community each year. Many of them have not received adequate treatment and are unprepared for life in conventional society. They provide a significant risk to communities; these risks include increases in child abuse, family violence, the spread of infectious diseases, homelessness, and community disorganization.[43] For example, only 13 percent of inmates who suffer addiction receive any kind of drug abuse treatment in prison. Petersilia argues that once back in the community, offenders may increase their criminal activity because they want to "make up for lost time" and resume their criminal careers. The majority leave prison with no savings, no immediate entitlement to unemployment benefits, and few employment prospects. One year after release, as many as 60 percent of former inmates are not employed in the regular labor market, and there is increasing reluctance among employers to hire ex-offenders. Unemployment is closely related to drug and alcohol abuse. Losing a job can lead to substance abuse, which in turn is related to child and family violence. Mothers released from prison have difficulty finding services such as housing, employment, and childcare, and this causes stress for them and their children. Children of incarcerated and released parents often suffer confusion, sadness, and social stigma. These feelings often result in school-related difficulties, low self-esteem, aggressive behavior, and general emotional dysfunction. If the parents are negative role models, children fail to develop positive attitudes about work and responsibility. Children of incarcerated parents are five times more likely to serve time in prison than are children whose parents are not incarcerated.

The situation will become more serious as more and more parolees are released back into the disorganized communities whose deteriorated conditions may have motivated their original crimes.

Community Fear Unstable and disorganized neighborhoods suffer social incivility—trash and litter, graffiti, burned-out buildings, drunks, vagabonds, loiterers, prostitutes, noise, congestion, angry words. Residents pass by parks and playgrounds and see teens hanging out, maybe drinking and taking drugs, and their presence contributes to fear.[44] This evidence of incivility convinces residents that their neighborhood is dangerous; not surprisingly, when crime rates are high in these areas, fear levels undergo a dramatic increase.[45] As crime flourishes, neighborhood fear increases, which in turn decreases a community's cohesion and thwarts its ability to exert social control over its residents.[46] Fear of crime is much higher in disorganized neighborhoods than in affluent suburbs.[47] Members of the underclass fear crime and have little confidence that the government can do anything to counter the drug dealers and gangs that terrorize the neighborhood.[48] People tell others of their experiences of being victimized, spreading the word that the neighborhood is dangerous. Such fear is not the property of any single racial or ethnic group but can paralyze members of any population, especially when they believe that they are in the minority and vulnerable to attack.[49]

People living in neighborhoods with high levels of crime and civil disorder become suspicious and mistrusting.[50] They report being fatalistic, and they anticipate a relatively short life expectancy. Why plan for the future when there is a significant likelihood that they may never see it? In such areas young boys and girls may adjust psychologically by taking risks and discounting the future. Teenage birth rates soar, and so do violence rates.[51]

The **Project Return** website is dedicated to providing successful reentry from prison life to free society: www.projectreturninc.org. For an up-to-date list of web links, go to http://cj.wadsworth.com/siegel_jd9e.

When fear grips a neighborhood, people do not want to leave their homes at night, so they withdraw from community life. Fear has been related to distress, inactivity, and decline in health.[52] High levels of fear are also related to deteriorating business conditions, increased population mobility, and the domination of street life by violent gangs.

Weak Social Controls Most neighborhood residents share the goal of living in a crime-free area. Some communities rely on institutions such as families and schools to regulate behavior. When these efforts are blunted, delinquency rates increase and neighborhood cohesiveness is weakened, setting the stage for deterioration.

Neighborhoods maintain a variety of agencies of social control. Some operate on the personal level and involve peers, families, and relatives. These sources exert informal control over behavior by either awarding or withholding approval and respect. Informal control mechanisms include criticism, ridicule, ostracism, and physical punishment.[53] Communities also use local institutions to control delinquency, such as business associations, schools, churches, and voluntary organizations.[54]

Disorganized neighborhoods cannot mount an effective social control effort. Because the population is transient, interpersonal relationships tend to be superficial and cannot help to reduce deviant behavior.

Social institutions cannot work effectively in a climate of mistrust. Residents who live in these high crime areas, where crime and drug abuse is common, also suffer. Their ability to maintain social ties with neighbors and friends becomes weak and attenuated; this may further reduce already weakened levels of informal social control.[55] In such neighborhoods, the absence of political power brokers limits access to external funding and police protection. In contrast, areas that can draw on outside help and secure external resources—a process referred to as public social control—are better able to reduce the effects of disorganization and maintain lower levels of crime and victimization.[56]

Social control is also weakened because unsupervised peer groups, which flourish in disorganized areas, disrupt the influence of neighborhood control agents.[57] Children in disorganized areas report that they are unable to become involved with conventional social institutions and are therefore vulnerable to aggression and delinquency.[58]

Rage, Distrust, and Hopelessness Kids in disorganized areas are socialized in a world where adults maintain a siege mentality, sometimes believing there are government plots to undermine the neighborhood ("the AIDS virus was created to kill us off"; "the government brings drugs into the neighborhood to keep people under control").[59] They fear the police and consider them violent and dangerous.[60]

Young people growing up in these areas become angry, convinced that no one cares about their plight. There is free-floating anger, which causes adolescents to strike out at the merest hint of provocation.[61] Children living in these conditions become "crusted over"; they do not let people get close to them. Their peer relations are exploitive, and they develop a sense of hopelessness. Parents and teachers seem to focus on children's failures rather than on their achievements, leaving them vulnerable to the lure of delinquent groups.[62]

Lack of Collective Efficacy Communities that are cohesive and maintain high levels of social control develop **collective efficacy**—mutual trust and a willingness to intervene in the supervision of children and the maintenance of public order.[63] It is the cohesion among neighborhood residents combined with a shared interest in maintaining social control over public space within the neighborhood that promotes collective efficacy.[64] Collective efficacy helps reduce fear and stabilize communities. In neighborhoods where people help each other out, residents are less likely to fear crime and be afraid of becoming a crime victim.[65]

Local organizations designed to control crime, such as neighborhood associations, may only be effective if they promote a sense of collective efficacy.[66] These institutions

collective efficacy
The ability of communities to regulate the behavior of their residents through the influence of community institutions, such as the family and school. Residents in these communities share mutual trust and a willingness to intervene in the supervision of children and the maintenance of public order.

can be effective in helping kids avoid gang membership, thereby lowering neighborhood crime rates.[67] Parents in these areas are able to call upon neighborhood resources to take up the task of controlling their children; single mothers do not have to face the burden of providing adequate supervision alone.[68]

As they learn to increase levels of collective efficacy, residents may be better equipped to draw on resources from their neighbors in more affluent surrounding communities.[69] The plight of poor neighborhoods, which lack the means of forming collective efficacy, is exacerbated because they are cut off from outside areas for support.[70]

Communities with high collective efficacy generally experience low crime rates and low levels of physical and social disorder (for example, drinking in the street, spray-painting graffiti, and breaking windows). [71] In contrast, neighborhoods with low collective efficacy suffer high rates of violence and significant physical and social disorder.

Summary of Social Disorganization Theory In sum, according to social disorganization theory: (1) Disorganized areas cannot exert social control over acting-out youth; (2) these areas can be identified by their relatively high levels of change, fear, instability, incivility, poverty, and deterioration; and (3) these factors have a direct influence on the area's delinquency rate. It is not, then, some individual property or trait that is the cause of delinquency, but the quality and ambience of the community in which adolescents are forced to reside. In areas where there is a sense of collective efficacy, delinquency rates will be controlled no matter what the immediate economic situation.

Anomie/Strain

strain theory
Links delinquency to the strain of being locked out of the economic mainstream, which creates the anger and frustration that lead to delinquent acts.

Strain theory, the second branch of social structure theory, holds that crime is a function of the conflict between the goals people have and the means they can use to legally obtain them. Strain theorists argue that while social and economic goals are common to people in all economic strata, the ability to obtain these goals is class dependent. Most people in the United States desire wealth, material possessions, power, prestige, and other life comforts. Members of the lower class are unable to achieve these symbols of success through conventional means. Consequently, they feel anger, frustration, and resentment, which is referred to as strain. Lower-class citizens can either accept their condition and live out their days as socially responsible, if unrewarded, citizens, or they can choose an alternative means of achieving success, such as theft, violence, or drug trafficking.

According to sociologist Robert Merton, although most people share common values and goals, the means for legitimate economic and social success are stratified by socioeconomic class.[72] Upper-class kids can achieve success because they have ready access to good education and prestigious jobs; kids in the lower class rarely have such opportunities. Without acceptable means for obtaining success, individuals feel social and psychological strain; Merton called this condition **anomie.** Consequently, these youths may either use deviant methods to achieve their goals (for example, stealing money), or reject socially accepted goals and substitute deviant ones (for example, becoming drug users or alcoholics). (See Figure 4.4.)

anomie
Normlessness produced by rapidly shifting moral values; according to Merton, anomie occurs when personal goals cannot be achieved using available means.

Relative Deprivation Feelings of anomie/strain are not typically found in middle- and upper-class communities, where education and prestigious occupations are readily obtainable. In lower-class areas, however, strain occurs because legitimate avenues for success are closed. One reason is that in these areas residents may experience **relative deprivation,** a pervasive, strain-producing sense of injustice that develops in communities in which the poor and the wealthy live in close proximity to one another.[73] In these areas, kids who feel they are less well off than others begin to form negative self-feelings and hostility, which motivates them to engage in delinquent and antisocial behaviors.[74] There is ample evidence that neighborhoods that experience high levels of relative deprivation have significantly higher rates of crime and delinquency.[75] The effect of inequality may be felt the most among minority kids who believe they are losing out in a society where the balance of economic and social power

relative deprivation
Condition that exists when people of wealth and poverty live in close proximity to one another; the relatively deprived are apt to have feelings of anger and hostility, which may produce criminal behavior.

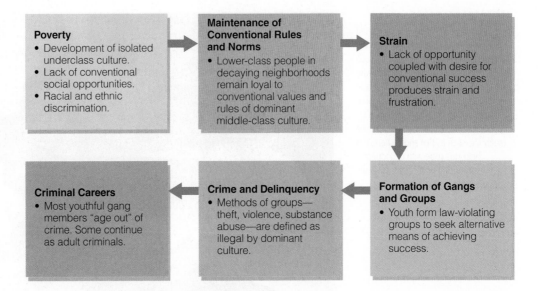

FIGURE 4.4
Strain Theory

Poverty
- Development of isolated underclass culture.
- Lack of conventional social opportunities.
- Racial and ethnic discrimination.

Maintenance of Conventional Rules and Norms
- Lower-class people in decaying neighborhoods remain loyal to conventional values and rules of dominant middle-class culture.

Strain
- Lack of opportunity coupled with desire for conventional success produces strain and frustration.

Criminal Careers
- Most youthful gang members "age out" of crime. Some continue as adult criminals.

Crime and Delinquency
- Methods of groups—theft, violence, substance abuse—are defined as illegal by dominant culture.

Formation of Gangs and Groups
- Youth form law-violating groups to seek alternative means of achieving success.

To read a little about **Merton's life,** go to either of these websites: www.utexas.edu/coc/journalism/SOURCE/j363/merton.html or www.umsl.edu/~etzkorn/400/NYT/Merton.html. For an up-to-date list of web links, go to http://cj.wadsworth.com/siegel_jd9e.

is shifting further toward the already affluent white middle class. Under these conditions, the likelihood that relatively poor kids will choose illegitimate life enhancing activities will increase.[76]

Considering the economic stratification of U.S. society, and the general emphasis on economic success above all else, anomie predicts that crime will prevail in lower-class culture, which it does. In a recent book entitled *Latino Homicide: Immigration, Violence, and Community,* sociologist Ramiro Martinez puts a new twist on the concept of relative deprivation. Martinez attempts to explain why the Latino homicide rate is relatively low despite the fact that many Latinos live in substandard communities. One reason is that Latino expectations for success and wealth are also relatively low, a world view that helps shield them from the influence of residence in deteriorated communities. Moreover, many Latinos are immigrants who have fled conditions in their homelands that are considerably worse than they find in the United States. Since they are now relatively less deprived, the "strain" of living in poverty has less impact.[77]

General Strain Theory (GST) An important reformulation of the strain concept is found in sociologist Robert Agnew's General Strain Theory (GST). Agnew has attempted to explain why kids who feel stress and strain are more likely to commit crimes, by offering a more general explanation of criminal activity among all elements of society rather than restricting his views to lower-class crime.[78]

Agnew suggests that criminality is the direct result of *negative affective states*—the anger, frustration, and adverse emotions that emerge in the wake of negative and destructive social relationships. He finds that negative affective states are produced by a variety of sources of strain:

▮ *Strain caused by the failure to achieve positively valued goals.* This category of strain, similar to what Merton speaks of in his theory of anomie, is a result of the disjunction between aspirations and expectations. This type of strain occurs when a youth aspires to wealth and fame but, lacking financial and educational resources, assumes that such goals are impossible to achieve.

▮ *Strain caused by the disjunction of expectations and achievements.* Strain can also be produced when there is a disjunction between expectations and achievements. When people compare themselves to peers who seem to be doing a lot better financially or socially (such as making more money or getting better grades), even those doing relatively well feel strain. For example, when a high school senior is accepted at a good college, but not a "prestige school" like some of her friends, she will feel strain. Perhaps she is not being treated fairly because the "playing field" is tilted against her: "Other kids have connections," she may say.

According to Agnew, strain may be caused by the presence of negative pain-inducing social interactions within the family, such as child abuse and neglect. Children who are abused at home may take their rage out on younger children at school or become involved in violent delinquency. On the other hand, a warm, supportive family life, such as that shown here, can help kids cope with delinquency-producing environmental strain.

▌ *Strain as the removal of positively valued stimuli from the individual.* Strain may occur because of the actual or anticipated removal or loss of a positively valued stimuli from the individual.[79] For example, the loss of a girl- or boyfriend can produce strain, as can the death of a loved one, moving to a new neighborhood, or the divorce or separation of parents.[80] Loss of positive stimuli may lead to delinquency as the adolescent tries to prevent the loss, retrieve what has been lost, obtain substitutes, or seek revenge against those responsible for the loss. For example, a child who experiences parental separation or divorce early in his life may seek out deviant peers to help fill his emotional needs and in so doing increases his chances of delinquency[81]

▌ *Strain as the presentation of negative stimuli.* Strain may also be caused by the presence of negative or noxious stimuli. Included within this category are such pain-inducing social interactions as child abuse and neglect, crime victimization, physical punishment, family and peer conflict, school failure, and interaction with stressful life experiences. For example, becoming the target of racism and discrimination may also trigger the anger and aggression predicted by Agnew.[82] Children who are abused at home may take their rage out on younger children at school or become involved in violent delinquency.[83] (See Figure 4.5.) According to Agnew, the greater the intensity and frequency of strain experiences, the greater their impact and the more likely they are to cause delinquency.

Each type of strain will increase the likelihood of experiencing negative emotions such as disappointment, depression, fear, and, most importantly, anger. Anger increases perceptions of being wronged and produces a desire for revenge, energizes individuals to take action, and lowers inhibitions. Violence and aggression seem justified if you have been wronged and are righteously angry.

There are a variety of sources of strain. Sometimes, a particular individual may be causing problems, such as an abusive parent or peer group rival. There are also social sources of strain. Kids may begin to feel strain because their membership in a peer or social group forces them into unwanted behavior patterns, such as using drugs.[84] These feelings may become magnified as compliance with peer group demands forces them to escalate their risky behaviors, for example, getting involved in a shoplifting spree to pay for drugs.[85]

Not all people who experience strain eventually resort to criminality. Some are able to marshal their emotional, mental, and behavioral resources to cope with the anger and frustration produced by strain. However, some cannot learn to cope ef-

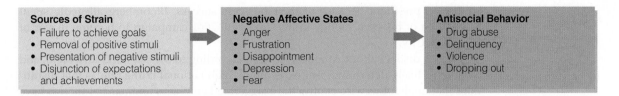

Sources of Strain	Negative Affective States	Antisocial Behavior
• Failure to achieve goals • Removal of positive stimuli • Presentation of negative stimuli • Disjunction of expectations and achievements	• Anger • Frustration • Disappointment • Depression • Fear	• Drug abuse • Delinquency • Violence • Dropping out

FIGURE 4.5
General Strain Theory (GST)

negative affective states
Anger, depression, disappointment, fear, and other adverse emotions that derive from strain.

fectively, and instead, these youths develop what Agnew calls **negative affective states,** as described earlier. The greater the intensity and frequency of strain experiences, the greater their impact and the more likely they are to cause delinquency. Research supports many of Agnew's claims: Kids who report feelings of stress and anger and have negative emotions are also more likely to engage in criminal behaviors;[86] people who fail to meet success goals are more likely to engage in illegal activities.[87]

Agnew's vision of strain seems particularly useful for explaining why crime rates peak during late adolescence. During this portion of the life course, social stress is maximized as parental supervision weakens and is replaced by relationships with a diverse peer group. Many kids going through the trauma of family breakup and frequent changes in family structure find themselves feeling a high degree of strain. For example, research shows that young girls of any social class are more likely to bear out-of-wedlock children if they themselves experienced an unstable family life.[88] Adolescence is also a period during which hormone levels peak and the behavior-moderating aspects of the brain have not fully developed, two factors that make adolescent males susceptible to environmental sources of strain.[89] They may react by becoming involved in precocious sexuality or by turning to substance abuse to mask the strain.

As they mature, children's expectations increase; some find that they are unable to meet academic and social demands. Adolescents are very concerned about their standing with peers. Those deficient in these areas may find they are social outcasts, another source of strain. In adulthood, crime rates drop because these sources of strain are reduced. New sources of self-esteem emerge, and adults seem more likely to bring their goals in line with reality.

In all its different modes, strain theory has proven to be an enduring vision of the cause of delinquency. Researchers have continued to show that kids who perceive strain are the ones most likely to engage in delinquent activity.[90]

Institutional Anomie Theory In their book *Crime and the American Dream*, Steven Messner and Richard Rosenfeld share their view that cultural and institutional influences in American society are the reason why American crime and delinquency rates are so high.[91]

Messner and Rosenfeld agree with Merton's view that the success goal is pervasive in American culture. They refer to this as the "American Dream," a term that they employ as both a goal and a process. As a goal, the American Dream involves the accumulation of material goods and wealth under conditions of open individual competition. As a process, it involves the socialization of youth to pursue material success above all else and to believe that prosperity is a universally achievable goal in the American culture. The desire to succeed at any cost drives people apart, weakens the collective sense of community, fosters ambition, and restricts the desirability of other kinds of achievement, such as a good name and respected reputation.

That Americans are conditioned to succeed at all costs should come as no surprise because the capitalist system encourages innovation in the pursuit of monetary rewards. Billionaire businessmen such as Michael Bloomberg, Bill Gates, and Donald Trump are considered national heroes whose wealth and lifestyle are universally admired. They have become cultural icons and leaders who many believe deserve to be elected president because of their business success. Bloomberg allegedly spent $45 million of his own money in his successful 2001 campaign to become mayor of New York City.

What is distinct about American society, according to Messner and Rosenfeld, and what most likely determines our exceedingly high national crime rate, is that institutions that might otherwise control the exaggerated emphasis on financial success have been rendered powerless or obsolete. There are three reasons social institutions have been undermined:

1. Noneconomic functions and roles have been devalued. Performance in other institutional settings—the family, school, or community—is assigned a lower priority than the goal of financial success. Human service jobs such as social work and teaching are considered significantly less important than entertainment or sports. Consider the following: Why does it seem normal and rational in American society for citizens to demand that the board of education ask public school teachers to take pay cuts or go for years without a raise, while the same people complain when the owner of a local baseball team allows a slugger to sign with another team rather than pay him $10 million per year?

2. When conflicts emerge, noneconomic roles become subordinate to and must accommodate economic roles. The schedules, routines, and demands of the workplace take priority over those of the home, the school, the community, and other aspects of social life. For example, many parents are willing to leave very young children in daycare for 10 hours or more per day in order to pursue the careers that can bring them increased levels of luxury.

3. Economic standards and norms penetrate into noneconomic realms. Economic terms become part of the common language: People want you to get to the "bottom line"; spouses view themselves as "partners" who "manage" the household. Business leaders run for public office promising to "run the country like a corporation."

According to Messner and Rosenfeld, the relatively high American delinquency rates can be explained by the interrelationship between culture and institutions. At the cultural level, the dominance of the American Dream mythology ensures that a great many kids will hunger for material goods that simply cannot be satisfied by legitimate means. Kids feel strain because no matter how much the typical American has, it's never enough: Kids always want the most stylish fashions, newest music, and hottest car. As soon as cultural values change, so does their need for material possessions.

At the institutional level, the dominance of economic concerns weakens the informal social control exerted by the family and school. Parents lose their authority when they cannot provide children with economic luxuries. Teachers lose their influence when adolescents no longer believe that education will get them what they want. Because the message "to succeed by any means necessary" has become a national icon, the result is high rates of theft and violence.

While institutional anomie theory has been the subject of relatively few research evaluations, those that have been conducted support its principal hypothesis.[92]

Cultural Deviance Theory

cultural deviance theory
Links delinquent acts to the formation of independent subcultures with a unique set of values that clash with the mainstream culture.

A third branch of structural theory, **cultural deviance theory,** holds that delinquency is a result of youths' desire to conform to lower-class neighborhood cultural values that conflict with those of the greater society. (See Figure 4.6.) Lower-class values include being tough, never showing fear, living for today, and disrespecting authority. In a socially disorganized neighborhood, conventional values such as honesty, obedience, and hard work make little sense to youths whose role models may include the neighborhood gunrunner, drug dealer, or pimp. Those adolescents who share lower-class values and admire criminals, drug dealers, and pimps find it difficult to impress authority figures such as teachers or employers. They experience a form of **culture**

culture conflict
When the values of a subculture clash with those of the dominant culture.

conflict and are rendered incapable of achieving success in a legitimate fashion; as

FIGURE 4.6
Cultural Deviance Theory

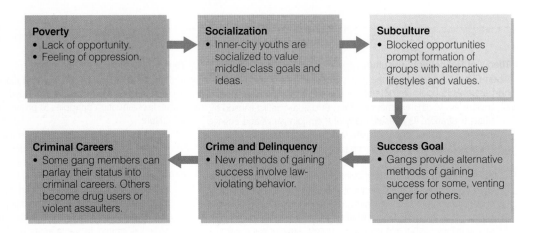

Poverty
- Lack of opportunity.
- Feeling of oppression.

Socialization
- Inner-city youths are socialized to value middle-class goals and ideas.

Subculture
- Blocked opportunities prompt formation of groups with alternative lifestyles and values.

Criminal Careers
- Some gang members can parlay their status into criminal careers. Others become drug users or violent assaulters.

Crime and Delinquency
- New methods of gaining success involve law-violating behavior.

Success Goal
- Gangs provide alternative methods of gaining success for some, venting anger for others.

a result, they join together in gangs and engage in behavior that is malicious and negativistic.[93]

Both legitimate and illegitimate opportunities are closed to youths in the most disorganized inner-city areas.[94] Consequently, they may join violent gangs to defend their turf, displaying their bravery and fighting prowess.[95] Instead of aspiring to be "preppies" or "yuppies," they want to be considered tough and street smart.

Youths living in disorganized areas consider themselves part of an urban underclass whose members must use their wits to survive or they will succumb to poverty, alcoholism, and drug addiction.[96] Exploitation of women abounds in a culture wracked by limited opportunity. Sexual conquest is one of the few areas open to lower-class males for achieving self-respect. The absence of male authority figures contributes to the fear that marriage will limit freedom. Peers heap scorn on anyone who allows himself to get "trapped" by a female, fueling the number of single-parent households. Youths who are committed to the norms of this deviant subculture are also more likely to disparage agents of conventional society such as police and teachers.[97] By joining gangs and committing crimes, lower-class youths are rejecting the culture that has already rejected them; they may be failures in conventional society, but they are the kings and queens of the neighborhood. Exhibit 4.1 sets out two prominent cultural deviance theories of delinquency.

The effect that culture has on young people living in a tough Hispanic neighborhood in the Bronx is the subject of the Focus on Delinquency box entitled "Random Family."

TO QUIZ YOURSELF ON THIS MATERIAL, go to the Juvenile Delinquency 9e website.

SOCIAL PROCESS THEORIES

Not all sociologists believe that merely living in an impoverished, deteriorated, lower-class area is a determinant of a delinquent career. Instead they argue that the root cause of delinquency may be traced to learning delinquent attitudes from peers, becoming detached from school, or experiencing conflict in the home. Although social position is important, socialization is considered to be the key determinant of behavior. If the socialization process is incomplete or negatively focused, it can produce an adolescent with a poor self-image who is alienated from conventional social institutions.

socialization

The process of learning the values and norms of the society or the subculture to which the individual belongs.

Socialization is the process of guiding people into acceptable behavior patterns through information, approval, rewards, and punishments. It involves learning the techniques needed to function in society. Socialization is a developmental process that is influenced by family and peers, neighbors, teachers, and other authority figures.

Socialization and Crime

Early socialization experiences have a lifelong influence on self-image, values, and behavior. Even children living in the most deteriorated inner-city environments will not get involved in delinquency if their socialization experiences are positive.[98] After all,

EXHIBIT **4.1**

Cultural Deviance Theories

Theory of Delinquent Subcultures

Albert Cohen first articulated the theory of delinquent subcultures in his classic 1955 book, *Delinquent Boys.*

I Lower-class youths experience a form of culture conflict caused by status frustration. As a result, many of them join gangs and engage in behavior that is "non-utilitarian, malicious, and negativistic."

I The delinquent gang is a separate subculture, possessing a value system directly opposed to that of the larger society. The subculture takes its norms from the larger culture, but turns them upside down.

I The development of the delinquent subculture is a consequence of socialization practices in lower-class environments. Lower-class children lack the basic skills, including a proper education, necessary to achieve social and economic success. Lower-class children are incapable of impressing authority figures, such as teachers, employers, or supervisors. In U.S. society, these positions tend to be held by members of the middle class, who have difficulty relating to the lower-class youngster. Cohen calls the standards set by these authority figures *middle-class measuring rods.*

I The conflict and frustration lower-class youths experience when they fail to meet these standards is a primary cause of delinquency.

I Rejected by middle-class decision makers, lower-class boys usually join one of three existing subcultures: the corner boy, the college boy, or the delinquent boy.

I The corner boy's main loyalty is to his peer group, on which he depends for support, motivation, and interest. The corner boy retreats into the comforting world of his lower-class peers and eventually becomes a stable member of his neighborhood, holding a menial job, marrying, and remaining in the community.

I The college boy embraces the cultural and social values of the middle class. Rather than scorning middle-class measuring rods, he actively strives to succeed by those standards. Cohen views this type of youth as one who is embarking on an almost hopeless path because he is ill-equipped academically, socially, and linguistically to achieve the rewards of middle-class life.

I The delinquent boy adopts a set of norms and principles that directly oppose middle-class values. He engages in short-run hedonism, living for today and letting tomorrow take care of itself. Frustrated by their inability to succeed, these boys resort to a process called *reaction formation,* including overly intense responses that seem disproportionate to the stimuli that trigger them. For the delinquent boy, this takes the form of irrational, malicious, and unaccountable hostility to the enemy, which in this case is "the norms of respectable middle-class society."

Theory of Differential Opportunity

In their classic work, *Delinquency and Opportunity,* written more than 40 years ago, Richard Cloward and Lloyd Ohlin combined strain and social disorganization principles to portray a gang-sustaining criminal subculture.

I According to the concept of differential opportunity, people in all strata of society share the same success goals; however, those in the lower class have limited means of achieving them.

I People who conclude that there is little hope for legitimate advancement may join like-minded peers to form a gang, which can provide them with emotional support.

I The opportunity for success in both conventional and criminal careers is limited. In stable areas, adolescents may be recruited by professional criminals, drug traffickers, or organized crime groups. Unstable areas, however, cannot support flourishing criminal opportunities. Opportunities for success, both illegal and conventional, are closed for the most disadvantaged youths.

Because of differential opportunity, young people are likely to join one of three types of gangs.

1. *Criminal gangs.* Criminal gangs exist in stable neighborhoods where close connections between adolescent, young adult, and adult offenders create an environment for successful criminal enterprise. Youths are recruited into established criminal gangs that provide training for a successful criminal career.

2. *Conflict gangs.* Conflict gangs develop in communities unable to provide either legitimate or illegitimate opportunities. These gangs attract tough adolescents who fight with weapons to win respect from rivals and engage in unpredictable and destructive assaults on people and property.

3. *Retreatist gangs.* Members of the retreatist subculture constantly search for ways of getting high—alcohol, pot, heroin, unusual sexual experiences, music. To feed their habits, retreatists develop a "hustle"—pimping, conning, selling drugs, or committing petty crimes.

Cloward and Ohlin's theory integrates cultural deviance and social disorganization variables and recognizes different modes of criminal adaptation. The fact that criminal cultures can be supportive, rational, and profitable seems to more realistically reflect the actual world of the delinquent.

SOURCES: Albert Cohen, *Delinquent Boys* (New York: Free Press, 1955); Richard Cloward and Lloyd Ohlin, *Delinquency and Opportunity* (New York: Free Press, 1960).

most inner-city youths do not commit serious crimes, and relatively few of those who do become career criminals.[99] More than 12 million youths live in poverty, but the majority do not become chronic offenders. Only those who experience improper socialization are at risk for crime. Research consistently shows a relationship between the elements of socialization and delinquency.

Family The primary influence on children is the family. When parenting is inadequate, a child's maturational processes will be interrupted and damaged. Although much debate still occurs over which elements of the parent-child relationship are most critical, there is little question that family relationships have a significant influence on behavior. One view is that youths socialized in families wracked by conflict and abuse are at risk for delinquency. For example, there is now evidence that children who grow up in homes where parents use severe discipline, yet lack warmth and are less involved in their children's lives, are prone to antisocial behavior.[100] In contrast, parents who are supportive and effectively control their children in a noncoercive fashion—*parental*

Random Family

In her book *Random Family*, talented journalist Adrian Nicole LeBlanc tells of the ten years she spent tracing the lives of a Puerto Rican family in the South Bronx, a journey which she begins in the mid-1980s, at the height of the crack epidemic, and concludes in 2001. Her book centers around the lives of Hispanic women who are forced to contend with the vicissitudes and hardships of an urban culture mired in poverty. There are two matriarchs, Foxy and Lourdes, beaten down by their environment, who become grandmothers by the age of 35. Foxy's daughter Coco is in turn tough and big hearted, ready to defend herself with a hidden razorblade but also willing to wait while the man she loves serves a prison sentence. Coco is smitten with Cesar, Lourdes's macho son who is an aspiring street hood. Cesar hops from jail to jail, never able to control his behavior or reign in his searing temper. At last, he is convicted of manslaughter. Lourdes's daughter, Jessica, is the neighborhood beauty who can get any man she wants. Her downfall begins when she is set up on a blind date with "Boy George," a bigtime dope dealer who reads *Yachting* magazine and was making over $100,000 a week dealing heroin by the time he was 21. Jessica loves or at least admires Boy George even though he beats her; she tattoos his name all over her body.

They live their lives in a neighborhood where going to prison is just like home in a different location; all your friends are there. Solitary confinement is not so bad, as it may be the first time some kids get a sense of peace and quiet. LeBlanc tells how residents view welfare as a scam but one that can be screwed up by getting caught in a variety of misdemeanors and offenses. Kids who cannot pass school and seem illiterate to teachers display fantastic organizational and financial skills when dealing drugs and running cartels. It is not uncommon for 13-year-old girls to have babies in a desperate attempt to keep their boyfriends involved.

Like so many girls in the neighborhood, Coco hooks up with men who are bad for her and has a wild streak herself. She loves Cesar and bears his child, a girl named Mercedes. But when Cesar is locked up, Coco gets pregnant by an old boyfriend named Kodak. Though Cesar is enraged by her infidelity, he and Coco get back together when he is released and have another daughter, Nautica. When Cesar is sent to jail once again for accidentally killing a friend, Coco again betrays him and has a child by a neighborhood boy named Wishman; true to form, Wishman shows little interest in the baby. Leaving the Bronx behind, Coco moves upstate to Troy with a drug dealer named Frankie, and has yet another child, a son, LaMonté. By the time she is in her 20s she has five children—one disabled—and spends her time shuttling between housing projects in the Bronx and in Troy. Despite her adversity she is devoted to her children.

By the time she was 19, Jessica had a baby with one boyfriend and a set of twins with the same guy's brother. She has little interest in taking care of her kids, who eventually wind up in the care of her friend Milagros after Lourdes refuses to care for her grandchildren (even when bribed with cocaine). Jessica works in Boy George's drug business helping to process and move heroin. She is attracted to his fleet of expensive cars, his lavish parties, and the fact that he sends his henchmen to Jessica's apartment to fill her family's refrigerator with food. He takes her to weekend getaways in the Poconos. When Boy George is busted by drug enforcement agents, Jessica refuses to testify against him and gets a 10-year prison sentence; Boy George gets a life sentence at age 23.

The book paints a bleak picture of inner-city Hispanic culture. There are few real options for mobility save drug dealing. People consider it a victory if their life today is slightly better than it was yesterday: There is food on the table and you haven't been beaten up; your kid is a heroin addict but has not taken crack. A girl who had four children by two boys is considered much better off than a girl who had four by three; a boy who deals drugs and gives the profits to his mother is better than one who spends it on himself. There is little hope and nowhere to go. Even a prison stay does not make Jessica any wiser, just older. There is not much optimism in this place because the demands of the culture overshadow every element of life, leaving little room for individual needs or choices.

Critical Thinking

1. Picture yourself growing up in the Bronx, hanging out with Boy George, Coco, and Jessica. Do you think you would be able to escape the cycle of poverty and crime they succumbed to or would you have the strength and drive to find a way out?

2. Does culture shape personality or does personality shape culture?

InfoTrac College Edition Research

To read critical reviews of *Random Family*, use the title in a keyword search on InfoTrac College Edition.

SOURCE: Adrian Nicole LeBlanc, *Random Family: Love, Drugs, Trouble, and Coming of Age in the Bronx* (New York: Scribner, 2003).

---

efficacy—are more likely to raise children who refrain from delinquency.[101] Delinquency will be reduced if parents provide the type of structure that integrates children into families while giving them the ability to assert their individuality and regulate their own behavior.[102] Children who have warm and affectionate ties to their parents report greater levels of self-esteem beginning in adolescence and extending into their adulthood; high self-esteem is inversely related to criminal behavior.[103] Conversely, when a parent exhibits deviant behavior, his or her children are more likely to follow

AP/Wide World Photos

suit. The family-crime relationship is significant across racial, ethnic, and gender lines, and is one of the most replicated findings in the criminological literature.[104]

Schools The literature linking delinquency to poor school performance and inadequate educational facilities is extensive. Youths who feel that teachers do not care, who consider themselves failures, and who do poorly in school are more likely to become involved in a delinquent way of life than adolescents who are educationally successful. Research findings based on studies done over the past two decades indicate that many school dropouts, especially those who have been expelled, face a significant chance of entering a criminal career.[105] In contrast, doing well in school and developing attachments to teachers has been linked to crime resistance.[106]

Peer Relations Still another suspected element of deviant socialization is peer group relations. Youths who become involved with peers who engage in antisocial behavior may learn the attitudes that support delinquency and soon find themselves cut off from conventional associates and institutions.[107] Chronic offenders surround themselves with peers who share their antisocial activities, and these relationships seem to be stable over time. People who maintain close relations with antisocial peers will sustain their own criminal behavior into their adulthood. Youths who become involved with peers who engage in antisocial behavior and hold antisocial attitudes may be deeply influenced by negative peer pressure. Peers may teach them the skills necessary to look and sound tough.[108]

Even productive activities such as an after-school job can promote crime if it means involving kids in unsupervised involvement with their peers who advocate that money earned be spent on *bling bling,* drugs, and alcohol rather than saving for a college education.[109] Kids who maintain close relations with antisocial peers will sustain their own criminal behavior into their adulthood. When peer influence diminishes, so does delinquent activity.[110]

Religion It has also been suggested that youths who are taught to hold high moral values and beliefs, who have learned to distinguish right from wrong, and who regularly attend religious services should also eschew crime and other antisocial behaviors.[111] Religion binds people together and forces them to confront the consequences of their behavior. Committing crimes would violate the principles of all organized religions. Kids living in disorganized high-crime areas who attend religious services are better able to resist illegal drug use and delinquency.[112] Kids who live in areas marked by strong religious values and who hold strong religious beliefs themselves are less likely to engage in delinquent activities themselves than adolescents who do not hold

Dare to Be You

Dare to Be You (DTBY) is a multilevel, primary prevention program for children 2 to 5 years old and their families whose main goal is to lower the risk of future substance abuse. Program founders suggest that a child's future high-risk activities can be curtailed by improving parent and child protective factors in the areas of communication, problem solving, self-esteem, and family skills.

HOW DOES IT WORK?

DTBY is a community-based program. Participants come from every social, racial, and ethnic background. The program targets low parental effectiveness that leads to insufficient readiness for their children entering school. The goals include

I   Improved parental competence
I   Increased satisfaction with and positive attitude about being a parent
I   Adoption and use of nurturing family management strategies
I   Increased and appropriate use of limit setting
I   Substantial decreases in parental use of harsh punishment
I   Significant increases in child developmental levels

The DTBY program focuses of three main components:

Family Component

The family component seeks to help families that are suffering from poor communication, unstable family environment, and family mental health problems. It offers parent, youth, and family training and activities for teaching self-responsibility, personal and parenting efficacy, communication, and social skills. The component consists of a 12-week family workshop series (30 hours) and semiannual 12-hour reinforcing family workshops.

School Component

The school component trains and supports teachers and child-care providers who work with the target youth.

Community Component

The community component trains community members who interact with target families, local health departments, social services agencies, probation officers, and counselors. This component targets community-level problems such as alcohol and drug use.

OUTCOMES AND RESULTS

The results of the prevention program have been quite successful. Families enrolled in the program have experienced an increase in parental effectiveness and satisfaction with the children. Other success indicators are a decrease in parent-child conflict, a reduction in the use of harsh punishment, and an increase in the children's developmental level. Researchers find that the addition of school and community components is necessary for a successful systems approach. Overall, the DTBY program builds on community strengths to establish collective efficacy.

Critical Thinking

Do you believe it is possible for a government sponsored program to overcome the negative outcomes of years of personal deprivation suffered by adolescents living in disorganized, deteriorated neighborhoods?

InfoTrac College Edition Research

To read about the operations of a similar program, look up the following on InfoTrac College Edition: Thomas Hanlon, Richard Bateman, Betsy Simon, Kevin O'Grady, and Steven Carswell, "An Early Community-Based Intervention for the Prevention of Substance Abuse and Other Delinquent Behavior," *Journal of Youth and Adolescence* 31:459–471 (2002).

SOURCE: Dare to Be You (Rockville, MD: Substance Abuse and Mental Health Services Administration, U.S. Department of Health and Human Services, 2004).

For more information, you can read a program fact sheet at http://modelprograms.samhsa.gov/pdfs/FactSheets/Dare.pdf. (Accessed on September 13, 2004.)

---

such beliefs or who live in less devout communities.[113] Communities with strong religious beliefs and involvement seem to have lower juvenile homicide rates than those that shun those values[114]

Interestingly, participation seems to be a more significant inhibitor of crime than merely having religious beliefs and values.[115] Cross-national research shows that countries with high rates of church membership and attendance have lower crime rates than less "devout" nations.[116]

Simply living in a violent neighborhood does not produce violent children; research shows that family, peer, and individual characteristics play a large role in predicting violence in childhood.[117] Only those who experience improper socialization are at risk for crime. This vision has been used to guide many delinquency prevention programs, including the Dare to Be You program, discussed in the Policy and Practice box above.

Theories of Socialization

Sociologists believe that the socialization process impacts delinquency in two ways. The first, **learning theory,** holds that delinquency is learned through close relationships with others. Both the techniques of crime and the attitudes necessary to support delinquency are learned. Learning theories assume that children are born "good" and then learn to be "bad." The second, **control theory,** views delinquency as a result of a weakened commitment to family, peers, and school. Because their bonds to these institutions of informal social control are severed, some adolescents feel free to exercise antisocial behavior. Unlike learning theories, control theories assume that people are born "bad" and then must be taught to control themselves through the efforts of parents and teachers.

Learning Theories

Learning theories hold that children living in even the most deteriorated areas can resist inducements to crime if they have learned proper values and behaviors. Delinquency, by contrast, develops by learning the values and behaviors associated with criminal activity (see Figure 4.7). Kids can learn deviant values from their parents, relatives, or peers. Social learning can involve the techniques of crime (how to hot-wire a car) as well as the psychological aspects (how to deal with guilt). The former are needed to commit crimes, whereas the latter are required to cope with the emotional turmoil that follows.

The best-known learning theory is Edwin Sutherland's **differential association theory,** which he first articulated in 1939 in *Principles of Criminology.*[118] Sutherland believed that as children are socialized, they are exposed to and learn prosocial and antisocial attitudes and behavior. Simply put, if the prodelinquency definitions they have learned outweigh the antidelinquency definitions, they will be vulnerable to choosing criminal behaviors over conventional ones. The basic principles of differential association theory are set out in Exhibit 4.2.

Another prominent learning approach, identified with David Matza and Gresham Sykes, suggests that delinquents hold values similar to those of law-abiding citizens, but they learn techniques that enable them to neutralize those values and drift back and forth between legitimate and delinquent behavior.[119] **Drift** is the process by which an individual moves from one behavioral extreme to another, behaving sometimes in an unconventional manner and at other times with constraint.

Sykes and Matza suggest that juveniles develop a distinct set of justifications for their behavior when it violates accepted social rules and norms. These **neutralization techniques** allow youths to drift away from the rules of the normative society and participate in delinquent behaviors. While most adolescents accept the rules of society, they learn these techniques to release themselves temporarily from moral constraints. The most prominent techniques of neutralization are described in Figure 4.8.[120]

Learning theory, then, portrays the delinquent as someone who, during the socialization process, has been consistently exposed not only to people who teach that "crime pays" but also to the techniques for becoming a successful criminal. Conversely, children living in the most highly disorganized neighborhood will be able to avoid the temptations of the streets if they are socialized in a warm, supportive family and have law-abiding peers.

---

learning theory
Hypothesizes that delinquency is learned through close relationships with others; asserts that children are born "good" and learn to be "bad" from others.

control theory
Posits that delinquency results from a weakened commitment to the major social institutions (family, peers, and school); lack of such commitment allows youths to exercise antisocial behavioral choices.

differential association theory
Asserts that criminal behavior is learned primarily within interpersonal groups and that youths will become delinquent if definitions they have learned favorable to violating the law exceed definitions favorable to obeying the law within that group.

drift
Idea that youths move in and out of delinquency and that their lifestyles can embrace both conventional and deviant values.

neutralization techniques
A set of attitudes or beliefs that allow would-be delinquents to negate any moral apprehension they may have about committing crime so that they may freely engage in antisocial behavior without regret.

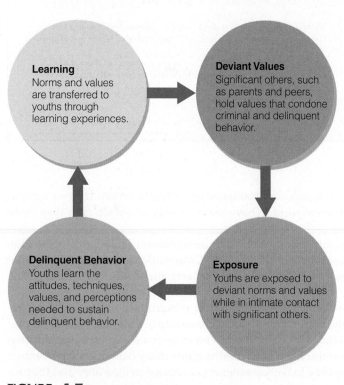

Learning
Norms and values are transferred to youths through learning experiences.

Deviant Values
Significant others, such as parents and peers, hold values that condone criminal and delinquent behavior.

Delinquent Behavior
Youths learn the attitudes, techniques, values, and perceptions needed to sustain delinquent behavior.

Exposure
Youths are exposed to deviant norms and values while in intimate contact with significant others.

FIGURE 4.7
Social Learning Theory of Delinquency

EXHIBIT **4.2**

Principles of Differential Association

1. Criminal behavior is learned. Learning criminal behavior involves all the mechanisms and techniques involved in any other learning.
2. Crime is learned in interactions with others, in a process of communication.
3. Learning occurs within close personal groups such as peers, families, work, sports, and so on. Observational learning in the media is not that important.
4. Learning includes the techniques, motives, drives, rationalizations, and attitudes that support behavior.
5. The specific direction of motives, drives, rationalizations, and attitudes is learned from legal codes as being favorable or unfavorable.
6. Kids engage in crime because of an excess of definitions favorable to law violation over definitions unfavorable to law breaking. This is the principle of differential association.
7. Differential association may vary in frequency, duration, priority, and intensity. For example, definitions acquired from parents may have a higher priority than those acquired from distant relatives; definitions that are constantly repeated over a long period of time are more important than those that occur in a single instance.

SOURCE: Edwin Sutherland, *Principles of Criminology* (Philadelphia: Lippincott, 1939).

FIGURE **4.8**
Techniques of Neutralization

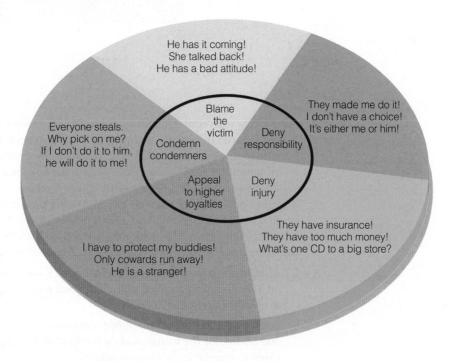

Control Theories

Control theories argue that delinquency can be pleasurable and exciting. Kids may enjoy flaunting the rules of society and engaging in antisocial behavior. According to control theorists, kids who obey the law and engage in conventional activities have been socialized to control their behavior. Maintaining control is a function of the close relationships with parents, friends, and teachers, which help form the ability to resist the lure of deviant behaviors. Kids who are socialized to develop a strong "commitment to conformity" will be able to resist pressures to violate the law.

social bond
Ties a person to the institutions and processes of society; elements of the bond include attachment, commitment, involvement, and belief.

Causes of Delinquency The most prominent control theory is one developed by sociologist Travis Hirschi. In his classic book *Causes of Delinquency*, Hirschi argues that the cause of delinquency lies in the strength of the relationships or **social bonds** a

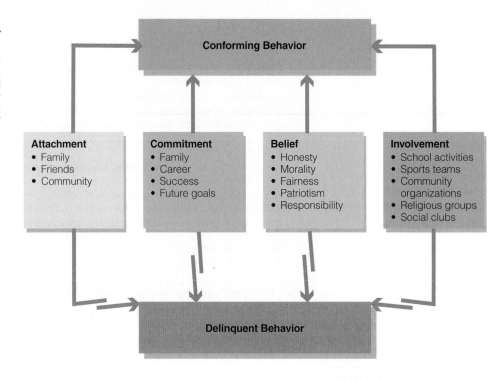

FIGURE 4.9

Elements of the Social Bond

If these bonds are weak or broken, an adolescent is more likely to engage in delinquent behavior. If they're strong and unbroken, they're more likely to participate in conforming and conventional behavior

Conforming Behavior

Attachment
- Family
- Friends
- Community

Commitment
- Family
- Career
- Success
- Future goals

Belief
- Honesty
- Morality
- Fairness
- Patriotism
- Responsibility

Involvement
- School activities
- Sports teams
- Community organizations
- Religious groups
- Social clubs

Delinquent Behavior

child forms with conventional individuals and groups.[121] If these bonds to society become fractured or broken, youths will feel free to violate the law; if caught, they have nothing to lose (see Figure 4.9). The youthful law violator, then, is someone who lacks a real commitment to social norms. The major elements of Hirschi's argument are (1) all people have the potential to commit crimes—for example, underage drinking—because they are pleasurable; (2) people are kept in check by their social bonds or attachments to society; and (3) weakened social bonds free people to engage in antisocial but personally desirable behaviors. Hirschi argues that the social bond a person maintains with society is divided into four main elements:

▌ *Attachment* to parents, peers, and schools. Kids who are attached to their families are less likely to get involved in a deviant peer group and consequently less likely to engage in criminal activities.[122]

▌ *Commitment* to the pursuit of conventional activities, such as getting an education and saving for the future. Kids who do well and are committed to school are less likely to engage in delinquent acts.[123]

▌ *Involvement* in conventional activities such as school, sports, and religion.

▌ *Belief* in values such as sensitivity to the rights of others and respect for the legal code.

Hirschi suggests that the elements of the social bond may be interrelated. For example, boys or girls who are attached to their parents and friends are also more likely to be committed to future goals. Youths who are unattached may lack commitment to conventional goals and are more likely to be involved in unconventional activities. Hirschi's vision of delinquency causation is one of the most influential of recent times.[124]

There has been significant empirical support for Hirschi's work. For example, research shows that positive attachments to family and peers help control delinquency.[125] Commitment has also been linked to delinquency: Kids who fail at school and are detached from the educational experience are at risk of criminality. Those who do well and are committed to school are less likely to engage in delinquent acts.[126]

There is also support for the effects of involvement on delinquent behaviors. Students who engage in a significant amount of extracurricular activities from 8th grade through 12th grade are more likely to experience high academic achievement and prosocial behaviors extending into young adulthood.[127]

Evaluating Social Control Theory While many research efforts support Hirschi's ideas, some important questions are still being raised about his views. For example, Hirschi argues that commitment to future success, such as an exciting career, reduces delinquent involvement. Research indicates that kids who are committed to success but actually fail to achieve it may be crime-prone.[128] Perhaps their failures produce feelings of strain that counterbalance the control of commitment. Questions have also been raised about the social relations of delinquents. Hirschi portrays them as "lone wolves," detached from family and friends. A number of research efforts show that delinquents do maintain close peer group ties.[129] Their friendship patterns seem similar to those of conventional youths.[130] In fact, there is some evidence that drug abusers maintain even more intimate relations with peers than do nonabusers.[131] Attachment to deviant peers seems to motivate the decision to commit crime; deviant friends facilitate delinquent acts.[132] While the issue of peer relations is troublesome, Hirschi's vision of control has remained one of the most influential models of delinquency for the past 25 years.

TO QUIZ YOURSELF ON THIS MATERIAL, go to the Juvenile Delinquency 9e website.

SOCIAL REACTION THEORIES

According to social reaction theories, the way society reacts to individuals and the way individuals react to society determines behavior. Social reactions determine which behaviors are considered criminal or conventional; they also determine individual behavior and can contribute to the formation of delinquent careers. Being **stigmatized,** or labeled, by agents of social control, including official institutions such as the police and the courts, and unofficial institutions, such as parents and neighbors, is what sustains delinquent careers.[133]

stigmatized
People who have been negatively labeled because of their participation, or alleged participation, in deviant or outlawed behaviors.

The Labeling Process

labeling theory
Posits that society creates deviance through a system of social control agencies that designate (or label) certain individuals as delinquent, thereby stigmatizing youths and encouraging them to accept this negative personal identity.

According to this view, also known as **labeling theory,** youths may violate the law for a variety of reasons, including poor family relationships, peer pressure, psychological abnormality, and prodelinquent learning experiences. Regardless of the cause, if individuals' delinquent behaviors are detected, the offenders will be given a negative label that can follow them throughout life. These labels include "troublemaker," "juvenile delinquent," "mentally ill," "junkie," and many more.

The way labels are applied is likely to have important consequences for the delinquent. The degree to which youngsters are perceived as deviants may affect their treatment at home and at school. Parents may consider them a detrimental influence on younger brothers and sisters. Neighbors may tell their children to avoid the "troublemaker." Teachers may place them in classes reserved for students with behavior problems, minimizing their chances of obtaining higher education. The delinquency label may also affect the attitudes of society in general, and youthful offenders are subjected to sanctions ranging from mild reprimands to incarceration.

Beyond these results, and depending on the visibility of the label and the manner in which it is applied, youths will have an increasing commitment to delinquent careers. As the negative feedback of law enforcement agencies, teachers, and other figures strengthens their commitment, delinquents may come to see themselves as "screwups." Thus, through a process of identification and sanctioning, reidentification, and increased sanctioning, young offenders are transformed. They are no longer children in trouble; they are "delinquents," and they accept that label as a personal identity—a process called **self-labeling** (see Figure 4.10).[134]

self-labeling
The process by which a person who has been negatively labeled accepts the label as a personal role or identity.

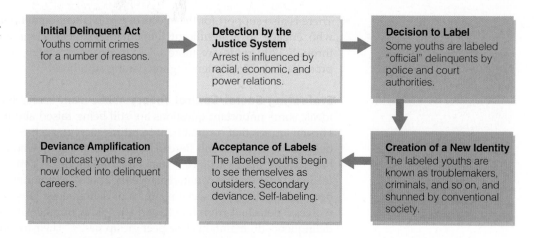

FIGURE 4.10
Labeling Theory

Initial Delinquent Act Youths commit crimes for a number of reasons.

Detection by the Justice System Arrest is influenced by racial, economic, and power relations.

Decision to Label Some youths are labeled "official" delinquents by police and court authorities.

Deviance Amplification The outcast youths are now locked into delinquent careers.

Acceptance of Labels The labeled youths begin to see themselves as outsiders. Secondary deviance. Self-labeling.

Creation of a New Identity The labeled youths are known as troublemakers, criminals, and so on, and shunned by conventional society.

The Effect of Labeling

We often form opinions of others based on first impressions.[135] If interactions involve perceptions of deviance, individuals may be assigned informal labels—"loser," "slut"—that both harm their social relationships and damage their self-image. Kids who are suspected of harboring such behavior problems are scrutinized by those with whom they interact; people search for signs of deviance, or simply shun them.[136]

When kids who have been rejected by society violate the criminal law, they may be given official labels, applied in "ceremonies"—for example, during trials or expulsion hearings in schools—that are designed to redefine the deviant's identity.[137] The effect of this process is a durable negative label and an accompanying loss of status. The labeled deviant becomes a social outcast who is prevented from enjoying higher education, well-paying jobs, and other societal benefits. Because this label is "official," few question the accuracy of the assessment. People who may have been merely suspicious now feel justified in their assessments: "I always knew he was a bad kid."

self-fulfilling prophecy
Deviant behavior patterns that are a response to an earlier labeling experience; youths act out these social roles even if they were falsely bestowed.

The Self-Fulfilling Prophecy The labeling process helps create a **self-fulfilling prophecy**.[138] If children continually receive negative feedback from parents, teachers, and others whose opinion they take to heart, they will interpret this rejection as accurate. Their behavior will begin to conform to the negative expectations; they will become the person others perceive them to be ("Teachers already think I'm stupid, so why should I bother to study"). The self-fulfilling prophecy leads to a damaged self-image and an increase in antisocial behaviors.[139] Research shows that adolescents who perceive labels from significant others also report more frequent delinquent involvement; perceptions of negative labels are significant predictors of serious delinquent behaviors.[140]

Self-Rejection Labeling helps create a deviant identity. Those exposed to negative sanctions experience both self-rejection and lowered self-image. Self-rejecting attitudes result in both a weakened commitment to conventional values and the acquisition of motives to deviate from social norms.[141] This transformation is amplified by the bonds social outcasts form with peers.[142] Labeled delinquents will seek out others who are similarly stigmatized.[143] Associating with deviant peers helps reinforce conventional society's negative evaluations: "We were right all along about him, look who his friends are!" (See Figure 4.11.)

Delinquent peers may help labeled youths "reject their rejectors." Teachers are "stupid"; cops are "dishonest"; parents "just don't understand."[144] Group identity enables outcast youths to show contempt for the sources of the labels and to distance themselves. These actions help solidify both the grip of deviant peers and the impact of the labels.[145] Those who have accepted these labels are more prone to engage in delinquent behaviors than those whose self-image has not been so tarnished.[146]

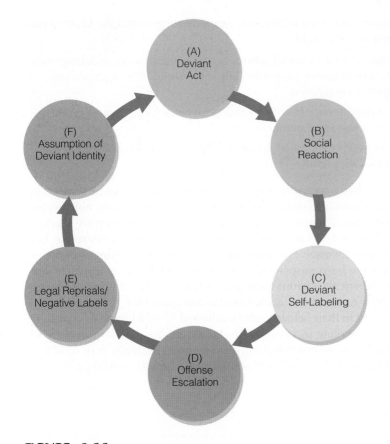

FIGURE 4.11
Lemert's Cycle of Secondary Deviance

According to sociologist Edwin Lemert, people who bear negative labels become secondary deviants—their label becomes a master status by which they are defined.

The figure shows a circular cycle with the following stages:
(A) Deviant Act
(B) Social Reaction
(C) Deviant Self-Labeling
(D) Offense Escalation
(E) Legal Reprisals/Negative Labels
(F) Assumption of Deviant Identity

The Juvenile Justice Process and Labeling

Processing through the juvenile justice system seems to unleash the labeling process. Here offenders find (perhaps for the first time) that authority figures consider them incorrigible outcasts who must be separated from the right-thinking members of society. To reach that decision, the judge relies on the testimony of witnesses—parents, teachers, police officers, social workers, and psychologists—who may testify that the offender is unfit to be part of conventional society. As the label *juvenile delinquent* is conferred on offenders, their identities may be transformed from kids who have done something bad to "bad kids."[147] This process has been observed in the United States and abroad, indicating that the labeling process is universal.[148] The justice system has long been accused of bestowing destructive labels on children who are suspected of being delinquents. Frank Tannenbaum first suggested that social typing, which he called **"dramatization of evil,"** transforms the offender's identity from a doer of evil to an "evil person."[149]

Delinquents, the argument goes, are the products of the juvenile justice assembly line.[150] Although youths enter as children in trouble, they emerge as bearers of criminal histories, which are likely to reinvolve them in criminal activity. Authority figures anticipate that these troublemakers will continue their life of crime.[151] Labeled delinquents are assumed to engage in a full range of violence, theft, and drug abuse. Although they have not necessarily demonstrated these characteristics, they become perennial suspects.[152] The system designed to reduce delinquency may help produce young criminals.

According to the social reaction perspective, the actions of the juvenile justice system turn the self-perception of a youthful suspect into that of a delinquent.[153] Harold Garfinkel addressed the reason this occurs when he described what he called a **"degradation ceremony,"** where the public identity of an offender is transformed in a solemn ritual during which the targeted person is thrust outside the social mainstream.[154] This process may be seen in juvenile court when a youngster goes before the court, is scolded by a judge, has charges read, and is officially labeled a delinquent; this process contains all the conditions for "successful degradation." Recognizing the role stigma plays in developing a delinquent career has prompted some juvenile justice agencies to create programs designed to limit delinquent labels.[155]

Evaluating Labeling Theory

Enthusiasm for the labeling approach diminished when its validity was heavily criticized. Some critics argued that the crime-controlling effects of punishment more than made up for the crime-producing effects of stigma. In *Beyond Probation*, Charles Murray and Louis Cox found that youths assigned to a program designed to reduce labels were more likely later to commit delinquent acts than a comparison group who were placed in a more punitive state training school. The implication was that the threat of punishment was deterrent and that the crime-producing influence of labels was minimal.[156]

dramatization of evil
The process of social typing that transforms an offender's identity from a doer of evil to an evil person.

degradation ceremony
Going to court, being scolded by a judge, or being found delinquent after a trial are examples of public ceremonies that can transform youthful offenders by degrading their self-image.

While these criticisms were damaging, other experts suggest that the labeling perspective can offer important insights:

▌ It identifies the role played by social control agents in the process of delinquency causation; delinquent behavior cannot be fully understood if the agencies empowered to control it are ignored.

▌ It recognizes that delinquency is not a pathological behavior; it focuses on the social interactions that shape behavior.

▌ It distinguishes between delinquent acts and delinquent careers and shows that they must be treated differently.[157]

Labeling theory has had a recent resurgence. As interest in criminal careers has escalated, labeling theory has taken on new relevance. Labeling theory may help explain why some youths continue down the path of antisocial behaviors (they are labeled), whereas most are able to desist from crime (they are free of stigma). For example, kids who are labeled may find themselves shut out of educational and employment opportunities. Those who have been suspended from school or labeled as troublemakers may find that these experiences haunt them a decade later when they seek employment as adults.[158] As a result, these labeled youths are more likely to sustain delinquent careers and persist in their behavior into adulthood.[159] In addition to explaining the continuity of crime, labeling theory may also help us understand why many hardcore offenders desist. Those who receive sufficient positive feedback may be able to transform their self-image and create a new self, helping them to go straight.[160]

TO QUIZ YOURSELF ON THIS MATERIAL, go to the Juvenile Delinquency 9e website.

SOCIAL CONFLICT THEORY

social conflict theory
Asserts that society is in a state of constant internal conflict, and focuses on the role of social and governmental institutions as mechanisms for social control.

The final branch of sociological theory, **social conflict theory,** finds that society is in a constant state of internal conflict, as different groups strive to impose their will on others. Those with money and power succeed in shaping the law to meet their needs and maintain their interests. Those adolescents whose behavior cannot conform to the needs of the power elite are defined as delinquents and criminals.

According to this view, those in power use the justice system to maintain their status while keeping others subservient: Men use their economic power to subjugate women; members of the majority want to stave off the economic advancement of minorities; capitalists want to reduce the power of workers to ensure they are willing to accept low wages. Conflict theory thus centers around a view of society in which an elite class uses the law as a means of meeting threats to its status. The ruling class is a self-interested collective whose primary interest is self-gain.[161] For example, conflict theorists suggest that while spending has been cut on social programs during the past few years, spending on the prison system has skyrocketed. Draconian criminal laws designed to curb terrorism, such as the USA PATRIOT Act, have been turned against political dissenters. Critical thinkers believe that they are responsible for informing the public about the dangers of these developments.[162]

Law and Justice

Social conflict theorists view the law and the justice system as vehicles for controlling the have-not members of society. Legal institutions help the powerful and rich to impose their standards of good behavior on the entire society. The law protects the property and physical safety of the haves from attack by the have-nots, and helps control the behavior of those who might otherwise threaten the status quo.[163] The ruling elite draws the lower-middle class into this pattern of control, leading it to believe it has a stake in maintaining the status quo.[164] According to social conflict theory, the poor may or may not commit more crimes than the rich, but they certainly are arrested more often.[165] It is not surprising to conflict theorists that complaints of police brutal-

Control of Law and Society
Those who hold economic power control the law and the agencies that administer it.

Application of the Law
The law is differentially administered to favor the rich and powerful and control the "have-not" members of society.

Delinquent Behavior
The rebellious behavior of lower-class youths is defined and controlled by State authorities.

Criminal Careers
Youths who will not conform and fulfill the roles of menial laborers are defined as criminals.

FIGURE 4.12
Social Conflict Theory

ity are highest in minority neighborhoods, especially those that experience relative deprivation. (African American residents earn significantly less money than the majority and therefore have less political and social power.[166]) Police misbehavior, which is routine in minority neighborhoods, would never be tolerated in affluent white areas. Consequently, a deep-rooted hostility is generated among members of the lower class toward a social order they may neither shape nor share.[167] (See Figure 4.12.)

The Conflict Concept of Delinquency

Conflict theorists view delinquency as a normal response to the conditions created by capitalism.[168] In fact, the creation of a legal category, delinquency, is a function of the class consciousness that occurred around the turn of the twentieth century.[169] In *The Child Savers*, Anthony Platt documented the creation of the delinquency concept and the role played by wealthy child savers in forming the philosophy of the juvenile court. Platt believed the child-saving movement's real goal was to maintain order and control while preserving the existing class system.[170] He and others have concluded that the child savers were powerful citizens who aimed to control the behavior of disenfranchised youths.

Conflict theorists still view delinquent behavior as a function of the capitalist system's inherent inequity. They argue that capitalism accelerates the trend toward replacing human labor with machines so that youths are removed from the labor force. From early childhood, the values of capitalism are reinforced. Social control agencies such as schools prepare youths for placement in the capitalist system by presenting them with behavior models that will help them conform to later job expectations. For example, rewards for good schoolwork correspond to the rewards a manager uses with employees. In fact, most schools are set up to reward youths who show promise in self-discipline and motivation and are therefore judged likely to perform well in the capitalist system. Youths who are judged inferior as potential job prospects become known as losers and punks and wind up in delinquent roles.

Class and Delinquency The capitalist system affects youths differently at each level of the class structure. In the lowest classes, youths form gangs, which can be found in the most desolated ghetto areas. These gangs serve as a means of survival in a system that offers no reasonable alternative. Lower-class youths who live in more stable areas are on the fringe of criminal activity because the economic system excludes them from meaningful opportunity.

Conflict theory also acknowledges middle-class delinquency. The alienation of individuals from one another, the competitive struggle, and the absence of human feeling, all qualities of capitalism, contribute to middle-class delinquency. Because capitalism is dehumanizing, it is not surprising that even middle-class youths turn to drugs, gambling, and illicit sex to find escape.

Controlling Delinquents Conflict theorists suggest that, rather than inhibiting delinquent behavior, the justice system may help to sustain such behavior. They claim that the capitalist state fails to control delinquents because it is in the state's interest to maintain a large number of outcast deviant youths. These youths can be employed as marginal workers, willing to work for minimum wage in jobs no one else wants. Thus, labeling by the justice system fits within the capitalist managers' need to maintain an underclass of cheap labor.

TO QUIZ YOURSELF ON THIS MATERIAL, go to the Juvenile Delinquency 9e website.

SOCIOLOGICAL THEORIES AND SOCIAL POLICY

Each of the various branches of sociological theory has had an impact on social policy designed to reduce or eliminate delinquency. The following sections describe a few of these efforts.

Social Structure Theories and Social Policy

Social structure–based delinquency prevention programs aim to improve conditions within broad areas of the community in order to reduce delinquency rates. The most prominent contemporary manifestation of a program based on social structure theory is Operation Weed and Seed, the federal multilevel action plan for revitalizing communities.[171] The concept of this program is that no single approach can reduce crime rates and that social service and law enforcement agencies must cooperate to be effective. Therefore there are four basic elements in this plan: law enforcement; community policing; prevention, intervention, and treatment; and neighborhood restoration. The last element, neighborhood restoration, is the one most closely attached to the social structure theory because it is designed to revitalize distressed neighborhoods and improve the quality of life in the target communities. The neighborhood restoration element focuses on economic development activities, such as economic opportunities for residents, improved housing conditions, enhanced social services, and improved public services in the target area. Programs are being developed that will improve living conditions; enhance home security; allow for low-cost physical improvements; develop long-term efforts to renovate and maintain housing; and provide educational, economic, social, recreational, and other vital opportunities. A key feature is the fostering of self-worth and individual responsibility among community members.

Social Process and Social Policy

Social process theories suggest that delinquency can be prevented by strengthening the socialization process. One approach has been helping social institutions improve their outreach. Educational programs have been improved by expanding preschool programs, developing curricula relevant to students' lives, and stressing teacher development. Counseling and remedial services have been aimed at troubled youth.

Prevention programs have also focused on providing services for youngsters who have been identified as delinquents or predelinquents. Such services usually include counseling, job placement, legal assistance, and more. Their aim is to reach out to troubled youths and provide them with the skills necessary to function in their environment before they get in trouble with the law. In addition to these local efforts, the federal government has sponsored several delinquency-prevention efforts using the principles of social process theory. These include vocational training programs, such as the Comprehensive Employment Training Act, as well as educational enrichment programs, such as Head Start for preschoolers. See Chapter 11 for more on these programs.

Prevention programs have also been aimed at strengthening families in crisis. Because attachment to parents is a cornerstone of all social process theories, developing good family relations is an essential element of delinquency prevention. Programs have been developed that encourage families to help children develop the positive self-image necessary to resist the forces promoting delinquency.[172]

Social Reaction and Social Policy

As the dangers of labeling became known, a massive effort was made to limit the interface of youths with the juvenile justice system. One approach was to divert youths from official processing at the time of their initial contact with police. The usual practice is to have police refer children to treatment facilities rather than to the juvenile court. In a similar vein, children who were petitioned to juvenile court might be eligible for alternative programs rather than traditional juvenile justice processing. For example, restitution allows children to pay back the victims of their crimes for the damage (or inconvenience) they have caused instead of receiving an official delinquency label.

If a youth was found delinquent, efforts were made to reduce stigma by using alternative programs such as boot camp or intensive probation monitoring. Alternative community-based sanctions substituted for state training schools, a policy known as **deinstitutionalization.** Whenever possible, anything producing stigma was to be avoided, a philosophy referred to as nonintervention.

While these programs were initially popular, critics claimed that the nonintervention movement created a new class of juvenile offenders who heretofore might have avoided prolonged contact with juvenile justice agencies; they referred to this phenomenon as widening the net.[173] Evaluation of existing programs did not indicate that they could reduce the recidivism rate of clients.[174] While these criticisms proved damaging, many nonintervention programs still operate.

Social Conflict and Social Policy

If conflict is the source of delinquency, conflict resolution may be the key to its demise.[175] This is the aim of **restorative justice,** an approach that relies on nonpunitive strategies for delinquency control.[176] The restorative justice movement has a number of sources. Negotiation, mediation, and peacemaking have been part of the dispute resolution process in European and Asian communities for centuries.[177] Native American and Native Canadian people have long used participation of community members in the adjudication process (sentencing circles, panels of elders).[178]

Restoration involves turning the justice system into a healing process rather than a distributor of retribution and revenge. An important aspect of achieving these goals is for the offenders to accept accountability for their actions and accept the responsibility for the harm those actions caused. Only then can they be restored as productive members of their community.

Most people involved in offender-victim relationships actually know one another or were related in some way before the criminal incident took place. Instead of treating one of the involved parties as a victim deserving of sympathy and the other as a criminal deserving of punishment, it is more productive to address the issues that produced conflict between these people. Rather than take sides and choose whom to isolate and punish, society should try to reconcile the parties involved in conflict.[179] The effectiveness of justice ultimately depends on the stake a person has in the community (or a

deinstitutionalization
Removing juveniles from adult jails and placing them in community-based programs to avoid the stigma attached to these facilities.

restorative justice
Nonpunitive strategies for dealing with juvenile offenders that make the justice system a healing process rather than a punishment process.

The restorative justice approach to delinquency prevention would have police officers talk to youngsters about the potential social harm caused by delinquent acts rather than acting as social control agents who rely on punishment and deterrence to control crime.

The Center for Restorative Justice & Peacemaking provides links and information on the ideals of restoration and programs based on its principles: http://2ssw.che.umn.edu/rjp/. For an up-to-date list of web links, go to http://cj.wadsworth.com/siegel_jd9e.

particular social group). If a person does not value his/her membership in the group, he/she will be unlikely to accept responsibility, show remorse, or repair the injuries caused by their actions. In contrast, people who have a stake in the community and its principal institutions, such as work, home, and school, find that their involvement enhances their personal and familial well-being.[180] Restorative justice stands in opposition to views of juvenile justice that limit consideration of the personal and social qualities of offenders.[181]

Even the most effective restorative justice programs will be unable to reach those who are disengaged from community institutions. Therefore, community involvement is an essential ingredient of the restorative justice approach. Gordon Bazemore and other policy experts helped formulate a version of restorative justice known as the balanced approach, which emphasizes that victims, offenders, and the community should all benefit from interactions with the justice system.[182] Restorative justice is covered more fully in Chapter 15.

Summary

- Social structure theories hold that delinquent behavior is an adaptation to conditions that predominate in lower-class environments.

- The social disorganization view suggests that economically deprived areas lose their ability to control the behavior of residents. Gangs flourish in these areas.

- Delinquency is a product of the socialization mechanisms within a neighborhood: Unstable neighborhoods have the greatest chance of producing delinquents. Such factors as fear, unemployment, change, and lack of cohesion help produce delinquent behavior patterns.

- Strain theories hold that lower-class youths may desire legitimate goals but that their unavailability causes frustration and deviant behavior.

- Robert Merton linked strain to anomie, a condition caused when there is a disjunction between goals and means.

- In his General Strain Theory, Robert Agnew identifies two more sources of strain: the removal of positive reinforcements and the addition of negative ones. He shows how strain causes delinquent behavior by creating negative affective states, and he outlines the means adolescents employ to cope with strain.

- Cultural deviance or subcultural theory maintains that the result of social disorganization and strain is the development of independent subcultures whose members hold values in opposition to mainstream society. These subcultures are the breeding ground of gangs and law-violating groups.

- Social process theories hold that improper socialization is the key to delinquency.

- One branch, called learning theories, holds that kids learn deviant behaviors and attitudes during interaction with family and peers.

- Social learning theory stresses that kids *learn* both how to commit crimes and the attitudes needed to support the behavior.

- People learn criminal behaviors much as they learn conventional behavior.

- Control theories suggest that kids are prone to delinquent behavior when they have not been properly socialized and lack a strong bond to society. Without a strong bond they are free to succumb to the lure of delinquent behavior.

- Labeling theory maintains that negative labels produce delinquent careers.

- Labels create expectations that the labeled person will act in a certain way; labeled people are always watched and suspected.

- Labeling and stigma may also reinforce delinquency. Kids who receive negative labels may internalize them and engage in self-labeling. This causes a self-fulfilling prophecy that breeds even more deviant behaviors and locks kids in a delinquent way of life.

- Social conflict theory views delinquency as an inevitable result of the class and racial conflict that pervades society. Delinquents are members of the "have-not" class that is shut out of the mainstream. The law benefits the wealthy over the poor.

- Social views of delinquency have had a great deal of influence on social policy. Programs have been designed to improve neighborhood conditions, help children be properly socialized, and reduce conflict.

Key Terms

culture of poverty, p. 108
underclass, p. 110
truly disadvantaged, p. 110
social disorganization theory, p. 112
transitional neighborhood, p. 112
cultural transmission, p. 112
social control, p. 112
gentrified, p. 113
poverty concentration effect, p. 113
collective efficacy, p. 115
strain theory, p. 116

anomie, p. 116
relative deprivation, p. 116
negative affective states, p. 118
cultural deviance theory, p. 120
culture conflict, p. 120
socialization, p. 121
learning theory, p. 126
control theory, p. 126
differential association theory, p. 126
drift, p. 126
neutralization techniques, p. 126

social bond, p. 127
stigmatized, p. 129
labeling theory, p. 129
self-labeling, p. 129
self-fulfilling prophecy, p. 130
dramatization of evil, p. 131
degradation ceremony, p. 131
social conflict theory, p. 132
deinstitutionalization, p. 135
restorative justice, p. 135

Questions for Discussion

1. Is there a transitional area in your town or city?

2. Is it possible that a distinct lower-class culture exists? Are lower-class values different from those of the middle class?

3. Have you ever perceived anomie? What causes anomie? Is there more than one cause of strain?

4. How does poverty cause delinquency?

5. Do middle-class youths become delinquent for the same reasons as lower-class youths?

6. Does relative deprivation produce delinquency?

Viewpoint

You have just been appointed as a presidential adviser on urban problems. The president informs you that he wants to initiate a demonstration project in a major city aimed at showing that government can do something to reduce poverty, crime, and drug abuse. The area he has chosen for development is a large inner-city neighborhood with more than 100,000 residents. The neighborhood suffers from disorganized community structure, poverty, and hopelessness. Predatory delinquent gangs run free and terrorize local merchants and citizens. The school system has failed to provide opportunities and education experiences sufficient to dampen enthusiasm for gang recruitment. Stores, homes, and public buildings are deteriorated and decayed. Commercial enterprise has fled the area, and civil servants are reluctant to enter the neighborhood. There is an uneasy truce among the various ethnic and racial groups that populate the area. Residents feel that little can be done to bring the neighborhood back to life.

You are faced with suggesting an urban redevelopment program that can revitalize the area and eventually bring down the crime rate. You can bring any element of the public and private sector to bear on this rather overwhelming problem—including the military! You can also ask private industry to help in the struggle, promising them tax breaks for their participation.

I Do you believe that living in such an area contributes to high delinquency rates? Or is poverty merely an excuse and delinquency a matter of personal choice?

I What programs do you feel could break the cycle of urban poverty?

I Would reducing the poverty rate produce a lowered delinquency rate?

I What role does the family play in creating delinquent behaviors?

Doing Research on the Web

Use "urban redevelopment" in a keyword search on Info-Trac College Edition.

A number of organizations are dedicated to breaking the cycle of urban poverty. Check out the website of Poverty USA (accessed on August 13, 2004):

www.nccbuscc.org/cchd/brakethecycle/pov_usa/.

Notes

1. Steven Messner and Richard Rosenfeld, *Crime and the American Dream* (Belmont, CA: Wadsworth, 1994), p. 11.
2. Gary LaFree, *Losing Legitimacy: Street Crime and the Decline of Social Institutions in America* (Boulder, CO: Westview, 1998).
3. Emilie Andersen Allan and Darrell Steffensmeier, "Youth, Underemployment, and Property Crime: Differential Effects of Job Availability and Job Quality on Juvenile and Young Adult Arrest Rates," *American Sociological Review* 54:107–123 (1989).
4. Edwin Lemert, *Human Deviance, Social Problems and Social Control* (Englewood Cliffs, NJ: Prentice-Hall, 1967).
5. U.S. Census Bureau News Release, September 26, 2003.
6. Oscar Lewis, "The Culture of Poverty," *Scientific American* 215:19–25 (1966).
7. Laura G. De Haan and Shelley MacDermid, "The Relationship of Individual and Family Factors to the Psychological Well-Being of Junior High School Students Living in Urban Poverty," *Adolescence* 33:73–90 (1998).
8. Julian Chow and Claudia Coulton, "Was There a Social Transformation of Urban Neighborhoods in the 1980s?" *Urban Studies* 35:135–175 (1998).
9. Rodrick Wallace, "Expanding Coupled Shock Fronts of Urban Decay and Criminal Behavior: How U.S. Cities Are Becoming 'Hollowed Out'," *Journal of Quantitative Criminology* 7:333–355 (1991).
10. Ken Auletta, *The Under Class* (New York: Random House, 1982).
11. Richard McGahey, "Economic Conditions, Organization, and Urban Crime," in Albert Reiss and Michael Tonry, eds., *Communities and Crime* (Chicago: University of Chicago Press, 1986), pp. 231–270.
12. Jeanne Brooks-Gunn and Greg J. Duncan, "The Effects of Poverty on Children." *The Future of Children* 7:34–39 (1997).
13. Gary Evans, Nancy Wells, and Annie Moch, "Housing and Mental Health: A Review of the Evidence and a Methodological and Conceptual Critique," *Journal of Social Issues* 59:475–501 (2003).
14. William Julius Wilson, *The Truly Disadvantaged* (Chicago: University of Chicago Press, 1987).
15. Maria Velez, Lauren Krivo, and Ruth Peterson, "Structural Inequality and Homicide: An Assessment of the Black-White Gap in Killings," *Criminology* 41:645–672 (2003).
16. James Ainsworth-Darnell and Douglas Downey, "Assessing the Oppositional Culture Explanation for Racial/Ethnic Differences on School Performances," *American Sociological Review* 63:536–553 (1998).
17. David Greenberg and Valerie West, "State Prison Populations and Their Growth, 1971–1991," *Criminology* 39:615–654 (2001).
18. Eric Lotke, "Hobbling a Generation: Young African-American Men in Washington, D.C.'s Criminal Justice System—Five Years Later," *Crime and Delinquency* 44:355–366 (1998).
19. Greenberg and West, "State Prison Populations and their Growth, 1971–1991," pp. 615–654.
20. William Julius Wilson, *The Bridge over the Racial Divide: Rising Inequality and Coalition Politics* (Wildavsky Forum Series, 2) (Berkeley: University of California Press, 1999).
21. Thomas McNulty and Paul Bellair, "Explaining Racial and Ethnic Differences in Serious Adolescent Violent Behavior," *Criminology* 41:709–748 (2003).
22. Clifford R. Shaw and Henry D. McKay, *Juvenile Delinquency and Urban Areas*, rev. ed. (Chicago: University of Chicago Press, 1972), p. 355.
23. Frederick Thrasher, *The Gang* (Chicago: University of Chicago Press, 1927).
24. Robert Bursik and Harold Grasmick, "The Multiple Layers of Social Disorganization," paper presented at the annual meeting of the American Society of Criminology, New Orleans, November 1992; Robert Bursik and Harold Grasmick, "Longitudinal Neighborhood Profiles in Delinquency: The Decomposition of Change," *Journal of Quantitative Criminology* 8:247–256 (1992).
25. Clifford R. Shaw and Henry D. McKay, *Juvenile Delinquency and Urban Areas*, rev. ed..
26. Steven Messner, Lawrence Raffalovich, and Richard McMillan, "Economic Deprivation and Changes in Homicide Arrest Rates for White and Black Youths, 1967–1998: A National Time Series—Analysis," *Criminology* 39:591–614 (2001).
27. Claire Valier, "Foreigners, Crime and Changing Mobilities," *British Journal of Criminology* 43:1–21 (2003).
28. D. Wayne Osgood and Jeff Chambers, "Social Disorganization Outside the Metropolis: An Analysis of Rural Youth Violence," *Criminology* 38:81–117 (2000).
29. Robert Bursik and Harold Grasmick, "Economic Deprivation and Neighborhood Crime Rates, 1960–1980," *Law and Society Review* 27:263–278 (1993).
30. Robert Sampson and W. Byron Groves, "Community Structure and Crime: Testing Social Disorganization Theory," *American Journal of Sociology* 94:774–802 (1989); Denise Gottfredson, Richard McNeill, and Gary Gottfredson, "Social Area Influences on Delinquency: A Multilevel Analysis," *Journal of Research in Crime and Delinquency* 28:197–206 (1991).
31. Ruth Peterson, Lauren Krivo, and Mark Harris, "Disadvantage and Neighborhood Violent Crime: Do Local Institutions Matter?" *Journal of Research in Crime and Delinquency* 37:31–63 (2000).
32. Ora Simcha-Fagan and Joseph Schwartz, "Neighborhood and Delinquency: An Assessment of Contextual Effects," *Criminology* 24:667–703 (1986).
33. Leo Scheurman and Solomon Kobrin, "Community Careers in Crime," in Albert Reiss and Michael Tonry, eds., *Communities and Crime* (Chicago: University of Chicago Press, 1986), pp. 67–100.
34. Ibid., p. 96.
35. Ellen Kurtz, Barbara Koons, and Ralph Taylor, "Land Use, Physical Deterioration, Resident-Based Control, and Calls for Service on Urban Streetblocks," *Justice Quarterly* 15:121–149 (1998).
36. Janet Heitgerd and Robert Bursik, Jr., "Extracommunity Dynamics and the Ecology of Delinquency," *American Journal of Sociology* 92:775–787 (1987).
37. Charis E. Kubrin, "Structural Covariates of Homicide Rates: Does Type of Homicide Matter?" *Journal of Research in Crime and Delinquency* 40:139–170 (2003).
38. Jeffrey Morenoff, Robert Sampson, and Stephen Raudenbush, "Neighborhood Inequality, Collective Efficacy, and the Spatial Dynamics of Urban Violence," *Criminology* 39:517–560 (2001).
39. Matthew Lee, Michael Maume and Graham Ousey, "Social Isolation and Lethal Violence Across the Metro/Nonmetro Divide: The Effects of Socioeconomic Disadvantage and Poverty Concentration on Homicide," *Rural Sociology* 68:107–131 (2003).
40. Richard Fowles and Mary Merva, "Wage Inequality and Criminal Activity: An Extreme Bounds Analysis for the United States 1975–1990," *Criminology* 34:163–182 (1996).
41. Karen Parker and Matthew Pruitt, "Poverty, Poverty Concentration, and Homicide," *Social Science Quarterly* 81:555–582 (2000).
42. Margo Wilson and Martin Daly, "Life Expectancy, Economic Inequality, Homicide, and Reproductive Timing in Chicago Neighbourhoods," *British Journal of Medicine* 314:1271–1274 (1997).
43. Joan Petersilia, "When Prisoners Return to Communities: Political, Economic, and Social Consequences," *Federal Probation* 65:3–9 (2001).
44. Pamela Wilcox, Neil Quisenberry, and Shayne Jones, "The Built Environment and Community Crime Risk Interpretation," *Journal of Research in Crime and Delinquency* 40:322–345 (2003).
45. Pamela Wilcox Rountree and Kenneth Land, "Burglary Victimization, Perceptions of Crime Risk, and Routine Activities: A Multilevel Analysis across Seattle Neighborhoods and Census Tracts," *Journal of Research in Crime and Delinquency* 33:147–180 (1996).
46. Fred Markowitz, Paul Bellair, Allen Liska, and Jianhong Liu, "Extending Social Disorganization Theory: Modeling the Relationships between Cohesion, Disorder, and Fear," *Criminology* 39:293–320 (2001).
47. See Wesley Skogan, "Fear of Crime and Neighborhood Change," in Albert Reiss and Michael Tonry, eds., *Communities and Crime* (Chicago: University of Chicago Press, 1986), pp. 191–232; Stephanie Greenberg, "Fear and Its Relationship to Crime, Neighborhood Deterioration, and Informal Social Control," in James Byrne and Robert Sampson, eds., *The Social Ecology of Crime* (New York: Springer-Verlag, 1985), pp. 47–62.
48. Jeffrey Will and John McGrath, "Crime, Neighborhood Perceptions, and the Underclass: The Relationship between Fear of Crime and Class Position," *Journal of Criminal Justice* 23:163–176 (1995).
49. Ted Chiricos, Ranee Mcentire, and Marc Gertz, "Social Problems, Perceived Racial and Ethnic Composition of Neighborhood and Perceived Risk of Crime," *Social Problems* 48:322–341 (2001).
50. Catherine E. Ross, John Mirowsky, and Shana Pribesh, "Powerlessness and the Amplification of Threat: Neighborhood Disadvantage, Disorder, and Mistrust," *American Sociological Review* 66:568–580 (2001).
51. Wilson and Daly, "Life Expectancy, Economic Inequality, Homicide, and Reproductive Timing in Chicago Neighborhoods."
52. Catherine Ross, "Fear of Victimization and Health," *Journal of Quantitative Criminology* 9:159–165 (1993).
53. Donald Black, "Social Control as a Dependent Variable," in D. Black, ed., *Toward a General Theory of Social Control* (Orlando, FL: Academic, 1990).
54. Bursik and Grasmick, "The Multiple Layers of Social Disorganization," pp. 8–10.
55. Barbara Warner, "The Role of Attenuated Culture in Social Disorganization Theory," *Criminology* 41:73–97 (2003).

56. Maria Velez, "The Role of Public Social Control in Urban Neighborhoods: A Multi-Level Analysis of Victimization Risk," *Criminology* 39:837–864 (2001).

57. Sampson and Groves, "Community Structure and Crime: Testing Social Disorganization Theory," pp. 774–802.

58. Gottfredson, McNeill, and Gottfredson, "Social Area Influences on Delinquency: A Multilevel Analysis," pp. 197–206.

59. Elijah Anderson, *Streetwise: Race, Class and Change in an Urban Community* (Chicago: University of Chicago Press, 1990), pp. 243–244.

60. William Terrill and Michael Reisig, "Neighborhood Context and Police Use of Force," *Journal of Research in Crime and Delinquency* 40:291–321 (2003).

61. Michael Greene, "Chronic Exposure to Violence and Poverty: Interventions that Work for Youth," *Crime and Delinquency* 39:106–124 (1993).

62. Ibid., pp. 110–111.

63. Chris Gibson, Jihong Zhao, Nicholas Lovrich, and Michael Gaffney, "Social Integration, Individual Perceptions of Collective Efficacy, and Fear of Crime in Three Cities," *Justice Quarterly* 19:537–564 (2002); Felton Earls, *Linking Community Factors and Individual Development* (Washington, DC: National Institute of Justice, 1998).

64. Robert J. Sampson and Stephen W. Raudenbush, *Disorder in Urban Neighborhoods: Does It Lead to Crime?* (Washington, DC: National Institute of Justice, 2001).

65. Matthew Lee and Terri Earnest, "Perceived Community Cohesion and Perceived Risk of Victimization: A Cross-National Analysis," *Justice Quarterly* 20:131–158 (2003).

66. Morenoff, Sampson, and Raudenbush, "Neighborhood Inequality, Collective Efficacy, and the Spatial Dynamics of Urban Violence," pp. 550–551.

67. George Capowich, "The Conditioning Effects of Neighborhood Ecology on Burglary Victimization," *Criminal Justice and Behavior* 30:39–62 (2003); Ruth Perterson, Lauren Krivo, and Mark Harris, "Disadvantage and Neighborhood Violent Crime: Do Local Institutions Matter?" *Journal of Research in Crime and Delinquency* 37:31–63 (2000).

68. Jennifer Beyers, John Bates, Gregory Pettit, and Kenneth Dodge, "Neighborhood Structure, Parenting Processes, and the Development of Youths' Externalizing Behaviors: A Multilevel Analysis," *American Journal of Community Psychology* 31:35–53 (2003).

69. Robert Sampson, Jeffrey Morenoff, and Felton Earls, "Beyond Social Capital: Spatial Dynamics of Collective Efficacy for Children," *American Sociological Review* 64:633–660 (1999).

70. Thomas McNulty, "Assessing the Race-Violence Relationship at the Macro Level: The Assumption of Racial Invariance and the Problem of Restricted Distribution," *Criminology* 39:467–490 (2001).

71. Capowich, "The Conditioning Effects of Neighborhood Ecology on Burglary Victimization," pp. 39–62.

72. Robert Merton, *Social Theory and Social Structure* (Glencoe, IL: Free Press, 1957).

73. Judith Blau and Peter Blau, "The Cost of Inequality: Metropolitan Structure and Violent Crime," *American Sociological Review* 147:114–129 (1982).

74. Beverly Stiles, Xiaoru Liu, and Howard Kaplan, "Relative Deprivation and Deviant Adaptations: The Mediating Effects of Negative Self-Feelings," *Journal of Research in Crime and Delinquency* 37:64–90 (2000).

75. Morenoff, Sampson, and Raudenbush, "Neighborhood Inequality, Collective Efficacy, and the Spatial Dynamics of Urban Violence."

76. Tomislav Kovandzic, Lynne Vieraitis, and Mark Yeisley, "The Structural Covariates of Urban Homicide: Reassessing the Impact of Income Inequality and Poverty in the Post-Reagan Era," *Criminology* 36:569–600 (1998); Scott South and Steven Messner, "Structural Determinants of Intergroup Association," *American Journal of Sociology* 91:1409–1430 (1986); Steven Messner and Scott South, "Economic Deprivation, Opportunity Structure and Robbery Victimization," *Social Forces* 64:975–991 (1986).

77. Ramiro Martinez, Jr., *Latino Homicide: Immigration, Violence, and Community* (New York: Routledge, 2002).

78. Robert Agnew, "Foundation for a General Strain Theory of Crime and Delinquency," *Criminology* 30:47–87 (1992).

79. Ibid., p. 57.

80. Tami Videon, "The Effects of Parent-Adolescent Relationships and Parental Separation on Adolescent Well-Being," *Journal of Marriage & the Family* 64:489–504 (2002).

81. Cesar Rebellon, "Reconsidering the Broken Homes/Delinquency Relationship and Exploring Its Mediating Mechanism(s)," *Criminology* 40:103–135 (2002).

82. Ronald Simons, Yi Fu Chen, and Eric Stewart, "Incidents of Discrimination and Risk for Delinquency: A Longitudinal Test of Strain Theory with an African American Sample," *Justice Quarterly* 20:827–854 (2003).

83. Timothy Brezina, "Adolescent Maltreatment and Delinquency: The Question of Intervening Processes," *Journal of Research in Crime and Delinquency* 35:71–99 (1998).

84. Paul Mazerolle, Velmer Burton, Francis Cullen, T. David Evans, and Gary Payne, "Strain, Anger, and Delinquent Adaptations Specifying General Strain Theory," *Journal of Criminal Justice* 28:89–101 (2000); Paul Mazerolle and Alex Piquero, "Violent Responses to Strain: An Examination of Conditioning Influences," *Violence and Victimization* 12:323–345 (1997).

85. George E. Capowich, Paul Mazerolle, and Alex Piquero, "General Strain Theory, Situational Anger, and Social Networks: An Assessment of Conditioning Influences," *Journal of Criminal Justice* 29:445–461 (2001).

86. Mazerolle, Burton, Cullen, Evans, and Payne, "Strain, Anger, and Delinquent Adaptations Specifying General Strain Theory."

87. Stephen Cernkovich, Peggy Giordano, and Jennifer Rudolph, "Race, Crime and the American Dream," *Journal of Research in Crime and Delinquency* 37:131–170 (2000).

88. Lawrence Wu, "Effects of Family Instability, Income and Income Instability on the Risk of Premarital Birth," *American Sociological Review* 61:386–406 (1996).

89. Anthony Walsh, "Behavior Genetics and Anomie/Strain Theory," *Criminology* 38:1075–1107 (2000).

90. Teresa LaGrange and Robert Silverman "Investigating the Interdependence of Strain and Self-Control," *Canadian Journal of Criminology and Criminal Justice* 45:431–464 (2003).

91. Messner and Rosenfeld, *Crime and the American Dream.*

92. Michale Maume and Matthew Lee, "Social Institutions and Violence: A Sub-National Test of Institutional Anomie Theory," *Criminology* 41:1137–1173 (2003).

93. Albert Cohen, *Delinquent Boys* (New York: Free Press, 1955).

94. Richard Cloward and Lloyd Ohlin, *Delinquency and Opportunity* (New York: Free Press, 1960).

95. See, for example, Irving Spergel, *Racketville, Slumtown, and Haulburg* (Chicago: University of Chicago Press, 1964).

96. James Short, "Gangs, Neighborhoods, and Youth Crime," *Criminal Justice Research Bulletin* 5:1–11 (1990).

97. Michael Leiber, Mahesh Nalla, and Margaret Farnworth, "Explaining Juveniles' Attitudes toward the Police," *Justice Quarterly* 15:151–173 (1998).

98. A. Leigh Ingram, "Type of Place, Urbanism, and Delinquency: Further Testing of the Determinist Theory," *Journal of Research in Crime and Delinquency* 30:192–212 (1993).

99. Alan Lizotte, Terence Thornberry, Marvin Krohn, Deborah Chard-Wierschem, and David McDowall, "Neighborhood Context and Delinquency: A Longitudinal Analysis," in H. J. Kerner and E. Weitekamp, eds., *Cross-National Longitudinal Research on Human Development and Criminal Behavior* (Dordrecht, The Netherlands: Kluwer Academic Publishers, 1993), pp. 1–11.

100. Ronald Simons, Chyi-In Wu, Kuei-Hsiu Lin, Leslie Gordon, and Rand Conger, "A Cross-Cultural Examination of the Link between Corporal Punishment and Adolescent Antisocial Behavior," *Criminology* 38:47–79 (2000).

101. John Paul Wright and Francis Cullen, "Parental Efficacy and Delinquent Behavior: Do Control and Support Matter?" *Criminology* 39:677–706 (2001).

102. Karol Kumpfer and Rose Alvarado, "Strengthening Approaches for the Prevention of Youth Problem Behaviors," *American Psychologist* 58:457–465 (2003); Carter Hay, "Parenting, Self-Control, and Delinquency: A Test of Self-Control Theory," *Criminology* 39:707–736 (2001).

103. Robert Roberts and Vern Bengston, "Affective Ties to Parents in Early Adulthood and Self-Esteem Across 20 Years," *Social Psychology Quarterly* 59:96–106 (1996).

104. Alexander Vazsonyi and Lloyd Pickering, "The Importance of Family and School Domains in Adolescent Deviance: African American and Caucasian Youth," *Journal of Youth and Adolescence* 32:115–129 (2003).

105. G. Roger Jarjoura, "Does Dropping Out of School Enhance Delinquent Involvement? Results from a Large-Scale National Probability Sample," *Criminology* 31:149–172 (1993); Terence Thornberry, Melaine Moore, and R. L. Christenson, "The Effect of Dropping Out of High School on Subsequent Criminal Behavior," *Criminology* 23:3–18 (1985).

106. Carolyn Smith, Alan Lizotte, Terence Thornberry, and Marvin Krohn, *Resilient Youth: Identifying Factors that Prevent High-Risk Youth from Engaging in Delinquency and Drug Use* (Albany, NY: Rochester Youth Development Study, 1994), pp. 19–21.

107. Thomas Berndt, "The Features and Effects of Friendship in Early Adolescence," *Child Development* 53:1447–1460 (1982).

108. Isabela Granic and Thomas Dishion, "Deviant Talk in Adolescent Friendships: A Step Toward Measuring a Pathogenic Attractor Process," *Social Development* 12:314–334 (2003).

109. Jeremy Staff and Christopher Uggen, "The Fruits of Good Work: Early Work Experiences and Adolescent Deviance," *Journal of Research in Crime and Delinquency* 40:263–290 (2003).

110. David Fergusson, L. John Horwood, and Daniel Nagin, "Offending Trajectories in a New Zealand Birth Cohort," *Criminology* 38:525–551 (2000).

111. Colin Baier and Bradley Wright, "If You Love Me, Keep My Commandments: A Meta-Analysis of the Effect of Religion on Crime," *Journal of Research in Crime and Delinquency* 38:3–21 (2001); Byron Johnson, Sung Joon Jang, David Larson, and Spencer De Li, "Does Adolescent Religious Commitment Matter? A Reexamination of the Effects of Religiosity on Delinquency," *Journal of Research in Crime and Delinquency* 38:22–44 (2001).

112. Sung Joon Jang and Byron Johnson, "Neighborhood Disorder, Individual Religiosity, and Adolescent Use of Illicit Drugs: A Test of Multilevel Hypothesis," *Criminology* 39:109–144 (2001).

113. Mark Regnerus, "Moral Communities and Adolescent Delinquency: Religious Contexts and Community Social Control," *The Sociological Quarterly* 44:523–554 (2003).

114. Matthew Lee and John Bartkowski, "Love Thy Neighbor? Moral Communities, Civic Engagement, and Juvenile Homicide in Rural Areas," *Social Forces* 82:1001–1035 (2004).

115. T. David Evans, Francis Cullen, R. Gregory Dunaway, and Velmer Burton, Jr., "Religion and Crime Reexamined: The Impact of Religion, Secular Controls, and Social Ecology on Adult Criminality," *Criminology* 33:195–224 (1995).

116. Lee Ellis and James Patterson, "Crime and Religion: An International Comparison among Thirteen Industrial Nations," *Personal Individual Differences* 20:761–768 (1996).

117. Eric Stewart, Ronald Simons, and Rand Conger, "Assessing Neighborhood and Social Psychological Influences on Childhood Violence in an African-American Sample," *Criminology* 40:801–830 (2002).

118. Edwin Sutherland, *Principles of Criminology* (Philadelphia: Lippincott, 1939).

119. Gresham Sykes and David Matza, "Techniques of Neutralization: A Theory of Delinquency," *American Sociological Review* 22:664–670 (1957); David Matza, *Delinquency and Drift* (New York: Wiley, 1964).

120. Ibid.

121. Travis Hirschi, *Causes of Delinquency* (Berkeley: University of California Press, 1969).

122. Helen Garnier and Judith Stein, "An 18-Year Model of Family and Peer Effects on Adolescent Drug Use and Delinquency," *Journal of Youth and Adolescence* 31:45–56 (2002).

123. Thomas Vander Ven, Francis Cullen, Mark Carrozza, and John Paul Wright, "Home Alone: The Impact of Maternal Employment on Delinquency," *Social Problems* 48:236–257 (2001).

124. For a review of existing research, see Kimberly Kempf, "The Empirical Status of Hirschi's Control Theory," in Bill Laufer and Freda Adler, eds., *Advances in Criminological Theory* (New Brunswick, NJ: Transaction, 1992).

125. Bobbi Jo Anderson, Malcolm Holmes, and Erik Ostresh, "Male and Female Delinquent's Attachments and Effects of Attachments on Severity of Self-Reported Delinquency," *Criminal Justice and Behavior* 26:425–452 (1999).

126. Vander Ven, Cullen, Carrozza, and Wright, "Home Alone: The Impact of Maternal Employment on Delinquency"; Patricia Jenkins, "School Delinquency and the School Social Bond," *Journal of Research in Crime and Delinquency* 34:337–367 (1997).

127. Jonathan Zaff, Kristin Moore, Angela Romano Papillo, and Stephanie Williams, "Implications of Extracurricular Activity Participation During Adolescence on Positive Outcomes," *Journal of Adolescent Research* 18:599–631 (2003).

128. Cernkovich, Giordano, and Rudolph, "Race, Crime and the American Dream."

129. Richard Lawrence, "Parents, Peers, School and Delinquency," paper presented at the American Society of Criminology meeting, Boston, November 1995.

130. Peggy Giordano, Stephen Cernkovich, and M. D. Pugh, "Friendships and Delinquency," *American Journal of Sociology* 91:1170–1202 (1986).

131. Denise Kandel and Mark Davies, "Friendship Networks, Intimacy, and Illicit Drug Use in Young Adulthood: A Comparison of Two Competing Theories," *Criminology* 29:441–467 (1991).

132. Leslie Samuelson, Timothy Hartnagel, and Harvey Krahn, "Crime and Social Control among High School Dropouts," *Journal of Crime and Justice* 18:129–161 (1990).

133. For a review of this position, see Anne R. Mahoney, "The Effect of Labeling upon Youths in the Juvenile Justice System: A Review of the Evidence," *Law and Society Review* 8:583–614 (1974); see also David Matza, *Becoming Deviant* (Englewood Cliffs, NJ: Prentice-Hall, 1974).

134. The self-labeling concept originated in Edwin Lemert, *Social Pathology* (New York: McGraw-Hill, 1951); see also Frank Tannenbaum, *Crime and the Community* (Boston: Ginn, 1936).

135. Nalini Ambady and Robert Rosenthal, "Half a Minute: Predicting Teacher Evaluations from Thin Slices of Nonverbal Behavior and Physical Attractiveness," *Journal of Personality and Social Psychology* 64:431–141 (1993).

136. Monica Harris, Richard Milich, Elizabeth Corbitt, Daniel Hoover, and Marianne Brady, "Self-Fulfilling Effects of Stigmatizing Information on Children's Social Interactions," *Journal of Personality and Social Psychology* 33:41–50 (1992).

137. Harold Garfinkel, "Conditions of Successful Degradation Ceremonies," *American Journal of Sociology* 61:420–424 (1956).

138. Charles H. Cooley, *Human Nature and the Social Order* (New York: Scribner's, 1902).

139. Ross Matsueda, "Reflected Appraisals, Parental Labeling, and Delinquency: Specifying a Symbolic Interactionist Theory," *American Journal of Sociology* 97:1577–1611 (1992).

140. Mike Adams, Craig Robertson, Phyllis Gray-Ray, Melvin Ray, "Labeling and Delinquency," *Adolescence* 38:171–186 (2003).

141. Howard Kaplan and Hiroshi Fukurai, "Negative Social Sanctions, Self-Rejection, and Drug Use," *Youth and Society* 23:275–298 (1992).

142. Howard Kaplan, *Toward a General Theory of Deviance: Contributions from Perspectives on Deviance and Criminality* (College Station, TX: Texas A & M University, n.d.).

143. Harris et al., "Self-Fulfilling Effects of Stigmatizing Information on Children's Social Interactions," pp. 48–50.

144. Kaplan, *Toward a General Theory of Deviance.*

145. Howard Kaplan, Robert Johnson, and Carol Bailey, "Deviant Peers and Deviant Behavior: Further Elaboration of a Model," *Social Psychology Quarterly* 30:277–284 (1987).

146. Adams, Robertson, Gray-Ray, and Ray, "Labeling and Delinquency," pp.171–86.

147. Lemert, *Human Deviance, Social Problems, and Social Control*, p. 15.

148. Lening Zhang, "Official Offense Status and Self-Esteem among Chinese Youths," *Journal of Criminal Justice* 31:99–105 (2003).

149. Tannenbaum, *Crime and the Community.*

150. Aaron Cicourel, *The Social Organization of Juvenile Justice* (New York: Wiley, 1968).

151. Matza, *Becoming Deviant.*

152. Ibid., p. 78.

153. Stanton Wheeler and Leonard Cottrell, "Juvenile Delinquency: Its Prevention and Control," in Donald Cressey and David Ward, eds., *Delinquency, Crime, and Social Processes* (New York: Harper & Row, 1969), p. 609.

154. Garfinkel, *Conditions of Successful Degradation Ceremonies*, p. 424.

155. Adams, Robertson, Gray-Ray, and Ray, "Labeling and Delinquency," pp. 171–86.

156. Charles A. Murray and Louis Cox, *Beyond Probation* (Beverly Hills: Sage Publications, 1979).

157. Raymond Paternoster and Leeann Iovanni, "The Labeling Perspective and Delinquency: An Elaboration of the Theory and an Assessment of the Evidence," *Justice Quarterly* 6:358–394 (1989).

158. Scott Davies and Julian Tanner, "The Long Arm of the Law: Effects of Labeling on Employment," *Sociological Quarterly* 44:385–404 (2003).

159. Jon Gunnar Bernburg and Marvin Krohn, "Labeling, Life Chances, and Adult Crime: The Direct and Indirect Effects of Official Intervention in Adolescence on Crime in Early Adulthood," *Criminology* 41:1287-1318 (2003).

160. Shadd Maruna, Thomas Lebel, Nick Mitchell, and Michelle Naples, "Pygmalion in the Reintegration Process: Desistance from Crime through the Looking Glass," *Psychology, Crime & Law* 10:271–281 (2004).

161. Meier, "The New Criminology," p. 463.

162. Tony Platt and Cecilia O'Leary "Patriot Acts," *Social Justice* 30:5–21 (2003).

163. Sykes, "The Rise of Critical Criminology," pp. 211–13.

164. Ibid.

165. Matthew Petrocelli, Alex Piquero, Michael Smith, "Conflict Theory and Racial Profiling: an Empirical Analysis of Police Traffic Stop Data," *Journal of Criminal Justice* 31:1–10 (2003).

166. Malcolm Homes, "Minority Threat and Police Brutality: Determinants of Civil Rights Criminal Complaints in U.S. Municipalities," *Criminology* 38:343–368 (2000).

167. Ibid.

168. Robert Gordon, "Capitalism, Class, and Crime in America," *Crime and Delinquency* 19:174 (1973).

169. Richard Quinney, *Class, State, and Crime* (New York: Longman, 1977), p. 52.

170. Anthony Platt, "The Triumph of Benevolence: The Origins of the Juvenile Justice System in the United States," in Richard Quinney, ed., *Criminal Justice in America: A Critical Understanding* (Boston: Little, Brown, 1974), p. 367; see also Anthony Platt, *The Child Savers* (Chicago: University of Chicago Press, 1969).

171. Operation Weed and Seed Executive Offices, U.S. Department of Justice, Washington, DC, 1998; Executive Office for Weed and Seed, Weed and Seed In-sites, Series: Volume VI, Number 5, August/September 1998.

172. Terence Thornberry, David Huizinga, and Rolf Loeber, "The Prevention of Serious Delinquency and Violence," in James Howell, Barry Krisberg, J. David Hawkins, and John Wilson, eds., *Sourcebook on Serious, Violent, and Chronic Juvenile Offenders* (Thousand Oaks, CA: Sage Publications, 1995).

173. James Austin and Barry Krisberg, "The Unmet Promise of Alternatives to Incarceration," *Crime and Delinquency* 28:3–19 (1982).

174. William Selke, "Diversion and Crime Prevention," *Criminology* 20:395–406 (1982).

175. Liz Walz, "One Blood," *Contemporary Justice Review* 6:25–36 (2003).

176. Kathleen Daly and Russ Immarigeon, "The Past, Present, and Future of Restorative Justice: Some Critical Reflections," *Contemporary Justice Review* 1:21–45 (1998).

177. Kay Pranis, "Peacemaking Circles: Restorative Justice in Practice Allows Victims and Offenders to Begin Repairing the Harm," *Corrections Today* 59:72–76 (1997).

178. Carol LaPrairie, "The 'New' Justice: Some Implications for Aboriginal Communities," *Canadian Journal of Criminology* 40:61–79 (1998).

179. Gene Stephens, "The Future of Policing: From a War Model to a Peace Model," in Brendan Maguire and Polly Radosh, eds., *The Past, Present and Future of American Criminal Justice* (Dix Hills, NY: General Hall Publishing, 1996), pp. 77–93.

180. Rick Shifley, "The Organization of Work as a Factor in Social Well-Being," *Contemporary Justice Review* 6:105–126 (2003).

181. Peter Cordella, "Justice," unpublished paper, St. Anselm College, Manchester, NH, 1997; see also Herbert Bianchi, *Justice as Sanctuary* (Bloomington: Indiana University Press, 1994); Nils Christie, "Conflicts as Property," *The British Journal of Criminology* 17:1–15 (1977); L. Hulsman, "Critical Criminology and the Concept of Crime," *Contemporary Crises* 10:63–80 (1986).

182. Gordon Bazemore, "What's New about the Balanced Approach?" *Juvenile and Family Court Journal* 48:1–23 (1997); Gordon Bazemore and Mara Schiff, "Community Justice/Restorative Justice: Prospects for a New Social Ecology for Community Corrections," *International Journal of Comparative and Applied Criminal Justice* 20:311–335 (1996).

5 Developmental Views of Delinquency

Chapter Outline

The Life-Course View

The Glueck Research

Contemporary Life Course Concepts

Age of Onset

Adolescent Limiteds vs. Life-Course Persisters

Problem Behavior Syndrome

POLICY AND PRACTICE: The Fast Track Project

Multiple Pathways

Continuity of Crime and Delinquency

Life-Course Theories

The Social Development Model

FOCUS ON DELINQUENCY: The Path to Delinquency

Interactional Theory

Sampson and Laub: Age-Graded Theory

FOCUS ON DELINQUENCY: Shared Beginnings,
Divergent Lives

Latent Trait Theories

General Theory of Crime

Analyzing the GTC

Evaluating the Developmental View

Chapter Objectives

1. Be familiar with the concept of developmental theory
2. Know the factors that influence the life course
3. Recognize that there are different pathways to delinquency
4. Be able to discuss the social development model
5. Describe what is meant by interactional theory
6. Be familiar with the "turning points in delinquency"
7. Be able to discuss the influence of social capital on delinquency
8. Know what is meant by a "latent trait"
9. Be able to discuss Gottfredson and Hirschi's general theory of delinquency
10. Be familiar with the concepts of "impulsivity" and "self-control"

CNN. View the CNN video clip of this story and answer related Critical Thinking questions on your Juvenile Delinquency 9e CD-ROM.

On April 26, 2004, an 8-year-old Georgia girl, Amy Michelle Yates, was found dead a few hours after she was reported missing by her family. The next day, a 12-year-old neighbor boy was arrested and charged with strangling Amy, who disappeared while riding her bicycle to a nearby friend's house. Because of his age, Amy's killer was only eligible for a relatively short institutional stay. Amy's distraught parents asked legislators to rewrite state law so a child 12 or younger who is convicted of murder could be sentenced to life in prison; they proposed calling it "Amy's Law."

The boy who was accused in Amy's death was one of those kids who seem at odds with the world. He hung out with older kids, bummed cigarettes, and was described by neighbors as being "rough" with girls. According to developmental theorists, the roots of his violent act can be traced back much earlier in his childhood and Amy's murder was the culmination of a long involvement with antisocial behavior. Few kids begin their offending career by getting involved in a murder plot. Most serious offenders have a long history of antisocial activities, beginning early in their childhood and continuing into adolescence and adulthood.

Because serious juvenile offending is rarely a "one shot deal," it has become important to chart the natural history of a delinquent career. We know that most young offenders do not become adult criminals. Why is it that some kids become delinquents and then abandon the delinquent way of life as they mature, whereas others persist in criminality into their adulthood? Why do some offenders escalate their delinquent activities while others decrease or limit their law violations? Why do some offenders specialize in a particular delinquency while others become generalists who shoplift, take drugs, engage in violence, steal cars, and so on? Why do some criminals reduce delinquent activity and then resume it later in life? Research now shows that some offenders begin their delinquent careers at a very early age, whereas others begin later. How can early- and late-onset criminality be explained? Focusing attention on these questions has produced what is known as the **developmental theory** of delinquency, a view that looks at the onset, continuity, and termination of a delinquent career. There

developmental theory
The view that criminality is a dynamic process, influenced by social experiences as well as individual characteristics.

Interested in **the concept of human development?**
Access the United Nation's website on the topic at www.undp.org/hdro/. For an up-to-date list of web links, go to http://cj.wadsworth.com/siegel_jd9e.

are actually two distinct developmental views. The first, referred to as the **life-course theory,** suggests that delinquent behavior is a dynamic process, influenced by individual characteristics as well as social experiences, and that the factors that cause antisocial behaviors change dramatically over a person's life span.

However, while their position is growing increasingly popular, the life-course theorists are challenged by another group of scholars who suggest that human development is controlled by a "master trait" that remains stable and unchanging throughout a person's lifetime. As people travel through their life course this trait is always there, directing their behavior. Because this master trait is enduring, the ebb and flow of delinquent behavior is shaped less by personal change and more by the impact of external forces such as delinquent opportunity. For example, delinquency may increase when an adolescent joins a gang, which provides him with more opportunities to steal, take drugs, and attack others. In other words, the propensity to commit delinquent acts is constant, but the opportunity to commit them is constantly fluctuating. The main points, similarities, and differences of both positions are set out in Concept Summary 5.1.

Concept Summary 5.1

Latent Trait vs. Life-Course Theories

Latent Trait Theory	People do not change, criminal opportunities change; maturity brings fewer opportunities
	People have a master trait: personality, intelligence, genetic makeup
	Early social control and proper parenting can reduce criminal propensity
Life-Course Theories	People have multiple traits: social, psychological, economic
	People change over the life course
	Family, job, peers influence behavior
Similarities	Criminal careers are a passage
	Personal and structural factors influence crime
	External change affects crime
Differences	Latent Trait: An unchanging master trait controls antisocial behavior
	Life Course: People are constantly evolving

THE LIFE-COURSE VIEW

According to the life-course view, even as toddlers, people begin relationships and behaviors that will determine their entire life course. As children they must learn to conform to social rules and function effectively in society. Later they are expected to begin thinking about careers, leave their parental homes, find permanent relationships, and eventually marry and begin their own families.[1] These transitions are expected to take place in an orderly fashion, beginning with finishing school, entering the workforce, getting married, and having children.

Some kids, however, are incapable of maturing in a reasonable and timely fashion because of family, environmental, or personal problems. In some cases transitions can occur too early—for example, when adolescents engage in precocious sex. In other cases transitions may occur too late, as when a student fails to graduate on time because of bad grades or too many incompletes. Sometimes disruption of one trajectory can harm another. For example, teenage childbirth will most likely disrupt educational and career development. These negative life transitions can become cumulative: as kids acquire more personal deficits, the chances of acquiring additional deficits increases.[2] The boy who experiences significant amounts of anger in early adolescence is the one more likely to become involved in antisocial behavior as a teen and mature into a depressed adult who abuses alcohol.[3]

Disruptions in life's major transitions can be destructive and ultimately can promote criminality. Those who are already at risk because of socioeconomic problems or

High school graduation is an important milestone in the life course. According to the developmental approach, life transitions are expected to take place in an orderly fashion, beginning with completing school, entering the workforce, getting married, and having children.

© Chuck Savage/Corbis

family dysfunction are the most susceptible to these awkward transitions. The cumulative impact of these disruptions sustains criminality from childhood into adulthood.

Because a transition from one stage of life to another can be a bumpy ride, the propensity to commit delinquent acts is neither stable nor constant; it is a developmental process. A positive life experience may help some kids desist from delinquency for a while, whereas a negative one may cause them to resume their activities. Delinquent careers are also said to be interactional because people are influenced by the behavior of those around them and, in turn, influence others' behavior. For example, a girl who is constantly in trouble may feel rejected by her friends, which causes her to (1) seek antisocial friends, (2) increase her involvement in antisocial behavior, and (3) experience even more rejection.

Life-course theories also recognize that as people mature, the factors that influence their behavior change. At first, family relations may be most influential; in later adolescence, school and peer relations predominate; in adulthood, vocational achievement and marital relations may be the most critical influences. For example, some antisocial children who are in trouble throughout their adolescence may manage to find stable work and maintain intact marriages as adults; these life events help them desist from delinquency. In contrast, the less fortunate adolescents who end up with arrest records and get involved with the wrong crowd may find themselves limited to menial jobs and at risk for delinquent careers.

The Glueck Research

One of the cornerstones of life-course theories has been a renewed interest in the research efforts of Sheldon and Eleanor Glueck. While at Harvard University in the 1930s, the Gluecks popularized research on the life cycle of delinquent careers. In a series of longitudinal research studies, they followed the careers of known delinquents to determine the factors that predicted persistent offending.[4] The Gluecks made extensive use of interviews and records in their elaborate comparisons of delinquents and nondelinquents.[5]

The Gluecks' research focused on early onset of delinquency as a harbinger of a delinquent career: "The deeper the roots of childhood maladjustment, the smaller the chance of adult adjustment."[6] They also noted the stability of offending careers: Children who are antisocial early in life are the most likely to continue their offending careers into adulthood.

Read more about **the life and work of Eleanor Glueck** at www.school.eb.com/women/articles/Glueck_Eleanor_Touroff.html. For an up-to-date list of web links, go to http://cj.wadsworth.com/siegel_jd9e.

TO QUIZ YOURSELF ON THIS MATERIAL, go to the Juvenile Delinquency 9e website.

The Gluecks identified a number of personal and social factors related to persistent offending. The most important of these factors was family relations, considered in terms of quality of discipline and emotional ties with parents. The adolescent raised in a large, single-parent family of limited economic means and educational achievement was the most vulnerable to delinquency.

The Gluecks did not restrict their analysis to social variables. When they measured such biological and psychological traits as body type, intelligence, and personality, they found that physical and mental factors also played a role in determining behavior. Children with low intelligence, a background of mental disease, and a powerful (mesomorph) physique were the most likely to become persistent offenders.

CONTEMPORARY LIFE-COURSE CONCEPTS

These pioneering efforts have produced views of delinquency causation that integrate both social and personal factors and also recognize that the factors that produce crime and delinquency are multidimensional and dynamic. Crime-producing elements that affect people at one point in the life cycle may not be relevant at another.[7] Because people are influenced by different factors as they mature, social and personal interactions that may have an important influence at one stage of life (like delinquent peers) may have little influence later on.[8]

People may show a propensity to offend early in their lives, but the nature and frequency of their activities are affected by outside forces beyond their control.[9] Although one factor may dominate, the cause of delinquency is essentially multidimensional. Why does one youth becomes a chronic offender while another may commit an occasional illegal act but later desists from crime? One possibility is that when faced with important life transitions such as becoming a student or getting a job, some kids have what it takes to succeed, while others are incapable of maturing in a reasonable and timely fashion because of family, environmental, or personal problems.

The next sections review some of the more important concepts associated with the developmental perspective.

The Program of Research on the Causes and Correlates of Delinquency, sponsored by the federal government, coordinates longitudinal projects that are often referred to in this text. You can reach their website at http://ojjdp.ncjrs.org/ccd/oview.html. For an up-to-date list of web links, go to http://cj.wadsworth.com/siegel_jd9e.

Age of Onset

Research shows that children who will later become delinquents begin their deviant careers at a very early (preschool) age, and the earlier the onset of criminality, the more frequent, varied, and sustained the criminal career.[10] In a thorough review of this issue, Rolf Loeber and David Farrington have found that the youngest criminals typically have a long history of disruptive behavior beginning in early childhood with truancy, cruelty to animals, lying, and theft.[11] Though most commit less serious forms of delinquency, since 1980 more than 600 murders have been committed by youngsters aged 12 or under; between 12 percent and 14 percent of all juveniles arrested for rape are between 7 and 12 years old.

Not all persistent offenders begin at an early age; some begin their journey at different times.[12] Some stay out of trouble in adolescence and do not violate the law until their teenage years. There are even a few who skip antisocial behavior in their childhood and adolescence altogether and begin their offending career in adulthood.[13]

Why do some kids get involved in delinquency at an early age and others wait until their late adolescence? Early starters, who begin offending before age 14, seem to follow a path going from (1) poor parenting to (2) deviant behaviors and then to (3) involvement with delinquent groups. Late starters, who begin offending after age 14, follow a somewhat different path: (1) Poor parenting leads to (2) identification with delinquent groups and then to (3) deviant behaviors. By implication, adolescents who suffer poor parenting and are at risk for deviant careers can avoid criminality if they can bypass involvement with delinquent peers.[14] While most adolescents eventually reduce their delinquent activity, some persist at a high rate into their 20s.[15]

The earlier the onset, the more likely kids will engage in serious delinquency and for a longer period of time. Studies of the juvenile justice system show that many incarcerated youth began their offending careers very early in life and that a significant number had engaged in heavy drinking and drug abuse at age 10 or younger.[16]

Adolescent-Limiteds vs. Life-Course Persisters

adolescent-limited
Offender who follows the most common delinquent trajectory, in which antisocial behavior peaks in adolescence and then diminishes.

life-course persister
One of the small group of offenders whose delinquent careers continue well into adulthood.

According to psychologist Terrie Moffitt, adolescents who repeatedly violate the law can be divided into two groups: **adolescent-limiteds** and **life-course persisters**.[17] Adolescent-limited offenders get involved with antisocial activities early in life and then begin to phase out of their delinquent behaviors as they mature. These kids may be considered "typical teenagers" who get into minor scrapes and engage in what might be considered rebellious teenage behavior with their friends, such as recreational drug use.[18] In contrast, life-course persisters remain high-rate offenders into young adulthood.[19] They combine family dysfunction with severe neurological problems that predispose them to antisocial behavior patterns. These problems can be the result of maternal drug abuse, poor nutrition, or exposure to toxic agents such as lead. Life-course persisters may have lower verbal ability, which inhibits reasoning skills, learning ability, and school achievement. They seem to mature faster and engage in early sexuality and drug use, referred to as **pseudomaturity**.[20]

pseudomaturity
Characteristic of life-course persisters, who tend to engage in early sexuality and drug use.

Recent research has found support for Moffitt's views.[21] There is evidence that life-course persisters manifest significantly more mental health problems, including psychiatric pathologies, than adolescent-limited offenders, a finding which may help explain their persistent offending patterns.[22]

Further research is warranted because Moffitt's work shows that there are two classes of delinquents and that social policy must recognize that delinquency is a multifaceted problem.

problem behavior syndrome (PBS)
A cluster of antisocial behaviors that may include family dysfunction, substance abuse, smoking, precocious sexuality and early pregnancy, educational underachievement, suicide attempts, sensation seeking, and unemployment, as well as delinquency.

Problem Behavior Syndrome

The life-course view is that delinquency is but one of many social problems faced by at-risk youth. Referred to collectively as **problem behavior syndrome (PBS),** these behaviors include family dysfunction, substance abuse, smoking, precocious sexuality and early pregnancy, educational underachievement, suicide attempts, sensation seeking, and unemployment (see Exhibit 5.1).[23] People who suffer from one of these conditions typically exhibit many symptoms of the others.[24] Research has found the following problem behaviors cluster together:

I Adolescents with a history of gang involvement are more likely to have been expelled from school, be a binge drinker, test positively for marijuana, have been in three or more fights in the past six months, have a nonmonogamous partner, and test positive for sexually transmitted diseases.[25]

I Kids who gamble at an early age also take drugs and commit delinquent acts.[26]

I Youths who drink in the late elementary school years, who are aggressive, and who have attention and other psychological problems are more likely to be offenders during adolescence.[27]

I Youths who are less attached to their parents and school and have antisocial friends are more likely to be offenders.

I Youths from neighborhoods where drugs are easily available are more likely to be offenders during adolescence.[28]

EXHIBIT 5.1

Problem Behaviors That Cluster Together

Social	I Family dysfunction
	I Unemployment
	I Educational underachievement
	I School misconduct
Personal	I Substance abuse
	I Suicide attempts
	I Early sexuality
	I Sensation seeking
	I Early parenthood
	I Accident proneness
	I Medical problems
	I Mental disease
	I Anxiety
	I Eating disorders (bulimia, anorexia)
Environmental	I High-delinquency area
	I Disorganized area
	I Racism
	I Exposure to poverty

The Fast Track Project

Fast Track is designed to prevent serious antisocial behavior and related adolescent problems in high-risk children entering first grade. The intervention is guided by a developmental approach that suggests that antisocial behavior is the product of the interaction of multiple social and psychological influences:

1. Residence in low-income, high-crime communities places stressors and influences on children and families that increase their risk levels. In these areas, families characterized by marital conflict and instability make consistent and effective parenting difficult to achieve, particularly with children who are impulsive and of difficult temperament.

2. Children of high-risk families usually enter the education process poorly prepared for its social, emotional, and cognitive demands. Their parents often are unprepared to relate effectively with school staff and a poor school-home bond often aggravates the child's adjustment problems. They may themselves be grouped with other children who are similarly unprepared. This peer group may be negatively influenced by disruptive classroom contexts and punitive teachers.

3. Over time, aggressive and disruptive children are rejected by families and peers, and tend to receive less support from teachers. All of these processes increase the risk of antisocial behaviors, in a process that begins in elementary school and lasts throughout adolescence. During this period, peer influences, academic difficulties, and dysfunctional personal identity development can contribute to serious conduct problems and related risky behaviors.

WHAT DOES FAST TRACK DO?

Fast Track provides intervention based on the assumption that improving child competencies, parenting effectiveness, school context, and school-home communications will, over time, contribute to preventing antisocial behavior in the period from early childhood through adolescence. To carry out this mission, in four sites across the United States, Fast Track coordinators selected a sample of 445 high-risk children in kindergarten who were identified by their conduct problems at home and at school; a matched control group of 446 youths was also identified. Treatment was provided in a number of phases stretching from 1st to 10th grade.

ELEMENTARY SCHOOL PHASE OF THE INTERVENTION PROGRAM (GRADES 1–5)

▌ Teacher-led classroom curricula (called PATHS) as a universal intervention directed toward the development of emotional concepts, social understanding, and self-control (including weekly teacher consultation about classroom management)

▌ Parent training groups designed to promote the development of positive family-school relationships and to teach parents behavior management skills, particularly in the use of praise, time out, and self-restraint

▌ Home visits for the purpose of fostering parents' problem-solving skills, self-efficacy, and life management

▌ Child social skill training groups (called Friendship Groups)

▌ Child tutoring in reading, and child friendship enhancement in the classroom (called Peer Pairing)

ADOLESCENT PHASE OF THE INTERVENTION PROGRAM (GRADES 6–10)

▌ Standard and individualized activities for high-risk youth and families. Group-based interventions were de-

---

▌ Juvenile delinquents with conduct disorder, who have experienced and observed violence, who have been traumatized, and who suffer from a wide spectrum of psychopathology also have high rates of suicidal thoughts and attempts.[29]

People who exhibit one of these conditions typically exhibit many of the others.[30] All varieties of delinquent behavior, including violence, theft, and drug offenses, may be part of a generalized PBS, indicating that all forms of antisocial behavior have similar developmental patterns.[31]

Now that delinquency experts understand the problem behavior view, they are beginning to design treatment prevention that provides multidimensional strategies. The Fast Track project discussed in the above Policy and Practice box is one such program.

Multiple Pathways

Life-course theorists recognize that delinquents may travel more than a single road in their delinquent career. Some are chronic offenders, while others may commit delinquent acts only once or twice; some increase their activities as they age while others de-emphasized, in order to avoid promoting engagement with deviant peers.

- Curriculum-based parent and youth group meetings were included in the intervention, to support children in their transition into middle school (grades 5–7).

- Individualized services, designed to strengthen protective factors and reduce risk factors in areas of particular need for each youth, which included academic tutoring, mentoring, support for positive peer-group involvement, home visiting and family problem-solving, and liaisons with school and community agencies.

EVALUATION OF THE FAST TRACK PROGRAM

The efficacy of the Fast Track prevention program is tested periodically, by comparing the group of children receiving intervention services to children in the control group, with regard to a wide range of problem-behavior outcomes and their development over time. Significant progress was made toward the goal of improving competencies of the children receiving intervention services and their parents. Compared to the control group, the intervention children improved their social-cognitive and academic skills, and their parents reduced their use of harsh discipline. These group differences also were reflected in behavioral improvements during the elementary school years and beyond. Compared with children in the control group, children in the intervention group displayed significantly less aggressive behavior at home, in the classroom, and on the playground. By the end of third grade, 37 percent of the intervention group had become free of conduct problems, in contrast with 27 percent of the control group. By the end of elementary school, 33 percent of the intervention group had a developmental trajectory of decreasing conduct problems, as compared with 27 percent of the control group. Furthermore, placement in special education by the end of elementary school was about one-fourth lower in the intervention group than in the control group.

Group differences continued through adolescence. Court records indicate that by eighth grade, 38 percent of the intervention group boys had been arrested, in contrast with 42 percent of the control group. Finally, psychiatric interviews after ninth grade indicate that the Fast Track program intervention has reduced serious conduct disorder by over a third, from 27 percent to 17 percent. These effects generalized across gender and ethnic groups, and across the wide range of child and family characteristics measured by Fast Track.

Critical Thinking

1. The success of the Fast Track program has led to its implementation in several school systems across the country, as well as in schools in Great Britain, Australia, and Canada. Would you want such a program implemented in your local school system?

2. Should the government devote significant resources to helping at-risk kids, or might the funds be better off spent on programs that provide advanced training to the academically gifted?

InfoTrac College Edition Research

To read a research study conducted within the Fast Track project, see David L. Rabiner and Patrick S. Malone, "The Impact of Tutoring on Early Reading Achievement for Children with and without Attention Problems," *Journal of Abnormal Child Psychology* 32:273–284 (2004).

SOURCES: Fast Track project overview, www.fasttrackproject.org/fasttrackoverview.htm, and Fast Track Data Center, www.fasttrackproject.org/datacenter.htm. Accessed on August 24, 2004.

---

escalate their antisocial behaviors.[32] Some may specialize in a single type of delinquent act, such as selling drugs, while others may engage in a variety of delinquent acts.

Rolf Loeber and his associates have identified three distinct paths to a delinquent career (see Figure 5.1):[33]

authority conflict pathway
Pathway to delinquent deviance that begins at an early age with stubborn behavior and leads to defiance and then to authority avoidance.

covert pathway
Pathway to a delinquent career that begins with minor underhanded behavior, leads to property damage, and eventually escalates to more serious forms of theft and fraud.

overt pathway
Pathway to a delinquent career that begins with minor aggression, leads to physical fighting, and eventually escalates to violent delinquency.

1. The **authority conflict pathway** begins at an early age with stubborn behavior. This leads to defiance (doing things one's own way, disobedience) and then to authority avoidance (staying out late, truancy, running away).

2. The **covert pathway** begins with minor, underhanded behavior (lying, shoplifting) that leads to property damage (setting nuisance fires, damaging property). This behavior eventually escalates to more serious forms of criminality, ranging from joyriding, pocket picking, larceny, and fencing to passing bad checks, using stolen credit cards, stealing cars, dealing drugs, and breaking and entering.

3. The **overt pathway** escalates to aggressive acts beginning with aggression (annoying others, bullying), leading to physical (and gang) fighting and then to violence (attacking someone, forced theft).

The Loeber research indicates that each of these paths may lead to a sustained deviant career. Some people enter two and even three paths simultaneously: They are

FIGURE 5.1
Loeber's Pathways to Crime

SOURCE: "Serious and Violent Offenders," *Juvenile Justice Bulletin*, May 1998.

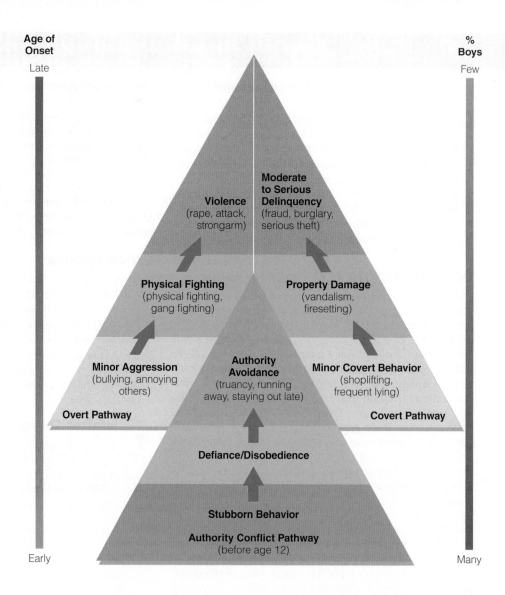

Age of Onset
Late
Early

% Boys
Few
Many

Violence (rape, attack, strongarm)

Moderate to Serious Delinquency (fraud, burglary, serious theft)

Physical Fighting (physical fighting, gang fighting)

Property Damage (vandalism, firesetting)

Minor Aggression (bullying, annoying others)

Authority Avoidance (truancy, running away, staying out late)

Minor Covert Behavior (shoplifting, frequent lying)

Overt Pathway

Covert Pathway

Defiance/Disobedience

Stubborn Behavior

Authority Conflict Pathway (before age 12)

To read about the highlights of the **Pittsburgh Youth Study,** which is directed by **Rolf Loeber,** go to www.ncjrs.org/txtfiles1/fs9995.txt. For an up-to-date list of web links, go to http://cj.wadsworth.com/siegel_jd9e.

stubborn, lie to teachers and parents, are bullies, and commit petty thefts. These adolescents are the most likely to become persistent offenders as they mature. Although some persistent offenders may specialize in one type of behavior, others engage in varied delinquent acts and antisocial behaviors as they mature. For example, they cheat on tests, bully kids in the schoolyard, take drugs, commit burglary, steal a car, and then shoplift from a store.

Some recent support for Loeber's "pathways" model was encountered by Sheila Royo Maxwell and Christopher Maxwell in their study of the career paths of young female offenders. One distinct group was made up of substance abusers who used drugs and engaged in a variety of illegal activities, including theft and prostitution, to generate capital for further drug purchases. The second group specialized in drug selling and avoided prostitution and other illegal activities.[34] The Maxwell research suggests the existence of a multitude of criminal career subgroupings with their own distinctive career paths.

Continuity of Crime and Delinquency

Another aspect of life-course theory is the continuity of delinquency: the best predictor of future criminality is past criminality. Children who are repeatedly in trouble during early adolescence will generally still be antisocial in their middle and late teens and as adults.[35] These kids are continually involved in theft offenses and aggression. As they emerge into adulthood, persisters report less emotional support, lower job satisfaction, distant peer relationships, and more psychiatric problems than those who desist.[36]

Early delinquent activity is likely to be sustained because these offenders seem to lack the social survival skills necessary to find work or to develop the interpersonal relationships needed to allow them to drop out of delinquency. Delinquency may be contagious: Kids at risk for delinquency may live in families and neighborhoods in which they are constantly exposed to deviant behavior. As they mature, having brothers, fathers, neighbors, and friends who engage in and support their activities reinforces their deviance.[37]

Gender Differences As they mature, both male and female delinquents who have early experiences with antisocial behavior are the ones most likely to be continually involved in antisocial behavior throughout the life course. Research shows that female delinquents, like male delinquents, often exhibit antisocial behavior that begins early in life and then persists through adolescence into adulthood. Girls with conduct problems at age 13 go on to experience poor school adjustment, substance use, mental health problems, and poor sexual health and behavior throughout adolescence. These delinquent girls continue to experience difficulties such as increased drug and alcohol use, psychiatric problems, higher rates of mortality, criminal behavior, insufficient parenting skills, relationship dysfunction, lower performance in academic and occupational environments, involvement with social service assistance, and adjustment difficulties as they enter young adulthood and beyond.[38]

Nonetheless, there are also some distinct gender differences in the effect. For males, the path runs from delinquency to problems at work and substance abuse. For females, antisocial behavior in youth leads to relationship problems, depression, tendency to commit suicide, and poor health in adulthood.[39] Males seem to be more deeply influenced by an early history of childhood aggression: Those who exhibited chronic physical aggression during the elementary school years exhibit the risk of continued physical violence and delinquency during adolescence. There is little evidence of any linkage between childhood physical aggression and adolescent offending among females.[40]

A famous study that investigated the path to delinquency is discussed in the following Focus on Delinquency box entitled "The Path to Delinquency."

To read more about **Farrington's findings,** go to www.criminology.fsu.edu/crimtheory/farrington95.htm. For an up-to-date list of web links, go to http://cj.wadsworth.com/siegel_jd9e.

TO QUIZ YOURSELF ON THIS MATERIAL, go to the Juvenile Delinquency 9e website.

LIFE-COURSE THEORIES

An ongoing effort has been made to track persistent offenders over their life course.[41] The early data seem to support what is already known about delinquent and delinquent career patterns: Juvenile offenders are likely to become adult criminals; early onset predicts more lasting delinquency; and chronic offenders commit a significant portion of all delinquent acts.[42] Based on these findings, criminologists have formulated a number of systematic theories that account for the onset, continuance, and desistance from delinquency.

The Social Development Model

social development model (SDM)
A developmental theory that attributes delinquent behavior patterns to childhood socialization and pro- or antisocial attachments over the life course.

In their **social development model (SDM),** Joseph Weis, Richard Catalano, J. David Hawkins, and their associates focus on the different factors affecting a child's social development over the life course.[43] According to their view, as children mature within their environment, elements of socialization control their developmental process and either insulate them from delinquency or encourage their antisocial activities. The theory has a number of important elements:

I Every child faces the risk of delinquent behavior, especially those forced to live in the poorest neighborhoods and attend substandard schools. If they are to avoid

The Path to Delinquency

One of the most important longitudinal studies tracking persistent offenders is the Cambridge Study in Delinquent Development, which has followed the offending careers of 411 London boys born in 1953. This cohort study, directed since 1982 by David Farrington, is one of the most serious attempts to isolate the factors that predict lifelong continuity of criminal behavior. The study uses self-report data as well as in-depth interviews and psychological testing. The boys have been interviewed eight times over 24 years, beginning at age 8 and continuing to age 32.

The results of the Cambridge study show that many of the same patterns found in the United States are repeated in a cross-national sample: the existence of chronic offenders, the continuity of offending, and early onset of criminal activity. Each of these patterns leads to persistent criminality.

Farrington found that the traits present in persistent offenders can be observed as early as age 8. The chronic criminal begins as a property offender, is born into a large low-income family headed by parents who have criminal records, and has delinquent older siblings. The future criminal receives poor parental supervision, including the use of harsh or erratic punishment and childrearing techniques; the parents are likely to divorce or separate. The chronic offender tends to associate with friends who are also future criminals. By age 8, the child exhibits antisocial behavior, including dishonesty and aggressiveness; at school the chronic offender tends to have low educational achievement and is restless, troublesome, hyperactive, impulsive, and often truant. After leaving school at age 18, the persistent criminal tends to take a relatively well paid but low-status job and is likely to have an erratic work history and periods of unemployment.

Farrington found that deviant behavior tends to be versatile rather than specialized. That is, the typical offender not only commits property offenses, such as theft and burglary, but also engages in violence, vandalism, drug use, excessive drinking, drunk driving, smoking, reckless driving, and sexual promiscuity—evidence of a generalized problem behavior syndrome. Chronic offenders are more likely to live away from home and have conflicts with their parents. They wear tattoos, go out most evenings, and enjoy hanging out with groups of their friends. They are much more likely than nonoffenders to get involved in fights, to carry weapons, and to use them in violent encounters. The frequency of offending reaches a peak in the teenage years (about 17 or 18) and then declines in the 20s, when offenders marry or live with a significant other.

By the 30s, the former delinquent is likely to be separated or divorced and be an absent parent. His employment record remains spotty, and he moves often between rental units. His life is still characterized by evenings out, heavy drinking, substance abuse, and more violent behavior than his contemporaries.

Because the typical offender provides the same kind of deprived and disrupted family life for his own children that he experienced, the social experiences and conditions that produce delinquency are carried on from one generation to the next. The following list summarizes the specific risk factors that Farrington associates with forming a delinquent career:

Prenatal and perinatal: Early childbearing increases the risk of such undesirable outcomes for children as low school attainment, antisocial behavior, substance use, and early sexual activity. An increased risk of offending among children of teenage mothers is associated with low income, poor housing, absent fathers, and poor childrearing methods.

Personality: Impulsiveness, hyperactivity, restlessness, and limited ability to concentrate are associated with low attainment in school and a poor ability to foresee the consequences of offending.

Intelligence and attainment: Low intelligence and poor performance in school, although important statistical predictors of offending, are difficult to disentangle from each other. One plausible explanation of the link between low intelligence and crime is its association with a poor ability to manipulate abstract concepts and to appreciate the feelings of victims.

Parental supervision and discipline: Harsh or erratic parental discipline and cold or rejecting parental attitudes have been linked to delinquency and are associated with children's lack of internal inhibitions against offending. Physical abuse by parents has been associated with an increased risk of the children themselves becoming violent offenders in later life.

Parental conflict and separation: Living in a home affected by separation or divorce is more strongly related to delinquency than when the disruption has been caused by the death of one parent. However, it may not be a "broken home" that creates an increased risk of offending

---

prosocial bonds
Socialized attachment to conventional institutions, activities, and beliefs.

the risk of antisocial behavior the child must develop and maintain **prosocial bonds.** These are developed within the context of family life, when parents routinely praise children and give them consistent, positive feedback.

Parental attachment affects a child's behavior for life, determining both school experiences and personal beliefs and values. For those with strong family relationships, the school experience will be meaningful, marked by academic success and commitment to education. Young people growing up in supportive homes are likely to develop conventional beliefs and values, become committed to conventional activities, form attachments to conventional others, and avoid delinquent entanglements.

so much as the parental conflict that leads to the separation.

Socioeconomic status: Social and economic deprivation are important predictors of antisocial behavior and crime, but low family income and poor housing are better measurements than the prestige of parents' occupations.

Delinquent friends: Delinquents tend to have delinquent friends. But it is not certain whether membership in a delinquent peer group leads to offending or whether delinquents simply gravitate toward each other's company (or both). Breaking up with delinquent friends often coincides with desisting from crime.

School influences: The prevalence of offending by pupils varies widely between secondary schools. But it is not clear how far schools themselves have an effect on delinquency (for example, by paying insufficient attention to bullying or providing too much punishment and too little praise), or whether it is simply that troublesome children tend to go to high-delinquency-rate schools.

Community influences: The risks of becoming criminally involved are higher for young people raised in disorganized inner-city areas, characterized by physical deterioration, overcrowded households, publicly subsidized renting, and high residential mobility. It is not clear, however, whether this is due to a direct influence on children, or whether environmental stress causes family adversities, which in turn cause delinquency.

NONOFFENDERS AND DESISTERS

Farrington has also identified factors that predict the discontinuity of criminal offenses. He found that people who exhibit these factors have backgrounds that put them at risk of becoming offenders; however, either they are able to remain nonoffenders, or they begin a criminal career and then later desist. The factors that protected high-risk youths from beginning criminal careers include having a somewhat shy personality, having few friends (at age 8), having nondeviant families, and being highly regarded by their mothers. Shy children with few friends avoided damaging relationships with other adolescents (members of a high-risk group) and were therefore able to avoid criminality.

WHAT CAUSED OFFENDERS TO DESIST?

Holding a relatively good job helped reduce criminal activity. Conversely, unemployment seemed to be related to the esca-

lation of theft offenses; violence and substance abuse were unaffected by unemployment. In a similar vein, getting married also helped diminish criminal activity. However, finding a spouse who was also involved in criminal activity and had a criminal record increased criminal involvement.

Physical relocation also helped some offenders desist because they were forced to sever ties with co-offenders. For this reason, leaving the city for a rural or suburban area was linked to reduced criminal activity. Although employment, marriage, and relocation helped potential offenders desist, not all desisters found success. At-risk youths who managed to avoid criminal convictions were unlikely to avoid other social problems. Rather than becoming prosperous home owners with flourishing careers, they tended to live in unkempt homes and have large debts and low-paying jobs. They were also more likely to remain single and live alone. Youths who experienced social isolation at age 8 were also found to experience it at age 32. Farrington's theory suggests that life experiences shape the direction and flow of behavior choices. He finds that while there may be continuity in offending, the factors that predict criminality at one point in the life course may not be the ones that predict criminality at another. Although most adult criminals begin their careers in childhood, life events may help some children forgo criminality as they mature.

Critical Thinking

Farrington finds that the traits present in persistent offenders can be observed as early as age 8. Should such young children be observed and monitored, even though they have not actually committed crimes? Would such monitoring create a self-fulfilling prophecy?

InfoTrac College Edition Research

Use the term "child development" as a subject guide on InfoTrac College Edition. A number of periodical articles provide information on development issues that influence behavior over the life course.

SOURCES: David Farrington, "Key Results from the First Forty Years of the Cambridge Study in Delinquent Development," in Terence Thornberry and Marvin Krohn, eds., *Taking Stock of Delinquency: An Overview of Findings from Contemporary Longitudinal Studies* (New York: Kluwer, 2002), pp. 137–185; David Farrington, "The Development of Offending and Anti-Social Behavior from Childhood: Key Findings from the Cambridge Study of Delinquent Development," *Journal of Child Psychology and Psychiatry* 36:2–36 (1995); David Farrington, *Understanding and Preventing Youth Crime* (London: Joseph Rowntree Foundation, 1996).

■ Children who cannot form prosocial bonds within their family are at risk for being exposed to deviant attitudes and behaviors (see Figure 5.2). Their ties to conventional institutions such as schools are weakened, and they are left unprotected from the lures of delinquent behavior. These youth will eventually believe that it is easy to get away with antisocial behavior and see it as "cool" and rewarding.[44]

■ Adolescents who perceive opportunities and rewards for antisocial behavior will form deep attachments to deviant peers and will become committed to a delinquent way of life. In contrast, those who perceive opportunities for prosocial

FIGURE 5.2

The Social Development Model of Antisocial Behavior

SOURCE: Adapted from Seattle Social Development Project.

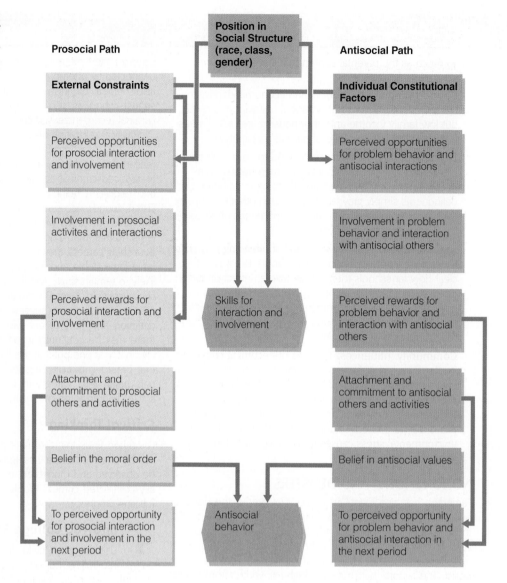

behavior will take a different path, getting involved in conventional activities and forming attachments to others who share their conventional lifestyle.

The SDM holds that commitment and attachment to conventional institutions, activities, and beliefs insulate youths from the delinquency-producing influences in their environment. They may meet peers who promote antisocial behaviors—smoking, drinking, and precocious sex. Without the proper level of bonding, adolescents can succumb to theses prodelinquency influences.[45] There has been research support for the SDM, and it is a significant example of developmental theory.[46]

Interactional Theory

Like the SDM, Terence Thornberry's **interactional theory** finds that the onset of delinquent behavior can be traced to a deterioration of the social bond during adolescence, marked by weakened attachment to parents, commitment to school, and belief in conventional values (see Figure 5.3).[47] The theory has a number of unique elements:

I Delinquency is a dynamic process that takes on different meanings and forms as a person matures.[48] During early adolescence, attachment to the family is the single most important determinant of whether a youth will adjust to conventional

To read more about the **social development model,** go to http://ojjdp.ncjrs.org/jjbulletin/9810_2/g1.html. For an up-to-date list of web links, go to http://cj.wadsworth.com/siegel_jd9e.

interactional theory
A developmental theory that attributes delinquent trajectories to mutual reinforcement between delinquents and significant others over the life course—family in early adolescence, school and friends in midadolescence, and social peers and one's own nuclear family in adulthood.

FIGURE 5.3

Overview of the Interactional
Theory of Delinquency

SOURCE: Terence Thornberry, Margaret
Farnworth, Alan Lizotte, and Susan
Stern, "A Longitudinal Examination of
the Causes and Correlates of
Delinquency," working paper No. 1,
Rochester Youth Development Study
(Albany, NY: Hindelang Criminal
Justice Research Center, 1987), p. 11.

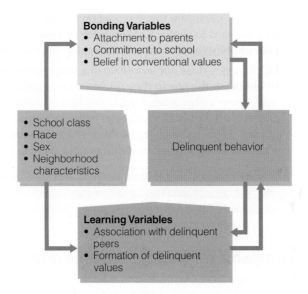

Bonding Variables
• Attachment to parents
• Commitment to school
• Belief in conventional values

• School class
• Race
• Sex
• Neighborhood
  characteristics

Delinquent behavior

Learning Variables
• Association with delinquent
  peers
• Formation of delinquent
  values

society and be shielded from delinquency. By mid-adolescence, the influence of the family is replaced by the "world of friends, school and youth culture."[49] In adulthood, a person's behavioral choices are shaped by her place in conventional society and her own nuclear family. So interactional theory finds that the root cause of delinquency and delinquency fluctuates according to a person's position in the life cycle.

▌ Delinquency is bidirectional: Weak bonds lead children to develop friendships with deviant peers and get involved in antisocial behaviors. Frequent delinquent involvement weakens bonds and makes it difficult to establish conventional relationships. By shutting the offender out of a conventional lifestyle, early criminality helps entrap him in a deviant lifestyle.[50]

▌ Delinquency-promoting factors tend to reinforce one another. Kids who go through stressful life events such as a family financial crises, death of a parent, parents' divorce, physical illness, breaking up with a boyfriend or girlfriend, changing schools, and getting into trouble with classmates at school are more likely to later get involved in antisocial behaviors and vice versa.[51]

According to the SDM, the onset of crime can be traced to a deterioration of the social bond during adolescence, marked by a weakening of attachment to parents, commitment to school, and belief in conventional values.

© Michael Newman/PhotoEdit

- Early and persistent involvement in antisocial behavior generates consequences that are hard to shake. Kids who are in trouble with the law find it difficult to later establish social bonds and develop positive social relations.

- Delinquency does not terminate in a single generation. An offender who is in trouble with the law in their adolescence is unlikely to develop the skills that will make them a nurturing parent. The lack of parental efficacy renders their own children susceptible to antisocial behaviors. It is not surprising then that delinquency seems to be intergenerational: Delinquent fathers produce delinquent sons who in turn produce delinquent grandsons.[52]

In sum, interactional theory suggests that delinquency is part of a dynamic social process and not just an outcome of that process. Although delinquents may be influenced by social forces, their behavior influences those around them in a never-ending cycle.[53]

Sampson and Laub: Age-Graded Theory

If there are various pathways to crime and delinquency, are there trails back to conformity? In an important 1993 work, *Crime in the Making,* Robert Sampson and John Laub identify **turning points** in a delinquent career.[54] Reanalyzing the original Glueck data, they found that the stability of delinquent behavior can be affected by events that occur later in life, even after a chronic delinquent career has been established. By calling their theory *age graded,* they refer to the fact that both continuity and change exist throughout the life course and that change in the direction of a person's behavior may occur at any age through new experiences or social circumstances. They agree that formal and informal social controls restrict criminality and that delinquency begins early in life and continues over the life course; they disagree that once this course is set, nothing can impede its progress.

Turning Points Sampson and Laub's most important contribution is identifying the life events that enable adult offenders to desist from delinquency. Two critical turning points are career and marriage:

- Adolescents who are at risk for delinquency can live conventional lives if they can find good jobs or achieve successful careers. Their success may hinge on a lucky break. Even those who have been in trouble with the law may turn from delinquency if employers are willing to give them a chance despite their records.

According to developmental theories, people change as they go through critical life transitions such as having a child and becoming a parent. Fifteen-month-old Brian Vides is held by his mother, Jasira Perlera, as they attend a rally March 14, 2001, at the Statehouse in Boston, in support of increased funding for teen parent families. Legislators and family advocate organizations say increased funding is necessary to reduce the level of homelessness among teen parents.

AP/Wide World Photos

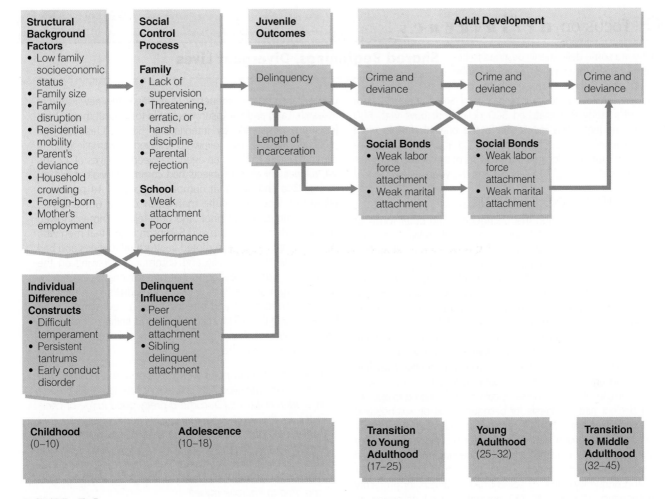

FIGURE **5.4**

Sampson and Laub's Age-Graded Theory

SOURCE: Robert Sampson and John Laub, *Crime in the Making: Pathways and Turning Points through Life* (Cambridge, MA: Harvard University Press, 1993), pp. 244–245.

Adolescents who have had significant problems with the law are also able to desist from delinquency if, as adults, they become attached to a spouse who supports and sustains them, regardless of their past.[55] Spending time in marital and family activities reduces exposure to deviant peers, which reduces the opportunity to become involved in delinquent activities.[56] People who cannot sustain secure marital relations are less likely to desist from delinquency.

social capital
Positive relations with individuals and institutions, as in a successful marriage or a successful career, that support conventional behavior and inhibit deviant behavior.

Social Capital A cornerstone of age-graded theory is the influence of **social capital** on behavior. Social scientists recognize that people build social capital—positive relations with individuals and institutions that are life sustaining. Social capital, which includes the resources accessed through interpersonal connections and relationships, is as critical as human capital (what a person or organization actually possesses) to individuals, social groups, organizations, and communities in obtaining their objectives.[57]

In the same manner that building financial capital improves the chances for economic success, building social capital supports conventional behavior and inhibits deviant behavior (see Figure 5.4).[58]

For example, a successful marriage creates social capital when it improves a person's stature, creates feelings of self-worth, and encourages others to trust the person. A successful career inhibits delinquency by creating a stake in conformity: Why commit delinquency when you are doing well at your job? The relationship is reciprocal. If people are chosen to be employees, they return the favor by doing the best job possible; if they are chosen as spouses, they blossom into devoted partners.

Shared Beginnings, Divergent Lives

Why are some delinquents destined to become persistent criminals as adults? John Laub and Robert Sampson have conducted a follow-up to their reanalysis of Sheldon and Eleanor Glueck's study that matched 500 delinquent boys with 500 nondelinquents. The individuals in the original sample were reinterviewed by the Gluecks at ages 25 and 32. Now Sampson and Laub have located the survivors of the delinquent sample, the oldest being 70 years old and the youngest 62.

PERSISTENCE AND DESISTANCE

Laub and Sampson find that delinquency and other forms of antisocial conduct in childhood are strongly related to adult delinquency and drug and alcohol abuse. Former delinquents also suffer consequences in other areas of social life, such as school, work, and family life. For example, delinquents are far less likely to finish high school than are nondelinquents and subsequently more likely to be unemployed, receive welfare, and experience separation or divorce as adults.

In their latest research, Laub and Sampson address one of the key questions posed by life-course theories: Is it possible for former delinquents to turn their lives around as adults? They find that most antisocial children do not remain antisocial as adults. For example, of men in the study cohort who survived to age 50, 24 percent had no arrests for delinquent acts of violence and property after age 17 (6 percent had no arrests for total delinquency); 48 percent had no arrests for predatory delinquency after age 25 (19 percent for total delinquency); 60 percent had no arrests for predatory delinquency after age 31 (33 percent for total delinquency); and 79 percent had no arrests for predatory delinquency after age 40 (57 percent for total delinquency). They conclude that desistance from delinquency is the norm and that most, if not all, serious delinquents desist from delinquency.

WHY DO DELINQUENTS DESIST?

Laub and Sampson's earlier research indicated that building social capital through marriage and jobs were key components of desistance from delinquency. However, in this new round of research, Laub and Sampson were able to find out more about long-term desistance by interviewing 52 men as they approached age 70. The follow-up showed a dramatic drop in criminal activity as the men aged: Between the ages of 17 and 24, 84 percent of the subjects had committed violent crimes; in their 30s and 40s, that number dropped to 14 percent; it fell to just 3 percent as the men reached their 60s and 70s. Property crimes and alcohol- and drug-related crimes showed significant decreases. Laub and Sampson found that men who desisted from crime were rooted in structural routines and had strong social ties to family and community. Drawing on the men's own words, they found that one important element for "going straight" is the "knifing off" of individuals from their immediate environment and offering them a new script for the future. Joining the military can provide this knifing-off effect, as does marriage, or changing one's residence. One former delinquent (age 69) told them:

I'd say the turning point was, number one, the Army. You get into an outfit, you had a sense of belonging, you made your friends. I think I became a pretty good judge of character. In the Army, you met some good ones, you met some foul balls. Then I met the wife. I'd say probably that would be the turning point. Got married, then naturally, kids come. So now you got to get a better job, you got to make more money. And that's how I got to the Navy Yard and tried to improve myself.

Former delinquents who "went straight" were able to put structure into their lives. Structure often led the men to disassociate from delinquent peers, reducing the opportunity to get into trouble. Getting married, for example, may limit the number of nights men can "hang with the guys." As one wife of a former delinquent said, "It is not how many beers you

---

In contrast, losing or wasting social capital increases both personal deficits and the likelihood of getting involved in delinquency. For example, moving to a new city reduces social capital by closing people off from long-term relationships.[59] Losing social capital has a cumulative effect. As kids develop more and more disadvantages, the likelihood of their entering a delinquent and criminal career increases.[60]

Testing Age-Graded Theory Several indicators support the validity of age-graded theory.[61] Research shows that children who grow up in two-parent families are more likely to have happier marriages than children whose parents were divorced or never married.[62] This finding suggests that the marriage-delinquency association may be intergenerational. If people with marital problems are more delinquency-prone, their children will also suffer a greater long-term risk of marital failure and antisocial activity.

Evidence now shows that once begun, delinquent career trajectories can be reversed if life conditions improve, an outcome predicted by age-graded theory.[63] At-risk youths who accumulate social capital in childhood (for example, by doing well in school or having a tightly knit family) are also the most likely to maintain steady work as adults. Kids who have long-term exposure to poverty will find that their involve-

have, it's who you drink with." Even multiple offenders who did time in prison were able to desist with the help of a stabilizing marriage.

Former delinquents who can turn their life around, who have acquired a degree of maturity by taking on family and work responsibilities, and who have forged new commitments are the ones most likely to make a fresh start and find new direction and meaning in life. It seems that men who desisted changed their identity as well, and this, in turn, affected their outlook and sense of maturity and responsibility. The ability to change did not reflect delinquency "specialty": violent offenders followed the same path as property offenders.

While many former delinquents desisted from delinquency, they still faced the risk of an early and untimely death. Thirteen percent ($n=62$) of the delinquent subjects, as compared to only 6 percent ($n=28$) of the nondelinquent subjects, died unnatural deaths such as violence, cirrhosis of the liver caused by alcoholism, poor self-care, or suicide. By age 65, 29 percent ($n=139$) of the delinquent and 21 percent ($n=95$) of the nondelinquent subjects had died from natural causes. Frequent delinquent involvement in adolescence and alcohol abuse were the strongest predictors of an early and unnatural death. So while many troubled youth are able to reform, their early excesses may haunt them across their lifespan.

POLICY IMPLICATIONS

Laub and Sampson find that youth problems—delinquency, substance abuse, violence, dropping out, teen pregnancy—often share common risk characteristics. Intervention strategies, therefore, should consider a broad array of antisocial, criminal, and deviant behaviors, and not limit the focus to just one subgroup or delinquency type. Because criminality and other social problems are linked, early prevention efforts that reduce delinquency will probably also reduce alcohol abuse, drunk driving, drug abuse, sexual promiscuity, and family violence. The best way to achieve these goals is through four significant life-changing events: marriage, joining the military,

getting a job, and changing one's environment or neighborhood. What appears to be important about these processes is that they all involve, to varying degrees, the following items: a knifing-off of the past from the present; new situations that provide both supervision and monitoring as well as new opportunities of social support and growth; and new situations that provide the opportunity for transforming identity. Prevention of delinquency must be a policy at all times and at all stages of life.

Critical Thinking

1. Do you believe that the factors that influenced the men in the original Glueck sample are still relevant for change—for example, a military career?

2. Would it be possible for men such as these to join the military today? Do you believe that some sort of universal service program might be beneficial and help people turn their lives around?

InfoTrac College Edition Research

Read a review of Laub and Sampson's *Crime in the Making* in Roland Chilton, "Crime in the Making: Pathways and Turning Points Through Life," *Social Forces* 74(1995):357–358. To learn more about these concepts, use "social capital" as a key term search on InfoTrac College Edition.

SOURCES: John Laub and Robert Sampson, *Shared Beginnings, Divergent Lives: Delinquent Boys to Age 70* (Cambridge, MA: Harvard University Press, 2003); John Laub and Robert Sampson, "Understanding Desistance from Delinquency" in Michael Tonry, ed., *Crime and Justice, A Review of Research* 28:1–71 (Chicago: University of Chicago Press, 2001); John Laub, "Delinquency over the Life Course," *Poverty Research News, the Newsletter of the Northwestern University/University of Chicago Joint Center for Poverty Research*, vol. 4, no. 3, May–June 2000; John Laub and George Vaillant, "Delinquency and Mortality: A 50-Year Follow-Up Study of 1,000 Delinquent and Nondelinquent Boys," *The American Journal of Psychiatry* 157:96–102 (2000).

ment in crime escalates. However, their involvement in crime will diminish if their life circumstances improve because their parents are able to escape poverty and move to more stable environments. Recent research by Ross Macmillan and his colleagues shows that children whose mothers were initially poor but escaped from poverty were no more likely to develop behavior problems than children whose mothers who were never poor. Gaining social capital then may help erase some of the damage caused by its absence.[64]

As predicted by age-graded theory, delinquent youth who enter the military, serve overseas, and receive veterans' benefits enhance their occupational status (social capital) while reducing delinquent involvement.[65] In contrast, people who are self-centered and present-oriented are less likely to accumulate social capital and more prone to commit delinquent acts.[66]

Laub and Sampson have conducted an important follow-up to their original research: finding and interviewing the survivors from the original Glueck research. Sampson and Laub have located the survivors, the oldest subject being 70 years old and the youngest 62. The results of their research are examined in the Focus on Delinquency box entitled "Shared Beginnings, Divergent Lives."

TO QUIZ YOURSELF ON THIS MATERIAL, go to the Juvenile Delinquency 9e website.

LATENT TRAIT THEORIES

latent trait
A stable feature, characteristic, property, or condition, such as defective intelligence or impulsive personality, that makes some people delinquency-prone over the life course.

In a popular 1985 book, *Delinquency and Human Nature*, two prominent social scientists, James Q. Wilson and Richard Herrnstein, argued that personal traits, such as genetic makeup, intelligence, and body build, operate in tandem with social variables such as poverty and family function. Together these factors influence people to "choose delinquency" over nondelinquent behavioral alternatives.[67]

Following their lead, David Rowe, D. Wayne Osgood, and W. Alan Nicewander proposed the concept of latent traits. Their model assumes that a number of people in the population have a personal attribute or characteristic that controls their inclination or propensity to commit delinquent acts.[68] This disposition, or **latent trait,** is either present at birth or established early in life, and it remains stable over time. Suspected latent traits include defective intelligence, impulsive personality, genetic abnormalities, the physical-chemical functioning of the brain, and environmental influences on brain function such as drugs, chemicals, and injuries.[69] Those who carry one of these latent traits are in danger of becoming career criminals; those who lack the traits have a much lower risk. Latent traits should affect the behavioral choices of all people equally, regardless of their gender or personal characteristics.[70]

According to this latent trait view, the propensity or inclination to commit delinquency is stable, but the opportunity to commit delinquency fluctuates over time. People age out of delinquency because, as they mature, there are simply fewer opportunities to commit delinquency and greater inducements to remain "straight." They may marry, have children, and obtain jobs. The former delinquents' newfound adult responsibilities leave them little time to hang with their friends, abuse substances, and get into scrapes with the law.

Assume, for example, that a stable latent trait such as low IQ causes some people to commit delinquency. Teenagers have more opportunity to commit delinquency than adults, so at every level of intelligence, adolescent delinquency rates will be higher. As they mature, however, teens with both high and low IQs will commit less delinquency because their adult responsibilities provide them with fewer delinquent opportunities. Thus, latent trait theories integrate concepts usually associated with trait theories (such as personality and temperament) and concepts associated with rational choice theories (such as delinquent opportunity and suitable targets).

While there are a number of latent trait type theories of crime and delinquency, the most well known is the General Theory of Crime.

General Theory of Crime

General Theory of Crime (GTC)
A developmental theory that modifies social control theory by integrating concepts from biosocial, psychological, routine activities, and rational choice theories.

Michael Gottfredson and Travis Hirschi's **General Theory of Crime (GTC)** modifies and redefines some of the principles articulated in Hirschi's social control theory (see Chapter 4) by integrating the concepts of control with those of biosocial, psychological, routine activities, and rational choice theories.[71]

The Act and the Offender In their General Theory of Crime, Gottfredson and Hirschi consider the delinquent offender and the delinquent act as separate concepts.

I Delinquent acts, such as robberies or burglaries, are illegal events or deeds that people engage in when they perceive them to be advantageous. For example, burglaries are typically committed by young males looking for cash, liquor, and entertainment; the delinquency provides "easy, short-term gratification."[72]

I Delinquency is rational and predictable: Kids break the law when it promises rewards with minimal threat of pain. Therefore, the threat of punishment can deter delinquency: If targets are well guarded, and guardians are present, delinquency rates will diminish.

I Delinquent offenders are predisposed to commit delinquencies. However, they are not robots who commit delinquency without restraint; their days are also filled with conventional behaviors, such as going to school, parties, concerts, and church. But given the same set of delinquent opportunities, such as having a lot of free time for mischief and living in a neighborhood with unguarded homes containing valuable merchandise, delinquency-prone people have a much higher probability of violating the law than do nondelinquents. The propensity to commit delinquent acts remains stable throughout a person's life. Change in the frequency of delinquent activity is purely a function of change in opportunity.

By recognizing that there are stable differences in people's propensity to commit delinquent acts, the GTC adds a biosocial element to the concept of social control. The biological and psychological factors that make people impulsive and delinquency-prone may be inherited or may develop through incompetent or absent parenting.

What Makes People Delinquency-Prone? What, then, causes people to become excessively delinquency-prone? Gottfredson and Hirschi attribute the tendency to commit delinquent acts to a person's level of self-control. Low self-control develops early in life and remains stable into and through adulthood.[73] People with limited self-control tend to be impulsive; they are insensitive to other people's feelings, physical (rather than mental), risk takers, shortsighted, and nonverbal.[74] They have a "here and now" orientation and refuse to work for distant goals; they lack diligence, tenacity, and persistence. Impulsive people tend to be adventuresome, active, and self-centered. As they mature, they often have unstable marriages, jobs, and friendships.[75] People lacking self-control are less likely to feel shame if they engage in deviant acts and are more likely to find them pleasurable.[76] They are also more likely to engage in dangerous behaviors such as drinking, smoking, and reckless driving; all of these behaviors are associated with criminality.[77] (See Concept Summary 5.2.)

Concept Summary 5.2
The General Theory of Crime

Impulsive Personality	Weakening of Social Bonds	Crime and Deviance
Physical	Attachment	Delinquency
Insensitive	Involvement	Smoking
Risk-taking	Commitment	Drinking
Short-sighted	Belief	Sex
Nonverbal		Crime
Low Self-Control	**Criminal Opportunity**	
Poor parenting	Gangs	
Deviant parents	Free time	
Lack of supervision	Drugs	
Active	Suitable targets	
Self-centered		

Because those with low self-control enjoy risky, exciting, or thrilling behaviors with immediate gratification, they are more likely to enjoy delinquent acts, which require stealth, agility, speed, and power, than conventional acts, which demand long-term study and cognitive and verbal skills. And, because they enjoy taking risks, they are more likely to get involved in accidents and suffer injuries than people who maintain self-control.[78] As Gottfredson and Hirschi put it, they derive satisfaction from "money without work, sex without courtship, revenge without court delays."[79] Although these acts are not illegal, they too provide immediate, short-term gratification. Exhibit 5.2 lists the elements of impulsivity, or low self-control.

Gottfredson and Hirschi trace the root cause of poor self-control to inadequate childrearing practices. Parents who are unwilling or unable to monitor a child's behavior, to recognize deviant behavior when it occurs, or to punish that behavior will

EXHIBIT 5.2

The Elements of Impulsivity: Signs that a Person Has Low Self-Control

- Insensitive
- Physical
- Shortsighted
- Nonverbal
- Here-and-now orientation
- Unstable social relations
- Enjoys deviant behaviors
- Risk taker
- Refuses to work for distant goals

- Lacks diligence
- Lacks tenacity
- Adventuresome
- Self-centered
- Shameless
- Imprudent
- Lacks cognitive and verbal skills
- Enjoys danger and excitement

produce children who lack self-control. Children who are not attached to their parents, who are poorly supervised, and whose parents are delinquent or deviant themselves are the most likely to develop poor self-control. In a sense, lack of self-control occurs naturally when steps are not taken to stop its development.[80] It comes as no shock to life-course theorists when research shows that antisocial behavior runs in families and that having delinquent relatives is a significant predictor of future misbehaviors.[81]

Self-Control and Delinquency Gottfredson and Hirschi claim that self-control theory can explain all varieties of delinquent behavior and all the social and behavioral correlates of delinquency. That is, such widely disparate delinquent acts such as burglary, robbery, embezzlement, drug dealing, murder, rape, and running away from home all stem from a deficiency of self-control. Likewise, gender, racial, and ecological differences in delinquency rates can be explained by discrepancies in self-control: If male delinquency rates are higher than female delinquency rates it is because males have lower levels of self-control than females.

Supporting Evidence for the GTC Following the publication of the General Theory of Crime, dozens of research efforts tested the validity of Gottfredson and Hirschi's theoretical views. One approach involved identifying indicators of impulsiveness and self-control to determine whether scales measuring these factors correlate with measures of delinquent activity. A number of studies conducted both in the United States and abroad have successfully showed this type of association.[82] Some of the most important findings are summarized in Exhibit 5.3.

Analyzing the GTC

By integrating the concepts of socialization and criminality, Gottfredson and Hirschi help explain why some people who lack self-control can escape criminality, and, conversely, why some people who have self-control might not escape criminality. People who are at risk because they have impulsive personalities may forgo delinquent careers because there are no opportunities to commit delinquency; instead they may find other outlets for their impulsive personalities. In contrast, if the opportunity is strong enough, even people with relatively strong self-control may be tempted to violate the law; the incentives to commit delinquency may overwhelm self-control. Integrating delinquent propensity and delinquent opportunity can explain why some children enter into chronic offending while others living in similar environments are able to resist delinquent activity.

Although the General Theory of Crime seems persuasive, several questions and criticisms remain unanswered. Among the most important are the following:

- *Circular reasoning.* Some critics argue that the theory involves circular reasoning. How do we know when people are impulsive? When they do commit delinquen-

EXHIBIT **5.3**

Empirical Evidence Supporting the General Theory of Crime

- Offenders lacking in self-control commit a garden variety of delinquent acts.[1]
- More mature and experienced criminals become more specialized in their choice of delinquency (e.g., robbers, burglars, drug dealers).[2]
- Male and female drunk drivers are impulsive individuals who manifest low self-control.[3]
- Repeat violent offenders are more impulsive than their less violent peers.[4]
- Incarcerated youth enjoy risk-taking behavior and hold values and attitudes that suggest impulsivity.[5]
- Kids who take drugs and commit delinquency are impulsive and enjoy engaging in risky behaviors.[6]
- Measures of self-control can predict deviant and antisocial behavior across age groups ranging from teens to adults age 50.[7]
- People who commit white-collar and workplace delinquency have lower levels of self-control than nonoffenders.[8]
- Gang members have lower levels of self-control than the general population; gang members report lower levels of parental management, a factor associated with lower self-control.[9]

- Low self-control shapes perceptions of delinquent opportunity and consequently conditions the decision to commit delinquent acts.[10]
- People who lack self-control expect to commit delinquency in the future.[11]
- Kids whose problems develop early in life are the most resistant to change in treatment and rehabilitation programs.[12]
- Gender differences in self-control are responsible for delinquency rate differences. Females who lack self-control are as delinquency-prone as males with similar personalities.[13]
- Parents who manage their children's behavior increase their self-control, which helps reduce their delinquent activities.[14]
- Having parents (or stepparents) available to control behavior may reduce the opportunity to commit delinquency.[15]
- Victims have lower self-control than non-victims. Impulsivity predicts both the likelihood that a person will engage in delinquent behavior and the likelihood that the person will become a victim of delinquency.[16]
- Low self-control has been significantly related to antisocial behavior in other cultures and nations.[17]

NOTES

1. Xiaogang Deng and Lening Zhang, "Correlates of Self-Control: An Empirical Test of Self-Control Theory," *Journal of Delinquency and Justice* 21:89–103 (1998).
2. Alex Piquero, Raymond Paternoster, Paul Mazeroole, Robert Brame, and Charles Dean, "Onset Age and Offense Specialization," *Journal of Research in Delinquency and Delinquency* 36:275–299 (1999).
3. Peter Muris and Cor Meesters "The Validity of Attention Deficit Hyperactivity and Hyperkinetic Disorder Symptom Domains in Nonclinical Dutch Children," *Journal of Clinical Child & Adolescent Psychology* 32:460–466 (2003); Carl Keane, Paul Maxim, and James Teevan, "Drinking and Driving, Self-Control, and Gender: Testing a General Theory of Delinquency," *Journal of Research in Delinquency and Delinquency* 30:30–46 (1993).
4. Judith DeJong, Matti Virkkunen, and Marku Linnoila, "Factors Associated with Recidivism in a Delinquent Population," *Journal of Nervous and Mental Disease* 180:543–550 (1992).
5. David Cantor, "Drug Involvement and Offending Among Incarcerated Juveniles," paper presented at the annual meeting of the American Society of Criminology, Boston, November 1995.
6. David Brownfield and Ann Marie Sorenson, "Self-Control and Juvenile Delinquency: Theoretical Issues and an Empirical Assessment of Selected Elements of a General Theory of Delinquency," *Deviant Behavior* 14:243–264 (1993); John Cochran, Peter Wood, and Bruce Arneklev, "Is the Religiosity-Delinquency Relationship Spurious? A Test of Arousal and Social Control Theories," *Journal of Research in Delinquency and Delinquency* 31:92–123 (1994).
7. Velmer Burton, T. David Evans, Francis Cullen, Kathleen Olivares, and R. Gregory Dunaway, "Age, Self-Control, and Adults' Offending Behaviors: A Research Note Assessing a General Theory of Delinquency," *Journal of Delinquent Justice* 27:45–54 (1999); John Gibbs and Dennis Giever, "Self-Control and Its Manifestations Among University Students: An Empirical Test of Gottfredson and Hirschi's General Theory," *Justice Quarterly* 12:231–255 (1995).

8. Carey Herbert, "The Implications of Self-Control Theory for Workplace Offending," paper presented at the annual meeting of the American Society of Criminology, San Diego, 1997.
9. Dennis Giever, Dana Lynskey, and Danette Monnet, "Gottfredson and Hirschi's General Theory of Delinquency and Youth Gangs: An Empirical Test on a Sample of Middle School Youth," paper presented at the annual meeting of the American Society of Criminology, San Diego, 1997.
10. Douglas Longshore, Susan Turner, and Judith Stein, "Self-Control in a Delinquent Sample: An Examination of Construct Validity," *Criminology* 34:209–228 (1996).
11. Deng and Zhang, "Correlates of Self-Control: An Empirical Test of Self-Control Theory."
12. Linda Pagani, Richard Tremblay, Frank Vitaro, and Sophie Parent, "Does Preschool Help Prevent Delinquency in Boys with a History of Perinatal Complications?" *Criminology* 36:245–268 (1998).
13. Velmer Burton, Francis Cullen, T. David Evans, Leanne Fiftal Alarid, and R. Gregory Dunaway, "Gender, Self-Control, and Delinquency," *Journal of Research in Crime and Delinquency* 35:123–147 (1998).
14. John Gibbs, Dennis Giever, and Jamie Martin, "Parental Management and Self-Control: An Empirical Test of Gottfredson and Hirschi's General Theory," *Journal of Research in Crime and Delinquency* 35:40–70 (1998).
15. Vic Bumphus and James Anderson, "Family Structure and Race in a Sample of Offenders," *Journal of Delinquent Justice* 27:309–320 (1999).
16. Christopher Schreck, "Delinquent Victimization and Low Self-Control: An Extension and Test of a General Theory of Delinquency," *Justice Quarterly* 16:633–654 (1999).
17. Alexander Vazsonyi, Lloyd Pickering, Marianne Junger, and Dick Hessing, "An Empirical Test of a General Theory of Delinquency: A Four-Nation Comparative Study of Self-Control and the Prediction of Deviance," *Journal of Research in Crime and Delinquency* 38:91–131 (2001).

cies, are all criminals impulsive? Of course, or else they would not have broken the law![83]

- *Personality disorder.* It is possible that a lack of self-control is merely a symptom of some broader, underlying personality disorder, such as an antisocial personality, which produces delinquency. Other personality traits such as low self-direction (the tendency not to act in one's long-term benefit) may be a better predictor of criminality than impulsivity or lack of self-control.[84]

■ *Ecological/individual differences.* The GTC also fails to address individual and ecological patterns in the delinquency rate. For example, if delinquency rates are higher in Los Angeles than in Albany, New York, can it be assumed that residents of Los Angeles are more impulsive than residents of Albany? Gottfredson and Hirschi might argue that there are more delinquent opportunities in L.A., hence the delinquency rate difference.

■ *Racial and gender differences.* Although distinct gender differences in the delinquency rate exist, there is little evidence that males are more impulsive than females.[85] The relationship between self-control and delinquency seems to be different for males and females and the theory predicts no such difference should occur.[86] Similarly, Gottfredson and Hirschi explain racial differences in the delinquency rate as a failure of childrearing practices in the African American community.[87] In so doing, they overlook issues of institutional racism, poverty, and relative deprivation, which have been shown to have a significant impact on delinquency rate differentials.

■ *People change.* The GTC assumes that delinquent propensity does not change; opportunities change. A number of research efforts show that factors that help control delinquent behavior, such as peer relations and school performance, vary over time. The social influences, which are dominant in early adolescence, such as the peer group, may fade and be replaced by others, such as the nuclear family, in adulthood.[88] Also, as people mature, they may be better able to control their impulsive behavior.[89] These findings contradict the GTC, which assumes that levels of self-control and therefore delinquent propensity are constant and independent of personal relationships.

■ *Modest relationship.* Some research results support the proposition that self-control is a causal factor in delinquent and other forms of deviant behavior, but that the association is quite modest.[90] There seems to be only modest association between measures of self-control and imprudent or risk-taking behaviors.[91] Low self-control alone cannot predict the onset of a delinquent or deviant career.

If delinquency experts are able to understand the developmental influences on behavior they may be better able to design multidimensional strategies for prevention and treatment. Intervention may occur either before kids start down the path to delinquency or after they have become involved in law-violating behavior. Here, an instructor introduces a recovering teen addict in a drug prevention class at the Orange County Youth Guidance Center in Santa Ana, California.

I **Cross-cultural differences.** There is some evidence that law violators in other countries do not lack self-control, indicating that the GTC may be culturally limited.[92] Behavior that may be considered imprudent in one culture may be socially acceptable in another and therefore cannot be viewed as lack of self-control.[93]

I **Different classes of criminals.** As you may recall, Moffitt has identified two classes of criminals—adolescent-limited and life-course persistent.[94] Other researchers have found that there may be different criminal paths or trajectories. People offend at a different pace, commit different kinds of crimes, and are influenced by different external forces.[95] For example, most criminals tend to be "generalists" who engage in a garden variety of criminal acts. However, people who commit violent crimes may be different than nonviolent offenders and maintain a unique set of personality traits and problem behaviors.[96]

Although questions like these remain, the strength of the general theory lies in its scope and breadth. It attempts to explain all forms of delinquency and deviance, from lower-class gang delinquency to sexual harassment in the business community.[97] By integrating concepts of delinquent choice, delinquent opportunity, socialization, and personality, Gottfredson and Hirschi make a plausible argument that all deviant behaviors may originate at the same source. Continued efforts are needed to test the GTC and establish the validity of its core concepts. It remains one of the key developments of modern criminological theory.

TO QUIZ YOURSELF ON THIS MATERIAL, go to the Juvenile Delinquency 9e website.

EVALUATING THE DEVELOPMENTAL VIEW

The developmental view is that a delinquent career must be understood as a passage along which people travel, that it has a beginning and an end, and that events and life circumstances influence the journey. The factors that affect a delinquent career may include structural factors, such as income and status; socialization factors, such as family and peer relations; biological factors, such as size and strength; psychological factors, including intelligence and personality; and opportunity factors, such as free time, inadequate police protection, and a supply of easily stolen merchandise.

Life-course theories emphasize the influence of changing interpersonal and structural factors (that is, people change along with the world they live in). Latent trait theories place more emphasis on the fact that behavior is linked less to personal change than to changes in the surrounding world.

These perspectives differ in their view of human development. Do people constantly change, as life-course theories suggest, or are they more stable, constant, and changeless, as the latent trait view indicates? Are the factors that produce criminality different at each stage of life, as the life-course view suggests, or does a master trait such as impulsivity or self-control steer the course of human behavior?

It is also possible that these two positions are not mutually exclusive and each may make a notable contribution to understanding the onset and continuity of a delinquent career. For example, recent research by Bradley Entner Wright and his associates found evidence supporting both latent trait and life-course theories.[98] Their research, conducted with subjects in New Zealand, indicates that low self-control in childhood predicts disrupted social bonds and delinquent offending later in life, a finding that supports latent trait theory. They also found that maintaining positive social bonds helps reduce criminality and that maintaining prosocial bonds could even counteract the effect of low self-control. Latent traits are an important influence on delinquency, but Wright's findings indicate that social relationships that form later in life appear to influence delinquent behavior "above and beyond" individuals' preexisting characteristics.[99] This finding may reflect the fact that there are two classes of criminals: a less serious group who are influenced by life events, and a more chronic group whose latent traits insulate them from any positive prosocial relationships.[100]

Summary

- Life-course theories argue that events that take place over the life course influence delinquent choices.

- The cause of delinquency constantly changes as people mature. At first, the nuclear family influences behavior; during adolescence, the peer group dominates; in adulthood, marriage and career are critical.

- There are a variety of pathways to delinquency: some kids are sneaky, others hostile, and still others defiant.

- Delinquency may be part of a variety of social problems, including mental health, physical, and interpersonal troubles.

- The social development model finds that living in a disorganized area helps weaken social bonds and sets people off on a delinquent path.

- According to interactional theory, delinquency influences social relations, which in turn influences delinquency; the relationship is interactive. The sources of delinquency evolve over time.

- Sampson and Laub's age-graded theory holds that the social sources of behavior change over the life course. People who develop social capital are best able to avoid antisocial entanglements. There are important life events or turning points that enable adult offenders to desist from delinquency. Among the most important are getting married and serving in the military.

- Latent trait theories hold that some underlying condition present at birth or soon after controls behavior. Suspect traits include low IQ, impulsivity, and personality structure. This underlying trait explains the continuity of offending because, once present, it remains with a person throughout his or her life.

- The General Theory of Crime, developed by Gottfredson and Hirschi, integrates choice theory concepts. People with latent traits choose delinquency over nondelinquency; the opportunity for delinquency mediates their choice.

Key Terms

developmental theory, p. 143
life-course theory, p. 144
adolescent-limited, p. 147
life-course persister, p. 147
pseudomaturity, p. 147
problem behavior syndrome (PBS), p. 147

authority conflict pathway, p. 149
covert pathway, p. 149
overt pathway, p. 149
social development model (SDM), p. 151
prosocial bonds, p. 152
interactional theory, p. 154

turning points, p. 156
social capital, p. 157
latent trait, p. 160
General Theory of Crime (GTC), p. 160

Questions for Discussion

1. Do you consider yourself the holder of "social capital"? If so, what form does it take?

2. A person gets a 1600 on the SAT. Without knowing this person, what personal, family, and social characteristics do you think he or she must have? Another person becomes a serial killer. Without knowing this person, what personal, family, and social characteristics must he or she have? If "bad behavior" is explained by multiple problems, is "good behavior" explained by multiple strengths?

3. Do you believe there is a latent trait that makes a person delinquency-prone, or is delinquency a function of environment and socialization?

4. Do you agree with Loeber's multiple pathway model? Do you know people who have traveled down those paths?

Viewpoint

Luis Francisco is the leader of the Almighty Latin Kings and Queens Nation. He was convicted of murder in 1998 and sentenced to life imprisonment plus 45 years. Luis Francisco's life has been filled with displacement, poverty, and chronic predatory delinquency. The son of a prostitute in Havana, at the age of 9 he was sent to prison for robbery. He had trouble in school, and teachers described him as having attention problems; he dropped out in the seventh grade. On his 19th birthday in 1980, he immigrated to the United States and soon after became a gang member in Chicago, where he joined the Latin Kings. After moving to the Bronx, he shot and killed his girlfriend in 1981. He fled to Chicago and was not apprehended until 1984. Sentenced to nine years for second-degree manslaughter, Luis Francisco ended up in a New York prison, where he started a New York prison chapter of the Latin Kings. As King Blood, Inka, First Supreme Crown, Francisco ruled the 2,000 Latin Kings in and out of prison. Disciplinary troubles erupted when some Kings were found stealing from the organization. Infuriated, King Blood wrote to his street lieutenants and ordered

their termination. Federal authorities, who had been monitoring Francisco's mail, arrested 35 Latin Kings. The other 34 pled guilty; only Francisco insisted on a trial, where he was found guilty of conspiracy to commit murder.

I Explain Luis's behavior patterns from a developmental perspective.

I How would a latent trait theorist explain his escalating delinquent activities?

Doing Research on the Web

The Seattle Social Development Project uses the Social Development model as a cornerstone for their treatment programs. You can visit their website (accessed on August 24, 2004) at

http://depts.washington.edu/ssdp/

The Life History Studies Program at the University of Pittsburgh is a longitudinal study designed to test the

principles of life-course theory. Read more about it (site accessed on October 11, 2004) at

www.wpic.pitt.edu/research/famhist/

You might also want to read some of the highlights of the Rochester Youth Study, another longitudinal study of the delinquent life course (site accessed on August 24, 2004):

www.ncjrs.org/pdffiles1/fs99103.pdf

Notes

1. Marvin Krohn, Alan Lizotte, and Cynthia Perez, "The Interrelationship Between Substance Use and Precocious Transitions to Adult Sexuality," *Journal of Health and Social Behavior* 38:87–103 (1997), at p. 88.

2. Peggy Giordano, Stephen Cernkovich, and Jennifer Rudolph "Gender, Delinquency, and Desistance: Toward a Theory of Cognitive Transformation?" *American Journal of Sociology* 107:990–1064 (2002).

3. John Hagan and Holly Foster, "S/He's a Rebel: Toward a Sequential Stress Theory of Delinquency and Gendered Pathways to Disadvantage in Emerging Adulthood," *Social Forces* 82:53–86 (2003).

4. See Sheldon Glueck and Eleanor Glueck, *500 Delinquent Careers* (New York: Knopf, 1930); Sheldon Glueck and Eleanor Glueck, *One Thousand Juvenile Delinquents* (Cambridge, MA: Harvard University Press, 1934); Sheldon Glueck and Eleanor Glueck, *Predicting Delinquency and Delinquency* (Cambridge, MA: Harvard University Press, 1967), pp. 82–83.

5. Sheldon Glueck and Eleanor Glueck, *Unraveling Juvenile Delinquency* (Cambridge, MA: Harvard University Press, 1950).

6. Ibid., p. 48.

7. G. R. Patterson, L. Crosby, and S. Vuchinich, "Predicting Risk for Early Police Arrest," *Journal of Quantitative Criminology* 8:335–355 (1992); Rolf Loeber, Magda Stouthamer-Loeber, Welmoet Van Kammen, and David Farrington, "Initiation, Escalation, and Desistance in Juvenile Offending and Their Correlates," *Journal of Criminal Law and Criminology* 82:36–82 (1991).

8. Paul Mazerolle, "Delinquent Definitions and Participation Age: Assessing the Invariance Hypothesis," *Studies on Crime and Crime Prevention* 6:151–168 (1997).

9. Raymond Paternoster, Charles Dean, Alex Piquero, Paul Mazerolle, and Robert Brame, "Generality, Continuity, and Change in Offending," *Journal of Quantitative Criminology* 13:231–266 (1997).

10. Alex R. Piquero and He Len Chung, "On the Relationships between Gender, Early Onset, and the Seriousness of Offending," *Journal of Delinquent Justice* 29:189–206 (2001); David Nurco, Timothy Kinlock, and Mitchell Balter, "The Severity of Preaddiction Criminal Behavior among Urban, Male Narcotic Addicts and Two Nonaddicted Control Groups," *Journal of Research in Crime and Delinquency* 30:293–316 (1993).

11. Rolf Loeber and David Farrington, "Young Children Who Commit Crime: Epidemiology, Developmental Origins, Risk Factors, Early Interventions, and Policy Implications," *Development and Psychopathology* 12:737–762 (2000).

12. Ick-Joong Chung, Karl G. Hill, J. David Hawkins, Lewayne Gilchrist, and Daniel Nagin, "Childhood Predictors of Offense Trajectories," *Journal of Research in Delinquency & Delinquency* 39:60–91 (2002).

13. Elaine Eggleston and John Laub, "The Onset of Adult Offending: A Neglected Dimension of the Delinquent Career," *Journal of Delinquent Justice* 30:603–622 (2002).

14. Ronald Simons, Chyi-In Wu, Rand Conger, and Frederick Lorenz, "Two Routes to Delinquency: Differences Between Early and Later Starters in the Impact of Parenting and Deviant Careers," *Criminology* 32:247–275 (1994).

15. Alex R. Piquero, Robert Brame, Paul Mazerolle, and Rudy Haapanen, "Crime in Emerging Adulthood," *Criminology* 40:137–169 (2002).

16. Ronald Prinz and Suzanne Kerns, "Early Substance Use by Juvenile Offenders," *Child Psychiatry & Human Development* 33:263–268 (2003).

17. Terrie Moffitt, "Natural Histories of Delinquency," in *Cross-National Longitudinal Research on Human Development and Delinquent Behavior*, Elmar Weitekamp and Hans-Jurgen Kerner, eds. (Dordrecht, Netherlands: Kluwer, 1994), pp. 3–65.

18. Alex Piquero and Timothy Brezina, "Testing Moffitt's Account of Adolescent-Limited Delinquency," *Criminology* 39:353–370 (2001).

19. Amy D'Unger, Kenneth Land, Patricia McCall, and Daniel Nagin, "How Many Latent Classes of Delinquent/Delinquent Careers? Results from Mixed Poisson Regression Analyses," *American Journal of Sociology* 103:1593–1630 (1998).

20. Michael Newcomb, "Pseudomaturity Among Adolescents: Construct Validation, Sex Differences, and Associations in Adulthood," *Journal of Drug Issues* 26:477–504 (1996).

21. Andrea Donker, Wilma Smeenk, Peter van der Laan, and Frank Verhulst, "Individual Stability of Antisocial Behavior from Childhood to Adulthood: Testing the Stability Postulate of Moffitt's Developmental Theory," *Criminology* 41:593–609 (2003).

22. Robert Vermeiren, "Psychopathology and Delinquency in Adolescents: A Descriptive and Developmental Perspective," *Clinical Psychology Review* 23:277–318 (2003).

23. Magda Stouthamer-Loeber and Evelyn Wei, "The Precursors of Young Fatherhood and Its Effect on Delinquency of Teenage Males," *Journal of Adolescent Health* 22:56–65 (1998); Richard Jessor, John Donovan, and Francis Costa, *Beyond Adolescence: Problem Behavior and Young Adult Development* (New York: Cambridge University Press, 1991).

24. Krohn, Lizotte, and Perez, "The Interrelationship Between Substance Use and Precocious Transitions to Adult Sexuality," p. 88; Richard Jessor, "Risk Behavior in Adolescence: A Psychosocial Framework for Understanding and Action," in *Adolescents at Risk: Medical and Social Perspectives*, D.E. Rogers and E. Ginzburg, eds. (Boulder, CO: Westview, 1992).

25. Gina Wingood, Ralph DiClemente, Rick Crosby, Kathy Harrington, Susan Davies, and Edward Hook, III, "Gang Involvement and the Health of African American Female Adolescents," *Pediatrics* 110:57 (2002).

26. David Husted, Nathan Shapira, and Martin Lazoritz, "Adolescent Gambling, Substance Use and Other Delinquent Behavior" *Psychiatric Times* 20:52–55 (2003).

27. Richard Dembo and James Schmeidler, "A Classification of High-Risk Youths," *Crime & Delinquency* 49:201–230 (2003).

28. Ick-Joong Chung, J. David Hawkins, Lewayne Gilchrist, Karl Hill, and Daniel Nagin, "Identifying and Predicting Offending Trajectories among Poor Children," *Social Service Review* 76:663–687 (2002).

29. Vladislav Ruchkin, Mary Schwab-Stone, Roman Koposov, Robert Vermeiren, and Robert King "Suicidal Ideations and Attempts in Juvenile Delinquents," *Child Psychology & Psychiatry & Allied Disciplines* 44:1058–1067 (2003).

30. Krohn, Lizotte, and Perez, "The Interrelationship Between Substance Use and Precocious Transitions to Adult Sexuality," p. 88; Richard Jessor, "Risk Behavior in Adolescence: A Psychosocial Framework for Understanding and Action."

31. Deborah Capaldi and Gerald Patterson, "Can Violent Offenders Be Distinguished from Frequent Offenders: Prediction from Childhood to Adolescence," *Journal of Research in Delinquency and Delinquency* 33:206–231 (1996); D. Wayne Osgood, "The Covariation among Adolescent Problem Behaviors," paper presented at the annual meeting of the American Society of Criminology, Baltimore, November 1990.

32. Margit Wiesner and Deborah Capaldi, "Relations of Childhood and Adolescent Factors to Offending Trajectories of Young Men," *Journal of Research in Delinquency and Delinquency* 40:231–262 (2003).

33. Rolf Loeber, Phen Wung, Kate Keenan, Bruce Giroux, Magda Stouthamer-Loeber, Wemoet Van Kammen, and Barbara Maughan, "Developmental Pathways in Disruptive Behavior," *Development and Psychopathology* 5:101–132 (1993).

34. Sheila Royo Maxwell and Christopher Maxwell, "Examining the 'Criminal Careers' of Prostitutes within the Nexus of Drug Use, Drug Selling, and Other Illicit Activities," *Criminology* 38:787–809 (2000).

35. Mark Lipsey and James Derzon, "Predictors of Violent or Serious Delinquency in Adolescence and Early Adulthood: A Synthesis of Longitudinal Research," in *Serious and Violent Juvenile Offenders: Risk Factors and Successful Interventions*, Rolf Loeber and David Farrington, eds. (Thousand Oaks, CA: Sage Publications, 1998).

36. Glenn Clingempeel and Scott Henggeler, "Aggressive Juvenile Offenders Transitioning into Emerging Adulthood: Factors Discriminating Persistors and Desistors," *American Journal of Orthopsychiatry* 73:310–323 (2003).

37. Marshall Jones and Donald Jones, "The Contagious Nature of Antisocial Behavior," *Criminology* 38:25–46 (2000).

38. Holly Hartwig and Jane Myers, "A Different Approach: Applying a Wellness Paradigm to Adolescent Female Delinquents and Offenders," *Journal of Mental Health Counseling* 25:57–76 (2003).

39. Terrie Moffitt, Avshalom Caspi, Michael Rutter, and Phil Silva, *Sex Differences in Antisocial Behavior: Conduct Disorder, Delinquency, and Violence in the Dunedin Longitudinal Study* (London, England: Cambridge University Press, 2001).

40. Lisa Broidy, Richard Tremblay, Bobby Brame, David Fergusson, John Horwood, Robert Laird, Terrie Moffitt, Daniel Nagin, John Bates, Kenneth Dodge, Rolf Loeber, Donald Lynam, Gregory Pettit, and Frank Vitaro, "Developmental Trajectories of Childhood Disruptive Behaviors and Adolescent Delinquency: A Six-Site, Cross-National Study," *Developmental Psychology* 39:222–245 (2003).

41. See, for example, the Rochester Youth Development Study, Hindelang Delinquent Justice Research Center, 135 Western Avenue, Albany, New York 12222.

42. David Farrington, "The Development of Offending and Antisocial Behavior from Childhood to Adulthood," paper presented at the Congress on Rethinking Delinquency, University of Minho, Braga, Portugal, July 1992.

43. Joseph Weis and J. David Hawkins, *Reports of the National Juvenile Assessment Centers: Preventing Delinquency* (Washington, DC: U.S. Department of Justice, 1981); Joseph Weis and John Sederstrom, *Reports of the National Juvenile Justice Assessment Centers: The Prevention of Serious Delinquency: What to Do* (Washington, DC: U.S. Department of Justice, 1981).

44. Bu Huang, Rick Kosterman, Richard Catalano, J. David Hawkins, and Robert Abbott, "Modeling Mediation in the Etiology of Violent Behavior in Adolescence: A Test of the Social Development Model," *Criminology* 39:75–107 (2001).

45. Todd Herrenkohl, Bu Huang, Rick Kosterman, J. David Hawkins, Richard Catalano, and Brian Smith, "A Comparison of Social Development Processes Leading to Violent Behavior in Late Adolescence for Childhood

46. Kenneth Laundra, Gary Kiger, and Stephen Bahr, "A Social Development Model of Serious Delinquency: Examining Gender Differences," *Journal of Primary Prevention* 22:389–407 (1993).

47. Terence Thornberry, "Toward an Interactional Theory of Delinquency," *Criminology* 25:863–891 (1987).

48. Ibid.

49. Ibid., p. 863.

50. Terence Thornberry and Marvin Krohn, "The Development of Delinquency: An Interactional Perspective" in Susan White, ed., *Handbook of Youth and Justice* (New York: Plenum, 2001), pp. 289–305.

51. Kee Jeong Kim, Rand Conger, Glen Elder, Jr., and Frederick Lorenz, "Reciprocal Influences between Stressful Life Events and Adolescent Internalizing and Externalizing Problems," *Child Development* 74:127–143 (2003).

52. Terence Thornberry, Adrienne Freeman-Gallant, Alan Lizotte, Marvin Krohn, and Carolyn Smith. "Linked Lives: The Intergenerational Transmission of Antisocial Behavior," *Journal of Abnormal Child Psychology* 31:171–185 (2003).

53. Terence Thornberry, Alan Lizotte, Marvin Krohn, Margaret Farnworth, and Sung Joon Jang, *Delinquent Peers, Beliefs, and Delinquent Behavior: A Longitudinal Test of Interactional Theory*, working paper no. 6, rev., Rochester Youth Development Study (Albany, NY: Hindelang Delinquent Justice Research Center, 1992), pp. 628–629.

54. Robert Sampson and John Laub, *Crime in the Making: Pathways and Turning Points Through Life* (Cambridge, MA: Harvard University Press, 1993); John Laub and Robert Sampson, "Turning Points in the Life Course: Why Change Matters to the Study of Delinquency," paper presented at the annual meeting of the American Society of Criminology, New Orleans, November 1992.

55. Terri Orbuch, James House, Richard Mero, and Pamela Webster, "Marital Quality over the Life Course," *Social Psychology Quarterly* 59:162–171 (1996); Lee Lillard and Linda Waite, "'Til Death Do Us Part: Marital Disruption and Mortality," *American Journal of Sociology* 100:1131–1156 (1995).

56. Mark Warr, "Life-Course Transitions and Desistance from Delinquency," *Criminology* 36:183–216 (1998).

57. Nan Lin, *Social Capital: A Theory of Social Structure and Action* (Cambridge, UK: Cambridge University Press, 2002).

58. Sampson and Laub, *Crime in the Making*, p. 249.

59. John Hagan, Ross MacMillan, and Blair Wheaton, "New Kid in Town: Social Capital and the Life Course Effects of Family Migration on Children," *American Sociological Review* 61:368–385 (1996).

60. Robert Sampson and John Laub. "A Life-Course Theory of Cumulative Disadvantage and the Stability of Delinquency," in Terence Thornberry, ed., *Developmental Theories of Delinquency and Delinquency* (Somerset, NJ: Transaction Publishing, 1997), pp. 138–62.

61. Raymond Paternoster and Robert Brame, "Multiple Routes to Delinquency? A Test of Developmental and General Theories of Delinquency," *Criminology* 35:49–84 (1997).

62. Pamela Webster, Terri Orbuch, and James House, "Effects of Childhood Family Background on Adult Marital Quality and Perceived Stability," *American Journal of Sociology* 101:404–432 (1995).

63. Robert Hoge, D. A. Andrews, and Alan Leschied, "An Investigation of Risk and Protective Factors in a Sample of Youthful Offenders," *Journal of Child Psychology and Psychiatry* 37:419–424 (1996).

64. Ross Macmillan, Barbara J. McMorris, and Candace Kruttschnitt, "Linked Lives: Stability and Change in Maternal Circumstances and Trajectories of Antisocial Behavior in Children," *Child Development* 75:205–220 (2004).

65. Robert Sampson and John Laub, "Socioeconomic Achievement in the Life Course of Disadvantaged Men: Military Service as a Turning Point, circa 1940–1965," *American Sociological Review* 61:347–367 (1996).

66. Daniel Nagin and Raymond Paternoster, "Personal Capital and Social Control: The Deterrence Implications of a Theory of Delinquent Offending," *Criminology* 32:581–606 (1994).

67. James Q. Wilson and Richard Herrnstein, *Delinquency and Human Nature* (New York: Simon and Schuster, 1985).

68. David Rowe, D. Wayne Osgood, and W. Alan Nicewander, "A Latent Trait Approach to Unifying Delinquent Careers," *Criminology* 28:237–270 (1990).

69. Lee Ellis, "Neurohormonal Bases of Varying Tendencies to Learn Delinquent and Delinquent Behavior," in *Behavioral Approaches to Delinquency and Delinquency*, E. Morris and C. Braukmann, eds. (New York: Plenum, 1988), pp. 499–518.

70. David Rowe, Alexander Vazsonyi, and Daniel Flannery, "Sex Differences in Delinquency: Do Means and Within-Sex Variation Have Similar Causes?" *Journal of Research in Delinquency and Delinquency* 32:84–100 (1995).

Initiators and Adolescent Initiators of Violence," *Journal of Research in Delinquency and Delinquency* 38:45–63 (2001).

71. Michael Gottfredson and Travis Hirschi, *A General Theory of Delinquency* (Stanford, CA: Stanford University Press, 1990).

72. Ibid., p. 27.

73. Robert Agnew, "The Contribution of Social-Psychological Strain Theory to the Explanation of Delinquency and Delinquency," *Advances in Criminological Theory* 6:211–213 (1994).

74. Gottfredson and Hirschi, *A General Theory of Delinquency*, p. 90.

75. Ibid., p. 89.

76. Alex Piquero and Stephen Tibbetts, "Specifying the Direct and Indirect Effects of Low Self-Control and Situational Factors in Offenders' Decision Making: Toward a More Complete Model of Rational Offending," *Justice Quarterly* 13:481–508 (1996).

77. David Forde and Leslie Kennedy, "Risky Lifestyles, Routine Activities, and the General Theory of Delinquency," *Justice Quarterly* 14:265–294 (1997).

78. Marianne Junger and Richard Tremblay, "Self-Control, Accidents, and Delinquency," *Delinquent Justice and Behavior* 26:485–501 (1999).

79. Gottfredson and Hirschi, *A General Theory of Delinquency*, p. 112.

80. Dennis Giever, "An Empirical Assessment of the Core Elements of Gottfredson and Hirschi's General Theory of Delinquency," paper presented at the annual meeting of the American Society of Criminology, Boston, November 1995.

81. David Farrington, Darrick Jolliffe, Rolf Loeber, Madga Southamer-Loeber, and Larry Kalb, "The Concentration of Offenders in Families, and Family Criminality in the Prediction of Boys' Delinquency," *Journal of Adolescence* 24:579–596 (2001).

82. Peter Muris and Cor Meesters, "The Validity of Attention Deficit Hyperactivity and Hyperkinetic Disorder Symptom Domains in Nonclinical Dutch Children," *Journal of Clinical Child & Adolescent Psychology* 32:460–466 (2003); David Brownfield and Ann Marie Sorenson, "Self-Control and Juvenile Delinquency: Theoretical Issues and an Empirical Assessment of Selected Elements of a General Theory of Delinquency," *Deviant Behavior* 14:243–264 (1993); Harold Grasmick, Charles Tittle, Robert Bursik, and Bruce Arneklev, "Testing the Core Empirical Implications of Gottfredson and Hirschi's General Theory of Delinquency," *Journal of Research in Delinquency and Delinquency* 30:5–29 (1993).

83. Ronald Akers, "Self-Control as a General Theory of Delinquency," *Journal of Quantitative Criminology* 7:201–211 (1991).

84. Richard Wiebe, "Reconciling Psychopathy and Low Self-Control," *Justice Quarterly* 20:297–336 (2003).

85. Alan Feingold, "Gender Differences in Personality: A Meta Analysis," *Psychological Bulletin* 116:429–456 (1994).

86. Charles Tittle, David Ward, and Harold Grasmick, "Gender, Age, and Crime/Deviance: A Challenge to Self-Control Theory," *Journal of Research in Crime & Delinquency* 40:426–453 (2003).

87. Gottfredson and Hirschi, *A General Theory of Delinquency*, p. 153.

88. Scott Menard, Delbert Elliott, and Sharon Wofford, "Social Control Theories in Developmental Perspective," *Studies on Delinquency and Delinquency Prevention* 2:69–87 (1993).

89. Charles R. Tittle and Harold G. Grasmick, "Delinquent Behavior and Age: A Test of Three Provocative Hypotheses," *Journal of Delinquent Law and Criminology* 88:309–342 (1997).

90. Travis Pratt and Frank Cullen, "The Empirical Status of Gottfredson and Hirschi's General Theory of Delinquency: A Meta-Analysis," *Criminology* 38:938–964 (2000); Douglas Longshore, "Self-Control and Delinquent Opportunity: A Prospective Test of the General Theory of Delinquency," *Social Problems* 45:102–114 (1998).

91. Charles Tittle, David Ward, and Harold Grasmick, "Self-Control and Crime/Deviance: Cognitive vs. Behavioral Measures," *Journal of Quantitative Criminology* 19:333–365 (2003).

92. Otwin Marenin and Michael Resig, "A General Theory of Delinquency and Patterns of Delinquency in Nigeria: An Exploration of Methodological Assumptions," *Journal of Delinquent Justice* 23:501–518 (1995).

93. Bruce Arneklev, Harold Grasmick, Charles Tittle, and Robert Bursik, "Low Self-Control and Imprudent Behavior," *Journal of Quantitative Criminology* 9:225–246 (1993).

94. Terrie Moffitt, "Adolescence-Limited and Life-Course Persistent Antisocial Behaviors: A Developmental Taxonomy," *Psychological Review* 100:674–701 (1993).

95. Alex Piquero, Robert Brame, Paul Mazerolle, and Rudy Haapanen, "Crime in Emerging Adulthood," *Criminology* 40:137–170 (2002).

96. Donald Lynam, Alex Piquero, Terrie Moffitt, "Specialization and the Propensity to Violence: Support from Self-Reports but Not Official Records," *Journal of Contemporary Criminal Justice* 20:215–228 (2004).

97. Kevin Thompson, "Sexual Harassment and Low Self-Control: An Application of Gottfredson and Hirschi's General Theory of Delinquency," paper presented at the annual meeting of the American Society of Criminology, Phoenix, Arizona, November 1993.

98. Bradley Entner Wright, Avashalom Caspi, Terrie Moffitt, and Phil Silva, "Low Self-Control, Social Bonds, and Delinquency: Social Causation, Social Selection, or Both?" *Criminology* 37:479–514 (1999).

99. Ibid., p. 504.

100. Stephen Cernkovich and Peggy Giordano, "Stability and Change in Antisocial Behavior: The Transition from Adolescence to Early Adulthood," *Criminology* 39:371–410 (2001).

PART

3

Social, Community, and Environmental Influences on Delinquency

Social, community, and environmental relations are thought to exert a powerful influence on an adolescent's involvement in delinquent activities. Kids who fail at home, at school, and in the neighborhood are considered in danger of developing and/or sustaining delinquent careers. Research indicates that chronic, persistent offenders are quite likely to experience educational failure, poor home life, substance abuse, and unsatisfactory peer relations.

Social, community, and environmental relations can also have a positive influence and shield at-risk children from involvement in a delinquent way of life. Consequently, many delinquency prevention efforts focus on improving family relations, supporting educational achievement, and utilizing community resources. Some begin early in childhood, others during the teen years, while a third type of prevention effort is designed to help those who have been involved in antisocial behavior to desist from further activities.

Part Three contains six chapters devoted to the influences critical social forces have on delinquency. Chapter 6 explores gender relations and their relationship to delinquency. Chapter 7 is devoted to the family, and Chapter 8 looks at peer relations including juvenile groups and gangs. Chapter 9 examines the relationship between education and delinquency, and Chapter 10 concerns substance abuse. Finally, Chapter 11 looks at how the community environment is being used to help youth avoid involvement in delinquent behaviors.

Chapter 6 Gender and Delinquency

Chapter 7 The Family and Delinquency

Chapter 8 Peers and Delinquency: Juvenile Gangs and Groups

Chapter 9 Schools and Delinquency

Chapter 10 Drug Use and Delinquency

Chapter 11 Delinquency Prevention: Social and Developmental Perspectives

Gender and Delinquency

6

Chapter Outline

Gender Differences in Development
Socialization Differences
Cognitive Differences
Personality Differences
What Causes Gender Differences?

Gender Differences and Delinquency
Gender Patterns in Delinquency
Violent Behavior

Trait Views: Are Female Delinquents Born that Way?
Early Psychological Explanations
Contemporary Trait Views
FOCUS ON DELINQUENCY: The Biosocial Study
of Female Delinquency

Socialization Views
Socialization and Delinquency
Contemporary Socialization Views
POLICY AND PRACTICE: Preventing Teen Pregnancy
FOCUS ON DELINQUENCY: Desisting from Delinquency:
Life Transformations

Liberal Feminist Views
Support for Liberal Feminism
Critiques of Liberal Feminism

Critical Feminist Views
Crime and Patriarchy
FOCUS ON DELINQUENCY: Power, Gender,
and Adolescent Dating Violence
Power-Control Theory

Gender and the Juvenile Justice System

Chapter Objectives

1. Be familiar with the changes in the female delinquency rate
2. Understand the cognitive differences between males and females
3. Be able to discuss the differences in socialization between boys and girls and how it may affect their behavior
4. Understand the psychological differences between the sexes
5. Be able to discuss the early work on gender, delinquency, and human traits
6. Know the elements contemporary trait theorists view as the key to understanding gender differences such as psychological makeup and hormonal differences
7. Know how socialization is thought to impact on female delinquency rates
8. Discuss contemporary socialization views of female delinquency
9. Understand the term "liberal feminism"
10. Discuss how critical feminists view female delinquency
11. Describe Hagan's power-control theory
12. Be familiar with how the treatment girls receive by the juvenile justice system differs from the treatment of boys

CNN. View the CNN video clip of this story and answer related Critical Thinking questions on your Juvenile Delinquency 9e CD-ROM.

On May 4, 2003, girls at a "powder puff" touch football game in Northbrook, Illinois, went on a rampage that was captured on videotape. Senior girls began the event by chugging beer straight from a keg provided by some parents. Then they began pounding some of the younger girls with their fists and bats, while pushing them down into the mud. They covered the novice football players with excrement, garbage, and food. The students apparently arranged the event in secret, making sure that school administrators were kept unaware of the time and place. In the aftermath, five girls were hospitalized, including one who broke an ankle and another who suffered a cut that required 10 stitches in her head. The attackers were suspended from school and criminal charges filed. The tape was circulated to the news media and it was shown repeatedly all around the country.

The Northbrook incident was shocking because it involved young girls in an extremely violent incident, an image that defies the traditional female image of being less aggressive than males. When the study of juvenile delinquency began, the female offender was viewed as an aberration who engaged in crimes that usually had a sexual connotation—prostitution, running away (which presumably leads to sexual misadventure), premarital sex, and crimes of sexual passion (killing a boyfriend or a husband).[1] Criminologists often ignored female offenders, assuming that they rarely violated the law, or, if they did, that their illegal acts were status-type offenses. Female delinquency was viewed as emotional or family-related, and such problems were not an important concern of criminologists. In fact, the few "true" female delinquents were considered anomalies whose criminal activity was a function of taking on masculine characteristics, a concept referred to as the "**masculinity hypothesis.**"[2]

Because female delinquency was considered unimportant, most early theories of delinquency focused on male misconduct. Quite often these models failed to adequately explain gender differences in the delinquency rate. For example, strain theory (see Chapter 4) holds that delinquency results from the failure to achieve socially desirable goals. Using this logic, females should be more criminal than males because they face *gender discrimination* and males do not. Some delinquency experts interpret such exceptions to the rules as an indication that separate explanations for male and female delinquency are required.[3]

masculinity hypothesis
View that women who commit crimes have biological and psychological traits similar to those of men who commit crimes.

173

Contemporary interest in the association between gender and delinquency has surged, fueled by observations that although the female delinquency rate is still much lower than the male rate, it is growing at a faster pace than male delinquency. Moreover, the types of delinquent acts young women are engaging in seem quite similar to those of young men. Larceny and aggravated assault, the crimes for which most young men are arrested, are also the most common offenses for which females are arrested. There is evidence that girls are getting more heavily involved in gangs and gang violence.[4] Ironically, recent research (2004) indicates that boys rather than girls are more likely to be arrested for sexually related offenses such as prostitution. When David Finkelhor and Richard Ormrod analyzed national arrest data, they found that juvenile prostitution offenders known to police were more often male (61 percent) than female (39 percent), a greater disproportion than among adult prostitution offenders (53 percent male and 47 percent female).[5]

Although girls still commit less crime than boys, members of both sexes are similar in the onset and development of their offending careers.[6] In societies with high rates of male delinquency, there are also high rates of female delinquency. Over time, male and female arrest rates rise and fall in a parallel fashion.[7]

Another reason for the interest in gender studies is that conceptions of gender differences have changed. A feminist approach to understanding crime is now firmly established. The stereotype of the female delinquent as a sexual deviant is no longer taken seriously.[8] The result has been an increased effort to conduct research that would adequately explain differences and similarities in male and female offending patterns.

This chapter provides an overview of gender factors in delinquency. We first discuss some of the gender differences in development and how they may relate to the gender differences in offending rates. Then we turn to some explanations for these differences: (1) the trait view, (2) the socialization view, (3) the liberal feminist view, and (4) the critical feminist view.

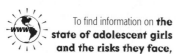
To find information on **the state of adolescent girls and the risks they face,** go to the website of the Commonwealth Fund at www.cmwf.org/programs/women/adoleshl.asp#RISKY. For an up-to-date list of web links, go to http://cj.wadsworth.com/siegel_jd9e.

GENDER DIFFERENCES IN DEVELOPMENT

Gender differences in cognition, socialization, and behavior may exist as early as infancy, when boys are able to express emotions at higher rates. Infant girls show greater control over their emotions, whereas boys are more easily angered and depend more on input from their mothers.[9] There are indications that gender differences in socialization and development do exist and that they may have an effect on juvenile offending patterns.[10]

Socialization Differences

Psychologists believe that differences in the way females and males are socialized affect their development. Males learn to value independence, whereas females are taught that their self-worth depends on their ability to sustain relationships. Girls, therefore, run the risk of losing themselves in their relationships with others, whereas boys may experience a chronic sense of alienation. Because so many relationships go sour, females also run the risk of feeling alienated because of the failure to achieve relational success.[11]

Although there are few gender differences in aggression during the first few years of life, girls are socialized to be less aggressive than boys and are supervised more closely.[12] Differences in aggression become noticeable between ages 3 and 6, when children are socialized into organized groups such as the daycare center. Males are more likely to display physical aggression, whereas females display relational aggression—for example, by excluding disliked peers from play groups.[13]

As they mature, girls learn to respond to provocation by feeling anxious, unlike boys, who are encouraged to retaliate.[14] Overall, women are much more likely to feel

Research shows that males are more likely than females to behave in an aggressive manner. Biosocial theorists find that qualities of male biological traits make males "naturally" more aggressive than females and therefore more likely to commit violent acts.

distressed than men.[15] Although females get angry as often as males, many have been taught to blame themselves for such feelings. Females are, therefore, much more likely than males to respond to anger with feelings of depression, anxiety, and shame. Females are socialized to fear that anger will harm relationships; males are encouraged to react with "moral outrage," blaming others for their discomfort.[16]

Females are also more likely than males to be targets of sexual and physical abuse. Female victims have been shown to suffer more seriously from these attacks, sustaining damage to their self-image; victims of sexual abuse find it difficult to build autonomy and life skills.

Cognitive Differences

There are also cognitive differences between adolescent males and females starting in childhood. Males excel in tasks that assess the ability to manipulate visual images in working memory, whereas females do better in tasks that require retrieval from long-term memory and the acquisition and use of verbal information.[17] Girls learn to speak earlier and faster, with better pronunciation, most likely because parents talk more to their infant daughters than to their infant sons. Girls are far less likely than boys to have reading problems, but boys do much better on standardized math tests, which is attributed by some experts to their strategies for approaching math problems. Boys in the United States are more likely than girls to be dyslexic.

In most cases cognitive differences are small, narrowing, and usually attributed to cultural expectations. When given training, girls can increase their visual-spatial skills. However, differences still exert a penalty on young girls. For example, performance on the mathematics portion of the Scholastic Aptitude Test (SAT) still favors males: twice as many boys as girls attain scores over 500 and 13 times as many boys as girls attain scores over 700.[18]

Personality Differences

Girls are often stereotyped as talkative, but research shows that in many situations boys spend more time talking than girls do. Females are more willing to reveal their

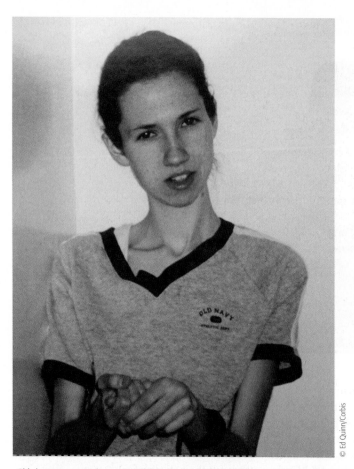
© Ed Quinn/Corbis

Girls learn to respond to provocation by feeling anxious and depressed. Their anxiety may lead to psychological turmoil manifested in eating conditions such as anorexia and bulimia. Jennifer Shortis, a young Massachusetts girl, developed anorexia and wasted away from 124 pounds to 70. After more than $100,000 in anorexia-related treatment costs, she is on the road to recovery.

feelings and more likely to express concern for others. Females are more concerned about finding the "meaning of life" and less interested in competing for material success.[19] Males are more likely to introduce new topics and to interrupt conversations.

Adolescent females use different knowledge than males and have different ways of interpreting their interactions with others; they have more empathy for others, which may help shield them from antisocial acts.[20]

These gender differences in empathy may have an impact on self-esteem and self-concept. Research shows that, as adolescents develop, male self-esteem and self-concept rise whereas female self-confidence is lowered.[21] One reason is that girls are more likely to stress about their weight and be more dissatisfied with the size and shape of their bodies.[22] Young girls are regularly confronted with unrealistically high standards of slimness that make them extremely unhappy with their own bodies; it is not surprising that the incidence of eating disorders such as *anorexia* and *bulimia* have increased markedly in recent years. Psychologist Carol Gilligan uncovered an alternative explanation for this decline in female self-esteem: As girls move into adolescence, they become aware of the conflict between the positive way they see themselves and the negative way society views females. Many girls respond by "losing their voices," that is, submerging their own feelings and accepting the negative view of women conveyed by adult authorities.[23]

These various gender differences are described in Concept Summary 6.1.

Concept Summary 6.1

Gender Differences

	Females	Males
Socialization	Sustain relationships Be less aggressive Blame self	Be independent Be aggressive Externalize anger
Cognitive	Have superior verbal ability Speak earlier Have better pronunciation Read better	Have superior visual/spatial ability Are better at math
Personality	Have lower self-esteem Are self-aware Have better attention span	Have higher self-esteem Are materialistic Have lower attention span

What Causes Gender Differences?

Why do these gender differences occur? Some experts suggest that gender differences may have a biological origin: males and females are essentially different. They have somewhat different brain organizations; females are more left brain–oriented and males more right brain–oriented. (The left-brain is believed to control language, and the right, spatial relations.) Others point to the hormonal differences between the sexes as the key to understanding their behavior.

Another view is that gender differences are a result of the interaction of socialization, learning, and enculturation. Boys and girls may behave differently because they have been exposed to different styles of socialization, learned different values, and had different cultural experiences. It follows, then, that if members of both sexes were equally exposed to the factors that produce delinquency, their delinquency rates would be equivalent.[24] According to psychologist Sandra Bem's **gender-schema theory,** our culture polarizes males and females by forcing them to obey mutually exclusive gender roles, or "scripts." Girls are expected to be "feminine," exhibiting traits such as being sympathetic and gentle. In contrast, boys are expected to be "masculine," exhibiting assertiveness and dominance. Children internalize these scripts and accept gender polarization as normal. Children's self-esteem becomes wrapped up in how closely their behavior conforms to the proper sex role stereotype. When children begin to perceive themselves as either *boys* or *girls* (which occurs at about age 3), they search for information to help them define their role; they begin to learn what behavior is appropriate for their sex.[25] Girls are expected to behave according to the appropriate script and to seek approval of their behavior: Are they acting as girls should at that age? Masculine behavior is to be avoided. In contrast, males look for cues from their peers to define their masculinity; aggressive behavior may be rewarded with peer approval, whereas sensitivity is viewed as nonmasculine.[26]

Biology or Socialization? In her book *The Two Sexes: Growing up Apart, Coming Together,* psychologist Eleanor Maccoby argues that gender differences are not a matter of individual personality or biological difference but the way kids socialize and how their relationships are structured.[27] Despite the best efforts of parents who want to break down gender boundaries, kids still segregate themselves by gender in their playgroups. Thus a "boy culture" and a "girl culture" develop side by side. Kids also take on different roles depending on whom they are with and who is being exposed to behavior. A boy will be all macho bravado when he is with his peers but may be a tender, loving big brother when asked to babysit his little sister. Little girls aren't "passive" as a result of some ingrained quality; they have learned to be passive only when boys are present. According to Maccoby, gender separation has partly biological and partly social causes. Though biological and cognitive differences do impact on behavior, Maccoby claims that gender distinctions arise mainly in social interactions and that peer groups are highly influential in greatly enhancing gender. Nonetheless, biological and social factors are so intertwined that it is erroneous to think of gender differences as having an independent social or physical origin.

gender-schema theory
Asserts that our culture polarizes males and females, forcing them into exclusive gender roles of "feminine" or "masculine"; these gender scripts provide the basis for deviant behaviors.

The mission of the **National Council for Research on Women** is to enhance the connections among research, policy analysis, advocacy, and innovative programming on behalf of women and girls. Visit their site at www.ncrw.org. For an up-to-date list of web links, go to http://cj.wadsworth.com/siegel_jd9e.

TO QUIZ YOURSELF ON THIS MATERIAL, go to the Juvenile Delinquency 9e website.

GENDER DIFFERENCES AND DELINQUENCY

Regardless of their origin, gender distinctions may partly explain the significant gender differences in the delinquency rate. Males seem more aggressive and less likely to form attachments to others, factors that might increase their crime rates. Males view aggression as an appropriate means to gain status. Boys are also more likely than girls to socialize with deviant peers and, when they do, they display personality traits that make them more susceptible to delinquency. Recent research by Jean Bottcher found that young boys perceive their roles as being more dominant than young girls. Male perceptions of power, their ability to have freedom and hang with their friends helped explain the gender differences in delinquency.[28]

Girls are shielded by their moral sense, which directs them to avoid harming others. Their moral sensitivity may counterbalance the effects of family problems.[29] Females display more self-control than males, a factor that has been related to criminality.[30]

Females are more verbally proficient, a skill that may help them deal with conflict without resorting to violence. They are taught to be less aggressive and view belligerence

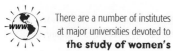
There are a number of institutes at major universities devoted to **the study of women's issues.** You can visit the site of the one at the University of Michigan at www.lsa.umich.edu/women/. For an up-to-date list of web links, go to http://cj.wadsworth.com/siegel_jd9e.

as a lack of self-control.[31] When girls are aggressive, they are more likely than boys to hide their behavior from adults; girls who bully others are less likely than boys to admit their behavior.[32]

Cognitive and personality differences are magnified when children internalize gender-specific behaviors. Boys who aren't tough are labeled sissies. Girls are expected to form closer bonds with their friends and to share feelings.

Gender Patterns in Delinquency

Over the past decades, females have increased their participation in delinquent behaviors at a faster rate than males. Arrest data indicate that juvenile females make up a greater percentage of the arrest statistics today than they did 30 years ago. In 1967, females constituted 13 percent of all juvenile index-crime arrests; today they make up about one third. The most recent arrest data show that between 1994 and 2003 the total teenage male arrest rate *decreased* by about 22 percent and the female rate decreased by only 3 percent.[33] Even more striking was the relative change in arrests for serious violent crimes. During the same period of falling crime rates, teenage male violent crime arrests declined 36 percent whereas female arrests declined a more modest 10 percent.

The Monitoring the Future self-report study also shows that patterns of male and female criminality appear to be converging. Self-report data indicate that the rank ordering of male and female deviant behaviors is similar. The illegal acts most common for boys—petty larceny, using a false ID, and smoking marijuana—are also the ones most frequently committed by girls.[34]

Violent Behavior

Gender differences in the delinquency rate may be narrowing, but males continue to be overrepresented in arrests for violent crimes. For example, almost all homicide offenders are males. In 2003, of the more than 773 juveniles arrested for murder, only 73 were female.[35]

One reason for the gender disparity in lethal violence is that males and females display differences in the victims they target and the weapons they use. The typical male juvenile kills a friend or acquaintance with a handgun during an argument. In contrast, the typical female is as likely to kill a family member as an acquaintance and is more likely to use a knife. Both males and females tend to kill males, generally their brothers, fathers, or friends.

Why do these differences occur, and why are girls increasing their involvement in delinquent activities at a faster pace than boys? The wide range of opinions on these questions will be presented in the remaining sections of this chapter.

TO QUIZ YOURSELF ON THIS MATERIAL, go to the Juvenile Delinquency 9e website.

TRAIT VIEWS: ARE FEMALE DELINQUENTS BORN THAT WAY?

There is a long tradition of tracing gender differences in delinquency to traits that are uniquely male or female. The argument that biological and psychological differences between males and females can explain differences in crime rates is not a new one. The earliest criminologists focused on physical characteristics believed to be precursors of crime. Cesare Lombroso's concept of the "born criminal" rested on male-oriented traits such as extraordinary strength and agility, lack of emotion, and insensitivity to pain. Female delinquents were treated as an aberration. Because the female crime rate was so low and most girls were not delinquents, those whose behavior deviated from what was considered appropriate for females were believed to be inherently evil or physically maladapted.

With the publication in 1895 of *The Female Offender,* Lombroso (with William Ferrero) extended his work on criminality to females.[36] Lombroso maintained that women were lower on the evolutionary scale than men, more childlike, and less intelligent.[37] Women who committed crimes could be distinguished from "normal" women by physical characteristics—excessive body hair, wrinkles, and an abnormal cranium, for example.[38] In appearance, delinquent females appeared closer to men than to other women. The masculinity hypothesis suggested that delinquent girls had excessive male characteristics.[39]

Lombrosian thought had a significant influence for much of the twentieth century. Delinquency rate differentials were explained in terms of gender-based differences. For example, in 1925 Cyril Burt linked female delinquency to menstruation.[40] Similarly, William Healy and Augusta Bronner suggested that males' physical superiority enhanced their criminality. Their research showed that about 70 percent of the delinquent girls they studied had abnormal weight and size, a finding that supported the "masculinity hypothesis."[41] In a later work (1950), *The Criminality of Women,* Otto Pollak linked the onset of female criminality to the impact of biological conditions—menstruation, pregnancy, and menopause:[42]

> *Thefts, particularly shoplifting, arson, homicide, and resistance against public officials seem to show a significant correlation between the menstruation of the offender and the time of the offense. The turmoil of the onset of menstruation and the puberty of girls appears to express itself in the relatively high frequency of false accusations and—where cultural opportunities permit—of incendiarism. Pregnancy in its turn is a crime-promoting influence with regard to attacks against the life of the fetus and the newborn. The menopause finally seems to bring about a distinct increase in crime, especially in offenses resulting from irritability such as arson, breaches of the peace, perjury, and insults.[43]*

Pollak argued that most female delinquency goes unrecorded because the female is the instigator, rather than the perpetrator, of illegal behavior.[44] Females first use their sexual charms to instigate crime and then beguile males in the justice system in order to obtain deferential treatment. This observation is referred to as the **chivalry hypothesis,** which holds that gender differences in the delinquency rate can be explained by the fact that female criminality is overlooked or forgiven by male agents of the criminal justice system. Those who believe in the chivalry hypothesis point to data

chivalry hypothesis (also known as paternalism hypothesis) View that low female crime and delinquency rates are a reflection of the leniency with which police treat female offenders.

According to the chivalry hypothesis, male police officers are less likely to arrest female offenders than male offenders because they have been socialized to be solicitous to women. As the percentage of women entering police work increases, the effects of chivalry may decline, serving to increase the female arrest rate.

© Richard Lord/PhotoEdit

To read more about the **chivalry hypothesis** and how it relates to gang delinquency, go to www.ngcrc.com/ngcrc/page16.htm. For an up-to-date list of web links, go to http://cj.wadsworth.com/siegel_jd9e.

showing that although women make up about 20 percent of all arrestees, they account for less than 5 percent of all inmates. Police and other justice system personnel may still be less willing to arrest and penalize female offenders than they are to arrest and penalize males.[45]

Early Psychological Explanations

Psychologists also viewed the physical differences between male and female as a basis for their behavior differentials. Sigmund Freud maintained that girls interpret their lack of a penis as a sign that they have been punished. Boys fear that they can be punished by having their penis cut off, and thus learn to fear women. From this conflict comes *penis envy*, which often produces an inferiority complex in girls, forcing them to make an effort to compensate for their "defect." One way to compensate is to identify with their mothers and accept a maternal role. Also, girls may attempt to compensate for their lack of a penis by dressing well and beautifying themselves.[46] Freud also claimed that "If a little girl persists in her first wish—to grow into a boy—in extreme cases she will end as a manifest homosexual, and otherwise she will exhibit markedly masculine traits in the conduct of her later life, will choose a masculine vocation, and so on."[47]

At mid-century, psychodynamic theorists suggested that girls are socialized to be passive, which helps explain their low crime rate. However, this condition also makes some females susceptible to being manipulated by men; hence, their participation in sex-related crimes such as prostitution. A girl's wayward behavior, psychoanalysts suggested, was restricted to neurotic theft (kleptomania) and overt sexual acts, which were symptoms of personality maladaption.[48]

According to these early versions of the psychoanalytic approach, gender differences in the delinquency rate can be traced to differences in psychological orientation. Male delinquency reflects aggressive traits, whereas female delinquency is a function of repressed sexuality, gender conflict, and abnormal socialization.

Contemporary Trait Views

Contemporary biosocial and psychological theorists have continued the tradition of attributing gender differences in delinquency to physical and emotional traits (see Figure 6.1). These theorists recognize that it is the interaction of biological and psychological traits with the social environment that produces delinquency.

precocious sexuality
Sexual experimentation in early adolescence.

Early Physical Maturity Early theorists linked female delinquency to early or **precocious sexuality.** According to this view, girls who experience an early onset of physical maturity are most likely to engage in antisocial behavior.[49] Female delinquents were believed to be promiscuous and more sophisticated than male delinquents.[50] Linking female delinquency to sexuality was responsible, in part, for the view that female delinquency is symptomatic of maladjustment.[51]

Equating female delinquency purely with sexual activity is no longer taken seriously, but early sexuality has been linked to other problems, such as higher risk of teen pregnancy and sexually transmitted diseases.[52] Empirical evidence suggests that girls who reach puberty at an early age are at the highest risk for delinquency.[53] One reason is that "early bloomers" may be more attractive to older adolescent boys, and increased contact with this high-risk group places the girls in jeopardy for antisocial behavior. Research shows that young girls who date boys three or more years older are more likely to engage in precocious sex, feel pressured into having sex, and engage in sex while under the influence of drugs and/or alcohol than girls who date more age-appropriate boys.[54]

Girls who are more developed relative to their peers are more likely to socialize at an early age and get involved in deviant behaviors, especially "party deviance" such

A longitudinal study that followed children born on the Hawaiian island of Kauai in 1955 for thirty-two years found that the most reliable traits for predicting delinquency in boys included these:

- Disordered care-taking

- Lack of educational stimulation in the home

- Reading problems

- A need for remedial education by age 10

- Late maturation

- An unemployed, criminal, or absent father

In addition, boys appeared to be particularly vulnerable to early childhood learning problems, leading to school failure. A combination of reaching puberty late and lack of a significant male role model also encouraged the persistence of antisocial behavior throughout adolescence.

In the same longitudinal study, researchers found that delinquent girls tend to have the following traits:

- A history of minor congenital defects

- Low development scores by age 2

- A need for mental health services by age 10

- Earlier-than-average onset of puberty

Researchers hypothesize that birth defects and slow early development could lead to poor self-esteem, whereas early sexual development may encourage sexual relationships with older males and conflict with parents.

FIGURE 6.1
Trait Differences in Male and Female Delinquents

SOURCE: Felton Earls and Albert Reiss, *Breaking the Cycle: Predicting and Preventing Crime* (Washington, DC: National Institute of Justice, 1994), pp. 24–25.

as drinking, smoking, and substance abuse. Early puberty is most likely to encourage delinquent activities that occur in the context of socializing with peers and having romantic relationships with boys.[55] The delinquency gap between early and late bloomers narrows when the latter group reaches sexual maturity and increases their exposure to boys.[56] Biological and social factors seem to interact to postpone or accelerate female delinquent activity.

Hormonal Effects As you may recall from Chapter 3, some biosocial theorists link antisocial behavior to hormonal influences.[57] One view is that hormonal imbalance may influence aggressive behavior. For example, changes in the level of the hormone **cortisol**, which is secreted by the adrenal glands in response to any kind of physical or psychological stress, has been linked to conduct problems in young girls.[58]

Another view is that excessive amounts of male hormones (androgens) are related to delinquency. The androgen most often related to antisocial behavior is testosterone.[59] In general, females who test higher for testosterone are more likely to engage in stereotypical male behaviors.[60] Females who have low androgen levels are less aggressive than males, whereas those who have elevated levels will take on characteristically male traits, including aggression.[61]

Some females are overexposed to male hormones in utero. Females affected this way may become "constitutionally masculinized." They may develop abnormal hair growth, large musculature, low voice, irregular menstrual cycle, and hyper-aggressiveness; this condition can also develop as a result of steroid use or certain medical disorders.[62] Diana Fishbein has reviewed the literature in this area and finds that, after holding constant a variety of factors (including IQ, age, and environment), females exposed to male hormones in utero are more likely to engage in aggressive behavior later in life.[63] The biosocial factors that shape female delinquency patterns are discussed in the accompanying Focus on Delinquency box.

cortisol
A hormone secreted by the adrenal glands in response to any kind of physical or psychological stress.

The Biosocial Study of Female Delinquency

The Biosocial Study followed nearly 1,000 Philadelphia residents from birth through early adulthood. Participants came from families involved in the Philadelphia Collaborative Perinatal Project at Pennsylvania Hospital between 1959 and 1966. This was part of a nationwide study of biological and environmental influences upon the pregnancies of 60,000 women, as well as the physical, neurological, and psychological development of their children. Upon registration for the Perinatal Project, each mother underwent a battery of interviews and physical examinations that provided data for each pregnancy, including the mother's reproductive history, recent and past medical history, and labor and delivery events. Data recorded for each child includes information on neurological examinations conducted at birth, throughout the hospital stay, at 4 months, and at ages 1 and 7. Additionally, the children had their speech, language, and hearing examined at ages 3 and 8. Philadelphia public school records were used to collect data on academic achievement and evidence of learning or disciplinary problems. In addition, official police records were collected for all subjects from ages 7 to 22.

The Biosocial Study found that nine factors, some social and some biological, had an important impact on the likelihood that a female would engage in delinquent behavior: disciplinary problems in school, lack of foster parents, abnormal movement, neurological abnormalities, left foot preference, father absence, low language achievement, normal intellectual status, and right eye preference.

The data yielded a number of surprises, including the discovery that foster care had a more positive effect on behavior than keeping a child with her own family! Many of the children who were placed in foster care in the Biosocial Study came from disruptive and abusive homes where at least one parent was absent. It appears then that their early family experiences had a significant effect on their later delinquency. The significant association found between father absence and delinquency confirms this conclusion.

The Biosocial Study also assessed neurological impairment and its relationship to delinquency. A number of different tests were used to measure abnormality. Researchers would ask a test child to hold out both arms horizontally for 30 seconds to ease the detection of abnormal posture, chorea (rapid involuntary jerks), and athetosis (slow, spasmodic repetitions). They recorded many different types of abnormal movements, including tremors, tics, and mirror movements. They also noted neurological abnormalities, which are conditions often related to central nervous system disorders, such as abnormalities of skull size and shape, spinal anomalies, and primary muscle disease. Neurological abnormalities and factors associated with attention deficit disorder were found to be important predictors of female delinquency and violence. Those physical factors—number of neurological abnormalities, mixed cerebral

dominance as indicated by left-footedness and right-eyedness, and abnormal movements—can interfere with language achievement. Poor language skills were found to have a positive correlation with female delinquency. The study found that for females, delinquency and violence are associated with learning difficulties and low achievement, but not with the more serious types of mental impairment such as mental retardation or abnormal intellectual status. This finding is consistent with other analyses, which indicate generally that the more violent and chronic delinquents had lower achievement test scores, but that they are not significantly represented in programs for the mentally retarded.

Which juvenile female delinquents later became adult offenders? Four factors showed direct effects on the number of adult offenses among females: seriousness of juvenile offenses, number of disciplinary problems in school, low number of juvenile offenses, and father's low educational level. As with males, the seriousness of delinquent offenses was significant; however, unlike males, those most apt to continue to commit crime during adulthood were not always those who committed the most crime during their youth. This result is not surprising, however, as females commit a relatively larger number of petty or status offenses, like shoplifting. Therefore, unlike males, chronic female offenders were not always the most serious offenders. In addition, disciplinary problems in school had a long-term effect on adult offending. This is evidence that early problem behavior is predictive of problems in adulthood.

Critical Thinking

The Biosocial Study is important because it involves careful and precise measurements of physical traits and conditions. It shows that both social factors and physical traits have important effects on female delinquency and, later, on their adult criminality. Can such physical traits be neutralized by social support, or do you believe that we cannot overcome our biological limitations?

InfoTrac College Edition Research

Is it possible that the traits that predispose people to crime may be developed before birth? To read about this process, go to InfoTrac College Edition, and access Amy Conseur, Frederick P. Rivara, Robert Barnoski, and Irvin Emanuel, "Maternal and Perinatal Risk Factors for Later Delinquency," *Pediatrics* 99(6):785 (June 1997).

SOURCES: Deborah W. Denno, *Biology and Violence: From Birth to Adulthood* (New York: Cambridge University Press, 1990); Deborah W. Denno, "Gender, Crime, and the Criminal Law Defenses," *Journal of Criminal Law and Criminology* 85:80–180 (1994).

Premenstrual Syndrome Early biotheorists suspected that premenstrual syndrome (PMS) was a direct cause of the relatively rare instances of female violence: "For several days prior to and during menstruation, the stereotype has been that 'raging hormones' doom women to irritability and poor judgment—two facets of premenstrual syndrome."[64] The link between PMS and delinquency was popularized by Katharina Dalton, whose studies of English women led her to conclude that females are more likely to commit suicide and be aggressive and otherwise antisocial before or during menstruation.[65]

Today there is conflicting evidence on the relationship between PMS and female delinquency. Diana Fishbein, an expert on biosocial theory, concludes that there is an association between elevated levels of female aggression and menstruation. Research shows that a significant number of incarcerated females committed their crimes during the premenstrual phase and that a small percentage of women appear vulnerable to cyclical hormonal changes that make them more prone to anxiety and hostility.[66] Fishbein notes that the majority of these women do not actually engage in criminal behavior.[67]

Existing research has been criticized on the basis of methodological inadequacy.[68] A valid test of the association must consider its time-ordering: It is possible that the stress of antisocial behavior produces early menstruation and not vice versa.[69]

Aggression According to some biosocial theorists, gender differences in the delinquency rate can be explained by inborn differences in aggression; males are inherently more likely to be aggressive.[70] Some psychologists have suggested that these differences are present very early in life, appearing before socialization can influence behavior. Males seem to be more aggressive in all societies for which data is available; gender differences in aggression can even be found in nonhuman primates.[71]

Some biosocial theorists argue that gender-based differences in aggression reflect the dissimilarities in the male and female reproductive systems. Males are more aggressive because they wish to possess as many sex partners as possible to increase their chances of producing offspring. Females have learned to control their aggressive impulses because multiple mates do not increase their chances of conception. Instead they concentrate on acquiring things that will help them rear their offspring, such as a reliable mate who will supply material resources.[72]

The weight of the evidence is that males are more aggressive than females. However, evidence also exists that females are more likely to act aggressively under some circumstances than others. For instance:

▌ Females may feel more freedom than males to express anger and aggression in the family setting.[73]

▌ Males are more likely than females to report physical aggression in their behavior, intentions, and dreams.

▌ Females are more likely to feel anxious or guilty about behaving aggressively, and these feelings tend to inhibit aggression.

▌ Females behave as aggressively as males when they have the means to do so and believe their behavior is justified.

▌ Females are more likely to empathize with the victim—to put themselves in the victim's place.

▌ Sex differences in aggression decrease when the victim is anonymous; anonymity may prevent females from empathizing with the victim.[74]

Psychological Problems Because girls are socialized to be less aggressive than boys, it is possible that the young women who do get involved in antisocial and violent behavior are suffering from some form of mental anguish or abnormality. Girls are also more likely than boys to be involved in status offenses such as running away and truancy, behaviors that may indicate underlying psychological distress.

Research indicates that antisocial adolescent girls do suffer a wide variety of mental-health problems and have dysfunctional and violent relationships.[75] Incarcerated adolescent female offenders have more acute mental health symptoms and psychological disturbances than male offenders.[76] Female delinquents score highly on psychological tests measuring such traits as psychopathic deviation, schizophrenia, paranoia, and psychasthenia (a psychological disorder characterized by phobias, obsessions, compulsions, or excessive anxiety).[77] Clinical interviews indicate that female delinquents are significantly more likely than males to suffer from mood disorders, including any disruptive disorder, major depressive disorder, and separation anxiety disorder.[78] For example, serious female delinquents have been found to have a relatively high incidence of **callous-unemotional** (**CU**) **traits,** an affective disorder described by a lack of remorse or shame, poor judgment, failure to learn by experience, and chronic lying.[79] In sum, there are some experts who believe that female delinquents suffer from some form of biological/psychological deficits ranging from early physical maturity to serious psychological impairments.[80] The most serious female offenders may endure a garden variety of these emotional, biological, and mental problems, from substandard intelligence to antisocial personality disorder.[81]

callous-unemotional (CU) traits
An affective disorder described by a lack of remorse or shame, poor judgment, failure to learn by experience, and chronic lying.

TO QUIZ YOURSELF ON THIS MATERIAL, go to the Juvenile Delinquency 9e website.

SOCIALIZATION VIEWS

Socialization views are based on the idea that a child's social development may be the key to understanding delinquent behavior. If a child experiences impairment, family disruption, and so on, the child will be more susceptible to delinquent associations and criminality.

Linking crime rate variations to gender differences in socialization is not a recent discovery. In a 1928 work, *The Unadjusted Girl,* W. I. Thomas suggested that some girls who have not been socialized under middle-class family controls can become impulsive thrill seekers. According to Thomas, female delinquency is linked to the wish for luxury and excitement.[82] Inequities in social class condemn poor girls from demoralized families to using sex as a means to gain amusement, pretty clothes, and other luxuries. Precocious sexuality makes these girls vulnerable to older men, who lead them down the path to decadence.[83]

Socialization and Delinquency

To read about **the socialization of female delinquents,** go to http://ojjdp.ncjrs.org/pubs/principles/ch1_4.html. For an up-to-date list of web links, go to http://cj.wadsworth.com/siegel_jd9e.

Scholars concerned with gender differences in crime are interested in the distinction between the lifestyles of males and females. Girls may be supervised more closely than boys. If girls behave in a socially disapproved fashion, their parents may be more likely to notice. Adults may be more tolerant of deviant behavior in boys and expect boys to act tough and take risks.[84] Closer supervision restricts the opportunity for crime and the time available to mingle with delinquent peers. It follows, then, that the adolescent girl who is growing up in a troubled home and lacks supervision may be more prone to delinquency.[85]

Focus on Socialization In the 1950s, a number of researchers began to focus on gender-specific socialization patterns. They made three assumptions about gender differences in socialization: Families exert a more powerful influence on girls than on boys; girls do not form close same-sex friendships but compete with their peers; and female criminals are primarily sexual offenders. First, parents are stricter with girls because they perceive them as needing control. In some families, adolescent girls rebel against strict controls. In others, where parents are absent or unavailable, girls may turn to the streets for companionship. Second, girls rarely form close relationships with female peers because they view them as rivals for males who would make eligible marriage partners.[86] Instead, girls enter into affairs with older men who exploit

According to contemporary socialization views, if a girl grows up in an atmosphere of sexual tension, where hostility exists between her parents or where the parents are absent, she likely will turn to outside sources for affection and support. In their reaction to loneliness, frustration, and parental hostility, girls begin to engage in the same activities as boys: staying out late at night, drinking, partying, and riding around with their friends.

them, involve them in sexual deviance, and father their illegitimate children.[87] The result is prostitution, drug abuse, and marginal lives. Their daughters repeat this pattern in a never-ending cycle of exploitation.

In a classic work, *The Adolescent Girl in Conflict* (1966), Gisela Konopka suggested that female delinquency has its roots in feelings of uncertainty and loneliness.[88] During adolescence, a girl's major emotional need is to be accepted by members of the opposite sex. If normal channels (such as family and friends) for receiving such approval are impaired, she may join a "crowd" or engage in gratuitous sexual relationships. This behavior leads to "rejection by the community, general experience of having no recognized success…and more behavior, which increases the feeling of worthlessness."[89] In fatherless homes, girls have an especially hard time because "the road to a healthy development toward womanhood through affection for the male and identification with the female simply does not exist."[90] The absence of socioeconomic mobility can also create problems. Delinquent girls are believed to suffer from lack of education. This locks them into low-paying jobs with little hope for advancement. These conditions lead girls to relieve their thwarted ambition through destructive behavior. The world presents a hostile environment to some girls; adult authority figures tell them what to do, but no one is there to listen to their needs.

Broken Homes/Fallen Women A number of experts shared Konopka's emphasis on the family as a primary influence on delinquent behavior. Male delinquents were portrayed as rebels who esteemed "toughness," "excitement," and other lower-class values. Males succumbed to the lure of delinquency when they perceived few legitimate opportunities. In contrast, female delinquents were portrayed as troubled adolescents who suffered inadequate home lives and, more often than not, were victims of sexual and physical abuse. Ruth Morris described delinquent girls as unattractive youths who reside in homes marked by family tensions.[91] In *The Delinquent Girl* (1970), Clyde Vedder and Dora Somerville suggest that female delinquency is usually a problem of adjustment to family pressure; an estimated 75 percent of institutionalized girls have family problems.[92] They also suggest that girls have serious problems in a male-dominated culture with rigid and sometimes unfair social practices.

Eleanor and Sheldon Glueck also distinguished between the causes of male and female delinquency. They linked male delinquency to muscular body type, a hostile attitude, and a poor home life.[93] Delinquent males had been reared in homes of "little understanding or affection, stability or moral fiber," by parents who were unfit to be role models.[94] In contrast, when they examined the life histories of institutionalized female offenders in *Five Hundred Delinquent Women,* they found that a majority of these women had been involved in sexual deviance that began early in their teens.[95] The Gluecks concluded that sexual delinquency and general maladjustment developed in girls simultaneously with unstable home lives.[96]

Other early efforts linked "rebellious" behavior to sexual conflicts in the home.[97] Broken or disrupted homes were found to predict female delinquency.[98] Females petitioned to juvenile court were more likely than males to be charged with ungovernable behavior and sex offenses. They also were more likely to reside in single-parent homes.[99] Studies of incarcerated juveniles found that most of the male delinquents were incarcerated for burglary and other theft-related offenses, but female delinquents tended to be involved in incorrigibility and sex offenses. The conclusion: Boys became delinquent to demonstrate their masculinity; girls were delinquent because of hostility toward parents and a consequent need to obtain attention from others.[100]

Contemporary Socialization Views

Investigators continue to support the view that female delinquents have more dysfunctional home lives than male offenders.[101] Institutionalized girls tell of lives filled with severe physical and sexual abuse. In addition to tragic home lives, delinquent girls report social experiences that were frustrating or even degrading.[102] Recent research efforts have found that girls who are the victims of child sexual abuse and physical abuse are the ones most likely to engage in violent and nonviolent criminal behavior.[103]

Girls seem to be more deeply affected than boys by child abuse, and the link between abuse and female delinquency seems stronger than it is for male delinquency.[104] A significant amount of female delinquency can be traced to abuse in the home.[105] Meda Chesney-Lind, a prominent feminist scholar, has described this association: "Young women on the run from homes characterized by sexual abuse and parental neglect are forced, by the very statutes designed to protect them, into the life of an escaped convict."[106] Girls may be forced into a life of sexual promiscuity because their sexual desirability makes them a valuable commodity in families living on the edge. For example, girls may be "lent out" to drug dealers so their parents or partners can get high. Girls on the streets are encouraged to sell their bodies because they have little else of value to trade.[107] Many of these girls may find themselves pregnant at a very young age. A number of programs have been created to help prevent teen pregnancy and to help girls who find themselves pregnant. This is the topic of the following Policy and Practice box entitled "Preventing Teen Pregnancy."

There is a significant body of literature linking abusive home lives to gang participation and crime. Joan Moore's analysis of gang girls in East Los Angeles found that many came from troubled homes. Sixty-eight percent of the girls she interviewed were afraid of their fathers, and 55 percent reported fear of their mothers.[108] Many of the girls reported that their parents were overly strict and controlling despite the fact that they engaged in criminality themselves. Moore also details accounts of sexual abuse; about 30 percent of the girls reported that family members had made sexual advances.[109] Emily Gaarder and Joanne Belknap's interviews with young women sent to adult prisons indicated that most had endured prolonged sexual abuse and violence. For example, Lisa, a young white woman serving time for attempted murder, had used drugs, alcohol, and joined gangs to escape the pain and troubles of her home life. Her mother was an alcoholic, and her father a convicted rapist. She had been sexually and physically abused by her stepfather from the ages of 9 to 11. Soon after Lisa began skipping school, started using alcohol and acid, and joined a gang when she was 12 years old. "They were like a family to me," she told Gaarder and Belknap. "But I became involved in a lot of stuff . . . I got high a lot, I robbed people, burglarized homes, stabbed people, and was involved in drive-bys." At age 15, she stabbed a woman in a fight. She is serving 7 to 15 years for the crime. She made this statement:

> I had just gotten out of this group home. The lady I stabbed had been messing with my sister's fiancé. This woman [had] a bunch of my sister's stuff, like her stereo and VCR, so me, my sister, her fiancé, and my boyfriend went over to pick up the stuff. We were all getting high beforehand. When we got the house, my sister and I went in . . . they [her sister and the victim] started fighting over him, and I started stabbing her with a knife. I always carried a knife with me because I was in a gang.[110]

Running Away Sometimes home life is so bad that young girls take the desperate step of running away from home. Sociologist Laurie Schaffner studied young runaways from a variety of backgrounds who were being held in a short-term residential facility in Massachusetts. She found that rather than being rebellious and antisocial, (1) adolescents actually resisted running away—it was actually a last option for them, and (2) each runaway had a plan of action that included "running to somebody" in search of the love and protection they needed from other people. She also found that running away can be viewed as a fixable problem—that healing and reconciliation do take place and running away was not necessarily a permanently disabling rupture for every family.[111]

Girls who become pregnant during their teen years often find that it is a rocky road. Many drop out of school, believing they will not be able to handle being a mother and a student at the same time. Those who do drop out find themselves without the necessary skills and educational degrees to obtain adequate employment. They may sink into persistent poverty, managing to survive on often-meager state support. Their plight is often intergenerational: Children of teen parents are also more likely to suffer educational deficiencies, be kept back in school, and are more likely to eventually drop out. Their daughters are significantly more likely to become teen mothers than the offspring of women who were older, married, and living in two-parent households. For these reasons, juvenile justice experts believe it is critical to help teen moms continue with their high school education while receiving help in developing their parenting skills. A number of programs have been developed to reach this objective.

LEARNING, EARNING AND PARENTING (LEAP)

One teen parenting program that has been popular is Ohio-based Learning, Earning and Parenting (LEAP). The LEAP program aims at requiring teen moms to either attend high school or attempt to earn a GED, in order to attain financial assistance from the state's Aid to Families with Dependant Children (AFDC). While they are in attendance they are also awarded an additional monthly stipend if they attend school and have an equal amount deducted if they drop out. In addition, upon graduation, the teen is awarded an additional stipend.

The LEAP program strives for teens to continue their high school education, to gain employment skills, and also to become familiar with effective parenting skills. Evaluations show that the program does in fact increase participants' school enrollment and attendance. However, graduation rates increased only for those teen moms who were already enrolled in school when the program was implemented and not those who entered after the program was announced. Nonetheless, four-year follow-up tests indicate that the program can be a big help, especially in boosting employment among teen mothers.

LEAP has proven so successful that it is being adopted across Canada. The Canadian program requires that each teen complete high school credits and fulfill 35 hours of parenting classes. Once both of these requirements are completed, the teen is awarded $500, which can either be put toward further education for the teen or put away for the child's future education.

GRADS

Graduation, Reality, and Dual-Role Skills (GRADS) program is a voluntary program for pregnant teenagers and/or teen parents who are in 7th to 12th grades. Also developed in Ohio, GRADS is comprised of four major areas: (1) pregnancy, (2) parenting, (3) balancing work and family, and (4) security and happiness. Participants attend classes taught by licensed and certified instructors, are placed in individual counseling, and also participate in group sessions with other teen parents. In addition, guest speakers from different organizations, such as Planned Parenthood, come in to enrich the classroom experience.

The GRADS program is aimed at strengthening the teens' bond with society. So far, it appears to be a success. The na-

Preventing Teen Pregnancy

tional dropout rate for teen mothers is approximately 60 percent, whereas the rate for those involved with the GRADS program is only about 14 percent. Repeat pregnancies by teen moms also dropped; 13 percent of those involved with the GRADS program became pregnant again, while 29 percent of teen mothers not in the program have had additional pregnancies. The program has proven so successful that GRADS is now implemented within 80 percent of Ohio's school districts, and 17 other states have also adopted the program.

ROAD

Reaching Out to Adolescent Dads (ROAD) is a Virginia-based program that targets young fathers between the ages of 13 and 20. The program strives to help the fathers continue their education by encouraging either high school attendance or participation in a GED program. ROAD helps participants develop job skills and explore career opportunities. Teens are taught to accept responsibility and are educated on preventing further pregnancies. The program teaches the participants the importance of father-child relationships and educates them on parenting skills that will benefit them in caring for their child. The program helps teens understand the importance of paying child support. Evaluations suggest that the ROAD is successful in increasing the levels of responsibility a father begins to take, improves school performance, helps them gain employment, and also reduces the chances of teens having more children.

Critical Thinking

1. The teen pregnancy rate has declined sharply during the past two decades. Do you believe that the programs described here and similar ones are responsible? Or are there other social and cultural factors that may explain the drop?

2. Should the parents of teen fathers be forced to pay child support for their son's offspring? If so, would that lower the teen birth rate?

InfoTrac College Edition Research

Use "teen pregnancy" as a key term on InfoTrac College Edition.

SOURCES: To access the LEAP program description online, go to www.cfcs.gov.on.ca/NR/MCFCS/OW/English/36_0.doc; Mike Bauer and Lorraine Graham-Watson, "Learning, Earning and Parenting Program (LEAP) 2001 Progress Report." (Ontario, Canada: Regional Municipality of Niagara, Social Assistance and Employment Opportunities Division, 2001), pp. 1–3; Johannes Bos and Veronica Fellerath, *LEAP Final Report on Ohio's Welfare Initiative to Improve School Attendance Among Teenage Parents* (New York: Manpower Demonstration Research Corporation, 1997); "Learning, Earning and Parenting Program." (Ontario, Canada: Ministry of Community, Family and Children's Services, 2003), pp. 29–30; U.S. Department of Education, "Compendium of School-Based and School-Linked Programs for Pregnant and Parenting Adolescents," National Institute on Early Childhood Development and Education, Office of Educational Research and Improvement (Washington, DC: U.S. Department of Education, 1999), www.ed.gov/pubs/Compendium/ title.html (accessed on August 25, 2004); ROAD Program, "Reaching Out to Adolescent Dads." (Roanoke, VA, 2002), p. 1.

Desisting from Delinquency: Life Transformations

The socialization view links female delinquency to a troubled home life, but how does it explain desistance from delinquent activities? In a recent study of adolescent motherhood, Trina Hope, Esther Wilder, and Toni-Terling Watt found that desistance may be linked to significant life changes that help create a commitment to conformity. Hope discovered that teens and young women who had multiple pregnancies were the ones most likely to have high rates of delinquent and antisocial behavior. However, adolescent mothers showed no evidence of delinquency levels higher than those of their never-pregnant peers. Hope and her colleagues found that in contrast to adolescent females who end their pregnancies with an abortion, those who keep their babies actually reduce deviant activities such as smoking and marijuana use. The birth of a child serves as a mechanism of social control and reduces the likelihood of delinquent behavior. Attachment to a child, even during difficult circumstances, may produce a commitment to conformity, which helps reduce delinquency.

In another important study, sociologists Peggy C. Giordano, Stephen Cernkovich, and Jennifer Rudolph link desistance to a process of cognitive change. They believe that under some circumstances changes in their environment help some people to construct a kind of psychic "scaffolding" that makes it possible for them to make significant life changes. These behavior changes can include desisting from crime.

To be eligible for desistance, individuals must discard their old bad habits, and begin the process of crafting a different way of life. Because at first the new lifestyle is usually only a distant dream or faint possibility, people who want to change must find it within themselves to resonate with, move toward, or select the various environmental catalysts for change.

COGNITIVE TRANSFORMATIONS

Giordano and her associates believe there are certain "hooks for change" within the environment. These hooks are positive life experiences that help people turn their lives around; people have to latch on to these opportunities when and if they become available. If they can manage to seize the right opportunity, the former offender may undergo a *cognitive transformation*—a process in which they reshape their thought and behavior patterns into a more conventional and rewarding life style. Giordano and her associates have identified four critical cognitive transformations that are the key to the healing process:

1. *A shift in the actor's basic openness to change.* In order to change a person must be ready and willing to change.

2. *Exposure to a particular hook or set of hooks for change.* Though a general openness to change is necessary, by itself it is often insufficient to produce meaningful results. There must also be some environmental catalyst available to "hook on to." The potential desistor must not only regard the new environmental situation as a positive development (e.g., experiencing high attachment to a spouse), but must also define the new state of affairs as fundamentally incompatible with continued deviation.

3. *Envisioning and beginning to fashion an appealing and conventional replacement self, which they can substitute for their older, damaged identity.* People can begin to escape their deviant lifestyle only when they begin to believe in their new personae and think, "It is inappropriate for someone like me to do something like that." The new identity must serve as a basis for decision making as they move into new and novel situations: "I may have smoked pot as a kid, but now that I am a husband the new me would never take the risk." The concept of a replacement self is critical when the actor faces stressful

The adolescent girls in her sample resisted fighting back against their parents and resisted breaking family rules. They seemed to struggle against running away, preferring instead to try to remain socially attached to intact family bonds. Runaways expressed resentment and hurt feelings at the loss of an interconnection between themselves and their parents. Though many told of the rage and anger that precipitated their escape, the young women also expressed fear, hurt, and pain over their fractured family relations.

According to Schaffner, the vision of runaways as incorrigible delinquents is a popular misconception. She found, instead, a much more complex picture of children who find it impossible to conform and comply with unevenly applied family rules and proscriptions; these emotionally abused girls use their running away as a desperate survival strategy. Runaway girls perceived their living arrangements as being so bad that they felt forced to run away, forced to go against what they really wished for or wanted: warm relationships with parents who could be trusted. Not surprisingly, Schaffner also found that in families where emotional and relational dynamics are deeply problematic, but not physical, youths often recounted wishful hopes for reconciliation.

life circumstances (e.g., divorce, unemployment) and he or she is forced to make decisions that differ from the ones made in the past (and which turned out to be destructive).

4. *There must be a transformation in the way the actor views the deviant behavior or lifestyle itself.* The desistance process can be seen as complete when the actor no longer sees their past life and behaviors as positive, viable, or even personally relevant. What they did in the past was foolish and destructive: It is no longer cool to get high, but selfish and destructive.

Using these cognitive shifts, the desistance process proceeds from (1) an overall "readiness" to change, to (2) encountering one or more environmental hooks for change, to (3) a shift in identity, and to (4) the maintenance of a positive identity that gradually decreases the desirability of the former deviant behavior.

Giordano and associates tested their views by using data collected from incarcerated delinquent youth who were first interviewed in 1982 and reinterviewed in 1995. They found that kids who desisted from crime as adults did in fact experience cognitive transformations. However, the hooks that got them to change were varied. For men, going to prison was a life-transforming event. For many women, having religious conversion served as a catalyst for change. Women also believed that having children was the hook that helped them reform. Some desistors told Giordano that having a romantic relationship was a key factor in their personal turnaround because supportive partners helped them raise their self-esteem: "He said I didn't belong where I was at." By seeking out conventional partners, desistors are demonstrating a cognitive shift ("I am the type of person who wants to associate with this respectable man/woman"). The potential desistor, tired of being dishonest, is helped when they are able to connect to someone who demonstrates what it means to be honest on a daily basis.

The Giordano research helps us better understand the life transforming processes which help some but not all people desist from crime.

Critical Thinking

1. Have you ever gone through a life transformation in which you radically altered some behavior that you found troubling, such as overeating, drinking, fighting with your parents, or doing poorly in school? Does the model set out by Giordano, Cernkovich, and Rudolph accurately describe the experiences you had during this period of your life?

2. Do you believe that there are significant differences in the way males and females approach change and transformation?

InfoTrac College Edition Research

To read the article on which this Focus on Delinquency is based, go to InfoTrac College Edition and read Peggy Giordano, Stephen Cernkovich, and Jennifer Rudolph, "Gender, Crime, and Desistance: Toward a Theory of Cognitive Transformation," *American Journal of Sociology* 107:990–1064 (2002). You may also want to use "cognitive transformation" in a key word search.

SOURCES: Trina Hope, Esther Wilder, Toni-Terling Watt, "The Relationships among Adolescent Pregnancy, Pregnancy Resolution, and Juvenile Delinquency," *The Sociological Quarterly* 44:555–576 (2003); Peggy Giordano, Stephen Cernkovich, and Jennifer Rudolph, "Gender, Crime, and Desistance: Toward a Theory of Cognitive Transformation," *American Journal of Sociology* 107:990–1064 (2002).

In summary, the socialization approach holds that a poor home life is likely to have an even more damaging effect on females than on males. Because girls are less likely than boys to have close-knit peer associations, they are more likely to need close parental relationships to retain emotional stability. In fact, girls may become sexually involved with boys to receive support from them, a practice that tends to magnify their problems.

Interaction is the key to understanding female delinquency. If a girl grows up in an atmosphere of sexual tension, where hostility exists between her parents, or where the parents are absent, she is likely to turn to outside sources for support. Girls are expected to follow narrowly defined behavioral patterns. In contrast, it is not unusual for boys to stay out late, drive around with friends, or get involved in other unstructured behaviors linked to delinquency. If, in reaction to loneliness and parental hostility, girls engage in the same "routine activities" as boys (staying out late, partying, and riding around with friends), they run the risk of engaging in similar types of delinquent behavior.[112]

Although the socialization approach describes the process in which girls get involved in delinquency, the question remains, why do most desist and lead conventional lifestyles as adults? This question is the topic of the above Focus on Delinquency box entitled "Desisting from Delinquency: Life Transformations."

TO QUIZ YOURSELF ON THIS MATERIAL, go to the Juvenile Delinquency 9e website.

LIBERAL FEMINIST VIEWS

The feminist movement has, from its origins, fought to help women break away from their traditional roles and secure economic, educational, and social advancement. There is little question that the women's movement has revised the way women perceive their roles in society, and it has altered the relationships of women to many social institutions.

liberal feminism
Asserts that females are less delinquent than males because their social roles provide them with fewer opportunities to commit crimes; as the roles of girls and women become more similar to those of boys and men, so too will their crime patterns.

Liberal feminism also has influenced thinking about delinquency. According to liberal feminists, females are less delinquent than males because their social roles provide fewer opportunities to commit crime. As the roles of women become more similar to those of men, so will their crime patterns. Female criminality is motivated by the same influences as male criminality. According to Freda Adler's important book *Sisters in Crime* (1975), by striving for independence, women have begun to alter the institutions that had protected males in their traditional positions of power.[113] Adler argued that female delinquency would be affected by the changing role of women. As females entered new occupations and participated in sports, politics, and other traditionally male endeavors, they would also become involved in crimes that had heretofore been male-oriented; delinquency rates would then converge. She noted that girls were becoming increasingly involved in traditionally masculine crimes such as gang activity and fighting.

Adler predicted that the women's movement would produce steeper increases in the rate of female delinquency because it created an environment in which the roles of girls and boys converge. She predicted that the changing female role will produce female criminals who are similar to their male counterparts.[114]

Support for Liberal Feminism

A number of studies support the feminist view of gender differences in delinquency.[115] More than 20 years ago, Rita Simon explained how the increase in female criminality is a function of the changing role of women. She claimed that as women were empowered economically and socially, they would be less likely to feel dependent and oppressed. Consequently, women would be less likely to attack their traditional targets: their husbands, their lovers, or even their own children.[116] Instead, their new role as breadwinner might encourage women to engage in traditional male crimes such as larceny and car theft.

Simon's view has been supported in part by research showing a significant correlation between the women's rights movement and the female crime rate.[117] If 1966 is used as a jumping-off point (because the National Organization for Women was founded in that year), there are indications that patterns of serious female crime (robbery and auto theft) correlate with indicators of female emancipation (the divorce rate and participation in the labor force). Although this research does not prove that female crime is related to social change, it identifies behavior patterns that support that hypothesis.

In addition to these efforts, self-report studies support the liberal feminist view by showing that gender differences in delinquency are fading; that is, the pattern of female delinquency, if not the extent, is now similar to that of male delinquency.[118] With few exceptions the factors that seem to motivate both male and female criminality seem similar.[119] For example, research shows that economic disadvantages are felt equally by both male and female residents of underprivileged inner-city neighborhoods.[120]

As the sex roles of males and females have become less distinct, their offending patterns have become more similar. Girls may be committing crimes to gain economic advancement and not because they lack parental support. Both of these patterns are predicted by liberal feminists.

Critiques of Liberal Feminism

Not all delinquency experts believe changing sex roles influence crime rates. Some argue that the delinquent behavior patterns of girls have remained static and have not been influenced by the women's movement. Females involved in violent crime more often than not have some connection to a male partner who influences their behavior. One study of women who kill in the course of their involvement in the drug trade found that they kill on behalf of a man or out of fear of a man.[121]

Others dispute that changes in female rates relate to the feminist movement. Self-report studies show that female participation in most crime has remained stable for the past 10 years.[122] It is possible that the women's movement has not influenced crime rates as much as previously thought.[123] Perhaps the greater participation by females in the Uniform Crime Report arrest data is more a function of how police are treating females than an actual change in female behavior patterns.

In summary, some critics believe that gender differences in crime have not changed as much as liberal feminist writers had predicted.[124] Consequently, the argument that female crime and delinquency will be shaped by the women's movement has not received unqualified support.

TO QUIZ YOURSELF ON THIS MATERIAL, go to the Juvenile Delinquency 9e website.

CRITICAL FEMINIST VIEWS

critical feminists (also known as Marxist feminists)
Hold that gender inequality stems from the unequal power of men and women and the subsequent exploitation of women by men; the cause of female delinquency originates with the onset of male supremacy and the efforts of males to control females' sexuality.

A number of writers take a more critical view of gender differences in crime. These scholars can be categorized as **critical feminists,** who believe gender inequality stems from the unequal power of men and women in a capitalist society and the exploitation of females by fathers and husbands: Women are a "commodity" like land or money.[125] Female delinquency originates with the onset of male supremacy (*patriarchy*), the subordination of women, male aggression, and the efforts of men to control females sexually.[126]

Critical feminists focus on the social forces that shape girls' lives.[127] They attempt to show how the sexual victimization of girls is often a function of male socialization and that young males learn to be exploitive of women. James Messerschmidt, an influential feminist scholar, has formulated a theoretical model to show how misguided concepts of "masculinity" flow from the inequities built into "patriarchal capitalism." Men dominate business in capitalist societies, and males who cannot function well within its parameters are at risk for crime. Women are inherently powerless in such a society, and their crimes reflect their limited access to both legitimate and illegitimate opportunity.[128] It is not surprising that research surveys have found that 90 percent of adolescent girls are sexually harassed in school, with almost 30 percent reporting having been psychologically pressured to "do something sexual," and 10 percent physically forced into sexual behaviors.[129]

According to the critical view, male exploitation acts as a trigger for female delinquent behavior. Female delinquents recount being so severely harassed at school that they were forced to carry knives. Some reported that boyfriends, sometimes in their 30s, who "knew how to treat a girl," would draw them into criminal activity such as drug trafficking, which eventually entangled them in the justice system.[130]

When female adolescents run away and use drugs, they may be reacting to abuse at home or at school. Their attempts at survival are then labeled delinquent.[131] Research shows that a significant number of girls who are victims of sexual and other forms of abuse later engage in delinquency.[132] All too often, school officials ignore complaints made by female students. Young girls therefore may feel trapped and desperate.

For more than 20 years, the **Center for Research on Women** has been in the forefront of research in which the central questions are shaped by the experiences and perspectives of women. Their website can be accessed at www.wcwonline.org. For an up-to-date list of web links, go to http://cj.wadsworth.com/siegel_jd9e.

Crime and Patriarchy

A number of theoretical models have attempted to use a critical or Marxist feminist perspective to explain gender differences in delinquency. For example, in *Capitalism, Patriarchy, and Crime,* James Messerschmidt argues that capitalist society is marked by both patriarchy and class conflict. Capitalists control workers, and men control women, both economically and biologically.[133] This "double marginality" explains why females in a capitalist society commit fewer crimes than males. They are isolated

Power, Gender, and Adolescent Dating Violence

Research on domestic violence among adults most often concludes that females are the primary targets of violence and when they fight back it is most often in self-defense. However, studies of adolescent dating violence often find equal or higher rates of female-perpetrated physical violence than male violence. How can this discrepancy be explained?

To find out, sociologists Jody Miller and Norman White conducted in-depth interviews with 70 African American youths, aged 12–19, in north St. Louis, Missouri. Rather than take a "gender-neutral" approach and treat gender simply as a category, either male or female, the researchers considered gender, and the conflict and power relationships it creates, as an important factor that shaped the direction and content of adolescent personal relationships.

Miller and White find significant differences in dating violence structured by gender relationships. Girls achieve status by having boyfriends but get less emotional support than might be imagined. Boys actually get more from relationships but must disguise their stake in order to conform to cultural norms. To gain status among their friends, they must take the role of being a "playa" (player)—guys who use girls for sex and have multiple sexual partners and conquests. Playas have little emotional attachment to their sexual partners, and adopt a detached, uninvolved "cool" attitude and demeanor. They bestow derogatory sexual labels on the girls they are with (e.g., "hood rats" or "ho's") especially if they "give in" too easily. This attitude seems to correspond with the fact that the boys are given strong messages from their male peers that "love equals softness"). Consequently, to avoid being labeled soft by their friends, they engage in aggressive behavior during their relationships. They are much more likely to cheat on their girlfriends, whereas girls are more likely to be loyal to their boyfriends. In addition, boys are more willing to share sexual details with their peers, mistreat their girlfriends openly in front of friends, and downplay the meaningfulness of their relationships.

Miller and White found significant differences in the motivation for domestic dating violence. Girls' violence is attributed to their emotionality, especially the anger they experience when they suspect their boyfriend is cheating. Though jealousy is considered emotional instability, its basis is tied to reality: Girls are much more likely to have been the actual victim of infidelity than boys. (If confronted by a jealous mate, boys are more likely to react to their accusations with a "cool" response, walking away or minimizing the damage caused by their infidelity. The cool response only makes girls angrier and more willing to cause a confrontation. Ironically, some girls attack their boyfriends to get an emotional response from them, to drive them out of their cool state, even if it means being struck back harder in return. Some are willing to interpret the violent response as an indicator that the boy actually likes them; any response is favorable even if it is violent.

In contrast, boys are taught not to use violence against girls, who are considered weaker; hitting them is unmanly: "If a boy hits a girl they a punk." However, violence against girlfriends is justifiable in retaliation for female-perpetrated violence: The boy cheats, the girl slaps him, and he slaps her back.

Though most dating violence is of the retaliatory type, some boys describe using violence to control a girlfriend or put her in her place. Some describe girls as deserving male violence when they are "runnin' they mouth" or "get all up in my face." Miller and White find that there are significant differences in the dynamics of dating violence. Girls' violence may actually be more frequent in incidence, but it is not considered dangerous. Its motives are the girls' desire to exercise control in their relationships—to keep their boyfriends from flirting, chatting, or showing off with other girls. When their anger escalates they become the target for retaliation because they typically lack the power to achieve these goals. Consequently, boys describe girls' violence as resulting from girls being emotionally "out of control" and they do not view it as posing a serious threat. This dynamic reveals the substantial gender-based inequalities in dating relationships.

Critical Thinking

1. Do you think that the description of girls' violence as "emotional" undermines their ability to challenge the inequality in their relationships? How can this inequality be addressed?

2. Are the relationships found by Miller and White normative? Do they exist in your own peer network? Are they universal or limited to the group they studied?

InfoTrac College Edition Research

To find out more about this subject, use "domestic violence" and "dating violence" in a key term search on InfoTrac College Edition.

SOURCE: Jody Miller and Norman White, "Gender and Adolescent Relationship Violence: A Contextual Examination," *Criminology* 41:1207–1248 (2003).

in the family and have fewer opportunities to engage in elite deviance (white-collar and economic crimes); they are also denied access to male-dominated street crimes. Because capitalism renders women powerless, they are forced to commit less serious crimes such as abusing drugs. The Focus on Delinquency box entitled "Power, Gender, and Adolescent Dating Violence" explores how gender inequality shapes dating violence among adolescents.

Power-Control Theory

John Hagan and his associates have speculated that gender differences in delinquency are a function of class differences that influence family life. Hagan, who calls his view **power-control theory,** suggests that class influences delinquency by controlling the quality of family life.[134] In paternalistic families, fathers assume the role of breadwinners, and mothers have menial jobs or remain at home. Mothers are expected to control the behavior of their daughters while granting greater freedom to sons. The parent-daughter relationship can be viewed as a preparation for the "cult of domesticity," which makes daughters' involvement in delinquency unlikely. Hence, males exhibit a higher degree of delinquent behavior than their sisters.

In **egalitarian families**—in which the husband and wife share similar positions of power at home and in the workplace—daughters gain a kind of freedom that reflects reduced parental control. These families produce daughters whose law-violating behaviors mirror those of their brothers. Ironically, these kinds of relationships also occur in households with absent fathers. Similarly, Hagan and his associates found that when both fathers and mothers hold equally valued managerial positions, the similarity between the rates of their daughters' and sons' delinquency is greatest. Therefore, middle-class girls are most likely to violate the law because they are less closely controlled than lower-class girls.

Research conducted by Hagan and his colleagues has tended to support the core relationship between family structure and gender differences in delinquency.[135] Other social scientists have produced tests of the theory, which have generally supported its hypothesis. For example, Brenda Sims Blackwell and Mark Reed found that the gap between brother-sister delinquency is greatest in patriarchal families and least in egalitarian families, a finding consistent with the core premise of power-control theory.[136]

However, some of the basic premises of power-control theory, such as the relationship between social class and delinquency, have been challenged. For example, some critics have questioned the assumption that upper-class youths may engage in more petty delinquency than lower-class youths because they are brought up to be "risk takers" who do not fear the consequences of their misdeeds.[137]

Power-control theory encourages a new approach to the study of delinquency, one that addresses gender differences, class position, and family structure. It also helps explain the relative increase in female delinquency by stressing the significance of changing feminine roles. With the increase in single-parent homes, the patterns Hagan

According to power-control theory, when girls grow up in egalitarian families, where the husband and the wife share similar positions of power at home and in the workplace, they achieve greater freedom and independence.

has identified may change. The decline of the patriarchal family may produce looser family ties on girls, changing sex roles, and increased delinquency. Ironically, this raises an interesting dilemma: The daughters of successful and powerful mothers are more at risk for delinquency than the daughters of stay-at-home moms! However, as sociologist Christopher Uggen points out, there may be a bright side to this dilemma. Not only are they more likely to commit delinquent acts, the daughters of independent working mothers may also be encouraged to take prosocial risks such as engaging in athletic competition and breaking into traditional male-dominated occupations, such as policing and the military.[138]

TO QUIZ YOURSELF ON THIS MATERIAL, go to the Juvenile Delinquency 9e website.

GENDER AND THE JUVENILE JUSTICE SYSTEM

Not only do gender differences have an effect on crime patterns, they also may have a significant impact on the way children are treated by the juvenile justice system. Several feminist scholars argue that girls are not only the victims of injustice at home but also risk being victimized by agents of the justice system.

The early juvenile court viewed female delinquency as sexual in nature and believed that the great majority of female delinquents' troubles could be linked to their being sexually precocious. When Mary Odem and Steven Schlossman studied the records of more than 200 girls petitioned to the Los Angeles Juvenile Court in 1920, they found that the majority were suspected of sexual activity; all were given a compulsory pelvic exam. Girls adjudged sexually delinquent on the basis of the exam were segregated from the merely incorrigible girls to prevent moral corruption. Of those found to be sexually active, *29 percent* were committed to custodial institutions, a high price to pay for moral transgressions.[139]

Are girls still victims of the juvenile justice system? Meda Chesney-Lind's well-regarded research found that police are more likely to arrest female adolescents for sexual activity and to ignore the same behavior among male delinquents.[140] Girls were also more likely to be sent to a detention facility before trial, and the length of their detention averaged three times that of boys. Girls are far more likely than boys to be picked up by police for status offenses and are more likely to be kept in detention for such offenses.[141]

Girls, more than boys, are still disadvantaged if their behavior is viewed as morally incorrect by government officials, or if they are considered beyond parental control.[142] Recent research conducted by John MacDonald and Meda Chesney-Lind found that the juvenile justice system still categorizes female offenders into two distinct groups: girls who momentarily strayed from the "good girl" path, and are therefore deserving of solicitous, humanitarian treatment, and dangerously wayward girls who have serious problems and must therefore be kept under strict control lest they stray further.[143]

Girls may also be feeling the brunt of the more punitive policies now being used in the juvenile justice system. For example, when Chesney-Lind and Vickie Paramore analyzed data from the city and county of Honolulu, they found that tougher juvenile justice standards meant that more cases were being handled formally within the juvenile justice system.[144] Though girls are actually committing fewer violent crimes, they are more likely to become enmeshed within the grasp of the juvenile justice system. Once in the system, girls may receive fewer benefits and services than their male counterparts. Institutionalized girls report that they receive fewer privileges and programs, less space and less equipment, and harsher treatment than institutionalized boys.[145]

Girls may still be subject to harsh punishments if they are considered dangerously immoral. They are more likely to be charged with being a status offender than boys, especially if they participate in behaviors which may lead them "astray."[146] For example, girls are more likely than boys to be arrested as runaways and for vice-related crimes such as prostitution, since running away and having sex are considered inappropriate and extremely dangerous for young girls; the sexual double standard still exists.[147]

In addition, there still appears to be an association between male standards of beauty and sexual behavior. Criminal justice professionals may look on attractive girls who engage in sexual behavior more harshly, overlooking some of the same behaviors in less attractive girls. In some jurisdictions, girls are still being incarcerated for status offenses because their behavior does not measure up to concepts of proper female behavior.[148] Even though girls are still less likely to be arrested than boys, those who fail to measure up to stereotypes of "proper" female behavior are more likely to be sanctioned than male offenders.[149]

Why do these differences persist? Perhaps because correctional authorities continue to subscribe to stereotyped beliefs about the needs of young girls. Randall Shelden and Meda Chesney-Lind found that court officials and policy makers still show a lack of concern about girls' victimization and instead are more concerned with controlling their behavior than addressing the factors that brought them to the attention of the juvenile justice system in the first place.[150] The role of girls in the juvenile justice system will be discussed further in Chapters 13–16.

TO QUIZ YOURSELF ON THIS MATERIAL, go to the Juvenile Delinquency 9e website.

Summary

- The relationship between gender and delinquency has become a topic of considerable interest to criminologists.

- At one time, attention was directed solely at male offenders, and the rare female delinquent was considered an oddity. The nature and extent of female delinquent activities have changed, and girls are now engaging in more frequent and serious illegal activity.

- Sociologists and psychologists recognize that there are differences in attitudes, values, and behavior between boys and girls.

- Females process information differently than males and have different cognitive and physical strengths. These differences may, in part, explain gender differences in delinquency.

- Girls are socialized differently, which causes them to internalize rather than externalize anger and aggression.

- There are also psychological differences between the sexes. Girls may actually be at risk for a greater level of mental anguish than boys.

- There are a number of different views of female delinquency.

- Trait views are concerned with biological and psychological differences between the sexes. Early efforts by Cesare Lombroso and his followers placed the blame for delinquency on physical differences between males and females. Girls who were delinquent had inherent masculine characteristics.

- Contemporary trait theorists view girls' psychological makeup, hormonal, and physical characteristics as key to their delinquent behavior.

- Socialization has also been identified as a cause of delinquency. Males are socialized to be tough and aggressive, females to be passive and obedient.

- Early socialization views portrayed the adolescent female offender as a troubled girl who lacked love at home and supportive peer relations.

- These theories treated female delinquents as sexual offenders whose criminal activities were linked to destructive relationships with men.

- Contemporary socialization views continue to depict female delinquents as being raised in hellish homes where they are the victims of sexual and physical abuse.

- More recent views of gender and delinquency incorporate the changes brought about by the women's movement. Liberal feminists argue that as the roles of women change, so will their crime patterns. Although a number of studies support this view, some theorists question its validity. The female crime rate has increased, and female delinquency patterns now resemble those of males, but the gender gap has not narrowed substantially after more than two decades.

- Critical feminists view female delinquency as a function of patriarchy and the mistreatment and exploitation of females in a male-dominated society.

- Hagan's power-control theory helps us understand why gender differences in the crime rate exist and whether change may be coming.

- The treatment girls receive by the juvenile justice system has also been the subject of debate. Originally, it was thought that police protected girls from the stigma of a delinquency label. Contemporary criminologists charge, however, that girls are discriminated against by agents of the justice system.

Key Terms

masculinity hypothesis, p. 173
gender-schema theory, p. 177
chivalry hypothesis, p. 179
precocious sexuality, p. 180

cortisol, p. 181
callous-unemotional (CU) traits, p. 184
liberal feminism, p. 190

critical feminists, Marxist feminists, p. 191
power-control theory, p. 193
egalitarian families, p. 193

Questions for Discussion

1. Are girls delinquent for different reasons than boys? Do girls have a unique set of problems?

2. As sex roles become more homogenous, do you believe female delinquency will become identical to male delinquency in rate and type?

3. Does the sexual double standard still exist?

4. Are lower-class girls more strictly supervised than upper- and middle-class girls? Is control stratified across class lines?

5. Are girls the victims of unfairness at the hands of the justice system, or do they benefit from "chivalry"?

Viewpoint

As the principal of a northeastern junior high school, you get a call from a parent who is disturbed because he has heard a rumor that the student literary digest plans to publish a story with a sexual theme. The work is written by a junior high school girl who became pregnant during the year and underwent an abortion. You ask for and receive a copy of the narrative.

The girl's story is actually a cautionary tale of young love that results in an unwanted pregnancy. The author details the abusive home life that led her to engage in an intimate relationship with another student, her pregnancy, her conflict with her parents, her decision to abort, and the emotional turmoil that the incident created. She tells students to use contraception if they are sexually active and recommends appropriate types of birth control. There is nothing provocative or sexually explicit in the work.

Some teachers argue that girls should not be allowed to read this material because it has sexual content from which they must be protected, and that in a sense it advocates defiance of parents. Also, some parents may object to a story about precocious sexuality because they fear it may encourage their children to "experiment." Such behavior is linked to delinquency and drug abuse. Those who advocate publication believe that girls have a right to read about such important issues and decide on their own course of action.

❙ Should you force the story's deletion because its theme is essentially sexual and controversial?

❙ Should you allow publication because it deals with the subject matter in a mature fashion?

❙ Do you think reading and learning about sexual matters encourages or discourages experimentation in sexuality?

❙ Should young girls be protected from such material? Would it cause them damage?

Doing Research on the Web

Inequalities still exist in the way boys and girls are socialized by their parents and treated by social institutions. Do these gender differences also manifest themselves in the delinquency rate? What effect do gender roles have on behavior choices?

To answer this question, you might want to first read: *Hazelwood School District et al. v. Kuhlmeier et al* (accessed on August 26, 2004):

www.bc.edu/bc_org/avp/cas/comm/free_speech/ hazelwood.html

The following website has more material on this and similar issues (accessed on August 26, 2004):

www.landmarkcases.org/hazelwood/home.html

To read more about school news and censorship issues, go to the National Scholastic Press Association website (accessed on August 26, 2004):

http://studentpress.journ.umn.edu/nspa/trends/

Notes

1. Cesare Lombroso, *The Female Offender* (New York: Appleton, 1920); W. I. Thomas, *The Unadjusted Girl* (New York: Harper & Row, 1923).

2. Cesare Lombroso and William Ferrero, *The Female Offender* (New York: Philosophical Library, 1895).

3. James Messerschmidt, *Masculinities and Crime: Critique and Reconceptualization of Theory* (Lanham, MD: Rowman and Littlefield, 1993).

4. Cheryl Maxson and Monica Whitlock, "Joining the Gang: Gender Differences in Risk Factors for Gang Membership," in C. Ronald Huff, ed., *Gangs in America III* (Thousand Oaks, CA: Sage Publications, 2002), pp. 19–35.

5. David Finkelhor and Richard Ormrod, "Prostitution of Juveniles: Patterns from NIBRS," *Juvenile Justice Bulletin*, June 2004 (Washington, DC: The Office of Juvenile Justice and Delinquency Prevention, 2004), www.ncjrs.org/html/ojjdp/203946/contents.html. (Accessed on August 25, 2004.)

6. Paul Mazerolle, Robert Brame, Ray Paternoster, Alex Piquero, and Charles Dean, "Onset Age, Persistence, and Offending Versatility: Comparisons across Sex," paper presented at the annual Society of Criminology meeting, San Diego, November 1997.

7. Kathleen Daly, "From Gender Ratios to Gendered Lives: Women's Gender in Crime and Criminological Theory," in Michael Tonry, ed., *The Handbook of Crime and Punishment* (New York: Oxford University Press, 1998).

8. Rita James Simon, *The Contemporary Woman and Crime* (Washington, DC: U.S. Government Printing Office, 1975).

9. Rolf Loeber and Dale Hay, "Key Issues in the Development of Aggression and Violence from Childhood to Early Adulthood," *Annual Review of Psychology* 48:371–410 (1997).

10. This section leans heavily on Spencer Rathus, *Voyages in Childhood* (Belmont, CA: Wadsworth, 2004); see also Darcy Miller, Catherine Trapani, Kathy Fejes-Mendoza, Carolyn Eggleston, and Donna Dwiggins, "Adolescent Female Offenders: Unique Considerations," *Adolescence* 30:429–435 (1995).

11. Allison Morris, *Women, Crime and Criminal Justice* (Oxford: Basil Blackwell, 1987).

12. Dennis Giever, "An Empirical Assessment of the Core Elements of Gottfredson and Hirschi's General Theory of Crime," paper presented at the American Society of Criminology meeting, Boston, November 1995.

13. Loeber and Hay, "Key Issues in the Development of Aggression and Violence from Childhood to Early Adulthood," p. 378.

14. John Mirowsky and Catherine Ross, "Sex Differences in Distress: Real or Artifact?" *American Sociological Review* 60:449–468 (1995).

15. Ibid., pp. 460–465.

16. For a review of this issue, see Anne Campbell, *Men, Women and Aggression* (New York: Basic Books, 1993).

17. Diane Halpern and Mary LaMay, "The Smarter Sex: A Critical Review of Sex Differences in Intelligence," *Educational Psychology Review*, 12:229–246 (2000).

18. Camilla Benbow, David Lubinski, Daniel Shea, and Hossain Eftekhari-Sanjani, "Sex Differences in Mathematical Reasoning Ability at Age 13: Their Status 20 Years Later," *Psychological Science*, 11:474–480 (2000).

19. Ann Beutel and Margaret Mooney Marini, "Gender and Values," *American Sociological Review* 60:436–448 (1995).

20. Lisa Broidy, Elizabeth Cauffman, and Dorothy Espelage, "Sex Differences in Empathy and Its Relation to Juvenile Offending," *Violence and Victims* 18:503–516 (2003).

21. American Association of University Women, *Shortchanging Girls, Shortchanging America: Executive Summary* (Washington, DC: American Association of University Women, 1991).

22. Spencer Rathus, *Voyages in Childhood* (Belmont, CA: Wadsworth, 2004).

23. Carol Gilligan, *In a Different Voice* (Cambridge, MA: Harvard University Press, 1982).

24. David Rowe, Alexander Vazsonyi, and Daniel Flannery, "Sex Differences in Crime: Do Means and Within-Sex Variation Have Similar Causes?" *Journal of Research in Crime and Delinquency* 32:84–100 (1995).

25. Sandra Bem, *The Lenses of Gender* (New Haven: Yale University Press, 1993).

26. Walter DeKeseredy and Martin Schwartz, "Male Peer Support and Woman Abuse," *Sociological Spectrum* 13:393–413 (1993).

27. Eleanor Maccoby, *The Two Sexes: Growing Up Apart, Coming Together* (Cambridge, MA: Belknap Press, 1999).

28. Jean Bottcher, "Social Practices of Gender: How Gender Relates to Delinquency in the Everyday Lives of High-Risk Youths," *Criminology* 39:893–932 (2001).

29. Daniel Mears, Matthew Ploeger, and Mark Warr, "Explaining the Gender Gap in Delinquency: Peer Influence and Moral Evaluations of Behavior," *Journal of Research in Crime and Delinquency* 35:251–266 (1998).

30. John Gibbs, Dennis Giever, and Jamie Martin, "Parental Management and Self-Control: An Empirical Test of Gottfredson and Hirschi's General Theory," *Journal of Research in Crime and Delinquency* 35:40–70 (1998); Velmer Burton, Francis Cullen, T. David Evans, Leanne Fiftal Alarid, and R. Gregory Dunaway, "Gender, Self-Control, and Crime," *Journal of Research in Crime and Delinquency* 35:123–147 (1998).

31. Messerschmidt, *Masculinities and Crime: Critique and Reconceptualization of Theory*.

32. D.J. Pepler and W.M. Craig, "A Peek Behind the Fence: Naturalistic Observations of Aggressive Children with Remote Audiovisual Recording," *Developmental Psychology* 31:548–553 (1995).

33. Federal Bureau of Investigation, *Crime in the United States, 2002* (Washington, DC: U.S. Government Printing Office, 2003) pp. 239.

34. Monitoring the Future 2002. Data supplied by the Institute for Social Research, Ann Arbor, MI, 2003.

35. Federal Bureau of Investigation, *Crime in the United States, 2002*, p. 248.

36. Lombroso and Ferrero, *The Female Offender*.

37. Ibid., p. 122.

38. Ibid., pp. 51–52.

39. For a review, see Anne Campbell, *Girl Delinquents* (Oxford: Basic Blackwell, 1981), pp. 41–48.

40. Cyril Burt, *The Young Delinquent* (New York: Appleton, 1925); see also Warren Middleton, "Is There a Relation between Kleptomania and Female Periodicity in Neurotic Individuals?" *Psychology Clinic* (December 1933), pp. 232–47.

41. William Healy and Augusta Bronner, *Delinquents and Criminals, Their Making and Unmaking* (New York: Macmillan, 1926).

42. Otto Pollak, *The Criminality of Women* (Philadelphia: University of Pennsylvania Press, 1950).

43. Ibid., p. 158.

44. Ibid., p. 10.

45. Miriam Sealock and Sally Simpson, "Unraveling Bias in Arrest Decisions: The Role of Juvenile Offender Type-Scripts," *Justice Quarterly* 15:427–457 (1998); Christina Polsenberg and Kenneth Jackson, "Putting Race into Context: Race, Juvenile Justice Processing and Urbanization," paper presented at the American Society of Criminology meeting, Boston, November 1995 (updated version, 1996). For a general review, see Carl Pope and William Feyerherm, "Minority Status and Juvenile Justice Processing (Part I)," *Criminal Justice Abstracts* 22:327–335 (1990); see also Douglas Smith and Jody Klein, "Police Control of Interpersonal Disputes," *Social Problems* 31:468–481 (1984).

46. Sigmund Freud, *An Outline of Psychoanalysis*, James Strachey, trans. (New York: Norton, 1949), p. 278.

47. Dorie Klein, "The Etiology of Female Crime: A Review of the Literature," in Freda Adler and Rita Simon, eds., *The Criminology of Deviant Women* (Boston: Houghton Mifflin, 1979), pp. 69–71.

48. Peter Blos, "Preoedipal Factors in the Etiology of Female Delinquency," *Psychoanalytic Studies of the Child* 12:229–242 (1957).

49. Sheldon Glueck and Eleanor Glueck, *Five Hundred Delinquent Women* (New York: Knopf, 1934).

50. J. Cowie, V. Cowie, and E. Slater, *Delinquency in Girls* (London: Heinemann, 1968).

51. Anne Campbell, "On the Invisibility of the Female Delinquent Peer Group," *Women and Criminal Justice* 2:41–62 (1990).

52. Carolyn Smith, "Factors Associated with Early Sexual Activity among Urban Adolescents," *Social Work* 42:334–346 (1997).

53. For a review, see Christy Miller Buchanan, Jacquelynne Eccles, and Jill Becker, "Are Adolescents the Victims of Raging Hormones? Evidence for Activational Effects of Hormones on Moods and Behavior at Adolescence," *Psychological Bulletin* 111:63–107 (1992).

54. L. Kris Gowen, S. Shirley Feldman, Rafael Diaz, and Donnovan Somera Yisrael, "A Comparison of the Sexual Behaviors and Attitudes of Adolescent Girls with Older vs. Similar-aged Boyfriends," *Journal of Youth and Adolescence* 33:167–176 (2004).

55. Dana Haynie "Contexts of Risk? Explaining the Link between Girls' Pubertal Development and Their Delinquency Involvement," *Social Forces* 82:355–397 (2003).

56. Avshalom Caspi, Donald Lyman, Terrie Moffitt, and Phil Silva, "Unraveling Girls' Delinquency: Biological, Dispositional, and Contextual Contributions to Adolescent Misbehavior," *Developmental Psychology* 29:283–289 (1993).

57. Eleanor Maccoby and Carol Jacklin, *The Psychology of Sex Differences* (Stanford, CA: Stanford University Press, 1974).
58. Kathleen Pajer, William Gardner, Robert Rubin, James Perel, and Stephen Neal, "Decreased Cortisol Levels in Adolescent Girls with Conduct Disorder," *Archives of General Psychiatry* 58:297–302 (2001).
59. Alan Booth and D. Wayne Osgood, "The Influence of Testosterone on Deviance in Adulthood: Assessing and Explaining the Relationship," *Criminology* 31:93–118 (1993).
60. D.H. Baucom, P.K. Besch, and S. Callahan, "Relationship between Testosterone Concentration, Sex Role Identity, and Personality among Females," *Journal of Personality and Social Psychology* 48:1218–1226 (1985).
61. Lee Ellis, "Evidence of Neuroandrogenic Etiology of Sex Roles from a Combined Analysis of Human, Nonhuman Primate and Nonprimate Mammalian Studies," *Personality and Individual Differences* 7:519–552 (1986).
62. Diana Fishbein, "Selected Studies on the Biology of Antisocial Behavior," in John Conklin, ed., *New Perspectives in Criminology* (Needham Heights, MA: Allyn & Bacon, 1996), pp. 26–38.
63. Diana Fishbein, "The Psychobiology of Female Aggression," *Criminal Justice and Behavior* 19:99–126 (1992).
64. Spencer Rathus, *Psychology,* 3rd ed. (New York: Holt, Rinehart & Winston, 1987), p. 88.
65. See Katharina Dalton, *The Premenstrual Syndrome* (Springfield, IL: Charles C Thomas, 1971).
66. Fishbein, "Selected Studies on the Biology of Antisocial Behavior."
67. Fishbein, "Selected Studies on the Biology of Antisocial Behavior"; Karen Paige, "Effects of Oral Contraceptives on Affective Fluctuations Associated with the Menstrual Cycle," *Psychosomatic Medicine* 33:515–537 (1971).
68. B. Harry and C. Balcer, "Menstruation and Crime: A Critical Review of the Literature from the Clinical Criminology Perspective," *Behavioral Sciences and the Law* 5:307–322 (1987).
69. Julie Horney, "Menstrual Cycles and Criminal Responsibility," *Law and Human Nature* 2:25–36 (1978).
70. Lee Ellis, "The Victimful-Victimless Crime Distinction and Seven Universal Demographic Correlates of Victimful Criminal Behavior," *Personality and Individual Differences* 9:525–548 (1988).
71. Eleanor Maccoby and Carol Jacklin, *The Psychology of Sex Differences* (Stanford, CA: Stanford University Press, 1974).
72. Ellis, "Evolutionary and Neurochemical Causes of Sex Differences in Victimizing Behavior," pp. 605–636.
73. Buchanan, Eccles, and Becker, "Are Adolescents the Victims of Raging Hormones?" p. 94.
74. Ann Frodi, J. Maccauley, and P. R. Thome, "Are Women Always Less Aggressive than Men? A Review of the Experimental Literature," *Psychological Bulletin* 84:634–660 (1977).
75. Kathleen Pajer, "What Happens to 'Bad' Girls? A Review of the Adult Outcomes of Antisocial Adolescent Girls," *American Journal of Psychiatry* 155:862–870 (1998).
76. Jan ter Laak, Martijn de Goede, Liesbeth Aleva, Gerard Brugman, Miranda van Leuven, and Judith Hussmann, "Incarcerated Adolescent Girls: Personality, Social Competence, and Delinquency," *Adolescence* 38:251–265 (2003).
77. Dorothy Espelage, Elizabeth Cauffman, Lisa Broidy, Alex Piquero, Paul Mazerolle, and Hans Steiner "A Cluster-Analytic Investigation of MMPI Profiles of Serious Male and Female Juvenile Offenders," *Journal of the American Academy of Child and Adolescent Psychiatry* 42:770–777 (2003).
78. Kristen McCabe, Amy Lansing, Ann Garland, Richard Hough, "Gender Differences in Psychopathology: Functional Impairment, and Familial Risk Factors among Adjudicated Delinquents," *Journal of the American Academy of Child and Adolescent Psychiatry* 41:860–867 (2002).
79. Paul Frick, Amy Cornell, Christopher Barry, Doug Bodin, and Heather Dane, "Callous-Unemotional Traits and Conduct Problems in the Prediction of Conduct Problem Severity, Aggression, and Self-Report of Delinquency," *Journal of Abnormal Child Psychology* 31:457–470 (2003).
80. Alex Mason and Michael Windle, "Gender, Self-Control, and Informal Social Control in Adolescence: A Test of Three Models of the Continuity of Delinquent Behavior," *Youth & Society* 33:479–514 (2002).
81. Dana Jones Hubbard and Travis Pratt, "A Meta-analysis of the Predictors of Delinquency among Girls," *Journal of Offender Rehabilitation* 34:1–13 (2002).
82. Thomas, *The Unadjusted Girl.*
83. Ibid., p. 109.
84. David Farrington, "Juvenile Delinquency," in John Coleman, ed., *The School Years* (London: Routledge, 1992), p. 133.
85. Ibid.
86. Ruth Morris, "Female Delinquents and Relational Problems," *Social Forces* 43:82–89 (1964).
87. Cowie, Cowie, and Slater, *Delinquency in Girls,* p. 27.
88. Gisela Konopka, *The Adolescent Girl in Conflict* (Englewood Cliffs, NJ: Prentice-Hall, 1966).
89. Ibid., p. 40.
90. Ibid., p. 50.
91. Morris, "Female Delinquency and Relational Problems."
92. Clyde Vedder and Dora Somerville, *The Delinquent Girl* (Springfield, IL: Charles C Thomas, 1970).
93. Sheldon Glueck and Eleanor Glueck, *Unraveling Juvenile Delinquency* (Cambridge, MA: Harvard University Press, 1950).
94. Ibid., pp. 281–282.
95. Glueck and Glueck, *Five Hundred Delinquent Women.*
96. Ibid., p. 90.
97. Ames Robey, Richard Rosenwal, John Small, and Ruth Lee, "The Runaway Girl: A Reaction to Family Stress," *American Journal of Orthopsychiatry* 34:763–767 (1964).
98. William Wattenberg and Frank Saunders, "Sex Differences among Juvenile Court Offenders," *Sociology and Social Research* 39:24–31 (1954).
99. Don Gibbons and Manzer Griswold, "Sex Differences among Juvenile Court Referrals," *Sociology and Social Research* 42:106–110 (1957).
100. Gordon Barker and William Adams, "Comparison of the Delinquencies of Boys and Girls," *Journal of Criminal Law, Criminology, and Police Science* 53:470–475 (1962).
101. George Calhoun, Janelle Jurgens, and Fengling Chen, "The Neophyte Female Delinquent: A Review of the Literature," *Adolescence* 28:461–471 (1993).
102. Joanne Belknap, Kristi Holsinger, and Melissa Dunn, "Understanding Incarcerated Girls: The Results of a Focus Group Study," *Prison Journal* 77:381–405 (1997).
103. Veronica. Herrera and Laura Ann McCloskey, "Sexual Abuse, Family Violence, and Female Delinquency: Findings from a Longitudinal Study," *Violence and Victims* 18:319–334 (2003).
104. Kimberly Barletto, "Who's at Risk: Delinquent Trajectories of Children with Attention and Conduct Problems," paper presented at the American Society of Criminology meeting, San Diego, November 1997; Veronica Herrera, "Equals in Risk? The Differential Impact of Family Violence on Male and Female Delinquency," paper presented at the annual Society of Criminology meeting, San Diego, November 1997.
105. Meda Chesney-Lind, "Girls' Crime and Women's Place: Toward a Feminist Model of Female Delinquency," paper presented at the American Society of Criminology meeting, Montreal, November 1987.
106. Ibid., p. 20.
107. Emily Gaarder and Joanne Belknap, "Tenuous Borders: Girls Transferred to Adult Court," *Criminology* 40:481–518 (2002).
108. Joan Moore, *Going Down to the Barrio: Homeboys and Homegirls in Change* (Philadelphia: Temple University Press, 1991), p. 93.
109. Ibid., p. 101.
110. Gaarder and Belknap, "Tenuous Borders: Girls Transferred to Adult Court," p. 498.
111. Laurie Schaffner, *Teenage Runaways: Broken Hearts and "Bad Attitudes"* (New York: Haworth Press, 1999).
112. D. Wayne Osgood, Janet Wilson, Patrick O'Malley, Jerald Bachman, and Lloyd Johnston, "Routine Activities and Individual Deviant Behaviors," *American Sociological Review* 61:635–655 (1996).
113. Adler, *Sisters in Crime.*
114. Ibid., pp. 10–11.
115. Rita James Simon, "Women and Crime Revisited," *Social Science Quarterly* 56:658–663 (1976).
116. Ibid., pp. 660–61.
117. Roy Austin, "Women's Liberation and Increase in Minor, Major, and Occupational Offenses," *Criminology* 20:407–430 (1982).
118. Martin Gold, *Delinquent Behavior in an American City* (Pacific Grove, CA: Brooks/Cole, 1970), p. 118; John Clark and Edward Haurek, "Age and Sex Roles of Adolescents and Their Involvement in Misconduct: A Reappraisal," *Sociology and Social Research* 50:495–508 (1966); Nancy Wise, "Juvenile Delinquency in Middle-Class Girls," in E. Vaz, ed., *Middle Class Delinquency* (New York: Harper & Row, 1967), pp. 179–88; Gary Jensen and Raymond Eve, "Sex Differences in Delinquency: An Examination of Popular Sociological Explanations," *Criminology* 13:427–448 (1976).
119. Beth Bjerregaard and Carolyn Smith, "Gender Differences in Gang Participation and Delinquency," *Journal of Quantitative Criminology* 9:329–350 (1993).
120. Darrell Steffensmeier and Dana Haynie, "Gender, Structural Disadvantage, and Urban Crime: Do Macrosocial Variables Also Explain Female Offending Rates?" *Criminology* 38:403–438 (2000).

121. Henry Brownstein, Barry Spunt, Susan Crimmins, and Sandra Langley, "Women Who Kill in Drug Market Situations," *Justice Quarterly* 12:472–498 (1995).

122. Darrell Steffensmeier and Renee Hoffman Steffensmeier, "Trends in Female Delinquency," *Criminology* 18:62–85 (1980); see also Steffensmeier and Steffensmeier, "Crime and the Contemporary Woman: An Analysis of Changing Levels of Female Property Crime, 1960–1975," *Social Forces* 57:566–584 (1978); Darrell Steffensmeier and Michael Cobb, "Sex Differences in Urban Arrest Patterns, 1934–1979," *Social Problems* 29:37–49 (1981).

123. Darrell Steffensmeier, "National Trends in Female Arrests, 1960–1990: Assessment and Recommendations for Research," *Journal of Quantitative Criminology* 9:411–437 (1993).

124. Carol Smart, "The New Female Offender: Reality or Myth?" *British Journal of Criminology* 19:50–59 (1979).

125. Julia Schwendinger and Herman Schwendinger, *Rape and Inequality* (Beverly Hills: Sage Publications, 1983).

126. For a review of feminist theory, see Sally Simpson, "Feminist Theory, Crime and Justice," *Criminology* 27:605–632 (1989).

127. Ibid., p. 611.

128. Messerschmidt, *Masculinities and Crime: Critique and Reconceptualization of Theory.*

129. Center for Research on Women, *Secrets in Public: Sexual Harassment in Our Schools* (Wellesley, MA: Wellesley College, 1993).

130. Belknap, Holsinger, and Dunn, "Understanding Incarcerated Girls: The Results of a Focus Group Study."

131. Kathleen Daly and Meda Chesney-Lind, "Feminism and Criminology," *Justice Quarterly* 5:497–538 (1988).

132. Jane Siegel and Linda Williams, "The Relationship between Child Sexual Abuse and Female Delinquency and Crime: A Prospective Study," *Journal of Research in Crime & Delinquency* 40:71–94 (2003).

133. James Messerschmidt, *Capitalism, Patriarchy and Crime* (Totowa, NJ: Rowman and Littlefield, 1986); for a critique of this work, see Herman Schwendinger and Julia Schwendinger, "The World According to James Messerschmidt," *Social Justice* 15:123–145 (1988).

134. John Hagan, A.R. Gillis, and John Simpson, "The Class Structure and Delinquency: Toward a Power-Control Theory of Common Delinquent Behavior," *American Journal of Sociology* 90:1151–1178 (1985); John Hagan, John Simpson, and A.R. Gillis, "Class in the Household: A Power-Control Theory of Gender and Delinquency," *American Journal of Sociology* 92:788–816 (1987).

135. John Hagan, A.R. Gillis, and John Simpson, "Clarifying and Extending Power-Control Theory," *American Journal of Sociology* 95:1024–1037 (1990).

136. Brenda Sims Blackwell and Mark Reed, "Power-Control as a Between- and Within-Family Model: Reconsidering the Unit of Analysis," *Journal of Youth and Adolescence* 32:385–400 (2003).

137. Gary Jensen and Kevin Thompson, "What's Class Got to Do with It? A Further Examination of Power-Control Theory," *American Journal of Sociol-
ogy* 95:1009–1023 (1990); Kevin Thompson, "Gender and Adolescent Drinking Problems: The Effects of Occupational Structure," *Social Problems* 36:30–44 (1989); for some critical research, see Simon Singer and Murray Levine, "Power-Control Theory, Gender and Delinquency: A Partial Replication with Additional Evidence on the Effects of Peers," *Criminology* 26:627–648 (1988).

138. Christopher Uggen, "Class, Gender, and Arrest: An Intergenerational Analysis of Workplace Power and Control," *Criminology* 38:835–862 (2001).

139. Mary Odem and Steven Schlossman, "Guardians of Virtue: The Juvenile Court and Female Delinquency in Early 20th-Century Los Angeles," *Crime and Delinquency* 37:186–203 (1991).

140. Meda Chesney-Lind, "Judicial Enforcement of the Female Sex Role: The Family Court and the Female Delinquent," *Issues in Criminology* 8:51–59 (1973).

141. Thomas J. Gamble, Sherrie Sonnenberg, John Haltigan, and Amy Cuzzola-Kern, "Detention Screening: Prospects for Population Management and the Examination of Disproportionality by Race, Age, and Gender," *Criminal Justice Policy Review*, 13:380–395 (2002); Kimberly Kempf-Leonard and Lisa Sample, "Disparity Based on Sex: Is Gender-Specific Treatment Warranted?" *Justice Quarterly* 17:89–128 (2000).

142. Meda Chesney-Lind and Randall Shelden, *Girls, Delinquency and Juvenile Justice* (Belmont, CA: West/Wadsworth, 1998).

143. John MacDonald and Meda Chesney-Lind, "Gender Bias and Juvenile Justice Revisited: A Multiyear Analysis," *Crime and Delinquency* 47:173–195 (2001).

144. Meda Chesney-Lind and Vickie Paramore, "Are Girls Getting More Violent? Exploring Juvenile Robbery Trends," *Journal of Contemporary Criminal Justice*, 17:142–166 (2001).

145. Joanne Belknap, Kristi Holsinger, and Melissa Dunn, "Understanding Incarcerated Girls: The Results of a Focus Group Study," *Prison Journal* 77:381–405 (1997).

146. Holly Hartwig and Jane Myers, "A Different Approach: Applying a Wellness Paradigm to Adolescent Female Delinquents and Offenders," *Journal of Mental Health Counseling* 25:57–75 (2003); Carol Pepi, "Children without Childhoods: A Feminist Intervention Strategy Utilizing Systems Theory and Restorative Justice in Treating Female Adolescent Offenders," *Women and Therapy* 20:85–101 (1997).

147. Jennifer Stevens Aubrey, "Sex and Punishment: An Examination of Sexual Consequences and the Sexual Double Standard in Teen Programming," *Sex Roles: A Journal of Research*, 50:505–514 (2004).

148. Jill Leslie Rosenbaum and Meda Chesney-Lind, "Appearance and Delinquency: A Research Note," *Crime and Delinquency* 40:250–261 (1994).

149. Sealock and Simpson, "Unraveling Bias in Arrest Decisions: The Role of Juvenile Offender Typescripts."

150. Chesney-Lind and Shelden, *Girls, Delinquency and Juvenile Justice*, p. 243.

7

The Family and Delinquency

Chapter Outline

The Changing American Family

Family Makeup

Childcare

Economic Stress

The Family's Influence on Delinquency

Family Breakup

Family Conflict

FOCUS ON DELINQUENCY: For Better or For Worse: Does Divorce Matter?

Family Efficacy

Family Deviance

Do Families Matter?

Child Abuse and Neglect

A Historical Perspective

Defining Abuse and Neglect

FOCUS ON DELINQUENCY: The Sexual Exploitation of Children

The Extent of Child Abuse

Causes of Child Abuse and Neglect

The Child Protection System: Philosophy and Practice

The Abused Child in Court

Disposition of Abuse and Neglect Cases

Abuse, Neglect, and Delinquency

Case Studies of the Effects of Child Abuse

Cohort Studies of the Effects of Child Abuse

The Abuse-Delinquency Link

The Family and Delinquency Control Policy

POLICY AND PRACTICE: Fathering After Violence Project

Chapter Objectives

1. Be familiar with the link between family relationships and juvenile delinquency

2. Understand the complex association between family breakup and delinquent behavior

3. Understand why families in conflict produce more delinquents than those that function harmoniously

4. Know the association between inconsistent discipline and supervision and juvenile crime

5. Be able to discuss how parental and sibling misconduct influences delinquent behaviors

6. Define the concept of child abuse

7. Know the nature and extent of abuse

8. List the factors that are seen as causing child abuse

9. Be familiar with the complex system of state intervention in abuse cases

10. Discuss the association between child abuse and delinquent behavior

CNN. View the CNN video clip of this story and answer related Critical Thinking questions on your Juvenile Delinquency 9e CD-ROM.

The small town of Lewisville, Texas, was stunned when a 15-year-old sister and 10-year-old brother gave police statements about their involvement in the death of their younger brother, Jackson Carr. The two held the 6-year-old down in muddy water until he was dead. Neighbors described the Carrs as strange children who were to be avoided. Some neighbors claimed the kids were starved for attention and that their folks, Michael and Rita, lacked parenting skills. But there was nothing in their prior histories that could explain their violent outburst. Could there have been something in their family life so traumatic that the Carr children were driven to engage in siblicide—the killing of a brother or sister. While extreme, siblicide claims about 100 victims each year.

The Carr case is of course extreme. But many kids today are being socialized in troubled homes. Some respond with violence, and some engage in self-destructive behavior ranging from substance abuse to suicide. Others, up to 3 million per year, run away from home. Why do they run? While some may be evading the law, suffering depression, or dealing with a personal crisis, most are running from a disturbed family or home life. They have problems with their parents' divorce or remarriage; there is conflict over rules and discipline; sibling conflicts have gotten out of control. Many of these kids simply want to remove themselves from a bad situation without any destination in mind or plans for the future. Most of these troubled youth stay with a friend for a few days and then return home. Others stay away longer, and some leave home never to return. Many find shelter with other kids living in similar circumstances, sleeping under bridges and in abandoned buildings, forming uneasy alliances for survival. Many abuse drugs and become the victims of predatory criminals. Few remain undamaged by their ordeal. Some teens repeatedly run away from home only to become an easy target for adult predators who try to lure them into prostitution, drug use, or both.

The problems faced by runaways illustrate the significant impact that family relationships have on adolescent development. Many experts believe that family dysfunction is a key ingredient in the development of emotional deficits that eventually lead to long-term social problems.[1] Interactions between parents and children, and between siblings, provide opportunities for children to acquire or inhibit antisocial behavior patterns.[2] Some kids are close to their parents and can confide in them,

© Joel Gordon

While estimates vary, somewhere between 1 and 3 million kids run away from home each year. Some runaways may be evading the law, suffering depression, or dealing with a personal crisis. Most, however, are running from a disturbed family or home life.

nuclear family
A family unit composed of parents and their children; this smaller family structure is subject to great stress due to the intense, close contact between parents and children.

A great deal of **information on families and children** can be found at the website of the David and Lucile Packard Foundation: www.futureofchildren.org. For an up-to-date list of web links, go to http://cj.wadsworth.com/siegel_jd9e.

whereas others engage in frequent patterns of lying and deceit.[3] The effect of a positive home life can be life affirming.

Even children living in high-crime areas are able to resist the temptation of the streets if they receive fair discipline and support from parents who provide them with positive role models.[4] However, children in affluent families who are being raised in a household characterized by abuse and conflict, or whose parents are absent or separated, will still be at risk for delinquency.[5] Nor is the relationship between family life and delinquency unique to U.S. culture; cross-national data support a significant association between family variables and delinquency.[6]

The assumed relationship between delinquency and family life is critical today because the American family is changing. Extended families, once common, are now for the most part anachronisms. In their place is the **nuclear family,** described as a "dangerous hothouse of emotions" because of the close contact between parents and children; in these families problems are unrelieved by contact with other kin living nearby.[7]

The nuclear family is showing signs of breakdown. Much of the responsibility for childrearing is delegated to television and daycare providers. Despite these changes, some families are able to continue functioning as healthy units, producing well-adjusted children. Others have crumbled under the stress, severely damaging their children.[8] This is particularly true when child abuse and neglect become part of family life.

Because these issues are critical for understanding delinquency, this chapter is devoted to an analysis of the family's role in producing or inhibiting delinquency. First, the changing face of the American family is covered, followed by a review of the way family structure and function influence delinquent behavior. The relationship among child abuse, neglect, and delinquency is covered in some depth. Finally, programs designed to improve family functioning are briefly reviewed.

THE CHANGING AMERICAN FAMILY

The so-called traditional family, with a male breadwinner and a female who cares for the home, is a thing of the past. No longer can this family structure be considered the norm. Changing sex roles have created a family in which women play a much greater role in the economic process; this has created a more egalitarian family structure. About three quarters of all mothers of school-age children are employed today, up from 50 percent in 1970 and 40 percent in 1960. The changing economic structure may be reflected in shifting sex roles. Fathers are now spending more time with their children on workdays than they did 20 years ago (2.3 hours versus 1.8), and women are spending somewhat less time (3.0 hours versus 3.3).[9] On their days off, both working men and women spend about an hour more with their children than they did 20 years ago, with women devoting about 8 hours and men 6. So, although the time spent with children may be less than would be desirable, it has increased over the past 20 years.

Family Makeup

The proportion of American households that have children living with both parents has declined substantially. The number of single mothers increased from 3 million to 10 million since 1970; over the same time frame, the number of single fathers increased also, from 393,000 to 2 million.[10] The percentage of children living in two-parent families has declined from 76 percent in 1980 to about 68 percent today. About 19.8 million children under 18 live with one parent: 16.5 million with their mother and 3.3 million with their father. About three in ten children living with their single father, or 1.1 million, reside in a household that includes dad's unmarried partner. In contrast, only one in ten children who live with their single mother, or 1.8 million, share the home with mom's unmarried partner.[11]

Family disruption takes its greatest toll on minority youth. Today about 37 percent of African American children live in families with two parents, compared to about 74 percent of white children.[12] As many 75 percent of African American children will experience parental separation or divorce before they reach age 16, and many of these children will experience multiple family disruptions over time.[13]

Though there has been a sharp decline in the teen birthrate (dropping more than 28 percent since 1990), more than 500,000 babies are born to teenage mothers every year, about 200,000 to girls under age 18. A significant number of children are still being born to unmarried women. Of the approximately 4 million annual births, about one third (1.3 million) are to unmarried women; this proportion has increased in every state since 1990.[14] One reason that the number of children living in mother-only homes is on the rise is simply because more single women than ever are deciding to keep and raise their children; about 30 percent of all births are to unmarried women.

Childcare

Charged with caring for children is a daycare system whose workers are often paid minimum wage. Of special concern are "family daycare homes," in which a single provider takes care of three to nine children. Several states neither license nor monitor these private providers. Even in states that mandate registration and inspection of daycare providers, it is estimated that 90 percent or more of the facilities operate "underground." It is not uncommon for one adult to care for eight infants, an impossible task regardless of training or concern.

Children from working poor families are most likely to suffer from inadequate childcare. These children often spend time in makeshift arrangements that allow their parents to work but lack the stimulating environment children need to thrive.[15] About 3.5 million children under age 13 spend some time at home alone each week while their parents are at work.

Economic Stress

The family is also undergoing economic stress. The majority of indigent families live in substandard housing without adequate health care, nutrition, or childcare. About 17 percent of all children live in poverty and about 7 percent live in extreme poverty—at least 50 percent below the poverty line. About 30 percent of all children live in families where no parent has full-time, year-round employment.[16] Those whose incomes place them above the poverty line are deprived of government assistance. Recent political trends suggest that the social "safety net" is under attack, and poor families can expect less government aid in the coming years.

Will this economic pressure be reduced in the future? The number of senior citizens is on the rise. As people retire, there will be fewer workers to cover the costs of Social Security, medical care, and nursing home care. These costs will put greater economic stress on families. Voter sentiment has an impact on the allocation of public funds, and there is concern that an older generation, worried about health care costs, may be reluctant to spend tax dollars on at-risk kids.

TO QUIZ YOURSELF ON THIS MATERIAL, go to the Juvenile Delinquency 9e website.

THE FAMILY'S INFLUENCE ON DELINQUENCY

Most experts believe a disturbed home environment can have a significant impact on delinquency. The family is the primary unit in which children learn the values and attitudes that guide their actions throughout their lives. Family disruption or change can have a long-lasting effect on children.

Four categories of family dysfunction seem to promote delinquent behavior: families disrupted by spousal conflict or breakup, families involved in interpersonal

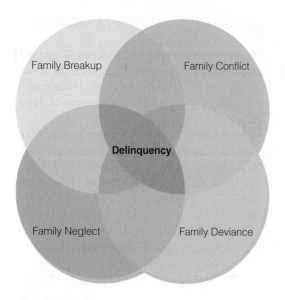

FIGURE 7.1

Family Influences on Behavior

Each of these four factors has been linked to antisocial behavior and delinquency. Interaction between these factors may escalate delinquent activity.

broken home
Home in which one or both parents are absent due to divorce or separation; children in such an environment may be prone to antisocial behavior.

blended families
Nuclear families that are the product of divorce and remarriage; blending one parent from each of two families and their combined children into one family unit.

conflict, negligent parents who are not attuned to their children's behavior and emotional problems (family efficacy), and families that contain deviant parents who may transmit their behavior to their children (see Figure 7.1).[17] These factors may interact; drug-abusing parents may be more likely to engage in family conflict, child neglect, and marital breakup. We now turn to the specific types of family problems that have been linked to delinquent behavior.

Family Breakup

One of the most enduring controversies in the study of delinquency is the relationship between a parent being absent from the home and the onset of delinquent behavior. Research indicates that parents whose marriage is secure produce children who are secure and independent.[18] In contrast, children growing up in homes with one or both parents absent may be prone to antisocial behavior.

A number of experts contend that a **broken home** is a strong determinant of a child's law-violating behavior. The connection seems self-evident because a child is first socialized at home. Any disjunction in an orderly family structure could be expected to have a negative impact on the child.

The suspected broken home–delinquency relationship is important because, if current trends continue, less than half of all children born today will live continuously with their own mother and father throughout childhood. And because stepfamilies, or so-called **blended families,** are less stable than families consisting of two biological parents, an increasing number of children will experience family breakup two or even three times during childhood.[19]

A number of studies indicate that children who have experienced family breakup are more likely to demonstrate behavior problems and hyperactivity than children in intact families.[20] Family breakup is often associated with conflict, hostility, and aggression; children of divorce are suspected of having lax supervision, weakened attachment, and greater susceptibility to peer pressure.[21] And, as a recent study of more than 4,000 youths in Denver, Pittsburgh, and Rochester found, the more often children are forced to go through family transitions, the more likely they are to engage in delinquent activity.[22]

Effects of Divorce The relationship between broken homes and delinquency was established in early research, which suggested that a significant association existed between parental absence and youthful misconduct.[23] Other efforts showed that parental absence seemed to affect girls, white youths, and the affluent more than it did males, minorities, and the indigent.[24] But the link was clear: Children growing up in broken homes were much more likely to fall prey to delinquency than those who lived in two-parent households. Considering this view, it is not surprising that as the number of single-parent households in the population surged, so too did the juvenile crime rate.[25]

Not all delinquency experts concur on the divorce-delinquency link. Some argue that the studies that show an association between broken homes and delinquency used the records of police, courts, and correctional institutions.[26] This research may be tainted by a sampling bias. Youths from broken homes may get arrested more often than youths from intact families, but this does not necessarily mean they engage in more frequent and serious delinquent behavior. Official statistics may reflect the fact that agents of the justice system treat children from disrupted households more severely because they cannot call on parents for support. The *parens patriae* philosophy of the juvenile courts calls for official intervention when parental supervision is considered inadequate.[27] Researchers concluded that the absence of parents has a greater effect on agents of the justice system than it does on the behavior of children.[28]

These suspicions are substantiated by numerous studies, using self-report data that have failed to establish any clear-cut relationship between broken homes and delin-

A mother helps her two children leave an abusive home and head toward a shelter for battered women and children. Family violence is a critical priority for juvenile justice officials, political leaders, and the public because it affects so many families each year.

quent behavior.[29] Boys and girls from intact families seem as likely to self-report delinquency as those whose parents are divorced or separated. And even when self-reports do show that children from intact homes commit less crime, there is evidence that their responses may be invalid. Kids from intact homes tend to underreport their antisocial activity, while kids from single-parent homes are more honest and accurate.[30]

Divorce Reconsidered Though some researchers still question the divorce-delinquency link, there is growing sentiment that family breakup is traumatic and most likely has a direct influence on factors related to adolescent misbehavior.[31] Research shows that kids whose parents divorce may increase their involvement in delinquency, especially if they have a close bond with the parent who is forced to leave.[32]

In her study of the effects of parental absence on children, sociologist Sara McLanahan finds that children who grow up apart from their fathers typically do less well than children who grow up in intact families. They are less likely to finish high school and attend college, less likely to find and keep a steady job, and more likely to become teen mothers. Although most children who grow up with a single parent do quite well, differences between children in one- and two-parent families are significant, and there is fairly good evidence that father absence per se is responsible for some social problems.[33] The McLanahan research has been supported by other studies showing that divorce is in fact related to delinquency and status offending, especially if a child had a close relationship with the parent who is forced to leave the home.[34] These studies also find that the effects of divorce seem gender-specific:

▌ Boys seem to be more affected by the post-divorce absence of the father. In post-divorce situations, fathers seem less likely to be around to solve problems, to discuss standards of conduct, or to enforce discipline. A divorced father who remains actively involved in his child's life reduces his son's chances of delinquency

▌ Girls are more affected by the quality of their mother's parenting and post-divorce parental conflict. It is possible that parents' fighting or extreme levels of parental conflict may serve as a model to young girls coping with the aftermath of their parents' separation.[35]

While the prevailing wisdom is that marriage is better than divorce and that kids living with single parents are more likely to get involved in delinquent behavior than kids living in intact families, the quality of both the marital and post-marital periods can significantly affect or mediate this outcome. In other words, even in a family heading for divorce, the quality of life and how parents handle their breakup can significantly

EXHIBIT 7.1

The Family Structure–Delinquency Link

I Children growing up in families disrupted by parental death are better adjusted than children of divorce. Parental absence is not a per se cause of antisocial behavior.

I Remarriage does not lessen the effects of divorce on youth. Children living with a stepparent exhibit as many problems as youths in divorce situations and considerably more problems than children living with both biological parents.

I Continued contact with the noncustodial parent has little effect on a child's well-being.

I Evidence that the behavior of children of divorce improves over time is inconclusive.

I Post-divorce conflict between parents is related to child maladjustment.

I Parental divorce raises the likelihood of teenage marriage.

I Parental divorce increases the risk of experiencing psychological problems, having a discordant marriage, seeing one's own marriage end in divorce, and having weak ties to parents (especially fathers) in adulthood. However, the overall effect may not be as strong as some critics believe.

SOURCES: Paul Amato, "Reconciling Divergent Perspectives: Judith Wallerstein, Quantitative Family Research and Children of Divorce," *Family Relations* 52:332–339 (2003); Nicholas Wolfinger, "Parental Divorce and Offspring Marriage: Early or Late?" *Social Forces* 82:337–354 (2003); Paul Amato and Bruce Keith, "Parental Divorce and the Well-Being of Children: A Meta-Analysis," *Psychological Bulletin* 110:26–46 (1991).

influence their children's subsequent adjustment.[36] Kids who can maintain attachments to their parents during the *Sturm und Drang* (storm and stress) of divorce are less likely to engage in delinquency than those who are alienated and detached.[37] For example, research by Sarah Jaffee and her associates shows that the quality of marriage may be more important than its makeup. Jaffee found that the less time fathers lived with their children, the more conduct problems their children had. However, when fathers engaged in high levels of antisocial behavior, the more time they lived with their children, the more conduct problems their children had. Marriage, they conclude, may not be the answer to the problems faced by children living in single-parent families unless fathers can refrain from deviant behaviors and become reliable sources of emotional and economic support.[38] Exhibit 7.1 summarizes some key findings on the association between divorce and children's behavior. The traumas resulting from divorce are the subject of the Focus on Delinquency box entitled "For Better or For Worse: Does Divorce Matter?"

Family Conflict

intrafamily conflict
An environment of discord and conflict within the family; children who grow up in dysfunctional homes often exhibit delinquent behaviors, having learned at a young age that aggression pays off.

Not all unhappy marriages end in divorce; some continue in an atmosphere of conflict. **Intrafamily conflict** is a common experience in many American families.[39] The link between parental conflict and delinquency was established almost 40 years ago when F. Ivan Nye found that a child's perception of his or her parents' marital happiness was a significant predictor of delinquency.[40] Contemporary studies have also found that children who grow up in maladapted homes and witness discord or violence later exhibit emotional disturbance and behavior problems.[41] There seems to be little difference between the behavior of children who merely *witness* intrafamily violence and those who are its *victims*.[42] In fact, some research efforts show that observing the abuse of a parent (mother) is a more significant determinant of delinquency than being the target of child abuse.[43]

Research efforts have consistently supported the relationship among family conflict, hostility, and delinquency.[44] Adolescents who are incarcerated report growing up in dysfunctional homes.[45] Parents of beyond-control youngsters have been found to be inconsistent rule setters, to be less likely to show interest in their children, and to display high levels of hostile detachment.[46] Kids who report having troubled home lives also exhibit lower levels of self-esteem and are more prone to antisocial behaviors.[47] How parents respond to conflict may influence their children's behavior. Even in a conflict-ridden home, parents who try to use positive tactics such as humor, support, physical and verbal affection, and problem solving to mediate conflict seem more successful than if they relied on negative tactics such as nonverbal hostility, defensiveness,

For Better or For Worse: Does Divorce Matter?

Does divorce matter? Are the children of divorced couples more at risk for antisocial behavior than those who reside in intact homes? Two well-received books reach startlingly opposite conclusions on this important matter.

In their 2000 book, *The Unexpected Legacy of Divorce,* Judith Wallerstein, Julia M. Lewis, and Sandra Blakeslee report on the findings of a longitudinal study, begun in the early 1970s, with 131 children whose parents divorced during their adolescence. Wallerstein and her associates check in with 93 of the original 131 children and extensively profile 5 children who most embody the common life experiences of the larger group. They follow their lives in detail through adolescence, delving into their love affairs, their marital successes and failures, and the parenting of their own children.

The researchers find that the effects of divorce on children are not short term and transient but long lasting and cumulative. Children of divorce develop lingering fears about their own ability to develop long-term relationships; these fears often impede their ability to marry and raise families. While most spouses are able to reduce their emotional pain and get on with their lives a few years after they divorce, this is not true of their children, whose emotional turmoil may last for decades. The children often find it emotionally draining to spend time with their noncustodial parents and resent the disruption for years afterward. Some of the children in the study felt they had been an "inconvenience" and that their parents fit them in around their schedules. Considering their emotional turmoil, it is not surprising that these kids exhibit high levels of drug and alcohol abuse and, for girls, precocious sexuality. Consequently, only 40 percent of the kids they follow, many in their late 20s to early 30s, have ever married (compared to 81 percent of men and 87 percent of women in the general population). Some subjects told the researchers that marriage seemed impossible because their traumatic home life gave them no clue what a loving relationship was actually like.

In some cases, the parents' intense love/hate relationship that developed during marriage never ends, and parents continue to battle for years after separating; some collapse emotionally and physically. The authors document how some kids cope with long-term psychological turmoil by taking on the job of family caregiver. They become nurse, analyst, mentor, and confidant to their parents. One told them how, at 10 years old, she would spend time with her insomniac mother watching television and drinking beer at midnight. She frequently stayed home from school to make sure that her mother would not become depressed and suicidal or take the car out when she was drinking. Such personal burdens compromise the child's ability to develop friendships and personal interests. Such children may feel both trapped and guilty when they put their own needs ahead of the needy parent.

Wallerstein and her associates find that adolescents who grew up in homes where they experienced divorce are now struggling with the fear that their relationships will fail like those of their parents. Lacking guidance and experience, they must invent their own codes of behavior in a culture that offers few guidelines on how to become successful, protective parents themselves. This development has serious consequences, considering the theoretical importance placed on the develop-ment of positive family relationships as an inhibitor of delinquency and adult criminality.

DIVORCE RECONSIDERED

In 2002, award-winning psychologist E. Mavis Hetherington and writing partner John Kelly presented data from her study conducted over a 30-year period of more than 1,400 families and 2,500 children. Rather than the tumultuous event described by Wallerstein, Hetherington sees divorce as part of a series of a life transitions that can be destructive in the short term but actually have positive benefits in the long run. Divorce creates an opportunity for long-term personal growth. If the ex-partners can bring a sense of maturity to the dissolution of their relationship and have enough material and personal strength to become autonomous, they will be able to weather the short-term upheaval of separation. Within five or six years of separating they stand a good chance of becoming much happier than they were while married. Of course, those ex-partners whose personalities render them impulsive and antisocial have a diminished chance of turning their lives around.

Hetherington finds that children of divorce may undergo some trauma, but for the most part they are much better off than those Wallerstein encountered. While children in single-parent families and stepfamilies have more psychological problems than those in intact families, more than 75 percent ultimately do as well as children from intact families. Though divorce is a painful experience, most go on to establish careers, create intimate relationships, and build meaningful lives.

Although Hetherington's picture of the aftermath of divorce is somewhat rosier than Wallerstein's, she too finds peril in family breakup. After six years, about one quarter of her sample had contact with their noncustodial father once a year or less. Many women report anxiety six years after the breakup, and stepfathers often find it difficult to connect with the kids in their blended families; many stop trying after a few years of frustration.

Critical Thinking

1. Considering the long-term effects of divorce, should we make it more difficult to dissolve marriages—for example, by doing away with the concept of no-fault divorce and requiring stringent reasons for obtaining a separation?

2. Should it be more difficult to get married? Should couples be forced to go through counseling and education programs before being granted a marriage license? We do it for driving, why not marriage?

3. Which researcher, Wallerstein or Hetherington, paints a more accurate picture of the aftermath of family dissolution?

InfoTrac College Edition Research

Use "divorce" as a keyword on InfoTrac College Edition to conduct research on its effect on children.

SOURCES: Judith S. Wallerstein, Julia M. Lewis, and Sandra Blakeslee, *The Unexpected Legacy of Divorce* (New York: Hyperion, 2000); E. Mavis Hetherington and John Kelly, *For Better or for Worse: Divorce Reconsidered* (New York: W. W. Norton, 2002).

physical distress, verbal hostility, threat, pursuit, personal insult, physical aggression, or withdrawal.[48]

Although damaged parent-child relationships are associated with delinquency, it is difficult to assess the relationship. It is often assumed that preexisting family problems cause delinquency, but it may also be true that children who act out put enormous stress on a family. Kids who are conflict-prone may actually help to destabilize households. To avoid escalation of a child's aggression, these parents may give in to their children's demands. The children learn that aggression pays off.[49]

Parents may feel overwhelmed and shut their child out of their lives. Adolescent misbehavior may be a precursor of family conflict; strife leads to more adolescent misconduct, producing an endless cycle of family stress and delinquency.[50]

Family Efficacy

parental efficacy
The ability of parents to effectively raise their children in a noncoercive fashion.

Many experts believe children need a warm, supportive relationship with their parents.[51] Parents who are supportive and effectively control their children in a noncoercive fashion—**parental efficacy**—are more likely to raise children who refrain from delinquency.[52] Delinquency will be reduced if parents provide the type of structure that integrates children into families while giving them the ability to assert their individuality and regulate their own behavior.[53] For example, parents who practice religion and bring their children to services reduce the probability of child misconduct. Religious parents have been found to be more likely to engage in warm, supportive parenting, which helps decrease the chances that a child will associate with deviant peers and engage in delinquent behavior.[54]

Evidence of the link between the quality of family life and delinquency comes in many forms. Children who feel inhibited with their parents and refuse to discuss important issues with them are more likely to engage in deviant activities. Poor child-parent communications have been related to dysfunctional activities such as running away, and in all too many instances these children enter the ranks of homeless street youths who get involved in theft and prostitution to survive.[55] In contrast, even children who appear to be at risk are better able to resist involvement in delinquent activity when they report a strong attachment to their parents.[56] The importance of close relations with the family may diminish as children reach late adolescence and develop stronger peer-group relations, but most experts believe family influence remains considerable throughout life.[57]

Physical Discipline The link between discipline and deviant behavior is uncertain. Most Americans still support the use of corporal punishment to discipline children. The use of physical punishment cuts across racial, ethnic, and religious groups.[58] However, despite this public support, there is growing evidence of a "violence begetting violence" cycle. Children who are subject to even minimal amounts of physical punishment may be more likely to use violence themselves; the effect seems greatest among Caucasian children and less among African American and Latino children. Recent research finds that white non-Hispanic children who were spanked more frequently before age 2 were substantially more likely to have behavior problems after entry into school; associations were not significant for Hispanic and black children.[59] Racial-ethnic differences may reflect greater acceptance of corporal punishment in minority families and less subsequent effect on a child's behavior.[60]

Murray Straus reviewed the concept of discipline in a series of surveys and found a powerful relationship between exposure to physical punishment and later aggression.[61] Physical punishment weakens the bond between parents and children, lowers the children's self-esteem, and undermines their faith in justice. It is not surprising, then, that Straus finds a high correlation between physical discipline and street crime. It is possible that physical punishment encourages children to become more secretive and dishonest.[62] Overly strict discipline may have an even more insidious link to antisocial behaviors: Abused children have a higher risk of neurological dysfunction than the nonabused, and brain abnormalities have been linked to violent crime.[63]

Improved parenting skills may be key to reducing the incidence of child abuse. Here, Nicholas, 9 (left), and his brother, Jared, 7, get help with homework from their mom, Wendy Hastie, at their home in Nashville, Tennessee. Wendy Hastie and her husband recently completed a Youth Village treatment program so they could learn to cope better with behavioral and health problems experienced by Jared. The program stresses early intervention in an attempt to head off problems before a juvenile breaks the law.

The corporal punishment–crime relationship has been supported by cross-national research studies. Nonviolent societies are also ones in which parents rarely punish their children physically; there is a link among corporal punishment, delinquency, spousal abuse, and adult crime.[64] Research conducted in 10 European countries shows that the degree to which parents and teachers approve of corporal punishment is related to the homicide rate.[65]

Although the evidence linking corporal punishment to delinquency seems overwhelming, recent research by Ronald Simons and his associates indicates that the effects may be mitigated if parents are otherwise warm and supportive. Using samples from the United States and Taiwan, Simons found that kids who are routinely physically punished are no more likely to engage in antisocial behavior than those who are never so punished, if parents also provide support, warmth, and care. When kids experience physical punishment in the absence of parental involvement, they feel angry and unjustly treated and are more willing to defy their parents and engage in antisocial behavior.[66]

Adequacy of Supervision Evidence also exists that inadequate or inconsistent supervision can promote delinquency. Youths who believe their parents care little about their activities are more likely to engage in criminal acts than those who believe their actions will be closely monitored.[67] Research shows that families in which children and parents spend more time together, and in which children approve of the fact that parents monitor their behavior, also experience lower levels of antisocial behavior.[68] In contrast, adolescents who spend long periods of time without adult supervision are much more likely to engage in risk-taking behavior such as precocious sex and drug taking. The effects of parental nonappearance are even greater if kids have limited opportunities to participate in activities monitored by other adults, such as after-school activities.[69]

Mother's Employment Parents who closely supervise their children, and have close ties with them, help reduce the likelihood of adolescent delinquent behavior.[70] When life circumstances prevent or interfere with adequate supervision, delinquent opportunities may increase. For example, some critics have suggested that even in intact homes, a working mother who is unable to adequately supervise her children will provide the opportunity for delinquency. This phenomenon may be aggravated by economic factors: In poor neighborhoods parents cannot call upon neighborhood resources to take up the burden of controlling children and, as a result, a greater burden is placed on families to provide adequate supervision.[71] While this finding is troubling, considering the fact that many indigent mothers are forced to seek employment outside the home, there is also research that finds that having a mother who is employed has little if any effect on youthful misbehavior, especially if the children are adequately supervised.[72] So the true relationship between mother's employment and child misbehavior remains unknown.

Family Size Parents may find it hard to control their children because they have such large families that resources, such as time, are spread too thin (referred to as **resource dilution**). Larger families are more likely than smaller ones to produce delinquents, and middle children are more likely than first- or last-born children to engage in delinquent acts.

Some sociologists assume that large family size has a direct effect on delinquency, attributing this phenomenon to stretched resources and the relatively limited supervision parents can provide for each child.[73] It is also possible that the relationship is indirect, caused by the connection of family size to some external factor; for example, resource dilution has been linked to educational underachievement, long considered a correlate of delinquency.[74] Middle children may suffer because they are most likely to be home when large numbers of siblings are also at home and economic resources are most stretched.[75]

The current trend is that affluent, two-wage-earner families are having fewer children, whereas indigent, single-parent households are growing larger. Children are at a greater risk of being both poor and delinquent because indigent families are the ones most likely to have more children.[76]

Family Deviance

A number of studies have found that parental deviance has a powerful influence on delinquent behavior.[77] Deviant behavior is intergenerational; the children of deviant parents produce delinquent children themselves.[78]

Parental deviance disrupts the family's role as an agent of social control.[79] Some of the most important data on parental deviance has been gathered by David P. Farrington and his associates as part of a long-term study of English youth called the Cambridge Study in Delinquent Development (CSDD). The data found that a significant number of delinquent youths have criminal fathers.[80] About 8 percent of the sons of non-criminal fathers became chronic offenders, compared to 37 percent of youths with criminal fathers.[81] Farrington has also found that one type of parental deviance, bullying, may be both inter- and intra-generational. Bullies have children who bully others, and these "second-generation bullies" grow up to become the fathers of children who are also bullies.[82] (See Chapter 9 for more on bullying.) Analysis of more recent data from the CSDD again confirms the intergenerational nature of antisocial behavior: Delinquent youth grow up to become the parents of antisocial children.[83]

The cause of intergenerational deviance is uncertain. Genetic, environmental, psychological, and childrearing factors may all play a role. One finding that supports a genetic basis is that fathers of youths who suffer attention deficit/hyperactivity disorder (ADHD), a condition linked to delinquency, are five times more likely to suffer antisocial personality disorder (APD) than fathers of non-ADHD youths.[84] This linkage may be evidence that aggressive tendencies are inherited. Similarly, research on the sons of alcoholics shows that they suffer from neurological impairments related to delinquency.[85] It is possible that parental alcoholism causes genetic problems related to developmental impairment or that the children of substance-abusing parents are more prone to neurological impairment.

As with other forms of contributors to delinquency, the quality of family life may also be key. Criminal parents may be least likely to have close relationships with their offspring, and research confirms that substance-abusing or criminal parents are more likely to use harsh and inconsistent discipline, a factor linked to delinquent behavior.[86] This association may be reinforced by stigmatization of children of known deviants. Social control agents may be quick to fix a "delinquent" label on the children of known law violators.[87]

Data from the CSDD may help shed some light on the association. Recent analysis shows that parental conflict and authoritarian parenting were related to early childhood conduct problems in two successive generations. In addition, males who were poorly supervised by their parents were themselves poor supervisors as fathers. These findings indicate that parenting styles may help explain antisocial behavior in children and that style is passed down from one generation to the next. CSDD data also found that antisocial males tend to partner with antisocial female peers and produce antisocial children. In sum then, the CSDD data indicate that the intergenerational transmission of antisocial behaviors may have both genetic and environmental dimensions.[88]

Sibling Influences Evidence exists that siblings may also influence behavior; this is referred to as the **contagion effect**.[89] Research shows that if one sibling is a delinquent there is a significant likelihood their brother or sister will engage in delinquent behaviors.[90] Siblings who report warm relationships and share friends are the most likely to behave in a similar fashion; those who maintain a close relationship also report similar rates of drug abuse and delinquency.[91]

A number of interpretations of this data are possible. Siblings who live in the same environment are influenced by similar social and economic factors. Another possibility is that deviant siblings grow closer because of shared interests. It is possible that the relationship is due to personal interactions: Younger siblings imitate older siblings.

The contagion effect may explain in part the higher concordance of deviant behaviors found in identical twins as compared to fraternal twins or mere siblings (see Chapter 3). The relationship between identical twins may be stronger and more enduring than the one between other sibling pairs so that contagion and not genetics explains their behavioral similarities. According to Marshall Jones and Donald Jones, the contagion effect may also help explain aspects of the aging-out process.[92] They suggest that a great deal of offending is done with peers, and peer influence has a significant effect on juvenile offending rates. Boys who commit delinquent acts with their friends may desist as adults because as people mature, they marry, get jobs, and their social group dissolves. If peer influence shapes delinquency, its effect wanes as youth groups and cliques split up in adulthood. In contrast, twin relationships are everlasting, and one twin's antisocial behavior legitimizes and supports the criminal behavior of the other twin, an effect that may grow even stronger in adulthood. What seems to be a genetic effect may actually be the result of sibling interaction with a brother or sister who engages in antisocial activity.

Do Families Matter?

In a controversial book, *The Nature Assumption*, psychologist Judith Rich Harris questioned the cherished belief that parents play an important, if not the most important, role in a child's upbringing. Instead of family influence, Harris claims that genetics and environment determine, to a large extent, how a child turns out. Children's own temperament and peer relations shape their behavior and modify the characteristics they were born with; their interpersonal relations determine the kind of people they will be when they mature.[93] While Harris's arguments are provocative, the prevailing research on delinquency and family relationships offers ample evidence that family life can be a potent force in a child's development. The delinquent child is likely to grow up in a large family with parents who may drink, participate in criminal acts, be harsh and inconsistent in their discipline, be cold and unaffectionate, have marital conflicts, and be poor role models. Overall, the quality of a child's family life seems to be more important than its structure.

CHILD ABUSE AND NEGLECT

Family violence is a critical priority for criminal justice officials, political leaders, and the public.[94] Concern about the quality of family life has increased because of reports that many children are physically abused or neglected by their parents and that this treatment has serious consequences for their behavior. Because of this topic's importance, the remainder of this chapter is devoted to the issue of child abuse and neglect and its relationship to delinquent behavior.

A Historical Perspective

Parental abuse and neglect are not modern phenomena. Maltreatment of children has occurred throughout history. Some concern for the negative effects of such maltreatment was voiced in the eighteenth century in the United States, but concerted efforts to deal with the problem did not begin until 1874. In that year, residents of a New York City apartment building reported to a public health nurse, Etta Wheeler, that a child in one of the apartments was being abused by her stepmother. The nurse found a young child named Mary Ellen Wilson, who had been repeatedly beaten and was malnourished from a diet of bread and water. Even though the child was seriously ill, the police agreed that the law entitled the parents to raise Mary Ellen as they saw fit. The New York City Department of Charities claimed it had no custody rights over Mary Ellen.

According to legend, Mary Ellen's removal from her parents had to be arranged through the Society for the Prevention of Cruelty to Animals (SPCA) on the grounds that she was a member of the animal kingdom. The truth, however, is less sensational: Mary Ellen's case was heard by a judge. Because the child needed protection, she was placed in an orphanage.[95] The SPCA was actually founded the following year.[96]

Little research into the problems of maltreated children occurred before that of C. Henry Kempe, at the University of Colorado. In 1962, Kempe reported the results of a survey of medical and law enforcement agencies that indicated the child abuse rate was much higher than had been thought. He coined a term, **battered child syndrome,** which he applied to cases of nonaccidental injury of children by their parents or guardians.[97]

battered child syndrome
Nonaccidental physical injury of children by their parents or guardians.

In 1874 Henry Bugh and Etta Angell Wheeler persuaded a New York court to take a child, Mary Ellen, away from her stepmother on the grounds of child abuse. This is the first recorded case in which a court was used to protect a child. Mary Ellen is shown at age 9 when she appeared in court showing bruises from a whipping and several gashes from a pair of scissors. The other photograph shows her a year later.

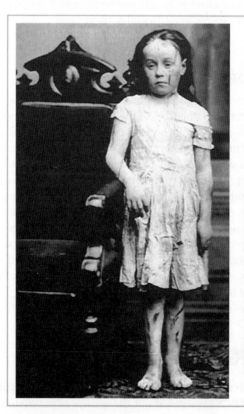

American Humane Society

Defining Abuse and Neglect

child abuse
Any physical, emotional, or sexual trauma to a child, including neglecting to give proper care and attention, for which no reasonable explanation can be found.

Kempe's pioneering work has been expanded in a more generic expression of **child abuse** that includes neglect as well as physical abuse. Specifically, it describes any physical or emotional trauma to a child for which no reasonable explanation, such as an accident, can be found. Child abuse is generally seen as a pattern of behavior rather than a single act. The effects of a pattern of behavior are cumulative. That is, the longer the abuse continues, the more severe the effect will be.[98]

neglect
Passive neglect by a parent or guardian, depriving children of food, shelter, health care, and love.

Although the terms *child abuse* and **neglect** are sometimes used interchangeably, they represent different forms of maltreatment. Neglect refers to deprivations children suffer at the hands of their parents (lack of food, shelter, health care, love). Abuse is a more overt form of aggression against the child, one that often requires medical attention. The distinction between the terms is often unclear because, in many cases, both abuse and neglect occur simultaneously.

Physical abuse includes throwing, shooting, stabbing, burning, drowning, suffocating, biting, or deliberately disfiguring a child. The greatest number of injuries result from beatings. *Physical neglect* results from parents' failure to provide adequate food, shelter, or medical care for their children, as well as failure to protect them from physical danger.

Emotional abuse or neglect is manifested by constant criticism and rejection of the child.[99] Those who suffer emotional abuse have significantly lower self-esteem as adults.[100] *Emotional neglect* includes inadequate nurturing, inattention to a child's emotional development, and lack of concern about maladaptive behavior.

abandonment
Parents physically leave their children with the intention of completely severing the parent-child relationship.

Sexual abuse refers to the exploitation of children through rape, incest, and molestation by parents, family members, friends, or legal guardians. Finally, **abandonment** refers to the situation in which parents leave their children with the intention of severing the parent-child relationship.[101]

There are a variety of legal definitions of abuse, but almost all contain concepts such as nonaccidental physical injury, physical neglect, emotional abuse or neglect, sexual abuse, and abandonment.[102] Regardless of how it is defined, the effects of abuse can be devastating. Children who have experienced some form of maltreatment possess mental representations characterized by a devalued sense of self, mistrust of others, a tendency toward attributing hostility toward others in situations where the intentions of others are ambiguous, a tendency to generate antagonistic solutions to social problems, and a suspicion of close relationships.[103]

Sexual Abuse Sexual abuse can vary in content and style. It may range from rewarding children for sexual behavior that is inappropriate for their level of development to using force or the threat of force for the purposes of sex. It can involve children who are aware of the sexual content of their actions and others too young to have any idea what their actions mean. It can involve a variety of acts, from inappropriate touching to forcible sexual penetration.

The effects of sexual abuse can be devastating. Abused children suffer disrupted ego and personality development.[104] Guilt and shame are common. The ego of the victim may be overwhelmed by rage and horror over the incident, and the experience can have long-lasting repercussions. Some victims find themselves sexualizing their own children in ways that lead those children to sexual or physical abuse. Several studies have found a close association between sexual abuse and adolescent prostitution.[105] Many sexually abused children later become involved in aggression and delinquency.[106] Girls who were sexually and physically abused as children are more often suicidal as adults than the non-abused.[107]

Research indicates a correlation between the severity of abuse and its long-term effects: The less serious the abuse, the more quickly the child can recover.[108] Children who are frequently abused over long periods and suffer actual sexual penetration are most likely to experience long-term trauma, including post-traumatic stress disorder (PTSD), precocious sexuality, and poor self-esteem.[109]

A recent national survey on the sexual exploitation of children conducted by researchers at the University of Pennsylvania indicates that the problem may be much

The Sexual Exploitation of Children

In a detailed study of child sexual exploitation in North America, Richard J. Estes and Neil Alan Weiner found that the problem of child sexual abuse is much more widespread than has been previously believed or documented. Estes and Weiner, two researchers at the School of Social Welfare at the University of Pennsylvania, relied on interviews with victims, child welfare workers, and law enforcement officials in 28 cities in the United States, Mexico, and Canada from January 1999 through March 2001. They also used the latest estimates on the number of runaway and homeless youths in the three countries and on estimates by law enforcement officials and child welfare authorities of the estimated number of sexually exploited children.

Their research indicated that each year in the United States 325,000 children are subjected to some form of sexual exploitation, including sexual abuse, prostitution, use in pornography, and molestation by adults. Most are likely to be white and middle class. Equal numbers of boys and girls are involved, but the activities of boys generally receive less attention from authorities. Many of these kids are runaways (more than 120,000), while others had fled mental hospitals and foster homes. More than 50,000 had been thrown out of their home by a parent or guardian.

Who were the sexual exploiters? Most of the sexual assaults had been committed by relatives and acquaintances, such as a teacher, coach, or a neighbor; and only 4 percent by strangers. Abusers were nearly all men and about a quarter of them were married with children.

Once they fled an abusive situation at home, the kids become vulnerable to life on the streets. Some get hooked into the sex trade, starting as strippers and lap dancers, and drifting into prostitution and pornography. Some meet pimps, who quickly turn them to a life of prostitution and beat them if they do not make their daily financial quotas. Others who fled to the streets exchange sex for money, food, and shelter. Some have been traded between prostitution rings, while others are shipped from city to city and even sent overseas as prostitutes. About 20 percent of sexually exploited children were involved in prostitution rings that worked across state lines. Table A lists some of the sexual exploitation endured by these children.

TABLE A EXPLOITATION OF CHILDREN

Girls	Boys	Both Sexes
Stripping, topless dancing	Gay sex paid for by adult males	Sexual molestation by family and acquaintances
Sex exploitations in gangs	Commercial sex, hustling	Pornography
Pimp-controlled prostitution		Participation in national and international crime networks that transport children for sexual purposes

Critical Thinking

1. Estes and Weiner maintain that there are serious gaps in policies and services to combat sexual exploitation and provide help to victims. They suggest increasing penalties, enforcing existing laws more vigorously, and expanding the federal government's role in combating abuse. Should special laws be created that would punish those who traffic in children more harshly than if their victims were adults? For example, would you recommend a life sentence for someone who exploits children in a prostitution ring?

2. Is the sexual exploitation of children essentially a hate crime?

InfoTrac College Edition Research

Juvenile prostitution and sexual exploitation are worldwide phenomena. To read more about them, use "prostitution, juvenile" as a subject guide on InfoTrac College Edition.

SOURCE: Richard J. Estes and Neil Alan Weiner, *The Commercial Sexual Exploitation of Children in the U.S., Canada and Mexico* (Philadelphia: University of Pennsylvania, 2001).

---

more widespread than previously thought. The Focus on Delinquency box entitled "The Sexual Exploitation of Children" looks at their research in depth.

The Extent of Child Abuse

It is almost impossible to estimate the extent of child abuse. Many victims are so young that they have not learned to communicate. Some are too embarrassed or afraid. Many incidents occur behind closed doors, and even when another adult witnesses inappropriate or criminal behavior, the adult may not want to get involved in a "family matter." There are a number of different ways of measuring the extent of child abuse, and some of the most important ones are discussed next.

Survey Data Some indications of the severity of the problem came from a 1980 survey conducted by sociologists Richard Gelles, Murray Straus, and Suzanne Steinmentz.[110] Gelles and Straus estimated that between 1.4 and 1.9 million children in the United

States were subject to physical abuse from their parents. This abuse was rarely a one-time act. The average number of assaults per year was 10.5, and the median was 4.5. Gelles and Straus also found that 16 percent of the couples in their sample reported spousal abuse; 50 percent of the multichild families reported attacks between siblings; 20 percent of the families reported incidents in which children attacked parents.[111]

The Gelles and Straus survey was a milestone in identifying child abuse as a national phenomenon. Surveys conducted in 1985 and 1992 indicated that the incidence of severe violence toward children had declined.[112] One reason was that parental approval of corporal punishment, which stood at 94 percent in 1968, decreased to 68 percent by 1994.[113] Recognition of the problem may have helped moderate cultural values and awakened parents to the dangers of physically disciplining children.

Nonetheless, more than 1 million children were still being subjected to severe violence annually. If the definition of "severe abuse" used in the survey had included hitting with objects such as a stick or a belt, the number of child victims would have been closer to 7 million per year.

Cases Reported to Child Protective Services Not all child abuse and neglect cases are reported to authorities, but those that are become the focus of state action. Child protective services (CPS) agencies receive referrals from educators, law enforcement personnel, social workers, parents, and concerned neighbors alleging that children have been abused or neglected. While some reports are considered unfounded, many others are "screened in" and investigated, indicating that the referral was deemed appropriate for investigation or assessment. The U.S. Department of Health and Human Services conducts annual surveys of CPS agencies in order to assess the nature and trends in reported abuse.[114] The most recent survey (2002) indicates that an estimated total of 2.6 million referrals concerning the welfare of approximately 4.5 million children were made to CPS agencies throughout the United States.[115] Of these, approximately two-thirds (an estimated 1.8 million) were accepted for investigation or assessment; one-third was not accepted. After investigation, an estimated 896,000 children were determined to be victims of child abuse or neglect; the rate of annual victimization per 1,000 children in the national population dropped from 13.4 children in 1990 to 12.3 children in 2002. Of the abused population, more than 60 percent of child victims experienced neglect, about 20 percent were physically abused, 10 percent were sexually abused, and 7 percent were emotionally maltreated. Children from birth to 3 years old had the highest rates of victimization at 16.0 per 1,000 children. Girls were slightly more likely to be victims than boys. Child fatalities are the most tragic consequence of maltreatment, and in 2002, an estimated 1,400 children died due to abuse or neglect.

Young children (aged 3 and younger) are the most frequent victims of child fatalities: Children younger than 1 year account for about 40 percent of fatalities, while children younger than 4 years accounted for more than 75 percent of fatalities. This population of children is the most vulnerable for many reasons, including their dependency, small size, and inability to defend themselves (see Figure 7.2).

Cases Reported to the Police There have also been attempts to review cases of child abuse reported to local police departments. Using data from 12 states, David Finkelhor and Richard Ormrod found that child abuse constituted a significant portion of all crimes against children and that parents and caretakers were responsible for the majority of these cases.[116] Their data show that large numbers of parental child abuse cases are, in fact, reported to the police. These incidents are predominantly physical assaults, involve more older than younger children, and involve more male than female caretakers. Only about one-half of these cases are associated with any recorded injury to the victim. The most important of Finkelhor and Ormrod's findings are contained in Exhibit 7.2.

Reports of Sexual Abuse Attempts to determine the extent of sexual abuse indicate that perhaps 1 in 10 boys and 1 in 3 girls have been the victim of some

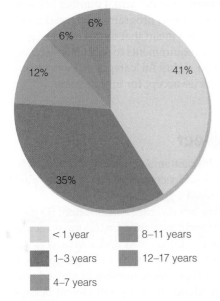

6%
6%
12%
41%
35%

■ < 1 year   ■ 8–11 years
■ 1–3 years   ■ 12–17 years
■ 4–7 years

FIGURE 7.2
Child Abuse and Neglect Fatalities, 2004

Investigators found that more than 80 percent of perpetrators were parents. Other relatives accounted for 7 percent, and unmarried partners of parents accounted for 3 percent of perpetrators. The remaining perpetrators include people with other (camp counselor, school employee, etc.) or unknown relationships to the child victims. The number of substantiated cases corresponds with the results of the surveys conducted by Gelles, Straus, and their associates.

EXHIBIT 7.2

Child Abuse Cases Reported to the Police

▌ Incidents of child abuse committed by parents and other caretakers make up about one-fifth (19 percent) of violent crimes against juveniles (age 0 to 17) reported to the police and 4 percent of violent crimes against people of any age.

▌ The majority (73 percent) of these parent and other caretaker crimes are physical assaults, and 23 percent are cases of sexual abuse.

▌ Child abuse constitutes more than one-half of the crimes against children age 2 or younger reported to the police.

▌ Male offenders are responsible for three-quarters of the child abuse incidents reported to the police, including 92 percent of sexual assaults and 68 percent of physical assaults.

▌ Thirteen percent of the episodes of parental assault against a child reported to the police are associated with an assault against a spouse or former spouse.

▌ In spite of protocols in some states that require police notification about child maltreatment, there is evidence that police data tally only a fraction of physical and sexual abuse investigated and substantiated by child welfare authorities.

SOURCE: David Finkelhor and Richard Ormrod, "Child Abuse Cases Reported to the Police," *Juvenile Justice Bulletin* (Washington, DC: Office of Juvenile Justice and Delinquency Prevention, 2001).

form of sexual exploitation. An oft-cited survey by Diana Russell found that 16 percent of women reported sexual abuse by a relative, and 4.5 percent reported abuse by a father or stepfather.[117] It has been estimated that 30 percent to 75 percent of women in treatment for substance abuse disorders experienced childhood sexual abuse.[118]

While sexual abuse is still quite prevalent, the number of reported cases has been in a significant decline. Research by Lisa Jones and David Finkelhor of the University of New Hampshire's Crimes Against Children Research Center shows that after a 15-year increase, substantiated child sexual-abuse cases in the United States dropped 31 percent between 1992 and 1998. Most states (36 out of the 47 they reviewed) showed declines of at least 30 percent.[119] This data could mean that the actual number of cases is truly in decline because of the effectiveness of prevention programs, increased prosecution, and public awareness campaigns. It could also mean that more cases are getting overlooked because of (1) increased evidentiary requirements to substantiate cases, (2) increased caseworker caution due to new legal rights for caregivers, and (3) increasing limitations on the types of cases that agencies accept for investigation.[120]

Causes of Child Abuse and Neglect

Maltreatment of children is a complex problem with neither a single cause nor a single solution. It cuts across racial, ethnic, religious, and socioeconomic lines. Abusive parents cannot be categorized by sex, age, or educational level.

Of all factors associated with child abuse, three are discussed most often: (1) parents who themselves suffered abuse tend to abuse their own children; (2) the presence of an unrelated adult increases the risk of abuse; and (3) isolated and alienated families tend to become abusive. A cyclical pattern of violence seems to be perpetuated from one generation to another. Evidence indicates that a large number of abused and neglected children grow into adulthood with a tendency to engage in violent behavior. The behavior of abusive parents can often be traced to negative experiences in their own childhood—physical abuse, emotional neglect, and incest. These parents become unable to separate their own childhood traumas from their relationships with their children. Abusive parents often have unrealistic perceptions of normal development. When their children are unable to act appropriately—when they cry or strike their parents—the parents may react in an abusive manner.[121] Parents may also become abusive if they are isolated from friends, neighbors, or relatives.

Many abusive parents describe themselves as alienated from their extended families, and they lack close relationships with people who could provide help in stressful situations.[122] The relationship between alienation and abuse may be particularly acute in homes where there has been divorce or separation, or in which parents have never actually married; abusive punishment in single-parent homes has been found to be twice that of two-parent families.[123] Parents who are unable to cope with stressful events—divorce, financial stress, recurring mental illness, drug addiction—are most at risk.[124]

Substance Abuse and Child Abuse Abusive families also suffer from severe stress, and it is therefore not surprising that they frequently harbor members who turn to drugs and alcohol.[125] Research clearly indicates a connection between substance abuse and child abuse. Among confirmed cases of child maltreatment, 40 percent involve the use of alcohol or other drugs. This suggests that, of the 1 million or so confirmed victims of child maltreatment each year, an estimated 480,000 children are mistreated by a caretaker with alcohol or other drug problems. Additionally, research suggests that alcohol and other drug problems are factors in a majority of cases of emotional abuse and neglect[126] Children of alcoholics are more likely than children in the general population to suffer a variety of physical, mental, and emotional health problems. They often have feelings of low self-esteem and failure and suffer from depression and anxiety. It is thought that exposure to violence in both alcohol-abusing and child-maltreating households increases the likelihood that the children will commit, and be recipients of, acts of violence.[127]

Stepparents and Abuse Research indicates that stepchildren share a greater risk for abuse than do biological offspring.[128] Stepparents may have less emotional attachment to someone else's children. Often the biological parent has to choose between the new mate and the child, sometimes even becoming an accomplice in the abuse.[129]

Stepchildren are overrepresented in cases of **familicide,** mass murders in which a spouse and one or more children are slain. It is also more common for fathers who kill their biological children to commit suicide than those who kill stepchildren, an indication that the biological parent's act was motivated by despair, the stepparent's by hostility.[130]

familicide
Mass murders in which a spouse and one or more children are slain.

Social Class and Abuse Surveys indicate a high rate of reported abuse and neglect among people in lower economic classes. Children from families earning less than $15,000 per year experience more abuse than children living in more affluent homes.[131] More than 40 percent of CPS workers indicate that most of their clients either live in poverty or face increased financial stress due to unemployment and economic recession.[132] These findings suggest that parental maltreatment of children is predominantly a lower-class problem. Is this conclusion valid?

It is possible that the statistics are generally accurate. Low-income families, especially those headed by a single parent, are often subject to greater environmental stress and have fewer resources for dealing with such stress than families with higher incomes.[133] A relationship seems to exist between the burdens of raising a child without adequate resources and the use of excessive force. Self-report surveys do show that indigent parents are more likely than affluent parents to hold attitudes that condone physical chastisement of children.[134]

Higher rates of maltreatment in low-income families reflect the stress caused by the limited resources lower-class parents have to help them in raising their children; in contrast, middle-class parents devote a smaller percentage of their total resources to raising a family.[135] This burden becomes especially onerous in families with emotionally and physically handicapped children. Stressed-out parents may consider special-needs children a drain on the family's finances with little potential for future success; research finds that children with disabilities are maltreated at a rate almost double that of other children.[136]

The Child Protection System: Philosophy and Practice

For most of the nation's history, courts have assumed that parents have the right to bring up their children as they see fit. In the 2000 case *Troxel v. Granville,* the Supreme Court ruled that the due process clause of the Constitution protects against government interference with certain fundamental rights and liberty interests, including parents' fundamental right to make decisions concerning the care, custody, and control of their children.[137] If the care a child receives falls below reasonable standards, the state may take action to remove a child from the home and place her or him in a less threatening environment. In these extreme circumstances, the rights of both parents and children are constitutionally protected. In the cases of *Lassiter v. Department of Social Services* and *Santosky v. Kramer,* the U.S. Supreme Court recognized the child's right to be free from parental abuse and set down guidelines for a termination-of-custody hearing, including the right to legal representation.[138] States provide a guardian *ad litem* (a lawyer appointed by the court to look after the interests of those who do not have the capacity to assert their own rights). States also ensure confidentiality of reporting.[139]

Though child protection agencies have been dealing with abuse and neglect since the late nineteenth century, recent awareness of the problem has prompted judicial authorities to take increasingly bold steps to ensure the safety of children.[140] The assumption that the parent-child relationship is inviolate has been challenged. In 1974 Congress passed the Child Abuse Prevention and Treatment Act (CAPTA), which provides funds to states to bolster their services for maltreated children and their parents.[141] The act provides federal funding to states in support of prevention, investigation, and treatment. It also provides grants to public agencies and nonprofit organizations for demonstration programs.

The Child Abuse Prevention and Treatment Act has been the impetus for the states to improve the legal frameworks of their child protection systems. Abusive parents are subject to prosecution under statutes against assault, battery, and homicide. Many states have child abuse statutes that make it a felony to injure and abuse children.

Investigating and Reporting Abuse Maltreatment of children can easily be hidden from public view. Although state laws require doctors, teachers, and others who work with children to report suspected cases to child protection agencies, many maltreated children are out of the law's reach because they are too young for school or because their parents do not take them to a doctor or a hospital. Parents abuse their children in private and, even when confronted, often accuse their children of lying, or blame the children's medical problems on accidents. Social service agencies must find more effective ways to locate abused children and to handle such cases once found.

All states have statutes requiring that people suspected of abuse and neglect be reported. Many have made failure to report child abuse a criminal offense. Though such statutes are rarely enforced, teachers and nurses have been criminally charged for failing to report abuse or neglect cases.[142]

Once reported to a child protection agency, the case is screened by an intake worker and then turned over to an investigative caseworker. Protective service workers often work with law enforcement officers. If the caseworker determines that the child is in imminent danger of severe harm, the caseworker may immediately remove the child from the home. A court hearing must be held shortly after to approve the custody. Stories abound of children erroneously taken from their homes, but it is much more likely that these "gatekeepers" will consider cases unfounded and take no action. More than 50 percent of all reported cases are so classified.[143] Among the most common reasons for screening out cases is that the reporting party is involved in a child custody case.[144]

Even when there is compelling evidence of abuse, most social service agencies will try to involve the family in voluntary treatment. Case managers will do periodic follow-ups to determine whether treatment plans are being followed. If parents are uncooperative or if the danger to the children is so great that they must be removed from the home, a complaint will be filed in the criminal, family, or juvenile court system.

The Process of State Intervention Although procedures vary from state to state, most follow a similar legal process once a social service agency files a court petition alleging abuse or neglect.[145] This process is diagrammed in Figure 7.3.

If the allegation of abuse is confirmed, the child may be placed in protective custody. Most state statutes require that the court be notified "promptly" or "immedi-

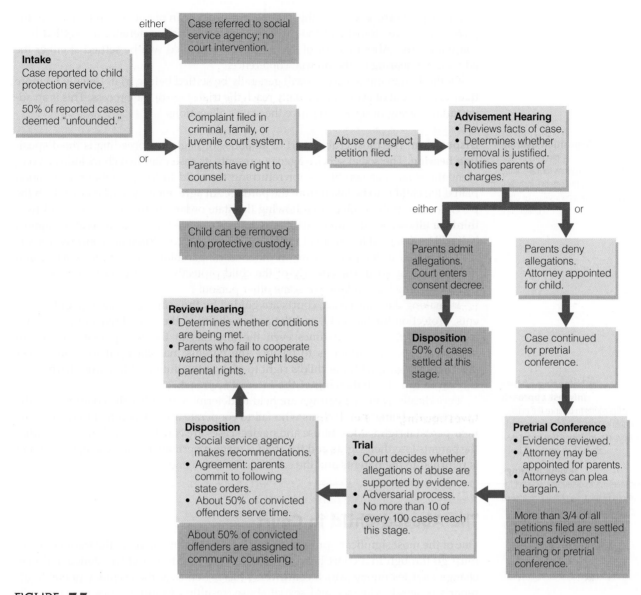

Intake
Case reported to child protection service.

50% of reported cases deemed "unfounded."

either → Case referred to social service agency; no court intervention.

or → Complaint filed in criminal, family, or juvenile court system.

Parents have right to counsel.

Child can be removed into protective custody.

Abuse or neglect petition filed.

Advisement Hearing
• Reviews facts of case.
• Determines whether removal is justified.
• Notifies parents of charges.

either → Parents admit allegations. Court enters consent decree.

or → Parents deny allegations. Attorney appointed for child.

Disposition
50% of cases settled at this stage.

Case continued for pretrial conference.

Review Hearing
• Determines whether conditions are being met.
• Parents who fail to cooperate warned that they might lose parental rights.

Disposition
• Social service agency makes recommendations.
• Agreement: parents commit to following state orders.
• About 50% of convicted offenders serve time.

About 50% of convicted offenders are assigned to community counseling.

Trial
• Court decides whether allegations of abuse are supported by evidence.
• Adversarial process.
• No more than 10 of every 100 cases reach this stage.

Pretrial Conference
• Evidence reviewed.
• Attorney may be appointed for parents.
• Attorneys can plea bargain.

More than 3/4 of all petitions filed are settled during advisement hearing or pretrial conference.

FIGURE 7.3
The Process of State Intervention in Cases of Abuse and Neglect

advisement hearing
A preliminary protective or temporary custody hearing in which the court will review the facts and determine whether removal of the child is justified and notify parents of the charges against them.

pretrial conference
The attorney for the social services agency presents an overview of the case, and a plea bargain or negotiated settlement can be agreed to in a consent decree.

ately" if the child is removed; some states, including Arkansas, North Carolina, and Pennsylvania, have gone as far as requiring that no more than 12 hours elapse before official action is taken. If the child has not been removed from the home, state authorities are given more time to notify the court of suspected abuse. For example, Louisiana and Maryland set a limit of 30 days to take action, whereas Wisconsin mandates that state action take no more than 20 days once the case has been investigated.

When an abuse or neglect petition is prosecuted, an **advisement hearing** (also called a *preliminary protective hearing* or *temporary custody hearing*) is held. The court will review the facts of the case, determine whether removal is justified, and notify the parents of the charges against them. Parents have the right to counsel in all cases of abuse and neglect, and many states require the court to appoint an attorney for the child as well. If the parents admit the allegations, the court enters a consent decree, and the case is continued for disposition. Approximately one-half of all cases are settled by admission at the advisement hearing. If the parents deny the petition, an attorney is appointed for the child and the case is continued for a pretrial conference.

At the **pretrial conference,** the attorney for the social service agency presents an overview of the case and the evidence. Such matters as admissibility of photos and written reports are settled. At this point the attorneys can negotiate a settlement of the case. About three-fourths of the cases that go to pretrial conference are settled by a consent decree. About 85 out of every 100 petitions filed will be settled at either the advisement hearing or the pretrial conference.

Of the 15 remaining cases, 5 will generally be settled before trial. Usually no more than 10 cases out of every 100 actually reach the trial stage of the process. This is an adversarial hearing designed to prove the state's allegations.

disposition hearing
The social service agency presents its case plan and recommendations for care of the child and treatment of the parents, including incarceration and counseling or other treatments.

Disposition The most crucial part of an abuse or neglect proceeding is the **disposition hearing.** The social service agency presents its case plan, which includes recommendations such as conditions for returning the child to the parents or a visitation plan if the child is to be taken from the parents. An agreement is reached by which the parents commit themselves to following the state orders. Between one-half and two-thirds of all convicted parents will be required to serve time in incarceration; almost half will be assigned to a form of treatment. As far as the children are concerned, some may be placed in temporary care; in other cases, parental rights are terminated and the child is placed in the custody of the child protective service. Legal custody can then be assigned to a relative or some other person.

In making their decisions, courts are guided by three interests: the role of the parents, protection for the child, and the responsibility of the state. Frequently, these interests conflict. In fact, at times even the interests of the two parents are not in harmony. The state attempts to balance the parents' natural right to control their child's upbringing with the child's right to grow into adulthood free from harm. This is referred to as the **balancing-of-the-interest approach.**

balancing-of-the-interest approach
Efforts of the courts to balance the parents' natural right to raise a child with the child's right to grow into adulthood free from physical abuse or emotional harm.

Periodically, **review hearings** are held to determine whether the conditions of the case plan are being met. Parents who fail to cooperate are warned that they may lose their parental rights. Most abuse and neglect cases are concluded within a year. Either the parents lose their rights and the child is given a permanent placement, or the child is returned to the parents and the court's jurisdiction ends.

review hearings
Periodic meetings to determine whether the conditions of the case plan for an abused child are being met by the parents or guardians of the child.

The Abused Child in Court

One of the most significant problems associated with abuse cases is the trauma a child must go through in a court hearing. Children get confused and frightened and may change their testimony. Much controversy has arisen over the accuracy of children's reports of family violence and sexual abuse, resulting in hung juries in some well-known cases, including the McMartin Day Care case in California.[146]

State jurisdictions have instituted procedures to minimize the trauma to the child. Most have enacted legislation allowing videotaped statements, or interviews with child witnesses, taken at a preliminary hearing or at a formal deposition, to be admissible in court. Videotaped testimony spares child witnesses the trauma of testifying in open court. States that allow videotaped testimony usually put some restrictions on its use. Some prohibit the government from calling the child to testify at trial if the videotape is used; some states require a finding that the child is "medically unavailable" because of the trauma of the case before videotaping can be used; some require that the defendant be present during the videotaping; a few specify that the child not be able to see or hear the defendant.[147]

Today, most states now allow a child's testimony to be given on closed-circuit television (CCTV). The child is able to view the judge and attorneys, and the courtroom participants are able to observe the child. The standards for CCTV testimony vary widely. Some states, such as New Hampshire, assume that any child witness under age 12 would benefit from not having to appear in court. Others require an independent examination by a mental health professional to determine whether there is a "compelling need" for CCTV testimony.

In addition to innovative methods of testimony, children in sexual abuse cases have been allowed to use anatomically correct dolls to demonstrate happenings that they cannot describe verbally. The Victims of Child Abuse Act of 1990 allows children to use these dolls when testifying in federal courts; at least eight states have passed similar legislation.[148] Similarly, states have relaxed their laws of evidence to allow out-of-court statements by the child to a social worker, teacher, or police officer to be used as evidence (such statements would otherwise be considered **hearsay**). Typically, corroboration is required to support these statements if the child does not also testify.

hearsay
Out-of-court statements made by one person and recounted in court by another; such statements are generally not allowed as evidence except in child abuse cases wherein a child's statements to social workers, teachers, or police may be admissible.

The prevalence of sexual abuse cases has created new problems for the justice system. Often accusations are made in conjunction with marital disputes. The fear is growing that children may become pawns in custody battles; the mere suggestion of sexual abuse is enough to affect the outcome of a divorce action. The justice system must develop techniques that can get at the truth without creating a lifelong scar on the child's psyche.

Legal Issues A number of cases have been brought before the Supreme Court, testing the right of children to present evidence at trial using nontraditional methods. Two issues stand out. One is the ability of physicians and mental health professionals to testify about statements made to them by children, especially when the children are incapable of testifying. The second concerns the way children testify in court.

In a 1992 case, *White v. Illinois,* the Court ruled that the state's attorney is required neither to produce young victims at trial nor to demonstrate the reason they were unavailable to serve as witnesses.[149] *White* involved statements given by the child to the child's babysitter and mother, a doctor, a nurse, and a police officer concerning the alleged assailant in a sexual assault case. The prosecutor twice tried to call the child to testify, but both times the 4-year-old experienced emotional difficulty and could not appear in court. The outcome hinged solely on the testimony of the five witnesses.

By allowing others to testify as to what the child said, *White* removed the requirement that prosecutors produce child victims in court. This facilitates the prosecution of child abusers in cases where a court appearance by a victim would prove too disturbing or where the victim is too young to understand the court process.[150] The Court noted that statements made to doctors during medical exams or those made when a victim is upset carry more weight than ones made after careful reflection. The Court ruled that such statements can be repeated during trial because the circumstances in which they were made could not be duplicated simply by having the child testify to them in court.

In-Court Statements Children who are victims of sexual or physical abuse often make poor witnesses. Yet their testimony may be crucial. In a 1988 case, *Coy v. Iowa,* the Court placed limitations on efforts to protect child witnesses in court. During a sexual assault case, a one-way glass screen was set up so that the child victims would not be able to view the defendant (the defendant, however, could view the witnesses).[151] The Iowa statute that allowed the protective screen assumed that children would be traumatized by their courtroom experience. The Court ruled that unless there was a finding that the child witness needs special protection, the Sixth Amendment of the Constitution grants defendants "face-to-face" confrontation with their accusers. In her dissenting opinion, Justice Sandra Day O'Connor suggested that if courts found it necessary, it would be appropriate to allow children to testify via CCTV or videotape.

Justice O'Connor's views became law in *Craig v. Maryland.*[152] In this case a day-care operator was convicted of sexually abusing a 6-year-old child; one-way CCTV testimony was used during the trial. The decision was overturned in the Maryland Court of Appeals on the ground that the procedures used were insufficient to show that the child could only testify in this manner because a trial appearance would be too traumatic. On appeal, the Court ruled that the Maryland statute that allows CCTV testimony is sufficient because it requires a determination that the child will suffer distress if forced to testify. The Court noted that CCTV could serve as the equivalent of in-court testimony and would not interfere with the defendant's right to confront witnesses.

The National Child Welfare Resource Center on Legal and Judicial Issues is dedicated to achieving safety, permanence and well-being for abused and neglected children through improved laws and judicial decision-making, at www.abanet.org/child/rclji/. For an up-to-date list of web links, go to http://cj.wadsworth.com/siegel_jd9e.

Disposition of Abuse and Neglect Cases

There is considerable controversy over what forms of intervention are helpful in abuse and neglect cases. Today, social service agents avoid removing children from the home whenever possible and instead try to employ techniques to control abusive relationships. In serious cases, the state may remove children from their parents and place them in shelter care or foster homes. All too often this action does not alleviate problems but creates new ones. Placement of children in foster care is intended to be temporary, but it is not uncommon for children to remain in foster care for three years or more. More troubling is that a recent survey by the Packard Foundation found that few states monitor how well foster families are meeting the educational, health care, and mental health needs of children in their care. Though reviews of foster care are mandated by the Child and Family Service Reviews (CFSRs) Act of 1994, only 32 states have completed the review process, and none of these has met all federal performance measures. Many children in the child welfare system are absent from school, less likely to be involved in extracurricular activities, and more likely to suffer inconsistent health care; many do not receive immunizations or even routine care.[153] Ultimately, the court has the power to terminate the rights of parents over their children, but because the effects of destroying the family unit are far-reaching, the court does so only in the most severe cases. Judicial hesitancy is illustrated in a Virginia appellate case in which grandparents contested a father's being awarded custody of his children. Even though he had a history of alcohol abuse, had already been found to be an unfit parent, and was awaiting appeal of his conviction for killing the children's mother, the trial court claimed that he had turned his life around and granted him custody.[154]

Despite such occurrences, efforts have been ongoing to improve the child protection system. Jurisdictions have expedited case processing, instituted procedures designed not to frighten child witnesses, coordinated investigations between social service and law enforcement agencies, and assigned an advocate or guardian *ad litem* to children in need of protection. Efforts are also being made to help prosecutors handle abuse cases. The Office of Juvenile Justice and Delinquency Prevention (OJJDP) now funds the National Center for Prosecution of Child Abuse (the Center) to enhance investigators' and prosecutors' skills and help them handle child and adolescent abuse cases. First established in 1985, by the National District Attorneys Association, the Center serves as the nation's main resource for training, expert legal assistance, court reform, and state-of-the-art information on criminal child abuse investigations and prosecutions.[155]

TO QUIZ YOURSELF ON THIS MATERIAL, go to the Juvenile Delinquency 9e website.

ABUSE, NEGLECT, AND DELINQUENCY

Mental health and delinquency experts have found that abused kids experience mental and social problems across their lifespan, ranging from substance abuse to possession of a damaged personality.[156] For example, victims of abuse are prone to suffer mental illness such as dissociative identity disorder (DID), formerly known as multiple personality disorder (MPD); research shows that child abuse is present in the histories of the vast majority of DID subjects.[157]

One particular area of concern is the child's own personal involvement with violence. Psychologists suggest that maltreatment encourages children to use aggression as a means of solving problems and prevents them from feeling empathy for others. It diminishes their ability to cope with stress and makes them vulnerable to the violence in the culture. Abused children have fewer positive interactions with peers, are less well liked, and are more likely to have disturbed social interactions.[158]

The link between maltreatment and delinquency is also supported by a number of criminological theories. For example:

I *Social control theory* By disrupting normal relationships and impeding socialization, maltreatment reduces the social bond and frees individuals to become involved in deviance.

- *Social learning theory* Maltreatment leads to delinquency because it teaches children that aggression and violence are justifiable forms of behavior.
- *General Strain Theory* Maltreatment creates the "negative affective states" that are related to strain, anger, and aggression.

A significant amount of literature suggests that abuse may have a profound effect on behavior in later years. Exposure to abuse in early life provides a foundation for violent and antisocial behavior.[159] Delinquent behavior is the means by which many abused children act out their hostility toward their parents. Some join gangs, which furnish a sense of belonging and allow pent-up anger to be expressed in group-approved delinquent acts.

Case Studies of the Effects of Child Abuse

Studies of juvenile offenders have confirmed that between 70 percent and 80 percent may have had abusive backgrounds. Many of these juveniles reported serious injury by a parent or guardian, including bruises, lacerations, fractures, and being knocked unconscious. Several studies have examined the incarcerated delinquent and criminal population and found that adult and juvenile inmates report much higher rates of childhood abuse and neglect than the general population.[160] National estimates indicate that approximately 4 to 8 percent of all children are reported to child welfare agencies as alleged victims of abuse or neglect, while more than 50 percent of court-referred juveniles have experienced abuse. For example, one study of high-risk male juvenile parolees in three states revealed that the proportion of juveniles who had allegedly been victims of abuse or neglect ranged from 29 percent in Virginia to 45 percent in Colorado to 53 percent in Nevada. Findings are similar for adult offenders. A recent study of adult offenders found that 16 percent of males and 57 percent of females in state prisons had experienced childhood physical or sexual abuse.[161]

Involvement in delinquent activity is not the only social problem for which abused kids are at risk. Compared with non-maltreated matched control groups, abused or neglected children are significantly more likely to engage in violent behavior, become pregnant during adolescence, use drugs, have lower GPAs, and/or experience mental health problems.[162] Girls who are psychologically, sexually, or physically abused as children are more likely to have lower self-esteem and be more suicidal as adults than those who were not abused.[163] Kids who are victimized in the home are more likely to run away in order to escape their environment, an action that puts them at risk for juvenile arrest and involvement with the justice system.[164]

Cohort Studies of the Effects of Child Abuse

These findings do not necessarily prove that maltreatment causes delinquency. It is possible that child abuse is a reaction to misbehavior and not vice versa. In other words, it is possible that angry parents attack their delinquent and drug-abusing children and that child abuse is a *result* of delinquency, not its cause.

One way of solving this dilemma is to follow a cohort of youths who had been reported as victims of abuse and compare them with a similar cohort of non-abused youths. A classic study conducted by Jose Alfaro in New York found that about half of all children reported to area hospitals as abused children later acquired arrest records. Conversely, a significant number of boys (21 percent) and girls (29 percent) petitioned to juvenile court had prior histories as abuse cases. Children treated for abuse were disproportionately involved in violent offenses.[165]

Cathy Spatz Widom followed the offending careers of 908 youths reported as abused from 1967 to 1971 and compared them with a control group of 667 nonabused youths. Widom found that the abuse involved a variety of perpetrators, including parents, relatives, strangers, and even grandparents. Twenty-six percent of the abused sample had juvenile arrests, compared to 17 percent of the comparison group; 29 percent of those who were abused had adult criminal records, compared to 21 percent of the control group. Race, gender, and age also affected the probability that abuse would lead to delinquency. The highest-risk group comprised older black males who had suffered abuse; about 67 percent of this group went on to become adult criminals. In contrast, only 4 percent of young, white, nonabused females became adult offenders.[166] Widom's conclusion: Being abused increased the likelihood of arrest both as a juvenile and as an adult.[167]

Widom and her colleagues are now conducting a second phase of research to determine why some victims of childhood abuse and neglect fare well, while others experience long-term negative consequences. They located a large number of subjects 20 to 25 years after they experienced childhood victimization. Interviews with formerly abused and neglected youths have found that child abuse in early life is related to the following negative outcomes over the life course:

I Mental health concerns (suicide attempts and post-traumatic stress disorder)

I Educational problems (extremely low IQ scores and reading ability)

I Occupational difficulties (lack of work, high rates of unemployment, and employment in low-level service jobs)

I Public health and safety issues (prostitution in males and females, and alcohol problems in females)[168]

Cohort research also shows that sexually abused youths are much more likely to suffer an arrest than nonabused children. The risk is greatest if the abuse took place when the child was less than 7 years of age and the offense was committed by a male.[169] Sexually abused girls share a significant risk of becoming violent over the life course. There is also evidence that sexual abuse victims are more likely to abuse others, especially if they were exposed to other forms of family violence.[170] Self-report studies also confirm that child maltreatment increases the likelihood of delinquency. The most severely abused youths are at the greatest risk for long-term serious delinquency.[171]

The Abuse-Delinquency Link

These findings do not necessarily mean that most abused children become delinquent. Many do not, and many delinquent youths come from what appear to be model homes. Though Widom found that more abused than non-abused children in her cohort became involved in delinquency, the majority of *both* groups did not.[172]

Although these studies suggest an abuse-delinquency link, others find that the association is either insignificant or inconsistent (for example, having a greater influence on girls than boys).[173] Abused adolescents seem to get involved in more status offenses than delinquent acts—perhaps indicating that abused children are more likely to "flee than fight."[174] Some researchers also suggest that if there is a link between abuse and antisocial behavior later in life, the connection is shaped by the nature and type of abuse. For example, research shows that sexual offenders have suffered a history of sexual abuse but that sexual abuse may not be related to other types of offenses; in contrast, physical abuse seems a significant variable in the history of nonsexual offenders.[175] However, some recent research by Timothy Ireland and his associates indicates that the abuse-delinquency link may be a function of when the abuse occurred. Kids who were maltreated solely during their early childhood are less likely to later engage in delinquent acts than those mistreated when they were older or those whose abuse occurred first in childhood and then persisted into later adolescence.[176] Ireland speculates that adolescents who have experienced persistent and long-term maltreatment are more likely to have families suffering an array of other social problem deficits, including poverty, parental mental illness, and domestic violence, which may make children more likely to engage in antisocial behavior. Persistent maltreatment also gives the victim little opportunity to cope or deal with their ongoing victimization.

TO QUIZ YOURSELF ON THIS MATERIAL, go to the Juvenile Delinquency 9e website.

THE FAMILY AND DELINQUENCY CONTROL POLICY

Counselors commonly work with the families of antisocial youths as part of a court-ordered treatment strategy. Family counseling and therapy are routine when the child's acting-out behavior is suspected to be the result of family-related problems such as child abuse or neglect.

Since the family is believed to play such an important role in the production of youth crime, it follows that improving family functioning can help prevent delinquency. Counselors commonly work with the families of antisocial youths as part of a court-ordered treatment strategy. Family counseling and therapy are almost mandatory when the child's acting-out behavior is suspected to be the result of family-related problems such as child abuse or neglect.[177] Some jurisdictions have integrated family counseling services into the juvenile court.[178]

Another approach to involving the family in delinquency prevention is to attack the problem before it occurs. Early childhood prevention programs that target at-risk youths can relieve some of the symptoms associated with delinquency.[179] Frequent home visits by trained nurses and social service personnel help reduce child abuse and other injuries to infants.[180] Evidence suggests that early intervention may be the most effective method and that the later the intervention, the more difficult the change process.[181]

Because the family plays such an important role in delinquency prevention and control policies, it is one of the focus areas in Chapter 11's discussion of delinquency prevention strategies. Since it is suspected that child abuse leads to a cycle of violence, there are also programs designed to help abusive parents refrain from repeating their violent episodes. One of these is discussed in the Policy and Practice box entitled "Fathering After Violence Project."

Summary

▌ The family is undergoing change, and an increasing number of children will not live with their birth parents during their entire childhood.

▌ Families are undergoing social and economic stress.

▌ A number of factors shape the family's influence on delinquency. Poor family relationships have been linked to juvenile delinquency.

▌ Early theories viewed the broken home as a cause of youthful misconduct, but subsequent research found that divorce and separation play a smaller role than was previously believed.

▌ However, contemporary studies now show that parental absence may have a significant influence on delinquency because it is more difficult for one parent to provide the same degree of discipline and support as two.

▌ The quality of family life also has a great influence on a child's behavior. Families in conflict produce more delinquents than those that function harmoniously.

▌ Kids who grow up in conflict-ridden households are more likely to become delinquent.

▌ Poor parent-child relations, including inconsistent discipline, have been linked to delinquency.

▌ Parents who commit crimes and use drugs are likely to have children who do the same.

▌ If one sibling is delinquent, her brothers and sisters are likely to be as well.

▌ Families who neglect their children are at risk for delinquency. Inconsistent discipline and poor supervision have also been linked to juvenile crime.

▌ Parental and sibling misconduct is another factor that predicts delinquent behaviors.

▌ Concern over the relationship between family life and delinquency has been heightened by reports of widespread child abuse.

▌ While the maltreatment of juveniles has occurred throughout history, the concept of child abuse is relatively recent.

▌ C. Henry Kempe first recognized the "battered child syndrome."

Fathering After Violence Project

The Fathering After Violence Project (FVPF) is aimed at encouraging abusive men to become better father figures for their children. Developed in Boston with Dorchester Community Roundtable, the Child Witness to Violence Project, EMERGE, Roxbury Comprehensive Community Health Services and Common Purpose, FVPF targets men who have used violence and children who have witnessed violence. Materials are now being developed that include:

▮ Exercises that could be incorporated into typical sessions in any batterers' intervention program

▮ Tools and homework for program participants to use with their children outside the program

▮ Outreach materials about fathering for men who have used violence

▮ Policy and practice recommendations that support the objectives of the project

▮ A monograph on considerations in working with fathers for child mental health practitioners

▮ A list of resources for batterers' intervention programs

▮ A safety and accountability guide for doing this work

The program asks abusive men to evaluate their own violent past and become aware of the long-term effects their violent behavior can have on their children. Abusers are taught to realize the importance of engaging in positive behaviors so children will have appropriate role models. The program uses an eight-point system designed to achieve nonviolent relationships in the home:

1. *Changing abusive behavior.* Violence must end immediately. Men must also realize that establishing a better relationship with their children may be an arduous procedure; patience by the abuser is critical.

2. *Modeling constructive behavior.* Children need role models. With the termination of abusive behavior, men must learn to adopt more positive actions. In addition, fathers must realize they can no longer disrespect the child's mother, since that would constitute negative behavior.

3. *Stopping denial, blaming, and justification.* Abusers must learn what happens to a child who witness violence, is blamed for violent actions, and who feels responsible for their father's actions.

4. *Being fully accountable.* Abusers must accept the consequences of their behavior. They must confront the fact that their children may not forgive or accept their attempts at rebuilding their relationship.

5. *Acknowledging damage.* Abusers must not only understand the effects of violence on their children, but they must also communicate to their child that they are aware of the damage they have caused.

6. *Not forcing the process.* Every child will react differently when an abusive father decides he wants to improve his relationship with his son/daughter; thus, it is important that the abuser be patient and not force unwanted contact with the child.

7. *Not trying to turn the page.* Abusers must be willing to revisit their violent past as often as necessary.

8. *Listening and validating.* Abusers must be ready to accept that their children may be angry, scared, sad, and/or rejecting.

The hope is that through these eight components men who have been abusive toward their families will be able to improve their family relations. In addition, the program is designed to send the message to abused children that using violence against others is wrong.

The Fathering After Violence Project has been implemented within various batterer intervention programs. Though the project is in its beginning stages, it is hoped that it can help fathers not only end their abusive behavior, but also become better parents.

Critical Thinking

Could a program such as Fathering After Violence help break the cycle of violence? Or are more severe measures needed, such as mandatory sentences for child abusers?

InfoTrac College Edition Research

To learn more about this topic, use "parental violence" in a key term search on InfoTrac College Edition.

SOURCES: Juan Carlos Arean, "The Fathering After Violence Project: Dealing with a Complex and Unavoidable Issue," Family Violence Prevention Fund (2003), pp. 1–5, www.endabuse.org (accessed on September 1, 2004); Family Violence Prevention Fund, "New Program Promotes Healthy Parenting for Fathers While Addressing Past Violence," pp. 1–2, http://library.adoption.com/Violence-and-Violence-Prevention/New-Program-Promotes-Healthy-Parenting-for-Fathers-While-Addressing-Past-Violence/article/8335/1.html (accessed on September 1, 2004).

- We now recognize sexual, physical, and emotional abuse, as well as neglect.
- It has been estimated that there are 3 million reported cases of child abuse each year, of which almost 1 million are confirmed by child welfare investigators.
- The number of reported sexual abuse cases has been in decline during the past decade.
- There are a number of suspected causes of child abuse, including parental substance abuse, isolation, and a history of physical and emotional abuse.
- Two factors are seen as causing child abuse. First, parents who themselves suffered abuse as children tend to abuse their own children. Second, isolated and alienated families tend to become abusive.
- Local, state, and federal governments have attempted to alleviate the problem of child abuse. All 50 states have statutes requiring that suspected cases of abuse be reported.
- There is a complex system of state intervention once allegations of child abuse are made. Thousands of youths are removed from their homes every year.
- A number of studies have linked abuse to delinquency. They show that a disproportionate number of court-adjudicated youths had been abused or neglected.
- Although the evidence is not conclusive, the data suggest that a strong relationship exists between child abuse and delinquent behavior.
- To make it easier to prosecute abusers, the Supreme Court has legalized the use of closed-circuit TV in some cases. Most states allow children to use anatomically correct dolls when testifying in court.

Key Terms

nuclear family, p. 202
broken home, p. 204
blended families, p. 204
intrafamily conflict, p. 206
parental efficacy, p. 208
resource dilution, p. 210
contagion effect, p. 211

battered child syndrome, p. 212
child abuse, p. 213
neglect, p. 213
abandonment, p. 213
familicide, p. 217
advisement hearing, p. 219
pretrial conference, p. 219

disposition hearing, p. 220
balancing-of-the-interest approach, p. 220
review hearings, p. 220
hearsay, p. 221

Questions for Discussion

1. What is the meaning of the terms *child abuse* and *child neglect*?
2. Social agencies, police departments, and health groups all indicate that child abuse and neglect are increasing. What is the incidence of such action by parents against children? Are the definitions of child abuse and child neglect the key elements in determining the volume of child abuse cases in various jurisdictions?
3. What causes parents to abuse their children?
4. What is meant by the child protection system? Do courts act in the best interest of the child when they allow an abused child to remain with the family?
5. Should children be allowed to testify in court via closed-circuit TV? Does this approach prevent defendants in child abuse cases from confronting their accusers?
6. Is corporal punishment ever permissible as a disciplinary method?

Viewpoint

You are an investigator with the county bureau of social services. A case has been referred to you by a middle school's head guidance counselor. It seems that a young girl, Emily M., has been showing up to school in a dazed and listless condition. She has had a hard time concentrating in class and seems withdrawn and uncommunicative. The 13-year-old has missed more than a normal share of school days and has often been late to class. Last week, she seemed so lethargic that her homeroom teacher sent her to the school nurse. A physical examination revealed that she was malnourished and in poor physical health. She also had evidence of bruising that could only come from a severe beating. Emily told the nurse that she had been punished by her parents for doing poorly at school and for failing to do her chores at home.

When her parents were called to school to meet with the principal and guidance counselor, they claimed to be members of a religious order that believes children should be punished severely for their misdeeds. Emily had been placed on a restricted diet as well as beaten with a belt to correct her misbehavior. When the guidance counselor asked them if they would be willing to go into family therapy, they were furious and told her to "mind her own business." "It's a sad day," they said, "when God-fearing American citizens cannot bring up their children according to their religious beliefs." The girl is in no immediate danger insofar as her punishment has not been life threatening.

The case is then referred to your office. When you go to see the parents at home, they refuse to make any change in their behavior. They claim they are in the right and that you represent all that is wrong with society. The "lax" discipline you suggest leads to drugs, sex, and other teenage problems.

I Would you get a court order removing Emily from her house and requiring the parents to go into counseling?

I Would you report the case to the district attorney's office so that criminal action could be taken against her parents under the state's Child Protection Act?

I Would you take no further action, reasoning that Emily's parents have the right to discipline their child as they see fit?

I Would you talk with Emily and see what she wants to happen?

Doing Research on the Web

Use "child abuse" in a key term search on InfoTrac College Edition.

The Child Abuse Prevention Network is a coalition of over a dozen organizations that work to end child abuse (site accessed on September 1, 2004):

www.child-abuse.com

Prevent Child Abuse America has been working at the national, state, and community levels to prevent

child abuse in all its forms (site accessed on September 1, 2004):

www.preventchildabuse.org

Childabuse.org is dedicated to breaking the cycle of child abuse and neglect, serving and strengthening children and families (site accessed on September 1, 2004):

www.childabuse.org

Notes

1. Paul Amato and Bruce Keith, "Parental Divorce and the Well-Being of Children: A Meta-Analysis," *Psychological Bulletin* 110:26–46 (1991).
2. Rolf Loeber and Magda Stouthamer-Loeber, "Development of Juvenile Aggression and Violence," *American Psychologist* 53:242–259 (1998), p. 250.
3. Lene Arnett Jensen, Jeffrey Jensen Arnett, S. Shirley Feldman, and Elizabeth Cauffman. "The Right to Do Wrong: Lying to Parents among Adolescents and Emerging Adults," *Journal of Youth and Adolescence* 33:101–113 (2004).
4. Joan McCord, "Family Relationships, Juvenile Delinquency, and Adult Criminality," *Criminology* 29:397–417 (1991); Scott Henggeler, ed., *Delinquency and Adolescent Psychopathology: A Family Ecological Systems Approach* (Littleton, MA: Wright–PSG, 1982).
5. For a general review of the relationship between families and delinquency, see Alan Jay Lincoln and Murray Straus, *Crime and the Family* (Springfield, IL: Charles C. Thomas, 1985); Rolf Loeber and Magda Stouthamer-Loeber, "Family Factors as Correlates and Predictors of Juvenile Conduct Problems and Delinquency," in Michael Tonry and Norval Morris, eds., *Crime and Justice*, vol. 7 (Chicago: University of Chicago Press, 1986), pp. 29–151.
6. David Farrington, "Juvenile Delinquency," in John Coleman, ed., *The School Years* (London: Routledge, 1992), pp. 139–40.
7. Ruth Inglis, *Sins of the Fathers: A Study of the Physical and Emotional Abuse of Children* (New York: St. Martin's Press, 1978), p. 131.
8. See Joseph J. Costa and Gordon K. Nelson, *Child Abuse and Neglect: Legislation, Reporting, and Prevention* (Lexington, MA: D.C. Heath, 1978), p. xiii.
9. Tamar Lewin, "Men Assuming Bigger Role at Home, New Survey Shows," *New York Times*, April 15, 1998, p. A18.
10. *America's Families and Living Arrangements* (U.S. Census Bureau, Washington, DC, 2001).
11. Census Bureau Press Release, "About 7-in-10 Children Live with Their Parents, According to Census Bureau Pre-Father's Day Release," Washington, DC, June 12, 2003.
12. U.S. Census Bureau, "Children's Living Arrangements and Characteristics: March 2002 Detailed Tables for Current Population Report, P20-547,"

www.census.gov/population/www/socdemo/hh-fam/cps2002.html. (Accessed on August 30, 2004.)
13. Terence P. Thornberry, Carolyn A. Smith, Craig Rivera, David Huizinga, and Magda Stouthamer-Loeber, *Family Disruption and Delinquency, Juvenile Justice Bulletin* (Washington, DC: Office of Juvenile Justice and Delinquency Prevention, 1999).
14. Department of Health and Human Services, "U.S. Pregnancy Rate Down from Peak; Births and Abortions on the Decline" (press release, Washington, DC, October 31, 2003); Department of Health and Human Services, "HHS Report Shows Teen Birth Rate Falls to New Record Low in 2001" (press release, Washington, DC, June 6, 2002).
15. Annie E. Casey Foundation, "Kids Count Survey 1998" (press release, Baltimore, May 5, 1998).
16. Annie E. Casey Foundation, Kids Count Data Book, online at www.aecf.org/kidscount/databook/. (Accessed on September 19, 2004.)
17. Loeber and Stouthamer-Loeber, "Family Factors," pp. 39–41.
18. Paul Howes and Howard Markman, "Marital Quality and Child Functioning: A Longitudinal Investigation," *Child Development* 60:1044–1051 (1989).
19. Barbara Dafoe Whitehead, "Dan Quayle Was Right," *Atlantic Monthly* 271:47–84 (1993).
20. C. Patrick Brady, James Bray, and Linda Zeeb, "Behavior Problems of Clinic Children: Relation to Parental Marital Status, Age, and Sex of Child," *American Journal of Orthopsychiatry* 56:399–412 (1986).
21. Scott Henggeler, *Delinquency in Adolescence* (Newbury Park, CA: Sage Publications, 1989), p. 48.
22. Thornberry et al., *Family Disruption and Delinquency*.
23. Sheldon Glueck and Eleanor Glueck, *Unraveling Juvenile Delinquency* (Cambridge: Harvard University Press, 1950); Ashley Weeks, "Predicting Juvenile Delinquency," *American Sociological Review* 8:40–46 (1943).
24. Jackson Toby, "The Differential Impact of Family Disorganization," *American Sociological Review* 22:505–512 (1957); Ruth Morris, "Female Delinquency and Relation Problems," *Social Forces* 43:82–89 (1964); Roland Chilton and Gerald Markle, "Family Disruption, Delinquent Conduct, and the Effects of Sub-Classification," *American Sociological Review* 37:93–99 (1972).
25. Jukka Savolainen, "Relative Cohort Size and Age-Specific Arrest Rates: A Conditional Interpretation of the Easterlin Effect," *Criminology* 38:117–136 (2000).

26. For a review of these early studies, see Thomas Monahan, "Family Status and the Delinquent Child: A Reappraisal and Some New Findings," *Social Forces* 35:250–258 (1957).

27. Clifford Shaw and Henry McKay, *Report on the Causes of Crime, Social Factors in Juvenile Delinquency*, vol. 2 (Washington, DC: U.S. Government Printing Office, 1931), p. 392.

28. Christina DeJong and Kenneth Jackson, "Putting Race into Context: Race, Juvenile Justice Processing, and Urbanization," *Justice Quarterly* 15:487–504 (1998).

29. John Laub and Robert Sampson, "Unraveling Families and Delinquency: A Reanalysis of the Gluecks' Data," *Criminology* 26:355–380 (1988); Lawrence Rosen, "The Broken Home and Male Delinquency," in M. Wolfgang, L. Savitz, and N. Johnston, eds., *The Sociology of Crime and Delinquency* (New York: Wiley, 1970), pp. 489–495.

30. Julia Yun Soo Kim, Michael Fendrich, and Joseph Wislar, "The Validity of Juvenile Arrestees' Drug Use Reporting: A Gender Comparison," *Journal of Research in Crime and Delinquency* 37:419–432 (2000).

31. Robert Johnson, John Hoffman, and Dean Gerstein, *The Relationship between Family Structure and Adolescent Substance Abuse* (Washington, DC: Office of Applied Studies, Substance Abuse and Mental Health Services Administration, 1996); Cesaro Rebellon, "Reconsidering the Broken Homes/Delinquency Relationship and Exploring Its Mediating Mechanism(s)," *Criminology* 40:103–135 (2002).

32. Tami Videon, "The Effects of Parent-Adolescent Relationships and Parental Separation on Adolescent Well-Being," *Journal of Marriage & the Family* 64:489–504 (2002).

33. Sara McLanahan, "Father Absence and the Welfare of Children," working paper prepared for the John D. and Catherine MacArthur Research Foundation, Chicago, 1998.

34. Rebellon, "Reconsidering the Broken Homes/Delinquency Relationship and Exploring Its Mediating Mechanism(s).

35. Ronald Simons, Kuei-Hsiu Lin, Leslie Gordon, Rand Conger, and Frederick Lorenz, "Explaining the Higher Incidence of Adjustment Problems Among Children of Divorce Compared to Those in Intact Families," *Journal of Marriage and the Family* 61:131–148 (1999).

36. Stephen Demuth and Susan Brown, "Family Structure, Family Processes, and Adolescent Delinquency: The Significance of Parental Absence versus Parental Gender," *Journal of Research in Crime and Delinquency* 41:58–81 (2004).

37. Christopher Kierkus and Douglas Baer, "A Social Control Explanation of the Relationship between Family Structure and Delinquent Behaviour," *Canadian Journal of Criminology* 44:425–458 (2002).

38. Sara Jaffee, Terrie Moffitt, Avshalom Caspi, and Alan Taylor, "Life with (or without) Father: The Benefits of Living with Two Biological Parents Depend on the Father's Antisocial Behavior," *Child Development* 74:109–117 (2003).

39. Judith Smetena, "Adolescents' and Parents' Reasoning about Actual Family Conflict," *Child Development* 60:1052–1067 (1989).

40. F. Ivan Nye, "Child Adjustment in Broken and Unhappy Unbroken Homes," *Marriage and Family* 19:356–361 (1957); idem, *Family Relationships and Delinquent Behavior* (New York: Wiley, 1958).

41. Michael Hershorn and Alan Rosenbaum, "Children of Marital Violence: A Closer Look at the Unintended Victims," *American Journal of Orthopsychiatry* 55:260–266 (1985).

42. Peter Jaffe, David Wolfe, Susan Wilson, and Lydia Zak, "Similarities in Behavior and Social Maladjustment among Child Victims and Witnesses to Family Violence," *American Journal of Orthopsychiatry* 56:142–146 (1986).

43. Veronica Herrera, "Equals in Risk? The Differential Impact of Family Violence on Male and Female Delinquency," paper presented at the Annual Society of Criminology meeting, San Diego, November 1997.

44. Henggeler, *Delinquency in Adolescence*, p. 39.

45. Jill Leslie Rosenbaum, "Family Dysfunction and Female Delinquency," *Crime and Delinquency* 35:31–44 (1989), at p. 41.

46. Paul Robinson, "Parents of 'Beyond Control' Adolescents," *Adolescence* 13:116–119 (1978).

47. Robert Vermeiren, Jef Bogaerts, Vladislav Ruchkin, Dirk Deboutte, and Mary Schwab-Stone, "Subtypes of Self-Esteem and Self-Concept in Adolescent Violent and Property Offenders," *Journal of Child Psychology and Psychiatry* 45:405–411 (2004).

48. E. Mark Cummings, Marcie C. Goeke-Morey, and Lauren M. Papp, "Everyday Marital Conflict and Child Aggression," *Journal of Abnormal Child Psychology* 32:191–203 (2004).

49. Loeber and Stouthamer-Loeber, "Development of Juvenile Aggression and Violence," p. 251.

50. Carolyn Smith, Sung Joon Jang, and Susan Stern, "The Effect of Delinquency on Families," *Family and Corrections Network Report* 13:1–11 (1997).

51. Adrian Raine, Patricia Brennan, and Sarnoff Mednick, "Interaction between Birth Complications and Early Maternal Rejection in Predisposing Individuals to Adult Violence: Specificity to Serious, Early-Onset Violence," *American Journal of Psychiatry* 154:1265–1271 (1997).

52. John Paul Wright and Francis Cullen, "Parental Efficacy and Delinquent Behavior: Do Control and Support Matter," *Criminology* 39:677–706 (2001).

53. Carter Hay, "Parenting, Self-Control, and Delinquency: A Test of Self-Control Theory," *Criminology* 39:707–736 (2001).

54. Leslie Gordon Simons, Ronald Simons, and Rand Conger, "Identifying the Mechanisms whereby Family Religiosity Influences the Probability of Adolescent Antisocial Behavior," *Journal of Comparative Family Studies*, 35:547–563 (2004).

55. Bill McCarthy and John Hagan, "Mean Streets: The Theoretical Significance of Situational Delinquency among Homeless Youth," *American Journal of Sociology* 98:597–627 (1992).

56. Carolyn Smith, Alan Lizotte, Terence Thornberry, and Marvin Krohn, "Resilience to Delinquency," *The Prevention Researcher* 4:4–7 (1997).

57. Sung Joon Jang and Carolyn Smith, "A Test of Reciprocal Causal Relationships among Parental Supervision, Affective Ties, and Delinquency," *Journal of Research in Crime and Delinquency* 34:307–336 (1997).

58. Christopher Ellison and Darren Sherkat, "Conservative Protestantism and Support for Corporal Punishment," *American Sociological Review* 58:131–144 (1993).

59. Eric Slade and Lawrence Wissow, "Spanking in Early Childhood and Later Behavior Problems: A Prospective Study of Infants and Young Toddlers," *Pediatrics* 113:1321–1330 (2004).

60. Ibid., p. 1327

61. Murray Straus, "Discipline and Deviance: Physical Punishment of Children and Violence and Other Crime in Adulthood," *Social Problems* 38:101–123 (1991).

62. Loeber and Stouthamer-Loeber, "Development of Juvenile Aggression and Violence," p. 251.

63. Nathaniel Pallone and James Hennessy, "Brain Dysfunction and Criminal Violence," *Society* 35:21–27 (1998).

64. Murray A. Straus, "Spanking and the Making of a Violent Society: The Short- and Long-Term Consequences of Corporal Punishment," *Pediatrics* 98:837–843 (1996).

65. Ibid.

66. Ronald Simons, Chyi-In Wu, Kuei-Hsiu Lin, Leslie Gordon, and Rand Conger, "A Cross-Cultural Examination of the Link between Corporal Punishment and Adolescent Antisocial Behavior," *Criminology* 38:47–79 (2000).

67. Lisa Broidy, "Direct Supervision and Delinquency: Assessing the Adequacy of Structural Proxies," *Journal of Criminal Justice* 23:541–554 (1995).

68. Robert Laird, Gregory Pettit, Kenneth Dodge, and John Bates, "Change in Parents' Monitoring Knowledge: Links with Parenting, Relationship Quality, Adolescent Beliefs, and Antisocial Behavior," *Social Development* 12:401–419 (2003).

69. Deborah Cohen, Thomas Farley, Stephanie Taylor, David Martin, and Mark Schuster, "When and Where Do Youths Have Sex? The Potential Role of Adult Supervision," *Pediatrics* 110:66 (2002).

70. Jang and Smith, "A Test of Reciprocal Causal Relationships among Parental Supervision, Affective Ties, and Delinquency," p. 60; Linda Waite and Lee Lillard, "Children and Marital Disruption," *American Journal of Sociology* 96:930–953 (1991).

71. Jennifer Beyers, John Bates, Gregory Pettit, and Kenneth Dodge, "Neighborhood Structure, Parenting Processes, and the Development of Youths' Externalizing Behaviors: A Multilevel Analysis," *American Journal of Community Psychology* 31:35–53 (2003).

72. Thomas Vander Ven and Francis Cullen, "The Impact of Maternal Employment on Serious Youth Crime: Does the Quality of Working Conditions Matter?" *Crime and Delinquency* 50:272–292 (2004); Thomas Vander Ven, Francis Cullen, Mark Carrozza, and John Paul Wright, "Home Alone: The Impact of Maternal Employment on Delinquency," *Social Problems* 48:236–257 (2001).

73. Douglas Downey, "Number of Siblings and Intellectual Development," *American Psychologist* 56:497–504 (2001); Douglas Downey, "When Bigger Is Not Better: Family Size, Parental Resources, and Children's Educational Performance," *American Sociological Review* 60:746–761 (1995).

74. G. Rahav, "Birth Order and Delinquency," *British Journal of Criminology* 20:385–395 (1980); D. Viles and D. Challinger, "Family Size and Birth Order of Young Offenders," *International Journal of Offender Therapy and Comparative Criminology* 25:60–66 (1981).

75. Ibid.

76. David Eggebeen and Daniel Lichter, "Race, Family Structure, and Changing Poverty among American Children," *American Sociological Review* 56:801–817 (1991).

77. For an early review, see Barbara Wooton, *Social Science and Social Pathology* (London: Allen and Unwin, 1959).

78. Daniel Shaw, "Advancing Our Understanding of Intergenerational Continuity in Antisocial Behavior," *Journal of Abnormal Child Psychology* 31:193–199 (2003).

79. Laub and Sampson, "Unraveling Families and Delinquency," p. 375.

80. D. J. West and D. P. Farrington, eds., "Who Becomes Delinquent?" in *The Delinquent Way of Life* (London: Heinemann, 1977); D. J. West, *Delinquency, Its Roots, Careers, and Prospects* (Cambridge, MA: Harvard University Press, 1982).

81. West, *Delinquency*, p. 114.

82. David Farrington, "Understanding and Preventing Bullying," in Michael Tonry, ed., *Crime and Justice*, vol. 17 (Chicago: University of Chicago Press, 1993), pp. 381–457.

83. Carolyn Smith and David Farrington, "Continuities in Antisocial Behavior and Parenting across Three Generations," *Journal of Child Psychology and Psychiatry* 45:230–247 (2004).

84. Leonore Simon, "Does Criminal Offender Treatment Work?" *Applied and Preventive Psychology*, Summer:1–22 (1998).

85. Philip Harden and Robert Pihl, "Cognitive Function, Cardiovascular Reactivity, and Behavior in Boys at High Risk for Alcoholism," *Journal of Abnormal Psychology* 104:94–103 (1995).

86. Laub and Sampson, "Unraveling Families and Delinquency," p. 370.

87. D. P. Farrington, Gwen Gundry, and D. J. West, "The Familial Transmission of Criminality," in Alan Lincoln and Murray Straus, eds., *Crime and the Family* (Springfield, IL: Charles C. Thomas, 1985), pp. 193–206.

88. Smith and Farrington, "Continuities in Antisocial Behavior and Parenting across Three Generations."

89. Marshall Jones and Donald Jones, "The Contagious Nature of Antisocial Behavior," *Criminology* 38:25–46 (2000).

90. Abigail Fagan and Jake Najman, "Sibling Influences on Adolescent Delinquent Behaviour: An Australian Longitudinal Study," *Journal of Adolescence* 26:546–558 (2003).

91. David Rowe and Bill Gulley, "Sibling Effects on Substance Use and Delinquency," *Criminology* 30:217–232 (1992); see also David Rowe, Joseph Rogers, and Sylvia Meseck-Bushey, "Sibling Delinquency and the Family Environment: Shared and Unshared Influences," *Child Development* 63:59–67 (1992).

92. Jones and Jones, "The Contagious Nature of Antisocial Behavior," p. 31.

93. Judith Rich Harris, *The Nature Assumption, Why Children Turn Out the Way They Do* (New York: Free Press, 1998).

94. Charles De Witt, director of the National Institute of Justice, quoted in National Institute of Justice, Research in Brief, *The Cycle of Violence* (Washington, DC: National Institute of Justice, 1992), p. 1.

95. Richard Gelles and Claire Pedrick Cornell, *Intimate Violence in Families*, 2nd ed. (Newbury Park, CA: Sage Publications, 1990), p. 33.

96. Lois Hochhauser, "Child Abuse and the Law: A Mandate for Change," *Harvard Law Journal* 18:200 (1973); see also Douglas J. Besharov, "The Legal Aspects of Reporting Known and Suspected Child Abuse and Neglect," *Villanova Law Review* 23:458 (1978).

97. C. Henry Kempe, F. N. Silverman, B. F. Steele, W. Droegemueller, and H. K. Silver, "The Battered-Child Syndrome," *Journal of the American Medical Association* 181:17–24 (1962).

98. Brian G. Fraser, "A Glance at the Past, a Gaze at the Present, a Glimpse at the Future: A Critical Analysis of the Development of Child Abuse Reporting Statutes," *Chicago-Kent Law Review* 54:643 (1977–78).

99. See, especially, Inglis, *Sins of the Fathers*, ch. 8.

100. William Downs and Brenda Miller, "Relationships between Experiences of Parental Violence during Childhood and Women's Self-Esteem," *Violence and Victims* 13:63–78 (1998).

101. Ruth S. Kempe and C. Henry Kempe, *Child Abuse* (Cambridge: Harvard University Press, 1978), pp. 6–7.

102. Ibid.

103. Joseph Price and Kathy Glad," Hostile Attributional Tendencies in Maltreated Children," *Journal of Abnormal Child Psychology* 31:329–344 (2003).

104. Herman Daldin, "The Fate of the Sexually Abused Child," *Clinical Social Work Journal* 16:20–26 (1988).

105. Magnus Seng, "Child Sexual Abuse and Adolescent Prostitution: A Comparative Analysis," *Adolescence* 24:665–675 (1989); Dorothy Bracey, *Baby Pros: Preliminary Profiles of Juvenile Prostitutes* (New York: John Jay Press, 1979).

106. Heather Swanston, Patrick Parkinson, and Brian O'Toole, "Juvenile Crime, Aggression and Delinquency after Sexual Abuse: A Longitudinal Study," *The British Journal of Criminology* 43:729–749 (2003).

107. Xavier Coll, Fergus Law, Aurelio Tobias, Keith Hawton, and Josep Tomas, "Abuse and Deliberate Self-Poisoning in Women: A Matched Case-Control Study," *Child Abuse and Neglect* 25:1291–1293 (2001).

108. Judith Herman, Diana Russell, and Karen Trocki, "Long-Term Effects of Incestuous Abuse in Childhood," *American Journal of Psychiatry* 143:1293–1296 (1986).

109. Kathleen Kendall-Tackett, Linda Meyer Williams, and David Finkelhor, "Impact of Sexual Abuse on Children: A Review and Synthesis of Recent Empirical Studies," *Psychological Bulletin* 113:164–180 (1993).

110. Murray Straus, Richard Gelles, and Suzanne Steinmetz, *Behind Closed Doors: Violence in the American Family* (Garden City, NY: Anchor Books, 1980); Richard Gelles and Murray Straus, "Violence in the American Family," *Journal of Social Issues* 35:15–39 (1979).

111. Gelles and Straus, "Violence in the American Family," p. 24.

112. Gelles and Straus, *Intimate Violence*, pp. 108–109; Murray A. Straus and Glenda Kaufman Kantor, "Trends in Physical Abuse by Parents from 1975 to 1992: A Comparison of Three National Surveys," paper presented at the American Society of Criminology meeting, Boston, November 1995.

113. Murray A. Straus and Anita K. Mathur, "Social Change and Trends in Approval of Corporal Punishment by Parents from 1968 to 1994," in D. Frehsee, W. Horn, and K. Bussman, eds., *Violence against Children* (New York: de Gruyter, 1996), pp. 91–105.

114. U.S. Department of Health and Human Services, Administration on Children, Youth and Families, *Child Maltreatment 1999* (Washington, DC: U.S. Government Printing Office, 2001).

115. National Clearinghouse on Child Abuse and Neglect Information, *Child Maltreatment 2002: Summary of Key Findings* (Washington, DC: U.S. Department of Health and Human Services, 2004).

116. David Finkelhor and Richard Ormrod, "Child Abuse Cases Reported to the Police," *Juvenile Justice Bulletin* (Washington, DC: Office of Juvenile Justice and Delinquency Prevention, 2001).

117. Diana Russell, *Sexual Exploitation: Rape, Child Sexual Abuse, and Workplace Harassment* (Beverly Hills, CA: Sage Publications, 1984).

118. Maria Root, "Treatment Failures: The Role of Sexual Victimization in Women's Addictive Behavior," *American Journal of Orthopsychiatry* 59:543–549 (1989).

119. Lisa Jones and David Finkelhor, *The Decline in Child Sexual Abuse Cases* (Washington, DC: Office of Juvenile Justice and Delinquency Prevention, 2001).

120. Lisa Jones, David Finkelhor, and Kathy Kopie, "Why Is Sexual Abuse Declining? A Survey of State Child Protection Administrators," *Child Abuse and Neglect* 25:1139–1141 (2001).

121. Carolyn Webster-Stratton, "Comparison of Abusive and Nonabusive Families with Conduct-Disordered Children," *American Journal of Orthopsychiatry* 55:59–69 (1985); Brandt F. Steele and Carl B. Pollock, "A Psychiatric Study of Parents Who Abuse Infants and Small Children," in Ray Helfer and C. Henry Kempe, eds., *The Battered Child* (Chicago: University of Chicago Press, 1968), pp. 103–145.

122. Brandt F. Steele, "Violence within the Family," in Ray E. Helfer and C. Henry Kempe, eds., *Child Abuse and Neglect: The Family and the Community* (Cambridge, MA: Ballinger, 1976), p. 13.

123. William Sack, Robert Mason, and James Higgins, "The Single-Parent Family and Abusive Punishment," *American Journal of Orthopsychiatry* 55:252–259 (1985).

124. Fontana, "The Maltreated Children of Our Times," pp. 450–451; see also Blair Justice and Rita Justice, *The Abusing Family* (New York: Human Sciences Press, 1976); Steele, "Violence within the Family," p. 12; Nanette Dembitz, "Preventing Youth Crime by Preventing Child Neglect," *American Bar Association Journal* 65:920–923 (1979).

125. Douglas Ruben, *Treating Adult Children of Alcoholics: A Behavioral Approach* (New York: Academic, 2000).

126. *The Relationship between Parental Alcohol or Other Drug Problems and Child Maltreatment* (Chicago, IL: Prevent Child Abuse America, 2000).

127. Anna Lau and John Weisz, "Reported Maltreatment among Clinic-Referred Children: Implications for Presenting Problems, Treatment Attrition, and Long-Term Outcomes," *Journal of the American Academy of Child and Adolescent Psychiatry* 42:1327–1334 (2003).

128. Martin Daly and Margo Wilson, "Violence against Stepchildren," *Current Directions in Psychological Science* 5:77–81 (1996).

129. Ibid.

130. Margo Wilson, Martin Daly, and Atonietta Daniele, "Familicide: The Killing of Spouse and Children," *Aggressive Behavior* 21:275–291 (1995).

131. Wang and Daro, *Current Trends in Child Abuse*, p. 10.

132. Ibid., p. 12.

133. Richard Gelles, "Child Abuse and Violence in Single-Parent Families: Parent Absence and Economic Deprivation," *American Journal of Orthopsychiatry* 59:492–501 (1989).

134. Susan Napier and Mitchell Silverman, "Family Violence as a Function of Occupation Status, Socioeconomic Class, and Other Variables," paper pre-

sented at the American Society of Criminology meeting, Boston, November 1995.

135. Robert Burgess and Patricia Draper, "The Explanation of Family Violence," in Lloyd Ohlin and Michael Tonry, eds., *Family Violence* (Chicago: University of Chicago Press, 1989), pp. 59–117.

136. Ibid., pp. 103–104.

137. *Troxel et vir. v. Granville* No. 99–138 (June 5, 2000).

138. 452 U.S. 18, 101 S.Ct. 2153 (1981); 455 U.S. 745, 102 S.Ct. 1388 (1982).

139. For a survey of each state's reporting requirements, abuse and neglect legislation, and available programs and agencies, see Costa and Nelson, *Child Abuse and Neglect*.

140. Linda Gordon, "Incest and Resistance: Patterns of Father-Daughter Incest, 1880–1930," *Social Problems* 33:253–267 (1986).

141. P.L. 93B247 (1974); P.L. 104B235 (1996).

142. The story of 2-year-old Dominic James made headlines, not only because of his tragic death, but because criminal charges were lodged against a nurse for failing to report his suspicious injuries. His story provides a cautionary tale. See Barbara Ryan, "Do You Suspect Child Abuse?" *RN* 66:73–76 (2003).

143. Debra Whitcomb, *When the Victim Is a Child* (Washington, DC: National Institute of Justice, 1992), p. 5.

144. "False Accusations of Abuse Devastating to Families," *Crime Victims Digest* 6(2):4–5 (1989).

145. Sue Badeau and Sarah Gesiriech, "A Child's Journey through the Child Welfare System," the Pew Commission on Children in Foster Care, Washington, DC December 13, 2003; Shirley Dobbin, Sophia Gatowski, and Margaret Springate, "Child Abuse and Neglect," *Juvenile and Family Court Journal* 48:43–54 (1997).

146. For an analysis of the accuracy of children's recollections of abuse, see Candace Kruttschnitt and Maude Dornfeld, "Will They Tell? Assessing Preadolescents' Reports of Family Violence," *Journal of Research in Crime and Delinquency* 29:136–147 (1992).

147. Ibid.

148. Whitcomb, *When the Victim Is a Child*, p. 33.

149. *White v. Illinois*, 502 U.S. 346; 112 S.Ct. 736 (1992).

150. Myrna Raeder, "White's Effect on the Right to Confront One's Accuser," *Criminal Justice*, Winter:2–7 (1993).

151. *Coy v. Iowa*, 487 U.S. 1012 (1988).

152. *Maryland v. Craig*, 110 S.Ct. 3157 (1990).

153. Sandra Bass, Margie Shields, Roselyn Lowe-Webb, and Teresa Lanz, "Children, Families, and Foster Care," Henry and Lucile Packard Foundation, *The Future of Children* 14 (2004). This report can be obtained online at www.futureofchildren.org/homepage2824/index.htm. (Accessed on August 31, 2004).

154. *Walker v. Fagg*, 400 S.E. 2d 708 (Va. App. 1991).

155. Robin V. Delany-Shabazz and Victor Vieth, "The National Center for Prosecution of Child Abuse" (Washington, DC: Office of Juvenile Justice and Delinquency Prevention, 2001).

156. Fred Rogosch and Dante Cicchetti, "Child Maltreatment and Emergent Personality Organization: Perspectives from the Five-Factor Model," *Journal of Abnormal Child Psychology* 32:123–145 (2004).

157. Wendy Fisk, "Childhood Trauma and Dissociative Identity Disorder," *Child and Adolescent Psychiatric Clinics of North America* 5:431–447 (1996).

158. Mary Haskett and Janet Kistner, "Social Interactions and Peer Perceptions of Young Physically Abused Children," *Child Development* 62:679–690 (1991).

159. Gelles and Straus, "Violence in the American Family."

160. This section is based on Richard Wiebush, Raelene Freitag, and Christopher Baird, *Preventing Delinquency through Improved Child Protection Services* (Washington, DC: Office of Juvenile Justice and Delinquency Prevention, 2001).

161. Caroline Wolf Harlow, "Prior Abuse Reported by Inmates and Probationers" (Washington, DC: U.S. Bureau of Justice Statistics, 1999).

162. Wiebush, Freitag, and Baird, *Preventing Delinquency through Improved Child Protection Services*.

163. Michael Wiederman, Randy Sansone, and Lori Sansone, "History of Trauma and Attempted Suicide among Women in a Primary Care Setting," *Violence and Victims* 13:3–11 (1998); Susan Leslie Bryant and Lillian

Range, "Suicidality in College Women Who Were Sexually and Physically Abused and Physically Punished by Parents," *Violence and Victims* 10:195–215 (1995); William Downs and Brenda Miller, "Relationships between Experiences of Parental Violence during Childhood and Women's Self-Esteem," *Violence and Victims* 13:63–78 (1998); Sally Davies-Netley, Michael Hurlburt, and Richard Hough, "Childhood Abuse as a Precursor to Homelessness for Homeless Women with Severe Mental Illness," *Violence and Victims* 11:129–142 (1996).

164. Jeanne Kaufman and Cathy Spatz Widom, "Childhood Victimization, Running Away, and Delinquency," *Journal of Research in Crime and Delinquency* 36:347–370 (1999).

165. Jose Alfaro, "Report of the Relationship between Child Abuse and Neglect and Later Socially Deviant Behavior," unpublished paper (Albany, NY: n.d.), pp. 175–219.

166. Cathy Spatz Widom, "Child Abuse, Neglect, and Violent Criminal Behavior," *Criminology* 27:251–271 (1989).

167. Cathy Spatz Widom, "The Cycle of Violence," *Science* 244:160–166 (1989).

168. Cathy Widom and Michael Maxfield, *An Update on the "Cycle of Violence"* (Washington, DC: National Institute of Justice, 2001).

169. Jane Siegel and Linda Meyer Williams, "Violent Behavior among Men Abused as Children," paper presented at the American Society of Criminology meeting, Boston, November 1995; Jane Siegel and Linda Meyer Williams, "Aggressive Behavior among Women Sexually Abused as Children," paper presented at the American Society of Criminology meeting, Phoenix, 1993 (rev. version).

170. David Skuse, Arnon Bentovim, Jill Hodges, Jim Stevenson, Chriso Andreou, Monica Lanyado, Michelle New, Bryn Williams, and Dean McMillan, "Risk Factors for Development of Sexually Abusive Behaviour in Sexually Victimised Adolescent Boys: Cross Sectional Study," *British Medical Journal* 317:175–180 (1998).

171. Carolyn Smith and Terence Thornberry, "The Relationship between Childhood Maltreatment and Adolescent Involvement in Delinquency," *Criminology* 33:451–477 (1995).

172. Widom, "Child Abuse, Neglect, and Violent Criminal Behavior," p. 267.

173. Bruce Rind, Philip Tromovitch, and Robert Bauserman, "A Meta-Analytic Examination of Assumed Properties of Child Sexual Abuse Using College Samples," *Psychological Bulletin* 124:22–53 (1998); Kimberly Barletto, "Who's at Risk: Delinquent Trajectories of Children with Attention and Conduct Problems," paper presented at the American Society of Criminology meeting, San Diego, November 1997; Veronica Herrera, "Equals in Risk? The Differential Impact of Family Violence on Male and Female Delinquency," paper presented at the Annual Society of Criminology meeting, San Diego, November 1997.

174. Matthew Zingraff, "Child Maltreatment and Youthful Problem Behavior," *Criminology* 31:173–202 (1993).

175. William Lindsay, Jacqueline Law, Kathleen Quinn, Nicola Smart, and Anne H.W. Smith, "A Comparison of Physical and Sexual Abuse: Histories of Sexual and Non-Sexual Offenders with Intellectual Disability," *Child Abuse and Neglect*, 25:989–996 (2001).

176. Timothy Ireland, Carolyn Smith, and Terence Thornberry, "Development Issues in the Impact of Child Maltreatment on Later Delinquency and Drug Use," *Criminology* 40:359–401 (2002).

177. Leonard Edwards and Inger Sagatun, "Dealing with Parent and Child in Serious Abuse Cases," *Juvenile and Family Court Journal* 34:9–14 (1983).

178. Susan McPherson, Lance McDonald, and Charles Ryer, "Intensive Counseling with Families of Juvenile Offenders," *Juvenile and Family Court Journal* 34:27–34 (1983).

179. The programs in this section are described in Edward Zigler, Cara Taussig, and Kathryn Black, "Early Childhood Intervention, a Promising Preventative for Juvenile Delinquency," *American Psychologist* 47:997–1006 (1992).

180. Lawrence W. Sherman, Denise C. Gottfredson, Doris L. MacKenzie, John Eck, Peter Reuter, and Shawn D. Bushway, *Preventing Crime: What Works, What Doesn't, What's Promising* (Washington, DC: National Institute of Justice, 1998).

181. Zigler, Taussig, and Black, "Early Childhood Intervention: A Promising Preventative for Juvenile Delinquency," pp. 1000–1004.

8

Peers and Delinquency: Juvenile Gangs and Groups

Chapter Outline

Adolescent Peer Relations

Peer Relations and Delinquency

The Structure of Peer Relations

Youth Gangs

What Are Gangs?

The Study of Juvenile Gangs and Groups

What Factors Explain Changes in Gang Activity?

Contemporary Gangs

Gang Names

Gang Types

FOCUS ON DELINQUENCY: Getting High and Getting By: Drug Dealing Gangs and Gang Boys in Southwest Texas

Location

Age

Gender

Formation

Leadership

Communications

Criminality

Ethnic and Racial Composition

Why Do Youths Join Gangs?

Anthropological View

Social Disorganization/Sociocultural View

Anomie View

Psychological View

Rational Choice View

Controlling Gang Activity

Law Enforcement Efforts

POLICY AND PRACTICE: Boston's Youth Violence Strike Force (YVSF)

Community Control Efforts

Why Gang Control Is Difficult

Chapter Objectives

1. Be familiar with the development of peer relations
2. Know the association between peers and delinquency
3. Be able to define the concept of the gang
4. Be familiar with the history of gangs
5. Know the nature and extent of gang activity
6. Recognize the various types of gangs
7. Understand how gangs are structured
8. Be familiar with the gender, racial, and ethnic makeup of gangs
9. Discuss the various theories of gang development
10. Know how police departments are undertaking gang prevention and suppression
11. Be familiar with community control efforts
12. Know why gang reduction is so difficult

CNN. View the CNN video clip of this story and answer related Critical Thinking questions on your Juvenile Delinquency 9e CD-ROM.

They called themselves the "Newington Mafia," but the gang consisted of just two boys, Darren Bennett and Christopher Alexander, who gained fame after going on a rampage of defacing public buildings and monuments. Their fame was not based on their delinquent acts but because they actually made the effort to videotape themselves while they were on their crime spree. Is their behavior unique? Aside from the videotaping, they were not dissimilar from most kids who get involved in crime. The majority of delinquent acts are committed in groups, a process known as co-offending. There is a need for teens to bond with a positive peer group. When teens fail to connect they may seek out damaging social relationships. Some join with deviant peers and form law-violating youth groups and gangs. While the "Newington Mafia" was as small as they come, some juvenile gangs have thousands of members.

Few issues in the study of delinquency are more important today than the problems presented by gangs, whether they are made up of a few loosely organized neighborhood youths or have thousands of members who cooperate in complex illegal enterprises.[1] A significant portion of all drug distribution in the nation's inner cities is believed to be gang controlled, and gang violence accounts for hundreds of homicides each year.[2] Gangs can put an entire community in fear. Their presence undermines community cohesiveness, especially in neighborhoods where residents believe they have few resources to call upon for protection and little in the way of government assistance.[3] Consequently, there has been an outcry from politicians to increase punishment for the "little monsters" and to save the "fallen angels," or the victimized youths, who are being threatened by gang members.[4]

Social service and law enforcement groups have made a concerted effort to contain gangs and reduce their criminal activity. Approaches range from introducing treatment-oriented settlement houses to deploying tactical gang control units. The problem of gang control is a difficult one: Gangs flourish in inner-city areas that offer lower-class youths few conventional opportunities. Members are resistant to the offers of help that cannot deliver legitimate economic hope. Though gang members may be subject to arrest, prosecution, and incarceration, a new crop of young recruits is always ready to take the place of their fallen comrades. Those sent to prison find that, upon release, their former gangs are only too willing to have them return to action.

To read a general overview of **gangs in America,** see www.ncjrs.org/pdffiles/167249.pdf. For an up-to-date list of web links, go to http://cj.wadsworth.com/siegel_jd9e.

This chapter discusses the nature and extent of gang and group delinquency. It begins with a discussion of peer relations and shows how group relations influence delinquent behavior. It then explores the definition, nature, and structure of delinquent gangs. In addition, theories of gang formation, the extent of gang activity, and gang-control efforts are presented.

ADOLESCENT PEER RELATIONS

Psychologists have long recognized that as children mature, the nature of their friendship patterns also evolves. While parents are the primary source of influence and attention in children's early years, between ages 8 and 14, children seek out a stable peer group; both the number and the variety of friendships increase as children go through adolescence. Friends soon begin having a greater influence over decision making than parents.[5] By their early teens, children report that their friends give them emotional support when they are feeling bad and that they can confide intimate feelings to peers without worrying about their confidences being betrayed.[6]

cliques
Small groups of friends who share intimate knowledge and confidences.

crowds
Loosely organized groups who share interests and activities.

As they go through adolescence, children form **cliques**—small groups of friends who share activities and confidences.[7] They also belong to **crowds,** which are loosely organized groups of children who share interests and activities. While clique members share intimate knowledge, crowds are brought together by mutually shared activities, such as sports, religion, and hobbies. Popular youths can be members of a variety of same-sex cliques and crowds, while also joining groups containing members of the opposite sex. Intimate friends play an important role in social development, but adolescents are also deeply influenced by this wider circle of friends. Adolescent self-image is in part formed by individuals' perceptions of their place in the social world, whether they are considered as an accepted insider or an unpopular outcast.[8]

In later adolescence, acceptance by peers has a major impact on socialization. Popular youths do well in school and are socially astute. In contrast, children who are rejected by their peers are more likely to display aggressive behavior and disrupt group activities by bickering or behaving antisocially.[9] Lower-class youths, lacking in educational and vocational opportunities, may place even greater emphasis on friendship than middle-class youths, who can easily replace friends as they change locale and involvements, such as when they go off to college.[10]

Peer relations, then, are a significant aspect of maturation. Some experts, such as Judith Rich Harris, believe that peers exert a powerful influence on youths and pressure them to conform to group values. Peer influence may be more important than parental nurturance in the development of long-term behavior.[11] Peers guide children and help them learn to share and cooperate, cope with aggressive impulses, and discuss feelings they would not dare bring up at home. With peers, youths can compare their own experiences and learn that others have similar concerns and problems; they realize that they are not alone.[12] As children begin to talk to their friends about deviant behavior—for example, getting together to use drugs—their levels of participation in antisocial behavior increase as well.[13] In later adolescence, acceptance by their peers has a major impact on socialization. Popular youths do well in school and are socially astute. In contrast, children who are rejected by their peers are more likely to display aggressive behavior and to disrupt group activities by bickering or behaving antisocially. Another group of kids—**controversial status youth**—are aggressive kids who are either highly liked or intensely disliked by their peers. These controversial youth are the ones most likely to become engaged in antisocial behavior. When they find themselves in leadership positions among their peers they get them involved in delinquent and problem behaviors.[14]

controversial status youth
Aggressive kids who are either greatly liked or intensely disliked by their peers.

It is clear that childhood peer status is an important contributor to children's social and emotional development that follows them across the life course.[15] Girls who engage in aggressive behavior with childhood peers later have more conflict-ridden relationships with their romantic partners. Boys who are highly aggressive and are therefore rejected by their peers in childhood are also more likely to engage in criminality and delinquency from adolescence into young adulthood.[16] Peer relations, then, are a signif-

To read more about **the effects of peer relations,** go to http://ianrpubs.unl.edu/family/nf211.htm. For an up-to-date list of web links, go to http://cj.wadsworth.com/siegel_jd9e.

icant aspect of maturation. Peer influence may be more important than parental nurturance in the development of long-term behavior.[17] Peers guide each other and help each other learn to share and cooperate, to cope with aggressive impulses, and to discuss feelings they would not dare bring up at home. Youths can compare their own experiences with peers and learn that others have similar concerns and problems.[18]

Peer Relations and Delinquency

Experts have long debated the exact relationship between peer group interaction and delinquency. Research shows that peer group relationships are closely tied to delinquent behaviors. Kids who report inadequate or strained peer relations, who say they are not popular with the opposite sex, are the ones most likely to become delinquent.[19] The weight of the empirical evidence indicates that youths who are loyal to delinquent friends, belong to gangs, and have "bad companions" are the ones most likely to commit crimes and engage in violence.[20] Reviews of the research show that delinquent acts tend to be committed in small groups, rather than alone—a process called **co-offending.**[21] The group process may involve family members as well as peers; brothers are likely to commit offenses with brothers of a similar age.[22]

co-offending
Committing criminal acts in groups.

Delinquent groups tend to be small and transitory.[23] Kids often belong to more than a single deviant group or clique and develop an extensive *network* of delinquent associates. Multiple memberships are desirable because delinquent groups tend to "specialize" in different types of delinquent activity. One group may concentrate on shoplifting, while another performs home invasions. Group roles can vary: An adolescent who assumes a leadership role in one group may be a follower in another.[24] A youth who may instigate the group to commit a criminal act in one context will be a follower in another.

Some kids are particularly susceptible to peer influence. In one recent study Richard Felson and Dana Haynie found that boys who go through puberty at an early age were more likely to later engage in violence, property crimes, drug use, and precocious sexual behavior. The boys who mature early were the most likely to develop strong attachments to delinquent friends and be influenced by peer pressure.[25] The conclusion: The earlier a youngster develops relationships with delinquent peers and the closer those relationships become, the more likely the youth will become a delinquent.

The Structure of Peer Relations

Though there seems little question peers help control adolescent behavior, there is still uncertainty over the structure and direction the influence takes. Does having antisocial peers cause delinquency, or are delinquents antisocial youths who seek out like-minded companions because they can be useful in committing crimes? There are actually five independent viewpoints on this question.

▌ According to the control theory approach articulated by Travis Hirschi (see Chapter 4), delinquents are as detached from their peers as they are from other elements of society.[26] While they appear to have close friends, delinquents actually lack the social skills to make their peer relations rewarding or fulfilling.[27] Antisocial adolescents seek out like-minded peers for criminal associations. If delinquency is committed in groups, it is because "birds of a feather flock together." Peers have less of an influence on delinquency than traditionally believed.

▌ Delinquent friends cause law-abiding youth to get in trouble. Kids who fall in with a bad crowd are at risk for delinquency. Youths who maintain friendships with antisocial peers are more likely to become delinquent regardless of their own personality or the type of supervision they receive at home.[28] Even previously law-abiding youths are more likely to get involved in delinquency if they become associated with friends who initiate them into delinquent careers.[29]

As children mature, the nature of their friendship patterns also evolves. While parents are the primary source of influence and attention in children's early years, both the number and the variety of friendships increase as children go through adolescence. Friends soon begin having a greater influence over decision making than parents. Girls like these share secrets and experiences, which help shape their lives and development.

© Yang Liu/Corbis

▌ Antisocial youths seek out and join up with like-minded friends; deviant peers sustain and amplify delinquent careers.[30] Those who choose aggressive or violent friends are more likely to begin engaging in antisocial behavior themselves and suffer psychological deficits.[31]

▌ As youths move through their life course, antisocial friends help them maintain delinquent careers and obstruct the aging-out process.[32] In contrast, nondelinquent friends moderate delinquency.[33] If adulthood brings close and sustaining ties to conventional friends, marriage, and family, the level of deviant behavior will decline.[34]

▌ Troubled kids choose delinquent peers out of necessity rather than desire. The social baggage they cart around prevents them from developing associations with conventional peers. Because they are impulsive they may hook up with friends who are dangerous and get them into trouble.[35] Deviant peers do not cause straight kids to go bad, but they amplify the likelihood of a troubled kid getting further involved in antisocial behaviors.[36]

While each of these scenarios has its advocates, the weight of the empirical evidence clearly indicates that regardless of why or how they are chosen, delinquent peers have a significant influence on behavior. Youths who are loyal to delinquent friends, belong to gangs, and have bad companions are the ones most likely to commit crimes and engage in violence.[37]

Are Delinquents Actually Close to Their Peers? Despite Hirschi's widely accepted view that delinquents are detached loners, there are numerous research studies that indicate that the friendship patterns of delinquents may not be dissimilar from those of nondelinquents. Delinquent youths report that their peer relations contain elements of caring and trust and that they could be open and intimate with their friends.[38] Delinquent youths also report getting more intrinsic rewards from their peers than do nondelinquents.

There are, however, some recorded differences between the peer relations of delinquents and nondelinquents. The former report more conflict than the latter with their friends, more feelings of jealousy and competition, and, not unexpectedly, more pronounced feelings of loyalty in the face of trouble. Taken as a whole, these findings support the view that delinquents' peer group relations play an important part in their lifestyle and stand in contrast to the viewpoint that youthful law violators are loners without peer group support.

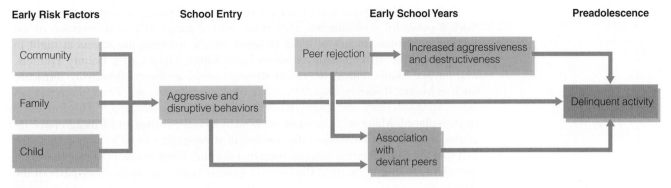

FIGURE 8.1

Development of Early Offending Behavior and Peer Influences

SOURCE: J. D. Cole and S. Miller-Johnson, "Peer Factors and Interventions," in R. Loeber and D. P. Farrington, eds., *Serious and Violent Juvenile Offenders: Risk Factors and Successful Interventions* (Thousand Oaks, CA: Sage Publications, 2001), pp. 191–209.

Peer Rejection/Peer Acceptance While most research looks at the influence of deviant peers, there is also evidence that conventional, law-abiding peers affect behavior.[39] By snubbing kids whom they consider wild and unruly, peer rejection helps lock aggressive kids into a cycle of persistent violence that is likely to continue into early adulthood. Peer rejection has also been found to magnify the effect of other delinquency-producing traits. For example, rejected kids who have attention and hyperactivity problems are more likely to suffer later conduct problems.

Peer rejection may help increase and sustain antisocial behaviors because outcast kids become suspicious of other people's motives, see them as hostile, and become more likely to respond in an antisocial manner. Because the most popular kids reject them, these troubled youth have fewer positive social options and may be drawn to lower status and deviant peer groups. Hoping to belong and be accepted in at least one peer group, no matter its damaged reputation, they feel compelled to engage in more antisocial activity in an effort to gain standing and approval. This relationship is illustrated in Figure 8.1.

If peer rejection promotes delinquency, can peer acceptance reverse its tide? As Sampson and Laub suggested in their age-graded theory (see Chapter 5) having prosocial friends who are committed to conventional success may help increase social capital, an end-product which helps shield kids from crime-producing inducements in their environment. Recently, using data from a national survey of youth, John Paul Wright and Francis Cullen found that, as predicted, associating with prosocial coworkers on the job helped lure kids away from delinquent peer networks, and consequently reduced their criminal behavior and drug use; the effect continued on to their adulthood.[40]

what are the attributes of a gang? Leaders initiation
difference between clique, crowd, gang?

TO QUIZ YOURSELF ON THIS MATERIAL, go to the Juvenile Delinquency 9e website.

YOUTH GANGS

As youths move through adolescence, they gravitate toward cliques that provide them with support, assurance, protection, and direction. Peer group membership allows them to devalue enemies, achieve status, and develop self-assurance. In some instances, the peer group provides the social and emotional basis for antisocial activity, including crime and substance abuse. In this instance, the clique is transformed into a *gang*.

Although the youth gang is sometimes viewed as a uniquely American phenomenon, youth gangs have also been reported in England, Germany, Italy, New Zealand, Australia, and other nations.[41] Nor are gangs a recent phenomenon. In the 1600s, London was terrorized by organized gangs who called themselves Hectors, Bugles, Dead Boys, and other colorful names. In the seventeenth and eighteenth centuries, English gangs wore distinctive belts and pins marked with serpents, animals, stars, and so on.[42]

Today, the delinquent gang is a topic of considerable interest to many Americans. Such a powerful mystique has grown up around gangs that mere mention of the word *gang* evokes images of black-jacketed youths roaming the streets at night in groups bearing such colorful names as Latin Kings, Mafia Crips, Bounty Hunters, and Savage Skulls. Films, television shows, novels, and even Broadway musicals, such as *Menace II Society, Boyz N the Hood, New Jack City, Trespass, Fresh, Clockers, Outsiders, West Side Story,* and *Colors,* have popularized the youth gang.[43] This interest is not misplaced: Major metropolitan areas such as Los Angeles and Chicago have reported a significant increase in the number of street-gang related killings despite the fact that the general crime rate has been in a decline. There is also evidence that gang members are migrating from the cities to smaller communities in many parts of the nation.[44]

Considering the suspected role gangs play in violent crime and drug activity, it is not surprising that they have recently become the target of a great deal of research interest.[45] The secretive, constantly changing nature of juvenile gangs makes them a difficult focus of study. Nonetheless, important attempts have been made to gauge their size, location, makeup, and activities.

What Are Gangs?

gangs
Groups of youths who collectively engage in delinquent behaviors.

What exactly are delinquent gangs? **Gangs** are groups of youths who collectively engage in delinquent behaviors. Yet there is a distinction between *group delinquency* and *gang delinquency.* The former consists of a short-lived alliance created to commit a particular crime or engage in a random violent act. In contrast, gang delinquency involves long-lived, complex institutions that have a distinct structure and organization, including identifiable leadership, division of labor (some members are fighters, others burglars, while some are known as deal makers), rules, rituals, and possessions (such as a headquarters and weapons).

Despite the familiarity of gangs to the American public, delinquency experts are often at odds over the precise definition of a gang. The term is sometimes used broadly to describe any congregation of youths who have joined together to engage in delinquent acts. Some police departments use narrower definitions, designating as gangs only cohesive groups that hold and defend territory, or turf.[46]

interstitial group
Delinquent group that fills a crack in the social fabric and maintains standard group practices.

Academic experts have also created a variety of definitions to distinguish delinquent gangs from groups and cliques. One of the core elements generally included in the concept of the gang is that it is an **interstitial group,** a phrase coined by pioneering gang expert Frederick Thrasher. He used the term to refer to the fact that gangs fill the "cracks" in the fabric of society. To be considered a gang, a group must maintain standard group processes, such as recruiting new members, setting goals (such as controlling the neighborhood drug trade), assigning roles (appointing someone to negotiate with rivals), and developing status (grooming young members for leadership roles).[47] Exhibit 8.1 provides definitions of teen gangs by leading experts on delinquency.

Although a great deal of divergence over the definition of *gang* exists, Malcolm Klein argues that two factors stand out as part of the concept of the youth gang:

▮ Members have self-recognition of their gang status, and use special vocabulary, clothing, signs, colors, graffiti, and names. Members set themselves apart from the community and are viewed as a separate entity by others. Once they get the label of gang, members eventually accept and take pride in their status.

▮ There is a commitment to criminal activity, though even the most criminal gang members spend the bulk of their time in noncriminal activities.[48]

The Study of Juvenile Gangs and Groups

The study of juvenile gangs and groups was prompted by the Chicago School sociologists in the 1920s. Researchers such as Clifford Shaw and Henry McKay were con-

EXHIBIT 8.1
Definitions of Teen Gangs

Frederick Thrasher

An interstitial group originally formed spontaneously and then integrated through conflict. It is characterized by the following types of behavior: meeting face to face, milling, movement through space as a unit, conflict, and planning. The result of this collective behavior is the development of tradition, unreflective internal structure, esprit de corps, solidarity, morale, group awareness, and attachment to local territory.

Malcolm Klein

Any denotable adolescent group of youngsters who (a) are generally perceived as a distinct aggregation by others in their neighborhood; (b) recognize themselves as a denotable group (almost invariably with a group name); and (c) have been involved in a sufficient number of delinquent incidents to call forth a consistent negative response from neighborhood residents and/or law enforcement agencies.

Desmond Cartwright

An interstitial and integrated group of people who meet face to face more or less regularly and whose existence and activities are considered an actual or potential threat to the prevailing social order.

Walter Miller

A self-formed association of peers, bound together by mutual interests, with identifiable leadership, well-developed lines of authority, and other organizational features, who act in concert to achieve a specific purpose or purposes, which generally include the conduct of illegal activity and control over a particular territory, facility, or type of enterprise.

G. David Curry and Irving Spergel

Groups containing law-violating juveniles and adults that are complexly organized, although sometimes diffuse, and sometimes cohesive, with established leadership and membership rules. The gang also engages in a range of crime (but with significantly more violence) within a framework of norms and values in respect to mutual support, conflict relations with other gangs, and a tradition of turf, colors, signs, and symbols. Subgroups of the gang may be deferentially committed to various delinquent or criminal patterns, such as drug trafficking, gang fighting, or burglary.

James Short

Gangs are groups of young people whose members meet together with some regularity, over time, on the basis of group-defined criteria of membership and group-defined organizational characteristics. In the simplest terms, gangs are unsupervised (by adults), self-determining groups that demonstrate continuity over time.

National Youth Gang Center

A youth gang is commonly thought of as a self-formed association of peers having the following characteristics: three or more members, generally ages 12 to 24; a gang name and some sense of identity, generally indicated by such symbols as style of clothing, graffiti, and hand signs; some degree of permanence and organization; and an elevated level of involvement in delinquent or criminal activity.

SOURCES: Frederick Thrasher, *The Gang* (Chicago: University of Chicago Press, 1927), p. 57; Malcolm Klein, *Street Gangs and Street Workers* (Englewood Cliffs, NJ: Prentice Hall, 1971), p. 13; Desmond Cartwright, Barbara Tomson, and Hersey Schwarts, eds., *Gang Delinquency* (Pacific Grove, CA: Brooks/Cole, 1975), pp. 149–150; Walter Miller, "Gangs, Groups, and Serious Youth Crime," in David Schicor and Delos Kelly, eds., *Critical Issues in Juvenile Delinquency* (Lexington, MA: Lexington Books, 1980); G. David Curry and Irving Spergel, "Gang Homicide, Delinquency, and Community," *Criminology* 26:382; James Short, Jr. and Fred Strodtbeck, *Group Process and Gang Delinquency* (Chicago: University of Chicago Press, 1965); National Youth Gang Center, www.iir.com/nygc/faq.htm (accessed on September 9, 2004).

cerned about the nature of the urban environment and how it influenced young people. Delinquency was believed to be a product of unsupervised groups made up of children of the urban poor and immigrants.

Frederick Thrasher initiated the study of the modern gang in his analysis of more than 1,300 youth groups in Chicago. His report on this effort, *The Gang*, was published in 1927.[49] Thrasher found that the social, economic, and ecological processes that affect the structure of great metropolitan cities create interstitial areas, or cracks, in the normal fabric of society, characterized by weak family controls, poverty, and social disorganization. According to Thrasher, groups of youths develop spontaneously to meet such childhood needs as play, fun, and adventure—activities that sometimes lead to delinquent acts.

The slum area presents many opportunities for conflict between groups of youths and between the groups and adult authority. If this conflict continues, the groups become more solidified, and their activities become primarily illegal. The groups thus develop into gangs, with a name and a structure oriented toward delinquent behavior.

To Thrasher, the gang provides the young, lower-class boy with an opportunity for success. Since adult society does not meet the needs of slum dwellers, the gang solves the problem by offering what society fails to provide—excitement, fun, and opportunity. The gang is not a haven for disturbed youths but rather an alternative lifestyle for normal boys.

Thrasher's work has had an important influence on the accepted view of the gang. Recent studies of delinquent gang behavior are similar to Thrasher's in their emphasis on the gang as a means for lower-class boys to achieve advancement and opportunity as well as to defend themselves and attack rivals.

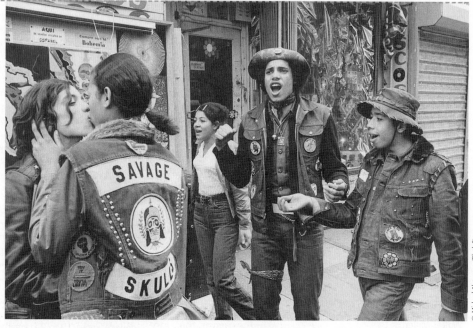

Gang activity by such groups as the Savage Skulls (pictured) reemerged in the 1970s in major cities, including New York, Detroit, El Paso, Los Angeles, and Chicago. In addition, such cities as Cleveland and Columbus, Ohio, and Milwaukee, Wisconsin, which had not experienced serious gang problems before, saw the development of local gangs.

Gangs in the 1950s and 1960s In the 1950s and early 1960s, the threat of gangs and gang violence swept the public consciousness. Rarely did a week go by without a major city newspaper featuring a story on the violent behavior of fighting gangs and their colorful leaders and names—the Egyptian Kings, the Vice Lords, the Blackstone Rangers. Social service and law enforcement agencies directed major efforts to either rehabilitate or destroy the gangs. Movies, such as *The Wild Ones* and *Blackboard Jungle,* were made about gangs, and the Broadway musical *West Side Story* romanticized violent gangs.

In his classic 1967 work, *Juvenile Gangs in Context,* Malcolm Klein summarized existing knowledge about gangs.[50] He concluded that gang membership was a way for individual boys to satisfy certain personal needs that were related to the development of youths caught up in the emotional turmoil typical of the period between adolescence and adulthood. A natural inclination to form gangs is reinforced by the perception that the gang represents a substitute for unattainable middle-class rewards.

The experience of being a member of a gang will dominate a youngster's perceptions, values, expectations, and behavior. Finally, the gang is self-reinforcing: It is within the gang more than anywhere else that a youngster may find forms of acceptance for delinquent behavior—rewards instead of negative sanctions. And as the gang strives for internal cohesion, the negative sanctions of the "outside world" become interpreted as threats to cohesion, thus providing secondary reinforcement for the values central to the legitimization of gang behavior.[51]

By the mid-1960s, the gang menace seemed to have disappeared. Some experts attribute the decline of gang activity to successful gang-control programs.[52] They believed that gangs were eliminated because police gang-control units infiltrated gangs, arrested leaders, and constantly harassed members.[53] Gang boys were more likely to be sanctioned by the juvenile justice system and receive more severe sentences than nongang youths.[54] Another explanation for the decline in gang activity was the increase in political awareness that developed during the 1960s. Many gang leaders became involved in the social or political activities of ethnic pride, civil rights, and antiwar groups. In addition, many gang members were drafted. Still another explanation is that gang activity diminished during the 1960s because many gang members became active users of heroin and other drugs, which curtailed their group-related criminal activity.[55]

Gangs Reemerge Interest in gang activity began anew in the early 1970s. Walter Miller comments on the New York scene:

> All was quiet on the gang front for almost 10 years. Then, suddenly and without advance warning, the gangs reappeared. Bearing such names as Savage Skulls and Black Assassins, they began to form in the South Bronx in the spring of 1971, quickly spread to other parts of the city, and by 1975 comprised 275 police-verified gangs with 11,000 members. These new and mysteriously merging gangs were far more lethal than their predecessors—heavily armed, incited and directed by violence-hardened older men, and directing their lethal activities far more to the victimization of ordinary citizens than to one another.[56]

Gang activity also reemerged in other major cities, including Detroit, El Paso, Los Angeles, and Chicago. Today, the number of gang youths appears, at least in these major cities, to be at an all-time high.[57] In addition, such cities as Cleveland and Columbus, Ohio, and Milwaukee, Wisconsin, which had not experienced serious gang problems before, saw the development of local gangs.[58] Large urban gangs sent representatives to organize chapters in distant areas or take over existing gangs. For example, Chicago gangs moved into Dade County, Florida, and demanded cooperation and obedience from local gangs. Two major Chicago gangs, the Gangster Disciples and their rivals, the Vice Lords, established branches in Milwaukee.[59] Members of the two largest gangs in Los Angeles, the Crips and the Bloods, began operations in Midwest cities with the result that local police departments with little experience in gang control were confronted with well-organized, established gang activities. Even medium-sized cities, such as Columbus, Ohio, saw gangs emerge from local dance and rap groups and neighborhood street-corner groups.[60]

In 1975, sociologist Walter Miller conducted the first national survey of gang membership, and estimated that 55,000 adolescents were members of youth gangs and groups; a second survey conducted in 1982 raised the number to 98,000.[61] This explosion of gang activities in the 1980s was reflected in the renewed media interest in gang activity. The *Los Angeles Times* printed 36 gang-related stories in 1977 and 15 in 1978; by 1988, 69 articles appeared, and in 1989, the number of stories concerning police sweeps, revenge shootings, and murder trials had risen to 267.[62] In some communities the fear of gangs, fanned by media attention, created a "moral panic," which prompted increased funding for police and prosecutors.[63] Clearly, gangs had captured the national attention.

Gangs Today How many gangs are there in the United States, and how many members do they contain? To answer these questions, the federal government sponsors an annual national assessment of gang activity.[64] According to the most recent survey data available (2002) gangs were present in the proportions shown in Table 8.1.

The latest national youth gang survey results estimate that youth gangs are active in more than 2,300 cities with a population of 2,500 or more and in more than 550 rural/suburban jurisdictions. Approximately 731,500 kids are active gang members in

TABLE **8.1**

Gang Presence by Population Size

Population	Presence of Gangs
250,000 or more	100%
100,000 and 249,999	87%
Suburban counties	38%
Smaller city agencies	27%
Rural county agencies	12%

SOURCE: Arlen Egley, Jr., and Aline Major, *Highlights of the 2002 National Youth Gang Survey* (Washington, DC: Office of Juvenile Justice and Delinquency Prevention, 2004).

The purpose of the **National Youth Gang Center** is to expand and maintain the body of critical knowledge about youth gangs and effective responses to them. To learn more about its activities, go to www.iir.com/nygc/PublicationLinks.htm#Surveys, Statistics, and Analysis. For an up-to-date list of web links, go to http://cj.wadsworth.com/siegel_jd9e.

21,500 gangs. The estimated number of gang members decreased 14 percent between 1996 and 2002, and the estimated number of jurisdictions experiencing gang problems decreased 32 percent. Most of the decline in reported gangs and gang membership has occurred in smaller cities and rural counties.[65]

Gang-problem cities are concentrated in a relatively small group of counties with high populations: Cook County, Illinois, including the city of Chicago, typically reports the largest number of gang cities, followed by Los Angeles County, California. Riverside and Orange Counties in California also reported high concentrations of gang cities. So while the national assessment finds that the number of gangs has declined somewhat, gang membership has been stable, possibly because kids are staying in gangs longer and swelling their membership rolls.[66]

What Factors Explain Changes in Gang Activity?

One compelling reason for the increase in gang activity between 1970 and the present may be the involvement of youth gangs in distribution and sales of illegal drugs.[67] While early gangs relied on group loyalty and protection of turf to encourage membership, modern gang boys are lured by the quest for drug profits. In some areas, gangs have replaced traditional organized crime families as the dominant suppliers of cocaine and crack. The traditional weapons of gangs—chains, knives, and homemade guns—have been replaced by the "heavy artillery" drug money can buy: Uzi and AK-47 automatic weapons.

Felix Padilla studied a Latino gang in Chicago and found that the gang represents a viable and persistent business enterprise within the U.S. economy, with its own culture, logic, and systematic means of transmitting and reinforcing its fundamental business virtues.[68]

To read more about **the connection between drug dealing and youth gangs,** go to www.ncjrs.org/pdffiles1/93920.pdf. For an up-to-date list of web links, go to http://cj.wadsworth.com/siegel_jd9e.

Ironically, efforts by the FBI and other federal agencies to crack down on traditional organized crime families in the 1980s have opened the door to more violent youth gangs that control the drug trade on a local level and will not hesitate to use violence to maintain and expand their authority. The division between organized crime and gang crime is becoming increasingly narrow.

Economic Conditions Drug trafficking may be an important reason for gang activity, but it is by no means the only one. Not all gang boys sell or use drugs, and many dealers are not gang members. Gang activity may also be on the rise because of economic and social dislocation. In her analyses of gangs in postindustrial America, Pamela Irving Jackson found that gang formation is the natural consequence of the evolution from a manufacturing economy with a surplus of relatively high-paying jobs to a low-wage service economy.[69] The American city, which traditionally required a large population base for its manufacturing plants, now faces incredible economic stress as these plants shut down. In this uneasy economic climate, gangs form and flourish while the moderating influence of successful adult role models and stable families declines.

Family Crisis The ongoing crisis in the American family was discussed earlier in Chapter 7. Many commentators link gang membership to the disorganization of the American family. Gang members come from families that are torn by parental absence, substance abuse, poverty, and criminality.[70] To some experts, the gang serves as a substitute family that contributes the same kind of support, security, and caring that the "traditional," intact nuclear family is supposed to provide.

This is a compelling argument, but at the same time, a sizable number of gang boys come from stable and adequate families, while a significant number of youths from dysfunctional families avoid gang involvement. In some families one brother or sister is ganged up (a member of a gang), while another evades gang membership. The gang may be a substitute family for some members, but it clearly does not have that appeal for all.

TO QUIZ YOURSELF ON THIS MATERIAL, go to the Juvenile Delinquency 9e website.

CONTEMPORARY GANGS

Thousands of gangs are operating around the country today with hundreds of thousands of members. The gang, however, cannot be viewed as a uniform or homogenous social concept. Gangs vary by activity, makeup, location, leadership style, and age. The following sections attempt to describe some of the most salient features of this heterogeneous social phenomenon.

Gang Names

When the early gangs were formed, they took their names from the neighborhoods where they started and carried on their activities (for example, Southside Raiders, Twelfth Street Locos, Jackson Park Boys).[71] Some used more colorful, non-locality-based names of their own choosing (Cobras, Warriors, Los Diablos, Mafia Emperors). During the 1960s, gang branches became popular in some cities, so local gangs used a variant of a common gang name. For example, many gangs in Chicago employed a variation of the Vice Lord name—the California Lords, War Lords, Fifth Avenue Lords, and Maniac Lords—so that they could claim to be part of and loyal to a common organization—the Vice Lord Nation. Beginning in the 1980s, gang federations expanded, and the two most prominent organizations—the Los Angeles–based Crips and Bloods—eventually spread. More than 1,100 gangs in 115 cities around the nation had Bloods or Crips in their names, with locality designations reflecting city neighborhoods (for example, Hoover Crips, East Side 40th Street Gangster Crips, Hacienda Village Bloods, and 42nd Street Piru Bloods).

Gang Types

Gangs have been categorized by their activity. Some are devoted to violence and protecting their neighborhood boundaries, or turf; others are devoted to theft. Some specialize in drug trafficking; others are primarily social groups concerned with recreation, rather than crime.[72]

retreatists
Gangs whose members actively engage in substance abuse.

In their early work, Richard Cloward and Lloyd Ohlin recognized that some gangs specialized in violent behavior; others were **retreatists,** whose members actively engaged in substance abuse; while a third type were criminal gangs that devoted their energy to crime for profit.[73] It has become increasingly difficult to make the *criminal-retreatist-conflict* distinction since so many gang members are involved in all three behaviors, but experts continue to find that on an aggregate level gangs can be characterized according to dominant behavioral activities. For example, Jeffrey Fagan analyzed gang behavior in Chicago, San Diego, and Los Angeles and found that most gangs fall into one of four categories:

I The *social gang* is involved in few delinquent activities and little drug use other than alcohol and marijuana. Membership is more interested in the social aspects of group behavior.

I The *party gang* concentrates on drug use and sales, forgoing most delinquent behavior except vandalism. Drug sales are designed to finance members' personal drug use.

I The *serious delinquent gang* engages in serious delinquent behavior while eschewing most drug use. Drugs are used only on social occasions.

I The *organized gang* is heavily involved in criminality and drug use and sales. Drug use and sales reflect a systemic relationship with other criminal acts. For example, violent acts are used to establish control over drug sale territories. Highly cohesive and organized, this gang is on the verge of becoming a formal criminal organization.[74]

Getting High and Getting By: Drug Dealing Gangs and Gang Boys in Southwest Texas

Avelardo Valdez and Stephen J. Sifaneck, two gang experts, have studied the role that Mexican American gangs and gang members play in drug markets, and the relationship between gang members' drug use and drug selling behaviors. Using an innovative research design, which involved identifying and observing gang members, creating focus groups (essentially group interviews, relying on in-group interaction, designed to obtain perceptions on a defined area of interest), and life history interviews, they gained in-depth knowledge of the lives of 160 males in 26 different Hispanic gangs operating in southwest Texas.

GANG CATEGORIES

Valdez and Sifaneck found that gangs could be divided into two separate categories according to their involvement in drug dealing criminal enterprise. One grouping, made up of 19 of the 26 gangs they identified, shun drug dealing and are organized as traditional, territory-based gangs. They engage in gang rituals such as identification with distinct colors, hand signs, and gang "placas" (symbols). They are involved in a variety of criminal acts, including auto theft, burglary, robbery, vandalism, criminal mischief, and petty crime; some members deal drugs on their own. Members of these types of gangs tend to act as individuals. Their violence is personal and random rather than collective and organized. Gang membership offers protection from rivals, other gang boys, or people in the community who threaten them. Protection is extended to those members who are involved in drug selling and dealing activities.

The second group was made up of the remaining seven gangs that were organized into criminal drug dealing enterprises. These have a more clearly defined leadership that takes a share of the profits generated from all gang members involved in the business. These gangs are not concerned with territorial issues or turf violations, and do not engage in random acts of violence such as drive-by shootings. Violence among these gangs tends to be more organized and related to drug distribution, though some members may be involved in other criminal enterprises such as auto theft and fencing stolen goods.

THE GANG MEMBER'S ROLE

The second dimension discovered by Valdez and Sifaneck was an individual gang member's role in selling and dealing drugs within the gang. The one extreme of this dimension is the user-seller who is primarily buying drugs for personal consumption, and selling a portion of the drugs to offset the costs associated with his own personal drug use. The other extreme of this dimension includes the dealers, gang members who deal drugs (marijuana, cocaine, and heroin) for their own profit. The cross-classification of drug style with gang type is illustrated in Figure 8-A.

Homeboys

Homeboys are gang members who belong to a street gang whose criminal behavior tends to be more individual, less organized, and less gang directed. Most of their violence is centered on interpersonal fights and random situational acts of violence often associated with male bravado. Most of these user-sellers usually buy just what they are going to use to get high and sell small remaining quantities to reduce the costs associated with their own consumption. These members usually score small amounts for themselves, friends, and other associates.

Hustlers: Drug Dealers in Non-Dealing Gangs

In this category gang members identified as hustlers are dealing drugs for profit within a street gang that is not characterized as a drug dealing organization. However, it does provide protection to hustlers within the territory controlled by the gang. Protection

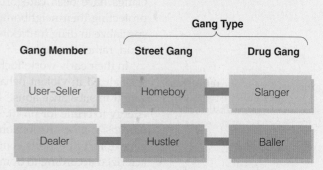

FIGURE 8-A A TYPOLOGY OF DRUG DEALERS AND USER-SELLERS IN STREET AND DRUG GANGS

Fagan's findings have been duplicated by other gang observations around the United States. After observing gangs in the Columbus, Ohio, area, C. Ronald Huff found that they could be organized into "hedonistic gangs" (similar to the party gangs), "instrumental gangs" (similar to the serious delinquent gang), and "predatory gangs," whose heavy crime and crack use make them similar to the organized gang found by Fagan in Chicago and on the West Coast.[75] Carl Taylor adds the *scavenger gang,* a group of impulsive kids who have no common bond beyond surviving in a tough urban environment. These kids are typically low achievers who prey on any target they encounter. Taylor contrasts the scavenger gang with the *organized/corporate gang,* whose structure and goal orientation make it similar to a Fortune 500 company in its relentless pursuit of profit and market share.[76]

is extended to those people because they are members of the organization rather than because of their drug selling activities. Profits generated by these hustlers are their own and are not used to support the collective activities of the street gang.

Slangers: Drug Users-Sellers in Drug Dealing Gangs

Gang members in this category are characterized as user-sellers in gangs that are organized as drug dealing enterprises. Slangers are members who either chose not to participate in the higher levels of the gang's organized drug dealing activities or who are excluded from those circles for various reasons. However, the slangers continue to use and sell drugs at an individual level mostly to help offset costs associated with their drug use and to support themselves economically. In the vernacular of the gangs, these members are dealing to "get high and get by." The slangers stand in contrast to the hard-core dealer members in the drug gang who are heavily involved in the gang's higher level organized drug distribution activities.

Ballers: Drug Dealers in Drug Dealing Gangs

Ballers are the individuals who control the drug distribution business in hard-core drug gangs. Ballers sit atop the gang's hierarchy and comprise a leadership structure that provides protection to members against rival gangs and predatory adult criminals. Among these gang members, heroin use was generally discouraged, although as the gangs began to deal heroin, many ballers began shabanging (non-injection use) and or picando (injecting), and some subsequently became addicted. One of the distinctions of ballers from seller-dealers, slangers, and homeboys is their generally lower visibility and the higher volume of drugs they deal. Furthermore, they avoid ostentatious aggressive behavior that attracts law enforcement, such as drive-by shootings. Violence among ballers is also more purposeful and revolves around business transactions.

GANGS IN CONTEXT

Valdez and Sifaneck found that gangs must be evaluated within the context of the community environment. Juvenile gang members' involvement in selling and dealing is influenced by the presence of adult criminals in the community. Many of these adult criminals were former juvenile gang members and later joined prison gangs. Their presence was a stabilizing force, giving the gang an intergenerational gang presence, which made it more cohesive.

An important part of gang membership is the protection it can give members in exchange for their commitment and obligation to the gang. Protection may often misperceived by police as evidence that a gang is a drug dealing enterprise when in reality members may be operating independently from the gang as an organization. Often law enforcement personnel indiscriminately extend this perception to all Mexican American youth living in these neighborhoods, resulting in continual harassment, shakedowns, and detainment of many innocent youth.

A serious consequence of this perception is very often drug law enforcement indiscriminately arrests and prosecutes offenders without distinguishing the differences that constitute the four distinct types of gang members. Consequently, when homeboys are arrested for minor violations of drug laws, such as possession of small amounts of marijuana, they are often treated like ballers, the big time dealers. If gangs and gang members are to be dealt with in a realistic fashion, these distinctions must be recognized by law enforcement agents engaged in anti-gang activities.

Critical Thinking

1. Of the four types of gang boys identified by Valdez and Sifaneck, which do you believe might be the easiest to wean away from the gang?
2. Is it realistic to believe that a government program could convince ballers to give up drug profits for some low-paying (albeit legitimate) job?

InfoTrac College Edition Research

To read more about Hispanic gangs in the Southwest, go to L. Thomas Winfree, Jr., Frances Bernat, and Finn-Aage Esbensen, "Hispanic and Anglo Gang Membership in Two Southwestern Cities," *The Social Science Journal* 38:105–118 (2001).

SOURCE: Avelardo Valdez and Stephen J. Sifaneck, "Getting High and Getting By: Dimensions of Drug Selling Behaviors Among U.S. Mexican Gang Members in South Texas," *Journal of Research in Crime and Delinquency* 41:82–105 (2004).

Cheryl Maxson, a noted gang researcher, finds that gangs can be organized into groups based on their size, age range, duration of existence, territory, and criminal acts. Maxson's findings are illustrated in Exhibit 8.2.[77] By far the most common gang is the compressed structure; the collective gang is the least common, followed by specialty gangs. Contrary to public opinion, less than half of the specialty gangs are involved in drug distribution.[78]

These more recent observations seem to validate Cloward and Ohlin's research findings from 40 years ago indicating that many gangs specialize in their activities. However, many gangs engage in a variety of criminal activities, ranging from violent turf battles to drug dealing, as well as social activities, including helping members' families and organizing parties.[79] The above Focus on Delinquency entitled "Getting High and Getting By"

EXHIBIT 8.2

Maxson's Gang Typology

▌ **Traditional gangs:** In existence for 20 years or more. Contain clear subgroups based on age. Sometimes subgroups are separated by neighborhoods rather than age. Have wide age range (members' ages are from 10 to 30) and are very large, with hundreds of members. Territorial, with well-defined home turf.

▌ **The neotraditional gang:** A territorial gang, smaller and newer than the traditional gang, which may evolve into a traditional gang over time.

▌ **The compressed gang:** A smaller gang, with less than 50 members, a short history, no subgroups, narrow age range, and less defined territory.

▌ **The collective gang:** A larger group resembling a "shapeless mass" of adolescent and young adult members that has not developed the distinguishing characteristics of other gangs.

▌ **The specialty gang:** A crime-focused gang that is more criminal than social and is smaller in size and age range than other gangs. It has a well-defined territory that can be based either on neighborhoods or the particular form of crime it specializes in, such as drug territories.

SOURCE: Cheryl Maxson, "Investigating Gang Structures," *Journal of Gang Research* 3:33–40 (1995).

presents research showing that not only are there different types of gangs, but there may also be different types of gang boys.

Location

The gang problem has traditionally been considered an urban, lower-class phenomenon. Two types of urban areas are gang-prone. The first is the transitional neighborhood, which is marked by rapid population change in which diverse ethnic and racial groups find themselves living side by side and in competition with one another.[80] Intergang conflict and homicide rates are high in these areas, which house the so-called urban underclass.[81]

The second gang area is the **stable slum,** a neighborhood where population shifts have slowed down, permitting patterns of behavior and traditions to develop over a number of years. Most typical of these areas are the slums in New York and Chicago and the Mexican American barrios of the Southwest and California.[82] The stable slum more often contains the large, structured gang clusters that are the most resistant to attempts by law enforcement and social service agencies to modify or disband them.

Shifting Gang Locales Transitional neighborhoods and the stable slum are not the only environments that produce gangs. In recent years, there has been a massive movement of people out of the central city into outlying suburbs. Many of these people have been from the upper or middle class, but lower-income residents have also been affected. In some cities, once-fashionable outlying neighborhoods have declined, and downtown, central city areas have undergone extensive urban renewal. Central, inner-city districts of major cities such as New York and Chicago have become devoted to finance, retail stores, restaurants, and entertainment.[83] Two aspects of this development inhibit gang formation: First, there are few residential areas and thus few adolescent recruits, and second, there is intensive police patrol. Consequently, in some urban communities, such as Miami and Boston, gang areas have shifted from the downtown areas to outer-city, ring-city, or suburban areas—that is, to formerly middle-class areas now in decay. Some midsize cities now contain the type of gangs that only a few years ago were restricted to large metropolitan areas.

The suburbs are not the only areas experiencing gang problems. A recent survey by Ralph A. Weisheit and L. Edward Wells found that half of rural areas surveyed have experienced some form of gang presence. Unlike urban gangs, which thrive in disorganized neighborhoods, rural gangs are more likely to be active in areas experi-

stable slum
A neighborhood where population shifts have slowed down, permitting patterns of behavior and traditions to develop over a number of years.

encing economic growth and prosperity. Weisheit and Wells speculate that as the local economy booms, it attracts inner-city families to remote outlying areas. These new arrivals bring with them their gang-affiliated children who help maintain and nourish a gang culture in their new communities. Most rural gangs can be found in the counties' largest communities (population of 2,500 or more), a fact that reinforces the effect of urban sprawl into formerly gang-free rural outlying areas.[84]

Migration Gang migration may also help to account for the national growth in gang activity. The National Gang Survey estimates that 18 percent of gang members were migrants from another jurisdiction. In rural areas, 34 percent of members had come from elsewhere; in small cities, 27 percent, and in suburban counties, 20 percent were outsiders. Larger cities had the smallest percentage of migrants (17 percent), indicating that the flow of gang members was from more- to less-populated areas, and not vice versa. Not surprisingly, law enforcement agents report that the appearance of gang members outside of large cities in the 1990s was caused by the migration of young people from central cities.[85]

About 700 U.S. cities have experienced some form of gang migration during the past decade, either short term—for example, to sell drugs—or long term to form permanent gangs. Most of the new arrivals were from Los Angeles gangs, though Chicago, New York, and Detroit are also the source of migrators. The most common motive for gang members to migrate was actually social: Their family relocated or they came to stay with relatives. Others had a specific criminal purpose, such as expanding drug sales and markets. Most of the migrators were African American or Hispanic males who maintained close ties with members of their original gangs "back home."[86] Although retention of gang identity is important, some migrants join local gangs, shedding old ties and gaining new affiliations. And while gang migration remains a serious problem, most cities had local gangs before the onset of migration and most likely would have had a gang problem regardless of migration. The number of migrants is relatively small in proportion to the overall gang population, supporting the contention that most gangs are actually "homegrown."

Neighborhood Reactions The presence of gangs in areas unaccustomed to delinquent group activity can have a devastating effect on community life. In his famous study of Milwaukee gangs, John Hagedorn found that a great deal of neighborhood hostility was evoked when gangs formed in this Midwestern city.[87] Community resistance to gangs arose for a number of reasons. First, Milwaukee's gangs had little neighborhood turf affiliation and were formed solely to profit from illegal gain and criminal activity. Second, the gangs were formed at the same time minority students were being bused to implement desegregation. Gang recruitment took place on the buses and in schools and not on neighborhood streets. Gang membership, therefore, cut across neighborhoods, rendering local social control ineffective. Finally, the neighborhoods most likely to be plagued by gang violence were strained economically. Residential segregation and a lack of affordable housing prevented many working-class residents from leaving. The result was mixed neighborhoods of struggling working-class and poor families coexisting with drug houses, gangs, and routine violence. Frightened residents had little recourse but to call police when they heard gunshots; neighborhoods became uneasy and unstable.

Hagedorn's study illustrates the dreadful impact gang activity can have on a neighborhood. As Lawrence Rosenthal points out, unlike any other crime, gang activity is frequently undertaken out in the open, on the public ways, and in full view of the rest of the community.[88] Brazen criminal activity undermines community solidarity because it signals that the police must be either corrupt or inept. The fact that gangs are willing to openly engage in drug sales and other types of criminal activity shows their confidence that they have silenced or intimidated law-abiding people in their midst. The police and community alike become hopeless about their ability to restore community stability.

Age

The ages of gang members range widely, perhaps from as young as 8 to as old as 55.[89] However, members of offending groups are usually no more than a few years apart in age, with a leader, or instigator, who may be more experienced and a few years older.[90]

A recent survey of 3,348 youths, including almost 2,000 gang members, conducted by the National Gang Crime Research Center, found that kids first hear about gangs at around 9 years old, get involved in violence at age 10 or 11, and join their first gang at age 12. By age 13, half of the gang boys interviewed had fired a pistol, seen someone killed or seriously injured by gang violence, gotten a permanent gang tattoo, and been arrested.[91]

Gang experts believe the average age of gang members has been increasing yearly, a phenomenon explained in part by the changing structure of the U.S. economy.[92] About half of all gang members today are aged 18 to 24, an increase from 46 percent in 1998 and 37 percent in 1996. In contrast, the proportion of gang members aged 15 to 17 decreased to 26 percent from a high of 34 percent in 1996.[93]

Why are gang members' ages increasing? Though the economy was robust during the 1990s, desirable unskilled factory jobs that would entice older boys to leave the gang have been lost to overseas competition. Replacing these legitimate jobs are low-level drug dealing opportunities that require a gang affiliation. William Julius Wilson found that the inability of inner-city males to obtain adequate employment prevents them from attaining adult roles; for example, they cannot afford to marry and raise families. Criminal records acquired at an early age quickly lock them out of the job market. Remaining in a gang into their adulthood has become an economic necessity.[94] The weakening economy should prolong gang membership even further.

In his Milwaukee research, John Hagedorn also found that economic deterioration has had an important impact on the age structure of gang membership. In the past, gangs had a shifting membership because older members could easily slip into the economic mainstream. Good-paying manufacturing jobs that required little education and few skills were an attractive alternative to gang activity. These jobs are simply no longer available, with the result that the economic lure of gangs continues past adolescence into young adulthood. Less than one in five founding members of the youth gangs Hagedorn studied were able to find full-time employment by their mid-20s; 86 percent had spent considerable time in prison. *Old heads*—older members with powerful street reputations—were held in high esteem by young gang boys. In the past, ex-members served as a moderating influence, helping steer gang boys into conventional roles and jobs. Today, young adults continue relationships with their old gangs and promote values of hustling, drug use, and sexual promiscuity. As a result, gang affiliations can last indefinitely, and it is not unusual to see intergenerational membership, with the children and even grandchildren of gang members affiliating with the same gang.[95] When Hagedorn and his associates interviewed 101 older gang members from 14 Milwaukee area gangs, they found that there are actually four types of adult gang members:

I *Legits* have left the gang and 'hood behind.

I *Dope fiends* are addicted to cocaine and need drug treatment.

I *New Jacks* have given up on the legitimate economy and see nothing wrong in selling cocaine to anyone.

I *Homeboys,* who are a majority of all adult gang members, work regular jobs, but when they cannot make enough money, they sell cocaine. They want out of the drug trade and wish to have a "normal" life, but believe that ganging is the only way to make ends meet.[96]

Gender

Traditionally, gang membership was a male-oriented activity. Of the more than 1,000 groups included in Thrasher's original survey, only half a dozen were female gangs. Today, national surveys indicate that about 94 percent of gang members are male and

6 percent female. However, while only about 2 percent of gangs are identified as predominantly female, about 39 percent of all gangs had female members.[97]

Some local gang surveys that rely on interview and self-report data, however, indicate that the number of female gang members may be on the rise in some areas of the country.[98] Carl Taylor's analysis of Detroit gangs found that girls were very much involved in gang activity.[99] And an important analysis of Denver youth found that the number of female gang members is higher than previously thought: Approximately 25 percent of the gang members they surveyed were female.[100] A recent survey of almost 6,000 youths in 42 schools located in 11 cities found that almost 40 percent of the gang members were females.[101] It is possible that law enforcement agencies undercount female gang membership and that in actuality more young girls are gang affiliated than previously believed.[102] Consequently, some experts claim that between one-fourth and one-third of all youth gang members are female.[103]

Structure of Female Gangs Females have traditionally been involved in gang activities in one of three ways: as auxiliaries, or branches, of male gangs; as part of sexually mixed gangs; and as autonomous gangs. Auxiliaries are a feminized version of the male gang name, such as the Lady Disciples of the Devil's Disciples. Some gangs are integrated, containing both male and female members. For example, Mary Glazier's study of a small-town Pennsylvania gang, "The Hit and Run," found that girls were invited to become gang members because it was considered unacceptable for male members to fight with females who gave them trouble; girl members were given that responsibility.[104]

Independent or autonomous female gangs are now becoming more common.[105] While initial female gang participation may be forged by links to male gang members, once in gangs, girls form close ties with other female members. Peer interactions form the basis for independent female gangs and group criminal activity.[106]

Why Do Girls Join Gangs? Are there any real benefits to female gang membership? According to the *liberation view,* ganging can provide girls a sense of sisterhood, independence, and solidarity as well as a chance to earn profit through illegal activity such

The number and extent of girl gangs is increasing. In the Grape Street area of Los Angeles, a female gang member is about to kick another young woman. This is not a random or spontaneous attack but part of the "court in" ceremony in which new members are initiated into the gang.

as drug dealing. Females join gangs in an effort to cope with a bleak and harsh life and the prospects of an equally dismal future.[107] Girls in gangs seem less violent than boys and more likely to engage in theft offenses than violent crimes.[108] This may indicate the desire for female gang members to use their status for economic gain in order to improve their lifestyle and enhance their future.

While the liberation view suggests there may be benefits to gang membership, the *social injury view* suggests that the deficits of gang membership are greater than its benefits. Female members are still sexually exploited by males and are sometimes forced to exploit other females. Girls who are members of male gang auxiliaries may be particularly prone to exploitation. They report that males in the gang not only control the girls in the auxiliary gangs by determining the arenas within which they can operate (for example, the extent to which they are allowed to become involved in intergang violence), but also play a divisive role in the girls' relationships with each other. Findings from a recent study of Texas gangs by Alan Turley substantiate the social injury view. He found that male gang members use coercion and peer pressure to recruit females in their neighborhood to join gangs. Young girls are given subordinate or auxiliary memberships in male gangs and are required to perform such minor or secondary functions as transporting or hiding drugs and guns.[109]

Why then do girls join gangs if they are exploitive and provide little opportunities for sisterhood? When criminologist Jody Miller studied female gangs in St. Louis, Missouri, and Columbus, Ohio, she found that girls in mixed-gangs expressed little evidence of sisterhood and solidarity with other female gang members.[110] Rather, female gang members expressed hostility to other women in the gang, believing, for example, that those who suffered sexual assault by males in the same gang actually deserved what they got. Instead of trying to create a sense of sisterhood, female gang members tried to identify with males and view themselves as "one of the guys" in the gang.

Miller found that even though being a gang member was not a walk in the park, most girls join gangs in an effort to cope with their turbulent personal life, which may provide them with an even harsher reality. They see the gang as an institution that can actually increase their status and improve their lifestyle. The gang provides them with an alternative to a tough urban life filled with the risk of violence and victimization. Many of the girl gang members had early exposure to neighborhood violence, encounters with girl gangs while growing up, experienced severe family problems (violence or abuse), and had close family members who were gang-involved.[111] Did they experience life benefits after they joined the gang? The evidence is mixed. Miller found that female gang members increased their delinquent activities and increased their risk of becoming a crime victim. They were more likely to suffer physical injury than those girls who shunned gang membership. The risk of being sexually assaulted by male members of their own gang was also not insignificant. However, female gang membership did have some benefits: It protected female gang members from sexual assault by nongang neighborhood men, which they viewed as a more dangerous and deadly risk.

Formation

It has long been suggested that gangs form in order to defend their turf from outsiders; thus, gang formation involves a sense of territoriality. Most gang members live in close proximity to one another, and their sense of belonging and loyalty extends only to their small area of the city. At first, a gang may form when members of an ethnic minority newly settled in the neighborhood join together for self-preservation. As the group gains numerical domination over an area, it may view the neighborhood as its territory or turf, which needs to be defended. Defending turf involves fighting rivals who want to make the territory their own.

Once formed, gangs grow when youths who admire the older gang boys and wish to imitate their lifestyle "apply" and are accepted for membership. Sometimes, the new members will be given a special, diminished identity within the gang that reflects their inexperience and apprenticeship status. Joan Moore and her associates found that once formed, youth cliques (*klikas*) in Hispanic gangs remain together as unique

klikas
Independent cliques contained within Hispanic gangs.

groups with separate names (for example, the Termites), separate identities, and distinct experiences; they also have more intimate relationships among themselves than among the general gang membership.[112] She likens *klikas* to a particular class in a university, such as the class of '94—not a separate organization, but one that has its own unique experiences.

Moore also found that gangs can expand by including members' kin, even if they do not live in the immediate neighborhood, and rival gang members who wish to join because they admire the gang's way of doing things. Adding outsiders gives the gang the ability to take over new territory. However, it also brings with it new problems, since outsider membership and the grasp for new territory usually result in greater conflicts with rival gangs.

Leadership

Most experts describe gang leaders as cool characters who have earned their position by demonstrating a variety of abilities—fighting prowess, verbal quickness, athletic distinction, and so on.[113] Experts emphasize that gang leadership is held by one person and varies with particular activities, such as fighting, sex, and negotiations. In fact, in some gangs, each age level of the gang has its own leaders. Older members may be looked up to, but they are not necessarily considered leaders by younger members. In his analysis of Los Angeles gangs, Malcolm Klein observed that many gang leaders shrink from taking a leadership role and actively deny leadership. Klein overheard one gang boy claim, "We got no leaders, man. Everybody's a leader, and nobody can talk for nobody else."[114] The most plausible explanation of this ambivalence is the boy's fear that during times of crisis, his decisions will conflict with those of other leaders and he will lose status and face.

There appears then to be a diverse concept of leadership depending on the organizational structure of the gang. Less organized gangs are marked by diffuse and shifting leadership. Larger and more organized gangs have a clear chain of command and leaders who are supposed to give orders, plan activities, and control members' behavior.[115]

Communications

Gangs today seek recognition both from their rivals and the community as a whole. Image and reputation depend on a gang's ability to communicate to the rest of the world. One major source of gang communication is **graffiti** (see Figure 8.2). These wall writings are especially elaborate among Latino gangs, who call their inscriptions *placasos* or *placa*, meaning sign or plaque.[116] Latino gang graffiti will usually contain the writer's street name and the name of the gang. Strength or power is frequently asserted through the use of the term *rifa*, which means to rule, and *controllo*, indicating that the gang controls the area. Another common inscription is "p/v," meaning *por vida*; this refers to the fact that the gang expects to control the area "for life." If the numeral 13 is used, it signifies that the gang is *loco*, or "wild." Crossed-out graffiti indicates that a territory is being contested by a rival gang, while undisturbed writing indicates that the gang's power has gone unchallenged.

Gangs also communicate by ritualistic argot (speech patterns). *Gangbangers* may refer to their *crew, posse, troop,* or *tribe.* Within larger gangs are *sets,* which hang in particular neighborhoods, and *tips,* which are small groups formed for particular purposes. Exhibit 8.3 illustrates a variety of gang argot.

Flashing or tossing gang signs in the presence of rivals is often viewed as a direct challenge that can escalate into a verbal or physical confrontation. In Chicago, gangs call this **representing.** Gang boys will proclaim their affiliation ("Latin King Love!" "Stone Killers!") and ask victims, "Who do you ride?" or "What do you be about?"; an incorrect response will provoke an attack.[117] False representing can be used to intentionally misinform witnesses and victims. It can be used to expose imposters or neutrals trying to make safe passage through gang-controlled territory.

graffiti
Inscriptions or drawings made on a wall or structure and used by delinquents for gang messages and turf definition.

To view **current examples of gang graffiti,** go to www.streetgangs.com/graffiti/. For an up-to-date list of web links, go to http://cj.wadsworth.com/siegel_jd9e.

representing
Tossing or flashing gang signs in the presence of rivals, often escalating into a verbal or physical confrontation.

Gangster Disciples
(GD)

New Breed Black Gangsters
LLL: Love, Life, Loyalty
III: Third Disciple Nation

Latin Kings
Use 3- or 5-pointed crowns

Latin Disciples

Cobra Stones
putting down
Gangster Disciples

Vice Lords

Ambrose

P R Stones

FIGURE 8.2
Gang Symbols Used in Graffiti

SOURCE: Illinois State Police, Springfield, IL, 2004.

Still another method of communication is clothing. In some areas, gang members communicate their membership by wearing jackets with the name of their gang embroidered on the back. In Boston neighborhoods, certain articles of clothing, for example, sneakers or sports jackets with a particular team logo, are worn to identify gang membership.[118] In Los Angeles, the two major black gangs are the Crips and the Bloods, each containing many thousands of members. Crips are identified with the color blue and will wear some article of blue clothing—hat, belt, or jacket—to communicate their allegiance; their rivals, the Bloods, identify with the color red.[119]

Criminality

In the 1600s, English gangs broke windows, demolished taverns, assaulted local watchmen, and fought intergang battles (dressed in colored ribbons so they could tell who was on their side).[120] Regardless of their type, gang members typically commit more crimes than any other youths in the social environment.[121] Members self-report significantly more crime than nonmembers and the more enmeshed a youth is in a gang the more likely they are to report criminal behavior, to have official records, and to get sent to juvenile court. The gang-membership/crime relationship begins as early as middle school.[122]

Today, gang criminality has numerous patterns.[123] Some gangs specialize; for example, drug-oriented gangs concentrate on the sale of marijuana, PCP, cocaine, crack, and amphetamines. Drug use is quite common. In one recent survey, Geoffrey Hunt and his associates found that 82 percent of the female gang members they surveyed were poly-drug users, using drugs such as cocaine, crack, LSD, PCP, methamphetamine, heroin, glue/inhalants, MDMA, and Quaaludes.[124]

EXHIBIT **8.3**

Gang Slang

13, XIII, X3, or trece: Thirteenth letter of the alphabet (M), which symbolizes or identifies gang affiliation of Mexican heritage. Also may refer to allegiance to Southern California gangs.

14, XIV, or X4: Fourteenth letter of the alphabet (N); refers to allegiance to Northern California or Norte Califas gangs.

5-O: The police.

8-ball: A quantity of cocaine.

AK: A semi-automatic assault rifle, such as AK47 or SKS rifles.

Baby G or BG: A very young gangster, approximately 9 to 12 years old; stands for "baby gangster."

BG, BD, or BGD: Refers to "sets" of large Midwestern gangs called Black Gangsters, Black Disciples, or Black Gangster Disciples, a coalition of criminal enterprises under the organized umbrella of the "Folk Nation."

BK: "Blood killer"; used by Crip gangs to threaten rival Blood gangs. The brand of athletic shoes called British Knights are popular with the Crip gang members because of the initials BK on the shoes.

Blood: The organized umbrella gang over numerous sets of California street gangs. They utilize the color red in clothing, graffiti, etc.

Bud: Marijuana.

Busted, popped a cap: Shot at someone.

CK: "Crip killer"; used by Blood gangs to threaten rival Crip gangs.

Chola: A girl involved in gang activity.

Cholo: A boy involved in gang activity.

Clica, clika: A set, clique, gang.

Clique: A set; a gang.

Clicking in: Getting initiated into a gang.

Colors: Gang colors. Flying colors means wearing a bandana or clothing that represents gang colors.

Crab: Bloods' derogatory nickname for Crip gang members.

Crib: A person's home, an inmate's cell, room.

Crip: The organized umbrella gang over numerous sets of California street gangs; they utilize the color blue in clothing, graffiti, etc.

Cuzz: Friendly slang term used for one another by Crips when talking with other Crips.

Double Deuce: A .22 caliber handgun.

Doo-rag: A handkerchief or bandanna wrapped around a gang member's head.

Dusted: Under the influence of PCP; often used to refer to a marijuana joint laced with PCP.

Flying your colors: Wearing your gang's colors.

G or gangster: How gang members see and describe themselves.

Gage: A shotgun.

Gangbanger: A gang member.

Gat: A gun.

Get down: Fight.

Hard: Someone who is strong-willed, unemotional, or uncaring.

Hater: A snitch.

Holmes: A person from a neighborhood, homeboy.

Homey, homeboy: A fellow gang member from the same neighborhood.

Hood: Neighborhood.

In the mix: Involved in gang activity.

Jack: To rob or assault someone.

Kicking it: Gangbanging or spending time with someone or some group.

Lighting up/lit up: Shot.

Mad dog: Staring or glaring at another person with intent to intimidate.

Mi vida loca: Spanish for "my crazy life." Symbolizes what the gang member thinks of their lifestyle. Live for now, don't worry about the consequences.

OG: "Original gangster"; one of the original members of a clique, set, or gang.

Pay back: Vendetta, retaliation.

Placas: Graffiti identifying a gang name.

People/People Nation: A coalition of Midwestern gangs, including the Vice Lords and affiliate groups that have formed an organized criminal group of gangs/sets. Rival of the Folks/Folk Nation.

Pipe head: A person addicted to cocaine.

Por vida: "For life." Means the gang member is in the gang for life.

Posse: East Coast term for gang.

Primo: Marijuana joint laced with cocaine.

Putting in work: A gang member doing a shooting; a murder.

R.I.P.: "Rest in peace." Often seen in graffiti and is a signal of pending violence or violence that has already occurred.

Rag: A handkerchief in gang's color.

Ride: A car.

Set: Neighborhood gangs; another term used for a gang by criminal street gang members. Most sets are loyal to and fall under a greater organized umbrella entity such as the Bloods, Crips, Folks, or People.

Shank: Prison terminology for homemade knife.

Shooter: A person who uses a gun.

Slob: Crip's insult for Blood gang member.

Smile now, cry later: Popular tattoo of a smiling face and frowning face. Depicts gangster life.

Smoked him: Shot someone.

Snitch: An informer.

Squab: An argument or fight.

Tag: A writer's name (moniker is his tag; to write graffiti is to tag).

Tagger: A person who writes graffiti.

Trey eight: A .38 caliber handgun.

Turf: Territory claimed by the gang.

Vato: A man, boy, guy.

Vato loco: A "crazy dude."

What it "B" like: Blood greeting.

What it "C" like: Crip greeting.

SOURCE: Robert Tagle, Project Coordinator City of Houston, Police Department, Mayor's Anti-Gang Office, personal communication, September 14, 2004.

Other gangs are eclectic, engaging in a wide range of criminal activity from felony assaults to drug dealing.[125] The National Youth Gang Survey found that offense types reported to be most prevalent among gang members are larceny/theft, aggravated assault, and burglary/breaking and entering, and estimated that 46 percent of youth gang members are involved in street drug sales to generate profits for the gang.[126] But not all gangs are major players in drug trafficking, and those that are tend to distribute small amounts of drugs at the street level. The world of major dealing belongs to adults, not to gang youths.[127]

Regardless of their type, gang members typically commit more crimes than any other youths in the social environment; gang membership enhances any preexisting propensity to commit crime.[128] Data from the Rochester Youth Development Study (RYDS), a longitudinal cohort study of 1,000 youths in upstate New York, supports the gang-crime association survey. While 30 percent of the youths in the sample report being a gang member, they account for 65 percent of all reported delinquent acts. The RYDS data show that gang members account for 86 percent of all serious crimes, 63 percent of alcohol use, and 61 percent of drug abuse.[129] Recent research by Rachel Gordon and her associates confirms that boys in Pittsburgh who joined gangs are more delinquent before entering the gang than nongang kids. Gordon also finds that once in gangs, boys increase their involvement in such delinquent activities as drug selling, drug use, violent behaviors and vandalism of property. However, once the youth decides to leave the gang, their involvement in crime and delinquency drops significantly, a finding that shows that gangs facilitate commission of criminal acts.[130]

Gang Violence The National Youth Gang Survey (NYGS) found that 84 percent of police in areas with a gang problem reported at least one occurrence of firearm use by one or more gang members in an assault crime. Thornberry and his associates found that gang kids in Rochester, New York, were about ten times more likely to carry handguns than nongang juvenile offenders. Gun toting gang members committed about ten times more violent crimes than nonmembers.[131] One reason may be that gang membership enhances the likelihood of owning a gun for protection. Current gang members are more likely than nonmembers to own guns for protection (30.9 percent versus 14.2 percent). However, once they leave gangs, former members are no more likely to own guns than nonmembers, a finding which suggests that (1) boys who do not want to participate in the violence and gun carrying associated with gangs choose to leave, and (2) once they leave, they feel less need to carry guns because they are no longer in a climate of conflict and violence.[132]

Research indicates that gang violence is impulsive and emotional and therefore comes in spurts. It typically involves defense of the gang and the gang memberships' reputation.[133] Once a spurt ends, the level of violence may recede, but it remains at a level higher than it was previously, constantly escalating with each battle. Spurts usually are not citywide but occur in specific neighborhoods during periods of intense competition over the expansion and defense of gang territory. Peaks in gang homicides tend to correspond to a series of escalating confrontations, usually over control of territory—either traditional street gang turf or an entrepreneurial drug market.[134] Violence often takes the form of boundary disputes. The most dangerous areas are along disputed boundaries where a drug hot spot intersects with a turf hot spot. There are also "marauder" patterns in which members of rival gangs travel to the hub of their enemy's territory in search of potential victims.[135]

Because of the violent nature of their vocation, gang boys are heavily armed, dangerous, and more violent than nonmembers. One nationwide survey of arrestees found that half of those who owned or carried guns claimed to be gang members.[136]

Violence is a core factor of gang formation and life; it is what causes gangs to spread from one neighborhood to another.[137] Gang members are always feeling threatened by other gangs and are wary of encroachments on their turf. It is not surprising that gang members are likely to increase gun ownership and possession once they join gangs.[138] Considering that gang boys are well armed and wary, members face a far greater chance of death at an early age than nongang boys.[139]

Those who are members of gangs are much more likely to carry weapons and to have peers—also gang members—who own guns for protection. Gun ownership is related to a wide range of undesirable delinquent behaviors, including gun carrying, gun crime, gang membership, and drug selling.[140]

Honor, Courage, and Prestige Scott Decker has studied gangs in St. Louis, Missouri, and found that violence is a central feature of gang life, essential to the transformation of a peer group into a gang. When asked why he calls the groups he belongs to a gang, one member replied, "Violence, I guess. There is more violence than a family. With a gang it's like fighting all the time, killing, shooting."[141] Decker found that gang violence can take on a number of different forms. When joining the gang, members may be forced to participate in violent rituals to prove their courage and reliability. Gang members are ready to fight when others attack them and/or when they believe their territory or turf is being encroached upon. Defacing gang signs or graffiti will demand a violent response. Retaliatory violence may be directed against rival gang boys accused of insults or who are involved in personal disputes. Gang boys also expect to fight when they go to certain locations that are off limits or attend events such as house parties where violence is routine.

Gang members are sensitive to any rivals who question their honor or courage. Once an insult is perceived or a challenge is offered, the gang's honor cannot be restored until the "debt" is repaid. Police efforts to cool down gang disputes only delay the inevitable revenge—a beating or a drive-by shooting. Random acts of revenge have become so common that physicians now consider the consequences of drive-by shootings as a significant health problem, one that is a major contributor to early morbidity and mortality among adolescents and children in Los Angeles and other major gang cities.[142]

Retaliation is often directed against gang members who step out of line. If subordinates disobey orders, perhaps by using rather than selling drugs, they may be subject to harsh disciplinary action by other gang members. Violence is used to maintain the gang's internal discipline and security.

Another common gang crime is extortion, called "turf tax," which involves forcing people to pay the gang to be protected from dangerous neighborhood youths (presumably themselves). **Prestige crimes** occur when a gang boy steals or assaults someone, even a police officer, to gain prestige in the gang and neighborhood. These crimes may be part of an initiation rite or an effort to establish a special reputation, a position of responsibility, or a leadership role; to prevail in an internal power struggle; or to respond to a challenge from a rival (proving the youth is not chicken).

prestige crimes
Stealing or assaulting someone to gain prestige in the neighborhood; often part of gang initiation rites.

Using violence to protect one's reputation is not restricted to boy gangs. Girl gang members may fight when they sense that a member of a rival gang is trying to hook up with their boyfriend. Gini Sykes spent two years with girl gangs in New York City in order to develop an understanding of their lives and lifestyle. One girl, Tiny, told her how ferociousness made up for her lack of stature:

> Tiny fixed me with a cold stare that wiped away any earlier impression of childish cuteness. "See, we smaller girls, we go for your weak spot." Her gaze moved across my features. "Your face. Your throat. Your eyes, so we can blind you. I don't care if you have more weight on me. I'll still try to kill you because, you know, I have a bad temper...."[143]

Tiny related the story of how she attacked a rival whom she caught in a sexual encounter with her boyfriend:

> "She was crying and begging, but she'd disrespected me in front of everybody. We started fighting and she pulled that blade out—" Tiny shrugged. "I just wasn't prepared. You can't tell when someone's got a razor in their mouth."

After she was cut, Tiny went into a defensive rage:

> "...frantically felt for the wound, blood seeping between her fingers. Suddenly, in self-preservation, she grabbed the girl's neck and, blinded by her own blood, began smashing her rival's head into the concrete until Isabel, hearing a siren, dragged her away. The girl had slashed Tiny's face eleven times."

Ethnic and Racial Composition

According to the National Youth Gang Survey respondents, nearly half (49 percent) of all gang members are Hispanic/Latino, 34 percent are African American/black, 10 percent are Caucasian/white, 6 percent are Asian, and the remainder are of some other race/ethnicity.[144]

The majority of gang observers view gangs as racially homogeneous groups: all white (English, Italian, Irish, and/or Slavic origin), all black (African origin), all Hispanic/Latino (Mexican, Puerto Rican, Panamanian, Colombian, and other Spanish-speaking people), or all Asian (Chinese, Japanese, Korean, Taiwanese, Samoan, and Vietnamese).[145] Most intergang conflict appears to be among groups of the same ethnic and racial background.[146]

The ethnic distribution of gangs corresponds to their geographic location. For example, in Philadelphia and Detroit, the overwhelming number of gang members are African American. In New York and Los Angeles, Latino gangs predominate, and San Francisco's small gang population is mostly Asian.[147] Newly emerging immigrant groups are making their presence felt in gangs. Authorities in Buffalo, New York, estimate that 10 percent of their gang population are Jamaicans. Cambodian and Haitian youths are joining gangs in Boston. A significant portion of Honolulu's gangs are Samoans and Filipinos.[148]

African American Gangs The first black youth gangs were organized in the early 1920s and specialized in common street crime activities.[149] Since they had few rival organizations in their inner-city locales, they were able to concentrate on criminal activity, rather than defending their turf. By the 1930s, the expanding number of rival gangs spawned competition, and inner-city gang warfare became commonplace.

In Los Angeles, which is today a hot spot of gang activity, the first black youth gang formed in the 1920s was the Boozies, named after a family that provided a significant portion of its membership. This gang virtually ran the inner city until the 1930s, when rivals began to challenge its criminal monopoly. In the next 20 years, a number of black gangs, including the Businessmen, Home Street, Slauson, and Neighborhood, emerged and met with varying degrees of criminal success.

In the 1970s, the dominant Crips gang was formed and began to spread over much of Los Angeles. Other neighborhood gangs merged into the Crips or affiliated with it by adding "Crips" to their name, so that the Main Street gang became the Main Street Crips. The Crips' dominance has since been challenged by its archrivals, the Bloods. Both of these groups, whose total membership exceeds 25,000 youths, have an organization that resembles an organized crime family and are heavily involved in drug trafficking.

In Chicago, the Blackstone Rangers dominated illicit activities for almost 25 years beginning in the 1960s and until the early 1990s, when their leader, Jeff Fort, and many of his associates were indicted and imprisoned.[150] The Rangers, who later evolved into the El Rukin gang, worked with "legitimate" businessmen to import and sell heroin. Earning millions in profits, they established businesses that helped them launder drug money. Among their enterprises was a security company, which allowed members to carry guns legally. Though many of the convictions were later overturned, the power of El Rukin was ended. (Fort remains in a high-security prison.)

The Rangers' chief rivals, the Black Gangster Disciples, are now the dominant gang in Chicago. While most street gangs are too disorganized to become stable crime groups, the Gangster Disciples have a structure, activities, and relationships similar to traditional organized gangs, such as the Mafia. Gangster Disciple members are actively involved in politics in an effort to gain power and support. Members meet together regularly, commit crime as a group, and maintain ongoing relationships with other street gangs and also with prison-based gangs. The Gangster Disciples have extensive ownership of "legitimate" private businesses and dealings with other businessmen. They offer protection against rival gangs and supply stolen merchandise to customers and employees.[151]

African American gang members, especially those in Los Angeles, have some unique behavioral characteristics. They frequently use nicknames to identify themselves, often based on a behavioral trait: "Little .45" might be used by someone whose favorite weapon is a large handgun. Although TV shows portray gangs as wearing distinctive attire and jackets, in reality, members usually favor nondescript attire in order to reduce police scrutiny; after all, a routine police search can turn up narcotics or weapons. However, gang boys do frequently use distinctive hairstyles, featuring shaving, cornrows, shaping, and/or braids that are designed to look like their leaders. Tattooing is popular, and members often wear colored scarves or "rags" to identify their gang affiliation. In Los Angeles, Crips use blue or black rags, while Bloods normally carry red.

It is also common for black gang members to mark their territory with distinctive graffiti. The messages are crude, rather than sophisticated: drawings of guns, dollar signs, proclamations of individual power, and profanity.

Hispanic Gangs The popularity of gangs and gang culture is relatively high among youths of Hispanic background, explaining in part their disproportionate participation in gang membership.[152]

barrio
A Latino term meaning neighborhood.

Latin or **barrio** gangs are not a recent development. Aggressive male youth groups have been a feature of the Mexican community in Los Angeles as far back as the nineteenth century.[153] The early barrio gangs were made up of young laborers whose behavior was more oriented around sports and socializing than criminality. Today these gangs are made up of kids whose ethnic ancestry can be traced to one of several Spanish-speaking cultures, such as Puerto Rico and Mexico. They are known for their fierce loyalty to their original or "home" gang; this affiliation is maintained even if they move to a new neighborhood that contains a rival gang. Admission to the gang usually involves an initiation ritual in which boys are required to show their fearlessness and prove their *machismo,* or manliness. The most common test requires novices to fight several established members or commit some crime, such as a purse snatching or robbery. The code of conduct associated with membership means never ratting on a brother or even a rival, facing death or prison without betraying their sense of honor.

cholo
A member of the Hispanic subculture of marginalized, antisocial youth.

Latino barrio gangs have evolved over time, sustained by continuous waves of immigrants from Mexico and Latin and South America. Some of these gangs are ethnically distinct—Dominican, Salvadoran, Mexican—while others may have members from a variety of nations. Each new wave of immigrants settles in existing barrios or creates new ones. There, youngsters subscribe to the *cholo* (marginalized) subculture, with its own set of slang, clothing, style, and values. The *cholo* subculture places a high value on friendship, often imputing family and kinship relationships to peers (by calling them "brother" or "cousin"). Unlike other immigrants, gang members are more likely to fight becoming acculturated in the American way of life and cling to the values of their land of origin, a process referred to as **choloization**.[154]

choloization
Becoming acculturated in the American way of life, but clinging to the values of their land of origin.

Scholastic achievement is devalued and replaced with "partying." Employment is valued only if it requires little effort and brings in enough cash to party. An important aspect of the culture is demonstrating *machismo*. Barrio youths try to impress their peers and rivals with their ability to drink more than others, their fighting and sexual prowess, and their heart.

In some areas, such as Miami, Hispanic gangs are rigidly organized with a fixed leadership hierarchy. However, in Southern California, which has the largest concentration of Hispanic youth gangs, leadership is fluid. No youth is elected to a post such as president or warlord. During times of crisis, those with particular skills will assume command on a situational basis.[155] For example, one boy will lead in combat, while another will negotiate drug deals.

In the 1940s, the *pachuco* fad swept through the Latino community; its advocates wore outlandish outfits (zoot suits) and spoke a unique Spanish-English slang. A well-publicized murder case and some urban disturbances helped brand the *pachucos* as vicious "rat packs." Though most zoot-suiters (who can be compared to members of the heavy metal music culture today) were not gang members or necessarily involved in crime, the press focused attention on them as a major social problem, and a popular stereotype was created. Hispanic gang boys are still known for their distinctive dress codes. Some wear knit, dark-colored watch caps pulled down over the ears with a small roll at the bottom. Others wear a folded bandana over the forehead and tied in back. Another popular headpiece is the "stingy brim" fedora or a baseball cap with the wearer's nickname and gang affiliation written on the cap's turned up bill. Members favor tank-style T-shirts or an open Pendleton shirt, which gives them quick access to weapons.

Reaching out to Asian gang members may involve innovative programming. The Venerable Khon Sao, a Buddhist monk, teaches young Cambodian youths, many of them gang members, how to meditate at a Buddhist temple in 2003. Lowell, Massachusetts, has a large Cambodian community and is trying to fight a surge in Cambodian street gangs with Buddhism. The temple, in conjunction with the police department, began a program that teaches fundamentals of Buddhist thought two evenings a week. Youths learn how to pray, meditate, and live peacefully.

© Spencer Platt/Getty Images

Members also proclaim their affiliations by marking off territory with colorful and intricate graffiti. Hispanic gang graffiti has very stylized lettering, frequently uses three-dimensional designs, and proclaims members' organizational pride and power.

Hispanic gangs have a strong sense of territory, or turf, and a great deal of gang violence is directed at warding off any threat to their control. Slights by rivals, including put-downs, stare-downs ("mad-dogging"), defacing gang insignia, and territorial intrusions, can set off a violent and bloody gang confrontation. Newer gangs will carry out this violence with high-powered automatic weapons, a far cry from the zip guns and gravity knives of the past.

Asian Gangs Asian gangs are prominent in such cities as New York, Los Angeles, San Francisco, Seattle, and Houston. The earliest gangs, *Wah Ching,* were formed in the nineteenth century by Chinese youth affiliated with adult crime groups (*tongs*). In the 1960s, two other gangs formed in San Francisco, the Joe Boys and Yu Li, now operate, along with the Wah Ching, in many major U.S. cities. National attention focused on the activities of these Chinese gangs in 1977, when a shootout in the Golden Dragon restaurant in San Francisco left 5 dead and 11 wounded. On the East Coast, prominent Asian gangs include Flying Dragon, Green Dragon, Ghost Shadows, Fu Ching, So on Leong, Tong So on, and Born to Kill (a Vietnamese gang).[156]

In an important work, Ko-Lin Chin has described the inner workings of Chinese youth gangs today.[157] Chin finds that these gangs have unique properties, such as their reliance on raising capital from the Chinese community through extortion and then investing this money in legitimate business enterprises. Chinese gangs recruit new members from the pool of disaffected youth who have problems at school and consider themselves among the few educational failures in a culture that prizes academic achievement.

In addition to Chinese gangs, Samoan gangs, primarily the Sons of Samoa, have operated on the West Coast, as have Vietnamese gangs whose influence has been felt in Los Angeles, New York, and Boston. James Diego Vigil and Steve Chong Yun studied Vietnamese gangs and found that their formation can be tied to such external factors as racism, economic problems, and school failure and such internal problems as family stress and failure to achieve the level of success enjoyed by other Asians. Vietnamese gangs are formed when youths feel they need their *ahns,* or brothers, for protection and have unsatisfied needs for belonging.[158]

Asian gangs tend to victimize members of their own ethnic group. Because of group solidarity and distrust of outside authorities, little is known about their activities.

Anglo Gangs The first American youth gangs were made up of white ethnic youths of European ancestry, especially Irish and Italian immigrants. During the 1950s such ethnic youth gangs commonly competed with African American and Hispanic gangs in the nation's largest cities.

Today, Anglo gang activity is not uncommon, especially in smaller towns.[159] Many are organized as derivatives of the English punk and **skinhead** movement of the 1970s. In England, these youths, generally the daughters and sons of lower-class parents, sported wildly dyed hair, often shaved into "mohawks," military clothes, iron cross earrings, and high-topped military boots. Music was a big part of their lives, and the band that characterized their lifestyle was the punk band the Sex Pistols, led by Johnny Rotten and Sid Vicious. Their creed was antiestablishment, and their anger was directed toward foreigners, who they believed were taking their jobs.

skinhead
A member of a white supremacist gang, identified by a shaved skull and Nazi or Ku Klux Klan markings.

The punker-skinhead style was brought over to the States by bands that replicated the Sex Pistols' antisocial music, stage presence, and dress. The music, philosophy, and lifestyle of these rock bands inspired the formation of a variety of white youth gangs. However, unlike their British brothers, American white gang members are often alienated middle-class youths, rather than poor, lower-class kids who are out of society's mainstream. These gang members include "punkers" or "stoners" who dress in the latest heavy metal rock fashions and engage in drug- and violence-related activities. Some of these gangs espouse religious beliefs involving the occult and satanic worship.[160] There are also skinhead groups that are devoted to racist, white supremacist activities. These kids are being actively recruited by adult hate groups. Another variety of white youth gang engages in satanic rituals and becomes obsessed with occult themes, suicide, ritual killings, and animal mutilations. Members of these gangs get seriously involved in devil worship, tattoo themselves with occult symbols, and gouge their bodies to draw blood for satanic rituals.

While national surveys do not show an upsurge in Anglo gang activity, a recent survey of almost 6,000 youths in 42 schools located in 11 cities found that about 25 percent of the kids who claimed to be gang members are white, a far higher number than found in national surveys.[161]

TO QUIZ YOURSELF ON THIS MATERIAL, go to the Juvenile Delinquency 9e website.

WHY DO YOUTHS JOIN GANGS?

Though gangs flourish in lower-class, inner-city areas, gang membership cannot be assumed to be solely a function of lower-class subcultural identity. Many lower-class youths do not join gangs, and middle-class kids are found in suburban skinhead and stoner groups. What are some of the suspected causes of gang delinquency?

Anthropological View

Writing about gangs in the 1950s, Herbert Block and Arthur Niederhoffer suggested that gangs appeal to adolescents' deep-seated longing for the tribal group process that sustained and nurtured their ancestors.[162] Block and Niederhoffer found that gang processes and functions do seem similar to the puberty rites of some tribal cultures; like their ancient counterparts, gang rituals help the child bridge the gap between childhood and adulthood. For example, uniforms, tattoos, and other identifying marks are an integral part of gang culture. Gang initiation ceremonies are similar to activities of young men in Pacific island cultures. Many gangs put new members through a hazing as an initiation to make sure they have "heart," a feature similar to tribal rites. In tribal societies, initiation into a cult is viewed as the death of childhood. By analogy, younger boys in lower-class urban areas yearn for the time when they can join the gang and really start to live. Membership in the adolescent gang "means the youth gives up his life as a child and assumes a new way of life."[163] Gang names are suggestive of "totemic ancestors" because they usually are symbolic (Cobras, Jaguars, and Kings, for example).

Evidence exists that contemporary gangs continue these traditions. The Gang Prevention and Intervention survey found that over two-thirds of gang kids have family members who are or were in gangs, and fully two-thirds of the gang kids reported having members in their gang whose parents are also active members. These data indicate that ganging has become a cultural family tradition passed on as a rite of passage from one generation to the next.[164] James Diego Vigil has described the rituals of gang initiation, which include physical pummeling to show that the gang boy is brave and ready to leave his matricentric (mother-dominated) household; this process seems reminiscent of tribal initiation rights.[165] For gang members, these rituals become an important part of gang activities. Hand signs and graffiti have a tribal flavor. Gang members adopt nicknames and street identities that reflect personality or physical traits: The more volatile are called "Crazy," "Loco," or "Psycho," while those who wear glasses or read books are dubbed "Professor."[166]

Social Disorganization/Sociocultural View

Sociologists have commonly viewed the shattering, destructive sociocultural forces in socially disorganized inner-city slum areas as the major cause of gang formation. Thrasher introduced this concept in his pioneering work on gangs, and it is a theme found in the classic studies of Richard Cloward and Lloyd Ohlin and of Albert K. Cohen.[167] Irving Spergel's consummate study *Racketville, Slumtown, and Haulburg,* found that Slumtown, the area with the lowest income and the largest population, also had the highest number of violent gangs.[168] According to Spergel, the gang gives lower-class youths a means of attaining personal reputations and peer group status. Malcolm Klein's oft-cited research of the late 1960s and 1970s again found that typical gang members came from dysfunctional and destitute families, had family members with criminal histories, and lacked adequate educational and vocational role models.[169]

The social disorganization/sociocultural view retains its prominent position today. Vigil paints a vivid picture of the forces that drive kids into gangs in his well-respected work *Barrio Gangs.*[170] Vigil's gang kids are pushed into membership because of poverty and minority status. Those who join gangs are the most marginal youths in their neighborhoods and are outcasts in their own families. Vigil finds that all barrio dwellers experience some forms of psychological, economic, cultural, or social "stressors," which hinder their lives. Gang kids are usually afflicted with more than one of these problems, causing them to suffer from "multiple marginality." Barrio youths join gangs because they seek a sense of belonging; gangs offer a set of peers with whom friendship and family-like relationships are expected.[171]

Overall, the sociocultural view assumes that gangs are a natural and normal response to the privations of lower-class life and that gangs are a status-generating medium for boys whose aspirations cannot be realized by legitimate means. Kids who join gangs may hold conventional values, such as the desire to become a financial success, but are either unwilling or unable to accomplish this goal through conventional means, such as schooling.[172] Gang boys have many positive social attributes which in some instances may be more positive than those held by nonmembers.[173] Gangs then are not solely made up of kids from dysfunctional families who seek deviant peers in order to compensate for parental brutality or incompetence. Gangs form in poor neighborhoods and recruit youths from many different kinds of families. Rather than an alternate family, the gang is a coalition of troubled kids who are socialized mainly by the streets rather than by conventional institutions.[174]

Anomie View

In his book on gangs, Irving Spergel suggests that youths are encouraged to join gangs during periods of social, economic, and cultural turmoil; conditions that are thought to produce anomie-like conditions.[175] For example, gangs were present during the Russian Revolution of 1917 and then again during the chaos following the crumbling of the Soviet Union in the early 1990s. The rise of right-wing youth gangs in Germany is associated with social and political change brought about by the unification of East and West Germany. Skinhead groups have formed in response to the immigrants coming from Turkey and North Africa. In the United States, Spergel makes note, gangs have formed in areas where rapid population changes have unsettled community norms.

Immigration or emigration, rapidly expanding or contracting populations, and/or the incursion of different racial/ethnic groups or even different segments or generations of the same racial/ethnic population, can create fragmented communities and gang problems.[176] These conditions may be present in the current upswing in gang activity in the United States. *Street Wars*, a recent (2004) book by California state senator Tom Hayden, the founder of SDS (Students for a Democratic Society), links the growth of gangs in Los Angeles, New York, and Chicago to the anomic conditions found in the poorest sections of these inner city areas. Hayden argues that gang members band together to find connection, understanding, and respect in a world where social norms are undergoing constant upheaval and the success goal is blocked by the actions of the affluent. Gangs are sustained by two anomie producing trends in modern society:

1. The reliance on overly harsh punishments to control the poor. The affluent are more willing to spend on building prisons to house the "incorrigible" than to create social programs that help them gain economic opportunities. Hayden shows that rather than deterring crime, the prison system reinforces gang identity through humiliation and punishment.

2. Globalization has created a force of unemployable men and women around the world who are defined as incorrigible and therefore, virtually unemployable. The gang is their only alternative.

For Hayden, the key to reducing gang activity is the economic restructuring of society and not reliance on harsh punishments, which serve to increase feelings of alienation and anomie.[177]

Psychological View

A minority position on the formation of gangs is that they serve as an outlet for psychologically diseased youths. One proponent of this view is Lewis Yablonsky, whose theory of violent-gang formation holds that violent gangs recruit their members among the more sociopathic youths living in disorganized slum communities.[178] Yablonsky views the sociopathic youth as one who lacks "social feelings." He "has not been trained to have human feelings or compassion or responsibility for another."[179] Yablonsky supports this contention by pointing to the eccentric, destructive, and hostile sexual attitudes and behavior of gang youths, who are often violent and sadistic. He sums up the sociopathic character traits of gang boys as (1) a defective social conscience marked by limited feelings of guilt for destructive acts against others; (2) limited compassion or empathy for others; (3) behavior dominated by egocentrism and self-seeking goals; and (4) the manipulation of others for immediate self-gratification (for example, sexually exploitative modes of behavior) without any moral concern or responsibility. Yablonsky's view is substantiated by cross-cultural studies, which have also found that gang members suffer from psychological deficits, including impulsivity and poor personality control.[180]

Malcolm Klein's more recent analysis of Los Angeles gangs finds that many street gang members suffer from psychological and neuropsychological deficits, including low self-concept, social disabilities or deficits, poor impulse control, and limited life skills. Adolescents who display conduct disorders, early onset of antisocial behavior, and violent temperaments are at the greatest risk for later gang membership.[181] Yet, Klein does not consider most gang youths to be abnormal or pathological. To help them, he believes that psychological therapy is less important than providing gang members with vocational training, educational skills, and improving their chances for legitimate opportunities.[182]

While these arguments are persuasive, other research have not found that gang boys exhibit a pattern of psychological pathology. Many report holding conventional attitudes and beliefs and have positive relationships with their parents and peers.[183] Though some gang boys may suffer serious emotional problems, many others do not.

Rational Choice View

Some youths may join gangs after making the rational choice that gang membership may benefit their law-violating careers and be a source of income. Members of the underclass, who perceive few opportunities in the legitimate economic structure, will turn to gangs as a way of obtaining desired goods and services, either directly through theft and extortion or indirectly through the profits generated by drug dealing and weapon sales. Joining a gang then can be viewed as an "employment decision": The gang can provide its "partners" with the security of knowing they can call on the services of talented "associates" to successfully carry out business ventures. Mercer Sullivan's study of Brooklyn gangs found that members call success at crime "getting paid," a term that imparts an economic edge to gang activity. Gang boys also refer to the rewards of crime as "getting over," which refers to their triumph and pride at "beating the system" and succeeding, even though they are way out of the economic mainstream.[184]

According to this view, the gang boy has long been involved in criminal activity *prior* to his gang membership and joins the gang as a means of improving his illegal "productivity."[185] Gang membership is *not* a necessary precondition for delinquency; kids who are already delinquent may join gangs because membership facilitates or enhances their criminal careers.

Felix Padilla found this when he studied the Diamonds, a Latino gang in Chicago.[186] Joining the gang was a decision made after a careful assessment of legitimate economic opportunities. The gang represented a means of achieving aspirations that were otherwise closed off. The Diamonds made collective business decisions; individuals who made their own deals were severely penalized. The gang maintained a distinct organizational structure and carried out other functions similar to those of legitimate enterprises, including personnel recruitment and financing business ventures with internal and external capital.

The rational choice view is also endorsed by Martin Sanchez-Jankowski in his important book *Islands in the Street*.[187] Sanchez-Jankowski found gangs to be organizations made up of adolescents who maintain a "defiant individualist character." These individuals maintain distinct personality traits: wariness or mistrust of the outside world; self-reliance; isolation from society; good survival instincts; defiance against authority; and a strong belief in the survival of the fittest, that only the strong survive. Kids holding these views and possessing these character traits make a rational decision to join a gang because the gang presents an opportunity to improve the quality of their lives. The gang offers otherwise unobtainable economic and social opportunities, including both support for crime and access to parties, social events, and sexual outlets. Gangs that last the longest and are the most successful are the ones that can offer incentives to these ambitious but destitute youths and can control their behaviors. Sanchez-Jankowski's views, important for understanding the economic and social incentives of gang membership, have been supported by independent research data.[188]

The rational choice view holds that gangs provide support for criminal opportunities that might not otherwise be available. Some recent research by Terence Thornberry and his colleagues at the Rochester Youth Development Study support this model. They found that before kids become gang members, their substance abuse and delinquency rates are no higher than nongang members. When they are in the gang, their crime and drug abuse rates increase significantly, only to decrease when they leave the gang. Thornberry concludes that gangs facilitate criminality, rather than provide a haven for youth who are disturbed or already highly delinquent. This research is also important because it lends support to the life course model: Events that take place during the life cycle, such as joining a gang, have significant impact on criminal behavior and drug abuse.[189] Criminal behavior is not determined solely by factors that are present at birth or soon after.

Personal Safety According to Spergel, some adolescents choose to join gangs from a "rational calculation" to achieve personal safety rather than profit.[190] Youths who are new to a community may believe they will become the targets of harassment or attack if they remain "unaffiliated." Motivation may have its roots in interracial or interethnic rivalry: Youths who are white, African American, Asian, or Hispanic who reside in an area dominated by a different racial or ethnic group may be persuaded that gang membership is an efficient means of collective protection. Ironically, gang members are more likely to be attacked than nonmembers. Girls also join gangs for protection. Though they may be exploited by male gang members, they are protected from assaults by nongang males in the neighborhood.[191]

Fun and Support Some youths join gangs simply to party and have fun.[192] They want to enjoy hanging out with kids like themselves and getting involved in exciting experiences. Kids can learn the meaning of friendship and loyalty through gang membership. There is evidence that kids learn pro-gang attitudes from their peers and that these attitudes direct them to join gangs.[193]

Some experts suggest that kids join gangs in an effort to obtain the family-like atmosphere all too often absent from their own homes. Many gang members report that they have limited contact with their fathers and mothers, many of whom are unskilled laborers or unemployed and battling with substance abuse problems.[194]

These positions are summarized in Concept Summary 8.1.

TO QUIZ YOURSELF ON THIS MATERIAL, go to the Juvenile Delinquency 9e website.

Concept Summary 8.1

Views of Gangs

View	Premise	Evidence
Anthropological	Gangs appeal to kids' tribal instincts.	Use of totems, signs, secret languages, and symbols.
Sociocultural	Gangs form because of destructive sociocultural forces in disorganized inner-city areas.	Concentration of gangs in inner-city areas.
Anomie	Alienated kids join gangs.	Upswing in gang activities after market forces create anomic conditions. Gangs activity increases with globalization.
Psychological	Kids with personality problems form gangs and become leaders.	Antisocial, destructive behavior patterns. Increase in violence.
Rational choice	Kids join gangs for protection, fun, and survival.	Presence of party gangs, gang members protect one another.

CONTROLLING GANG ACTIVITY

Two basic methods are used to control gang activity. The first involves priority targeting by local criminal justice agencies; the second operates through a variety of social service efforts. Each of these methods will be discussed below.

Law Enforcement Efforts

In recent years, gang control has often been left to local police departments. Gang control takes three basic forms:

1. The youth service program, in which traditional police personnel, usually from the youth unit, are given responsibility for gang control. No personnel are assigned exclusively or mainly to gang-control work.

2. The gang detail, in which one or more police officers, usually from youth or detective units, are assigned exclusively to gang-control work.

3. The gang unit, established solely to deal with gang problems, to which one or more officers are assigned exclusively to gang-control work.[195]

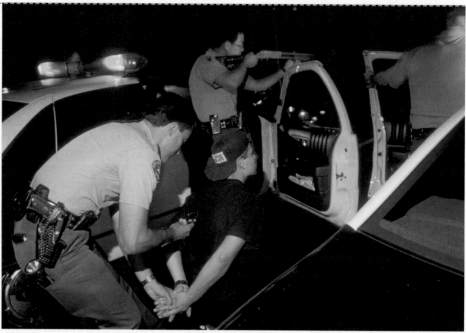

© A. Ramey/PhotoEdit

Most police departments surveyed maintain separate gang-control units. They are involved in such activities as processing information on youth gangs and gang leaders; prevention efforts, such as mediation programs; enforcement efforts to suppress criminal activity and apprehend those who are believed to have committed crimes; and follow-up investigations directed at apprehending gang members alleged to have committed crimes. Most of these units have special training in gang control for their personnel, have specific policies directed at dealing with gang boys, and enforce special laws designed to control gang activity.[196]

A good example of these units is the Chicago Police Department's 400-plus officer gang crime section, which maintains intelligence on gang problems and trains officers in dealing with those problems. Through its gang target program, it identifies street gang members and enters their names in a computer bank that is programmed to alert the unit if the youths are picked up or arrested. Some departments also sponsor general prevention programs that can help control gang activities, including school-based lectures, police-school liaisons, information dissemination, recreation programs, and street worker programs that offer counseling, assistance to parents, and community organization, among other services.

Some police departments engage in *gang-breaking* activities, in which police will focus on the gang leaders and make special efforts to arrest, prosecute, convict, and incarcerate them whenever possible. For example, Los Angeles police conduct intensive anti-gang sweeps, in which more than 1,000 officers are put on the street to round up and intimidate gang boys. Police say that the sweeps let the gangs know "who the streets belong to" and show neighborhood residents that someone cares.[197] Few departments have written policies or procedures on how to deal with youths, and many do not provide gang-control training.

Gang sweeps and other traditional police tactics may not work on today's drug gangs. It might be more appropriate to view gangs as organized criminal enterprises and deal with them as traditional organized crime families. It might be useful to (1) develop informants through criminal prosecutions, payments, and witness protection programs; (2) rely heavily on electronic surveillance and long-term undercover investigations; and (3) use special statutes that create criminal liabilities for conspiracy, extortion, or engaging in criminal enterprises.[198] Of course, such policies are expensive and difficult to implement because they may be needed only against the most sophisticated gangs. However, the gangs that present the greatest threat to urban life may be

Boston's Youth Violence Strike Force (YVSF)

The Youth Violence Strike Force (YVSF) is one of the primary enforcement strategies that Boston is pursuing to combat youth gang violence. The YVSF is a multi-agency coordinated task force made up of 45 to 50 full-time Boston police officers and 15 officers from outside agencies. The membership of the YVSF includes the Massachusetts State Police, the Department of Treasury's Bureau of Alcohol, Tobacco, and Firearms (ATF), police departments from neighboring jurisdictions, Massachusetts Corrections, Probation, Parole, and Division of Youth Service (juvenile corrections) officers, and other agencies as appropriate. It works closely with the Suffolk County District Attorney's and state Attorney General's offices, and participates in the Department of Justice's Anti-Violent Crime Initiative (AVCI) led locally by the United States Attorney. The YVSF investigates youth crimes, arrests those responsible, and breaks up the environment for crime. One important accomplishment of the YVSF was the creation of a comprehensive computer database, which has allowed tough enforcement efforts against the leaders of gangs, and positive intervention in the lives of those who are at risk of becoming hard-core gang members.

In addition, the Youth Violence Strike Force, in cooperation with the city of Boston and the Department of Justice, has used criminal and civil forfeiture laws to help secure the safety of the community by taking over drug dens and renovating them as new homes. Drug dens have been closed through joint federal-state-local cooperation. Some former drug houses have been renovated in order to provide low-income elderly housing.

The Youth Violence Strike Force takes tough action every day against gangs and gang members across Boston. Yet many of the strike force officers view their work in prevention as equally important, and many of these officers help to sponsor numerous prevention activities in the community. For example, members of the YVSF work in partnership with law enforcement, social service, and private institutions to raise funds for a series of "Kids at Risk" programs, including camping programs, membership at the Boys and Girls Clubs and YMCAs, and attendance at basketball camp or the Boston Police's Teen Summer Academy.

Another program, Operation Night Life, puts the YVSF together with concerned clergy members, youth outreach workers, and social service professionals to prevent youth and gang violence of probationers by regularly visiting their homes.

Critical Thinking

Is it possible to reduce gang membership without providing youth with a reasonable legitimate alternative, including first-rate schools and job opportunities?

InfoTrac College Edition Research

To read more about Operation Night Life, read James T. Jordan, "Boston's Operation Night Light: New Roles, New Rules," *The FBI Law Enforcement Bulletin* 67:1–5 (1998).

SOURCE: *Youth Violence: A Community-based Response: One City's Success Story* (Washington, DC: Office of the Attorney General, 1996); updated, personal communication with the Boston Police Department, January 5, 2004.

---

suitable targets for more intensive police efforts. In addition, as new community-policing strategies are implemented in which police officers are assigned to keep the peace in local neighborhoods (see Chapter 13 for more on community policing), it may be possible to garner sufficient local support and information to counteract gang influences. The Policy and Practice box entitled "Boston's Youth Violence Strike Force" describes one of the more successful police-sponsored gang control efforts.

Community Control Efforts

In addition to law enforcement activities, there have been a number of community-based gang-control efforts. Some have involved directing social intervention efforts at gang members. In these programs, social welfare professionals offer direct assistance to at-risk youth. This is actually not a new initiative. During the late nineteenth century, social workers of the YMCA worked with youths in Chicago gangs.[199] During the 1950s, at the height of perceived gang activity, the **detached street worker** program was developed in major centers of gang activity.[200] This unique approach sent social workers into the community to work with gangs on their own turf. The worker attached him- or herself to a gang, participated in its activities, and tried to get to know its members. The purpose was to act as an advocate of the youths, to provide them with a positive role model, to help orient their activities in a positive direction, and to treat individual problems.

detached street workers
Social workers who go out into the community and establish close relationships with juvenile gangs with the goal of modifying gang behavior to conform to conventional behaviors and to help gang members get jobs and educational opportunities.

EXHIBIT 8.4

Elements of Spergel's Community Gang-Control Program

1. Community mobilization, including citizens, youth, community groups, and agencies.
2. Provision of academic, economic, and social opportunities. Special school training and job programs are especially critical for older gang members who are not in school but may be ready to leave the gang or decrease participation in criminal gang activity for many reasons, including maturation and the need to provide for family.
3. Social intervention, using street outreach workers to engage gang-involved youth.
4. Gang suppression, including formal and informal social control procedures of the juvenile and criminal justice systems and community agencies and groups. Community-based agencies and local groups must collaborate with juvenile and criminal justice agencies in the surveillance and sharing of information under conditions that protect the community and the civil liberties of youth.
5. Organizational change and development, that is, the appropriate organization and integration of the above strategies and potential reallocation of resources.

SOURCES: Irving Spergel and Candice Kane, *Community-Based Youth Agency Model* (Washington, DC: Office of Juvenile Justice and Delinquency Prevention, 1990); Jim Burch and Candice Kane, *Implementing the OJJDP Comprehensive Gang Model* (Washington, DC: Office of Juvenile Justice and Delinquency Prevention, 1999).

Detached street worker programs are sometimes credited with curbing gang activities in the 1950s and 1960s, although their effectiveness has been challenged on the ground that they helped legitimize delinquent groups by turning them into neighborhood organizations.[201] Some critics believed that the detached street workers helped maintain group solidarity, and as a result, new members were drawn to gangs.

Today there are numerous community-level programs designed to limit gang activity. Some, such as the Neutral Zone in Mountlake Terrace, Washington (a Seattle suburb), open recreation areas in the evening hours to provide supervised activities as an alternative to street life.[202] In some areas, citywide coordinating groups help orient gang-control efforts. For example, the Chicago Intervention Network operates field offices around the city in low-income, high-crime areas that provide a variety of services, including neighborhood watches, parent patrols, alternative youth programming, and family support efforts.

Some community efforts are partnerships with juvenile justice agencies. In Los Angeles County the Gang Alternative Prevention Program (GAPP) provides intensive supervision of at-risk juveniles who are on probation for relatively minor crimes. GAPP provides prevention services to juveniles before they become entrenched in gangs. GAPP's services include individual and group counseling; bicultural and bilingual services that are not being provided in the community for adolescents and their parents; and special programs such as tutoring, parent training, job development, and recreational, educational, and cultural experiences.[203]

Sociologist Irving Spergel, a leading expert on gangs, has developed a model for helping communities deal with gang-involved youth that has become the basis for gang-control efforts around the nation. His model includes the five distinct strategies contained in Exhibit 8.4. The Spergel model is now being tested in a number of communities around the country.

Why Gang Control Is Difficult

The era of the massive urban-based opportunity program has ended in the face of budget shortfalls and the deficit economy. Experts have charged that the lack of legitimate economic opportunity for unskilled adolescents creates a powerful incentive for them to become involved in the illegal economy. Even if police departments develop effective anti-gang methods, as seems to be the case in Los Angeles, gang boys may migrate to other surrounding towns and cities whose police departments may suddenly find themselves ill equipped to handle a crime problem which heretofore was unknown in the area. For example, when L.A. cracked down on gangs in 2003 and

2004, nearby jurisdictions saw a spike in gang activity. As a result the Los Angeles Regional Gang Information Network was launched in 2004 by five regional districts in order to enhance coordination of anti-gang strategies. The new system involves a database that can eliminate conflicts between two jurisdictions tracking the same gang boys and issue warnings to federal and local law enforcement about gang sweeps or drug busts being planned.[204]

Gang experts Jodi Lane and James Meeker find that policies that focus only on eradicating gangs and creating harsher suppression and punishment strategies cannot eradicate fear of gang crime. Though get-tough programs may be a safe and successful political strategy, they are costly in both financial and human terms and have not substantially decreased the number of gangs or gang members in the United States.[205]

Alternative strategies may be necessary to reduce the gang problem. A more reasonable approach may be to provide economic opportunities, a policy that might prove to be particularly effective because surveys of gang boys reveal that many might leave gangs if education and vocational opportunities existed.[206]

This solution does not seem practical or probable. As you may recall from Chapter 4, the more embedded youth become in criminal enterprise, the less likely they are to find meaningful adult work. It is unlikely that gang youths can suddenly be transformed into highly paid professionals. A more reasonable and effective alternative would be to devote a greater degree of available resources to the most deteriorated urban areas, even if it requires pulling funds from groups that have traditionally been recipients of government aid, such as the elderly.[207]

While social solutions to the gang problem seem elusive, the evidence shows that gang involvement is a socio-ecological phenomenon and must therefore be treated as such. Kids join gangs when they live in deteriorated areas, where their need for economic growth and self-fulfillment cannot be met by existing social institutions, and when gang members are there to recruit them at home or at school.[208] Social causes demand social solutions. Programs that enhance the lives of adolescents at school or in the family are the key to reducing gang delinquency.

Summary

- Peer relations are a critical element of maturation.

- Many experts believe that maintaining delinquent friends is a significant cause of antisocial behaviors.

- Some experts believe that criminal kids seek each other out.

- Gangs are law-violating youth groups that use special vocabulary, clothing, signs, colors, graffiti, and names, and whose members are committed to antisocial behavior.

- Gangs are a serious problem in many cities.

- Gangs have been around since the eighteenth century.

- The gang problem died down for a while and re-emerged in the 1970s.

- There are now thousands of gangs, containing more than 750,000 members.

- Most gang members are males, aged 14 to 21, who live in urban areas.

- Gangs can be classified by their structure, behavior, or status. Some are believed to be social groups, others are criminally oriented, and still others are violent.

- Hundreds of thousands of crimes are believed to be committed annually by gangs. While some gangs specialize in drug dealing, gang kids engage in a wide variety of criminal offenses.

- Violence is an important part of being a gang member.

- Although most gang members are male, the number of females in gangs is growing at a faster pace. African American and Hispanic gangs predominate, but Anglo and Asian gangs are also quite common.

- We are still not sure what causes gangs. One view is that they serve as a bridge between adolescence and adulthood when adult control is lacking. Another view suggests that gangs serve as an alternative means of advancement for disadvantaged youths. Still another view is that some gangs are havens for disturbed youths.

- Police departments' gang-control efforts have not been well organized. A recent national survey found relatively few training efforts designed to help police officers deal with the gang problem.

Key Terms

cliques, p. 234
crowds, p. 234
controversial status youth, p. 234
co-offending, p. 235
gangs, p. 238
interstitial group, p. 238

retreatists, p. 243
stable slum, p. 246
klikas, p. 250
graffiti, p. 251
representing, p. 251
prestige crimes, p. 255

barrio, p. 257
cholo, p. 257
choloization, p. 257
skinhead, p. 259
detached street workers, p. 265

Questions for Discussion

1. Do gangs serve a purpose? Differentiate between a gang and a fraternity.

2. Discuss the differences between violent, criminal, and drug-oriented gangs.

3. How do gangs in suburban areas differ from inner-city gangs?

4. Do delinquents have cold and distant relationships with their peers?

5. Can gangs be controlled without changing the economic opportunity structure of society? Are there any truly meaningful alternatives to gangs today for lower-class youths?

6. Can you think of other rituals in society that reflect an affinity or longing for more tribal times? Hint: Have you ever pledged a fraternity or sorority, gone to a wedding, or attended a football game?

Viewpoint

You are a professor who teaches courses on delinquent behavior at a local state university. One day you are approached by the director of the President's National Task Force on Gangs (NTFG). This group has been formed to pool resources from a variety of federal agencies, ranging from the FBI to Health and Human Services, in order to provide local jurisdictions with a comprehensive plan for fighting gangs. The director claims that the gang problem is big and becoming bigger. Thousands of gangs, with hundreds of thousands of members, are operating around the country. Government sources, he claims, indicate that there has been a significant growth in gang membership over the past 20 years. So far the government has not been able to do anything at either a state or national level to stem this growing tide of organized criminal activity. They would like you to be part of the team that provides state and local jurisdictions with a gang-control activity model, which, if implemented, would provide a cost-effective means of reducing both gang membership and gang activity.

▌ Would you recommend that police employ anti-gang units that use tactics developed in the fight against organized crime families?

▌ Would you recommend the redevelopment of deteriorated neighborhoods in which gangs flourish?

▌ Would you try to educate kids about the dangers of gang membership?

▌ Would you tell the director that gangs have always existed and there is probably not much the government can do to reduce their numbers?

Doing Research on the Web

To read more about gang prevention efforts, go to Info-Trac College Edition and check out Lonnie Jackson, "Understanding and Responding to Youth Gangs: a Juvenile Corrections Approach," *Corrections Today* 16:62 (August 1999). Also see John M. Hagedorn, Jose Torres, and Greg Giglio, "Cocaine, Kicks, and Strain: Patterns of Substance Use in Milwaukee Gangs," *Contemporary Drug Problems* 25(1):113–145 (Spring 1998).

Notes

1. For a general review, see Scott Cummings and Daniel Monti, *Gangs: The Origin and Impact of Contemporary Youth Gangs in the United States* (Albany, NY: State University of New York Press, 1993); this chapter also makes extensive use of George Knox et al., *Gang Prevention and Intervention: Preliminary Results from the 1995 Gang Research Task Force* (Chicago, IL: National Gang Research Center, 1995).

2. George Knox et al., *Preliminary Results of the 1995 Adult Corrections Survey* (Chicago, IL: National Gang Research Center, 1995); G. David Curry, Robert J. Fox, Richard Ball, and Daryl Stone, *National Assessment of Law Enforcement Anti-Gang Information Resources, Final Report* (Morgantown, WV: National Assessment Survey, 1992), Table 6, pp. 36–37. Hereinafter cited as *National Assessment*.

3. Jodi Lane and James Meeker, "Social Disorganization Perceptions, Fear of Gang Crime, and Behavioral Precautions among Whites, Latinos, and Vietnamese," *Journal of Criminal Justice* 32:49–62 (2004).

4. Paul Perrone and Meda Chesney-Lind, "Representations of Gangs and Delinquency: Wild in the Streets?" *Social Justice* 24:96–117 (1997).

5. Thomas Berndt, "The Features and Effects of Friendships in Early Adolescence," *Child Development* 53:1447–1469 (1982).

6. Thomas Berndt and T. B. Perry, "Children's Perceptions of Friendships as Supportive Relationships," *Developmental Psychology* 22:640–648 (1986).

7. Spencer Rathus, *Understanding Child Development* (New York: Holt, Rinehart and Winston, 1988), p. 462.

8. Peggy Giordano, "The Wider Circle of Friends in Adolescence," *American Journal of Sociology* 101:661–697 (1995).

9. Judith Rich Harris, *The Nurture Assumption: Why Children Turn Out the Way They Do* (New York: Free Press, 1998).

10. See Penelope Eckert, *Jocks and Burnouts: Social Categories and Identity in the High School* (New York: Teachers College Press, 1989).

11. Harris, *The Nurture Assumption*.

12. Ibid.

13. Isabela Granic and Thomas Dishion, "Deviant Talk in Adolescent Friendships: A Step Toward Measuring a Pathogenic Attractor Process," *Social Development* 12:314–334 (2003).

14. Shari Miller-Johnson, Philip Costanzo, John Coie, Mary Rose, Dorothy Browne, and Courtney Johnson, "Peer Social Structure and Risk-Taking Behaviors among African American Early Adolescents," *Journal of Youth and Adolescence* 32:375–384 (2003).

15. John Coie and Shari Miller-Johnson, "Peer Factors in Early Offending Behavior," in Rolf Loeber and David Farrington, eds., *Child Delinquents* (Thousand Oaks, CA: Sage Publications, 2001), pp. 191–210.

16. Shari Miller-Johnson, John Coie, and Patrick Malone, "Do Aggression and Peer Rejection in Childhood Predict Early Adult Outcomes?" Paper presented at the biennial meeting of the Society for Research in Child Development, Tampa, FL (April 2003).

17. Harris, *The Nurture Assumption*.

18. Ibid., p. 463.

19. Robert Agnew and Timothy Brezina, "Relational Problems with Peers, Gender and Delinquency," *Youth and Society* 29:84–111 (1997).

20. David Farrington and Rolf Loeber, "Epidemiology of Juvenile Violence," *Child and Adolescent Psychiatric Clinics of North America* 9:733–748 (2000); Cindy Hanson, Scott Henggeler, William Haefele, and J. Douglas Rodick, "Demographic, Individual, and Family Relationship Correlates of Serious Repeated Crime among Adolescents and Their Siblings," *Journal of Consulting and Clinical Psychology* 52:528–538 (1984).

21. Albert Reiss, "Co-Offending and Criminal Careers," in Michael Tonry and Norval Morris, eds., *Crime and Justice*, vol. 10 (Chicago: University of Chicago Press, 1988).

22. David Farrington and Donald West, "The Cambridge Study in Delinquent Development: A Long-Term Follow-Up of 411 London Males," in H. J. Kerner and G. Kaiser, eds., *Criminality: Personality, Behavior, and Life History* (Berlin: Springer-Verlag, 1990).

23. Mark Warr, "Organization and Instigation in Delinquent Groups," *Criminology* 34:11–37 (1996).

24. Ibid., pp. 31–33.

25. Richard Felson and Dana Haynie, "Pubertal Development, Social Factors, and Delinquency among Adolescent Boys," *Criminology* 40:967–989 (2002).

26. See Travis Hirschi, *Causes of Delinquency* (Berkeley: University of California Press, 1969).

27. James Short and Fred Strodtbeck, *Group Process and Gang Delinquency* (Chicago: Aldine, 1965).

28. Kate Keenan, Rolf Loeber, Quanwu Zhang, Magda Stouthamer-Loeber, and Welmoet Van Kammen, "The Influence of Deviant Peers on the Development of Boys' Disruptive and Delinquent Behavior: A Temporal Analysis," *Development and Psychopathology* 7:715–726 (1995).

29. John Cole, Robert Terry, Shari-Miller Johnson, and John Lochman, "Longitudinal Effects of Deviant Peer Groups on Criminal Offending in Late Adolescence," paper presented at the American Society of Criminology meeting, Boston, November 1995.

30. Terence Thornberry and Marvin Krohn, "Peers, Drug Use and Delinquency," in David Stoff, James Breiling, and Jack Maser, eds., *Handbook of Antisocial Behavior* (New York: Wiley, 1997), pp. 218–233; Thomas Dishion, Deborah Capaldi, Kathleen Spracklen, and Fuzhong Li, "Peer Ecology of Male Adolescent Drug Use," *Development and Psychopathology* 7:803–824 (1995).

31. Sylive Mrug, Betsy Hoza, and William Bukowski, "Choosing or Being Chosen by Aggressive-Disruptive Peers: Do They Contribute to Children's Externalizing and Internalizing Problems?" *Journal of Abnormal Child Psychology* 32:53–66 (2004).

32. Mark Warr, "Age, Peers and Delinquency," *Criminology* 31:17–40 (1993).

33. Sara Battin, Karl Hill, Robert Abbott, Richard Catalano, and J. David Hawkins, "The Contribution of Gang Membership to Delinquency Beyond Delinquent Friends," *Criminology* 36:93–116 (1998).

34. Mark Warr, "Life-Course Transitions and Desistance from Crime," *Criminology* 36:502–536 (1998).

35. Stephen W. Baron, "Self-Control, Social Consequences, and Criminal Behavior: Street Youth and the General Theory of Crime," *Journal of Research in Crime and Delinquency* 40:403–425 (2003).

36. Daneen Deptula and Robert Cohen, "Aggressive, Rejected, and Delinquent Children and Adolescents: A Comparison of Their Friendships," *Aggression & Violent Behavior* 9:75–104 (2004).

37. Farrington and Loeber, "Epidemiology of Juvenile Violence."

38. Peggy Giordano, Stephen Cernkovich, and M. D. Pugh, "Friendships and Delinquency," *American Journal of Sociology* 91:1170–1202 (1986).

39. This section is adapted from Gail Wasserman, Kate Keenan, Richard Tremblay, John Coie, Todd Herrenkohl, Rolf Loeber, and David Petechuk, "Risk and Protective Factors of Child Delinquency," *Child Delinquency Bulletin Series* (Washington, DC: Office of Juvenile Justice and Delinquency Prevention, 2003).

40. John Paul Wright and Francis Cullen, "Employment, Peers, and Life-Course Transitions," *Justice Quarterly* 21:183–205 (2004).

41. Irving Spergel, *The Youth Gang Problem, A Community Approach* (New York: Oxford University Press, 1995). Hereinafter cited as *Youth Gang Problem*.

42. Ibid., p.3.

43. Other well-known movie representations of gangs include *The Wild Ones* and *Hell's Angels on Wheels*, which depicted motorcycle gangs, and *Saturday Night Fever*, which focused on neighborhood street toughs. See also David Dawley, *A Nation of Lords* (Garden City, NY: Anchor, 1973).

44. Fox Butterfield, "Rise in Killings Spurs New Steps to Fight Gangs," *New York Times*, January 17, 2004, pA1.

45. For a recent review of gang research, see James Howell, "Recent Gang Research: Program and Policy Implications," *Crime and Delinquency* 40:495–515 (1994).

46. Walter Miller, *Violence by Youth Gangs and Youth Groups as a Crime Problem in Major American Cities* (Washington, DC: Government Printing Office, 1975). Hereinafter cited as *Violence by Youth Gangs*.

47. Ibid., p. 20.

48. Malcolm Klein, *The American Street Gang, Its Nature, Prevalence and Control* (New York: Oxford University Press, 1995), p. 30.

49. Frederic M. Thrasher, *The Gang: A Study of 1,313 Gangs in Chicago* (Chicago: University of Chicago Press, 1927).

50. Malcolm Klein, ed., *Juvenile Gangs in Context* (Englewood Cliffs, NJ: Prentice-Hall, 1967), pp. 1–12.

51. Ibid., p. 6.

52. Irving Spergel, *Street Gang Work: Theory and Practice* (Reading, MA: Addison-Wesley, 1966).

53. Miller, *Violence by Youth Gangs*, p. 2.

54. Marjorie Zatz, "*Los Cholos:* Legal Processing of Chicago Gang Members," *Social Problems* 33:13–30 (1985).

55. Miller, *Violence by Youth Gangs*, pp. 1–2.

56. Ibid.

57. "LA Gang Warfare Called Bloodiest in 5 Years," *Boston Globe*, December 18, 1986, p. A4.

58. John Hagedorn, *People and Folks: Gangs, Crime and the Underclass in a Rustbelt City* (Chicago: Lake View Press, 1988).

59. National School Safety Center, *Gangs in Schools, Breaking Up Is Hard to Do* (Malibu, CA: Pepperdine University, 1988), p. 8. Hereinafter cited as *Gangs in Schools*.

60. C. Ronald Huff, "Youth Gangs and Public Policy," *Crime and Delinquency* 35:524–537 (1989).

61. Miller, *Violence by Youth Gangs*; Miller, *Crime by Youth Gangs and Groups in the United States* (Washington, DC: Office of Juvenile Justice Delinquency Prevention, 1982).

62. Joan Moore, *Going Down to the Barrio: Homeboys and Homegirls in Change* (Philadelphia: Temple University Press, 1991), p. 3.

63. Richard McCorkle and Terance Miethe, "The Political and Organizational Response to Gangs: An Examination of a 'Moral Panic' in Nevada," *Justice Quarterly* 15(9):41–64 (1998).

64. Arlen Egley, Jr., and Aline Major, *Highlights of the 2002 National Youth Gang Survey* (Washington, DC: Office of Juvenile Justice and Delinquency Prevention, 2004); for more, see Walter Miller, *The Growth of the Youth Gang Problem in the United States, 1970–1998* (Washington, DC: Office of Juvenile Justice and Delinquency Prevention, 2001).

65. Egley and Major, *Highlights of the 2002 National Youth Gang Survey.*

66. Arlen Egley, Jr., and Mehala Arjunan, *Highlights of the 2000 National Youth Gang Survey* (Washington, DC: Office of Juvenile Justice and Delinquency Prevention, 2002).

67. Irving Spergel, *Youth Gangs: Problem and Response* (Chicago: University of Chicago, School of Social Service Administration, 1989).

68. Felix Padilla, *The Gang as an American Enterprise* (New Brunswick, NJ: Rutgers University Press, 1992), p. 3.

69. Pamela Irving Jackson, "Crime, Youth Gangs, and Urban Transition: The Social Dislocations of Postindustrial Economic Development," *Justice Quarterly* 8:379–397 (1991).

70. Moore, *Going Down to the Barrio*, pp. 89–101.

71. Walter B. Miller, *The Growth of Youth Gang Problems in the United States.*

72. Jeffery Fagan, "The Social Organization of Drug Use and Drug Dealing among Urban Gangs," *Criminology* 27:633–669 (1989).

73. Richard Cloward and Lloyd Ohlin, *Delinquency and Opportunity* (New York: Free Press), pp. 1–12.

74. Fagan, "The Social Organization of Drug Use and Drug Dealing among Urban Gangs."

75. Huff, "Youth Gangs and Public Policy," pp. 528–529.

76. Carl Taylor, *Dangerous Society* (East Lansing: Michigan State University Press, 1990).

77. Cheryl Maxson, "Investigating Gang Structures," *Journal of Gang Research* 3:33–40 (1995).

78. Personal communication with Malcolm Klein, December 12, 1995.

79. Scott Decker, Tim Bynum, and Deborah Weisel, "A Tale of Two Cities: Gangs and Organized Crime Groups," *Justice Quarterly* 15:395–425 at 410 (1998).

80. Saul Bernstein, *Youth in the Streets: Work with Alienated Youth Gangs* (New York: Associated Press, 1964).

81. William Julius Wilson, *The Truly Disadvantaged* (Chicago: University of Chicago Press, 1987).

82. James Diego Vigil, *Barrio Gangs: Street Life and Identity in Southern California* (Austin: University of Texas Press, 1988).

83. Miller, *Violence by Youth Gangs*, pp. 17–20.

84. Ralph A. Weisheit and L. Edward Wells, "Youth Gangs in Rural America," *NIJ Journal* 251:1–6 (2004).

85. 1999 National Youth Gang Survey.

86. Cheryl Maxson, Kristi Woods, and Malcolm Klein, *Street Migration in the United States: Executive Summary* (Los Angeles: Center for the Study of Crime and Social Control, University of Southern California, 1995).

87. John Hagedorn, "Gangs, Neighborhoods and Public Policy," *Social Problems* 20:529–541 (1991).

88. Lawrence Rosenthal, "Gang Loitering and Race," *Journal of Criminal Law and Criminology*, 91:99–160 (2000).

89. *Gangs in Schools*, p. 7.

90. Warr, "Organization and Instigation in Delinquent Groups."

91. *Gang Prevention and Intervention*, p. vii.

92. Wilson, *The Truly Disadvantaged.*

93. 1999 Youth Gang Survey.

94. Wilson, *The Truly Disadvantaged.*

95. *Gangs in Schools*, p. 7.

96. John Hagedorn, Jerome Wonders, Angelo Vega, and Joan Moore, *The Milwaukee Drug Posse Study* (unpublished leaflet, undated).

97. Egley, *National Youth Gang Survey Trends from 1996 to 2000.*

98. Gary Jensen, "Defiance and Gang Identity: Quantitative Tests of Qualitative Hypothesis," paper presented at the American Society of Criminology meeting, Boston, November 1995.

99. Taylor, *Dangerous Society*, p. 109.

100. Finn-Aage Esbensen and David Huizinga, "Gangs, Drugs and Delinquency in a Survey of Urban Youth," *Criminology* 31:565–587 (1993).

101. Finn-Aage Esbensen, "Race and Gender Differences between Gang and Nongang Youths: Results from a Multisite Survey" *Justice Quarterly* 15:504–525 (1998).

102. G. David Curry, "Female Gang Involvement," *Journal of Research in Crime and Delinquency*, 35:100–119 (1998).

103. Cheryl Maxson and Monica Whitlock, "Joining the Gang: Gender Differences in Risk Factors for Gang Membership," in C. Ronald Huff, ed., *Gangs in America III* (Thousand Oaks, CA: Sage Publications 2002), pp. 19–35.

104. Mary Glazier, "Small Town Delinquent Gangs: Origins, Characteristics and Activities," paper presented at the American Society of Criminology meeting, Boston, November 1995.

105. Curry, "Female Gang Involvement."

106. Moore, *Going Down to the Barrio*; Anne Campbell, *The Girls in the Gang* (Cambridge, MA: Basil Blackwood, 1984).

107. Karen Joe and Meda Chesney-Lind, "'Just Every Mother's Angel': An Analysis of Gender and Ethnic Variations in Youth Gang Membership," *Gender and Society* 9:408–430 (1995).

108. Curry, "Female Gang Involvement."

109. Alan Turley, "Female Gangs and Patterns of Female Delinquency in Texas," *Journal of Gang Research* 10:1–12 (2003).

110. Jody Miller, *One of the Guys: Girls, Gangs and Gender* (New York, Oxford University Press, 2001).

111. Ibid.

112. Joan Moore, James Diego Vigil, and Robert Garcia, "Residence and Territoriality in Chicano Gangs," *Social Problems* 31:182–194 (1983).

113. William F. Whyte, *Street Corner Society* (Chicago: University of Chicago Press, 1955).

114. Malcolm Klein, "Impressions of Juvenile Gang Members," *Adolescence* 3:59 (1968).

115. Decker, Bynum, and Weisel, "A Tale of Two Cities."

116. Los Angeles County Sheriff's Department, *Street Gangs of Los Angeles County, White Paper* (Los Angeles: LACSD, n.d.), p. 14.

117. LeRoy Martin, *Collecting, Organizing and Reporting Street Gang Crime* (Chicago: Chicago Police Department, 1988).

118. Patricia Wen, "Boston Gangs: A Hard World," *Boston Globe*, May 10, 1988, p. 1.

119. Rick Graves and Ed Allen, *Black Gangs and Narcotics and Black Gangs* (Los Angeles: Los Angeles County Sheriff's Department, n.d.).

120. *Youth Gang Problem*, p. 3.

121. Terence Thornberry and James Burch, *Gang Members and Delinquent Behavior* (Washington, DC: Office of Juvenile Justice and Delinquency Prevention, 1997).

122. G. David Curry, Scott Decker, and Arlen Egley, Jr., "Gang Involvement and Delinquency in a Middle School Population," *Justice Quarterly* 19: 275–292 (2002).

123. Joseph Sheley, Joshua Zhang, Charles Brody, and James Wright, "Gang Organization, Gang Criminal Activity, and Individual Gang Members' Criminal Behavior," *Social Science Quarterly* 76:53–68 (1995).

124. Geoffrey Hunt; Karen Joe-Laidler, and Kristy Evans, "The Meaning and Gendered Culture of Getting High: Gang Girls and Drug Use Issues," *Contemporary Drug Problems* 29:375–415 (2002).

125. Kevin Thompson, David Brownfield, and Ann Marie Sorenson, "Specialization Patterns of Gang and Nongang Offending: A Latent Structure Analysis," *Journal of Gang Research* 3:25–35 (1996).

126. 1999 National Youth Gang Survey.

127. Thompson, Brownfield, and Sorenson, "Specialization Patterns of Gang and Nongang Offending."

128. Sara Battin, Karl Hill, Robert Abbott, Richard Catalano, and J. David Hawkins, "The Contribution of Gang Membership to Delinquency Beyond Delinquent Friends," *Criminology* 36:93–116 (1998).

129. Terence Thornberry and James Burch, *Gang Members and Delinquent Behavior* (Washington, DC: Office of Juvenile Justice and Delinquency Prevention, 1997).

130. Rachel Gordon, Benjamin Lahey, Eriko Kawai, Rolf Loeber, Magda Stouthamer-Loeber, and David Farrington, "Antisocial Behavior and Youth Gang Membership," *Criminology* 42:55–88 (2004).

131. Terence Thornberry, Marvin Krohn, Alan Lizotte, Carolyn Smith, and Kimberly Tobin, *Gangs and Delinquency in Developmental Perspective* (New York, NY: Cambridge University Press, 2003).

132. Alan Lizotte and David Sheppard, *Gun Use by Male Juveniles* (Washington, DC: Office of Juvenile Justice and Delinquency Prevention, 2001).

133. James C. Howell, "Youth Gang Drug Trafficking and Homicide: Policy and Program Implications," *Juvenile Justice Journal* 4:3–5 (1997).

134. Ibid.

135. Ibid.

136. Scott Decker, Susan Pennell, and Ami Caldwell, *Arrestees and Guns: Monitoring the Illegal Firearms Market* (Washington, DC: National Institute of Justice, 1996).

137. Scott Decker, "Collective and Normative Features of Gang Violence," *Justice Quarterly* 13:243–264 (1996).

138. Beth Bjerregaard and Alan Lizotte, "Gun Ownership and Gang Membership," *Journal of Criminal Law and Criminology* 86:37–53 (1995).

139. Pamela Lattimore, Richard Linster, and John MacDonald, "Risk of Death among Serious Young Offenders," *Journal of Research in Crime and Delinquency* 34:187–209 (1997).

140. Alan Lizotte and David Sheppard, *Gun Use by Male Juveniles* (Washington, DC: Office of Juvenile Justice and Delinquency Prevention, 2001).

141. Decker, "Collective and Normative Features of Gang Violence," p. 253.

142. H. Range Hutson, Deirdre Anglin, and Michale Pratts, Jr., "Adolescents and Children Injured or Killed in Drive-By Shootings in Los Angeles," *The New England Journal of Medicine* 330:324–327 (1994).

143. Gini Sykes, *8 Ball Chicks: A Year in the Violent World of Girl Gangsters* (New York: Doubleday, 1998), pp. 2–11.

144. *2001 Youth Gang Survey* (Washington, DC: Office of Juvenile Justice and Delinquency Prevention, 2001).

145. Miller, *Violence by Youth Gangs*, pp. 2–26.

146. Malcolm Klein, "Violence in American Juvenile Gangs," in Donald Muvihill, Melvin Tumin, and Lynn Curtis, eds., *Crimes of Violence, National Commission on the Causes and Prevention of Violence*, vol. 13 (Washington, DC: U.S. Government Printing Office, 1969), p. 1429.

147. Kevin Cullen, "Gangs Are Seen as Carefully Organized," *Boston Globe*, January 7, 1987, p. 17.

148. *National Assessment*, pp. 60–61.

149. The following description of ethnic gangs leans heavily on the material developed in *Gangs in Schools*, pp. 11–23.

150. *The Youth Gang Problem*, pp. 136–37.

151. Decker, Bynum, and Weisel, "A Tale of Two Cities."

152. Thomas Winfree, Jr., Frances Bernat, and Finn-Aage Esbensen, "Hispanic and Anglo Gang Membership in Two Southwestern Cities," *The Social Science Journal* 38:105–118 (2001).

153. See Joan Moore, "Isolation and Stigmatization in the Development of an Underclass: The Case of Chicano Gangs in East Los Angeles," *Social Problems* 33:1–12 (1985); Joan Moore, *Homeboys: Gangs, Drugs and Prison in the Barrios of Los Angeles* (Philadelphia: Temple University Press, 1979); Joan Moore, *Going Down to the Barrio: Homeboys and Homegirls in Change* (Philadelphia: Temple University Press, 1991); James Diego Vigil, *Barrio Gangs: Street Life and Identity in Southern California* (Austin: University of Texas Press, 1988); James Diego Vigil and John Long, "Emic and Etic Perspectives on Gang Culture: The Chicano Case," in C. Ronald Huff, ed., *Gangs in America* (Newbury Park, CA: Sage Publications, 1990), pp. 55–70; James Diego Vigil, "Cholos and Gangs: Culture Change and Street Youth in Los Angeles," in Huff, ed., *Gangs in America*, pp. 116–28.

154. D. A. Lopez and Patricia O'Donnell Brummett, "Gang Membership and Acculturation: ARSMA-II and Choloization," *Crime and Delinquency* 49:627–642 (2004).

155. Los Angeles County Sheriff's Department, *Street Gangs of Los Angeles County*.

156. Zheng Wang, Indiana University of Pennsylvania, personal communication, February 3, 1993.

157. Ko-Lin Chin, *Chinese Subculture and Criminality: Non-Traditional Crime Groups in America* (Westport, CO: Greenwood Press, 1990).

158. James Diego Vigil and Steve Chong Yun, "Vietnamese Youth Gangs in Southern California," in C. Ronald Huff, ed., *Gangs in America* (Newbury Park, CA: Sage Publications, 1990), pp. 146–63.

159. See Glazier, "Small Town Delinquent Gangs."

160. For a review, see Lawrence Trostle, *The Stoners, Drugs, Demons and Delinquency* (New York: Garland, 1992).

161. Esbensen, "Race and Gender Differences between Gang and Nongang Youths."

162. Herbert Block and Arthur Niederhoffer, *The Gang: A Study in Adolescent Behavior* (New York: Philosophical Library, 1958).

163. Ibid., p. 113.

164. *Gang Prevention and Intervention*, p. 44.

165. James Diego Vigil, "Group Processes and Street Identity: Adolescent Chicano Gang Members," *Ethos* 16:421–445 (1988).

166. Vigil and Long, "Emic and Etic Perspectives on Gang Culture: The Chicano Case," p. 66.

167. Albert Cohen, *Delinquent Boys* (New York: Free Press, 1955), pp. 1–19.

168. Irving Spergel, *Racketville, Slumtown, and Haulburg: An Exploratory Study of Delinquent Subcultures* (Chicago: University of Chicago Press, 1964).

169. Malcolm Klein, *Street Gangs and Street Workers* (Englewood Cliffs, NJ: Prentice-Hall, 1971), pp. 12–15.

170. Vigil, *Barrio Gangs*.

171. Vigil and Long, "Emic and Etic Perspectives on Gang Culture," p. 61.

172. David Brownfield, Kevin Thompson, and Ann Marie Sorenson, "Correlates of Gang Membership: A Test of Strain, Social Learning, and Social Control," *Journal of Gang Research* 4:11–22 (1997).

173. Carl Taylor, Richard Lerner, Alexander von Eye, Deborah Bobek, Aida Balsano, Elizabeth Dowling, and Pamela Anderson, "Positive Individual and Social Behavior among Gang and Nongang African American Male Adolescents," *Journal of Adolescent Research* 18:548–574 (2003).

174. John Hagedorn, Jose Torres, and Greg Giglio, "Cocaine, Kicks, and Strain: Patterns of Substance Use in Milwaukee Gangs," *Contemporary Drug Problems*, 25:113–145 (1998).

175. Spergel, *The Youth Gang Problem*, pp. 4–5.

176. Ibid.

177. Tom Hayden, *Street Wars: Gangs and the Future of Violence* (New York: New Press, 2004).

178. Lewis Yablonsky, *The Violent Gang* (Baltimore, MD: Penguin Books, 1984), p. 237.

179. Ibid., pp. 239–41.

180. Marc Le Blanc and Nadine Lanctot, "Social and Psychological Characteristics of Gang Members According to the Gang Structure and Its Subcultural and Ethnic Making," paper presented at the American Society of Criminology meeting, Miami, 1994.

181. Malcolm Klein, *The American Street Gang* (New York: Oxford, 1995).

182. Ibid., p. 163.

183. Christopher Thomas, Charles Holzer, and Julie Wall, "Serious Delinquency and Gang Membership," *Adolescent Psychiatry* 27:59–81 (2004).

184. Mercer Sullivan, *Getting Paid: Youth Crime and Work in the Inner City* (Ithaca, NY: Cornell University Press, 1989), pp. 244–45.

185. Esbensen and Huizinga, "Gangs, Drugs and Delinquency in a Survey of Urban Youth," p. 583; G. David Curry and Irving Spergel, "Gang Involvement and Delinquency among Hispanic and African American Adolescent Males," *Journal of Research in Crime and Delinquency* 29:273–291 (1992).

186. Padilla, *The Gang as an American Enterprise*, p. 103.

187. Martin Sanchez-Jankowski, *Islands in the Street: Gangs and American Urban Society* (Berkeley: University of California Press, 1991).

188. Jensen, "Defiance and Gang Identity: Quantitative Tests of Qualitative Hypothesis."

189. Terence Thornberry, Marvin Krohn, Alan Lizotte, and Deborah Chard-Wierschem, "The Role of Juvenile Gangs in Facilitating Delinquent Behavior," *Journal of Research in Crime and Delinquency* 30:55–87 (1993).

190. *The Youth Gang Problem*, pp. 93–94.

191. Miller, *One of the Guys: Girls, Gangs and Gender*.

192. Ibid., p. 93.

193. L. Thomas Winfree, Jr., Teresa Vigil Backstrom, and G. Larry Mays, "Social Learning Theory, Self-Reported Delinquency and Youth Gangs: A New Twist on a General Theory of Crime and Delinquency," *Youth and Society* 26:147–177 (1994).

194. Karen Joe Laidler and Geoffrey Hunt, "Violence and Social Organization in Female Gangs," *Social Justice* 24:148–187 (1997).

195. Needle and Stapleton, *Police Handling of Youth Gangs*, p. 19.

196. *National Assessment*, p. 65.

197. Scott Armstrong, "Los Angeles Seeks New Ways to Handle Gangs," *Christian Science Monitor*, April 23, 1988, p. 3.

198. Mark Moore and Mark A. R. Kleiman, *The Police and Drugs* (Washington, DC: National Institute of Justice, 1989), p. 8.

199. Barry Krisberg, "Preventing and Controlling Violent Youth Crime: The State of the Art," in Ira Schwartz, ed., *Violent Juvenile Crime* (Minneapolis: University of Minnesota, Hubert Humphrey Institute of Public Affairs, n.d.).

200. See Spergel, *Street Gang Work*.

201. For a revisionist view of gang delinquency, see Hedy Bookin-Weiner and Ruth Horowitz, "The End of the Youth Gang," *Criminology* 21:585–602 (1983).

202. Quint Thurman, Andrew Giacomazzi, Michael Reisig, and David Mueller, *Crime and Delinquency* 42:279–296 (1996).

203. Michael Agopian, "Evaluation of the Gang Alternative Prevention Program," paper presented at the American Society of Criminology meeting, Boston, November 1995.

204. Daniel Wood "As Gangs Rise, So Do Calls for U.S.-Wide Dragnet," *Christian Science Monitor* 96:2 (2004).

205. Jodi Lane and James Meeker, "Fear of Gang Crime: A Look at Three Theoretical Models," *Law and Society Review* 37:425–457 (2003).

206. James Houston, "What Works: The Search for Excellence in Gang Intervention Programs," paper presented at the American Society of Criminology meeting, Boston, November 1995.

207. Hagedorn, "Gangs, Neighborhoods and Public Policy."

208. Curry and Spergel, "Gang Involvement and Delinquency among Hispanic and African-American Adolescent Males."

Schools and Delinquency

9

Chapter Outline

The School in Modern American Society
Socialization and Status
Education in Crisis

Academic Performance and Delinquency
School Failure and Delinquency
The Causes of School Failure
School Climate

Delinquency within the School
FOCUS ON DELINQUENCY: Dropping Out
School Shootings
FOCUS ON DELINQUENCY: Bullying in School
The Community and School Crime
Reducing School Crime
Improving School Climate
POLICY AND PRACTICE: Safe Harbor: A School-Based
    Victim Assistance and Violence Prevention Program

Legal Rights within the School
Compulsory School Attendance
Free Speech
School Prayer
School Discipline
Privacy
JUVENILE LAW IN REVIEW: *Board of Education of
    Independent School District No. 92 of Pottawatomie
    County et al., v. Earls et al.*
Academic Privacy

The Role of the School in Delinquency Control Policy

Chapter Objectives

1. Be familiar with the crisis in the American education system
2. Be able to discuss the role education plays in the lives of contemporary youth
3. Know about the role education plays in socialization
4. Point to the linkages between the delinquent behavior of juveniles and their experiences within the educational system
5. Discuss the factors that influence school failure
6. Know the causes of student alienation from the educational experience
7. Discuss the dropout problem
8. Know what "bullying" means and how it can be prevented
9. Discuss how school administrators are attempting to eliminate school crime and prevent delinquency
10. Be familiar with legal rights within the school
11. Know about school-based delinquency prevention efforts

CNN. View the CNN video clip of this story and answer related Critical Thinking questions on your Juvenile Delinquency 9e CD-ROM.

Debra Beasley Lafave was a popular teacher at the Greco Middle School in Temple Terrace, Florida, a few miles north of Tampa. In 2004, she was charged with two counts of lewd and lascivious battery and one count of lewd and lascivious exhibition when the parents of a 14-year-old student told authorities that she had sex with the student in the back of her sport utility vehicle while the student's 15-year-old cousin drove them around the Ocala area. Lafave, 23, who had been married less than a year, was suspended pending investigation of the incident. At a bail hearing the judge reduced her bail from $15,000 to $5,000 after her attorney, Fred Vollrath, noted that she had no criminal history and had ties to the community. According to Florida statutes, if Lafave is convicted, each charge could bring up to 15 years in prison and a fine of up to $10,000.

While the Lafave incident is unusual, it is not unique. Students today are faced with many difficult choices. Some are the victims of school yard bullies; others are being placed in remedial academic tracks while others contemplate dropping out. The case also illustrates the varied and complex issues faced by school administrators. They must be able to address such questions as: What factors influence school climate? What can be done to improve education? How serious is the threat of school violence? School officials, whose interest and training may be focused on education and learning, must make daily decisions on discipline and crime prevention.

Because the schools are responsible for educating virtually everyone during most of their formative years and because so much of an adolescent's time is spent in school, some relationship would seem logical between delinquent behavior and what is happening—or not happening—in classrooms throughout the United States. This relationship was pointed out as early as 1939, when a study by the New Jersey Delinquency Commission found that of 2,021 inmates of prisons and correctional institutions in that state, two out of every five had first been committed for **truancy.**[1]

truancy
Staying out of school without permission.

academic achievement
Being successful in a school environment.

Numerous studies have confirmed that delinquency is related to **academic achievement,** and experts have concluded that many of the underlying problems of delinquency, as well as their prevention and control, are intimately connected with the nature and quality of the school experience. Research shows that school-related variables are among the most important contributing factors to delinquent behavior.[2] Although there are differences of opinion, most theorists agree that the educational system bears some responsibility for the high rate of juvenile crime.

This chapter examines the relationship between the school and delinquency. We first explore how educational achievement and delinquency are related and what factors in the school experience appear to contribute to delinquent behavior. Next, we turn to delinquency within the school setting itself—vandalism, theft, violence, and so on. Finally, we look at the educational system's attempts to prevent and control delinquency.

THE SCHOOL IN MODERN AMERICAN SOCIETY

The school plays a significant role in shaping the values and norms of American children.[3] In contrast to earlier periods, when formal education was a privilege of the upper classes, the American system of compulsory public education has made schooling a legal obligation. Today more than 90 percent of the school-age population attends school, compared with only 7 percent in 1890.[4] As Figure 9.1 shows, significantly more American citizens are finishing high school and going to college today than in the past. However, only about 25 of the population has earned a bachelor's and/or graduate degree (see Figure 9.2).

In contrast to the earlier, agrarian days of U.S. history, when most adolescents shared in the work of the family and became socialized into adulthood as part of the work force, today's young people, beginning as early as age 3 or 4, spend most of their time in school. The school has become the primary instrument of **socialization,** the "basic conduit through which the community and adult influences enter into the lives of adolescents."[5]

socialization
The process of learning the values and norms of the society or the subculture to which the individual belongs.

Because young people spend a longer time in school, the period of their adolescence is prolonged. As long as students are still economically dependent on their families and have not entered the work world, they are not considered adults, either in their own minds or in the estimation of the rest of society. The responsibilities of adulthood come later to modern-day youths than those in earlier generations, and some experts see this prolonged childhood as a factor that contributes to the irresponsible, childish, often irrational, behavior of many juveniles who commit delinquent acts.

Socialization and Status

Another significant aspect of the educational experience of American youths is that it is overwhelmingly a peer encounter. Children spend their school hours with their

FIGURE 9.1
Years of School Completed by Persons 25 to 29 Years of Age: 1940–2001

SOURCE: *1960 Census of Population,* Volume 1, part 1 (Washington, DC: U.S. Department of Commerce, Bureau of the Census); *Current Population Reports, Series P-20* (Washington, DC: U.S. Department of Commerce, Bureau of the Census, 2003); *Current Population Survey* (Washington, DC: Department of Labor, Bureau of Labor Statistics, Office of Employment and Unemployment Statistics, unpublished data, 2004).

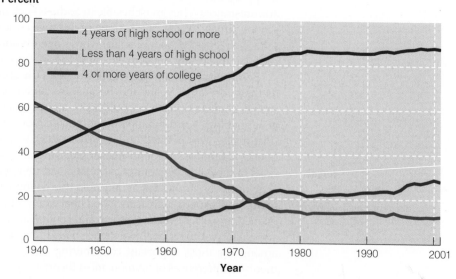

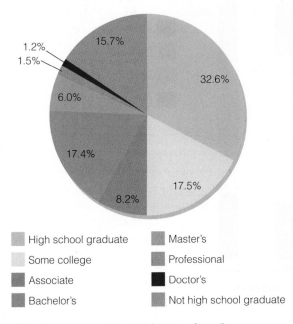

Total persons age 25 and over = 177.0 million

1.2%
1.5%
15.7%
32.6%
6.0%
17.4%
8.2%
17.5%

■ High school graduate   ■ Master's
□ Some college   ■ Professional
■ Associate   ■ Doctor's
■ Bachelor's   ■ Not high school graduate

NOTE: Detail may not add to totals because of rounding.

FIGURE 9.2

Highest Level of Education Attained by Persons 25 Years and Older: 2001

SOURCE: *Current Population Reports, Series P-20* (Washington, DC: U.S. Department of Commerce, Bureau of the Census, 2003); *Current Population Survey* (Washington, DC: Department of Labor, Bureau of Labor Statistics, Office of Employment and Unemployment Statistics, unpublished data, 2004).

peers, and most of their activities after school take place with school friends. Young people rely increasingly on school friends and consequently become less and less interested in adult role models. The norms and values of the peer culture are often at odds with those of adult society, and a pseudo-culture with a distinct social system develops, offering a united front to the adult world. Law-abiding behavior or conventional norms may not be among the values promoted in such an atmosphere. Youth culture may instead admire bravery, defiance, piercing and tattooing, and having fun much more.

In addition to its role as an instrument of socialization, the school has become a primary determinant of economic and social status in American society. In this highly technological age, education is the key to a job that will mark its holder as successful. No longer can parents ensure the status of their children through social-class origin alone. Educational achievement has become of equal, if not greater, importance as a determinant of economic success.

Schools, then, are geared toward success defined in terms of academic achievement, which provides the key to profit and position in society. Adolescents derive much of their identity out of what happens to them in school. Virtually all adolescents must participate in the educational system, not only because it is required by law but also because the notion of success is defined in terms of the possession of a technical or professional skill that can be acquired only through formal education.

The value of education is fostered by parents, the media, and the schools themselves. Regardless of their social or economic background, most children grow up believing that education is the key to success. Despite their apparent acceptance of the value of education, many youths do not meet acceptable standards of school achievement. Whether failure is measured by test scores, not being promoted, or dropping out, its incidence continues to be a major social problem of American society. A single school failure often leads to patterns of chronic academic failure. The links between school failures, academic and social aspirations, and delinquency will be explored more fully in the following sections.

Education in Crisis

The critical role schools play in adolescent development is underscored by the problems faced by the American education system. Budget cutting has severely reduced educational resources in many communities and curtailed state support for local school systems. As a result, the most recent government surveys indicate that improvement in educational achievement is a mixed bag. For example, while reading performance of eighth graders has improved over the past decade, that of fourth graders has not. As Figure 9.3 shows, the writing performance of fourth and eighth graders has improved during the past decade while twelfth graders have not shown similar progress.

Spending in the United States on elementary and secondary education (as a percent of the gross national product) trails that of many other nations. Though there has been some improvement in measured performance in reading, math, and science achievement during the past decade, the U.S. still lags many nations in key educational achievement measures. However, there are some encouraging signs: Fourth graders in the U.S. are better readers than children in most other nations, though they are no better than kids in some extremely poor nations such as Bulgaria and Latvia (see Table 9.1).

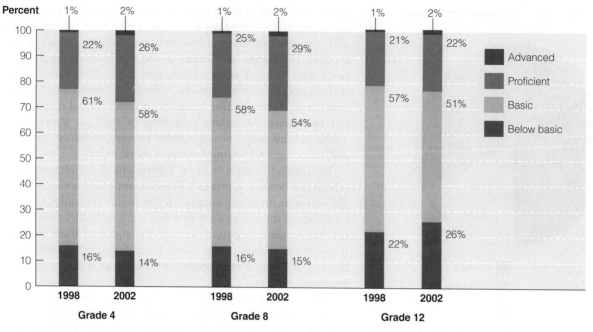

Percent

NOTE: Detail may not add to totals because of rounding.

FIGURE 9.3

Percentage Distribution of Students Performing at Each Writing Achievement Level, by Grade: 1998 and 2002

SOURCE: National Center for Education Statistics (Washington, DC: National Center for Education Statistics, Institute of Education Sciences, U.S. Department of Education).

TABLE 9.1

Average Score Relative to the United States	Average Combined Reading Literacy Scale Score of Fourth Graders, by Country, 2001					
	Country and Score					
Significantly higher	Sweden	561	Netherlands[1]	554	England[1]	553
Not significantly different	Bulgaria	550	Hungary	543	Italy	541
	Latvia	545	Lithuania[1]	543	Germany	539
	Canada[2]	544	United States	542	Czech Republic	537
Significantly lower	New Zealand	529	Iceland	512	Turkey	449
	Hong Kong SAR[3]	528	Romania	512	Macedonia, Republic of	442
	Russian Federation[1]	528	Israel[1]	509	Columbia	422
	Scotland[1]	528	Slovenia	502	Argentina	420
	Singapore	528	International average	500	Iran, Islamic Republic of	414
	France	525	Norway	499	Kuwait	396
	Greece[1]	524	Cyprus	494	Morocco[1]	350
	Slovak Republic	518	Moldova, Republic of	492	Belize	327

NOTES:

[1]Country did not meet the international sampling and/or other guidelines.

[2]Canada is represented by the provinces of Ontario and Quebec only.

[3]Hong Kong SAR is a Special Administrative Region (SAR) of the People's Republic of China.

The target population was the upper of the two adjacent grades with the most 9-year-olds. In most countries, this was fourth grade. The international average (500) is the weighted average of the national averages of the 35 countries, with a standard deviation of 100.

SOURCE: I. V. S. Mullis, M. O. Martin, E. J. Gonzalez, and A. M. Kennedy. *PIRLS 2001 International Report: IEA's Study of Reading Literacy Achievement in Primary Schools in 35 Countries,* exhibit 1.1 (2003). Data from the International Association for the Evaluation of Educational Achievement (IEA), Progress in International Reading Literacy Study, 2001. Online at http://nces.ed.gov/programs/coe/2003/section2/indicator10.asp#info (accessed on September 20, 2004).

© AP/Wide World Photos

Budget cutting has severely reduced educational resources in many communities and curtailed state support for local school systems. Some systems are finding it difficult to recruit qualified teachers. Some districts now employ dedicated people who lack the proper qualifications, such as Xochitl Rodriguez, shown here, handing back homework to her students in Sepulveda, California. Rodriguez left her job in human services and was hired by the school district, even though she lacked experience and had not taken teaching courses. In this case, dedication and hard work have been a plus for the district.

To get more educational data, go to the **NCES website** at http://nces.ed.gov/. For an up-to-date list of web links, go to http://cj.wadsworth.com/siegel_jd9e.

TO QUIZ YOURSELF ON THIS MATERIAL, go to the Juvenile Delinquency 9e website.

Recognizing the need to improve school performance, the U.S. government implemented the No Child Left Behind Act in 2001. The NCLB requires states to implement accountability systems covering all public schools and students. These systems are designed to improve state standards in reading and mathematics, create annual testing for all students in grades 3 through 8, and mandate annual statewide progress objectives ensuring that all students reach proficiency within 12 years. School districts and schools that fail to make adequate yearly progress (AYP) toward statewide proficiency goals will be required to restructure their learning measures in order to get them back on course to meet state standards. Schools that meet or exceed AYP objectives or close achievement gaps will be eligible for State Academic Achievement Awards.

ACADEMIC PERFORMANCE AND DELINQUENCY

The general path towards occupational prestige is education, and when youth are deprived of this avenue of success through poor school performance there is a greater likelihood of delinquent behavior.[6]

underachievers
Those who do not achieve success in school at the level of their expectations.

school failure
Failing to achieve success in school can result in frustration, anger, and reduced self-esteem, which may contribute to delinquent behavior.

Poor academic performance has been directly linked to delinquent behavior: There is general consensus that students who are chronic **underachievers** in school are also among the most likely to be delinquent.[7] In fact, researchers commonly find that **school failure** is a stronger predictor of delinquency than such personal variables as economic class membership, racial or ethnic background, or peer group relations. Studies that compare the academic records of delinquents and nondelinquents, including their scores on standardized tests of basic skills, failure rate, teacher ratings, and other academic measures, have found that delinquents are often academically deficient, a condition that may lead to their leaving school and becoming involved in antisocial activities. Kids who report that they do not like school, do not do well in school, and do not concentrate on their homework are also the ones most likely to self-report delinquent acts.[8] In contrast, at-risk kids, even those with histories of abuse and neglect, who do well in school are often able to avoid delinquent involvement.[9]

The academic failure–delinquency association is commonly found among chronic offenders. Those leaving school without a diploma were significantly more likely to become involved in chronic delinquency than graduates.[10] Only 9 percent of the chronic offenders in Wolfgang's Philadelphia cohort graduated from high school, compared with 74 percent of nonoffenders.[11] Chronic offenders also had significantly more disciplinary actions and remedial/disciplinary placements than nonoffenders.[12]

The relationship between school achievement and persistent offending is supported by surveys of prison inmates that indicate that only 40 percent of incarcerated felons had twelve or more years of education, compared with about 80 percent of the general population.[13]

School Failure and Delinquency

While there is general agreement that school failure and delinquency are related, some question exists over the nature and direction the relationship takes. One view is that the school experience is a *direct cause* of delinquent behavior. Children who fail at school soon feel frustrated, angry, and rejected. Believing they will never achieve success through conventional means, they seek out like-minded companions and together engage in antisocial behaviors. Educational failure, beginning early in the life course, evokes negative responses from important people in the child's life, including teachers, parents, and perspective employers. These reactions help solidify feelings of social inadequacy and, in some cases, lead the underachieving student into a pattern of chronic delinquency.

A second view is that school failure leads to psychological and behavioral dysfunction, which is the actual cause of antisocial behavior. For example, academic failure helps reduce self-esteem; studies using a variety of measures of academic competence and self-esteem clearly demonstrate that good students have a better attitude about themselves than do poor students.[14] Reduced self-esteem has also been found to contribute to delinquent behavior.[15] The association then runs from school failure to low self-concept to delinquency. The school failure–delinquency association may be mediated then by efforts to stabilize or improve the self-image of academically challenged children.

A third view is that school failure and delinquency share a *common cause*; they are all part of the problem behavior syndrome (PBS). It would be therefore erroneous to conclude that school failure *precedes* antisocial behavior. The research evidence that the association between school failure and delinquency is a function of a PBS includes the issues described in Exhibit 9.1.[16]

To read more about the **school failure–delinquency link,** go to www.juvjustice.org/publications/jjmonitor/5-4-007.html. For an up-to-date list of web links, go to http://cj.wadsworth.com/siegel_jd9e.

The Causes of School Failure

While disagreement still exists over the direction the relationship takes, there is little argument that delinquent behavior is linked to a child's educational experiences. A number of factors have been linked to the onset of school failure; the most prominent are discussed in some detail on the following page.

EXHIBIT 9.1

The Correlates of School Failure

I Delinquents may have lower IQs than nondelinquents, a factor that might also explain their poor academic achievement.

I Delinquent behavior has also been associated with a turbulent family life, a condition that most likely leads to academic underachievement.

I Delinquency has been associated with low self-control and impulsivity, traits that also may produce school failure.

I The adolescent who both fails at school and engages in delinquency may be experiencing drug use, depression, malnutrition, abuse, and disease, all symptoms of a generally troubled lifestyle.

SOURCE: J. D. McKinney, "Longitudinal Research on the Behavioral Characteristics of Children with Learning Disabilities," *Journal of Learning Disabilities* 22:141–150 (1998).

To read about **teaching strategies designed to help kids with attention disorders,** go to www.ldonline. org/ld_indepth/teaching_techniques/ adhd_strategies.html. For an up-to-date list of web links, go to http://cj.wadsworth.com/ siegel_jd9e.

Attention Problems and School Failure Research shows a linkage between school failure and attention. Kids with attention problems may find it not only difficult to concentrate in class, but their condition may also impede efforts to help their academic advancement, such as tutoring programs.[17] Between 25 percent and 40 percent of kids who manifest attention problems typically suffer reading disabilities, a critical factor in determining academic performance.[18]

Social Class and School Failure During the 1950s, Albert Cohen referred to the failure of lower-class kids to live up to "middle-class measuring rods" as a significant cause of delinquency.[19] These views have been supported by the greater than average retention and dropout rates among lower class children.

Recent surveys by the National Center for Educational Statistics show that as the number of family socioeconomic risk factors (household below poverty level, non-English primary home language, mother's highest education less than a high school diploma/GED, and single-parent household) increase, school achievement declines. As economic status declines, kids may be forced to take part-time jobs to help support the family. Working while in school seems to lower commitment to educational achievement and is associated with higher levels of delinquent behavior.[20] Some theorists contend that the high incidence of failure among lower-class youths is actually fostered by the schools themselves.[21] Kids from an impoverished background often find that the school experience can be a frightening one in which constant testing and the threat of failure are clear and ever-present dangers.[22] Research data confirm not only that such children begin school at lower levels of achievement but also that without help, their performance progressively deteriorates the longer they are in school. If this is true, the school itself becomes an active force in the generation of delinquency insofar as it is linked to failure.[23]

Not all experts, however, agree with the social class–school failure–delinquency hypothesis. There is evidence that affluent students are equally or even more deeply affected by school failure than lower-class kids and that middle-class youths who did poorly in school were actually more likely to become delinquent than their lower-class peers.[24] Referred to as the *disadvantage-saturation thesis,* this view suggests that poor youth are faced with so many social deficits that school failure and/or delinquency has less of an impact on them than it has on their overachieving middle-class peers. Because lower-class youth are significantly less likely to indicate that getting good grades or going to college is important, they most likely feel less pressure to perform well and less strain if they fail.[25] School failure may cause more damage to more affluent youth when their limited ability conflicts with their overinflated expectations (a finding which jibes with Agnew's General Strain theory; see Chapter 4).[26]

Tracking

Placement in noncollege tracks of the contemporary high school means consignment to an educational oblivion without apparent purpose or meaning.[27]

tracking
Dividing students into groups according to their ability and achievement levels.

Most researchers have looked at academic **tracking**—dividing the students into groups according to ability and achievement level—as a contributor to delinquency.[28] Studies overwhelmingly indicate that, compared with those in college tracks, non-college preparatory students experience greater academic failure and progressive deterioration of achievement, participate less frequently in extracurricular activities, have an increased tendency to drop out, engage in more frequent misbehavior in school, and commit more delinquent acts. These differences are at least partially caused by assignment to a low academic track, whereby the student is effectively locked out of a chance to achieve educational success. Some effects of tracking as it relates to delinquency are illustrated in Exhibit 9.2.[29]

Some school officials begin stereotyping and tracking students in the lowest grade levels.[30] Educators separate youths into special groups that have innocuous names (e.g., "special enrichment program") but may carry with them the taint of failure and academic incompetence. Junior and senior high school students may be tracked within

EXHIBIT **9.2**

The Effects of Tracking

I **Self-fulfilling prophecy:** Low-track students, from whom little achievement and more misbehavior are expected, tend to live up to these often unspoken assumptions about their behavior.

I **Stigma:** The labeling effect of placement in a low track leads to loss of self-esteem, which increases the potential for academic failure and troublemaking both in and out of school.

I **Student subculture:** Students segregated in lower tracks develop a value system that often rewards misbehavior, rather than the academic success they feel they can never achieve.

I **Teacher effectiveness:** Teachers of high-ability students make more of an effort to teach in an interesting and challenging manner than those who instruct lower-level students.

I **Future rewards:** Low-track students are less inclined to conform. Because they see no future rewards for their schooling, their futures are not threatened by a record of deviance or low academic achievement.

I **Grading policies:** Low-track students tend to receive lower grades than other students, even for work of equal quality, based on the rationale that students who are not college-bound are "obviously" less bright and do not need good grades to get into college.

self-fulfilling prophecy
Deviant behavior patterns that are a response to an earlier labeling experience; youths act out these social roles even if they were falsely bestowed.

student subculture
The independent, self-contained high school culture that controls the behavior and attitudes of American youth.

individual subjects based on their perceived ability. Classes may be labeled in descending order, such as advanced placement, academically enriched, average, basic, and remedial. It is common for students to have all their courses in only one or two tracks.[31]

The effects of negative school labels (for example, "failure," "slow," or "special needs") accumulate over time. Thus, if a student fails academically, this often means that he or she is probably destined to fail again. Over time, the repeated instances of failure can help to produce the career of the misfit, delinquent, or **dropout.**[32] Consequently, a tracking system keeps certain students from having any hope of achieving academic success, thereby causing a lack of motivation, failure, and rebellion, all of which may foster delinquent behavior.[33]

dropouts
Youths who leave school before completing their required program of education.

Another disturbing outcome of tracking is that students are often **stigmatized** as academically backward if they voluntarily attend a program or institution designed to help underachievers.[34] Teachers consider remedial reading programs to be dumping grounds for youths with a bad attitude; consequently, they expect youths who attended special-education programs to be disruptive in the classroom.[35] Those who oppose tracking also believe it retards the academic progress of many students, especially those in average and low groups.[36] Tracking may lead to lower self-esteem, school misbehavior, and dropping out. Tracking also appears to lower the aspirations of students who are not in the top groups. And perhaps most important is that tracking separates students along socioeconomic lines, separating rich from poor, whites from minorities: Research shows that as tracks become more defined, interracial friendships decline.[37]

stigmatized
People who have been negatively labeled because of their participation, or alleged participation, in deviant or outlawed behaviors.

The end result is that poor and minority children are found far more often than others in the bottom tracks and as a result, are likely to suffer far more negative consequences of schooling than are their more fortunate peers.

For a **detailed analysis of tracking,** go to www. edexcellence.net/foundation/ publication/publication.cfm?id=127. For an up-to-date list of web links, go to http://cj.wadsworth.com/siegel_jd9e.

School Climate

School climate has also been related to school failure.[38] While it is difficult to define "school climate," the term generally refers to a broad range of concepts that include the culture of the school, how the school is structured and administered, its design, and its rule structure. Schools with a positive culture will maintain unwritten rules of conduct that encourage communication between students and also with faculty and administration. The schools' norms should discourage negative actions such as bullying and discrimination. Rules are fair and clearly written and disseminated to students.

Positive climate is enhanced by administrations that are sensitive to student needs. This can be manifested in curriculum designed to provide a relevant classroom experience—for example, English courses that include multicultural literature and/or

EXHIBIT 9.3

Sources of Student Alienation

- **School size:** Schools are getting larger because smaller school districts have been consolidated into multi-jurisdictional district schools. In 1900, there were 150,000 school districts; today there are approximately 16,000. Larger schools are often impersonal, and relatively few students can find avenues for meaningful participation. Teachers and other school personnel do not have the opportunity to deal with early indications of academic or behavior problems and thus act to prevent delinquency.

- **Irrelevant curriculum:** Some students may be unable to see the relevance or significance of what they are taught in school. The gap between their education and the real world leads them to feel that the school experience is little more than a waste of time.

- **Lack of payoff:** Many students, particularly those from low-income families, believe that school has no payoff in terms of their future. Because the legitimate channel of education appears to be meaningless, illegitimate alternatives become increasingly more attractive for students who did not plan to attend college or to use their high school educations directly in their careers.

- **Middle- and upper-class bias:** The preeminent role of the college preparatory curriculum and the second-class position of vocational and technical programs in many school systems alienates some lower-class students. Furthermore, methods of instruction as well as curriculum materials reflect middle-class mores, language, and customs and have little meaning for the disadvantaged child.

technology courses that include Internet web page design. Schools that can offer relevant courses with reasonable student-teacher ratios will produce a more positive culture than those that ignore such critical needs.

School climate has been found to be a critical determinate of delinquency within the schools.[39] Both boys and girls who perceive a positive school climate are less likely to manifest psychological and behavioral problems than those who fail to share such positive perceptions.[40] Even schools located in high crime areas report relatively less crime when they maintain a positive and supportive climate. School stability then may help neutralize the delinquency-producing effect of neighborhood disorganization and high crime rates.

Student Alienation Schools that do not maintain a positive school climate are at risk for producing large numbers of cynical, alienated students who report they neither like school nor care about their teachers' opinions. In contrast, kids who like school and report greater involvement in school activities also are less likely to engage in delinquent behaviors.[41] Commitment to school coupled with the belief that their school is being fairly run and that school rules are being consistently applied helps kids resist criminality.[42] Attachment to teachers also helps insulate high-risk adolescents from delinquency.[43] Some of the suspected causes of **alienation** are listed in Exhibit 9.3.

Alienated students attending isolated, impersonal schools that have curriculums irrelevant to their needs may want to drop out, a step that may make them even more prone to antisocial behaviors, as can be seen in the Focus on Delinquency box entitled "Dropping Out."

alienation
Feelings of separation and distance from mainstream society.

TO QUIZ YOURSELF ON THIS MATERIAL, go to the Juvenile Delinquency 9e website.

DELINQUENCY WITHIN THE SCHOOL

The nation was shocked when on March 24, 1998, a 13-year-old boy, who had vowed to kill all the girls who had broken up with him, and his 11-year-old cousin, opened fire on students outside a middle school in Jonesboro, Arkansas, killing four girls and a teacher and wounding 11 other people.[44] The Jonesboro killings were premeditated murder: The two boys, dressed in camouflage clothing, apparently lay in wait in a wooded area near the school after setting off a fire alarm, forcing students and faculty members outside. There have been similar multiple school shootings in the past few years, including well-publicized ones in West Paducah, Kentucky, and Littleton, Colorado (see Exhibit 9.4 on page 284). How is it possible that students so young have access to guns and feel free to carry them in school? These terrible incidents may be occurring because it is now

Dropping Out

Though dropout rates are in decline, more than 10 percent of Americans aged 16 to 24 have left school permanently without a diploma; of these, more than 1 million withdrew before completing 10th grade. According to a recent report by the non-profit Urban Institute, the national graduation rate is 68 percent, with nearly one-third of all public high school students failing to graduate. Among the report's most important findings:

I Tremendous racial gaps are found for graduation rates.

I Students from historically disadvantaged minority groups (American Indian, Hispanic, African American) have little more than a 50-50 chance of finishing high school with a diploma.

I By comparison, graduation rates for whites and Asians are 75 and 77 percent nationally.

I Males graduate from high school at a rate 8 percent lower than female students.

I Graduation rates for students who attend school in high-poverty, racially segregated, and urban school districts lag from 15 to 18 percent behind their peers.

I A great deal of variation in graduation rates and gaps among student groups is found across regions of the country as well as the states.

Dropping out is a serious issue, because once kids leave school they are more likely to engage in drug abuse and anti-social behavior and to persist in criminal behavior throughout adulthood. For example, national surveys of substance-abuse levels among people who had been arrested by police find that juvenile arrestees who no longer attended school were more likely to abuse drugs than those who did attend school. Data from Phoenix, Arizona, show that 70 percent of male arrestees who had dropped out tested positively for drugs as compared to 57 percent who were still in school. Among females, 70 percent of arrestees who had dropped out tested positive as compared to 36 percent who were still in school.

WHY DO KIDS DROP OUT?

When surveyed, most dropouts say they left either because they did not like school or because they wanted to get a job. Others could not get along with teachers, had been expelled, or were under suspension. Almost half of all female dropouts left school because they were pregnant or had already given birth.

Poverty and family dysfunction increase the chances of dropping out among all racial and ethnic groups. Dropouts are more likely than graduates to have lived in single-parent families headed by parents who were educational underachievers.

Some youths have no choice but to drop out. They are pushed out of school because they lack attention or have poor attendance records. Teachers label them troublemakers, and school administrators use suspensions, transfers, and other means to "convince" them that leaving school is their only option. Because minority students often come from circumstances that interfere with their attendance, they are more likely to be labeled disobedient.

RACE AND DROPPING OUT

Race-based disciplinary practices may help sustain high minority dropout rates. Although the African American dropout rate has declined faster than the white dropout rate over the past two decades, minority students still drop out at a high rate. About 14 percent of African Americans aged 16 to 24 are dropouts; the Hispanic dropout rate for this age group is 29 percent.

In his thoughtful book *Creating the Dropout,* Sherman Dorn shows that graduation rates slowly but steadily rose during the twentieth century and that regional, racial, and ethnic differences in graduation rates declined. Nonetheless, Dorn argues that the relatively high dropout rate among minorities is the legacy of disciplinary policies instituted more than 40 years ago when educational administrators opposed to school desegregation employed a policy of race-based suspension and expulsion directed at convincing minority students to leave previously all-white high school districts. The legacy of these policies still infects contemporary school districts. Dorn believes that the dropout problem is a function of inequality of educational opportunity rather than the failure of individual students. The proportion of blacks who fail to graduate from high school remains high compared to the proportion of whites failing to graduate

commonplace for students to carry weapons in school. Research efforts have shown that students most likely to own guns and bring them to school are the ones who have engaged in other forms of deviant behavior, including selling drugs, assault, and battery.[45] Nor is the presence of weapons and violence lost on the average student. Data from a recent (2004) survey of high school students in Brownsville, Texas, found that almost half reported having seen other students carry knives at school, roughly 1 in 10 reported having seen other students carry guns at school, and more than 1 in 5 reported being fearful of weapon-associated victimization at school.[46]

Attention was first brought to focus on school crime in school when, more than 20 years ago, the federal government published its pioneering study of the school system, *Violent Schools—Safe Schools* (1977).[47] This survey found that although teenagers spend only 25 percent of their time in school, 40 percent of the robberies and 36 percent of the physical attacks involving this age group occur there.

because the educational system still fails to provide minority group members with the services and support they need.

NOT ALL DROPOUTS ARE EQUAL

The reasons students choose to drop out may have a significant impact on their future law violations. Research by Roger Jarjoura shows that youths who left school because of problems at home, for financial reasons, or because of poor grades were unlikely to increase their delinquent activity after leaving school. In contrast, those who dropped out to get married or because of pregnancy were more likely to increase their violent activities; this pattern may be linked to abuse. Those who were expelled did not increase their violent activity but were more likely to engage in theft and drug abuse.

Leaving school, then, is not a cause of misconduct per se, but youths with a history of misconduct in school often continue their antisocial behavior after dropping out. Dropouts engaged in more antisocial activity than graduates, but the reason youths dropped out influenced their offending patterns.

DROPPING OUT AND SCHOOL POLICY

This debate has serious implications for educational policy. Evidence that delinquency rates decline after students leave school has caused some educators to question the wisdom of compulsory education. Some experts, such as Jackson Toby, argue that the effort to force teenagers to stay in school is counterproductive and that delinquency might be lessened by allowing them to assume a productive position in the workforce. For many youths, leaving school can have the effect of escape from a stressful situation. Toby proposes a radical solution: Make high schools voluntary, and require students to justify the expenses allocated for their education.

Critical Thinking

1. Do you believe that efforts to keep children in school, provide tutoring, and create programs conducive to educational achievement should be continued to lower both dropout and delinquency rates or would the money be better spent on motivated students?

2. Do you believe that a free high school education is a privilege that must be earned and therefore unmotivated and/or disruptive students should be asked to leave school before graduation?

InfoTrac College Edition Research

Is it possible that school climate is the cause behind both school failure and the likelihood that some students will drop out? To research this topic, use "school climate" as a subject guide on InfoTrac College Edition.

SOURCES: Christopher B. Swanson, *Who Graduates? Who Doesn't? A Statistical Portrait of Public High School Graduation, Class of 2001* (Washington, DC: Urban Institute, 2004); National Center for Education Statistics, *Drop Out Rates in the United States* (Washington, DC, 2000); Terence Thornberry, Melanie Moore, and R. L. Christenson, "The Effect of Dropping Out of High School on Subsequent Criminal Behavior," *Criminology* 23:3–18 (1985); Marvin Krohn, Terence Thornberry, Lori Collins-Hall, and Alan Lizotte, "School Dropout, Delinquent Behavior, and Drug Use," in Howard Kaplan, ed., *Drugs, Crime, and other Deviant Adaptations: Longitudinal Studies* (New York: Plenum Press, 1995), pp. 163–183; ADAM, *1999 Annual Report on Drug Use Among Adult and Juvenile Arrestees* (Washington, DC: United States Government Printing Office, 2000); Howard Snyder and Melissa Sickmund, *Juvenile Offenders and Victims: A National Report* (Washington, DC: Office of Juvenile Justice and Delinquency Prevention, 1995), p. 15; Jay Teachman, Kathleen Paasch, and Karen Carver, "Social Capital and the Generation of Human Capital," *Social Forces* 75:1343–1360 (1997); Michel Janosz, Marc Le Blanc, Bernard Boulerice, and Richard Tremblay, *What Information Is Really Needed to Predict School Dropout? A Replication on Two Longitudinal Samples* (University of Montreal, School of Psychoeducation, 1995); Christine Bowditch, "Getting Rid of Troublemakers: High School Disciplinary Procedures and the Production of Dropouts," *Social Problems* 40:493–508 (1993); Sherman Dorn, *Creating the Dropout* (New York: Praeger, 1996); G. Roger Jarjoura, "Does Dropping Out of School Enhance Delinquent Involvement? Results from a Large-Scale National Probability Sample," *Criminology* 31:149–172 (1993); Jackson Toby, "Getting Serious about School Discipline," *The Public Interest* 133:68–74 (1998).

The federal government has continued to conduct national surveys on school crime and violence. Each year the School Survey on Crime and Safety uses a variety of data sources, including surveys of public school principals, to compile information on the number and seriousness of school crimes.[48] The latest survey (2003) estimates that about 1.5 million violent incidents occur in public elementary and secondary schools each year. Few schools are immune: More than 70 percent of public schools experienced one or more violent incidents, and 36 percent of schools reported one or more such incidents to the police. Twenty percent of schools experienced one or more serious violent incidents, including rape and armed robbery; almost half of all public schools experienced one or more thefts. These translate into an estimated 61,000 serious violent incidents and 218,000 thefts at public schools each year. About 15 percent of public schools reported one or more serious violent incidents to the police and 28 percent reported one or more thefts to the police.

EXHIBIT 9.4

Recent School Shootings

▌ **February 2, 2004.** James Richardson, aged 17, was shot to death in Ballou Senior High School in Washington, D.C. The shooting resulted from a confrontation with another student, who was arrested.

▌ **September 24, 2003.** John Jason McLaughlin, aged 15, killed one student and wounded another at Rocori High School in Cold Spring, Minnesota.

▌ **April 14, 2003.** In a gang-related shooting, one 15-year-old was killed and three students were wounded at John McDonogh High School in New Orleans, Louisiana, by gunfire from four teenagers (none were students at the school).

▌ **March 5, 2001.** A student in Santee, California, an alleged victim of schoolyard bullies, killed two students.

▌ **February 29, 2000.** A first-grader in Michigan shot and killed a fellow student, a 6-year-old girl with whom he had quarreled.

▌ **May 20, 1999.** A 15-year-old, upset over a broken romance, opened fire at Heritage High School in Conyers, Georgia, injuring six students.

▌ **April 20, 1999.** Two young men killed 13 students and injured 20 others before committing suicide at Columbine High School in Colorado.

▌ **April 16, 1999.** A high school sophomore fired two shotgun blasts in a school hallway in Notus, Idaho.

▌ **May 21, 1998.** Two teenagers were fatally shot and more than 20 people hurt when a 15-year-old boy allegedly opened fire at a high school in Springfield, Oregon. His parents were found slain at their home.

▌ **May 19, 1998.** Three days before his graduation, an 18-year-old honor student allegedly opened fire in a parking lot at a high school in Fayetteville, Tennessee, killing a classmate who was dating his ex-girlfriend.

▌ **April 24, 1998.** A science teacher was shot to death in front of students at the eighth-grade graduation dance in Edinboro, Pennsylvania.

To access the **school crime survey,** go to http://nces. ed.gov/pubsearch/pubsinfo. asp?pubid=2004004. For an up-to-date list of web links, go to http://cj.wadsworth.com/ siegel_jd9e.

School level and size of the school have a significant impact on the likelihood of experiencing theft and violence. Secondary schools were more likely to have a violent incident than elementary, middle, or combined schools. Likewise, larger schools were more likely to have a violent incident and report one or more violent incidents to the police than smaller schools. About 90 percent of all schools with 1,000 students or more had a violent incident, compared with 60 percent of schools with fewer than 300 students. School location also seems to have a significant influence on school crime. Urban schools were more likely than suburban and rural schools to experience crime or report it to the police.

One of the more disturbing aspects of school crime is bullying. Because this issue of bullying is so important, it is the topic of the Focus on Delinquency box entitled "Bullying in School."

School Shootings

Though incidents of school-based crime and violence are not uncommon, it is the highly publicized incidents of fatal school shootings that have helped focus attention on school crime. Upwards of 10 percent of students report bringing weapons to school on a regular basis. Many of these kids have a history of being abused and bullied; many perceive a lack of support from peers, parents, and teachers.[49] Kids who have been the victims of crime themselves and who hang with peers who carry weapons are the ones most likely to bring guns to school.[50] Troubled kids who have little social support but carry deadly weapons make for an explosive situation.

Nature and Extent of Shootings Social scientists are now conducting studies of these events in order to determine their trends and patterns. One study examined all school-related shootings occurring between July 1, 1994, through June 30, 1999.[51] Of the 220 shooting incidents, 172 were homicides, 30 were suicides, 11 were homicide-suicides, 5 were legal intervention deaths, and 2 were unintentional firearm-related

Bullying in School

Experts define bullying among children as repeated, negative acts committed by one or more children against another. These negative acts may be physical or verbal in nature—for example, hitting or kicking, teasing or taunting—or they may involve indirect actions such as manipulating friendships or purposely excluding other children from activities. Implicit in this definition is an imbalance in real or perceived power between the bully and victim.

Bullying is a sad but common occurrence in the United States educational system. It occurs in most school systems, and research by Catherine Dulmus indicates that it may actually be more pervasive in rural rather than in urban schools. Research by Tonja Nansel and her associates found that more than 16 percent of U.S. schoolchildren say they have been bullied by other students during the current school term, and approximately 30 percent of 6th- through 10th-grade students reported being involved in some aspect of moderate-to-frequent bullying, either as a bully, the target of bullying, or both.

Studies of bullying suggest that there are short- and long-term consequences for both the perpetrators and the victims of bullying. Students who are chronic victims of bullying experience more physical and psychological problems than their peers who are not harassed by other children and they tend not to grow out of the role of victim. Young people mistreated by peers may not want to be in school and may thereby miss out on the benefits of school connectedness as well as educational advancement. Longitudinal studies have found that victims of bullying in early grades also reported being bullied several years later. Studies also suggest that chronically victimized students may, as adults, be at increased risk for depression, poor self-esteem, and other mental health problems, including schizophrenia.

It is not only victims who are at risk for short- and long-term problems; bullies also are at increased risk for negative outcomes. One researcher found that those elementary students who were bullies attended school less frequently and were more likely to drop out than other students. Several studies suggest that bullying in early childhood may be a critical risk factor for the development of future problems with violence and delinquency. For example, bullies are more likely to carry weapons in and out of school. Research conducted in Scandinavia found that, in addition to threatening other children, bullies were several times more likely than their nonbullying peers to commit antisocial acts, including vandalism, fighting, theft, drunkenness, and truancy, and to have an arrest by young adulthood. Another study of more than 500 children found that aggressive behavior at the age of 8 was a powerful predictor of criminality and violent behavior at the age of 30.

CAN BULLYING BE PREVENTED?

The first and best-known intervention to reduce bullying among school children was launched by Dan Olweus in Norway and Sweden in the early 1980s. Prompted by the suicides of several severely victimized children, Norway supported the development and implementation of a comprehensive program to address bullying among children in school. The program involved interventions at multiple levels:

▌ **Schoolwide interventions:** A survey of bullying problems at each school, increased supervision, schoolwide assem-

blies, and teacher in-service training to raise the awareness of children and school staff regarding bullying.

▌ **Classroom-level interventions:** The establishment of classroom rules against bullying, regular class meetings to discuss bullying at school, and meetings with all parents.

▌ **Individual-level interventions:** Discussions with students identified as bullies and victims.

The program was found to be highly effective in reducing bullying and other antisocial behavior among students in primary and junior high schools. Within two years of implementation, both boys' and girls' self-reports indicated that bullying had decreased by half. These changes in behavior were more pronounced the longer the program was in effect. Moreover, students reported significant decreases in rates of truancy, vandalism, and theft, and indicated that their school's climate was significantly more positive as a result of the program. Not surprisingly, those schools that had implemented more of the program's components experienced the most marked changes in behavior. The core components of the Olweus anti-bullying program have been adapted for use in several other cultures, including Canada, England, and the United States. Results of the anti-bullying efforts in these countries have been similar to the results experienced in the Scandinavian countries, with the efforts in Toronto schools showing somewhat more modest results. Again, as in the Scandinavian study, schools that were more active in implementing the program observed the most marked changes in reported behaviors.

Critical Thinking

Should schoolyard bullies be expelled from school? Would such a measure make a bad situation worse? For example, might expelled bullies shift their aggressive behavior from the schoolyard to the community?

⚲ InfoTrac College Edition Research

To learn more about the cause and effect of bullying, use "school bullying" in a key word search on InfoTrac College Edition.

SOURCES: Catherine Dulmus, Matthew Theriot, Karen Sowers, James Blackburn, "Student Reports of Peer Bullying Victimization in a Rural School," *Stress, Trauma & Crisis: An International Journal* 7:1–15 (2004); Anna Baldry and David Farrington, "Evaluation of an Intervention Program for the Reduction of Bullying and Victimization in Schools," *Aggressive Behavior* 30:1–14 (2004); Marcel van der Wal, Cees A. M. de Wit, and Remy Hirasing, "Psychosocial Health among Young Victims and Offenders of Direct and Indirect Bullying," *Pediatrics* 111:1312–1317 (2003); Marla Eisenberg, Dianne Neumark-Sztainer, and Cheryl Perry, "Peer Harassment, School Connectedness, and Academic Achievement," *Journal of School Health* 73:311–316 (2003); Michael Reiff, "Bullying and Violence," *Journal of Developmental & Behavioral Pediatrics* 24:296–297 (2003); Susan Limber and Maury Nation, "Bullying among Children and Youth," in June L. Arnette and Marjorie C. Walsleben, *Combating Fear and Restoring Safety in Schools* (Washington, DC: Office of Juvenile Justice and Delinquency Prevention, 1998); Tonja Nansel, Mary Overpeck, and Ramani Pilla, "Bullying Behaviors among U.S. Youth: Prevalence and Association with Psychosocial Adjustment," *JAMA* 285:2094–3100 (2001); Dan Olweus, "Victimization by Peers: Antecedents and Long-Term Outcomes," in K. H. Rubin and J. B. Asendorf, eds., *Social Withdrawal, Inhibitions, and Shyness* (Hillsdale, NJ: Erlbaum, 1993), pp. 315–341.

School shootings have become sadly routine. Here, students exit from Rocori High School in Cold Spring, Minnesota, on September 24, 2003, to be released to school buses and waiting parents after a shooting at the school. Two students were shot, one fatally (the second died later). Coach and teacher Mark Johnson persuaded the shooter to lay down his gun.

deaths. While the media would have us believe school violence is epidemic, this amounted to 0.068 per 100,000 students.

The research discovered that most shooting incidents occur around the start of the school day, the lunch period, or the end of the school day. In most of the shootings (55 percent), a note, threat, or other action indicating risk for violence occurred prior to the event. Shooters were also likely to have expressed some form of suicidal behavior prior to the event and to report having been bullied by their peers. These patterns may help school officials to one day identify potential risk factors and respond in a timely fashion.

Who Is the School Shooter? The United States Secret Service has developed a profile of school shootings and shooters after evaluating 41 school shooters who participated in 37 incidents.[52] They found that most attacks were neither spontaneous nor impulsive. Shooters typically developed a plan of attack well in advance; more than half had considered the attack for at least two weeks and had a plan for at least two days.

The attackers' mental anguish was well known, and they had come to the attention of someone (school officials, police, fellow students) because of their bizarre and disturbing behavior before the attack took place. One student told more than 20 friends beforehand about his plans, which included killing students and planting bombs. Threats were communicated in more than three-fourths of the cases, and in more than half the incidents the attacker told more than one person. Some people knew detailed information, while others knew "something spectacular" was going to happen on a particular date. In less than one-fourth of the cases did the attacker make a direct threat to the target.

The Secret Service found that shooters came from such a wide variety of backgrounds that no accurate or useful profile of at-risk kids could be developed. They ranged in age from 11 to 21 and came from a wide variety of ethnic and racial backgrounds; about 25 percent of the shooters were minority-group members. Some lived in intact families with strong ties to the community, while others were reared in foster homes with histories of neglect. Some were excellent students, while others were poor academic performers. Shooters could not be characterized as isolated and alienated; some had many friends and were considered popular. There was no evidence that shootings were a result of the onset of mental disorder. Drugs and alcohol seemed to have little involvement in school violence.

What the Secret Service determined was that many of the shooters had a history of feeling extremely depressed or desperate because they had been picked on or bullied. About three-fourths of shooters threatened to kill themselves, made suicidal gestures, or tried to kill themselves before the attack; six of the students studied killed themselves during the incident. The most frequent motivation was revenge. More than three-fourths were known to hold a grievance, real or imagined, against the target and/or others. In most cases, this was the first violent act against the target. Two-thirds of the attackers described feeling persecuted, and in more than three-fourths of the incidents the attackers had difficulty coping with a major change in a significant relationship or a loss of status, such as a lost love or a humiliating failure. Not surprisingly, most shooters had experience with guns and weapons and had access to them at home.

The Community and School Crime

A number of researchers have observed that school crime is a function of the community in which the school is located. In other words, crime in schools does not occur in isolation from crime in the community.[53]

Poverty and Disorganization Schools experiencing crime and drug abuse are most likely to be found in socially disorganized neighborhoods with a high proportion of students behind grade level in reading, with many students from families on welfare, and with high unemployment and poverty rates.[54] Neighborhoods with high population density and transient populations also have problem-prone schools.[55] In contrast, schools located in more stable areas, with high-achieving students, drug-free environments, and involved parents have fewer behavioral problems within the student body.[56]

When Wayne Welsh, Robert Stokes, and Jack Greene studied community influences on school crime, they found that community influences may undermine school stability and climate.[57] Poverty in a school's surrounding area influences the social characteristics of students. They may lack the readiness and interest to learn when compared with students from more affluent neighborhoods. Poor areas may find it difficult to hire and retain the most qualified faculty and/or provide students with the most up-to-date equipment and books. Because poor communities have lower tax bases, they are handcuffed when they want to provide remedial programs for students with learning issues, or conversely, enrichment programs for the gifted. Finally, parents and other students have neither the time nor resources to become involved in school activities or participate in governance. These factors may eventually undermine school climate and destabilize the educational environment, which leads to school crime and disorder.

Cross-national research efforts confirm the community influences on school crime. One study of violent crimes in the schools of Stockholm, Sweden, found that, although only one-fifth of schools were located in areas of social instability and disorganization, almost a third of school crime happened in these schools.[58]

Neighborhood Crime There is also evidence that crime in schools reflects the patterns of antisocial behavior that exist in the surrounding neighborhood.[59] Schools in high-crime areas experience more crime than schools in safer areas. Students who report being afraid in school are actually more afraid of being in city parks, streets, or subway. Because of this fear, students in high crime areas may carry weapons for self-protection as they go from their homes to school.[60]

Research also shows that many perpetrators of school crime have been victims of delinquency themselves.[61] It is possible that school-based crimes have "survival value"—striking back against a weaker victim is a method of regaining lost possessions or self-respect.[62] This would imply that areas with high crime rates produce a large pool of student victims who will also manifest high rates of school crime. It may be futile to attempt to eliminate school crime without considering the impact of communities. The Welsh research found that schools that are stable and have a positive climate manifest lower rates of criminal activity on school grounds.

Reducing School Crime

Schools around the country have mounted a campaign to reduce the incidence of delinquency on campus. In fact, some school officials have been accused of over-reacting to school crime, by adopting a "zero tolerance" policy, which requires suspensions or

Some school systems have adopted a "zero tolerance" approach in order to reduce school crime. This means that kids may be suspended or expelled for a first offense, even one that may seem trivial or minor. Taylor Hess, a Hurst, Texas, high school honors student with dreams of college, was expelled for a year after school officials found a bread knife in the bed of his pickup. Hess's original punishment was reduced to five days spent in a disciplinary alternative education program when a public uproar over the severity of the punishment caused the expulsion to be reconsidered. How far should school officials go to reduce campus crime?

even expulsion for seemingly minor acts. As a result, more than 3 million students are now being suspended yearly and nearly 100,000 more expelled. At least 40 states now require that certain violations committed in school be reported to the police, where before they were handled internally. Some commentators believe that boys and minority group members are being unfairly targeted by school administrators, increasing their chances of dropping out and engaging in delinquency.[63] What steps are now being taken to eliminate crime in schools?

Control Gangs Some schools have initiated on-campus anti-gang initiatives. For example, Gang Resistance Education and Training (G.R.E.A.T.) is an officer-taught education program. Class topics include crime and victimization, prejudice and cultural sensitivity, conflict resolution skills, drugs and neighborhoods, personal responsibility, and setting goals. G.R.E.A.T. is a national program that has been used in middle schools across the country. Research indicates that it is successful and has helped reduce levels of delinquency and gang affiliation while increasing student involvement in prosocial activities.[64] There will be more on G.R.E.A.T. in Chapter 13.

Safe School Zone Nearly all states have developed some sort of crime-free, weapon-free, or safe-school zone statute.[65] Most have defined these zones to include school transportation and school-sponsored functions. Schools are also cooperating with court officials and probation officers to share information and monitor students who have criminal records. School districts are formulating crisis prevention and intervention policies and are directing individual schools to develop safe-school plans.

Control Student Activity Some schools have instituted strict controls over student activity—for example, conducting locker searches, preventing students from having lunch off campus, and using patrols to monitor drug use. According to one national survey, a majority of schools have adopted a zero tolerance policy that mandates predetermined punishments for specific offenses, most typically possession of drugs, weapons, and/or tobacco, and also for engaging in violent behaviors.[66]

Increase Security Almost every school attempts to restrict entry of dangerous persons by having visitors sign in before entering, and most close the campus for lunch.[67] Schools have attempted to ensure the physical safety of students and staff by using mechanical security devices such as surveillance cameras, electronic barriers to keep out intruders, random metal detectors, and roving security guards. Some districts have gone so far as to infiltrate undercover detectives on school grounds. These detectives attend classes, mingle with students, contact drug dealers, make buys, and arrest campus dealers.[68] Some administrators keep buildings dark at night, believing that brightly illuminated schools give the buildings too high a profile and attract vandals who might have not bothered the facility, or even noticed it, if the premises are not illuminated; others believe a well-lit school is a deterrent to crime.[69]

Law and order approaches have relied on such measures as metal detectors to identify gun-wielding students. About 4 percent of schools now use random metal detector checks and 1 percent employ daily checks; metal detectors are much more common in large schools (15 percent), especially where serious crime has taken place.[70] One program in New York City uses random searches with inexpensive handheld detectors at the start of the school day; students report a greater sense of security and attendance has increased.[71]

Schools have employed a variety of security setups. Some have independent security divisions, others hire private guards, while still others cooperate with local law enforcement agencies. For example, in cities such as Houston, it is routine to employ armed guards in full uniform during the day. Nor does security end in the evening. In San Diego, an elaborate security system makes use of infrared beams and silent alarms to protect school grounds from vandals and unwelcome visitors.[72] Rather than suspending violators, some school districts now send them to a separate center for evaluation and counseling so they are kept separate from the law-abiding students.[73] In New York City, the school board maintains a force of about 4,000 officers in its Division of School Safety, who now patrol the more than 1,000 public schools armed only with handcuffs.[74]

While these measures seem extreme, they are by no means unique to the United States. School districts in Australia report that local schools are installing spy cameras and hiring security guards. Security is warranted because of arson, assaults or threats against school staff and students, repeated burglaries, theft and criminal damage of computers, gang fights spilling onto school grounds, student violence over teenage relationships, and stress claims by teachers, partly due to clashes with parents and students.[75] Exhibit 9.5 illustrates some of the security measures now being used in U.S. schools.

The effectiveness of school security measures has received mixed reviews. Research based on findings from national surveys find that security measures are not really effective in reducing the incidence of school crime or the likelihood of school yard victimization.[76] Some critics complain that even when security methods are effective, they reduce staff and student morale. Tighter security may reduce acts of crime and violence in school, only to displace them to the community. Similarly, expelling or suspending troublemakers puts them on the street with nothing to do, so that, in the end, lowering the level of crime in schools may not reduce the total amount of crime committed by young people. A more realistic approach might involve early identification of at-risk students and teaching them prosocial skills rather than threatening them with consequence-based punishments.[77]

Improving School Climate

Some school districts have reduced school crime by reducing disorganization and improving the educational climate. For example, to improve school safety, New York City instituted a program in 2003 that focused on reducing crime in the city's 12 most dangerous schools. Though these few schools constituted less than 1 percent of the city's enrollment, they accounted for 13 percent of all serious crimes and 11 percent of the total safety incidents. To reduce delinquency, the NYPD doubled the number of officers assigned to each school site and formed a 150-member task force of officers to focus on danger zones such as hallways and cafeterias. The police also monitored the perimeters of the schools and organized truancy sweeps. Each school received frequent visits from

EXHIBIT **9.5**

Security Measures Being Used to Reduce School Crime

Outsiders on campus

- Posted signs regarding penalties for trespassing
- Enclosed campus (fencing)
- Guard at main entry gate to campus
- Greeters in strategic locations
- Vehicle parking stickers
- Uniforms or dress codes
- Exterior doors locked from the outside
- A challenge procedure for anyone out of class
- Cameras in remote locations
- School laid out so all visitors must pass through front office
- Temporary "fading" badges issued to all visitors
- Designating one main door entry to school, equipping exits with push bars, and locking all other doors to outside entry
- Installing bulletproof windows
- Equipping the school with closed-circuit video surveillance systems to reduce property crime such as break-ins, theft, vandalism, and assaults
- Designing landscaping to create an inviting appearance without offering a hiding place for trespassers or criminals
- Installing motion-sensitive lights to illuminate dark corners in hallways or on campus
- Mounting convex mirrors to monitor blind spots in school hallways
- Requiring photo identification badges for students, teachers, and staff and identification cards for visitors on campus

Fights on campus

- Cameras
- Duress alarms
- Whistles

Vandalism

- Graffiti-resistant sealers
- Glass-break sensors
- Aesthetically pleasing wall murals (these usually are not hit by graffiti)
- Law enforcement officers living on campus
- Eight-foot fencing
- Well-lit campus

Theft

- Interior intrusion detection sensors
- Property marking (including microdots) to deter theft
- Bars on windows
- Reinforced doors
- Elimination of access points up to rooftops
- Cameras
- Doors with hinge pins on secure side
- Bolting down computers and TVs
- Locating high-value assets in interior rooms

- Key control
- Biometric entry into rooms with high-value assets
- Law enforcement officer living on campus

Drugs

- Drug detection swipes
- Hair analysis kits for drug use detection (intended for parental application)
- Drug dogs
- Removal of lockers
- Random searches
- Vapor detection of drugs

Alcohol

- No open campus at lunch
- Breathalyzer test equipment
- No access to vehicles
- No lockers
- Clear or open mesh backpacks
- Saliva test kits

Weapons

- Walk-through metal detectors
- Handheld metal detectors
- Vapor detection of gunpowder
- Crime stopper hotline with rewards for information
- Gunpowder detection swipes
- Random locker, backpack, and vehicle searches
- X-ray inspection of bookbags and purses

Malicious acts

- Distancing school buildings from vehicle areas
- Inaccessibility of air intake and water source
- All adults on campus required to wear badges
- Vehicle barriers near main entries and student gathering areas

Parking lot problems

- Cameras
- Parking decals
- Fencing
- Card identification systems for parking lot entry
- Parking lots sectioned off for different student schedules
- Sensors in parking areas that should have no access during school day
- Roving guards
- Bike patrol

False fire alarms

- Sophisticated alarm systems that allow assessment of alarms (and cancellation if false) before they become audible
- Boxes installed over alarm pulls that alarm locally (screamer boxes)

Bomb threats

- Caller I.D. on phone system
- Crime stopper program with big rewards for information
- Recording all phone calls, with a message regarding this at the beginning of each incoming call
- All incoming calls routed through a district office
- Phone company support
- No pay phones on campus
- Policy to extend the school year when plagued with bomb threats and subsequent evacuations

Bus problems

- School bus drivers tested for drug and alcohol use
- Video cameras and recorders within enclosures on buses
- Identification required to ride school buses
- Security aides on buses
- Smaller buses
- Duress alarm system or radios for bus drivers

Teacher safety

- Duress alarms
- Roving patrols
- Classroom doors left open during class
- Cameras in black boxes in classrooms
- Controlled access to classroom areas
- Equipping classrooms with intercom systems connected to the central school office
- Issuing two-way radios to security patrols or campus staff members
- Purchasing cellular phones for use in crises or emergency situations

Campus safety

- Establishing Neighborhood Watch programs in areas near schools
- Recruiting parents to provide safe houses along school routes and to monitor "safe corridors" or walkways to and from school
- Enlisting parent volunteers to monitor hallways, cafeterias, playgrounds, and school walkways in order to increase visibility of responsible adults
- Creating block safety watch programs carried out by area residents at school bus stops as a crime deterrent for school children and area residents
- Fencing school grounds to secure campus perimeters
- Replacing bathroom doors with zigzag entrances, to make it easier to monitor sounds, and installing roll-down doors to secure bathrooms after hours

SOURCES: Adapted from Mary W. Green, *The Appropriate and Effective Use of Security Technologies in U.S. Schools* (Washington, DC: National Institute of Justice, 1999); Arnette and Walsleben, *Combating Fear and Restoring Safety in Schools.*

Safe Harbor: A School-Based Victim Assistance and Violence Prevention Program

All too many school officials have witnessed students being drawn into a cycle of violence. First, they are victimized by other students, they then retaliate against weaker or younger peers, only to be victimized once again. To help remedy this troubling situation, Safe Harbor, a violence prevention and victim assistance program for schools, was developed. This multifaceted program attempts to prevent school crime and victimization while providing assistance to curb future victimization.

The Safe Harbor program has five core components:

1. A 10-lesson violence prevention and victim assistance curriculum.

2. Individual and group counseling with social workers and school counselors for victims.

3. Prevention workshops in parenting and stress management to strengthen relationships with children and/or students in order to help parents and teachers understand what students are facing in today's society.

4. Group activities (art, physical, and relaxation programs) and discussion groups for students. These are aimed at helping them understand and discuss current issues and also how to resolve conflict with their peers in a nonviolent fashion.

5. Poster campaigns, school assemblies, and/or arts and crafts projects that are all geared toward a schoolwide antiviolence stand. These activities provide students with opportunities for leadership in their community without violence.

So far Safe Harbor seems very successful. Preliminary evaluations show that students enrolled in the program improve their conflict resolution skills and change their attitudes about violence.

Critical Thinking

1. If you were called upon to design a school-based delinquency prevention program, what activities would you suggest?

2. Do you think that school bullies and troublemakers would make themselves available for help in a school-based program? If not, why?

InfoTrac College Edition Research

Use "delinquency prevention" in a key word search on InfoTrac College Edition.

SOURCE: U.S. Department of Justice, Office for Victims of Crime, "Safe Harbor: A School Based Victim Assistance/Violence Prevention Program" (Washington, DC: *OVC Bulletin*, January, 2003).

The National School Safety and Security Services is a Cleveland, Ohio–based consulting firm specializing in school security and crisis-preparedness training, security assessments, and related safety consulting for K–12 schools, law enforcement, and other youth safety providers. Their site contains a lot of information on school security. Visit it at www.schoolsecurity.org. For an up-to-date list of web links, go to http://cj.wadsworth.com/siegel_jd9e.

school-safety teams made up of police officers, community workers, and educators. Evaluations showed that the schools receiving the extra enforcement averaged 3.02 criminal incidents per day, down nearly 9 percent from 3.3 incidents per day before the program began.[78]

Another approach to improving the school climate is to increase educational standards. Programs have been designed to improve the standards of the teaching staff and administrators and the educational climate in the school, increase the relevance of the curriculum, and provide law-related education classes. The Policy and Practice box entitled "Safe Harbor" discusses one such program.

Efforts to improve school climate should be encouraged. Recent research efforts have found preliminary support for the linkage between climate and delinquency. Schools that encourage order, organization, and student bonding may also experience a decline in disorder and crime.[79]

Social Programs Controlling school crime is ultimately linked to the community and family conditions. When communities undergo such changes as increases in unemployment and the number of single-parent households, both school disruption and community crime rates may rise.[80] The school environment can be made safer only if community issues are addressed: for example, by taking steps to keep intruders out of school buildings, putting pressure on local police to develop community safety programs, increasing correctional services, strengthening laws on school safety, and making parents bear greater responsibility for their children's behavior.[81]

Schools must also use the resources of the community when controlling school crime. Most school districts refer problem students to social services outside the school. About 70 percent of public schools provide outside referrals for students with substance abuse problems, while 90 percent offer drug education within the school.[82]

TO QUIZ YOURSELF ON THIS MATERIAL, go to the Juvenile Delinquency 9e website.

As educational officials have attempted to restore order within the school, their actions often have run into opposition from the courts, which are concerned with maintaining the legal rights of minors. The U.S. Supreme Court has sought to balance the civil liberties of students with the school's mandate to provide a reasonable and safe educational environment. In some instances, the Court has sided with students, while in others the balance has shifted toward the educational establishment. The main issues concerning the rights of children and the schools include compulsory attendance, free speech in school, and school discipline.

Compulsory School Attendance

In the United States, compulsory school attendance statutes have been in effect for more than half a century.[83] Children are required by law to attend school until a given age, normally 16 or 17.[84] Violations of compulsory attendance laws generally result in complaints that can lead to court action. Often, however, children are truant because of emotional problems or learning disabilities. They are then brought into the court system for problems beyond their control. Many of them might be better off leaving school at an earlier age than the compulsory education law allows. On the other hand, emotionally disturbed and nonconforming children are pushed out of many school systems and thereby deprived of an education. Whether these children have a right to attend school is unclear. Many school systems ignore the difficult student, who may be classified as "bad" or "delinquent."

In 1925, the Supreme Court determined that compulsory education did not necessarily have to be provided by a public school system and that parochial schools could be a reasonable substitute.[85] From that time through the 1970s, the courts upheld the right of the state to make education compulsory. Then, in 1972, in the case of *Wisconsin v. Yoder*, the Supreme Court made an exception to the general compulsory education law by holding that traditional Amish culture was able to give its children the skills that would prepare them for adulthood within Amish society. Thus, the removal of Amish children from school after the completion of the eighth grade was justified.[86] It is not clear, however, whether this decision speaks directly to the issue of compulsory education or whether it is simply an instance of freedom of religion. Therefore, the state's role in requiring school attendance is still unsettled.

Free Speech

Freedom of speech is granted and guaranteed in the First Amendment to the U.S. Constitution. The right has been divided into two major categories as it affects children in schools. The first category involves what is known as *passive speech*, a form of expression not associated with the actual speaking of words. Examples include wearing armbands or political protest buttons. The most important U.S. Supreme Court decision concerning a student's right to passive speech was in 1969 in the case of *Tinker v. Des Moines Independent Community School District*.[87] This case involved the right to wear black armbands to protest the war in Vietnam. Two high school students, aged 16 and 17, were told they would be suspended if they demonstrated their objections to the Vietnam War by wearing black armbands. They attended school wearing the armbands and were suspended. According to the Court, in order for the state (in the person of a school official) to justify prohibiting an expression of opinion, it must be able to show that its action was caused by something more than a mere desire to avoid the discomfort and unpleasantness that accompany the expression of an unpopular view. Unless it can be shown that the forbidden conduct will interfere with the discipline required to operate the school, the prohibition cannot be sustained. In the *Tinker* case, the Court said there was no evidence that the school authorities had reason to believe

Students in Rochester, New York, are shown protesting a school ruling over the presence of metal detectors. The Supreme Court allows school officials to control student speech while on school premises if it interferes with the school's mission to implant "the shared values of a civilized social order." Student protest off-campus is still an open question. In the future, the courts may be asked to rule whether schools can control such forms of speech or whether they are shielded by the First Amendment.

that the wearing of armbands would substantially interfere with the work of the school or infringe on the rights of the students.[88]

This decision is significant because it recognizes the child's right to free speech in a public school system. Justice Abe Fortas stated in his majority opinion, "Young people do not shed their constitutional rights at the schoolhouse door."[89] *Tinker* established two things: (1) a child is entitled to free speech in school under the First Amendment of the U.S. Constitution and (2) the test used to determine whether the child has gone beyond proper speech is whether he or she materially and substantially interferes with the requirements of appropriate discipline in the operation of the school.

The concept of free speech articulated in *Tinker* was used again in the 1986 case *Bethel School District No. 403 v. Fraser.*[90] This case upheld a school system's right to suspend or otherwise discipline a student who uses obscene or profane language and gestures. Matthew Fraser, a Bethel high school student, used sexual metaphors in making a speech nominating a friend for student office. His statement included these remarks:

> *I know a man who is firm—he's firm in his pants, he's firm in his shirt, his character is firm— but most . . . of all, his belief in you, the students of Bethel, is firm.*
>
> *Jeff Kuhlman is a man who takes his point and pounds it in. If necessary, he'll take an issue and nail it to the wall. He doesn't attack things in spurts—he drives hard, pushing and pushing until finally—he succeeds.*
>
> *Jeff is a man who will go to the very end—even the climax, for each and every one of you.*
>
> *So vote for Jeff for A.S.B. vice-president—he'll never come between you and the best our high school can be.*

The Court found that a school has the right to control lewd and offensive speech that undermines the educational mission. The Court drew a distinction between the sexual content of Fraser's remarks and the political nature of Tinker's armband. It ruled that the pervasive sexual innuendo of the speech interfered with the school's mission to implant "the shared values of a civilized social order" in the student body.

In a 1988 case, *Hazelwood School District v. Kuhlmeier*, the Court extended the right of school officials to censor "active speech" when it ruled that the principal could censor articles in a student publication.[91] In this case, students had written about their personal experiences with pregnancy and parental divorce. The majority ruled that censorship was justified in this case because school-sponsored publications, activities, and productions were part of the curriculum and therefore designed to impart knowledge. Control over such school-supported activities could be differentiated from the action the Tinkers initiated on their own accord. In a dissent, Justice William J. Brennan accused school officials of favoring "thought control."

While the Court has dealt with of speech on campus, it may now be asked to address off-campus speech issues. Students have been suspended for posting messages on their Internet web pages that school officials consider defamatory.[92] In the future, the Court may be asked to rule whether schools can control such forms of speech or whether they are shielded by the First Amendment.

School Prayer

One of the most divisive issues involving free speech is school prayer. While some religious-minded administrators, parents, and students want to have prayer sessions in schools or have religious convocations, others view the practice both as a violation of the principle of separation of church and state and as an infringement on the First Amendment caution against creating a state-approved religion. The 2000 case of *Santa Fe Independent School District, Petitioner v. Jane Doe* helps clarify the issue.[93]

Prior to 1995, the Santa Fe High School student who occupied the school's elective office of student council chaplain delivered a prayer over the public address system before each varsity football game for the entire season. After the practice was challenged in federal district court, the school district adopted a different policy that permitted, but did not require, prayer initiated and led by a student at all home games. The district court entered an order modifying that policy to permit only nonsectarian, nonproselytizing prayer. However, a federal appellate court held that, even as modified, the football prayer policy was invalid. This decision was appealed to the United States Supreme Court, which ruled that prayers led by an elected student undermines the protection of minority viewpoints. Such a system encourages divisiveness along religious lines and threatens the students not desiring to participate in a religious exercise.

Though the Santa Fe case severely limits school-sanctioned prayer at public events, the Court has not totally ruled out the role of religion in schools. In its ruling in *Good News Club v. Milford Central School* (2001), the Supreme Court required an upstate New York school district to provide space for an after-school Bible club for elementary students.[94] The Court ruled that it was a violation of the First Amendment's free speech clause to deny the club access to the school's space on the ground that the club was religious in nature; the school routinely let secular groups use its space. The Court reasoned that because the club's meetings were to be held after school hours, not sponsored by the school, and open to any student who obtained parental consent, it could not be perceived that the school was endorsing the club or that students might feel coerced to participate in its activities. In 2001, the Court let stand a Virginia statute that mandates that each school division in the state establish in its classrooms a "minute of silence" so that "each pupil may, in the exercise of his or her individual choice, meditate, pray, or engage in any other silent activity which does not interfere with, distract, or impede other pupils in the like exercise of individual choice."[95] The Court refused to hear an appeal filed by several Virginia students and their parents, which contended that a "moment of silence" establishes religion in violation of the First Amendment.[96] In its most recent statement on the separation of church and state, the Court refused to hear a case brought by a California father contesting the recital of the Pledge of Allegiance because it contains the phrase "under God."[97] Though the Court dismissed the case on a technical issue, some of the justices felt the issue should have been dealt with and dismissed. Chief Justice Rehnquist wrote in his opinion:

> To give the parent of such a child a sort of "heckler's veto" over a patriotic ceremony willingly participated in by other students, simply because the Pledge of Allegiance contains the descriptive phrase "under God," is an unwarranted extension of the establishment clause, an extension which would have the unfortunate effect of prohibiting a commendable patriotic observance.[98]

School Discipline

Most states have statutes permitting teachers to use corporal punishment to discipline students in public school systems. Under the concept of *in loco parentis*, discipline is one of the assumed parental duties given to the school system. In two decisions, the Supreme Court upheld the school's right to use corporal punishment. In the case of *Baker v. Owen*, the Court stated:

> We hold that the Fourteenth Amendment embraces the right of parents generally to control the means and discipline of their children, but that the state has a countervailing interest in the maintenance of order in the schools...sufficient to sustain the right of teachers, and school officials must accord to students minimal due process in the course of inflicting such punishment.[99]

In 1977, the Supreme Court again spoke on the issue of corporal punishment in school systems in the case of *Ingraham v. Wright*, which upheld the right of teachers to use corporal punishment.[100] In this case, students James Ingraham and Roosevelt Andrews sustained injuries as a result of paddling in the Charles Drew Junior High School in Dade County, Florida. The legal problems raised in the case were (1) whether corporal punishment by teachers was a violation in this case of the Eighth Amendment against cruel and unusual punishment and (2) whether the due process clause of the Fourteenth Amendment required that the students receive proper notice and a hearing prior to receiving corporal punishment. The Court held that neither the Eighth Amendment nor the Fourteenth Amendment was violated in this case. Even though Ingraham suffered hematomas on his buttocks as a result of twenty blows with a wooden paddle and Andrews was hurt in the arm, the Supreme Court ruled that such punishment was not a constitutional violation. The Court established the standard that only reasonable discipline is allowed in school systems, but it accepted the degree of punishment administered in this case. The key principle in *Ingraham* is that the reasonableness standard that the Court articulated represents the judicial attitude that the scope of the school's right to discipline a child is by no means more restrictive than the rights of the child's own parents to impose corporal punishment. Today 24 states still use physical punishment.

Other issues involving the legal rights of students include their due process rights when interrogated, if corporal punishment is to be imposed, and when suspension and expulsion are threatened. When students are questioned by school personnel, no warning as to their legal rights to remain silent or right to counsel need be given. However, when school security guards, on-campus police officials, and public police officers question students, such constitutional warnings are required. In the area of corporal punishment, procedural due process established with the case of *Baker v. Owen* requires that students at least be forewarned about the possibility of corporal punishment as a discipline. In addition, the *Baker* case requires that there be a witness to the administration of corporal punishment and allows the student and the parent to elicit reasons for the punishment.

With regard to suspension and expulsion, the Supreme Court ruled in 1976 in the case of *Goss v. Lopez* that any time a student is to be suspended for up to a period of ten days, he or she is entitled to a hearing.[101] The hearing would not include a right to counsel or a right to confront or cross-examine witnesses. The Court went on to state in *Goss* that the extent of the procedural due process requirements would be established on a case-by-case basis. That is, each case would represent its own facts and have its own procedural due process elements.

In sum, schools have the right to discipline students, but students are protected from unreasonable, excessive, and arbitrary discipline.

Privacy

Do students maintain the right to privacy while on school grounds or can they be searched, tested, and questioned at the whim of teachers and school administrators? Are their school records private or part of the public record?

The Right to Personal Privacy One major issue is the right of school officials to search students and their possessions on school grounds. Drug abuse, theft, assault and battery, and racial conflicts in schools have increased the need to take action against troublemakers. School administrators have questioned students about their illegal activities, conducted searches of students' persons and possessions, and reported suspicious behavior to the police.

In 1984, in *New Jersey v. T.L.O.*, the Supreme Court helped clarify a vexing problem: whether the Fourth Amendment's prohibition against unreasonable searches and seizures applies to school officials as well as to police officers.[102] In this case, the Court found that students are in fact constitutionally protected from illegal searches but that school officials are not bound by the same restrictions as law enforcement agents. Police need "probable cause" before they can conduct a search, but educators can legally search students when there are reasonable grounds to believe the students have violated the law or broken school rules. In creating this distinction, the Court recognized the needs of school officials to preserve an environment conducive to education and to secure the safety of students.

One question left unanswered by *New Jersey v. T.L.O.* is whether teachers and other school officials can search lockers and desks. Here, the law has been controlled by state decisions, and each jurisdiction may create its own standards. Some allow teachers a free hand in opening lockers and desks.[103]

Drug Testing Another critical issue concerning privacy is the drug testing of students. In 1995, the Supreme Court extended schools' authority to search by legalizing a random drug testing policy for student athletes. The Supreme Court's decision in *Vernonia School District 47J v. Acton* expanded the power of educators to ensure safe learning environments.[104]

As a result of *Vernonia*, schools may employ safe-school programs such as drug testing procedures so long as the policies satisfy the reasonableness test. *Vernonia* may bring forth a spate of suspicionless searches in public schools across the country. Metal-detection procedures, the use of drug-sniffing dogs, and random locker searches will be easier to justify. In upholding random, suspicionless drug testing for student athletes, the Supreme Court extended one step further the schools' authority to search, despite court-imposed constitutional safeguards for children. Underlying this decision, like that of *New Jersey v. T.L.O.*, is a recognition that the use of drugs is a serious threat to public safety and to the rights of children to receive a decent and safe education. The Juvenile Law in Review box entitled "*Board of Education of Independent School District No. 92 of Pottawatomie County et al., v. Earls et al.*" reviews a case extending the *Vernonia* doctrine to almost all school children.

FACTS

Board of Education of Independent School District No. 92 of Pottawatomie County et al., v. Earls et al.

Tecumseh, Oklahoma, School District adopted a student activities drug testing policy that requires all middle and high school students to consent to urinalysis testing for drugs in order to participate in any extracurricular activity. The policy was a response to increased perceptions of student drug use by faculty and administrators. Teachers saw students who appeared to be under the influence of drugs and heard students speaking openly about using drugs. A drug dog found marijuana near the school parking lot, and police found drugs or drug paraphernalia in a car driven by an extracurricular club member. The school board president reported that people in the community were calling the board to discuss the drug situation.

In practice, the policy was applied only to competitive extracurricular activities sanctioned by the Oklahoma Secondary Schools Activities Association (OSSAA). A group of students and their parents filed suit against the policy, arguing that it infringed on a student's right to personal privacy. The Tenth Circuit Court of Appeals agreed and held that before imposing a suspicionless drug testing program a school must demonstrate some identifiable drug abuse problem among a sufficient number of students so that testing that group will actually redress its drug problem. The federal court held that the school district had failed to demonstrate such a problem among Tecumseh students participating in competitive extracurricular activities. However, the Supreme Court reversed their decision and ruled that the policy is a reasonable means of furthering the school district's important interest in preventing and deterring drug use among its schoolchildren and does not violate the Fourth Amendment.

DECISION

The Court ruled that drug testing policies had to be "reasonable." However, in contrast to searches for criminal evidence, school authorities could search students (to determine whether they used drugs) without "probable cause" because the need for that level of evidence interferes with maintaining swift and informal disciplinary procedures that are needed to maintain order in a public school. Because the schools' responsibility for children cannot be disregarded, it would not be unreasonable to search students for drug usage even if no single student was suspected of abusing drugs.

The Court also ruled that within this context, students have a limited expectation of privacy. In their complaint, the students argued that children participating in nonathletic extracurricular activities have a stronger expectation of privacy than athletes who regularly undergo physicals as part of their participation in sports. However, the Court disagreed, maintaining that students who participate in competitive extracurricular activities voluntarily subject themselves to many of the same intrusions on their privacy as do athletes. Some of these clubs and activities require off-campus travel and communal undress, and all of them have their own rules and requirements that do not apply to the student body as a whole. Each of them must abide by OSSAA rules, and a faculty sponsor monitors students for compliance with the various rules dictated by the clubs and activities. Such regulation diminishes the student's expectation of privacy.

Finally, the Court concluded that the means used to enforce the drug policy was not overly invasive or an intrusion on the students' privacy. Under the policy, a faculty monitor would wait outside a closed restroom stall for the student to produce a sample and must listen for the normal sounds of urination to guard against tampered specimens and ensure an accurate chain of custody. This procedure is virtually identical to the "negligible" intrusion concept that was approved in an earlier case, *Vernonia vs. Acton,* that applied to student athletes. The policy requires that test results be kept in confidential files separate from a student's other records and released to school personnel only on a "need to know" basis. Moreover, the test results are not turned over to any law enforcement authority. Nor do the test results lead to the imposition of discipline or have any academic consequences. Rather, the only consequence of a failed drug test is to limit the student's privilege of participating in extracurricular activities.

SIGNIFICANCE

In *Pottawatomie County,* the Court concluded that a drug testing policy effectively serves a school district's interest in protecting its students' safety and health. It reasoned that preventing drug use by schoolchildren is an important governmental concern. School districts need not show that kids participating in a particular activity have a drug problem in order to test them for usage. The need to prevent and deter the substantial harm of childhood drug use itself provides the necessary immediacy for a school testing policy. Given what it considers a "nationwide epidemic of drug use," it was entirely reasonable for the school district to enact a drug testing policy.

Critical Thinking

Pottawatomie County extends the drug testing allowed in the *Vernonia* case from athletes to all students who participate in any form of school activity. Do you believe this is a reasonable exercise of state authority or a violation of due process? After all, the students being tested have not shown any evidence of drug abuse, nor do nonathletic school activities provide the same degree of danger as athletics, during the course of which an impaired participant may suffer serious injury.

InfoTrac College Edition Research

To read what former drug czar and values guru William Bennett has to say about the case, go to InfoTrac College Edition and read "Statement of Empower America Co-Director William J. Bennett on the Supreme Court's Decision in *Pottawatomie County v. Earls,*" US Newswire, June 27, 2002, p. 1008178n9466.

SOURCE: *Board of Education of Independent School District No. 92 of Pottawatomie County et al. v. Earls et al.* #01.332 (2002).

Academic Privacy

Students have the right to expect that their records will be kept private. Although state laws govern the disclosure of information from juvenile court records, a 1974 federal law—the Family Educational Rights and Privacy Act (FERPA)—restricts disclosure of information from a student's education records without parental consent.[105] The act defines an education record to include all records, files, and other materials, such as photographs, containing information related to a student that an education agency maintains. In 1994, Congress passed the Improving America's Schools Act, which allowed educational systems to disclose education records under these circumstances: (1) state law authorizes the disclosure, (2) the disclosure is to a juvenile justice agency, (3) the disclosure relates to the justice system's ability to provide preadjudication services to a student, and (4) state or local officials certify in writing that the institution or individual receiving the information has agreed not to disclose it to a third party other than another juvenile justice system agency.[106]

TO QUIZ YOURSELF ON THIS MATERIAL, go to the Juvenile Delinquency 9e website.

THE ROLE OF THE SCHOOL IN DELINQUENCY CONTROL POLICY

Can the American school system, viewed by critics as overly conservative and archaic, play a significant role in delinquency prevention? Some experts contend that no significant change in the lives of youths is possible by merely changing the schools; the entire social and economic structure of society must be altered if schools are to help students realize their full potential.[107] Others suggest that smaller, alternative schools, which create a positive learning environment with low student-teacher ratios, informal classroom structure, and individualized, self-paced learning, may be the answer. While in theory such programs may help promote academic performance and reduce delinquency, evaluations suggest that attending alternative programs have little effect on delinquency rates.[108]

A danger also exists that the pressure being placed on schools to improve the educational experience of students can produce unforeseen problems for staff members. For example, there have been recent reports of teachers being prosecuted for encouraging students to cheat on tests and providing them with answer sheets. The pressure

The young girls shown here are participating in the baby-sitting class run by Rise and Shine, a summer program that is part of Alternatives for Girls and the Mercy Education Project in Detroit. This after-school program is run by the religious order the Sisters of Mercy and is aimed at enhancing social skills, expanding horizons, and building self-esteem and decision-making skills. The girls gathered at St. Vincent Middle School are taught that raising a baby isn't child's play and that there are healthy alternatives to teen pregnancy.

© Ricardo Thomas/The Detroit News

to improve student performance on standardized tests was the motive for the faculty cheating.[109]

School-Based Prevention Programs Education officials have instituted numerous programs to make schools more effective instruments of delinquency prevention.[110] Among the most prevalent strategies are:

▎ *Cognitive.* Increase students' awareness about the dangers of drug abuse and delinquency.

▎ *Affective.* Improve students' psychological assets and self-image, giving them the resources to resist antisocial behavior.

▎ *Behavioral.* Train students in techniques to resist peer pressure.

▎ *Environmental.* Establish school management and disciplinary programs that deter crime, such as locker searches.

▎ *Therapeutic.* Treat youths who have already manifested problems.[111]

More specific suggestions include creating special classes or schools with individualized educational programs that foster success, rather than failure, for nonadjusting students.[112] Efforts can be made to help students learn to deal constructively with academic failure when it does occur. More personalized student-teacher relationships have been recommended. This effort to provide young persons with a caring, accepting adult role model will, it is hoped, strengthen the controls against delinquency.

It has been proposed that experiments be undertaken to integrate job training and experience with the usual classroom instruction so that students may see education as a meaningful and relevant prelude to their future careers. Job training programs could emphasize public service, so that students could gain a sense of attachment to their communities while they are acquiring useful vocational training.

Schools may not be able to reduce delinquency single-handedly, but a number of viable alternatives to their present operations could aid a communitywide effort to lessen the problem of juvenile crime. Because this issue is so critical, it is discussed in greater detail in Chapter 11.

Summary

▎ The American education system has been in crisis because of budget cutbacks.

▎ We put relatively less money into education than many other nations.

▎ Contemporary youths spend much of their time in school because education has become increasingly important as a determinant of social and economic success.

▎ Educational institutions are one of the primary instruments of socialization, and it is believed that this role is bound to affect the amount of delinquent behavior by school-age children.

▎ Research points to many definite links between the delinquent behavior of juveniles and their experiences within the educational system.

▎ Some kids fail because they have learning and attention problems.

▎ There is some question whether social class affects the educational experience.

▎ Alienation from the educational experience is the result of the impersonal nature of schools, the traditionally passive role assigned to students, and students' perception of their education as irrelevant to their future lives.

▎ Dissatisfaction with the educational experience frequently sets the stage for more serious forms of delinquency both in and out of school.

▎ Some dissatisfied students choose to drop out of school as soon as they reach the legal age. While some dropouts lower their delinquency rates, others may increase their antisocial behaviors. The reasons kids drop out has been linked to changes in their antisocial behavior.

I Student misbehavior, which may have its roots in the school experience itself, ranges from minor infractions of school rules (for example, smoking and loitering in halls) to serious crimes, such as assault, burglary, arson, drug abuse, and vandalism of school property.

I Bullying has become a significant problem in schools.

I School administrators have attempted to eliminate school crime and prevent delinquency.

I Among the measures taken are security squads, electronic surveillance, and teacher training.

I Curriculums are being significantly revised to make the school experience more meaningful and improve the educational climate. School climate has been linked to delinquency.

I The school has also become the focus of delinquency prevention efforts.

I Students maintain legal rights within the school. Issues include right to privacy, freedom of expression, and protection against unreasonable disciplinary measures.

Key Terms

truancy, p. 273
academic achievement, p. 273
socialization, p. 274
underachievers, p. 277

school failure, p. 277
tracking, p. 279
self-fulfilling prophecy, p. 280
student subculture, p. 280

dropout, p. 280
stigmatized, p. 280
alienation, p. 281

Questions for Discussion

1. Was there a delinquency problem in your high school? If so, how was it dealt with?

2. Should disobedient youths be suspended from school? Does this solution hurt or help?

3. What can be done to improve the delinquency prevention capabilities of schools?

4. Is school failure responsible for delinquency, or are delinquents simply school failures?

Viewpoint

On March 16, 2001, security officer Cathy Jones was patrolling the halls of a Los Angeles high school between classes when she noticed that two students were standing in an area off-limits to students. When Jones approached the pair, one student, Randy G., put his hand in his pocket and appeared nervous. Jones asked if the two were OK and told them to go to class. Randy G. finished adjusting his pocket and went to class. Jones followed Randy because she felt he was acting "very paranoid and nervous." Jones notified her supervisor and summoned another security officer to the scene. The officers then went to Randy G.'s classroom and asked him to step outside into the hallway. They asked if he had any weapons in his possession. Randy said that he did not have weapons and consented to a search of his bag and a pat-down search of his person. The officers found a knife in the student's pocket.

When Randy was charged with possession of a knife on school property, his attorney claimed that the evidence of the knife be excluded because the officers who discovered the knife had violated the Fourth Amendment, which provides for freedom from unlawful search and seizure. The defense claimed that the discovery of the knife was unreasonable because Officer Jones had no reasonable suspicion that the student had a knife or had violated a criminal statute or a school rule. Merely looking nervous is not reasonable grounds to search a person.

I Should the search of Randy be permitted?

I Should the evidence seized be used against Randy in a court of law?

I Should schools employ security guards such as Officer Jones, who act as cops on campus?

Doing Research on the Web

This scenario is based upon an actual California case, *The People v. Randy G.*, (Supreme Court of California, No. S089733, 2001). The Court ruled that school administrators have broad authority over student behavior and school safety. "...school officials have the power to stop a minor student in order to ask questions or conduct an investigation even in the absence of reasonable suspicion, so long as such authority is not exercised in an arbitrary, capricious, or harassing manner."

Read the case at this site (accessed on September 23, 2004):

http://caselaw.lp.findlaw.com/data2/californiastatecases/s089733.pdf

For an analysis, go to this site (accessed on September 23, 2004):

www.securitymanagement.com/library/People_Randy1101.html

To read more about the case, go to InfoTrac College Edition and read: Teresa Anderson, "School Security," *Security Management* 45:96–98 (2001).

Notes

1. *Justice and the Child in New Jersey,* report of the New Jersey Juvenile Delinquency Commission (1939), p. 110, cited in Paul H. Hahn, *The Juvenile Offender and the Law* (Cincinnati: Anderson, 1978).
2. Alexander Vazsonyi and Lloyd Pickering, "The Importance of Family and School Domains in Adolescent Deviance: African American and Caucasian Youth," *Journal of Youth and Adolescence* 32:115–129 (2003).
3. See Richard Lawrence, *School Crime and Juvenile Justice* (New York: Oxford University Press, 1998).
4. U.S. Office of Education, *Digest of Educational Statistics* (Washington, DC: Government Printing Office, 1969), p. 25.
5. Kenneth Polk and Walter E. Schafer, eds., *Schools and Delinquency* (Englewood Cliffs, NJ: Prentice–Hall, 1972), p. 13.
6. Simon Singer and Susyan Jou, "Specifying the SES/Delinquency Relationship by Subjective and Objective Indicators of Parental and Youth Social Status," paper presented at the annual meeting of the American Society of Criminology, New Orleans, November 1992.
7. For reviews, see Bruce Wolford and LaDonna Koebel, "Kentucky Model for Youths at Risk" *Criminal Justice* 9:5–55 (1995); J. David Hawkins, Richard Catalano, Diane Morrison, Julie O'Donnell, Robert Abbott, and L. Edward Day, "The Seattle Social Development Project," in Joan McCord and Richard Tremblay, eds., *The Prevention of Antisocial Behavior in Children* (New York: Guilford, 1992), pp. 139–160.
8. Terence Thornberry, Alan Lizotte, Marvin Krohn, Margaret Farnworth, and Sung Joon Jang, "Testing Interactional Theory: An Examination of Reciprocal Causal Relationships among Family, School and Delinquency," *Journal of Criminal Law and Criminology* 82:3–35 (1991).
9. Carolyn Smith, Alan Lizotte, Terence Thornberry, and Marvin Krohn, "Resilience to Delinquency," *The Prevention Researcher* 4:4–7 (1997); Matthew Zingraff, Jeffrey Leiter, Matthew Johnsen, and Kristen Myers, "The Mediating Effect of Good School Performance on the Maltreatment-Delinquency Relationship," *Journal of Research in Crime and Delinquency* 31:62–91 (1994).
10. Lyle Shannon, *Assessing the Relationship of Adult Criminal Careers to Juvenile Careers: A Summary* (Washington, DC: Government Printing Office, 1982).
11. Marvin Wolfgang, Robert Figlio, and Thorsten Sellin, *Delinquency in a Birth Cohort* (Chicago: University of Chicago Press, 1972).
12. Ibid., p. 94.
13. Bureau of Justice Statistics, *Prisons and Prisoners* (Washington, DC: Government Printing Office, 1982), p. 2.
14. Martin Gold, "School Experiences, Self-Esteem, and Delinquent Behavior: A Theory for Alternative Schools," *Crime and Delinquency* 24:294–295 (1978).
15. Ibid.
16. Michael Gottfredson and Travis Hirschi, *A General Theory of Crime* (Stanford, CA: Stanford University Press, 1990); J. D. McKinney, "Longitudinal Research on the Behavioral Characteristics of Children with Learning Disabilities," *Journal of Learning Disabilities* 22:141–150.
17. David Rabiner and Patrick. Malone, "The Impact of Tutoring on Early Reading Achievement for Children with and without Attention Problems," *Journal of Abnormal Child Psychology* 32:273–285 (2004).
18. Stefan Samuelsson, Ingvar Lundberg, and Birgitta Herkner, "ADHD and Reading Disability in Male Adults: Is There a Connection?" *Journal of Learning Disabilities* 37:155–168 (2004).
19. Albert K. Cohen, *Delinquent Boys* (New York: Free Press, 1955). See also Kenneth Polk, Dean Frease, and F. Lynn Richmond, "Social Class, School Experience, and Delinquency," *Criminology* 12:84–85 (1974).
20. John Paul Wright, Francis Cullen, and Nicolas Williams, "Working While in School and Delinquent Involvement: Implications for Social Policy," *Crime and Delinquency* 43:203–221 (1997).
21. William Glaser, *Schools without Failure* (New York: Harper & Row, 1969).
22. Gold, "School Experiences, Self Esteem, and Delinquent Behavior," p. 292.
23. Ibid., pp. 283–285.
24. Lance Hannor, "Poverty, Delinquency, and Educational Attainment: Cumulative Disadvantage or Disadvantage Saturation?" *Sociological Inquiry* 73:575–594 (2003).
25. Singer and Jou, "Specifying the SES/Delinquency Relationship by Subjective and Objective Indicators of Parental and Youth Social Status," p. 11.
26. Robert Agnew, "Foundation for a General Strain Theory of Crime and Delinquency," *Criminology* 30:47–87 (1992), at p. 48.
27. Kenneth Polk, "Class, Strain, and Rebellion among Adolescents," in Polk and Schafer, eds., *Schools and Delinquency.*
28. For an opposing view, see Michael Waitrowski, Stephen Hansell, Charles Massey, and David Wilson, "Curriculum Tracking and Delinquency," *American Sociological Review* 47:151–160 (1982).
29. Based on Walter E. Schafer, Carol Olexa, and Kenneth Polk, "Programmed for Social Class: Tracking in High School," in Polk and Schafer, eds., *Schools and Delinquency,* pp. 34–54.
30. Delos Kelly and William Pink, "School Crime and Individual Responsibility: The Perpetuation of a Myth," *Urban Review* 14:47–63 (1982).
31. Jeannie Oakes, *Keeping Track, How Schools Structure Inequality* (New Haven, CT: Yale University Press, 1985), p. 48.
32. Ibid., p. 57.
33. Delos Kelly, *Creating School Failure, Youth Crime, and Deviance* (Los Angeles: Trident Shop, 1982), p. 11.
34. Delos Kelly and W. Grove, "Teachers' Nominations and the Production of Academic Misfits," *Education* 101:246–263 (1981).
35. Delos Kelly, "The Role of Teachers' Nominations in the Perpetuation of Deviant Adolescent Careers," *Education* 96:209–217 (1976).
36. Oakes, *Keeping Track,* p. 48.
37. Elizabeth Stearns, "Interracial Friendliness and the Social Organization of Schools," *Youth & Society* 35:395–419 (2004).
38. David Anderson, "Curriculum, Culture, and Community: The Challenge of School Violence," in Michael Tonry and Mark Moore, eds., *Youth Violence: Crime and Justice, An Annual Review of Research* (Chicago: University of Chicago Press, 1998), pp. 317–363.

39. Wayne Welsh, "The Effects of School Climate on School Disorder," *The Annals of the American Academy of Political and Social Science* 567:88–107 (2000).

40. Alexandra Loukas and Sheri Robinson, "Examining the Moderating Role of Perceived School Climate in Early Adolescent Adjustment," *Journal of Research on Adolescence* 14:209–234 (2004).

41. Richard Lawrence, "Parents, Peers, School, and Delinquency," paper presented at the American Society of Criminology meeting, Boston, November 1995.

42. Patricia Jenkins, "School Delinquency and the School Social Bond," *Journal of Research in Crime and Delinquency* 34:337–367 (1997).

43. Carolyn Smith, Alan Lizotte, Terence Thornberry, and Marvin Krohn, "Resilience to Delinquency," *The Prevention Researcher* 4:4–7 (1997); Matthew Zingraff, Jeffrey Leiter, Matthew Johnsen, and Kristen Myers, "The Mediating Effect of Good School Performance on the Maltreatment-Delinquency Relationship," *Journal of Research in Crime and Delinquency* 31:62–91 (1994).

44. Rick Bragg, "4 Girls and a Teacher Are Shot to Death in an Ambush at a Middle School in Arkansas," *New York Times*, March 25, 1998, p.1.

45. Charles Callahan and Frederick Rivara, "Urban High School Youth and Handguns," *Journal of the American Medical Association* 267:3038–3042 (1992).

46. Ben Brown and William Reed Benedict, "Bullets, Blades, and Being Afraid in Hispanic High Schools: An Exploratory Study of the Presence of Weapons and Fear of Weapon-Associated Victimization among High School Students in a Border Town," *Crime and Delinquency* 50:372–395 (2004).

47. National Institute of Education, U.S. Department of Health, Education and Welfare, *Violent Schools—Safe Schools: The Safe Schools Study Report to the Congress*, vol. 1 (Washington, DC: Government Printing Office, 1977).

48. Jill DeVoe, Katharin Peter, Sally Ruddy, Amanda Miller, Mike Planty, Thomas Snyder, and Michael Rand, *Indicators of School Crime and Safety, 2003* (Washington, DC: U.S. Department of Education and Bureau of Justice Statistics, 2004).

49. Christine Kerres Malecki and Michelle Kilpatrick Demaray, "Carrying a Weapon to School and Perceptions of Social Support in an Urban Middle School," *Journal of Emotional and Behavioral Disorders* 11:169–178 (2003).

50. Pamela Wilcox and Richard Clayton, "A Multilevel Analysis of School-Based Weapon Possession," *Justice Quarterly* 18:509–542 (2001).

51. Mark Anderson, Joanne Kaufman, Thomas Simon, Lisa Barrios, Len Paulozzi, George Ryan, Rodney Hammond, William Modzeleski, Thomas Feucht, Lloyd Potter, and the School-Associated Violent Deaths Study Group, "School-Associated Violent Deaths in the United States, 1994–1999," *Journal of the American Medical Association* 286:2695–2702 (2001).

52. Bryan Vossekuil, Marisa Reddy, Robert Fein, Randy Borum, and William Modzeleski, *Safe School Initiative, An Interim Report on the Prevention of Targeted Violence in Schools* (Washington, DC: United States Secret Service, 2000).

53. James Q. Wilson, "Crime in Society and Schools," in J. M. McPartland and E. L. McDill, eds., *Violence in Schools: Perspective, Programs and Positions* (Lexington, MA: D.C. Heath, 1977), p. 48.

54. Gary Gottfredson and Denise Gottfredson, *Victimization in Schools* (New York: Plenum Press, 1985), p. 18.

55. Daryl Hellman and Susan Beaton, "The Pattern of Violence in Urban Public Schools: The Influence of School and Community," *Journal of Research in Crime and Delinquency* 23:102–127 (1986).

56. Nancy Weishew and Samuel Peng, "Variables Predicting Students' Problem Behaviors," *Journal of Educational Research* 87:5–17 (1993).

57. Wayne Welsh, Robert Stokes, and Jack Greene, "A Macro-Level Model of School Disorder," *Journal of Research in Crime and Delinquency* 37:243–283 (2000).

58. Peter Lindstrom, "Patterns of School Crime: A Replication and Empirical Extension," *British Journal of Criminology* 37:121–131 (1997).

59. Richard Lawrence, *School Crime and Juvenile Justice* (New York: Oxford University Press, 1998).

60. Wayne Welsh, Robert Stokes, and Jack Greene, "A Macro-Level Model of School Disorder," p. 270.

61. Joan McDermott, "Crime in the School and in the Community: Offenders, Victims, and Fearful Youth," *Crime and Delinquency* 29:270–283 (1983).

62. Ibid.

63. Annette Fuentes, "Discipline and Punish," *Nation* 277:17–21 (2003).

64. Finn-Aage Esbensen and D. Wayne Osgood, "Gang Resistance Education and Training (GREAT): Results from the National Evaluation," *Journal of Research in Crime and Delinquency* 36:194–225 (1999).

65. June L. Arnette and Marjorie C. Walsleben, *Combating Fear and Restoring Safety in Schools* (Washington, DC: Office of Juvenile Justice and Delinquency Prevention, 1998).

66. Heaviside and Burns, *Violence and Discipline Problems in U.S. Public Schools*.

67. Ibid., p. 20.

68. Bruce Jacobs, "Anticipatory Undercover Targeting in High Schools," *Journal of Criminal Justice* 22:445–457 (1994).

69. Mike Kennedy, "Fighting Crime by Design," *American School & University* 73:46–47 (2001).

70. Ibid.

71. American Academy of Pediatrics Committee on School Health, "Violence in Schools: Current Status and Prevention," in P. R. Nader, ed., *School Health: Policy and Practice* (Elk Grove Village, IL: American Academy of Pediatrics Committee on School Health), pp. 363–380 at 369.

72. Kevin Bushweller, "Guards with Guns," *The American School Board Journal* 180:34–36 (1993).

73. Bella English, "Hub Program to Counsel Violent Pupils," *Boston Globe*, February 24, 1987, p. 1.

74. Randal C. Archibold, "City Schools Tentatively Agree to Let the Police Run Security," *New York Times*, August 29, 1998.

75. Robyn Colman and Adrian Colman, "School Crime," *Youth Studies Australia* 23:6–7 (2004).

76. Christopher Schreck, J. Mitchell Miller, and Chris Gibson, "Trouble in the School Yard: A Study of the Risk Factors of Victimization at School," *Crime and Delinquency* 49:460–484 (2003).

77. Stuart Tremlow, "Preventing Violence in Schools," *Psychiatric Times* 21: 61–65 (2004).

78. Darcia Harris Bowman, "Curbing Crime," *Education Week* 23(30) (2004).

79. Allison Ann Payne, Denise Gottfredson, and Gary Gottfredson, "Schools as Communities: The Relationships among Communal School Organization, Student Bonding, and School Disorder," *Criminology* 41:749–777 (2003).

80. Hellman and Beaton, "The Pattern of Violence in Public Schools," pp. 122–23.

81. Julius Menacker, Ward Weldon, and Emanuel Hurwitz, "Community Influences on School Crime and Violence," *Urban Education* 25:68–80 (1990).

82. Mansfield and Farris, *Public School Principal Survey*, p. iii.

83. S. Arons, "Compulsory Education: The Plain People Resist," *Saturday Review* 15:63–69 (1972).

84. Ibid.

85. See *Pierce v. Society of Sisters*, 268 U.S. 610, 45 S.Ct. 571, 69 L.Ed. 1070 (1925).

86. 406 U.S. 205, 92 S.Ct. 1526, 32 L.Ed.2d 15 (1972).

87. 393 U.S. 503, 89 S.Ct. 733 (1969).

88. Ibid.

89. Ibid., p. 741.

90. *Bethel School District No. 403 v. Fraser*, 478 U.S. 675, 106 S.Ct. 3159, 92 L.Ed.2d 549 (1986).

91. *Hazelwood School District v. Kuhlmeier*, 484 U.S. 260, 108 S.Ct. 562, 98 L.Ed.2d 592 (1988).

92. Terry McManus, "Home Web Sites Thrust Students into Censorship Disputes," *New York Times*, August 13, 1998, p. E9.

93. *Santa Fe Independent School District, Petitioner v. Jane Doe*, individually and as next friend for her minor children, Jane and John Doe, et al., No. 99–62 (June 19, 2000).

94. *Good News Club et al. v. Milford Central School No. 99–2036* (2001).

95. Va. Code Ann. S 22.1-203 (Michie 2000).

96. *Brown v. Gilmore*, 01-384 (Case heard on October 29, 2001).

97. *Elk Grove Unified School District v. Newdow*, case no. 02-1624 (2004).

98. Ibid.

99. 423 U.S. 907, 96 S.Ct. 210, 46 L.Ed.2d 137 (1975).

100. 430 U.S. 651, 97 S.Ct. 1401 (1977).

101. 419 U.S. 565, 95 S.Ct. 729 (1976).

102. *New Jersey v. T.L.O.*, 469 U.S. 325, 105 S.Ct. 733 (1985).

103. *People v. Overton*, 24 N.Y.2d 522, 301 N.Y.S.2d 479, 249 N.E.2d 366 (1969); Brenda Walts, "*New Jersey v. T.L.O.*: Questions the Court Did Not Answer about School Searches," *Law and Education Journal* 14:421 (1985).

104. *Vernonia School District 47J v. Acton*, 115 S.Ct. 2394 (1995); Bernard James and Jonathan Pyatt, "Supreme Court Extends School's Authority to Search," *National School Safety Center News Journal* 26:29 (1995).

105. Michael Medaris, *A Guide to the Family Educational Rights and Privacy Act* (Washington, DC: Office of Juvenile Justice and Delinquency Prevention, 1998).

106. Ibid.

107. Alexander Liazos, "Schools, Alienation, and Delinquency," *Crime and Delinquency* 24:355–361 (1978).

108. Stephen Cox, William Davidson, and Timothy Bynum, "A Meta-Analytic Assessment of Delinquency-Related Outcomes of Alternative Education Programs," *Crime and Delinquency* 41:219–234 (1995).

109. Gary Putka, "Cheaters in Schools May Not Be Students but Their Teachers," *Wall Street Journal,* November 2, 1989, p. 1.

110. U.S. Senate Subcommittee on Delinquency, *Challenge for the Third Century,* p. 95.

111. William Bukoski, "School–Based Substance Abuse Prevention: A Review of Program Research," *Journal of Children in Contemporary Society* 18:95–116 (1985).

112. See J. David Hawkins and Denise Lishner, "Schooling and Delinquency," in E. H. Johnson, ed., *Handbook on Crime and Delinquency* (Westport, Conn.: Greenwood Press, 1987).

Drug Use and Delinquency

10

Chapter Outline

Frequently Abused Drugs
Marijuana and Hashish
Cocaine
Heroin
Alcohol
Other Drug Categories

Trends in Teenage Drug Use
The Monitoring the Future (MTF) Survey
The PRIDE Survey
The National Survey on Drug Use and Health
Are the Survey Results Accurate?

Why Do Youths Take Drugs?
Social Disorganization
Peer Pressure
Family Factors
Genetic Factors
Emotional Problems
Problem Behavior Syndrome
Rational Choice

Pathways to Drug Abuse
Adolescents Who Distribute Small Amounts of Drugs
FOCUS ON DELINQUENCY: Problem Behaviors and
    Substance Abuse
Adolescents Who Frequently Sell Drugs
Teenage Drug Dealers Who Commit Other Delinquent Acts
Losers and Burnouts
Persistent Offenders

Drug Use and Delinquency
Drugs and Chronic Offending
Explaining Drug Use and Delinquency

Drug Control Strategies
Law Enforcement Efforts
Education Strategies
Community Strategies
POLICY AND PRACTICE: Drug Abuse Resistance
    Education (D.A.R.E.)
Treatment Strategies
Harm Reduction

What Does the Future Hold?

Chapter Objectives

1. Know which are the drugs most frequently abused by American youth
2. Understand the extent of the drug problem among American youth today
3. Be able to discuss how teenage drug use in this country has changed over time
4. Know the main explanations for why youths take drugs
5. Recognize the different behavior patterns of drug-involved youths
6. Understand the relationship between drug use and delinquency
7. Be familiar with the major drug-control strategies
8. Be able to argue the pros and cons of government use of different drug-control strategies

CNN. View the CNN video clip of this story and answer related Critical Thinking questions on your Juvenile Delinquency 9e CD-ROM.

Surveys indicate that more than half of all high school–age kids have used drugs. Although this is a troubling statistic, these surveys also show that teen drug use is down from five and ten years ago. Many programs have been implemented over the years to help children and teens avoid taking drugs, such as educating them about the dangers of drug use and developing skills to "Just Say No." Some of these programs take place in the school and the community, and some involve police and other juvenile justice agencies. But what role can families play in helping to prevent teen drug use? A study by the Center on Addiction and Substance Abuse suggests that parents play an important role. The study found that teens whose parents set down rules about what they can watch and listen to, care about how they are doing at school, and generally take an active interest in their lives are the least likely group to use drugs. In contrast, teens with hands-off parents were found to be more likely to try drugs.

substance abuse
Using drugs or alcohol in such a way as to cause physical, emotional and/or psychological harm to yourself.

The Lindesmith Center is one of the leading independent drug policy institutes in the United States. View its website at www.lindesmith.org. For an up-to-date list of web links, go to http://cj.wadsworth.com/ siegel_jd9e.

There is little question that adolescent **substance abuse** and its association with delinquency are vexing problems. Almost every town, village, and city in the United States has confronted some type of teenage substance abuse problem.

Self-report surveys indicate that more than half of high school seniors have tried drugs and more than 75 percent use alcohol.[1] Adolescents at high risk for drug abuse often come from the most impoverished communities and experience a multitude of problems, including school failure and family conflict.[2] Equally troubling is the association between drug use and crime.[3] Research indicates that more than half of all juvenile arrestees in some cities test positive for cocaine.[4] Self-report surveys show that drug abusers are more likely to become delinquents than are nonabusers.[5] The pattern of drug use and crime makes teenage substance abuse a key national concern.[6]

This chapter addresses some important issues involving teenage substance abuse, beginning with a review of the kinds of drugs children and adolescents are using and how often they are using them. Then we discuss who uses drugs and what causes substance abuse. After describing the association between drug abuse and delinquent behavior, the chapter concludes with a review of efforts to control the use of drugs in the United States.

FREQUENTLY ABUSED DRUGS

A wide variety of substances referred to as "drugs" are used by teenagers. Some are addicting, others not. Some create hallucinations, others cause a depressed stupor, and a few give an immediate uplift. This section identifies the most widely used substances and discusses their effects. All of these drugs can be abused, and because of the danger they present, many have been banned from private use. Others are available legally only with a physician's supervision, and a few are available to adults but prohibited for children.

Marijuana and Hashish

hashish
A concentrated form of cannabis made from unadulterated resin from the female cannabis plant.

marijuana
The dried leaves of the cannabis plant.

Commonly called "pot" or "grass," marijuana is produced from the leaves of *Cannabis sativa*. **Hashish** (hash) is a concentrated form of cannabis made from unadulterated resin from the female plant. The main active ingredient in both marijuana and hashish is tetrahydrocannabinol (THC), a mild hallucinogen. **Marijuana** is the drug most commonly used by teenagers.

Smoking large amounts of pot or hash can cause distortions in auditory and visual perception, even producing hallucinatory effects. Small doses produce an early excitement ("high") that gives way to drowsiness. Pot use is also related to decreased activity, overestimation of time and space, and increased food consumption. When the user is alone, marijuana produces a dreamy state. In a group, users become giddy and lose perspective.

Marijuana is not physically addicting, but its long-term effects have been the subject of much debate. During the 1970s, it was reported that smoking pot caused a variety of physical and mental problems, including brain damage and mental illness. Although the dangers of pot and hash may have been overstated, use of these drugs does present some health risks, including an increased risk of lung cancer, chronic bronchitis, and other diseases. Marijuana smoking should be avoided by prospective parents because it lowers sperm count in male users, and females experience disrupted ovulation and a greater chance of miscarriage.[7]

Cocaine

cocaine
A powerful natural stimulant derived from the coca plant.

Cocaine is an alkaloid derivative of the coca plant. When first isolated in 1860, it was considered a medicinal breakthrough that could relieve fatigue, depression, and other symptoms, and it quickly became a staple of patent medicines. When its addictive qualities and dangerous side effects became apparent, its use was controlled by the Pure Food and Drug Act of 1906.

Cocaine is the most powerful natural stimulant. Its use produces euphoria, restlessness, and excitement. Overdoses can cause delirium, violent manic behavior, and possible respiratory failure. The drug can be sniffed, or "snorted," into the nostrils, or it can be injected. The immediate feeling of euphoria, or "rush," is short-lived, and heavy users may snort coke as often as every 10 minutes. Another dangerous practice is "speedballing"—injecting a mixture of cocaine and heroin.

crack
A highly addictive crystalline form of cocaine containing remnants of hydrochloride and sodium bicarbonate, which emits a crackling sound when smoked.

Crack is processed street cocaine. Its manufacture involves using ammonia or baking soda (sodium bicarbonate) to remove the hydrochlorides and create a crystalline form of cocaine that can be smoked. In fact, crack gets its name from the fact that the sodium bicarbonate often emits a crackling sound when the substance is smoked. Also referred to as "rock," "gravel," and "roxanne," crack gained popularity in the mid-1980s. It is relatively inexpensive, can provide a powerful high, and is highly addictive psychologically. Crack cocaine use has been in decline in recent years. Heavy criminal penalties, tight enforcement, and social disapproval have helped to lower crack use.

Heroin

heroin

A narcotic made from opium and then cut with sugar or some other neutral substance until it is only 1 to 4 percent pure.

addict

A person with an overpowering physical or psychological need to continue taking a particular substance or drug.

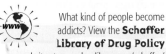

What kind of people become addicts? View the **Schaffer Library of Drug Policy** website at www.druglibrary.org/schaffer/Library/studies/cu/cu4.html. For an up-to-date list of web links, go to http://cj.wadsworth.com/siegel_jd9e.

Narcotic drugs have the ability to produce insensibility to pain and to free the mind of anxiety and emotion. Users experience relief from fear and apprehension, release of tension, and elevation of spirits. This short period of euphoria is followed by a period of apathy, during which users become drowsy and may nod off. **Heroin,** the most commonly used narcotic in the United States, is produced from opium, a drug derived from the opium poppy flower. Dealers cut the drug with neutral substances (sugar or lactose), and street heroin is often only 1 to 4 percent pure.

Heroin is probably the most dangerous commonly used drug. Users rapidly build up a tolerance for it, fueling the need for increased doses to obtain the desired effect. At first heroin is usually sniffed or snorted; as tolerance builds, it is "skin popped" (shot into skin, but not into a vein); and finally it is injected into a vein, or "mainlined."[8] Through this progressive use, the user becomes an **addict**—a person with an overpowering physical and psychological need to continue taking a particular substance by any means possible. If addicts cannot get enough heroin to satisfy their habit, they will suffer withdrawal symptoms, which include irritability, depression, extreme nervousness, and nausea.

Alcohol

alcohol

Fermented or distilled liquids containing ethanol, an intoxicating substance.

The drug of choice for most teenagers continues to be **alcohol.** Seventy percent of high school seniors reported using alcohol in the past year, and 77 percent say they have tried it at some time during their lifetime; by the 12th grade just under three-fifths of American youth report that they have "been drunk."[9] More than 20 million Americans are estimated to be problem drinkers, and at least half of these are alcoholics.

Alcohol may be a factor in nearly half of all murders, suicides, and accidental deaths.[10] Alcohol-related deaths number 100,000 a year, far more than all other illegal drugs combined. Just over 1.4 million drivers are arrested each year for driving under the influence (including 13,400 teens), and around 1.2 million more are arrested for other alcohol-related violations.[11] The economic cost is staggering. An estimated $185 billion is lost each year, including $36 billion from premature deaths, $88 billion in reduced work effort, and $19 billion arising from short- and long-term medical problems.[12]

According to the gateway model of drug abuse, drug involvement begins with drinking alcohol at an early age, which progresses to experimentation with recreational drugs such as marijuana, and finally, to using hard drugs such as cocaine and even heroin.

© Richard Hutchings/PhotoEdit

To learn more about the **causes of alcoholism,** go to the National Council on Alcoholism and Drug Dependence, Inc. (NCADD), a group that advocates prevention, intervention, research, and treatment of alcoholism and other drug addictions: www.ncadd.org. For an up-to-date list of web links, go to http://cj.wadsworth.com/siegel_jd9e.

Considering these problems, why do so many youths drink to excess? Youths who use alcohol report that it reduces tension, enhances pleasure, improves social skills, and transforms experiences for the better.[13] Although these reactions may result from limited use of alcohol, alcohol in higher doses acts as a depressant. Long-term use has been linked with depression and physical ailments ranging from heart disease to cirrhosis of the liver. Many teens also think drinking stirs their romantic urges, but scientific evidence indicates that alcohol decreases sexual response.[14]

Other Drug Categories

Other drug categories include anesthetic drugs, inhalants, sedatives and barbiturates, tranquilizers, hallucinogens, stimulants, steroids, designer drugs, and cigarettes.

anesthetic drugs
Central nervous system depressants.

Anesthetic Drugs Anesthetic drugs are central nervous system (CNS) depressants. Local anesthetics block nervous system transmissions; general anesthetics act on the brain to produce loss of sensation, stupor, or unconsciousness. The most widely abused anesthetic drug is phencyclidine (PCP), known as "angel dust." Angel dust can be sprayed on marijuana or other leaves and smoked, drunk, or injected. Originally developed as an animal tranquilizer, PCP creates hallucinations and a spaced-out feeling that causes heavy users to engage in violent acts. The effects of PCP can last up to two days, and the danger of overdose is high.

inhalants
Volatile liquids that give off a vapor, which is inhaled, producing short-term excitement and euphoria followed by a period of disorientation.

Inhalants Some youths inhale vapors from lighter fluid, paint thinner, cleaning fluid, or model airplane glue to reach a drowsy, dizzy state that is sometimes accompanied by hallucinations. **Inhalants** produce a short-term euphoria followed by a period of disorientation, slurred speech, and drowsiness. Amyl nitrite ("poppers") is a commonly used volatile liquid packaged in capsule form, which is inhaled when the capsule is broken open.

sedatives
Drugs of the barbiturate family that depress the central nervous system into a sleeplike condition.

Sedatives and Barbiturates Sedatives, the most commonly used drugs of the barbiturate family, depress the central nervous system into a sleeplike condition. On the illegal market, sedatives are called "goofballs" or "downers" and are often known by the color of the capsules: "reds" (Seconal), "blue devils" (Amytal), and "rainbows" (Tuinal).

Sedatives can be prescribed by doctors as sleeping pills. Illegal users employ them to create relaxed, sociable feelings; overdoses can cause irritability, repellent behavior, and unconsciousness. Barbiturates are the major cause of drug-overdose deaths.

tranquilizers
Drugs that reduce anxiety and promote relaxation.

Tranquilizers Tranquilizers reduce anxiety and promote relaxation. Legally prescribed tranquilizers, such as Ampazine, Thorazine, Pacatal, and Sparine, were originally designed to control the behavior of people suffering from psychoses, aggressiveness, and agitation. Less powerful tranquilizers, such as Valium, Librium, Miltown, and Equanil, are used to combat anxiety, tension, fast heart rate, and headaches. The use of illegally obtained tranquilizers can lead to addiction, and withdrawal can be painful and hazardous.

hallucinogens
Natural or synthetic substances that produce vivid distortions of the senses without greatly disturbing consciousness.

Hallucinogens Hallucinogens, either natural or synthetic, produce vivid distortions of the senses without greatly disturbing the viewer's consciousness. Some produce hallucinations, and others cause psychotic behavior in otherwise normal people.

One common hallucinogen is mescaline, named after the Mescalero Apaches, who first discovered its potent effect. Mescaline occurs naturally in the peyote, a small cactus that grows in Mexico and the southwestern United States. After initial discomfort, mescaline produces vivid hallucinations and out-of-body sensations.

A second group of hallucinogens are synthetic alkaloid compounds. These can be transformed into lysergic acid diethylamide, commonly called LSD. This powerful substance stimulates cerebral sensory centers to produce visual hallucinations, intensify hearing, and increase sensitivity. Users often report a scrambling of sensations; they may "hear colors" and "smell music." Users also report feeling euphoric and mentally superior, although to an observer they appear disoriented. Anxiety and panic may occur, and overdoses can produce psychotic episodes, flashbacks, and even death.

stimulants
Synthetic substances that produce an intense physical reaction by stimulating the central nervous system.

Stimulants Stimulants ("uppers," "speed," "pep pills," "crystal") are synthetic drugs that stimulate action in the central nervous system. They produce increased blood pressure, breathing rate, and bodily activity, and mood elevation. One widely used amphetamine produces psychological effects such as increased confidence, euphoria, impulsive behavior, and loss of appetite. Commonly used stimulants include Benzedrine ("bennies"), Dexedrine ("dex"), Dexamyl, Bephetamine ("whites"), and Methedrine ("meth," "speed," "crystal meth").

Methedrine is probably the most widely used and most dangerous amphetamine. Some people swallow it; heavy users inject it. Long-term heavy use can result in exhaustion, anxiety, prolonged depression, and hallucinations. Another form of methamphetamine is a crystallized substance with the street name of "ice" or "crystal." Smoking this crystal causes weight loss, kidney damage, heart and respiratory problems, and paranoia.[15]

anabolic steroids
Drugs used by athletes and bodybuilders to gain muscle bulk and strength.

Steroids Teenagers use highly dangerous **anabolic steroids** to gain muscle bulk and strength.[16] Black-market sales of these drugs approach $1 billion annually. Although not physically addicting, steroids can become an "obsession" among teens who desire athletic success. Long-term users may spend up to $400 a week on steroids and may support their habit by dealing the drug.

Steroids are dangerous because of the health problems associated with their long-term use: liver ailments, tumors, kidney problems, sexual dysfunction, hypertension, and mental problems such as depression. Steroid use runs in cycles, and other drugs—Clomid, Teslac, and Halotestin, for example—that carry their own dangerous side effects are often used to curb the need for high dosages of steroids. Finally, steroid users often share needles, which puts them at high risk for contracting HIV, the virus that causes AIDS.

designer drugs
Lab-made drugs designed to avoid existing drug laws.

Designer Drugs Designer drugs are lab-created synthetics that are designed to get around existing drug laws, at least temporarily. The most widely used designer drug is "ecstasy," which is derived from speed and methamphetamine. After being

Club drugs are primarily synthetic substances commonly used at nightclubs, bars, and raves. The most widely used designer drug is ecstasy, or MDMA, which combines an amphetamine-like rush with hallucinogenic experiences. It produces mood swings, disturbs sleeping and eating habits, alters thinking processes, and creates aggressive behavior.

© Amy Etra/PhotoEdit

swallowed, snorted, injected, or smoked, it acts simultaneously as a stimulant and a hallucinogen, producing mood swings, disturbing sleeping and eating habits, altering thinking processes, creating aggressive behavior, interfering with sexual function, and affecting sensitivity to pain. The drug can also increase blood pressure and heart rate. Teenage users taking ecstasy at raves have died from heat stroke because the drug can cause dehydration.

Cigarettes Approximately 25 countries have established laws to prohibit the sale of cigarettes to minors. The reality, however, is that in many countries children and adolescents have easy access to tobacco products.[17] In the United States, the Synar Amendment, enacted in 1992, requires states to enact and enforce laws restricting the sale of tobacco products to youths under the age of 18. States are required to reduce illegal sales rates to minors to no more than 20 percent within several years. The FDA rules require age verification for anyone under the age of 27 who is purchasing tobacco products. The FDA has also banned cigarette vending machines and self-service displays except in adult-only facilities. Despite all of these measures, just over 5 out of 10 high school seniors in America—54 percent of them—report having smoked cigarettes over their lifetime. However, in recent years cigarette use by high school students has been on the decline.[18]

TO QUIZ YOURSELF ON THIS MATERIAL, go to the Juvenile Delinquency 9e website.

TRENDS IN TEENAGE DRUG USE

Has America's decade-long war on drugs paid off? Has drug use declined, or is it on the upswing? A number of national surveys conduct annual reviews of teen drug use by interviewing samples of teens around the nation. What do national surveys tell us about the extent of drug use, and what have been the recent trends in teen usage?

The Monitoring the Future (MTF) Survey

One of the most important and influential surveys of teen substance abuse is the annual Monitoring the Future survey conducted by the Institute for Social Research at the University of Michigan. In all, about 45,000 students located in 433 secondary schools participate in the study.[19]

The most recent MTF survey indicates that, with a few exceptions, drug use among American adolescents held steady in 2003, but declined from the recent peak levels reached in 1996 and 1997. As Figure 10.1 shows, drug use peaked in the late 1970s and early 1980s and then began a decade-long decline until showing an uptick in the mid-1990s; usage for most drugs has been stable or in decline since then. Especially encouraging has been a significant drop in the use of crack cocaine among younger kids. There has also been a continuing decline in cigarette smoking, as well as the use of smokeless tobacco products. More troubling is the use of ecstasy, which, because of its popularity at dance clubs and raves, rose among older teens (10th- and 12th-graders) for much of the late 1990s and up to 2001, but has since dropped sharply. In 2003, 3 percent of 10th-graders reported some use of ecstasy during the previous 12 months (down from 4.9 percent in 2002); 4.5 percent of the 12th-graders also reported some use (down from 7.4 percent in 2001). Heroin use has also dropped sharply in the last couple of years (just under 1 percent of 12th-grade boys are users) after the rates had roughly doubled between 1991 and 1995, when noninjectable forms of heroin use became

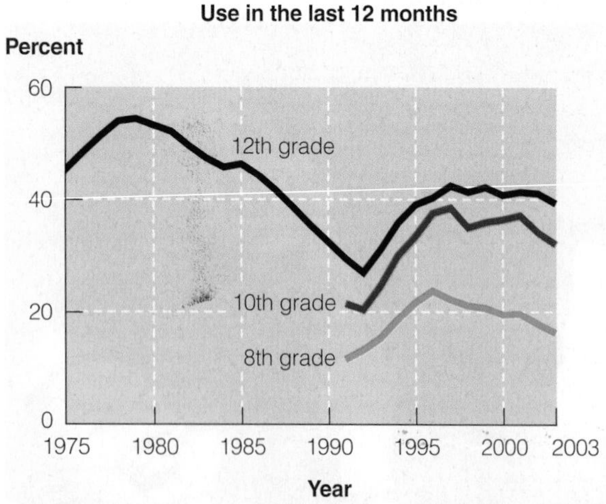

Use in the last 12 months

Percent

12th grade

10th grade

8th grade

FIGURE 10.1

Trends in Annual Prevalence of an Illicit Drug Use Index

SOURCE: Lloyd D. Johnson, Patrick M. O'Malley, Jerald G. Bachman, and John E. Schulenberg, *Monitoring the Future: National Results on Adolescent Drug Use. Overview of Key Findings, 2003* (Bethesda, MD: National Institute on Drug Abuse, 2004), Table 1.

Table 10.1

Annual Drug Use, 1998–99 versus 2002–03, Grades 6–12

	1998–99	2002–03	% rate of decrease
Cigarettes	37.9	27.3	28.0
Any alcohol	56.8	50.1	11.8
Any illicit drug	27.1	24.3	10.3

SOURCE: PRIDE Surveys (Bowling Green, KY: Pride, Inc., 2003).

popular. It is possible that widely publicized overdose deaths of musicians and celebrities may have helped stabilize heroin abuse. Alcohol use among teens has been fairly stable over the past several years. Nonetheless, nearly one-fifth of 8th-graders, and almost half of 12th-graders use alcohol regularly.

The PRIDE Survey

A second source of information on teen drug and alcohol abuse is the National Parents' Resource Institute for Drug Education (PRIDE) survey, which is also conducted annually.[20] Typically, findings from the PRIDE survey correlate highly with the MTF drug survey. The most recent PRIDE survey (for the 2002–03 school year) indicates slight increases in drug activity over the previous school year, but substantial decreases over the last five years. For example, about 24 percent of students in grades 6 to 12 claimed to have used drugs during the past year, down from 27 percent in the 1998–99 school year (see Table 10.1). Cigarette smoking and alcohol use are also down from five years ago. The fact that two surveys generate roughly the same pattern in drug abuse helps bolster their validity and give support to a decline in teenage substance abuse.

The National Survey on Drug Use and Health

Conducted by the Department of Health and Human Services' National Institute on Drug Abuse (NIDA), the National Survey on Drug Use and Health (formerly called the National Household Survey of Drug Abuse) interviews approximately 70,000 people at home each year.[21] Like the MTF and PRIDE surveys, this survey shows that drug and alcohol use, though still a significant problem, has stabilized or declined.

Although teen drug and alcohol use stabilized in recent years, it is still a significant problem. For example, *heavy drinking* (defined as having five or more alcoholic drinks on the same occasion on at least five different days in the past 30 days) was reported by 6.7 percent of the population aged 12 and older, or 15.9 million people. Among youths aged 12 to 17, 2.5 percent were heavy drinkers and 10.7 percent engaged in *binge drinking,* defined as having five or more alcoholic beverages on the same occasion at least once in the past 30 days.[22]

Are the Survey Results Accurate?

Student drug surveys must be interpreted with caution. First, it may be overly optimistic to expect that heavy users are going to cooperate with a drug-use survey, especially one conducted by a government agency. Even if willing, these students are likely to be absent from school during testing periods. Also, drug abusers are more likely to be forgetful and to give inaccurate accounts of their substance abuse.

Another problem is the likelihood that the most drug-dependent portion of the adolescent population is omitted from the sample. In some cities, almost half of all youths arrested dropped out of school before the 12th grade, and more than half of these arrestees are drug users.[23] Juvenile detainees (those arrested and held in a lockup) test positively for cocaine at a rate many times higher than those reporting recent use in the MTF and PRIDE surveys.[24] The inclusion of eighth-graders in the MTF sample is one way of getting around the dropout problem. Nonetheless, high school surveys may be excluding some of the most drug-prone young people in the population.

There is evidence that the accuracy of reporting may be affected by social and personal traits: Girls are more willing than boys to admit taking drugs; kids from two-parent homes are less willing to admit taking drugs than kids growing up in single-parent homes. Julia Yun Soo Kim, Michael Fendrich, and Joseph Wislar speculate that it is culturally unacceptable for some subgroups in the population, such as Hispanic females, to use drugs, and therefore, in self-report surveys, they may underrepresent their involvement.[25]

Although these problems are serious, they are consistent over time and therefore do not hinder the *measurement of change* or trends in drug usage. That is, prior surveys also omitted dropouts and other high-risk individuals and were biased because of cultural issues. However, because these problems are built into every wave of the surveys, any change recorded in the annual substance abuse rate is probably genuine. So, although the *validity* of these surveys may be questioned, they are probably *reliable* indicators of trends in substance abuse.

TO QUIZ YOURSELF ON THIS MATERIAL, go to the Juvenile Delinquency 9e website.

WHY DO YOUTHS TAKE DRUGS?

Why do youths engage in an activity that is sure to bring them overwhelming problems? It is hard to imagine that even the youngest drug users are unaware of the problems associated with substance abuse. Although it is easy to understand dealers' desires for quick profits, how can we explain users' disregard for long- and short-term consequences? Concept Summary 10.1 reviews some of the most likely reasons.

Concept Summary 10.1
Key Reasons Why Youths Take Drugs

Social Disorganization	Poverty; growing up in disorganized urban environment
Peer Pressure	Associating with youths who take drugs
Family Factors	Poor family life, including harsh punishment, neglect
Genetic Factors	Parents abuse drugs
Emotional Problems	Feelings of inadequacy; blame others for failures
Problem Behavior Syndrome	Drug use is one of many problem behaviors
Rational Choice	Perceived benefits, including relaxation, greater creativity

Social Disorganization

One explanation ties drug abuse to poverty, social disorganization, and hopelessness. Drug use by young minority group members has been tied to factors such as racial prejudice, low self-esteem, poor socioeconomic status, and the stress of living in a harsh urban environment.[26] The association between drug use, race, and poverty has been linked to the high level of mistrust and defiance found in lower socioeconomic areas.[27] Despite the long-documented association between social disorganization and drug use, the empirical data on the relationship between class and crime has been inconclusive. For example, the National Youth Survey (NYS), a longitudinal study of delinquent behavior conducted by Delbert Elliott and his associates, found little if any association between drug use and social class. The NYS found that drug use is higher among urban youths, but there was little evidence that minority youths or members of the lower class were more likely to abuse drugs than white youths and the more affluent.[28] Research by the Rand Corporation indicates that many drug-dealing youths had legitimate jobs at the time they were arrested for drug trafficking.[29] Therefore, it would be difficult to describe drug abusers simply as unemployed dropouts.

Peer Pressure

Research shows that adolescent drug abuse is highly correlated with the behavior of best friends, especially when parental supervision is weak.[30] Youths in inner-city areas where feelings of alienation run high often come in contact with drug users who teach them that drugs provide an answer to their feelings of inadequacy and stress.[31] Perhaps they join with peers to learn the techniques of drug use; their friendships with other drug-dependent youths give them social support for their habit. Empirical research efforts show that a youth's association with friends who are substance abusers increases the probability of drug use.[32] The relationship is reciprocal: Adolescent substance abusers seek friends who engage in these behaviors, and associating with drug abusers leads to increased levels of drug abuse.

Peer networks may be the most significant influence on long-term substance abuse. Shared feelings and a sense of intimacy lead youths to become enmeshed in what has been described as the "drug-use subculture."[33] Research indicates that drug users do in fact have warm relationships with substance-abusing peers who help support their behaviors.[34] This lifestyle provides users with a clear role, activities they enjoy, and an opportunity for attaining status among their peers.[35] One reason it is so difficult to treat hard-core users is that quitting drugs means leaving the "fast life" of the streets.

Family Factors

Poor family life is also offered as an explanation for drug use. Studies have found that the majority of drug users have had an unhappy childhood, which included harsh punishment and parental neglect.[36] The drug abuse and family quality association

Shared feelings and a sense of intimacy lead youths to become fully enmeshed in the "drug-use subculture." Drug users do in fact have intimate and warm relationships with substance-abusing peers, which help support their habits and behaviors.

© Joel Gordon

may involve both racial and gender differences: Females and whites who were abused as children are more likely to have alcohol and drug arrests as adults; abuse was less likely to affect drug use in males and African Americans.[37] It is also common to find substance abusers within large families and where parents are divorced, separated, or absent.[38]

Social psychologists suggest that drug abuse patterns may also result from observation of parental drug use.[39] Youths who learn that drugs provide pleasurable sensations may be most likely to experiment with illegal substances; a habit may develop if the user experiences lower anxiety and fear.[40] Research shows, for example, that gang members raised in families with a history of drug use were more likely than other gang members to use cocaine and to use it seriously. And even among gang members, parental abuse was found to be a key factor in the onset of adolescent drug use.[41] Observing drug abuse may be a more important cause of drug abuse than other family-related problems.

Other family factors associated with teen drug abuse include parental conflict over childrearing practices, failure to set rules, and unrealistic demands followed by harsh punishments. Low parental attachment, rejection, and excessive family conflict have all been linked to adolescent substance abuse.[42]

Genetic Factors

The association between parental drug abuse and adolescent behavior may have a genetic basis. Research has shown that biological children of alcoholics reared by non-alcoholic adoptive parents develop alcohol problems more often than the natural children of the adoptive parents.[43] A number of studies comparing alcoholism among identical and fraternal twins have found that the degree of concordance (both siblings behaving identically) is twice as high among the identical twin groups.[44]

A genetic basis for drug abuse is also supported by evidence showing that future substance abuse problems can be predicted by behavior exhibited as early as 6 years of age. The traits predicting future abuse are independent from peer relations and environmental influences.[45]

To read more about the **concept of addiction,** go to the Psychedelic Library and read www.psychedelic-library.org/davies/myth4.htm. For an up-to-date list of web links, go to http://cj.wadsworth.com/siegel_jd9e.

Emotional Problems

As we have seen, not all drug-abusing youths reside in lower-class urban areas. To explain drug abuse across social classes, some experts have linked drug use to emotional problems that can strike youths in any economic class. Psychodynamic explanations of substance abuse suggest that drugs help youths control or express unconscious needs. Some psychoanalysts believe adolescents who internalize their problems may use drugs to reduce their feelings of inadequacy. Introverted people may use drugs as an escape from real or imagined feelings of inferiority.[46] Another view is that adolescents who externalize their problems and blame others for their perceived failures are likely to engage in antisocial behaviors, including substance abuse. Research exists to support each of these positions.[47]

Drug abusers are also believed to exhibit psychopathic or sociopathic behavior characteristics, forming what is called an **addiction-prone personality.**[48] Drinking alcohol may reflect a teen's need to remain dependent on an overprotective mother or an effort to reduce the emotional turmoil of adolescence.[49]

Research on the psychological characteristics of narcotics abusers does, in fact, reveal the presence of a significant degree of pathology. Personality testing of users suggests that a significant percentage suffer from psychotic disorders. Studies have found that addicts suffer personality disorders characterized by a weak ego, a low frustration tolerance, and fantasies of omnipotence. Up to half of all drug abusers may also be diagnosed with antisocial personality disorder (ASPD), which is defined as a pervasive pattern of disregard for the rights of others.[50]

addiction-prone personality
A personality that has a compulsion for mood-altering drugs, believed by some to be the cause of substance abuse.

For a **web-based antidrug education campaign,** see Freevibe at www.freevibe.com. For an up-to-date list of web links, go to http://cj.wadsworth.com/siegel_jd9e.

Problem Behavior Syndrome

For some adolescents, substance abuse is one of many problem behaviors that begin early in life and remain throughout the life course.[51] Longitudinal studies show that youths who abuse drugs are maladjusted, emotionally distressed, and have many social problems.[52] Having a deviant lifestyle means associating with delinquent peers, living in a family in which parents and siblings abuse drugs, being alienated from the dominant values of society, and engaging in delinquent behaviors at an early age.[53]

Youths who abuse drugs lack commitment to religious values, disdain education, and spend most of their time in peer activities.[54] Youths who take drugs do poorly in school, have high dropout rates, and maintain their drug use after they leave school.[55] This view of adolescent drug taking is discussed in the Focus on Delinquency box entitled "Problem Behaviors and Substance Abuse."

Rational Choice

TO QUIZ YOURSELF ON THIS MATERIAL, go to the Juvenile Delinquency 9e website.

Youths may choose to use drugs because they want to get high, relax, improve their creativity, escape reality, or increase their sexual responsiveness. Research indicates that adolescent alcohol abusers believe getting high will increase their sexual performance and facilitate their social behavior; they care little about negative consequences.[56] Substance abuse, then, may be a function of the rational, albeit mistaken, belief that substance abuse benefits the user.

PATHWAYS TO DRUG ABUSE

gateway drug
A substance that leads to use of more serious drugs; alcohol use has long been thought to lead to more serious drug abuse.

There is no single path to becoming a drug abuser, but it is generally believed that most users start at a young age using alcohol as a **gateway drug** to harder substances. That is, drug involvement begins with drinking alcohol at an early age, which progresses to experimentation with marijuana, and finally, to using cocaine and even heroin. Research on adolescent drug users in Miami found that youths who began their substance abuse careers early—by experimenting with alcohol at age 7, getting drunk at age 8, having alcohol with an adult present by age 9, and becoming regular drinkers by the time they were 11 years old—later became crack users.[57] Drinking with an adult present was a significant precursor of substance abuse and delinquency.[58]

Although the gateway concept is still being debated, there is little disagreement that serious drug users begin their involvement with alcohol.[59] Though most recreational users do not progress to "hard stuff," most addicts first experiment with recreational alcohol and recreational drugs before progressing to narcotics. By implication, if teen drinking could be reduced, the gateway to hard drugs would be narrowed.

What are the patterns of teenage drug use? Are all abusers similar, or are there different types of drug involvement? Research indicates that drug-involved youths do take on different roles, lifestyles, and behavior patterns, some of which are described in the next sections.[60]

Adolescents Who Distribute Small Amounts of Drugs

Many adolescents who use and distribute small amounts of drugs do not commit any other serious delinquent acts. They occasionally sell marijuana, "crystal," and PCP to support their own drug use. Their customers include friends, relatives, and acquaintances. Deals are arranged over the phone, in school, or at public meeting places; however, the actual distribution takes place in more private arenas, such as at home or in cars.

Petty dealers do not consider themselves "seriously" involved in drugs. One girl commented, "I don't consider it dealing. I'll sell hits of speed to my friends, and joints

Problem Behaviors and Substance Abuse

According to the problem behavior syndrome model, substance abuse may be one of a constellation of social problems experienced by at-risk youth. There is significant evidence to substantiate the view that kids who abuse substances are also more likely to experience an array of social problems. For example, a recent study examined the relationship among adolescent illicit-drug use, physical abuse, and sexual abuse with a sample of Mexican American and non-Hispanic white youths living in the southwestern United States. The research found that youths who report physical and/or sexual abuse are significantly more likely to report illicit drug use than those who have never been abused. About 40 percent of youths who have experienced physical abuse report using marijuana in the previous month, while only 28 percent of youths who have

never been abused report using the drug within that time. These findings were independent of factors such as academic achievement and family structure, and they suggest that treatment directed at abused adolescents should include drug-use prevention, intervention, and education components (see Figure 10-A).

Kids who abuse drugs and alcohol are also more likely to have educational problems. A recent study of substance use among Texas students in grades 7 through 12 found that those who were absent 10 or more days during the previous school year were more likely to report alcohol, tobacco, and other drug use. For example, twice as many students with high absentee

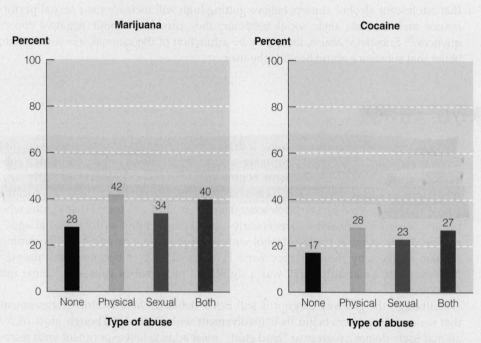

FIGURE 10-A PERCENTAGE OF YOUTHS REPORTING PAST-MONTH MARIJUANA OR PAST-YEAR COCAINE USE, BY TYPE OF ABUSE SUFFERED (N = 2,468)

NOTE: These analyses were based on data collected between 1988 and 1992 for the Mexican-American Drug Use and Dropout Survey, a yearly survey of Mexican-American and non-Hispanic white school dropouts and a comparison group of enrolled students from one school district in each of three communities in the southwestern United States.

SOURCES: Deanna Pérez, "The Relationship between Physical Abuse, Sexual Victimization, and Adolescent Illicit Drug Use," *Journal of Drug Issues* 30:641–662 (2000).

and nickel bags [of marijuana] to my friends, but that's not dealing." Petty dealers are insulated from the justice system because their activities rarely result in apprehension. In fact, few adults notice their activities because these adolescents are able to maintain a relatively conventional lifestyle. In several jurisdictions, however, agents of the justice system are cooperating in the development of educational programs to provide nonusers with the skills to resist the "sales pitch" of petty dealers.

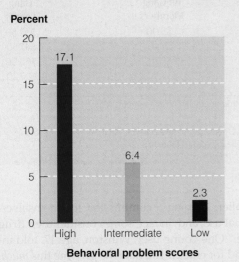

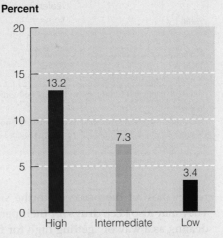

FIGURE 10-B PERCENTAGE OF YOUTHS AGED 12 TO 17 REPORTING DEPENDENCE ON ALCOHOL OR ILLICIT DRUGS, BY BEHAVIORAL AND EMOTIONAL PROBLEM SCORES, 1994–1996

NOTE: Severity levels (high, intermediate, and low) for the behavioral and emotional problem scale were determined using values set in the Youth Self-Report (YSR), an instrument extensively used in adolescent studies to assess psychological difficulties.

SOURCE: Substance Abuse and Mental Health Services Administration, Office of Applied Studies, "The Relationship between Mental Health and Substance Abuse among Adolescents," Analytic Series A-9, 1999.

rates reported using marijuana in the previous month (29% vs. 14%, respectively) than students who did not miss school.

There is also a connection between substance abuse and serious behavioral and emotional problems. One national study found that behaviorally troubled youth are seven times more likely than those with less serious problems to report that they were dependent on alcohol or illicit drugs (17.1% vs. 2.3%). In addition, youths with serious emotional problems were nearly four times more likely to report dependence (13.2% vs. 3.4%) (see Figure 10-B).

Critical Thinking

These studies provide dramatic evidence that drug abuse is highly associated with other social problems—abuse, school failure, and emotional disorders. They imply that getting kids off drugs may take a lot more effort than relying on some simple solution like "Just Say No." What would it take to get kids to refrain from using drugs?

InfoTrac College Edition Research

To find out more about the relationship between problem behaviors and adolescent substance abuse, go to InfoTrac College Edition and read Lisa H. Jaycox, Andrew R. Morral, and Jaana Juvonen, "Mental Health and Medical Problems and Service Use among Adolescent Substance Users," *Journal of the American Academy of Child & Adolescent Psychiatry* 42(6):701 (June 2003).

SOURCES: Deanna Pérez, "The Relationship between Physical Abuse, Sexual Victimization, and Adolescent Illicit Drug Use," *Journal of Drug Issues* 30:641–662 (2000); Texas Commission on Alcohol and Drug Abuse, "Substance Use among Youths at High Risk of Dropping Out: Grades 7–12 in Texas, 1998," *Texas Commission on Alcohol and Drug Abuse Research Brief,* June 2000; Substance Abuse and Mental Health Services Administration, Office of Applied Studies, "The Relationship between Mental Health and Substance Abuse among Adolescents," Analytic Series: A-9, 1999. Data and tables supplied by the Center for Substance Abuse Research, University of Maryland, College Park (2001).

Adolescents Who Frequently Sell Drugs

A small number of adolescents are high-rate dealers who bridge the gap between adult drug distributors and the adolescent user. Though many are daily users, they take part in many normal activities, including going to school and socializing with friends.

Frequent dealers often have adults who "front" for them—that is, sell them drugs for cash. The teenagers then distribute the drugs to friends and acquaintances. They

TABLE 10.2

Estimated Hourly Wages of Members in a Drug-Selling Gang

	Drug Dealers	All Gang Members	Gang Leader
Year 1	$2.50	$5.90	$32.50
Year 2	$3.70	$7.40	$47.50
Year 3	$3.30	$7.10	$65.90
Year 4	$7.10	$11.10	$97.20

NOTES: Estimated hourly wages include both official and unofficial income sources. All wages are in 1995 dollars.

SOURCE: Adapted from Steven D. Levitt and Sudhir A. Venkatesh, "An Economic Analysis of a Drug-Selling Gang's Finances," *Quarterly Journal of Economics* 115:755–789 (2000), Table III.

return most of the proceeds to the supplier, keeping a commission for themselves. They may also keep drugs for their personal use, and, in fact, some consider their drug dealing as a way of "getting high for free." One young user, Winston, age 17, told investigators, "I sell the cracks for money and for cracks. The man, he give me this *much*. I sell most of it and I get the rest for me. I like this much. Every day I do this."[61] James Inciardi and his associates found that about 80 percent of the youths who dealt crack regularly were daily users.[62]

Frequent dealers are more likely to sell drugs in parks, schools, or other public places. Deals occur irregularly, so the chance of apprehension is not significant, nor is the payoff substantial. Robert MacCoun and Peter Reuter found that drug dealers make about $30 per hour when they are working and clear on average about $2,000 per month. These amounts are greater than most dealers could hope to have earned in legitimate jobs, but they are not enough to afford a steady stream of luxuries. Most small-time dealers also hold conventional jobs.[63]

In a more recent analysis of the financial activities of a drug-selling street gang over a four-year period in which the gang was active, economists Steven Levitt and Sudhir Venkatesh found that the average hourly wage of drug dealers or "foot soldiers" was between $2.50 and $7.10 (see Table 10.2).[64] As an average wage per month, this comes to $140 to $470.[65] In a typical month, drug dealers worked just over 50 hours. As shown in Table 10.2, the hourly wage of drug dealers is substantially lower than the average wage for all gang members and the gang leader. These more recent findings suggest that, at least for drug dealers, factors other than income may explain participation in this activity.

Teenage Drug Dealers Who Commit Other Delinquent Acts

A more serious type of drug-involved youth is the one who distributes multiple substances and commits both property and violent crimes. These youngsters make up about 2 percent of the teenage population, but they may commit up to 40 percent of robberies and assaults and about 60 percent of all teenage felony thefts and drug sales. Few gender or racial differences exist among these youths: Girls are as likely as boys to become persistent drug-involved offenders, white youths as likely as black youths, and middle-class adolescents raised outside cities as likely as lower-class city children.[66]

In cities, these youths frequently are hired by older dealers to act as street-level drug runners. Each member of a crew of 3 to 12 youths will handle small quantities of drugs; the supplier receives 50 to 70 percent of the drug's street value. The crew members also act as lookouts, recruiters, and guards. Although they may be recreational drug users themselves, crew members refrain from using addictive drugs such as heroin. Between drug sales, the young dealers commit robberies, burglaries, and other thefts.

Most youngsters in the street drug trade either terminate their dealing or become drug dependent. A few, however, develop entrepreneurial skills. Those who are rarely apprehended by police advance in the drug business. They develop their own crews and may handle more than half a million dollars a year.

In many instances, these drug dealer–delinquents are members of teenage gangs. The gangs maintain "rock houses," or "stash houses," that receive drug shipments arranged by members who have the overseas connections and financial backing needed to wholesale drugs. The wholesalers pay the gang for permission to deal in their territory. Lower-echelon gang members help transport the drugs and work the houses, retailing cocaine and other drugs to neighborhood youths. Each member makes a profit for every ounce of rock sold. Police estimate that youths who work in rock houses will earn $700 and up for a 12-hour shift.[67]

Some experts question whether gangs are responsible for as much drug dealing as the media would have us believe. Some believe that the tightly organized "super" gangs are being replaced with loosely organized neighborhood groups. The turbulent environment of drug dealing is better handled by flexible organizations than by rigid, vertically organized gangs with a leader who is far removed from the action.[68]

Losers and Burnouts

Some drug-involved youths do not have the savvy to join gangs or groups and instead begin committing unplanned crimes that increase their chances of arrest. Their heavy drug use increases their risk of apprehension and decreases their value for organized drug distribution networks.

Drug-involved "losers" can earn a living by steering customers to a seller in a "copping" area, touting drug availability for a dealer, or acting as a lookout. However, they are not considered trustworthy or deft enough to handle drugs or money. Though these offenders get involved in drugs at an early age, they receive little attention from the justice system until they have developed an extensive arrest record. By then they are approaching the end of their minority and will either desist or become so entrapped in the drug-crime subculture that little can be done to deter their illegal activities.

Persistent Offenders

About two-thirds of substance-abusing youths continue to use drugs in adulthood, but about half desist from other criminal activities. Those who persist in both substance abuse and crime maintain these characteristics:

- They come from poor families.
- Other criminals are members of their families.
- They do poorly in school.
- They started using drugs and committing other delinquent acts at an early age.
- They use multiple types of drugs and commit crimes frequently.
- They have few opportunities in late adolescence to participate in legitimate and rewarding adult activities.[69]

TO QUIZ YOURSELF ON THIS MATERIAL, go to the Juvenile Delinquency 9e website.

Some evidence exists that these drug-using persisters have low nonverbal IQs and poor physical coordination. Nonetheless, there is little evidence to explain why some drug-abusing youths drop out of crime while others remain active.

An association between drug use and delinquency has been established, and this connection can take a number of forms. Crime may be an instrument of the drug trade: Violence erupts when rival gangs use weapons to settle differences and establish territorial monopolies. In New York City, authorities report that crack gangs will burn down their rivals' headquarters. It is estimated that between 35 and 40 percent of New York's homicides are drug related.[70]

Drug users may also commit crimes to pay for their habits.[71] One study conducted in Miami found that 573 narcotics users *annually* committed more than 200,000 crimes to obtain cash. Similar research with a sample of 356 addicts accounted for 118,000 crimes annually.[72] If such proportions hold true, then the nation's estimated 700,000 heroin addicts alone may be committing more than 100 million crimes each year.

Drug users may be more willing to take risks because their inhibitions are lowered by substance abuse. Cities with high rates of cocaine abuse are also more likely to experience higher levels of armed robbery. It is possible that crack and cocaine users are more willing to engage in a risky armed robbery to get immediate cash than a burglary, which requires more planning and effort.[73]

The relationship between alcohol and drug abuse and delinquency has been substantiated by a number of studies. Some have found that youths who abuse alcohol are most likely to engage in violence; as adults, those with long histories of drinking are more likely to report violent offending patterns.[74]

The National Institute of Justice's Arrestee Drug Abuse Monitoring (ADAM) program tracks trends in drug use among arrestees in urban areas. Some, but not all, of its 36 sites collect data on juveniles. Due to a lack of funding, the Department of Justice ended this program in 2004.[75] The most recent report (2002) found that, among juvenile detainees, almost 60 percent of juvenile males and 30 percent of juvenile females tested positive for marijuana, the most commonly used drug, and its prevalence was ten and six times higher than cocaine use for juvenile males and females, respectively.[76] With the exception of methamphetamines, male detainees were more likely to test positive for the use of any drug than were female detainees. While males and minority-group members have somewhat higher positive test rates than females and Caucasians, drug use is prevalent among juvenile arrestees, reaffirming the close association between substance abuse and criminality.

There is evidence that incarcerated youths are much more likely to be involved in substance abuse than adolescents in the general population. For example, research by David Cantor on incarcerated youths in Washington, D.C., found their drug involvement more than double that of nonincarcerated area youths.[77]

Drugs and Chronic Offending

It is possible that most delinquents are not drug users but that police are more likely to apprehend muddle-headed substance abusers than clear-thinking abstainers. A second, more plausible, interpretation of the existing data is that the drug abuse–crime connection is so powerful because many delinquents are in fact substance abusers. Research by Bruce Johnson and his associates confirms this suspicion. Using data from a national self-report survey, these researchers found that less than 2 percent of the youths who responded to the survey (1) report using cocaine or heroin, and (2) commit two or more index crimes each year. However, these drug-abusing adolescents accounted for 40 to 60 percent of all the index crimes reported in the sample. Less than one-quarter of these delinquents committed crimes solely to support a drug habit. These data suggest that a small core of substance-abusing adolescents commits a significant proportion of all serious crimes. It is also evident that a behavior—drug abuse—that develops late in adolescence influences the extent of delinquent activity through the life course.[78]

The relationship between drug abuse and chronic offending is illustrated by Inciardi, Horowitz, and Pottieger's interviews with crack-involved youths in Miami. The 254 kids in their sample reported committing 223,439 criminal offenses during the 12 months prior to their interviews. It is not surprising that 87 percent of the sample had been arrested. The greater the involvement in the crack business, the greater the likelihood of committing violent crime. About 74 percent of the dealers committed robbery, and 17 percent engaged in assault. Only 12 percent of the nondealers committed robbery, and 4 percent engaged in assault.[79]

Explaining Drug Use and Delinquency

The association between delinquency and drug use has been established in a variety of cultures.[80] It is far from certain, however, whether (a) drug use *causes* delinquency, (b) delinquency *leads* youths to engage in substance abuse, or (c) both drug abuse and delinquency are *functions* of some other factor.[81]

Some of the most sophisticated research on this topic has been conducted by Delbert Elliott and his associates at the Institute of Behavioral Science at the University of Colorado.[82] Using data from the National Youth Survey, a longitudinal study of self-reported delinquency and drug use, Elliott and his colleagues David Huizinga and Scott Menard found a strong association between delinquency and drug use.[83] However, the direction of the relationship is unclear. As a general rule, drug abuse appears to be a *type* of delinquent behavior and not a *cause* of delinquency. Most youths become involved in delinquent acts *before* they are initiated into drugs; it is difficult, therefore, to conclude that drug use causes crime.

According to the Elliott research, both drug use and delinquency seem to reflect developmental problems; they are both part of a disturbed lifestyle. This research reveals some important associations between substance abuse and delinquency:

1. Alcohol abuse seems to be a cause of marijuana and other drug abuse because most drug users started with alcohol, and youths who abstain from alcohol almost never take drugs.

2. Marijuana use is a cause of multiple-drug use: About 95 percent of youths who use more serious drugs started on pot; only 5 percent of serious drug users never smoked pot.

3. Youths who commit felonies started off with minor delinquent acts. Few delinquents (1%) report committing felonies only.

The Elliott research has been supported by other studies also indicating that delinquency and substance abuse are part of a general pattern of deviance or problem behavior syndrome, such as association with an antisocial peer group and educational failure.[84] There seems to be a pattern in which troubled youths start by committing petty crimes and drinking alcohol and proceed to harder drugs and more serious crimes. Kids who drink at an early age later go on to engage in violent acts in their adolescence; violent adolescents increase their alcohol abuse as they mature.[85] Both their drug abuse and the delinquency are part of an urban underclass lifestyle involving limited education, few job skills, unstable families, few social skills, and patterns of law violations.[86]

TO QUIZ YOURSELF ON THIS MATERIAL, go to the Juvenile Delinquency 9e website.

DRUG CONTROL STRATEGIES

Billions of dollars are being spent each year to reduce the importation of drugs, deter drug dealers, and treat users. Yet although the overall incidence of drug use has declined, drug use has concentrated in the nation's poorest neighborhoods, with a consequent association between substance abuse and crime.

A number of drug-control strategies have been tried. Some are designed to deter drug use by stopping the flow of drugs into the country, apprehending dealers, and cracking down on street-level drug deals. Another approach is to prevent drug use by educating would-be users and convincing them to "say no" to drugs. A third approach is to treat users so that they can terminate their addictions. These and other drug control strategies efforts are discussed in the following sections. Concept Summary 10.2 reviews the key strategies.

Concept Summary 10.2

Key Drug Control Strategies

Law Enforcement	Preventing drugs from entering the country; destroying crops used to make drugs; arresting members of drug cartels and street-level dealers
Education	Informing children about the dangers of drug use; teaching children to resist peer pressure
Community-Based	Community organizations and residents taking action to deter drug dealing; engaging youth in prosocial activities
Treatment	Intervening with drug users, including counseling and experiential activities
Harm Reduction	Minimizing the harmful effects caused by drug use and some of the more punitive responses to drug use

Law Enforcement Efforts

Law enforcement strategies are aimed at reducing the supply of drugs and, at the same time, deterring would-be users from drug abuse.

Source Control One approach to drug control is to deter the sale of drugs through apprehension of large-volume drug dealers, coupled with enforcement of drug laws that carry heavy penalties. This approach is designed to punish known dealers and users and to deter those who are considering entering the drug trade.

A major effort has been made to cut off supplies of drugs by destroying overseas crops and arresting members of drug cartels; this approach is known as *source control*. The federal government has been encouraging exporting nations to step up efforts to destroy drug crops and to prosecute dealers. Other less aggressive source control approaches, such as crop substitution and alternative development programs for the largely poor farmers in other countries, have also been tried, and a recent review of international efforts suggests that "some success can be achieved in reduction of narcotic crop production."[87] Three South American nations—Peru, Bolivia, and Colombia—have agreed to coordinate control efforts with the United States. However, translating words into deeds is a formidable task. Drug lords fight back through intimidation, violence, and corruption. The United States was forced to invade Panama with 20,000 troops in 1989 to stop its leader, General Manuel Noriega, from trafficking in cocaine.

Even when efforts are successful in one area, production may shift to another. For example, between 1994 and 1999, enforcement efforts in Peru and Bolivia were so successful that they altered cocaine cultivation patterns. As a consequence, Colombia became the premier coca-cultivating country when the local drug cartels encouraged growers to cultivate coca plants. When the Colombian government mounted an effective eradication campaign in the traditional growing areas, the cartel linked up with rebel groups in remote parts of the country for their drug supply.[88] Leaders in neighboring countries expressed fear when, in August 2000, the United States announced $1.3 billion in military aid to fight Colombia's rural drug dealers/rebels, assuming that success would drive traffickers over the border.[89] Another unintended effect of

To find out more about the **federal government's drug control strategies,** go to www.whitehousedrugpolicy.gov. For an up-to-date list of web links, go to http://cj.wadsworth.com/siegel_jd9e.

this campaign has been a recent shift by drug cartels to exploit new crops, from a traditional emphasis on coca to opium poppy, the plant used to make heroin. It is estimated that Latin American countries, including Mexico, now supply upwards of 80 percent of the heroin consumed in the U.S.[90]

Border Control Law enforcement efforts have also been directed at interdicting drug supplies as they enter the country. Border patrols and military personnel have been involved in massive interdiction efforts, and many billion-dollar seizures have been made. It is estimated that between one-quarter and one-third of the annual cocaine supply shipped to the United States is seized by drug enforcement agencies. Yet U.S. borders are so vast and unprotected that meaningful interdiction is impossible. In 2001, U.S. law enforcement agencies seized 233,000 pounds of cocaine and almost 5,500 pounds of heroin.[91] Global rates of interception of cocaine indicate that only one-third of all imports are being seized by law enforcement.[92]

In recent years, another form of border control to interdict drugs entering the country has emerged: targeting Internet drug traffickers in foreign countries. With the increasing popularity of the Internet, some offenders are now turning to this source to obtain designer-type drugs. In 2001, U.S. Customs in Buffalo, New York, discovered that a steady flow of packages containing the drug gamma-butyrolactone or GBL, an ingredient of GBH (gamma hydroxybutyrate) or the date-rape drug, were entering the country from Canada; the drug was disguised as a cleaning product. Operation Webslinger, a joint investigation of federal law enforcement agencies in the U.S. and Canada, was put in place to track down the suppliers. Within a year, Operation Webslinger had shut down four Internet drug rings operating in the U.S. and Canada, made 115 arrests in 84 cities, and seized the equivalent of 25 million doses of GBH and other related drugs.[93] In 2003, another federal task force, known as Operation Gray Lord and involving the Food and Drug Administration and the Drug Enforcement Administration, was set up to combat illegal sales of narcotics on the Internet.[94]

If all importation were ended, homegrown marijuana and lab-made drugs such as ecstasy could become the drugs of choice. Even now, their easy availability and relatively low cost are increasing their popularity; they are a $10 billion business in the United States today. In 2003, 8,000 illegal methamphetamine laboratories were seized by authorities across the United States. Many of these labs were operated out of homes, putting children—3,300 children were found in these 8,000 labs—at grave risk of being burned or injured, not to mention exposing them to illegal drugs.[95]

Targeting Dealers Law enforcement agencies have also made a concerted effort to focus on drug trafficking. Efforts have been made to bust large-scale drug rings. The long-term consequence has been to decentralize drug dealing and to encourage teenage gangs to become major suppliers. Ironically, it has proven easier for federal agents to infiltrate traditional organized crime groups than to take on drug-dealing gangs.

Police can also intimidate and arrest street-level dealers and users in an effort to make drug use so much of a hassle that consumption is cut back. Some street-level enforcement efforts have had success, but others are considered failures. "Drug sweeps" have clogged correctional facilities with petty offenders while proving a drain on police resources. These sweeps are also suspected of creating a displacement effect: Stepped-up efforts to curb drug dealing in one area or city may encourage dealers to seek friendlier territory.[96] People arrested on drug-related charges are the fastest growing segment of both the juvenile and adult justice systems. National surveys have found that juvenile court judges are prone to use a get-tough approach on drug-involved offenders. They are more likely to be processed formally by the court and to be detained between referral to court and disposition than other categories of delinquent offenders, including those who commit violent crimes.[97] Despite these efforts, juvenile drug use continues, indicating that a get-tough policy is not sufficient to deter drug use.

The Drug Abuse Resistance Education (D.A.R.E.) program is an elementary school course designed to give students the skills for resisting peer pressure to experiment with tobacco, drugs, and alcohol. It employs uniformed police officers to deliver the antidrug message to students before they enter junior high school. While reviews have been mixed, the program continues to be used around the nation.

Education Strategies

Another approach to reducing teenage substance abuse relies on educational programs. Drug education now begins in kindergarten and extends through the 12th grade. More than 80 percent of public school districts include these components: teaching students about the causes and effects of alcohol, drug, and tobacco use; teaching students to resist peer pressure; and referring students for counseling and treatment.[98] Education programs such as Project ALERT, based in middle schools in California and Oregon, appear to be successful in training youths to avoid recreational drugs and to resist peer pressure to use cigarettes and alcohol.[99] Drug Abuse Resistance Education (D.A.R.E.) is an elementary school course designed to give students the skills for resisting peer pressure to experiment with tobacco, drugs, and alcohol. It is unique because it employs uniformed police officers to carry the antidrug message to the students before they enter junior high school. Critics question whether the program is actually as effective as advertised. Because of its importance, D.A.R.E. is discussed in the accompanying Policy and Practice box.

Two recent large-scale studies demonstrate the effectiveness of antidrug messages targeted at youth. An evaluation of the National Youth Anti-Drug Media Campaign, which features ads showing the dangers of marijuana use, reported that almost half of students in grades 6 to 12 with "high exposure" to the ads said the ads made them less likely to try or use drugs compared with 38 percent of students who had little or no exposure to the ads. Importantly, the study also reported that past-year marijuana use among youth was down by 9 percent between 2002 and 2003.[100] The second study, the National Survey on Drug Use and Health, which asked young people (aged 12 to 17) about antidrug messages they had heard or seen outside of school hours, reported that past-month drug use by those exposed to the messages was 15 percent lower than those who had not been exposed to the messages.[101] These are encouraging findings given the limited effectiveness of D.A.R.E.

To go to the official site of **D.A.R.E.,** check out www. dare-america.com. For an up-to-date list of web links, go to http://cj.wadsworth.com/siegel_jd9e.

Community Strategies

Another type of drug-control effort relies on local community groups. Representatives of local government agencies, churches, civic organizations, and similar institutions are being brought together to create drug-prevention programs. Their activities

Drug Abuse Resistance Education (D.A.R.E.)

The most widely known drug education program, Drug Abuse Resistance Education (D.A.R.E.), is an elementary school course designed to give students the skills they need to resist peer pressure to try tobacco, drugs, and alcohol. Uniformed police officers run the D.A.R.E. program, targeting students before they enter junior high school. The program focuses on five major areas:

1. Providing accurate information about tobacco, alcohol, and drugs
2. Teaching students techniques to resist peer pressure
3. Teaching students to respect the law and law enforcers
4. Giving students ideas for alternatives to drug use
5. Building the self-esteem of students

The D.A.R.E. program is based on the concept that the young students need specific analytical and social skills to resist peer pressure and "say no" to drugs. Instructors work with children to raise their self-esteem, provide them with decision-making tools, and help them identify positive alternatives to substance abuse.

The D.A.R.E. approach has been adopted so rapidly since its founding in 1983 that it is now taught in almost 80 percent of school districts nationwide and in 54 other countries. In 2002 alone, 26 million children in the United States and 10 million children in other countries participated in the program. More than 40 percent of all school districts incorporate assistance from local law enforcement agencies in their drug-prevention programming. New community policing strategies commonly incorporate the D.A.R.E. program into their efforts to provide services to local neighborhoods at the grassroots level.

DOES D.A.R.E. WORK?

Although D.A.R.E. is popular with both schools and police agencies, a number of evaluations have not found it to have an impact on student drug usage. For example, in a highly sophisticated evaluation of the program, Donald Lynam and his colleagues found the program to be ineffective over the short and long term. They followed a cohort of sixth-grade children who attended a total of 31 schools. Twenty-three of the schools were randomly assigned to receive D.A.R.E. in the sixth grade, while the other eight received whatever drug education was routinely provided in their classes. The research team assessed the participants yearly through the tenth grade and then recontacted them when they were 20 years old. They found that D.A.R.E. had no effect on students' drug use at any time through tenth grade. The 10-year follow-up failed to find any hidden or "sleeper" effects that were delayed in developing. At age 20, there were no differences between those who received D.A.R.E. and those who did not in their use of cigarettes, alcohol, marijuana, or other drugs; the only difference was that those who had participated in D.A.R.E. reported slightly lower levels of self-esteem at age 20, an effect that proponents were not aiming for. In the most rigorous and comprehensive review so far on the effectiveness of D.A.R.E, the General Accountability Office (GAO, formerly the General Accounting Office), the research arm of Congress, found that the program neither prevents student drug use nor changes student attitudes toward drugs.

CHANGING THE D.A.R.E. CURRICULUM

Although national evaluations and independent reviews have questioned the validity of D.A.R.E. and a few communities have discontinued its use, it is still widely employed in school districts around the United States. To meet criticism head-on, D.A.R.E. began testing a new curriculum in 2001. The new program aims at older students and relies more on having them question their assumptions about drug use than on listening to lectures on the subject. The new program works largely on changing social norms, teaching students to question whether they really have to use drugs to fit in with their peers. Emphasis shifted from fifth-grade students to those in the seventh grade, and a booster program will be added in the ninth grade, when kids are more likely to experiment with drugs. Police officers now serve more as coaches than as lecturers, encouraging students to challenge the social norm of drug use in discussion groups. Students also do more role-playing in an effort to learn decision-making skills. There is also an emphasis on the role of media and advertising in shaping behavior. The new curriculum underwent tests in 80 high schools and 176 middle schools—half the schools continue using the original curriculum, and the other half use the new D.A.R.E. program—so that the new curriculum may be scientifically evaluated.

Critical Thinking

1. Do you believe that an education program such as D.A.R.E. can turn kids from drugs, or are the reasons for teenage drug use so complex that a single school-based program is doomed to fail?
2. If you ran D.A.R.E., what experiences would you give to the children? Do you think it would be effective to have current or former addicts address classes about how drugs influenced their lives?

InfoTrac College Edition Research

For more information on the enhanced D.A.R.E. program, go to InfoTrac College Edition and read "Enhanced D.A.R.E. Program More Effective for Adolescent Boys," *Brown University Child and Adolescent Behavior Letter* 19:1 (April 2003).

SOURCES: *Youth Illicit Drug Use Prevention: D.A.R.E. Long-Term Evaluations and Federal Efforts to Identify Effective Programs* (Washington, DC: U.S. General Accountability Office, 2003), p. 2; Brian Vastag, "GAO: DARE Does Not Work," *Journal of the American Medical Association* 289:539 (2003); Kate Zernike, "Antidrug Program Says It Will Adopt a New Strategy," *New York Times*, February 15, 2001, p.1; Donald R. Lynam, Rich Milich, Rick Zimmerman, Scott Novak, T.K. Logan, Catherine Martin, Carl Leukefeld, and Richard Clayton, "Project D.A.R.E.: No Effects at 10-Year Follow-Up," *Journal of Consulting and Clinical Psychology* 67:590–593 (1999).

Tyler Anter, 15, kisses his grandmother and teasingly puts on her hat. Anter is a successful participant in Clark County, Nevada's juvenile drug court program, the first in the nation when it began in 1985. Drug courts have proven so successful that there are more than 90 being used today.

© AP/Wide World Photos

include drug-free school zones, which encourage police to keep drug dealers away from schools; neighborhood watch programs, which are geared to reporting drug dealers; citizen patrols, which frighten dealers away from public-housing projects; and community centers, which provide an alternative to the street culture.

Community-based programs reach out to high-risk youths, getting them involved in after-school programs; offering counseling; delivering clothing, food, and medical care when needed; and encouraging school achievement. Community programs also sponsor drug-free activities involving the arts, clubs, and athletics. Evaluations of community programs have shown that they may encourage antidrug attitudes and help insulate participating youths from an environment that encourages drugs.[102]

Treatment Strategies

Each year more than 131,000 youths aged 12 to 17 are admitted to treatment facilities in the United States, with over half being referred through the juvenile justice system. Just over 60 percent of all admissions involved marijuana as the primary drug of abuse.[103]

Several approaches are available to treat users. Some efforts stem from the perspective that users have low self-esteem, and they use various techniques to build up the user's sense of self. Some use psychological counseling, and others, such as the **multisystemic therapy (MST)** technique developed by Scott Henggeler, direct attention to family, peer, and psychological problems by focusing on problem solving and communication skills.[104] In a long-term evaluation of MST, Henggeler found that adolescent substance abusers who went through the program were significantly less likely to recidivate than youths who received traditional counseling services. However, mixed treatment effects were reported for future substance abuse by those who received MST compared with those who did not.[105]

Another approach is to involve users in outdoor activities, wilderness training, and after-school community programs.[106] More intensive efforts use group therapy, in which leaders try to give users the skills and support that can help them reject the so-

multisystemic therapy (MST)
Addresses a variety of family, peer, and psychological problems by focusing on problem-solving and communication skills training.

cial pressure to use drugs. These programs are based on the Alcoholics Anonymous philosophy that users must find the strength to stay clean and that support from those who understand their experiences can be a successful way to achieve a drug-free life.

Residential programs are used with more heavily involved drug abusers. Some are detoxification units that use medical procedures to wean patients from the more addicting drugs. Others are therapeutic communities that attempt to deal with the psychological causes of drug use. Hypnosis, aversion therapy (getting users to associate drugs with unpleasant sensations, such as nausea), counseling, biofeedback, and other techniques are often used.

There is little evidence that these residential programs can efficiently terminate teenage substance abuse.[107] Many are restricted to families whose health insurance will pay for short-term residential care; when the coverage ends, the children are released. Adolescents do not often enter these programs voluntarily, and most have little motivation to change.[108] A stay can stigmatize residents as "addicts," even though they never used hard drugs; while in treatment, they may be introduced to hard-core users with whom they will associate upon release. One residential program that holds promise for reducing teenage substance abuse is UCLA's Comprehensive Residential Education, Arts, and Substance Abuse Treatment (CREASAT) program, which integrates "enhanced substance abuse services" (group therapy, education, vocational skills) and visual and performing arts programming.[109]

Balanced and Restorative Justice Model Another approach to treating drug-involved juveniles is referred to as the *balanced and restorative justice* (BARJ) method. This model integrates the traditional rehabilitative philosophy of the juvenile court with increasing societal concern about victims' rights and community safety.[110]

BARJ programs attempt to make offenders more accountable by having them make amends to the victim and community, while at the same time improving their competency development by changing their behaviors and improving functional skills. BARJ programs also focus on community safety and stress protecting the community by carefully monitoring the juvenile's behavior. BARJ has become the guiding philosophy in juvenile justice system change in at least 12 states. An important aspect of the BARJ philosophy is a system of graduated sanctions that hold juveniles accountable for their actions and reward them for positive progress toward rehabilitation. Good behavior results in increased freedom or other rewards, while negative behavior results in more severe restrictions or a more intensive therapeutic environment. If the offender lapses into alcohol or drug (AOD) use and/or delinquent behavior at any point in the treatment process, graduated sanctions involving placing the juvenile in a higher-security, more intense therapeutic environment are applied. This approach may be applied in a specialized juvenile drug court, where the juvenile's progress is generally monitored by a judge who relies on a variety of professionals in assessing needs, recommending services, monitoring behaviors, and applying sanctions when a lack of improvement is evident.

Harm Reduction

harm reduction
Efforts to minimize the harmful effects caused by drug use.

A **harm reduction** approach involves lessening the harms caused to youths by drug use and by some of the more punitive responses to drug use. Harm reduction encapsulates some of the efforts advanced under the community and treatment strategies noted above, but maintains as its primary focus efforts to minimize the harmful effects of drug use. This approach includes the following components:

1. The availability of drug treatment facilities so that all addicts who wish to do so can overcome their habits and lead drug-free lives.

2. The use of health professionals to administer drugs to addicts as part of a treatment and detoxification program.

3. Needle exchange programs that will slow the transmission of HIV and educate drug users about how HIV is contracted and spread.

4. Special drug courts or pretrial diversion programs that compel drug treatment.[111] (Juvenile drug courts are discussed in Chapter 12.)

Needle exchange programs—providing drug users with clean needles in exchange for used ones—have been shown to maintain the low prevalence of HIV transmission among drug users and lower rates of hepatitis C. Methadone maintenance clinics in which heroin users receive doctor-prescribed methadone (a non-addictive substance that satisfies the cravings caused by heroin) have been shown to reduce illegal heroin use and criminal activity.[112]

Critics of the harm reduction approach warn that it condones or promotes drug use, "encouraging people either to continue using drugs or to start using drugs, without recognizing the dangers of their addiction."[113] Advocates, on the other hand, refer to harm reduction as a valuable interim measure in dealing with drug use: "There are safer ways of using drugs, and harm reduction for patients is a valuable interim measure to help them make informed choices and improve their overall health."[114] Advocates also call for this approach to replace the "War on Drugs," and claim that this change in drug policy will go a long way toward solving two key problems caused by punitive responses. First, it will reduce the number of offenders, both juvenile and adult, being sent to already overcrowded institutionalized settings for what amounts to less serious offenses. Second, it will discourage police crackdowns in minority neighborhoods that result in racial minorities being arrested and formally processed at much higher rates for drug offenses.[115]

The War on Drugs has been a major source of the racial discrimination that occurs in the juvenile justice system. (For more on racial discrimination in the juvenile justice system, see Chapters 13, 14, and 15.) The latest data (1999) show that African Americans make up only 15 percent of the juvenile population, but account for 27 percent (50,900) of all drug law violations referred to juvenile court. This is down from 44 percent in 1990 and 33 percent in 1995. African American juveniles involved in drug offense cases are also more likely to be detained (held in a detention facility or in shelter care to await court appearances) than white juveniles.[116]

To learn more about the **harm reduction** approach to teenage drug use, check out the Harm Reduction Coalition at www.harmreduction.org. For an up-to-date list of web links, go to http://cj.wadsworth.com/siegel_jd9e.

TO QUIZ YOURSELF ON THIS MATERIAL, go to the Juvenile Delinquency 9e website.

WHAT DOES THE FUTURE HOLD?

The United States appears willing to go to great lengths to fight the drug war.[117] Law enforcement efforts, along with prevention programs and treatment projects, have been stepped up. Yet all drug-control strategies are doomed to fail as long as youths want to take drugs and drugs remain widely available and accessible. Prevention, deterrence, and treatment strategies ignore the core reasons for the drug problem: poverty, alienation, and family disruption. As the gap between rich and poor widens and the opportunities for legitimate advancement decrease, it should come as no surprise that adolescent drug use continues.

Despite all efforts, drug control is difficult because there can be a great deal of money to be made in drug trafficking. For example, the profits involved in the sale of a single drug such as ecstasy are enormous. Ecstasy, or MDMA, is manufactured clandestinely in western Europe, primarily in the Netherlands and Belgium. A typical clandestine laboratory is capable of producing 70,000 to 100,000 tablets per day; one laboratory raided by Dutch police was producing 350,000 tablets per day. The cost of producing a tablet runs as little as 50 cents, and they sell for up to about $2, giving the lab owners a potential profit of between $100,000 and $150,000 per day. Once the MDMA reaches the United States, a domestic cell distributor will charge from $6 to $8 per tablet. The MDMA retailer will, in turn, distribute the MDMA for $25 to $40 per tablet.[118]

legalization of drugs

Decriminalizing drug use to reduce the association between drug use and crime.

Some commentators have called for the **legalization of drugs.** This approach can have the short-term effect of reducing the association between drug use and crime (as, presumably, the cost of drugs would decrease), but it may have grave consequences. Drug use would most certainly increase, creating an overflow of unproductive people who must be cared for by the rest of society. The problems of teenage alcoholism should serve as a warning of what can happen when controlled substances are made readily available. However, the implications of decriminalization should be further studied: What effect would a policy of partial decriminalization (for example, legalizing small amounts of marijuana) have on drug-use rates? Does a get-tough policy on drugs "widen the net"? Are there alternatives to the criminalization of drugs that could help reduce their use?[119]

The Rand Corporation study of drug dealing in Washington, D.C., suggests that law enforcement efforts can have little influence on drug-abuse rates as long as dealers can earn more than the minimal salaries they might earn in the legitimate world. Only by giving youths legitimate future alternatives can hard-core users be made to forgo drug use willingly.[120]

Summary

- Alcohol is the most frequently abused drug by American teens. Other popular drugs include marijuana; cocaine and its derivative, crack; and designer drugs such as ecstasy.

- Self-report surveys indicate that more than half of all high school–age kids have tried drugs. Surveys of arrestees indicate that a significant proportion of teenagers are drug users and many are high school dropouts. The number of drug users may be even higher than surveys suggest, because surveys of teen abusers may be missing the most delinquent youths.

- Although the national survey conducted by PRIDE shows that teenage drug use increased slightly in the past year, this survey, the Monitoring the Future survey, and the National Survey on Drug Use and Health, both also national, report that drug and alcohol use are much lower today than 5 and 10 years ago.

- There are many explanations for why youths take drugs, including growing up in disorganized areas in which there is a high degree of hopelessness, poverty, and despair; peer pressure; parental substance abuse; emotional problems; or suffering from general problem behavior syndrome.

- A variety of youths use drugs. Some are occasional users who might sell to friends. Others are seriously involved in both drug abuse and delinquency; many of these are gang members. There are also "losers," who filter in and out of the juvenile justice system. A small percentage of teenage users remain involved with drugs into adulthood.

- It is not certain whether drug abuse causes delinquency. Some experts believe there is a common cause for both delinquency and drug abuse—perhaps alienation and rage.

- Many attempts have been made to control the drug trade. Some try to inhibit the importation of drugs, others to close down major drug rings, and a few to stop street-level dealing. There are also attempts to treat users through rehabilitation programs, to reduce juvenile use by educational efforts, and implement hard reduction measures. Some communities have mounted grassroots drives. These efforts have not been totally successful, although overall use of drugs may have declined somewhat.

- It is difficult to eradicate drug abuse because there is so much profit to be made in the drug trade. One suggestion: legalize drugs. But critics warn that such a step may produce greater numbers of substance abusers.

Key Terms

substance abuse, p. 305
hashish, p. 306
marijuana, p. 306

cocaine, p. 306
crack, p. 306
heroin, p. 307

addict, p. 307
alcohol, p. 307
anesthetic drugs, p. 308

inhalants, p. 308
sedatives, p. 308
tranquilizers, p. 308
hallucinogens, p. 308

stimulants, p. 309
anabolic steroids, p. 309
designer drugs, p. 309
addiction-prone personality, p. 314

gateway drug, p. 315
multisystemic therapy (MST), p. 326
harm reduction, p. 327
legalization of drugs, p. 329

Questions for Discussion

1. Discuss the differences among the various categories and types of substances of abuse. Is the term *drugs* too broad to have real meaning?

2. Why do you think youths take drugs? Do you know anyone with an addiction-prone personality?

3. What policy might be the best strategy to reduce teenage drug use: Source control? Reliance on treatment? National education efforts? Community-level enforcement? Harm reduction measures?

4. Under what circumstances, if any, might the legalization or decriminalization of drugs be beneficial to society?

5. Do you consider alcohol a drug? Should greater controls be placed on the sale of alcohol?

6. Do TV shows and films glorify drug usage and encourage youths to enter the drug trade? Should all images of drinking and smoking be banned from TV? What about advertisements that try to convince youths how much fun it is to drink beer or smoke cigarettes?

Viewpoint

The president has appointed you the new "drug czar." You have $10 billion under your control with which to wage your campaign. You know that drug use is unacceptably high, especially among poor, inner-city kids, that a great deal of criminal behavior is drug-related, and that drug-dealing gangs are expanding around the United States.

At an open hearing, drug control experts express their policy strategies. One group favors putting the money into hiring new law enforcement agents who will patrol borders, target large dealers, and make drug raids here and abroad. They also call for such get-tough measures as the creation of strict drug laws, the mandatory waiver of young drug dealers to the adult court system, and the death penalty for drug-related gang killings.

A second group believes the best way to deal with drugs is to spend the money on community treatment

programs, expanding the number of beds in drug detoxification units, and funding research on how to reduce drug dependency clinically.

A third group argues that neither punishment nor treatment can restrict teenage drug use and that the best course is to educate at-risk kids about the dangers of substance abuse and then legalize all drugs but control their distribution. This course of action will help reduce crime and violence among drug users and also balance the national debt, because drugs could be heavily taxed.

▌ Do you believe drugs should be legalized? If so what might be the negative consequences of legalization?

▌ Can any law enforcement strategies reduce drug consumption?

▌ Is treatment an effective drug-control technique?

Doing Research on the Web

To research this topic, use "youth and drugs" as a key term on InfoTrac College Edition.

The following organizations provide more information on different approaches to reducing teenage drug use. Before you answer the questions here, check out their websites (sites accessed on August 17, 2004):

The Open Society Institute

www.soros.org

Centers for Disease Control and Prevention Health Programs

www.cdc.gov/programs/health.htm

National Institute on Drug Abuse
www.nida.nih.gov
National Center on Addiction and Substance Abuse at Columbia University
www.casacolumbia.org

Partnership for a Drug-Free America
www.drugfreeamerica.org
The U.S. Bureau of Customs and Border Protection
www.customs.gov

Notes

1. Lloyd D. Johnston, Patrick M. O'Malley, Jerald G. Bachman, and John E. Schulenberg, *Monitoring the Future: National Results on Adolescent Drug Use. Overview of Key Findings, 2003* (Bethesda, MD: National Institute on Drug Abuse, 2004), Table 1.
2. Peter Greenwood, "Substance Abuse Problems among High-Risk Youth and Potential Interventions," *Crime and Delinquency* 38:444–458 (1992).
3. U.S. Department of Justice, *Drugs and Crime Facts, 1988* (Washington, DC: Bureau of Justice Statistics, 1989), pp. 3–4.
4. *Preliminary Data on Drug Use & Related Matters Among Adult Arrestees and Juvenile Detainees, 2002* (Washington, DC: Arrestee Drug Abuse Monitoring Program, National Institute of Justice, 2003).
5. Mary Ellen Macksey-Amiti and Michael Fendrich, "Delinquent Behavior and Inhalant Use among High School Students," paper presented at the American Society of Criminology meeting, Boston, November 1995.
6. National Institute on Drug Abuse, Community Epidemiology Work Group, *Epidemiological Trends in Drug Abuse* (Washington, DC: National Institute on Drug Abuse, 1997).
7. Dennis Coon, *Introduction to Psychology* (St. Paul, MN: West, 1992), p. 178.
8. Alan Neaigus et al., "Trends in the Noninjected Use of Heroin and Factors Associated with the Transition to Injecting," in James Inciardi and Lana Harrison, eds., *Heroin in the Age of Crack-Cocaine* (Thousand Oaks, CA: Sage Publications, 1998), pp. 108–30.
9. Johnston, O'Malley, Bachman, and Schulenberg, *Monitoring the Future: National Results on Adolescent Drug Use. Overview of Key Findings, 2003*, Tables 1 and 2.
10. Special Issue, "Drugs—The American Family in Crisis," *Juvenile and Family Court* 39:45–46 (1988).
11. Federal Bureau of Investigation, *Crime in the United States, 2001* (Washington, DC: U.S. Government Printing Office, 2002), Tables 29, 38.
12. Henrick J. Harwood, *Updating Estimates of the Economic Costs of Alcohol Abuse in the United States: Estimates, Update Methods, and Data,* report prepared by the Lewin Group for the National Institute of Alcohol Abuse and Alcoholism (Rockville, MD: U.S. Department of Health and Human Services, 2000), Table 3.
13. D. J. Rohsenow, "Drinking Habits and Expectancies about Alcohol's Effects for Self versus Others," *Journal of Consulting and Clinical Psychology* 51:75–76 (1983).
14. Spencer Rathus, *Psychology,* 4th ed. (New York: Holt, Rinehart & Winston, 1990), p. 161.
15. Mary Tabor, "'Ice' in an Island Paradise," *Boston Globe,* December 8, 1989, p. 3.
16. Paul Goldstein, "Anabolic Steroids: An Ethnographic Approach," unpublished paper (Narcotics and Drug Research, Inc., March 1989).
17. Centers for Disease Control, *Center Facts about Access to Tobacco by Minors* (Atlanta: Centers for Disease Control, May 23, 1997).
18. Johnston, O'Malley, Bachman, and Schulenberg, *Monitoring the Future,* Table 1.
19. Ibid.
20. *PRIDE Questionnaire Report for Grades 6 through 12: 2002–2003 PRIDE Surveys National Summary/Total* (Bowling Green, Kentucky: PRIDE Surveys, August 29, 2003), Tables 2.9 and 2.10.
21. Data in this section come from Substance Abuse and Mental Health Services Administration, *Overview of Findings from the 2002 National Survey on Drug Use and Health* (Rockville, MD: Office of Applied Studies, NHSDA Series H-21, Department of Health and Human Services, 2003).
22. Ibid., pp. 23–24.
23. Diana C. Noone, "Drug Use Among Juvenile Detainees," in National Institute of Justice, *Arrestee Drug Abuse Monitoring: 2000 Annual Report* (Washington, DC: National Institute of Justice, 2003), p. 135.
24. *Preliminary Data on Drug Use & Related Matters Among Adult Arrestees and Juvenile Detainees, 2002.*
25. Julia Yun Soo Kim, Michael Fendrich, and Joseph Wislar, "The Validity of Juvenile Arrestees' Drug Use Reporting: A Gender Comparison," *Journal of Research in Crime and Delinquency* 37:419–432 (2000).
26. G. E. Vallant, "Parent-Child Disparity and Drug Addiction," *Journal of Nervous and Mental Disease* 142:534–539 (1966).
27. Charles Winick, "Epidemiology of Narcotics Use," in D. Wilner and G. Kassenbaum, eds., *Narcotics* (New York: McGraw-Hill, 1965), pp. 3–18.
28. Delbert Elliott, David Huizinga, and Scott Menard, *Multiple Problem Youth: Delinquency, Substance Abuse and Mental Health Problems* (New York: Springer-Verlag, 1989).
29. Peter Reuter, Robert MacCoun, and Patrick Murphy, *Money from Crime: A Study of the Economics of Drug Dealing in Washington, D.C.* (Santa Monica: Rand, 1990).
30. Thomas Dishion, Deborah Capaldi, Kathleen Spracklen, and Fuzhong Li, "Peer Ecology of Male Adolescent Drug Use," *Development and Psychopathology* 7:803–824 (1995).
31. C. Bowden, "Determinants of Initial Use of Opioids," *Comprehensive Psychiatry* 12:136–140 (1971).
32. Terence Thornberry and Marvin Krohn, "Peers, Drug Use and Delinquency," in David Stoff, James Breiling, and Jack Maser, eds., *Handbook of Antisocial Behavior* (New York: Wiley, 1997), pp. 218–33.
33. Richard Cloward and Lloyd Ohlin, *Delinquency and Opportunity: A Theory of Delinquent Gangs* (Glencoe, IL: Free Press, 1960).
34. Denise Kandel and Mark Davies, "Friendship Networks, Intimacy and Illicit Drug Use in Young Adulthood: A Comparison of Two Competing Theories," *Criminology* 29:441–471 (1991).
35. James Inciardi, Ruth Horowitz, and Anne Pottieger, *Street Kids, Street Drugs, Street Crime: An Examination of Drug Use and Serious Delinquency in Miami* (Belmont, CA: Wadsworth, 1993), p. 43.
36. D. Baer and J. Corrado, "Heroin Addict Relationships with Parents during Childhood and Early Adolescent Years," *Journal of Genetic Psychology* 124:99–103 (1974).
37. Timothy Ireland and Cathy Spatz Widom, *Childhood Victimization and Risk for Alcohol and Drug Arrests* (Washington, DC: National Institute of Justice, 1995).
38. See S. F. Bucky, "The Relationship between Background and Extent of Heroin Use," *American Journal of Psychiatry* 130:709–710 (1973); I. Chien, D. L. Gerard, R. Lee, and E. Rosenfield, *The Road to H: Narcotics Delinquency and Social Policy* (New York: Basic Books, 1964).
39. J. S. Mio, G. Nanjundappa, D. E. Verlur, and M. D. DeRios, "Drug Abuse and the Adolescent Sex Offender: A Preliminary Analysis," *Journal of Psychoactive Drugs* 18:65–72 (1986).
40. G. T. Wilson, "Cognitive Studies in Alcoholism," *Journal of Consulting and Clinical Psychology* 55:325–331 (1987).
41. John Hagedorn, Jose Torres, and Greg Giglio, "Cocaine, Kicks, and Strain: Patterns of Substance Use in Milwaukee Gangs," *Contemporary Drug Problems* 25:113–145 (1998).
42. For a thorough review, see Karol Kumpfer, "Impact of Maternal Characteristics and Parenting Processes on Children of Drug Abusers," paper presented at the American Society of Criminology meeting, Boston, November 1995.
43. D. W. Goodwin, "Alcoholism and Genetics," *Archives of General Psychiatry* 42:171–174 (1985).
44. Ibid.
45. Patricia Dobkin, Richard Tremblay, Louise Masse, and Frank Vitaro, "Individual and Peer Characteristics in Predicting Boys' Early Onset of Substance Abuse: A Seven-Year Longitudinal Study," *Child Development* 66:1198–1214 (1995).

46. Ric Steele, Rex Forehand, Lisa Armistead, and Gene Brody, "Predicting Alcohol and Drug Use in Early Adulthood: The Role of Internalizing and Externalizing Behavior Problems in Early Adolescence," *American Journal of Orthopsychiatry* 65:380–387 (1995).

47. Ibid., pp. 380–381.

48. Jerome Platt and Christina Platt, *Heroin Addiction* (New York: Wiley, 1976), p. 127.

49. Rathus, *Psychology*, p. 158.

50. Eric Strain, "Antisocial Personality Disorder, Misbehavior and Drug Abuse," *Journal of Nervous and Mental Disease* 163:162–165 (1995).

51. Dobkin, Tremblay, Masse, and Vitaro, "Individual and Peer Characteristics in Predicting Boys' Early Onset of Substance Abuse."

52. J. Shedler and J. Block, "Adolescent Drug Use and Psychological Health: A Longitudinal Inquiry," *American Psychologist* 45:612–630 (1990).

53. Greenwood, "Substance Abuse Problems among High-Risk Youth and Potential Interventions," p. 448.

54. John Wallace and Jerald Bachman, "Explaining Racial/Ethnic Differences in Adolescent Drug Use: The Impact of Background and Lifestyle," *Social Problems* 38:333–357 (1991).

55. Marvin Krohn, Terence Thornberry, Lori Collins-Hall, and Alan Lizotte, "School Dropout, Delinquent Behavior, and Drug Use," in Howard Kaplan, ed., *Drugs, Crime and Other Deviant Adaptations: Longitudinal Studies* (New York: Plenum Press, 1995), pp. 163–183.

56. B. A. Christiansen, G. T. Smith, P. V. Roehling, and M. S. Goldman, "Using Alcohol Expectancies to Predict Adolescent Drinking Behavior after One Year," *Journal of Counseling and Clinical Psychology* 57:93–99 (1989).

57. Inciardi, Horowitz, and Pottieger, *Street Kids, Street Drugs, Street Crime*, p. 135.

58. Ibid., p. 136.

59. Mary Ellen Mackesy-Amiti, Michael Fendrich, and Paul Goldstein, "Sequence of Drug Use among Serious Drug Users: Typical vs. Atypical Progression," *Drug and Alcohol Dependence* 45:185–196 (1997).

60. The following sections lean heavily on Marcia Chaiken and Bruce Johnson, *Characteristics of Different Types of Drug-Involved Youth* (Washington, DC: National Institute of Justice, 1988).

61. Ibid., p. 100.

62. Inciardi, Horowitz, and Pottieger, *Street Kids, Street Drugs, Street Crime*.

63. Robert MacCoun and Peter Reuter, "Are the Wages of Sin $30 an Hour? Economic Aspects of Street-Level Drug Dealing," *Crime and Delinquency* 38:477–491 (1992).

64. Steven D. Levitt and Sudhir A. Venkatesh, "An Economic Analysis of a Drug-Selling Gang's Finances," *Quarterly Journal of Economics* 115:755–789 (2000), Table III.

65. Ibid., Table II.

66. Chaiken and Johnson, *Characteristics of Different Types of Drug-Involved Youth*, p. 12.

67. Rick Graves and Ed Allen, *Narcotics and Black Gangs* (Los Angeles: Los Angeles County Sheriff's Department, n.d.).

68. John Hagedorn, "Neighborhoods, Markets, and Gang Drug Organization," *Journal of Research in Crime and Delinquency* 31:264–294 (1994).

69. Chaiken and Johnson, *Characteristics of Different Types of Drug-Involved Youth*, p. 14.

70. Eric Baumer, Janet Lauritsen, Richard Rosenfeld, and Richard Wright, "The Influence of Crack Cocaine on Robbery, Burglary, and Homicide Rates: A Cross-City, Longitudinal Analysis," *Journal of Research in Crime and Delinquency* 35:316–340 (1998).

71. Ibid.

72. James Inciardi, "Heroin Use and Street Crime," *Crime and Delinquency* 25:335–346 (1979); James Inciardi, *The War on Drugs* (Palo Alto, CA: Mayfield, 1986); see also W. McGlothlin, M. Anglin, and B. Wilson, "Narcotic Addiction and Crime," *Criminology* 16:293–311 (1978); George Speckart and M. Douglas Anglin, "Narcotics Use and Crime: An Overview of Recent Research Advances," *Contemporary Drug Problems* 13:741–769 (1986); Charles Faupel and Carl Klockars, "Drugs-Crime Connections: Elaborations from the Life Histories of Hard-Core Heroin Addicts," *Social Problems* 34:54–68 (1987).

73. Eric Baumer, "Poverty, Crack and Crime: A Cross-City Analysis," *Journal of Research in Crime and Delinquency* 31:311–327 (1994).

74. Marvin Dawkins, "Drug Use and Violent Crime among Adolescents," *Adolescence* 32:395–406 (1997); Robert Peralta, "The Relationship between Alcohol and Violence in an Adolescent Population: An Analysis of the Monitoring the Future Survey," paper presented at the annual Society of Criminology meeting, San Diego, November 1997; Helene Raskin White and Stephen Hansell, "The Moderating Effects of Gender and Hostility on the Alcohol-Aggression Relationship," *Journal of Research in Crime and Delinquency* 33:450–470 (1996); D. Wayne Osgood, "Drugs, Alcohol, and Adolescent Violence," paper presented at the annual meeting of the American Society of Criminology, Miami, 1994.

75. Fox Butterfield, "Justice Department Ends Testing of Criminals for Drug Use," *New York Times,* January 28, 2004.

76. *Preliminary Data on Drug Use & Related Matters Among Adult Arrestees and Juvenile Detainees, 2002,* Tables 2 and 3.

77. David Cantor, "Drug Involvement and Offending of Incarcerated Youth," paper presented at the American Society of Criminology meeting, Boston, November 1995.

78. B. D. Johnson, E. Wish, J. Schmeidler, and D. Huizinga, "Concentration of Delinquent Offending: Serious Drug Involvement and High Delinquency Rates," *Journal of Drug Issues* 21:205–229 (1991).

79. Inciardi, Horowitz, and Pottieger, *Street Kids, Street Drugs, Street Crime.*

80. W. David Watts and Lloyd Wright, "The Relationship of Alcohol, Tobacco, Marijuana, and Other Illegal Drug Use to Delinquency among Mexican-American, Black, and White Adolescent Males," *Adolescence* 25:38–54 (1990).

81. For a general review of this issue, see Helene Raskin White, "The Drug Use–Delinquency Connection in Adolescence," in Ralph Weisheit, ed., *Drugs, Crime and Criminal Justice* (Cincinnati: Anderson, 1990), pp. 215–256; Speckart and Anglin, "Narcotics Use and Crime"; Faupel and Klockars, "Drugs-Crime Connections."

82. Delbert Elliott, David Huizinga, and Susan Ageton, *Explaining Delinquency and Drug Abuse* (Beverly Hills: Sage Publications, 1985).

83. David Huizinga, Scott Menard, and Delbert Elliott, "Delinquency and Drug Use: Temporal and Developmental Patterns," *Justice Quarterly* 6:419–455 (1989).

84. Helene Raskin White, Robert Padina, and Randy LaGrange, "Longitudinal Predictors of Serious Substance Use and Delinquency," *Criminology* 25:715–740 (1987).

85. Bu Huang, Helene White, Rick Kosterman, Richard Catalano, and J. David Hawkins, "Developmental Associations between Alcohol and Interpersonal Aggression during Adolescence," *Journal of Research in Crime and Delinquency* 38:64–83 (2001).

86. Eric Wish, "U.S. Drug Policy in the 1990s: Insights from New Data from Arrestees," *International Journal of the Addictions* 25:1–15 (1990).

87. Graham Farrell, "Drugs and Drug Control," in Graeme Newman, ed., *Global Report on Crime and Justice* (New York: Oxford University Press, 1999), p. 177.

88. U.S. Department of State, 1998 International Narcotics Control Strategy Report, February 1999.

89. Clifford Krauss, "Neighbors Worry about Colombian Aid," *New York Times,* August 25, 2000, p. A3.

90. Juan Forero with Tim Weiner, "Latin America Poppy Fields Undermine U.S. Drug Battle," *New York Times,* August 8, 2003, p. A1.

91. *National Drug Threat Assessment 2003* (Washington, DC: National Drug Intelligence Center, U.S. Department of Justice, 2003).

92. Farrell, "Drugs and Drug Control," pp. 179–180.

93. "Operation Webslinger Targets Illegal Internet Trafficking of Date-Rape Drug," *U.S. Customs Today* 38 (2002).

94. Gardiner Harris, "Two Agencies to Fight Online Narcotics Sales," *New York Times,* October 18, 2003.

95. Fox Butterfield, "Home Drug-Making Laboratories Expose Children to Toxic Fallout," *New York Times,* February 23, 2004.

96. Mark Moore, *Drug Trafficking* (Washington, DC: National Institute of Justice, 1988).

97. Melissa Sickmund, *Juveniles in Court* (Washington, DC: OJJDP National Report Series Bulletin, 2003), pp. 18 and 20; Anne L. Stahl, *Drug Offense Cases in Juvenile Courts, 1990–1999,* fact sheet (Washington, DC: Office of Juvenile Justice and Delinquency Prevention, 2003).

98. Ibid.

99. Phyllis Ellickson, Robert Bell, and K. McGuigan, "Preventing Adolescent Drug Use: Long-Term Results of a Junior High Program," *American Journal of Public Health* 83:856–861 (1993).

100. *Partnership Attitude Tracking Study 2003 Teens Study: Survey of Teens' Attitudes and Behaviors Toward Marijuana* (Washington, DC: RoperASW, 2003), pp. 11 and 12.

101. Substance Abuse and Mental Health Services Administration, *Overview of Findings from the 2002 National Survey on Drug Use and Health* (Rockville, MD: Office of Applied Studies, 2003).

102. Brandon C. Welsh and Akemi Hoshi, "Communities and Crime Prevention," in Lawrence W. Sherman, David P. Farrington, Brandon C. Welsh, and Doris Layton MacKenzie, eds., *Evidence-Based Crime Prevention* (New York: Routledge, 2002), pp. 184–186.

103. Michele Spiess, *Juveniles and Drugs* (Washington, DC: Executive Office of the President, Office of National Drug Control Policy Fact Sheet, 2003), p. 5.

104. Scott W. Henggeler, Sonja K. Schoenwald, Charles M. Borduin, Melisa D. Rowland, and Phillippe B. Cunningham, *Multisystemic Treatment of Antisocial Behavior in Children and Adolescents* (New York: Guilford, 1998).

105. Scott W. Henggeler, W. Glenn Clingempeel, Michael J. Brondino, and Susan G. Pickrel, "Four-Year Follow-Up of Multisystemic Therapy with Substance-Abusing and Substance-Dependent Juvenile Offenders," *Journal of the American Academy of Child and Adolescent Psychiatry* 41:868–874 (2002).

106. Eli Ginzberg, Howard Berliner, and Miriam Ostrow, *Young People at Risk: Is Prevention Possible?* (Boulder: Westview Press, 1988), p. 99.

107. James C. Howell, *Preventing and Reducing Juvenile Delinquency: A Comprehensive Framework* (Thousand Oaks, CA: Sage Publications, 2003), p. 139.

108. Ginzberg, Berliner, and Ostrow, *Young People at Risk: Is Prevention Possible?*

109. Donnie W. Watson, Lorrie Bisesi, Susie Tanamly, and Noemi Mai, "Comprehensive Residential Education, Arts, and Substance Abuse Treatment (CREASAT): A Model Treatment Program for Juvenile Offenders," *Youth Violence and Juvenile Justice* 1:388–401 (2003).

110. The following section is adapted from Curtis J. Vander Waal, Duane C. McBride, Yvonne M. Terry-McElrath, and Holly VanBuren, *Breaking the Juvenile Drug-Crime Cycle* (Washington, DC: National Institute of Justice, 2001).

111. Steven R. Donziger, ed., *The Real War on Crime: The Report of the National Criminal Justice Commission* (New York: HarperPerennial, 1996), pp. 201 and 202.

112. Charlotte Allan and Nat Wright, "Harm Reduction: The Least Worst Treatment of All; Tackling Drug Addiction Has Few Easy Solutions," *Student British Medical Journal* 12:92–93 (2004), p. 92.

113. Ibid., p. 92.

114. Ibid., p. 92; see also Erik K. Laursen and Paul Brasler, "Is Harm Reduction a Viable Choice for Kids Enchanted with Drugs?" *Reclaiming Children and Youth*, 11:181–183 (2002).

115. Donziger, *The Real War on Crime*, p. 201.

116. Stahl, *Drug Offense Cases in Juvenile Courts, 1990–1999*, pp. 1 and 2.

117. Eric L. Jensen, Jurg Gerber, and Clayton Mosher, "Social Consequences of the War on Drugs: The Legacy of Failed Policy," *Criminal Justice Policy Review* 15: 100–121 (2004).

118. Donnie R. Marshall, DEA congressional testimony, Senate Caucus on International Narcotics Control, March 21, 2001.

119. Kathryn Ann Farr, "Revitalizing the Drug Decriminalization Debate," *Crime and Delinquency* 36:223–237 (1990).

120. Reuter, MacCoun, and Murphy, *Money from Crime*, pp. 165–168.

Delinquency Prevention: Social and Developmental Perspectives

11

Chapter Outline

The Many Faces of Delinquency Prevention
Costs of Delinquency: A Justification for Prevention
A Brief History of Delinquency Prevention
Classifying Delinquency Prevention
POLICY AND PRACTICE: Head Start

Early Prevention of Delinquency
Home-Based Programs
Improving Parenting Skills
Daycare Programs
Preschool
School Programs in the Primary Grades

Prevention of Delinquency in the Teenage Years
Mentoring
School Programs for Teens
After-School Programs
Job Training
Comprehensive Community-Based Programs

Future of Delinquency Prevention
POLICY AND PRACTICE: Blueprints for Violence Prevention

Chapter Objectives

1. Know the difference between delinquency prevention and delinquency control

2. Have an understanding of the magnitude of cost to society caused by juvenile crime and violence

3. Be able to identify some of the major historical events that gave rise to the present focus on delinquency prevention

4. Be familiar with different approaches to classifying delinquency prevention programs

5. Know the key features of the developmental perspective of delinquency prevention

6. Have an understanding of the many different types of effective delinquency prevention programs for children and teens

7. Be able to identify some of the key factors of effective programs

8. Be able to discuss some of the other benefits that are produced by delinquency prevention programs

9. Be able to identify and comment on pressing issues facing the future of delinquency prevention

View the CNN video clip of this story and answer related Critical Thinking questions on your Juvenile Delinquency 9e CD-ROM.

On her way home from high school, after celebrating the last day of classes by drinking alcohol and smoking marijuana with friends, Carla Wagner lost control of her car and hit Helen Marie Witty, age 16, who was rollerblading on the sidewalk. The impact of the collision instantly killed the young victim. Wagner was convicted of manslaughter while driving under the influence and was sentenced to six years at a women's prison in Florida. As part of her sentence she is required to speak to high school students about the dangers of drinking and driving and the lifelong consequences that this criminal action can cause to victims and their families, as well as offenders. The victim's parents, Helen and John Witty, also speak to the same high school students to tell their story of their tragic loss. These educational campaigns have become more widespread in recent years, along with teen-focused antidrug and antiviolence workshops, which help youths to learn more about what works and how they can play a role in preventing drug use and violence.

Public officials faced with the problem of juvenile delinquency in their cities have many options. For some, it will be a clear choice of getting tough on juvenile delinquency and implementing punitive or justice-oriented measures. For others, it will be a matter of getting tough on the causes of juvenile delinquency and implementing prevention programs to ward off delinquency before it takes place. Still others will combine justice and nonjustice measures to combat the problem. Ideally, decisions about which approach or which combination of measures to use will be based on the needs of the community and the highest quality available evidence on what works best in preventing juvenile delinquency.

This chapter begins with a discussion of key features of delinquency prevention, which include the differences between prevention and other approaches to tackle delinquent behavior, the financial costs that delinquency imposes on society, and efforts to make sense of the many different types of prevention programs and measures. The history of delinquency prevention in the United States is also discussed. Next, we review the effectiveness of delinquency prevention programs that are provided in the childhood years. Daycare, preschool, and primary school programs are among the different types of prevention programs covered. This is followed by a review of the effectiveness of a wide range of delinquency prevention programs implemented in the teenage years, including school-based, after-school, and job training programs. The chapter concludes with a look at key issues to be faced in the ongoing efforts to prevent delinquency.

THE MANY FACES OF DELINQUENCY PREVENTION

delinquency control or delinquency repression
Involves any justice program or policy designed to prevent the occurrence of a future delinquent act.

delinquency prevention
Involves any nonjustice program or policy designed to prevent the occurrence of a future delinquent act.

Preventing juvenile delinquency means many different things to many different people. Programs or policies designed to prevent juvenile delinquency can include the police making an arrest as part of an operation to address gang problems, a juvenile court sanction to a secure correctional facility, or, in the extreme case, a death penalty sentence. These measures are often referred to as **delinquency control** or **delinquency repression.** More often, though, **delinquency prevention** refers to intervening in young people's lives before they engage in delinquency in the first place—that is, preventing the first delinquent act. Both forms of delinquency prevention have a common goal of trying to prevent the occurrence of a future delinquent act, but what distinguishes delinquency prevention from delinquency control is that prevention typically does not involve the juvenile justice system. Instead, programs or policies designed to prevent delinquency involve daycare providers, nurses, teachers, social workers, recreation staff at the YMCA, counselors at Boys and Girls Clubs of America, other young people in school, and parents. This form of delinquency prevention is sometimes referred to as nonjustice delinquency prevention or alternative delinquency prevention. Exhibit 11.1 lists examples of programs to prevent and control delinquency.

Delinquency prevention programs are not designed with the intention of excluding juvenile justice personnel. Many types of delinquency prevention programs, especially those that focus on adolescents, involve juvenile justice personnel such as the police. In these cases, the juvenile justice personnel work in close collaboration with those from such areas as education, health care, recreation, and social services. In this chapter, we focus on delinquency prevention programs that are driven or led by these non–juvenile justice agencies.

An important issue facing delinquency prevention is cost: Programs cost money to run. Expenses include staff salaries, equipment, and sometimes rent for the facilities in which programs take place. Though prevention programs can be costly, they are beneficial because they save money that would otherwise be spent in the justice system.

Costs of Delinquency: A Justification for Prevention

The impacts of juvenile delinquency on society, which include such things as damaged property, pain and suffering to victims, and the involvement of police and other agencies of the juvenile justice system, can be converted into dollars and cents. The damaged property will need to be repaired or replaced, and it is the victim who will often have to pay for this, as many crime victims do not have insurance. The pain and suffering inflicted on an individual from an assault or robbery can result not only in immediate costs of medical care and lost wages from missing work, but also in re-

EXHIBIT 11.1

Delinquency Prevention vs. Control

Prevention	Control
Home visitation	Anti-gang police task force
Preschool	Boot camps
Child skills training	Wilderness programs
Mentoring	Probation
After-school recreation	Electronic monitoring
Job training	Secure confinement

FIGURE 11.1

Costs to Crime Victims

SOURCE: Adapted from Ted R. Miller,
Mark A. Cohen, and Brian Wiersema,
*Victim Costs and Consequences: A New
Look* (Washington, DC: National
Institute of Justice, U.S. Department of
Justice, 1996), p. 9, Table 2.

Costs to crime victims (dollars)

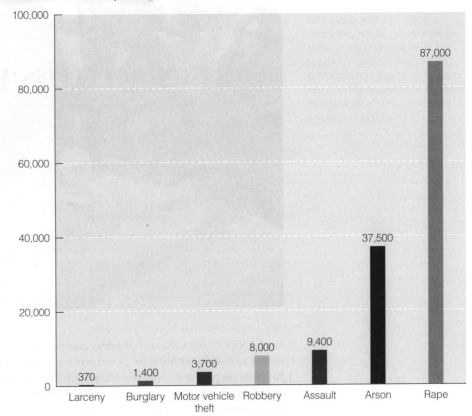

Type of crime

duced quality of life from debilitating injuries or fear of being victimized again, which can result in not being able to go to work, long-term medical care, and counseling.

Here again it is the crime victim and also the victim's family, employer, and many services, such as Medicaid, welfare, and mental health, that incur the dollar costs associated with these services. Victim costs resulting from an assault are as high as $9,400, and are even higher for rape and arson (see Figure 11.1). The average murder costs around $3 million.[1] Another study puts the total cost of a murder, which includes victim costs plus costs to the justice system, at just under $10 million.[2] Then there is the cost of the involvement of the police, courts, and corrections agencies. While some of the costs incurred by the juvenile justice system go toward addressing the needs of victims, such as follow-up interviews by police and court-based victim assistance programs, the majority of the costs are directed at the processing of offenders. Police arrest, public defender costs, court appearances, serving a sentence—whether it be probation or incarceration—and aftercare programs upon release into the community are all costly steps in the justice system. There are also costs incurred by society in efforts to prevent juvenile delinquency, through different types of prevention programs.

The typical criminal career over the juvenile (ages 14 to 17) and adult (ages 18 to 23) years costs society between $1.3 and $1.5 million.[3] Adding the costs of drug use and dropping out of high school brings the total cost to $1.7 to $2.3 million. Just focusing on juveniles, it has been estimated that a typical juvenile criminal career imposes costs on society in the range of $80,000 to $325,000.

Studies have looked at the costs of juvenile delinquency to different states and the nation as a whole.

State Costs Ted Miller and his associates examined the costs of juvenile violence in the state of Pennsylvania.[4] The study was based on the violent offenses of murder,

The financial costs of juvenile violence are immense. One study estimates that juvenile violence costs the United States $158 billion each year. Costs to victims, including pain, suffering, and reduced quality of life, account for the majority of these costs. Here, teenage girls lay flowers on the coffin of a drive-by shooting victim in Glendora, California.

rape, robbery, assault, and physical and sexual abuse. Violence by juveniles was estimated to cost $2.6 billion in victim costs and $46 million in perpetrator costs per year. Juvenile perpetrator costs were made up of costs to the juvenile and adult justice systems, which included costs from probation, detention, juvenile treatment programs, and incarceration in adult prisons. Interestingly, this study also reported on the costs of violence against juveniles that was committed by adults and other juveniles. Compared to the victim costs of violence committed by juveniles, the victim costs of violence committed against juveniles was much higher: $4.5 billion versus $2.6 billion. The main reason for this difference was because juveniles suffered more sexual abuse—a very costly offense—at the hands of adults, but there was very little sexual abuse by juveniles against adults.

National Costs The only national estimate of the costs of juvenile delinquency focuses on juvenile violence. Violent crime by juveniles costs the United States $158 billion each year.[5] This estimate includes some of the costs incurred by federal, state, and local governments to assist victims of juvenile violence, such as medical treatment for injuries and services for victims. These tangible, or out-of-pocket, victim costs of juvenile violence came to $30 billion. But the majority of the costs of juvenile violence, the remaining $128 billion, were due to losses suffered by victims, such as lost wages, pain, suffering, and reduced quality of life. Missing from this $158 billion price tag of juvenile violence are the costs from society's response to juvenile violence, which include early prevention programs, services for juveniles, and the juvenile justice system. These costs are unknown.

Considering these costs, it is not surprising that there has been a long-standing effort to prevent juvenile delinquency.

To read more about the **costs of juvenile violence in the United States,** go to www.edarc.org/pubs/tables/youth-viol.htm. For an up-to-date list of web links, go to http://cj.wadsworth.com/siegel_jd9e.

A Brief History of Delinquency Prevention

The history of the prevention of juvenile delinquency in the United States is closely tied to the history of juvenile justice in this country. From the House of Refuge, which opened in New York in 1825, to more contemporary events, such as amendments to the federal Juvenile Justice and Delinquency Prevention Act of 1974, child saving organizations and lawmakers have had an interest in both the prevention and control of delinquency. However, many social scientists have noted that efforts to prevent juveniles from engaging in delinquency in the first place were secondary to and often overlooked in favor of interventions with juveniles who had already committed delinquent acts.[6] This imbalance between prevention and control of juvenile delinquency remains in place to this day.

Chicago Area Project One of the earliest juvenile delinquency prevention programs was the Chicago Area Project, which was started in 1933 by Clifford Shaw and Henry McKay.[7] This project was designed to produce social change in communities that suffered from high delinquency rates and gang activity. As part of the project, qualified local leaders coordinated social service centers that promoted community solidarity and counteracted social disorganization. More than 20 different programs were developed, featuring discussion groups, counseling services, hobby groups, school-related activities, and recreation. There is still some question of whether these programs had a positive influence on the delinquency rate. Some evaluations indicated positive results, but others showed that the Chicago Area Project efforts did little to reduce juvenile delinquency.[8]

Cambridge-Somerville Youth Study Another well-known delinquency prevention program that was implemented around the same time as the Chicago project was the Cambridge-Somerville (Massachusetts) Youth Study.[9] The focus of this program was more on improving individuals than their surroundings. One interesting feature of this program is that it was one of the first delinquency prevention programs to be evaluated using a **randomized experimental design.** Prior to the start of the program, 650 boys (325 matched pairs) were assigned to receive the program (the **experimental group**) or not to receive the program (the **control group**). The experimental group boys received regular friendly attention from counselors for an average of five years, and whatever medical and educational services were needed. The counselors talked to the boys, took them on trips and to recreational activities, tutored them in reading and arithmetic, played games with them at the project's center, encouraged them to attend church, and visited their families to give advice and general support. The program was to have continued for 10 years, but when America became involved in World War II, many of the adult counselors were drafted.[10] An evaluation of the program 30 years after it ended, when the men were 45 years old, found that those in the experimental group committed more crime than those in the control group.[11] One possible reason

randomized experimental design
Considered the "gold standard" of evaluation designs to measure the effect of a program on delinquency or other outcomes. Involves randomly assigning subjects either to receive the program (the experimental group) or not receive it (the control group).

experimental group
The group of subjects that receives the program.

control group
The comparison group of subjects that does not receive the program.

After identifying that the highest delinquency rates in early 1930s Chicago were in the poverty-stricken, transitional, inner-city zones, sociologists Clifford Shaw and Henry McKay set out to design and implement a program to target key community-level determinants of the delinquency problem. The result was the Chicago Area Project, an early innovative model of delinquency prevention. Shown here are youths of the Boy Scout Troop at Camp Reinberg in 1946, one of the programs offered by the Chicago Area Project.

Courtesy of Chicago Area Project

for this negative result was that the program was done in groups instead of one-on-one. The group format was thought to have resulted in minor delinquents being influenced by more involved or serious delinquents.[12]

Detached Street Workers In the 1950s, a major focus of delinquency prevention programs was to reach out to youths who were unlikely to use community centers. Instead of having troubled youths come to them, detached street workers were sent into inner-city neighborhoods, creating close relationships with juvenile gangs and groups in their own milieu.[13] The best-known detached street worker program was Boston's Mid-City Project, which dispatched trained social workers to seek out and meet with youth gangs three to four times a week on the gangs' own turf. Their goal was to modify the organization of the gang and allow gang members a chance to engage in more conventional behaviors. The detached street workers tried to help gang members get jobs and educational opportunities. They acted as go-betweens for gang members with agents of the power structure—lawyers, judges, parole officers, and the like. Despite these efforts, an evaluation of the program by Walter Miller failed to show that it resulted in a significant reduction in criminal activity.[14]

Federally Funded Programs The 1960s ushered in a tremendous interest in the prevention of delinquency. Much of this interest was in programs based on social structure theory. This approach seemed quite compatible with the rehabilitative policies of the Kennedy (New Frontier) and Johnson (Great Society/War on Poverty) administrations. Delinquency prevention programs received a great deal of federal funding. The most ambitious of these was the New York City–based Mobilization for Youth (MOBY). Funded by more than $50 million, MOBY attempted an integrated approach to community development. Based on Cloward and Ohlin's concept of providing opportunities for legitimate success, MOBY created employment opportunities in the community, coordinated social services, and sponsored social action groups such as tenants' committees, legal action services, and voter registration. But MOBY ended for lack of funding amid questions about its utility and use of funds.

Improving the socialization of lower-class youths to reduce their potential for future delinquency was also an important focus of other federally funded programs during the 1960s. The largest and best-known of these programs was Head Start, a national program for preschoolers that continues to this day. (See the accompanying Policy and Practice box.)

To read more about **Head Start,** go to www.acf.dhhs.gov/programs/hsb/. For an up-to-date list of web links, go to http://cj.wadsworth.com/siegel_jd9e.

Contemporary Preventive Approaches The emphasis on large-scale federally funded programs aimed at the prevention of delinquency continued into the 1970s and 1980s, and these types of programs are still important today. But in recent years the focus of delinquency prevention efforts has shifted from neighborhood reclamation projects of the 1960s to more individualized, family-centered treatments.[15]

Classifying Delinquency Prevention

Just as there are a number of different ways to define delinquency prevention and very little agreement on the best way to do so,[16] the organization or classification of delinquency prevention is equally diverse, and there is very little agreement on the most effective way to do this.

Public Health Approach One of the first efforts to classify the many different types of delinquency prevention activities drew upon the public health approach to preventing diseases and injuries.[17] This method divided delinquency prevention activities into three categories: primary prevention, secondary prevention, and tertiary prevention. Primary prevention focuses on improving the general well-being of individuals through such measures as access to health care services and general prevention education, and modifying conditions in the physical environment that are

Head Start

Head Start is probably the best-known effort to help lower-class youths achieve proper socialization and, in so doing, reduce their potential for future criminality. Head Start programs were instituted in the 1960s as part of President Lyndon Johnson's War on Poverty. In the beginning, Head Start was a two-month summer program for children who were about to enter a school that was aimed at embracing the "whole child." In embracing the whole child, the school offered comprehensive programming that helped improve physical health, enhance mental processes, and improve social and emotional development, self-image, and interpersonal relationships. Preschoolers were provided with an enriched educational environment to develop their learning and cognitive skills. They were given the opportunity to use pegs and pegboards, puzzles, toy animals, dolls, letters and numbers, and other materials that middle-class children take for granted. These opportunities provided the children a leg up in the educational process.

Today, with annual funding approaching $7 billion, the Head Start program is administered by the Head Start Bureau, the Administration on Children, Youth, and Families (ACYF), the Administration for Children and Families (ACF), and the Department of Health and Human Services (DHHS). Head Start teachers strive to provide a variety of learning experiences appropriate to the child's age and development. These experiences encourage the child to read books, to understand cultural diversity, to express feelings, and to play with and relate to peers in an appropriate fashion. Students are guided in developing gross and fine motor skills, and self-confidence. Health care is also an issue, and most children enrolled in the program receive comprehensive health screening, physical and dental examinations, and appropriate follow-up. Many programs provide meals, and in so doing help children receive proper nourishment.

Head Start programs now serve parents in addition to their preschoolers. Some programs allow parents to enroll in classes, which cover parenting, literacy, nutrition/weight loss, domestic violence prevention, and other social issues; social services, health, nutrition, and educational services are also available.

Considerable controversy has surrounded the success of the Head Start program. In 1970, the Westinghouse Learning Corporation issued a definitive evaluation of the Head Start effort and concluded that there was no evidence of lasting cognitive gains on the part of the participating children. Initial gains seemed to fade away during the elementary school years, and by the third grade, the performance of the Head Start children was no different than their peers.

While disappointing, this evaluation focused on IQ levels and gave short shrift to improvement in social competence and other survival skills. More recent research has produced dramatically different results. One report found that by age 5, children who experienced the enriched daycare offered by Head Start averaged more than 10 points higher on their IQ scores than their peers who did not participate in the program. Other research that carefully compared Head Start children to similar youngsters who did not attend the program found that the former made significant intellectual gains. Head Start children were less likely to have been retained in a grade or placed in classes for slow learners; they outperformed peers on achievement tests; and they were more likely to graduate from high school.

Head Start kids also made strides in nonacademic areas: They appear to have better health, immunization rates, nutrition, and enhanced emotional characteristics after leaving the program. Research also shows that the Head Start program can have important psychological benefits for the mothers of participants, such as decreasing depression and anxiety and increasing feelings of life satisfaction. While findings in some areas may be tentative, they are all in the same direction: Head Start enhances school readiness and has enduring effects on social competence.

If, as many experts believe, there is a close link among school performance, family life, and crime, programs such as Head Start can help some potentially criminal youths avoid problems with the law. By implication, their success indicates that programs that help socialize youngsters can be used to combat urban criminality.

Despite these views and the research findings, Head Start faces a number of challenges on a number of fronts. Some proposals for change include turning the program over to state control, focusing more narrowly on improving children's literacy, and mandating more qualified teachers but not providing the necessary resources to improve their low pay. Experts and advocates alike argue that these measures threaten to "water down" one of the most successful national programs for children and families in need.

Critical Thinking

1. Head Start reaches only one-third of all children and families in need. In addition to spending more money, what does the U.S. government need to do to expand Head Start's reach?

2. What changes could be made to Head Start to make it more effective in improving the lives of children and families?

InfoTrac College Edition Research

To read more about Head Start, go to Matthew Neff, "Study Shows Positive Results from Early Head Start Program," *American Family Physician* 66:194 (July 15, 2002), and Maris A. Vinovskis, "Do Federal Compensatory Programs Really Work? A Brief Historical Analysis of Title I and Head Start," *American Journal of Education* 107:187 (May 1999). To find further information, use "Head Start" as a key term on InfoTrac College Edition.

SOURCES: Carol H. Ripple and Edward Zigler, "Research, Policy, and the Federal Role in Prevention Initiatives for Children," *American Psychologist* 58:482–490 (2003); *New York Times*, "Tinkering with Head Start," editorial, *New York Times*, June 16, 2003; Edward Zigler and Sally Styfco, "Head Start, Criticisms in a Constructive Context," *American Psychologist* 49:127–132 (1994); Nancy Kassebaum, "Head Start, Only the Best for America's Children," *American Psychologist* 49:123–126 (1994); Faith Lamb Parker, Chaya Piorkowski, and Lenore Peay, "Head Start as Social Support for Mothers: The Psychological Benefits of Involvement," *American Journal of Orthopsychiatry* 57:220–233 (1987).

conducive to delinquency through such measures as removing abandoned vehicles and improving the appearance of buildings. Secondary prevention focuses on intervening with children and young people who are potentially at risk for becoming offenders, as well as the provision of neighborhood programs to deter known delinquent activity. Tertiary prevention focuses on intervening with adjudicated juvenile offenders through such measures as substance abuse treatment and imprisonment. Here, the goal is to reduce repeat offending or recidivism.[18]

Developmental Perspective Another popular approach to classifying delinquency prevention activities is the developmental perspective. Developmental prevention refers to interventions, especially those targeting **risk and protective factors,** designed to prevent the development of criminal potential in individuals.[19] Developmental prevention of juvenile delinquency is informed generally by motivational or human development theories on juvenile delinquency, and specifically by longitudinal studies that follow samples of young persons from their early childhood experiences to the peak of their involvement with delinquency in their teens and crime in their 20s.[20] The developmental perspective claims that delinquency in adolescence (and later criminal offending in adulthood) is influenced by "behavioral and attitudinal patterns that have been learned during an individual's development."[21] Concept Summary 11.1 lists key features of the developmental perspective. From this perspective, prevention activities are organized around different stages of the life course. We divide our discussion of developmental prevention of juvenile delinquency into two stages: childhood and adolescence.

For the most part, we have adopted the developmental perspective in discussing the effectiveness of different types of delinquency prevention programs in the rest of this chapter. This approach has several advantages: It allows for assessing the success of programs at different life-course stages; its coverage of the types of delinquency prevention programs that have been implemented is vast; and it is a well-recognized approach that has been used by other social scientists in reviews of the effectiveness of delinquency prevention.[22]

Concept Summary 11.1

Developmental Perspective on Delinquency Prevention

- Informed by human development theories and longitudinal studies
- Designed to prevent the development of criminal potential in individuals
- Targeted at risk factors for delinquency and protective factors against delinquency
- Provided to children and families
- Implemented at different stages over the life course: childhood, early school years, adolescence, and transition to work

EARLY PREVENTION OF DELINQUENCY

In the effort to address juvenile delinquency, early childhood interventions—initiated before delinquency occurs—have received much interest and have come to be seen as an important part of an overall strategy to reduce the harm caused by juvenile delinquency. Early childhood delinquency prevention programs aim at positively influencing the early risk factors or "root causes" of delinquency and criminal offending that may continue into the adult years. These early risk factors are many, some of which include growing up in poverty, a high level of hyperactivity or impulsiveness, inadequate parental supervision, and harsh or inconsistent discipline. Early childhood interventions are often multidimensional, targeted at more than one risk factor, because they take a variety of different forms, including cognitive development, child skills training, and family support. The following sections examine early childhood

Early prevention programs that stress family support can reduce child abuse and neglect and juvenile delinquency. The most effective early family support programs provide infants with regular pediatrician checkups and provide parents with advice about care for the child, infant development, and local services. Here, Arlington, Texas, nurse practitioner Marilyn Graham gives 3-month-old Donovan Washington a checkup, as his father, Guy Washington, holds him.

delinquency prevention programs that have been implemented in the four most influential settings: home, daycare, preschool, and the school. Most of the programs have been carried out in the United States.

Home-Based Programs

In a supportive and loving home environment, parents care for their children's health and general well-being, help instill in their children positive values such as honesty and respect for others, and nurture prosocial behaviors. One of the most important types of home-based programs to prevent juvenile delinquency involves the provision of support for families. Support for families in their homes can take many different forms. A popular and effective form of family support is home visitation.[23]

Home Visitation One of the best-known home visitation programs is the Prenatal/Early Infancy Project (PEIP) that was started in Elmira, New York.[24] This program was designed with three broad objectives:

1. To improve the outcomes of pregnancy

2. To improve the quality of care that parents provide to their children (and their children's subsequent health and development)

3. To improve the women's own personal life-course development (completing their education, finding work, and planning future pregnancies)[25]

The program targeted first-time mothers-to-be who were under 19 years of age, unmarried, or poor. In all, 400 women were enrolled in the program. The mothers-to-be received home visits from nurses during pregnancy and during the first two years of the child's life. Each home visit lasted about one and one-quarter hours, and the mothers were visited on average every two weeks. The home visitors gave advice to the mothers about care of the child, infant development, and the importance of proper nutrition and avoiding smoking and drinking during pregnancy. Fifteen years after the program started, children of the mothers who received home visits had half as many arrests as children of mothers who received no home visits (the control group).[26] It was also found that these children, compared to those in the control group, had fewer

FIGURE 11.2

Costs and Benefits of Home Visits for High-Risk Families

SOURCE: Adapted from Peter W. Greenwood et al., "Estimating the Costs and Benefits of Early Childhood Interventions: Nurse Home Visits and the Perry Preschool," in Brandon C. Welsh, David P. Farrington, and Lawrence W. Sherman, eds., *Costs and Benefits of Preventing Crime* (Boulder, CO: Westview Press, 2001), Table 4.3.

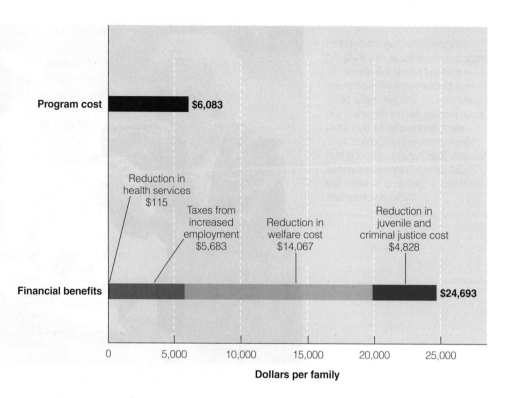

convictions and violations of probation, were less likely to run away from home, and were less likely to drink alcohol. In addition to the program's success in preventing juvenile crime and other delinquent activities, it also produced a number of improvements in the lives of the mothers, such as lower rates of child abuse and neglect, crime in general, and substance abuse, as well as less reliance on welfare and social services.[27] A Rand study found that the program's desirable effects, for both the children and the mothers, translated into substantial financial benefits for government and taxpayers, and that the total amount of these benefits was more than four times the cost of the program (see Figure 11.2).[28]

There are many other home visitation programs across the United States, such as one very similar to the Elmira program that was implemented in Memphis, Tennessee,[29] and the Hawaii Healthy Start program.[30] Because none have been around long enough to test their effectiveness in preventing juvenile delinquency, it is difficult to say with much certainty whether home visitation services achieve their goal. The claim can, however, be made that home visitation can be very effective in reducing child abuse and neglect and child injuries, and in improving the lives of families, particularly young mothers.[31]

Improving Parenting Skills

Another form of family support that has shown some success in preventing juvenile delinquency is improving parenting skills. Although the main focus of parent training programs is on the parents, many of these programs also involve children with the aim of improving the parent-child bond.

Oregon Social Learning Center The most widely cited parenting skills program is one created at the Oregon Social Learning Center (OSLC) by Gerald Patterson and his colleagues.[32] Patterson's research convinced him that poor parenting skills were associated with antisocial behavior in the home and at school. Family disruption and coercive exchanges between parents and children led to increased family tension, poor academic performance, and negative peer relations. The primary cause of the problem seemed to be that parents did not know how to deal effectively with their children. Parents sometimes ignored their children's behavior, but at other times the same actions would trigger explosive rage. Some parents would discipline their children for reasons that had little to do with the children's behavior, instead reflecting their own frustrations.

The children reacted in a regular progression, from learning to be noncompliant to learning to be assaultive. Their "coercive behavior," which included whining, yelling, and temper tantrums, would sometimes be acquired by other family members. Eventually family conflict would flow out of the home and into the school and social environment.

The OSLC program uses behavior modification techniques to help parents acquire proper disciplinary methods. Parents are asked to select several behaviors for change and to count the frequency of their occurrence. OSLC personnel teach social skills to reinforce positive behaviors, and constructive disciplinary methods to discourage negative ones. Incentive programs are initiated in which a child can earn points for desirable behaviors. Points can be exchanged for allowance, prizes, or privileges. Parents are also taught disciplinary techniques that stress firmness and consistency rather than "nattering" (low-intensity behaviors, such as scowling or scolding) or explosive discipline, such as hitting or screaming. One important technique is the "time out," in which the child is removed for brief isolation in a quiet room. Parents are taught the importance of setting rules and sticking to them. A number of evaluation studies carried out by Patterson and his colleagues showed that improving parenting skills can lead to reductions in juvenile delinquency.[33]

The parent training method used by the OSLC may be the most cost-effective method of early intervention. A Rand study found that parent training costs about one-twentieth what a home visit program costs and is more effective in preventing serious crimes. The study estimates that 501 serious crimes could be prevented for every million dollars spent on parent training (or $2,000 per crime), a far cheaper solution than long-term incarceration, which would cost about $16,000 to prevent a single crime.[34]

To read more about the **OSLC parenting skills program,** go to www.oslc.org. For an up-to-date list of web links, go to http://cj.wadsworth.com/siegel_jd9e.

Daycare Programs

Daycare services are available to children as young as 6 weeks old in the United States and other Western countries.[35] In addition to allowing parents to return to work, daycare serves to provide children with a number of important benefits, including social interaction with other children and stimulation of their cognitive, sensory, and motor control skills. The effectiveness of early childhood intervention has been studied in two programs described here—one in Syracuse, New York, and one in Houston, Texas.

Among the best-known of early childhood intervention programs that provides high-quality daycare services is the Syracuse University Family Development Research Program. This program involved high-risk women during the later stages of their pregnancies. After the women gave birth, paraprofessionals were assigned to work with them, encouraging sound parent-child relationships, providing nutrition information, and helping them establish relationships with social service agencies. In addition, the children received free full-time daycare, designed to develop their intellectual abilities, up to age 5. A 10-year follow-up compared children involved in the program with a control group and found that those who received the intervention were less likely to be referred to the juvenile court for delinquency offenses, more likely to express positive feelings about themselves, and able to take a more active role in dealing with personal problems. Girls seemed especially to benefit, doing better in school; parents were more likely to express prosocial attitudes.[36]

Another high-quality daycare program was that of the Houston Parent-Child Development Center. Like the Syracuse University program, both mothers and their children received services. In the first year of the program, the mothers received home visits from social service professionals, for the purpose of informing them about child development and parenting skills and helping them to develop prosocial bonds with their children. In the second year of the program, the mothers and their children attended a child development center four mornings a week. Here, children were provided with day services to foster cognitive skills and encourage positive interactions with other children. Mothers participated in classes on family communication and child management. Eight years after the program ended, children who received the program were less involved in fighting and other delinquent activities when compared to a control group.[37]

The success of these programs rests in their targeting of important individual- and family-level risk factors for delinquency, such as low intelligence, impulsiveness, and inconsistent and poor parenting. Social scientists point to a package of child- and parent-centered interventions targeted at multiple risk factors as a core ingredient of successful delinquency prevention programs.[38]

Preschool

Preschool programs differ from daycare programs in that preschool is geared more toward preparing children for school. Preschool is typically provided to children aged 3 to 5 years. These are the formative years of brain development; more learning takes place during this developmental stage than at any other stage over the life course. Low intelligence and school failure are important risk factors for juvenile delinquency.[39] (See Chapter 5 for why these are risk factors for juvenile delinquency.) For these reasons, highly structured, cognitive-based preschool programs give young children a positive start in life. A preschool in Michigan, a program in Chicago, and Head Start centers in Washington provide some positive findings on the benefits of early intervention.

Started in the mid-1960s, the Perry Preschool in Ypsilanti, Michigan, provided disadvantaged children with a program of educational enrichment supplemented with weekly home visits. The main hypothesis of the program was that "good preschool programs can help children in poverty make a better start in their transition from home to community and thereby set more of them on paths to becoming economically self-sufficient, socially responsible adults."[40] The main intervention was high-quality, active-learning preschool programming administered by professional teachers for two years. Preschool sessions were one-half day long and were provided 5 days a week for the duration of the 30-week school year. The educational approach focused on supporting the development of the children's cognitive and social skills through individualized teaching and learning.

A number of assessments were made of the program at important stages of development. The first assessment of juvenile delinquency, when the participants were age 15, found that those who received the program reported one-third fewer offenses than a control group.[41] By the age of 27, program participants had accumulated half the arrests of the control group. The researchers also found that the preschoolers had achieved many other significant benefits compared to their control group counterparts, including higher monthly earnings, higher percentages of home ownership and second car ownership, a higher level of schooling completed, and a lower percentage receiving welfare benefits.[42] All of these benefits translated into substantial dollar cost savings. It was estimated that for each dollar it cost to run and administer the program, more than $7 was saved to taxpayers, potential crime victims, and program participants.[43] An independent study by Rand also found that Perry Preschool was a very worthwhile investment.[44]

The most recent assessment of the effectiveness of Perry Preschool—when the subjects were age 40—found that it continues to make an important difference in the lives of those who were enrolled in the program. Compared to the control group, program group members had achieved many significant benefits, including

- Fewer lifetime arrests for violent crimes (32% vs. 48%), property crimes (36% vs. 58%), and drug crimes (14% vs. 34%)

- Higher levels of schooling completed (79% vs. 60% graduated from high school or completed a college degree)

- Higher annual earnings (57% vs. 43% had earnings in the top half of the sample)[45]

An assessment of the costs and benefits of the 40-year follow-up of the program has not yet been carried out.

The Child-Parent Center (CPC) program in Chicago, like Perry Preschool, provided disadvantaged children, aged 3 to 4 years, with high-quality, active-learning preschool supplemented with family support. However, unlike Perry, CPC continued to provide the children with the educational enrichment component into elementary school, up to the age of 9 years. Just focusing on the effect of the preschool, it was found that, compared to a control group, those who received the program were less likely to be arrested for nonviolent offenses (17% vs. 25%) and violent offenses (9% vs. 15%) by the time they were 18. Preschool participants, compared to a control group, were also less likely to be arrested more than once (10% vs. 13%). Other significant benefits realized by the preschool participants compared to the control group included

I A higher rate of high school completion (50% vs. 39%)

I More years of completed education (11 vs. 10)

I A lower rate of dropping out of school (47% vs. 55%)[46]

The success of the CPC program in preventing juvenile delinquency and improving other life-course outcomes produced substantial cost savings. For each dollar spent on the program, $7.14 was saved to taxpayers, potential crime victims, and program participants.[47]

Another early intervention that closely resembles these preschool programs is Head Start. (See the Policy and Practice box earlier in the chapter.) Head Start provides children with, among other things, an enriched educational environment to develop their learning and cognitive skills. One study of Head Start centers in Seattle, Washington, found that very young children who were enrolled in the program were less likely to misbehave than children in the control group.[48]

Overall, high-quality, intensive preschool programs show strong support for preventing delinquency and improving the lives of young people.[49] The provision of family support services combined with preschool programming likely adds to the strength of the Perry and CPC programs in preventing delinquency, but it is clear that preschool was the most important element. The intellectual enrichment component of preschool helps prepare children for the academic challenges of elementary and later grades; reducing the chances of school failure is a significant factor in reducing delinquency. Another notable point about the positive findings of Perry and CPC is that these two programs were implemented many years apart, yet the CPC, as a semi-replication of Perry, demonstrates that preschool programs today can still be effective in preventing delinquency.

School Programs in the Primary Grades

Schools are a critical social context for delinquency prevention efforts, from the early to later grades.[50] (See Chapter 9.) All schools work to produce vibrant and productive members of society. The school's role in preventing delinquency in general, which is the focus of this section, differs from measures taken to make the school a safer place. In this case, a school may adopt a greater security orientation and implement such measures as metal detectors, police in school, and closed circuit television cameras. A number of experimental programs have attempted to prevent or reduce delinquency by manipulating factors in the learning environment; two are discussed here.

The Seattle Social Development Project (SSDP) used a method in which teachers learn techniques that reward appropriate student behavior and minimize disruptive behavior. The program started in first grade and continued through sixth grade. Students were taught in small groups. Students were also provided with skills training to help them master problem solving, communication, and conflict resolution skills. Family training classes were offered, teaching parents how to reward and encourage desirable behavior and provide negative consequences for undesirable behavior in a consistent fashion. Other parent training focused on improving their children's academic performance while reducing at-risk behaviors such as drug abuse. In short, the program was extremely comprehensive, targeting an array of important risk factors for delinquency.

A long-term evaluation of the Seattle program found that children who received the program reported more commitment and attachment to school, better academic achievement, less alcohol abuse, and fewer violent delinquent acts compared to a control group.[51] One study found that the program's success in preventing delinquency alone—not including the other important successes—produced cost savings to the criminal justice system and victims of crime that outweighed the costs of running the program.[52]

In Montreal, child psychologist Richard Tremblay set up an experiment to investigate the effects of an early preventive intervention program for 6-year-old boys who were aggressive and hyperactive and from poor neighborhoods. Known as the Montreal Longitudinal-Experimental Study, the program lasted for two years and had two components: school-based social skills training and home-based parent training. Social skills training for the children focused predominantly on improving social interactions with peers. The parent-training component was based on the social learning principles of Gerald Patterson and involved training parents in how to provide positive reinforcement for desirable behavior, use nonpunitive and consistent discipline practices, and develop family crisis management techniques. The program was successful in reducing delinquency. By age 12, boys in the experimental group compared to those in the control group committed less burglary and theft and were less likely to be involved in fights. At every age from 10 to 15, self-reported delinquency was lower for the boys in the experimental group compared to those in the control group.[53]

Schools may not be able to reduce delinquency single-handedly, but a number of viable alternatives to their present operations could aid a communitywide effort to reduce the problem of juvenile crime. A recent review of school-based programs was conducted by Denise Gottfredson and her colleagues as part of a study to determine the best methods of delinquency prevention. Some of their findings are contained in Exhibit 11.2. The main difference between the programs that work and those that do

To read more about **SSDP,** go to http://depts.washington.edu/ssdp/. For an up-to-date list of web links, go to http://cj.wadsworth.com/siegel_jd9e.

EXHIBIT 11.2

School-Based Delinquency Prevention Programs that Work

What Works for Delinquency?

- Programs aimed at building school capacity to initiate and sustain innovation
- Programs aimed at clarifying and communicating norms about behaviors by establishing school rules, improving the consistency of their enforcement (particularly when they emphasize positive reinforcement of appropriate behavior), or communicating norms through schoolwide campaigns (for example, antibullying campaigns) or ceremonies
- Comprehensive instructional programs that focus on a range of social competency skills (such as developing self-control and skills in stress management, responsible decision making, social problem solving, and communication) and that are delivered over a long period of time to continually reinforce skills

What Does Not Work for Delinquency?

- Instructional programs that do not focus on social competency skills or do not make use of cognitive-behavioral teaching methods

What Is Promising for Delinquency?

- Programs that group youths into smaller "schools within schools" to create smaller units, more supportive interactions, or greater flexibility in instruction
- Classroom or instructional management

SOURCE: Denise C. Gottfredson, David B. Wilson, and Stacy Skroban Najaka, "School-Based Crime Prevention," in Lawrence W. Sherman, David P. Farrington, Brandon C. Welsh, and Doris Layton MacKenzie, eds., *Evidence-Based Crime Prevention* (New York: Routledge, 2002).

not is that successful programs target an array of important risk factors. Often it is not enough to improve only the school environment or only the family environment; for example, a youth who has a troubled family life may find it more difficult to do well at school, regardless of the improvements made at school. Some effective early school-based delinquency prevention programs also show that greater gains are made with those who are at the highest risk for future delinquency. An evaluation of Peace-Builders, a school-based violence prevention program for kindergarteners to fifth graders, found that decreases in aggression and improvements in social competence were larger for the highest risk kids compared to those at medium and low levels of risk.[54] Another important ingredient of successful school-based programs is that they be intensive; two or three sessions a semester often does not cut it.

TO QUIZ YOURSELF ON THIS MATERIAL, go to the Juvenile Delinquency 9e website.

PREVENTION OF DELINQUENCY IN THE TEENAGE YEARS

Like early childhood interventions, delinquency prevention programs started in the teenage years also play an important role in an overall strategy to reduce juvenile delinquency. A wide range of non–juvenile justice delinquency prevention programs attempt to address such risk factors as parental conflict and separation, poor housing, dropping out of high school, and antisocial peers. The following sections examine the five main delinquency prevention approaches targeted at teenagers: mentoring, school-based programs, after-school programs, job training, and comprehensive community-based programs.

Mentoring

Mentoring programs usually involve nonprofessional volunteers spending time with young people at risk for delinquency, dropping out of school, school failure, and other social problems. Mentors behave in a supportive, nonjudgmental manner while acting as role models.[55] In recent years, there has been a large increase in the number of mentoring programs, many of which are aimed at preventing delinquency.[56]

Juvenile Mentoring Program The Office of Juvenile Justice and Delinquency Prevention (OJJDP) has supported mentoring for many years in all parts of the United States, most notably through the Juvenile Mentoring Program (JUMP). The program, which has provided more than 9,200 youths with mentors,[57] relies on responsible and caring adults to volunteer their time as mentors to young people who are exposed to some risk factors, including delinquency, dropping out of school, and problems in school. The most common areas of increased risk, based on a large number of male and female youths enrolled in JUMP, are school and social/family domains. (See Table 11.1.) Mentors work one-on-one with young people.[58] Research has shown that mentoring and other types of delinquency prevention programs offered in group settings, particularly for high-risk youths, may end up causing more harm than good. By participating in these types of programs in groups, young people who are more chronically involved in delinquency may negatively affect those who are marginally involved in delinquency.[59] OJJDP's two-year evaluation of JUMP suggests that strengthening the role of mentoring as a component of youth programming may pay handsome dividends in improved school performance and reduced antisocial behavior, including alcohol and other drug abuse.[60]

To read more about **JUMP**, go to http://ojjdp.ncjrs.org/jump/. For an up-to-date list of web links, go to http://cj.wadsworth.com/siegel_jd9e.

Quantum Opportunities Program One of the most successful mentoring programs in preventing juvenile delinquency is the Quantum Opportunities Program (QOP). QOP was implemented in five sites across the country: Milwaukee, Oklahoma City, Philadelphia, Saginaw (Michigan), and San Antonio. At each of the five sites, 25 young people received the program, while another 25 young people served as the comparison group. The main goal of the program was to improve the life course opportunities

TABLE 11.1

Risk Factors of Young People in the Juvenile Mentoring Program (JUMP)

Risk Domain	Percentage of Enrolled Youth*	
	Male (n = 3,592)	Female (n = 3,807)
School Problems	74.6%	63.0%
School behavior	39.5	23.5
Poor grades	53.6	45.9
Truancy	10.4	9.1
Social/Family Problems	51.7	56.4
Delinquency	17.5	8.5
Fighting	12.8	6.3
Property crime	2.8	0.5
Gang activity	3.0	1.0
Weapons	1.1	0.4
Alcohol Use	3.2	1.5
Drug Use	4.0	1.8
Tobacco Use	2.3	1.9
Pregnancy/Early Parenting	0.2	1.5

*Percentage of total JUMP enrollment for each gender. For 23 youths, no gender was reported in the database.

SOURCE: Laurence C. Novotney, Elizabeth Mertinko, James Lange, and Tara Kelly Baker, *Juvenile Mentoring Program: A Progress Review* (Washington, DC: *OJJDP Juvenile Justice Bulletin*, 2000), p. 5.

of disadvantaged, at-risk youths during the high school years. The program ran for four years or up to grade 12, and was designed around the provision of three "quantum opportunities":

1. Educational activities (peer tutoring, computer-based instruction, homework assistance)

2. Service activities (volunteering with community projects)

3. Development activities (curricula focused on life and family skills, and college and career planning)

Incentives in the form of cash and college scholarships were also offered to students for work carried out in these three areas. These incentives served to provide short-run motivation for school completion and future academic and social achievement. Staff also received cash incentives and bonuses for keeping youths involved in the program.[61]

An evaluation of the program six months after it ended found that those who received the program were less likely to be arrested compared to the control group (17% vs. 58%). A number of other significant effects were observed. For example, compared to the control group, QOP group members were

I More likely to have graduated from high school (63% vs. 42%)

I More likely to be enrolled in some form of postsecondary education (42% vs. 16%)

I Less likely to have dropped out of high school (23% vs. 50%)[62]

Big Brothers Big Sisters Program Another effective mentoring program is offered by Big Brothers Big Sisters (BBBS) of America, a national youth mentoring organization, founded in 1904 and committed to improving the life chances of at-risk children and teens. The BBBS program brings together unrelated pairs of adult volunteers and youths, ages 6 to 18. Rather than trying to address particular problems facing a youth, the program focuses on providing a youth with an adult friend. The premise behind this is that "[t]he friendship forged with a youth by the Big Brother or Big Sister creates the framework through which the mentor can support and aid the youth."[63] The program also stresses that this friendship needs to be long lasting. To this end, men-

Research demonstrates that the Big Brothers Big Sisters (BBBS) program is an effective form of mentoring for preventing delinquency involvement, improving school achievement, and forging prosocial relationships. Here, Ariel Kritz, 10, and her "Big Sister," Gloria Ruotsala, take part in the annual party of the BBBS of Washington County in West Bend, Wisconsin, August 21, 2003.

To learn more about **Big Brothers Big Sisters of America,** go to www.bbbsa.org. For an up-to-date list of web links, go to http://cj.wadsworth.com/siegel_jd9e.

tors meet with youths on average three or four times a month (for three to four hours each time) for at least one year. An evaluation of the program took place at eight sites across the country and involved randomly assigning more than 1,100 youths to a program group that received mentoring or to a control group that did not. Eighteen months after the start of the program, it was found that those youths who received the program, compared to their control counterparts, were significantly less likely to have hit someone, initiated illegal drug use, or been truant from school. The program group members were also more likely than the controls to do better in school and have better relationships with their parents and peers.[64]

Despite the findings of these three mentoring programs, the overall evidence of the impact of mentoring on delinquency remains mixed.[65] Furthermore, other mentoring programs have not had success in other areas, such as academic achievement, school attendance, school dropout, and employment.[66] So, why do some mentoring programs work and not others? The biggest issue has to do with what the mentors actually do and how they do it. In all three of the profiled programs, mentors are a source of support and guidance to help young people deal with a broad range of issues that have to do with their family, school, and future career. They work one-on-one with young people, in many cases forming strong bonds. Care is taken in matching the mentor and young person. For future mentoring programs to be successful they should follow the approaches adopted by these programs.

School Programs for Teens

Safety of students in middle schools and high schools takes on a much higher profile than in the early grades because of a larger number of school shootings and other violent incidents. However, the role of schools in the prevention of delinquency in the wider community remains prominent. A wide range of programs to deal with juvenile delinquency in the community have been set up in middle schools and high schools across the United States and in other countries. We review just a couple of the most influential school-based delinquency prevention programs.

Project PATHE Positive Action Through Holistic Education, or PATHE, is a comprehensive program used in secondary schools that reduces school disorder and aims to improve the school environment. The goal is to enhance students' experiences and attitudes about school by increasing students' bonds to the school, increasing their self-concept, and improving educational and occupational attainment. These improvements will help reduce juvenile delinquency.

PATHE was operated in four middle schools and three high schools in South Carolina. It focused on four elements: strengthening students' commitment to school, providing successful school experiences, encouraging attachment to the educational community, and increasing participation in school activities. By increasing students' sense of belonging and usefulness, the project sought to promote a positive school experience. The PATHE program has undergone extensive evaluation by sociologist Denise Gottfredson, who found that the schools in which it was used experienced a moderate reduction in delinquency. Replications of the project are currently under development.[67]

Violence Prevention Curriculum for Adolescents Violence prevention curricula as part of health education classes is one type of school-based prevention program that has received much attention in recent years in the United States.[68] However, few rigorous evaluations of these programs or other instructional-based violence prevention programs in schools have assessed effects on juvenile violence.[69] One of these evaluations assessed the impact of this type of program on high school students in a number of locations across the country. The curriculum was designed to do five main things in the following order:

1. Provide statistical information on adolescent violence and homicide

2. Present anger as a normal, potentially constructive emotion

3. Create a need in the students for alternatives to fighting by discussing the potential gains and losses from fighting

4. Have students analyze the precursors to a fight and practice avoiding fights using role-play and videotape

5. Create a classroom ethos that is nonviolent and values violence prevention behavior[70]

The curriculum was administered in 10 sessions. The sessions were very interactive between the teacher and the students, relying on many different techniques, including brainstorming and role-playing. Like many school-based delinquency prevention programs, the violence prevention curriculum was concerned with reducing delinquency, specifically fighting, in schools and in the larger community. An evaluation of the program in four major urban areas showed that fighting had been significantly reduced among the young people who attended the sessions compared to a control group that did not receive the curriculum.[71]

The review of what works in preventing delinquency in schools by Denise Gottfredson and her colleagues (see Exhibit 11.2) is not limited to the early grades, but also includes programs in middle schools and high schools. And the conclusion on the effectiveness of school-based delinquency prevention programs in the later grades is the same as for the early grades: Some programs work and some programs do not work. But what are the key features of successful school-based delinquency prevention programs? As with the successful school programs in the early grades, successful programs in the later grades are those that target a number of important risk factors. For the two programs described here, this meant a focus on reducing school disorder and improving the school environment. Two additional components of successful school-based delinquency prevention programs in the later grades are improving the family environment by engaging parents in helping the student to learn, and reducing negative peer influences through information about the downsides of gun carrying, drug use, and gang involvement.

After-School Programs

More than two-thirds of all married couples with school-age children (ages 6 to 17) have both parents working outside the home, and the proportion of single parents with school-age children working outside the home is even higher.[72] This leaves many unsupervised young people in communities during the after-school hours (2:00 P.M. to 6:00 P.M.), which is believed to be the main reason for the elevated rates of delinquency during this period of time.[73] After-school programs have become a popular response to this problem in recent years. In the United States in 1999, $200 million in federal grants were made to enable schools to establish after-school programs called Twenty-First Century Community Learning Centers. While recreation is just one form of after-school programs—other types include drop-in clubs, dance groups, and tutoring services—it plays an important role in young people's lives, especially for a large number who do not have access to organized sport and other recreational opportunities.

Research shows that younger children (ages 5 to 9) and those in low-income neighborhoods gain the most from after-school programs, showing improvement in work habits, behavior with peers and adults, and performance in school. Young teens who attend after-school activities achieve higher grades in school and engage in less risky behavior. These findings must be interpreted with caution. Because after-school programs are voluntary, participants may be the more motivated youngsters in a given population and the least likely to engage in antisocial behavior.[74]

Boys and Girls Clubs of America One of the most successful after-school programs in preventing delinquency (and substance abuse) is provided by the Boys and Girls Clubs of America. Founded in 1902, the Boys and Girls Clubs of America is a nonprofit organization with a membership today of more than 1.3 million boys and girls nationwide. Boys and Girls Clubs (BGC) provide programs in six main areas:

- Cultural enrichment
- Health and physical education
- Social recreation
- Personal and educational development
- Citizenship and leadership development
- Environmental education[75]

One study examined the effectiveness of BGCs for high-risk youths in public housing developments at five sites across the country. The usual services of BGCs, which include reading classes, sports, and homework assistance, were offered, as well as a program to prevent substance abuse, known as SMART Moves (Self-Management and Resistance Training). This program targets the specific pressures that young people face to try drugs and alcohol. It also provides education to parents and the community at large to assist young people in learning about the dangers of substance abuse and strategies for resisting the pressures to use drugs and alcohol.[76] Evaluation results showed that housing developments with BGCs, with and without SMART Moves, had fewer damaged units and less delinquency in general than housing developments without the clubs. There was also an overall reduction in substance abuse, drug trafficking, and other drug-related delinquency activity.[77]

To learn more about the **Boys and Girls Clubs of America,** go to www.bgca.org. For an up-to-date list of web links, go to http://cj.wadsworth.com/siegel_jd9e.

Participate and Learn Skills A Canadian program implemented in a public housing development in the nation's capital, Ottawa, recruited low-income young people to participate in after-school activities, such as sports (ice hockey), music, dance, and scouting. Known as Participate and Learn Skills (PALS), the program ran for almost three years and aimed to advance young people toward higher skill levels in the activities they chose and to integrate them into activities in the wider community. PALS was based on the belief that skill development in sports, music, dance, and so on, could affect other areas of young people's lives, such as prosocial attitudes and behaviors, which in turn could help them avoid engaging in delinquent activities.

At the end of the program, it was found that those who participated in the after-school activities were much better off than their control counterparts on a range of measures. The strongest impact of the program was found for juvenile delinquency, with an 80 percent reduction in police arrests. This positive effect was diminished somewhat in the 16 months after the program ended. The researchers speculated that the effects of the program may wear off. Substantial gains were also observed in skill acquisition, as measured by the number of levels advanced in an activity, and in integration in the wider community. These benefits translated into impressive cost savings. For every dollar that was spent on the program, more than $2.50 was saved to the juvenile justice system (fewer arrests), the housing development (less need for private security services), and the city government.[78]

Overall, after-school recreation represents a promising approach to preventing juvenile delinquency. It works because it engages young people in productive, fun, and rewarding activities. For some young people, this is enough to keep them occupied and out of trouble. These programs are also successful in reducing delinquency because they instill in young people important messages about the downsides of drug use and gang membership.

Not enough of these programs have been evaluated to say that after-school recreation is a success, but it does deserve further testing.[79] The fact that violent juvenile delinquency is at its peak in the after-school hours underscores the importance of high-quality after-school programs.

Job Training

Having a job means having money to pay for necessities as well as to spend on leisure activities. It can bring a sense of pride and accomplishment, and it can be a protective factor against involvement in delinquency. Job training programs improve the chances of obtaining jobs in the legal economy and thereby may reduce delinquency.[80] The developmental stage of transition to work is difficult for many young people. Coming from a disadvantaged background, having poor grades in school or perhaps dropping out of school, and having some involvement in delinquency can all pose difficulties in securing a steady, well-paying job in early adulthood. Programs like the two described here are concerned not only with providing young people with employable skills, but also with helping them overcome some of these immediate obstacles.

Job Corps The best-known and largest job training program in the United States is Job Corps, which was established in 1964 as a federal training program for disadvantaged, unemployed youths. The designers of the national program, the Department of Labor, were hopeful that spin-off benefits in the form of reduced dependence on social assistance and a reduction in delinquency would occur as a result of empowering at-risk youth to achieve stable, long-term employment opportunities. The program is still active today, operating out of 119 centers across the nation, and each year provides services to more than 60,000 new young people at a cost of over $1 billion.[81]

Job Corps' main goal is to improve the employability of participants by offering a comprehensive set of services that largely includes vocational skills training, basic education (the ability to obtain graduate equivalent degrees), and health care. Job Corps is provided to young people between the ages of 16 and 24 years. Most of the young people enrolled in the program are at high risk for delinquency, substance abuse, and social assistance dependency. Two out of five youths come from families on social assistance, four out of five have dropped out of school, and the average family income is $6,000 per year.[82] Almost all of the Job Corps centers require the participants to live there while taking the program.

A large-scale evaluation of Job Corps, involving almost 12,000 young people, found that the program was successful in reducing delinquency. Arrest rates were 16 percent

Job Corps is a national program serving more than 60,000 at-risk young people each year. It seeks to help them improve their vocational skills and education, find sustainable jobs, serve their communities, and avoid lives of crime. Pictured here are teen Job Corps students removing graffiti from the Tatum Waterway near Biscayne Bay, Florida.

© Jeff Greenberg/Alamy

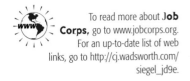

To read more about **Job Corps,** go to www.jobcorps.org. For an up-to-date list of web links, go to http://cj.wadsworth.com/siegel_jd9e.

lower for those who received the program compared to a comparison group. Program group members were less likely to be convicted and serve jail time upon conviction. Also, there were higher employment rates and greater earnings for those who received the program.[83] An earlier evaluation of Job Corps found it to be a worthwhile investment of public resources: For each dollar that was spent on the program, $1.45 was saved to government or taxpayers, crime victims, and program participants.[84] A more recent analysis of the program's costs and benefits also found it to be worthwhile investment of public resources, saving society at large $2 for each dollar spent on the program.[85]

YouthBuild U.S.A. Another job training program for disadvantaged, unemployed youths is YouthBuild U.S.A. Started in 1978 by a group of young people in New York City, YouthBuild has become a national program, each year serving approximately 6,500 young people between the ages of 16 and 24 years in the 200 programs across the country.[86] The program's focus is on building or renovating affordable housing, and through this young people learn skills in carpentry and construction. YouthBuild also provides educational services—for example, to achieve a high school diploma or prepare for college—and promotes the development of leadership skills. The program's impact on delinquency varies from site to site, with some sites reporting reductions as high as 40 percent among youths enrolled in the program compared to similar youths who did not receive the program.[87] The program has also proven tremendously successful in helping a large percentage of participants find work in the construction industry and get into college.[88]

Comprehensive Community-Based Programs

Experimentation with comprehensive community-based delinquency prevention programs began as early as the 1930s, with Shaw and McKay's Chicago Area Project. The Mobilization for Youth program of the 1960s is another example of this type of initiative to prevent juvenile delinquency. Neither of these programs was found to be overly successful in reducing delinquency, but few of these types of programs have been evaluated. Typically implemented in neighborhoods with high delinquency and crime rates, they are made up of a range of different types of interventions and usually involve an equally diverse group of community and government agencies that are concerned with the problem of juvenile delinquency, such as the YM/YWCA, Boys and Girls Clubs of America, and social and health services. The three programs discussed here rely on a systematic approach or comprehensive planning model to develop preventive interventions. This includes analyzing the delinquency problem, identifying available resources in the community, developing priority delinquency problems, and identifying successful programs in other communities and tailoring them to local conditions and needs.[89] Not all comprehensive community-based prevention programs follow this model, but there is evidence to suggest that this approach will produce the greatest reductions in juvenile delinquency.[90] One of the main drawbacks of this approach is the difficulty of sustaining the level of resources and multiagency cooperation necessary to lower the rates of juvenile delinquency across a large geographical area such as a city.

Children At Risk Program One contemporary example of a comprehensive community-based delinquency prevention program that has been evaluated is the Children At Risk (CAR) program. CAR was set up to help improve the lives of young people at high risk for delinquency, gang involvement, substance abuse, and other problem behaviors. It was delivered to a large number of young people in poor and high-crime neighborhoods in five cities across the country. It involved a wide range of preventive measures, including case management and family counseling, family skills training, tutoring, mentoring, after-school activities, and community policing. The program was different in each neighborhood. A study of all five cities showed that one year after the program ended the young people who received the program, compared to a control group, were less likely to have committed violent delinquent acts and to

EXHIBIT 11.3

SafeFutures Program to Reduce Juvenile Delinquency and Youth Violence

SafeFutures is made up of nine program areas:

1. After-school programs
2. Juvenile mentoring programs (JUMP)
3. Family strengthening and support services
4. Mental health services for at-risk and adjudicated youth
5. Delinquency prevention programs in general
6. Comprehensive communitywide approaches to gang-free schools and communities
7. Community-based day treatment programs
8. Continuum-of-care services for at-risk and delinquent girls
9. Serious, violent, and chronic juvenile offender programs (with an emphasis on enhancing graduated sanctions)

SOURCE: Elaine Morley, Shelli B. Rossman, Mary Kopczynski, Janeen Buck, and Caterina Gouvis, *Comprehensive Responses to Youth at Risk: Interim Findings from the SafeFutures Initiative* (Washington, DC: Office of Juvenile Justice and Delinquency Prevention, 2000), p. x.

have used or sold drugs. Other beneficial results for those in the program included less association with delinquent peers, less peer pressure to engage in delinquency, and more positive peer support.[91]

Communities That Care and SafeFutures Initiative Other large-scale comprehensive community-based delinquency prevention programs include Communities That Care (CTC)[92] and the SafeFutures Initiative.[93] Both programs are funded by OJJDP. The CTC strategy emphasizes the reduction of risk factors for delinquency and the enhancement of protective factors against delinquency for different developmental stages from birth through adolescence.[94] CTC follows a rigorous, multilevel planning process that includes drawing upon interventions that have previously demonstrated success and tailoring them to the needs of the community.[95] Two recent case studies of CTC demonstrate its ability to help mobilize communities to plan and implement delinquency prevention programs based on the highest quality research evidence on what works best.[96]

The SafeFutures Initiative operates much like CTC; for example, by emphasizing the reduction of risk factors for delinquency and protective factors against delinquency, using what works, and following a rigorous planning model to implement different interventions. It also works to build or strengthen existing collaborations among the many community groups and government departments working to prevent delinquency. Unlike CTC, the SafeFutures Initiative is only targeted at youths who are both at high risk for delinquency and adjudicated offenders. (See Exhibit 11.3.)

TO QUIZ YOURSELF ON THIS MATERIAL, go to the Juvenile Delinquency 9e website.

FUTURE OF DELINQUENCY PREVENTION

The success of delinquency prevention is shown by evaluations of individual programs (as described throughout this chapter) and larger efforts to assess what works, such as the Blueprints for Violence Prevention initiative, discussed in the accompanying Policy and Practice box. Despite the success of many different types of delinquency prevention programs—from preschool to mentoring—these programs receive a fraction of what is spent on the juvenile justice system to deal with young people once they have broken the law.[97] This is also true in the adult criminal justice system.[98] To many juvenile justice officials, policy makers, and politicians, prevention is tantamount to being soft on crime, and delinquency prevention programs are often referred to as "pork," otherwise known as pork barrel, or wasteful, spending.[99] Aside from these views, delinquency prevention programs face a number of very real obstacles, including

Blueprints for Violence Prevention

In 1996 the Center for the Study and Prevention of Violence (CSPV) at the University of Colorado at Boulder launched the Blueprints for Violence Prevention initiative. The principal aim of the Blueprints initiative is to "identify and replicate effective youth violence prevention programs across the nation." For programs to be labeled as effective, they must adhere to a set of strict scientific standards. The key standards include

▌ Statistical evidence of effectiveness in reducing violent behavior

▌ Evaluations using the most rigorous designs (for example, randomized experiment)

▌ Large sample size to allow for any changes to be detected

▌ Low attrition of subjects

▌ Use of reliable and accepted instruments to assess impact on violence

▌ Sustained reductions in violence for at least one year after the end of the program

▌ Replication: implementation of the program in at least two different sites

More than 600 programs have been reviewed. There are 11 model programs, or Blueprints, that have proven to be effective in reducing juvenile violence or risk factors for juvenile violence. Another 23 programs have been designated as promising. Not all of the model programs are designed to prevent violence before it takes place; some are designed for offenders and involve the juvenile justice system. The 11 model programs are

1. Prenatal and infancy home visitation by nurses
2. Promotion of social competence and reduction of child conduct problems
3. Promotion of alternative thinking strategies
4. Prevention of bullying
5. Big Brothers Big Sisters of America
6. Life skills training
7. Comprehensive substance abuse prevention
8. Functional family therapy: brings together families and juvenile offenders to address family problems and unlearn aggressive behavior

9. Multisystemic therapy: multiple component treatment for chronic and violent juvenile offenders, which may involve individual, family, peer, school, and community interventions
10. Multidimensional treatment foster care: an alternative to incarceration that matches juvenile offenders with trained foster families
11. Project Toward No Drug Abuse

These model programs are distributed to communities and serve as a prevention menu, allowing communities to select proven programs that are best suited to their needs. An OJJDP survey of state juvenile justice specialists found that 40 states have implemented one or more of these model programs, with the most widely implemented programs being multisystemic therapy (30 states), functional family therapy (21 states), Big Brothers Big Sisters of America (15 states), and the prevention of bullying (12 states).

Critical Thinking

1. What is the importance of replicating delinquency prevention programs in multiple sites?
2. How is the Blueprints initiative helpful to communities faced with a delinquency problem?

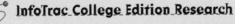 **InfoTrac College Edition Research**

To read more about youth violence prevention on InfoTrac College Edition, use "violence-prevention" as a key term.

SOURCES: Sharon F. Mihalic, Abigail Fagan, Katherine Irwin, Diane Ballard, and Delbert Elliott, *Blueprints for Violence Prevention* (Washington, DC: OJJDP Report, 2004); Sharon F. Mihalic and Katherine Irwin, "Blueprints for Violence Prevention: From Research to Real-World Settings—Factors Influencing the Successful Replication of Model Programs," *Youth Violence and Juvenile Justice* 1:307–329 (2003); *OJJDP News @ A Glance*, "Implementing Blueprints for Violence Prevention" (Washington, DC: Office of Juvenile Justice and Delinquency Prevention, U.S. Department of Justice, 2003), p. 4; Sharon F. Mihalic, Katherine Irwin, Delbert Elliott, Abigail Fagan, and Diane Hansen, *Blueprints for Violence Prevention* (Washington, DC: OJJDP Juvenile Justice Bulletin, 2001).

▌ Ethical concerns about early intervention:[100] Is it right to intervene in the lives of children and young people using methods that may or may not be successful?

▌ Labeling and stigmatization associated with programs that target high-risk populations:[101] Children and families receiving support may be called hurtful names and/or looked down upon by fellow community members.

▌ Long delay before early childhood programs can have an impact on delinquency:[102] While the saying "pay now, save later" is true for early childhood delinquency prevention programs, the length of time for this benefit to be felt can act as a deterrent. In a society and political system that demand immediate results, the building of a juvenile corrections facility is often seen as a more tangible measure than the building of a preschool.

 To learn more about the **Blueprints program,** go to www.colorado.edu/cspv/blueprints/. For an up-to-date list of web links, go to http://cj.wadsworth.com/siegel_jd9e.

The future of delinquency prevention programs depends on educating the public and key decision makers about the value of preventing delinquency. One example of this is discussing the success of prevention programs in financial terms.[103] For the handful of programs that have measured costs and benefits, some of which are discussed in this chapter, the savings are substantial.[104] The costs of running prevention programs are low relative to the costly nature of delinquency. Notwithstanding these important issues, the future of delinquency prevention is likely to be bright. With many local efforts, state initiatives, and a growing list of national programs showing positive results, the prevention of delinquency is proving its worth.

Summary

- Prevention is distinguished from control or repression in that prevention seeks to reduce the risk factors for delinquency before antisocial behavior or delinquency becomes a problem. Delinquency control programs, which involve the juvenile justice system, intervene in the lives of juvenile offenders with the aim of preventing the occurrence of future delinquent acts.

- The costs of juvenile delinquency are considerable. These costs include the responses of the juvenile justice system, losses to victims of delinquent acts, and the financial impact on offenders and their families. One approach to reduce these costs that has garnered a great deal of attention in recent years is prevention.

- The history of the prevention of juvenile delinquency in the United States is closely tied to the history of the juvenile justice system in this country. A number of key events, including the Chicago Area Project and federally funded initiatives, helped shape the development of delinquency prevention today.

- There are a number of different ways to classify or organize delinquency prevention programs, including the public health approach and the developmental perspective.

- Some of the key features of the developmental perspective of delinquency prevention include the target-

ing of risk factors and the promotion of protective factors, the provision of services to children and families, and programs provided over the life course.

- Many different types of delinquency prevention programs have been targeted at children and teens, and many of these programs show positive results in reducing delinquency as well as other problem behaviors, such as substance abuse and truancy.

- Theory-driven, targeting multiple risk factors for delinquency, intensity, and successful implementation are among the key factors of effective delinquency prevention programs.

- Delinquency prevention programs have also been shown to lead to improvements in other areas of life, such as educational achievement, health, and employment. These benefits often translate into substantial cost savings.

- Efforts to better understand what works in preventing delinquency and to address some of the concerns with prevention programs need more attention. Intervening in the lives of children, young people, and their families to prevent delinquency before it takes place is a key component of an overall strategy to address the problem of juvenile delinquency.

Key Terms

delinquency control or delinquency repression, p. 336
delinquency prevention, p. 336

randomized experimental design, p. 339
experimental group, p. 339

control group, p. 339
risk factor, p. 342
protective factor, p. 342

Questions for Discussion

1. Prevention and control are the two broad-based approaches that can be used to reduce delinquency. How do these approaches differ?

2. The costs of juvenile delinquency are wide-ranging and substantial. Do you think these costs justify spending money on delinquency prevention programs?

3. What are some of the benefits of implementing prevention programs in childhood compared to adolescence?

4. In addition to reducing delinquency, many prevention programs also have a positive impact on other social problems. Identify four of these problems, and give an example of a program that was successful in reducing each of them.

5. What are comprehensive community-based delinquency prevention programs?

6. Many programs have been successful in preventing delinquency, but many have not been successful. What are some of the reasons why a program may fail to reduce delinquency?

Viewpoint

You are the mayor of a medium-sized city. Juvenile delinquency is on the rise, and there have been disturbing reports of increased gang activity. The police chief informs you that some urban gangs, seeking to migrate to your city, have sent members to recruit local youth. Their appeal appears to have been working, and several local chapters of the Crips, Bloods, and Latin Kings have now been formed. Street shootings, thefts of cars, and other serious delinquency problems have risen in recent weeks, and all have been linked to this new gang activity. The police, business groups in the downtown core of the city, and the public are all calling for you to take immediate action to deal with these problems.

When you meet with local community leaders they inform you that the gangs appeal to many local kids who come from troubled homes and have no real hope of success in the conventional world. Some are doing poorly in school and receive little educational support. Others who have left school have trouble finding jobs. The gangs also appeal to kids with emotional and developmental problems.

The police chief suggests that you cannot coddle these hoodlums. He tells you to put more police on the streets and hire more police officers. He also argues that you should lobby the governor and legislature to pass new laws making it mandatory that kids involved in gang violence are transferred to the adult court for trial.

In contrast, community advocates ask you to spend more money on disadvantaged families so they have access to childcare and health care. They suggest you beef up the educational budget to reduce class sizes, reduce dropout rates, and improve attendance rates.

| Would you spend more money on community-based services for young people, or would you order the chief to crack down on the gangs?

| If you choose to spend money on prevention, which programs would you support?

| When should prevention begin? Should kids be given special help even before they get in trouble with the law?

Doing Research on the Web

To research this topic, use "prevention" as a keyword on InfoTrac College Edition.

The following organizations provide more information on different approaches to preventing juvenile delinquency (sites accessed on October 15, 2004):

The American Youth Policy Forum
www.aypf.org

Fight Crime: Invest in Kids
www.fightcrime.org

The National Crime Prevention Council
www.ncpc.org

The Child Welfare League of America
www.cwla.org

The Office of Juvenile Justice and Delinquency Prevention

http://ojjdp.ncjrs.org/

Notes

1. Ted R. Miller, Mark A. Cohen, and Brian Wiersema, *Victim Costs and Consequences: A New Look* (Washington, DC: NIJ, 1996), p. 9, table 2.

2. Mark A. Cohen, Roland T. Rust, Sara Steen, and Simon T. Tidd, "Willingness-To-Pay for Crime Control Programs," *Criminology* 42: 89–109 (2004), p. 98, table 2.

3. Mark A. Cohen, "The Monetary Value of Saving a High-Risk Youth," *Journal of Quantitative Criminology* 14:5–33 (1998).

4. Ted R. Miller, Deborah A. Fisher, and Mark A. Cohen, "Costs of Juvenile Violence: Policy Implications," *Pediatrics* 107(1):1–7 (2001), http://pediatrics.aappublications.org; see also Joint State Government Commission, General Assembly of the Commonwealth of Pennsylvania, *The Cost*

of Juvenile Violence in Pennsylvania, staff report to the Task Force to Study the Issues Surrounding Violence as a Public Health Concern (Harrisburg, PA: Author, January 1995).

5. Children's Safety Network, "State Costs of Violence Perpetrated by Youth," www.edarc.org/pubs/tables/youth-viol.htm (July 12, 2000). (Accessed on August 16, 2004.)

6. Barry Krisberg and James Austin, *The Children of Ishmael: Critical Perspectives on Juvenile Justice* (Palo Alto, CA: Mayfield, 1978), pp. 7–45; Joseph G. Weis and J. David Hawkins, *Preventing Delinquency* (Washington, DC: Office of Juvenile Justice and Delinquency Prevention, 1981), pp. 1–6; Richard J. Lundam, *Prevention and Control of Juvenile Delinquency,* 3rd ed. (New York: Oxford University Press, 2001), pp. 23 and 25.

7. Clifford R. Shaw and Henry D. McKay, *Juvenile Delinquency and Urban Areas: A Study of Rates of Delinquents in Relation to Differential Characteristics of Local Communities in American Cities* (Chicago: University of Chicago Press, 1942).

8. For an intensive look at the Chicago Area Project, see Steven Schlossman and Michael Sedlack, "The Chicago Area Project Revisited," *Crime and Delinquency* 29:398–462 (1983).

9. Joan McCord and William McCord, "A Follow-Up Report on the Cambridge-Somerville Youth Study," *Annals of the American Academy of Political and Social Science* 322:89–96 (1959).

10. Richard J. Lundman, *Prevention and Control of Juvenile Delinquency,* 3rd ed. (New York: Oxford University Press, 2001), p. 50.

11. Joan McCord, "A Thirty-Year Follow-Up of Treatment Effects," *American Psychologist* 33:284–289 (1978).

12. Thomas J. Dishion, Joan McCord, and François Poulin, "When Interventions Harm: Peer Groups and Problem Behavior," *American Psychologist* 54:755–764 (1999). See also Joan McCord, "Counterproductive Juvenile Justice," *Australian and New Zealand Journal of Criminology* 35:230–237 (2002); Joan McCord, "Cures That Harm: Unanticipated Outcomes of Crime Prevention Programs," *Annals of the American Academy of Political and Social Science* 587:16–30 (2003).

13. See New York City Youth Board, *Reaching the Fighting Gang* (New York: New York City Youth Board, 1960).

14. Walter Miller, "The Impact of a 'Total Community' Delinquency Control Project," *Social Problems* 10:168–191 (1962).

15. See Karol L. Kumpfer and Rose Alvarado, "Family-Strengthening Approaches for the Prevention of Youth Problem Behaviors," *American Psychologist* 58:457–465 (2003).

16. Trevor Bennett, "Crime Prevention," in Michael Tonry, ed., *The Handbook of Crime and Punishment* (New York: Oxford University Press, 1998).

17. Paul J. Brantingham and Frederick L. Faust, "A Conceptual Model of Crime Prevention," *Crime and Delinquency* 22:284–296 (1976).

18. See Brandon C. Welsh, "Public Health and the Prevention of Juvenile Criminal Violence," *Youth Violence and Juvenile Justice* 3:1–18 (2005).

19. David P. Farrington, "Early Developmental Prevention of Juvenile Delinquency," *Criminal Behaviour and Mental Health* 4:209–227 (1994).

20. David P. Farrington, "The Development of Offending and Antisocial Behaviour from Childhood: Key Findings from the Cambridge Study in Delinquent Development," *Journal of Child Psychology and Psychiatry* 36:929–964 (1995).

21. Richard E. Tremblay and Wendy M. Craig, "Developmental Crime Prevention," in Michael Tonry and David P. Farrington, eds., *Building a Safer Society: Strategic Approaches to Crime Prevention. Crime and Justice: A Review of Research,* vol. 19 (Chicago: University of Chicago Press, 1995), p. 151.

22. Tremblay and Craig, "Developmental Crime Prevention"; Gail A. Wasserman and Laurie S. Miller, "The Prevention of Serious and Violent Juvenile Offending," in Rolf Loeber and David P. Farrington, eds., *Serious and Violent Juvenile Offenders: Risk Factors and Successful Interventions* (Thousand Oaks, CA: Sage Publications, 1998); Joan McCord, Cathy Spatz Widom, and Nancy A. Crowell, eds., *Juvenile Crime, Juvenile Justice,* panel on Juvenile Crime: Prevention, Treatment, and Control (Washington, DC: National Academy Press, 2001); Patrick Tolan, "Crime Prevention: Focus on Youth," in James Q. Wilson and Joan Petersilia, eds., *Crime: Public Policies for Crime Control* (Oakland, CA: Institute for Contemporary Studies, 2002).

23. Deanna S. Gomby, Patti L. Culross, and Richard E. Behrman, "Home Visiting: Recent Program Evaluations—Analysis and Recommendations," *The Future of Children* 9(1):4–26 (1999).

24. David L. Olds, Charles R. Henderson, Robert Chamberlin, and Robert Tatelbaum, "Preventing Child Abuse and Neglect: A Randomized Trial of Nurse Home Visitation," *Pediatrics* 78:65–78 (1986).

25. David L. Olds, Charles R. Henderson, Charles Phelps, Harriet Kitzman, and Carole Hanks, "Effects of Prenatal and Infancy Nurse Home Visitation on Government Spending," *Medical Care* 31:155–174 (1993).

26. David L. Olds et al., "Long-Term Effects of Nurse Home Visitation on Children's Criminal and Antisocial Behavior: 15-Year Follow-Up of a Randomized Controlled Trial," *Journal of the American Medical Association* 280:1238–1244 (1998).

27. David L. Olds et al., "Long-Term Effects of Home Visitation on Maternal Life Course and Child Abuse and Neglect: Fifteen-Year Follow-Up of a Randomized Trial," *Journal of the American Medical Association* 278:637–643 (1997).

28. Peter W. Greenwood, Lynn A. Karoly, Susan S. Everingham, Jill Houbé, M. Rebecca Kilburn, C. Peter Rydell, Matthew Sanders, and James Chiesa, "Estimating the Costs and Benefits of Early Childhood Interventions: Nurse Home Visits and the Perry Preschool," in Brandon C. Welsh, David P. Farrington, and Lawrence W. Sherman, eds., *Costs and Benefits of Preventing Crime* (Boulder, CO: Westview Press, 2001), p. 133.

29. Harriet Kitzman et al., "Effect of Prenatal and Infancy Home Visitation by Nurses on Pregnancy Outcomes, Childhood Injuries, and Repeated Childbearing: A Randomized Controlled Trial," *Journal of the American Medical Association* 278:644–652 (1997).

30. Anne K. Duggan et al., "Evaluation of Hawaii's Healthy Start Program," *The Future of Children* 9(1):66–90 (1999); Anne K. Duggan, Amy Windham, Elizabeth McFarlane, Loretta Fuddy, Charles Rohde, Sharon Buchbinder, and Calvin Sia, "Hawaii's Healthy Start Program of Home Visiting for At-Risk Families: Evaluation of Family Identification, Family Engagement, and Service Delivery," *Pediatrics* 105:250–259 (2000).

31. David P. Farrington and Brandon C. Welsh, "Family-Based Prevention of Offending: A Meta-Analysis," *Australian and New Zealand Journal of Criminology* 36:127–151 (2003); David P. Farrington and Brandon C. Welsh, "Family-Based Crime Prevention," in Lawrence W. Sherman, David P. Farrington, Brandon C. Welsh, and Doris Layton MacKenzie, eds., *Evidence-Based Crime Prevention* (New York: Routledge, 2002).

32. See Gerald R. Patterson, "Performance Models for Antisocial Boys," *American Psychologist* 41:432–444 (1986); Gerald R. Patterson, *Coercive Family Process* (Eugene, OR: Castalia, 1982).

33. Gerald R. Patterson, Patricia Chamberlain, and John B. Reid, "A Comparative Evaluation of a Parent-Training Program," *Behavior Therapy* 13:638–650 (1982); Gerald R. Patterson, John B. Reid, and Thomas J. Dishion, *Antisocial Boys* (Eugene, OR: Castalia, 1992).

34. Peter W. Greenwood, Karyn E. Model, C. Peter Rydell, and James Chiesa, *Diverting Children from a Life of Crime: Measuring Costs and Benefits* (Santa Monica: Rand, 1996).

35. Sonya Michel, *Children's Interests/Mother's Rights: The Shaping of America's Child Care Policy* (New Haven, CT: Yale University Press, 1999).

36. J. Ronald Lally, Peter L. Mangione, and Alice S. Honig, "The Syracuse University Family Development Research Program: Long-Range Impact of an Early Intervention with Low-Income Children and their Families," in D. R. Powell, ed., *Parent Education as Early Childhood Intervention: Emerging Directions in Theory, Research and Practice* (Norwood, NJ: Ablex, 1988).

37. Dale L. Johnson and Todd Walker, "Primary Prevention of Behavior Problems in Mexican-American Children," *American Journal of Community Psychology* 15:375–385 (1987).

38. Tremblay and Craig, "Developmental Crime Prevention."

39. Farrington, "Early Developmental Prevention of Juvenile Delinquency," pp. 216–217.

40. Lawrence J. Schweinhart, Helen V. Barnes, and David P. Weikart, *Significant Benefits: The High/Scope Perry Preschool Study Through Age 27* (Ypsilanti, MI: High/Scope Press, 1993), p. 3.

41. Lawrence J. Schweinhart and David P. Weikart, *Young Children Grow Up: The Effects of the Perry Preschool Program through Age 15* (Ypsilanti, MI: High/Scope Press, 1980).

42. Schweinhart, Barnes, and Weikart, *Significant Benefits: The High/Scope Perry Preschool Study through Age 27,* p. xv.

43. W. Steven Barnett, *Lives in the Balance: Age 27 Benefit-Cost Analysis of the High/Scope Perry Preschool Program* (Ypsilanti, MI: High/Scope Press, 1996); W. Steven Barnett, "Cost-Benefit Analysis," in Schweinhart, Barnes, and Weikart, *Significant Benefits: The High/Scope Perry Preschool Study Through Age 27* (Ypsilanti, MI: High/Scope Press, 1993).

44. Greenwood et al., "Estimating the Costs and Benefits of Early Childhood Interventions: Nurse Home Visits and the Perry Preschool."

45. Lawrence J. Schweinhart and Zongping Xiang, "Evidence that the High/Scope Perry Preschool Program Prevents Adult Crime," paper presented at the American Society of Criminology meeting, Denver, November 2003.

46. Arthur J. Reynolds, Judy A. Temple, Dylan L. Robertson, and Emily A. Mann, "Long-Term Effects of an Early Childhood Intervention on Educational Achievement and Juvenile Arrest: A 15-Year Follow-up of Low-Income Children in Public Schools," *Journal of the American Medical Association* 285:2339–2346 (2001).

47. Arthur J. Reynolds, Judy A. Temple, and Suh-Ruu Ou, "School-Based Early Intervention and Child Well-Being in the Chicago Longitudinal Study," *Child Welfare* 82:633–656 (2003).

48. Carolyn Webster-Stratton, "Preventing Conduct Problems in Head Start Children: Strengthening Parenting Competencies," *Journal of Consulting and Clinical Psychology* 66:715–730 (1998).

49. Edward Zigler and Sally J. Styfco, "Extended Childhood Intervention Prepares Children for School and Beyond," *Journal of the American Medical Association* 285:2378–2380 (2001).

50. Delbert S. Elliott, Beatrix Hamburg, and Kirk R. Williams, "Violence in American Schools: An Overview," in Delbert S. Elliott, Beatrix Hamburg, and Kirk R. Williams, eds., *Violence in American Schools: A New Perspective* (New York: Cambridge University Press, 1998), p. 16.

51. J. David Hawkins, Richard F. Catalano, Rick Kosterman, Robert Abbott, and Karl G. Hill, "Preventing Adolescent Health-Risk Behaviors by Strengthening Protection during Childhood," *Archives of Pediatrics and Adolescent Medicine* 153:226–234 (1999).

52. Steve Aos, Polly Phipps, Robert Barnoski, and Roxanne Lieb, "The Comparative Costs and Benefits of Programs to Reduce Crime: A Review of Research Findings with Implications for Washington State," in Brandon C. Welsh, David P. Farrington, and Lawrence W. Sherman, eds., *Costs and Benefits of Preventing Crime* (Boulder: Westview Press, 2001).

53. Richard E. Tremblay et al., "Parent and Child Training to Prevent Early Onset of Delinquency: The Montréal Longitudinal-Experimental Study," in Joan McCord and Richard E. Tremblay, eds., *Preventing Antisocial Behavior: Interventions from Birth through Adolescence* (New York: Guilford, 1992); Richard E. Tremblay, Linda Pagani-Kurtz, Louise C. Mâsse, Frank Vitaro, and Robert O. Pihl, "A Bimodal Preventive Intervention for Disruptive Kindergarten Boys: Its Impact through Mid-Adolescence," *Journal of Consulting and Clinical Psychology* 63:560–568 (1995); Richard E. Tremblay, Louise C. Mâsse, Linda Pagani-Kurtz, and Frank Vitaro, "From Childhood Physical Aggression to Adolescent Maladjustment: The Montreal Prevention Experiment," in R. De V. Peters and R. J. McMahon, eds., *Preventing Childhood Disorders: Substance Abuse, and Delinquency* (Thousand Oaks, CA: Sage Publications, 1996).

54. Alexander T. Vazsonyi, Lara B. Belliston, and Daniel J. Flannery, "Evaluation of a School-Based, Universal Violence Prevention Program: Low-, Medium-, and High-Risk Children," *Youth Violence and Juvenile Justice* 2:185–206 (2004).

55. James C. Howell, ed., *Guide for Implementing the Comprehensive Strategy for Serious, Violent, and Chronic Juvenile Offenders* (Washington, DC: Office of Juvenile Justice and Delinquency Prevention, U.S. Department of Justice, 1995), p. 90.

56. Joan McCord, Cathy Spatz Widom, and Nancy A. Crowell, eds., *Juvenile Crime, Juvenile Justice*, panel on Juvenile Crime: Prevention, Treatment, and Control (Washington, DC: National Academy Press, 2001), p. 147.

57. *OJJDP News @ A Glance*, "Mentoring Makes a Difference" (Washington, DC: Office of Juvenile Justice and Delinquency Prevention, U.S. Department of Justice, 2003), p. 1.

58. Laurence C. Novotney, Elizabeth Mertinko, James Lange, and Tara Kelly Baker, *Juvenile Mentoring Program: A Progress Review* (Washington, DC: OJJDP Juvenile Justice Bulletin, 2000).

59. Thomas J. Dishion, Joan McCord, and François Poulin, "When Interventions Harm: Peer Groups and Problem Behavior," *American Psychologist* 54:755–764 (1999).

60. Jean Grossman and Eileen Gary, *Mentoring—A Proven Delinquency Prevention Strategy* (Washington, DC: OJJDP Juvenile Justice Bulletin, 1997).

61. Andrew Hahn, "Extending the Time of Learning," in Douglas J. Besharov, ed., *America's Disconnected Youth: Toward a Preventive Strategy* (Washington, DC: Child Welfare League of America Press, 1999).

62. Andrew Hahn, *Evaluation of the Quantum Opportunities Program (QOP): Did the Program Work?* (Waltham, MA: Brandeis University, 1994).

63. Jean Baldwin Grossman and Joseph P. Tierney, "Does Mentoring Work? An Impact Study of the Big Brothers Big Sisters Program," *Evaluation Review* 22:403–426 (1998), p. 405.

64. Ibid., p. 422.

65. David L. DuBois, Bruce E. Holloway, Jeffrey C. Valentine, and Harris Cooper, "Effectiveness of Mentoring Programs for Youth: A Meta-Analytic Review," *American Journal of Community Psychology* 30:157–197 (2002); Brandon C. Welsh and Akemi Hoshi, "Communities and Crime Prevention," in Lawrence W. Sherman, David P. Farrington, Brandon C. Welsh, and Doris Layton MacKenzie, eds., *Evidence-Based Crime Prevention* (New York: Routledge, 2002); Joan McCord, Cathy Spatz Widom, and Nancy A. Crowell, eds., *Juvenile Crime, Juvenile Justice*.

66. McCord, Spatz Widom, and Crowell, eds., *Juvenile Crime, Juvenile Justice*, p. 147.

67. Denise C. Gottfredson, "An Empirical Test of School-Based Environmental and Individual Interventions to Reduce the Risk of Delinquent Behavior," *Criminology* 24:705–731 (1986); Denise C. Gottfredson, "Changing School Structures to Benefit High-Risk Youth," in Peter Leone, ed., *Understanding Troubled and Troubling Youth* (Newbury Park, CA: Sage Publications, 1990); Denise C. Gottfredson, *Schools and Delinquency* (New York: Cambridge University Press, 2001).

68. Debra Galant, "Violence Offers Its Own Lessons," *New York Times*, June 15, 2003.

69. Gottfredson et al., "School-Based Crime Prevention."

70. James Larson, "Violence Prevention in the Schools: A Review of Selected Programs and Procedures," *School Psychology Review* 23:151–164 (1994).

71. Ibid., p. 153.

72. Denise C. Gottfredson, Gary D. Gottfredson, and Stephanie A. Weisman, "The Timing of Delinquent Behavior and Its Implications for After-School Programs," *Criminology & Public Policy* 1:61–86 (2001), p. 61.

73. Ibid., p. 63.

74. Executive Summary, "When School Is Out," *The Future of Children* 9:Fall 1999 (Los Altos, CA: The David and Lucile Packard Foundation).

75. Steven P. Schinke, Mario A. Orlandi, and Kristin C. Cole, "Boys & Girls Clubs in Public Housing Developments: Prevention Services for Youth at Risk," *Journal of Community Psychology, Office of Substance Abuse Prevention* Special Issue:118–128 (1992).

76. Ibid., p. 120.

77. Ibid., pp. 125–127.

78. Marshall B. Jones and David R. Offord, "Reduction of Anti-Social Behaviour in Poor Children by Nonschool Skill Development," *Journal of Child Psychology and Psychiatry* 30:737–750 (1989).

79. Lawrence W. Sherman et al., *Preventing Crime: What Works, What Doesn't, What's Promising* (Washington, DC: NIJ, 1997); Lawrence W. Sherman et al., *Preventing Crime: What Works, What Doesn't, What's Promising* (Washington, DC: NIJ Research in Brief, 1998). (Note: The 1998 publication is a summary of the 1997 publication.)

80. McCord, Widom, and Crowell, eds., *Juvenile Crime, Juvenile Justice*, pp. 150–151.

81. Peter Z. Schochet, John Burghardt, and Steven Glazerman, *National Job Corps Study: The Impacts of Job Corps on Participants' Employment and Related Outcomes* (Washington, DC: Employment and Training Administration, U.S. Department of Labor, 2001), p. xxv.

82. Lynn A. Curtis, *The State of Families: Family, Employment and Reconstruction: Policy Based on What Works* (Milwaukee, WI: Families International, 1995).

83. Schochet, Burghardt, and Glazerman, *National Job Corps Study.*

84. David A. Long, Charles D. Mallar, and Craig V. D. Thornton, "Evaluating the Benefits and Costs of the Job Corps," *Journal of Policy Analysis and Management* 1:55–76 (1981).

85. Sheena McConnell and Steven Glazerman, *National Job Corps Study: The Benefits and Costs of Job Corps* (Washington, DC: Employment and Training Administration, U.S. Department of Labor, 2001).

86. Tim Cross and Daryl Wright, "What Works with At-Risk Youths," *Corrections Today* 66:64–68 (2004), p. 64.

87. Ibid, p. 65.

88. Rudy Hernandez, *YouthBuild U.S.A.* (Washington, DC: OJJDP Youth in Action Fact Sheet, 2001).

89. J. David Hawkins, Richard F. Catalano, and Associates, *Communities That Care: Action for Drug Abuse* (San Francisco: Jossey-Bass, 1992).

90. Richard F. Catalano, Michael W. Arthur, J. David Hawkins, Lisa Berglund, and Jeffrey J. Olson, "Comprehensive Community- and School-Based Interventions to Prevent Antisocial Behavior," in Rolf Loeber and David P. Farrington, eds., *Serious and Violent Juvenile Offenders: Risk Factors and Successful Interventions* (Thousand Oaks, CA: Sage Publications, 1998), p. 281.

91. Adele V. Harrell, Shannon E. Cavanagh, and Sanjeev Sridharan, *Evaluation of the Children At Risk Program: Results 1 Year after the End of the Program* (Washington, DC: NIJ Research in Brief, 1999).

92. Hawkins, Catalano, and Associates, *Communities That Care: Action for Drug Abuse Prevention.*

93. Elaine Morley, Shelli B. Rossman, Mary Kopczynski, Janeen Buck, and Caterina Gouvis, *Comprehensive Responses to Youth at Risk: Interim Findings from the Safe Futures Initiative* (Washington, DC: Office of Juvenile Justice and Delinquency Prevention, 2000).

94. Catalano, Arthur, Hawkins, Berglund, and Olson, "Comprehensive Community- and School-Based Interventions to Prevent Antisocial Behavior."

95. James C. Howell and J. David Hawkins, "Prevention of Youth Violence," in Michael Tonry and Mark H. Moore, eds., *Youth Violence: Crime and Justice: A Review of Research*, vol. 24 (Chicago: University of Chicago Press, 1998), pp. 303–304.

96. Tracy W. Harachi, J. David Hawkins, Richard F. Catalano, Andrea M. Lafazia, Brian H. Smith, and Michael W. Arthur, "Evidence-Based Community Decision Making for Prevention: Two Case Studies of Communities That Care," *Japanese Journal of Sociological Criminology* 28:26–38 (2003).

97. Bryan J. Vila, "Human Nature and Crime Control: Improving the Feasibility of Nurturant Strategies," *Politics and the Life Sciences* 16:3–21 (1997).

98. Irvin Waller and Brandon C. Welsh, "International Trends in Crime Prevention: Cost-Effective Ways to Reduce Victimization," in Graeme Newman, ed., *Global Report on Crime and Justice* (New York: Oxford University Press, 1999).

99. Richard A. Mendel, *Prevention or Pork? A Hard-Headed Look at Youth-Oriented Anti-Crime Programs* (Washington, DC: American Youth Policy Forum, 1995), p. 1.

100. McCord, "Cures That Harm: Unanticipated Outcomes of Crime Prevention Programs." See also Thomas Gabor, "Prevention into the Twenty-First Century: Some Final Remarks," *Canadian Journal of Criminology* 32:197–212 (1990).

101. David R. Offord, Helena Chmura Kraemer, Alan E. Kazdin, Peter S. Jensen, and Richard Harrington, "Lowering the Burden of Suffering from Child Psychiatric Disorder: Trade-Offs Among Clinical, Targeted, and Universal Interventions," *Journal of the American Academy of Child and Adolescent Psychiatry* 37:686–694 (1998).

102. Farrington and Welsh, "Delinquency Prevention Using Family-Based Interventions."

103. National Crime Prevention Council, "Saving Money While Stopping Crime," *Topics in Crime Prevention* (Washington, DC: NCPC, Fall 1999).

104. Brandon C. Welsh, "Economic Costs and Benefits of Early Developmental Prevention," in Rolf Loeber and David P. Farrington, eds., *Child Delinquents: Development, Intervention, and Service Needs* (Thousand Oaks, CA: Sage Publications, 2001); Brandon C. Welsh, David P. Farrington, and Lawrence W. Sherman, eds., *Costs and Benefits of Preventing Crime* (Boulder: Westview Press, 2001).

The Juvenile Justice System

Since 1900, a separate juvenile justice system has been developed that features its own rules, institutions, laws, and processes. The separation of juvenile and adult offenders reflects society's concern for the plight of children. Ideally, care, protection, and treatment are the bywords of the juvenile justice system. However, because of public fear of violent youth, there have been efforts to "toughen up" the juvenile justice system and treat some delinquents much more like adult offenders. Because of these concerns, the treatment of delinquents has become an American dilemma. Severe punishment seems to have little deterrent effect on teenagers—if anything, it may prepare them for a life of adult criminality. Many incarcerated adult felons report that they were institutionalized as youths. The juvenile justice system is caught between the futility of punishing juveniles and the public's demand that something be done about serious juvenile crime. Yet, the rehabilitative ideal of the juvenile justice system has not been totally lost. Even though the nation seems to be in the midst of a punishment cycle, juvenile justice experts continue to press for judicial fairness, rehabilitation, and innovative programs for juvenile offenders.

Part Four provides a general overview of the juvenile justice system, including its process, history, and legal rules. Chapter 12 reviews the history and development of juvenile justice and provides an overview of its major components, processes, goals, and institutions. Chapter 13 deals with police handling of delinquent and status offenders. It contains information on the police role, the organization of police services, legal rights of minors in police custody, and prevention efforts. Chapter 14 is concerned with the juvenile court process. It describes such issues and programs as diversion, the transfer of youths to adult courts, legal rights during trial, the role of the prosecutor, the juvenile court judge, and the defense attorney, and the sentencing of juvenile offenders.

Chapter 15 discusses efforts to treat juveniles who have been found to be delinquent. It reviews the history and practices of probation, community corrections, and juvenile institutions. Chapter 16 reviews international efforts to treat delinquent offenders. It compares how other nations organize their juvenile justice systems and treat juvenile offenders with methods used in the United States. Finally, Chapter 17 looks at the future of delinquency and juvenile justice. It highlights critical issues that present challenges to the understanding of delinquency and society's efforts to bring about its prevention and control.

Chapter 12 Juvenile Justice: Then and Now

Chapter 13 Police Work with Juveniles

Chapter 14 Juvenile Court Process: Pretrial, Trial, and Sentencing

Chapter 15 Juvenile Corrections: Probation, Community Treatment, and Institutionalization

Chapter 16 Delinquency and Juvenile Justice Abroad

Chapter 17 The Future of Delinquency and Juvenile Justice

12 Juvenile Justice: Then and Now

Chapter Outline

Juvenile Justice in the Nineteenth Century

Urbanization

The Child-Saving Movement

House of Refuge

Were They Really Child Savers?

Development of Juvenile Institutions

Children's Aid Society

Society for the Prevention of Cruelty to Children

A Century of Juvenile Justice

The Illinois Juvenile Court Act and Its Legacy

Reforming the System

Juvenile Justice Today

The Juvenile Justice Process

Conflicting Values in Juvenile Justice

Criminal Justice vs. Juvenile Justice

FOCUS ON DELINQUENCY: Similarities and Differences Between Juvenile and Adult Justice Systems

A Comprehensive Juvenile Justice Strategy

Prevention

Intervention

Graduated Sanctions

Institutional Programs

Alternative Courts

POLICY AND PRACTICE: Teen Courts

Future of Juvenile Justice

POLICY AND PRACTICE: Abolish the Juvenile Court?

Chapter Objectives

1. Understand the major social changes leading to creation of the first modern juvenile court in Chicago in 1899

2. Be familiar with some of the landmark Supreme Court decisions that have influenced present-day juvenile justice procedures

3. Be able to comment on the nature of delinquency cases being processed in juvenile court

4. Know how children are processed by the juvenile justice system, beginning with arrest and concluding with reentry into society

5. Understand the conflicting values in contemporary juvenile justice

6. Recognize key similarities and differences between the adult and juvenile justice systems

7. Be able to argue the pros and cons of the juvenile justice system's goal to treat rather than punish and assess if this goal is being met today

8. Understand the need for and be aware of the key elements of a comprehensive juvenile justice strategy to deal with juvenile delinquency

9. See the difference between prevention and intervention efforts to reduce juvenile delinquency

10. Be able to identify and comment on pressing issues in the future of juvenile justice

CNN. View the CNN video clip of this story and answer related Critical Thinking questions on your Juvenile Delinquency 9e CD-ROM.

From the development of the first juvenile court in 1899 to the introduction of graduated sanctions, the history of the juvenile justice system is rife with innovations. One of the more recent innovations is the teen court, also called the youth court. Developed to relieve overcrowding and provide an alternative to traditional forms of juvenile courts, hundreds of jurisdictions across the country have set up these special courts. Teen courts differ from other juvenile justice programs because youths rather than adults determine the disposition in a case. In the South Bronx, New York, one teen court for first-time juvenile offenders includes a 16-year-old judge and a prosecutor, defense attorney, and jury who are all teenagers. In addition to being well received by youths, the program claims success in reducing rearrests.

This chapter begins with a discussion of the major social changes leading to creation of the first modern juvenile court in Chicago in 1899. We then cover the reform efforts of the twentieth century, including the movement to grant children the procedural rights typically given to adult offenders. This discussion includes descriptions of some landmark Supreme Court decisions that have influenced present-day juvenile justice procedures.

The second part of this chapter presents an overview of the contemporary juvenile justice system and the various philosophies, processes, organizations, and legal constraints that dominate its operations. The chapter describes the process that takes a youthful offender through a series of steps, beginning with arrest and concluding with reentry into society. What happens to young people who violate the law? Do they have legal rights? How are they helped? How are they punished? Should juvenile killers be released from custody prior to their 18th birthday? Should the goal of the system be rehabilitation or punishment?

To help address such questions, we have included a discussion of the similarities and differences between the adult and juvenile justice systems. This discussion draws attention to the principle that children are treated separately. By segregating delinquent children from adult offenders, society has placed greater importance on the delinquent being a *child* rather than being a *criminal*. Consequently, rehabilitation rather than punishment has traditionally been the goal. Today, with children committing more serious crimes, the juvenile justice system is having great difficulty handling these offenders.

In the final section, we discuss the need for a comprehensive juvenile justice strategy and the role of the federal government in juvenile justice reform—the key element in funding state juvenile justice and delinquency prevention efforts.

JUVENILE JUSTICE IN THE NINETEENTH CENTURY

At the beginning of the nineteenth century, delinquent, neglected, and runaway children in the United States were treated the same as adult criminal offenders.[1] Like children in England, when convicted of crimes they received harsh sentences similar to those imposed on adults. The adult criminal code applied to children, and no juvenile court existed.

During the early nineteenth century, various pieces of legislation were introduced to humanize criminal procedures for children. The concept of probation, introduced in Massachusetts in 1841, was geared toward helping young people avoid imprisonment. Many books and reports written during this time heightened public interest in juvenile care.

Despite this interest, no special facilities existed for the care of youths in trouble with the law, nor were there separate laws or courts to control their behavior. Youths who committed petty crimes, such as stealing or vandalism, were viewed as wayward children or victims of neglect and were placed in community asylums or homes. Youths who were involved in more serious crimes were subject to the same punishments as adults—imprisonment, whipping, or death.

Several events led to reforms and nourished the eventual development of the juvenile justice system: (1) urbanization, (2) the child saving movement and growing interest in the concept of *parens patriae*, and (3) development of institutions for the care of delinquent and neglected children.

Urbanization

Especially during the first half of the nineteenth century, the United States experienced rapid population growth, primarily due to an increased birthrate and expanding immigration. The rural poor and immigrant groups were attracted to urban commercial centers that promised jobs in manufacturing. In 1790, 5 percent of the

The House of Refuge was one of the earliest juvenile institutions in the United States to offer residents vocational training.

To learn more about the **early urbanization movement in America,** go to the Library of Congress web page devoted to American history at www.americaslibrary.gov/cgi-bin/page.cgi. For an up-to-date list of web links, go to http://cj.wadsworth.com/siegel_jd9e.

population lived in cities. By 1850, the share of the urban population had increased to 15 percent; it jumped to 40 percent in 1900, and 51 percent in 1920.[2] New York had more than quadrupled its population in the 30-year stretch between 1825 and 1855—from 166,000 in 1825 to 630,000 in 1855.[3]

Urbanization gave rise to increased numbers of young people at risk, who overwhelmed the existing system of work and training. To accommodate destitute youths, local jurisdictions developed poorhouses (almshouses) and workhouses. The poor, the insane, the diseased, and vagrant and destitute children were housed there in crowded and unhealthy conditions.

By the late eighteenth century, the family's ability to exert control over children began to be questioned. Villages developed into urban commercial centers, and work began to center around factories, not the home. Children of destitute families left home or were cast loose to make out as best they could; wealthy families could no longer absorb vagrant youth as apprentices or servants.[4] Chronic poverty became an American dilemma. The affluent began to voice concern over the increase in the number of people in what they considered the "dangerous classes"—the poor, single, criminal, mentally ill, and unemployed.

Urbanization and industrialization also generated the belief that certain segments of the population (youths in urban areas, immigrants) were susceptible to the influences of their decaying environment. The children of these classes were considered a group that might be "saved" by a combination of state and community intervention.[5] Intervention in the lives of these so-called dangerous classes became acceptable for wealthy, civic-minded citizens. Such efforts included *settlement houses,* a term used around the turn of the twentieth century to describe shelters or nonsecure residential facilities for vagrant children.

The Child-Saving Movement

The problems generated by urban growth sparked interest in the welfare of the "new" Americans, whose arrival fueled this expansion. In 1816, prominent New Yorkers formed the Society for the Prevention of Pauperism. Although they concerned themselves with shutting down taverns, brothels, and gambling parlors, they also were concerned that the moral training of children of the dangerous classes was inadequate. Soon other groups concerned with the plight of poor children began to form. Their focus was on extending government control over youthful activities (drinking, vagrancy, and delinquency) that had previously been left to private or family control.

These activists became known as *child savers.* Prominent among them were penologist Enoch Wines; Judge Richard Tuthill; Lucy Flowers, of the Chicago Women's Association; Sara Cooper, of the National Conference of Charities and Corrections; and Sophia Minton, of the New York Committee on Children.[6] Poor children could become a financial burden, and the child savers believed these children presented a threat to the moral fabric of society. Child saving organizations influenced state legislatures to enact laws giving courts the power to commit children who were runaways or criminal offenders to specialized institutions.

To read more about the **child savers,** go to www.ncjrs.org/criminal_justice2000/vol_2/02b2.pdf. For an up-to-date list of web links, go to http://cj.wadsworth.com/siegel_jd9e.

House of Refuge

House of Refuge
A care facility developed by the child savers to protect potential criminal youths by taking them off the street and providing a family-like environment.

The most prominent of the care facilities developed by child savers was the **House of Refuge**.[7] Its creation was effected by prominent Quakers and influential political leaders, such as Cadwallader Colden and Stephen Allen. In 1816, they formed the Society for the Prevention of Pauperism, which was devoted to the concept of protecting indigent youths who were at risk to crime by taking them off the streets and reforming them in a family-like environment.

The first House of Refuge, constructed in New York City, was the product of their reform efforts. Though the House was privately managed, the state legislature began providing funds, partly through a head tax on arriving transatlantic passengers and seamen, plus the proceeds from license fees for New York City's taverns, theaters, and circuses. These revenue sources were deemed appropriate, since supporters blamed immigration, intemperance, and commercial entertainment for juvenile crime!

The reformatory opened January 1, 1825, with only six boys and three girls, but within the first decade of its operation 1,678 inmates were admitted. Most kids were sent because of vagrancy and petty crimes and were sentenced or committed indefinitely until they reached adulthood. Originally, the institution accepted inmates from across the state of New York, but when a Western House of Refuge was opened in Rochester, New York, in 1849, residents came mostly from the New York City environs.

Once a resident, the adolescent's daily schedule was devoted for the most part to supervised labor, which was regarded as beneficial to education and discipline. Inmate labor also supported operating expenses for the reformatory. Male inmates worked in shops that produced brushes, cane chairs, brass nails, and shoes. The female inmates sewed uniforms, did laundry, and carried out other domestic work. A badge system was used to segregate inmates according to their behavior. Although students received rudimentary educational skills, greater emphasis was placed on evangelical religious instruction; non-Protestant clergy were excluded. The reformatory had the authority to bind out inmates through indenture agreements to private employers; most males were farm workers and females were domestic laborers.

The Refuge Movement Spreads When the House of Refuge opened, the majority of children admitted were status offenders placed there because of vagrancy or neglect. Children were placed in the institution by court order, sometimes over parents' objections. Their length of stay depended on need, age, and skill. Critics complained that the institution was run like a prison, with strict discipline and absolute separation of the sexes. Such a harsh program drove many children to run away, and the House of Refuge was forced to take a more lenient approach. Despite criticism, the concept enjoyed expanding popularity. In 1826, the Boston City Council founded the House of Reformation for juvenile offenders.[8] The courts committed children found guilty of criminal violations, or found to be beyond the control of their parents, to these schools. Because the child savers considered parents of delinquent children to be as guilty as convicted offenders, they sought to have the reform schools establish control over the children. Refuge managers believed they were preventing poverty and crime by separating destitute and delinquent children from their parents and placing them in an institution.[9]

The earliest institutions resembled the New York House of Refuge and housed a small number of children in relatively small buildings. But by the 1850s, the number of incarcerated children began to climb, resulting in the construction of larger institutions removed from the urban environment. For example, in New York the number of youthful residents expanded from 9 at the outset to more than 1,000 housed on Randall's Island in the East River in an institution indistinguishable from an adult prison.[10]

Despite ongoing criticism and scandal, the Houses of Refuge hung on for more than 100 years. After the Civil War, the urban Refuge began to be replaced by state institutions located in rural areas. In 1935, the institution on Randall's Island closed forever.

Were They Really Child Savers?

Debate continues over the true objectives of the early child savers. Some historians conclude that they were what they seemed—concerned citizens motivated by humanitarian ideals.[11] Modern scholars, however, have reappraised the child saving movement. In *The Child Savers*, Anthony Platt paints a picture of representatives of the ruling class who were galvanized by immigrants and the urban poor to take action to preserve their own way of life.[12] He claims

> The child savers should not be considered humanists: (1) their reforms did not herald a new system of justice but rather expedited traditional policies which had been informally developed during the nineteenth century; (2) they implicitly assumed the natural dependence of adolescents and created a special court to impose sanctions on premature independence and behavior

unbecoming to youth; (3) their attitudes toward delinquent youth were largely paternalistic and romantic but their commands were backed up by force; (4) they promoted correctional programs requiring longer terms of imprisonment, longer hours of labor, and militaristic discipline, and the inculcation of middle class values and lower class skills.[13]

Other critical thinkers followed Platt in finding that child saving was motivated more by self-interest than by benevolence. For example, Randall Shelden and Lynn Osborne traced the child saving movement in Memphis, Tennessee, and found that its leaders were a small group of upper-class citizens who desired to control the behavior and lifestyles of lower-class youth. The outcome was ominous. Most cases petitioned to the juvenile court (which opened in 1910) were for petty crimes and status offenses, yet 25 percent of the youths were committed to some form of incarceration; more than 96 percent of the actions with which females were charged were status offenses.[14]

In summary, these scholars believe that the reformers applied the concept of *parens patriae* for their own purposes, including the continuance of middle- and upper-class values and the furtherance of a child labor system consisting of marginal and lower-class skilled workers.

In the course of "saving children" by turning them over to houses of refuge, the basic legal rights of children were violated: Children were simply not granted the same constitutional protections as adults.

Development of Juvenile Institutions

State intervention in the lives of children continued well into the twentieth century. The child savers influenced state and local governments to create special institutions, called *reform schools*, which would house delinquent youths who would have otherwise been sent to adult prisons. The first institutions opened in Westboro, Massachusetts, in 1848 and in Rochester, New York, in 1849.[15] Institutional programs began in Ohio in 1850 and in Maine, Rhode Island, and Michigan in 1906. The Houses of Refuge began to be replaced by rural facilities, which used cottages to house residents rather than large prisonlike facilities. In New York, for example, the legislature authorized a State Training School for Boys at Warwick for inmates under 16, and the State Vocational School at Coxsackie for those 16 to 19.[16]

Children spent their days working in the institution, learning a trade where possible, and receiving some basic education. They were racially and sexually segregated, discipline was harsh, and their physical care was poor. Some were labeled as criminal, but were in reality abused and neglected. They too were subject to harsh working conditions, strict discipline, and intensive labor.[17] Although some people viewed reform schools as humanitarian answers to poorhouses and prisons, many were opposed to such programs.

Children's Aid Society

Children's Aid Society
Child saving organization that took children from the streets of large cities and placed them with farm families on the prairie.

orphan trains
The name for trains in which urban youths were sent West by the Children's Aid Society for adoption with local farm couples.

To read more about **the life of Charles Loring Brace,** go to www.trailblazerbooks.com/books/roundup/Roundup-bio.html. For an up-to-date list of web links, go to http://cj.wadsworth.com/siegel_jd9e.

As an alternative to secure correctional facilities, New York philanthropist Charles Loring Brace helped develop the **Children's Aid Society** in 1853.[18] Brace's formula for dealing with delinquent youths was to rescue them from the harsh environment of the city and provide them with temporary shelter.

Deciding there were simply too many needy children to care for in New York City, and believing the urban environment was injurious to children, Brace devised what he called his *placing-out plan* to send these children to western farms where they could be cared for and find a home. They were placed on what became known as **orphan trains**, which made preannounced stops in western farming communities. Families wishing to take in children would meet the train, be briefly introduced to the passengers, and leave with one of the children. Brace's plan was activated in 1854 and very soon copied by other childcare organizations. Though the majority of the children benefited from the plan and did find a new life, others were less successful, and some were exploited

RESCUED.

HOMELESS.

OFF FOR THE WEST.

THE YOUNG FARMER.

ADOPTED.

and harmed by the experience. By 1930, political opposition to Brace's plan, coupled with the negative effects of the economic depression, spelled the end of the orphan trains, but not before 150,000 children were placed in rural homesteads. Concept Summary 12.1 describes those first juvenile institutions and organizations.

Society for the Prevention of Cruelty to Children

Society for the Prevention of Cruelty to Children
First established in 1874, these organizations protected children subjected to cruelty and neglect at home or at school.

In 1874, the first **Society for the Prevention of Cruelty to Children** (SPCC) was established in New York. Agents of the society were granted power to remove children from their homes and arrest anyone who interfered with their work; they also assisted the court in making placement decisions.[19] By 1890, the society controlled the intake

Concept Summary 12.1
The First Juvenile Institutions and Organizations

Reform Schools	Devoted to the care of vagrant and delinquent youths
Children's Aid Society	Designed to protect delinquent youths from the city's dangers through the provision of temporary shelter
Orphan Trains	The practice of using trains to place delinquent urban youths with families in western farming communities
Society for the Prevention of Cruelty to Children	Designed to protect abused and neglected children by placing them with other families and advocating for criminal penalties for negligent parents

and disposition of an annual average of 15,000 poor and neglected children. By 1900, there were 300 such societies in the United States.[20]

Leaders of the SPCCs were concerned that abused boys would become lower-class criminals and that mistreated young girls might become sexually promiscuous women. A growing crime rate and concern about a rapidly changing population served to swell SPCC membership. In addition, these organizations protected children who had been subjected to cruelty and neglect at home and at school.

SPCC groups influenced state legislatures to pass statutes protecting children from parents who did not provide them with adequate food and clothing or made them beg or work in places where liquor was sold.[21] Criminal penalties were created for negligent parents, and provisions were established for removing children from the home. In some states, agents of the SPCC could actually arrest abusive parents; in others, they would inform the police about suspected abuse cases and accompany officers when they made an arrest.[22]

The organization and control of SPCCs varied widely. For example, the New York City SPCC was a city agency supported by municipal funds. It conducted investigations of delinquent and neglected children for the court. In contrast, the Boston SPCC emphasized delinquency prevention and worked with social welfare groups; the Philadelphia SPCC emphasized family unity and was involved with other charities.[23]

TO QUIZ YOURSELF ON THIS MATERIAL, go to the Juvenile Delinquency 9e website.

A CENTURY OF JUVENILE JUSTICE

Although reform groups continued to lobby for government control over children, the committing of children under the doctrine of *parens patriae* without due process of law began to be questioned. Could the state incarcerate children who had not violated the criminal law? Should children be held in the same facilities that housed adults? Serious problems challenged the effectiveness of the existing system. Institutional deficiencies, the absence of due process for poor, ignorant, and noncriminal delinquents, and the treatment of these children by inadequate private organizations all spurred the argument that a juvenile court should be established.

Increasing delinquency rates also hastened the development of a juvenile court. Theodore Ferdinand's analysis of the Boston juvenile court found that in the 1820s and 1830s very few juveniles were charged with serious offenses. By 1850, juvenile delinquency was the fastest growing component of the local crime problem.[24] Ferdinand concluded that the flow of juvenile cases strengthened the argument that juveniles needed their own court.

The Illinois Juvenile Court Act and Its Legacy

The child saving movement culminated in passage of the Illinois Juvenile Court Act of 1899, which established the nation's first independent juvenile court. Interpretations of its intentions differ, but unquestionably the Illinois Juvenile Court Act established juvenile delinquency as a legal concept. For the first time the distinction was made between children who were neglected and those who were delinquent. Delinquent children were those under the age of 16 who violated the law. Most important, the act established a court and a probation program specifically for children. In addition, the legislation allowed children to be committed to institutions and reform programs under the control of the state. The key provisions of the act were these:

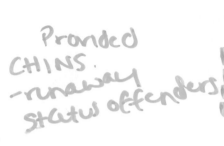
Provided CHINS. —runaway status offenders

- A separate court was established for delinquent and neglected children.
- Special procedures were developed to govern the adjudication of juvenile matters.
- Children were to be separated from adults in courts and in institutional programs.
- Probation programs were to be developed to assist the court in making decisions in the best interests of the state and the child.

Following passage of the Illinois Juvenile Court Act, similar legislation was enacted throughout the nation. The special courts these laws created maintained jurisdiction over predelinquent (neglected and dependent) and delinquent children. Juvenile court jurisdiction was based primarily on a child's noncriminal actions and status, not strictly on a violation of criminal law. The *parens patriae* philosophy predominated, ushering in a form of personalized justice that still did not provide juvenile offenders with the full array of constitutional protections available to adult criminal offenders. The court's process was paternalistic rather than adversarial. Attorneys were not required, and hearsay evidence, inadmissible in criminal trials, was admissible in the adjudication of juvenile offenders. Verdicts were based on a *preponderance of the evidence* instead of the stricter standard used by criminal courts, *beyond a reasonable doubt*, and children were often not granted any right to appeal their convictions.

The principles motivating the Illinois reformers were these:

1. Children should not be held as accountable as adult transgressors;
2. The objective of the juvenile justice system is to treat and rehabilitate rather than punish;
3. Disposition should be predicated on analysis of the youth's special circumstances and needs; and
4. The system should avoid the trappings of the adult criminal process with all its confusing rules and procedures.

This was a major event in the juvenile justice movement. Its significance was such that by 1917, juvenile courts had been established in all but three states.

The Legacy of Illinois Just what were the ramifications of passage of the Illinois Juvenile Court Act? The traditional interpretation is that the reformers were genuinely motivated to pass legislation that would serve the best interests of the child. U.S. Supreme Court Justice Abe Fortas took this position in the landmark 1967 *In re Gault* case:

> The early reformers were appalled by adult procedures and penalties and by the fact that children could be given long prison sentences and mixed in jails with hardened criminals. They were profoundly convinced that society's duty to the child could not be confined by the concept of justice alone. . . . The child—essentially good, as they saw it—was to be made to feel that he was the object of the state's care and solicitude, not that he was under arrest or on trial. . . . The idea of crime and punishment was to be abandoned. The child was to be treated and rehabilitated and the procedures from apprehension through institutionalization were to be clinical rather than punitive.[25]

The child savers believed that children were influenced by their environments. Society was to be concerned with what their problems were and how these problems could be handled in the interests of the children and the state.

Nowhere can this procedural informality be seen more fully than in the Denver Juvenile Court presided over by Judge Benjamin Lindsey.[26] He viewed the children who came before him as "his boys" who were fundamentally good human beings led astray by their social and psychological environment. While Lindsey had no specific statutory authority to do so, he adopted a social worker–friend approach to the children who had been petitioned to court. The need for formal adjudication of the charges was unimportant compared to an effort to treat and rehabilitate these wayward youth. He condemned the criminal justice system, which he saw operating as a "medieval torture chamber" that victimized children.[27]

The Early Juvenile Court The major functions of the juvenile justice system were to prevent juvenile crime and to rehabilitate juvenile offenders. The roles of the judge and the probation staff were to diagnose the child's condition and prescribe programs to alleviate it; judgments about children's actions and consideration for their constitutional rights were secondary.

By the 1920s, noncriminal behavior in the form of incorrigibility and truancy from school was added to the jurisdiction of many juvenile court systems. Of particular interest was the sexual behavior of young girls, and the juvenile court enforced a strict moral code on working-class girls, not hesitating to incarcerate those who were sexually active.[28] Programs of all kinds, including individualized counseling and institutional care, were used to *cure* juvenile criminality.

By 1925, juvenile courts existed in virtually every jurisdiction in every state. Although the juvenile court concept expanded rapidly, it cannot be said that each state implemented it thoroughly. Some jurisdictions established elaborate juvenile court systems, whereas others passed legislation but provided no services. Some courts had trained juvenile court judges; others had nonlawyers sitting in juvenile cases. Some courts had extensive probation departments; others had untrained probation personnel. In 1920, a U.S. Children's Bureau survey found that only 16 percent of these new juvenile courts held separate calendars or hearings for children's cases or had an officially established probation service, and recorded social information about the children coming through the court. In 1926, it was reported that five out of six of these courts in the United States failed to meet the minimum standards of the Children's Bureau.[29]

Great diversity also marked juvenile institutions. Some maintained a lenient orientation, but others relied on harsh punishments, including beatings, straitjacket restraints, immersion in cold water, and solitary confinement with a diet of bread and water.

These conditions were exacerbated by the rapid growth in the juvenile institutional population. Between 1890 and 1920, the number of institutionalized youths jumped 112 percent, a rise that far exceeded the increase in the total number of adolescents in the United States.[30] Although social workers and court personnel deplored the increased institutionalization of youth, the growth was due in part to the successful efforts by reformers to close poorhouses, thereby creating a need for institutions to house their displaced populations. In addition, the lack of a coherent national policy on needy children allowed private entrepreneurs to fill the void.[31] Although the increase in institutionalization seemed contrary to the goal of rehabilitation, such an approach was preferable to the poorhouse and the streets.

Reforming the System

Reform of this system was slow in coming. In 1912, the U.S. Children's Bureau was formed as the first federal child welfare agency. By the 1930s, the bureau began to investigate the state of juvenile institutions and tried to expose some of their more repressive aspects.[32] After World War II, critics such as Paul Tappan and Francis Allen began to identify problems in the juvenile justice system, among which were the neglect of procedural rights and the warehousing of youth in ineffective institutions. Status offenders commonly were housed with delinquents and given sentences that were more punitive than those given to delinquents.[33]

From its origin, the juvenile court system denied children procedural rights normally available to adult offenders. Due-process rights, such as representation by counsel, a jury trial, freedom from self-incrimination, and freedom from unreasonable search and seizure, were not considered essential for the juvenile court system because its primary purpose was not punishment but rehabilitation. However, the dream of trying to rehabilitate children was not achieved. Individual treatment approaches failed, and delinquency rates soared.

Reform efforts, begun in earnest in the 1960s, changed the face of the juvenile justice system. In 1962, New York passed legislation creating a family court system.[34] The new court assumed responsibility for all matters involving family life, with emphasis on delinquent and neglected children. In addition, the legislation established the PINS classification (person in need of supervision). This category included individuals involved in such actions as truancy and incorrigibility. By using labels like PINS and CHINS (children in need of supervision) to establish jurisdiction over children, juvenile courts expanded their role as social agencies. Because noncriminal children were now involved in the juvenile court system to a greater degree, many juvenile courts had to improve their social services. Efforts were made to personalize the system of justice for children. These reforms were soon followed by a due-process revolution, which ushered in an era of procedural rights for court-adjudicated youth.

In the 1960s and 1970s, the U.S. Supreme Court radically altered the juvenile justice system when it issued a series of decisions that established the right of juveniles to receive due process of law.[35] The Court established that juveniles had the same rights as adults in important areas of trial process, including the right to confront witnesses, notice of charges, and the right to counsel. Exhibit 12.1 illustrates some of the most important legal cases bringing procedural due process to the juvenile justice process.

Federal Commissions In addition to the legal revolution brought about by the Supreme Court, a series of national commissions sponsored by the federal government helped change the shape of juvenile justice. In 1967, the President's Commission

EXHIBIT 12.1

Leading Constitutional Cases in Juvenile Justice

Kent v. United States (1965) determined that a child has due process rights, such as having an attorney present at waiver hearings.

In re Gault (1967) ruled that a minor has basic due process rights including: (1) notice of the charges with respect to their timeliness and specificity, (2) right to counsel, (3) right to confrontation and cross-examination, (4) privilege against self-incrimination, (5) right to a transcript of the trial record, and (6) right to appellate review.

McKeiver v. Pennsylvania (1971) held that trial by jury in a juvenile court's adjudicative stage is not a constitutional requirement.

Breed v. Jones (1975) ruled that a child has the protection of the double-jeopardy clause of the Fifth Amendment and cannot be tried twice for the same crime.

Fare v. Michael C. (1979) held that a child's request to see his probation officer at the time of interrogation did not operate to invoke his Fifth Amendment right to remain silent. According to the Court, the probation officer cannot be expected to offer the type of advice that an accused would expect from an attorney. The landmark *Miranda v. Arizona* case ruled that a request for a lawyer is an immediate invocation of a person's right to silence, but this rule is not applicable for a request to see the probation officer.

Eddings v. Oklahoma (1982) ruled that a defendant's age should be a mitigating factor in deciding whether to apply the death penalty.

Schall v. Martin (1984) upheld a statute allowing for the placement of children in preventive detention before their adjudication. The

Court concluded that it was not unreasonable to detain juveniles for their own protection.

New Jersey v. T.L.O. (1985) determined that the Fourth Amendment applies to school searches. The Court adopted a "reasonable suspicion" standard, as opposed to the stricter standard of "probable cause," to evaluate the legality of searches and seizures in a school setting.

Thompson v. Oklahoma (1988) ruled that imposing capital punishment on a juvenile murderer who was 15 years old at the time of the offense violated the Eighth Amendment's constitutional prohibition against cruel and unusual punishment.

Stanford v. Kentucky and Wilkins v. Missouri (1989) concluded that the imposition of the death penalty on a juvenile who committed a crime between the ages of 16 and 18 was not unconstitutional and that the Eighth Amendment's cruel and unusual punishment clause did not prohibit capital punishment.

Vernonia School District v. Acton (1995) held that the Fourth Amendment's guarantee against unreasonable searches is not violated by the suspicionless drug testing of all students choosing to participate in interscholastic athletics. The Supreme Court expanded power of public educators to ensure safe learning environments in schools.

United States v. Lopez (1995) ruled that Congress exceeded its authority under the Commerce Clause when it passed the Gun-Free School Zone Act, which made it a federal crime to possess a firearm within 1,000 feet of a school.

SOURCES: *Kent v. United States*, 383 U.S. 541, 86 S.Ct. 1045, 16 L.Ed.2d 84 (1966); *In re Gault*, 387 U.S. 1; 87 S.Ct. 1248 (1967); *McKeiver v. Pennslyvania*, 403 U.S. 528, 91 S.Ct. 1976 (1971); *Breed v. Jones*, 421 U.S. 519, 95 S.Ct. 1779 (1975); *Fare v. Michael C.*, 442 U.S. 707, 99 S.Ct. 2560 (1979); *Eddings v. Oklahoma*, 455 U.S. 104, 102 S.Ct. 869, 71 L.Ed.2d 1 (1982); *Schall v. Martin*, 467 U.S. 253, 104 S.Ct. 2403 (1984); *New Jersey v. T.L.O.*, 469 U.S. 325, 105 S.Ct. 733 (1985); *Thompson v. Oklahoma*, 487 U.S. 815, 108 S.Ct. 2687, 101 L.Ed.2d 702 (1988); *Stanford v. Kentucky*, 492 U.S. 361, 109 S.Ct. 2969 (1989); *Wilkins v. Missouri*, 492 U.S. 361, 109 S.Ct. 2969 (1989); *Vernonia School District v. Acton*, 515 U.S. 646, 115 S.Ct. 2386, 132 L.Ed.2d 564 (1995); *United States v. Lopez*, 115 S.Ct. 1624 (1995).

on Law Enforcement and the Administration of Justice, organized by President Lyndon Johnson, suggested that the juvenile justice system must provide underprivileged youths with opportunities for success, including jobs and education. The commission also recognized the need to develop effective law enforcement procedures to control hard-core offenders, while at the same time granting them due process. The commission's report acted as a catalyst for passage of the federal Juvenile Delinquency Prevention and Control (JDP) Act of 1968. This law created a Youth Development and Delinquency Prevention Administration, which concentrated on helping states develop new juvenile justice programs, particularly those involving diversion of youth, decriminalization, and decarceration. In 1968, Congress also passed the Omnibus Safe Streets and Crime Control Act.[36] Title I of this law established the **Law Enforcement Assistance Administration (LEAA)** to provide federal funds for improving the adult and juvenile justice systems. In 1972, Congress amended the JDP Act to allow the LEAA to focus its funding on juvenile justice and delinquency prevention programs. State and local governments were required to develop and adopt comprehensive plans to obtain federal assistance.

Because crime continued to receive much publicity, a second effort called the National Advisory Commission on Criminal Justice Standards and Goals was established in 1973 by the Nixon administration.[37] Its report identified such strategies as (1) preventing delinquent behavior, (2) developing diversion activities, (3) establishing dispositional alternatives, (4) providing due process for all juveniles, and (5) controlling violent and chronic delinquents. This commission's recommendations formed the basis for the Juvenile Justice and Delinquency Prevention Act of 1974.[38] This act eliminated the Youth Development and Delinquency Prevention Administration and replaced it with the Office of Juvenile Justice and Delinquency Prevention (OJJDP) within the LEAA. In 1980, the LEAA was phased out, and the OJJDP became an independent agency in the Department of Justice. Throughout the 1970s, its two most important goals were (1) removing juveniles from detention in adult jails, and (2) eliminating the incarceration together of delinquents and status offenders. During this period, the OJJDP stressed the creation of formal diversion and restitution programs.

The latest effort was the Violent Crime Control and Law Enforcement Act of 1994.[39] The largest piece of crime legislation in the history of the United States, it provided 100,000 new police officers and billions of dollars for prisons and prevention programs for both adult and juvenile offenders. A revitalized juvenile justice system would need both a comprehensive strategy to prevent and control delinquency and a consistent program of federal funding.[40]

Law Enforcement Assistance Administration (LEAA)
Unit in the U.S. Department of Justice established by the Omnibus Crime Control and Safe Streets Act of 1968 to administer grants and provide guidance for crime prevention policy and programs.

To read about the **Juvenile Justice and Delinquency Prevention Act of 1974,** go to http://ojjdp.ncjrs.org/about/ojjjact.txt. For an up-to-date list of web links, go to http://cj.wadsworth.com/siegel_jd9e.

TO QUIZ YOURSELF ON THIS MATERIAL, go to the Juvenile Delinquency 9e website.

JUVENILE JUSTICE TODAY

Today the juvenile justice system exercises jurisdiction over two distinct categories of offenders—delinquents and status offenders.[41] *Delinquent children* are those who fall under a jurisdictional age limit, which varies from state to state, and who commit an act in violation of the penal code. *Status offenders* are commonly characterized in state statutes as persons or children in need of supervision (PINS or CHINS). Most states distinguish such behavior from delinquent conduct to reduce the effect of any stigma on children as a result of their involvement with the juvenile court. In addition, juvenile courts generally have jurisdiction over situations involving conduct directed at (rather than committed by) juveniles, such as parental neglect, deprivation, abandonment, and abuse.

The states have also set different maximum ages below which children fall under the jurisdiction of the juvenile court. Most states (and the District of Columbia) include all children under 18, others set the upper limit at 17, and still others include children under 16 (see Table 12.1).

Some states exclude certain classes of offenders or offenses from the juvenile justice system. For example, youths who commit serious violent offenses such as rape and/or murder may be automatically excluded from the juvenile justice system and treated as adults, on the premise that they stand little chance of rehabilitation within the confines

Some states exclude certain classes of offenders or offenses from the juvenile justice system—for example, youths who commit serious violent offenses such as rape and/or murder—while others retain even the most serious cases in the juvenile justice system. Here, 12-year-old Michael Nichols is led from an Arkansas court on July 25, 2000, after a juvenile court judge refused to consider an insanity defense in his case. Nichols was tried on charges of shooting a police officer who stopped him while he was heading toward his school with a shotgun.

---

juvenile justice process
Under the paternal (*parens patriae*) philosophy, juvenile justice procedures are informal and nonadversarial, invoked for the juvenile offender rather than against him or her; a petition instead of a complaint is filed; courts make findings of involvement or adjudication of delinquency instead of convictions; and juvenile offenders receive dispositions instead of sentences.

of the juvenile system. Juvenile court judges may also transfer, or *waive,* repeat offenders who they deem untreatable by the juvenile authorities.

Today's juvenile justice system exists in all states by statute. Each jurisdiction has a juvenile code and a special court structure to accommodate children in trouble. Nationwide, the juvenile justice system consists of thousands of public and private agencies, with a total budget amounting to hundreds of millions of dollars. Most of the nation's police agencies have juvenile components, and there are more than 3,000 juvenile courts and about an equal number of juvenile correctional facilities.

Figure 12.1 depicts the numbers of juvenile offenders removed at various stages of the juvenile justice process. These figures do not take into account the large number of children who are referred to community diversion and mental health programs. There are thousands of these programs throughout the nation. This multitude of agencies and people dealing with juvenile delinquency has led to the development of what professionals view as an incredibly expansive and complex system.

The Juvenile Justice Process

How are children processed by the juvenile justice system?[42] Most children come into the justice system as a result of contact with a police officer. When a juvenile commits a serious crime, the police are empowered to make an arrest. Less serious offenses may also require police action, but in these instances, instead of being arrested, the child may be warned or a referral may be made to a social service program. A little more than 70 percent of all children arrested are referred to the juvenile court. Figure 12.2 outlines the **juvenile justice process,** and a detailed analysis of this process is presented in the next sections.

Police Investigation When youths commit a crime, police have the authority to investigate the incident and decide whether to release the youths or commit them to the juvenile court. This is often a discretionary decision, based not only on the nature of the offense but also on conditions existing at the time of the arrest. Such factors as the seriousness of the offense, the child's past contacts with the police, and whether the child denies committing the crime determine whether a petition is filed. Juveniles in custody have constitutional rights similar to those of adult offenders. Children are protected against unreasonable search and seizure under the Fourth and Fourteenth Amendments of the Constitution. The Fifth Amendment places limitations on police interrogation procedures.

TABLE 12.1

Oldest Age for Juvenile Court Jurisdiction in Delinquency Cases

Age	State (Total Number)
15	Connecticut, New York, North Carolina (3)
16	Georgia, Illinois, Louisiana, Massachusetts, Michigan, Missouri, New Hampshire, South Carolina, Texas, Wisconsin (10)
17	Alabama, Alaska, Arizona, Arkansas, California, Colorado, Delaware, Florida, Hawaii, Idaho, Indiana, Iowa, Kansas, Kentucky, Maine, Maryland, Minnesota, Mississippi, Montana, Nebraska, Nevada, New Jersey, New Mexico, North Dakota, Ohio, Oklahoma, Oregon, Pennsylvania, Rhode Island, South Dakota, Tennessee, Utah, Vermont, Virginia, Washington, West Virginia, Wyoming (37) and the District of Columbia

SOURCE: Melissa Sickmund, *Juveniles in Court* (Washington, DC: Office of Juvenile Justice and Delinquency Prevention, U.S. Department of Justice, 2003), p. 5.

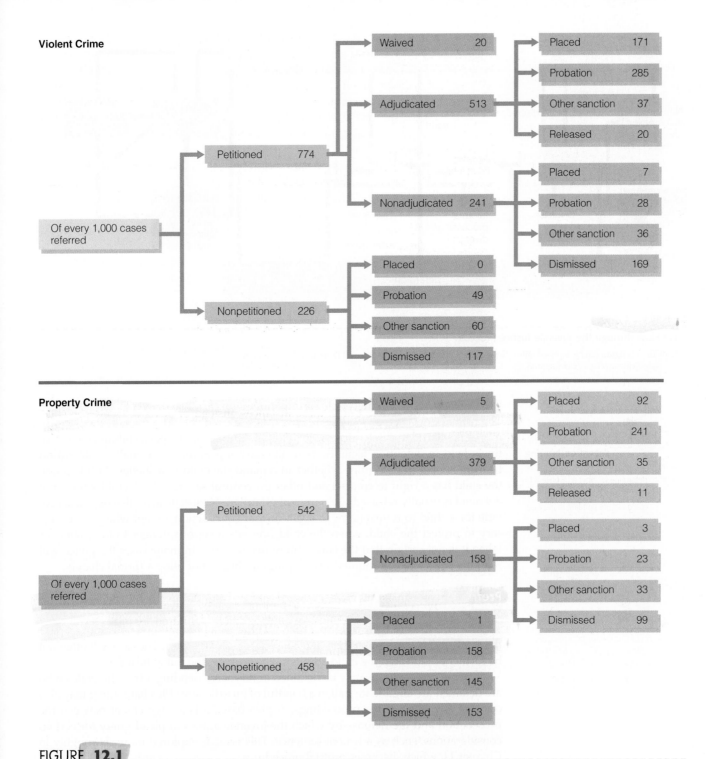

Violent Crime

- Of every 1,000 cases referred
  - Petitioned 774
    - Waived 20
    - Adjudicated 513
      - Placed 171
      - Probation 285
      - Other sanction 37
      - Released 20
    - Nonadjudicated 241
      - Placed 7
      - Probation 28
      - Other sanction 36
      - Dismissed 169
  - Nonpetitioned 226
    - Placed 0
    - Probation 49
    - Other sanction 60
    - Dismissed 117

Property Crime

- Of every 1,000 cases referred
  - Petitioned 542
    - Waived 5
    - Adjudicated 379
      - Placed 92
      - Probation 241
      - Other sanction 35
      - Released 11
    - Nonadjudicated 158
      - Placed 3
      - Probation 23
      - Other sanction 33
      - Dismissed 99
  - Nonpetitioned 458
    - Placed 1
    - Probation 158
    - Other sanction 145
    - Dismissed 153

FIGURE 12.1

Case Processing of Typical Violent Crime and Property Crime in the Juvenile Justice System

NOTE: The likelihood of adjudication varied within the general offense categories. For example, within violent offenses, 67% of petitioned aggravated assault cases were adjudicated in 1999, compared with 63% of petitioned simple assault cases. In general, the more serious the charge, the more likely the case was to result in adjudication.

SOURCE: Charles Puzzanchera, Anne L. Stahl, Terrence A. Finnegan, Nancy Tierney, and Howard N. Snyder, *Juvenile Court Statistics 1999* (Pittsburgh, PA: National Center for Juvenile Justice, 2003).

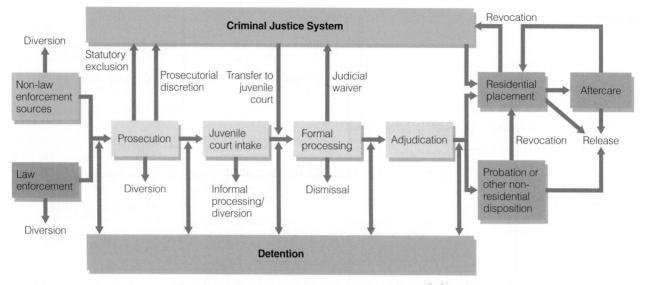

FIGURE 12.2

Case Flow through the Juvenile Justice Process

SOURCE: This figure can be accessed online through the Office of Juvenile Justice and Delinquency Prevention at www.ojjdp.ncjrs.org/facts/casejpg.html.

detention hearing
A hearing by a judicial officer of a juvenile court to determine whether a juvenile is to be detained or released while juvenile proceedings are pending in the case.

Detention If the police decide to file a petition, the child is referred to juvenile court. The primary decision at this point is whether the child should remain in the community or be placed in a detention facility or shelter home. In the past, children were routinely held in detention facilities to await court appearances. Normally, a **detention hearing** is held to determine whether to remand the child to a shelter. At this point, the child has a right to counsel and other procedural safeguards. A child who is not detained is usually released to a parent or guardian. Most state juvenile-court acts provide for a child to return home to await further court action, except when it is necessary to protect the child, when the child presents a serious danger to the public, or when it is not certain that the child will return to court. In many cases the police will refer the child to a community service program instead of filing a formal charge.

Pretrial Procedures In most jurisdictions, the adjudication process begins with some sort of hearing. At this hearing, juvenile court rules normally require that juveniles be informed of their right to a trial, that the plea or admission be voluntary, and that they understand the charges and consequences of the plea. The case will often not be further adjudicated if a child admits to the crime at the initial hearing.

In some cases, youths may be detained at this stage pending a trial. Juveniles who are detained are eligible for bail in a handful of jurisdictions. Plea bargaining may also occur at any stage of the proceedings. A plea bargain is an agreement between the prosecution and the defense by which the juvenile agrees to plead guilty for certain considerations, such as a lenient sentence. This issue is explored more thoroughly in Chapter 14, which discusses pretrial procedures.

adjudicatory hearing
The fact-finding process wherein the juvenile court determines whether there is sufficient evidence to sustain the allegations in a petition.

If the child denies the allegation of delinquency, an **adjudicatory hearing** or trial is scheduled. Under extraordinary circumstances, a juvenile who commits a serious crime may be transferred or waived to an adult court. Today, most jurisdictions have laws providing for such transfers. Whether such a transfer occurs depends on the type of offense, the youth's prior record, the availability of treatment services, and the likelihood that the youth will be rehabilitated in the juvenile court system.

Adjudication Adjudication is the trial stage of the juvenile court process. If the child does not admit guilt at the initial hearing and is not transferred to an adult court, an adjudication hearing is held to determine the facts of the case. The court hears evidence on the allegations in the delinquency petition. This is a trial on the merits (dealing with issues of law and facts), and rules of evidence similar to those of criminal proceedings generally apply. At this stage, the juvenile offender is entitled to many of the procedural guarantees given adult offenders. These include the right to counsel, freedom from self-incrimination, the right to confront and cross-examine witnesses, and, in certain instances, the right to a jury trial. In addition, many states have their own procedures concerning rules of evidence, competence of witnesses, pleadings, and pretrial motions. At the end of the adjudicatory hearing, the court enters a judgment against the juvenile.

Disposition If the adjudication process finds the child delinquent, the court must decide what should be done to treat the child. Most juvenile court acts require a dispositional hearing separate from the adjudication. This two-stage decision is often referred to as a **bifurcated process.** The dispositional hearing is less formal than adjudication. Here, the judge imposes a **disposition** on the offender in light of the offense, the youth's prior record, and his or her family background. The judge can prescribe a wide range of dispositions, ranging from a reprimand to probation to institutional commitment. In theory, the judge's decision serves the best interests of the child, the family, and the community.

Treatment After disposition in juvenile court, delinquent offenders may be placed in some form of correctional treatment. Probation is the most commonly used formal sentence for juvenile offenders, and many states require that a youth fail on probation before being sent to an institution (unless the criminal act is extremely serious). Probation involves placing the child under the supervision of the juvenile probation department for the purpose of community treatment. The most severe of the statutory dispositions available to the juvenile court involves commitment of the child to an institution. The committed child may be sent to a state training school or a private residential treatment facility. These are usually minimum-security facilities with small populations and an emphasis on treatment and education. Some states, however, maintain facilities with populations of over 1,000 youths. Currently there are more than 100,000 youths in some form of correctional institution.

Some jurisdictions allow for a program of juvenile aftercare or parole. A youth can be paroled from an institution and placed under the supervision of a parole officer. This means that he or she will complete the period of confinement in the community and receive assistance from the parole officer in the form of counseling, school referral, and vocational training.

Juveniles who are committed to programs of treatment and control have a legal right to treatment. States are required to provide suitable rehabilitation programs that include counseling, education, and vocational services. Appellate courts have ruled

bifurcated process
The procedure of separating adjudicatory and dispositionary hearings so different levels of evidence can be heard at each.

disposition
For juvenile offenders, the equivalent of sentencing for adult offenders; however, juvenile dispositions should be more rehabilitative than retributive.

Although juvenile offenders have a legal right to treatment, is correctional treatment more rhetoric than reality? Many experts argue that there is more punishment than rehabilitation in juvenile treatment programs. Shown here is one type of juvenile treatment, the Juvenile Justice Alternative Education Program in Denton County, Texas. Students expelled from regular school attend daily course instruction in math, English, and social studies, as well as receiving psychological counseling and transition services.

EXHIBIT 12.2

Time Line of Juvenile Justice Ideology

Time Frame	Activity
Prior to 1899	Juveniles treated similarly to adult offenders. No distinction by age or capacity to commit criminal acts.
1899 to 1950s	Children treated differently, beginning with the Illinois Juvenile Court Act of 1899. By 1925 juvenile court acts are established in virtually every state.
1950s to 1970s	Recognition by experts that the rehabilitation model and the protective nature of *parens patriae* have failed to prevent delinquency.
1960s to 1970s	Constitutional due process is introduced into the juvenile justice system. The concept of punishing children or protecting them under *parens patriae* is under attack by the courts.
1970s to 1980s	Failure of rehabilitation and due-process protections to control delinquency leads to a shift to a crime control and punishment philosophy similar to that of the adult criminal justice system.
Early 1990s	Mixed constitutional protections with some treatment. Uncertain goals and programs; the juvenile justice system relies on punishment and deterrence.
Mid-1990s to present	Attention given to strategy that focuses on reducing the threat of juvenile crime and expanding options for handling juvenile offenders. Emphasis is placed on "what works" and implementing the best intervention and control programs. Effort is made to utilize the restorative justice model, which involves balancing the needs of the victim, the community, and the juvenile.

that if such minimum treatment is not provided, individuals must be released from confinement.

Conflicting Values in Juvenile Justice

This overview of the juvenile justice process hints at the often-conflicting values at the heart of the system. Efforts to ensure that juveniles are given appropriate treatment are consistent with the doctrine of *parens patriae* that predominated in the first half of the twentieth century. (See Exhibit 12.2 for a time line of ideologies of juvenile justice during the twentieth century.)

Over the past century, the juvenile court struggled to provide treatment for juvenile offenders while guaranteeing them constitutional due process. But the system has been so overwhelmed by the increase in violent juvenile crime and family breakdown that some judges and politicians have suggested abolishing the juvenile system. Even those experts who want to retain an independent juvenile court have called for its restructuring. Crime-control advocates want to reduce the court's jurisdiction over juveniles charged with serious crimes and liberalize the prosecutor's ability to try them in adult courts. In contrast, child advocates suggest that the court scale back its judicial role and transfer its functions to community groups and social service agencies.[43]

Criminal Justice vs. Juvenile Justice

The components of the adult and juvenile criminal processes are similar. However, the juvenile system has a separate organizational structure. In many communities, juvenile justice is administered by people who bring special skills to the task. Also, more kinds of facilities and services are available to juveniles than to adults.

One concern of the juvenile court reform movement was to make certain that the stigma attached to a convicted offender would not be affixed to young people in juvenile proceedings. Thus, even the language used in the juvenile court differs from that used in the adult criminal court (see Exhibit 12.3 on page 382). Juveniles are not indicted for a crime; they have a **petition** filed against them. Secure pretrial holding facilities are called *detention centers* rather than jails. Similarly, the criminal trial is called a *hearing* in the juvenile justice system. (See the Focus on Delinquency box entitled "Similarities and Differences Between Juvenile and Adult Justice Systems.")

petition
Document filed in juvenile court alleging that a juvenile is a delinquent, a status offender, or a dependent and asking that the court assume jurisdiction over the juvenile.

TO QUIZ YOURSELF ON THIS MATERIAL, go to the Juvenile Delinquency 9e website.

Since its creation, the juvenile justice system has sought to maintain its independence from the adult justice system. Yet there are a number of similarities that characterize the institutions, processes, and law of the two systems.

Similarities and Differences Between Juvenile and Adult Justice Systems

SIMILARITIES

▮ Police officers, judges, and correctional personnel use discretion in decision making in both the adult and the juvenile systems.

▮ The right to receive *Miranda* warnings applies to juveniles as well as to adults.

▮ Juveniles and adults are protected from prejudicial lineups or other identification procedures.

▮ Similar procedural safeguards protect juveniles and adults when they make an admission of guilt.

▮ Prosecutors and defense attorneys play equally critical roles in juvenile and adult advocacy.

▮ Juveniles and adults have the right to counsel at most key stages of the court process.

▮ Pretrial motions are available in juvenile and criminal court proceedings.

▮ Negotiations and plea bargaining exist for juvenile and adult offenders.

▮ Juveniles and adults have a right to a hearing and an appeal.

▮ The standard of evidence in juvenile delinquency adjudications, as in adult criminal trials, is proof beyond a reasonable doubt.

▮ Juveniles and adults can be placed on probation by the court.

▮ Both juveniles and adults can be placed in pretrial detention facilities.

▮ Juveniles and adults can be kept in detention without bail if they are considered dangerous.

▮ After trial, both can be placed in community treatment programs.

▮ Juveniles and adults can be required to undergo drug testing.

▮ Boot camp correctional facilities are now being used for both juveniles and adults.

DIFFERENCES

▮ The primary purpose of juvenile procedures is protection and treatment. With adults, the aim is to punish the guilty.

▮ Age determines the jurisdiction of the juvenile court. The nature of the offense determines jurisdiction in the adult system. Juveniles can be ordered to the criminal court for trial as adults.

▮ Juveniles can be apprehended for acts that would not be criminal if committed by an adult (status offenses).

▮ Juvenile proceedings are not considered criminal; adult proceedings are.

▮ Juvenile court procedures are generally informal and private. Those of adult courts are more formal and are open to the public.

▮ Courts cannot release identifying information about a juvenile to the press, but they must release information about an adult.

▮ Parents are highly involved in the juvenile process but not in the adult process.

▮ The standard of arrest is more stringent for adults than for juveniles.

▮ Juveniles are released into parental custody. Adults are generally given the opportunity for bail.

▮ Juveniles have no constitutional right to a jury trial. Adults have this right. Some state statutes provide juveniles with a jury trial.

▮ Juveniles can be searched in school without probable cause or a warrant.

▮ A juvenile's record is generally sealed when the age of majority is reached. The record of an adult is permanent.

▮ A juvenile court cannot sentence juveniles to county jails or state prisons; these are reserved for adults.

▮ The U.S. Supreme Court has declared that the Eighth Amendment does not prohibit the death penalty for crimes committed by juveniles aged 16 and 17, but it is not a sentence given to children under age 16.

Critical Thinking

1. What are some of the key principles of the juvenile justice system that distinguish it from the adult justice system and that have come under increased scrutiny of late?

2. What can be done to ensure that these key principles are protected so that the juvenile justice system remains distinct from the adult system?

InfoTrac College Edition Research

For more information on how the juvenile justice system is becoming increasingly like the adult justice system, go to InfoTrac College Edition and read L. Mara Dodge, "Our Juvenile Court Has Become More Like a Criminal Court: A Century of Reform at the Cook County (Chicago) Juvenile Court," *Michigan Historical Review* 26(2):51 (2000).

EXHIBIT **12.3**

Comparison of Terms Used in Adult and Juvenile Justice Systems

	Juvenile Terms	Adult Terms
The Person and the Act	Delinquent child	Criminal
	Delinquent act	Crime
Preadjudicatory Stage	Take into custody	Arrest
	Petition	Indictment
	Agree to a finding	Plead guilty
	Deny the petition	Plead not guilty
	Adjustment	Plea bargain
	Detention facility; childcare shelter	Jail
Adjudicatory Stage	Substitution	Reduction of charges
	Adjudication or fact-finding hearing	Trial
	Adjudication	Conviction
Postadjudicatory Stage	Dispositional hearing	Sentencing hearing
	Disposition	Sentence
	Commitment	Incarceration
	Youth development center; treatment; training school	Prison
	Residential childcare facility	Halfway house
	Aftercare	Parole

A COMPREHENSIVE JUVENILE JUSTICE STRATEGY

At a time when much attention is focused on serious juvenile offenders, a comprehensive strategy has been called for to deal with all aspects of juvenile crime. This strategy focuses on crime prevention and expanding options for handling juvenile offenders. It addresses the links among crime and poverty, child abuse, drugs, weapons, and school behavior. Programs are based on a continuum of care that begins in early childhood and progresses through late adolescence. The components of this strategy include (1) prevention in early childhood; (2) intervention for at-risk teenage youths; (3) graduated sanctions to hold juvenile offenders accountable for crimes; (4) proper utilization of detention and confinement; and (5) placement of serious juvenile offenders in adult courts.[44] There are many expected benefits from the use of this comprehensive strategy (see Exhibit 12.4).

Prevention

Research has identified certain factors that may suggest future delinquency. For young children, these include abuse and neglect, domestic violence, educational underachievement, and health problems.[45] Early childhood services may prevent delinquency and make a child less vulnerable to future criminality.[46] The federal Head Start program provides children in poverty with, among other things, an enriched educational environment to develop learning and cognitive skills to be better prepared for the early school years. Low intelligence and school failure are important risk factors for juvenile delinquency. Home-visiting programs target families at risk because of child abuse and neglect. Chapter 11 discusses these programs in greater detail.

Intervention

Intervention programs are focused on teenage youths considered to be at higher risk for engaging in petty delinquent acts, using drugs or alcohol, or associating with antisocial peers.[47] Interventions at this stage are designed to ward off involvement in more serious delinquency. Many jurisdictions are developing new intervention programs for teenage youths. An example is the Big Brother Big Sister program, which matches a volunteer adult with a youngster. Similarly, in the Office of Juvenile Justice and Delin-

EXHIBIT 12.4

Benefits of Using the Comprehensive Strategy

1. Increased prevention of delinquency (and thus fewer young people enter the juvenile justice system)
2. Enhanced responsiveness from the juvenile justice system
3. Greater accountability on the part of youth
4. Decreased costs of juvenile corrections
5. A more responsible juvenile justice system
6. More effective juvenile justice programs
7. Less delinquency
8. Fewer delinquents become serious, violent, and chronic offenders
9. Fewer delinquents become adult offenders

SOURCE: James C. Howell, *Preventing and Reducing Juvenile Delinquency: A Comprehensive Framework* (Thousand Oaks, CA: Sage Publications, 2003), p. 245

quency Prevention's Juvenile Mentoring Program (JUMP), responsible and caring adults volunteer their time as mentors to youths at risk for delinquency and dropping out of school. The mentors work one-on-one with the youths, offering support and guidance.[48] Job training, through the likes of Job Corps and YouthBuild U.S.A., is another important intervention that receives government funding. These programs improve the chances of young people obtaining jobs in the legal economy and thereby may reduce delinquency. Efforts are also being made to deter them from becoming involved with gangs, because gang members ordinarily have higher rates of serious violent behavior. Chapter 11 discusses some of these programs in greater detail.

Graduated Sanctions

Graduated sanction programs for juveniles are another solution being explored by states across the country. Types of graduated sanctions include immediate sanctions for nonviolent offenders (these consist of community-based diversion and day treatment); intermediate sanctions such as probation and electronic monitoring, which target repeat minor offenders and first-time serious offenders; and secure institutional care, which is reserved for repeat serious offenders and violent offenders. The philosophy behind this approach is to limit the most restrictive sanctions to the most dangerous offenders, while increasing restrictions and intensity of treatment services as offenders move from minor to serious offenses.[49]

Institutional Programs

Another key to a comprehensive strategy is improving institutional programs. Many experts believe juvenile incarceration is overused, particularly for nonviolent offenders. That is why the concept of deinstitutionalization—removing as many youths from secure confinement as possible—was established by the Juvenile Justice and Delinquency Prevention Act of 1974. Considerable research supports the fact that warehousing juveniles without proper treatment does little to deter criminal behavior. The most effective secure corrections programs are those that provide individual services for a small number of participants.[50]

Alternative Courts

New venues of juvenile justice that provide special services to youth while helping to alleviate the case flow problems that plague overcrowded juvenile courts are being implemented across the United States. For example, as of 2003, there were 285 juvenile drug courts (another 110 are in the planning process) with 12,500 juveniles enrolled.[51] These special courts have jurisdiction over the burgeoning number of cases involving

drug courts
Courts whose focus is providing treatment for youths accused of drug-related acts.

Teen Courts

Teen courts differ from other juvenile justice programs because young people rather than adults determine the disposition in a case. Cases handled in these courts typically involve young juveniles (ages 10 to 15) with no prior arrest records, who are being charged with minor law violations, such as shoplifting, vandalism, and disorderly conduct. Usually, young offenders are asked to volunteer to have their case heard in a teen court instead of the more formal court of the traditional juvenile justice system.

As in a regular juvenile court, teen court defendants may go through an intake process, a preliminary review of charges, a court hearing, and disposition. In a teen court, however, other young people are responsible for much of the process. Charges may be presented to the court by a 15-year-old "prosecutor." Defendants may be represented by a 16-year-old "defense attorney." Other youth may serve as jurors, court clerks, and bailiffs. In some teen courts, a youth "judge" (or panel of youth judges) may choose the best disposition or sanction for each case. In a few teen courts, teens even determine whether the facts in a case have been proven by the prosecutor (similar to a finding of guilt). Offenders are often ordered to pay restitution or perform community service. Some teen courts require offenders to write formal apologies to their victims; others require offenders to serve on a subsequent teen court jury. Many courts use other innovative dispositions, such as requiring offenders to attend classes designed to improve their decision-making skills, enhance their awareness of victims, and deter them from future theft.

Though decisions are made by juveniles, adults are also involved in teen courts. They often administer the programs, and they are usually responsible for essential functions, such as budgeting, planning, and personnel. In many programs, adults supervise the courtroom activities, and they often coordinate the community service placements where the young offenders work to fulfill the terms of their dispositions. In some programs, adults act as the judges while teens serve as attorneys and jurors.

Proponents of teen court argue that the process takes advantage of one of the most powerful forces in the life of an adolescent—the desire for peer approval and the reaction to peer pressure. According to this argument, youth respond better to prosocial peers than to adult authority figures. Thus, teen courts are seen as a potentially effective alternative to traditional juvenile courts that are staffed with paid professionals, such as lawyers, judges, and probation officers. Teen courts may benefit the volunteer youth attorneys and judges, who probably learn more about the legal system than they ever could in a classroom. The presence of a teen court may also encourage the entire community to take a more active role in responding to juvenile crime. In sum, teen courts offer at least four potential benefits:

- **Accountability:** Teen courts may help to ensure that young offenders are held accountable for their illegal behavior, even when their offenses are relatively minor and would not likely result in sanctions from the traditional juvenile justice system.

- **Timeliness:** An effective teen court can move young offenders from arrest to sanctions within a matter of days rather than the months that may pass with traditional juvenile courts. This rapid response may increase the positive impact of court sanctions, regardless of their severity.

- **Cost savings:** Teen courts usually depend heavily on youth and adult volunteers. If managed properly, they may

---

substance abuse and trafficking. Although juvenile drug courts operate under a number of different frameworks, the aim is to place nonviolent first offenders into intensive treatment programs rather than placing them in a custodial institution.[52]

In a **systematic review** and **meta-analysis** of the effects of drug courts, David Wilson and his colleagues found that drug courts are an effective alternative crime control measure to reducing recidivism rates among drug-involved offenders. Of the 38 studies included in the review, only three were of juvenile drug courts. This is explained, in part, by the relatively recent interest of juvenile justice agencies in experimenting with drug courts. The findings of the three juvenile drug courts were mixed. On the one hand, their overall effectiveness was significantly greater than the adult drug courts for all offenses measured. On the other hand, they were no more effective in reducing drug offenses than traditional juvenile court processing or adult drug courts.[53]

Similar findings were found in a recent three-year evaluation of a juvenile drug court in Maricopa County, Arizona. (This study was not included in the above review; it was published after the review was completed.) Drug-involved juvenile offenders assigned to drug court, compared to similar youths who received a disposition of probation, were less likely to commit further criminal offenses, but there was no difference in marijuana use between the two groups and cocaine use was higher among drug court youths. The authors found that family stability, school attendance, and

systematic review
A type of review that uses rigorous methods for locating, appraising, and synthesizing evidence from prior evaluation studies.

meta-analysis
A statistical analysis technique that synthesizes results from prior evaluation studies.

To read more about **juvenile drug courts,** go to www.ncjrs.org/pdffiles/173425.pdf. For an up-to-date list of web links, go to http://cj.wadsworth.com/siegel_jd9e.

handle a substantial number of offenders at relatively little cost to the community.

- ▌ **Community cohesion:** A well-structured and expansive teen court program may affect the entire community by increasing public appreciation of the legal system, enhancing community-court relationships, encouraging greater respect for the law among youth, and promoting volunteerism among both adults and youth.

The teen court movement is one of the fastest growing delinquency intervention programs in the country, with more than 900 of these courts in operation in 46 states and the District of Columbia. Recent evaluations of teen courts have found that they did not "widen the net" of justice by handling cases that in the absence of the teen court would have been subject to a lesser level of processing. Also, in the OJJDP Evaluation of Teen Courts Project, which covered four states—Alaska, Arizona, Maryland, and Missouri—and compared 500 first-time offending youths referred to teen court with 500 similar youths handled by the regular juvenile justice system, it was found that six-month recidivism rates were lower for those who went through the teen court program in three of the four jurisdictions. Importantly, in these three teen courts, the six-month recidivism rates were under 10 percent. A similar finding was reported in another rigorous evaluation of a teen court in Florida. On the other hand, other recent evaluations of teen courts in Kentucky, New Mexico, and Delaware indicate that short-term recidivism rates range from 25 percent to 30 percent. The conclusions from the OJJDP teen court evaluation may be the best guide for future experimentation with teen courts:

Teen courts and youth courts may be preferable to the normal juvenile justice process in jurisdictions that do not, or cannot, provide meaningful sanctions for all young, first-time juvenile offenders. In jurisdictions that do not provide meaningful sanctions and services for these offenders, youth court may still perform just as well as a more traditional, adult-run program.

Critical Thinking

1. Could teen courts be used to try serious criminal acts, such as burglary and robbery?
2. Is a conflict of interest created when teens judge the behavior of other teens? Does the fact that they themselves may one day become defendants in a teen court influence decision-making?

InfoTrac College Edition Research

To read more about teen courts, go to InfoTrac College Edition and read Kathiann M. Kowalski, "Courtroom Justice for Teens—by Teens," *Current Health* 2, a *Weekly Reader* publication, 25 (8):29 (April 1999).

SOURCES: Jeffrey A. Butts and Janeen Buck, "Teen Courts: A Focus on Research," *Juvenile Justice Bulletin October 2000* (Washington, DC: Office of Juvenile Justice and Delinquency Prevention, 2000); Jeffrey A. Butts, "Encouraging Findings from the OJJDP Evaluation," *In Session: The Newsletter of the National Youth Court Center* 2(3):1, 7 (Summer 2002); Kevin Minor, James Wells, Irinia Soderstrom, Rachel Bingham, and Deborah Williamson, "Sentence Completion and Recidivism among Juveniles Referred to Teen Courts," *Crime & Delinquency* 45:467–480 (1999); Paige Harrison, James R. Maupin, and G. Larry Mays, "Teen Court: An Examination of Processes and Outcomes," *Crime and Delinquency* 47:243–264 (2001); Arthur H. Garrison, "An Evaluation of a Delaware Teen Court," *Juvenile and Family Court Journal* 52:11–21 (2001); Anthony P. Logalbo and Charlene M. Callahan, "An Evaluation of a Teen Court as a Juvenile Crime Diversion Program," *Juvenile and Family Court Journal* 52:1–11 (2001); Office of Juvenile Justice and Delinquency Prevention, "September Is First National Youth Court Month," *OJJDP News @ a Glance* 1(4):1, 3 (July/ August 2002).

---

teen courts
Courts that make use of peer juries to decide nonserious delinquency cases.

TO QUIZ YOURSELF ON THIS MATERIAL, go to the Juvenile Delinquency 9e website.

legal indicators were important to the effectiveness of the drug court in reducing recidivism.[54]

Teen courts, also called youth courts, are another alternative to traditional forms of juvenile court that have received increased attention of late in an effort to relieve overcrowding and provide a more effective response to reducing recidivism. The Policy and Practice box entitled "Teen Courts" discusses this alternative.

FUTURE OF JUVENILE JUSTICE

The future of the juvenile court is now being debated. Some experts, including Barry Feld, believe that over the years the juvenile justice system has taken on more of the characteristics of the adult courts, which he refers to as the "criminalizing" of the juvenile court,[55] or in a more stern admonition: "Despite juvenile courts' persisting rehabilitative rhetoric, the reality of *treating* juveniles closely resembles *punishing* adult criminals."[56]

Robert Dawson suggests that because the legal differences between the juvenile and criminal systems are narrower than they ever have been, it may be time to abolish the

In teen courts, used across the country as alternatives to traditional forms of juvenile courts, youths play the roles of attorney and prosecutor and sometimes judge. Shown here are members of a teen court, demonstrating what happens during a real session of the court.

juvenile court.[57] This value conflict has led some experts to advocate the actual abolition of the juvenile court, a topic discussed in the accompanying Policy and Practice box.

These concerns reflect the changes that have been ongoing in the juvenile justice system. There has been a nationwide effort to modify the system in response to the public's perceived fear of predatory juvenile offenders and the reaction to high-profile cases such as the Columbine tragedy. As a result, states have begun to institute policies that critics believe undermine the true purpose of the juvenile court movement.[58] Some have made it easier to transfer children to the adult courts. During the 1990s, at least four states lowered the age limit for transfer to adult court—today there are 23 states and the District of Columbia where no minimum age is specified (see Table 12.2)—seven added crimes, and four added or modified prior-record provisions. As a result, more juvenile offenders are being sentenced as adults and incarcerated in adult prisons.[59]

Getting tough on juvenile crime is the primary motivation for moving cases to the adult criminal justice system.[60] Some commentators argue that waiving juveniles is a statement that juvenile crime is taken seriously by society; others believe the fear of being transferred serves as a deterrent.[61] Some states, such as Arizona, have initiated legislation that significantly restricts eligibility for juvenile justice processing and criminalizing acts that heretofore would have fallen under the jurisdiction of the juvenile court. For example, the Arizona legislation provides for the statutory exclusion for 15-, 16-, or 17-year-olds charged with violent crimes or if they had two prior felony adjudications and were charged with any third felony. It also added the provision, "once an

TABLE 12.2

Minimum Age Specified in Statute for Transferring Juveniles to Adult Court

Age	State (Total Number)
None	Alaska, Arizona, Delaware, Florida, Georgia, Hawaii, Idaho, Indiana, Maine, Maryland, Montana, Nebraska, Oklahoma, Oregon, Pennsylvania, Rhode Island, South Carolina, South Dakota, Tennessee, Texas, Washington, West Virginia, Wisconsin (23) and the District of Columbia
10	Kansas, Vermont (2)
12	Colorado, Missouri (2)
13	Illinois, Mississippi, New Hampshire, New York, North Carolina, Wyoming (6)
14	Alabama, Arkansas, California, Connecticut, Iowa, Kentucky, Louisiana, Massachusetts, Michigan, Minnesota, Nevada, New Jersey, North Dakota, Ohio, Utah, Virginia (16)
15	New Mexico (1)

SOURCE: Melissa Sickmund, *Juveniles in Court* (Washington, DC: Office of Juvenile Justice and Delinquency Prevention, U.S. Department of Justice, 2003), p. 9.

Abolish the Juvenile Court?

In an important work, *Bad Kids: Race and the Transformation of the Juvenile Court*, legal expert Barry Feld makes the rather controversial suggestion that the juvenile court system should be discontinued and/or replaced by an alternative method of justice. He suggests that the current structure makes it almost impossible for the system to fulfill or achieve the purpose for which it was originally intended.

Feld maintains that the juvenile court was developed in an effort to create a more lenient atmosphere and process than the one used against adult criminals. Although a worthwhile goal, the juvenile court system was doomed to failure even from the beginning, because it was thrown into the role of providing child welfare at the same time that it was an instrument of law enforcement. These two missions are often at cross-purposes. During its history, various legal developments have further undermined its purpose—most notably the *In re Gault* ruling, which ultimately led to juveniles receiving similar legal protections as adults and led to children being treated like adults in all respects. The juvenile court's vision of leniency was further undercut by the fear and consequent racism created by postwar migration and economic trends that led to the development of large enclaves of poor and underemployed African Americans living in northern cities. Then in the 1980s, the sudden rise in gang membership, gun violence, and homicide committed by juveniles further undermined the juvenile court mission and resulted in legislation that created mandatory sentences for juvenile offenders and mandatory waiver to the adult court. As a result, the focus of the court has been on dealing with the offense rather than treating the offender. In Feld's words, the juvenile court has become a "deficient second-rate criminal court." The welfare and rehabilitative purposes of the juvenile court have been subordinated to its role of law enforcement agent.

Can juvenile courts be reformed? Feld maintains that it is impossible because of their conflicting purposes and shifting priorities. The money spent on serving the court and its large staff would be better spent on child welfare, which would target a larger audience and prevent children's antisocial acts before they occur. In lieu of juvenile court, youths who violate the law should receive full procedural protections in the criminal court system. The special protections given youths in the juvenile court could be provided by altering the criminal law and recognizing age as a factor in the creation of criminal liability. Because youths have had a limited opportunity to develop self-control, their criminal liability should also be curtailed or restricted.

Is Feld's rather dour assessment of the juvenile court valid, and should it in fact be abolished? Not so, according to John Johnson Kerbs, who suggests that Feld makes assumptions that may not be wedded to the reality of the American legal system. First, Kerbs finds that it is naïve to assume the criminal courts can provide the same or greater substantive and procedural protections as the juvenile court. Many juvenile court defendants are indigent, especially those coming from the minority community, and it may be impossible for them to obtain adequate legal defense in the adult system. Second, Feld's assumption that criminal courts will take a defendant's age into close consideration may be illusory. In this get-tough era, it is likely that criminal courts will provide harsher sentences, and the brunt of these draconian sentences will fall squarely on the shoulders of minority youth. Research efforts routinely show that African American adults are unduly punished in adult courts. Sending juvenile offenders to these venues will most likely further enmesh them in an already unfair system. Finally, Kerbs finds that the treatment benefits of the juvenile courts should not be overlooked or abandoned. There is ample research, he maintains, that shows that juvenile courts can create lower recidivism rates than criminal courts. Though the juvenile court is far from perfect and should be improved, it would be foolish to abandon a system aimed at helping kids find alternatives to crime. The alternative is one that produces higher recidivism rates, lowers their future prospects, and has a less than stellar record of providing due process and equal protection for the nation's most needy citizens.

Critical Thinking

What's your take on this issue? Should the juvenile court be abolished? Since the trend has been to transfer the most serious criminal cases to the adult court, is there still a purpose for an independent juvenile court? Should the juvenile court be reserved for nonserious first offenders?

InfoTrac College Edition Research

Before you make up your mind about the future of juvenile court, read Joseph V. Penn, "Justice for Youth? A History of the Juvenile and Family Court," *The Brown University Child and Adolescent Behavior Letter* 17(9):1 (September 2001).

SOURCES: Barry C. Feld, *Bad Kids: Race and the Transformation of the Juvenile Court* (New York: Oxford University Press, 1999); John Johnson Kerbs, "(Un)equal Justice: Juvenile Court Abolition and African Americans," *Annals of the American Academy of Political and Social Science* 564:109–125 (1999).

adult, always an adult," where, if a juvenile was previously tried and convicted in criminal court, any future offenses involving that juvenile will be tried in adult court.[62] Thirty-three other states also have the once an adult, always an adult provision.[63] While there is no mistaking the intention of this provision—to get tough on juvenile crime—some experts point out that inconsistencies that it created between the two justice systems may have inadvertently also produced a number of legal loopholes.[64]

There is other evidence of this get-tough movement. More states are now permitting juvenile court judges to commit a juvenile to the corrections department for a longer period of time than the court's original jurisdiction, typically to age 21. In recent years, at least five states (Florida, Kansas, Kentucky, Montana, and Tennessee) increased the age for extended juvenile court jurisdiction for serious and violent juvenile offenders.[65]

These changes concern juvenile justice advocates such as Hunter Hurst, director of the National Center for Juvenile Justice, who warns:

> How could the wholesale criminalization of children possibly be a wise thing? If their vulnerability to predation in jails and prisons does not destroy them, won't the so-called taint of criminality that they carry with them for the rest of their lives be an impossible social burden for them and us? ... Have our standards of decency devolved to the point where protection of children is no longer a compelling state interest? In many ways the answer is yes.[66]

The National Research Council and Institute of Medicine's Panel on Juvenile Crime also expressed alarm over an increasingly punitive juvenile justice system and called for a number of changes to uphold the importance of treatment for juveniles. One of their recommendations is particularly noteworthy:

> The federal government should assist the states through federal funding and incentives to reduce the use of secure detention and secure confinement, by developing community-based alternatives. The effectiveness of such programs both for the protection of the community and the benefit of the youth in their charge should be monitored.[67]

Although calling for reforms to the juvenile justice system was a key element of the national panel's final report, panel members were equally, and perhaps more, concerned with the need to prevent delinquency before it occurs and intervene with at-risk children and adolescents. Importantly, there is growing public support for prevention and intervention programs designed to reduce delinquency.[68] The panel also called attention to the need for more rigorous experimentation with prevention and intervention programs with demonstrated success in reducing risk factors associated with delinquency.[69] Some states, like Washington, have begun to incorporate a research-based approach to guide juvenile justice programming and policy.[70]

Those who support the juvenile justice concept believe that it is too soon to write off the rehabilitative ideal that has always underpinned the separate treatment of juvenile offenders. They note that fears of a juvenile crime wave are misplaced and that the actions of a few violent children should not mask the needs of millions who can benefit from solicitous treatment rather than harsh punishments. Authors Alida Merlo, Peter Benekos, and William Cook note that a child is more likely to be hit by lightning than shot in a school.[71] And while a get-tough approach may be able to reduce the incidence of some crimes, economic analysis indicates that the costs incurred by placing children in more punitive secure facilities outweigh the benefits accrued in crime reduction.[72]

Summary

- Urbanization created a growing number of at-risk youth in the nation's cities. The juvenile justice system was established at the turn of the twentieth century after decades of effort by child-saving groups. These reformers sought to create an independent category of delinquent offender and keep their treatment separate from adults.

- Over the past four decades, the U.S. Supreme Court and lower courts have granted procedural safeguards and the protection of due process in juvenile courts. Major court decisions have laid down the constitutional requirements for juvenile court proceedings. In years past the protections currently afforded to both adults and children were not available to children.

- For both violent and property offenses, more than half of all formally processed delinquency cases in 1999 resulted in the youth being adjudicated delinquent.

- The juvenile justice process consists of a series of steps: the police investigation, the intake procedure in the juvenile court, the pretrial procedures used for juvenile offenders, and the adjudication, disposition, and postdispositional procedures.

- There are conflicting values in juvenile justice. Some experts want to get tough with young criminals, while others want to focus on rehabilitation.

- The adult and juvenile justice systems have a number of key similarities and differences. One of the similarities is the right to receive *Miranda* warnings; this applies to juveniles as well as adults. One of the differences is that juvenile proceedings are not considered criminal, while adult proceedings are.

I There has been a movement to toughen the juvenile justice system, and because of this many view the importance of treatment as having been greatly diminished. Proponents of treatment argue that it is best suited to the developmental needs of juveniles. Critics contend that treatment simply serves to mollycoddle juveniles and reduces the deterrent value of the juvenile court.

I A comprehensive juvenile justice strategy has been developed to preserve the need for treatment services for juveniles while at the same time using appropriate sanctions to hold juveniles accountable for their actions. Elements of this strategy include delinquency prevention, intervention programs, graduated sanctions, improvement of institutional programs, and

treating juveniles like adults. New courts, such as drug courts and teen courts, are now in place.

I Prevention efforts are targeted at children and teens in an effort to prevent the onset of delinquency. Intervention efforts are targeted at children and teens considered at higher risk for delinquency and are designed to ward off involvement in more serious delinquent behavior.

I The future of the juvenile justice system is in doubt. A number of state jurisdictions are now revising their juvenile codes to restrict eligibility in the juvenile justice system and remove the most serious offenders. At the same time there are some promising signs, such as public support for prevention and intervention programs and some states beginning to incorporate research-based initiatives to guide juvenile justice programming and policy.

Key Terms

House of Refuge, p. 367
Children's Aid Society, p. 369
orphan trains, p. 369
Society for the Prevention of Cruelty
   to Children, p. 370
Law Enforcement Assistance
   Administration (LEAA), p. 375

juvenile justice process, p. 376
detention hearing, p. 378
adjudicatory hearing, p. 378
bifurcated process, p. 379
disposition, p. 379
petition, p. 380
drug courts, p. 383

systematic review, p. 384
meta-analysis, p. 384
teen courts, p. 385

Questions for Discussion

1. What factors precipitated the development of the Illinois Juvenile Court Act of 1899?

2. One of the most significant reforms in dealing with the juvenile offender was the opening of the New York House of Refuge in 1825. What were the social and judicial consequences of this reform on the juvenile justice system?

3. The child savers have been accused of wanting to control the lives of poor and immigrant children for their own benefit. Are there any parallels to the child saving movement in modern-day America?

4. Should there be a juvenile justice system, or should juveniles who commit serious crimes be treated as adults, while the others are handled by social welfare agencies?

5. The Supreme Court has made a number of major decisions in the area of juvenile justice. What are these

decisions? What is their impact on the juvenile justice system?

6. What is the meaning of the term *procedural due process of law*? Explain why and how procedural due process has had an impact on juvenile justice.

7. The formal components of the criminal justice system are often considered to be the police, the court, and the correctional agency. How do these components relate to the major areas of the juvenile justice system? Is the operation of justice similar in the juvenile and adult systems?

8. How would the rehabilitation model and the restorative justice model consider the use of capital punishment as a criminal sanction for first-degree murder by a juvenile offender?

9. What role has the federal government played in the juvenile justice system over the last 25 years?

Viewpoint

Fourteen-year-old Daphne A., a product of New York City's best private schools, lives with her wealthy family in a luxury condo in a fashionable neighborhood. Her fa-

ther is an executive at a local financial services conglomerate and earns close to a million dollars per year. Daphne, however, is always in trouble at school, and teachers report she is impulsive and has poor self-control. At times she can be kind and warm, but on other occasions she is obnoxious, unpredictable, insecure, and demanding of attention. She is overly self-conscious about her body and has a drinking problem.

Despite repeated promises to get her life together, Daphne likes to hang out at night in a local park, drinking with neighborhood kids. On more than one occasion she has gone to the park with her friend and confidant Chris G., a quiet boy with his own personal problems. His parents have separated and he is prone to suffer severe anxiety attacks. He has been suspended from school and diagnosed with depression, for which he takes two drugs—an antidepressant and a sedative.

One night, the two met up with Michael M., a 44-year-old man with a long history of alcoholism. After a night of drinking, a fight broke out and Michael was stabbed, his throat cut, and his body dumped in a pond. Soon after the attack, Daphne called 911, telling police that a friend "jumped in the lake and didn't come out." Police searched the area and found Michael's slashed and stabbed body in the water; the body had been disemboweled in an attempt to sink it. When the authorities traced the call, Daphne was arrested, and she confessed to police that she had helped Chris murder the victim.

During an interview with court psychiatrists, Daphne admits she participated in the killing but cannot articulate what caused her to get involved. She had been drinking and remembers little of the events. She said she was flirting with Michael and Chris stabbed him in a jealous rage. She speaks in a flat, hollow voice and shows little remorse for her actions. It was a spur-of-the-moment thing, she claims, and after all it was Chris who had the knife and not she. Later, Chris claims that Daphne instigated the fight, egged him on, taunting him that he was too scared to kill someone. Chris says that Daphne, while drunk, often talked of killing an adult because she hates older people, especially her parents.

If Daphne is tried as a juvenile she can be kept in institutions until she is 17; the sentence could be expanded to age 21, but only if she is a behavior problem in custody and demonstrates conclusive need for further secure treatment.

I Should the case of Daphne A. be dealt with in the juvenile court, even though the maximum possible sentence she can receive is 2 to 6 years? If not, over what kind of cases should the juvenile court have jurisdiction?

I How does the concept of *parens patriae* apply in cases such as that of Daphne A.?

I If you believe that the juvenile court is not equipped to handle cases of extremely violent youth, then should it be abolished?

I What reforms must be made in the juvenile justice system to rehabilitate adolescents like Daphne? Or should it even try?

Doing Research on the Web

Before you answer these questions, you may want to learn more about this topic by checking out the following websites (sites accessed on October 15, 2004):

National Center for Juvenile Justice
http://ncjj.servehttp.com/NCJJWebsite/main.htm

Office of Juvenile Justice and Delinquency Prevention
http://ojjdp.ncjrs.org/

Office of the Surgeon General
www.surgeongeneral.gov

Urban Institute
www.urban.org/content/PolicyCenters/Justice/Overview.htm

Washington State Institute for Public Policy
www.wsipp.wa.gov

To research the debate on the most effective strategies to address serious and violent juvenile offending, use "juvenile and violence" in a keyword search on InfoTrac College Edition.

Notes

1. Robert M. Mennel, "Origins of the Juvenile Court: Changing Perspectives on the Legal Rights of Juvenile Delinquents," *Crime and Delinquency* 18:68–78 (1972).
2. Anthony Salerno, "The Child Saving Movement: Altruism or Conspiracy," *Juvenile and Family Court Journal* 42:37 (1991).
3. Frank J. Coppa and Philip C. Dolce, *Cities in Transition: From the Ancient World to Urban America* (Chicago: Nelson Hall, 1974), p. 220.
4. Robert Mennel, "Attitudes and Policies toward Juvenile Delinquency," *Crime and Justice*, vol. 5 (Chicago: University of Chicago Press, 1983), p. 198.
5. Anthony M. Platt, *The Child Savers: The Invention of Delinquency* (Chicago: University of Chicago Press, 1969).
6. See Anne Meis Knupfer, *Reform and Resistance: Gender, Delinquency, and America's First Juvenile Court* (London: Routledge, 2001).
7. This section is based on material from the New York State Archives, *The Greatest Reform School in the World: A Guide to the Records of the New York House of Refuge: A Brief History 1824–1857* (Albany, NY, 2001); Sanford J. Fox, "Juvenile Justice Reform: A Historical Perspective," *Stanford Law Review* 22:1187 (1970).
8. Robert S. Pickett, *House of Refuge—Origins of Juvenile Reform in New York State, 1815–1857* (Syracuse, NY: Syracuse University Press, 1969).
9. Mennel, "Origins of the Juvenile Court," pp. 69–70.
10. Sanford Fox, "The Early History of the Court" from *The Future of Children* (Los Altos, CA: David and Lucille Packard Foundation, 1996).
11. Salerno, "The Child Saving Movement," p. 37.
12. Platt, *The Child Savers*.
13. Ibid., p. 116.

14. Randall Shelden and Lynn Osborne, "'For Their Own Good': Class Interests and the Child Saving Movement in Memphis, Tennessee, 1900–1917," *Criminology* 27:747–767 (1989).

15. U.S. Department of Justice, Juvenile Justice and Delinquency Prevention, *Two Hundred Years of American Criminal Justice: An LEAA Bicentennial Study* (Washington, DC: LEAA, 1976).

16. New York State Law Ch. 412, Laws of 1929; Ch. 538, Laws of 1932.

17. Beverly Smith, "Female Admissions and Paroles of the Western House of Refuge in the 1880s, An Historical Example of Community Corrections," *Journal of Research in Crime and Delinquency* 26:36–66 (1989).

18. Fox, "Juvenile Justice Reform," p. 1229.

19. Fox, "The Early History of the Court."

20. Elizabeth Pleck, "Criminal Approaches to Family Violence, 1640–1980," in Lloyd Ohlin and Michael Tonry, eds., *Family Violence* (Chicago: University of Chicago Press, 1989), pp. 19–58.

21. Elizabeth Pleck, *Domestic Tyranny: The Making of Social Policy against Family Violence from Colonial Times to the Present* (New York: Oxford University Press, 1987), pp. 28–30.

22. Linda Gordon, *Family Violence and Social Control* (New York: Viking, 1988).

23. Kathleen Block and Donna Hale, "Turf Wars in the Progressive Era of Juvenile Justice: The Relationship of Private and Public Child Care Agencies," *Crime and Delinquency* 37:225–241 (1991).

24. Theodore Ferdinand, "Juvenile Delinquency or Juvenile Justice: Which Came First?" *Criminology* 27:79–106 (1989).

25. *In re Gault*, 387 U.S. 1, 87 S.Ct. 1428, 18 L.Ed.2d 527 (1967).

26. Fox, "The Early History of the Court," p. 4.

27. Ibid.

28. Mary Odem and Steven Schlossman, "Guardians of Virtue: The Juvenile Court and Female Delinquency in Early 20th-Century Los Angeles," *Crime and Delinquency* 37:186–203 (1991).

29. Fox, "The Early History of the Court," p. 4.

30. John Sutton, "Bureaucrats and Entrepreneurs: Institutional Responses to Deviant Children in the United States, 1890–1920," *American Journal of Sociology* 95: 1367–1400 (1990).

31. Ibid., p. 1383.

32. Marguerite Rosenthal, "Reforming the Juvenile Correctional Institution: Efforts of the U.S. Children's Bureau in the 1930s," *Journal of Sociology and Social Welfare* 14:47–74 (1987); see also David Steinhart, "Status Offenses," The Center for the Future of Children, The Juvenile Court (Los Altos, CA: David and Lucille Packard Foundation, 1996).

33. For an overview of these developments, see Theodore Ferdinand, "History Overtakes the Juvenile Justice System," *Crime and Delinquency* 37:204–224 (1991).

34. N.Y. Fam.Ct. Act, Art. 7, Sec. 712 (Consol. 1962).

35. *Kent v. United States*, 383 U.S. 541, 86 S.Ct. 1045, 16 L.Ed.2d 84 (1966); *In re Gault*, 387 U.S. 1, 87 S.Ct. 1428, 18 L.Ed.2d 527 (1967): Juveniles have the right to notice, counsel, confrontation, and cross-examination, and to the privileges against self-incrimination in juvenile court proceedings. *In re Winship*, 397 U.S. 358, 90 S.Ct. 1068, 25 L.Ed.2d 368 (1970): Proof beyond a reasonable doubt is necessary for conviction in juvenile proceedings. *Breed v. Jones*, 421 U.S. 519, 95 S.Ct. 1779, 44 L.Ed.2d 346 (1975): Jeopardy attaches in a juvenile court adjudicatory hearing, thus barring subsequent prosecution for the same offense as an adult.

36. Public Law 90–351, Title I—Omnibus Safe Streets and Crime Control Act of 1968, 90th Congress, June 1968.

37. National Advisory Commission on Criminal Justice Standards and Goals, *A National Strategy to Reduce Crime* (Washington, DC: U.S. Government Printing Office, 1973).

38. Juvenile Justice and Delinquency Prevention Act of 1974, Public Law 93–415 (1974). For a critique of this legislation, see Ira Schwartz, *Justice for Juveniles—Rethinking the Best Interests of the Child* (Lexington, MA: D.C. Heath, 1989), p. 175.

39. For an extensive summary of the Violent Crime Control and Law Enforcement Act of 1994, see *Criminal Law Reporter* 55:2305–2430 (1994).

40. Shay Bilchik, "A Juvenile Justice System for the 21st Century," *Crime and Delinquency* 44:89 (1998).

41. For a comprehensive view of juvenile law, see Joseph J. Senna and Larry J. Siegel, *Juvenile Law: Cases and Comments*, 2nd ed. (St. Paul, MN: West, 1992).

42. For an excellent review of the juvenile process, see Adrienne Volenik, *Checklists for Use in Juvenile Delinquency Proceedings* (Washington, DC: American Bar Association, 1985); see also Jeffrey Butts and Gregory Halemba, *Waiting for Justice—Moving Young Offenders through the Juvenile Court Process* (Pittsburgh: National Center for Juvenile Justice, 1996).

43. Fox Butterfield, "Justice Besieged," *New York Times*, July 21, 1997, p. A16.

44. National Conference of State Legislatures, *A Legislator's Guide to Comprehensive Juvenile Justice, Juvenile Detention, and Corrections* (Denver: National Conference of State Legislators, 1996).

45. Joan McCord, Cathy Spatz Widom, and Nancy A. Crowell, eds., *Juvenile Crime, Juvenile Justice* (Washington, DC: National Academy Press, Panel on Juvenile Crime: Prevention, Treatment, and Control, 2001).

46. Brandon C. Welsh and David P. Farrington, "Effective Programmes to Prevent Delinquency," in Joanna Adler, ed., *Forensic Psychology* (Cullompton, Devon, England: Willan, 2004).

47. *Youth Violence: A Report of the Surgeon General* (Rockville, MD: U.S. Department of Health and Human Services, 2001).

48. Laurence C. Novotney, Elizabeth Mertinko, James Lange, and Tara Kelly Baker, *Juvenile Mentoring Program: A Progress Review* (Washington, DC: OJJDP Juvenile Justice Bulletin, 2000).

49. James C. Howell, *Preventing and Reducing Juvenile Delinquency: A Comprehensive Framework* (Thousand Oaks, CA: Sage Publications, 2003), p. 248.

50. Peter W. Greenwood, "Juvenile Crime and Juvenile Justice," in James Q. Wilson and Joan Petersilia, eds., *Crime: Public Policies for Crime Control* (Oakland, CA: Institute for Contemporary Studies, 2002), pp. 90–91.

51. "Implementation Status of Drug Court Programs" (Washington, DC: Office of Justice Programs Drug Court Clearinghouse at American University, September 8, 2003).

52. *Juvenile Drug Courts: Strategies in Practice* (Washington, DC: Bureau of Justice Assistance, 2003).

53. David B. Wilson, Ojmarrh Mitchell, and Doris Layton MacKenzie, "A Systematic Review of Drug Court Effects on Recidivism" (Manassas, VA: Administration of Justice, George Mason University, 2004).

54. Nancy Rodriguez and Vincent J. Webb, "Multiple Measures of Juvenile Drug Court Effectiveness: Results of a Quasi-Experimental Design," *Crime and Delinquency* 50:292–314 (2004).

55. Barry Feld, "Criminology and the Juvenile Court: A Research Agenda for the 1990s," in Ira M. Schwartz, *Juvenile Justice and Public Policy—Toward a National Agenda* (New York: Lexington Books, 1992), p. 59.

56. Barry C. Feld, "Juvenile and Criminal Justice Systems' Responses to Youth Violence," in Michael Tonry and Mark H. Moore, eds., *Youth Violence: Crime and Justice: A Review of Research. Vol. 24* (Chicago: University of Chicago Press, 1998), p. 222.

57. Robert O. Dawson, "The Future of Juvenile Justice: Is It Time to Abolish the System?" *Journal of Criminal Law and Criminology* 81:136–155 (1990); see also Leonard P. Edwards, "The Future of the Juvenile Court: Promising New Directions," *The Future of Children: The Juvenile Court* (Los Altos, CA: David and Lucille Packard Foundation, 1996).

58. Hunter Hurst, "Juvenile Court: As We Enter the Millennium," *Juvenile and Family Court Journal* 50:21–27 (1999).

59. Carol J. DeFrances and Kevin Strom, *Juveniles Prosecuted in the State Criminal Courts* (Washington, DC: Bureau of Justice Statistics, 1997).

60. Franklin E. Zimring, *American Youth Violence* (New York: Oxford University Press, 1998).

61. Bilchik, "A Juvenile Justice System for the 21st Century."

62. Patricia Torbet and Linda Szymanski, *State Legislative Responses to Violent Crime: 1996–97 Update* (Washington, DC: Office of Juvenile Justice and Delinquency Prevention, 1998).

63. Melissa Sickmund, *Juveniles in Court* (Washington, DC: Office of Juvenile Justice and Delinquency Prevention, U.S. Department of Justice, 2003), p. 7.

64. Stacy C. Moak and Lisa Hutchinson Wallace, "Legal Changes in Juvenile Justice: Then and Now," *Youth Violence and Juvenile Justice* 1:289–299 (2003), p. 292.

65. Torbet and Szymanski, *State Legislative Responses to Violent Crime*.

66. Hurst, "Juvenile Court: As We Enter the Millennium," p. 25.

67. McCord, Spatz Widom, and Crowell, *Juvenile Crime, Juvenile Justice*, p. 224.

68. Melissa M. Moon, Francis T. Cullen, and John Paul Wright, "It Takes a Village: Public Willingness to Help Wayward Youths," *Youth Violence and Juvenile Justice* 1:32–45 (2003).

69. McCord, Spatz Widom, and Crowell, *Juvenile Crime, Juvenile Justice*, p. 152.

70. Greenwood, "Juvenile Crime and Juvenile Justice."

71. Alida Merlo, Peter Benekos, and William Cook, "The Juvenile Court at 100 Years: Celebration or Wake?" *Juvenile and Family Court Journal* 50:1–9 at 7 (1999).

72. Simon M. Fass and Chung-Ron Pi, "Getting Tough on Juvenile Crime: An Analysis of Costs and Benefits," *Journal of Research in Crime and Delinquency* 39:363–399 (2002).

13 Police Work with Juveniles

Chapter Objectives

History of Juvenile Policing

Community Policing in the New Millennium

The Community Policing Model

The Police and Juvenile Offenders

Police Services

Police Roles

Police and Violent Juvenile Crime

Police and the Rule of Law

The Arrest Procedure

Search and Seizure

Custodial Interrogation

Discretionary Justice

Environmental Factors

Police Policy

Situational Factors

Bias and Police Discretion

FOCUS ON DELINQUENCY: Juvenile Race, Gender, and Ethnicity in Police Decision Making

Limiting Police Discretion

Police Work and Delinquency Prevention

Aggressive Law Enforcement

Police in Schools

Community-Based Policing Services

Problem-Oriented Policing

POLICY AND PRACTICE: Boston's Operation Ceasefire

Chapter Objectives

1. Be able to identify key historical events that have shaped juvenile policing in America today

2. Understand key roles and responsibilities of the police in responding to juvenile offenders

3. Be able to comment on the organization and management of police services for juveniles

4. Be aware of major court cases that have influenced police practices

5. Understand key legal aspects of police work, including search and seizure and custodial interrogation, and how they apply to juveniles

6. Be able to describe police use of discretion and factors that influence discretion

7. Understand the importance of police use of discretion with juveniles and some of the associated problems

8. Be familiar with the major policing strategies to prevent delinquency

9. See the pros and cons of police using different delinquency prevention strategies

CNN. View the CNN video clip of this story and answer related Critical Thinking questions on your Juvenile Delinquency 9e CD-ROM.

More than 60 percent of the homicides committed by juveniles involve guns. Juvenile gang killings, high-profile shootings in schools, and accidental shootings involving children have led to numerous proposals to crack down on guns getting into the hands of kids. Some of these proposals include tougher gun laws and new methods for law enforcement to trace guns. The federal agency now known as the Bureau of Alcohol, Tobacco, Firearms, and Explosives or ATF estimates that one-third of the guns used in crimes by juveniles were originally purchased from federally licensed dealers, but resold to juveniles. Police are on the front line in an effort to reduce juvenile gun crimes. Problem-oriented policing strategies, often involving other juvenile justice agencies, targeting juvenile gangs and high gun-crime areas in cities have been implemented across the country. In Boston, a comprehensive police-led strategy to reduce the flow of guns to youths substantially reduced juvenile gun homicides and other gun crimes across the city.

This chapter focuses on police work in juvenile justice. It first takes a brief look at the history of policing juveniles, from the time of the Norman conquest of England up to today. Community policing in modern times is the focus of the next section. Here the relationship between police and community efforts to prevent crime is explored. We then look at the roles and responsibilities of the police and the organization and management of police-juvenile operations. Legal aspects of police work, including the arrest procedure, search and seizure, and custodial interrogation, are reviewed. We also examine the concept of police discretion in light of the broad authority that police have in dealing with juveniles. The chapter ends with a review of police work and delinquency prevention. A wide range of police techniques in preventing delinquency are discussed, including those that rely on the deterrent powers of police and those that engage schools and the community.

HISTORY OF JUVENILE POLICING

pledge system
Early English system in which neighbors protected each other from thieves and warring groups.

watch system
Replaced the pledge system in England; watchmen patrolled urban areas at night to provide protection from harm.

Providing specialized police services for juveniles is a relatively recent phenomenon. At one time citizens were responsible for protecting themselves and maintaining order.

The origin of police agencies can be traced to early English society.[1] Before the Norman conquest of England, the **pledge system** assumed that neighbors would protect each other from thieves and warring groups. Individuals were entrusted with policing themselves and resolving minor problems. By the thirteenth century, however, the **watch system** was created to police larger communities. Men were organized in church parishes to patrol areas at night and guard against disturbances and breaches of the peace. This was followed by establishment of the constable, who was responsible for dealing with more serious crimes. By the seventeenth century, the constable, the justice of the peace, and the night watchman formed the nucleus of the police system in England.

When the Industrial Revolution brought thousands of people from the countryside to work in factories, the need for police protection increased. As a result, the first organized police force was established in London in 1829. The British "bobbies" (so-called after their founder, Sir Robert Peel) were not successful at stopping crime and were influenced by the wealthy for personal and political gain.[2]

In the American colonies, the local sheriff became the most important police official. By the mid-1800s, city police departments had formed in Boston, New York, and Philadelphia. Officers patrolled on foot, and conflicts often arose between untrained officers and the public.

By this time, children began to be treated as a distinguishable group (see Chapter 1). When children violated the law they were often treated the same as adult offenders. But even at this stage a belief existed that the enforcement of criminal law should be applied differently to children.

During the late nineteenth century and into the twentieth, the problems associated with growing numbers of unemployed and homeless youths increased. Groups such as the Wickersham Commission of 1931 and the International Association of Chiefs of Police became the leading voices for police reform.[3] Their efforts resulted in creation of specialized police units, known as delinquency control squads.

The most famous police reformer of the 1930s was August Vollmer. As the police chief of Berkeley, California, Vollmer instituted numerous reforms, including university training, modern management techniques, prevention programs, and juvenile aid bureaus.[4] These bureaus were the first organized police services for juvenile offenders.

In the 1960s, policing entered a turbulent period.[5] The U.S. Supreme Court handed down decisions designed to restrict police operations and discretion. Civil unrest produced growing tensions between police and the public. Urban police departments were unable to handle the growing crime rate. Federal funding from the Law Enforcement Assistance Administration (LEAA), an agency set up to fund justice-related programs, was a catalyst for developing hundreds of new police programs and enhancement of police services for children. By the 1980s, most urban police departments recognized that the problem of juvenile delinquency required special attention.

Today, the role of the juvenile police officer—an officer assigned to juvenile work—has taken on added importance, particularly with the increase in violent juvenile crime. Most of the nation's urban law enforcement agencies now have specialized juvenile police programs. Typically, such programs involve prevention (police athletic leagues, D.A.R.E. programs, community outreach), and law enforcement work (juvenile court, school policing, gang control). Other concerns of the programs include child abuse, domestic violence, and missing children.

To gain a comprehensive history of the **London Metropolitan Police** from 1829 to 2004, go to www.met.police.uk/history/. For an up-to-date list of web links, go to http://cj.wadsworth.com/siegel_jd9e.

TO QUIZ YOURSELF ON THIS MATERIAL, go to the Juvenile Delinquency 9e website.

COMMUNITY POLICING IN THE NEW MILLENNIUM

In the minds of most citizens, the primary responsibility of the police is to protect the public. While the image depicted in films, books, and TV shows is one of crime fight-

One of the main functions of the police is to deter juvenile crime. But in recent decades policing has taken on many new functions, including being a visible and accessible component of the community and working with residents to address delinquency problems. This has come to be known as community policing.

© Cleve Bryant/PhotoEdit

ers who always get their man, since the 1960s, the public has become increasingly aware that the reality of police work is substantially different from its fictional glorification. When police departments failed to bring the crime rate down despite massive government subsidies, when citizens complained of civil rights violations, and when tales of police corruption became widespread, it was evident that a crisis was imminent in American policing.

Recently, a new view of policing has emerged. Discarding the image of crime fighters who track down serious criminals or stop armed robberies in progress, many police departments have adopted the concept that the police role should be to maintain order and be a visible and accessible component of the community. The argument is that police efforts can be successful only when conducted in partnership with concerned citizens. This movement is referred to as **community policing**.[6]

community policing
Police strategy that emphasizes reducing fear, organizing the community, and maintaining order rather than fighting crime.

Interest in community policing does not mean that the crime control model of law enforcement is history. An ongoing effort is being made to improve the crime-fighting capability of police agencies and there are some indications that the effort is paying off. Research indicates that aggressive action by police can help reduce the incidence of repeat offending, and innovations such as computerized fingerprinting systems may bring about greater efficiency.[7] Nonetheless, little conclusive evidence exists that merely improving police officers' crime-fighting skills alone can lower crime rates.[8] Thus, the emergence of the community policing model of crime prevention, regarded as one of the most important changes in U.S. law enforcement, warrants further exploration.

Working with juvenile offenders may be especially challenging for police officers because the desire to help young people and to steer them away from crime seems to conflict with the traditional police duties of crime prevention and maintenance of order. In addition, the police are faced with a nationwide adolescent drug problem and renewed gang activity. Although the need to help troubled youths may conflict with traditional police roles, it fits nicely with the newly emerging community policing models. Improving these relationships is critical because many juveniles do not have a high regard for the police; minority teens are especially critical of police performance.[9] A recent, large-scale study carried out to investigate juveniles' attitudes toward police confirmed this long-held finding. While African American teens rated the police less favorably than all other racial groups for all questions asked (for example, Are police friendly? Are police courteous?), the most striking racial differences pertained to the question about police honesty: only 15 percent of African American youths said the police were honest. In contrast, 57 percent of whites, 51 percent of Asians, 31 percent of Hispanics, and 30 percent of Native Americans said they were.[10]

The Community Policing Model

The premise of the community policing model of crime prevention is that the police can carry out their duties more effectively by gaining the trust and assistance of concerned citizens. Under this model, the main police role is to increase feelings of community safety and encourage area residents to cooperate with their local police agencies.[11] Advocates of community policing regard the approach as useful in juvenile justice for a number of reasons:

1. Direct engagement with a community gives police more immediate information about problems unique to a neighborhood and better insight into their solutions.

2. Freeing officers from the emergency response system permits them to engage more directly in proactive crime prevention.

3. Making police operations more visible increases police accountability to the public.

4. Decentralizing operations allows officers to develop greater familiarity with the needs of various constituencies in the community and to adapt procedures to accommodate those needs.

5. Encouraging officers to view citizens as partners improves relations between police and the public.

6. Moving decision making to patrol officers places more authority in the hands of the people who best know the community's problems and expectations.[12]

The community policing model has been translated into a number of policy initiatives. It has encouraged police departments to get officers out of patrol cars, where they were insulated from the community, and into the streets via foot patrol.[13] A recent survey of policing in the United States—the Law Enforcement Management and Administrative Statistics (LEMAS) survey—reports that two-thirds (66%) of local police departments, employing 86 percent of all officers, had full-time community policing officers. Across the country, local police departments employ about 103,000 community policing officers.[14]

One community policing program, the Youth Firearms Violence Initiative (YFVI) of the federal Office of Community Oriented Policing Services (COPS), is running in 10 cities across the United States with the aim of reducing juvenile gun violence. Each city was provided with up to $1 million to pay for interventions that incorporated community policing strategies.[15] These strategies include:

I   Working in partnership with other city agencies to promote education, prevention, and intervention programs related to handguns and their safety

I   Developing community-based programs focused on youth handgun violence

I   Developing programs involving and assisting families in addressing youth handgun problems[16]

To learn more about **COPS,** go to www.cops.usdoj.gov. For an up-to-date list of web links, go to http://cj.wadsworth.com/siegel_jd9e.

The YFVI programs also include some traditional law enforcement measures, such as new enforcement units within the police department and standard surveillance and intelligence-gathering techniques.

An evaluation of the YFVI was conducted in all 10 cities, but program effectiveness in reducing gun violence was measured in only 5 cities (Baltimore; Cleveland; Inglewood, California; Salinas, California; and San Antonio). Police-reported gun crimes were reduced in each of the five cities and in every target area of the cities, with the ex-

TABLE 13.1

Impact of YFVI Programs on Gun Crimes

	Number of Gun Crimes in 12-Month Period before YFVI Began	Number of Gun Crimes in 12-Month Period after YFVI Began	Change (%)
Baltimore, MD	8,764	8,581	−2
Cherry Hill	104	105	0
Park Heights	643	594	−8
Cleveland, OH	3,149	2,672	−15
Three RAPP houses*	26	16	−38
Inglewood, CA	945	730	−23
Darby-Dixon	43	22	−49
Salinas, CA			
Citywide	552	490	−11
San Antonio, TX	2,895	1,716	−41
Four target areas	523	328	−37

*RAPP = Residential Area Policing Program

SOURCE: Adapted from Terence Dunworth, *National Evaluation of the Youth Firearms Violence Initiative* (Washington, DC: NIJ Research in Brief, 2000), p. 8, exhibit 6.

ception of Cherry Hill in Baltimore. (See Table 13.1 for the impact of the program on gun crimes.) The evaluation also examined the percentage change of gun crimes involving young people in the before and after periods. The results were not as encouraging. Only San Antonio demonstrated a significant reduction in the percentage of gun crimes involving youths, from 57 percent to 55 percent.

The Office of Community Oriented Policing Services is also involved in other initiatives to reduce gun violence by serious juvenile offenders.[17] One of these initiatives is Project Safe Neighborhoods, which brings together federal, state, and local law enforcement, prosecutors, and community leaders to deter and punish gun crime.[18]

Efforts are being made by police departments to involve citizens in delinquency control. Community policing is a philosophy that promotes community, government, and police partnerships that address juvenile crime, as well as adult crime.[19] Although there is not a great deal of evidence that these efforts can lower crime rates,[20] they do seem to be effective methods of improving perceptions of community safety and the quality of community life,[21] and involving citizens in the juvenile justice network. Under the community policing philosophy, prevention programs may become more effective crime control measures. Programs that combine the reintegration of youths into the community after institutionalization with police surveillance and increased communication are vital for improving police effectiveness with juveniles.[22]

TO QUIZ YOURSELF ON THIS MATERIAL, go to the Juvenile Delinquency 9e website.

THE POLICE AND JUVENILE OFFENDERS

The alarming increase in serious juvenile crime in recent decades has made it obvious that the police can no longer neglect youthful antisocial behavior. Departments need to assign resources to the problem and have the proper organization for coping with it. The theory and practice of police organization have undergone many changes, and as a result, police departments are giving greater emphasis to the juvenile function. The organization of juvenile work depends on the size of the police department, the kind of community in which the department is located, and the amount and quality of resources available in the community.

Prevention programs

- Community Relations
- Police Athletic League (PAL)
- D.A.R.E. programs (drug prevention)
- Officer Friendly

Juvenile crimes

- Detective Bureau
- Juvenile Court Processing
- School Liaison
- Gang Control Unit

FIGURE 13.1

Typical Urban Police Department Organization with Juvenile Justice Component

Police Services

Police who work with juvenile offenders usually have skills and talents that go beyond those generally associated with regular police work. In large urban police departments, juvenile services are often established through a special unit. Ordinarily this unit is the responsibility of a command-level police officer, who assigns officers to deal with juvenile problems throughout the police department's jurisdiction. Police departments with very few officers have little need for an internal division with special functions. Most small departments make one officer responsible for handling juvenile matters for the entire community. A large proportion of justice agencies have written policy directives for handling juvenile offenders. Figure 13.1 illustrates the major elements of a police department organization dealing with juvenile offenders. However, in both large and small departments, officers assigned to work with juveniles will not necessarily be the only ones involved in handling juvenile offenses. When officers on patrol encounter a youngster committing a crime, they are responsible for dealing with the problem initially; they generally refer the case to the juvenile unit or to a juvenile police officer for follow-up.

juvenile officers
Police officers who specialize in dealing with juvenile offenders; they may operate alone or as part of a juvenile police unit within the department.

role conflicts
Conflicts police officers face that revolve around the requirement to perform their primary duty of law enforcement and a desire to aid in rehabilitating youthful offenders.

Police Roles

Juvenile officers operate either as specialists within a police department or as part of the juvenile unit of a police department. Their role is similar to that of officers working with adult offenders: to intervene if the actions of a citizen produce public danger or disorder. Most juvenile officers are appointed after having had some general patrol experience. A desire to work with juveniles as well as an aptitude for the work are considered essential for the job. Officers must also have a thorough knowledge of the law, especially the constitutional protections available to juveniles.

Most officers regard the violations of juveniles as nonserious unless they are committed by chronic troublemakers or involve significant damage to persons or property. Police encounters with juveniles are generally the result of reports made by citizens, and the bulk of such encounters pertain to matters of minor legal consequence.[23] Of course, police must also deal with serious juvenile offenders whose criminal acts are similar to those of adults; these are a minority of the offender population. Thus, police who deal with delinquency must concentrate on being peacekeepers and crime preventers.[24]

Handling juvenile offenders can produce major **role conflicts** for police. They may experience a tension between their desire to perform what they consider their primary duty, law enforcement,

Police officers must deal with serious offenders whose violent acts are similar to those of adults, but these are a small minority of the offender population. Shown here is Kayla La Sala, 14, accused of murdering her father in West Virginia in 2004. She later fled to Florida where she is being held in the Seminole Juvenile Detention Center and faces extradition to West Virginia.

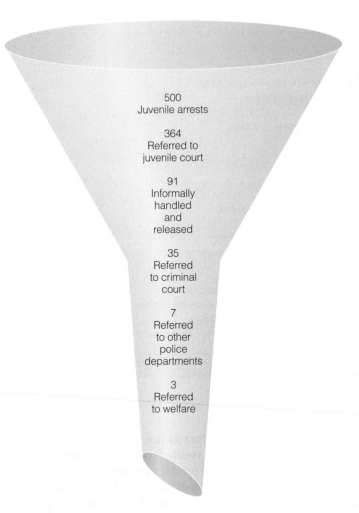

500
Juvenile arrests

364
Referred to
juvenile court

91
Informally
handled
and
released

35
Referred
to criminal
court

7
Referred
to other
police
departments

3
Referred
to welfare

FIGURE 13.2
Police Response to Juvenile Crime

To understand how police deal with juvenile crime, picture a funnel, with the result shown here. For every 500 juveniles taken into custody, a little more than 70 percent are sent to juvenile court, and around 20 percent are released.

SOURCE: FBI, *Crime in the United States 2002* (Washington, DC: U.S. Government Printing Office, 2003), p. 291, table 68.

and the need to aid in the rehabilitation of youthful offenders. Police officers' actions in cases involving adults are usually controlled by the law and their own judgment or discretion. (The concept of discretion is discussed later in this chapter.) In contrast, a case involving a juvenile often demands that the officer consider the "best interests of the child" and how the officer's actions will influence the child's future well-being. However, in recent years police have become more likely to refer juvenile offenders to courts. It is estimated that 73 percent of all juvenile arrests are referred to juvenile court, while around 20 percent of all juvenile arrests are handled informally within the police department or are referred to a community-service agency (see Figure 13.2). These informal dispositions are the result of the police officer's discretionary authority.[25]

Police intervention in situations involving juveniles can be difficult and emotional. The officer often encounters hostile behavior from the juvenile offender, as well as agitated witnesses. Overreaction by the officer can result in a violent incident. Even if the officer succeeds in quieting or dispersing the witnesses, they will probably reappear the next day, often in the same place.[26]

Role conflicts are common, because most police-juvenile encounters are brought about by loitering and rowdiness rather than by serious law violations. Public concern has risen about out-of-control youth. Yet, because of legal constraints and family interference, the police are often limited in the ways they can respond to such offenders.[27]

What role should the police play in mediating problems with youths—law enforcer or delinquency prevention worker? The answer may lie somewhere in between. Most police departments operate juvenile programs that combine law enforcement and delinquency prevention roles, and the police work with the juvenile court to determine a role most suitable for their community.[28] Police officers may even act as prosecutors in some rural courts when attorneys are not available. Thus, the police-juvenile role extends from the on-the-street encounter to the station house to the court. For juvenile matters involving minor criminal conduct or incorrigible behavior, the police ordinarily select the least restrictive alternative, which includes such measures as temporary assistance or referral to community agencies. In contrast, violent juvenile crime requires that the police arrest youths while providing constitutional safeguards similar to those available to adult offenders.

Police and Violent Juvenile Crime

Violent juvenile offenders are defined as those adjudicated delinquent for crimes of homicide, rape, robbery, aggravated assault, and kidnapping. Juveniles typically account for nearly 20 percent of all violent crime arrests. Though the juvenile violence rate has recently declined, the future is uncertain. Some experts believe that a surge of violence will occur as the children of baby boomers enter their "prime crime" years. Some experts predict that juvenile arrests for violent crime will double by the year 2010.[29]

EXHIBIT 13.1

Policing Programs

What Works

I   Increased directed patrols in street-corner hot spots of crime
I   Proactive arrests of serious repeat offenders
I   Proactive arrests of drunk drivers
I   Arrests of employed suspects for domestic assault
I   Problem-oriented policing

What Does Not Work

I   Neighborhood block watch
I   Arrests of some juveniles for minor offenses
I   Arrests of unemployed suspects for domestic assault
I   Drug market arrests
I   Community policing that is not targeted at risk factors
I   Adding extra police to cities with no regard to assignment or activity

What Is Promising

I   Police traffic enforcement patrols targeting illegally carried handguns
I   Community policing when the community is involved in setting priorities
I   Community policing focused on improving police legitimacy
I   Warrants for arrest of suspect absent when police respond to domestic violence

SOURCE: Lawrence W. Sherman and John E. Eck, "Policing for Crime Prevention," in Lawrence W. Sherman, David P. Farrington, Brandon C. Welsh, and Doris Layton MacKenzie, eds., *Evidence-Based Crime Prevention* (New York: Routledge, 2002), pp. 321–322.

As a result of these predictions, police and other justice agencies are experimenting with different methods of controlling violent youth. Some of these methods, such as placing more officers on the beat, have existed for decades; others rely on state-of-the-art technology to pinpoint the locations of violent crimes and develop immediate countermeasures. Research shows that there are a number of effective policing practices, including increased directed patrols in street-corner hot spots of crime; proactive arrests of serious repeat offenders; and **problem-oriented policing.**[30] (See Exhibit 13.1 for a complete list of policing practices that work, do not work, or are promising.) These strategies address problems of community disorganization and can be effective deterrents when combined with other laws and policies, such as restricting the possession of firearms.[31] Although many of these policing strategies are not new, implementing them as one element of an overall police plan may have an impact on preventing juvenile violence.

Finally, one key component of any innovative police program dealing with violent juvenile crime is improved communications between the police and the community.

problem-oriented policing
Law enforcement that focuses on addressing the problems underlying incidents of juvenile delinquency rather than the incidents only.

TO QUIZ YOURSELF ON THIS MATERIAL, go to the Juvenile Delinquency 9e website.

POLICE AND THE RULE OF LAW

When police are involved with criminal activity of juvenile offenders, their actions are controlled by statute, constitutional case law, and judicial review. Police methods of investigation and control include (1) the arrest procedure, (2) search and seizure, and (3) custodial interrogation.

The Arrest Procedure

When a juvenile is apprehended, the police must decide whether to release the youngster or make a referral to the juvenile court. Cases involving serious crimes against property or persons are often referred to court. Less serious cases, such as disputes be-

EXHIBIT **13.2**

Uniform Juvenile Court Act, Section 13 (Taking into Custody)

a. A child may be taken into custody:
   1. pursuant to an order of the court under this Act;
   2. pursuant to the laws of arrest;
   3. by a law enforcement officer (or duly authorized officer of the court) if there are reasonable grounds to believe that the child is suffering from illness or injury or is in immediate danger from his surroundings, and that his removal is necessary; or
   4. by a law enforcement officer (or duly authorized officer of the court) if there are reasonable grounds to believe that the child has run away from his parents, guardian, or other custodian.

b. The taking of a child into custody is not an arrest, except for the purpose of determining its validity under the constitution of this State or of the United States.

SOURCE: National Conference of Commissioners on Uniform State Laws, *Uniform Juvenile Court Act* (Chicago: National Conference on Uniform State Laws, 1968), Sect. 13.

---

tween juveniles, petty shoplifting, runaways, and assaults of minors, are often diverted from court action.

arrest
Taking a person into the custody of the law to restrain the accused until he or she can be held accountable for the offense in court proceedings.

Most states require that the law of **arrest** be the same for both adults and juveniles. To make a legal arrest, an officer must have probable cause to believe that an offense took place and that the suspect is the guilty party. **Probable cause** is usually defined as falling somewhere between a mere suspicion and absolute certainty. In misdemeanor cases the police officer must personally observe the crime in order to place a suspect in custody. For a felony, the police officer may make the arrest without having observed the crime if the officer has probable cause to believe the crime occurred and the person being arrested committed it. A felony is a serious offense; a misdemeanor is a minor or petty crime. Crimes such as murder, rape, and robbery are felonies; crimes such as petty larceny and disturbing the peace are misdemeanors.

probable cause
Reasonable grounds to believe that an offense was committed and that the accused committed that offense.

The main difference between arrests of adult and juvenile offenders is the broader latitude police have to control youthful behavior. Most juvenile codes, for instance, provide broad authority for the police to take juveniles into custody.[32] Such statutes are designed to give the police the authority to act *in loco parentis* (Latin for "in place of the parent"). Accordingly, the broad power granted to police is consistent with the notion that a juvenile is not arrested but taken into custody, which implies a protective rather than a punitive form of detention.[33] Once a juvenile is arrested, however, the constitutional safeguards of the Fourth and Fifth Amendments available to adults apply to the juvenile as well.

Section 13 of the Uniform Juvenile Court Act is an example of the provisions used in state codes regarding juvenile arrest procedures (see Exhibit 13.2). There is currently a trend toward treating juvenile offenders more like adults. Related to this trend are efforts by the police to provide a more legalistic and less informal approach to the arrest process, and a more balanced approach to case disposition.[34]

Search and Seizure

search and seizure
The U.S. Constitution protects citizens from any search and seizure by police without a lawfully obtained search warrant; such warrants are issued when there is probable cause to believe that an offense has been committed.

Do juveniles have the same right to be free from unreasonable **search and seizure** as adults? In general, a citizen's privacy is protected by the Fourth Amendment of the Constitution, which states

> *The right of the people to be secure in their persons, houses, papers, and effects, against unreasonable searches and seizures, shall not be violated, and no warrants shall issue, but upon probable cause, supported by oaths or affirmation, and particularly describing the place to be searched, and the persons or things to be seized.*[35]

Most courts have held that the Fourth Amendment ban against unreasonable search and seizure applies to juveniles and that illegally seized evidence is inadmissible in a

Officers search students at a high school. The Supreme Court allows police officers and security agents greater latitude in searching students than they would have with other citizens, on the grounds that the campus must be a safe and crime-free environment.

juvenile trial. To exclude incriminating evidence, a juvenile's attorney makes a pretrial motion to suppress the evidence, the same procedure that is used in the adult criminal process.

A full discussion of search and seizure is beyond the scope of this book, but it is important to note that the Supreme Court has ruled that police may stop a suspect and search for evidence without a warrant under certain circumstances. A person may be searched after a legal arrest, but then only in the immediate area of the suspect's control. For example, after an arrest for possession of drugs, the pockets of a suspect's jacket may be searched;[36] an automobile may be searched if there is probable cause to believe a crime has taken place;[37] a suspect's outer garments may be frisked if police are suspicious of his or her activities;[38] and a search may be conducted if a person volunteers for the search.[39] These rules are usually applied to juveniles as well as to adults. Concept Summary 13.1 reviews when warrantless searches are allowed.

Concept Summary 13.1

Warrantless Searches

Action	Scope of Search
Stop-and-frisk	Pat-down of a suspect's outer garments.
Search incident to arrest	Full body search after a legal arrest.
Automobile search	If probable cause exists, full search of car, including driver, passengers, and closed containers found in trunk. Search must be reasonable.
Consent search	Warrantless search of person or place is justified if suspect knowingly and voluntarily consents to search.
Plain view	Suspicious objects seen in plain view can be seized without a warrant.
Electronic surveillance	Material can be seized electronically without a warrant if suspect has no expectation of privacy.

Custodial Interrogation

custodial interrogation
Questions posed by the police to a suspect held in custody in the prejudicial stage of the juvenile justice process; juveniles have the same rights against self-incrimination as adults do when being questioned.

In years past, police often questioned juveniles without their parents or even an attorney present. Any incriminating statements arising from such **custodial interrogation** could be used at trial. However, in the 1966 *Miranda* case, the Supreme Court placed constitutional limitations on police interrogation procedures with adult offenders. *Miranda* held that persons in police custody must be told the following:

- They have the right to remain silent.
- Any statements they make can be used against them.
- They have the right to counsel.
- If they cannot afford counsel, it will be furnished at public expense.[40]

The *Miranda* **warning** has been made applicable to juveniles taken into custody. The Supreme Court case of *In re Gault* stated that constitutional privileges against self-incrimination apply in juvenile as well as adult cases. Because *In re Gault* implies that *Miranda* applies to custodial interrogation in criminal procedures, state court jurisdictions apply the requirements of *Miranda* to juvenile proceedings as well. Since the *Gault* decision in 1967, virtually all courts that have ruled on the question of the *Miranda* warning have concluded that the warning does apply to the juvenile process.

One problem associated with custodial interrogation of juveniles has to do with waiver of *Miranda* rights: Under what circumstances can juveniles knowingly and willingly waive the rights given them by *Miranda v. Arizona*? Does a youngster, acting alone, have sufficient maturity to appreciate the right to remain silent?

Most courts have concluded that parents or attorneys need not be present for juveniles effectively to waive their rights.[41] In a frequently cited California case, *People v. Lara*, the court said that the question of a juvenile's waiver is to be determined by the totality of the circumstances doctrine.[42] This means that the validity of a waiver rests not only on the age of the youth but also on a combination of other factors, including the child's education, the child's knowledge of the charge, whether the child was allowed to consult with family or friends, and the method of interrogation.[43] The general rule is that juveniles can waive their rights to protection from self-incrimination, but that the validity of this waiver is determined by the circumstances of each case.

The waiver of *Miranda* rights by a juvenile is one of the most controversial legal issues addressed in the state courts. It has also been the subject of federal constitutional review. In two cases, *Fare v. Michael C.* and *California v. Prysock*, the Supreme Court has attempted to clarify children's rights when they are interrogated by the police. In *Fare v. Michael C.*, the Court ruled that a child's asking to speak to his probation officer was not the equivalent of asking for an attorney; consequently, statements he made to the police absent legal counsel were admissible in court.[44] In *California v. Prysock*, the Court was asked to rule on the adequacy of a *Miranda* warning given to Randall Prysock, a youthful murder suspect.[45] After reviewing the taped exchange between the police interrogator and the boy, the Court upheld Prysock's conviction when it ruled that even though the *Miranda* warning was given in slightly different language and out of exact context, its meaning was easily understandable, even to a juvenile.

Taken together, *Fare* and *Prysock* make it seem indisputable that juveniles are at least entitled to receive the same *Miranda* rights as adults. *Miranda v. Arizona* is a historic decision that continues to protect the rights of all suspects placed in custody.[46]

To read more about the ***Miranda* decision,** go to www.tourolaw.edu/patch/Miranda/. For an up-to-date list of web links, go to http://cj.wadsworth.com/siegel_jd9e.

TO QUIZ YOURSELF ON THIS MATERIAL, go to the Juvenile Delinquency 9e website.

DISCRETIONARY JUSTICE

Today, juvenile offenders receive nearly as much procedural protection as adult offenders. However, the police have broader authority in dealing with juveniles than with adults. Granting such **discretion** to juvenile officers raises some important questions: Under what circumstances should an officer arrest status offenders? Should a summons be used in lieu of arrest? Under what conditions should a juvenile be taken into protective custody?

When police confront a case involving a juvenile offender, they rely on their discretion to choose an appropriate course of action. Police discretion is selective enforcement of the law by authorized police agents. Discretion gives officers a choice among possible courses of action within the limits on their power.[47] It is a prime example of *low-visibility decision making*—a public official making decisions that the public is not in a position to regulate or criticize.[48]

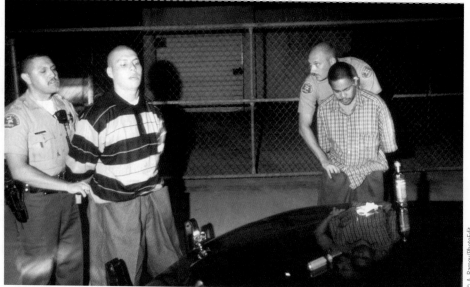

Two teenage gang members are arrested for possession of drugs and firearms by officers of the Los Angeles Police Department. Police have discretion to take formal action against youthful offenders, to release them with a warning, or take some other informal action.

To read about **trends in juvenile arrests,** go to www.ncjrs.org/pdffiles1/ ojjdp/191729.pdf. For an up-to-date list of web links, go to http://cj.wadsworth.com/ siegel_jd9e.

Discretion exists not only in the police function but also in prosecutorial decision making, judicial judgments, and corrections. Discretion results in the law being applied differently in similar situations. For example, two teenagers are caught in a stolen automobile; one is arrested, the other released. Two youths are drunk and disorderly; one is sent home, the other to juvenile court. A group of youngsters is involved in a gang fight; only a few are arrested, the others are released.

Much discretion is exercised in juvenile work because of the informality that has been built into the system in an attempt to individualize justice.[49] Furthermore, officials in the juvenile justice system make decisions that are often without oversight or review. The daily procedures of juvenile personnel are rarely subject to judicial review, except when they clearly violate a youth's constitutional rights. As a result, discretion sometimes deteriorates into discrimination and other abuses on the part of the police. The real danger in discretion is that it allows the law to discriminate against precisely those elements in the population—the poor, the ignorant, the unpopular—who are least able to draw attention to their plight.[50]

The problem of discretion in juvenile justice is one of extremes. Too little discretion provides insufficient flexibility to treat juvenile offenders as individuals. Too much discretion can lead to injustice. Guidelines and controls are needed to structure the use of discretion.

Generally, the first contact a youth has with the juvenile justice system is with the police. Research indicates that most police decisions arising from this initial contact involve discretion.[51] These studies show that many juvenile offenders are never referred to juvenile court.

In a classic 1963 study, Nathan Goldman examined the arrest records of more than 1,000 juveniles from four communities in Pennsylvania.[52] He concluded that more than 64 percent of police contacts with juveniles were handled informally. Subsequent research offered additional evidence of informal disposition of juvenile cases.[53] For example, in the 1970s, Paul Strasburg found that about 50 percent of all children who come in contact with the police do not get past the initial stage of the juvenile justice process.[54]

A recent study analyzed juvenile data collected as part of the Project on Policing Neighborhoods—a comprehensive study of police patrols in Indianapolis, Indiana, and St. Petersburg, Florida. This study indicated that police still use discretion.[55] It found that 13 percent of police encounters with juveniles resulted in arrest.[56] As shown in Table 13.2, the most likely disposition of police encounters with juveniles is a command or threat to arrest (38%), and the second most likely is search or interrogation of the suspects (24%).

TABLE 13.2

Disposition of Police Encounters with Juveniles

Disposition	Juveniles (%)
Release	14
Advise	11
Search/interrogate	24
Command/threaten	38
Arrest	13

SOURCE: Robert E. Worden and Stephanie M. Myers, *Police Encounters with Juvenile Suspects* (Albany, NY: Hindelang Criminal Justice Research Center and School of Criminal Justice, University at Albany, SUNY, 2001), Table 3.

After arrest, the most current data show an increase in the number of cases referred to the juvenile court. The FBI estimates that almost three-quarters of all juvenile arrests are referred to juvenile court.[57] Despite the variations between the estimates, these studies indicate that the police use significant discretion in their decisions regarding juvenile offenders. Research shows that differential decision making goes on without clear guidance.

If all police officers acted in a fair and just manner, the seriousness of the crime, the situation in which it occurred, and the legal record of the juvenile would be the factors that affect decision making. Research does show that police are much more likely to take formal action if the crime is serious and has been reported by a victim who is a respected member of the community, and if the offender is well known to them.[58] However, there are other factors that are believed to shape police discretion; they are discussed next.

Environmental Factors

How does a police officer decide what to do with a juvenile offender? The norms of the community are a factor in the decision. Some officers work in communities that tolerate a fair amount of personal freedom. In liberal environments, the police may be inclined to release juveniles rather than arrest them. Other officers work in conservative communities that expect a no-nonsense approach to police enforcement. Here, police may be more inclined to arrest a juvenile.

Police officers may be influenced by their perception of community alternatives to police intervention. Some officers may use arrest because they believe nothing else can be done.[59] Others may favor referring juveniles to social service agencies, particularly if they believe a community has a variety of good resources. These referrals save time and effort; records do not have to be filled out, and court appearances can be avoided. The availability of such options allows for greater latitude in police decision making.[60]

Police Policy

The policies and customs of the local police department also influence decisions. Juvenile officers may be pressured to make more arrests or to refrain from making arrests under certain circumstances. Directives instruct officers to be alert to certain types of juvenile violations. The chief of police might initiate policies governing the arrest practices of the juvenile department. For example, if local merchants complain that youths congregating in a shopping center parking lot are inhibiting business, police may be called on to make arrests. Under other circumstances, an informal warning might be given. Similarly, a rash of deaths caused by teenage drunk driving may galvanize the local media to demand police action. The mayor and the police chief, sensitive to possible voter dissatisfaction, may then demand that formal police action be taken in cases of drunk driving.

Another source of influence is pressure from supervisors. Some supervising officers may believe it is important to curtail disorderly conduct or drug use. In addition, officers may be influenced by the discretionary decisions made by their peers.

Situational Factors

In addition to the environment, a variety of situational factors affect a police officer's decisions. Situational factors are those attached to a particular crime, such as specific traits of offenders. Traditionally, it was believed that police officers rely heavily on the demeanor and appearance of the juvenile in making decisions. Some research shows that the decision to arrest is often based on factors such as dress, attitude, speech, and level of hostility toward the police.[61] Kids who display "attitude" were believed to be the ones more likely to be arrested than those who are respectful and contrite.[62] However, more recent research has challenged the influence of demeanor on police decision making, suggesting that it is delinquent behavior and actions that occur during police detention that influence the police decision to take formal action.[63] For example, a person who struggles or touches police during a confrontation is a likely candidate for arrest, but those who merely sport a bad attitude or negative demeanor are as likely to suffer an arrest as the polite and contrite.[64] It is possible that the earlier research reflected a time when police officers demanded absolute respect and were quick to take action when their authority was challenged. The more recent research may indicate that police, through training or experience, are now less sensitive to slights and confrontational behavior and view them as part of the job. Most studies conclude that the following variables are important in the police discretionary process:[65]

I The attitude of the complainant

I The type and seriousness of the offense

I The race, sex, and age of the offender

I The attitude of the offender

I The offender's prior contacts with the police

I The perceived willingness of the parents to assist in solving the problem (in the case of a child)

I The setting or location in which the incident occurs

I Whether the offender denies the actions or insists on a court hearing (in the case of a child)

I The likelihood that a child can be served by an agency in the community

Bias and Police Discretion

Do police allow bias to affect their decisions on whether to arrest youths? Do they routinely use "racial profiling" when they decide to make an arrest? A great deal of debate has been generated over this issue. Some experts believe that police decision making is deeply influenced by the offender's personal characteristics, whereas others maintain that crime-related variables are more significant.

Racial Bias It has long been charged that police are more likely to act formally with African American suspects and use their discretion to benefit whites.[66] In the context of traffic stops by police, the phrase "driving while black" has been coined to refer to the repeated findings of many studies that African American drivers are disproportionately stopped by police and that race is the primary reason for this practice.[67] As Table 13.3 shows, African American youths are arrested at a rate disproportionate to their representation in the population. Research on this issue has yielded mixed con-

TABLE 13.3

African American Representation in Arrest Statistics

Most Serious Offense	African American Juvenile Arrests in 2002 (%)
Murder	50
Forcible rape	34
Robbery	54
Aggravated assault	34
Burglary	28
Larceny/theft	29
Motor vehicle theft	37
Weapons	36
Drug abuse violations	33
Curfew and loitering	29
Runaways	18

NOTE: Percentage is of all juvenile arrests.

SOURCE: FBI, *Crime in the United States 2002* (Washington, DC: U.S. Government Printing Office, 2003), p. 252, table 43.

clusions. One view is that while discrimination may have existed in the past, there is no longer a need to worry about racial discrimination because minorities now possess sufficient political status to protect them within the justice system.[68] As Harvard University law professor Randall Kennedy forcefully argues, even if a law enforcement policy exists that disproportionately affects African American suspects, it might be justified as a "public good" because law-abiding African Americans are statistically more often victims of crimes committed by other African Americans.[69]

In contrast to these views, several research efforts do show evidence of police discrimination against African American youths.[70] Donna Bishop and Charles Frazier found that race can have a direct effect on decisions made at several junctures of the juvenile justice process.[71] According to Bishop and Frazier, African Americans are more likely than whites to be recommended for formal processing, referred to court, adjudicated delinquent, and given harsher dispositions for comparable offenses. In the arrest category, specifically, being African American increases the probability of formal police action.[72]

Similarly, a study by the National Council on Crime and Delinquency revealed significant overrepresentation by black youths at every point in the California juvenile justice system. Although they make up less than 9 percent of the state youth population, black youths accounted for 19 percent of juvenile arrests. According to the study, the causes for the disparity included (1) institutional racism, (2) environmental factors, (3) family dysfunction, (4) cultural barriers, and (5) school failure.[73]

In summary, studies of bias in police decision making have revealed the following:

1. Some researchers have concluded that the police discriminate against minority youths.

2. Other researchers do not find evidence of discrimination.

3. Racial disparity is most often seen at the arrest stage but probably exists at other stages.

4. The higher arrest rates of minorities are related to interpersonal, family, community, and organizational differences. Other influences may include police discretion, street crime visibility, and high crime rates within a particular group. Such factors, however, may also be linked to general societal discrimination.

For further information on racial bias in police decisions, see the Focus on Delinquency box entitled "Juvenile Race, Gender, and Ethnicity in Police Decision Making." Further research is needed to better understand and document what appears to be findings of disproportional arrests of minority juvenile offenders.[74]

Juvenile Race, Gender, and Ethnicity in Police Decision Making

Does police discretion work against the young, males, the poor, and minority group members, or does it favor special interest groups? Current research has uncovered information supporting both sides.

Although the police are involved in at least some discrimination against racial minorities who are juveniles, the frequency and scope of such discrimination may be less than anticipated. Some of today's literature shows that the police are likely to interfere with or arrest poor African American youths. The police frequently stop and question youths of color walking down the streets of their neighborhoods or hanging around street corners. If this is the case, then race plays a role in police discretion.

In contrast to these findings, data from other studies indicate that racial bias does not influence the decision to arrest and move a youngster through the juvenile justice system. The attitude of the youth, prior record, seriousness of crime, setting or location of the crime, and other variables control police discretion, not race, ethnicity, or gender. Another problem in determining the impact of race or gender on police discretion is that the victim's race, not the juvenile offender's, may be the key to racial bias. Police officers may take different action when the victim is white rather than when the victim is a minority group member.

Police bias may also be a result of organizational and administrative directions as opposed to bias by an individual officer "on the beat" or in a cruiser. For example, the police departments have been found to use racial profiles for stopping and questioning suspects.

Obviously, not all officers operate unfairly or with a racial bias. Quite possibly the impact of juvenile race on police discretion varies from jurisdiction to jurisdiction and from one group of juveniles to another. Many African American youngsters, for example, view their gang affiliation as a means of survival. Teenage gang members and their families often feel frustrated about the lack of opportunities and their experiences as being targets of discrimination.

Despite all the research findings, uncertainty about the extent and degree of racial bias continues to plague the juvenile justice system. Unfortunately, minority youths are involved in a disproportionate percentage of all juvenile arrests. This often gives the impression that racial, gender, and ethnic bias exists in urban police departments.

Critical Thinking

What do you think? Do the police take race into account when making decisions to arrest juveniles suspected of violating the law?

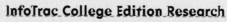

InfoTrac College Edition Research

To read more about racial bias on the part of police toward juveniles, go to Jim Leitzel, "Race and Policing," *Society* 38:38 (March 2001).

SOURCES: For an extensive review of research on police discretion (adult and juvenile) since 1980, see Eric Riksheim and Steven Chermak, "Causes of Police Behavior Revisited," *Journal of Criminal Justice* 21:353–382 (1993); also Carl E. Pope and Howard N. Snyder, *Race as a Factor in Juvenile Arrests* (Washington, DC: OJJDP Juvenile Justice Bulletin, 2003); William Brown, "The Fight for Survival: African American Gang Members and Their Families in a Segregated Society," *Juvenile and Family Court Journal* 49:1–15 (1998); Bohsui Wu, "The Effect of Race on Juvenile Justice Processing," *Juvenile and Family Court Journal* 48:43–53 (1997); Richard Sutphen, David Kurtz, and Martha Giddings, "The Influence of Juveniles' Race on Police Decision-Making: An Exploratory Study," *Juvenile and Family Court Journal* 44:69–78 (1997).

Gender Bias Is there a difference between police treatment of male and female offenders? Some experts favor the *chivalry hypothesis,* which holds that police are likely to act paternally toward young girls and not arrest them. Others believe that police may be more likely to arrest female offenders because their actions violate officers' stereotypes of the female.

There is some research support for various forms of gender bias. The nature of this bias may vary according to the seriousness of the offense and the age of the offender. Studies offer a variety of conclusions, but there seems to be general agreement that police are less likely to process females for delinquent acts and that they discriminate against them by arresting them for status offenses. Examples of the conclusions reached by some of these studies follow:

❚ Police tend to be more lenient toward females than males with regard to acts of delinquency. Merry Morash found that boys who engage in "typical male" delinquent activities are much more likely to develop police records than females.[75]

❚ Females who have committed minor or status offenses seem to be referred to juvenile court more often than males. Meda Chesney-Lind has found that adolescent female status offenders are arrested for less-serious offenses than boys.[76]

Recent evidence has confirmed earlier studies showing that the police, and most likely the courts, apply a double standard in dealing with male and female juvenile offenders. Bishop and Frazier found that both female status offenders and male delinquents are differently disadvantaged in the juvenile justice system in that, for status offenses, females are more likely to be arrested, and for other offenses, males are more likely to be arrested.[77] Chesney-Lind and Shelden report that in many other countries female teens are also more likely than male teens to be arrested for status offenses and referred to juvenile court for status offenses.[78]

Organizational Bias The policies of some police departments may result in biased practices. Research has found that police departments can be characterized by their professionalism (skills and knowledge) and bureaucratization.[79] Departments that are highly bureaucratized (high emphasis on rules and regulations) and at the same time unprofessional are most likely to be insulated from the communities they serve. Organizational policy may be influenced by the perceptions of police decision makers. A number of experts have found that law-enforcement administrators have a stereotyped view of the urban poor as troublemakers who must be kept under control.[80] Consequently, lower-class neighborhoods experience much greater police scrutiny than middle-class areas, and their residents face a proportionately greater chance of arrest. For example, there is a significant body of literature that shows that police are more likely to "hassle" or arrest African American males in poor neighborhoods than white males in middle-class neighborhoods.[81] It is therefore not surprising, as criminologist Robert Sampson has found, that teenage residents of neighborhoods in low socioeconomic areas have a significantly greater chance of acquiring police records than youths living in higher socioeconomic areas, regardless of the actual crime rates in these areas.[82] Sampson's research indicates that although police officers may not discriminate on an individual level, departmental policy that focuses on lower-class areas may result in class and racial bias in the police processing of delinquent youth.

Not all experts believe there is rampant police organizational bias. For example, when Ronald Weitzer surveyed people in three Washington, D.C., neighborhoods, he found that residents in primarily African American neighborhoods value racially integrated police services.[83] Similarly, Thomas Priest and Deborah Brown Carter have found that the African American community is supportive of the local police, especially when they respond quickly to calls for service. It is unlikely that African Americans would appreciate rapid service, or the presence of white officers, if police routinely practiced racial discrimination.[84]

One reason for these contrasting views is that racial influences on police decision making are often quite subtle and hard to detect. Data suggest that to be valid, any study of police discretion must take into account both victim and offender characteristics.

In summary, the policies, practices, and customs of the local police department influence discretion. Conditions vary from department to department and depend on the judgment of the chief and others in the organizational hierarchy. Because the police retain a large degree of discretionary power, the ideal of nondiscrimination is often difficult to achieve in practice. However, policies to limit police discretion can help eliminate bias.

To read about **what is being done to reduce racial profiling,** go to www.usdoj. gov/crt/split/documents/guidance_ on_race.htm. For an up-to-date list of web links, go to http://cj.wadsworth.com/ siegel_jd9e.

Limiting Police Discretion

A number of leading organizations have suggested the use of guidelines to limit police discretion. The American Bar Association (ABA) states, "Since individual police officers may make important decisions affecting police operations without discretion, with limited accountability and without any uniformity within a department, police discretion should be structured and controlled."[85] There is an almost unanimous opinion that steps must be taken to provide better control and guidance over police discretion in street and station house adjustments of juvenile cases.

One leading exponent of police discretion is Kenneth Culp Davis, who has done much to raise the consciousness of criminal justice practitioners about discretionary decision making. Davis recommends controlling administrative discretion through (1) the use of more narrowly defined laws, (2) the development of written policies, and (3) the recording of decisions by criminal justice personnel.[86] Narrowing the scope of juvenile codes, for example, would limit and redefine the broad authority police officers currently have to take youths into custody for criminal and noncriminal behavior. Such practices would provide fair criteria for arrests, adjustment, and police referral of juvenile offenders and would help eliminate largely personal judgments based on race, attitude, or demeanor of the juvenile.[87] Discretionary decision making in juvenile police work can be better understood by examining Figure 13.3.

TO QUIZ YOURSELF ON THIS MATERIAL, go to the Juvenile Delinquency 9e website.

POLICE WORK AND DELINQUENCY PREVENTION

Police have taken the lead in delinquency prevention. They have used a number of strategies: some rely on their deterrent powers; others rely on their relationship with schools, the community, and other juvenile justice agencies; and others rely on a problem-solving model. Concept Summary 13.2 lists the main police strategies to prevent delinquency.

Concept Summary 13.2
Police Strategies to Prevent Delinquency

Strategy	Scope
Aggressive law enforcement	High visibility; making arrests for minor and serious infractions.
Police in schools	Collaborate with school staff to create a safer school environment and develop programs.
Problem-oriented policing	Focus on problems underlying criminal incidents; often engage community and other juvenile justice agencies.
Community-based policing services and community policing	Engage citizens and community-based organizations.

Aggressive Law Enforcement

One method of contemporary delinquency prevention relies on aggressive patrolling targeted at specific patterns of delinquency. Police departments in Chicago and Los Angeles have at one time used saturation patrols, targeting gang areas and arresting members for any law violations. These tactics have not proven to be effective against gangs. For example, in 1996 the Dallas Police Department initiated a successful gang-control effort that employed such tactics as saturating known gang areas with anti-gang units, as well as aggressive enforcement of curfew and truancy laws. Targeting truancy and curfew laws led to a significant reduction in gang activity, whereas the saturation patrols proved ineffective.[88]

Police in Schools

You can visit **G.R.E.A.T.'s website** at www.great-online. org. For an up-to-date list of web links, go to http://cj.wadsworth.com/ siegel_jd9e.

One of the most important institutions playing a role in delinquency prevention is the school (see Chapter 9). In schools across the country, there are almost 14,000 full-time police working as school resource officers. In addition to helping make the school environment safe for students and teachers, school resource officers work closely with

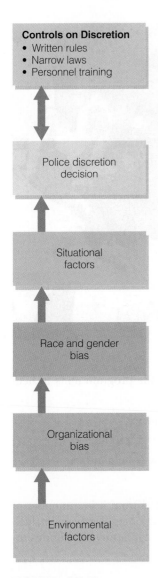

Controls on Discretion
- Written rules
- Narrow laws
- Personnel training

Police discretion decision

Situational factors

Race and gender bias

Organizational bias

Environmental factors

FIGURE **13.3**
Discretionary Justice with Juveniles

staff and administrators in developing delinquency prevention programs.[89] For example, these officers and liaison officers from schools and police departments have played a leadership role in developing recreational programs for juveniles. In some instances, police have actually operated such programs. In others, they have encouraged community support for recreational activities, including Little League baseball, athletic clubs, camping outings, and police athletic and scouting programs.

The Gang Resistance Education and Training (G.R.E.A.T.) program is one example of a police and school partnership to reduce delinquency. Modeled after D.A.R.E. (Drug Abuse and Resistance Education; see Chapter 10), G.R.E.A.T. was developed among a number of Arizona police departments in an effort to reduce adolescent involvement in criminal behavior. Today the program is in school curricula in all 50 states and the District of Columbia.[90] The program's primary objective is the prevention of delinquency and gang involvement. Trained police officers administer the program in school classrooms about once a week. The program consists of four components: a 13-week middle school curriculum (see Exhibit 13.3 for its 13 lessons), a 6-week elementary school curriculum, a summer program, and family training.

Evaluations of G.R.E.A.T. when it was just an eight-week program for middle school students showed mixed results in reducing delinquency and gang involvement. One evaluation found that students who completed the curriculum developed more prosocial attitudes and had lower rates of gang membership and delinquency than those in a comparison group who were not exposed to G.R.E.A.T.[91] Another evaluation of the program, four years after students completed the curriculum, did not find any significant differences for gang membership or delinquency compared to a control group. The evaluation did find that those who took the program held more prosocial attitudes than those who did not.[92] These evaluations contributed to the new and more comprehensive program, which was implemented on a national scale in 2003. Future evaluations will tell if these changes improve G.R.E.A.T.'s impact on delinquency, youth violence, and gang involvement.

Another example of police working in close collaboration with schools is the Community Outreach Through Police in Schools Program. This program brings together Yale University's Child Study Center and the New Haven Police Department to address the mental health and emotional needs of middle-school students who have

EXHIBIT **13.3**

Lessons of the Middle School G.R.E.A.T. Program

1. **Welcome to G.R.E.A.T.** Students get acquainted with the program.
2. **What's the Real Deal?** Students learn facts and myths about gangs and violence.
3. **It's About Us.** Students learn about their roles and responsibilities to their community and what they can do about gangs.
4. **Where Do We Go from Here?** Students are taught how to set realistic and achievable goals.
5. **Decisions, Decisions, Decisions.** Students learn the impact of decisions on goals.
6. **Do You Hear What I Am Saying?** Students are taught effective communication skills.
7. **Walk in Someone Else's Shoes.** Students learn about expressing empathy for others.
8. **Say It Like You Mean It.** Students learn about self-expression.
9. **Getting Along Without Going Along.** Students become acquainted with negative influences and peer pressure and how to resist them.
10. **Keeping Your Cool.** Students are taught techniques to control anger.
11. **Keeping It Together.** Students are taught techniques to recognize anger in others and how to diffuse that anger.
12. **Working It Out.** Students learn about resolving interpersonal conflict and where to go for help.
13. **Looking Back.** Students review what they have learned and think about how to make their school safe.

SOURCE: Bureau of Justice Assistance, Gang Resistance Education and Training (Washington, DC: Office of Justice Programs, Bureau of Justice Assistance, 2004, retrieved from www.great-online.org).

Increased youth gang and violence problems have given rise to many innovative police-led delinquency prevention programs. One of these is the Gang Resistance Education and Training (G.R.E.A.T.) program, which aims to reduce gang activity. Partnering with schools across the country, trained police officers instruct middle-school students on conflict resolution, social responsibility, and the dangers of gang life.

Bureau of Justice Assistance, U.S. Department of Justice

been exposed to violence in the community. Specifically, the program aims to help these students:

I Better understand the way their feelings affect their behavior.

I Develop constructive means of responding to violence and trauma.

I Change their attitudes toward police and learn how to seek help in their community.[93]

An evaluation of the program found that students benefited from it in a number of ways, including improved emotional and psychological functioning (for example, feeling less nervous, having fewer thoughts of death), as well as improved attitudes toward and relationships with the police.[94]

Community-Based Policing Services

Some police departments are now replacing more aggressive measures with cooperative community-based efforts. Because police officers are responsible for the care of juveniles taken into custody, it is essential that they work closely with social service groups day by day. In addition, the police are assuming a leadership role in identifying the needs of children in the community and helping the community meet those needs. In helping to develop delinquency prevention programs, the police are working closely with youth service bureaus, schools, recreational facilities, welfare agencies, and employment programs.

Using community services for juveniles has many advantages. Such services allow young people to avoid the stigma of being processed by a police agency. They also improve the community's awareness of the needs of young people and make it possible to restrict court referral to cases involving serious crime.

Curfews represent a community-based policing service. Curfew laws vary with respect to the locale affected, the time frame, and the sanctions. Most restrict minors to their homes or property between the hours of 11:00 P.M. and 6:00 A.M. Sanctions for curfew violations by youths range from fines to being charged with a misdemeanor violation, and may include participation in diversion programs or, in some jurisdictions, jail time for parents.

Curfew enforcement activities are implemented through regular law enforcement and special policing units. High quality evaluation studies of the impact of juvenile curfew ordinances are limited, but a recent assessment of the empirical evidence, including an evaluation of a curfew law in Charlotte, North Carolina, suggests that on their own, curfews are not effective in managing juveniles or reducing juvenile delinquency.[95] A recent systematic review of the existing empirical research on juvenile curfew laws reached the same conclusion.[96] The review also found that juvenile curfew laws had no lasting impact on reducing juvenile victimization, an important community justification for these laws.

Problem-Oriented Policing

Also referred to as problem-solving policing, problem-oriented policing involves a systematic analysis and response to the problems or conditions underlying criminal incidents rather than the incidents themselves.[97] The theory is that by attending to the underlying problems that cause criminal incidents, the police will have a greater chance of preventing the crimes from reoccurring—the main problem with reactive or "incident-driven policing."[98] However, as noted by Harvard criminologist Mark Moore, "This is not the same as seeking out the root causes of the crime problem in general. It is a much shallower, more situational approach."[99]

The systematic nature of problem-oriented policing is characterized by its adherence to a four-step model, often referred to as S.A.R.A., which stands for Scanning, Analysis, Response, and Assessment. Descriptions of the four steps are as follows:

1. Scanning involves identifying a specific crime problem through various data sources (for example, victim surveys, 911 calls).

2. Analysis involves carrying out an in-depth analysis of the crime problem and its underlying causes.

3. Response brings together the police and other partners to develop and implement a response to the problem based on the results produced in the analysis stage.

4. Assessment is the stage in which the response to the problem is evaluated.[100]

Like community policing, problem-oriented policing is viewed as a proactive delinquency prevention strategy. Unlike community policing, however, the engagement of the community in problem-oriented policing is not imperative, but more often than not these operations involve close collaborations with the community. Collaborations with other juvenile justice agencies are also common in problem-oriented policing operations.

As you may recall, problem-oriented policing has been shown to be effective in reducing juvenile delinquency in some circumstances. One of the most successful applications of this policing strategy is Boston's Operation Ceasefire,[101] which is the subject of the Policy and Practice box.

Following on the success of the Boston program, the Office of Juvenile Justice and Delinquency Prevention (OJJDP) launched a comprehensive initiative to reduce juvenile gun violence in four other cities (Baton Rouge and Shreveport, Louisiana; Oakland, California; and Syracuse, New York). Called the Partnerships to Reduce Juvenile Gun Violence Program, problem-oriented policing strategies are at the center of the program, but other intervention strategies are also important. These include specific delinquency prevention strategies (job training and mentoring), juvenile justice sanctions, and a public information campaign designed to communicate the dangers and consequences of gun violence to juveniles, families, and community residents.[102] An evaluation of the implementation of the program found that

To learn about other **problem-oriented policing programs**, go to www.popcenter.org. For an up-to-date list of web links, go to http://cj.wadsworth.com/siegel_jd9e.

Boston's Operation Ceasefire

One of the most successful examples of problem-oriented policing focused on reducing juvenile crime and violence is the program known as Operation Ceasefire. Implemented in Boston, this program aims to reduce youth homicide victimization and youth gun violence. Although it is a police-led program, Operation Ceasefire involves many other juvenile and criminal justice and social agencies, including probation and parole, the Bureau of Alcohol, Tobacco, Firearms, and Explosives (ATF), gang outreach and prevention street workers, and the Drug Enforcement Administration (DEA). This group of agencies has become known as the Ceasefire Working Group.

The program has two main elements:

1. A direct law enforcement focus on illicit gun traffickers who supply youth with guns
2. An attempt to generate a strong deterrent to gang violence

A wide range of measures have been used to reduce the flow of guns to youth, including pooling the resources of local, state, and federal justice authorities to track and seize illegal guns and targeting traffickers of the types of guns most used by gang members. The response to gang violence has been to pull every deterrence "lever" available, including shutting down drug markets, serving warrants, enforcing probation restrictions, and making disorder arrests. The Ceasefire Working Group delivered its message clearly to gang members: "We're ready, we're watching, we're waiting: Who wants to be next?" An example of how the Working Group communicated this message to gang members is shown by the following poster, which was displayed throughout known gang areas in the city.

FREDDIE CARDOZA

Problem:
Violent Gang Member

"Given his extensive criminal record,
if there was a Federal law against
jaywalking, we'd indict him for that."

—Don Stern, U.S. Attorney

Solution:
Armed Career Criminal Conviction

Arrested with one bullet
Sentence: 19 years, 7 months
No possibility of parole

Address:

Otisville Federal Correctional Institute
Maximum Security Facility, New York

An evaluation from before the program started to the time it ended showed a 63 percent reduction in the mean monthly number of youth homicide victims across the city. The program was also associated with significant decreases in the mean monthly number of gun assaults and overall gang violence across the city. In a comparison with other New England cities and large cities across the United States, most of which also experienced a reduction in youth homicides over the same period, it was found that the significant reduction in youth homicides in Boston was due to Operation Ceasefire.

Maintaining the level of intensity of this program and cooperation of the many agencies involved, which are essential ingredients of its success, has not been easy. In recent years, there have been cutbacks in local policing, fewer federal criminal justice resources made available to the program, and a perception that the deterrence strategy is no longer focused on the most dangerous suspects. Recent research suggests that in order for the program to maintain its success it will also have to adapt to changes in the nature of gang and youth violence across the city.

While the city of Boston works to improve its program, similar problem-oriented policing programs have been established in cities across the country. Of great interest is the replication of this program in an area of Los Angeles that suffers from exceptionally high rates of juvenile violence. The implementation of this program shows much promise, and an evaluation of the program is planned.

Critical Thinking

1. What is the importance of having a multidisciplinary team as part of the program?
2. With comprehensive programs it is often difficult to assess the independent effects of the different program elements. In your opinion, what is the most important element of this program? Why?

InfoTrac College Edition Research

For more information on problem-oriented policing and juvenile delinquency, go to InfoTrac College Edition and read Terry Eisenberg and Bruce Glassoock, "Looking Inward with Problem-Oriented Policing," *FBI Law Enforcement Bulletin* 70:1 (July 2001).

SOURCES: Anthony A. Braga, David M. Kennedy, Elin J. Waring, and Anne Morrison Piehl, "Problem-Oriented Policing Deterrence, and Youth Violence: An Evaluation of Boston's Operation Ceasefire," *Journal of Research in Crime and Delinquency* 38:195–225 (2001); Fox Butterfield, "Killing of Girl, 10, and Increase in Homicides Challenge Boston's Crime-Fighting Model," *New York Times*, July 14, 2002; David M. Kennedy, Anthony A. Braga, and Anne Morrison Piehl, "Developing and Implementing Operation Ceasefire," in *Reducing Gun Violence: The Boston Gun Project's Operation Ceasefire* (Washington, DC: NIJ Research Report, 2001); David M. Kennedy, "Pulling Levers: Chronic Offenders, High-Crime Settings, and a Theory of Prevention," *Valparaiso University Law Review* 31:449–484 (1997); David M. Kennedy, "Pulling Levers: Getting Deterrence Right," *National Institute of Justice Journal* (July):2–8 (1998), p. 6; Jack McDevitt, Anthony A. Braga, Dana Nurge, and Michael Buerger, "Boston's Youth Violence Prevention Program: A Comprehensive Community-Wide Approach," in Scott H. Decker, ed., *Policing Gangs and Youth Violence* (Belmont, CA: Wadsworth, 2003); George Tita, K. Jack Riley, and Peter Greenwood, "From Boston to Boyle Heights: The Process and Prospects of a 'Pulling Levers' Strategy in a Los Angeles Barrio," in Decker, ed., *Policing Gangs and Youth Violence*.

To read more about the **Partnerships to Reduce Juvenile Gun Violence Program,** go to www.ojjdp.ncjrs.org/pubs/gun_violence/profile08.html. For an up-to-date list of web links, go to http://cj.wadsworth.com/siegel_jd9e.

three of the four cities were successful in developing comprehensive strategies.[103] An evaluation of the effectiveness of the program in reducing juvenile gun violence is underway.[104] With successful implementation and inclusion of many of the components of the Boston program, this program offers promise in reducing juvenile violence.

Around the same time in the late-1990s, the federal COPS Office initiated a national Problem-Solving Partnerships (PSP) program with the objective of assisting police agencies to "solve recurrent crime and disorder problems by helping them form community partnerships and engage in problem-solving activities."[105] Various case studies to emerge out of a national evaluation of this program by the Police Executive Research Forum identify a wide range of successful efforts to reduce delinquency.[106]

Today, many experts consider delinquency prevention efforts to be crucial to the development of a comprehensive approach to youth crime. Although such efforts cut across the entire juvenile justice system, police programs have become increasingly popular.

Summary

- Modern policing developed in England at the beginning of the nineteenth century. The Industrial Revolution, recognition of the need to treat children as a distinguishable group, and growing numbers of unemployed and homeless youths were among some of the key events that helped shape juvenile policing in America.

- The role of juvenile officers is similar to that of officers working with adult offenders: to intervene if the actions of a citizen produce public danger or disorder. Juvenile officers must also have a thorough knowledge of the law, especially the constitutional protections available to juveniles.

- Juvenile officers operate either as specialists in a police department or as part of the juvenile unit of a police department.

- Through the *Miranda v. Arizona* decision, the U.S. Supreme Court established a clearly defined procedure for custodial interrogation.

- Most courts have held that the Fourth Amendment ban against unreasonable search and seizure applies to juveniles and that illegally seized evidence is inadmissible in a juvenile trial. Most courts have concluded that parents or attorneys need not be present for chil-

dren effectively to waive their right to remain silent.

- Discretion is a low-visibility decision made in the administration of adult and juvenile justice. Discretionary decisions are made without guidelines from the police administrator. Numerous factors influence the decisions police make about juvenile offenders, including the seriousness of the offense, the harm inflicted on the victim, and the likelihood that the juvenile will break the law again.

- Discretion is essential in providing individualized justice, but problems such as discrimination, unfairness, and bias toward particular groups of juveniles must be controlled.

- Police have taken the lead in delinquency prevention. Major policing strategies to prevent delinquency include aggressive law enforcement, police in schools, community-based and community policing, and problem-oriented policing.

- The ever-changing nature of juvenile delinquency calls for further experimentation and innovation in policing strategies to prevent delinquency. Tailoring policing activities to local conditions and engaging the community and other stakeholders are important first steps.

Key Terms

pledge system, p. 394
watch system, p. 394
community policing, p. 395
juvenile officers, p. 398

role conflicts, p. 398
problem-oriented policing, p. 400
arrest, p. 401
probable cause, p. 401

search and seizure, p. 401
custodial interrogation, p. 402
Miranda warning, p. 403
discretion, p. 403

Questions for Discussion

1. The term discretion is often defined as selective decision making by police and others in the juvenile justice system who are faced with alternative modes of action. Discuss some of the factors affecting the discretion of the police when dealing with juvenile offenders.

2. What role should police organizations play in delinquency prevention and control? Is it feasible to expect police departments to provide social services to children and families? How should police departments be better organized to provide for the control of juvenile delinquency?

3. What qualities should a juvenile police officer have? Should a college education be a requirement?

4. In light of the traditional and protective roles assumed by law enforcement personnel in juvenile justice, is there any reason to have a *Miranda* warning for youths taken into custody?

5. Can the police and community be truly effective in forming a partnership to reduce juvenile delinquency? Discuss the role of the juvenile police officer in preventing and investigating juvenile crime.

6. The experience of Boston's successful Operation Ceasefire program suggests that it may be difficult to sustain the needed intensity and problem-solving partnerships to keep violent juvenile crime under control over the long term. What other innovative problem-oriented policing measures could be employed to achieve this?

Viewpoint

You are a newly appointed police officer assigned to a juvenile unit of a medium-sized urban police department. Wayne G. is an 18-year-old white male who was caught shoplifting with two male friends of the same age. Wayne attempted to leave a large department store with a $25 shirt and was apprehended by a police officer in front of the store.

Wayne seemed quite remorseful about the offense. He said several times that he didn't know why he did it and that he had not planned to do it. He seemed upset and scared, and while admitting the offense, did not want to go to court. Wayne had three previous contacts with the police as a juvenile: one for malicious mischief when he destroyed some property, another involving a minor assault on a boy, and a third involving another shoplifting charge. In all three cases, Wayne promised to refrain from ever committing such acts again, and as a result was not required to go to court. The other shoplifting incident involved a small baseball worth only $3.

Wayne appeared at the police department with his mother. His parents are divorced. The mother did not seem overly concerned about the case and felt that her son was not really to blame. She argued that he was always getting in trouble and she was not sure how to control him. She blamed most of his troubles with the law on his being in the wrong crowd. Besides, a $25 shirt was "no big deal" and she offered to pay back the store. The store had left matters in the hands of the police and would support any decision you make.

Deciding what to do in a case like Wayne's is a routine activity for most police officers. When dealing with juveniles, they must consider not only the nature of the offense but also the needs of the juvenile. Police officers realize that actions they take can have a long-term effect on an adolescent's future.

- Would you submit Wayne's case for prosecution, release him with a warning, or use some other tactic?

- Should police officers be forced to act as counselors for troubled youth?

Doing Research on the Web

Before you answer, you may want to learn more about this topic by checking out the following websites (sites accessed on October 15, 2004):

International Association of Chiefs of Police
www.theiacp.org

Police Foundation
www.policefoundation.org

Police Executive Research Forum
http://policeforum.mn-8.net

National Academy of Science's Panel on Police Policies and Practices
http://books.nap.edu/catalog/10419.html

To research police handling of juveniles suspected of committing crimes, use "police and discretion" in a key word search on InfoTrac College Edition.

Notes

1. This section relies on sources such as Malcolm Sparrow, Mark Moore, and David Kennedy, *Beyond 911, A New Era for Policing* (New York: Basic Books, 1990); Daniel Devlin, *Police Procedure, Administration, and Organization* (London: Butterworth, 1966); Robert Fogelson, *Big City Police* (Cambridge: Harvard University Press, 1977); Roger Lane, *Policing the City, Boston 1822–1885* (Cambridge: Harvard University Press, 1967); Roger Lane, "Urban Police and Crime in Nineteenth-Century America," in Norval Morris and Michael Tonry, eds., *Crime and Justice*, vol. 2 (Chicago: University of Chicago Press, 1980), pp. 1–45; J. J. Tobias, *Crime and Industrial Society in the Nineteenth Century* (New York: Schocken, 1967); Samuel Walker, *A Critical History of Police Reform: The Emergence of Professionalism* (Lexington, MA: Lexington Books, 1977); idem, *Popular Justice* (New York: Oxford University Press, 1980); President's Commission on Law Enforcement and the Administration of Justice, *Task Force Report: The Police* (Washington, DC: U.S. Government Printing Office, 1967), pp. 1–9.

2. See Walker, *Popular Justice*, p. 61.

3. Law Enforcement Assistance Administration, *Two Hundred Years of American Criminal Justice* (Washington, DC: U.S. Government Printing Office, 1976).

4. August Vollmer, *The Police and Modern Society* (Berkeley: University of California Press, 1936).

5. O. W. Wilson, *Police Administration*, 2nd ed. (New York: McGraw-Hill, 1963).

6. Herman Goldstein, "Toward Community-Oriented Policing: Potential Basic Requirements and Threshold Questions," *Crime and Delinquency* 33:630 (1987); see also Janet Reno, "Taking America Back for Our Children," *Crime and Delinquency* 44:75 (1998).

7. Lawrence W. Sherman and Richard Berk, "The Specific Deterrent Effects of Arrest for Domestic Assault," *American Sociological Review* 49:261–272 (1984).

8. John E. Eck and Edward R. Maguire, "Have Changes in Policing Reduced Violent Crime? An Assessment of the Evidence," in Alfred Blumstein and Joel Wallman, eds., *The Crime Drop in America* (New York: Cambridge University Press, 2000); Lawrence W. Sherman, "Fair and Effective Policing," in James Q. Wilson and Joan Petersilia, eds., *Crime: Public Policies for Crime Control* (Oakland, CA: Institute for Contemporary Studies, 2002); Lawrence W. Sherman and John E. Eck, "Policing for Crime Prevention," in Lawrence W. Sherman, David P. Farrington, Brandon C. Welsh, and Doris Layton MacKenzie, eds., *Evidence-Based Crime Prevention* (New York: Routledge, 2002).

9. Yolander Hurst, James Frank, and Sandra Lee Browning, "The Attitudes of Juveniles toward the Police: A Comparison of Black and White Youth," *Policing* 23:37–53 (2000).

10. Terrance J. Taylor, K.B. Turner, Finn-Aage Esbensen, and L. Thomas Winfree, Jr., "Coppin' an Attitude: Attitudinal Differences among Juveniles Toward Police," *Journal of Criminal Justice* 29:295–305 (2001), p. 300.

11. For an analysis of this position, see George Kelling and James Q. Wilson, "Broken Windows: The Police and Neighborhood Safety," *Atlantic Monthly* 249:29–38 (1982).

12. U.S. Department of Justice, "Community Policing," *National Institute of Justice Journal* 225:1–32 (1992).

13. Robert Trojanowicz and Hazel Harden, *The Status of Contemporary Community Policing Programs* (East Lansing, MI: Michigan State University Neighborhood Foot Patrol Center, 1985).

14. Matthew J. Hickman and Brian A. Reaves, *Local Police Departments, 2000* (Washington, DC: Bureau of Justice Statistics, 2003), p. 15.

15. Terence Dunworth, *National Evaluation of the Youth Firearms Violence Initiative* (Washington, DC: NIJ Research in Brief, 2000), p. 1.

16. Ibid., p. 4.

17. See Anthony A. Braga, *Gun Violence Among Serious Young Offenders* (Washington, DC: Office of Community Oriented Policing Services, U.S. Department of Justice, 2004).

18. *Project Safe Neighborhoods: America's Network Against Gun Violence* (Washington, DC: Bureau of Justice Assistance Program Brief, 2004).

19. Susan Guarino-Ghezzi, "Reintegrative Police Surveillance of Juvenile Offenders: Forging an Urban Model," *Crime and Delinquency* 40:131–153 (1994).

20. See David Weisburd and John E. Eck, "What Can Police Do to Reduce Crime, Disorder, and Fear?" *Annals of the American Academy of Political and Social Science* 593:42–65 (2004), p. 57, Table 1.

21. Michael D. Reisig and Roger B. Parks, "Community Policing and Quality of Life," in Wesley G. Skogan, ed., *Community Policing: Can It Work?* (Belmont, CA: Wadsworth, 2004).

22. The President's Crime Prevention Council, *Preventing Crime and Promoting Responsibility: 50 Programs that Help Communities Help Their Youth* (Washington, DC: U.S. Government Printing Office, 1995).

23. Donald Black and Albert J. Reiss, Jr., "Police Control of Juveniles," *American Sociological Review* 35:63 (1970); Richard Lundman, Richard Sykes, and John Clark, "Police Control of Juveniles: A Replication," *Journal of Research on Crime and Delinquency* 15:74 (1978).

24. American Bar Association, *Standards Relating to Police Handling of Juvenile Problems* (Cambridge, MA: Ballinger, 1977), p. 1.

25. FBI, *Crime in the United States 2002* (Washington, DC: U.S. Government Printing Office, 2003), p. 291.

26. Samuel Walker, *The Police of America* (New York: McGraw-Hill, 1983), p. 133.

27. Karen A. Joe, "The Dynamics of Running Away, Deinstitutionalization Policies and the Police," *Juvenile Family Court Journal* 46:43–45 (1995).

28. Richard J. Lundman, *Prevention and Control of Delinquency*, 3rd ed. (New York: Oxford University Press, 2001), p. 23.

29. National Conference of State Legislatures, *A Legislator's Guide to Comprehensive Juvenile Justice, Interventions for Youth at Risk* (Denver: NCSL, 1996).

30. Sherman and Eck, "Policing for Crime Prevention," p. 321; for "hot spots" policing, see also Wesley G. Skogan and Kathleen Frydl, eds., *Fairness and Effectiveness in Policing: The Evidence* (Washington, DC: National Academy Press, Committee to Review Research on Police Policy and Practices, 2004); Anthony A. Braga, "The Effects of Hot Spots Policing on Crime," *Annals of the American Academy of Political and Social Science* 578:104–125 (2001).

31. See, for example, Edmund F. McGarrell, Steven Chermak, Alexander Weiss, and Jeremy Wilson, "Reducing Firearms Violence through Directed Police Patrol," *Criminology and Public Policy* 1:119–148 (2001).

32. Linda Szymanski, *Summary of Juvenile Code Purpose Clauses* (Pittsburgh: National Center for Juvenile Justice, 1988); see also, for example, GA Code Ann. 15; Iowa Code Ann. 232.2; Mass. Gen. Laws, ch. 119, 56.

33. Samuel M. Davis, *Rights of Juveniles—The Juvenile Justice System* (New York: Clark-Boardmen, rev. June 1989), Sec. 3.3.

34. National Council of Juvenile and Family Court Judges, *Juvenile and Family Law Digest* 29:1–2 (1997).

35. See Fourth Amendment, U.S. Constitution.

36. *Chimel v. Cal.*, 395 U.S. 752, 89 S.Ct. 2034 (1969).

37. *United States v. Ross*, 456 U.S. 798, 102 S.Ct. 2157 (1982).

38. *Terry v. Ohio*, 392 U.S.1, 88 S.Ct. 1868 (1968).

39. *Bumper v. North Carolina*, 391 U.S. 543, 88 S.Ct. 1788 (1968).

40. *Miranda v. Arizona*, 384 U.S. 436, 86 S.Ct. 1602 (1966).

41. *Commonwealth v. Gaskins*, 471 Pa. 238, 369 A.2d 1285 (1977); *In re E.T.C.*, 141 Vt. 375, 449 A.2d 937 (1982).

42. *People v. Lara*, 67 Cal.2d 365, 62 Cal.Rptr. 586, 432 P.2d 202 (1967).

43. *West v. United States*, 399 F.2d 467 (5th Cir. 1968).

44. *Fare v. Michael C.*, 442 U.S. 707, 99 S.Ct. 2560 (1979).

45. *California v. Prysock*, 453 U.S. 355, 101 S.Ct. 2806 (1981).

46. See, for example, Larry Holtz, "*Miranda* in a Juvenile Setting—A Child's Right to Silence," *Journal of Criminal Law and Criminology* 79:534–556 (1987).

47. Kenneth C. Davis, *Discretionary Justice: A Preliminary Inquiry* (Baton Rouge: Louisiana State University Press, 1969); H. Ted Rubin, *Juvenile Justice: Police, Practice and Law* (Santa Monica: Goodyear, 1979).

48. Joseph Goldstein, "Police Discretion Not to Invoke the Criminal Process: Low-Visibility Decisions in the Administration of Justice," *Yale Law Journal* 69:544 (1960).

49. Victor Streib, *Juvenile Justice in America* (Port Washington, NY: Kennikat, 1978).

50. Herbert Packer, *The Limits of the Criminal Sanction* (Palo Alto, CA: Stanford University Press, 1968).

51. Black and Reiss, "Police Control of Juveniles"; Richard J. Lundman, "Routine Police Arrest Practices," *Social Problems* 22:127–141 (1974); Robert E. Worden and Stephanie M. Myers, *Police Encounters with Juvenile Suspects* (Albany, NY: Hindelang Criminal Justice Research Center and School of Criminal Justice, University at Albany, SUNY, 2001).

52. Nathan Goldman, *The Differential Selection of Juvenile Offenders for Court Appearance* (Washington, DC: National Council on Crime and Delinquency, 1963).

53. Irving Piliavin and Scott Briar, "Police Encounters with Juveniles," *American Journal of Sociology* 70:206–214 (1964); Theodore Ferdinand and Elmer Luchterhand, "Inner-City Youth, the Police, Juvenile Court, and Justice," *Social Problems* 8:510–526 (1970).

54. Paul Strasburg, *Violent Delinquents: Report to Ford Foundation from Vera Institute of Justice* (New York: Monarch, 1978), p. 11; Robert Terry, "The Screening of Juvenile Offenders," *Journal of Criminal Law, Criminology, and Police Science* 58:173–181 (1967).

55. Joan McCord, Cathy Spatz Widom, and Nancy A. Crowell, eds., *Juvenile Crime, Juvenile Justice.* Panel on Juvenile Crime: Prevention, Treatment, and Control (Washington, DC: National Academy Press, 2001), p. 163.

56. Worden and Myers, *Police Encounters with Juvenile Suspects.*

57. FBI, *Crime in the United States 2002.*

58. Douglas Smith and Christy Visher, "Street-Level Justice: Situational Determinants of Police Arrest Decisions," *Social Problems* 29:167–178 (1981).

59. Douglas Smith and Jody Klein, "Police Control of Interpersonal Disputes," *Social Problems* 31:468–481 (1984).

60. Goldman, *The Differential Selection of Juvenile Offenders for Court Appearance*, p. 25; Norman Werner and Charles Willie, "Decisions of Juvenile Officers," *American Journal of Sociology* 77:199–214 (1971).

61. Aaron Cicourel, *The Social Organization of Juvenile Justice* (New York: Wiley, 1968).

62. Piliavin and Briar, "Police Encounters with Juveniles," p. 214.

63. David Klinger, "Demeanor or Crime? Why 'Hostile' Citizens Are More Likely to Be Arrested," *Criminology* 32:475–493 (1994).

64. Richard Lundman, "Demeanor or Crime? The Midwest City Police-Citizen Encounters Study," *Criminology* 32:631–653 (1994); Robert Worden and Robin Shepard, "On the Meaning, Measurement, and Estimated Effects of Suspects' Demeanor toward the Police." Paper presented at the American Society of Criminology meeting, Miami, November 1994.

65. James Fyfe, David Klinger, and Jeanne Flaving, "Differential Police Treatment of Male-on-Female Spousal Violence," *Criminology* 35:455–473 (1997).

66. Dale Dannefer and Russel Schutt, "Race and Juvenile Justice Processing in Police and Court Agencies," *American Journal of Sociology* 87:1113–1132 (1982); Smith and Visher, "Street-Level Justice: Situational Determinants of Police Arrest Decisions"; also, Ronald Weitzer, "Racial Discrimination in the Criminal Justice System: Findings and Problems in the Literature," *Journal of Criminal Justice* 24:309–322 (1996); Ronald Weitzer and Steven A. Tuch, "Perceptions of Racial Profiling: Race, Class, and Personal Experience," *Criminology* 40:435–456 (2002).

67. Richard J. Lundman and Robert L. Kaufman, "Driving While Black: Effects of Race, Ethnicity, and Gender on Citizen Self-Reports of Traffic Stops and Police Actions," *Criminology* 41:195–220 (2003).

68. Dan M. Kahan and Tracey L. Meares, "The Coming Crisis of Criminal Procedure," *Georgetown Law Journal* 86:1153–1184 (2000).

69. Randall Kennedy, *Race, Crime and the Law* (New York: Vintage, 1998).

70. Terence Thornberry, "Race, Socioeconomic Status, and Sentencing in the Juvenile Justice System," *Journal of Criminal Law and Criminology* 70:164–171 (1979); Dannefer and Schutt, "Race and Juvenile Justice Processing in Police and Court Agencies"; Jeffrey Fagan, Ellen Slaughter, and Eliot Hartstone, "Blind Justice? The Impact of Race on the Juvenile Justice Process," *Crime and Delinquency* 33:224–258 (1987).

71. Donna M. Bishop and Charles E. Frazier, "The Influence of Race in Juvenile Justice Processing," *Journal of Research in Crime and Delinquency* 25:242–261 (1988).

72. Ibid., p. 258; see also Howard N. Snyder and Melissa Sickmund, *Juvenile Offenders and Victims: 1999 National Report* (Pittsburgh: National Center for Juvenile Justice, 1999), p. 192.

73. National Council on Crime and Delinquency, *The Over-Representation of Minority Youth in the California Juvenile Justice System* (San Francisco: NCCD, 1992).

74. See Samuel Walker, Cassie Spohn, and Miriam DeLone, *The Color of Justice: Race, Ethnicity, and Crime in America* (Belmont, CA: Wadsworth, 1996).

75. Merry Morash, "Establishment of a Juvenile Record: The Influence of Individual and Peer Group Characteristics," *Criminology* 22:97–112 (1984).

76. Meda Chesney-Lind, "Judicial Enforcement of the Female Sex Role: The Family Court and Female Delinquency Issues," *Criminology* 8:51–71 (1973); idem, "Young Women in the Arms of Law," in L. Bowker, ed., *Women, Crime, and the Criminal Justice System*, 2nd ed. (Lexington, MA: Lexington Books, 1978).

77. Donna Bishop and Charles Frazier, "Gender Bias in Juvenile Justice Processing: Implications of the JJDP Act," *Journal of Criminal Law and Criminology* 82:1162–1186 (1992).

78. Meda Chesney-Lind and Randall G. Shelden, *Girls, Delinquency, and Juvenile Justice*, 3rd ed. (Belmont, CA: Wadsworth, 2004), p. 35.

79. Douglas Smith, "The Organizational Context of Legal Control," *Criminology* 22:19–38 (1984); see also Stephen Mastrofski and Richard Ritti, "Police Training and the Effects of Organization on Drunk Driving Enforcement," *Justice Quarterly* 13:291–320 (1996).

80. John Irwin, *The Jail: Managing the Underclass in American Society* (Berkeley: University of California Press, 1985).

81. Darlene Conley, "Adding Color to a Black and White Picture: Using Qualitative Data to Explain Racial Disproportionality in the Juvenile Justice System," *Journal of Research in Crime and Delinquency* 31:135–148 (1994).

82. Robert Sampson, "Effects of Socioeconomic Context of Official Reaction to Juvenile Delinquency," *American Sociological Review* 51:876–885 (1986).

83. Ronald Weitzer, "White, Black, or Blue Cops? Race and Citizen Assessments of Police Officers," *Journal of Criminal Justice* 28:313–324 (2000).

84. Thomas Priest and Deborah Brown Carter, "Evaluations of Police Performance in an African American Sample," *Journal of Criminal Justice* 27:457–465 (1999); see also Matt De Lisi and Bob Regoli, "Race, Conventional Crime, and Criminal Justice: The Declining Importance of Skin Color," *Journal of Criminal Justice* 27:549–557 (1999).

85. American Bar Association, *Standards of Criminal Justice: Standards Relating to Urban Police Function* (New York: Institute of Judicial Administration, 1972), Standard 4.2, p. 121.

86. Kenneth C. Davis, *Police Discretion* (St. Paul, MN: West, 1975).

87. Robert Shepard, Jr., ed., *Juvenile Justice Standards Annotated—A Balanced Approach* (Chicago: ABA, 1996).

88. Eric Fritsch, Tory Caeti, and Robert Taylor, "Gang Suppression through Saturation Patrol, Aggressive Curfew, and Truancy Enforcement: A Quasi-Experimental Test of the Dallas Anti-Gang Initiative," *Crime and Delinquency* 45:122–139 (1999).

89. Hickman and Reaves, *Local Police Departments, 2000*, p. 15.

90. Finn-Aage Esbensen, D. Wayne Osgood, Terrance J. Taylor, Dana Peterson, and Adrienne Freng, "How Great Is G.R.E.A.T.? Results from a Longitudinal Quasi-Experimental Design," *Criminology and Public Policy* 1:87–118 (2001), p. 88.

91. Finn-Aage Esbensen and D.Wayne Osgood, "Gang Resistance Education and Training (G.R.E.A.T.): Results from the National Evaluation," *Journal of Research in Crime and Delinquency* 36:194–225 (1999).

92. Esbensen, Osgood, Taylor, Peterson, and Freng, "How Great Is G.R.E.A.T.?"

93. Yale University Child Study Center, *Community Outreach Through Police in Schools* (Washington, DC: Office for Victims of Crime Bulletin, 2003), p. 2.

94. Ibid, p. 3.

95. J. David Hirschel, Charles W. Dean, and Doris Dumond, "Juvenile Curfews and Race: A Cautionary Note," *Criminal Justice Policy Review* 12:197–214 (2001), p. 209; see also McCord, Spatz Widom, and Crowell, eds., *Juvenile Crime, Juvenile Justice*, p. 145.

96. Kenneth Adams, "The Effectiveness of Juvenile Curfews at Crime Prevention," *Annals of the American Academy of Political and Social Science* 587:136–159 (2003).

97. Mark H. Moore, "Problem-Solving and Community Policing," in Michael Tonry and Norval Morris, eds., *Modern Policing. Crime and Justice: A Review of Research*, vol. 15 (Chicago: University of Chicago Press, 1992), p. 99.

98. Anthony A. Braga, *Problem-Oriented Policing and Crime Prevention* (Monsey, NY: Criminal Justice Press, 2002), p. 10.

99. Moore, "Problem-Solving and Community Policing," p. 120.

100. Debra Cohen, *Problem-Solving Partnerships: Including the Community for a Change* (Washington, DC: Office of Community Oriented Policing Services, 2001), p. 2.

101. Anthony A. Braga, David M. Kennedy, Elin J. Waring, and Anne Morrison Piehl, "Problem-Oriented Policing Deterrence, and Youth Violence: An Evaluation of Boston's Operation Ceasefire," *Journal of Research in Crime and Delinquency* 38:195–225 (2001).

102. David Sheppard, Heath Grant, Wendy Rowe, and Nancy Jacobs, *Fighting Juvenile Gun Violence* (Washington, DC: OJJDP Juvenile Justice Bulletin, 2000), p. 2.

103. Ibid, p. 10.

104. Alan Lizotte and David Sheppard, *Gun Use by Male Juveniles: Research and Prevention* (Washington, DC: OJJDP Juvenile Justice Bulletin, 2001), p. 7.

105. Cohen, *Problem-Solving Partnerships: Including the Community for a Change*, p. 2.

106. Ibid, pp. 5–7.

14

Juvenile Court Process: Pretrial, Trial, and Sentencing

Chapter Outline

The Juvenile Court and Its Jurisdiction
Court Case Flow
The Actors in the Juvenile Courtroom
Juvenile Court Process
Release or Detain?
POLICY AND PRACTICE: The Detention Diversion
   Advocacy Program
Bail for Children
The Intake Process
JUVENILE LAW IN REVIEW: *Schall v. Martin*
Diversion
The Petition
The Plea and Plea Bargaining
Transfer to the Adult Court
Waiver Procedures
Due Process in the Juvenile Waiver Procedure
Should Youths Be Transferred to Adult Court?
JUVENILE LAW IN REVIEW: *Kent v. United States*
   and *Breed v. Jones*
Juvenile Court Trial
Constitutional Rights at Trial
Disposition
JUVENILE LAW IN REVIEW: *In re Gault*
Juvenile Sentencing Structures
Sentencing Reform
The Death Penalty for Juveniles
The Child's Right to Appeal
Confidentiality in Juvenile Proceedings

Chapter Objectives

1. Understand the roles and responsibilities of the main players in the juvenile court

2. Be able to discuss key issues of the preadjudicatory stage of juvenile justice, including detention, intake, diversion, pretrial release, plea bargaining, and waiver

3. Be able to argue the pros and cons of transferring youths to adult court

4. Understand key issues of the trial stage of juvenile justice, including constitutional rights of youths and disposition

5. Be familiar with major U.S. Supreme Court decisions that have influenced the handling of juveniles at the preadjudicatory and trial stages

6. Know the most common dispositions for juvenile offenders

7. Know the major arguments opposed to and in favor of the death penalty for juveniles

8. Be able to argue the pros and cons of confidentiality in juvenile proceedings and privacy of juvenile records

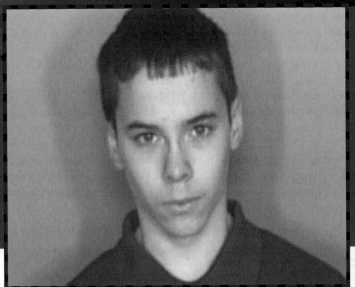

CNN. View the CNN video clip of this story and answer related Critical Thinking questions on your Juvenile Delinquency 9e CD-ROM.

According to the Miami, Florida, state attorney's office, Michael Hernandez, age 14, acted alone and with premeditation in slashing the throat of his friend and classmate, Jaime Gough, also 14, in a bathroom at the Southwood Middle School. Hernandez then returned to class in his blood-soaked clothes. The knife used in the killing, along with a bloody latex glove, was later found in the accused's book bag. Hernandez's waiver to adult court was never in question. Nor will be his sentence if he is convicted of first-degree murder: life without parole. In Florida and in many other states across the country this is a mandatory sentence that the judge must impose. But although this sentence has the support of many, there is growing opposition to its severity for juveniles who are so young and who may benefit from early treatment. One proposal is that juvenile killers under the age of 16 with clean records be eligible for parole after serving a minimum of eight years in a secure juvenile institution. Advocates of this and similar proposals argue that this is in keeping with the juvenile justice system's treatment philosophy and the need to separate juveniles from adult offenders.

Because the judicial process is one of the most critical points in the juvenile justice process, it is covered here in some detail. We begin with a discussion of the juvenile court and its jurisdiction. We then turn to issues involving the preadjudicatory stage of juvenile justice: detention, intake, diversion, pretrial release, plea bargaining, and waiver. The trial stage is examined next, looking at the rights of the child at trial—particularly those rights dealing with counsel and trial by jury—through a detailed analysis of U.S. Supreme Court decisions. Procedural rules that govern the adjudicatory and dispositional hearings are also reviewed. We conclude with a discussion of dispositional alternatives and trends in sentencing.

Today's juvenile delinquency cases are sometimes handled as part of a criminal trial court jurisdiction, or even within the probate court. Also called surrogate court in some states, probate court is a court of special jurisdiction that handles wills, administration of estates, and guardianship of minors and incompetents. However, in most jurisdictions they are treated in the structure of a family court or an independent juvenile court (14 states use more than one method to process juvenile cases).[1] The independent juvenile court is a specialized court for children, designed to promote rehabilitation of youths within a framework of procedural due process. It is concerned with acting both in the best interest of the child and in the best interest of public protection, two often-incompatible goals. Family courts, in contrast, have broad jurisdiction over a wide range of personal and household problems, including delinquency, paternity, child support, and custody issues. The major advantages of such a system are that it can serve sparsely populated areas, it permits judicial personnel and others to deal exclusively with children's matters, and it can obtain legislative funding more readily than other court systems.

Court Case Flow

Today, more than 1.6 million delinquency cases are adjudicated annually. Between 1990 and 1999 (the latest data available), case flow increased 27 percent. The increasing numbers of cases were the product of a significant rise in the number of drug law violation cases (up 169 percent), public order offense cases (up 74 percent), and cases involving personal offenses (up 55 percent); property offense cases, on the other hand, decreased 19 percent.[2]

There were distinct gender- and race-based differences in the juvenile court population. In 1999, 76 percent of delinquency cases involved a male and 24 percent a female. However, the number of females processed by juvenile courts has increased from 1990, when less than 20 percent of the cases involved females. Similarly, 28 percent of the juvenile court population was comprised of African American youth, although African Americans make up only about 15 percent of the general population.[3]

The Actors in the Juvenile Courtroom

The key players in the juvenile court are prosecutors, judges, and defense attorneys.

The Defense Attorney As a result of a series of Supreme Court decisions, the right of a delinquent youth to have counsel at state trials has become a fundamental part of the juvenile justice system.[4] Today, courts must provide counsel to indigent defendants who face the possibility of incarceration. Over the past three decades, the rules of juvenile justice administration have become extremely complex. Preparation of a case for juvenile court often involves detailed investigation of a crime, knowledge of court procedures, use of rules of evidence, and skills in trial advocacy. The right to counsel is essential if children are to have a fair chance of presenting their cases in court.

juvenile defense attorney
Represents children in juvenile court and plays an active role at all stages of the proceedings.

In many respects, the role of **juvenile defense attorney** is similar to that in the criminal and civil areas. Defense attorneys representing children in the juvenile court play an active and important part in virtually all stages of the proceedings. For example, the defense attorney helps to clarify jurisdictional problems and to decide whether there is sufficient evidence to warrant filing a formal petition. The defense attorney helps outline the child's position regarding detention hearings and bail, and explores the opportunities for informal adjustment of the case. If no adjustment or diversion occurs, the defense attorney represents the child at adjudication, presenting

Juvenile defense attorneys play an active and important part in virtually all stages of the juvenile court proceedings, ranging from representing youths in police custody to filing their final appeals.

evidence and cross-examining witnesses to see that the child's position is made clear to the court. Defense attorneys also play a critical role in the dispositional hearing. They present evidence bearing on the treatment decision and help the court formulate alternative plans for the child's care. Finally, defense attorneys pursue any appeals from the trial, represent the child in probation revocation proceedings, and generally protect the child's right to treatment.

Important to these roles is the attorney-juvenile relationship and the competence of the attorney. Some studies report that many juvenile offenders do not trust their attorney,[5] but juvenile offenders represented by private attorneys are more trusting in their attorney than those represented by court-appointed attorneys.[6] One possible reason for this difference may be the belief among juveniles that because court-appointed attorneys work for the "system" they might share information with the judge, police, or others.[7] Another important dimension of the attorney-juvenile relationship is effective participation of the juvenile as a defendant, which "requires a personally relevant understanding of the lawyer's advocacy role and the confidential nature of the attorney-client relationship."[8] A recent study investigating effective participation among juvenile and adult defendants concluded that juveniles are in need of extra procedural safeguards, such as training for lawyers on how to be more effective counselors.[9] There may also be a need to improve the competency of juvenile defense attorneys, as well as to overcome some of the time constraints they face in case preparation. In a study of legal representation of juveniles charged with felonies in three juvenile courts in Missouri, it was found that they were more likely to receive an out-of-home placement disposition (instead of a less punitive disposition) if they had an attorney, even after controlling for other legal and individual factors.[10] (See the following section for other problems specific to public defenders.)

In some cases, a **guardian *ad litem*** may be appointed by the court.[11] The guardian *ad litem*—ordinarily seen in abuse, neglect, and dependency cases—may be appointed in delinquency cases where there is a question of a need for a particular treatment (for example, placement in a mental health center), and offenders and their attorneys resist placement. The guardian *ad litem* may advocate for the commitment on the basis that it is in the child's best interests. This individual fulfills many roles, ranging from legal advocate to concerned individual, who works with parents and human service professionals in developing a proper treatment plan that best serves the interests of the minor child.[12]

guardian *ad litem*
A court-appointed attorney who protects the interests of the child in cases involving the child's welfare.

public defender
An attorney who works in a public agency or under private contractual agreement as defense counsel to indigent defendants.

Court Appointed Special Advocates (CASA) Court Appointed Special Advocates (CASA) employ volunteers who advise the juvenile court about child placement. The CASA programs (*casa* is Spanish for "home") have demonstrated that volunteers can investigate the needs of children and provide a vital link among the judge, the attorneys, and the child in protecting the juvenile's right to a safe placement.[13]

Public Defender Services for Children To satisfy the requirement that indigent children be provided with counsel, the federal government and the states have expanded **public defender** services. Three alternatives exist for providing children with legal counsel: (1) an all–public defender program, (2) an appointed private-counsel system, and (3) a combination system of public defenders and appointed private attorneys.

The public defender program is a statewide program established by legislation and funded by the state government to provide counsel to children at public expense. This program allows access to the expertise of lawyers, who spend a considerable amount of time representing juvenile offenders every day. Defender programs generally provide separate office space for juvenile court personnel, as well as support staff, and training programs for new lawyers.

In many rural areas, where individual public defender programs are not available, defense services are offered through appointed private counsel. Private lawyers are assigned to individual juvenile court cases, and they receive compensation for the time and services they provide. When private attorneys are used in large urban areas, they are generally selected from a list established by the court, and they often operate in conjunction with a public defender program. The weaknesses of a system of assigned private counsel include assignment to cases for which the lawyers are unqualified, inadequate compensation, and lack of supportive or supervisory services.

Though efforts have been made to supply juveniles with adequate legal representation, many juveniles still go to court unrepresented, or with an overworked lawyer who provides inadequate representation. Many juvenile court defense lawyers work on more than 500 cases per year, and more than half leave their jobs in under two years.[14] Other problems facing public defenders include (1) lack of resources for independent evaluations, expert witnesses, and investigatory support; (2) lack of computers, telephones, files, and adequate office space; (3) juvenile public defenders' inexperience, lack of training, low morale, and salaries lower than those of their counterparts who defend adults or serve as prosecutors; and (4) inability to keep up with rapidly changing juvenile codes.[15] In a six-state study of access to counsel and quality of legal representation for indigent juveniles, the American Bar Association found these and many other problems,[16] as shown in Exhibit 14.1. With juvenile offenders facing the prospect of much longer sentences, mandatory minimum sentences, and time in adult prisons, the need for quality defense attorneys for juveniles has never been greater.

juvenile prosecutor
Government attorney responsible for representing the interests of the state and bringing the case against the accused juvenile.

The Prosecutor The **juvenile prosecutor** is the attorney responsible for bringing the state's case against the accused juvenile. Depending on the level of government and the jurisdiction, the prosecutor can be called a district attorney, a county attorney, a state attorney, or a United States attorney. Prosecutors are members of the bar selected for their positions by political appointment or popular election.

Ordinarily, the juvenile prosecutor is a staff member of the prosecuting attorney's office. If the office of the district attorney is of sufficient size, the juvenile prosecutor may work exclusively on juvenile and other family law matters. If the caseload of juvenile offenders is small, the juvenile prosecutor may also have criminal prosecution responsibilities.

For the first 60 years of its existence, the juvenile court did not include a prosecutor, because the concept of an adversary process was seen as inconsistent with the philosophy of treatment. The court followed a social service helping model, and informal proceedings were believed to be in the best interests of the child. Today, in a more legalistic juvenile court, almost all jurisdictions require by law that a prosecutor be present in the juvenile court.

EXHIBIT 14.1

Selected Problems in Public Defender Services for Indigent Juveniles in Six States

Maine

- Juvenile defenders are paid $50 per hour, with a cap of $315; therefore, defenders are expected to spend only a little over six hours on each case.
- In 2002, only two hours of juvenile justice–related training were available to defenders.

Maryland

- In one jurisdiction, juvenile public defenders handle about 360 cases each year; this is almost double the ABA standard's recommended maximum of 200.
- In 10 of the jurisdictions studied, more than a third of juveniles waived their right to counsel.

Montana

- Nearly all of the interviewed youth revealed that their attorneys had done no investigation into their cases.
- There are no minimum requirements for attorneys seeking appointment to defend children and youth in the justice system.

North Carolina

- Some 44 percent of juvenile defense attorneys surveyed reported that they rarely or never see the police report or other investigative material prior to their first meeting with a client.
- Some 44 percent also said they had no or inadequate access to investigators.

Pennsylvania

- About 94 percent of juvenile defense attorneys do not have access to independent investigators or social workers.
- Of the 40 public defender offices that confirmed representing youth at dispositional reviews, only 9 percent usually interview the youth before hearings.

Washington

- In some counties, up to 30 percent of children appear without counsel.
- Juvenile defenders working full-time reported that they are assigned an average of nearly 400 cases annually.

SOURCES: Adapted from American Bar Association, *Statistics: Juvenile Indigent Defense Reports by the Numbers* (Chicago: Juvenile Justice Center, 2003); American Bar Association, *Montana: An Assessment of Access to Counsel and Quality of Representation in Delinquency Proceedings* (Chicago: American Bar Association, 2003), p. 5.

A number of states have passed legislation giving prosecutors control over intake and waiver decisions. Some have passed concurrent-jurisdiction laws that allow prosecutors to decide in which court to bring serious juvenile cases. In some jurisdictions, it is the prosecutor and not the juvenile court judge who is entrusted with the decision of whether to transfer a case to adult court. Consequently, the role of juvenile court prosecutor is now critical in the juvenile justice process. Including a prosecutor in juvenile court balances the interests of the state, the defense attorney, the child, and the judge, preserving the independence of each party's functions and responsibilities.

The prosecutor has the power either to initiate or to discontinue delinquency or status offense allegations. Like police officers, prosecutors have broad discretion in the exercise of their duties. Because due-process rights have been extended to juveniles, the prosecutor's role in the juvenile court has in some ways become similar to the prosecutor's role in the adult court.

Because children are committing more serious crimes today and because the courts have granted juveniles constitutional safeguards, the prosecutor is likely to play an increasingly significant role in the juvenile court system. According to authors James Shine and Dwight Price, the prosecutor's involvement will promote a due process model that should result in a fairer, more just system for all parties. But they also point out that, to meet current and future challenges, prosecutors need more information on such issues as (1) how to identify repeat offenders, (2) how to determine which programs are most effective, (3) how early-childhood experiences relate to delinquency, and (4) what measures can be used in place of secure placements without reducing public safety.[17]

To read more about the **players in the court system,** go to the website of the **American Judicature Society,** a nonpartisan organization with a membership of judges, lawyers, and nonlegally trained citizens interested in the administration of justice: www.ajs.org. For an up-to-date list of web links, go to http://cj.wadsworth.com/siegel_jd9e.

EXHIBIT **14.2**

Duties of the Juvenile Court Judge

I Rule on pretrial motions involving such legal issues as arrest, search and seizure, interrogation, and lineup identification

I Make decisions about the continued detention of children prior to trial

I Make decisions about plea bargaining agreements and the informal adjustment of juvenile cases

I Handle trials, rule on the appropriateness of conduct, settle questions of evidence and procedure, and guide the questioning of witnesses

I Assume responsibility for holding dispositional hearings and deciding on the treatment accorded the child

I Handle waiver proceedings

I Handle appeals where allowed by statute

Today, prosecutors are addressing the problems associated with juvenile crime. A balanced approach has been recommended—one that emphasizes enforcement, prosecution, and detention of serious offenders and the use of proven prevention and intervention programs.[18]

The Juvenile Court Judge Even with the elevation of the prosecutor's role, the **juvenile court judge** is still the central character in a court of juvenile or family law. Her or his responsibilities have become far more extensive and complex in recent years. Juvenile or family court judges perform the functions listed in Exhibit 14.2.

In addition, judges often have extensive influence over other agencies of the court: probation, the court clerk, the law enforcement officer, and the office of the juvenile prosecutor. Juvenile court judges exercise considerable leadership in developing solutions to juvenile justice problems. In this role they must respond to the pressures the community places on juvenile court resources. According to the *parens patriae* philosophy, the juvenile judge must ensure that the necessary community resources are available so that the children and families who come before the court can receive the proper care and help.[19] This may be the most untraditional role for the juvenile court judge, but it may also be the most important.

In some jurisdictions juvenile court judges handle family-related cases exclusively. In others they preside over criminal and civil cases as well. Traditionally, juvenile court judges have been relegated to a lower status than other judges. Judges assigned to juvenile courts have not ordinarily been chosen from the highest levels of the legal profession. Such groups as the American Judicature Society have noted that the field of juvenile justice has often been shortchanged by the appointment of unqualified judges. In some jurisdictions, particularly major urban areas, juvenile court judges may be of the highest caliber, but many courts continue to function with mediocre judges.

Inducing the best-trained individuals to accept juvenile court judgeships is a very important goal. Where the juvenile court is part of the highest general court of trial jurisdiction, the problem of securing qualified personnel is not as great. However, if the juvenile court is of limited or specialized jurisdiction and has the authority to try only minor cases, it may attract only poorly trained personnel. Lawyers and judges who practice in juvenile court receive little respect. The juvenile court has a negative image, because even though what it does is of great importance to parents, children, and society in general, it has been placed at the lowest level of the judicial hierarchy.

juvenile court judge
A judge elected or appointed to preside over juvenile cases and whose decisions can only be reviewed by a judge of a higher court.

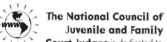
The National Council of Juvenile and Family Court Judges is dedicated to serving the nation's children and families by improving the courts of juvenile and family jurisdictions. Their website can be found at www.ncjfcj.org. For an up-to-date list of web links, go to http://cj.wadsworth.com/siegel_jd9e.

TO QUIZ YOURSELF ON THIS MATERIAL, go to the Juvenile Delinquency 9e website.

JUVENILE COURT PROCESS

Now that we have briefly described the setting of the juvenile court and the major players who control its operations, we turn to a discussion of the procedures that shape the contours of juvenile justice—the pretrial process and the juvenile trial and disposition. Many critical decisions are made at this stage in the juvenile justice system: whether to detain a youth or release the youth to the community; whether to waive youths to the adult court or retain them in the juvenile justice system; whether to treat them in the community or send them to a secure treatment center. Each of these can have a profound influence on the child, with effects lasting throughout the life course. What are these critical stages, and how are decisions made within them?

Release or Detain?

After a child has been taken into custody and a decision is made to treat the case formally (that is, with a juvenile court hearing), a decision must be made either to release the child into the custody of parents or to detain the child in the temporary care of the state, in physically restrictive facilities pending court disposition or transfer to another agency.[20] Nationally, about 70 percent of all states have detention centers administered at the county level; about 34 percent have state-level facilities, 16 percent have court-administered facilities, and 11 percent contract with private vendors to operate facilities.[21]

Detention can be a traumatic experience because many facilities are prisonlike, with locked doors and barred windows. Consequently, most experts in juvenile justice advocate that detention be limited to alleged offenders who require secure custody for the protection of themselves and others. However, children who are neglected and dependent, runaways, and those who are homeless may under some circumstances be placed in secure detention facilities along with violent and dangerous youths until more suitable placements can be found.[22] Others have had a trial but have not been sentenced, or are awaiting the imposition of their sentence. Some may have violated probation and are awaiting a hearing while being kept alongside a severely mentally ill adolescent for whom no appropriate placement can be found. Another group are adjudicated delinquents awaiting admittance to a correctional training school.[23] Consequently, it is possible for nonviolent status offenders to be housed in the same facility with delinquents who have committed felony-type offenses.

To remedy this situation, an ongoing effort has been made to remove status offenders and neglected or abused children from detention facilities that also house juvenile delinquents. In addition, alternatives to detention centers—temporary foster

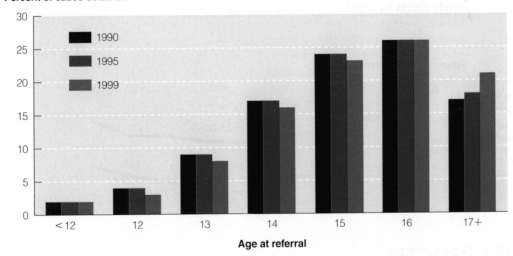

Percent of cases detained

Legend: 1990, 1995, 1999

Age at referral: < 12, 12, 13, 14, 15, 16, 17+

FIGURE 14.1

Profile of Detainees by Age

NOTE: Detail may not total 100% because of rounding.

SOURCE: Charles Puzzanchera, Anne L. Stahl, Terrence A. Finnegan, Nancy Tierney, and Howard N. Snyder, *Juvenile Court Statistics 1999* (Pittsburgh, PA: National Center for Juvenile Justice, 2003), p. 23.

homes, detention boarding homes, and programs of neighborhood supervision—have been developed. These alternatives, referred to as **shelter care,** enable youths to live in a more homelike setting while the courts dispose of their cases.

National Detention Trends Despite an ongoing effort to limit detention, juveniles are still being detained in 20 percent of all delinquency cases, with some variation across the major offense categories: violent (23 percent), property (16 percent), drugs (23 percent), and public order (23 percent). Although the detention rate for delinquency cases is down from 23 percent in 1990, over the 10-year period of 1990 to 1999, the total number of juveniles held in short-term detention facilities increased 11 percent, from 302,800 to 336,200.[24]

The typical delinquent detainee is male, over 15 years of age (see Figure 14.1), and charged with a violent crime;[25] whereas the typical status offender is female, under 16 years of age, and a runaway.[26] Racial minorities are heavily overrepresented in detention (see Figure 14.2), especially those who are indigent and whose families may be receiving public assistance. Minority overrepresentation is particularly vexing, considering that detention may increase the risk of a youth being adjudicated and eventually confined.[27]

Why Is Detention Increasing? The recent increase in detention use among juvenile offenders may result from the steady growth in the number of offenders.[28] However, some things about juvenile detention have not changed: There remains a serious problem of overrepresentation of minorities in secure detention.[29] In a study of the extent of racial discrimination and disparity among male juvenile property offenders in six Missouri counties at four stages of juvenile justice (decision to file a petition, pretrial detention, adjudication, and disposition), it was found that African American youth were more likely than white youth to be detained prior to adjudication (40 percent compared to 22 percent).[30] The study also found that African American youth were more likely to be formally referred and white youth were more likely to be adjudicated. The authors speculate that a "correction of biases" may be one of the reasons for white youth being more likely than African American youth to be adjudicated; that is, "judges may dismiss black youths because they feel that a detained youth has been punished enough already."[31]

The Decision to Detain Most children taken into custody by the police are released to their parents or guardians. Some are held overnight until their parents can be notified of the arrest. Police officers normally take a child to a place of detention only after

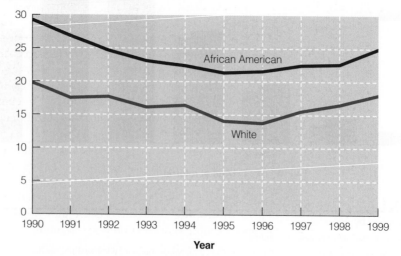

FIGURE 14.2

Cases Involving Detention of African American Juveniles vs. White Juveniles

SOURCE: Charles Puzzanchera, Anne L. Stahl, Terrence A. Finnegan, Nancy Tierney, and Howard N. Snyder, *Juvenile Court Statistics 1999* (Pittsburgh, PA: National Center for Juvenile Justice, 2003), p. 24.

other alternatives have been exhausted. Many juvenile courts in urban areas have staff members, such as intake probation officers, on duty 24 hours a day to screen detention admissions.

Ordinarily, delinquent children are detained if the police believe they are inclined to run away while awaiting trial, or if they are likely to commit an offense dangerous to the parent. There is evidence that some decision makers are more likely to detain minority youth, especially if they live in dangerous lower-class areas.[32]

Generally, children should not be held in a detention facility or shelter care unit for more than 24 hours without a formal petition (a written request to the court) being filed to extend the detention period. To detain a juvenile, there must be clear evidence of probable cause that the child has committed the offense and that he or she will flee if not detained. Although the requirements for detention hearings vary, most jurisdictions require that they occur almost immediately after the child's admission to a detention facility and provide the youth with notice and counsel.

New Approaches to Detention Efforts have been ongoing to improve the process and conditions of detention. Experts maintain that detention facilities should provide youth with education, visitation, private communications, counseling, continuous supervision, medical and health care, nutrition, recreation, and reading. Detention should also include, or provide, a system for clinical observation and diagnosis that complements the wide range of helpful services.[33]

The consensus today is that juvenile detention centers should be reserved for youths who present a clear threat to the community. In some states, nonsecure facilities are being used to service juveniles for a limited period. Alternatives to secure detention include in-home monitoring, home detention, day-center electronic monitoring, high-intensity community supervision, and comprehensive case management programs. The successful Detention Diversion Advocacy Program (DDAP) relies on a case management strategy. Because this is an important development, it is covered in more detail in the accompanying Policy and Practice feature.

Undoubtedly, juveniles pose special detention problems, but some efforts are being made to improve programs and to reduce pretrial detention use, especially in secure settings. Of all the problems associated with detention, however, none is as critical as the issue of placing youths in adult jails.

Restricting Detention in Adult Jails A significant problem in juvenile justice is placing youths in adult jails. This is usually done in rural areas where no other facility exists. Almost all experts agree that placing children under the age of 18 in any type of jail facility should be prohibited because youngsters can easily be victimized by other inmates and staff, be forced to live in squalid conditions, and be subject to physical and sexual abuse.

Until a few years ago, placing juveniles in adult facilities was common, but efforts have been made to change this situation. In 1989, the Juvenile Justice and Delinquency Prevention Act (JJDPA) of 1974 was amended to require that the states remove all juveniles from adult jails and lockups. According to federal guidelines, all juveniles in state custody must be separated from adult offenders, or the state could lose federal juvenile justice funds. The OJJDP defines separation as the condition in which juvenile detainees have either totally independent facilities or shared facilities that are designed so that juveniles and adults neither have contact nor share programs or staff.[34]

Much debate has arisen over whether the initiative to remove juveniles from adult jails has succeeded. Most indications are that the number of youths being held in adult facilities has declined significantly from the almost 500,000 a year recorded in 1979.[35] Today, fewer than 100,000 juveniles are detained annually in adult jails. These figures may be misleading, however, because they do not include youths held in urban jails for under 6 hours, or in rural ones for under 24 hours; youths transferred to adult courts; or youths in states that consider anyone over 16 or 17 to be an adult.

The Detention Diversion Advocacy Program

The concept behind the Detention Diversion Advocacy Program (DDAP) approach is case advocacy employing the efforts of a staff of laypersons or nonlegal experts acting on behalf of youthful offenders at disposition hearings. It relies on a case management strategy that involves coordination of human services, opportunities, or benefits. Case management efforts are designed to integrate services across a cluster of organizations, to ensure continuity of care, and to facilitate development of client skills (for example, job interviewing, or reading and writing skills) by involving a variety of social networks and service providers (social agencies that provide specific services to youth, such as drug counseling and crisis intervention).

Detention advocacy involves identifying youths likely to be detained pending their adjudication. Detention Diversion Advocacy Program clients are identified primarily through referrals from the public defender's office, the probation department, community agencies, and parents. Admission to DDAP is restricted to youths currently held, or likely to be held, in secure detention. Once a potential client is identified, DDAP case managers present a release plan to the judge that includes a list of appropriate community services (tutoring, drug counseling, family counseling) that will be made available on the youth's behalf. Additionally, the plan includes specified objectives (improved grades, victim restitution, drug-free status) as a means of evaluating the youth's progress in the program. Emphasis is placed on allowing the youth to live at home while going through the program. If home placement is not a viable option, program staff will identify and secure a suitable alternative. If the judge deems the release plan acceptable, the youth is released to DDAP supervision.

The DDAP case management model provides frequent and consistent support and supervision to youths and their families. Case managers link youths to community-based services and closely monitor their progress. The DDAP program requires the case manager to have daily contact with the youth, the family, and significant others, including a minimum of three in-person meetings a week with the youth. The youth's family members, particularly parents and guardians, are provided with additional services that typically include assistance in securing employment, daycare, drug treatment services, and income support (for example, food stamps).

Evaluations of the DDAP program have indicated that it is very successful:

- The overall recidivism rate of the DDAP group is 34 percent, compared with 60 percent for the comparison group.
- Fourteen percent of the DDAP group have two or more subsequent referrals, compared with 50 percent of the comparison group.
- Nine percent of the DDAP group return to court on a violent crime charge, compared with 25 percent of the comparison group.
- Five percent of the DDAP group have two or more subsequent petitions, compared with 22 percent of the comparison group.

Critical Thinking

1. Should adolescents be detained for nonviolent offenses such as substance abuse and/or theft?
2. Do you believe that the decision to detain a child is based on an evaluation of the child's behavior or his/her parent's behavior and ability to provide care and supervision? If the latter, is that a violation of due process? In other words, why should children be punished for the shortcomings of their parents?

InfoTrac College Edition Research

To learn more about this concept, use "juvenile detention" as a subject guide on InfoTrac College Edition.

SOURCE: Randall G. Shelden, "Detention Diversion Advocacy: An Evaluation," *Juvenile Justice Bulletin* (Washington, DC: Office of Juvenile Justice and Delinquency Prevention, 1999).

With federal help, some progress appears to have been made in removing juveniles from adult facilities, but thousands each year continue to be held in close contact with adults, and thousands more are held in facilities that, although physically separate, put them in close proximity to adults. To the youths held within their walls, there may appear to be little difference between the juvenile detention facilities and the adult jail.

Removing Status Offenders Along with removing all juveniles from adult jails, the OJJDP has made deinstitutionalization of status offenders a cornerstone of its policy. The Juvenile Justice and Delinquency Prevention Act of 1974 prohibits the placement of status offenders in secure detention facilities.

Removing status offenders from secure facilities serves two purposes: (1) It reduces interaction with serious offenders, and (2) it insulates status offenders from the stigma associated with being a detainee in a locked facility. Efforts appear to be working, and the number of status offenders being held in some sort of secure confinement has been on a two-decade decline. Nonetheless, the debate over the most effective way to handle juvenile status offenders continues, and some critics have argued that if the juvenile court is unable to take effective action in status offender cases, it should be stripped of jurisdiction over these youths. Most judges would prefer to retain jurisdiction so they can help children and families resolve problems that cause runaways, truancy, and other status offense behaviors.[36]

Bail for Children

bail
Amount of money that must be paid as a condition of pretrial release to ensure that the accused will return for subsequent proceedings. Bail is normally set by the judge at the initial appearance, and if unable to make bail, the accused is detained in jail.

One critical pretrial issue is whether juveniles can be released on **bail**. Adults retain the right, via the Eighth Amendment to the Constitution, to reasonable bail in noncapital cases. Most states, however, refuse juveniles the right to bail. They argue that juvenile proceedings are civil, not criminal, and that detention is rehabilitative, not punitive. In addition, they argue that juveniles do not need a constitutional right to bail because statutory provisions allow children to be released into parental custody.

State juvenile bail statutes fall into three categories: (1) those guaranteeing the right to bail, (2) those that grant the court discretion to give bail, and (3) those that deny a juvenile the right to bail.[37] This disparity may be a function of the lack of legal guidance on the matter. The U.S. Supreme Court has never decided the issue of juvenile bail. Some courts have stated that bail provisions do not apply to juveniles. Others rely on the Eighth Amendment against cruel and unusual punishment, or on state constitutional provisions or statutes, and conclude that juveniles do have a right to bail.

preventive detention
Keeping the accused in custody prior to trial because the accused is suspected of being a danger to the community.

Preventive Detention Although the U.S. Supreme Court has not yet decided whether juveniles have a right to traditional money bail, they have concluded that the state has a right to detain dangerous youths until their trial, a practice called **preventive detention**. On June 4, 1984, the U.S. Supreme Court dealt with this issue in *Schall v. Martin*, when it upheld the State of New York's preventive detention statute.[38] Because this is a key case in juvenile justice, it is the subject of the accompanying Juvenile Law in Review. Today, most states allow "dangerous" youths to be held indefinitely before trial. Because preventive detention may attach a stigma of guilt to a child presumed innocent, the practice remains a highly controversial one, and the efficacy of such laws remains unknown.[39]

The Intake Process

intake
Process during which a juvenile referral is received and a decision is made to file a petition in juvenile court to release the juvenile, to place the juvenile under supervision, or to refer the juvenile elsewhere.

The term **intake** refers to the screening of cases by the juvenile court system. The child and his or her family are screened by intake officers to determine whether the services of the juvenile court are needed. Intake officers may (1) send the youth home with no further action, (2) divert the youth to a social agency, (3) petition the youth to the juvenile court, or (4) file a petition and hold the youth in detention. The intake process reduces demands on court resources, screens out cases that are not within the court's jurisdiction, and enables assistance to be obtained from community agencies without court intervention. Juvenile court intake is provided for by statute in almost all of the states.

After reviewing the case, justice system authorities decide whether to dismiss, informally handle, or formally process the case by taking the matter before a judge. About 17 percent (279,100) of all delinquency cases in 1999 were dismissed at intake, often because they were not legally sufficient. Another 26 percent (432,000) were processed informally, with the juvenile voluntarily agreeing to the recommended disposition (for example, voluntary treatment).[40]

Intake screening allows juvenile courts to enter into consent decrees with juveniles without filing petitions and without formal adjudication. The consent decree is a court order authorizing disposition of the case without a formal label of delinquency. It is based on an agreement between the intake department of the court and the juvenile who is the subject of the complaint.

FACTS

Schall v. Martin

Gregory Martin was arrested in New York City on December 13, 1977, on charges of robbery, assault, and criminal possession of a weapon.

Because he was arrested at 11:30 P.M. and lied about his residence, Martin was kept overnight in detention and brought to juvenile court the next day for an "initial appearance" accompanied by his grandmother.

The family court judge, citing possession of a loaded weapon, the false address given to police, and the fact that Martin was left unsupervised late in the evening, ordered him detained before trial under section 320.5(3)(6) of the New York State code, which authorizes pretrial detention of an accused juvenile delinquent if "there is a substantial probability that he will not appear in court on the return date or there is a serious risk that he may before the return date commit an act which if committed by an adult would constitute a crime." Later, at trial, Martin was found to be a delinquent and sentenced to two years' probation.

While he was in pretrial detention, Martin's attorneys filed a class action on behalf of all youths subject to preventive detention in New York, charging that this form of detention was a denial of due-process rights under the Fifth and Fourteenth Amendments. The New York appellate courts upheld Martin's claim on the ground that because, at adjudication, most delinquents are released or placed on probation it was unfair to incarcerate them before trial. The prosecution brought the case to the U.S. Supreme Court for final judgment.

DECISION

The U.S. Supreme Court upheld the state's right to place juveniles in preventive detention, holding that the practice serves the legitimate objective of protecting both the juvenile and society from pretrial crime. Pretrial detention need not be considered punishment merely because the juvenile is eventually released or put on probation. In addition, there are procedural safeguards, such as notice and a hearing, and a statement of facts that must be given to juveniles before they are placed in detention. The Court also found that detention based on prediction of future behavior was not a violation of due process. Many decisions are made in the justice system, such as the decision to sentence or grant parole, that are based in part on a prediction of future behavior, and these have all been accepted by the courts as legitimate exercises of state power.

SIGNIFICANCE OF THE CASE

Schall v. Martin established the right of juvenile court judges to deny youths pretrial release if they perceive them to be dangerous. However, the case also established a due-process standard for detention hearings that includes notice and a statement of substantial reasons for the detention. Despite these measures, opponents hold that preventive detention deprives offenders of their freedom because guilt has not been proven. It is also unfair, they claim, to punish people for what judicial authorities believe they may do in the future, as it is impossible to predict who will be a danger to the community. Moreover, because judges are able to use discretion in their detention decisions, an offender could unfairly be deprived of freedom without legal recourse.

Critical Thinking

1. Is the use of pretrial detention warranted for all juveniles charged with violent crimes? Explain.
2. Should judicial discretion be limited in decisions on pretrial release or detention?

InfoTrac College Edition Research

To learn more about innovations in pretrial detention for juveniles, read Amanda Paulson, "Chicago's Alternative to Locking Up Youth," *Christian Science Monitor*, January 21, 2004, p. 1.

SOURCE: *Schall v. Martin*, 104 S.Ct. 2403 (1984).

But intake also suffers from some problems. Although almost all state juvenile court systems provide intake and diversion programs, there are few formal criteria for selecting children for such alternatives. There are also legal problems associated with the intake process. Among them are whether the child has a right to counsel, whether the child is protected against self-incrimination, and to what degree the child needs to consent to nonjudicial disposition as recommended by the intake officer. Finally, intake dispositions are often determined by the prior record rather than by the seriousness of the offense or the social background of the child. This practice departs from the philosophy of *parens patriae*.[41]

The shift from rehabilitation has led to changes in the intake process. One trend has been the increased influence of prosecutors. Traditionally, the intake process has been controlled by probation personnel whose decisions influenced the judge's view of which cases to handle formally and which should be settled without court action. This

The majority of children taken into custody by the police are released to their parents or guardians. Some are held overnight until their parents can be notified of the arrest. Police officers normally take a child to a place of detention only after other alternatives have been exhausted. Many juvenile courts in urban areas have staff members, such as intake probation officers, who are on duty twenty-four hours a day to screen detention admissions.

© Rich Graulieh/Palm Beach Post

approach to intake, in which probation personnel seek to dispense the least disruptive amount of rehabilitative justice, is being replaced in some jurisdictions by a model in which a prosecutor is the central figure. Some states now require that intake officers get approval from the prosecutor before either accepting or rejecting a delinquency petition. Other states allow the complaining party to appeal petitions rejected by intake officers to the prosecutor.[42]

Diversion

One of the most important alternatives chosen at intake is nonjudicial disposition or, as it is variously called, nonjudicial adjustment, handling or processing, informal disposition, adjustment, or (most commonly) **diversion.** Juvenile diversion is the process of placing youths suspected of law-violating behavior into treatment-oriented programs prior to formal trial and disposition in order to minimize their penetration into the justice system and thereby avoid stigma and labeling.

Diversion implies more than simply screening out cases for which no additional treatment is needed. Screening involves abandoning efforts to apply coercive measures to a defendant. In contrast, diversion encourages an individual to participate in some specific program or activity to avoid further prosecution.

Most court-based diversion programs employ a particular formula for choosing youths for diversion. Criteria such as being a first offender, a nonviolent offender, or a status offender, or being drug or alcohol dependent, are used to select clients. In some programs, youths will be asked to partake of services voluntarily in lieu of a court appearance. In other programs, prosecutors will agree to defer, and then dismiss, a case once a youth has completed a treatment program. Finally, some programs can be initiated by the juvenile court judge after an initial hearing. Concept Summary 14.1 lists the factors considered in diversion decisions.

diversion
Official halting or suspending of a formal criminal or juvenile justice proceeding at any legally prescribed processing point after a recorded justice system entry, and referral of that person to a treatment or care program or a recommendation that the person be released.

Concept Summary 14.1

Who Gets Diversion?

Factors Considered	Criteria for Eligibility
Past criminal record	It is the juvenile's first offense.
Type of offense	It is a nonviolent or status offense.
Other circumstances	The juvenile abuses drugs or alcohol.

In sum, diversion programs have been created to remove nonserious offenders from the justice system, provide them with nonpunitive treatment services, and help them avoid the stigma of a delinquent label.

Issues in Diversion: Widening the Net Diversion has been viewed as a promising alternative to official procedures, but over the years its basic premises have been questioned.[43] The most damaging criticism has been that diversion programs are involving children in the juvenile justice system who previously would have been released without official notice. This is referred to as **widening the net.** Various studies indicate that police and court personnel are likely to use diversion programs for youths who ordinarily would have been turned loose at the intake or arrest stage.[44] Why does net-widening occur? One explanation is that police and prosecutors find diversion a more attractive alternative than both official processing and outright release—diversion helps them resolve the conflict between doing too much and doing too little.

> **widening the net**
> Phenomenon that occurs when programs created to divert youths from the justice system actually involve them more deeply in the official process.

Diversion has also been criticized as ineffective; that is, youths being diverted make no better adjustment in the community than those who go through official channels. However, not all experts are critical of diversion. Some challenge the net-widening concept as naive: How do we know that diverted youths would have had less interface with the justice system if diversion didn't exist?[45] Even if juveniles escaped official labels for their current offense, might they not eventually fall into the hands of the police? The rehabilitative potential of diversion should not be overlooked.[46] Juvenile diversion programs represent one alternative to the traditional process.

The Petition

> **complaint**
> Report made by the police or some other agency to the court that initiates the intake process.

A **complaint** is the report made by the police or some other agency to the court to initiate the intake process. Once the agency makes a decision that judicial disposition is required, a petition is filed. The petition is the formal complaint that initiates judicial action against a juvenile charged with delinquency or a status offense. The petition includes basic information such as the name, age, and residence of the child; the parents' names; and the facts alleging the child's delinquency. The police officer, a family member, or a social service agency can file a petition.

If after being given the right to counsel, the child admits the allegation in the petition, an initial hearing is scheduled for the child to make the admission before the court, and information is gathered to develop a treatment plan. If the child does not admit to any of the facts in the petition, a date is set for a hearing on the petition. This hearing, whose purpose is to determine the merits of the petition, is similar to the adult trial. Once a hearing date has been set, the probation department is normally asked to prepare a social study report. This predisposition report contains relevant information about the child, along with recommendations for treatment and service.

When a date has been set for the hearing on the petition, parents or guardians and other persons associated with the petition (witnesses, the arresting police officer, and victims) are notified. On occasion, the court may issue a summons—a court order requiring the juvenile or others involved in the case to appear for the hearing. The statutes in a given jurisdiction govern the contents of the petition. Some jurisdictions, for instance, allow for a petition to be filed based on the information of the complainant alone. Others require that the petition be filed under oath or that an affidavit accompany the petition.

Some jurisdictions authorize only one official, such as a probation officer or prosecutor, to file the petition. Others allow numerous officials, including family and social service agencies, to set forth facts in the petition.

The Plea and Plea Bargaining

plea bargaining
The exchange of prosecutorial and judicial concessions for a guilty plea by the accused; plea bargaining usually results in a reduced charge or a more lenient sentence.

In the adult criminal justice system, the defendant normally enters a plea of guilty or not guilty. More than 90 percent of all adult defendants plead guilty. A large proportion of those pleas involve **plea bargaining,** the exchange of prosecutorial and judicial concessions for guilty pleas.[47] Plea bargaining permits a defendant to plead guilty to a less-serious charge in exchange for an agreement by the prosecutor to recommend a reduced sentence to the court. In the case of juvenile justice, it involves a discussion between the child's attorney and the prosecutor by which the child agrees to plead guilty to obtain a reduced charge or a lenient sentence.

Few juvenile codes require a guilty or not-guilty plea when a petition is filed against a child. In most jurisdictions an initial hearing is held at which the child either submits to a finding of the facts or denies the petition.[48] If the child admits to the facts, the court determines an appropriate disposition. If the child denies the allegations, the case normally proceeds to trial. When a child enters no plea, the court ordinarily imposes a denial of the charges. This may occur where a juvenile doesn't understand the nature of the complaint or isn't represented by an attorney.

A high percentage of juvenile offenders enter guilty pleas; that is, they admit to the facts of the petition. How many of these pleas involve plea bargaining is unknown. In the past it was believed that plea bargaining was unnecessary in the juvenile justice system because there was little incentive to bargain in a system that does not have jury trials or long sentences. In addition, because the court must dispose of cases in the best interests of the child, plea negotiation seemed unnecessary. Consequently, there has long been a debate over the appropriateness of plea bargaining in juvenile justice. The arguments in favor of plea bargaining include lower court costs and efficiency. Counterarguments hold that plea bargaining with juveniles is an unregulated and unethical process. When used, experts believe the process requires the highest standards of good faith by the prosecutor.[49]

Growing concern about violent juvenile crime has spurred attorneys increasingly to seek to negotiate a plea rather than accept the so-called good interests of the court judgment—a judgment that might result in harsher sanctions. The extension of the adversary process to children has led to an increase in plea bargaining, creating an informal trial process that parallels the adult system. Other factors in the trend toward juvenile plea bargaining include the use of prosecutors rather than probation personnel and police officers in juvenile courts, and the ever-increasing caseloads in such courts.

Plea bargaining negotiations generally involve one or more of the following: (1) reduction of a charge, (2) change in the proceedings from that of delinquency to a status offense, (3) elimination of possible waiver to the criminal court, and (4) agreements regarding dispositional programs for the child. In states where youths are subject to long mandatory sentences, reduction of the charges may have a significant impact on the outcome of the case. In states where youths may be waived to the adult court for committing certain serious crimes, a plea reduction may result in the juvenile courts maintaining jurisdiction.

Little clear evidence exists of how much plea bargaining there is in the juvenile justice system, but it is apparent that such negotiations do take place and seem to be increasing. Joseph Sanborn found that about 20 percent of the cases processed in Philadelphia resulted in a negotiated plea. Most were for reduced sentences, typically probation in lieu of incarceration. Sanborn found that plea bargaining was a complex process, depending in large measure on the philosophy of the judge and the court staff. In general, he found it to have greater benefit for the defendants than for the court.[50]

In summary, the majority of juvenile cases that are not adjudicated seem to be the result of admissions to the facts rather than actual plea bargaining. Plea bargaining is less common in juvenile courts than in adult courts because incentives such as dropping multiple charges or substituting a misdemeanor for a felony are unlikely. Nonetheless, plea bargaining is firmly entrenched in the juvenile process. Any plea bargain, however, must be entered into voluntarily and knowingly; otherwise, the conviction may be overturned on appeal.

TO QUIZ YOURSELF ON THIS MATERIAL, go to the Juvenile Delinquency 9e website.

TRANSFER TO THE ADULT COURT

transfer process
Transfer of a juvenile offender from the jurisdiction of juvenile court to adult criminal court.

One of the most significant actions that can occur in the early court processing of a juvenile offender is the **transfer process.** Otherwise known as waiver, bindover, or removal, this process involves transferring a juvenile from the juvenile court to the adult criminal court. Virtually all state statutes allow for this kind of transfer.

The number of delinquency cases judicially waived to criminal court peaked in 1994 with 12,100 cases, an increase of almost 50 percent over the number of cases waived in 1990 (8,300). From 1994 to 1999 (the latest data available), however, the number of cases waived to criminal court has actually declined 38 percent to 7,500 cases, representing less than 1 percent of the formally processed delinquency caseload.[51] A 2003 federal study of juveniles waived to criminal court in the nation's 40 largest counties found that 7,100 juvenile felony defendants were adjudicated in adult criminal court.[52] Figure 14.3 shows numbers of delinquency cases waived to criminal court during the 1990s.

Waiver Procedures

Today, all states allow juveniles to be tried as adults in criminal courts in one of three ways:

1. *Concurrent jurisdiction.* In about 15 states, the prosecutor has the discretion of filing charges for certain offenses in either juvenile or criminal court.

2. *Statutory exclusion policies.* In about 29 states, certain offenses are automatically excluded from juvenile court. These offenses can be minor, such as traffic violations,

FIGURE 14.3

Delinquency Cases Waived to Criminal Court, 1990–1999

SOURCE: Charles M. Puzzanchera, Anne L. Stahl, Terrence A. Finnegan, Nancy Tierney, and Howard N. Snyder, *Juvenile Court Statistics 1999* (Pittsburgh, PA: National Center for Juvenile Justice, 2003), p. 29.

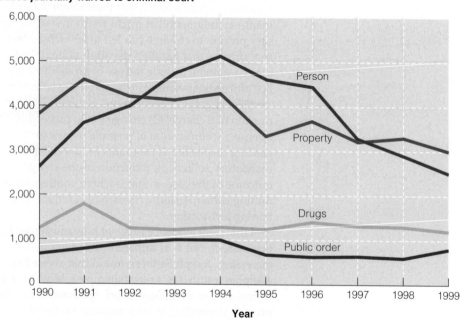

Cases judicially waived to criminal court

or serious, such as murder or rape. Statutory exclusion accounts for the largest number of juveniles tried as adults.

3. *Judicial waiver.* In the waiver (or bindover or removal) of juvenile cases to criminal court, a hearing is held before a juvenile court judge, who then decides whether jurisdiction should be waived and the case transferred to criminal court. All but four states (Massachusetts, Nebraska, New Mexico, and New York) offer provisions for juvenile waivers.[53]

Due Process in the Juvenile Waiver Procedure

The standards for waiver procedures are set by state statute. Some jurisdictions allow for transfer between the ages of 14 and 17. Others restrict waiver proceedings to mature juveniles and specify particular offenses. In a few jurisdictions, any child can be sentenced to the criminal court system, regardless of age.

Those states that have amended their waiver policies with statutory exclusion policies now exclude certain serious offenses from juvenile court jurisdiction. For example, Indiana excludes cases involving 16- and 17-year-olds charged with kidnapping, rape, or robbery. In Illinois, youths ages 15 and 16 who are charged with murder, assault, or robbery with a firearm are automatically sent to criminal court; in Pennsylvania, any child accused of murder, regardless of age, is tried before the criminal court.[54] Other jurisdictions use exclusion to remove traffic offenses and public-ordinance violations.

The trend toward excluding serious violent offenses from juvenile court jurisdictions is growing in response to the demand to get tough on crime. In addition, large numbers of youth under age 18 are tried as adults in states where the upper age of juvenile court jurisdiction is 15 or 16.

In a minority of states, statutes allow prosecutors to file particularly serious cases in either the juvenile court or the adult court.[55] Prosecutor discretion may occasionally be a more effective transfer mechanism than the waiver process, because the prosecutor can file a petition in criminal or juvenile court without judicial approval.

Since 1966, the U.S. Supreme Court and other federal and state courts have attempted to ensure fairness in the judicial waiver process by handing down decisions that spell out the need for due process. Two Supreme Court decisions, *Kent v. United States* (1966) and *Breed v. Jones* (1975), are relevant.[56] The *Kent* case declared a District of Columbia transfer statute unconstitutional and attacked the subsequent conviction of the child by granting him the specific due-process rights of having an attorney present at the hearing and access to the evidence that would be used in the case. In *Breed v. Jones,* the U.S. Supreme Court declared that the child was to be granted the protection of the double jeopardy clause of the Fifth Amendment after he was tried as a delinquent in the juvenile court: Once found to be a delinquent, the youth can no longer be tried as an adult. The accompanying Juvenile Law in Review feature discusses these two important cases in more detail.

transfer hearing
Preadjudicatory hearing in juvenile court for the purpose of determining whether juvenile court should be retained over a juvenile or waived and the juvenile transferred to adult court for prosecution.

Today, as a result of *Kent* and *Breed*, states that have **transfer hearings** provide (1) a legitimate transfer hearing, (2) sufficient notice to the child's family and defense attorney, (3) the right to counsel, and (4) a statement of the reason for the court order regarding transfer. These procedures recognize that the transfer process is critical in determining the statutory rights of the juvenile offender.

Should Youths Be Transferred to Adult Court?

Most juvenile justice experts oppose waiver because it clashes with the rehabilitative ideal. Basing waiver decisions on type and seriousness of offense rather than on the rehabilitative needs of the child has advanced the *criminalization* of the juvenile court and interfered with its traditional mission of treatment and rehabilitation.[57] And despite this sacrifice, there is little evidence that strict waiver policies can lower crime rates.[58] While it is true that some juvenile offenders commit crimes that deserve

KENT v. UNITED STATES   *Kent v. United States* and *Breed v. Jones*

FACTS

Morris Kent was arrested at the age of 16 in connection with charges of housebreaking, robbery, and rape. As a juvenile, he was subject to the exclusive jurisdiction of the District of Columbia Juvenile Court. The District of Columbia statute declared that the court could transfer the petitioner "after full investigation" and remit him to trial in the U.S. District Court. Kent admitted his involvement in the offenses and was placed in a receiving home for children. Subsequently, his mother obtained counsel, and they discussed with the social service director the possibility that the juvenile court might waive its jurisdiction.

Kent was detained at the receiving home for almost a week. There was no arraignment, no hearing, and no hearing for petitioner's apprehension. Kent's counsel arranged for a psychiatric examination, and a motion requesting a hearing on the waiver was filed. The juvenile court judge did not rule on the motion and entered an order stating, "After full investigation, the court waives its jurisdiction and directs that a trial be held under the regular proceedings of the criminal court." The judge made no finding and gave no reasons for his waiver decision. It appeared that the judge denied motions for a hearing, recommendations for hospitalization for psychiatric observation, requests for access to the social service file, and offers to prove that the petitioner was a fit subject for rehabilitation under the juvenile court.

After the juvenile court waived its jurisdiction, Kent was indicted by the grand jury and was subsequently found guilty of housebreaking and robbery and not guilty by reason of insanity on the charge of rape. Kent was sentenced to serve a period of 30 to 90 years on his conviction.

DECISION

The petitioner's lawyer appealed the decision on the basis of the infirmity of the proceedings by which the juvenile court waived its jurisdiction. He further attacked the waiver on statutory and constitutional grounds, stating, "(1) no hearing occurred, (2) no findings were made, (3) no reasons were stated before the waiver, and (4) counsel was denied access to the social service file." The U.S. Supreme Court found that the juvenile court order waiving jurisdiction and remitting the child to trial in the district court was invalid. Its arguments were based on the following criteria:

- The theory of the juvenile court act is rooted in social welfare procedures and treatments.
- The philosophy of the juvenile court, namely *parens patriae*, is not supposed to allow procedural unfairness.
- Waiver proceedings are critically important actions in the juvenile court.
- The juvenile court act requiring full investigation in the District of Columbia should be read in the context of constitutional principles relating to due process of law. These principles require at a minimum that the petitioner be entitled to a hearing, access to counsel, access by counsel to social service records, and a statement of the reason for the juvenile court decision.

SIGNIFICANCE OF THE CASE

This examined for the first time the substantial degree of discretion associated with a transfer proceeding in the District of Columbia. Thus, the Supreme Court significantly limited its holding to the statute involved but justified its reference to constitutional principles relating to due process and the assistance of counsel. In addition, it said that the juvenile court waiver hearings need to measure up to the essentials of due process and fair treatment. Furthermore, in an appendix to its opinion, the Court set up criteria concerning waiver of the jurisdictions. These are

punishment, and that rehabilitation programs will not be effective with all juveniles, the fact remains that most kids who remain in the juvenile justice system do not become adult offenders.

Waiver can also create long-term harm. Waived children may be stigmatized by a conviction in the criminal court. Labeling children as adult offenders early in life may seriously impair their future educational, employment, and other opportunities. Youthful offenders convicted in adult courts are more likely to be incarcerated and to receive longer sentences than had they remained in the juvenile court. In one study in Pennsylvania, the average sentence length for juvenile offenders sentenced in adult court was found to be significantly longer than for a similar group of young adult offenders (18 months compared to 6 months).[59] And these children may be incarcerated under conditions so extreme, and in institutions where they may be physically and sexually exploited, that they will become permanently damaged.[60] In a small-scale study of female youths transferred to criminal court and subsequently placed in a

- The seriousness of the alleged offense to the community
- Whether the alleged offense was committed in an aggressive, violent, or willful manner
- Whether the alleged offense was committed against persons or against property
- The prosecutive merit of the complaint
- The sophistication and maturity of the juvenile
- The record and previous history of the juvenile
- Prospects for adequate protection of the public and the likelihood of reasonable rehabilitation

BREED v. JONES

FACTS

In 1971, a petition in the juvenile court of California was filed against Jones, who was then 17, alleging that he had committed an offense that if committed by an adult, would constitute robbery. The petitioner was detained pending a hearing. At the hearing the juvenile court took testimony, found that the allegations were true, and sustained the petition.

The proceedings were continued for a disposition hearing, at which point Jones was found unfit for treatment in the juvenile court. It was ordered that he be prosecuted as an adult offender. At a subsequent preliminary hearing, the petitioner was held for criminal trial, an information was filed against him for robbery, and he was tried and found guilty. He was committed to the California Youth Authority over objections that he was being subjected to double jeopardy.

Petitioner Jones sought an appeal in the federal district court on the basis of the double jeopardy argument that jeopardy attaches at the juvenile delinquency proceedings. The **writ of habeas corpus** was denied.

DECISION

The U.S. Supreme Court held that the prosecution of Jones as an adult in the California Superior Court, after an adjudicatory finding in the juvenile court that he had violated a criminal statute and a subsequent finding that he was unfit for treatment as a juvenile, violated the double jeopardy clause of the Fifth Amendment to the U.S. Constitution as applied to the states through the Fourteenth Amendment. Thus, Jones's trial in the California Superior Court for the same offense as that for which he was tried in the juvenile court violated the policy of the double jeopardy clause, even if he never faced the risk of more than one punishment. Double jeopardy refers to the risk or potential risk of trial and conviction, not punishment.

SIGNIFICANCE OF THE CASE

The *Breed* case provided answers on several important transfer issues: (1) *Breed* prohibits trying a child in an adult court when there has been a prior adjudicatory juvenile proceeding; (2) probable cause may exist at a transfer hearing, and this does not violate subsequent jeopardy if the child is transferred to the adult court; (3) because the same evidence is often used in both the transfer hearing and subsequent trial in either the juvenile or adult court, a different judge is often required for each hearing.

Critical Thinking

Do you believe that some cases should be automatically waived to the adult system, or should all juvenile offenders be evaluated for the possibility of treatment in the juvenile court before a waiver decision is made?

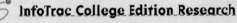

InfoTrac College Edition Research

Use "juvenile waiver" as a subject guide on InfoTrac College Edition to find out more about this issue.

SOURCES: *Kent v. United States*, 383 U.S. 541, 86 S.Ct. 1045, 16 L.Ed.2d 84 (1966); *Breed v. Jones*, 421 U.S. 519, 95 S.Ct. 1779 (1975).

---

writ of habeas corpus
Judicial order requesting that a person detaining another produce the body of the prisoner and give reasons for his or her capture and detention.

prison for adult women, it was found that the prison was severely limited in its ability to care for and provide needed treatment services for these youths compared with the adults.[61]

Waivers don't always support the goal of increased public protection. Because juveniles may only serve a fraction of the prison sentence imposed by the criminal court, the actual treatment of delinquents in adult court is similar to what they might have received had they remained in the custody of juvenile authorities.[62] Also, transferred juveniles convicted of felonies are not more likely to be sentenced to prison than similarly charged felons who are under the age of 18 but considered adults by the state.[63] Once they are released, waived juveniles have a higher recidivism rate than those kept in juvenile court.[64] This has prompted some critics to ask: Why bother transferring these children?

Sometimes waiver can add an undue burden to youthful offenders. Studies have found that although transfer to criminal court was intended for the most serious

Bucks County Courier Times © Jay Crawford

juvenile offenders, many transferred juveniles were not violent offenders but repeat property offenders.[65] Cases involving waiver take significantly longer than a comparable juvenile court case, during which time the waived youth is more likely to be held in a **detention** center. This finding is vexing, considering that some research shows that many waived youths were no more dangerous than youths who remain in juvenile courts.[66]

Transfer decisions are not always carried out fairly or equitably, and there is evidence that minorities are waived at a rate that is greater than their representation in the population.[67] Just over two-fifths (44%) of all waived youth are African Americans, even though they represent 28 percent of the juvenile court population.[68] The federal study of transfer in the nation's 40 largest counties found that 62 percent of waived youth were African American.[69] However, between 1990 and 1999, the number of judicially waived cases involving African American youth decreased 24 percent compared with a 9 percent increase for white youth.[70]

In Support of Waiver Not all experts challenge the waiver concept. Waiver is attractive to conservatives because it jibes with the get-tough policy currently popular. Some have argued that the increased use of waiver can help get violent offenders off the streets and should be mandatory for juveniles committing serious violent crimes.[71] Others point to studies that show that, for the most part, transfer is reserved for the most serious cases and the most serious juvenile offenders. Kids are most likely to be transferred to criminal court if they have injured someone with a weapon or if they have a long juvenile court record.[72] The most recent federal study of waiver found that 27 percent of juveniles tried in criminal court were sent to prison. This outcome might be expected because those waived to criminal court were more likely (64 percent) than adults (24 percent) to be charged with a violent felony. These juvenile defendants were generally regarded as serious offenders, because 52 percent did not receive pretrial release, 63 percent were convicted of a felony, and 43 percent of those convicted received a prison sentence.[73] Clearly, many waived juveniles might be considered serious offenders.

Author Franklin Zimring argues that, despite its faults, waiver is superior to alternative methods for handling the most serious juvenile offenders.[74] Some cases involving serious offenses, he argues, require a minimum criminal penalty greater than that available to the juvenile court. It is also possible that some juveniles take advantage of decisions to transfer them to the adult court. Although the charge against a child may be considered serious in the juvenile court, the adult criminal court will not find it so; consequently, a child may have a better chance for dismissal of the charges or acquittal after a jury trial.

In sum, though the use of waiver has been in decline, it is still an important strategy for attacking serious youth crime.[75] Its continued use can be attributed to the get-tough attitude toward the serious juvenile offender.

Some kids who commit the most serious crimes are routinely waived to adult court. Here, 14-year-old Kareem Watts is led from court in Doylestown, Pennsylvania, where he was tried as an adult for the murder of a neighbor, Darlyne Jules. A troubled young man, Watts started hearing voices in his head at age 8 and began to self-medicate by smoking pot and snorting household chemicals at age 11. When he stabbed Jules he was high on pot laced with embalming fluid. After his conviction, Watts was sent to a special unit within the juvenile justice system that houses young convicted offenders who need special psychiatric care. He will be released in seven years, on his 21st birthday, following an evaluation of his mental condition.

TO QUIZ YOURSELF ON THIS MATERIAL, go to the Juvenile Delinquency 9e website.

JUVENILE COURT TRIAL

detention
Temporary care of a child alleged to be delinquent who requires secure custody in physically restricting facilities pending court disposition or execution of a court order.

If the case cannot be decided during the pretrial stage, it will be brought forth for a trial in the juvenile court. An adjudication hearing is held to determine the merits of the petition claiming that a child is either a delinquent youth or in need of court supervision. The judge is required to make a finding based on the evidence and arrive at a judgment. Adjudication is comparable to an adult trial. Rules of evidence in adult

To get **information on juvenile courts,** go to the website of the **National Center for State Courts** at www.ncsconline.org. For an up-to-date list of web links, go to http://cj.wadsworth.com/siegel_jd9e.

criminal proceedings are generally applicable in juvenile court, and the standard of proof used—*beyond a reasonable doubt*—similar to that used in adult trials.

State juvenile codes vary with regard to the basic requirements of due process and fairness. Most juvenile courts have bifurcated hearings—that is, separate hearings for adjudication and disposition (sentencing). At disposition hearings, evidence can be submitted that reflects nonlegal factors such as the child's home life.

Most state juvenile codes provide specific rules of procedure, which have several purposes: They require that a written petition be submitted to the court, ensure the right of a child to have an attorney, provide that the adjudication proceedings be recorded, allow the petition to be amended, and provide that a child's plea be accepted. Where the child admits to the facts of the petition, the court generally seeks assurance that the plea is voluntary. If plea bargaining is used, prosecutors, defense counsel, and trial judges take steps to ensure the fairness of such negotiations.

At the end of the adjudication hearing, most juvenile court statutes require the judge to make a factual finding on the legal issues and evidence. In the criminal court, this finding is normally a prelude to reaching a verdict. In the juvenile court, however, the finding itself is the verdict—the case is resolved in one of three ways:

1. The juvenile court judge makes a finding of fact that the child or juvenile is not delinquent or in need of supervision.

2. The juvenile court judge makes a finding of fact that the juvenile is delinquent or in need of supervision.

3. The juvenile court judge dismisses the case because of insufficient or faulty evidence.

In some jurisdictions, informal alternatives are used, such as filing the case with no further consequences or continuing the case without a finding for a period of time, such as six months. If the juvenile does not get into further difficulty during that time, the case is dismissed. These alternatives involve no determination of delinquency or noncriminal behavior. Because of the philosophy of the juvenile court that emphasizes rehabilitation over punishment, a delinquency finding is not the same thing as a criminal conviction. The disabilities associated with conviction, such as disqualifications for employment or being barred from military service, do not apply in an adjudication of delinquency.

There are other differences between adult and juvenile proceedings. For instance, while adults are entitled to public trials by a jury of their peers, these rights are not extended to juveniles.[76] Because juvenile courts are treating some defendants similar to adult criminals, an argument can be made that the courts should extend to these youths the Sixth Amendment right to a public jury trial.[77] For the most part, however, state juvenile courts operate without recognizing a juvenile's constitutional right to a jury trial.

Constitutional Rights at Trial

In addition to mandating state juvenile code requirements, the U.S. Supreme Court has mandated the application of constitutional due-process standards to the juvenile trial. **Due process** is addressed in the Fifth and Fourteenth Amendments to the U.S. Constitution. It refers to the need for rules and procedures that protect individual rights. Having the right to due process means that no person can be deprived of life, liberty, or property without such protections as legal counsel, an open and fair hearing, and an opportunity to confront those making accusations against him or her.

For many years, children were deprived of their due-process rights because the *parens patriae* philosophy governed their relationship to the juvenile justice system. Such rights as having counsel and confronting one's accusers were deemed unnecessary. After all, why should children need protection from the state when the state was seen as acting in their interest? As we have seen, this view changed in the 1960s, when the U.S. Supreme Court began to grant due-process rights and procedures to minors. The key case was that of Gerald Gault; it articulated the basic requirements of due process that

due process
Basic constitutional principle based on the concept of the primacy of the individual and the complementary concept of limitation on governmental power; safeguards the individual from unfair state procedures in judicial or administrative proceedings. Due-process rights have been extended to juvenile trials.

For a review of **due process issues in juvenile justice,** go to www.ncjrs.org/ txtfiles/fs9749.txt. For an up-to-date list of web links, go to http://cj.wadsworth.com/ siegel_jd9e.

must be satisfied in juvenile court proceedings. Because *Gault* remains the key constitutional case in the juvenile justice system, it is set forth in the accompanying Juvenile Law in Review.

The *Gault* decision reshaped the constitutional and philosophical nature of the juvenile court system and, with the addition of legal representation, made it more similar to the adult system.[78] Following the *Gault* case, the U.S. Supreme Court decided *in re Winship* that the amount of proof required in juvenile delinquency adjudications is "beyond a reasonable doubt," a level equal to the requirements in the adult system.[79]

Although the ways in which the juvenile court operates were altered by *Gault* and *Winship,* the trend toward increased rights for juveniles was somewhat curtailed by the U.S. Supreme Court's decision in *McKeiver v. Pennsylvania* (1971), which held that trial by jury in a juvenile court's adjudicative stage is not a constitutional requirement.[80] This decision does not prevent states from giving the juvenile a trial by jury, but in the majority of states a child has no such right.

Once an adjudicatory hearing has been completed, the court is normally required to enter a judgment or finding against the child. This may take the form of declaring the child delinquent, adjudging the child to be a ward of the court, or possibly even suspending judgment so as to avoid the stigma of a juvenile record. After a judgment has been entered, the court can begin its determination of possible dispositions.

Disposition

The sentencing step of the juvenile justice process is called disposition. At this point the court orders treatment for the juvenile.[81] According to prevailing juvenile justice philosophy, dispositions should be in the *best interest of the child,* which in this context means providing the help necessary to resolve or meet the adolescent's personal needs, while at the same time meeting society's needs for protection.

As already mentioned, in most jurisdictions, adjudication and disposition hearings are separated, or bifurcated, so that evidence that could not be entered during the juvenile trial can be considered at the dispositional hearing. At the hearing, the defense counsel represents the child, helps the parents understand the court's decision, and influences the direction of the disposition. Others involved at the dispositional stage include representatives of social service agencies, psychologists, social workers, and probation personnel.

The Predisposition Report After the child has admitted to the allegations, or the allegations have been proved in a trial, the judge normally orders the probation department to complete a predisposition report. The predisposition report, which is similar to the presentence report of the adult justice system, has a number of purposes:

▌ It helps the judge decide which disposition is best for the child.

▌ It aids the juvenile probation officer in developing treatment programs where the child is in need of counseling or community supervision.

▌ It helps the court develop a body of knowledge about the child that can aid others in treating the child.[82]

Sources of dispositional data include family members, school officials, and statements from the juvenile offenders themselves. The results of psychological testing, psychiatric evaluations, and intelligence testing may be relevant. Furthermore, the probation officer might include information about the juvenile's feelings concerning his or her case.

Some state statutes make the predisposition report mandatory. Other jurisdictions require the report only when there is a probability that the child will be institutionalized. Some appellate courts have reversed orders institutionalizing children where the juvenile court did not use a predisposition report in reaching its decision. Access to predisposition reports is an important legal issue.

In the final section of the predisposition report, the probation department recommends a disposition to the presiding judge. This is a critical aspect of the report

FACTS

In re Gault

Gerald Gault, 15 years of age, was taken into custody by the sheriff of Gila County, Arizona, because a woman complained that he and another boy had made an obscene telephone call to her. At the time, Gerald was under a six-month probation disposition after being found delinquent for stealing a wallet. As a result of the woman's complaint, Gerald was taken to a children's home. His parents were not informed that he was being taken into custody. His mother appeared in the evening and was told by the superintendent of detention that a hearing would be held in the juvenile court the following day. On the day in question, the police officer who had taken Gerald into custody filed a petition alleging his delinquency. Gerald, his mother, and the police officer appeared before the judge in his chambers. Mrs. Cook, the complainant, was not at the hearing. Gerald was questioned about the telephone calls and was sent back to the detention home and subsequently released a few days later.

On the day of Gerald's release, Mrs. Gault received a letter indicating that a hearing would be held on Gerald's delinquency a few days later. A hearing was held, and the complainant again was not present. There was no transcript or recording of the proceedings, and the juvenile officer stated that Gerald had admitted making the lewd telephone calls. Neither the boy nor his parents were advised of any right to remain silent, right to be represented by counsel, or any other constitutional rights. At the conclusion of the hearing, the juvenile court committed Gerald as a juvenile delinquent to the state industrial school for the period of his minority.

This meant that at the age of 15, Gerald Gault was sentenced to remain in the state school until he reached the age of 21, unless he was discharged sooner. An adult charged with the same crime would have received a maximum punishment of no more than a $50 fine or two months in prison.

DECISION

Gerald's attorneys filed a writ of habeas corpus, which was denied by the Superior Court of the State of Arizona. That decision was subsequently affirmed by the Arizona Supreme Court. On appeal to the U.S. Supreme Court, Gerald's counsel argued that the juvenile code of Arizona under which Gerald was found delinquent was invalid because it was contrary to the due-process clause of the Fourteenth Amendment. In addition, Gerald was denied the following basic due-process rights: (1) notice of the charges with respect to their timeliness and specificity, (2) right to counsel, (3) right to confrontation and cross-examination, (4) privilege against self-incrimination, (5) right to a transcript of the trial record, and (6) right to appellate review. In deciding the case, the U.S. Supreme Court had to determine whether procedural due process of law within the context of fundamental fairness under the Four-

teenth Amendment applied to juvenile delinquency proceedings in which a child is committed to a state industrial school.

The Court, in a far-reaching opinion, agreed that Gerald's constitutional rights had been violated. Notice of charges was an essential ingredient of due process of law, as was the right to counsel, the right to cross-examine and to confront witnesses, and the privilege against self-incrimination. The questions of appellate review and a right to a transcript were not answered by the Court in this case.

SIGNIFICANCE OF THE CASE

The *Gault* case established that a child has the due-process constitutional rights listed here in delinquency adjudication proceedings, where the consequences were that the child could be committed to a state institution. It was confined to rulings at the adjudication state of the juvenile process.

This decision was significant not only because of the procedural reforms it initiated but also because of its far-reaching impact throughout the entire juvenile justice system. *Gault* instilled in juvenile proceedings the development of due-process standards at the pretrial, trial, and post-trial stages of the juvenile process. While recognizing the history and development of the juvenile court, it sought to accommodate the motives of rehabilitation and treatment with children's rights. It recognized the principle of fundamental fairness of the law for children as well as for adults. Judged in the context of today's juvenile justice system, *Gault* redefined the relationships among juveniles, their parents, and the state. It remains the single most significant constitutional case in the area of juvenile justice.

Critical Thinking

The *Gault* case is hailed as a milestone for giving juveniles due-process rights. Does the provision of those rights actually harm youth? In other words, would it have been advisable to keep attorneys and legal process out of the juvenile court? Is it too late to transform the system so that it reflects its original ideals?

InfoTrac College Edition Research

How has the *Gault* case shaped the philosophy of the juvenile court? To find out, read Lise A. Young, "Suffer the Children: The Basic Principle of Juvenile Justice Is to Treat the Child, Not Punish the Offense," *America* 185(12):19 (October 22, 2001).

SOURCE: *In re Gault,* 387 U.S. 1; 87 S.Ct. 1248 (1967).

When making disposition decisions, juvenile court judges may select programs that will enhance life skills and help youths form a positive bond with society. Here, a juvenile offender stands before a juvenile court judge at the Juvenile Justice Center of the Ninth Judicial Circuit court in Orlando, Florida; other youths look on as they wait their turn.

because it has been estimated that the court follows more than 90 percent of all probation department recommendations.

Juvenile Court Dispositions Historically, the juvenile court has had broad discretionary power to make dispositional decisions. The major categories of dispositional choices are (1) community release, (2) out-of-home placements, (3) fines or restitution, (4) community service, and (5) institutionalization. A more detailed list of the dispositions open to the juvenile court judge appears in Exhibit 14.3.[83]

Most state statutes allow the juvenile court judge to select whatever disposition seems best suited to the child's needs, including institutionalization. In some states the court determines commitment to a specific institution; in other states the youth corrections agency determines where the child will be placed. In addition to the dispositions in Exhibit 14.3, some states grant the court the power to order parents into treatment or to suspend a youth's driver's license.

It is common for juvenile court judges to employ a graduated sanction program for juveniles: (1) immediate sanctions for nonviolent offenders, which consist of community-based diversion and day treatment imposed on first-time, nonviolent offenders; (2) intermediate sanctions, which target repeat minor offenders and first-time serious offenders; and (3) secure care, which is reserved for repeat serious offenders and violent offenders.[84]

In 1999, juveniles were adjudicated delinquent in two-thirds (66 percent) of the 962,000 cases brought before a judge. Once adjudicated, the majority of these juveniles (62 percent or 398,200 cases) were placed on formal probation, one-quarter (24 percent or 155,200 cases) were placed in a residential facility, and 10 percent (or 64,000 cases) were given another disposition, such as referral to an outside agency, community service, or restitution.[85]

Although the juvenile court has been under pressure to get tough on youth crime, these figures show that probation is the disposition of choice, even in the most serious cases,[86] and its use has grown in recent years. Between 1990 and 1999, the number of cases in which the court ordered an adjudicated delinquent to be placed on formal probation increased 80 percent, while the number of cases involving placement in a residential facility increased 24 percent.[87] Figure 14.4 (page 446) shows recent changes in juvenile court placement of adjudicated youths for different crime types.

EXHIBIT 14.3

Common Juvenile Dispositions

Disposition	Action Taken
Informal consent decree	In minor or first offenses, an informal hearing is held, and the judge will ask the youth and his or her guardian to agree to a treatment program, such as counseling. No formal trial or disposition hearing is held.
Probation	A youth is placed under the control of the county probation department and is required to obey a set of probation rules and participate in a treatment program.
Home detention	A child is restricted to his or her home in lieu of a secure placement. Rules include regular school attendance, curfew observance, avoidance of alcohol and drugs, and notification of parents and the youth worker of the child's whereabouts.
Court-ordered school attendance	If truancy was the problem that brought the youth to court, a judge may order mandatory school attendance. Some courts have established court-operated day schools and court-based tutorial programs staffed by community volunteers.
Financial restitution	A judge can order the juvenile offender to make financial restitution to the victim. In most jurisdictions, restitution is part of probation (see Chapter 15), but in a few states, such as Maryland, restitution can be a sole order.
Fines	Some states allow fines to be levied against juveniles age 16 and over.
Community service	Courts in many jurisdictions require juveniles to spend time in the community working off their debt to society. Community service orders are usually reserved for victimless crimes, such as possession of drugs, or crimes against public order, such as vandalism of school property. Community service orders are usually carried out in schools, hospitals, or nursing homes.
Outpatient psychotherapy	Youths who are diagnosed with psychological disorders may be required to undergo therapy at a local mental health clinic.
Drug and alcohol treatment	Youths with drug- or alcohol-related problems may be allowed to remain in the community if they agree to undergo drug or alcohol therapy.
Commitment to secure treatment	In the most serious cases a judge may order an offender admitted to a long-term treatment center, such as a training school, camp, ranch, or group home. These may be either state or privately run institutions, usually located in remote regions. Training schools provide educational, vocational, and rehabilitation programs in a secure environment (see Chapter 15).
Commitment to a residential community program	Youths who commit crimes of a less serious nature but who still need to be removed from their homes can be placed in community-based group homes or halfway houses. They attend school or work during the day and live in a controlled, therapeutic environment at night.
Foster home placement	Foster homes are usually used for dependent or neglected children and status offenders. Judges place delinquents with insurmountable problems at home in state-licensed foster care homes.

Juvenile Sentencing Structures

For most of the juvenile court's history, disposition was based on the presumed needs of the child. Although critics have challenged the motivations of early reformers in championing rehabilitation, there is little question that the rhetoric of the juvenile court has promoted that ideal.[88] For example, in their classic work *Beyond the Best Interest of the Child*, Joseph Goldstein, Anna Freud, and Albert Solnit say that placement of children should be based on the **least detrimental alternative** available in order to foster the child's development.[89] Most states have adopted this ideal in their sentencing efforts, and state courts usually insist that the purpose of disposition must be rehabilitation and not punishment.[90] Consequently, it is common for state courts to require judges to justify their sentencing decisions if it means that juveniles are to be incarcerated in a residential treatment center: They must set forth in writing the reasons for the placement, address the danger the child poses to society, and explain why a less-restrictive alternative has not been used.[91]

Traditionally, states have used the **indeterminate sentence** in juvenile court. In about half of the states, this means having the judge place the offender with the state department of juvenile corrections until correctional authorities consider the youth ready to return to society or until the youth reaches legal majority. A preponderance of states consider 18 to be the age of release; others peg the termination age at 19; a few can retain minority status until their 21st birthday. In practice, few youths remain in

least detrimental alternative
Choice of a program for the child that will best foster the child's growth and development.

indeterminate sentence
Does not specify the length of time the juvenile must be held; rather, correctional authorities decide when the juvenile is ready to return to society.

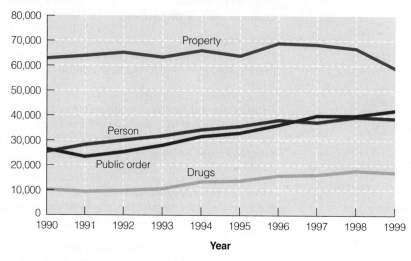

Number of cases

FIGURE 14.4

Juvenile Court Placement of Adjudicated Youths

NOTES: In 1999, one in four (24%) adjudicated delinquency cases resulted in out-of-home placement (i.e., placement in a residential treatment center, juvenile corrections facility, foster home, or group home); 62% resulted in an order of probation; 10% resulted in some other disposition, such as restitution, fines, community service, or referral to other treatment agencies; and 3% were released at disposition without sanction.

Placement cases grew 24% between 1990 and 1999.

There were racial differences in out-of-home placements. In 1999, about 23% of adjudicated cases involving white youths resulted in out-of-home placements, compared with 28% of cases involving black youths and 24% involving other minority youths.

SOURCE: Charles M. Puzzanchera, Anne L. Stahl, Terrence A. Finnegan, Nancy Tierney, and Howard N. Snyder, *Juvenile Court Statistics 1999* (Pittsburgh, PA: National Center for Juvenile Justice, 2003), p. 34.

custody for the entire statutory period; juveniles are usually released if their rehabilitation has been judged to have progressed satisfactorily. This practice is referred to as the **individualized treatment model.**

Another form of the indeterminate sentence allows judges to specify a maximum term. Under this form of sentencing, youths may be released if the corrections department considers them to be rehabilitated or they reach the automatic age of termination (usually 18 or 21). In states that stipulate a maximum sentence, the court may extend the sentence, depending on the youth's progress in the institutional facility.

A number of states have changed from an indeterminate to a **determinate sentence.** This means sentencing juvenile offenders to a fixed term of incarceration that must be served in its entirety. Other states have passed laws creating **mandatory sentences** for serious juvenile offenders. Juveniles receiving mandatory sentences are usually institutionalized for the full sentence and are not eligible for early parole. The difference between mandatory and determinate sentences is that the mandatory sentence carries a statutory requirement that a certain penalty be set in all cases on conviction for a specified offense.

individualized treatment model
Each sentence must be tailored to the individual needs of the child.

determinate sentence
Specifies a fixed term of detention that must be served.

mandatory sentence
Defined by a statutory requirement that states the penalty to be set for all cases of a specific offense.

Sentencing Reform

During the past decade there have been a number of attempts to create rational sentencing within juvenile justice. In some instances the goal has been to reduce judicial discretion, in others to toughen sentencing practices and create mandatory periods of incarceration for juveniles who commit serious crimes. However, not all statutory changes have had the desired effect. For instance, New York state has implemented a juvenile offender law requiring that juveniles accused of violent offenses be tried in criminal court as a get-tough-on-crime measure. Evaluations found many youths ended up receiving lighter sentences than they would have in the family court.[92]

Probably the best-known effort to reform sentencing in the juvenile court is the state of Washington's Juvenile Justice Reform Act of 1977. This act created a mandatory sentencing policy requiring juveniles aged 8 to 17 who are adjudicated delinquent to be confined in an institution for a minimum time.[93] The intent of the act was to make juveniles accountable for criminal behavior and to provide for punishment commensurate with the (1) age, (2) crime, and (3) prior history of the offender. Washington's approach is based on the principle of *proportionality*. How much time a youth must spend in confinement is established by the Juvenile Dispositions Standards Commission, based on the three stated criteria. The introduction of such mandatory-sentencing procedures reduces disparity in the length of sentences, according to advocates of a more punitive juvenile justice system.

The growing realization that the juvenile crime rate has stabilized may slow the tide of legislative change in juvenile justice. What is more likely is that states will continue to pass legislation making it easier to transfer youths to the adult court or giving the adult court original jurisdiction over serious cases. Thus, rather than toughening juvenile law for everyone, the system may reserve the harshest measures for the few more serious cases.

Blended Sentences State sentencing trends indicate that punishment and accountability, in addition to rehabilitation, have become equally important in juvenile justice policy. As a result, many states have created blended sentencing structures for cases involving serious offenders. Blended sentencing allows the imposition of juvenile and adult sanctions for juvenile offenders adjudicated in juvenile court or convicted in criminal court. In other words, this expanded sentencing authority allows criminal and juvenile courts to impose either a juvenile or an adult sentence, or both, in cases involving juvenile offenders. When both sentences are imposed simultaneously, the court suspends the adult sanction. If the youth follows the conditions of the juvenile sentence and commits no further violation, the adult sentence is revoked. This type of statute has become popular in recent years, with Connecticut, Kentucky, and Minnesota among the states adopting it since 1994.[94]

The Death Penalty for Juveniles

Juveniles who have been waived to adult court can receive the death penalty. The execution of minor children has not been uncommon in our nation's history; at least 366 juvenile offenders have been executed since 1642.[95] This represents about 2 percent of the total of more than 18,000 executions carried out since colonial times.

During the past 20 years, 196 juvenile death sentences have been imposed (about 3 percent of the almost 6,900 total U.S. death sentences). Approximately two-thirds of these have been imposed on 17-year-olds and nearly one-third on 15- and 16-year-olds.[96] As of 2003, 21 states permitted the juvenile death penalty[97] and 78 juvenile offenders were on death row. Since the death penalty was reinstated in 1976, 22 juvenile offenders have been executed in seven states, with Texas accounting for 13 of these 22 executions (see Table 14.1). All 22 of the executed juvenile offenders were male, 21 committed their crimes at age 17, and just over half (12 of them) were minorities.[98]

Legal Issues In *Thompson v. Oklahoma* (1988), the U.S. Supreme Court prohibited the execution of persons *under age 16*, but left open the age at

© AP/Wide World Photos

The death penalty for juveniles is one of the most controversial issues facing juvenile justice today. Supporters of the death penalty and those who oppose it counter with arguments over whether it has any deterrent effect and if it amounts to cruel and unusual punishment. Here, Rena and Ireland Beazley hold a photo of their son Napolean Beazley, who was 17 when it was alleged that he killed the father of a federal judge during a carjacking. Napolean was convicted and received the death sentence for this crime. He was executed in Huntsville, Texas, on May 28, 2002.

TABLE 14.1

Juveniles Executed or Facing Execution, by State, 1976–2003

State	Juvenile Offenders on Death Row	Juvenile Offenders Executed
Alabama	13	0
Arizona	5	0
Arkansas	0	0
Delaware	0	0
Florida	2	0
Georgia	2	1
Idaho	0	0
Kentucky	1	0
Louisiana	7	1
Mississippi	5	0
Missouri	2	1
Nevada	1	0
New Hampshire	0	0
North Carolina	5	0
Oklahoma	0	2
Pennsylvania	3	0
South Carolina	3	1
South Dakota	0	0
Texas	28	13
Utah	0	0
Virginia	1	3
Wyoming	0	0
Total	78	22

SOURCE: *Factsheet: The Juvenile Death Penalty* (Chicago: American Bar Association Juvenile Justice Center, 2003), p. 2.

which execution would be legally appropriate.[99] They then answered this question in two 1989 cases, *Wilkins v. Missouri* and *Stanford v. Kentucky,* in which they ruled that states were free to impose the death penalty for murderers who committed their crimes after they reached age 16 or 17.[100] In August 2003, the Supreme Court of Missouri declared the death penalty to be unconstitutional for offenders under the age of 18. The state petitioned the U.S. Supreme Court to take up this matter, and in January 2004 the U.S. Supreme Court agreed to decide whether the death penalty for 16- and 17-year-olds violates the Constitution.[101] According to the majority opinion, society has not formed a consensus that the execution of such minors constitutes a cruel and unusual punishment.

Those who oppose the death penalty for children find that it has little deterrent effect on youngsters who are impulsive and do not have a realistic view of the destructiveness of their misdeeds or their consequences. Victor Streib, the leading critic of the death penalty for children, argues that such a practice is cruel and unusual punishment because (1) the condemnation of children makes no measurable contribution to the legitimate goals of punishment; (2) condemning any minor to death violates contemporary standards of decency; (3) the capacity of the young for change, growth, and rehabilitation makes the death penalty particularly harsh and inappropriate; and (4) both legislative attitudes and public opinion reject juvenile executions.[102] Those who oppose the death penalty for children also refer to a growing body of research that shows that the brain continues to develop through the late teen years, as well as important mental functions, such as planning, judgment, and emotional control.[103] Supporters of the death penalty hold that people, regardless of their age, can form criminal intent and therefore should be responsible for their actions. If the death penalty is legal for adults, they argue, then it can also be used for children who commit serious crimes.

The fact that the United States is not alone in executing criminals appears to support retention of the death penalty. However, the fact that many countries have abolished capital punishment encourages those who want capital punishment to be abandoned.[104]

The Child's Right to Appeal

final order
Order that ends litigation between two parties by determining all their rights and disposing of all the issues.

appellate process
Allows the juvenile an opportunity to have the case brought before a reviewing court after it has been heard in juvenile or family court.

Regardless of the sentence imposed, juveniles may want to appeal the decision made by the juvenile court judge. Juvenile court statutes normally restrict appeals to cases where the juvenile seeks review of a **final order,** one that ends the litigation between two parties by determining all their rights and disposing of all the issues.[105] The **appellate process** gives the juvenile the opportunity to have the case brought before a reviewing court after it has been heard in the juvenile or family court. Today, the law does not recognize a federal constitutional right of appeal. In other words, the U.S. Constitution does not require any state to furnish an appeal to a juvenile charged and found to be delinquent in a juvenile or family court. Consequently, appellate review of a juvenile case is a matter of statutory right in each jurisdiction. However, the majority of states do provide juveniles with some method of statutory appeal.

The appeal process was not always part of the juvenile law system. In 1965, few states extended the right of appeal to juveniles.[106] Even in the *Gault* case in 1967, the U.S. Supreme Court refused to review the Arizona juvenile code, which provided no appellate review in juvenile matters. It further rejected the right of a juvenile to a transcript of the original trial record.[107] Today, however, most jurisdictions that provide a child with some form of appeal also provide for counsel and for securing a record and transcript, which are crucial to the success of any appeal.

Because juvenile appellate review is defined by individual statutes, each jurisdiction determines for itself what method of review will be used. There are two basic methods of appeal: the direct appeal and the collateral attack.

The *direct appeal* normally involves an appellate court review to determine whether, based on the evidence presented at the trial, the rulings of law and the judgment of the court were correct. The second major area of review involves the collateral attack of a case. The term *collateral* implies a secondary or indirect method of attacking a final judgment. Instead of appealing the juvenile trial because of errors, prejudice, or lack of evidence, *collateral review* uses extraordinary legal writs to challenge the lower-court position. One such procedural device is the writ of habeas corpus. Known as the *Great Writ,* the writ of habeas corpus refers to a procedure for determining the validity of a person's custody. In the context of the juvenile court, it is used to challenge the custody of a child in detention or in an institution. This writ is often the method by which the Supreme Court exercises its discretionary authority to hear cases regarding constitutional issues. Even though there is no constitutional right to appeal a juvenile case and each jurisdiction provides for appeals differently, juveniles have a far greater opportunity for appellate review today than in years past.

Confidentiality in Juvenile Proceedings

confidentiality
Restriction of information in juvenile court proceedings in the interest of protecting the privacy of the juvenile.

Along with the rights of juveniles at adjudication and disposition, the issue of **confidentiality** in juvenile proceedings has also received attention in recent years. The debate on confidentiality in the juvenile court deals with two areas: (1) open versus closed hearings, and (2) privacy of juvenile records. Confidentiality has become moot in some respects, as many legislatures have broadened access to juvenile records.

Open vs. Closed Hearings Generally, juvenile trials are closed to the public and the press, and the names of the offenders are kept secret. The U.S. Supreme Court has ruled on the issue of privacy in three important decisions. In *Davis v. Alaska,* the

Court concluded that any injury resulting from the disclosure of a juvenile's record is outweighed by the right to completely cross-examine an adverse witness.[108] The *Davis* case involved an effort to obtain testimony from a juvenile probationer who was a witness in a criminal trial. The Supreme Court held that a juvenile's interest in confidentiality was secondary to the constitutional right to confront adverse witnesses.

The decisions in two subsequent cases, *Oklahoma Publishing Co. v. District Court* and *Smith v. Daily Mail Publishing Co.,* sought to balance juvenile privacy with freedom of the press. In the *Oklahoma* case, the Supreme Court ruled that a state court was not allowed to prohibit the publication of information obtained in an open juvenile proceeding.[109] The case involved an 11-year-old boy suspected of homicide, who appeared at a detention hearing where photographs were taken and published in local newspapers. When the local district court prohibited further disclosure, the publishing company claimed that the court order was a restraint in violation of the First Amendment, and the Supreme Court agreed.

The *Smith* case involved the discovery and publication of the identity of a juvenile suspect in violation of a state statute prohibiting publication. The Supreme Court, however, declared the statute unconstitutional because the Court believed the state's interest in protecting the child's identity was not of such a magnitude as to justify the use of such a statute.[110] Therefore, if newspapers lawfully obtain pictures or names of juveniles, they may publish them. Based on these decisions, it appears that the Supreme Court favors the constitutional rights of the press over the right to privacy of the juvenile offender.

None of the decisions, however, give the press or public access to juvenile trials. Some jurisdictions still bar the press from juvenile proceedings unless they show at a hearing that their presence will not harm the youth. However, the trend has been to make it easier for the press and the public to have open access to juvenile trials. For example, in 1995 Georgia amended its juvenile code to allow the public access to juvenile hearings in cases in which a juvenile is charged with certain designated felonies, such as kidnapping and attempted murder. Also in 1995, Missouri passed legislation that "removes the veil of secrecy that once kept juvenile court proceedings private—in the hope that allowing names and photos in newspapers will discourage teen crime and alert school officials." Michigan has granted public access to court proceedings and documents in cases involving delinquents, truants, runaways, and abuse victims. During the past decade 17 jurisdictions have amended their laws to provide for greater openness in juvenile courts.[111]

Privacy of Juvenile Records For most of the twentieth century, juvenile records were kept confidential.[112] Today, however, the record itself, or information contained in it, can be opened by court order in many jurisdictions on the basis of statutory exception. The following groups can ordinarily gain access to juvenile records: (1) law enforcement personnel, (2) the child's attorney, (3) the parents or guardians, (4) military personnel, and (5) public agencies such as schools, court-related organizations, and correctional institutions.

Many states have enacted laws authorizing a central repository for juvenile arrest records. About 30 states have enacted provisions to allow open hearings in at least some juvenile cases. Forty-two states have enacted legislation authorizing the release and publication of the names and addresses of juvenile offenders in some cases. States also began to allow more juveniles to be fingerprinted and photographed. Nearly all states now allow juvenile fingerprints to be included in criminal history records, and nearly all states authorize juveniles to be photographed for later identification.[113] Some states allow a juvenile adjudication for a criminal act to be used as evidence in an adult criminal proceeding for the same act, to show predisposition or criminal nature.

Today, most states recognize the importance of juvenile records in sentencing. Many first-time adult offenders committed numerous crimes as juveniles, and evidence of these crimes may not be available to sentencing for the adult offenses unless states pass statutes allowing access. Knowledge of a defendant's juvenile record may help prosecutors and judges determine appropriate sentencing for offenders aged 18 to 24, the age group most likely to be involved in violent crime.

According to experts such as Ira Schwartz, the need for confidentiality to protect juveniles is far less than the need to open up the courts to public scrutiny.[114] The problem of maintaining confidentiality of juvenile records will become more acute in the future as electronic information storage makes these records both more durable and more accessible.

In conclusion, virtually every state provides prosecutors and judges access to the juvenile records of adult offenders. There is great diversity, however, regarding provisions for the collection and retention of juvenile records.[115]

Summary

- Prosecutors, judges, and defense attorneys are the key players in the juvenile court. The juvenile prosecutor is the attorney responsible for bringing the state's case against the accused juvenile. The juvenile judge must ensure that the children and families who come before the court receive the proper help. Defense attorneys representing children in the juvenile court play an active and important part in virtually all stages of the proceedings.

- Many decisions about what happens to a child may occur prior to adjudication. Key issues include detention, intake, diversion, pretrial release, plea bargaining, and waiver. Because the juvenile justice system is not able to try every child accused of a crime or status offense due to personnel limitations, diversion programs seem to hold greater hope for the control of delinquency. As a result, such subsystems as statutory intake proceedings, plea bargaining, and other informal adjustments are essential ingredients in the administration of the juvenile justice system.

- Each year, thousands of youths are transferred to adult courts because of the seriousness of their crimes. This process, known as waiver, is an effort to remove serious offenders from the juvenile process and into the more punitive adult system. Most juvenile experts oppose waiver because it clashes with the rehabilitative ideal. Supporters argue that its increased use can help get violent juvenile offenders off the street, and they point to studies that show that, for the most part, transfer is reserved for the most serious cases and the most serious juvenile offenders.

- Most jurisdictions have a bifurcated juvenile code system that separates the adjudication hearing from the dispositional hearing. Juveniles alleged to be delinquent have virtually all the rights given a criminal defendant at trial—except possibly the right to a trial by jury. In addition, juvenile proceedings are generally closed to the public.

- *In re Gault* is the key legal case that set out the basic requirements of due process that must be satisfied in juvenile court proceedings. In *Wilkins v. Missouri* and *Stanford v. Kentucky*, the U.S. Supreme Court ruled that states were free to impose the death penalty for murderers who committed their crimes after they reached age 16 or 17.

- The major categories of dispositional choice in juvenile cases are community release, out-of-home placements, fines or restitution, community service, and institutionalization. Although the traditional notion of rehabilitation and treatment as the proper goals for disposition is being questioned, many juvenile codes do require that the court consider the least-restrictive alternative.

- Juveniles who have been waived to adult court can receive the death penalty. Those who oppose the death penalty for juveniles find that it has little deterrent effect on youngsters who are impulsive and do not have a realistic view of the destructiveness of their misdeeds or their consequences. Supporters of the death penalty hold that people, regardless of their age, can form criminal intent and therefore should be responsible for their actions.

- Many state statutes require that juvenile hearings be closed and that the privacy of juvenile records be maintained to protect the child from public scrutiny and to provide a greater opportunity for rehabilitation. This approach may be inconsistent with the public's interest in taking a closer look at the juvenile justice system.

Key Terms

juvenile defense attorney, p. 422
guardian *ad litem*, p. 423
public defender, p. 424
juvenile prosecutor, p. 424
juvenile court judge, p. 426
shelter care, p. 428
bail, p. 431
preventive detention, p. 431
intake, p. 431

diversion, p. 433
widening the net, p. 434
complaint, p. 434
plea bargaining, p. 435
transfer process, p. 436
transfer hearing, p. 437
writ of habeas corpus, p. 439
detention, p. 440
due process, p. 441

least detrimental alternative, p. 445
indeterminate sentence, p. 445
individualized treatment model,
   p. 446
determinate sentence, p. 446
mandatory sentence, p. 446
final order, p. 449
appellate process, p. 449
confidentiality, p. 449

Questions for Discussion

1. Discuss and identify the major participants in the juvenile adjudication process. What are each person's role and responsibilities in the course of a juvenile trial?

2. The criminal justice system in the United States is based on the adversarial process. Does the same adversary principle apply in the juvenile justice system?

3. Children have certain constitutional rights at adjudication, such as the right to an attorney and the right to confront and cross-examine witnesses. But they do not have the right to a trial by jury. Should juvenile offenders have a constitutional right to a jury trial? Should each state make that determination? Discuss the legal decision that addresses this issue.

4. What is the point of obtaining a predisposition report in the juvenile court? Is it of any value in cases where the child is released to the community? Does it have a significant value in serious juvenile crime cases?

5. The standard of proof in juvenile adjudication is to show that the child is guilty beyond a reasonable doubt. Explain the meaning of this standard of proof in the U.S. judicial system.

6. Should states adopt get-tough sentences in juvenile justice or adhere to the individualized treatment model?

7. What are blended sentences?

8. Do you agree with the principle of imposing the death penalty on juveniles found to have committed certain capital crimes?

9. Should individuals who committed murder while under age 16 be legally executed?

Viewpoint

As an experienced family court judge, you are often faced with difficult decisions, but few are more difficult than the case of John M., arrested at age 14 for robbery and rape. His victim, a young neighborhood girl, was badly injured in the attack and needed extensive hospitalization; she is now in counseling. Even though the charges are serious, because of his age John can still be subject to the jurisdiction of the juvenile division of the state family court. However, the prosecutor has filed a petition to waive jurisdiction to the adult court. Under existing state law, a hearing must be held to determine whether there is sufficient evidence that John cannot be successfully treated in the juvenile justice system and therefore warrants transfer to the adult system; the final decision on the matter is yours alone.

At the waiver hearing, you discover that John is the oldest of three siblings living in a single-parent home. He has had no contact with his father for more than 10 years. His psychological evaluation showed hostility, anger toward females, and great feelings of frustration. His intelligence is

below average, and his behavioral and academic records are poor. In addition, he seems to be involved with a local youth gang, although he denies any association with them. This is his first formal involvement with the juvenile court. Previous contact was limited to a complaint for disorderly conduct at age 13, which was dismissed by the court's intake department. During the hearing, John verbalizes what you interpret to be superficial remorse for his offenses.

To the prosecutor, John seems to be a youth with poor controls who is likely to commit future crimes. The defense attorney argues that there are effective treatment opportunities within the juvenile justice system that can meet John's needs. Her views are supported by an evaluation of the case conducted by the court's probation staff, which concludes that the case can be dealt with in the confines of juvenile corrections.

If the case remains in the juvenile court, John can be kept in custody in a juvenile facility until age 18; if transferred to felony court, he could be sentenced to up to 20 years in a maximum-security prison. As the judge, you recognize the seriousness of the crimes committed by John and realize that it is very difficult to predict or assess his future behavior and potential dangerousness.

▌ Would you authorize a waiver to adult court or keep the case in the juvenile justice system?

▌ Can 14-year-olds truly understand the seriousness of their behavior?

▌ Should a juvenile court judge consider the victim in making a disposition decision?

Doing Research on the Web

Before you answer these questions, research waivers to adult court using "juveniles and waivers" in a key word search on InfoTrac College Edition. To get further information on this topic, go to the following websites (sites accessed on September 26, 2004):

The American Bar Association Juvenile Justice Center

www.abanet.org/crimjust/juvjus/

OJJDP Statistical Briefing Book

http://ojjdp.ncjrs.org/ojstatbb/

American Youth Policy Forum on Juvenile Justice

www.aypf.org/subcats/juvjust.htm

The Juvenile Justice Division of the Child Welfare League of America

www.cwla.org/programs/juvenilejustice/

The National Council on Crime and Delinquency and Children's Research Center

www.nccd-crc.org

Notes

1. Kelly Dedel, "National Profile of the Organization of State Juvenile Corrections Systems," *Crime and Delinquency* 44:507–525 (1998). Hereinafter cited as National Profile.
2. Anne L. Stahl, *Delinquency Cases in Juvenile Courts, 1999* (Washington, DC: OJJDP Fact Sheet, 2003), p. 1.
3. Ibid, p. 2.
4. *Powell v. Alabama* 287 U.S. 45, 53 S.Ct. 55, 77, L.Ed.2d 158 (1932); *Gideon v. Wainright* 372 U.S. 335, 83 S.Ct. 792, 9 L.Ed.2d 799 (1963); *Argersinger v. Hamlin* 407 U.S. 25, 92 S.Ct. 2006, 32 L.Ed.2d 530 (1972).
5. For a review of these studies, see T. Grisso, "The Competence of Adolescents as Trial Defendants," *Psychology, Public Policy, and Law* 3:3–32 (1997).
6. Christine Schnyder Pierce and Stanley L. Brodsky, "Trust and Understanding in the Attorney-Juvenile Relationship," *Behavioral Sciences and the Law* 20:89–107 (2002), p. 102.
7. Ibid, p. 102.
8. Melinda G. Schmidt, N. Dickon Reppucci, and Jennifer L. Woolard, "Effectiveness of Participation as a Defendant: The Attorney-Juvenile Client Relationship," *Behavioral Sciences and the Law* 21:175–198 (2003), p. 177.
9. Ibid, p. 193.
10. George W. Burruss, Jr., and Kimberly Kempf-Leonard, "The Questionable Advantage of Defense Counsel in Juvenile Court," *Justice Quarterly* 19:37–67 (2002), pp. 60–61.
11. Howard Davidson, "The Guardian *ad Litem:* An Important Approach to the Protection of Children," *Children Today* 10:23 (1981); Daniel Golden, "Who Guards the Children?" *Boston Globe Magazine,* December 27, 1992, p. 12.
12. Chester Harhut, "An Expanded Role for the Guardian *ad Litem,*" *Juvenile and Family Court Journal* 51:31–35 (2000).
13. Steve Riddell, "CASA, Child's Voice in Court," *Juvenile and Family Justice Today* 7:13–14 (1998).
14. American Bar Association, *A Call for Justice: An Assessment of Access to Counsel and Quality of Representation in Delinquency Proceedings* (Washington, DC: ABA Juvenile Justice Center, 1995).
15. Douglas C. Dodge, *Due Process Advocacy* (Washington, DC: Office of Juvenile Justice and Delinquency Prevention, 1997).
16. American Bar Association, "News Release: ABA President Says New Report Shows 'Conveyor Belt Justice' Hurting Children and Undermining Public Safety," Washington, DC, October 21, 2003.
17. James Shine and Dwight Price, "Prosecutor and Juvenile Justice: New Roles and Perspectives," in Ira Schwartz, ed., *Juvenile Justice and Public Policy* (New York: Lexington Books, 1992), pp. 101–133.
18. James Backstrom and Gary Walker, "A Balanced Approach to Juvenile Justice: The Work of the Juvenile Justice Advisory Committee," *The Prose-*

cutor 32:37–39 (1988); see also *Prosecutors' Policy Recommendations on Serious, Violent, and Habitual Youthful Offenders* (Alexandria, VA: American Prosecutors' Institute, 1997).
19. Leonard P. Edwards, "The Juvenile Court and the Role of the Juvenile Court Judge," *Juvenile and Family Court Journal* 43:3–45 (1992); Lois Haight, "Why I Choose to Be a Juvenile Court Judge," *Juvenile and Family Justice Today* 7:7 (1998).
20. American Correctional Association, *Standards for Juvenile Detention Facilities* (Laurel, MD: ACA, 1991).
21. National Profile, p. 514.
22. Madeline Wordes and Sharon Jones, "Trends in Juvenile Detention and Steps Toward Reform," *Crime and Delinquency* 44:544–560 (1998).
23. Robert Shepard, *Juvenile Justice Standards Annotated: A Balanced Approach* (Chicago: ABA, 1997).
24. Anne L. Stahl, *Delinquency Cases in Juvenile Courts, 1999* (Washington, DC: OJJDP Fact Sheet, 2003), p. 2.
25. Paul Harms, *Detention in Delinquency Cases, 1990–1999* (Washington, DC: OJJDP Fact Sheet, 2003), pp. 1–2.
26. Paul Harms, *Detention in Delinquency Cases, 1989–1998* (Washington, DC: Office of Juvenile Justice and Delinquency Prevention, 2002).
27. Bohsiu Wu and Angel Ilarraza Fuentes, "The Entangled Effects of Race and Urban Poverty," *Juvenile and Family Court Journal* 49:41–51 (1998).
28. Harms, *Detention in Delinquency Cases, 1990–1999,* p. 2.
29. Ira M. Schwartz and William H. Barton, eds., *Reforming Juvenile Detention—No More Hidden Closets* (Columbus: Ohio State University Press, 1994), p. 176.
30. Katherine E. Brown and Leanne Fiftal Alarid, "Examining Racial Disparity of Male Property Offenders in the Missouri Juvenile Justice System," *Youth Violence and Juvenile Justice* 2:107–128 (2004), p. 116.
31. Ibid, p. 119.
32. James Maupin and Lis Bond-Maupin, "Detention Decision-Making in a Predominantly Hispanic Region: Rural and Non-Rural Differences," *Juvenile and Family Court Journal* 50:11–21 (1999).
33. Earl Dunlap and David Roush, "Juvenile Detention as Process and Place," *Juvenile and Family Court Journal* 46:1–16 (1995).
34. "OJJDP Helps States Remove Juveniles from Jails," *Juvenile Justice Bulletin* (Washington, DC: U.S. Department of Justice, 1990).
35. Community Research Associates, *The Jail Removal Initiative: A Summary Report* (Champaign, IL: Community Research Associates, 1987).
36. David Steinhart, "Status Offenders," *The Future of Children: The Juvenile Court,* vol. 6 (Los Altos, CA: David and Lucile Packard Foundation, 1996), pp. 86–96.

37. Mark Soler et al., *Representing the Child Client* (New York: Matthew Bender, 1989), sec. 5.03b.

38. *Schall v. Martin*, 467 U.S. 253 (1984).

39. Jeffrey Fagan and Martin Guggenheim, "Preventive Detention for Juveniles: A Natural Experiment," *Journal of Criminal Law and Criminology*, 86:415–428 (1996).

40. Anne L. Stahl, *Delinquency Cases in Juvenile Courts, 1999.*

41. Leona Lee, "Factors Influencing Intake Disposition in a Juvenile Court," *Juvenile and Family Court Journal* 46:43–62 (1995).

42. H. Ted Rubin, "The Emerging Prosecutor Dominance of the Juvenile Court Intake Process," *Crime and Delinquency* 26:299–318 (1980).

43. Edwin E. Lemert, "Diversion in Juvenile Justice: What Hath Been Wrought?" *Journal of Research in Crime and Delinquency* 18:34–46 (1981).

44. Don C. Gibbons and Gerald F. Blake, "Evaluating the Impact of Juvenile Diversion Programs," *Crime and Delinquency Journal* 22:411–419 (1976); Richard J. Lundman, "Will Diversion Reduce Recidivism?" *Crime and Delinquency Journal* 22:428–437 (1976); B. Bullington, J. Sprowls, D. Katkin, and M. Phillips, "A Critique of Diversionary Juvenile Justice," *Crime and Delinquency* 24:59–71 (1978); Thomas Blomberg, "Diversion and Accelerated Social Control," *Journal of Criminal Law and Criminology* 68:274–282 (1977); Sharla Rausch and Charles Logan, "Diversion from Juvenile Court: Panacea or Pandora's Box," in J. Klugel, ed., *Evaluating Juvenile Justice* (Beverly Hills: Sage Publications, 1983), pp. 19–30.

45. Arnold Binder and Gilbert Geis, "Ad Populum Argumentation in Criminology: Juvenile Diversion as Rhetoric," *Criminology* 30:309–333 (1984).

46. Mark Ezell, "Juvenile Diversion: The Ongoing Search for Alternatives," in Ira M. Schwartz, ed., *Juvenile Justice and Public Policy* (New York: Lexington Books, 1992), pp. 45–59.

47. Albert W. Alschuler, "The Prosecutor's Role in Plea Bargaining," *University of Chicago Law Review* 36:50–112 (1968); Joyce Dougherty, "A Comparison of Adult Plea Bargaining and Juvenile Intake," *Federal Probation* June:72–79 (1988).

48. Sanford Fox, *Juvenile Courts in a Nutshell* (St. Paul, MN: West, 1985), pp. 154–56.

49. See Darlene Ewing, "Juvenile Plea Bargaining: A Case Study," *American Journal of Criminal Law* 6:167 (1978); Adrienne Volenik, *Checklists for Use in Juvenile Delinquency Proceedings* (Chicago: American Bar Association, 1985); Bruce Green, "Package Plea Bargaining and the Prosecutor's Duty of Good Faith," *Criminal Law Bulletin* 25:507–550 (1989).

50. Joseph Sanborn, *Plea Negotiations in Juvenile Court* (Ph.D. thesis, State University of New York at Albany, 1984); Joseph Sanborn, "Philosophical, Legal, and Systematic Aspects of Juvenile Court Plea Bargaining," *Crime and Delinquency* 39:509–527 (1993).

51. Charles M. Puzzanchera, *Delinquency Cases Waived to Criminal Court, 1990–1999* (Washington, DC: OJJDP Fact Sheet, 2003), p. 1.

52. Gerard Rainville and Steven K. Smith, *Juvenile Felony Defendants in Criminal Courts: Survey of 40 Counties, 1998* (Washington, DC: Bureau of Justice Statistics, 2003).

53. Puzzanchera, *Delinquency Cases Waived to Criminal Court, 1990–1999*, p. 1.

54. Ind. Code Ann. 31-6-2(d) 1987; Ill.Ann.Stat. Ch. 37 Sec. 805 (1988); Penn. Stat. Ann. Title 42 6355(a) (1982); Patrick Griffin et al., *Trying Juveniles as Adults in Criminal Court: An Analysis of State Transfer Provisions* (Washington, DC: OJJDP, 1998).

55. Joseph White, "The Waiver Decision: A Judicial, Prosecutorial, or Legislative Responsibility?" *Justice for Children* 2:28–30 (1987).

56. *Kent v. United States*, 383 U.S. 541, 86 S.Ct. 1045, 16 L.Ed.2d 84 (1966); *Breed v. Jones*, 421 U.S. 519, 95 S.Ct. 1179, 44 L.Ed.2d 346 (1975).

57. Barry Feld, "The Juvenile Court Meets the Principle of the Offense: Legislative Changes in Juvenile Waiver Statutes," *Journal of Criminal Law and Criminology* 78:471–534 (1987); Paul Marcotte, "Criminal Kids," *American Bar Association Journal* 76:60–66 (1990); Dale Parent et al., *Transferring Serious Juvenile Offenders to Adult Courts* (Washington, DC: U.S. Department of Justice, National Institute of Justice, 1997).

58. Richard Redding, "Juvenile Offenders in Criminal Court and Adult Prison: Legal, Psychological and Behavioral Outcomes," *Juvenile and Family Court Journal* 50:1–15 (1999); Craig A. Mason, Derek A. Chapman, Chang Shau, and Julie Simons, "Impacting Re-Arrest Rates Among Youth Sentenced in Adult Court: An Epidemiology Examination of the Juvenile Sentencing Advocacy Project," *Journal of Clinical Child & Adolescent Psychology* 32:205–214 (2003); David L. Myers, "The Recidivism of Violent Youths in Juvenile and Adult Court: A Consideration of Selection Bias," *Youth Violence and Juvenile Justice* 1:79–101 (2003).

59. Megan C. Kurlychek and Brian D. Johnson, "The Juvenile Penalty: A Comparison of Juvenile and Young Adult Sentencing Outcomes in Criminal Court," *Criminology* 42:485–517 (2004), p. 498.

60. Redding, "Juvenile Offenders in Criminal Court and Adult Prison: Legal, Psychological and Behavioral Outcomes," p. 11; see also Richard E. Redding, "The Effects of Adjudicating and Sentencing Juveniles as Adults: Research and Policy Implications," *Youth Violence and Juvenile Justice* 1:128–155 (2003).

61. Emily Gaarder and Joanne Belknap, "Tenuous Borders: Girls Transferred to Adult Court," *Criminology* 40:481–518 (2002), p. 508.

62. Redding, "Juvenile Offenders in Criminal Court and Adult Prison."

63. Howard N. Snyder and Melissa Sickmund, *Juvenile Offenders and Victims: 1999 National Report* (Washington, DC: U.S. Department of Justice, Office of Juvenile Justice and Delinquency Prevention, 1999), p. 177.

64. See Mason et al., "Impacting Re-Arrest Rates Among Youth Sentenced in Adult Court: An Epidemiology Examination of the Juvenile Sentencing Advocacy Project"; Myers, "The Recidivism of Violent Youths in Juvenile and Adult Court: A Consideration of Selection Bias."

65. James Howell, "Juvenile Transfers to the Criminal Justice System: State of the Art," *Law & Policy* 18:17–60 (1996).

66. M. A. Bortner, "Traditional Rhetoric, Organizational Realities: Remand of Juveniles to Adult Court," *Crime and Delinquency* 32:53–73 (1986).

67. Puzzanchera, *Delinquency Cases Waived to Criminal Court, 1988–1998*; Jeffrey Fagan, Martin Forst, and T. Scott Vivona, "Racial Determinants of the Judicial Transfer Decision: Prosecuting Violent Youth in Criminal Court," *Crime and Delinquency* 33:359–386 (1987); J. Fagan, E. Slaughter, and E. Hartstone, "Blind Justice: The Impact of Race on the Juvenile Justice Process," *Crime and Delinquency* 53:224–258 (1987); J. Fagan and E. P. Deschenes, "Determinants of Judicial Waiver Decisions for Violent Juvenile Offenders," *Journal of Criminal Law and Criminology* 81:314–347 (1990); see also James Howell, "Juvenile Transfers to Criminal Court," *Juvenile and Family Justice Journal* 6:12–14 (1997).

68. Anne L. Stahl, *Delinquency Cases in Juvenile Courts, 1999*, p. 2; Puzzanchera, *Delinquency Cases Waived to Criminal Court, 1990–1999*, p. 2.

69. Rainville and Smith, *Juvenile Felony Defendants in Criminal Courts: Survey of 40 Counties, 1998.*

70. Puzzanchera, *Delinquency Cases Waived to Criminal Court, 1990–1999*, p. 2.

71. Barry Feld, "Delinquent Careers and Criminal Policy," *Criminology* 21:195–212 (1983).

72. Howard N. Snyder, Melissa Sickmund, and Eileen Poe-Yamagata, *Juvenile Transfers to Criminal Court in the 1990s: Lessons Learned from Four Studies* (Washington, DC: Office of Juvenile Justice and Delinquency Prevention, 2000).

73. Rainville and Smith, *Juvenile Felony Defendants in Criminal Courts.*

74. Franklin E. Zimring, "Treatment of Hard Cases in American Juvenile Justice: In Defense of the Discretionary Waiver," *Notre Dame Journal of Law, Ethics and Policy* 5:267–280 (1991); Lawrence Winner, Lonn Kaduce, Donna Bishop, and Charles Frazier, "The Transfer of Juveniles to Criminal Courts: Reexamining Recidivism over the Long Term," *Crime and Delinquency* 43:548–564 (1997).

75. Robert Shepard, "The Rush to Waive Children to Adult Courts," *American Bar Association Journal of Criminal Justice* 10:39–42 (1995); see also Rainville and Smith, *Juvenile Felony Defendants in Criminal Courts.*

76. Institute of Judicial Administration, American Bar Association Joint Commission on Juvenile Justice Standards, *Standards Relating to Adjudication* (Cambridge, MA: Ballinger, 1980).

77. Joseph B. Sanborn, Jr., "The Right to a Public Jury Trial—A Need for Today's Juvenile Court," *Judicature* 76:230–238 (1993). In the context of delinquency convictions to enhance criminal sentences, see Barry C. Feld, "The Constitutional Tension Between *Apprendi* and *McKeiver*: Sentence Enhancement Based on Delinquency Convictions and the Quality of Justice in Juvenile Courts," *Wake Forest Law Review* 38:1111–1224 (2003).

78. Linda Szymanski, *Juvenile Delinquents' Right to Counsel* (Pittsburgh: National Center for Juvenile Justice, 1988).

79. *In re Winship*, 397 U.S. 358, 90 S.Ct. 1068 (1970).

80. *McKeiver v. Pennsylvania*, 403 U.S. 528, 91 S.Ct. 1976 (1971).

81. See R. T. Powell, "Disposition Concepts," *Juvenile and Family Court Journal* 34:7–18 (1983).

82. Sanford Fox, *Juvenile Courts in a Nutshell* (St. Paul, MN: West, 1984), p. 221.

83. This section is adapted from Jack Haynes and Eugene Moore, "Particular Dispositions," *Juvenile and Family Court Journal* 34:41–48 (1983); see also Grant Grissom, "Dispositional Authority and the Future of the Juvenile Justice System," *Juvenile and Family Court Journal* 42:25–34 (1991).

84. Barry Krisberg, Elliot Currie, and David Onek, "What Works with Juvenile Offenders," *American Bar Association Journal on Criminal Justice* 10:20–24 (1995).

85. Anne L. Stahl, *Delinquency Cases in Juvenile Courts, 1999*, p. 2.

86. Charles M. Puzzanchera, *Person Offenses in Juvenile Court, 1990–1999*, OJJDP Fact Sheet (Washington, DC: U.S. Department of Justice, Office of Juvenile Justice and Delinquency Prevention, 2003).

87. Anne L. Stahl, *Delinquency Cases in Juvenile Courts, 1999*, p. 2.

88. Anthony Platt, *The Child Savers: The Invention of Delinquency* (Chicago: University of Chicago Press, 1969); David Rothman, *Conscience and Convenience: The Asylum and the Alternative in Progressive America* (Boston: Little, Brown, 1980).

89. Joseph Goldstein, Anna Freud, and Albert Solnit, *Beyond the Best Interests of the Child* (New York: Free Press, 1973).

90. See, for example, *in Interest on M.P.* 697 N.E.2d 1153 (Il. App. 1998); *Matter of Welfare of CAW* 579 N.W.2d 494 (MN. App. 1998).

91. See, for example, *Matter of Willis Alvin M.* 479 S.E.2d. 871 (WV 1996).

92. Simon Singer and David McDowall, "Criminalizing Delinquency: The Deterrent Effects of NYJO Law," *Law and Society Review* 22:Sections 21–37 (1988).

93. Washington Juvenile Justice Reform Act of 1977, Chap. 291; Wash.Rev.Code Ann. Title 9A, Sec. 1–91 (1977).

94. National Criminal Justice Association, *Juvenile Justice Reform Initiatives in the States, 1994–1996* (Washington, DC: U.S. Department of Justice, 1997).

95. Victor L. Streib, *The Juvenile Death Penalty Today: Death Sentences and Executions for Juvenile Crimes, January 1, 1973 – September 30, 2003* (Ada, OH: The Claude W. Pettit College of Law, Ohio Northern University, October 6, 2003), p. 3.

96. Lynn Cothern, *Juveniles and the Death Penalty* (Washington, DC: Office of Juvenile Justice and Delinquency Prevention, 2000).

97. Erica Goode, "Young Killer: Bad Seed or Work in Progress?" *New York Times*, November 25, 2003.

98. Streib, *The Juvenile Death Penalty Today*.

99. Steven Gerstein, "The Constitutionality of Executing Juvenile Offenders, *Thompson v. Oklahoma*," *Criminal Law Bulletin* 24:91–98 (1988); *Thompson v. Oklahoma*, 108 S.Ct. 2687 (1988).

100. 109 S.Ct. 2969 (1989); for a recent analysis of the *Wilkins* and *Stanford* cases, see the note in "*Stanford v. Kentucky* and *Wilkins v. Missouri:* Juveniles, Capital Crime, and Death Penalty," *Criminal Justice Journal* 11:240–266 (1989).

101. Linda Greenhouse, "Supreme Court to Review Using Executions in Juvenile Cases," *New York Times*, January 27, 2004.

102. Victor Streib, "Excluding Juveniles from New York's Impendent Death Penalty," *Albany Law Review* 54:625–679 (1990).

103. Goode, "Young Killer: Bad Seed or Work in Progress?"

104. David Stout, "Dozens of Nations Weigh In on Death Penalty Case," *New York Times*, July 20, 2004.

105. Paul Piersma, Jeanette Ganousis, Adrienne E. Volenik, Harry F. Swanger, and Patricia Connell, *Law and Tactics in Juvenile Cases* (Philadelphia: American Law Institute, American Bar Association, Committee on Continuing Education, 1977), p. 397.

106. J. Addison Bowman, "Appeals from Juvenile Courts," *Crime and Delinquency Journal* 11:63–77 (1965).

107. *In re Gault*, 387 U.S. 1 87 S.Ct. 1428 (1967).

108. *Davis v. Alaska*, 415 U.S. 308 (1974); 94 S.Ct. 1105.

109. *Oklahoma Publishing Co. v. District Court*, 430 U.S. 97 (1977); 97 S.Ct. 1045.

110. *Smith v. Daily Mail Publishing Co.*, 443 U.S. 97, 99 S.Ct. 2667, 61 L.Ed.2d 399 (1979).

111. Thomas Hughes, "Opening the Doors to Juvenile Court: Is There an Emerging Right of Public Access?" *Communications and the Law* 19:1–50 (1997).

112. Linda Szymanski, *Confidentiality of Juvenile Court Records* (Pittsburgh: National Center for Juvenile Justice, 1989).

113. Jeffrey A. Butts, *Can We Do Without Juvenile Justice?* (Washington, DC; Urban Institute, 2000).

114. Ira M. Schwartz, *Justice for Juveniles: Rethinking the Best Interests of the Child* (Lexington, MA: D. C. Heath, 1989), p. 172.

115. National Institute of Justice Update, "State Laws on Prosecutors' and Judges' Use of Juvenile Records" (Washington, DC: Office of Justice Programs, 1995).

15 Juvenile Corrections: Probation, Community Treatment, and Institutionalization

Chapter Outline

Juvenile Probation

Historical Development

Expanding Community Treatment

Contemporary Juvenile Probation

Organization and Administration

Duties of Juvenile Probation Officers

Probation Innovations

Intensive Supervision

Electronic Monitoring

Restorative Justice

Balanced Probation

Restitution

Residential Community Treatment

Nonresidential Community Treatment

POLICY AND PRACTICE: Three Model Nonresidential
Programs

Secure Corrections

History of Juvenile Institutions

Juvenile Institutions Today: Public and Private

Population Trends

Physical Conditions

The Institutionalized Juvenile

Male Inmates

Female Inmates

Correctional Treatment for Juveniles

Individual Treatment Techniques: Past and Present

Group Treatment Techniques

Educational, Vocational, and Recreational Programs

Wilderness Programs

Juvenile Boot Camps

The Legal Right to Treatment

The Struggle for Basic Civil Rights

Juvenile Aftercare and Reentry

Supervision

POLICY AND PRACTICE: Using the Intensive Aftercare
Program (IAP) Model

Aftercare Revocation Procedures

Chapter Objectives

1. Be able to distinguish between community treatment and institutional treatment for juvenile offenders

2. Be familiar with the disposition of probation, including how it is administered and by whom and recent trends in its use compared with other dispositions

3. Be aware of new approaches for providing probation services to juvenile offenders and comment on their effectiveness in reducing recidivism

4. Understand key historical developments of secure juvenile corrections in this country, including the principle of *least restrictive alternative*

5. Be familiar with recent trends in the use of juvenile institutions for juvenile offenders and how their use differs across states

6. Understand key issues facing the institutionalized juvenile offender

7. Be able to identify the various juvenile correctional treatment approaches that are in use today and comment on their effectiveness in reducing recidivism

8. Know the nature of aftercare for juvenile offenders and comment on recent innovations in juvenile aftercare and reentry programs

CNN. View the CNN video clip of this story and answer related Critical Thinking questions on your Juvenile Delinquency 9e CD-ROM.

Started in the late 1980s, juvenile boot camps were introduced as a way to get tough on youthful offenders through rigorous military-style training, while at the same time providing them with treatment programs. In theory, a successful boot camp program should rehabilitate juvenile offenders, reduce the number of beds needed in secure institutional programs, and thus reduce the overall cost of care. However, evaluations of these programs across the country found this not to be the case, and some found juveniles in boot camps to have higher recidivism rates than similar youths in other institutional settings. Research shows that one of the main reasons for their ineffectiveness is that the treatment component is often left out. In New Jersey, juvenile justice administrators are trying to change this trend. Here, juvenile boot camps combine rigorous physical training with a strong emphasis on education, drug counseling, job skills training, and other treatment programs to help them prepare for their return to the community. One other change that administrators point to as promising is that boot camp leaders are trained to act as mentors or role models to the juvenile offenders.

community treatment
Using nonsecure and noninstitutional residences, counseling services, victim restitution programs, and other community services to treat juveniles in their own communities.

There is a wide choice of correctional treatments available for juveniles, which can be subdivided into two major categories: community treatment and institutional treatment. **Community treatment** refers to efforts to provide care, protection, and treatment for juveniles in need. These efforts include probation, treatment services (such as individual and group counseling), restitution, and other programs. Community treatment also refers to the use of privately maintained residences, such as foster homes, small-group homes, and boarding schools, which are located in the community. Nonresidential programs, where youths remain in their own homes but are required to receive counseling, vocational training, and other services, also fall under the rubric of community treatment.

Institutional treatment facilities are correctional centers operated by federal, state, and county governments; these facilities restrict the movement of residents through staff monitoring, locked exits, and interior fence controls. A variety of functions within juvenile corrections are served by these facilities, including (1) reception centers that screen juveniles and assign them to an appropriate facility; (2) specialized facilities that provide specific types of care, such as drug treatment; (3) training schools or reformatories for youths needing a long-term secure setting; (4) ranch or forestry camps that provide long-term residential care; and (5) boot camps, which seek to rehabilitate youths through the application of rigorous physical training.

Choosing the proper mode of juvenile corrections can be difficult. Some experts believe that any hope for rehabilitating juvenile offenders and resolving the problems of juvenile crime lies in community treatment programs. Such programs are smaller than secure facilities for juveniles, operate in a community setting, and offer creative approaches to treating the offender. In contrast, institutionalizing young offenders may do more harm than good. It exposes them to prisonlike conditions and to more-experienced delinquents without giving them the benefit of constructive treatment programs.

Those who favor secure treatment are concerned about the threat that violent young offenders present to the community and believe that a stay in a juvenile institution may have a long-term deterrent effect. They point to the findings of Charles Murray and Louis B. Cox, who uncovered what they call a **suppression effect**—a reduction in the number of arrests per year following release from a secure facility—which is not achieved when juveniles are placed in less-punitive programs.[1] Murray and Cox concluded that the justice system must choose which outcome its programs are aimed at achieving: prevention of delinquency, or the care and protection of needy youths. If the former is a proper goal, institutionalization or the threat of institutionalization is desirable. Not surprisingly, secure treatment is still being used extensively, and the populations of these facilities continue to grow as state legislators pass more stringent and punitive sentencing packages aimed at repeat juvenile offenders.

We begin this chapter with a detailed discussion of community treatment, examining both traditional probation and new approaches for providing probation services to juvenile offenders. Next, we trace the development of alternatives to incarceration, including community-based, nonsecure treatment programs and graduated sanctions (programs that provide community-based options while reserving secure care for violent offenders). The current state of secure juvenile corrections is then reviewed, beginning with some historical background, followed by a discussion of life in institutions, treatment issues, legal rights, and aftercare and reentry programs.

suppression effect
A reduction in the number of arrests per year for youths who have been incarcerated or otherwise punished.

JUVENILE PROBATION

probation
Nonpunitive, legal disposition for juveniles emphasizing community treatment in which the juvenile is closely supervised by an officer of the court and must adhere to a strict set of rules to avoid incarceration.

Probation and other forms of community treatment generally refer to nonpunitive legal disposition for delinquent youths, emphasizing treatment without incarceration. Probation is the primary form of community treatment used by the juvenile justice system. A juvenile who is on probation is maintained in the community under the supervision of an officer of the court. Probation also encompasses a set of rules and conditions that must be met for the offender to remain in the community. Juveniles on probation may be placed in a wide variety of community-based treatment programs that provide services ranging from group counseling to drug treatment.

Community treatment is based on the idea that the juvenile offender is not a danger to the community and has a better chance of being rehabilitated within the community. It provides offenders with the opportunity to be supervised by trained personnel who can help them reestablish forms of acceptable behavior in a community setting. When applied correctly, community treatment (1) maximizes the liberty of the individual while vindicating the authority of the law and protecting the public; (2) promotes rehabilitation by maintaining normal community contacts; (3) avoids the negative effects of confinement, which often severely complicate the reintegration of the offender into the community; and (4) greatly reduces the financial cost to the public.[2]

Historical Development

Although the major developments in community treatment have occurred in the twentieth century, its roots go back much farther. In England specialized procedures for dealing with youthful offenders were recorded as early as 1820, when the magistrates of the Warwickshire quarter sessions (periodic court hearings held in a county, or shire, of England) adopted the practice of sentencing youthful criminals to prison terms of one day, then releasing them conditionally under the supervision of their parents or masters.[3]

In the United States, juvenile probation developed as part of the wave of social reform characterizing the latter half of the nineteenth century. Massachusetts took the first step. Under an act passed in 1869, an agent of the state board of charities was authorized to appear in criminal trials involving juveniles, to find them suitable homes, and to visit them periodically. These services were soon broadened, so that by 1890 probation had become a mandatory part of the court structure.[4]

Probation was a cornerstone in the development of the juvenile court system. In fact, in some states, supporters of the juvenile court movement viewed probation as the first step toward achieving the benefits that the new court was intended to provide. The rapid spread of juvenile courts during the first decades of the twentieth century encouraged the further development of probation. The two were closely related and, to a large degree, both sprang from the conviction that the young could be rehabilitated and that the public was responsible for protecting them.

Expanding Community Treatment

By the mid-1960s, juvenile probation had become a complex institution that touched the lives of an enormous number of children. To many experts, institutionalization of even the most serious delinquent youths is a mistake. Reformers believed that confinement in a high-security institution could not solve the problems that brought a youth into a delinquent way of life, and that the experience could actually help amplify delinquency once the youth returned to the community.[5] Surveys indicating that 30 to 40 percent of adult prison inmates had prior experience with the juvenile court, and that many had been institutionalized as youths, gave little support to the argument that an institutional experience can be beneficial or reduce recidivism.[6]

The Massachusetts Experience The expansion of community programs was energized by correctional reform in the state of Massachusetts. Since the early 1970s, Massachusetts has led the movement to keep juvenile offenders in the community. After decades of documenting the failures of the youth correctional system, Massachusetts, led by its juvenile correctional commissioner Jerome Miller, closed most of its secure juvenile facilities.[7] Today, 30 years later, the Massachusetts Department of Youth Services still operates a community-based correctional system. The majority of youths are serviced in nonsecure community settings, and only a few dangerous or unmanageable youths are placed in some type of secure facilities.

Many of the early programs suffered from residential isolation and limited services. Over time, however, many of the group homes and unlocked structured residential settings were relocated in residential community environments and became highly successful in addressing the needs of juveniles, while presenting little or no security risk to themselves or others. For example, the Roxbury Youthworks is an inner-city program in Boston that aims to control delinquency through a comprehensive range of resources that include (1) evaluation and counseling at a local court clinic, (2) employment and training, (3) detention diversion, and (4) outreach and tracking to help youths reenter the community. Contracting with the state, Roxbury Youthworks provides intensive community supervision for almost 90 percent of the youths under its jurisdiction.[8]

Though the efforts to turn juvenile corrections into a purely community-based system has not been adopted elsewhere, the Massachusetts model encouraged development of nonpunitive programs, which have proliferated across the nation. The concept of probation has been expanded, and new programs have been created.

Juvenile probation officers provide supervision and treatment in the community. The treatment plan is a product of the intake, diagnostic, and investigative aspects of probation. Treatment plans vary in terms of approach and structure. Some juveniles simply report to the probation officer and follow the conditions of probation. In other cases, juvenile probation officers will supervise young people more intensely, monitor their daily activities, and work with them in directed treatment programs. Here, a juvenile probation officer and police officer talk with Crips gang members in California.

Contemporary Juvenile Probation

Traditional probation is still the backbone of community-based corrections. As Figure 15.1 shows, almost 400,000 juveniles were placed on formal probation in 1999, which amounts to more than 60 percent of all juvenile dispositions. The use of probation has increased significantly since 1990, when around 220,000 adjudicated youths were being placed on probation.[9] These figures show that regardless of public sentiment, probation continues to be a popular dispositional alternative for judges. Here are the arguments in favor of probation:

1. For youths who can be supervised in the community, probation represents an appropriate disposition.

2. Probation allows the court to tailor a program to each juvenile offender, including those involved in person-oriented offenses.

3. The justice system continues to have confidence in rehabilitation, while accommodating demands for legal controls and public protection, even when caseloads may include many more serious offenders than in the past.

4. Probation is often the disposition of choice, particularly for status offenders.[10]

The Nature of Probation In the majority of jurisdictions, probation is a direct judicial order that allows a youth who is found to be a delinquent or status offender to remain in the community under court-ordered supervision. A probation sentence implies a contract between the court and the juvenile. The court promises to hold a period of institutionalization in abeyance; the juvenile promises to adhere to a set of rules mandated by the court. If the rules are violated—and especially if the juvenile commits another offense—the probation may be revoked. In that case, the contract is terminated and the original commitment order may be enforced. The rules of probation vary, but they typically involve conditions such as attending school or work, keeping regular hours, remaining in the jurisdiction, and staying out of trouble.

In the juvenile court, probation is often ordered for an indefinite period. Depending on the statutes of the jurisdiction, the seriousness of the offense, and the juvenile's adjustment on probation, youths can remain under supervision until the court no longer has jurisdiction over them (that is, when they reach the age of majority). State statutes determine whether a judge can specify how long a juvenile may be placed under an order of probation. In most jurisdictions, the status of probation is reviewed

FIGURE 15.1

Probation and Correctional
Population Trends

NOTE: There has been a substantial
increase in the number of cases in
which adjudicated juveniles were
placed on probation or ordered to
a residential facility between 1990
and 1999.

SOURCE: Charles Puzzanchera, Anne
L. Stahl, Terrence A. Finnegan, Nancy
Tierney, and Howard N. Snyder, *Juvenile
Court Statistics 1999* (Pittsburgh, PA:
National Center on Juvenile
Justice, 2003).

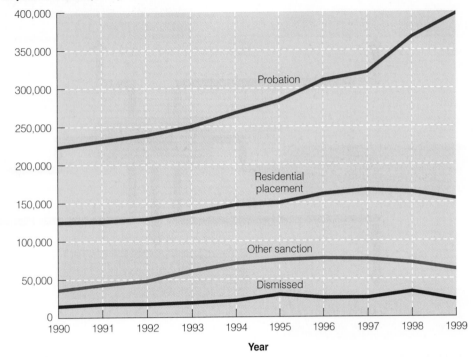

Adjudicated delinquency cases

regularly to ensure that a juvenile is not kept on probation needlessly. Generally, discretion lies with the probation officer to discharge youths who are adjusting to the treatment plan.

Conditions of Probation Probation conditions are rules mandating that a juvenile on probation behave in a particular way. They can include restitution or reparation, intensive supervision, intensive counseling, participation in a therapeutic program, or participation in an educational or vocational training program. In addition to these specific conditions, state statutes generally allow courts to insist that probationers lead law-abiding lives, maintain a residence in a family setting, refrain from associating with certain types of people, and remain in a particular area unless they have permission to leave. (See Figure 15.2 for different probation options.)

Although probation conditions vary, they are never supposed to be capricious, cruel, or beyond the capacity of the juvenile to satisfy. Furthermore, conditions of probation should relate to the crime that was committed and to the conduct of the youth. Courts have invalidated probation conditions that were harmful or that violated the juvenile's due-process rights. Restricting a young person's movement, insisting on a mandatory program of treatment, ordering indefinite terms of probation, and demanding financial reparation where this is impossible are all grounds for appellate court review. For example, it would not be appropriate for a probation order to bar a youth from visiting his girlfriend (unless he had threatened or harmed her) merely because her parents objected to the relationship.[11] However, courts have ruled that it is permissible to bar juveniles from such sources of danger as a "known gang area" in order to protect them from harm.[12]

If a youth violates the conditions of probation—and especially if the juvenile commits another offense—the court can revoke probation. In this case, the contract is terminated and the original commitment order may be enforced. The juvenile court ordinarily handles a decision to revoke probation upon recommendation of the probation officer. Today, as a result of Supreme Court decisions dealing with the rights of adult probationers, a juvenile is normally entitled to legal representation and a hearing when a violation of probation occurs.[13]

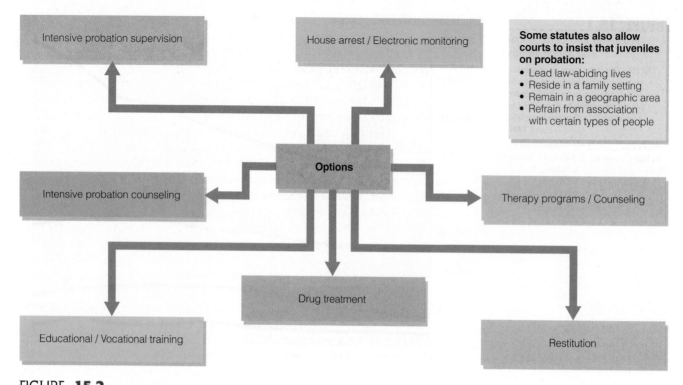

FIGURE 15.2
Conditions of Probation

Organization and Administration

Probation services are administered by the local juvenile court, or by the state administrative office of courts, in 23 states and the District of Columbia. In another 14 states, juvenile probation services are split, with the juvenile court having control in urban counties and a state executive serving in smaller counties. About 10 states have a statewide office of juvenile probation located in the executive branch. In 3 states, county executives administer probation.[14] These agencies employ an estimated 18,000 juvenile probation officers throughout the United States.

In the typical juvenile probation department, the chief probation officer is central to its effective operation. In addition, large probation departments include one or more assistant chiefs, each of whom is responsible for one aspect of probation service. One assistant chief might oversee training, another might supervise special offender groups, and still another might act as liaison with police or community-service agencies.

Although juvenile probation services continue to be predominantly organized under the judiciary, recent legislative activity has been in the direction of transferring those services from the local juvenile court judge to a state court administrative office. Whether local juvenile courts or state agencies should administer juvenile probation services is debatable. In years past, the organization of probation services depended primarily on the size of the program and the number of juveniles under its supervision. Because of this momentum to develop unified court systems, many juvenile court services are being consolidated into state court systems.

Duties of Juvenile Probation Officers

juvenile probation officer
Officer of the court involved in all four stages of the court process—intake, predisposition, postadjudication, and postdisposition—who assists the court and supervises juveniles placed on probation.

The **juvenile probation officer** plays an important role in the justice process, beginning with intake and continuing throughout the period in which a juvenile is under court supervision. Probation officers are involved at four stages of the court process. At *intake*, they screen complaints by deciding to adjust the matter, refer the juvenile to an agency for service, or refer the case to the court for judicial action. During the *predisposition* stage, they participate in release or detention decisions. At the *postadjudication* stage, they assist the court in reaching its dispositional decision. During *postdisposition,* they supervise juveniles placed on probation.

At intake, the probation staff has preliminary discussions with the juvenile and the family to determine whether court intervention is necessary or whether the matter can be better resolved by some form of social service. If the juvenile is placed in a detention facility, the probation officer helps the court decide whether the juvenile should continue to be held or released pending the adjudication and disposition of the case.

The probation officer exercises tremendous influence over the youth and the family by developing a **social investigation,** or **predisposition, report** and submitting it to the court. This report is a clinical diagnosis of the youth's problems and of the need for court assistance based on an evaluation of social functioning, personality, and environmental issues. The report includes an analysis of the child's feelings about the violations and his or her capacity for change. It also examines the influence of family members, peers, and other environmental influences in producing and possibly resolving the problems. All of this information is brought together in a complex but meaningful picture of the offender's personality, problems, and environment.

Juvenile probation officers also provide the youth with supervision and treatment in the community. Treatment plans vary in terms of approach and structure. Some juveniles simply report to the probation officer and follow the **conditions of probation.** In other cases, the probation officer may need to provide extensive counseling to the youth and family or, more typically, refer them to other social service agencies, such as a drug treatment center. Figure 15.3 provides an overview of the juvenile probation

social investigation report, predisposition report
Developed by the juvenile probation officer, this report consists of a clinical diagnosis of the juvenile and his or her need for court assistance, relevant environmental and personality factors, and any other information that would assist the court in developing a treatment plan for the juvenile.

conditions of probation
The rules and regulations mandating that a juvenile on probation behave in a particular way.

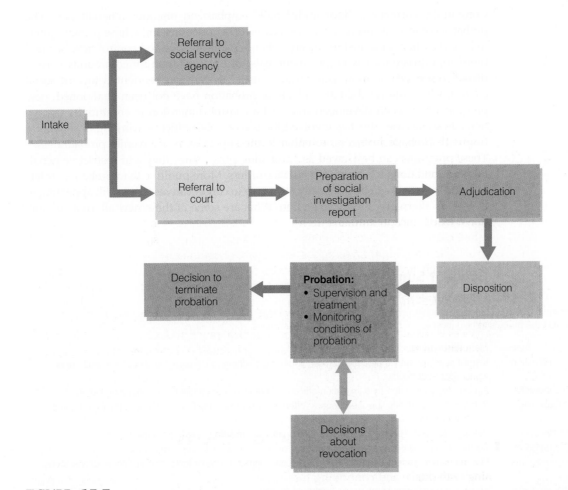

FIGURE 15.3
The Juvenile Probation Officer's Influence

EXHIBIT **15.1**

Duties of the Juvenile Probation Officer

I Provide direct counseling and casework services
I Interview and collect social service data
I Make diagnostic recommendations
I Maintain working relationships with law enforcement agencies
I Use community resources and services
I Direct volunteer case aides
I Write predisposition or social investigation reports
I Work with families of children under supervision
I Provide specialized services, such as group therapy
I Supervise specialized caseloads involving children with special problems
I Make decisions about the revocation of probation and its termination

TO QUIZ YOURSELF ON THIS MATERIAL, go to the Juvenile Delinquency 9e website.

officer's sphere of influence. Exhibit 15.1 summarizes the probation officer's role. Performance of such a broad range of functions requires thorough training. Today, juvenile probation officers have legal or social work backgrounds or special counseling skills.

PROBATION INNOVATIONS

Community corrections have traditionally emphasized offender rehabilitation. The probation officer has been viewed as a caseworker or counselor, whose primary job is to help the offender adjust to society. Offender surveillance and control have seemed more appropriate for law enforcement, jails, and prisons than for community corrections.[15] Since 1980, a more conservative justice system has reoriented toward social control. While the rehabilitative ideals of probation have not been abandoned, new programs have been developed that add a control dimension to community corrections. In some cases this has involved the use of police officers, working in collaboration with probation officers, to enhance the supervision of juvenile probationers.[16] These programs can be viewed as "probation plus," since they add restrictive penalties and conditions to community-service orders. More punitive than probation, intermediate sanctions can be politically attractive to conservatives, while still appealing to liberals as alternatives to incarceration. What are some of these new alternative sanctions? (See Concept Summary 15.1.)

Concept Summary 15.1

Community-Based Corrections

Although correctional treatment in the community generally refers to nonpunitive legal dispositions, in most cases there are still restrictions designed to protect the public and hold juvenile offenders accountable for their actions.

Type	Main Restrictions
Probation	Regular supervision by a probation officer; youth must adhere to conditions such as attend school or work, stay out of trouble.
Intensive supervision	Almost daily supervision by a probation officer; adhere to similar conditions as regular probation.
House arrest	Remain at home during specified periods; often there is monitoring through random phone calls, visits, or electronic devices.
Restorative justice	Restrictions may be prescribed by community members to help repair harm done to victim.
Balanced probation	Restrictions are tailored to the risk the juvenile offender presents to the community.
Residential programs	Placement in a residential, nonsecure facility such as group home or foster home; adhere to conditions; close monitoring.
Nonresidential programs	Remain in own home; comply with treatment regime.

Intensive Supervision

juvenile intensive probation supervision (JIPS)
A true alternative to incarceration that involves almost daily supervision of the juvenile by the probation officer assigned to the case.

Juvenile intensive probation supervision (JIPS) involves treating offenders who would normally have been sent to a secure treatment facility as part of a very small probation caseload that receives almost daily scrutiny.[17] The primary goal of JIPS is *decarceration*; without intensive supervision, youngsters would normally be sent to secure juvenile facilities that are already overcrowded. The second goal is control; high-risk juvenile offenders can be maintained in the community under much closer security than traditional probation efforts can provide. A third goal is maintaining community ties and reintegration. Offenders can remain in the community and complete their education while avoiding the pains of imprisonment.

Intensive probation programs get mixed reviews. Some jurisdictions find that they are more successful than traditional probation supervision and come at a much cheaper cost than incarceration.[18] However, most research indicates that the failure rate is high and that younger offenders who commit petty crimes are the most likely to fail when placed in intensive supervision programs.[19] It is not surprising that intensive probation clients fail more often because, after all, they are more serious offenders who might otherwise have been incarcerated and are now being watched and supervised more closely than other probationers.

An innovative experiment in three Mississippi counties examined the differential effects on juvenile justice costs for intensive supervision and monitoring, regular probation, and cognitive behavioral treatment, which involved sessions on problem solving, social skills, negotiation skills, the management of emotion, and values enhancement, to improve the thinking and reasoning ability of juvenile offenders. After one year of the program the intensive supervision treatment was found to be less cost effective than the other two treatments, with the cognitive behavioral treatment imposing the fewest costs on the juvenile justice system.[20]

Electronic Monitoring

house arrest
An offender is required to stay at home during specified periods of time; monitoring is done by random phone calls and visits or by electronic devices.

electronic monitoring
Active monitoring systems consist of a radio transmitter worn by the offender that sends a continuous signal to the probation department computer, alerting officials if the offender leaves his or her place of confinement. Passive systems employ computer-generated random phone calls that must be responded to in a certain period of time from a particular phone or other device.

Another program, which has been used with adult offenders and is finding its way into the juvenile justice system, is **house arrest,** which is often coupled with **electronic monitoring.** This program allows offenders sentenced to probation to remain in the community on condition that they stay at home during specific periods (for example, after school or work, on weekends, and in the evenings). Offenders may be monitored through random phone calls, visits, or, in some jurisdictions, electronic devices.

Two types of electronic systems are used: active and passive. *Active systems* monitor the offender by continuously sending a signal back to the central office. If an offender leaves home at an unauthorized time, the signal is broken and the failure recorded. In some cases, the control officer is automatically notified through a beeper. In contrast, *passive systems* usually involve random phone calls generated by computers to which the juvenile offender must respond within a particular time (for example, 30 seconds). Some passive systems require the offender to place the monitoring device in a verifier box that sends a signal back to the control computer; another approach is to have the arrestee repeat words that are analyzed by a voice verifier and compared with tapes of the juvenile's voice.

Most systems employ radio transmitters that receive a signal from a device worn by the offender and relay it back to the computer via telephone lines. Probationers are fitted with an unremovable monitoring device that alerts the probation department's computers if they leave their place of confinement.[21]

Joseph B. Vaughn conducted one of the first surveys of juvenile electronic monitoring in 1989, examining eight programs in five different probation departments.[22] Vaughn found that all the programs adopted electronic monitoring to reduce institutional overcrowding and that most agencies reported success in reducing the number of days juveniles spent in detention. In addition, the programs allowed the youths, who would otherwise be detained, to remain in the home and participate in counseling, educational, or vocational activities. Of particular benefit to pretrial detainees

A number of probation innovations have been experimented with to keep juvenile offenders from being sent to secure juvenile facilities. One of these is electronic monitoring, which, in addition to requiring juveniles to follow regular conditions of probation, monitors their movements to keep them confined to specified areas such as home, school, or work. Pictured here is a juvenile probationer with an electronic monitoring device strapped to his ankle.

© Joel Gordon

was the opportunity to remain in a home environment with supervision. This experience provided the court with a much clearer picture of how the juvenile would eventually reintegrate into society. However, Vaughn found that none of the benefits of the treatment objective in the programs had been empirically validated. The potential for behavior modification and the lasting effects of any personal changes remain unknown.

Recent indications are that electronic monitoring can be effective. Evaluations show that recidivism rates are no higher than in traditional programs, costs are lower, and overcrowding is reduced. Also, electronic monitoring seems to work better with some individuals than others: Serious felony offenders, substance abusers, repeat offenders, and people serving the longest sentences are the most likely to fail.[23]

Electronic monitoring combined with house arrest is being hailed as one of the most important developments in correctional policy. Its supporters claim that it has the benefits of relatively low cost and high security, while at the same time it helps offenders avoid imprisonment in overcrowded, dangerous state facilities. Furthermore, fewer supervisory officers are needed to handle large numbers of offenders.

Despite these strengths, electronic monitoring has its drawbacks:

I Existing systems can be affected by faulty telephone equipment.

I Most electronic monitoring/house arrest programs do not provide rehabilitation services.

I Some believe electronic monitoring is contrary to a citizen's right to privacy.[24]

Restorative Justice

Restorative justice is a nonpunitive strategy for delinquency control that attempts to address the issues that produce conflict between two parties (offender and victim) and, hence, reconcile the parties. Restoration rather than retribution or punishment is at the heart of the restorative justice approach. Seven core values characterize restorative justice:

I Crime is an offense against human relationships.

I Victims and the community are central to justice processes.

I The first priority of justice processes is to assist victims.

I The second priority of justice processes is to restore the community, to the degree possible.

I The offender has a personal responsibility to victims and to the community for crimes committed.

- The offender will develop improved competency and understanding as a result of the restorative justice experience.
- Stakeholders share responsibilities for restorative justice through partnerships for action.[25]

Researchers Heather Strang and Lawrence Sherman carried out a systematic review and meta-analysis of the effects of restorative justice on juvenile reoffending and victim satisfaction. The review involved two studies from Australia and one from the United States that evaluated the restorative justice practice of face-to-face conferences. (The main reason for the small number of studies is that the authors used only those studies that employed the highest quality evaluation design—randomized controlled experiments—to assess program effects.) The conferences proceeded as follows:

> *Any victims (or their representatives) present have the opportunity to describe the full extent of the harm a crime has caused, offenders are required to listen to the victims and to understand the consequences of their own actions, and all participants are invited to deliberate about what actions the offender could take to repair them. The precondition of such a conference is that the offender does not dispute the fact that he is responsible for the harm caused, and the conference cannot and will not become a trial to determine what happened.[26]*

The review found evidence that this form of restorative justice can be an effective strategy in reducing repeat offending by juveniles who have committed violent crimes. The type of violence includes minor offenses of battery to middle-level offenses of assault and aggravated assault. The review also found that face-to-face conferences can be effective in preventing victims from committing crimes of retaliation against their perpetrators. Perhaps not surprisingly, across all studies victim satisfaction levels strongly favored restorative justice compared to traditional juvenile justice proceedings.[27]

To learn more about the **Australian restorative justice experiments,** go to www.aic.gov.au/rjustice/rise/index.html. For an up-to-date list of web links, go to http://cj.wadsworth.com/siegel_jd9e.

Balanced Probation

balanced probation
Programs that integrate community protection, accountability of the juvenile offender, competency, and individualized attention to the juvenile offender; based on the principle that juvenile offenders must accept responsibility for their behavior.

In recent years some jurisdictions have turned to a **balanced probation** approach in an effort to enhance the success of probation.[28] Balanced probation systems build on the principles of restorative justice, by integrating community protection, the accountability of the juvenile offender, and individualized attention to the offender (see Figure 15.4). These programs are based on the view that juveniles are responsible for their actions and have an obligation to society whenever they commit an offense. The probation officer establishes a program tailored to the offender while helping the offender accept responsibility for his or her actions. The balanced approach is promising because it specifies a distinctive role for the juvenile probation system.[29] The balanced approach has been implemented with some success, as these examples demonstrate:

- In Pittsburgh, probationers in an intensive day treatment program solicit suggestions from community organizations about service projects they would like to see completed. They work with community residents on projects such as home repair and gardening for the elderly, voter registration, painting homes and public buildings, and cultivating community gardens.

- In Florida, in a program sponsored by the Florida Department of Juvenile Justice and supervised by The 100 Black Men of Palm Beach County, Inc., offenders create shelters for abused, abandoned, and HIV-positive infants. Victims' rights advocates also train juvenile justice staff on sensitivity in their interaction with victims and help prepare victim awareness curricula for youths in residential programs.

- In cities and towns in Pennsylvania, Montana, and Minnesota, family members and other citizens acquainted with a juvenile offender, or the victim of a juvenile crime, gather to determine the best response to the offense. Held in schools, churches, or other community facilities, these conferences ensure that offenders hear community disapproval of their behavior. Participants develop an agreement for repairing the damage to the victim and the community and define a plan for reintegrating the offender.[30]

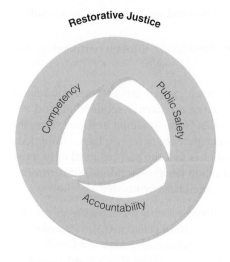

FIGURE 15.4
Balanced Approach Mission

SOURCE: Gordon Bazemore and Mark Umbreit, *Balanced and Restorative Justice for Juveniles—A Framework for Juvenile Justice in the 21st Century* (Washington, DC: Office of Juvenile Justice and Delinquency Prevention, 1997), p. 14.

Another promising program that adheres to a balanced probation approach is the California 8% Solution, which is run by the Orange County Probation Department. The "8%" refers to the percentage of juvenile offenders who are responsible for the majority of crime: In the case of Orange County, 8 percent of first-time offenders were responsible for 55 percent of repeat cases over a three-year period. This 8 percent problem has become the 8 percent solution, by the Probation Department initiating a comprehensive, multiagency program targeting this group of offenders.[31]

Once the probation officer identifies an offender for the program—the 8% Early Intervention Program—the youth is referred to the Youth and Family Resource Center. Here the youth's needs are assessed and an appropriate treatment plan is developed. Some of the services provided to youths include

I An outside school for students in junior and senior high school

I Transportation to and from home

I Counseling for drug and alcohol abuse

I Employment preparation and job placement services

I At-home, intensive family counseling[32]

Although balanced probation programs are still in their infancy and their effectiveness remains to be tested, they have generated great interest because of their potential for relieving overcrowded correctional facilities and reducing the pain and stigma of incarceration. There seems to be little question that the use of these innovations, and juvenile probation in general, will increase in the years ahead. Given the $40,000 cost of a year's commitment to a typical residential facility, it should not be a great burden to develop additional probation services.

Restitution

monetary restitution
A requirement that juvenile offenders compensate crime victims for out-of-pocket losses caused by the crime, including property damage, lost wages, and medical expenses.

victim service restitution
The juvenile offender is required to provide some service directly to the crime victim.

community service restitution
The juvenile offender is required to assist some worthwhile community organization for a period of time.

Victim restitution is another widely used method of community treatment. In most jurisdictions, restitution is part of a probationary sentence and is administered by the county probation staff. In many jurisdictions, independent restitution programs have been set up by local governments; in others, restitution is administered by a private nonprofit organization.[33]

Restitution can take several forms. A juvenile can reimburse the victim of the crime or donate money to a charity or public cause; this is referred to as **monetary restitution.** In other instances, a juvenile may be required to provide some service directly to the victim (**victim service restitution**) or to assist a community organization (**community service restitution**).

Requiring youths to reimburse the victims of their crimes is the most widely used method of restitution in the United States. Less widely used, but more common in Europe, is restitution to a charity. In the past few years numerous programs have been set up for the juvenile offender to provide service to the victim or to participate in community programs—for example, working in schools for children with development delays. In some cases, juveniles are required to contribute both money and community service. Other programs emphasize employment.[34]

Restitution programs can be employed at various stages of the juvenile justice process. They can be part of a diversion program prior to conviction, a method of informal adjustment at intake, or a condition of probation. Restitution has a number of advantages: It provides alternative sentencing options; it offers monetary compensation or service to crime victims; it allows the juvenile the opportunity to compensate the victim and take a step toward becoming a productive member of society; it helps relieve overcrowded juvenile courts, probation caseloads, and detention facilities. Finally, like other alternatives to incarceration, restitution has the potential for allowing vast savings in the operation of the juvenile justice system. Monetary restitution programs in particular may improve the public's attitude toward juvenile justice by offering equity to the victims of crime and ensuring that offenders take responsibility for their actions.

Despite its many advantages, some believe restitution supports retribution rather than rehabilitation because it emphasizes justice for the victim and criminal responsibility for illegal acts. There is some concern that restitution creates penalties for juvenile offenders where none existed before.

The use of restitution is increasing. In 1977 there were fewer than 15 formal restitution programs around the United States. By 1985, formal programs existed in 400 jurisdictions, and 35 states had statutory provisions that gave courts the authority to order juvenile restitution.[35] Today, all 50 states, as well as the District of Columbia, have statutory restitution programs.

Does Restitution Work? How successful is restitution as a treatment alternative? Most evaluations have shown that it is reasonably effective and should be expanded.[36] In an analysis of federally sponsored restitution programs, Peter Schneider and his associates found that about 95 percent of youths who received restitution as a condition of probation successfully completed their orders.[37] Factors related to success were family income, good school attendance, few prior offenses, minor current offense, and size of restitution order. Schneider found that the youths who received restitution as a sole sanction (without probation) were those originally viewed by juvenile court judges as the better risks, and consequently they had lower failure and recidivism rates than youths ordered to make restitution after being placed on probation.

Anne Schneider conducted a thorough analysis of restitution programs in four different states and found that participants had lower recidivism rates than youths in control groups (regular probation caseloads).[38] Although Schneider's data indicate that restitution may reduce recidivism, the number of youths who had subsequent involvement in the justice system still seemed high. In short, there is evidence that most restitution orders are successfully completed and that youths who make restitution are less likely to become recidivists. However, the number of repeat offenses committed by juveniles who made restitution suggests that, by itself, restitution is not the answer to the delinquency problem.

Restitution programs may be difficult to implement in some circumstances. Offenders may find it difficult to make monetary restitution without securing new employment, which can be difficult during periods of high unemployment. Problems also arise when offenders who need jobs suffer from drug abuse or emotional problems. Public and private agencies are likely sites for community service restitution, but their directors are sometimes reluctant to allow delinquent youths access to their organizations. Beyond these problems, some juvenile probation officers view restitution programs as a threat to their authority and to the autonomy of their organizations.

Another criticism of restitution programs is that they foster involuntary servitude. Indigent clients may be unfairly punished when they are unable to make restitution payments or face probation violations. To avoid such bias, probation officers should first determine why payment has stopped and then suggest appropriate action, rather than simply treating nonpayment as a matter of law enforcement.

Finally, restitution orders are subject to the same abuses as traditional sentencing methods. Restitution orders given to one delinquent offender may be quite different from those given another in a comparable case. To remedy this situation, a number of jurisdictions have been using guidelines to encourage standardization of orders.

Restitution programs may be an important alternative to incarceration, benefiting the child, the victim, and the juvenile justice system. H. Ted Rubin, a leading juvenile justice expert, even advocates that courts placing juveniles in day treatment and community-based residential programs also include restitution requirements in their orders and expect that these requirements be fulfilled during placement.[39] However, all restitution programs should be evaluated carefully to answer these questions:

I   What type of offenders would be most likely to benefit from restitution?

I   When is monetary restitution more desirable than community service?

I What is the best point in the juvenile justice process to impose restitution?

I What is the effect of restitution on the juvenile justice system?

I How successful are restitution programs?

Residential Community Treatment

As noted earlier, many experts believe that institutionalization of even the most serious delinquent youths is a mistake. Confinement in a high-security institution usually cannot solve the problems that brought a youth into a delinquent way of life, and the experience may actually amplify delinquency once the youth returns to the community. Many agree that warehousing juveniles without attention to their treatment needs does little to prevent their return to criminal behavior. Research has shown that the most effective secure-corrections programs provided individualized services for a small number of participants. Large training schools have not proved to be effective.[40] This realization has produced a wide variety of residential community treatment programs to service youths who need a more secure environment than can be provided by probation services, but who do not require placement in a state-run juvenile correctional facility.

How are community corrections implemented? In some cases, youths are placed under probation supervision, and the probation department maintains a residential treatment facility. Placement can also be made to the department of social services or juvenile corrections with the direction that the youth be placed in a residential facility. **Residential programs** are typically divided into four major categories: (1) group homes, including boarding schools and apartment-type settings, (2) foster homes, (3) family group homes, and (4) rural programs.

Group homes are nonsecure residences that provide counseling, education, job training, and family living. They are staffed by a small number of qualified persons, and generally house 12 to 15 youngsters. The institutional quality of the environment is minimized, and youths are given the opportunity to build a close relationship with the staff. Youths reside in the home, attend public schools, and participate in community activities in the area.

Foster care programs involve one or two juveniles who live with a family—usually a husband and wife who serve as surrogate parents. The juveniles enter into a close relationship with the foster parents and receive the attention and care they did not receive at home. The quality of the foster home experience depends on the foster parents. Foster care for adjudicated juvenile offenders has not been extensive in the United States. Welfare departments generally handle foster placements, and funding of this treatment option has been a problem for the juvenile justice system. However, foster home services have expanded as a community treatment approach.

One example of a successful foster care program is the multidimensional treatment foster care (MTFC) program, developed by social scientists at the Oregon Social Learning Center. Designed for the most serious and chronic male young offenders, this program combines individual therapy such as skill building in problem solving for the youths, and family therapy for the biological or adoptive parents. The foster care families receive training by program staff so they can provide the young people with close supervision, fair and consistent limits and consequences, and a supportive relationship with an adult.[41] Foster care families also receive close supervision and are consulted regularly on the progress of the youth by program staff. An experiment of MTFC found that one year after the completion of the program, participating youths were significantly less likely to be arrested than a control group.[42]

Family group homes combine elements of foster care and group home placements. Juveniles are placed in a group home that is run by a family rather than by a professional staff. Troubled youths have an opportunity to learn to get along in

residential programs
Placement of a juvenile offender in a residential, nonsecure facility such as a group home, foster home, family group home, or rural home where the juvenile can be closely monitored and develop close relationships with staff members.

group homes
Nonsecured, structured residences that provide counseling, education, job training, and family living.

foster care programs
Juveniles who are orphans or whose parents cannot care for them are placed with families who provide the attention, guidance, and care they did not receive at home.

family group homes
A combination of foster care and a group home in which a juvenile is placed in a private group home run by a single family rather than by professional staff.

a family-like situation, and at the same time the state avoids the startup costs and neighborhood opposition often associated with establishing a public institution.

rural programs
Specific recreational and work opportunities provided for juveniles in a rural setting such as a forestry camp, a farm, or a ranch.

Rural programs include forestry camps, ranches, and farms that provide recreational activities or work for juveniles. Programs typically handle from 30 to 50 youths. Such programs have the disadvantage of isolating juveniles from the community, but reintegration can be achieved if the youth's stay is short and if family and friends are allowed to visit.

Most residential programs use group counseling as the major treatment tool. Although group facilities have been used less often than institutional placements, there is a trend toward developing community-based residential facilities.

Nonresidential Community Treatment

nonresidential programs
Juveniles remain in their own homes but receive counseling, education, employment, diagnostic, and casework services through an intensive support system.

In **nonresidential programs** youths remain in their homes and receive counseling, education, employment, diagnostic, and casework services. A counselor or probation officer gives innovative and intensive support to help the youth remain at home. Family therapy, educational tutoring, and job placement may all be part of the program.

Nonresidential programs are often modeled on the Provo experiment, begun in 1959 in Utah, and on the Essexfields Rehabilitation Project, started in the early 1960s in Essex County, New Jersey.[43] Today, one of the best-known approaches is multisystemic therapy (MST), which has been replicated at a number of sites around the United States. MST and two other innovative programs are the subject of the Policy and Practice box entitled "Three Model Nonresidential Programs."

Pros and Cons of Residential Community Treatment The community treatment approach has limitations. The public may have a negative impression of community treatment, especially when it is offered to juvenile offenders who pose a threat to society. Institutionalization may be the only answer for violent, chronic offenders. Even if the juvenile crime problem abates, society may be unwilling to accept the outcomes of reform-minded policies and practices. For example, it is not uncommon for neighborhood groups to oppose the location of corrections programs in their community. But is their fear realistic?

Much of the early criticism of community treatment was based on poor delivery of services, shabby operation, and haphazard management, follow-up, and planning. In the early 1970s, when Massachusetts deinstitutionalized its juvenile correction system, a torrent of reports revealed the inadequate operation of community treatment programs, based in part on the absence of uniform policies and procedures and the lack of accountability. The development of needed programs was hampered, and available resources were misplaced. Today's community treatment programs have generally overcome their early deficiencies and operate more efficiently than in the past.

Despite such criticisms, community-based programs continue to present the most promising alternative to the poor results of reform schools for these reasons:

1. Some states have found that residential and nonresidential settings produce comparable or lower recidivism rates. Some researchers have found that youths in nonsecure settings are less likely to become recidivists than those placed in more secure settings (although this has not been proven conclusively).

2. Community-based programs have lower costs and are especially appropriate for large numbers of nonviolent juveniles and those guilty of lesser offenses.

3. Public opinion of community corrections remains positive. Many citizens prefer community-based programs for all but the most serious juvenile offenders.[44]

As jurisdictions continue to face high rates of violent juvenile crime and ever-increasing costs for juvenile justice services, community-based programs will play an important role in providing rehabilitation of juvenile offenders and ensuring public safety.

MULTISYSTEMIC THERAPY

Three Model Nonresidential Programs

Multisystemic therapy (MST), a nonresidential delinquency treatment program developed by Dr. Scott Henggeler of the Medical University of South Carolina, views individuals as being "nested" within a complex of interconnected systems, including the family, community, school, and peers. The MST treatment team may target problems in any of these systems for change and use the individual's strengths in these systems to effect that change. Treatment teams, which usually include three counselors, provide services over a four-month period for about 50 families per year.

In one evaluation of the effectiveness of MST in Missouri, 176 high-risk juvenile offenders were randomly assigned either to MST or to a control group that received individual therapy that focused on personal, family, and academic issues. Four years later, only 29 percent of the MST offenders had been rearrested, compared with 74 percent of the control group. Significant reductions were also found in the severity of offenses for the MST group compared to the control group. Meta-analyses that include many evaluations of MST also provide evidence of its effectiveness in treating juvenile offenders. In one of the meta-analyses, MST was found to have reduced recidivism by about 20 percent. This corresponds approximately to a decrease in recidivism from 50 percent in the control group to 30 percent in the MST group. Cost-benefit analyses of MST show that it produces substantial financial savings to the juvenile justice system.

PROJECT NEW PRIDE

Begun in 1973 in Denver, Colorado, Project New Pride has been a model for similar programs around the country. The target group for Project New Pride is serious or violent youthful offenders from 14 to 17 years of age who have at least two prior convictions for serious misdemeanors or felonies and are formally charged or convicted of another offense when they are referred to New Pride. The only youths not eligible for participation are those who have committed forcible rape or are diagnosed as severely psychotic. New Pride believes this restriction is necessary in the interest of the safety of the community and of the youths themselves. The project's specific goals are to steer these hard-core offenders back into the mainstream of their communities and to reduce the number of rearrests. Generally, reintegration into the community means enrolling in school, getting a job, or both.

Each participant in New Pride has six months of intensive involvement and a six-month follow-up period during which the youth slowly reintegrates into the community. During the

follow-up period, the youth continues to receive as many services as necessary, such as schooling and job placement, and works closely with counselors.

THE BETHESDA DAY TREATMENT CENTER PROGRAM

The Bethesda Day Treatment Center Program in West Milton, Pennsylvania, is another model day-treatment program. The center's services include intensive supervision, counseling, and coordination of a range of services necessary for youths to develop skills to function effectively in the community. The program provides delinquent and dependent youths, ages 10 to 17, with up to 55 hours of services a week without removing them from their homes. A unique program feature requires work experience for all working-age clients, with 75 percent of their paychecks directed toward payment of fines, court costs, and restitution. A preliminary study revealed recidivism rates far lower than state and national norms.

Critical Thinking

1. What are some of the differences between residential and nonresidential treatment programs for juvenile offenders?
2. What are the features that are characteristic of all three of these successful nonresidential treatment programs?

InfoTrac College Edition Research

To read more about nonresidential programs for juvenile offenders, go to Diane Hirth, "Early Intensive Help for High-Risk Juveniles," *Corrections Today* 63:80 (December 2001). To find further information, use "juvenile corrections" as a key term.

SOURCES: Shay Bilchik, *A Juvenile Justice System for the 21st Century* (Washington, DC: OJJDP, 1998); Charles M. Borduin et al., "Multisystemic Treatment of Serious Juvenile Offenders: Long-Term Prevention of Criminality and Violence," *Journal of Consulting and Clinical Psychology* 63:569–587 (1995); David P. Farrington and Brandon C. Welsh, "Family-Based Prevention of Offending: A Meta-Analysis," *Australian and New Zealand Journal of Criminology* 36:127–151 (2003); Scott W. Henggeler, *Treating Serious Anti-Social Behavior in Youth: The MST Approach* (Washington, DC: OJJDP Juvenile Justice Bulletin, 1997); Project New Pride (Washington, DC: U.S. Government Printing Office, 1985); Susan R. Woolfenden, K. Williams, and J. K. Peat, "Family and Parenting Interventions for Conduct Disorder and Delinquency: A Meta-Analysis of Randomized Controlled Trials," *Archives of Disease in Childhood* 86:251–256 (2002).

Experts have confirmed the decline of rehabilitation in juvenile justice throughout much of the United States over the last 25 years.[45] But several recent meta-analysis studies have refuted the claim that "nothing works" with juvenile offenders and have given support to community rehabilitation.[46] According to Barry Krisberg and his associates, the most successful community-based programs seem to share at least some of these characteristics: (1) comprehensiveness, dealing with many aspects of youths'

TO QUIZ YOURSELF ON THIS MATERIAL, go to the Juvenile Delinquency 9e website.

lives; (2) intensivity, involving multiple contacts; (3) operation outside the justice system; (4) foundation upon youths' strengths; and (5) adoption of a socially grounded approach to understanding a juvenile's situation rather than an individual-level (medical or therapeutic) approach.[47]

SECURE CORRECTIONS

When the court determines that community treatment can't meet the special needs of a delinquent youth, a judge may refer the juvenile to a secure treatment program. Today, correctional institutions operated by federal, state, and county governments are generally classified as either secure or open facilities. Secure facilities restrict the movement of residents through staff monitoring, locked exits, and interior fence controls. Open institutions generally do not restrict the movement of the residents and allow much greater freedom of access to the facility.[48] In the following sections, we analyze the state of secure juvenile corrections, beginning with some historical background. This is followed by a discussion of life in institutions, the juvenile client, treatment issues, legal rights, and aftercare and reentry programs.

History of Juvenile Institutions

reform schools
Institutions in which educational and psychological services are used in an effort to improve the conduct of juveniles who are forcibly detained.

Until the early 1800s, juvenile offenders, as well as neglected and dependent children, were confined in adult prisons. The inhumane conditions in these institutions were among the factors that led social reformers to create a separate children's court system in 1899.[49] Early juvenile institutions were industrial schools modeled after adult prisons but designed to protect children from the evil influences in adult facilities. The first was the New York House of Refuge, established in 1825. Not long after this, states began to establish **reform schools** for juveniles. Massachusetts was the first, opening the Lyman School for Boys in Westborough in 1846. New York opened the State Agricultural and Industrial School in 1849, and Maine opened the Maine Boys' Training School in 1853. By 1900, 36 states had reform schools.[50] Although it is difficult to determine exact populations of these institutions, by 1880 there were approximately 11,000 youths in correctional facilities, a number that more than quadrupled by 1980.[51] Early reform schools were generally punitive in nature and were based on the concept of rehabilitation (or reform) through hard work and discipline.

cottage system
Housing juveniles in a compound containing a series of small cottages, each of which accommodates 20 to 40 children and is run by a set of cottage parents who create a homelike atmosphere.

In the second half of the nineteenth century, emphasis shifted to the **cottage system.** Juvenile offenders were housed in compounds of cottages, each of which could accommodate 20 to 40 children. A set of parents ran each cottage, creating a homelike atmosphere. This setup was believed to be more conducive to rehabilitation.

The first cottage system was established in Massachusetts in 1855, the second in Ohio in 1858.[52] The system was held to be a great improvement over training schools. The belief was that by moving away from punishment and toward rehabilitation, not only could offenders be rehabilitated, but also crime among unruly children could be prevented.[53]

Twentieth-Century Developments The early twentieth century witnessed important changes in juvenile corrections. Because of the influence of World War I, reform schools began to adopt a militaristic style. Living units became barracks; cottage groups became companies; house fathers became captains; and superintendents became majors or colonels. Military-style uniforms were standard wear.

In addition, the establishment of the first juvenile court in 1899 reflected the expanded use of confinement for delinquent children. As the number of juvenile offenders increased, the forms of juvenile institutions varied to include forestry camps, ranches, and vocational schools. Beginning in the 1930s, camps modeled after those run by the Civilian Conservation Corps became a part of the juvenile correctional system. These camps centered on conservation activities and work as a means of rehabilitation.

Young boys, watched by their master, are shown working in the Carpentry and Joinery Department of the New York State Industrial School, Rochester, 1886. The boys were required to work six and a half hours a day.

Los Angeles County was the first to use camps during this period.[54] Southern California was experiencing problems with transient youths who came to California with no money and then got into trouble with the law. Rather than filling up the jails, the county placed these offenders in conservation camps, paid them low wages, and released them when they had earned enough money to return home. The camps proved more rehabilitative than training schools, and by 1935 California had established a network of forestry camps for delinquent boys. The idea soon spread to other states.[55]

Also during the 1930s, the U.S. Children's Bureau sought to reform juvenile corrections. The bureau conducted studies to determine the effectiveness of the training school concept. Little was learned from these programs because of limited funding and bureaucratic ineptitude, and the Children's Bureau failed to achieve any significant change. But such efforts recognized the important role of positive institutional care.[56]

Another innovation came in the 1940s with passage of the American Law Institute's Model Youth Correction Authority Act. This act emphasized reception/classification centers. California was the first to try out this idea, opening the Northern Reception Center and Clinic in Sacramento in 1947. Today, there are many such centers scattered around the United States.

Since the 1970s, a major change in institutionalization has been the effort to remove status offenders from institutions housing juvenile delinquents. This includes removing status offenders from detention centers and removing all juveniles from contact with adults in jails. This *decarceration* policy mandates that courts use the **least restrictive alternative** in providing services for status offenders. A noncriminal youth should not be put in a secure facility if a community-based program is available. In addition, the federal government prohibits states from placing status offenders in separate facilities that are similar in form and function to those used for delinquent offenders. This is to prevent states from merely shifting their institutionalized population around so that one training school houses all delinquents and another houses all status offenders, but actual conditions remain the same.

Throughout the 1980s and into the 1990s, admissions to juvenile correctional facilities grew substantially.[57] Capacities of juvenile facilities also increased, but not enough to avoid overcrowding. Training schools became seriously overcrowded in some states, causing private facilities to play an increased role in juvenile corrections. Reliance on incarceration became costly to states: Inflation-controlled juvenile corrections expenditures for public facilities grew to more than $2 billion in 1995, an increase

least restrictive alternative
Choosing a program with the least restrictive or secure setting that will best benefit the child.

of 20 percent from 1982.[58] A 1994 report issued by the OJJDP said that crowding, inadequate health care, lack of security, and poor control of suicidal behavior was widespread in juvenile corrections facilities. Despite new construction, crowding persisted in more than half the states.[59]

TO QUIZ YOURSELF ON THIS MATERIAL, go to the Juvenile Delinquency 9e website.

JUVENILE INSTITUTIONS TODAY: PUBLIC AND PRIVATE

Most juveniles are housed in public institutions administered by state agencies: child and youth services, health and social services, corrections, or child welfare.[60] In some states these institutions fall under a centralized system that covers adults as well as juveniles. Recently, a number of states have removed juvenile corrections from an existing adult corrections department or mental health agency. However, the majority of states still place responsibility for the administration of juvenile corrections within social service departments.

Supplementing publicly funded institutions are private facilities that are maintained and operated by private agencies funded or chartered by state authorities. The majority of today's private institutions are relatively small facilities holding fewer than 30 youths. Many have a specific mission or focus (for example, treating females who display serious emotional problems). Although about 80 percent of public institutions can be characterized as secure, only 20 percent of private institutions are high-security facilities.

Population Trends

Whereas most delinquents are held in public facilities, most status offenders are held in private facilities. At last count, there were slightly less than 109,000 juvenile offenders being held in public (70%) and private (30%) facilities in the United States.[61] Between 1997 and 1999, the number of juveniles held in custody increased 3 percent.[62] The juvenile custody rate varies widely among states: South Dakota makes the greatest use of custodial treatment, incarcerating around 630 delinquents in juvenile facilities per 100,000 juveniles in the population, while Vermont and Hawaii have the lowest juvenile custody rates (less than 100). Although not a state, the District of Columbia actually has the highest juvenile custody rate in the nation, at over 700 per 100,000 juveniles. This is almost twice the national average (see Table 15.1).[63] Some states rely heavily on privately run facilities, while others place many youths in out-of-state facilities.

Although the number of institutionalized youths appears to have stabilized in the last few years, the data may reveal only the tip of the iceberg. The data do not include many minors who are incarcerated after they are waived to adult courts or who have been tried as adults because of exclusion statutes. Most states place underage juveniles convicted of adult charges in youth centers until they reach the age of majority, whereupon they are transferred to an adult facility. In addition, there may be a hidden, or subterranean, correctional system that places wayward youths in private mental hospitals and substance abuse clinics for behaviors that might otherwise have brought them a stay in a correctional facility or community-based program.[64] These data suggest that the number of institutionalized children may be far greater than reported in the official statistics.[65] Studies also show that large numbers of youths are improperly incarcerated because of a lack of appropriate facilities. A nationwide survey carried out by congressional investigators as part of the House Committee on Government Reform found that 15,000 children with psychiatric disorders who were awaiting mental health services were improperly incarcerated in secure juvenile detention facilities in 2003.[66] In New Jersey, investigations into the state's child welfare system found that large numbers of teenage foster children were being held in secure juvenile detention facilities. Other states resort to similar practices, citing a lack of appropriate noncorrectional facilities.[67]

TABLE 15.1

State Comparison of Numbers and Rates of Juvenile Offenders in Custody, 1999

State of offense	Number	Rate	State of offense	Number	Rate
U.S. total	*108,931*	*371*	Oklahoma	1,123	273
Upper age 17			Oregon	1,549	404
Alabama	1,589	333	Pennsylvania	3,819	285
Alaska	382	419	Rhode Island	310	284
Arizona	1,901	334	South Dakota	603	632
Arkansas	705	234	Tennessee	1,534	256
California	19,072	514	Utah	985	320
Colorado	1,979	407	Vermont	67	96
Delaware	347	431	Virginia	3,085	415
Dist. of Columbia	259	704	Washington	2,094	307
Florida	6,813	427	West Virginia	388	202
Hawaii	118	96	Wyoming	310	488
Idaho	360	220	**Upper age 16**		
Indiana	2,650	384	Georgia	3,729	475
Iowa	1,017	296	Illinois	3,885	322
Kansas	1,254	383	Louisiana	2,745	580
Kentucky	1,188	270	Massachusetts	1,188	206
Maine	242	167	Michigan	4,324	417
Maryland	1,579	269	Missouri	1,161	205
Minnesota	1,760	290	New Hampshire	216	167
Mississippi	784	229	South Carolina	1,650	441
Montana	246	220	Texas	7,954	370
Nebraska	720	342	Wisconsin	1,924	338
Nevada	789	378	**Upper age 15**		
New Jersey	2,386	273	Connecticut	1,466	513
New Mexico	855	378	New York	4,813	334
North Dakota	235	297	North Carolina	1,429	221
Ohio	4,531	345			

NOTE: The rate is the number of juvenile offenders in residential placement in 1999 per 100,000 juveniles aged 10 through the upper age of original juvenile court jurisdiction in each state. The U.S. total includes 2,645 juvenile offenders in private facilities for whom state of offense was not reported and 174 juvenile offenders in tribal facilities.

SOURCE: Melissa Sickmund, *Juveniles in Corrections* (Washington, DC: Office of Juvenile Justice and Delinquency Prevention, 2004), p. 7.

Physical Conditions

The physical plants of juvenile institutions vary in size and quality. Many older training schools still place all offenders in a single building, regardless of the offense. More acceptable structures include a reception unit with an infirmary, a security unit, and dormitory units or cottages. Planners have concluded that the most effective design for training schools is to have facilities located around a community square. The facilities generally include a dining hall and kitchen area, a storage warehouse, academic and vocational training rooms, a library, an auditorium, a gymnasium, an administration building, and other basic facilities.

The individual living areas also vary, depending on the type of facility and the progressiveness of its administration. Most traditional training school conditions were appalling. Today, however, most institutions provide toilet and bath facilities, beds, desks, lamps, and tables. New facilities usually provide a single room for each individual. However, the Juvenile Residential Facility Census, which collects information about the facilities in which juvenile offenders are held, found that 39 percent of the 2,875 facilities that reported information were overcrowded—that is, they had more residents than available standard beds.[68] Some states, such as Massachusetts and Rhode Island, report that upwards of 75 percent of all their facilities for juvenile offenders are overcrowded. It was also found that overcrowded facilities were signifi-

The physical condition of some juvenile facilities is far less than ideal. An inmate looks out the window of his cell at the New Jersey Training School for Boys. The state budget includes a special $1 million appropriation to renovate cells for suicide prevention due to a growing problem of mentally ill inmates. The toilet and sink will be replaced with safer versions as part of the numerous changes being made during the renovation.

cantly more likely than other facilities (45 percent versus 38 percent) to report having transported juveniles to emergency rooms because of injuries sustained in fights.[69]

Most experts recommend that juvenile facilities have leisure areas, libraries, education spaces, chapels, facilities where youths can meet with their visitors, windows in all sleeping accommodations, and fire-safety equipment and procedures. Because institutions for delinquent youths vary in purpose, it is not necessary that they meet identical standards. Security measures used in some closed institutions, for instance, may not be required in a residential program.

The physical conditions of secure facilities for juveniles have come a long way from the training schools of the turn of the century. However, many administrators realize that more modernization is necessary to comply with national standards for juvenile institutions.[70] Although some improvements have been made, there are still enormous problems to overcome.

TO QUIZ YOURSELF ON THIS MATERIAL, go to the Juvenile Delinquency 9e website.

THE INSTITUTIONALIZED JUVENILE

The typical resident of a juvenile facility is a 15- to 16-year-old white male incarcerated for an average stay of five months in a public facility or six months in a private facility. Private facilities tend to house younger children, while public institutions provide custodial care for older children, including a small percentage of youths between 18 and 21 years of age. Most incarcerated youths are person, property, or drug offenders.

To read about **life in a secure Canadian facility,** go to the website maintained by the Prince George Youth Custody Center in British Columbia, which provides a range of programs to allow youths to make maximal constructive use of their time while in custody: http://members.pgonline.com/~pgycc/index.html. For an up-to-date list of web links, go to http://cj.wadsworth.com/siegel_jd9e.

Minority youths are incarcerated at a rate two to five times that of white youths. The difference is greatest for African American youths, with a custody rate of 1,004 per 100,000 juveniles; for white youths the rate is 212.[71] In a number of states, such as Illinois, New Jersey, and Wisconsin, the difference in custody rates between African American and white youths is considerably greater (see Table 15.2). Research has found that this overrepresentation is not a result of differentials in arrest rates, but often stems from disparity at early stages of case processing.[72] Of equal importance, minorities are more likely to be confined in secure public facilities rather than in open private facilities that might provide more costly and effective treatment.[73] Among

TABLE 15.2

State Comparison of Custody Rates Between White and African American Juvenile Offenders, 1999

State of offense	White	African American	State of offense	White	African American
U.S average	*212*	*1,004*	Missouri	146	554
Alabama	208	588	Montana	148	1,463
Alaska	281	612	Nebraska	220	1,552
Arizona	234	957	Nevada	305	1,019
Arkansas	139	575	New Hampshire	150	1,278
California	269	1,666	New Jersey	701	108
Colorado	257	1,436	New Mexico	211	1,011
Connecticut	160	2,143	New York	169	1,119
Delaware	203	1,143	North Carolina	123	466
Dist. of Columbia	173	855	North Dakota	204	1,136
Florida	306	964	Ohio	221	1,038
Georgia	273	878	Oklahoma	194	821
Hawaii	39	87	Oregon	353	1,689
Idaho	203	871	Pennsylvania	123	1,230
Illinois	152	1,005	Rhode Island	155	1,363
Indiana	280	1,260	South Carolina	244	772
Iowa	240	1,726	South Dakota	436	2,908
Kansas	239	1,691	Tennessee	170	576
Kentucky	192	1,030	Texas	204	965
Louisiana	223	1,127	Utah	267	1,043
Maine	166	390	Vermont	93	698
Maryland	136	575	Virginia	225	1,024
Massachusetts	93	648	Washington	232	1,507
Michigan	243	1,058	West Virginia	166	1,060
Minnesota	183	1,504	Wisconsin	164	1,965
Mississippi	118	300	Wyoming	396	2,752

NOTE: The custody rate is the number of juvenile offenders in residential placement on October 27, 1999, per 100,000 juveniles age 10 through the upper age of original juvenile court jurisdiction in each state. The U.S. total includes 2,645 juvenile offenders in private facilities for whom state of offense was not reported and 174 juvenile offenders in tribal facilities.

SOURCE: Melissa Sickmund, *Juveniles in Corrections* (Washington, DC: Office of Juvenile Justice and Delinquency Prevention, 2004), p. 10.

minority groups, African American youths are more likely to receive punitive treatment—throughout the juvenile justice system—compared with others.[74]

Minority youths accused of delinquent acts are less likely than white youths to be diverted from the court system into informal sanctions and are more likely to receive sentences involving incarceration. Racial disparity in juvenile disposition is a growing problem that demands immediate public scrutiny.[75] In response, some jurisdictions have initiated studies of racial disproportion in their juvenile justice systems,[76] along with federal requirements to reduce disproportionate minority confinement, as contained in the Juvenile Justice and Delinquency Prevention Act of 2002.[77] Today, more than 6 in 10 juveniles in custody belong to racial or ethnic minorities, and 7 in 10 youths held in custody for a violent crime are minorities.[78]

For more than two decades, shocking exposés, sometimes resulting from investigations by the U.S. Department of Justice's civil rights division, continue to focus public attention on the problems of juvenile corrections.[79] Today, more so than in past years, some critics believe public scrutiny has improved conditions in training schools. There is greater professionalism among the staff, and staff brutality seems to have diminished. Status offenders and delinquents are, for the most part, held in separate facilities. Confinement length is shorter, and rehabilitative programming has increased. However, there are significant differences in the experiences of male and female delinquents within the institution.

Male Inmates

Males make up the great bulk of institutionalized youth, accounting for six out of every seven juvenile offenders in residential placement,[80] and most programs are directed toward their needs. In many ways their experiences mirror those of adult offenders. In an important paper, Clement Bartollas and his associates identified an inmate value system that they believed was common in juvenile institutions:

Exploit whomever you can.

Don't play up to staff.

Don't rat on your peers.

Don't give in to others.[81]

In addition to these general rules, the researchers found that there were separate norms for African American inmates ("exploit whites; no forcing sex on blacks; defend your brother") and for whites ("don't trust anyone; everybody for himself").

Other research efforts confirm the notion that residents do in fact form cohesive groups and adhere to an informal inmate culture.[82] The more serious the youth's record and the more secure the institution, the greater the adherence to the inmate social code. Male delinquents are more likely to form allegiances with members of their own racial group and to attempt to exploit those outside the group. They also scheme to manipulate staff and take advantage of weaker peers. However, in institutions that are treatment oriented, and where staff-inmate relationships are more intimate, residents are less likely to adhere to a negativistic inmate code.

Female Inmates

The growing involvement of girls in criminal behavior and the influence of the feminist movement have drawn more attention to the female juvenile offender. This attention has revealed a double standard of justice. For example, girls are more likely than boys to be incarcerated for status offenses. Institutions for girls are generally more restrictive than those for boys, and they have fewer educational and vocational programs and fewer services. Institutions for girls also do a less-than-adequate job of rehabilitation. It has been suggested that this double standard operates because of a male-dominated justice system that seeks to "protect" young girls from their own sexuality.[83]

Over the years, the number of females held in public institutions has declined. This represents the continuation of a long-term trend to remove girls, many of whom are nonserious offenders, from closed institutions and place them in private or community-based facilities. In 1999, 35 percent of all female youths in residential placement were held in private facilities; for male youths it was 28 percent.[84]

The same double standard that brings a girl into an institution continues to exist once she is in custody. Females tend to be incarcerated for longer terms than males. In addition, institutional programs for girls tend to be oriented toward reinforcing traditional roles for women. How well these programs rehabilitate girls is questionable.

Many of the characteristics of juvenile female offenders are similar to those of their male counterparts, including poor social skills and low self-esteem. Other problems are more specific to the female juvenile offender (sexual abuse issues, victimization histories, lack of placement options).[85] In addition, there have been numerous allegations of emotional and sexual abuse by correctional workers, who either exploit vulnerable young women or callously disregard their emotional needs. A 1998 interview survey conducted by the National Council on Crime and Delinquency uncovered numerous incidents of abuse, and bitter resentment by the young women over the brutality of their custodial treatment.[86]

Although there are more coed institutions for juveniles than in the past, most girls remain incarcerated in single-sex institutions that are isolated in rural areas and rarely offer adequate rehabilitative services. Several factors account for the different treatment of girls. One is sexual stereotyping by administrators, who believe that teaching girls "appropriate" sex roles will help them function effectively in society. These beliefs are often held by the staff as well, many of whom hold highly sexist ideas of what is appropriate behavior for adolescent girls. Another factor that accounts for the different treatment of girls is that staff are often not adequately trained to understand and address the unique needs of this population.[87] Girls' institutions tend to be smaller than boys' institutions and lack the money to offer as many programs and services as do the larger male institutions.[88]

It appears that although society is more concerned about protecting girls who act out, it is less concerned about rehabilitating them because the crimes they commit are not serious. These attitudes translate into fewer staff, older facilities, and poorer educational and recreational programs than those found in boys' institutions.[89] To help address these and other problems facing female juveniles in institutions, the American Bar Association and the National Bar Association recommend a number of important changes, including these:

▌ Identify, promote, and support effective gender-specific, developmentally sound, culturally sensitive practices with girls.

▌ Promote an integrated system of care for at-risk and delinquent girls and their families based on their competencies and needs.

▌ Assess the adequacy of services to meet the needs of at-risk or delinquent girls and address gaps in service.

▌ Collect and review state and local practices to assess the gender impact of decision making and system structure.[90]

TO QUIZ YOURSELF ON THIS MATERIAL, go to the Juvenile Delinquency 9e website.

CORRECTIONAL TREATMENT FOR JUVENILES

Nearly all juvenile institutions implement some form of treatment program: counseling, vocational and educational training, recreational programs, or religious counseling. In addition, most institutions provide medical programs as well as occasional legal service programs. Generally, the larger the institution, the greater the number of programs and services offered.

The purpose of these programs is to rehabilitate youths to become well-adjusted individuals and send them back into the community to be productive citizens. Despite good intentions, however, the goal of rehabilitation is rarely attained, due in large part to programs being poorly implemented.[91] A significant number of juvenile offenders commit more crimes after release and some experts believe that correctional treatment has little effect on recidivism.[92] However, a careful evaluation of both community-based and institutional treatment services found that juveniles who receive treatment have recidivism rates about 10 percent lower than untreated juveniles, and that the best programs reduced recidivism between 20 and 30 percent.[93] The most successful programs provide training designed to improve interpersonal skills, self-control, and school achievement. These programs also tend to be the most intensive in terms of the amount and duration of attention to youths. Programs of a more psychological orientation, such as individual, family, and group counseling, showed only moderate positive effects on delinquents. Education, vocational training, and specific counseling strategies can be effective if they are intensive, relate to program goals, and meet the youth's individual needs.[94]

What are the drawbacks to correctional rehabilitation? One of the most common problems in efforts to rehabilitate juveniles is a lack of well-trained staff members. Budgetary limitations are a primary concern.[95] It costs a substantial amount of money per year to keep a child in an institution, which explains why institutions generally do not employ large professional staffs.

If you want to learn more about **improving the conditions for children in custody,** go to www.ojjdp. ncjrs.org/pubs/walls/contents.html. For an up-to-date list of web links, go to http://cj.wadsworth.com/siegel_jd9e.

The most glaring problem with treatment programs is that they are not being administered as intended. Although the official goals of many institutions may be treatment and rehabilitation, the actual programs may center around security and punishment. The next sections describe some treatment approaches that aim to rehabilitate offenders.

Individual Treatment Techniques: Past and Present

individual counseling
Counselors help juveniles understand and solve their current adjustment problems.

In general, effective individual treatment programs are built around combinations of psychotherapy, reality therapy, and behavior modification. **Individual counseling** is one of the most common treatment approaches, and virtually all juvenile institutions use it to some extent. This is not surprising, as psychological problems such as depression are prevalent in juvenile institutions.[96] Individual counseling does not attempt to change a youth's personality. Rather, it attempts to help individuals understand and solve their current adjustment problems. Some institutions employ counselors who are not professionally qualified, which subjects offenders to a superficial form of counseling.

psychotherapy
Highly structured counseling in which a skilled therapist helps a juvenile solve conflicts and make a more positive adjustment to society.

reality therapy
A form of counseling that emphasizes current behavior and that requires the individual to accept responsibility for all of his or her actions.

Professional counseling may be based on **psychotherapy,** which requires extensive analysis of the individual's childhood experiences. A skilled therapist attempts to help the individual make a more positive adjustment to society by altering negative behavior patterns learned in childhood. Another frequently used treatment is **reality therapy.**[97] This approach, developed by William Glasser during the 1970s, emphasizes current, rather than past, behavior by stressing that offenders are completely responsible for their own actions. The object of reality therapy is to make individuals more responsible people. This is accomplished by giving youths confidence through developing their ability to follow a set of expectations as closely as possible. The success of reality therapy depends greatly on the warmth and concern of the counselor. Many institutions rely heavily on this type of therapy because they believe trained professionals aren't needed to administer it. Actually, a skilled therapist is essential to the success of this form of treatment.

behavior modification
A technique for shaping desired behaviors through a system of rewards and punishments.

Behavior modification is used in many institutions.[98] It is based on the theory that all behavior is learned and that current behavior can be shaped through rewards and punishments. This type of program is easily used in an institutional setting that offers privileges as rewards for behaviors such as work, study, or the development of skills. It is reasonably effective, especially when a contract is formed with the youth to modify certain behaviors. When youths know what is expected of them, they plan their actions to meet these expectations and then experience the anticipated consequences. In this way, youths can be motivated to change. Behavior modification is effective in controlled settings where a counselor can manipulate the situation, but once the youth is back in the real world it becomes difficult to use.

To learn more about **reality therapy,** go to William Glasser's website at www.wglasser.com/whoweare.htm. For an up-to-date list of web links, go to http://cj.wadsworth.com/siegel_jd9e.

Group Treatment Techniques

group therapy
Counseling several individuals together in a group session; individuals can obtain support from other group members as they work through similar problems.

Group therapy is more economical than individual therapy because one therapist can counsel more than one individual at a time. Also, the support of the group is often valuable to individuals in the group, and individuals derive hope from other members of the group who have survived similar experiences. Another advantage of group therapy is that a group can often solve a problem more effectively than an individual.

One disadvantage of group therapy is that it provides little individual attention. Everyone is different, and some group members may need more individualized treatment. Others may be afraid to speak up in the group and thus fail to receive the benefits of the group experience. Conversely, some individuals may dominate group interaction, making it difficult for the leader to conduct an effective session. In addition, group condemnation may seriously hurt a participant. Finally, there is also the concern that by providing therapy in a group format, those who are more chronically involved in delinquency may negatively affect those who are marginally involved.[99] This can also happen with non–juvenile justice delinquency prevention programs (see Chapter 11).

More than any other group treatment technique, group psychotherapy probes into an individual's personality and attempts to restructure it. Relationships in these groups tend to be intense. The group is used to facilitate expression of feelings, solve problems, and teach members to empathize with one another.

Unfortunately, the ingredients for an effective group session—interaction, cooperation, and tolerance—are in conflict with the antisocial and antagonistic orientation of delinquents. This technique can be effective when the members of the group are in attendance voluntarily, but such is not the case with institutionalized delinquents. Consequently, the effectiveness of these programs is questionable.

Guided group interaction (GGI) is a fairly common method of group treatment. It is based on the theory that through group interactions, a delinquent can acknowledge and solve personal problems. A leader facilitates interaction, and a group culture develops. Individual members can be mutually supportive and can reinforce acceptable behavior. In the 1980s, a version of GGI called **positive peer culture (PPC)** became popular. These programs used groups in which peer leaders encourage other youths to conform to conventional behaviors. The rationale is that if negative peer influence can encourage youths to engage in delinquent behavior, then positive peer influence can help them conform.[100] Though research results are inconclusive, there is evidence that PPC may facilitate communication ability for incarcerated youth.[101]

Another common group treatment approach, **milieu therapy,** seeks to make all aspects of the inmates' environment part of their treatment and to minimize differences between custodial staff and treatment personnel. Based on psychoanalytic theory, milieu therapy was developed during the late 1940s and early 1950s by Bruno Bettelheim.[102] This therapy attempted to create a conscience, or superego, in delinquent youths by getting them to depend on their therapists to a great extent and then threatening them with loss of the caring relationship if they failed to control their behavior. Today, milieu therapy more often makes use of peer interactions and attempts to create an environment that encourages meaningful change, growth, and satisfactory adjustment. This is often accomplished through peer pressure to conform to group norms.

Today, group counseling often focuses on drug and alcohol issues, self-esteem development, or role-model support. In addition, because greater numbers of violent juveniles are entering the system than in years past, group sessions often deal with appropriate expressions of anger and methods for controlling such behavior.

Educational, Vocational, and Recreational Programs

Because educational programs are an important part of social development and have therapeutic as well as instructional value, they are an essential part of most treatment programs. What takes place through education is related to all other aspects of the institutional program—work activities, cottage life, recreation, and clinical services.

Educational programs are probably the best-staffed programs in training schools, but even at their best, most are inadequate. Training programs must contend with a myriad of problems. Many of the youths coming into these institutions are mentally challenged, have learning disabilities, and are far behind their grade levels in basic academics. Most have become frustrated with the educational experience, dislike school, and become bored with any type of educational program. Their sense of frustration often leads to disciplinary problems.

Ideally, institutions should allow the inmates to attend a school in the community or offer programs that lead to a high school diploma or GED. Unfortunately, not all institutions offer these types of programs. Secure institutions, because of their large size, are more likely than group homes or day treatment centers to offer programs such as

---

guided group interaction (GGI)
Through group interactions a delinquent can acknowledge and solve personal problems with support from other group members.

positive peer culture (PPC)
Counseling program in which peer leaders encourage other group members to modify their behavior, and peers help reinforce acceptable behaviors.

milieu therapy
All aspects of the environment are part of the treatment, and meaningful change, increased growth, and satisfactory adjustment are encouraged; this is often accomplished through peer pressure to conform to the group norms.

To see how **positive peer culture** can be used effectively, go to www.nida.nih.gov/MeetSum/CODA/Youth.html. For an up-to-date list of web links, go to http://cj.wadsworth.com/siegel_jd9e.

remedial reading, physical education, and tutoring. Some offer computer-based learning and programmed learning modules.

Vocational training has long been used as a treatment technique for juveniles. Early institutions were even referred to as "industrial schools." Today, vocational programs in institutions include auto repair, printing, woodworking, mechanical drawing, food service, cosmetology, secretarial training, and data processing. A common drawback of vocational training programs is sex-typing. The recent trend has been to allow equal access to all programs offered in institutions that house girls and boys. Sex-typing is more difficult to avoid in single-sex institutions, because funds aren't usually available for all types of training.

These programs alone are not panaceas. Youths need to acquire the kinds of skills that will give them hope for advancement. The Ventura School for Female Juvenile Offenders, established under the California Youth Authority, has been a pioneer in the work placement concept. Private industry contracts with the Youth Authority to establish businesses on the institution's grounds. The businesses hire, train, and pay for work. Wages are divided into a victim's restitution fund, room and board fees, and forced savings, with a portion given to the juvenile to purchase canteen items.[103] A study by the National Youth Employment Coalition (NYEC) finds that employment- and career-focused programs can do a great deal to prepare youths involved in the juvenile justice system for a successful transition to the workforce as long as they are comprehensive, last for a relatively long time, and are connected to further education or long-term career opportunities.[104]

Recreational activity is also an important way to help relieve adolescent aggressions, as evidenced by the many programs that focus on recreation as the primary treatment technique.

In summary, treatment programs that seem to be most effective for rehabilitating juvenile offenders are those that use a combination of techniques. Programs that are comprehensive, build on a juvenile's strengths, and adopt a socially grounded position have a much greater chance for success. Successful programs address issues relating to school, peers, work, and community.

Wilderness Programs

wilderness probation
Programs involving outdoor expeditions that provide opportunities for juveniles to confront the difficulties of their lives while achieving positive personal satisfaction.

Wilderness probation programs involve troubled youths in outdoor activities as a mechanism to improve their social skills, self-concept, and self-control. Typically, wilderness programs maintain exposure to a wholesome environment; where the concepts of education and the work ethic are taught and embodied in adult role models, troubled youth can regain a measure of self-worth.

A few wilderness programs for juvenile offenders have been evaluated for their effects on recidivism. In a detailed review of the effects of wilderness programs on recidivism, Doris MacKenzie concludes that these programs do not work.[105] Although some of the programs show success, such as the Spectrum Wilderness Program in Illinois,[106] others had negative effects; that is, the group that received the program had higher arrest rates than the comparison group that did not receive the program. Taken together, the programs suffered from

I Poor implementation

I Weak evaluation designs or problems with too few subjects or large dropout rates

I Failure to adhere to principles of successful rehabilitation, such as targeting high-risk youths and lasting for a moderate period of time[107]

boot camps
Juvenile programs that combine get-tough elements from adult programs with education, substance abuse treatment, and social skills training.

Juvenile Boot Camps

Correctional **boot camps** combine the get-tough elements of adult programs with education, substance abuse treatment, and social skills training. In theory, a successful

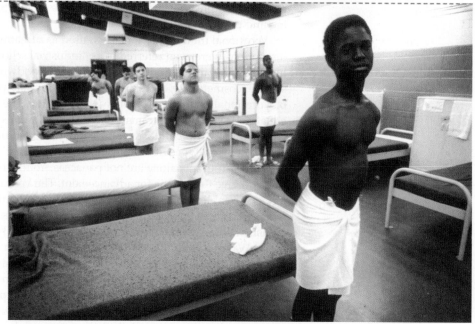

Juvenile boot camps apply rigorous, military-style training and discipline in an attempt to reshape the attitudes and behavior of unruly youth. Here, juveniles in Camp Holton, California, stand at attention as they wait to be inspected by boot camp officers.

© A. Ramey/PhotoEdit

boot camp program should rehabilitate juvenile offenders, reduce the number of beds needed in institutional programs, and thus reduce the overall cost of care. The Alabama boot camp program for youthful offenders estimated savings of $1 million annually when compared with traditional institutional sentences.[108] However, no one seems convinced that participants in these programs have lower recidivism rates than those who serve normal sentences. Ronald Corbett and Joan Petersilia do note, however, that boot camp participants seem to be less antisocial upon returning to society.[109]

Some juvenile corrections agencies feature shock incarceration programs, with high-intensity military discipline and physical training for short periods. The expectation is that the offender will be "shocked" into going straight. These programs are being used with young adult offenders and juveniles who have been waived to the adult system in many jurisdictions.

Some experts point out that (1) boot camps cannot save money unless they have hundreds of beds and the stay is limited to three months, conditions that would make the programs pointless; (2) boot camps often keep costs down by leaving aftercare to overloaded parole officers; and (3) no documentation exists that boot camps decrease delinquency.[110]

Other successes of juvenile boot camps are revealed in a national study comparing the environments of boot camps with more traditional secure correctional facilities for juveniles. Some of the main findings include these:

- Boot camp youths report more positive attitudes to their environment.
- Initial levels of depression are lower for boot camp youths, but initial levels of anxiety are higher; both of these declined over time for youths in both facilities.
- Staff at boot camps report more favorable working conditions, such as less stress and better communication among staff.[111]

However, the bottom line for juvenile boot camps, like other correctional sanctions, is whether or not they reduce recidivism. A recent meta-analysis of the effects of juvenile boot camps on recidivism found this to be an ineffective correctional approach to reducing recidivism; from the 16 different program samples, the control groups had, on average, lower recidivism rates than the treatment groups.[112] Interestingly, when compared to the effects of 28 program samples of boot camps for adults, the juvenile

To read more about **boot camps,** go to www.ncjrs.org/ txtfiles1/nij/197018.txt. For an up-to-date list of web links, go to http://cj.wadsworth.com/siegel_jd9e.

boot camps had a higher average recidivism rate, although the difference was not significant.[113]

Why do boot camps for juveniles fail to reduce future offending? The main reason is that they provide little in the way of therapy or treatment to correct offending behavior. Experts have also suggested that part of the reason for not finding differences in recidivism between boot camps and other correctional alternatives (the control groups) may be due to juveniles in the control groups receiving enhanced treatment while juveniles in the boot camps are spending more time on physical activities.[114]

The ineffectiveness of boot camps to reduce reoffending in the community by juvenile offenders (and adult offenders) appears to have resulted in this approach falling into disfavor with some correctional administrators. At the height of its popularity in the mid-1990s, more than 75 state-run boot camps were in operation in more than 30 states across the country; today, 51 remain.[115] Despite this, boot camps appear to still have a place among the array of sentencing options, if for no other reason than to appease the public with the promise of tougher sentences and lower costs.[116] If boot camps are to become a viable alternative for juvenile corrections, they must be seen, not as a panacea that provides an easy solution to the problems of delinquency, but as part of a comprehensive approach to juvenile care that is appropriate to a select group of adolescents.[117]

TO QUIZ YOURSELF ON THIS MATERIAL, go to the Juvenile Delinquency 9e website.

THE LEGAL RIGHT TO TREATMENT

The primary goal of placing juveniles in institutions is to help them reenter the community successfully. Therefore, lawyers claim that children in state-run institutions have a legal right to treatment.

right to treatment
Philosophy espoused by many courts that juvenile offenders have a statutory right to treatment while under the jurisdiction of the courts.

The concept of a **right to treatment** was introduced to the mental health field in 1960 by Morton Birnbaum, who argued that individuals deprived of their liberty because of a mental illness are entitled to treatment to correct that condition.[118] The right to treatment has expanded to include the juvenile justice system, an expansion bolstered by court rulings that mandate that rehabilitation and not punishment or retribution be the basis of juvenile court dispositions.[119] It stands to reason then, that if incarcerated, juveniles are entitled to the appropriate social services that will promote their rehabilitation.

One of the first cases to highlight this issue was *Inmates of the Boys' Training School v. Affleck* in 1972.[120] In its decision, a federal court argued that rehabilitation is the true purpose of the juvenile court and that without that goal, due-process guarantees are violated. It condemned such devices as solitary confinement, strip cells, and lack of educational opportunities, and held that juveniles have a statutory right to treatment. The court also established the following minimum standards for all juveniles confined in training schools:

❙ A room equipped with lighting sufficient for an inmate to read until 10:00 P.M.

❙ Sufficient clothing to meet seasonal needs

❙ Bedding, including blankets, sheets, pillows, pillowcases, and mattresses, to be changed once a week

❙ Personal hygiene supplies, including soap, toothpaste, towels, toilet paper, and toothbrush

❙ A change of undergarments and socks every day

❙ Minimum writing materials: pen, pencil, paper, and envelopes

❙ Prescription eyeglasses, if needed

❙ Equal access to all books, periodicals, and other reading materials located in the training school

- Daily showers
- Daily access to medical facilities, including provision of a 24-hour nursing service
- General correspondence privileges[121]

In 1974, in the case of *Nelson v. Heyne,* the First Federal Appellate Court affirmed that juveniles have a right to treatment and condemned the use of corporal punishment in juvenile institutions.[122] In *Morales v. Turman,* the court held that all juveniles confined in training schools in Texas have a right to treatment, including development of education skills, delivery of vocational education, medical and psychiatric treatment, and adequate living conditions.[123] In a more recent case, *Pena v. New York State Division for Youth,* the court held that the use of isolation, hand restraints, and tranquilizing drugs at Goshen Annex Center violated the Fourteenth Amendment right to due process and the Eighth Amendment right to protection against cruel and unusual punishment.[124]

The right to treatment has also been limited. For example, in *Ralston v. Robinson,* the Supreme Court rejected a youth's claim that he should continue to be given treatment after he was sentenced to a consecutive term in an adult prison for crimes committed while in a juvenile institution.[125] In the *Ralston* case, the offender's proven dangerousness outweighed the possible effects of rehabilitation. Similarly, in *Santana v. Callazo,* the U.S. First Circuit Court of Appeals rejected a suit brought by residents at the Maricao Juvenile Camp in Puerto Rico on the ground that the administration had failed to provide them with an individualized rehabilitation plan or adequate treatment. The circuit court concluded that it was a legitimate exercise of state authority to incarcerate juveniles solely to protect society if they are dangerous.

To learn more about **the right to treatment,** read "Meeting the Needs of the Mentally Ill—A Case Study of the 'Right to Treatment' as Legal Rights Discourse in the USA," by Michael McCubbin and David N. Weisstub, available on the Web at www.academyanalyticarts.org/mccweiss.html. For an up-to-date list of web links, go to http://cj.wadsworth.com/siegel_jd9e.

The Struggle for Basic Civil Rights

Several court cases have led federal, state, and private groups—for example, the American Bar Association, the American Correctional Association, and the National Council on Crime and Delinquency—to develop standards for the juvenile justice system. These standards provide guidelines for conditions and practices in juvenile institutions and call on administrators to maintain a safe and healthy environment for incarcerated youths.

For the most part, state-sponsored brutality has been outlawed, although the use of restraints, solitary confinement, and even medication for unruly residents has not been eliminated. The courts have ruled that corporal punishment in any form violates standards of decency and human dignity.

There are a number of mechanisms for enforcing these standards. For example, the federal government's Civil Rights of Institutionalized Persons Act (CRIPA) gives the Civil Rights Division of the U.S. Department of Justice (DOJ) the power to bring actions against state or local governments for violating the civil rights of persons institutionalized in publicly operated facilities.[126] CRIPA does not create any new substantive rights; it simply confers power on the U.S. Attorney General to bring action to enforce previously established constitutional or statutory rights of institutionalized persons; about 25 percent of cases involve juvenile detention and correctional facilities. There are many examples in which CRIPA-based litigation has helped ensure that incarcerated adolescents obtain their basic civil rights. For example, in November 1995, a federal court in Kentucky ordered state officials to remedy serious deficiencies in Kentucky's 13 juvenile treatment facilities. The decree required the state to take a number of steps to protect juveniles from abuse, mistreatment, and injury; to ensure adequate medical and mental health care; and to provide adequate educational, vocational, and aftercare services. Another CRIPA consent decree, ordered by a federal court in Puerto Rico in October 1994, addressed life-threatening conditions at eight juvenile detention and correction facilities. These dire conditions included juveniles committing and attempting suicide without staff intervention or treatment, widespread infection-control problems caused by rats and other vermin, and defective plumbing that forced juveniles to drink from their toilet bowls.

What provisions does the juvenile justice system make to help institutionalized offenders return to society? The remainder of this chapter is devoted to this topic.

TO QUIZ YOURSELF ON THIS MATERIAL, go to the Juvenile Delinquency 9e website.

JUVENILE AFTERCARE AND REENTRY

aftercare
Transitional assistance to juveniles, equivalent to adult parole, to help youths adjust to community life.

Aftercare in the juvenile justice system is the equivalent of parole in the adult criminal justice system. When juveniles are released from an institution, they may be placed in an aftercare program of some kind, so that youths who have been institutionalized are not simply returned to the community without some transitional assistance. Whether individuals who are in aftercare as part of an indeterminate sentence remain in the community or return to the institution for further rehabilitation depends on their actions during the aftercare period. Aftercare is an extremely important stage in the juvenile justice process because few juveniles age out of custody.[127]

reentry
The process and experience of returning to society upon release from a custody facility postadjudication.

Reentry involves aftercare services, but includes preparation for release from confinement, also called prerelease planning.[128] Reentry is further distinguished from aftercare in that reentry is seen as the whole process and experience of the transition of juveniles from "juvenile and adult correctional settings back into schools, families, communities, and society at large."[129] The concept of reentry, which is also the term given to it in the adult criminal justice system, is by no means new.[130] Recently, however, it has come to characterize the larger numbers of juvenile and adult offenders returning to communities each year and the increased needs these offenders exhibit with respect to employment, education, and mental health and substance abuse problems.[131] For juvenile offenders, reentry goes beyond the all-too-common practice of juveniles being placed in aftercare programs that are the same as adult parole programs, which "fail to take account of their unique needs and the challenges they face."[132]

Howard Snyder, research director for the National Center for Juvenile Justice, estimates that each year about 100,000 juvenile offenders are released from custody facilities following adjudication (or conviction in the adult system) and return to the communities from which they came.[133] A brief profile of these juveniles shows that:

I 88 percent were male.

I 19 percent were age 14 or younger and 36 percent were age 17 or older.

I 39 percent were white, 39 percent were black, and 17 percent were Hispanic.

I 38 percent were committed for a violent offense, 33 percent for a property offense, 14 percent for a public order offense, 11 percent for a drug offense, and 5 percent for a status offense.[134]

Aftercare and reentry services play an important role in their successful reintegration to society.

In a number of jurisdictions, a paroling authority, which may be an independent body or part of the corrections department or some other branch of state services, makes the release decision. Juvenile aftercare authorities, like adult parole officers, review the youth's adjustment within the institution, whether there is chemical dependence, what the crime was, and other specifics of the case. Some juvenile authorities are even making use of **parole guidelines** first developed with adult parolees. Each youth who enters a secure facility is given a recommended length of confinement that is explained at the initial interview with parole authorities. The stay is computed on the basis of the offense record, influenced by aggravating and mitigating factors. The parole authority is not required to follow the recommended sentence but uses it as a

parole guidelines
Recommended length of confinement and kinds of aftercare assistance most effective for a juvenile who committed a specific offense.

tool in making parole decisions.[135] Whatever approach is used, several primary factors are considered by virtually all jurisdictions when recommending a juvenile for release: (1) institutional adjustment, (2) length of stay and general attitude, and (3) likelihood of success in the community.

Risk classifications have also been designed to help parole officers make decisions about which juveniles should receive aftercare services.[136] The risk-based system uses an empirically derived risk scale to classify youths. Juveniles are identified as most likely or least likely to commit a new offense based on factors such as prior record, type of offense, and degree of institutional adjustment.

Supervision

One purpose of aftercare and reentry is to provide support during the readjustment period following release. First, individuals whose activities have been regimented for some time may not find it easy to make independent decisions. Second, offenders may perceive themselves as scapegoats, cast out by society. Finally, the community may view the returning minor with a good deal of prejudice; adjustment problems may reinforce a preexisting need to engage in deviant behavior.

Juveniles in aftercare programs are supervised by parole caseworkers or counselors whose job is to maintain contact with the juvenile, make sure that a corrections plan is followed, and show interest and caring. The counselor also keeps the youth informed of services that may assist in reintegration and counsels the youth and his or her family. Unfortunately, aftercare caseworkers, like probation officers, often carry such large caseloads that their jobs are next to impossible to do adequately.

Recent state legislation underscores the importance of aftercare and reentry for juvenile offenders. For example, the Texas Youth Commission operates an "independent living program" that provides prerelease and transition assistance to male and female offenders aged 16 to 18 who are returning to the community. An aftercare program in Cuyahoga County, Ohio, begins with education and employment training while a youth is incarcerated and continues after the youth is released. A reintegration program for youths released from the New Mexico Boys' School has been successful because clients spend less time in secure correction.[137]

The Intensive Aftercare Program (IAP) Model New models of aftercare and reentry have been aimed at the chronic and/or violent offender. The **Intensive Aftercare Program (IAP)** model developed by David Altschuler and Troy Armstrong offers a continuum of intervention for serious juvenile offenders returning to the community following placement.[138] The IAP model begins by drawing attention to five basic principles, which collectively establish a set of fundamental operational goals:

1. Preparing youth for progressively increased responsibility and freedom in the community

2. Facilitating youth-community interaction and involvement

3. Working with both the offender and targeted community support systems (families, peers, schools, employers) on qualities needed for constructive interaction and the youth's successful community adjustment

4. Developing new resources and supports where needed

5. Monitoring and testing the youth and the community on their ability to deal with each other productively

These basic goals are then translated into practice, which incorporates individual case planning with a family and community perspective. The program stresses a mix of intensive surveillance and services, and a balance of incentives and graduated consequences coupled with the imposition of realistic, enforceable conditions. There is also

To learn about the federal government's **Serious and Violent Offender Reentry Initiative,** go to www.ojp.usdoj.gov/reentry/. For an up-to-date list of web links, go to http://cj.wadsworth.com/siegel_jd9e.

How has the IAP model been used around the nation?

Using the Intensive Aftercare Program (IAP) Model

COLORADO

Although adolescents are still institutionalized, community-based providers begin weekly services (including multifamily counseling and life-skills services) that continue during aftercare. Sixty days prior to release, IAP youths begin a series of step-down measures, including supervised trips to the community and, 30 days before release, overnight or weekend home passes. Upon release to parole, most program youths go through several months of day treatment programming that, in addition to services, provides a high level of structure during the day. Trackers provide evening and weekend monitoring during this period of reentry. As a youth's progress warrants, the frequency of supervision decreases. The planned frequency of contact is once a week during the first few months of supervision, with gradual reductions to once a month in later stages of supervision.

NEVADA

Once the parole plan is finalized, all IAP youths begin a 30-day prerelease phase, during which IAP staff provide a series of services that continue through the early months of parole. These consist primarily of two structured curriculums on life skills (Jettstream) and substance abuse (Rational Recovery). In addition, a money management program (The Money Program) is initiated. Youths are provided with mock checking accounts from which "bills" must be paid for rent, food, insurance, and other necessities. Youths can also use their accounts to purchase recreation and other privileges, but each youth must have a balance of at least $50 at the end of the 30 days to purchase his bus ticket home. The initial 30 days of release are considered an institutional furlough (youths are still on the institutional rolls) that involves intensive supervision and service; any time during this period the youth may be returned to the institution for significant program infractions. During furlough, youths are involved in day programming and are subject to frequent drug testing and evening and weekend surveillance. Upon successful completion of the furlough, the IAP transition continues through the use of phased levels of supervision. During the first three months, three contacts per week with the case manager or field agent are required. This level of supervision is reduced to two contacts per week for the next two months, and then to once per week during the last month of parole.

VIRGINIA

Virginia's transition differs from the other two sites in that its central feature is the use of group home placements as a bridge between the institution and the community. Immediately after release from the institution, youths enter one of two group homes for a 30- to 60-day period. The programs and services in which they will be involved in the community are initiated shortly after placement in the group home. Virginia uses a formal step-down system to ease the intensity of parole supervision gradually. In the two months following the youth's release from the group home, staff are required to contact him five to seven times per week. This is reduced to three to five times per week during the next two months, and again to three times per week during the final 30 days.

Critical Thinking

1. What is the importance of reducing the number of supervision contacts with the juvenile offender toward the end of the aftercare program?

2. Should juvenile offenders who have committed less serious offenses also have to go through intensive aftercare programs?

InfoTrac College Edition Research

To read more about aftercare programs for juvenile offenders, go to Kit Glover and Kurt Bumby, "Re-Entry at the Point of Entry," *Corrections Today* 63:68 (December 2001). To find further information, use "juvenile corrections" as a key term.

SOURCE: Steve V. Gies, *Aftercare Services* (Washington, DC: OJJDP Juvenile Justice Bulletin, 2003); Richard G. Wiebush, Betsie McNulty, and Thao Le, *Implementation of the Intensive Community-Based Aftercare Program* (Washington, DC: OJJDP Juvenile Justice Bulletin, 2000).

"service brokerage," in which community resources are used and linkage with social networks established.[139]

The IAP initiative was designed to help correctional agencies implement effective aftercare programs for chronic and serious juvenile offenders. After more than 12 years of testing, the program is now being aimed at determining how juveniles are prepared for reentry into their communities, how the transition is handled, and how the aftercare in the community is provided.[140] The Policy and Practice box entitled "Using the Intensive Aftercare Program (IAP) Model" illustrates how the model is being used in three state jurisdictions.

Aftercare Revocation Procedures

Juvenile parolees are required to meet established standards of behavior, which generally include but are not limited to the following:

I Adhere to a reasonable curfew set by youth worker or parent.

I Refrain from associating with persons whose influence would be detrimental.

I Attend school in accordance with the law.

I Abstain from drugs and alcohol.

I Report to the youth worker when required.

I Refrain from acts that would be crimes if committed by an adult.

I Refrain from operating an automobile without permission of the youth worker or parent.

I Refrain from being habitually disobedient and beyond the lawful control of parent or other legal authority.

I Refrain from running away from the lawful custody of parent or other lawful authority.

If these rules are violated, the juvenile may have his parole revoked and be returned to the institution. Most states have extended the same legal rights enjoyed by adults at parole revocation hearings to juveniles who are in danger of losing their aftercare privileges, as follows:

I Juveniles must be informed of the conditions of parole and receive notice of any obligations.

I Juveniles have the right to legal counsel at state expense if necessary.

I They maintain the right to confront and cross-examine witnesses against them.

I They have the right to introduce documentary evidence and witnesses.

I They have the right to a hearing before an officer who shall be an attorney but not an employee of the revoking agency.[141]

Summary

I Community treatment encompasses efforts to keep offenders in the community and spare them the stigma of incarceration. The primary purpose is to provide a nonrestrictive or home setting, employing educational, vocational, counseling, and employment services. Institutional treatment encompasses provision of these services but in more restrictive and sometimes secure facilities.

I The most widely used method of community treatment is probation. Youths on probation must obey rules given to them by the court and participate in some form of treatment program. Behavior is monitored by probation officers. If rules are violated, youths may have their probation revoked.

I It is now common to enhance probation with more restrictive forms of treatment, such as intensive supervision and house arrest with electronic monitoring. Restitution programs involve having juvenile offenders either reimburse their victims or do community service.

I Residential community treatment programs allow youths to live at home while receiving treatment in a nonpunitive, community-based center. There are also residential programs that require that youths reside in group homes while receiving treatment.

I The secure juvenile institution was developed in the mid-nineteenth century as an alternative to placing youths in adult prisons. Youth institutions evolved from large, closed institutions to cottage-based education- and rehabilitation-oriented institutions. The concept of "least restrictive alternative" is applicable in decisions on placing juvenile offenders to institutions to ensure that the setting benefits the juvenile's treatment needs.

I The juvenile institutional population appears to have stabilized in recent years, but an increasing number of youths are "hidden" in private medical centers and drug treatment clinics. There are wide variations in juvenile custody rates across states.

- A disproportionate number of minorities are incarcerated in more secure, state-run youth facilities. Compared to males, female juvenile inmates are faced with many hardships.

- Most juvenile institutions maintain intensive treatment programs featuring individual or group therapy. Little evidence has been found that any single method is effective in reducing recidivism, yet rehabilitation remains an important goal of juvenile practitioners.

- The right to treatment is an important issue in juvenile justice. Legal decisions have mandated that a juvenile cannot simply be warehoused in a correctional center but must receive proper care and treatment to aid rehabilitation. What constitutes proper care is still being debated, however, and recent court decisions have backed off from the belief that every youth can be rehabilitated.

- Juveniles released from institutions are often placed on parole, or aftercare. There is little evidence that community supervision is more beneficial than simply releasing youths. Many jurisdictions are experiencing success with halfway houses and reintegration centers and other reentry programs.

Key Terms

community treatment, p. 457
suppression effect, p. 458
probation, p. 458
juvenile probation officer, p. 462
social investigation report, predisposition report, p. 463
conditions of probation, p. 463
juvenile intensive probation supervision (JIPS), p. 465
house arrest, p. 465
electronic monitoring, p. 465
balanced probation, p. 467
monetary restitution, p. 468
victim service restitution, p. 468

community service restitution, p. 468
residential programs, p. 470
group homes, p. 470
foster care programs, p. 470
family group homes, p. 470
rural programs, p. 471
nonresidential programs, p. 471
reform schools, p. 473
cottage system, p. 473
least restrictive alternative, p. 474
individual counseling, p. 481
psychotherapy, p. 481
reality therapy, p. 481
behavior modification, p. 481

group therapy, p. 481
guided group interaction (GGI), p. 482
positive peer culture (PPC), p. 482
milieu therapy, p. 482
wilderness probation, p. 483
boot camps, p. 483
right to treatment, p. 485
aftercare, p. 487
reentry, p. 487
parole guidelines, p. 487
Intensive Aftercare Program (IAP), p. 488

Questions for Discussion

1. Would you want a community treatment program in your neighborhood? Why or why not?

2. Is widening the net a real danger, or are treatment-oriented programs simply a method of helping troubled youths?

3. If youths violate the rules of probation, should they be placed in a secure institution?

4. Is juvenile restitution fair? Should a poor child have to pay back a wealthy victim, such as a store owner?

5. What are the most important advantages to community treatment for juvenile offenders?

6. What is the purpose of juvenile probation? Identify some conditions of probation and discuss the responsibilities of the juvenile probation officer.

7. Has community treatment generally proven successful?

8. Why have juvenile boot camps not been effective in reducing recidivism?

Viewpoint

As a local juvenile court judge you have been assigned the case of Jim Butler, a 13-year-old juvenile so short he can barely see over the bench. On trial for armed robbery, the boy has been accused of threatening a woman with a knife and stealing her purse. Barely a teenager, he has already had a long history of involvement with the law. At age 11 he was arrested for drug possession and placed on probation; soon after, he stole a car. At age 12 he was arrested for shoplifting. Jim is accompanied by his legal guardian, his maternal grandmother. His parents are unavailable because his father abandoned the family years ago and his mother is currently undergoing inpatient treatment at a local drug clinic. After talking with his attorney, Jim decides to admit to the armed robbery. At a dispositional hearing, his court-appointed attorney tells you of the tough life Jim has been forced to endure. His grandmother states that, although she loves the boy, her advanced age makes it impossible for her to provide the care he needs to stay out of trouble. She says that Jim is a good boy who has developed a set of bad companions; his current scrape was precipitated by his friends. A representative of the school system testifies that Jim has above-average intelligence and is actually respectful of teachers. He has potential, but his life circumstances have short-circuited his academic success. Jim himself shows remorse and appears to be a sensitive youngster who is easily led astray by older youths.

You must now make a decision. You can place Jim on probation and allow him to live with his grandmother while being monitored by county probation staff. You can place him in a secure incarceration facility for up to three years. You can also put him into an intermediate program such as a community-based facility, which would allow him to attend school during the day while residing in a halfway house and receiving group treatment in the evenings. Although Jim appears salvageable, his crime was serious and involved the use of a weapon. If he remains in the community he may offend again; if he is sent to a correctional facility he will interact with older, tougher kids. What mode of correctional treatment would you choose?

▮ Would you place Jim on probation and allow him to live with his grandmother while being monitored?

▮ Would you send him to a secure incarceration facility for up to three years?

▮ Would you put him into an intermediate program such as a community-based facility?

Doing Research on the Web

Before you answer these questions, you may want to research the effectiveness of different types of correctional treatment for juvenile offenders. Use "juvenile correctional treatment" in a key word search on InfoTrac College Edition. To learn more about juvenile treatment options, visit the following websites (sites accessed on September 28, 2004):

California Department of the Youth Authority
www.cya.ca.gov

Center for the Study and Prevention of Violence
www.colorado.edu/cspv/

Washington State Institute for Public Policy on Juvenile Justice
www.wsipp.wa.gov/crime/JuvJustice.html

The National Council on Crime and Delinquency and Children's Research Center
www.nccd-crc.org

The Urban Institute
www.urban.org/content/PolicyCenters/Justice/overview.htm

Notes

1. Charles Murray and Louis B. Cox, *Beyond Probation* (Beverly Hills, CA: Sage Publications, 1979).
2. Robert Shepard, Jr., ed., *Juvenile Justice Standards, A Balanced Approach* (Chicago: ABA, 1996).
3. George Killinger, Hazel Kerper, and Paul F. Cromwell, Jr., *Probation and Parole in the Criminal Justice System* (St. Paul, MN: West, 1976), p. 45; National Advisory Commission on Criminal Justice Standards and Goals, *Corrections* (Washington, DC: U.S. Government Printing Office, 1983), p. 75.
4. Ibid.
5. Jerome Miller, *Last One over the Wall: The Massachusetts Experiment in Closing Reform Schools* (Columbus: Ohio State University Press, 1998).
6. Bureau of Justice Statistics, *Report to the Nation on Crime and Justice* (Washington, DC: U.S. Government Printing Office, 1988), pp. 44–45; Peter Greenwood, "What Works with Juvenile Offenders: A Synthesis of the Literature and Experience," *Federal Probation* 58:63–67 (1994).
7. Robert Coates, Alden Miller, and Lloyd Ohlin, *Diversity in a Youth Correctional System* (Cambridge, MA: Ballinger, 1978); Barry Krisberg, James Austin, and Patricia Steele, *Unlocking Juvenile Corrections* (San Francisco: National Council on Crime and Delinquency, 1989).
8. Personal correspondence, Taneekah Freeman, executive assistant, January 3, 2001; "Roxbury Agency Offers a Map for Youths at the Crossroads," *Boston Globe*, February 18, 1990, p. 32.
9. Charles Puzzanchera, Anne L. Stahl, Terrence A. Finnegan, Nancy Tierney, and Howard N. Snyder, *Juvenile Court Statistics 1999* (Pittsburgh, PA: National Center for Juvenile Justice, 2003).

10. Ibid.
11. *In re J.G.* 692 N.E.2d 1226 (Ill.App. 1998).
12. *In re Michael D*, 264 CA Rptr 476 (CA App. 1989).
13. *Morrissey v. Brewer*, 408 U.S. 471, 92 S.Ct. 2593, 33 L.Ed.2d 484 (1972); *Gagnon v. Scarpelli*, 411 U.S. 778, 93 S.Ct. 1756, 36 L.Ed.2d 655 (1973).
14. Patricia McFall Torbet, *Juvenile Probation: The Workhorse of the Juvenile Justice System* (Washington, DC: Office of Juvenile Justice and Delinquency Prevention, 1996).
15. Richard Lawrence, "Reexamining Community Corrections Models," *Crime and Delinquency* 37:449–464 (1991).
16. See Matthew J. Giblin, "Using Police Officers to Enhance the Supervision of Juvenile Probationers: An Evaluation of the Anchorage CAN Program," *Crime and Delinquency* 48:116–137 (2002).
17. See Richard G. Wiebush, "Juvenile Intensive Supervision: The Impact on Felony Offenders Diverted from Institutional Placement," *Crime and Delinquency* 39:68–89 (1993); James Byrne, "The Control Controversy: A Preliminary Examination of Intensive Probation Supervision Programs in the United States," *Federal Probation* 50:4–16 (1986).
18. For a review of these programs, see James Byrne, ed., "Introduction," *Federal Probation* 50:2 (1986); see also Emily Walker, "The Community Intensive Treatment for Youth Program: A Specialized Community-Based Program for High-Risk Youth in Alabama," *Law and Psychology Review* 13:175–199 (1989).
19. James Ryan, "Who Gets Revoked? A Comparison of Intensive Supervision Successes and Failures in Vermont," *Crime and Delinquency* 43:104–118 (1997).

20. Angela A. Robertson, Paul W. Grimes, and Kevin E. Rogers, "A Short-Run Cost-Benefit Analysis of Community-Based Interventions for Juvenile Offenders," *Crime and Delinquency* 47:265–284 (2001).

21. Richard Ball and J. Robert Lilly, "A Theoretical Examination of Home Incarceration," *Federal Probation* 50:17–25 (1986); Joan Petersilia, "Exploring the Option of House Arrest," *Federal Probation* 50:50–56 (1986); Annesley Schmidt, "Electronic Monitors," *Federal Probation* 50: 56–60 (1986); Michael Charles, "The Development of a Juvenile Electronic Monitoring Program," *Federal Probation* 53:3–12 (1989).

22. Joseph B. Vaughn, "A Survey of Juvenile Electronic Monitoring and Home Confinement Programs," *Juvenile and Family Court Journal* 40:1–36 (1989).

23. Sudipto Roy, "Five Years of Electronic Monitoring of Adults and Juveniles in Lake County, Indiana: A Comparative Study on Factors Related to Failure," *Journal of Crime and Justice* 20:141–160 (1997).

24. Joseph Papy and Richard Nimer, "Electronic Monitoring in Florida," *Federal Probation* 55:31–33 (1991); Annesley Schmidt, "Electronic Monitors—Realistically, What Can Be Expected?" *Federal Probation* 55:47–53 (1991).

25. Anne Seymour and Trudy Gregorie, "Restorative Justice for Young Offenders and Their Victims," *Corrections Today* 64(1):90–92 (2002), p. 90.

26. Heather Strang and Lawrence W. Sherman, "Restorative Justice to Reduce Victimization," in Brandon C. Welsh and David P. Farrington, eds., *Preventing Crime: What Works for Children, Offenders, Victims, and Places* (Belmont, CA: Wadsworth, forthcoming).

27. Ibid.

28. Dennis Mahoney, Dennis Romig, and Troy Armstrong, "Juvenile Probation: The Balanced Approach," *Juvenile and Family Court Journal* 39:1–59 (1988).

29. Gordon Bazemore, "On Mission Statements and Reform in Juvenile Justice: The Case of the Balanced Approach," *Federal Probation* 61:64–70 (1992); Gordon Bazemore and Mark Umbreit, *Balanced and Restorative Justice* (Washington, DC: Office of Juvenile Justice and Delinquency Prevention, 1994).

30. Gordon Bazemore, *Guide for Implementing the Balanced and Restorative Justice Model* (Washington, DC: Office of Juvenile Justice and Delinquency Prevention, 1998).

31. Office of Juvenile Justice and Delinquency Prevention, *The 8% Solution* (Washington, DC: OJJDP Fact Sheet, 2001).

32. Ibid., pp. 1–2.

33. Anne L. Schneider, ed., *Guide to Juvenile Restitution* (Washington, DC: Department of Justice, 1985); Anne Schneider and Jean Warner, *National Trends in Juvenile Restitution Programming* (Washington, DC: U.S. Government Printing Office, 1989).

34. Gordon Bazemore, "New Concepts and Alternative Practice in Community Supervision of Juvenile Offenders: Rediscovering Work Experience and Competency Development," *Journal of Crime and Justice* 14:27–45 (1991); Jeffrey Butts and Howard Snyder, *Restitution and Juvenile Recidivism* (Washington, DC: U.S. Department of Justice, 1992).

35. Anne Schneider, "Restitution and Recidivism Rates of Juvenile Offenders: Results from Four Experimental Studies," *Criminology* 24:533–552 (1986).

36. Shay Bilchik, *A Juvenile Justice System for the 21st Century* (Washington, DC: Office of Juvenile Justice and Delinquency Prevention, 1998).

37. Peter Schneider, William Griffith, and Anne Schneider, *Juvenile Restitution as a Sole Sanction or Condition of Probation: An Empirical Analysis* (Eugene, OR: Institute for Policy Analysis, 1980); S. Roy, "Juvenile Restitution and Recidivism in a Midwestern County," *Federal Probation* 57:55–62 (1995).

38. Anne Schneider, "Restitution and Recidivism Rates of Juvenile Offenders," *Directory of Restitution Programs* (Washington, DC: OJJDP Juvenile Justice Clearinghouse, 1996). This directory contains information on more than 500 restitution programs across the country.

39. H. Ted Rubin, "Fulfilling Juvenile Restitution Requirements in Community Correctional Programs," *Federal Probation* 52:32–43 (1988).

40. Peter Greenwood, "What Works with Juvenile Offenders: A Synthesis of the Literature and Experience," *Federal Probation* 58:63–67 (1994).

41. Sharon Mihalic, Katherine Irwin, Delbert Elliott, Abigail Fagan, and Dianne Hansen, *Blueprints for Violence Prevention* (Washington, DC: OJJDP Juvenile Justice Bulletin, 2001), p. 10.

42. Patricia Chamberlain and John B. Reid, "Comparison of Two Community Alternatives to Incarceration," *Journal of Consulting and Clinical Psychology* 66:624–633 (1998).

43. Lamar T. Empey and Maynard Erickson, *The Provo Experiment* (Lexington, MA: D.C. Heath, 1972); Paul Pilnick, Albert Elias, and Neale Clapp, "The Essexfields Concept: A New Approach to the Social Treatment of Juvenile Delinquents," *Journal of Applied Behavioral Sciences* 2:109–121 (1966); Yitzhak Bakal, "Reflections: A Quarter Century of Reform in Massachusetts Youth Corrections," *Crime and Delinquency* 40:110–117 (1998).

44. Ira Schwartz, *Juvenile Justice and Public Policy* (New York: Lexington Books, 1992), p. 217.

45. Dan Macallair, "Reaffirming Rehabilitation in Juvenile Justice," *Youth and Society* 25:104–123 (1993).

46. Mark W. Lipsey and David B. Wilson, "Effective Intervention for Serious Juvenile Offenders: A Synthesis of Research," in Rolf Loeber and David P. Farrington, eds., *Serious & Violent Juvenile Offenders: Risk Factors and Successful Interventions* (Thousand Oaks, CA: Sage, 1998); Mark W. Lipsey, "What Do We Learn from 400 Research Studies on the Effectiveness of Treatment with Juvenile Delinquents?," in James McGuire, ed., *What Works: Reducing Reoffending* (New York: Wiley, 1995).

47. Barry Krisberg, Elliot Currie, and David Onek, "New Approaches in Corrections," *American Bar Association Journal of Criminal Justice* 10:51 (1995).

48. U.S. Department of Justice, *Children in Custody 1975–85: Census of Public and Private Juvenile Detention, Correctional, and Shelter Facilities* (Washington, DC: U.S. Department of Justice, 1989), p. 4.

49. For a detailed description of juvenile delinquency in the 1800s, see J. Hawes, *Children in Urban Society: Juvenile Delinquency in Nineteenth Century America* (New York: Oxford University Press, 1971).

50. D. Jarvis, *Institutional Treatment of the Offender* (New York: McGraw-Hill, 1978), p. 101.

51. Margaret Werner Cahalan, *Historical Corrections Statistics in the United States, 1850–1984* (Washington, DC: U.S. Department of Justice, 1986), pp. 104–105.

52. Clemons Bartollas, Stuart J. Miller, and Simon Dinitiz, *Juvenile Victimization: The Institutional Paradox* (New York: Wiley, 1976), p. 6.

53. LaMar T. Empey, *American Delinquency—Its Meaning and Construction* (Homewood, IL: Dorsey, 1978), p. 515.

54. Edward Eldefonso and Walter Hartinger, *Control, Treatment, and Rehabilitation of Juvenile Offenders* (Beverly Hills: Glencoe, 1976), p. 151.

55. Ibid., p. 152.

56. M. Rosenthal, "Reforming the Justice Correctional Institution: Efforts of U.S. Children's Bureau in the 1930s," *Journal of Sociology and Social Welfare* 14:47–73 (1987).

57. Bureau of Justice Statistics, *Fact Sheet on Children in Custody* (Washington, DC: U.S. Department of Justice, 1989); Barbara Allen-Hagen, *Public Juvenile Facilities—Children in Custody, 1989* (Washington, DC: Office of Juvenile Justice and Delinquency Prevention, 1991); James Austin et al., *Juveniles Taken into Custody, 1993* (Washington, DC: Office of Juvenile Justice and Delinquency Prevention, 1995).

58. National Conference of State Legislatures, *A Legislator's Guide to Comprehensive Juvenile Justice, Juvenile Detention and Corrections* (Denver: National Conference of State Legislators, 1996).

59. Ibid.

60. Hunter Hurst and Patricia Torbet, *Organization and Administration of Juvenile Services: Probation, Aftercare, and State Delinquent Institutions* (Pittsburgh: National Center for Juvenile Justice, 1993), p. 4.

61. Melissa Sickmund, *Juveniles in Corrections* (Washington, DC: Office of Juvenile Justice and Delinquency Prevention, 2004); Melissa Sickmund, *Juvenile Residential Facility Census, 2000: Selected Findings* (Washington, DC: Office of Juvenile Justice and Delinquency Prevention, 2002), p. 2.

62. Sickmund, *Juveniles in Corrections.*

63. Ibid.

64. Ira Schwartz, Marilyn Jackson-Beck, and Roger Anderson, "The 'Hidden' System of Juvenile Control," *Crime and Delinquency* 30:371–385 (1984).

65. Rebecca Craig and Andrea Paterson, "State Involuntary Commitment Laws: Beyond Deinstitutionalization," *National Conference of State Legislative Reports* 13:1–10 (1988).

66. Robert Pear, "Many Youths Reported Held Awaiting Mental Help," *New York Times,* July 8, 2004.

67. Richard Lezin Jones and Leslie Kaufman, "New Jersey Youths Out of Foster Homes End Up in Detention," *New York Times,* May 31, 2003.

68. Sickmund, *Juvenile Residential Facility Census, 2000: Selected Findings,* p. 3.

69. Ibid., p. 3.

70. John M. Broder, "Dismal California Prisons Hold Juvenile Offenders: Reports Document Long List of Maltreatment," *New York Times,* February 15, 2004, p. 12.

71. Sickmund, *Juveniles in Corrections.*

72. Howard N. Snyder and Melissa Sickmund, *Juvenile Offenders and Victims: 1999 National Report* (Pittsburgh: National Center for Juvenile Justice, 1999), p. 192.

73. Ibid., p. 195.

74. Rodney L. Engen, Sara Steen, and George S. Bridges, "Racial Disparities in the Punishment of Youth: A Theoretical and Empirical Assessment of the Literature," *Social Problems* 49:194–220 (2002).

75. Barry Krisberg, Ira Schwartz, G. Fishman, Z. Eisikovits, and E. Gitman, "The Incarceration of Minority Youth," *Crime and Delinquency* 33:173–205 (1987).

76. Craig Fischer, ed., "Washington State Moves to End Juvenile Justice Race Disparity," *Criminal Justice Newsletter* 27:1–8 (1996).

77. Heidi M. Hsia, George S. Bridges, and Rosalie McHale, *Disproportionate Minority Confinement, 2003 Update* (Washington, DC: OJJDP, 2003).

78. Sickmund, *Juveniles in Corrections*.

79. See David M. Halbfinger, "Care of Juvenile Offenders in Mississippi Is Faulted," *New York Times*, September 1, 2003.

80. Sickmund, *Juveniles in Corrections*, p. 14.

81. Bartollas, Miller, and Dinitz, *Juvenile Victimization*.

82. Christopher Sieverdes and Clemens Bartollas, "Security Level and Adjustment Patterns in Juvenile Institutions," *Journal of Criminal Justice* 14:135–145 (1986).

83. Several authors have written of this sexual double standard. See E. A. Anderson, "The Chivalrous Treatment of the Female Offender in the Arms of the Criminal Justice System: A Review of the Literature," *Social Problems* 23:350–357 (1976); G. Armstrong, "Females under the Law: Protected but Unequal," *Crime and Delinquency* 23:109–120 (1977); M. Chesney-Lind, "Judicial Enforcement of the Female Sex Role: The Family Court and the Female Delinquent," *Issues in Criminology* 8:51–59 (1973); M. Chesney-Lind, "Juvenile Delinquency: The Sexualization of Female Crime," *Psychology Today* 19:43–46 (1974); Allan Conway and Carol Bogdan, "Sexual Delinquency: The Persistence of a Double Standard," *Crime and Delinquency* 23:13–35 (1977); Medna Chesney-Lind and Randall G. Shelden, *Girls, Delinquency, and the Juvenile Justice System*, 3rd ed. (Belmont, CA: Wadsworth, 2004).

84. Sickmund, *Juveniles in Corrections*, p. 14.

85. See Emily Gaarder and Joanne Belknap, "Tenuous Borders: Girls Transferred to Adult Court," *Criminology* 40:481–518 (2002).

86. Leslie Acoca, "Outside/Inside: The Violation of American Girls at Home, on the Streets, and in the Juvenile Justice System," *Crime and Delinquency* 44:561–589 (1998).

87. Barbara Bloom, Barbara Owen, Elizabeth Piper Deschenes, and Jill Rosenbaum, "Improving Juvenile Justice for Females: A Statewide Assessment in California," *Crime and Delinquency* 48:526–552 (2002), p. 548.

88. For a historical analysis of a girls' reformatory, see Barbara Brenzel, *Daughters of the State* (Cambridge, MA: MIT Press, 1983).

89. Ilene R. Bergsmann, "The Forgotten Few Juvenile Female Offenders," *Federal Probation* 53:73–79 (1989).

90. *Justice by Gender: The Lack of Appropriate Prevention, Diversion and Treatment Alternatives for Girls in the Justice System: A Report* (Chicago: American Bar Association and National Bar Association, 2001), pp. 27–29.

91. Doris Layton MacKenzie, "Reducing the Criminal Activities of Known Offenders and Delinquents: Crime Prevention in the Courts and Corrections," in Lawrence W. Sherman, David P. Farrington, Brandon C. Welsh, and Doris Layton MacKenzie, eds., *Evidence-Based Crime Prevention* (New York: Routledge, 2002), p. 352.

92. For an interesting article highlighting the debate over the effectiveness of correctional treatment, see John Whitehead and Steven Lab, "Meta-Analysis of Juvenile Correctional Treatment," *Journal of Research in Crime and Delinquency* 26:276–295 (1989).

93. National Conference of State Legislatures, *A Legislator's Guide to Comprehensive Juvenile Justice, 1996.*

94. Robert Shepard, Jr., "State Pen or Playpen? Is Prevention 'Pork' or Simply Good Sense?" *American Bar Association Journal of Criminal Justice* 10:34–37 (1995); James Howell, ed., *Guide for Implementing the Comprehensive Strategy for Serious, Violent and Chronic Juvenile Offenders* (Washington, DC: OJJDP, 1995).

95. Broder, "Dismal California Prisons Hold Juvenile Offenders."

96. Louise Sas and Peter Jaffe, "Understanding Depression in Juvenile Delinquency: Implications for Institutional Admission Policies and Treatment Programs," *Juvenile and Family Court Journal* 37:49–58 (1985–1986).

97. See William Glasser, "Reality Therapy: A Realistic Approach to the Young Offender," in Robert Schaste and Jo Wallach, eds., *Readings in Delinquency and Treatment* (Los Angeles: Delinquency Prevention Training Project, Youth Studies Center, University of Southern California, 1965); see also Richard Rachin, "Reality Therapy: Helping People Help Themselves," *Crime and Delinquency* 16:143 (1974).

98. Helen A. Klein, "Toward More Effective Behavior Programs for Juvenile Offenders," *Federal Probation* 41:45–50 (1977); Albert Bandura, *Principles of Behavior Modification* (New York: Holt, Rinehart & Winston, 1969); H. A. Klein, "Behavior Modification as Therapeutic Paradox," *American Journal of Orthopsychiatry* 44:353 (1974).

99. Thomas J. Dishion, Joan McCord, and François Poulin, "When Interventions Harm: Peer Groups and Problem Behavior," *American Psychologist* 54:755–764 (1999); Joan McCord, "Cures that Harm: Unanticipated Outcomes of Crime Prevention Programs," *Annals of the American Academy of Political and Social Science* 587:16–30 (2003).

100. Larry Brendtero and Arlin Ness, "Perspectives on Peer Group Treatment: The Use and Abuses of Guided Group Interaction/Positive Peer Culture," *Child and Youth Services Review* 4:307–324 (1982).

101. Elaine Traynelis-Yurek and George A. Giacobbe, "Communication Rehabilitation Regime for Incarcerated Youth: Positive Peer Culture," *Journal of Offender Rehabilitation* 26:157–167 (1998).

102. Bruno Bettelheim, *The Empty Fortress* (New York: Free Press, 1967).

103. California Youth Authority, "Ventura School for Juvenile Female Offenders," *CYA Newsletter* (Ventura, CA: author, 1988).

104. Kate O'Sullivan, Nancy Rose, and Thomas Murphy, *PEPNet: Connecting Juvenile Offenders to Education and Employment* (Washington, DC: OJJDP Fact Sheet, 2001), p. 1.

105. Doris Layton MacKenzie, "Reducing the Criminal Activities of Known Offenders and Delinquents," p. 355; Doris Layton MacKenzie, "Evidence-Based Corrections: Identifying What Works," *Crime and Delinquency* 46:457–471 (2000), p. 466.

106. Thomas Castellano and Irina Soderstrom, "Therapeutic Wilderness Programs and Juvenile Recidivism: A Program Evaluation," *Journal of Offender Rehabilitation* 17:19–46 (1992).

107. MacKenzie, "Reducing the Criminal Activities of Known Offenders and Delinquents," p. 355.

108. Jerald Burns and Gennaro Vito, "An Impact Analysis of the Alabama Boot Camp Program," *Federal Probation* 59:63–67 (1995).

109. Ronald Corbett and Joan Petersilia, eds., "The Results of a Multi-Site Study of Boot Camps," *Federal Probation* 58:60–66 (1995).

110. Margaret Beyer, "Juvenile Boot Camps Don't Make Sense," *American Bar Association Journal of Criminal Justice* 10:20–21 (1996).

111. Doris Layton MacKenzie, Angela R. Gover, Gaylene Styve Armstrong, and Ojmarrh Mitchell, *A National Study Comparing the Environments of Boot Camps with Traditional Facilities for Juvenile Offenders* (Washington, DC: NIJ Research in Brief, 2001), pp. 1–2.

112. Doris Layton MacKenzie, David B. Wilson, and Suzanne B. Kider, "Effects of Correctional Boot Camps on Offending," in David P. Farrington and Brandon C. Welsh, eds., "What Works in Preventing Crime? Systematic Reviews of Experimental and Quasi-Experimental Research," *Annals of the American Academy of Political and Social Science* 578:126–143 (2001).

113. Ibid., p. 134.

114. MacKenzie, "Reducing the Criminal Activities of Known Offenders and Delinquents," p. 348.

115. Dale G. Parent, *Correctional Boot Camps: Lessons Learned from a Decade of Research* (Washington, DC: National Institute of Justice, 2003).

116. Anthony Salerno, "Boot Camps—A Critique and Proposed Alternative," *Journal of Offender Rehabilitation* 20:147–158 (1994).

117. Joanne Ardovini-Brooker and Lewis Walker, "Juvenile Boot Camps and the Reclamation of Our Youth: Some Food for Thought," *Juvenile and Family Court Journal* 51:12–28 (2000).

118. Morton Birnbaum, "The Right to Treatment," *American Bar Association Journal* 46:499 (1960).

119. See, for example, *Matter of Welfare of CAW* 579 N.W.2d 494 (MN App. 1998).

120. *Inmates of the Boys' Training School v. Affleck,* 346 F. Supp. 1354 (D.R.I. 1972).

121. Ibid., p. 1343.

122. *Nelson v. Heyne,* 491 F.2d 353 (1974).

123. *Morales v. Turman,* 383 F.Supp. 53 (E.D. Texas 1974).

124. *Pena v. New York State Division for Youth,* 419 F. Supp. 203 (S.D.N.Y. 1976).

125. *Ralston v. Robinson,* 102 S.Ct. 233 (1981).

126. Patricia Puritz and Mary Ann Scali, *Beyond the Walls: Improving Conditions of Confinement for Youth in Custody* (Washington, DC: Office of Juvenile Justice and Delinquency Prevention, 1998).

127. Joan McCord, Cathy Spatz Widom, and Nancy A. Crowell, *Juvenile Crime, Juvenile Justice,* Panel on Juvenile Crime: Prevention, Treatment, and Control (Washington, DC: National Academy Press, 2001), p. 194.

128. David M. Altschuler and Rachel Brash, "Adolescent and Teenage Offenders Confronting the Challenges and Opportunities of Reentry," *Youth Violence and Juvenile Justice* 2:72–87 (2004), p. 72.

129. Daniel P. Mears and Jeremy Travis, "Youth Development and Reentry," *Youth Violence and Juvenile Justice* 2:3–20 (2004), p. 3.

130. Edward J. Latessa, "Homelessness and Reincarceration: Editorial Introduction," *Criminology & Public Policy* 3:137–138 (2004).

131. Joan Petersilia, *When Prisoners Come Home: Parole and Prisoner Reentry* (New York: Oxford University Press, 2003).

132. Margaret Beale Spencer and Cheryl Jones-Walker, "Interventions and Services Offered to Former Juvenile Offenders Reentering Their Communities: An Analysis of Program Effectiveness," *Youth Violence and Juvenile Justice* 2:88–97 (2004), p. 91.

133. Howard N. Snyder, "An Empirical Portrait of the Youth Reentry Population," *Youth Violence and Juvenile Justice* 2:39–55 (2004).

134. Ibid., p. 43.

135. Michael Norman, "Discretionary Justice: Decision Making in a State Juvenile Parole Board," *Juvenile and Family Court Journal* 37:19–26 (1985–1986).

136. James Maupin, "Risk Classification Systems and the Provisions of Juvenile Aftercare," *Crime and Delinquency* 39:90–105 (1993).

137. National Conference of State Legislatures, *A Legislator's Guide to Comprehensive Juvenile Justice.*

138. David M. Altschuler and Troy L. Armstrong, "Juvenile Corrections and Continuity of Care in a Community Context – The Evidence and Promising Directions," *Federal Probation* 66:72–77 (2002).

139. David M. Altschuler and Troy L. Armstrong, "Intensive Aftercare for High-Risk Juveniles: A Community Care Model" (Washington, DC: Office of Juvenile Justice and Delinquency Prevention, 1994).

140. David M. Altschuler and Troy Armstrong, "Reintegrating Juvenile Offenders: Translating the Intensive Aftercare Program Model into Performance Standards." paper presented at the American Society of Criminology meeting, San Francisco, November 2000.

141. See *Morrissey v. Brewer,* 408 U.S. 471, 92 S.Ct. 2593, 33 L.Ed.2d 484 (1972).

16 Delinquency and Juvenile Justice Abroad

Chapter Outline

Delinquency around the World

Europe

The Americas

Australia and New Zealand

Asia

Africa

FOCUS ON DELINQUENCY: Youth Violence on the Rise in Japan

International Comparisons

Problems of Cross-National Research

Benefits of Cross-National Research

Juvenile Violence

Juvenile Property Crime

Juvenile Drug Use

Conclusion: What Do the Trends Tell Us?

Juvenile Justice Systems across Countries

Juvenile Policing

Age of Criminal Responsibility: Minimum and Maximum

Presence of Juvenile Court

Transfers to Adult Court

Sentencing Policies

POLICY AND PRACTICE: Precourt Diversion Programs around the World

Incarcerated Juveniles

POLICY AND PRACTICE: The Changing Nature of Youth Justice in Canada

Aftercare

A Profile of Juvenile Justice in England

Apprehension and Charge

Bail

Precourt Diversion

Prosecution

Youth Court

Sentencing

Chapter Objectives

1. Have a grasp of some of the different delinquency problems facing the regions of the world

2. Be able to identify the main challenges of conducting international comparisons of delinquency

3. Be able to identify the benefits of international comparative research

4. Be able to comment on trends in juvenile violence, property crime, and drug use in Europe and North America

5. Understand the key explanations for changes in these types of delinquency in Europe and North America

6. Know about the work of the United Nations to get countries to improve their juvenile justice systems

7. Be familiar with differences and similarities on key issues of juvenile justice across the world

8. Understand the key stages of juvenile justice in England

9. Be able to comment on the differences and similarities in juvenile justice in the United States and in England

CNN. View the CNN video clip of this story and answer related Critical Thinking questions on your Juvenile Delinquency 9e CD-ROM.

In some countries, rapid social and economic change are at the root of recent increases in juvenile crime rates. In Russia, the fall of Communism and economic market reforms have brought new opportunities for many youths, but have brought hardships for others. Desperate economic situations in smaller towns, family violence, abuse and neglect, among other social problems have caused thousands of Russian youths, some as young as 8 and 9 years old, to leave their homes for Moscow and other large urban centers. There they have the prospect of safety from family members and the chance to earn money, albeit from low-paying, menial jobs. But with these prospects comes the reality of living on the streets, and for many a life of crime becomes their only means of survival. Youths who are arrested face a punitive juvenile justice system, while others wind up in state-run halfway houses to await their parents to come for them; few parents ever arrive, however.

developed countries
Recognized by the United Nations as the richest countries in the world.

This state of affairs facing Russian youths aptly illustrates that juvenile delinquency is not unique to the United States. Many nations around the world are experiencing an upsurge in juvenile problem behavior, including gang violence, prostitution, and drug abuse. In response to the growing number of delinquent acts, some nations are now in the process of revamping their juvenile justice systems in an effort to increase their effectiveness and efficiency. This chapter addresses these issues by looking at international perspectives of delinquency and juvenile justice systems. The chapter begins by providing a snapshot of juvenile delinquency around the world. We discuss the challenges and benefits of making comparisons across nations and examine trends in delinquency rates in different countries compared with the United States. Next we provide a review of juvenile justice systems in **developed countries,** organized around important issues facing juvenile justice today, such as minimum age of criminal responsibility, transfers to adult court, and maximum length of sentence for incarcerated juveniles. The chapter concludes with a profile of the juvenile justice system in England, examining the many different stages that juveniles may face as they go through the system.

DELINQUENCY AROUND THE WORLD

There has been a noted upswing in juvenile delinquency around the world. Where has this occurred, and what has been the cause? Examples are found in all major areas of the world, and though there are many reasons, some common themes emerge.

Europe

Teen crime has been on the rise in Europe. One of the most alarming developments has been the involvement of children in the international sex trade. Russia is plagued with Internet sex rings that involve youths in pornographic pictures. In May 2001, more than 800 tapes and videos were seized in Moscow during Operation Blue Orchid, a joint operation conducted by Russian police and U.S. Customs agents.[1] Operation Blue Orchid led to criminal investigations against people who ordered child pornography in more than 20 nations. Equally disturbing has been the involvement of European youths in global prostitution rings. Desperate young girls and boys in war-torn areas such as the former Yugoslavia and in impoverished areas such as Eastern Europe have become involved with gangs that ship them around the world. In one case, an organized crime group involved in wildlife smuggling of tiger bones and skins to Asian markets began a sideline of supplying sex clubs with young Russian women.[2] In another case, as a result of a 12-nation crackdown on the trafficking of women for sex commerce, the Southeast European Cooperative Initiative in Bucharest, Romania, identified 696 victims of trafficking and 831 suspected traffickers.[3] Illicit drug use has also become more problematic in Eastern Europe, and is partly responsible for a large-scale increase in H.I.V. infection in Estonia.[4]

Western Europe has also experienced a surprising amount of teen violence. On April 26, 2002, in Erfurt, Germany, a 19-year-old male, armed with a pump-action shotgun and a handgun, entered his high school and shot dead 14 teachers, two students, and a police officer; he then took his own life. The youth had just been expelled from the school. It was the worst mass killing in Germany since World War II.[5] In May 2001, race riots broke out in England when young native-born Britons attacked groups of Asian immigrants. The young rioters were the sons of mill workers whose livelihoods were disrupted when the mills closed, leaving them with little chance of advancement.[6]

Violent hate crimes are not unique to England. Germany has been plagued with skinhead violence since reunification in 1989. Most German skinheads are social misfits, with minimal education and few employment opportunities. Because unemployment is high, they feel helpless and hopeless regarding their future, and many resort to physical violence in reaction to their plight.[7] Most of the increase in German youth violence has been encountered in what was Communist East Germany before the reunification. Youth violence in the East is 70 percent higher than in the West, a factor linked to the exposure of Eastern youth to greater poverty and unemployment than their West German peers.[8] France too has experienced a surge in violent hate crimes, as well as (to a lesser extent) street crime in Paris.[9] These events propelled crime to the number one issue in the 2002 French presidential election.[10]

What has fueled this increase in teen violence? Although each nation is quite different, all share an explosive mix of racial tension, poverty, envy, drug abuse, broken families, unemployment, and alienation. Some of the areas hardest hit have been undergoing rapid social and economic change—the fall of communism, the end of the Cold War, the effects of the global economy, an influx of multinational immigration—as they move toward increased economic integration, privatization, and diminished social services. In Europe, the main reason for skyrocketing teen violence is believed to be the tremendous growth in immigrant youth populations. This is not because immigrants are more prone to violence, but rather because of the relative poverty and social disintegration they face upon arriving in very homogenous countries such as Sweden, the Netherlands, and Germany.[11] This view has also been advanced as one of the main reasons for the growth in rates of total violent crime (adult plus juvenile) in Europe during the early to mid-1990s.[12] The result of these rapid changes has been the development of personal alienation in an anomic environment. (See Chapter 4 for more on the effect of anomie.) Kids become susceptible to violence when institutional and interpersonal sources of stability, such as schools and parents, are weak and/or absent.[13]

The Americas

Shocking stories of teen violence are also not uncommon in North America and South America. In Canada, there has been a rash of school shootings in recent years. Many have resulted in death and serious injury of other students and teachers. School shootings in Canada increased substantially following the massacre at Columbine High School in the United States in 1999, prompting some Canadian social scientists to speculate that these were copycat crimes. But other research points to the growing number of students who have access to guns and carry them to school,[14] as well as an increase in school violence in general.[15]

In Mexico, violent crime is one of the biggest problems facing the country. One study found more than 1,500 street gangs in Mexico City, the country's capital. Gang names include *Verdugos* (Executioners), *Malditos Ratas* (Wicked Punks), *Niños Podridos* (Bad Boys), and *Cerdos* (Pigs). Most of the gangs are made up of teenagers, and each gang is accompanied by what is referred to as their "diaper brigade," the equivalent of a "minor league" for children under age 12.[16]

South America has a long history of violent uprisings, police abuse, and political unrest. Some countries are more violent than others. In Brazil, violence is the second leading cause of death behind heart disease; there are more deaths each year by murder than by cancer. Young people are responsible for a disproportionate amount of these homicides.[17] Drug trafficking gangs are largely responsible for the violence. In Rio de Janeiro, the country's "showcase" city, these heavily armed gangs, referred to as "organized terrorist groups" by the head police authority, have taken to bombing government buildings, shopping centers, and tourist attractions. This is being done to cause the government to ease up on its long-standing campaign against these criminal groups.[18]

Among the more recent atrocities in South America is a government cover-up of killings of juvenile and other gang members in a prison in El Porvenir, Honduras.[19] The killing of street children continues to take place in many South American cities. These are children who leave home at a very young age because of abuse, neglect, or the loss of their parents, and earn their living largely by committing petty delinquent acts, begging, and selling garbage. In Rio de Janeiro, killings of street children are commonplace. **Death squads,** drug lords, juvenile gangs, and sometimes the police are behind these killings.[20]

death squads
Common to South America, organized government or criminal groups that selectively kill members of opposing groups and incite fear in those groups and among their supporters.

Australia and New Zealand

Although not normally associated with high crime and delinquency rates, these island nations have had their share of youth crime, ranging from graffiti to homicide. In fact, the graffiti problem has become so serious in New Zealand that some police departments have been forced to use photographs to prepare victim damage estimates. In one police office, 135 different incidents were investigated before the culprits, a youth group, were finally arrested.[21]

Australia has experienced a wide range of juvenile crime. Like Europe, child prostitution has become a significant problem, and an estimated 4,000 children, some as young as 10 years old, are involved in selling sex for money and drugs.[22] Australia has also experienced juvenile violence. Youths are the offenders (and/or victims) in about one-third of all the murders occurring in Australia.[23] Youth homicides tend to occur among strangers, with the youngest offenders (10 to 14 years) killing people they had never met before and older teens victimizing acquaintances. One reason for this trend is that the Australian juvenile is more likely to kill while committing another crime such as a robbery. Juveniles are also more likely to kill for revenge than are adults.

Asia

Crime rates are at an all-time high in Japan, with more than 3.5 million crimes committed in 2001.[24] According to the National Police Agency in Japan, juvenile crime and foreign criminal gangs are the "twin causes" of the rising crime rates.[25] In December 2001, police in the Fukushima Prefecture, located north of Tokyo, arrested a 15-year-old boy for killing his father. The 15-year-old punched his 61-year-old father in the face and stomped on his stomach until he was dead. The incident was extremely shocking because it occurred one day after a 13-year-old was arrested for beating his mother to death because he objected to the meal she had cooked![26] Japanese teen violence is at its highest level in more than 30 years, and the term *hikikomori* (those who isolate themselves) has been coined to describe troubled youth who commit crimes and engage in other antisocial acts.[27] The Japanese experience with delinquency and youth violence is the topic of the accompanying Focus on Delinquency.

Japan is not the only Asian nation experiencing an uptick in juvenile crime. Chinese authorities have found that juvenile delinquency has been on the increase for several years, though it is still relatively lower than adult crime.[28] The rise in delinquency has been linked to China's ongoing social and economic upheaval that began in 1979 when the country first adopted its reform policies and embraced the outside world.[29] Though the rapid economic growth has transformed society, rapid change has strained traditional norms, values, and ethics. Although China is often known for its ruthless suppression of crime and liberal use of the death penalty, the government has adopted a more humane approach to treating delinquents. The aim is to act as a wise and concerned pseudoparent, emphasizing prevention and education rather than punishment and repression.

Africa

Juvenile crime and gang violence are growing problems in many African countries. In the city of Dakar, Senegal, on the western coast of the continent, youth gang problems are out of control. Youth gangs here, with English names taken from American television and movies, like The Hooligan Boys, The Mafia Boys, and The Eagles, prey on different segments of the population. The Hooligans, for example, are best known for the violence they inflict at dance parties organized by other young people. This gang has also developed a type of violence market in which they "buy a fight." This involves gang members offering to take over a fight that has already started and then fighting the weaker of the two parties. Many of the younger boys growing up in Dakar look up to gang members; this admiration serves as an important tool in recruiting future gang members.[30]

Abject poverty, ethnic tensions, and an ever-growing gap between the haves and have-nots underlie much of the violence throughout Africa. In Nairobi, the capital of Kenya and one of the largest cities in Africa, up to 70 percent of residents live in slums on the outskirts of the city; 80 percent of residents are low-income earners; the rich occupy 60 percent of the city's land; and two-thirds of the population does not have access to clean water.[31]

© Eric Miller/Africanpictures.net

Few African nations have the resources to expend on treatment programs for juvenile offenders, let alone separate correctional facilities for adult and juvenile offenders. Here, South African juvenile offenders bide their time in the juvenile pretrial wing of Pollsmoor prison in Capetown.

Youth Violence on the Rise in Japan

Japan has long been considered a low-crime country. Despite its industrial might and highly urbanized population—trademarks of high-crime countries in the developed world—Japan has maintained extremely low delinquency and crime rates in the post–World War II era. But in recent years this trend has changed, with a dramatic upsurge in violence among young people. As shown in Figure 16-A, police arrests of 15- to 19-year-olds for violent offenses started to climb in 1996, following years of stability. (Although these figures are not expressed as rates per juvenile population, the increase in arrests between 1995 and 1998 far surpasses any increase in the juvenile population.) In 1997, the peak year, 2,300 arrests were made for juvenile violence.

Shocking events, rarely experienced before in Japan, are starting to become more common. Japanese youth gangs have started to carry out what they call "uncle hunting," whereby four or five gang members single out a lone businessman walking home and beat him to the ground. Victim reports claim that gangs are not only doing this for the money, but also for the thrill of inflicting pain on others. Other events include a 13-year-old boy murdering his female schoolteacher and a 16-year-old boy stabbing his girlfriend when she tried to end the relationship.

So what is causing this rise in youth violence in Japan? Japanese social scientists, politicians, leaders of business, and the public are all weighing in on the debate. One of the more controversial views is that the increase in juvenile violence and crime in general is being fueled by an increase in the number of multinational immigrants, which are overwhelmingly other Asians, who have come to find work in Japan. As in Europe, it is not that these new populations are more prone to violence, but rather that they are less well off financially, due in part to work being scarce, and are disconnected from familial and social groups.

Other views point to a decline in cultural values and societal norms, which are widely regarded as being fundamental to the economic success and crime-free lifestyle that Japan has long enjoyed. Conformity, sense of community, belonging to a group, honor or "face," and respect for authority are all believed to have declined in recent years, especially among young people. Economic stagnation has also played a role in the rise in youth violence. A higher unemployment rate and fewer opportunities have left many young people feeling marginalized and frustrated. It is also estimated that 45 percent of all crimes in Japan are committed by people under age 20, about double what it is in the United States. Because so much of Japanese crime is committed by youths and the rate of juvenile crime and violence is escalating, experts predict no slowdown in the present trends in youth violence.

Critical Thinking

1. What are some other possible reasons for Japan's increase in youth violence?
2. What type of action should Japan take to address this rise in youth violence? And how can young people be part of the solution?

InfoTrac College Edition Research

To read more about changes in youth violence in Japan, go to "Insecure; Crime in Japan," *The Economist* 369:40 (October 25, 2003). To find further information, use "crime and international" as a key term.

SOURCES: Aki Roberts and Gary LaFree, "Explaining Japan's Postwar Violent Crime Trends," *Criminology* 42:179–209 (2004); Norimitsu Onishi, "Crime Rattles Japanese Calm, Attracting Politicians' Notice," *New York Times*, September 6, 2003; Calvin Sims, "Shaken Japan Tries to Face Aftermath of School Attack," *New York Times*, June 10, 2001; Doug Struck, "Surge in Violent Crime Worries Japan," *Washington Post*, February 10, 2000; Nobuo Komiya, "A Cultural Study of the Low Crime Rate in Japan," *British Journal of Criminology* 39:369–390 (1999); Howard W. French, "Japan's Teen Crime Wave," *New York Times Upfront* 132:12 (November 15, 1999); Minoru Yokoyama, "Juvenile Justice and Juvenile Crime: An Overview of Japan," in John Winterdyk, ed., *Juvenile Justice Systems: International Perspectives*, 2nd ed. (Toronto: Canadian Scholars' Press, 2002); Hans Joachim Schneider, "Crime and Its Control in Japan and the Federal Republic of Germany," *International Journal of Offender Therapy and Comparative Criminology* 36:307–321 (1992); Freda Adler, *Nations Not Obsessed with Crime* (Littleton, CO: Rothman, 1983).

FIGURE 16-A ARRESTS FOR VIOLENT OFFENSES, 1988–1998

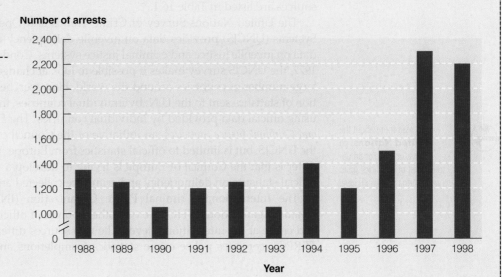

How does youth crime around the world compare to what we are experiencing here in the United States? There have been numerous efforts to compare delinquency across different countries.[32] Social scientists have carried out international comparisons for many reasons, including to test theories of delinquency; to compare delinquency and punishment over long periods of time; to investigate the effects of government policies on delinquency, such as gun control or child welfare benefits; to examine why some countries have very low delinquency rates; or just for general interest.[33] (Concept Summary 16.1 reviews the key reasons for making cross-national comparisons.) Advocacy organizations as well as governments sometimes point to events or trends in other countries to show how the United States is doing better or sometimes worse than other countries.

Concept Summary 16.1
Key Reasons for Cross-National Comparisons

Focus	Scope
Delinquency	To assess which countries have high and low delinquency rates
Theories of delinquency	To assess if similar theories can be used to explain delinquency in different countries
Juvenile justice system	To compare differences in juvenile justice philosophy and administration
Treatment and prevention	To compare different responses to juvenile delinquency and evaluate their effectiveness across countries

Problems of Cross-National Research

Unlike comparisons of delinquency in different cities or parts of the same country, international comparisons involving two or more countries demand that researchers pay a great deal more attention to what is being compared, what countries are being compared, and so on.[34] Comparing delinquency rates across countries can be difficult because of three main problems:

▌ The legal definitions of juvenile crime vary from country to country.[35]

▌ The measurement of juvenile crime varies across countries. In the United States, arrests are used to measure juvenile crime, while in many European countries, the number of cases solved by the police measures crime.[36]

▌ The age group defined as "juvenile" is not always the same.[37]

Despite these problems, valid comparisons of delinquency across different countries can still be made. The key is to acquire valid data and then make comparisons between nations that utilize similar methods of measuring youth crime. The best data sources are listed in Table 16.1.[38]

The United Nations Survey of Crime Trends and Operations of Criminal Justice Systems (UNCJS) provides data on juvenile delinquency and adult crime, as well as data on juvenile justice and criminal justice systems. Conducted every five years since 1977, the UNCJS survey makes it possible to look at changes over time, and for a very large number of countries around the world. However, because the data are a collection of statistics sent to the U.N. by individual countries, they are really no better than using official data provided by individual countries. The *European Sourcebook of Crime and Criminal Justice Statistics,* an initiative of the Council of Europe, is very similar to the UNCJS, but is limited to official statistics from Europe. Where the two data sources differ is that the Council of Europe is trying to develop a uniform system in the way official statistics on delinquency and crime are collected and reported.

The International Criminal Police Organization (INTERPOL) and the World Health Organization (WHO) are two other sources of official statistics on delinquency and crime at the international level. The two sources differ in a number of ways. INTERPOL compiles police crime statistics (completions and attempts) received from

To read more about the **United Nations,** go to www.un.org. For an up-to-date list of web links, go to http://cj.wadsworth.com/siegel_jd9e.

TABLE 16.1

International Sources of Delinquency Data

Data Source	Type of Delinquency Data Collected	Organization in Charge of Data Collection	Number of Countries Represented	Frequency of Data Collection
UNCJS	Police statistics	United Nations	103	Every five years (since 1977)
INTERPOL	Police statistics	International Criminal Police Organization	179	Annually
WHO	Medical certified homicides	World Health Organization	191	Annually
European Sourcebook of Crime and Criminal Justice Statistics	Police statistics	Council of Europe	36 European countries	Annually
International Self-Report Delinquency Study	Self-reports	Netherlands Ministry of Justice	12	One time only (early 1990s)

SOURCES: Josine Junger-Tas, Gert-Jan Terlouw, and Malcolm W. Klein, eds., *Delinquent Behavior among Young People in the Western World: First Results of the International Self-Report Delinquency Study* (New York: Kugler Publications, 1994); Graeme Newman and Gregory J. Howard, "Introduction: Data Sources and Their Use," in Graeme Newman, ed., *Global Report on Crime and Justice* (New York: Oxford University Press, 1999), pp. 3–12; European Committee on Crime Problems, *European Sourcebook of Crime and Criminal Justice Statistics* (Strasbourg, Germany: Council of Europe, 1999); Martin Killias and Marcelo F. Aebi, "Crime Trends in Europe from 1990 to 1996: How Europe Illustrates the Limits of the American Experience," *European Journal on Criminal Policy and Research* 8:43–63 (2000).

countries that are members of the organization. WHO, on the other hand, compiles homicide statistics (completions only) based on medical records received from countries that are affiliated with the organization. WHO's measure of homicide, which is based on the "classification of causes of death worldwide" and determined by medical practitioners,[39] is considered the most accurate source of homicide statistics[40] and is used in many international studies of homicide.[41] The main reason for WHO being the most accurate source of homicide data is that medical doctors and coroners are trained to determine cause of death.

To read more about **INTERPOL**, go to www.interpol.com. For an up-to-date list of web links, go to http://cj.wadsworth.com/siegel_jd9e.

The International Self-Report Delinquency (ISRD) study, which was carried out in 12 developed countries in the early 1990s, was the first attempt to measure self-reported delinquency at an international level using a standard questionnaire.[42] Because the same questionnaire was used for all subjects, delinquency rates could be compared in a more valid way across countries. Because the study has not been repeated, it is not possible to look at changes over time. A second sweep of the ISRD is planned.[43]

Benefits of Cross-National Research

Are juvenile offenders in the United States more violent than those in Japan? Are delinquents in Western Europe more likely to steal cars? How does Australia's juvenile justice system differ from that of the United States? Knowledge of the nature of juvenile delinquency and how juvenile justice systems operate in other countries is not only beneficial for the concerned citizen, but also important to social scientists and government policy makers. Investigating whether juvenile offenders in the United States are more violent than, say, juveniles in Canada may lead to important discoveries to help explain any differences that exist. These discoveries may in turn be useful to policy makers and lead to action; for example, more funding for problem solving policing tactics to reduce gun violence by juveniles.[44] (See Chapter 13 for examples of police efforts to reduce juvenile gun violence.)

Another value served by cross-national comparisons, whether it is delinquency rates or the treatment of incarcerated juvenile offenders, is to let a country know how well or how poorly it is doing relative to other countries. On the one hand, a poor international rating for the United States on juvenile homicides by an international agency, such as the United Nations, may prompt the U.S. government to take action to address this problem. On the other hand, a good international rating on, say, the legal rights afforded to detained juveniles demonstrates that the United States is on the right track. This, in turn, could lead to other countries making changes to follow the U.S. example.

Other benefits from cross-national comparisons can come from studying low-crime countries.[45] Examining these countries to find out how they maintain low delinquency rates may yield important insights for countries with higher delinquency rates. According to Erika Fairchild and Harry Dammer, another good reason to make cross-national comparisons is the need to address **transnational** and **international crime** problems.[46] Transnational crimes are those activities that extend into two or more countries and violate the laws of those countries, such as illegal migration, trafficking in body parts, trafficking in illegal drugs and weapons, and theft and trafficking in automobiles.[47] Through the National Institute of Justice's International Center, the United States is playing an important role in addressing transnational crime problems.[48]

International crimes are those that are recognized by international law, such as war crimes.[49] Criminal activities that take place across borders have grown considerably in the last two decades. "The end of the Cold War, the collapse of state authority in some countries and regions, and the process of globalization—of trade, finance, communications and information—have all provided an environment in which many criminal organizations find it more profitable and preferable to operate across national borders than confine their activities to one country."[50] This phenomenon has become known as the globalization of delinquency and crime.[51]

The best method of comparing the level of delinquency across countries is to use data that have been collected in a uniform way; for example, using a standard questionnaire that asks young people in different countries the same questions about their involvement in delinquency. At present, the best and most up-to-date source of delinquency rates is police statistics available from individual countries.

German social scientist Christian Pfeiffer examined trends in juvenile crime and violence in 10 European countries and the United States.[52] The 10 European countries were England, Sweden, Germany, the Netherlands, Italy, Austria, France, Denmark, Switzerland, and Poland. Delinquency data were available from police statistics from the mid-1980s to the mid-1990s. Three main findings emerged from the study:

1. Juvenile violence, especially robbery and offenses involving serious bodily harm, increased substantially over this period of time in almost all of the countries.

2. Total juvenile crime, which includes burglary, motor vehicle theft, larceny, and vandalism, increased very little over this period of time, with some countries showing no increase or an actual decrease.

3. Crimes of violence committed by young adults (18–20) or by adults in general have increased far less rapidly since the mid-1980s than have those committed by juveniles, and in some countries they have not increased at all.[53]

What does this international data tell us about the differences in delinquency trends between the United States and similar nations?

Juvenile Violence

The increase in juvenile violence between the mid-1980s and the mid-1990s was greater in most European countries than it was in the United States. (See Table 16.2.) Canada, the other North American country for which data was available to add to this comparison, showed a substantial increase in juvenile violence over this period. Between 1986 and 1995, the rates of all categories of youth violence in Canada increased substantially: homicide, +50 percent; assault, +150 percent; sexual assault, +40 percent; and robbery, +160 percent.[54]

This substantial increase in all violence categories was not the case in all of the European countries, with the increase in juvenile violence rates being largely driven by robbery and offenses involving serious bodily harm.[55] For example, in the Netherlands, increases in the rates of robbery (+297 percent) and violence against the person (+123 percent) were the driving forces behind the substantial increase in juvenile violence.[56] Russia too has experienced a significant increase in juvenile violence over this period of time.[57]

More recent data from some of the countries for which it is available show some marked changes in juvenile violence rates. For example, between 1996 and 2000, juvenile violence rates decreased by 13 percent in the Netherlands.[58] In Canada, a smaller 4 percent decrease was reported in juvenile violence rates between 1996 and 1999, while in the United States rates dropped by about 40 percent over the period of 1995 to 2001.[59] On the other hand, in Germany and Italy, rates of juvenile violence continued to climb into the late 1990s.[60]

Juvenile Property Crime

Juvenile property crime rates (including burglary, motor vehicle theft, larceny, and vandalism) increased very little in Europe and North America from the mid-1980s to the mid-1990s, and in the case of England, Denmark, and Switzerland, rates decreased or did not change at all (see Table 16.3). On the other hand, like juvenile violence, property crime rates increased substantially in two countries during this period of time: Germany with a 75 percent increase and Italy with a 140 percent increase. It is not altogether clear why total juvenile crime rates in these two countries increased as much as this. Perhaps the factors that were driving the increases in juvenile violence in these countries were also having an effect on less serious forms of delinquency, such as theft, burglary, and motor vehicle theft.

More recent data on juvenile property crime in Canada show that the slight increase in rates during the mid-1980s to mid-1990s changed to a 16 percent decrease between 1996 and 1999.[61] This reversal was also found in the United States, whereby juvenile property crime rates decreased by about 39 percent between 1995 and 2001.[62]

© AP/Wide World Photos

Juvenile violence is a problem in all parts of the world. Here, two American teens, covering their faces on the tables, sit by their lawyers in the Darmstadt, Germany, state court before hearing their sentence. The teenagers were convicted of murder for dropping stones from a highway overpass onto passing cars. Two women were killed, and four other motorists were injured.

Juvenile Drug Use

The first comparative study of teenage drug use in the United States and Europe found that 1 in 4 American students compared to 1 in 10 European students had used illicit drugs over their lifetime.[63] Comparisons across European countries of the percentage of students who have ever used illicit drugs are just as striking, ranging from a low of 2 percent in Finland and Cyprus to a high of 12 percent in the United Kingdom (see Figure 16.1). Carried out in conjunction with the Council of Europe and the University of Michigan's "Monitoring the Future" project, about 14,000 10th-grade students in the United States and approximately 95,000 10th-grade students in 30 European countries responded to the survey.

Although American students are more likely to use marijuana and other illicit drugs over their lifetime, European students are more likely to smoke cigarettes and use alcohol in the previous month. In England, underage drinking (the legal drinking age is 18) and drinking overall has become a "national crisis," which has resulted in the government considering a range of new measures, including tougher penalties for drunken behavior and making pubs pay for some of the costs of extra police officers.[64] In the United States, 40 percent of students report any alcohol use in the previous month, while in Denmark, the country with the highest rate, 85 percent of students report using alcohol in the previous month. Of the 31 countries, the United States has the second lowest rate of teenage alcohol use and the third lowest rate of cigarette smoking.[65]

TABLE 16.2

Juvenile Violence in Europe and North America

Country	Years	Age of Juveniles (years)	Percentage Change in Rate
England	1986–1994	10–16	+53
Germany	1984–1995	14–17	+150
Netherlands	1986–1995	12–17	+163
Italy	1986–1993	14–17	+175
Austria	1991–1995	14–18	+20
France	1984–1994	10–17	+87
Denmark	1980–1994	15–17	+146
Switzerland	1980–1995	15–17	+200
United States	1985–1994	10–17	+75
Canada	1986–1995	12–17	+130

SOURCES: Rebecca Kong, *Canadian Crime Statistics, 1996* (Ottawa: Canadian Centre for Justice Statistics Juristat, 1997), p. 17, Table 4; Christian Pfeiffer, "Juvenile Crime and Violence in Europe," in Michael Tonry, ed., *Crime and Justice: A Review of Research*, Volume 23 (Chicago: University of Chicago Press, 1998), pp. 263–291.

TABLE 16.3

Juvenile Property Crime in Europe and North America

Country	Years	Age of Juveniles (years)	Percentage Change in Rate
England	1986–1994	10–16	−9
Germany	1984–1995	14–17	+75
Netherlands	1985–1995	12–17	+4
Italy	1986–1993	14–17	+140
Austria	1991–1995	14–18	+31
France	1974–1992	10–18	+30
Denmark	1980–1994	15–19	−30
Switzerland	1980–1995	15–17	0
United States	1985–1994	10–17	+28
Canada	1986–1995	12–17	+5

SOURCES: Rebecca Kong, *Canadian Crime Statistics, 1996* (Ottawa: Canadian Centre for Justice Statistics Juristat, 1997), p. 17, Table 4; Christian Pfeiffer, "Juvenile Crime and Violence in Europe," in Michael Tonry, ed., *Crime and Justice: A Review of Research*, Volume 23 (Chicago: University of Chicago Press, 1998), pp. 263–291.

Past studies of teenage drug use in Europe show rates climbing (between 1995 and 1999), particularly in Eastern European countries,[66] while in the United States, the rate of teenage drug use held steady in 2003, but declined from the recent peak years of 1996 and 1997 (see Chapter 10).

Conclusion: What Do the Trends Tell Us?

Throughout the world, juvenile delinquency is a serious problem. Although there are many differences in the nature and character of juvenile delinquency in the different regions and countries of the world, there are a number of common threads. One is that juveniles account for a disproportionate amount of total crime. A second is the presence of violent youth gangs. The most important commonality is that a good number of countries report that juvenile delinquency, especially violence, is much higher in recent years than it was a decade ago. The question of greatest interest is why has this occurred?

FIGURE 16.1
Lifetime Teenage Illicit Drug Use (Other than Marijuana) in the United States and Europe

SOURCE: Thor Bjarnason, "European School Survey Project on Alcohol and Drugs," press release issued by the State University of New York at Albany, February 20, 2001, Figure 8.

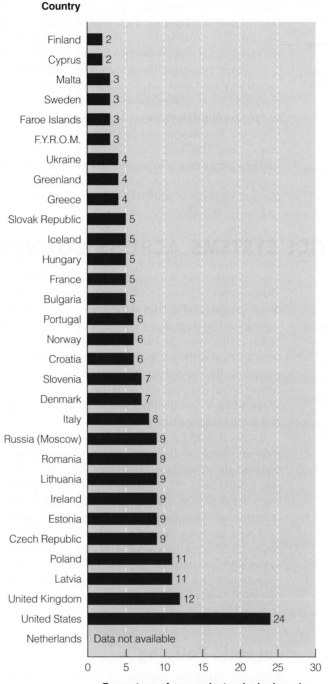

As noted above, all countries share an explosive mix of racial tension, poverty, envy, drug abuse, broken families, unemployment, and alienation. Some countries are also feeling the impacts of rapid social and economic change. The end of apartheid in South Africa has left many broken promises for its youth, with access to education being severely limited and unemployment at an all-time high. The transition from communism to democracy in many Eastern European countries has had profound effects. For example, neighboring countries have had to cope with a tremendous increase in immigrant youth populations in search of jobs and better lives, but because of difficulties in finding jobs and social isolation from family and friends, many of

To read more about **delinquency across countries** and what is being done to prevent it, go to www.crime-prevention-intl.org. For an up-to-date list of web links, go to http://cj.wadsworth.com/siegel_jd9e.

TO QUIZ YOURSELF ON THIS MATERIAL, go to the Juvenile Delinquency 9e website.

these youths turn to delinquency. Over the same period of time in the United States, rates of juvenile violence increased, but not as much as in most European countries. One possible explanation for this is that the United States did not experience some of the rapid social and economic changes that took place in Europe.

In some countries these trends in delinquency have begun to change. In other countries these trends have continued, and it is very likely that these trends will not be reversed unless governments are willing to tackle the many causal factors that give rise to juvenile delinquency. In some cases, this will mean countries working together to control the flow of immigration and providing assistance to new populations. In other cases, this will mean investing greater resources in education, employment training programs, and assistance programs for unemployed young people. It will also be important for countries to have effective and fair juvenile justice systems. In the next section we look at juvenile justice systems in different countries.

JUVENILE JUSTICE SYSTEMS ACROSS COUNTRIES

developing countries
Recognized by the U.N. as countries that are showing signs of improved economic growth and are making the transition from low income to high income.

least developed countries
Recognized by the U.N. as being the poorest countries in the world and suffering from long-term barriers to economic growth.

Many countries in the world have formal juvenile justice systems, but many do not. The presence of juvenile justice systems is strongly associated with a country's level of development; that is, developed or industrialized countries all have juvenile justice systems, while a smaller number of **developing** or **least developed countries** have juvenile justice systems. Part of the reason for countries not having separate justice systems to deal with juvenile delinquency and adult crime is the lack of importance placed on the special needs of juveniles who come in conflict with the law. Another reason is that developing and least developed countries have fewer financial resources to spend on a juvenile justice system, especially the building of separate correctional and treatment facilities.

In an effort to get more countries around the world to develop juvenile justice systems and improve the administration of juvenile justice, in 1985 the United Nations adopted the "Standard Minimum Rules for the Administration of Juvenile Justice" (see Exhibit 16.1). Also known as the "Beijing Rules" of juvenile justice because they were developed at a meeting in Beijing, these rules set out minimum standards for countries to follow in the administration of juvenile justice.[67]

There are many features of juvenile justice that are of interest to compare across countries. This section looks at the key features of juvenile justice systems in a number of developed countries: specialized police services for juveniles, age of criminal responsibility, presence of juvenile court, transfers to adult court, sentencing, treatment of incarcerated juveniles, and aftercare services.

Juvenile Policing

Specialized policing services for juveniles is an important but relatively recent addition to the repertoire of services offered by juvenile justice systems in many developed countries. The number of police officers assigned to juvenile work has increased in recent years. The International Association of Chiefs of Police found that approximately 500 departments, of the 1,400 surveyed in 1960, had juvenile units. By 1970, the number of police departments with a juvenile specialist doubled.[68] Few developing or least developed countries have police officers trained specifically to deal with juvenile offenders.

In the United States, juvenile officers operate either as specialists within a police department or as part of the juvenile unit of a police department. Their role is similar to that of officers working with adult offenders: to intervene if the actions of a citizen produce public danger or disorder. (See Chapter 13 for more information on juvenile policing in the United States.) In Austria an innovative delinquency prevention project involves specially trained police to deal with violent juvenile gangs. The gang unit works to establish an open dialogue with juvenile gangs to help get leaders of oppos-

EXHIBIT 16.1

Highlights of the "Standard Minimum Rules for the Administration of Juvenile Justice"

These rules were adopted by the U.N. General Assembly on November 29, 1985, on the recommendation of the Seventh U.N. Congress on the Prevention of Crime and the Treatment of Offenders (resolution 40/33).

Part 1: General Principles

Member states shall seek to further the well-being of juveniles and their families.

Member states shall try to develop conditions to ensure meaningful lives in the community for juveniles.

Sufficient attention should be given to positive measures involving mobilization of resources, such as the family, volunteers and community groups, to promote the well-being of juveniles.

Juvenile justice shall be an integral part of the national development process of each country.

In legal systems recognizing the concept of an age of criminal responsibility for juveniles, such an age level shall not be fixed too low, bearing in mind emotional, mental and physical maturity.

Any reaction by the juvenile justice system to juvenile offenders shall be in proportion to both the offenders and the offense.

Appropriate scope for the exercise of discretionary powers shall be allowed at all stages of legal processing affecting juveniles.

Efforts shall be made to ensure sufficient accountability at all stages in the exercise of such discretion.

Basic procedural safeguards, such as the presumption of innocence, the right to be notified of charges, the right to remain silent, the right to counsel, the right to the presence of a parent or guardian, the right to confront and cross-examine witnesses and the right to appeal, shall be guaranteed at all stages of proceedings.

The juvenile's right to privacy shall be respected at all stages.

Part 2: Investigation and Prosecution

Upon the apprehension of a juvenile, parents or guardians shall be notified as soon as possible.

Consideration shall be given to dealing with juvenile offenders without resort to trial, and any diversion to appropriate community or other services shall require consent of the juvenile or parents.

Part 3: Adjudication and Disposition

The placement of a juvenile in an institution shall always be a disposition of last resort and for the minimum necessary period.

Part 4: Non-Institutional Treatment

Efforts shall be made to provide necessary assistance, such as lodging, education, vocational training and employment, to facilitate the rehabilitation process.

Part 5: Institutional Treatment

Juveniles in institutions shall be kept separate from adults, and special attention shall be used to the greatest extent possible.

Part 6: Aftercare

Efforts shall be made to provide semi-institutional arrangements, such as halfway houses, educational homes and daytime training centers, to assist juveniles in their re-integration into society.

SOURCE: Abridged from United Nations, *The United Nations and Crime Prevention: Seeking Security and Justice for All* (New York: United Nations, 1996), pp. 78–82.

---

ing gangs to meet and work out their conflicts in a nonviolent way. A four-year assessment of the program found that it was extremely successful in reducing juvenile violence.[69]

Canada has also developed special juvenile gang units as part of police departments. Juvenile gang units exist in all of the police departments of the biggest Canadian cities, such as Montreal, Toronto, Vancouver, and Halifax, as well as in many medium-sized and smaller cities and towns.[70] In Japan, police boxes (*Koban*) in urban areas and police houses (*Chuzaisho*) in rural areas have special officers who deal with juvenile delinquency. Because of the sheer number of these police stations in the country—about 6,600 *Koban*s and 8,100 *Chuzaisho*s—the police have a very good understanding of conditions that might give rise to juvenile delinquency and violence problems in the community. This knowledge assists them in intervening before problems get out of control. In addition to juvenile police officers, there is a police-established system of volunteers to aid the police in dealing with juvenile delinquency. There are three types of voluntary systems:

I Guidance volunteers

I Police helpers for juveniles

I Instructors for juveniles

Guidance volunteers work with the police in providing advice to young people about the dangers of being involved in gangs or using drugs; they also provide some counseling services to young people in trouble with the law. Police helpers are mostly retired police officers in charge of dispersing large groups of juvenile delinquents, such as gangs. They are not a riot squad, but simply assist the police in dealing with large groups of young people who may be looking for trouble or are involved in delinquent acts. Instructors are authorized by the 1985 Law on Regulation of Business Affecting

Public Morals to protect juveniles from unsafe environments; that is, where young people are being abused or neglected.[71] In many ways, these individuals act as child or juvenile protection agents.

Age of Criminal Responsibility: Minimum and Maximum

Across the world there is a great deal of variation in the minimum age a person can be held responsible for his or her criminal actions, ranging from a low of 6 years in Sri Lanka to a high of under 21 years in Indonesia. In the majority of countries across the world, full adult criminal responsibility begins at age 18 years or older.[72] This general pattern is the same for the developed countries listed in Table 16.4. Switzerland has the lowest minimum age of criminal responsibility at 7 years, and Belgium has the highest at 16 to 18 years. Interestingly, in the United States, 36 states have no set minimum age that a young person can be held criminally responsible. By common law, states may use 7 years as the minimum, but in practice children under the age of 10 are rarely brought before a juvenile court.[73]

In those countries in which the minimum age is quite high, such as Belgium (16 to 18 years), Denmark (15 years), or Sweden (15 years), what happens to young people below the minimum age who commit delinquent acts? Doing nothing is not an option in any of the developed countries. Instead, these young people are dealt with under various forms of child or social welfare or child protection legislation. Under these laws young people may be placed in state-run homes, undergo counseling, or report to a social worker on a regular basis.

In some countries the minimum age can be lowered. This is typically done when the offense is very serious; for example, in New Zealand, the minimum age is 14, but if the offense is murder or manslaughter, the minimum age becomes 10. In Romania, the minimum age can be dropped from 16 to 14 if the young person is capable of understanding right from wrong.[74]

Presence of Juvenile Court

The majority of the developed countries have courts specifically for juveniles (see Table 16.4), and they operate pretrial diversion programs. (See the Policy and Practice box entitled "Precourt Diversion Programs around the World.") Only Denmark, Russia, and Sweden do not have juvenile courts. In each of these countries, juveniles appear before regular adult criminal courts. However, in Denmark, the Administration of Justice Act provides special rights for juveniles who appear in court; for example, closing the proceedings to the public and press.[75] Swedish courts also try to protect the identity of juvenile offenders if the court believes that publicity may be harmful to the juvenile.[76] In Russia too there are some protections afforded the juvenile: Age must be taken into account as a mitigating factor, the juvenile's living conditions must be considered, and whether or not the offense was committed with an adult.[77]

Transfers to Adult Court

Transfers of juvenile offenders to adult court are a widely accepted practice in developed countries (see Table 16.4). In all of the countries in which transfers are allowed, the main criterion is that the offense was of a very serious or violent nature. Other criteria can include the youth's record of delinquency and the use of weapons. But in these cases, the evidence must be particularly strong for a transfer to take place.

In the developed countries of Austria, France, Hungary, Italy, and Switzerland, transfers of juveniles to adult court are not permissible. Typically, this is because youths can receive an adult sentence while still under the authority of the juvenile court. This is also the case in Canada, where, until recently, transfers of juveniles to adult court were allowed. Under the new Youth Criminal Justice Act there is a proce-

TABLE 16.4

International Comparisons of Juvenile Justice Systems

Country	Minimum Age of Criminal Responsibility	Age of Adult Criminal Responsibility	Court That Handles Juveniles	Transfer to Adult Court Allowable?	Maximum Length of Sentence for a Juvenile	Separation of Incarcerated Juveniles from Adults
Australia	10*	16–17**	Children's courts	Yes, for serious felonies	2–7 years	Not mandatory, generally separated in practice
Austria	14	19	Special sections in local and regional courts; youth courts	No	Half of adult sentence	Yes
Belgium	16–18	18	Special juvenile courts	Yes	No juvenile incarcerations in juvenile court	Not mandatory, generally separated in practice
Canada	12	18	Youth courts	Yes	10 years	Yes
Denmark	15	18	No juvenile court	N/A	8 years	Yes
England	10	18	Youth courts	Yes	2 years	Yes
France	13 (unofficial)	18	Children's tribunals; youth courts of assizes	No	Half of adult sentence	Yes
Germany	14	18	Single-sitting judge; juvenile court; juvenile chamber	Yes	10 years	Yes
Hungary	14	18	Special sections of regular court	No	15 years	Yes
Italy	14	18	Separate juvenile courts	No	One-third of adult sentence	Yes
Japan	14	20	Family courts	Yes	Lifetime sentence	Yes
The Netherlands	12	18	Special juvenile courts	Yes	Lifetime sentence	Yes
New Zealand	14; 10 for murder and manslaughter	18	Youth courts	Yes	No juvenile incarcerations in youth court	No (some exceptions)
Russia	16; 14 for certain crimes	18	No juvenile court	N/A	10 years	Yes
Sweden	15	18	No juvenile court	N/A	No lifetime sentence	Yes
Switzerland	7	18	Special juvenile courts and/or juvenile prosecutors	No	One year	Yes
United States	6–10 for 14 states; 36 other states have no set minimum but may use age 7	15 for 3 states; 16 for 10 states; 17 for 37 states	Juvenile courts	Yes	Lifetime, death penalty sentences	Yes

NOTES: *The lower age limit is 7 in Tasmania; ** Age of full criminal responsibility differs by state; N/A = not available.

SOURCES: Adapted from Joan McCord, Cathy Spatz Widom, and Nancy Crowell, eds., *Juvenile Crime, Juvenile Justice.* Panel on Juvenile Crime: Prevention, Treatment, and Control (Washington, DC: National Academy Press, 2001), pp. 18–20, Table 1-1. Canadian data adapted from Brandon C. Welsh and Mark H. Irving, "Crime and Punishment in Canada, 1981–1999," in David P. Farrington and Michael Tonry, eds., *Cross-National Studies in Crime and Justice. Crime and Justice: A Review of Research*, Volume 33 (Chicago: University of Chicago Press, 2005). U.S. data adapted from Janet K. Wig, "Legal Issues," in Rolf Loeber and David P. Farrington, eds., *Child Delinquents: Development, Intervention, and Service Needs* (Thousand Oaks, CA: Sage Publications, 2001), p. 324.

dure that allows a juvenile to stay in youth court and be dealt with as a juvenile, and in the case of serious offenses the juvenile can receive an adult sentence.[78]

Sentencing Policies

The maximum sentence length for juvenile offenders varies considerably across developed countries. In Belgium and New Zealand there can be no sentence of incarceration for youths who appear before juvenile court; instead, youths must be transferred

Precourt Diversion Programs around the World

Keeping youths who have become involved in minor delinquent acts from being formally processed through the juvenile justice system is a top priority of many countries around the world. This is because they recognize the need to protect young people against the stigma and labeling that can occur from being "processed" through a juvenile court. In many ways, entering the juvenile justice system is viewed as a last resort to dealing with juvenile delinquency. Informal processing or precourt diversion programs, which vary from country to country, also represent a cost savings from the expense of paying for juvenile court judges, prosecutors, public defenders, and other justice personnel and administrative costs. These alternative approaches are more often used in European, particularly Western European, countries than in the United States. These programs are also very popular in Australia and New Zealand. Part of the reason for the greater use of these programs outside of the United States is that these countries are less punitive toward juvenile offenders than the United States. What follows are profiles of the use of precourt diversion programs in the Netherlands, France, and Australia.

NETHERLANDS

In response to a sharp rise in juvenile vandalism and its associated costs, the government of the Netherlands implemented a precourt diversion program called HALT, or *Het Alternatief*, which means "stop" in Dutch. Begun in the 1970s in the city of Rotterdam, the program quickly spread throughout the country and is now a national program in 65 locations. Accountability and assistance are at the center of the program. Young people aged 12 to 18 years caught for the first or second time committing an act of vandalism (the program is now used for other offenses as well) are offered the chance to avoid formal prosecution by participating in the program. Juveniles who go through the program must repair the vandalism damage they have caused, and counselors work with the young people to assist them with employment, housing, and education issues. If the program is successfully completed, police charges are dropped and the case is dismissed, and in those cases that are not successful, an official report is sent to the prosecutor. An evaluation of the program in three cities (Rotterdam, Eindoven, and Dordrecht) found the program to be very effective in reducing future acts of vandalism. Juvenile offenders in the treatment group were 63 percent less likely to be rearrested versus a comparison group that were 25 percent less likely to be rearrested.

FRANCE

Maisons de justice, or community justice centers, is one of the most well known pretrial diversion programs for juvenile offenders in France. Set up by the Ministry of Justice and community associations across the country, the centers address minor offenses and other legal problems through alternative justice approaches. One of these alternative approaches is victim-offender mediation, whereby a trained staff member works with the offender, the victim, and sometimes the victim's family to settle a dispute without the need for formal justice proceedings. An apology or an order of restitution or compensation is commonly reached as part of victim-offender mediation. Although there has been no formal evaluation of community justice centers, they are widely credited as helping to relieve some of the backlog in the courts and to settle cases much faster than traditional means.

AUSTRALIA

Precourt diversion programs have gone through extensive changes in Australia in recent years. Up to the early 1990s, there were two types of juvenile diversion programs: police cautions, which involve the police more or less warning offenders that the next time they are caught, formal action will be taken; and children's panels, made up of police and social workers who admonish a young person for his or her delinquent behavior. Today, precourt diversion programs for juvenile offenders include an expanded use of police cautions and the addition of restorative justice–based programs known as "family group conferences." Family group conferences (FGCs) bring together the juvenile offender and his or her family, the victim, and a professional coordinator to discuss the problem caused by the juvenile offender and to agree on a mutually acceptable resolution that will benefit all parties and the wider community. FGCs attempt to provide the victim with restoration and restitution and the offender with rehabilitation and reintegration. An evaluation of an FGC program in South Australia showed that the overwhelming majority of offenders complied with the program, and more than 9 out of 10 victims were pleased with the process of FGCs and the resulting resolutions.

Critical Thinking

1. What are some of the problems with precourt diversion programs?
2. Should these programs also be used for serious and violent juvenile offenders? Explain.

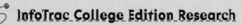

InfoTrac College Edition Research

To read more about pretrial diversion programs for juvenile offenders, use "juvenile-corrections" as a key term.

SOURCES: Josine Junger-Tas, "Youth Justice in the Netherlands," in Michael Tonry and Anthony N. Doob, eds., *Youth Crime and Youth Justice: Comparative and Cross-National Perspectives. Crime and Justice: A Review of Research*, Volume 31 (Chicago: University of Chicago Press, 2004); Irvin Waller and Brandon C. Welsh, "International Trends in Crime Prevention: Cost-Effective Ways to Reduce Victimization," in Graeme Newman, ed., *Global Report on Crime and Justice* (New York: Oxford University Press, 1999); Lynn Atkinson, "Juvenile Justice in Australia," in John A. Winterdyk, ed., *Juvenile Justice Systems: International Perspectives*, 1st edition (Toronto: Canadian Scholars' Press, 1997).

In China, juvenile crime rates are on the rise. In an effort to combat this problem, justice officials are resorting to more punitive-oriented dispositions, even for minor infractions. One example of this is public shaming or humiliation. Shown here are Chinese police in Guangzhou Province publicly displaying juvenile petty offenders as part of their disposition.

to adult court to receive custodial sentences. Some countries, such as Austria, France, and Italy, specify that sentences can only be for one-half or one-third of what an adult would receive for a similar offense. In Italy, juveniles who are sentenced to custody can receive up to one-third of the same sentence for adults but, unlike adults, can be conditionally released at any stage of the sentence regardless of the amount of time spent in custody.[79]

The country with the harshest sentence for juvenile offenders is the United States; here, juvenile offenders can be sentenced to death. Japan and the Netherlands have the next harshest sentences for juvenile offenders: lifetime sentences. In Japan, a life sentence may mean spending between 10 and 15 years in a correctional facility with or without forced labor, while in the Netherlands, a life sentence may mean serving as much as 20 years.[80] In Russia, the maximum sentence length for juveniles is 10 years, and in recent years it has made extensive use of incarceration (or commitment), with 50 to 60 percent of all adjudicated juvenile offenders receiving some form of this disposition.[81] Switzerland, on the other hand, is the most lenient country: One year is the longest period of time that a juvenile offender can be sentenced to custody, and transfers to adult court are not allowed.

Finding an appropriate balance between punishment (in the form of secure commitment) and treatment for juvenile offenders is more difficult for some countries than others. This is the subject of the next Policy and Practice box, which profiles changes in youth justice laws in Canada.

Incarcerated Juveniles

The separation of juveniles from adults in correctional facilities is an important rule under the U.N.'s "Standard Minimum Rules for the Administration of Juvenile Justice" because juveniles are susceptible to negative influences of more seasoned and crime-prone adult offenders. In many ways, juvenile offenders become the apprentices of adult offenders, learning about new techniques to commit delinquent and criminal acts. Another reason for separating adults and juveniles in correctional institutions is for the physical safety of juveniles. With the average juvenile offender having less physical strength than the average adult offender, adults often prey upon juveniles.

The Changing Nature of Youth Justice in Canada

Canada, a welfare state that has an extensive social safety network that includes among other benefits universal health care coverage and year-long maternity leave, is well known for its liberal views on social issues. Some of these include efforts to limit the use of prisons for offenders, the implementation of a national gun registry and other tough gun control laws, partial legalization of marijuana use, and support for same-sex marriage. But this liberal view may be changing somewhat with respect to the government's response to juvenile delinquency.

In 1984, the Young Offenders Act (YOA) replaced the Juvenile Delinquents Act (JDA), which had been the legislative framework for youth justice in Canada since 1908. In addition to numerous legal and procedural changes, the movement from the JDA to the YOA marked a change in principles of youth justice, from a welfare orientation to a more legalistic orientation. (Like the United States, Canada adheres to the *parens patriae* treatment philosophy. This did not change under the new law and continues to this day.) Some of the YOA's important provisions included:

▍ A minimum age of criminal responsibility of 12 years (it was 7 years) and a uniform age of adult criminal responsibility of 18 years.

▍ Youthful offenders are entitled to childcare/youth care experts as well as lawyers for counsel.

▍ The primary purpose of intervention is a balance between penalizing delinquent behavior and providing appropriate treatment.

Over the years, academics and juvenile justice practitioners alike criticized the YOA for not providing clear legislative direction to guide appropriate implementation in several key areas, such as transfers to adult court. This lack of clear legislative direction was thought to be an important factor contributing to problems and deficiencies in Canada's youth justice system. Furthermore, as Canadian criminologists Anthony Doob and Jane Sprott point out,

> there are two substantial problems with the YOA on which almost all policy and academic observers agreed: the youth justice system is being overused for minor offenses, and too many youths are going to custody, especially for relatively minor offenses.

These concerns were at the heart of the federal government's new youth justice law, the Youth Criminal Justice Act (YCJA), which was proclaimed into force in April 2003. Also important to this new law was a get-tough approach or at least the appearance of this. Some of these get-tough measures included a greater focus on holding youths accountable for their actions, making it easier to impose adult sanctions on the most serious and violent juvenile offenders, and publishing the offender's identity, again in the most serious cases.

The YCJA also greatly expanded aftercare programs for juvenile offenders. For example, it is now mandatory that all periods of time spent in an institution be followed by a period of intensive supervision in the community. The length of time of supervision is also stipulated in the law: It must be no less than half the time spent in custody. Thus, a juvenile offender who spends 12 months in an institution must then spend 6 months in intensive supervision while in the community. Under the old law, there were no requirements for supervision following a custodial sentence.

Another important change to the juvenile aftercare system introduced by the new law is that there are a number of conditions, both mandatory and optional, that the judge can impose on the youth as part of supervision orders. Mandatory conditions include keeping the peace and reporting to authorities. Optional conditions include attending school, getting a job, adhering to a curfew, abstaining from alcohol and drugs, and not associating with gang members.

Critical Thinking

1. How would you characterize the changes in Canada's youth justice laws over the last century?

2. Could juvenile justice in the United States benefit from incorporating some of the recent changes to Canada's youth justice laws? Explain.

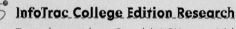

InfoTrac College Edition Research

To read more about Canada's YCJA, go to Nicholas Bala and Sanjeev Anand, "The First Months Under the Youth Criminal Justice Act: A Survey and Analysis of Case Law," *Canadian Journal of Criminology and Criminal Justice* 46:251–271 (2004). To find further information, use "youth crime and Canada" as a key term.

SOURCES: Anthony N. Doob and Jane B. Sprott, "Youth Justice in Canada," in Michael Tonry and Anthony N. Doob, eds, *Youth Crime and Youth Justice: Comparative and Cross-National Perspectives. Crime and Justice: A Review of Research*, Volume 31 (Chicago: University of Chicago Press, 2004), pp. 224–225; Brandon C. Welsh and Mark H. Irving, "Crime and Punishment in Canada, 1981–1999," in David P. Farrington and Michael Tonry, eds., *Cross-National Studies in Crime and Justice. Crime and Justice: A Review of Research*, Volume 33 (Chicago: University of Chicago Press, 2005); John A. Winterdyk, "Juvenile Justice and Young Offenders: An Overview of Canada," in John A. Winterdyk, ed., *Juvenile Justice Systems: International Perspectives*, 2nd edition (Toronto: Canadian Scholars' Press, 2002), pp. 66–68; Department of Justice Canada, "Fact Sheets: *Youth Criminal Justice Act*" (Ottawa: Department of Justice, March 1999).

In almost all of the developed countries, incarcerated juveniles are kept separate from incarcerated adults. In Australia and Belgium, separate incarceration is not mandatory, but in practice this is generally done. In New Zealand, the practice differs from all of the other countries. Incarcerated juveniles are not separated from incarcerated adults. But there are a few exceptions. For example, a juvenile offender that has

To read more about **juvenile justice in Australia,** go to www.aic.gov.au. For an up-to-date list of web links, go to http://cj. wadsworth.com/siegel_jd9e.

been transferred to adult court and sentenced to a term of imprisonment may be held at the discretion of the Director General of Social Welfare and the Secretary for Justice in a social welfare facility until age 17. The reason for the government generally not housing juvenile and adult inmates in separate facilities is that there are no separate correctional facilities for juvenile offenders. The government claims that the country is too small and there are too few juvenile inmates to justify building a separate correctional facility.[82]

Aftercare

When juveniles are released from an institution, they may be placed in an aftercare program of some kind, rather than simply returned to the community without transitional assistance. This transitional assistance can take the form of halfway houses, educational homes, and daytime training centers. The U.N.'s "Standard Minimum Rules for the Administration of Juvenile Justice" recommends that all countries implement aftercare programs to help juveniles prepare for their return to the community.

All developed countries provide juveniles with a wide range of aftercare programs. In Hong Kong, now part of the People's Republic of China, supervision orders are the most commonly used aftercare program to help juvenile offenders make a successful transition from the correctional institution to their community. Juveniles are first granted early release from a correctional facility, with the provision that they must abide by a number of conditions. These conditions differ according to the nature of the delinquent act they committed, but almost always involve regular visits with their parole officer. Some juveniles will have to attend drug addiction treatment centers.[83]

In many developed countries, juvenile offenders are eligible for early release or parole much earlier than adult offenders sentenced to the same amount of time in institutions. In Germany, for example, a juvenile may be released to the community upon serving one-third of his or her sentence, while an adult must serve at least half of the sentence before being paroled.[84]

The next section profiles the juvenile justice system in England. It looks at the many different stages that juveniles may face as they go through the system, from arrest through sentencing. Comparisons are made with the U.S. juvenile justice system. One reason for making England the subject of this profile is that like the United States, it is a highly developed industrialized country and so comparisons are more meaningful. Another reason is the long-standing shared history between the two countries: Much of U.S. common law is derived from English law.

TO QUIZ YOURSELF ON THIS MATERIAL, go to the Juvenile Delinquency 9e website.

A PROFILE OF JUVENILE JUSTICE IN ENGLAND

In 1908, England passed legislation that established for the first time that young offenders were to be treated separately from adult offenders; the law was known as the Children Act. Like the United States, England adheres to the *parens patriae* treatment philosophy, which recognizes that youth are in need of special consideration and assistance.

The Children Act was founded on three main principles:

1. Juvenile offenders should be kept *separate* from adult criminals and should receive *treatment* differentiated to suit their special needs.

2. Parents should be made more responsible for the wrongdoing of their children.

3. The imprisonment of juveniles should be abolished.[85]

Many changes have since taken place in juvenile justice in England. The following discussion of the different stages that juveniles may face as they go through the system reflects the way things are today. (See Figure 16.2.)

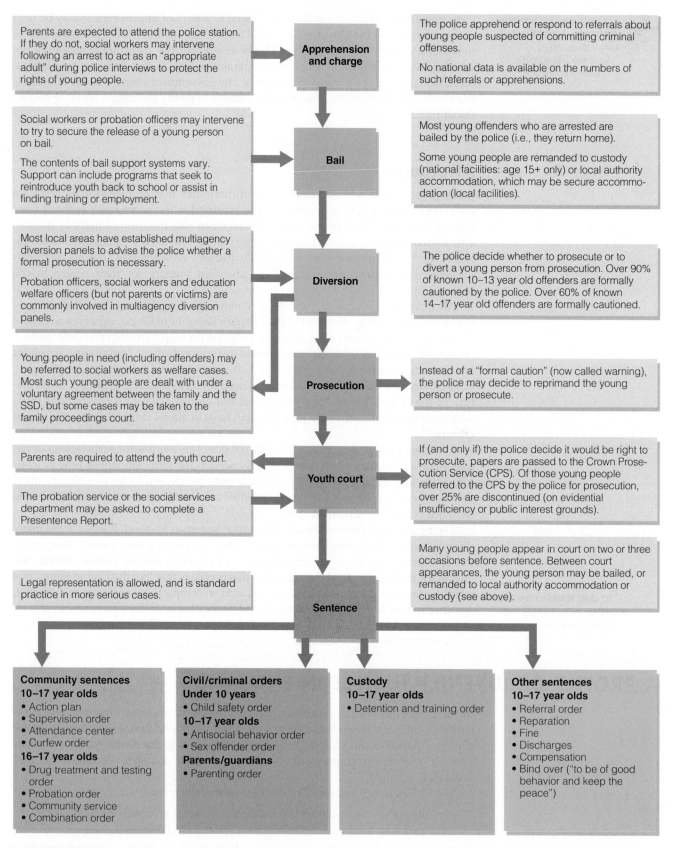

Apprehension and charge

Parents are expected to attend the police station. If they do not, social workers may intervene following an arrest to act as an "appropriate adult" during police interviews to protect the rights of young people.

The police apprehend or respond to referrals about young people suspected of committing criminal offenses.

No national data is available on the numbers of such referrals or apprehensions.

Bail

Social workers or probation officers may intervene to try to secure the release of a young person on bail.

The contents of bail support systems vary. Support can include programs that seek to reintroduce youth back to school or assist in finding training or employment.

Most young offenders who are arrested are bailed by the police (i.e., they return home).

Some young people are remanded to custody (national facilities: age 15+ only) or local authority accommodation, which may be secure accommodation (local facilities).

Diversion

Most local areas have established multiagency diversion panels to advise the police whether a formal prosecution is necessary.

Probation officers, social workers and education welfare officers (but not parents or victims) are commonly involved in multiagency diversion panels.

The police decide whether to prosecute or to divert a young person from prosecution. Over 90% of known 10–13 year old offenders are formally cautioned by the police. Over 60% of known 14–17 year old offenders are formally cautioned.

Prosecution

Young people in need (including offenders) may be referred to social workers as welfare cases. Most such young people are dealt with under a voluntary agreement between the family and the SSD, but some cases may be taken to the family proceedings court.

Instead of a "formal caution" (now called warning), the police may decide to reprimand the young person or prosecute.

Youth court

Parents are required to attend the youth court.

The probation service or the social services department may be asked to complete a Presentence Report.

If (and only if) the police decide it would be right to prosecute, papers are passed to the Crown Prosecution Service (CPS). Of those young people referred to the CPS by the police for prosecution, over 25% are discontinued (on evidential insufficiency or public interest grounds).

Many young people appear in court on two or three occasions before sentence. Between court appearances, the young person may be bailed, or remanded to local authority accommodation or custody (see above).

Sentence

Legal representation is allowed, and is standard practice in more serious cases.

Community sentences
10–17 year olds
- Action plan
- Supervision order
- Attendance center
- Curfew order
16–17 year olds
- Drug treatment and testing order
- Probation order
- Community service
- Combination order

Civil/criminal orders
Under 10 years
- Child safety order
10–17 year olds
- Antisocial behavior order
- Sex offender order
Parents/guardians
- Parenting order

Custody
10–17 year olds
- Detention and training order

Other sentences
10–17 year olds
- Referral order
- Reparation
- Fine
- Discharges
- Compensation
- Bind over ("to be of good behavior and keep the peace")

FIGURE 16.2

The Juvenile Justice System in England

SOURCE: Loraine Gelsthorpe and Vicky Kemp, "Comparative Juvenile Justice: England and Wales," in John A. Winterdyk, ed., *Juvenile Justice Systems: International Perspectives*, 2nd edition (Toronto: Canadian Scholars' Press, 2002), Figures 5.1, 5.2, pp. 129, 146.

Apprehension and Charge

The process of juvenile justice begins when police apprehend and charge a young person suspected of committing a delinquent act. The police are not the only ones involved at this stage. Parents or guardians of the young person are contacted and requested to attend the police station. If they cannot attend, social workers may offer assistance to the juvenile once an arrest has been made. The role of social workers at this stage is to act as an "appropriate adult" to help safeguard the legal rights of the juvenile. Alternatively, the juvenile may be represented by a defense attorney. The right to have legal representation exists throughout all stages of the juvenile justice system.[86] This is the same as in the U.S. juvenile justice system.

Bail

Once a decision has been made by the police to charge the juvenile, a bail hearing must take place to determine whether the juvenile can go home or be remanded to custody. This differs from the practice in the United States, where relatively few juveniles hold the right to be released on bail; in fact, most states refuse juveniles the right to bail. This is because detention is seen as rehabilitative, not punitive, and statutory provisions allow juveniles to be released into the custody of their parents. (See Chapter 14 for more information on bail for juveniles in the United States.)

In England, most juvenile offenders who are arrested are granted bail. For those who are denied bail, there are two options for where they will be held. National custody facilities can be used for juveniles 15 years and older, or local authority (local government) facilities may be used. For juveniles without legal representation, social workers or probation officers may assist the juvenile to be released on bail.

Precourt Diversion

Police "cautions"—the police issuing a warning to a young person involved or suspected of being involved in a delinquent act—is by far the most widely used and important precourt diversion measure in England. Begun in the 1970s, police cautions quickly became an essential component of the juvenile justice system. Although important administratively, so as to avoid the youth courts from becoming backlogged, police cautions were designed first and foremost with the best interests of the young person in mind: "Prosecution should not occur unless it was 'absolutely necessary' or as 'a last resort' and that the prosecution of first-time offenders where the offence was not serious was unlikely to be 'justifiable' unless there were 'exceptional circumstances.' Prosecution was to be regarded as a 'severe step.'"[87]

Between 1992 and 2001 (the latest data available), about half of all 15- to 17-year-old male juvenile offenders were given formal cautions by the police for indictable offenses (the equivalent of felony offenses); for females in the same age range and for younger male and female juvenile offenders the rates were much higher (see Table 16.5). Over this same period of time, police cautioning rates declined for all age groups and both male and female juvenile offenders, with the largest decrease (29 percent) occurring for 15- to 17-year-old males. British criminologists Anthony Bottoms and James Dignan report that this trend was a result of growing backlash from political and nonpolitical sources against the "minimum intervention" philosophy of England's youth justice system.[88]

Instead of a formal caution (now called a warning under the new "final warning scheme"), the police may issue a "reprimand" to a suspected juvenile delinquent or prosecute. Reprimands involve the police making a verbal admonition. They may go something like this: "I want you to behave properly from now on and do not get yourself involved in anything that requires us to bring you down to the station." These are not recorded by police and, therefore, cannot be used in court.

In the United States, police do not use a system of formal or other cautions per se; instead, they must rely on their discretionary authority. (See Chapter 13 for more

TABLE 16.5

Police Cautioning Rates for Young Offenders for Indictable Offenses in England, 1992–2001

Year	Age 10–11		Age 12–14		Age 15–17	
	Males	Females	Males	Females	Males	Females
1992	96	99	86	96	59	81
1993	96	99	83	95	59	80
1994	95	100	81	94	56	77
1995	94	99	79	93	54	76
1996	94	99	77	91	51	72
1997	93	98	74	89	49	68
1998	91	97	72	88	48	67
1999	87	96	69	87	45	64
2000	86	95	68	86	43	63
2001	86	95	66	85	42	64

NOTE: The "cautioning rate" is the number of persons cautioned, divided by the number of persons found guilty or cautioned, multiplied by 100.

SOURCE: Abridged from Anthony Bottoms and James Dignan, "Youth Justice in Great Britain," in Michael Tonry and Anthony N. Doob, eds., *Youth Crime and Youth Justice: Comparative and Cross-National Perspectives. Crime and Justice: A Review of Research*, Volume 31 (Chicago: University of Chicago Press, 2004), Table 1, p. 35.

details.) Upon the arrest of a juvenile, the police have the following options: refer to juvenile court; handle informally and release; refer to criminal court; refer to welfare; or refer to another police department. It is estimated that around 20 percent of all juvenile arrests are handled informally within the police department or are referred to a community service agency.

Prosecution

Crown Prosecution Service
The national agency in England that is in charge of all criminal prosecutions of juveniles and adults.

In England the prosecution of a juvenile offender is the mandate of the **Crown Prosecution Service.** The CPS is a national agency established by statute in 1985. It is headed by the director of public prosecutions, who is accountable to the attorney general.[89] In the United States, each jurisdiction has its own prosecuting attorney who oversees public prosecutions; with England having a central government system (there are no states), the reporting structure is somewhat different.

Importantly, in England a prosecution can only take place once the police have recommended to the CPS that it be done. This differs slightly from the practice in the United States in that the prosecutor has the power either to initiate or discontinue allegations against a juvenile. In England the prosecutor does, however, have the right to dismiss a case (allegation), and this is done in more than 25 percent of the cases that the police recommend to the CPS. There are two reasons that a prosecutor may dismiss a case: (1) There is insufficient evidence, or (2) it is not in the public interest. The latter is done when it is felt that the harm to the offender that comes from prosecuting him or her will outweigh any benefit to society from doing so. In the event that the prosecution dismisses a case because it is not in the public interest, the prosecution may recommend to the police that they issue a formal caution.[90]

Youth Court

Like the United States and most other developed countries, England has a special court that handles juveniles; it is called a youth court. Even before the commencement of trial a juvenile may have already had a number of hearings before youth court, such as a bail hearing or a hearing on transfer to adult court. In most instances, trials of juveniles are presided over by a three-member panel of youth court lay magistrates or judges. In urban areas it is common for a trial to be presided over by a single professional or more qualified judge. Juries are not used in English youth courts. The lay or nonprofessional youth court judges are elected to a three-year term by and from the court district in which they presently serve. These judges receive special training in the juvenile offender laws. During trials they are often assisted by a legally trained court clerk.[91]

In the United States only one juvenile court judge presides over a trial in the juvenile courtroom. Judges are assisted by court clerks, but unlike in England, court clerks in the United States rarely have law degrees and do not advise judges on legal matters. In the United States, juvenile court judges are either elected or appointed to that position, but when they are elected, it is by the public, not their fellow judges, as in England. In the United States, trial by jury in a juvenile court is seldom used; the majority of states do not allow for it.

Social workers and probation officers are other important actors in the English juvenile courtroom. Once a finding of guilt has been rendered, either party may be asked by the court to prepare a presentence report to assist the judge in sentencing. This is similar to a predisposition report in the U.S. juvenile justice system. As in the United States, plea bargaining is allowed for juveniles in England and is used extensively.

Crown Court
In England, the criminal court that deals with adult offenders or juveniles who have been transferred from youth court.

As in the United States, juveniles in England can be transferred to adult court—what is referred to as **Crown Court.** A juvenile can be transferred to Crown Court for two main reasons: (1) The juvenile is charged with a heinous crime, such as murder, or (2) the juvenile is charged with a serious crime in conjunction with an adult.[92]

Sentencing

Once the juvenile has been convicted, the youth court judge passes sentence, either immediately following conviction or at a special hearing a short time later. As in the United States, sentences (dispositions) for juvenile offenders are much more punitive in England today than they were 10 or 20 years ago. In the early 1980s, England changed its approach to the sentencing of juvenile offenders dramatically, moving away from a focus on institutional placements toward community-based sanctions. The murder of James Bulger by two 10-year-olds and an upsurge of juvenile violence in the country led to the passage of the Criminal Justice and Public Order Act in 1994. This made incarceration of juvenile offenders the preferred choice once again; it also increased the maximum sentence length and made it easier for very young juvenile offenders to be placed in correctional facilities. This punitive approach to dealing with juvenile offending, especially serious and violent juvenile offending, was continued with the passage of the Crime and Disorder Act in 1998 and the Youth Justice and Criminal Evidence Act in 1999.

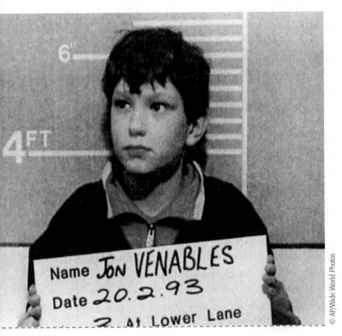

© AP/Wide World Photos

Jon Venables poses for a police photograph, which was taken eight days after he and Robert Thompson, both 10 years old, abducted and brutally murdered 2-year-old James Bulger in northern England. This picture was released to the media on June 22, 2001, the day the British government announced that the two child killers, now 18, would be released from prison and given new identities. This case sparked national and international attention over the administration of juvenile justice, with some countries reexamining the minimum age at which children can be held responsible for their delinquent or criminal actions and the maximum sentence length for serious offenses.

As shown in Figure 16.2, a wide range of sentencing options is available to the youth court judge, including custodial sentences, community sentences, civil/criminal orders, and a general category of other sentences, which includes fines and compensation. Interestingly, juvenile boot camps modeled on the U.S. experience have received some interest in England, with two being introduced on a demonstration basis. One offered a high intensity treatment regime coupled with work or training placement on release, while the other offered more of a military-style regime. The former program showed more favorable recidivism results and was more cost-effective,[93] but public support for boot camps proved unfavorable, and the programs were shut down.

England's punitive approach to juvenile offending is somewhat tempered by the availability of a wide range of community sentences like probation and aftercare services. For example, attendance center orders require juvenile offenders to report to a specified place in the community once a week for a range of activities, including recreation, social skills training, and vocational skills training. There are also community service orders (now called community punishment orders), which require juvenile offenders to perform various work-related activities in the community, and combination orders (now called community punishment and rehabilitation orders) that combine community service with increased supervision.[94]

In recent years, many developed countries have taken measures to "get tough" on juvenile offending. In some cases, this is being done because of a real increase in delinquency, particularly violence. In other cases, this is being done because of a perceived increase in delinquency coupled with a political response to a "punitive public" (at least for violent juvenile offenders).[95] Although more punitive juvenile justice systems seem to be the future for many countries, these countries are also making concerted efforts to reserve punitive sanctions for only the most serious and violent juvenile offenders and to provide more effective treatment and aftercare services.

Summary

- There is a long history of comparing delinquency and juvenile justice systems across different countries, but many important issues need to be considered in making international comparisons. Differences in legal systems, culture, language, and so on, demand that close attention be paid to what is being compared and what countries are being compared.

- Comparing delinquency rates across countries has three main challenges: (1) The legal definitions of juvenile crime vary from country to country; (2) the measurement of juvenile crime varies across countries; and (3) the age group defined as "juvenile" is not always the same.

- Knowledge of the nature of juvenile delinquency and how juvenile justice systems operate in other countries can be useful for concerned citizens, social scientists, and policy makers.

- Juvenile delinquency poses a serious problem to all regions of the world. Juvenile violence in Europe and North America increased substantially between the mid-1980s and the mid-1990s. During this same period, juvenile property crime increased very little, with some countries showing no increase or an actual decrease.

- More recent figures for teenage drug use show rates to be on the rise in Europe, but holding steady in the United States.

- Explanations for the increase in teen violence include an explosive mix of racial tension, poverty, envy, drug abuse, broken families, unemployment, and alienation.

- Many countries in the world have formal juvenile justice systems, but many do not. In an effort to get more countries around the world to develop juvenile justice systems and improve the administration of juvenile justice, in 1985 the United Nations adopted the "Standard Minimum Rules for the Administration of Juvenile Justice."

- Juvenile justice systems in developed countries have many commonalities but also differ in many respects. Examined are juvenile policing, age of criminal responsibility, presence of juvenile court, transfers to adult court, sentencing, treatment of incarcerated juveniles, and aftercare programs.

- The juvenile justice system in England was developed at the beginning of the twentieth century. Like the United States, England adheres to the treatment philosophy known as *parens patriae*, which recognizes that youth are in need of special consideration and assistance.

- There are many similarities between the British and U.S. juvenile justice systems, such as the use of bail hearings, plea bargaining, and the ability to transfer youths to adult court. There are also a number of important differences. As in the United States, sentences for juvenile offenders are much more punitive in England today than they were 10 or 20 years ago.

Key Terms

developed countries, p. 497
death squads, p. 499
transnational crime, p. 504

international crime, p. 504
developing countries, p. 508
least developed countries, p. 508

Crown Prosecution Service, p. 518
Crown Court, p. 519

Questions for Discussion

1. International comparisons of delinquency and juvenile justice systems are best done "like-with-like." What are some of the things that need to be considered in order to produce valid comparisons across countries?

2. What are some of the benefits and challenges in making international comparisons of delinquency?

3. Between the mid-1980s and the mid-1990s, juvenile violence increased substantially in most developed countries. What are some of the reasons for this rise in juvenile violence?

4. Across the world there is a great deal of variation in the minimum age a person can be held responsible for his or her criminal actions. What are the advantages and disadvantages of having a low minimum age?

5. Which developed countries appear to be the most lenient in their treatment of juvenile offenders, and which appear to be the most punitive?

6. What are some of the differences between juvenile justice systems in the United States and England? Identify two or three key differences and discuss how these differences could benefit the other country.

Viewpoint

As the recently elected prime minister of England you are faced with having to deal with national and international implications arising from the following case. In August 2001, two British teenagers, Jon Venables and Robert Thompson, were granted parole after serving eight years for the brutal murder of 2-year-old James Bulger. On February 12, 1993, these two boys, then 10 years old, abducted James from a mall just outside Liverpool, England. James's mother had stopped to look at a display window of one of the stores, letting go of James's hand for a few seconds. When she turned around James was gone. The whole event was caught on the mall's surveillance system. The horrifying video showed the two boys walking up to James and calmly leading him out of the mall. The 2-year-old's badly beaten body was found a short time later near railway tracks, a short distance from the mall. Because of the video, the two child killers were quickly apprehended and taken into custody. Throughout England there was a kind of collective agony for the death of the boy and the mother's loss of her infant son.

The capture and subsequent trial of these two boys sparked national and international attention and debate. Immediately, England and other countries began to reconsider the minimum age when children can be held responsible for their delinquent or criminal actions. Fortunately for England, the minimum age was 10 years. But in other countries like Canada, Italy, Japan, and Russia, the minimum age is much higher.

Like the capture and trial of these child killers, their release and events leading up to it caused national and international debate over the administration of juvenile justice. In January 1994, it was learned that the decision of Lord Justice Morland to detain the boys at Her Majesty's Pleasure—the equivalent of a life sentence—had been recommended to be no higher than eight years. As a discretionary sentence, this was legal, but was it too lenient for the crime? England and other countries were soon contemplating mandatory minimum sentences for juvenile offenders, and in England the then home secretary, Michael Howard, tried unsuccessfully to have the boys serve a minimum of 15 years. Then, in the early months of 2001, the public learned that the two boys were to be paroled sometime in the summer. In addition, their identities were to be changed to protect them from reprisal from the public, and there were rumors about them being sent to another country.

These events put England's juvenile offender laws and juvenile justice system to an extreme test in trying to balance the rights of the offender with the rights of the community and the moral and public outrage caused by this violent act. The international implications of these events were wide reaching, causing some countries to reexamine their juvenile offender laws and how they deal with violent juvenile offenders. As prime minister, how would you answer these questions from the media?

▮ Did the English juvenile justice system fail the victim's family and society as a whole?

▮ Should England have done more to keep these juveniles locked up for a longer time, or was the sentence appropriate?

▮ What can England do to try to prevent this from happening again? Should they change their juvenile offender laws and policies?

Doing Research on the Web

Before you answer these questions, you may want to research how other Western countries respond to juvenile violence and delinquency. Use "crime and international" in a key word search on InfoTrac College Edition. To learn more about juvenile treatment options, visit the following websites (sites accessed on September 30, 2004):

Campbell Collaboration Crime and Justice Group
www.aic.gov.au/campbellcj/

International Centre for the Prevention of Crime
www.crime-prevention-intl.org

European Institute for Crime Prevention and Control
www.heuni.fi

World Health Organization Department of Injuries and Violence Prevention
www.who.int/violence_injury_prevention/en/

United Nations Centre for International Crime Prevention
www.uncjin.org/CICP/cicp.html

Notes

1. "Pornography Cartel Broken," *Crime and Justice International* 17:13 (2001).
2. Sarah Shannon, "The Global Sex Trade: Humans as the Ultimate Commodity," *Crime and Justice International* 17:5–7 (2001).
3. David Binder, "12 Nations in Southeast Europe Pursue Traffickers in Sex Trade," *New York Times*, October 19, 2003, p. 6.
4. Lizette Alvarez, "H.I.V. Surge Catches Tradition-Bound Estonia Off Guard," *New York Times*, February 15, 2004, p. 6.
5. Reuters, "18 Dead in Shooting at High School in Eastern Germany," *New York Times*, April 26, 2002; Edmund L. Andrews, "Deep Shock in Germany, Where Guns Are Rare," *New York Times*, April 28, 2002, p. 15.
6. "Race Riots," *Crime and Justice International* 17:17 (2001).
7. Stephan Lhotzky, "Will Kai Become a Skinhead? Cultures of Hate Germany the New Europe," *Reclaiming Children and Youth* 10:86–91 (2001).
8. Christian Pfeiffer, "The Impoverishment of the Lower Classes Is Increasing Juvenile Aggressivity," *European Education* 32:95–100 (2000).
9. John Tagliabue, "Synagogue in Paris Firebombed; Raids Go On," *New York Times*, April 5, 2002, p. 5; John Tagliabue, "Paris Takes Aim at Its Crime Rate," *New York Times*, August 24, 2003, p. 3, section 5.
10. Donald G. McNeil, Jr., "Whodunnit? In Europe, Often the Immigrant," *New York Times*, April 28, 2002, p. 4, week in review section.
11. Richard Bernstein, "Crimes Most Outlandish, but Why in Germany?" *New York Times*, February 11, 2004; Christian Pfeiffer, "Juvenile Crime and Violence in Europe," in Michael Tonry, ed., *Crime and Justice: A Review of Research*, volume 23 (Chicago: University of Chicago Press, 1998), p. 300.
12. Martin Killias and Marcelo F. Aebi, "Crime Trends in Europe from 1990 to 1996: How Europe Illustrates the Limits of the American Experience," *European Journal on Criminal Policy and Research* 8:43–63 (2000).
13. John Hagan, Hans Merkens, and Klaus Boehnke, "Delinquency and Disdain: Social Capital and the Control of Right-Wing Extremism among East and West Berlin Youth," *The American Journal of Sociology* 100:1028–1053 (1995).
14. Sandra Gail Walker, *Weapons Use in Canadian Schools* (Ottawa: Solicitor General Canada, 1994).
15. Thomas Gabor, "Trends in Youth Crime: Some Evidence Pointing to Increases in the Severity and Volume of Violence on the Part of Young People," *Canadian Journal of Criminology* 41:385–392 (1999), p. 389; Thomas Gabor, *Responding to School Violence: An Assessment of Zero Tolerance and Related Policies* (Ottawa: Solicitor General Canada, 1995).
16. Héctor Castillo Berthier, "Popular Culture among Mexican Teenagers," *The Urban Age* 1:14–15 (Summer 1993).
17. Franz Vanderschueren, "From Violence to Justice and Security in Cities," *Environment and Urbanization* 8: 93–112 (1996).
18. Larry Rohter, "Rio's Drug Wars Begin to Take Toll on Tourism," *New York Times*, April 27, 2003, p. 3, section 5; Larry Rohter, "As Crime and Politics Collide in Rio, City Cowers in Fear," *New York Times*, May 8, 2003.
19. Tim Weiner, "Cover-Up Found in Honduras Prison Killings," *New York Times*, May 20, 2003.
20. José Carvalho de Noronha, "Drug Markets and Urban Violence in Rio de Janeiro: A Call for Action," *The Urban Age* 1:9 (Summer 1993).
21. "Graffiti, New York to New Zealand," *Crime and Justice International* 14:22 (1998).
22. "Child Prostitution on the Rise," *Crime and Justice International* 18:21 (2002).
23. Carlos Carcach, "Youth as Victims and Offenders of Homicide," *Crime and Justice International* 14:10–14 (1998).
24. The Associated Press, "Japan Crime Rate Rises," *New York Times*, November 19, 2002.
25. Norimitsu Onishi, "Crime Rattles Japanese Calm, Attracting Politician's Notice," *New York Times*, September 6, 2003.
26. "Japan Again Hit by Incidents of Violent Teen Crime," *Crime and Justice International* 17:15 (2001).
27. Horace Lyons, "Hikikomori and Youth Crime," *Crime and Justice International* 17:9–10 (2001).
28. Dai Yisheng, "Are the 'Wolves' Really Coming? An Alternative View of Juvenile Delinquency," *Crime and Justice International* 14:13–14 (1998).
29. Liling Yue, "Youth Injustice in China," in John A. Winterdyk, ed., *Juvenile Justice Systems: International Perspectives*, second edition (Toronto, Canada: Canadian Scholars' Press, 2002).
30. Mademba Ndiaye, "Dakar: Youth Groups and the Slide toward Violence," *The Urban Age* 1:7–8 (Summer 1993).
31. Otula Owuor, "City Residents Meet in Nairobi," *The Urban Age* 1:8 (Summer 1993).
32. For a general overview, see Piers Beirne, "Cultural Relativism and Comparative Criminology," *Contemporary Crises* 7:371–391 (1983); James Lynch, "Crime in International Perspective," in James Q. Wilson and Joan Petersilia, eds., *Crime: Public Policies for Crime Control* (Oakland, CA: Institute for Contemporary Studies, 2002).
33. John Henry Sloan et al., "Handgun Regulation, Crime, Assaults, and Homicide: A Tale of Two Cities," *New England Journal of Medicine* 319:1256–1262 (1988); Martin Killias, John van Kesteren, and Martin Rindlisbacher, "Guns, Violent Crime, and Suicide in 21 Countries," *Canadian Journal of Criminology* 43:429–448 (2001); Richard R. Bennett, "Constructing Cross-Cultural Theories in Criminology," *Criminology* 18:252–268 (1980); David Shichor, "Crime Patterns and Socioeconomic Development: A Cross-National Analysis," *Criminal Justice Review* 15:64–77 (1990); David P. Farrington, Patrick A. Langan, and Per-Olof H. Wikström, "Changes in Crime and Punishment in America, England and Sweden between the 1980s and the 1990s," *Studies on Crime and Crime Prevention* 3:104–131 (1994); Patrick A. Langan and David P. Farrington, *Crime and Justice in the United States and in England and Wales, 1981–96* (Washington, DC: Bureau of Justice Statistics, 1998); Joanne Savage and Bryan Vila, "Lagged Effects of Nuturance on Crime: A Cross-National Comparison," *Studies on Crime and Crime Prevention* 6:101–120 (1997); Marshall B. Clinard, *Cities with Little Crime: The Case of Switzerland* (New York: Cambridge University Press, 1978); Freda Adler, *Nations Not Obsessed with Crime* (Littleton, CO: Rothman, 1983); Manuel Eisner, "Crime, Problem Drinking, and Drug Use: Patterns of Problem Behavior in Cross-National Perspective," *Annals of the American Academy of Political and Social Science* 580:201–225 (2002).
34. Graeme Newman and Gregory J. Howard, "Introduction: Data Sources and Their Use," in Graeme Newman, ed., *Global Report on Crime and Justice* (New York: Oxford University Press, 1999), p. 18.
35. Jan van Dijk and Kristiina Kangaspunta, "Piecing Together the Cross-National Crime Puzzle," *National Institute of Justice Journal*:34–41 (January 2000).
36. Joan McCord, Cathy Spatz Widom, and Nancy Crowell, eds., *Juvenile Crime, Juvenile Justice*. Panel on Juvenile Crime: Prevention, Treatment, and Control (Washington, DC: National Academy Press, 2001), p. 17.
37. Pfeiffer, "Juvenile Crime and Violence in Europe," p. 261.

38. For more detail on the different international sources, see Gregory J. Howard, Graeme Newman, and William Alex Pridemore, "Theory, Method, and Data in Comparative Criminology," in David Duffee, ed., *Measurement and Analysis of Crime and Justice: Volume 4. Criminal Justice 2000* (Washington, DC: National Institute of Justice, 2000).

39. Newman and Howard, "Introduction: Data Sources and Their Use."

40. Gary LaFree, *Losing Legitimacy: Street Crime and the Decline of Social Institutions in America* (Boulder: Westview Press, 1997), p. 29.

41. See, for example, Franklin E. Zimring and Gordon Hawkins, *Crime Is Not the Problem: Lethal Violence in America* (New York: Oxford University Press, 1997).

42. Josine Junger-Tas, Gert-Jan Terlouw, and Malcolm W. Klein, eds., *Delinquent Behavior among Young People in the Western World: First Results of the International Self-Report Delinquency Study* (New York: Kugler Publications, 1994).

43. Rosemary Barberet, Benjamin Bowling, Josine Junger-Tas, Cristina Rechea-Alberola, John van Kesteren, and Andrew Zurawan, *Self-Reported Juvenile Delinquency in England and Wales, the Netherlands and Spain* (Helsinki, Finland: European Institute for Crime Prevention and Control, 2004), p. iii; see also Josine Junger-Tas, Ineke Haen Marshall, and Denis Ribeaud, *Delinquency in International Perspective: The International Self-Reported Delinquency Study* (Monsey, NY: Criminal Justice Press, 2003).

44. See also Philip L. Reichel, *Comparative Criminal Justice Systems: A Topical Approach*, 3rd edition (Upper Saddle River, NJ: Prentice Hall, 2002), pp. 4–5.

45. See, for example, Clinard, *Cities with Little Crime: The Case of Switzerland*; Adler, *Nations Not Obsessed with Crime*.

46. Erika Fairchild and Harry R. Dammer, *Comparative Criminal Justice Systems*, 2nd ed. (Belmont, CA: Wadsworth, 2001), p. 9.

47. Phil Williams, "Emerging Issues: Transnational Crime and Its Control," in Graeme Newman, ed., *Global Report on Crime and Justice* (New York: Oxford University Press, 1999), p. 222.

48. James O. Finckenauer, "Meeting the Challenge of Transnational Crime," *National Institute of Justice Journal*:2–7 (July 2000).

49. Williams, "Emerging Issues: Transnational Crime and Its Control," p. 222.

50. Ibid., p. 221.

51. Mark Findlay, *The Globalisation of Crime: Understanding Transnational Relationships in Context* (Cambridge, England: Cambridge University Press, 1999).

52. Pfeiffer, "Juvenile Crime and Violence in Europe."

53. Ibid., p. 256.

54. Rebecca Kong, *Canadian Crime Statistics, 1996* (Ottawa: Canadian Centre for Justice Statistics Juristat, 1997), p. 17, Table 4.

55. Pfeiffer, "Juvenile Crime and Violence in Europe," p. 256.

56. Ibid., p. 279.

57. James O. Finckenauer, *Russian Youth: Law, Deviance, and the Pursuit of Freedom* (New Brunswick, NJ: Transaction Publishers, 1995), pp. 71–73.

58. Josine Junger-Tas, "Youth Justice in the Netherlands," in Michael Tonry and Anthony N. Doob, eds., *Youth Crime and Youth Justice: Comparative and Cross-National Perspectives. Crime and Justice: A Review of Research*, Volume 31 (Chicago: University of Chicago Press, 2004).

59. Anthony N. Doob and Jane B. Sprott, "Youth Justice in Canada," in Michael Tonry and Anthony N. Doob, eds., *Youth Crime and Youth Justice: Comparative and Cross-National Perspectives. Crime and Justice: A Review of Research*, Volume 31 (Chicago: University of Chicago Press, 2004); Howard N. Snyder, *Juvenile Arrests 2001* (Washington, DC: OJJDP Juvenile Justice Bulletin, 2003).

60. Hans-Jörg Albrecht, "Juvenile Crime and Juvenile Law in the Federal Republic of Germany," in John A. Winterdyk, ed., *Juvenile Justice Systems: International Perspectives*, 2nd edition (Toronto: Canadian Scholars' Press, 2002); Uberto Gatti and Alfredo Verde, "Comparative Juvenile Justice: An Overview of Italy," in John A. Winterdyk, ed., *Juvenile Justice Systems: International Perspectives*, 2nd edition (Toronto: Canadian Scholars' Press, 2002).

61. John A. Winterdyk, "Juvenile Justice and Young Offenders: An Overview of Canada," in John A. Winterdyk, ed., *Juvenile Justice Systems: International Perspectives*, 2nd edition (Toronto: Canadian Scholars' Press, 2002).

62. Snyder, *Juvenile Arrests 2001*.

63. Kate Zernike, "Study Finds Teenage Drug Use Higher in U.S. than in Europe," *New York Times*, February 21, 2001.

64. Sarah Lyall, "British Worry that Drinking has Gotten Out of Hand," *New York Times*, July 22, 2004.

65. Thor Bjarnason, "European School Survey Project on Alcohol and Drugs," press release issued by the State University of New York at Albany, February 20, 2001.

66. Zernike, "Study Finds Teenage Drug Use Higher in U.S. than in Europe."

67. Elmar G. M. Weitekamp, Hans-Juergen Kerner, and Gernot Trueg, *International Comparison of Juvenile Justice Systems: Report to the National Academy of Sciences Commission on Behavioral and Social Sciences and Education* (Tuebingen, German: Institute of Criminology, University of Tuebingen, July 1999), p. 13.

68. National Advisory Commission on Criminal Justice Standards and Goals, *Task Force Report on Juvenile Justice and Delinquency Prevention* (Washington DC: Law Enforcement Assistance Administration, 1976), p. 258.

69. Pfeiffer, "Juvenile Crime and Violence in Europe," p. 314.

70. John A. Winterdyk, "Juvenile Justice and Young Offenders: An Overview of Canada," in John Winterdyk, ed., *Juvenile Justice Systems: International Perspectives*, 2nd edition (Toronto: Canadian Scholars' Press, 2002), p. 91.

71. Minoru Yokoyama, "Juvenile Justice and Juvenile Crime: An Overview of Japan," in John A. Winterdyk, ed., *Juvenile Justice Systems: International Perspectives*, 2nd edition (Toronto: Canadian Scholars' Press, 2002), pp. 337–338.

72. Satyanshu Mukherjee and Philip Reichel, "Bringing to Justice," in Graeme Newman, ed., *Global Report on Crime and Justice* (New York: Oxford University Press, 1999), p. 79.

73. McCord, Spatz Widom, and Crowell, eds., *Juvenile Crime, Juvenile Justice*, p. 20.

74. Winterdyk, ed., *Juvenile Justice Systems: International Perspectives*, p. xviii.

75. Weitekamp, Kerner, and Trueg, *International Comparison of Juvenile Justice Systems*, p. 83.

76. Ibid., p. 268.

77. Ibid., p. 253.

78. Doob and Sprott, "Youth Justice in Canada," p. 232.

79. Uberto Gatti and Alfredo Verde, "Comparative Juvenile Justice: An Overview of Italy," in John A. Winterdyk, ed., *Juvenile Justice Systems: International Perspectives*, 2nd edition (Toronto: Canadian Scholars' Press, 2002), p. 305.

80. Weitekamp, Kerner, and Trueg, *International Comparison of Juvenile Justice Systems*, pp. 208, 223.

81. James L. Williams and Daniel G. Rodeheaver, "Punishing Juvenile Offenders in Russia," *International Criminal Justice Review* 12:93–110 (2002), p. 104.

82. Weitekamp, Kerner, and Trueg, *International Comparison of Juvenile Justice Systems*, p. 243.

83. Harold Traver, "Juvenile Delinquency in Hong Kong," in John A. Winterdyk, ed., *Juvenile Justice Systems: International Perspectives*, 2nd edition (Toronto: Canadian Scholars' Press, 2002), p. 211.

84. Hans-Jörg Albrecht, "Youth Justice in Germany," in Michael Tonry and Anthony N. Doob, eds., *Youth Crime and Youth Justice: Comparative and Cross-National Perspectives. Crime and Justice: A Review of Research*, Volume 31 (Chicago: University of Chicago Press, 2004), p. 473.

85. Loraine Gelsthorpe and Vicky Kemp, "Comparative Juvenile Justice: England and Wales," in John A. Winterdyk, ed., *Juvenile Justice Systems: International Perspectives*, 2nd edition (Toronto: Canadian Scholars' Press, 2002), p. 130.

86. Weitekamp, Kerner, and Trueg, *International Comparison of Juvenile Justice Systems*, p. 90.

87. Gelsthorpe and Kemp, "Comparative Juvenile Justice: England and Wales," p. 138.

88. Anthony Bottoms and James Dignan, "Youth Justice in Great Britain," in Michael Tonry and Anthony N. Doob, eds., *Youth Crime and Youth Justice: Comparative and Cross-National Perspectives. Crime and Justice: A Review of Research*, Volume 31 (Chicago: University of Chicago Press, 2004), p. 36.

89. Weitekamp, Kerner, and Trueg, *International Comparison of Juvenile Justice Systems*, p. 90.

90. Ibid., p. 103.

91. Ibid., p. 100.

92. Ibid., p. 90.

93. David P. Farrington, John Ditchfield, Gareth Hancock, Philip Howard, Darrick Jolliffe, Mark S. Livingston, and Kate A. Painter, *Evaluation of Two Intensive Regimes for Young Offenders*, Home Office Research Study No. 239 (London: Home Office, 2002).

94. Gelsthorpe and Kemp, "Comparative Juvenile Justice: England and Wales," pp. 149–150.

95. Julian V. Roberts, "Public Opinion and Youth Justice," in Michael Tonry and Anthony N. Doob, eds., *Youth Crime and Youth Justice: Comparative and Cross-National Perspectives. Crime and Justice: A Review of Research*, Volume 31 (Chicago: University of Chicago Press, 2004), pp. 509–510.

17

The Future of Delinquency and Juvenile Justice

Chapter Outline

The Concept of Delinquency

Theories of Delinquency

Social, Community, and Environmental Influences on Delinquency

The Juvenile Justice System

> POLICY AND PRACTICE: Targeted Community
> Action Planning (TCAP)

Crisis in the U.S. Juvenile Justice System

Juvenile Justice Abroad

Chapter Objectives

1. Be able to discuss the future of the statutory concept of juvenile delinquency
2. Discuss the future of status offending
3. Be familiar with the trends in delinquency theory
4. Understand the direction of gender differences in delinquency
5. Comprehend the future of ecological factors on delinquency
6. Know the key issues that delinquency prevention faces in the years ahead
7. Be familiar with the different stages of juvenile justice reform over the last 100 years and some of the possible reforms in store ahead
8. Know what policing strategies are making a difference in reducing juvenile crime
9. Understand the major pressing problems facing the juvenile court process, such as detention and role of attorney, and discuss what is needed to rectify these problems in the coming years
10. Be able to comment on the significance of restorative justice and innovations in correctional treatment as part of an ongoing effort to reduce juvenile recidivism rates and limit institutionalization
11. Be able to identify the main reasons behind some industrialized countries considering more punitive juvenile justice systems

CNN. View the CNN video clip of this story and answer related Critical Thinking questions on your Juvenile Delinquency 9e CD-ROM.

In 2003, a Minnesota high school student, Jeffrey Lee Parson, was charged in connection with spreading a version of the "Blaster" virus. In a 12-page complaint filed in federal court, Parson was charged with one count of "intentionally causing and attempting to cause damage to a protected computer." The virus targeted a flaw in Microsoft's Windows XP and 2000 operating systems, with an estimated 400,000 computers infected worldwide. Described in the media as a heavyset loner who was depressed and angry, Parson refuted those assumptions during a *Today Show* interview (accessible on http://msnbc.msn.com/id/3078578/):

Today: In cases like this, there are a lot of quick, simple characterizations of the accused given to the media—for example, he was a loner, he didn't have friends, he was reckless, and so on. How would you describe yourself?

Parson: I'm the complete opposite of the way I've been portrayed in the press. I'm not a loner. I have a very supportive close group of friends. I'm not reckless, I don't do drugs, smoke, or drink. This is the first time I have ever had a run-in with the law. It's hurtful to see the accounts of me. I'm not depressed, embarrassed about my weight, or a misfit.

The Parson case illustrates the changing face of juvenile delinquency. In the future, young offenders may be less inclined to steal cars and use drugs than they are to participate in Internet fraud and identity theft. The case further illustrates the view that many youthful offenders are not irrational or angry, but clever, intelligent, and calculating. Some delinquency experts believe that the decision to commit an illegal act is a product of an individual decision-making process that may be shaped by the personal characteristics of the decision maker. They reject the notion that delinquents are a "product of their environment." But if social and economic factors alone determine behavior, how is it that many youths residing in dangerous neighborhoods live law-abiding lives? According to the U.S. Census Bureau, more than thirty-four million Americans live in poverty yet the vast majority do not become delinquents and criminals.[1] Research indicates that relatively few youths in any population, even the most economically disadvantaged, actually become hard-core, chronic delinquents.[2] The quality of neighborhood and family life may have little impact on the choices individuals make.[3]

We have reviewed in this text the current knowledge of the nature, causes, and correlates of juvenile delinquency and society's efforts to bring about its prevention and control. We have analyzed research programs, theoretical models, governmental policies, and legal cases. Taken in sum, this information presents a rather broad and complex picture of the youth crime problem and the most critical issues confronting the juvenile justice system. Delinquents come from a broad spectrum of society; kids of every race, gender, class, region, family type, and culture are involved in delinquent behaviors. To combat youthful law violations, society has tried a garden variety of intervention and control strategies: tough law enforcement; counseling, treatment, and rehabilitation; provision of legal rights; community action; educational programs; family change strategies. Yet, despite decades of intense effort and study, it is still unclear why delinquency occurs and what, if anything, can be done to control its occurrence. One thing is certain: Juvenile crime is one of the most serious domestic problems faced by Americans.

Though uncertainty prevails, it is possible to draw some inferences about youth crime and its control. After reviewing the material contained in this volume, certain conclusions seem self-evident. Some involve social facts; that is, particular empirical relationships and associations have been established that have withstood multiple testing and verification efforts. Other conclusions involve social questions; there are issues that need clarification, and the uncertainty surrounding them has hampered progress in combating delinquency and treating known delinquents.

In sum, we have reviewed some of the most important social facts concerning delinquent behavior and posed some of the critical questions that still remain to be answered.

THE CONCEPT OF DELINQUENCY

The statutory concept of juvenile delinquency is in need of review and modification. Today, the legal definition of a juvenile delinquent is a minor child, usually under the age of 17, who has been found to have violated the criminal law (juvenile code). The concept of juvenile delinquency still occupies a legal position falling somewhere between criminal and civil law; juveniles still enjoy more rights, protections, and privileges than adults. Nonetheless, concerns about teen violence may eventually put an end to the separate juvenile justice system. If kids are equally or even more violent as adults, why should they be given a special legal status consideration? Because juvenile violence rates have trended downward, calls for abolishing the juvenile justice system have been muted. However, recent gang violence may be a precursor of increases in both the number of violent acts and also their seriousness. As the number of poor children increases, so too may crime rates. If the teen violence rate begins to rise again, so too may calls for the abolition of a separate juvenile justice system.

Restructuring the Definition of Status Offender The concept of the status offender (PINS, CHINS, and MINS) may be in for revision. Special treatment for the status offender conforms with the *parens patriae* roots of the juvenile justice system. Granting the state authority to institutionalize noncriminal youth in order "to protect the best interest of the child" cannot be considered an abuse of state authority. While it is likely that the current system of control will remain in place for the near future, it is not beyond the realm of possibility to see the eventual restructuring of the definition of status offenders, with jurisdiction of "pure" noncriminal first-time offenders turned over to a department of social services, and chronic status offenders and those with prior records of delinquency petitioned to juvenile court as delinquency cases.

Juvenile Delinquency Rates in the Future The juvenile delinquency rate may slowly begin to increase. Official delinquency data suggests that there has been a decade-long decline in the juvenile delinquency rate. Overall, the number of juveniles arrested for violent crimes has declined almost 30 percent since 1993, the number of kids arrested for murder dropping an astounding 64 percent during this period. Juvenile property crime arrests have declined 34 percent. A number of prognosticators who had predicted a significant increase in the juvenile crime rate and the emerging danger of the juvenile "super predator" are busy wiping egg of their faces. Of course, the current decline may be a brief respite before juvenile delinquency rates begin to tick upward.

Immigration Trends The United States is one of the few industrialized nations whose population is predicted to increase over the coming decades. We should be a nation of 420 million people within 50 years, up from 290 million today. Much of the increase will be due to immigration, and many of the newest Americans may be forced to live in disorganized, poverty stricken areas. We can already detect evidence of this trend: Despite the booming economy of the 1990s, the number of children living in severely distressed neighborhoods increased 18 percent between 1990 and 2000. While the number of these needy kids may rapidly increase, the resources to help them may now be in permanent decline.

The Economy and Globalization The national debt is skyrocketing and the government is now forced to spend more than 175 billion per year on interest rate payments. That number is bound to rise in the future. Military spending is at an all-time high and the continuing war on terror holds out little hope that it will decline in the near future.

More than 60 percent of the homicides committed by juveniles involve guns. High-powered, large-capacity assault weapons are the guns of choice for some juvenile gangs and have been used in many of the nation's high-profile school shootings. Shown here is Montgomery County police chief Tom Manager displaying an M-16 assault rifle with a 30-round clip at a news conference in Bethesda, Maryland, on the day before federal legislation banning the sale of assault weapons was set to expire. On September 14, 2004, the 10-year assault weapons ban ended.

The graying of the population means that Social Security and Medicare payments should increase. All this means that there will be fewer resources to help kids, support educational reform, and target families in need. Coupled with these budgetary problems is the effect of globalization on the manufacturing economy: there will be fewer high-paying jobs in manufacturing; wages may decline because of foreign competition. More kids, less work, and reduced social support may add up to increases in juvenile crime.

Gun Control Easy availability of guns is a significant contributor to teen violence. Research indicates a close tie among gun use, control of drug markets, and teen violence. Unless efforts are made to control the spread of handguns or devise programs to deter handgun use, teenage violence rates will rise. While gun control has its passionate advocates, the powerful gun lobby has resisted efforts to reduce the number of guns or to even ban their sale and distribution outright.

Chronic Juvenile Offenders The chronic violent juvenile offender is a serious social problem for society and the juvenile justice system. Chronic male delinquent offenders commit a disproportionate amount of violent behavior including a significant amount of the most serious juvenile crimes, such as homicides, rapes, robberies, and aggravated assaults. Many chronic offenders become adult criminals and eventually end up in the criminal court system. How to effectively deal with chronic juvenile offenders and drug users remains a high priority for the juvenile justice system.

While it is possible that severe punishments may be created within the juvenile justice system to deal specifically with the chronic offender, it is more likely that they will be waived to adult court and punished as adults.

THEORIES OF DELINQUENCY

We have noted a trend to create multifaceted, multidimensional theories of delinquency that incorporate personal and social variables in a complex web. One reason is the proliferation of highly sophisticated statistical programs that allow researchers to use advanced data analysis techniques, which were unknown to an earlier generation of social scientists.

Emerging Theories In the future, more attention will be paid to personal traits and qualities. While the first theories of delinquency focused on individual traits, by the mid-twentieth century this view was abandoned for more sociological explanations. Most delinquency experts focused on the social factors and institutions that produced criminality: It was not who you were, but where you lived. Travis Hirschi began to change all that when his book *Causes of Delinquency* became the dominant view of delinquency causation in the 1970s and beyond. His view suggested that social psychological processes can direct delinquent activities (his "bonds" of commitment, attachment, involvement, and belief are essentially psychological processes). Today it is common for theorists to incorporate a psychological dimension in their work and many consider biological factors as well. This trend should continue in the future. We expect that the next theoretical model may rest on the growing science of **neuropsychology,** which is the study of brain behavior relationships. Neuropsychologists bring their training in anatomy, physiology, and pathology of the nervous system to the study of human behavior. Their clinical focus is on evaluating and treating people who are thought to have something wrong with the way in which their nervous system is operating. It is possible that in the near future kids who are experiencing trouble at home and at school will be routinely evaluated and treated based upon their mental functioning.

neuropsychology
The branch of psychology that involves the study of human behavior as it relates to normal and abnormal functioning of the central nervous system.

Recent Dominance of Developmental Theories There is still debate about whether the propensity to commit crime changes as people mature. Delinquency experts are now researching such issues as the onset, escalation, termination, and continuation of a delinquent career. There is an ongoing debate concerning change in delinquent behavior patterns. One position is that people do not change—conditions and opportunities do. A second view is that real human change is conditioned by life events. If the former position holds true, there is little hope of using treatment strategies to change known offenders. A more productive approach would be to limit their criminal opportunities through the use of long-term incarceration. If the latter position is accurate, effective treatment and provision of legitimate opportunities might produce real behavioral changes.

The developmental/life course vision appears to be gaining popularity as the dominant theoretical view on delinquency. If this position is maintained it would not be surprising to see kids at risk for delinquency being placed in quasi-military experiences where character building is stressed over punishment and discipline.

Go to the **National Academy of Neuropsychology** to learn more about this topic: www.nanonline.org. For an up-to-date list of web links, go to http://cj.wadsworth.com/siegel_jd9e.

TO QUIZ YOURSELF ON THIS MATERIAL, go to the Juvenile Delinquency 9e website.

SOCIAL, COMMUNITY, AND ENVIRONMENTAL INFLUENCES ON DELINQUENCY

A child's social, community, and environmental relations are now known to exert a potent influence on his/her behavior. Kids who fail at home and at school, who are persistently involved with deviant peer group members, are considered most at risk for delinquent careers over their life course. Chronic offenders are the ones most likely to experience educational failure, poor home life, substance abuse, and unsatisfactory peer relations.

At the same time, positive social, community, and environmental relations can protect at-risk children from involvement in a delinquent way of life. It comes as no sur-

© A. Ramey/PhotoEdit

prise that many delinquency prevention efforts focus on improving family relations, supporting educational achievement, and utilizing community resources. How will these factors evolve in the future?

The Rise in Female Delinquency Female delinquency has been increasing at a faster pace than male delinquency. The nature and extent of female delinquent activities changed in the late 1980s, and it now appears that the pace of girls' antisocial activities is increasing at a relatively faster pace than male antisocial behavior. Girls are now engaging in more frequent and serious illegal activity and female gang membership is on the rise.

While gender differences in the rate of the most serious crimes such as murder still persist, it is possible that further convergence will occur. Gender differences in education and work are narrowing and will continue to do so. As social differences narrow, so too may crime differences. On the other hand, if delinquency is a biological/psychological phenomenon, as some experts believe, there may not be the convergence that gender experts expect.

The Influence of the Family Environment There is little question that family environment affects patterns of juvenile behavior. Family relationships have been linked to the problem of juvenile delinquency by many experts. Broken homes, for instance, are not in and of themselves a cause of delinquency, but some evidence indicates that single-parent households are more inclined to contain children who manifest behavioral problems. Limited resource allocations limit the single parent's ability to control and supervise children. In addition, there seems to be a strong association in family relationships between child abuse and delinquency. Cases of abuse and neglect have been found in every level of the economic strata, and a number of studies have linked child abuse and neglect to juvenile delinquency. While the evidence is not conclusive, it does suggest that a strong relationship exists between child abuse and subsequent delinquent behavior.

Some experts believe a major effort is needed to reestablish parental accountability and responsibility. Ironically, if those groups lobbying hard to end choice and criminalize abortion succeed in their efforts they may actually be contributing to long-term increases in the delinquency rate. The number of children born out of wedlock to teen girls has been on the decline. If abortion (and birth control) were no longer available the trend will reverse, eventually producing a large pool of unwanted children born to mothers who may find it difficult to provide adequate care. A large cohort of unwanted and uncared-for children will help drive up future delinquency rates.

Juvenile Gangs in the United States Juvenile gangs have become a serious and growing problem in many major metropolitan areas throughout the United States. Ethnic youth gangs, mostly males aged 14 to 21, appear to be increasing in such areas as Los Angeles, Chicago, Boston, and New York. National surveys of gang activity now estimate that there are more than 700,000 members in the United States, up sharply over the previous 20 years. One view of gang development is that such groups serve as a bridge between adolescence and adulthood in communities where adult social control is not available. Another view suggests that gangs are a product of lower-class social disorganization and that they serve as an alternative means of economic advancement for poorly motivated and uneducated youth. Today's gangs are often more commercially than culturally oriented, and the profit motive may be behind increasing memberships. It is unlikely that gang control strategies can be successful as long as legitimate economic alternatives are lacking. Look for rapid growth in ganging when the current adolescent population matures and limited job opportunities encourage gang members to prolong their involvement in illegal activities. While jobs may be outsourced, gangs are a homegrown commodity.

School Failure and School-Based Crime Many of the underlying problems of youth crime and delinquency are directly related to education. Numerous empirical studies have confirmed that lack of educational success is an important contributing factor in delinquency. Dropping out of school is now being associated with long-term antisocial behavior. A large-scale study of school crime by the U.S. Departments of Education and Justice reports substantial declines over the last decade, but draws attention to ongoing school problems such as bullying, fighting, and drugs.[4] About 10 percent of all victimizations occur on school grounds. School-based crime control projects have not been very successful, and a great deal more effort is needed in the critical area of delinquency prevention in schools. In the future, look for increases in school-based crime as the number of children in need of services increases while school budgets are trimmed.

Substance Abuse Juvenile crime and delinquency are closely associated with substance abuse. Self-report surveys indicate that more than half of all high school kids have tried drugs. Surveys of arrestees indicate that a significant proportion of teenagers are drug users and many are high school dropouts. While one national survey shows that teenage drug use increased slightly in the past year, all three national surveys report that drug and alcohol use are much lower today than 5 and 10 years ago.

The Costs of Juvenile Violence The costs of delinquency are immense and wide-ranging. It is estimated that juvenile violence costs the United States $158 billion each year. The majority of this cost is due to losses suffered by victims, such as lost wages, pain, suffering, and reduced quality of life. Also included are costs incurred by federal, state, and local governments to assist victims of juvenile violence, such as medical treatment for injuries and services for victims. Missing from this estimate are the costs from society's response to juvenile violence, which include early prevention programs, services for juveniles, and the juvenile justice system. These costs are unknown. Many experts argue that the financial cost of juvenile delinquency is an important justification for greater delinquency prevention measures. We believe that costs should swell in the coming years because such required expenses as medical care for incarcerated youth are skyrocketing.

Delinquency Prevention Programs Prevention is a key component of an overall strategy to address the problem of juvenile delinquency. In recent years, many types of delinquency prevention programs have been targeted at children, young people, and families, and many of these programs show positive results in reducing delinquency as well as other problem behaviors, such as substance abuse and truancy. They have also been shown to lead to improvements in other areas of life, such as educational achievement, health, and employment. These benefits often translate into substantial cost savings.[5]

Despite the success of many different delinquency prevention programs—from preschool to mentoring—these programs receive a small fraction of what is spent on the juvenile justice system to deal with young people once they have broken the law. To many juvenile justice officials, policymakers, and politicians, prevention is tantamount to being soft on crime, and delinquency prevention programs are often referred to as "pork barrel" or wasteful spending. There is concern about the labeling and stigmatization associated with programs that target high-risk populations: Children and families receiving support may be called hurtful names or looked down upon by fellow community members. Overcoming these obstacles will require prevention programs tailored to the specific needs of juveniles and their families, further experimentation with universal programs, and educating the public and key decision makers about the value of preventing delinquency.

strategic planning
A disciplined effort to produce fundamental decisions and actions that shape and guide an organization and direct the focus of its future.

Notwithstanding these important issues, the future of delinquency prevention is likely to be very bright. With many local efforts, state initiatives, and a growing list of national programs showing positive results, the prevention of delinquency is proving its worth.

In the future, delinquency prevention programs will be designed to use technology, technical assistance, and tight organization to make the most out of every dollar. OJJDP's recent attempt at streamlining prevention by focusing it on specific problems and using **strategic planning** is described in the Policy and Practice box entitled "Targeted Community Action Planning (TCAP)."

TO QUIZ YOURSELF ON THIS MATERIAL, go to the Juvenile Delinquency 9e website.

THE JUVENILE JUSTICE SYSTEM

An analysis of the history of juvenile justice over the past 100 years shows how our policy regarding delinquency has gone through cycles of reform. Many years ago, society primarily focused on the treatment of youth who committed criminal behavior, often through no fault of their own. Early in the nineteenth century, juveniles were tried in criminal courts, like everyone else. Reformers developed the idea of establishing separate institutions for juvenile offenders in which the rehabilitation idea could proceed without involvement with criminal adults. As a result, the House of Refuge movement was born.

By the late 1890s the system proved unworkable because delinquent juveniles, minor offenders, and neglected children weren't benefiting from institutional placement. The 1899 Illinois Juvenile Court Act was an effort to regulate the treatment of children and secure institutional reform. *Parens patriae* was the justification to ignore legal formalities in the juvenile courts up until the early twentieth century. In the 1960s, the *Gault* decision heralded the promise of legal rights for children and interrupted the goal of individualized rehabilitation. The 1970s yielded progress in the form of the Juvenile Justice and Delinquency Prevention Act. Throughout the 1980s and 1990s, the juvenile justice system seemed suspended between the assurance of due process and efforts to provide services for delinquent children and their families. Today, society is concerned with the control of serious juvenile offenders and the development of firm sentencing provisions in the juvenile courts. These cycles represent the shifting philosophies of the juvenile justice system.

Conflicting Views of the Juvenile Justice System Today no single ideology or view dominates the direction, programs, and policies of the juvenile justice system. Throughout the past decade, numerous competing positions regarding juvenile justice have emerged. As the liberal program of the 1970s has faltered, more restrictive sanctions have been imposed. The "crime control" position seems most formidable as we enter the new millennium. However, there remains a great deal of confusion over

The Targeted Community Action Planning (TCAP) initiative is a new technical assistance initiative being made available to states and communities interested in developing targeted responses to their most pressing juvenile justice and delinquency prevention needs. A goal of comprehensive strategic planning is to promote a seamless continuum of services for children, youth, and families that is capable of providing the right resources to children and families at the appropriate time. As the program is implemented, 10 to 15 communities will receive intensive technical assistance (TA) in developing and implementing targeted responses using a streamlined community-based planning process.

The TCAP technical assistance program will support the delinquency prevention efforts of states, communities, and federally recognized Indian tribes and Alaska Native groups. Communities eligible for TCAP assistance will have the following characteristics:

▌ An identified high rate of juvenile crime and delinquency.

▌ A population of no more than 250,000. (Note: In a city larger than 250,000, the community population may be defined as that of a specific quadrant or zip code area within the city.)

▌ An existing local decision-making component or community champion who can convene key community leaders.

TCAP will be implemented in a number of distinct stages:

1. DIAGNOSTIC ASSESSMENT

During this stage, juvenile crime and court data will be analyzed to assess the juvenile crime problem in the community. The second part of the diagnostic assessment involves reviewing existing community plans, state directions (legislative mandates), and information on weaknesses and gaps in a community's comprehensive continuum of services for youth. During this stage, key community leaders will be interviewed to augment the data analysis, and a key leader summit will be held to develop a consensus on the identified targeted offender population.

2. PROBLEM ANALYSIS

The problem analysis stage identifies the specific nature of the offender problem in the community. The TCAP consultants will identify the causal nature of the problem behavior using both the diagnostic assessment and current research on the developmental pathways of delinquent behavior. Finally, the report will be reviewed in an executive briefing by the key leaders for final agreement.

3. RESPONSE DEVELOPMENT

Developing a targeted response brings the community together to work toward achieving a solution to the identified

Targeted Community Action Planning (TCAP)

problem. The targeted response will use "best practice" programs and strategies. The response plan will include identified goals, clear roles and responsibilities, measurable objectives, and evaluation components. In addition, the targeted response will integrate a comprehensive strategic planning framework into the ongoing operations of the continuum of services for youth and their families.

4. RESPONSE IMPLEMENTATION

This stage involves the implementation of the targeted response plan. A consultant assists the community in finding resources, with an emphasis on the reallocation of existing funds from at least one program area to the targeted response. The TCAP consultant will remain in contact with the locality to ensure that problems relating to implementation are solved and that an evaluation plan is followed. A plan can also be developed at this juncture to ensure continuing capacity to maintain momentum.

The TCAP plan includes the following components:

▌ Involvement and commitment of community leaders

▌ Community responses based on the most effective program models

▌ Addressing problems by reallocating existing resources

▌ Multifaceted responses that involve the full continuum of youth services

▌ Reliance on technology more than onsite training and technical assistance

▌ Access to resources and tools that support community planning

▌ Identification of communities' existing resources and capacity to collect and map data on problem behaviors, crime, and risk factors

▌ Identification of local infrastructure that can support community planning

Critical Thinking

1. Will such a structured procedure as TCAP provide an organizational model that can effectively reduce delinquency?

2. Could such a model work if delinquent behavior was a function of personal traits and characteristics?

InfoTrac College Edition Research

Use "delinquency prevention" in a key word search on InfoTrac College Edition.

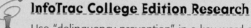

SOURCE: Office of Juvenile Justice and Delinquency Prevention, Targeted Community Action Planning (TCAP), www.ojjdp.ncjrs.org/tcap/ (accessed on October 4, 2004).

what the juvenile justice system does, what it should do, and how it should deal with youthful antisocial behavior. The juvenile justice system operates on distinctly different yet parallel tracks. On the one hand, modest funding is available for prevention and treatment strategies. At the same time, states are responding to anxiety about youth crime by devising more punitive measures.

Social Control vs. Crime Control Today's problems in the juvenile justice system can often be traced to the uncertainty of its founders, the "child savers." Such early twentieth-century groups formed the juvenile justice system on the misguided principle of reforming wayward youth and remodeling their behavior. The "best interest of the child" standard has long been the guiding light in juvenile proceedings, calling for the strongest available rehabilitative services. Today's juvenile justice system is often torn between playing the role of social versus crime control agent.

Juvenile Justice and the U.S. Supreme Court In recent years, the juvenile justice system has become more legalistic by virtue of U.S. Supreme Court decisions that have granted children procedural safeguards in various court proceedings. The case of *In re Gault* in the 1960s motivated state legislators to revamp their juvenile court legal procedures. Today, the Supreme Court is continuing to struggle with making distinctions between the legal rights of adults and those of minors. Recent Court decisions that allowed children to be searched by teachers and denied their right to a jury trial showed that the Court continues to recognize a legal separation between adult and juvenile offenders.

Constitutional Protection for Juvenile Offenders Despite some dramatic distinctions, juveniles have gained many of the legal due process rights enjoyed by adults. Among the more significant elements of due process are the right to counsel, evidence efficiency, protection from double jeopardy and self-incrimination, and the right to appeal. While the public continues to favor providing juveniles with the same due process and procedural guarantees accorded to adults, it is likely that constitutional protections that adults receive are not actually provided to juvenile offenders. High caseloads, poor pretrial preparation and trial performance, and the lack of dispositional representation are issues where juveniles are being denied due process of law. More resources are needed to implement constitutional procedures so that legal protections are not discarded.

The key area in which due process is required by *Gault* is the right to counsel. While progress has been made in improving the availability and quality of legal counsel afforded youths in delinquency proceedings in the three decades since *Gault*, much remains to be done.

State Laws Regarding Juvenile Records States are increasingly taking legislative action to ensure that juvenile arrest and disposition records are available to prosecutors and judges. Knowledge of defendants' juvenile records may help determine appropriate sentencing for offenders aged 18 to 24, the age group most likely to be involved in violent crime. Laws that are being passed include (1) police fingerprinting of juveniles charged with crimes that are felonies if committed by an adult; (2) centralized juvenile arrest and disposition record-holding and dissemination statutes; (3) prosecutor and court access to juvenile disposition records; and (4) limitations on expungement of juvenile records when there are subsequent adult convictions.

The Focus on Juvenile Court The Juvenile Court is the focal point of the contemporary juvenile justice system. Created at the turn of the century, it was adopted as an innovative solution to the problem of wayward youth. In the first half of the century, these courts (organized by the states and based on the historic notion of *parens patriae*) were committed to the treatment of the child. They functioned without procedures employed in the adult criminal courts. When the system was reviewed by the U.S.

Supreme Court in 1966, due process was imposed on the juvenile court system. Almost 40 years have since passed, and numerous reform efforts have been undertaken. But the statement of Justice Abe Fortas that "the child receives the worst of both worlds—neither the protection afforded adults nor the treatment needed for children" still rings true. Reform efforts have been disappointing.

More Specialized Juvenile Courts What are the remedies for the current juvenile court system? Some suggest abolishing the delinquency-status jurisdiction of the courts. This is difficult to do because the organization of the courts is governed by state law. Others want to strengthen the legal rights of juveniles by improving the quality of services of legal counsel. The majority of experts believe there is an urgent need to develop meaningful dispositional programs and expand treatment services. Over the last 50 years, the juvenile court system has been transformed from a rehabilitative to a quasi-criminal court. With limited resources and procedural deficiencies, there is little likelihood of much change in the near future. One area of change has been the development of specialized courts, such as drug courts, which focus attention on specific problems, and teen or youth courts, which use peer jurors and other officers of the court to settle less-serious matters. With many states faced with growing budget deficits and less federal funding for various juvenile justice programs, and looking for innovative ways to make juvenile justice more cost-effective, these specialized courts are becoming increasingly popular.[6]

The Juvenile Death Penalty The death penalty for children has been upheld by the Supreme Court. In the 1989 cases *Wilkens v. Missouri* and *Sanford v. Kentucky*, the Supreme Court concluded that states are free to impose the death penalty for murderers who commit their crimes while age 16 or 17. According to the majority decision written by Justice Antonin Scalia, society has not formed a consensus that such executions are a violation of the cruel and unusual punishment clause of the Eighth Amendment. In August 2003, the Supreme Court of Missouri declared the death penalty to be unconstitutional for offenders under the age of 18, and petitioned the U.S. Supreme Court to take up this matter. In January 2004, the Supreme Court agreed to decide whether the death penalty for 16- and 17-year-olds violates the Constitution.

Changes in Law Enforcement New approaches to policing juvenile delinquency show promising results in reducing serious offenses, such as gang activity and gun crimes. Some of these new approaches include aggressive law enforcement, community-based policing services, and police in schools. One of the most successful approaches has involved the police working closely with other juvenile justice agencies and the community. Operation Ceasefire in Boston, which brought together a broad range of juvenile justice and social agencies and community groups, produced substantial reductions in youth homicide victims, youth gun assaults, and gang violence throughout the city. Versions of this successful program are now being replicated in other cities across the country. With the research evidence demonstrating that targeted problem-solving policing strategies of this type are the most effective in reducing serious urban crime problems,[7] continued use of these strategies holds much promise in maintaining record low rates of juvenile violence.

Juvenile Detention The use of detention in the juvenile justice system continues to be a widespread problem. After almost three decades of work, virtually all jurisdictions

© Gabe Palmer/Corbis

Some community-based policing services assign police officers to outreach programs for youths to promote a positive work ethic, emphasize the values of community involvement, and help create a positive image of the police department.

have passed laws requiring that status offenders be placed in shelter care programs rather than detention facilities. Another serious problem related to the use of juvenile detention is the need to remove young people from lockups in adult jails. The Office of Juvenile Justice and Delinquency Prevention continues to give millions of dollars in aid to encourage the removal of juveniles from such adult lockups. But eliminating the confinement of children in adult institutions remains an enormously difficult task in the juvenile justice system. Although most delinquency cases do not involve detention, its use is more common for cases involving males, minorities, and older juveniles. Juvenile detention is one of the most important elements of the justice system and one of the most difficult to administer. It is experiencing a renewed emphasis on programs linked to short-term confinement.

Increasing Waivers of Serious Offenders to Adult Court The use of waiver, bind-over, and transfer provisions in juvenile court statutes is now more common. This trend has led toward a **criminalization** of the juvenile system. Because there are major differences between the adult and juvenile court systems, transfer to an adult court exposes youths to more serious consequences of their antisocial behavior and is a strong recommendation of those favoring a crime control model. Waiver of serious offenders is one of the most significant developments in the trend to criminalize the juvenile court. According to the National Conference of State Legislatures, every state has transfer proceedings. Many states are considering legislation that makes it easier to transfer juveniles into adult courts. States continue to modify age and offense criteria, allowing more serious offenders to be tried as criminals; some are considering new transfer laws, such as mandatory and presumptive waiver provisions. We believe that while the waiver rate has actually declined in recent years it will increase in the future as the juvenile crime rates trend upward.

Attorneys and the Juvenile Justice System The role of the attorney in the juvenile justice process requires further research and analysis. Most attorneys appear to be uncertain whether they should act as adversaries or advocates in the juvenile process. In addition, the role of the juvenile prosecutor has become more significant as a result of new and more serious statutory sentencing provisions, as well as legal standards promulgated by such organizations as the American Bar Association and the National District Attorneys Association. Juvenile defendants also need and are entitled to effective legal representation. Through creative and resourceful strategies, many more states are providing comprehensive representation for delinquent youth. These programs include law internships, attorney mentoring, and neighborhood defender services.

Sentencing Procedures in Juvenile Court Juvenile sentencing procedures now reflect the desire to create uniformity and limited discretion in the juvenile court, and this trend is likely to continue. Many states have now developed programs such as mandatory sentences, sentencing guidelines, and limited-discretion sentencing to bring uniformity into the juvenile justice system. As a result of the public's fear about serious juvenile crime, legislators have amended juvenile codes to tighten up juvenile sentencing provisions. Graduated sanctions are the latest type of sentencing solution being explored by states. The most popular piece of juvenile crime legislation in the near future will be tougher sentences for violent and repeat offenders. Perhaps the most dramatic impact on sentencing will be felt by the imposition of "blended sentences" that combine juvenile and adult sentences. More than a dozen states now use blended sentencing statutes, which allow courts to impose juvenile and/or adult correctional sanctions on certain young offenders.

Community Sentencing and Probation In the area of community sentencing, new forms of probation supervision have received greater attention in recent years. Intensive probation supervision, balanced probation, wilderness probation, and electronic monitoring have become important community-based alternatives over the last few years. Some studies report mixed results for these new forms of probation, but more

To read about **the future of detention,** go to www.co.multnomah.or.us/dcj/AR03_overview.pdf. For an up-to-date list of web links, go to http://cj.wadsworth.com/siegel_jd9e.

criminalization
The process during which a person becomes enmeshed in first a delinquent and then a criminal way of life.

What happens to **waived juveniles?** To find out, go to www.colorado.edu/cspv/publications/factsheets/cspv/FS-008.html. For an up-to-date list of web links, go to http://cj.wadsworth.com/siegel_jd9e.

experimentation is needed. Probation continues to be the single most significant intermediate sanction available to the juvenile court system. We believe that the cost and effectiveness of probation will underpin its usefulness in the coming years. In the future, look for probation caseloads to increase.

Community vs. Institutional Treatment for Juveniles There exists much debate about the effectiveness of community versus institutional treatment. Considerable research shows that warehousing juveniles without proper treatment does little to prevent future delinquent activities. The most effective secure corrections programs are those that provide individual services for a small number of participants.[8] Evaluations of community treatment provide evidence of a number of successful ways to prevent delinquency without jeopardizing the safety of community residents.

There is also a long-standing debate about the effectiveness of correctional treatments compared with other delinquency prevention measures. In their assessment of the full range of interventions to prevent serious and violent juvenile offending, Rolf Loeber and David Farrington found that it is never too early and never too late to make a difference.[9] Though some critics believe that juveniles are being coddled, in the future it is likely that innovative treatment methods will be applied continually within the juvenile justice system.

Restorative Justice Programs Restorative community juvenile justice is a new designation that refers to a preference for neighborhood-based, more accessible, and less formal juvenile services. The restorative justice idea focuses on the relationships among the victim, the community, and the offender. For the victim, restorative justice offers the hope of restitution or other forms of reparation, information about the case, support for healing, the opportunity to be heard, and input into the case, as well as expanded opportunities for involvement and influence. For the community, there is the promise of reduced fear and safer neighborhoods, a more accessible justice process, and accountability, as well as the obligation for involvement and participation in sanctioning crime, supporting victim restoration, reintegrating offenders, and crime prevention and control. For the offender, restorative justice requires accountability in the form of obligations to repair the harm to individual victims and victimized communities, and the opportunity to develop new competencies, social skills, and the capacity to avoid future crime. We believe that the restorative justice movement is in its infancy and will blossom and expand in years to come.

The Deinstitutionalization Movement Deinstitutionalization has become an important goal of the juvenile justice system. The Office of Juvenile Justice and Delinquency Prevention has provided funds to encourage this process. In the early 1980s, the deinstitutionalization movement seemed to be partially successful. Admissions to public juvenile correctional facilities declined in the late 1970s and early 1980s. In addition, the number of status offenders being held within the juvenile justice system was reduced. However, the number of institutionalized children in the 1990s and the early 2000s has increased, and the deinstitutionalization movement has failed to meet all of its optimistic goals. Nonetheless, the majority of states have achieved compliance with the DSO mandate (Deinstitutionalizing Status Offenders). Because juvenile crime is a high priority, the challenge to the states will be to retain a focus on prevention despite societal pressures for more punitive approaches. If that can be achieved, deinstitutionalization will remain a central theme in the juvenile justice system.

Incarceration Rates The number of incarcerated youths remains high. While the juvenile institutional population appears to have stabilized in recent years, there are slightly less than 109,000 youths in some type of correctional institution. The juvenile courts seem to be using the most severe of the statutory dispositions—that is, commitment to the juvenile institution—rather than the "least restrictive statutory alternative." There is also wide variation in juvenile custody rates across the nation. The District of Columbia has the highest juvenile incarceration rate at over 700 per 100,000 juveniles, which is almost twice the national average.

Incarceration Rates for Minority Youths A disproportionate number of minority youths are incarcerated in youth facilities. The difference is greatest for black youths, with the incarceration rate being almost five times greater than that for whites. Of equal importance, minorities are more likely to be placed in secure public facilities rather than in open private facilities that might provide more costly and effective treatment. The OJJDP is committed to ensuring that the country address situations where there is disproportionate confinement of minority offenders in the nation's juvenile justice system. In the future, we expect that this initiative will result in a more fair and balanced juvenile justice system.

Boot Camps Juvenile boot camps don't work. Correctional boot camps, which combine get-tough elements of adult programs with education, substance abuse treatment, and social skills training, are used to shock the offender into going straight. Systematic reviews and meta-analyses of the research evidence show that juvenile boot camps fail to reduce future offending. Despite their poor results, many states continue to use boot camps as a correctional option for juvenile offenders. However, we believe that negative reviews may doom the boot camp movement.

The Legal Right to Treatment for Juveniles The future of the legal right to treatment for juveniles remains uncertain. The appellate courts have established minimum standards of care and treatment on a case-by-case basis, but it does not appear that the courts can be persuaded today to expand this constitutional theory to mandate that incarcerated children receive adequate treatment. Eventually, this issue must be clarified by the Supreme Court. Reforms in state juvenile institutions often result from class-action lawsuits filed on behalf of incarcerated youth.

TO QUIZ YOURSELF ON THIS MATERIAL, go to the Juvenile Delinquency 9e website.

CRISIS IN THE U.S. JUVENILE JUSTICE SYSTEM

A serious crisis exists in the U.S. juvenile justice system. How to cope with the needs of large numbers of children in trouble remains one of the most controversial and frustrating issues in our society. The magnitude of the problem is such that around 2 million youths are arrested each year; over 1.6 million delinquency dispositions and 150,000 status offense cases are heard in court. Today, the system and the process seem more concerned with crime control and more willing to ignore the rehabilitative ideal. Perhaps the answer lies outside the courtroom in the form of greater job opportunities, improved family relationships, and more effective education. Much needs to be done in delinquency prevention. One fact is also certain: According to many experts, the problem of violent juvenile crime is a national crisis. While the good news is that the juvenile crime rate declined in recent years, violence by juveniles is still too prevalent and remains an issue of great concern. Developing programs to address juvenile violence seems to overshadow all other juvenile justice objectives.

Federal Funding Federal funding for juvenile delinquency is essential to improving state practices and programs. The Juvenile Justice and Delinquency Prevention Act of 1974 has had a tremendous impact on America's juvenile justice system. Its mandates to deinstitutionalize status offenders and remove juveniles from adult jails have spurred change for over two decades. The survival of many state programs will likely depend on this federal legislation. Because the act has contributed to a wide range of improvements, Congress will most likely approve future financial incentives.

Recommendations Today, the 100-year-old juvenile justice system and court are under attack more than ever before. Yet the system has weathered criticism for failing to control and rehabilitate juveniles. It is a unique American institution duplicated in many other countries as being the best model for handling juveniles who commit crime. The major recommendations of such important organizations as the National Council of Juvenile Court Judges, the American Bar Association, and the Office of

Juvenile Justice and Delinquency Prevention for the new century are (1) the court should be a leader for juvenile justice in the community; (2) people (judges, attorneys, and probation officers) are the key to the health of the juvenile justice system; (3) public safety and rehabilitation are the goals of the juvenile justice system; (4) juvenile court workloads are shaped today and in the future by the increase of substance abuse cases that must be resolved; and (5) the greatest future needs of the juvenile court in particular are resources and funding for more services, more staff, and more treatment facilities.

TO QUIZ YOURSELF ON THIS MATERIAL, go to the Juvenile Delinquency 9e website.

JUVENILE JUSTICE ABROAD

Juvenile delinquency is not just a problem in the United States; it poses a serious problem to all regions of the world. Many nations are experiencing an upsurge in juvenile problem behavior, including gang violence, prostitution, and drug abuse. Although each nation is quite different, all share an explosive mix of racial tension, poverty, envy, drug abuse, broken families, unemployment, and alienation. Some of the areas hardest hit have been undergoing rapid social and economic change—the fall of communism, the end of the Cold War, the effects of the global economy, an influx of multinational immigration—as they move toward increased economic integration, privatization, and diminished social services.

Standard Minimum Rules for the Administration of Juvenile Justice
Developed in 1985 by the United Nations to encourage countries to develop juvenile justice systems and improve the administration of juvenile justice.

Many countries in the world have formal juvenile justice systems, but many do not. The United Nations' **Standard Minimum Rules for the Administration of Juvenile Justice** were initiated in 1985 to encourage more countries around the world to develop juvenile justice systems and improve the administration of juvenile justice. Despite some differences, all industrialized nations have separate justice systems for juvenile and adult offenders.

In recent years, many developed countries have taken measures to get tough on juvenile offending. In some cases, this is being done because of a real increase in delinquency, particularly violence. In other cases, this is being done because of a perceived increase in delinquency coupled with a political response to a "punitive public" (at least for violent juvenile offenders). Although more punitive juvenile justice systems seem to be the future for many countries, these countries are also making concerted efforts to reserve punitive sanctions for only the most serious and violent juvenile offenders and to provide more effective treatment and aftercare services.[10]

Summary

- The future of the statutory concept of juvenile delinquency is undergoing change, and some experts are calling for it to be eliminated or merged with adult criminality.

- The future of the status offender is in doubt. Repeat offenders may be considered delinquents.

- Delinquency theory is undergoing change. More complex developmental theories seem the wave of the future.

- Gender differences in delinquency may be evaporating as the gap in gender roles narrows.

- Delinquency prevention is becoming more cost effective. Prevention programs are being designed to use technology, technical assistance, strategic planning, and tight organization to make the most out of every dollar.

- Juvenile justice is incorporating new innovations such as specialized courts.

- Policing strategies are making a difference in reducing juvenile crime. One of the most successful approaches has involved the police working closely with other juvenile justice agencies and the community.

- There are pressing problems facing the juvenile court process, such as the use of detention and waiver. In the future, more kids may be waived to adult court.

- Restorative justice is one of the more important innovations in correctional treatment and is viewed as a long-term solution to reduce juvenile recidivism rates and limit institutionalization.

- Industrialized countries are now considering more punitive juvenile justice systems.

Key Terms

neuropsychology, p. 528
strategic planning, p. 531
criminalization, p. 535

Standard Minimum Rules for the
Administration of Juvenile Justice,
p. 538

Questions for Discussion

1. With declining federal resources for after-school and other prevention programs for at-risk teens, can we expect a rise in juvenile delinquency rates in the years ahead? Or are there other factors that may keep delinquency rates in check?

2. What does the future hold for juvenile correctional treatment? Many experts argue that treatment is more rhetoric than reality and more closely resembles punishment for adults. Is this a good thing or do we need to uphold the core principles of juvenile treatment?

3. How will the emerging role of technology influence delinquency rates? Are kids more likely to get involved in Internet crime because they possess technical skills that are lacking in adults?

4. Should the status offense concept be abolished? Have we moved past the time when a child should be punished for behaviors allowed for adults?

Viewpoint

The governor of your state has asked you to come up with a report on future trends in juvenile delinquency and what the government's response should be to this ongoing social problem. She wants you to list five significant trends that may occur over the next five years. What are your predictions for the future and what would you do to combat any potential problem areas in your assessment?

Doing Research on the Web

Before you answer, read this material on the future of children (sites accessed on October 4, 2004)

www.futureofchildren.org

www.globalchange.com/books/rpl6b.htm

www.packard.org/index.cgi?page=cfc

Notes

1. U.S. Census Bureau, "Current Population Survey (CPS)," *2003 Annual Social & Economic Supplement (ASEC), 2003.* http://www.census.gov/hhes/poverty/poverty02/pov02hi.html.

2. Marvin Wolfgang, Robert Figlio, and Thorsten Sellin, *Delinquency in a Birth Cohort* (Chicago: University of Chicago Press, 1972).

3. Alan Lizotte, Terence Thornberry, Marvin Krohn, Deborah Chard-Wierschem, and David McDowall, "Neighborhood Context and Delinquency: A Longitudinal Analysis," in H. J. Kerner and E. Weitekamp, eds., *Cross-National Longitudinal Research on Human Development and Criminal Behavior* (Dordrecht, The Netherlands: Kluwer Academic Publishers, 1993), pp. 11–15.

4. Jill F. DeVoe et al., *Indicators of School Crime and Safety: 2004* (Washington, DC: U.S. Departments of Education and Justice, 2004), NCES 2005-002.

5. Brandon C. Welsh and David P. Farrington, "Monetary Costs and Benefits of Crime Prevention Programs," in Michael Tonry, ed., *Crime and Justice: A Review of Research,* volume 27 (Chicago: University of Chicago Press, 2000); Brandon C. Welsh, David P. Farrington, and Lawrence W. Sherman, eds., *Costs and Benefits of Preventing Crime* (Boulder, CO: Westview Press, 2001).

6. Fox Butterfield, "Proposed White House Budget Cuts Imperil a Lifeline for Troubled Oregon Teenagers," *New York Times,* March 9, 2003, p. 20; Jef-

frey A. Butts, "Encouraging Findings from the OJJDP Evaluation," *In Session: Newsletter of the National Youth Court Center* 2(3):1, 7 (Summer 2002).

7. David Weisburd and John E. Eck, "What Can Police Do to Reduce Crime, Disorder, and Fear?" *Annals of the American Academy of Political and Social Science* 593:42–65 (2004); Wesley G. Skogan and Kathleen Frydl, eds., *Fairness and Effectiveness in Policing: The Evidence.* Committee to Review Research on Police Policy and Practices (Washington, DC: National Academy Press, 2004).

8. Peter W. Greenwood, "Juvenile Crime and Juvenile Justice," in James Q. Wilson and Joan Petersilia, eds., *Crime: Public Policies for Crime Control* (Oakland, CA: Institute for Contemporary Studies, 2002), pp. 90–91.

9. Rolf Loeber and David P. Farrington, "Never Too Early, Never Too Late: Risk Factors and Successful Interventions for Serious and Violent Juvenile Offenders," *Studies on Crime and Crime Prevention* 7:7–30 (1998).

10. Michael Tonry and Anthony N. Doob, eds., *Youth Crime and Youth Justice: Comparative and Cross-National Perspectives. Crime and Justice: A Review of Research,* volume 31 (Chicago: University of Chicago Press, 2004).

Appendix

Excerpts from the U.S. Constitution

Amendment I (1791)

Congress shall make no law respecting an establishment of religion, or prohibiting the free exercise thereof; or abridging the freedom of speech, or of the press; or the right of the people peaceably to assemble, and to petition the government for a redress of grievances.

Amendment II (1791)

A well regulated militia, being necessary to the security of a free state, the right of the people to keep and bear arms, shall not be infringed.

Amendment III (1791)

No soldier shall, in time of peace, be quartered in any house, without the consent of the owner, nor in time of war, but in a manner to be prescribed by law.

Amendment IV (1791)

The right of the people to be secure in their persons, houses, papers, and effects, against unreasonable searches and seizures, shall not be violated, and no warrants shall issue, but upon probable cause, supported by oath or affirmation, and particularly describing the place to be searched, and the persons or things to be seized.

Amendment V (1791)

No person shall be held to answer for a capital, or otherwise infamous, crime unless on a presentment or indictment of a grand jury, except in cases arising in the land or naval forces, or in the militia, when in actual service in time of war or public danger; nor shall any person be subject for the same offense to be twice put in jeopardy of life or limb; nor shall be compelled in any criminal case to be a witness against himself, nor be deprived of life, liberty, or property; without due process of law; nor shall private property be taken for public use without just compensation.

Amendment VI (1791)

In all criminal prosecutions, the accused shall enjoy the right to a speedy and public trial, by an impartial jury of the state and district wherein the crime shall have been committed, which district shall have been previously ascertained by law, and to be informed of the nature and cause of the accusation; to be confronted with the witnesses against him; to have compulsory process for obtaining witnesses in his favor, and to have the assistance of counsel for his defense.

Amendment VII (1791)

In suits at common law, where the value in controversy shall exceed twenty dollars, the right of trial by jury shall be preserved, and no fact tried by a jury shall be otherwise reexamined in any court of the United States, than according to the rules of common law.

Amendment VIII (1791)

Excessive bail shall not be required, nor excessive fines imposed, nor cruel and unusual punishment inflicted.

Amendment IX (1791)

The enumeration in the Constitution of certain rights shall not be construed to deny or disparage others retained by the people.

Amendment X (1791)

The powers not delegated to the United States by the Constitution, nor prohibited by it to the states, are reserved to the states respectively, or to the people.

Amendment XIV (1868)

Section I. All persons born or naturalized in the United States, and subject to the jurisdiction thereof, are citizens of the United States and of the state wherein they reside. No state shall make or enforce any laws which abridge the privilege or immunities of citizens of the United States; nor shall any state deprive any person of life, liberty, or property, without due process of law; nor deny to any person within its jurisdiction the equal protection of the laws.

Glossary

abandonment Parents physically leave their children with the intention of completely severing the parent-child relationship.

academic achievement Being successful in a school environment.

active speech Expressing an opinion by speaking or writing; freedom of speech is a protected right under the First Amendment to the U.S. Constitution.

addict A person with an overpowering physical or psychological need to continue taking a particular substance or drug.

addiction-prone personality A personality that has a compulsion for mood-altering drugs, believed by some to be the cause of substance abuse.

adjudicatory hearing The fact-finding process wherein the juvenile court determines whether there is sufficient evidence to sustain the allegations in a petition.

adolescent-limited Offender who follows the most common delinquent trajectory, in which antisocial behavior peaks in adolescence and then diminishes.

advisement hearing A preliminary protective or temporary custody hearing in which the court will review the facts and determine whether removal of the child is justified and notify parents of the charges against them.

aftercare Transitional assistance to juveniles, equivalent to adult parole, to help youths adjust to community life.

age of consent Age at which youths are legally adults and may be independent of parental control. When an adolescent reaches the age of consent, he or she may engage in sexual behaviors prohibited to youths.

age of onset Age at which youths begin their delinquent careers; early onset is believed to be linked with chronic offending patterns.

aging-out process (also known as **desistance** or **spontaneous remission**) The tendency for youths to reduce the frequency of their offending behavior as they age; aging-out is thought to occur among all groups of offenders.

alcohol Fermented or distilled liquids containing ethanol, an intoxicating substance.

alienation Feelings of separation and distance from mainstream society.

anabolic steroids Drugs used by athletes and bodybuilders to gain muscle bulk and strength.

androgen The principal male sex hormone.

anesthetic drugs Central nervous system depressants.

anomie Normlessness produced by rapidly shifting moral values; according to Merton, anomie occurs when personal goals cannot be achieved using available means.

appellate process Allows the juvenile an opportunity to have the case brought before a reviewing court after it has been heard in juvenile or family court.

arousal theorists Delinquency experts who believe that aggression is a function of the level of an individual's need for stimulation or arousal from the environment. Those who require more stimulation may act in an aggressive manner to meet their needs.

arrest Taking a person into the custody of the law to restrain the accused until he or she can be held accountable for the offense in court proceedings.

at-risk youths Young people who are extremely vulnerable to the negative consequences of school failure, substance abuse, and early sexuality.

authority conflict pathway Pathway to delinquent deviance that begins at an early age with stubborn behavior and leads to defiance and then to authority avoidance.

bail Amount of money that must be paid as a condition of pretrial release to ensure that the accused will return for subsequent proceedings. Bail is normally set by the judge at the initial appearance, and if unable to make bail, the accused is detained in jail.

balanced probation Programs that integrate community protection, accountability of the juvenile offender, competency, and individualized attention to the juvenile offender; based on the principle that juvenile offenders must accept responsibility for their behavior.

balancing-of-the-interest approach Efforts of the courts to balance the parents' natural right to raise a child with the child's right to grow into adulthood free from physical abuse or emotional harm.

barrio A Latino term meaning neighborhood.

battered child syndrome Nonaccidental physical injury of children by their parents or guardians.

behavior modification A technique for shaping desired behaviors through a system of rewards and punishments.

behaviorism Branch of psychology concerned with the study of observable behavior rather than unconscious processes; focuses on particular stimuli and responses to them.

best interests of the child A philosophical viewpoint that encourages the state to take control of wayward children and provide care, custody, and treatment to remedy delinquent behavior.

bifurcated process The procedure of separating adjudicatory and dispositionary hearings so different levels of evidence can be heard at each.

bindover *See* **waiver.**

biosocial theory The view that both thought and behavior have biological and social bases.

blended families Nuclear families that are the product of divorce and remarriage; blending one parent from each of two families and their combined children into one family unit.

boot camps Juvenile programs that combine get-tough elements from adult programs with education, substance abuse treatment, and social skills training.

broken home Home in which one or both parents are absent due to divorce or separation; children in such an environment may be prone to antisocial behavior.

callous-unemotional traits (CU) An affective disorder described by a lack of remorse or shame, poor judgment, failure to learn by experience, and chronic lying.

capital punishment Use of the death penalty to punish offenders.

chancery courts Court proceedings created in fifteenth-century England to oversee the lives of high-born minors who were orphaned or otherwise could not care for themselves.

child abuse Any physical, emotional, or sexual trauma to a child, including neglecting to give proper care and attention, for which no reasonable explanation can be found.

child savers Nineteenth-century reformers who developed programs for troubled youth and influenced legislation creating the juvenile justice system; today some critics view them as being more concerned with control of the poor than with their welfare.

Children's Aid Society Child saving organization that took children from the streets of large cities and placed them with farm families on the prairie.

chivalry hypothesis (also known as **paternalism hypothesis**) View that low female crime and delinquency rates are a reflection of the leniency with which police treat female offenders.

choice theory Holds that youths will engage in delinquent and criminal behavior after weighing the consequences and benefits of their actions; delinquent behavior is a rational choice made by a motivated offender who perceives that the chances of gain outweigh any possible punishment or loss.

cholo A member of the Hispanic subculture of marginalized, antisocial youth.

choloization Becoming acculturated in the American way of life, but clinging to the values of their land of origin.

chronic delinquent *See* **chronic delinquent offender.**

chronic delinquent offender (also known as **chronic juvenile offenders, chronic delinquents,** or **chronic recidivists**) Youths who have been arrested four or more times during their minority and perpetuate a striking majority of serious criminal acts. This small group, known as the "chronic 6 percent," is believed to engage in a significant portion of all delinquent behavior; these youths do not age out of crime but continue their criminal behavior into adulthood.

chronic juvenile offender *See* **chronic delinquent offender.**

chronic recidivist *See* **chronic delinquent offender.**

classical criminology Holds that decisions to violate the law are weighed against possible punishments, and to deter crime the pain of punishment must outweigh the benefit of illegal gain; led to graduated punishments based on seriousness of the crime (let the punishment fit the crime).

cliques Small groups of friends who share intimate knowledge and confidences.

club drugs Synthetic substances (such as ecstasy and Rohypnol) commonly used at nightclubs, bars, and raves.

cocaine A powerful natural stimulant derived from the coca plant.

cognitive theory The branch of psychology that studies the perception of reality and the mental processes required to understand the world we live in.

collective efficacy The ability of communities to regulate the behavior of their residents through the influence of community institutions, such as the family and school. Residents in these communities share mutual trust and a willingness to intervene in the supervision of children and the maintenance of public order.

college boy Strives to conform to middle-class values and to move up the social ladder, but is ill-equipped to succeed and fated to become frustrated and disappointed.

commitment to conformity The strength of the ties of youths to conventional social institutions predicts their likely behavior; those with poor or negative ties are more likely to indulge in delinquent acts.

community policing Police strategy that emphasizes reducing fear, organizing the community, and maintaining order rather than fighting crime.

community service restitution The juvenile offender is required to assist some worthwhile community organization for a period of time.

community services Local delinquency prevention services such as recreational programs and drug and alcohol information programs in schools that help meet the community's needs for youths.

community treatment Using nonsecure and noninstitutional residences, counseling services, victim restitution programs, and other community services to treat juveniles in their own communities.

complaint Report made by the police or some other agency to the court that initiates the intake process.

conditions of probation The rules and regulations mandating that a juvenile on probation behave in a particular way.

confidentiality Restriction of information in juvenile court proceedings in the interest of protecting the privacy of the juvenile.

contagion effect The negative, crime-promoting influence of deviant siblings on their brothers and sisters.

containment theory Asserts that a strong self-image insulates youths from the pressure to engage in illegal acts; youths with poor self-concepts and low self-esteem are more likely to engage in crime.

continuity of crime The idea that chronic juvenile offenders are likely to continue violating the law as adults.

control group The comparison group of subjects that does not receive the program.

control theory Posits that delinquency results from a weakened commitment to the major social institutions (family, peers, and school); lack of such commitment allows youths to exercise antisocial behavioral choices.

controversial status youth Aggressive kids who are either greatly liked or intensely disliked by their peers.

co-offending Committing criminal acts in groups.

corner boy Not a delinquent but may engage in marginal behavior; eventually will marry a local girl and obtain a menial job with few prospects for advancement or success.

cortisol A hormone secreted by the adrenal glands in response to any kind of physical or psychological stress.

cottage system Housing juveniles in a compound containing a series of small cottages, each of which accommodates 20 to 40 children and is run by a set of cottage parents who create a homelike atmosphere.

Court Appointed Special Advocates (CASA) Volunteers appointed by the court to investigate the needs of the child and help officers of the court ensure a safe placement for the child.

covert pathway Pathway to a delinquent career that begins with minor underhanded behavior, leads to property damage, and eventually escalates to more serious forms of theft and fraud.

crack A highly addictive crystalline form of cocaine containing remnants of hydrochloride and sodium bicarbonate, which emits a crackling sound when smoked.

crack down A law enforcement operation that is designed to reduce or eliminate a particular criminal activity through the application of aggressive police tactics, typically involving a larger than usual contingent of police officers.

criminal atavism The idea that delinquents manifest physical anomalies that make them biologically and physiologically similar to our primitive ancestors, savage throwbacks to an earlier stage of human evolution.

criminalization The process during which a person becomes enmeshed in first a delinquent and then a criminal way of life.

critical criminologists Analysts who review historical and current developments in law and order to expose the interests of the power elite and ruling classes.

critical feminists (also known as **Marxist feminists**) Hold that gender inequality stems from the unequal power of men and women and the subsequent exploitation of women by men; the cause of female delinquency originates with the onset of male supremacy and the efforts of males to control females' sexuality.

crowds Loosely organized groups who share interests and activities.

Crown Court In England, the criminal court that deals with adult offenders or juveniles who have been transferred from youth court.

Crown Prosecution Service The national agency in England that is in charge of all criminal prosecutions of juveniles and adults.

cultural deviance theory Links delinquent acts to the formation of independent subcultures with a unique set of values that clash with the mainstream culture.

cultural transmission Cultural norms and values that are passed down from one generation to the next.

culture conflict When the values of a subculture clash with those of the dominant culture.

culture of poverty View that lower-class people form a separate culture with their own values and norms, which are sometimes in conflict with conventional society.

custodial interrogation Questions posed by the police to a suspect held in custody in the prejudicial stage of the juvenile justice process; juveniles have the same rights against self-incrimination as adults do when being questioned.

D.A.R.E. (Drug Abuse Resistance Education) An elementary school program designed to prevent teenage drug abuse by giving youths the skills they need to resist peer pressure to experiment with drugs.

dark figures of crime Incidents of crime and delinquency that go undetected by police.

death squads Common to South America, organized government or criminal groups that selectively kill members of opposing groups and incite fear in those groups and among their supporters.

degradation ceremony Going to court, being scolded by a judge, or being found delinquent after a trial are examples of public ceremonies that can transform youthful offenders by degrading their self-image.

deinstitutionalization Removing juveniles from adult jails and placing them in community-based programs to avoid the stigma attached to these facilities.

delinquency control (also known as **delinquency repression**) Involves any justice program or policy designed to prevent the occurrence of a future delinquent act.

delinquency prevention Involves any nonjustice program or policy designed to prevent the occurrence of a future delinquent act.

delinquency repression *See* **delinquency control.**

delinquent Juvenile who has been adjudicated by a judicial officer of a juvenile court as having committed a delinquent act.

delinquent boy Adopts a set of norms and values in direct opposition to middle-class society and resists control efforts by authority figures.

designer drugs Lab-made drugs designed to avoid existing drug laws.

detached street workers Social workers who go out into the community and establish close relationships with juvenile gangs with the goal of modifying gang behavior to conform to conventional behaviors and to help gang members get jobs and educational opportunities.

detention Temporary care of a child alleged to be delinquent who requires secure custody in physically restricting facilities pending court disposition or execution of a court order.

detention hearing A hearing by a judicial officer of a juvenile court to determine whether a juvenile is to be detained or released while juvenile proceedings are pending in the case.

determinate sentence Specifies a fixed term of detention that must be served.

developed countries Recognized by the United Nations as the richest countries in the world.

developing countries Recognized by the U.N. as countries that are showing signs of improved economic growth and are making the transition from low income to high income.

developmental process At different stages of the life course a variety of factors can influence behavior; factors influential at one stage of life may not be significant at a later stage.

developmental theory The view that criminality is a dynamic process, influenced by social experiences as well as individual characteristics.

developmental view The view that factors present at birth and events that unfold over a person's lifetime influence behavior; developmental theory focuses on the onset, escalation, desistance, and amplification of delinquent behaviors.

differential association theory Asserts that criminal behavior is learned primarily within interpersonal groups and that youths will become delinquent if definitions they have learned favorable to violating the law exceed definitions favorable to obeying the law within that group.

differential reinforcement theory A refinement of differential association theory that asserts that behavior is shaped by the reactions of others to that behavior; youths who receive more rewards than punishments for conforming behavior will be the most likely to remain nondelinquent.

disaggregated Analyzing the relationship between two or more independent variables (such as murder convictions and death sentence) while controlling for the influence of a dependent variable (such as race).

discretion Use of personal decision making and choice in carrying out operations in the criminal justice system, such as deciding whether to make an arrest or when to accept a plea bargain.

disorganized neighborhood Inner-city areas of extreme poverty where the critical social control mechanisms have broken down.

disposition For juvenile offenders, the equivalent of sentencing for adult offenders; however, juvenile dispositions should be more rehabilitative than retributive.

disposition hearing The social service agency presents its case plan and recommendations for care of the child and treatment of the parents, including incarceration and counseling or other treatments.

diversion Official halting or suspending of a formal criminal or juvenile justice proceeding at any legally prescribed processing point after a recorded justice system entry, and referral of that person to a treatment or care program or a recommendation that the person be released.

dramatization of evil The process of social typing that transforms an offender's identity from a doer of evil to an evil person.

drift Idea that youths move in and out of delinquency and that their lifestyles can embrace both conventional and deviant values.

dropouts Youths who leave school before completing their required program of education.

drug courts Courts whose focus is providing treatment for youths accused of drug-related acts.

due process Basic constitutional principle based on the concept of the primacy of the individual and the complementary concept of limitation on governmental power; safeguards the individual from unfair state procedures in judicial or administrative proceedings. Due-process rights have been extended to juvenile trials.

early onset The outbreak of deviant or delinquent behavior in preadolescence, which is generally viewed as a precursor of chronic offending in adolescence and which generally continues into adulthood.

egalitarian families Husband and wife share power at home; daughters gain a kind of freedom similar to that of sons, and their law-violating behaviors mirror those of their brothers.

ego identity According to Erik Erikson, ego identity is formed when a person develops a firm sense of who he is and what he stands for.

electronic monitoring Active monitoring systems consist of a radio transmitter worn by the offender that sends a continuous signal to the probation department computer, alerting officials if the offender leaves his or her place of confinement. Passive systems employ computer-generated random phone calls that must be responded to in a certain period of time from a particular phone or other device.

equipotentiality View that all people are equal at birth and are thereafter influenced by their environment.

evolutionary theory Explaining the existence of aggression and violent behavior as positive adaptive behaviors in human evolution; these traits allowed their bearers to reproduce disproportionately, which has had an effect on the human gene pool.

excluded offenses Offenses, some minor and others very serious, that are automatically excluded from juvenile court.

experimental group The group of subjects that receives the program.

extravert A person who behaves impulsively and doesn't have the ability to examine motives and behavior.

familicide Mass murders in which a spouse and one or more children are slain.

family group homes A combination of foster care and a group home in which a juvenile is placed in a private group home run by a single family rather than by professional staff.

Federal Bureau of Investigation (FBI) Arm of the U.S. Department of Justice that investigates violations of federal law, gathers crime statistics, runs a comprehensive crime laboratory, and helps train local law enforcement officers.

feminist theory Asserts that the patriarchal social system oppresses women, creating gender bias and encouraging violence against women.

final order Order that ends litigation between two parties by determining all their rights and disposing of all the issues.

focal concerns The value orientation of lower-class culture that is characterized by a need for excitement, trouble, smartness, fate, and personal autonomy.

foot patrol Police patrolling an area by walking around the community rather than driving about in patrol cars.

foster care programs Juveniles who are orphans or whose parents cannot care for them are placed with families who provide the attention, guidance, and care they did not receive at home.

free will View that youths are in charge of their own destinies and are free to make personal behavior choices unencumbered by environmental factors.

freebase Purified cocaine crystals that are crushed and smoked to provide a more powerful high than cocaine.

gangs Groups of youths who collectively engage in delinquent behaviors.

gateway drug A substance that leads to use of more serious drugs; alcohol use has long been thought to lead to more serious drug abuse.

gender identity The gender characteristics individuals identify in their own behaviors; members of both sexes who identify with "masculine" traits are more likely to engage in delinquent acts.

gender-schema theory Asserts that our culture polarizes males and females, forcing them into exclusive gender roles of "feminine" or "masculine"; these gender scripts provide the basis for deviant behaviors.

general deterrence Crime control policies that depend on the fear of criminal penalties, such as long prison sentences for violent crimes; the aim is to convince law violators that the pain outweighs the benefit of criminal activity.

General Theory of Crime (GTC) A developmental theory that modifies social control theory by integrating concepts from biosocial, psychological, routine activities, and rational choice theories.

gentrified The process of transforming a lower-class area into a middle-class enclave through property rehabilitation.

graffiti Inscriptions or drawings made on a wall or structure and used by delinquents for gang messages and turf definition.

group autonomy Maintaining subcultural values and attitudes that reinforce the independence of the group and separate it from other cultural groups.

group homes Nonsecured, structured residences that provide counseling, education, job training, and family living.

group therapy Counseling several individuals together in a group session; individuals can obtain support from other group members as they work through similar problems.

guardian *ad litem* A court-appointed attorney who protects the interests of the child in cases involving the child's welfare.

guided group interaction (GGI) Through group interactions a delinquent can acknowledge and solve personal problems with support from other group members.

hallucinogens Natural or synthetic substances that produce vivid distortions of the senses without greatly disturbing consciousness.

harm reduction Efforts to minimize the harmful effects caused by drug use.

hashish A concentrated form of cannabis made from unadulterated resin from the female cannabis plant.

hearsay Out-of-court statements made by one person and recounted in court by another; such statements are generally not allowed as evidence except in child abuse cases wherein a child's statements to social workers, teachers, or police may be admissible.

heroin A narcotic made from opium and then cut with sugar or some other neutral substance until it is only 1 to 4 percent pure.

hot spot A particular location or address that is the site of repeated and frequent criminal activity.

house arrest An offender is required to stay at home during specific periods of time; monitoring is done by random phone calls and visits or by electronic devices.

House of Refuge A care facility developed by the child savers to protect potential criminal youths by taking them off the street and providing a family-like environment.

identity crisis Psychological state, identified by Erikson, in which youth face inner turmoil and uncertainty about life roles.

Illinois Juvenile Court Act of 1899 A major event in the history of juvenile justice, this act served as a model for other states, establishing the special status of juveniles and the emphasis on helping to treat rather than punish young offenders.

in loco parentis In the place of the parent; rights given to schools that allow them to assume parental duties in disciplining students.

indeterminate sentence Does not specify the length of time the juvenile must be held; rather, correctional authorities decide when the juvenile is ready to return to society.

index crimes *See* **Part 1 offenses.**

individual counseling Counselors help juveniles understand and solve their current adjustment problems.

individualized treatment model Each sentence must be tailored to the individual needs of the child.

inhalants Volatile liquids that give off a vapor, which is inhaled, producing short-term excitement and euphoria followed by a period of disorientation.

inheritance school An early form of biological theory that held that deviant behavior was inherited and therefore ran in families, being passed on from generation to generation.

intake Process during which a juvenile referral is received and a decision is made to file a petition in juvenile court to release the juvenile, to place the juvenile under supervision, or to refer the juvenile elsewhere.

Intensive Aftercare Program (IAP) A balanced, highly structured, comprehensive continuum of intervention for serious and violent juvenile offenders returning to the community.

interactional theory A developmental theory that attributes delinquent trajectories to mutual reinforcement between delinquents and significant others over the life course—family in early adolescence, school and friends in mid-adolescence, and social peers and one's own nuclear family in adulthood.

international crime Crime that is punishable under international law.

interstitial group Delinquent group that fills a crack in the social fabric and maintains standard group practices.

intrafamily conflict An environment of discord and conflict within the family; children who grow up in dysfunctional homes often exhibit delinquent behaviors, having learned at a young age that aggression pays off.

judicial waiver When the juvenile court waives its jurisdiction over a juvenile and transfers the case to adult criminal court.

jurisdiction Every kind of judicial action; the authority of courts and judicial officers to decide cases.

juvenile court Court that has original jurisdiction over persons defined by statute as juveniles and alleged to be delinquents, status offenders, or dependents.

juvenile court judge A judge elected or appointed to preside over juvenile cases and whose decisions can only be reviewed by a judge of a higher court.

juvenile defense attorney Represents children in juvenile court and plays an active role at all stages of the proceedings.

juvenile delinquency Participation in illegal behavior by a minor who falls under a statutory age limit.

juvenile intensive probation supervision (JIPS) A true alternative to incarceration that involves almost daily supervision of the juvenile by the probation officer assigned to the case.

Juvenile Justice and Delinquency Prevention Act of 1974 This act established the OJJDP as an independent agency charged with developing and implementing programs to prevent and reduce juvenile crime.

juvenile justice process Under the paternal (*parens patriae*) philosophy, juvenile justice procedures are informal and non-adversarial, invoked for the juvenile offender rather than against him or her; a petition instead of a complaint is filed; courts make findings of involvement or adjudication of delinquency instead of convictions; and juvenile offenders receive dispositions instead of sentences.

Juvenile Justice Reform Act of 1977 A Washington state statute that created mandatory sentencing for juvenile offenders based on their age, the crime, and their prior history as an offender.

juvenile justice system The segment of the justice system, including law enforcement officers, the courts, and correctional agencies, designed to treat youthful offenders.

juvenile officers Police officers who specialize in dealing with juvenile offenders; they may operate alone or as part of a juvenile police unit within the department.

juvenile probation officer Officer of the court involved in all four stages of the court process—intake, predisposition, postadjudication, and postdisposition—who assists the court and supervises juveniles placed on probation.

juvenile prosecutor Government attorney responsible for representing the interests of the state and bringing the case against the accused juvenile.

klikas Independent cliques contained within Hispanic gangs.

labeling theory Posits that society creates deviance through a system of social control agencies that designate (or label) certain individuals as delinquent, thereby stigmatizing youths and encouraging them to accept this negative personal identity.

latchkey children Children left unsupervised after school by working parents.

latent delinquents Youths whose troubled family life leads them to seek immediate gratification without consideration of right and wrong or the feelings of others.

latent trait A stable feature, characteristic, property, or condition, such as defective intelligence or impulsive personality, that makes some people delinquency-prone over the life course.

law enforcement The primary duty of all police officers to fight crime and keep the peace.

Law Enforcement Assistance Administration (LEAA) Unit in the U.S. Department of Justice established by the Omnibus Crime Control and Safe Streets Act of 1968 to administer grants and provide guidance for crime prevention policy and programs.

learning disability (LD) Neurological dysfunction that prevents an individual from learning to his or her potential.

learning theory Posits that delinquency is learned through close relationships with others; asserts that children are born "good" and learn to be "bad" from others.

least detrimental alternative Choice of a program for the child that will best foster the child's growth and development.

least developed countries Recognized by the U.N. as being the poorest countries in the world and suffering from long-term barriers to economic growth.

least restrictive alternative Choosing a program with the least restrictive or secure setting that will best benefit the child.

left realism Asserts that crime is a function of relative deprivation and that criminals prey on the poor.

legalization of drugs Decriminalizing drug use to reduce the association between drug use and crime.

liberal feminism Asserts that females are less delinquent than males because their social roles provide them with fewer opportunities to commit crimes; as the roles of girls and women become more similar to those of boys and men, so too will their crime patterns.

life-course persister One of the small group of offenders whose delinquent careers continue well into adulthood.

life-course theory Theory that focuses on changes in criminality over the life course; developmental theory.

lifestyle violent juveniles Juveniles who become more violent when exposed to more serious offenders in institutions.

longitudinal studies A research design that entails repeated measures over time; for example, a cohort may be measured at several points over their life course to determine risk factors for chronic offending.

low-visibility decision making Decisions made by public officials in the criminal or juvenile justice system that the public is not in a position to understand, regulate, or criticize.

mandatory sentence Defined by a statutory requirement that states the penalty to be set for all cases of a specific offense.

marijuana The dried leaves of the cannabis plant.

Marxist feminists *See* **critical feminists**.

masculinity hypothesis View that women who commit crimes have biological and psychological traits similar to those of men.

meta-analysis A statistical analysis technique that synthesizes results from prior evaluation studies.

middle-class measuring rods Standards by which teachers and other representatives of state authority evaluate students' behavior; when lower-class youths cannot meet these standards they are subject to failure, which brings on frustration and anger at conventional society.

milieu therapy All aspects of the environment are part of the treatment, and meaningful change, increased growth, and satisfactory adjustment are encouraged; this is often accomplished through peer pressure to conform to the group norms.

minimal brain dysfunction (MBD) Damage to the brain itself that causes antisocial behavior injurious to the individual's lifestyle and social adjustment.

Miranda warning Supreme Court decisions require police officers to inform individuals under arrest of their constitutional rights; warning must also be given when suspicion begins to focus on an individual in the accusatory stage.

Missouri Plan Sets out how juvenile court judges are chosen and specifies that a commission should nominate candidates, an elected official should make the appointment, and the incumbent judge should run uncontested on his or her record in a nonpartisan election, usually every three years.

monetary restitution A requirement that juvenile offenders compensate crime victims for out-of-pocket losses caused by the crime, including property damage, lost wages, and medical expenses.

moral entrepreneurs Interest groups that attempt to control social life by promoting their own personal set of moral values and establishing them as law.

multisystemic therapy (MST) Addresses a variety of family, peer, and psychological problems by focusing on problem-solving and communication skills training.

National Advisory Commission on Criminal Justice Standards and Goals Established in 1973, the commission's report identified major strategies for juvenile justice and delinquency prevention.

National Council of Juvenile and Family Court Judges An organization that sponsors research and continuing legal education to help juvenile court judges master their field of expertise.

natural areas for crime Inner-city areas of extreme poverty where the critical social control mechanisms have broken down.

nature theory Holds that low intelligence is genetically determined and inherited.

near groups Relatively unstructured short-term groups with fluid membership.

need for treatment The criteria on which juvenile sentencing is based. Ideally, juveniles are treated according to their need for treatment and not the seriousness of the delinquent act they committed.

negative affective states Anger, depression, disappointment, fear, and other adverse emotions that derive from strain.

neglect Passive neglect by a parent or guardian, depriving children of food, shelter, health care, and love.

neurological Pertaining to the brain and nervous system structure.

neuropsychology The branch of psychology that involves the study of human behavior as it relates to normal and abnormal functioning of the central nervous system.

neuroticism A personality trait marked by unfounded anxiety, tension, and emotional instability.

neutralization techniques A set of attitudes or beliefs that allow would-be delinquents to negate any moral apprehension they may have about committing crime so that they may freely engage in antisocial behavior without regret.

neutralization theory Holds that youths adhere to conventional values while "drifting" into periods of illegal behavior; for drift to occur, youths must first neutralize conventional legal and moral values.

nonresidential programs Juveniles remain in their own homes but receive counseling, education, employment, diagnostic, and casework services through an intensive support system.

nuclear family A family unit composed of parents and their children; this smaller family structure is subject to great stress due to the intense, close contact between parents and children.

nurture theory Holds that intelligence is partly biological but mostly sociological; negative environmental factors encourage delinquent behavior and depress intelligence scores for many youths.

Office of Juvenile Justice and Delinquency Prevention (OJJDP) Branch of the U.S. Justice Department charged with shaping national juvenile justice policy through disbursement of federal aid and research funds.

official delinquency Delinquent acts that result in arrest by local police. These are included in the FBI's arrest data.

orphan trains The name for trains in which urban youths were sent West by the Children's Aid Society for adoption with local farm couples.

overt pathway Pathway to a delinquent career that begins with minor aggression, leads to physical fighting, and eventually escalates to violent delinquency.

parens patriae Power of the state to act on behalf of the child and provide care and protection equivalent to that of a parent.

parental efficacy The ability of parents to effectively raise their children in a noncoercive fashion.

parole guidelines Recommended length of confinement and kinds of aftercare assistance most effective for a juvenile who committed a specific offense.

Part I offenses (also known as **index crimes**) Offenses including homicide and non-negligent manslaughter, forcible rape, robbery, aggravated assault, burglary, larceny, arson, and motor vehicle theft; recorded by local law enforcement officers, these crimes are tallied quarterly and sent to the FBI for inclusion in the UCR.

Part II offenses All crimes other than Part I offenses; recorded by local law enforcement officers, arrests for these crimes are tallied quarterly and sent to the FBI for inclusion in the UCR.

passive speech A form of expression protected by the First Amendment but not associated with actually speaking words; examples include wearing symbols or protest messages on buttons or signs.

paternalism hypothesis *See* **chivalry hypothesis.**

paternalistic family A family style wherein the father is the final authority on all family matters and exercises complete control over his wife and children.

peacemakers Assert that peace and humanism can reduce crime and offers a new approach to crime control through mediation.

penis envy According to Freud, women are envious of the male sex organ and unconsciously wish that they were men.

persistence The process by which juvenile offenders persist in their delinquent careers rather than aging out of crime.

petition Document filed in juvenile court alleging that a juvenile is a delinquent, a status offender, or a dependent and asking that the court assume jurisdiction over the juvenile.

plea bargaining The exchange of prosecutorial and judicial concessions for a guilty plea by the accused; plea bargaining usually results in a reduced charge or a more lenient sentence.

pledge system Early English system in which neighbors protected each other from thieves and warring groups.

Poor Laws English statutes that allowed the courts to appoint overseers over destitute and neglected children, allowing placement of these children as servants in the homes of the affluent.

positive peer culture (PPC) Counseling program in which peer leaders encourage other group members to modify their behavior, and peers help reinforce acceptable behaviors.

poverty concentration effect According to sociologist William Julius Wilson, the consolidation of poor minority group members in urban areas.

power-control theory Holds that gender differences in the delinquency rate are a function of class differences and economic conditions that influence the structure of family life.

precocious sexuality Sexual experimentation in early adolescence.

predatory crime Violent crimes against people, and crimes in which an offender attempts to steal an object directly from its holder.

predisposition report *See* **social investigation report.**

predispositional investigation An investigation usually carried out by a member of the probationary staff to acquire information about the child that will allow the judge to make a decision in the best interest of the child.

premenstrual syndrome (PMS) A set of symptoms related to hormonal changes just prior to menstruation that may contribute to mood swings in women.

President's Commission on Law Enforcement and the Administration of Justice This 1967 commission suggested that we must provide juveniles with opportunities for success, including jobs and education, and that we must develop effective law enforcement procedures to control hard-core youthful offenders.

prestige crimes Stealing or assaulting someone to gain prestige in the neighborhood; often part of gang initiation rites.

pretrial conference The attorney for the social services agency presents an overview of the case, and a plea bargain or negotiated settlement can be agreed to in a consent decree.

preventive detention Keeping the accused in custody prior to trial because the accused is suspected of being a danger to the community.

primary deviance Deviant acts that do not redefine the self- and public-image of the offender.

primary sociopaths Individuals with an inherited trait that predisposes them to antisocial behavior.

primogeniture During the Middle Ages, the right of first-born sons to inherit lands and titles, leaving their brothers the option of a military or religious career.

probable cause Reasonable ground to believe that an offense was committed and that the accused committed that offense.

probation Nonpunitive, legal disposition for juveniles emphasizing community treatment in which the juvenile is closely supervised by an officer of the court and must adhere to a strict set of rules to avoid incarceration.

problem behavior syndrome (PBS) A cluster of antisocial behaviors that may include family dysfunction, substance abuse, smoking, precocious sexuality and early pregnancy, educational underachievement, suicide attempts, sensation seeking, and unemployment, as well as delinquency.

problem-oriented policing Law enforcement that focuses on addressing the problems underlying incidents of juvenile delinquency rather than the incidents only.

prosecutorial discretion Allowing the prosecutor to determine the jurisdiction by selecting the charge to be filed or by choosing to file the complaint in either juvenile or adult court.

prosocial bonds Socialized attachment to conventional institutions, activities, and beliefs.

protective factor A positive prior factor in an individual's life that decreases the risk of occurrence of a future delinquent act.

pseudomaturity Characteristic of life-course persisters, who tend to engage in early sexuality and drug use.

psychodynamic theory Branch of psychology that holds that the human personality is controlled by unconscious mental processes developed early in childhood.

psychopathic personality (also known as **sociopathic personality**) A person lacking in warmth and affection, exhibiting inappropriate behavior responses, and unable to learn from experience.

psychotherapy Highly structured counseling in which a skilled therapist helps a juvenile solve conflicts and make a more positive adjustment to society.

public defender An attorney who works in a public agency or under private contractual agreement as defense counsel to indigent defendants.

randomized experimental design Considered the "gold standard" of evaluation designs to measure the effect of a program on delinquency or other outcomes. Involves randomly assigning subjects either to receive the program (the experimental group) or not receive it (the control group).

reaction formation Rejecting conventional goals and standards that seem impossible to attain.

reality therapy A form of counseling that emphasizes current behavior and that requires the individual to accept responsibility for all of his or her actions.

reentry The process and experience of returning to society upon release from a custody facility postadjudication.

reflective role-taking A process whereby youths take on antisocial roles assigned to them by others.

reform schools Institutions in which educational and psychological services are used in an effort to improve the conduct of juveniles who are forcibly detained.

relative deprivation Condition that exists when people of wealth and poverty live in close proximity to one another; the relatively deprived are apt to have feelings of anger and hostility, which may produce criminal behavior.

removal *See* **waiver.**

representing Tossing or flashing gang signs in the presence of rivals, often escalating into a verbal or physical confrontation.

residential programs Placement of a juvenile offender in a residential, nonsecure facility such as a group home, foster home, family group home, or rural home where the juvenile can be closely monitored and develop close relationships with staff members.

resource dilution As the number of children in a family increases, the social and economic resources available to raise them are spread thinner and become less effective.

restorative justice Nonpunitive strategies for dealing with juvenile offenders that make the justice system a healing process rather than a punishment process.

retreatists Gangs whose members actively engage in substance abuse.

review hearings Periodic meetings to determine whether the conditions of the case plan for an abused child are being met by the parents or guardians of the child.

right to treatment Philosophy espoused by many courts that juvenile offenders have a statutory right to treatment while under the jurisdiction of the courts.

risk factor A negative prior factor in an individual's life that increases the risk of occurrence of a future delinquent act.

role conflicts Conflicts police officers face that revolve around the requirement to perform their primary duty of law enforcement and a desire to aid in rehabilitating youthful offenders.

role diffusion According to Erik Erikson, role diffusion occurs when youths spread themselves too thin, experience personal uncertainty, and place themselves at the mercy of leaders who promise to give them a sense of identity they cannot develop for themselves.

routine activities theory View that crime is a "normal" function of the routine activities of modern living; offenses can be expected if there is a motivated offender and a suitable target that is not protected by capable guardians.

rural programs Specific recreational and work opportunities provided for juveniles in a rural setting such as a forestry camp, a farm, or a ranch.

school failure Failing to achieve success in school can result in frustration, anger, and reduced self-esteem, which may contribute to delinquent behavior.

search and seizure The U.S. Constitution protects citizens from any search and seizure by police without a lawfully obtained search warrant; such warrants are issued when there is probable cause to believe that an offense has been committed.

secondary deviance Deviant acts that redefine the offender's self- and public image, forming the basis for the youth's self-concept.

secondary prevention (also known as **special prevention**) Psychological counseling, psychotropic medications, and other rehabilitation treatment programs designed to prevent repeat offenses.

secondary sociopaths Individuals who are biologically normal but exhibit antisocial behavior due to negative life experiences.

sedatives Drugs of the barbiturate family that depress the central nervous system into a sleeplike condition.

self-control Ability to control impulsive and often imprudent behaviors that offer immediate short-term gratification.

self-fulfilling prophecy Deviant behavior patterns that are a response to an earlier labeling experience; youths act out these social roles even if they were falsely bestowed.

self-labeling The process by which a person who has been negatively labeled accepts the label as a personal role or identity.

self-reports Questionnaire or survey technique that asks subjects to reveal their own participation in delinquent or criminal acts.

shelter care A place for temporary care of children in physically unrestricting facilities.

situational crime prevention Crime prevention method that relies on reducing the opportunity to commit criminal acts by (1) making them more difficult to perform, (2) reducing their reward, and (3) increasing their risks.

skinhead A member of a white supremacist gang, identified by a shaved skull and Nazi or Ku Klux Klan markings.

social bond Ties a person to the institutions and processes of society; elements of the bond include attachment, commitment, involvement, and belief.

social capital Positive relations with individuals and institutions, as in a successful marriage or a successful career, that support conventional behavior and inhibit deviant behavior.

social conflict theory Asserts that society is in a state of constant internal conflict, and focuses on the role of social and governmental institutions as mechanisms for social control.

social control Ability of social institutions to influence human behavior; the justice system is the primary agency of formal social control.

social development model (SDM) A developmental theory that attributes delinquent behavior patterns to childhood socialization and pro- or antisocial attachments over the life course.

social disorganization Neighborhood or area marked by culture conflict, lack of cohesiveness, a transient population, and insufficient social organizations; these problems are reflected in the problems at schools in these areas.

social disorganization theory Posits that delinquency is a product of the social forces existing in inner-city, low-income areas.

social ecology Theory focuses attention on the influence social institutions have on individual behavior and suggests that law-violating behavior is a response to social rather than individual forces operating in an urban environment.

social investigation report (also known as **predisposition report**) Developed by the juvenile probation officer, this report consists of a clinical diagnosis of the juvenile and his or her need for court assistance, relevant environmental and personality factors, and any other information that would assist the court in developing a treatment plan for the juvenile.

social learning theory The view that behavior is modeled through observation, either directly through intimate contact with others, or indirectly through media; interactions that are rewarded are copied, whereas those that are punished are avoided.

social process theories Posit that the interactions a person has with key elements of the socialization process determine his or her future behavior.

social structure theories Explain delinquency using socioeconomic conditions and cultural values.

socialization The process of learning the values and norms of the society or the subculture to which the individual belongs.

socially disorganized neighborhood Neighborhood or area marked by culture conflict, lack of cohesiveness, a transient population, and insufficient social organizations; these problems are reflected in the problems at schools in these areas.

Society for the Prevention of Cruelty to Children First established in 1874, these organizations protected children subjected to cruelty and neglect at home or at school.

sociopathic personality *See* **psychopathic personality.**

somatotype school Argued that delinquents manifest distinct physiques that make them susceptible to particular types of delinquent behavior.

special prevention *See* **secondary prevention.**

specific deterrence Sending convicted offenders to secure incarceration facilities so that punishment is severe enough to convince offenders not to repeat their criminal activity.

stable slum A neighborhood where population shifts have slowed down, permitting patterns of behavior and traditions to develop over a number of years.

Standard Minimum Rules for the Administration of Juvenile Justice Developed in 1985 by the United Nations to encourage countries to develop juvenile justice systems and improve the administration of juvenile justice.

status offense Conduct that is illegal only because the child is under age.

stigmatized People who have been negatively labeled because of their participation, or alleged participation, in deviant or outlawed behaviors.

stimulants Synthetic substances that produce an intense physical reaction by stimulating the central nervous system.

strain theory Links delinquency to the strain of being locked out of the economic mainstream, which creates the anger and frustration that lead to delinquent acts.

strategic planning A disciplined effort to produce fundamental decisions and actions that shape and guide an organization and direct the focus of its future.

stratification Grouping society into classes based on the unequal distribution of scarce resources.

student subculture The independent, self-contained high school culture that controls the behavior and attitudes of American youth.

subculture of violence An identified urban-based subculture in which young males are expected to respond with violence to the slightest provocation.

subcultures Groups that are loosely part of the dominant culture but that maintain a unique set of values, beliefs, and traditions.

substance abuse Using drugs or alcohol in such a way as to cause physical, emotional and/or psychological harm to yourself.

subterranean values The ability of youthful law violators to repress social norms.

suppression effect A reduction in the number of arrests per year for youths who have been incarcerated or otherwise punished.

swaddling The practice during the Middle Ages of completely wrapping newborns in long bandage-like clothes in order to restrict their movements and make them easier to manage.

systematic review A type of review that uses rigorous methods for locating, appraising, and synthesizing evidence from prior evaluation studies.

target-hardening technique Crime prevention technique that makes it more difficult for a would-be delinquent to carry out the illegal act, for example, by installing a security device in a home.

teen courts Courts that make use of peer juries to decide nonserious delinquency cases.

TOP program Police and community prevention effort in which teens are hired to patrol the city's parks and recreation areas.

totality of the circumstances doctrine Legal doctrine that mandates that a decision maker consider all the issues and circumstances of a case before judging the outcome; the suspect's age, intelligence, and competency may be issues that influence his or her understanding and judgment.

tracking Dividing students into groups according to their ability and achievement levels.

trait theory Holds that youths engage in delinquent or criminal behavior due to aberrant physical or psychological traits that govern behavioral choices; delinquent actions are impulsive or instinctual rather than rational choices.

tranquilizers Drugs that reduce anxiety and promote relaxation.

transfer hearing Preadjudicatory hearing in juvenile court for the purpose of determining whether juvenile court should be retained over a juvenile or waived and the juvenile transferred to adult court for prosecution.

transfer process Transfer of a juvenile offender from the jurisdiction of juvenile court to adult criminal court.

transitional neighborhood Area undergoing a shift in population and structure, usually from middle-class residential to lower-class mixed use.

transnational crime Crime that is carried out across the borders of two or more countries and violates the laws of those countries.

trial de novo A review procedure in which there is a complete retrial of the original case.

truancy Staying out of school without permission.

truly disadvantaged According to William Julius Wilson, those people who are left out of the economic mainstream and reduced to living in the most deteriorated inner-city areas.

turning points Critical life events, such as career and marriage, that may enable adult offenders to desist from delinquency.

underachievers Those who do not achieve success in school at the level of their expectations.

underclass Group of urban poor whose members have little chance of upward mobility or improvement.

Uniform Crime Report (UCR) Compiled by the FBI, the UCR is the most widely used source of national crime and delinquency statistics.

utilitarians Those who believe that people weigh the benefits and consequences of their future actions before deciding on a course of behavior.

victim service restitution The juvenile offender is required to provide some service directly to the crime victim.

victimizations The number of people who are victims of criminal acts; young teens are 15 times more likely than older adults (age 65 and over) to be victims of crimes.

Violent Crime Control and Law Enforcement Act of 1994 This act made available increased funding for juvenile justice and delinquency prevention.

Violent Juvenile Offender (VJO) program Specialized programs in small, secure settings where youths are gradually reintegrated into the community with intensive supervision.

waiver (also known as **bindover** or **removal**) Transferring legal jurisdiction over the most serious and experienced juvenile offenders to the adult court for criminal prosecution.

watch system Replaced the pledge system in England; watchmen patrolled urban areas at night to provide protection from harm.

wayward minors Early legal designation of youths who violate the law because of their minority status; now referred to as status offenders.

widening the net Phenomenon that occurs when programs created to divert youths from the justice system actually involve them more deeply in the official process.

wilderness probation Programs involving outdoor expeditions that provide opportunities for juveniles to confront the difficulties of their lives while achieving positive personal satisfaction.

writ of certiorari Order of a superior court requesting that the record of an inferior court (or administrative body) be brought forward for review or inspection.

writ of habeas corpus Judicial order requesting that a person detaining another produce the body of the prisoner and give reasons for his or her capture and detention.

zero tolerance policy Mandating specific consequences or punishments for delinquent acts and not allowing anyone to avoid these consequences.

Case Index

Baker v. Owen, *295*
   423 U.S. 907, 96 S.Ct. 210, 46 L.Ed.2d
   137 (1975)
Bethel School District No. 403 v. Fraser,
   293
   478 U.S. 675, 106 S.Ct. 3159, 92 L.Ed.2d
   549 (1986)
Board of Education of Independent
   School District No. 92 of
   Pottawatomie County et al., v. Earls
   et al., *296–97*
   (01–332) 536 U.S. 822 (2002) 242 F.3d
   1264, reversed
Breed v. Jones, *374, 437, 438–39*
   421 U.S. 519, 95 S.Ct. 1779 (1975)

California v. Prysock, *403*
   453 U.S. 355, 101 S.Ct. 2806 (1981)
Coy v. Iowa, *221*
   487 U.S. 1012 (1988)
Craig v. Maryland, *221*
   110 S.Ct. 3157 (1990)

Davis v. Alaska, *449–50*
   415 U.S. 308 (1974); 94 S.Ct. 1105

Eddings v. Oklahoma, *374*
   455 U.S. 104, 102 S.Ct. 869, 71 L.Ed.2d 1
   (1982)

Fare v. Michael C., *374, 403*
   442 U.S. 707, 99 S.Ct. 2560 (1979)

Good News Club v. Milford Central
   School, *294*
   533 U.S. 98 (2001)
Goss v. Lopez, *296*
   419 U.S. 565, 95 S.Ct. 729 (1976)

Hazelwood School District v.
   Kuhlmeier, *294*
   484 U.S. 260, 108 S.Ct. 562, 98 L.Ed.2d
   592 (1988)

In re Gault, *372, 374, 403, 441–42, 443,*
   449, 451, 531, 533
   387 U.S. 1, 87 S.Ct. 1428, 18 L.Ed.2d 527
   (1967)

In re Winship, *442*
   397 U.S. 358, 90 S.Ct. 1068 (1970)
Ingraham v. Wright, *295*
   430 U.S. 651, 97 S.Ct. 1401 (1977)
Inmates of the Boys' Training School v.
   Affleck, *485*
   346 F. Supp. 1354 (D.R.I. 1972)

Kent v. United States, *374, 437, 438–39*
   383 U.S. 541, 86 S.Ct. 1045, 16 L.Ed.2d
   84 (1966)

Lassiter v. Department of Social
   Services, *218*
   452 U.S. 18, 101 S.Ct. 2153 (1981)

McKeiver v. Pennsylvania, *374, 442*
   403 U.S. 528, 91 S.Ct. 1976 (1971)
Miranda v. Arizona, *374, 381, 388–89,*
   402–3, 415
   384 U.S. 436, 86 S.Ct. 1602 (1966)
Morales v. Turman, *486*
   383 F.Supp. 53 (E.D. Texas 1974)

Nelson v. Heyne, *486*
   491 F.2d 353 (1974)
New Jersey v. T.L.O., *296, 374*
   469 U.S. 325, 105 S.Ct. 733 (1985)

Oklahoma Publishing Co. v. District
   Court, *450*
   430 U.S. 97, 99 S.Ct. 2667, 61 L.Ed.2d
   399 (1979)

Pena v. New York State Division for
   Youth, *486*
   419 F. Supp. 203 (S.D.N.Y. 1976)
People v. Lara, *403*
   67 Cal.2d 365, 62 Cal.Rptr. 586, 432
   P.2d 202 (1967)

Ralston v. Robinson, *486*
   102 S.Ct. 233 (1981)
Roe v. Wade, *39*
   314 F.Supp. 1217 (1973), 410 U.S. 113

Santa Fe Independent School District v.
   Doe, *294*
   No. 99–62 (June 19, 2000)

Santana v. Callazo, *486*
   714 F.2d 451 (D.C. Cir. 1966)
Santosky v. Kramer, *218*
   455 U.S. 745, 102 S.Ct. 1388 (1982)
Schall v. Martin, *374, 431, 432*
   467 U.S. 253, 104 S.Ct. 2403 (1984)
Smith v. Daily Mail Publishing Co., *450*
   443 U.S. 97, 99 S.Ct. 2667, 61 L.Ed.2d
   399 (1979)
Stanford v. Kentucky, *374, 448, 451, 534*
   492 U.S. 361, 109 S.Ct.2969 (1989)

Thompson v. Oklahoma, *374, 447–48*
   487 U.S. 815, 108 S.Ct. 2687, 101
   L.Ed.2d 702 (1988)
Tinker v. Des Moines Independent
   Community School District, *292–94*
   393 U.S. 503, 89 S.Ct. 733 (1969)
Troxel v. Granville, *217*
   530 U.S. 57, 137 Wash. 2d 1, 969 P.2d 21
   (2000)

United States v. Lopez, *374*
   115 S.Ct. 1624 (1995)

Vernonia School District 47J v. Acton,
   296, 297
   115 S.Ct. 2394 (1995)
Vernonia School District v. Acton, *374*
   515 U.S. 646, 115 S.Ct. 2386, 132
   L.Ed.2d 564 (1995)

White v. Illinois, *221*
   502 U.S. 346, 112 S.Ct. 736 (1992)
Wilkins v. Missouri, *374, 448, 451, 534*
   492 U.S. 361, 109 S.Ct. 2969 (1989)
Wisconsin v. Yoder, *292*
   406 U.S. 205, 92 S.Ct. 1526, 32 L.Ed.2d
   15 (1972)

Name Index

Note: Page number entries with an "n" refer to names in Notes sections.

A

Abbott, Robert, 168n44, 269n33, 270n128, 301n7, 361n51
Aber, Mark S., 9
Ablow, Jennifer, 103n118
Acoca, Leslie, 494n86
Adams, Kenneth, 26, 27, 418n96
Adams, Mike, 140n140, n146, n155
Adams, William, 198n100
Adler, Freda, 140n124, 190, 197n47, 198n113, n114, 501, 522n33
Adler, Joanna, 391n46
Aebi, Marcelo, 503, 522n12
Ageton, Suzanne, 60n46, 332n82
Agnew, Robert, 60n41, 117–19, 136, 139n78, n79, 169n73, 269n19, 301n26
Agopian, Michael, 271n203
Aichorn, August, 88
Aickin, Mikel, 31n56, n57
Ainsworth-Darnell, James, 138n16
Akers, Ronald, 60n13, 169n83
Alarid, Leanne Fiftal, 163n13, 197n30, 453n30, n31
Albrecht, Hans-Jörg, 523n60, n84
Aleva, Liesbeth, 198n76
Alfaro, Jose, 223, 231n165
Allan, Charlotte, 333n111, n112, n113
Allan, David, 36
Allan, Emilie Andersen, 138n3
Allen, Ed, 270n119, 332n67
Allen, Francis, 373
Allen-Hagen, Barbara, 493n57
Allen, Stephen, 367
Alschuler, Albert, 454n47
Altschuler, David, 488, 494n128, 495n138, n139, n140
Alvarado, Rose, 139n102, 360n15
Alvarez, Lizette, 522n4
Amato, Paul, 206, 228n1
Andenaes, Johannes, 102n32
Anderson, Bobbi Jo, 140n125
Anderson, Craig, 38, 39, 91
Anderson, David, 301n38
Anderson, E. A., 494n83
Anderson, Elijah, 139n59
Anderson, James, 163n15
Anderson, Mark, 302n51
Anderson, Pamela, 271n173
Anderson, Roger, 493n64
Andreou, Chriso, 231n170
Andrews, D. A., 168n63
Andrews, Edmund, 522n5

Andrews, Roosevelt, 295
Anglin, Deirdre, 271n142, 332n72
Anglin, M. Douglas, 332n72, n81
Anter, Tyler, 326
Aos, Steve, 361n52
Apel, Robert, 101n15
Archerm, John, 102n67
Archibold, Randal, 302n74
Ardovini-Brooker, Joanne, 494n117
Arean, Juan Carlos, 226
Aries, Philippe, 12, 31n28, n30
Arjunan, Mehala, 270n66
Armistead, Lisa, 332n46, n47
Armstrong, Gaylene Styve, 494n83, 494n111
Armstrong, Scott, 271n197
Armstrong, Troy, 488, 493n28, 495n138, n139, n140
Arneklev, Bruce, 163n6, 169n82, n93
Arnett, Jeffrey Jensen, 228n3
Arnette, June, 285, 290, 302n65
Arnold, Tim, 31n68
Arons, S., 302n83, n84
Arseneault, Louise, 103n118
Arthur, Lindsay, 31n76
Arthur, Michael, 361n90, 94, 362n96
Asendorf, J. B., 285
Atkinson, Lynn, 512
Aubrey, Jennifer Stevens, 199n147
Auletta, Ken, 138n10
Austin, James, 141n173, 360n6, 492n7, 493n57
Austin, Roy, 198n117
Austin, Stephen, 27, 31n51
Austin, Timothy W., 102n60

B

Bachman, Jerald, 60n9, n16, 61n49, 101n12, 198n112, 310, 331n1, n9, n18, n19, 332n54
Backstrom, James, 453n18
Backstrom, Teresa Vigil, 271n193
Badeau, Sue, 231n145
Baer, Douglas, 229n37, 331n36
Bahr, Stephen, 168n46
Baier, Colin, 140n111
Bailey, Carol, 140n145
Baird, Christopher, 231n160, n162
Bakal, Yitzhak, 493n43
Baker, Myriam, 25
Baker, Tara Kelly, 350, 361n58, 391n48
Balcer, C., 198n68
Baldry, Anna, 285
Ball, Richard, 39, 269n2, 493n21
Ballard, Diane, 357
Balsano, Aida, 271n173

Balter, Mitchell, 61n60, 167n10
Bandura, Albert, 90, 494n98
Bannister, Andra, 26, 27
Barberet, Rosemary, 523n43
Bard, Barbara, 103n92
Barker, Gordon, 198n100
Barkley, Russell, 81
Barletto, Kimberly, 198n104, 231n173
Barnard, John, 31n38
Barnes, Helen, 360n40, n42, n43
Barnes, Julie Ann, 11
Barnett, Arnold, 61n64
Barnett, W. Steven, 360n43
Barnoski, Robert, 182, 361n52
Baron, Stephen, 269n35
Barrios, Lisa, 302n51
Barry, Christopher, 198n79
Bartkowski, John, 140n114
Bartollas, Clemons, 479, 493n52, 494n81, n82
Barton, William, 453n29
Bass, Sandra, 231n153
Bateman, Richard, 125
Bates, John, 139n68, 168n40, 229n68, n71
Battin, Sara, 269n33, 270n128
Baucom, D. H., 198n60
Bauer, Mike, 187
Baumer, Eric, 332n70, n71, n73
Baumhover, Lorin, 102n29
Bauserman, Robert, 231n173
Bazemore, Gordon, 136, 141n182, 468, 493n29, n30, n34
Beaton, Susan, 302n55, n80
Beazley, Ireland, 447
Beazley, Napolean, 447
Beazley, Rena, 447
Beccaria, Cesare, 66, 67, 101n8, 102n31
Becker, Jill, 103n83, 197n53, 198n73
Beckwith, Leila, 103n89
Behrman, Richard, 360n23
Beirne, Piers, 522n32
Belenko, Steven, 60n21
Belknap, Joanne, 186, 198n102, n107, n110, 199n130, n145, 454n61, 494n85
Bell, Robert, 332n99
Bellair, Paul, 60n37, 102n25, 138n21, n46
Belliston, Lara, 361n54
Bem, Sandra, 177
Benbow, Camilla, 197n18
Benedict, William Reed, 302n46
Benekos, Peter, 388, 391n71
Bengston, Vern, 139n103
Bennett, Neil, 102n70
Bennett, Richard, 522n33
Bennett, Treyor, 360n16
Bennett, William, 297

Bensley, Lillian S., 9
Bentham, Jeremy, 66, 101n4
Bentovim, Amon, 231n170
Berglund, Lisa, 361n90, n94
Bergsmann, Ilene, 494n89
Berk, Richard, 417n7
Berliner, Howard, 333n105, n107
Bern, Sandra, 197n25
Bernard, Thomas, 59n2
Bernat, Frances, 245, 271n152
Bernburg, Jon Gunnar, 140n159
Berndt, Thomas, 139n107, 269n5, n6
Bernstein, Gail A., 25
Bernstein, Richard, 522n11
Bernstein, Saul, 270n80
Berthier, Héctor Castillo, 522n16
Besch, P. K., 198n60
Besharov, Douglas, 31n35, 230n96, 361n61
Bettelheim, Bruno, 482, 494n102
Beutel, Ann, 197n19
Beyer, Margaret, 494n110
Beyers, Jennifer, 139n68, 229n71
Bhana, Arvinkumar, 9
Bianchi, Herbert, 141n181
Bier, Ian, 79
Bilchik, Shay, 31n47, 391n40, n61, 472, 493n36
Binder, Arnold, 27, 454n45
Binder, David, 522n3
Bingham, Rachel, 385
Bingham, Raymond, 9
Birmaher, Boris, 88
Birnbaum, Morton, 485, 494n118
Bisesi, Lorrie, 333n108
Bishop, Donna, 60n24, 407, 409, 418n71, n77, 454n74
Bjarnason, Thor, 507, 523n65
Bjerregaard, Beth, 198n119, 270n138
Blachman, D. R., 81
Black, Donald, 138n53, 417n23, n51
Black, Kathryn, 231n179, n181
Blackburn, James, 285
Blackwell, Brenda Sims, 101n13, 193, 199n136
Blake, Gerald, 454n44
Blakeslee, Sandra, 207
Blau, Judith, 139n73
Blau, Peter, 139n73
Block, Hebert, 259, 271n162, n163
Block, J., 332n52
Block, Kathleen, 391n23
Blomberg, Thomas, 454n44
Bloom, Barbara, 494n87
Bloomberg, Michael, 119–20
Blos, Peter, 197n48
Blumstein, Alfred, 61n49, n64
Bobek, Deborah, 271n173
Bodin, Doug, 198n79
Bodine, George, 60n7
Boehnke, Klaus, 522n13
Bogaerts, Jef, 229n47
Bogdan, Carol, 494n83
Bonati, Lisa, 102n27, n58
Bond-Maupin, Lis, 453n32
Bookin-Weiner, Hedy, 271n201
Booth, Alan, 198n59
Borduin, Charles, 332n103, 472
Bortner, M. A., 454n66

Borum, Randy, 302n52
Bos, Johannes, 187
Bottcher, Jean, 177, 197n28
Bottoms, Anthony, 517, 518, 523n88
Boulerice, Bernard, 103n95, 283
Bowden, C., 331n31
Bowditch, Christine, 283
Bowling, Benjamin, 523n43
Bowman, Darcia Harris, 302n78
Bowman, J. Addison, 455n106
Boy George (*Random Family* character), 123
Brace, Charles Loring, 369–70
Bracey, Dorothy, 230n105
Brackmann, C., 168n69
Brady, C. Patrick, 228n20
Brady, Marianne, 140n136, n143
Braga, Anthony, 414, 417n17, n30, 418n98, 419n101
Bragg, Rick, 302n44
Braithwaite, John, 60n46
Brame, Robert, 101n15, 163n2, 167n9, n15, 168n40, n61, 169n95, 197n6
Brantingham, Paul, 360n17
Brash, Rachel, 494n128
Brasler, Paul, 333n113
Bray, James, 228n20
Bremner, Robert H., 31n38
Brendtero, Larry, 494n100
Brennan, Patricia, 103n90, 229n51
Brennan, William, 294
Brenzel, Barbara, 494n88
Brezina, Timothy, 61n54, 68–69, 103n84, 139n83, 167n18, 269n19
Briar, Scott, 418n53, n62
Bridges, George, 60n20, n25, 493n74, 494n77
Broder, James, 493n70, 494n95
Broder, Paul, 103n100
Brodsky, Stanley, 453n6, n7
Brody, Charles, 270n123
Brody, Gene, 332n46, n47
Broidy, Lisa, 168n40, 197n20, 198n77, 229n67
Brondino, Michael, 333n104
Bronner, Augusta, 96, 179, 197n41
Brooks-Gunn, Jeanne, 138n12
Brown, Ben, 302n46
Brown, Katherine, 453n30, n31
Brown, Susan, 229n36
Brown, William, 408
Browne, Dorothy, 269n14
Brownfield, David, 163n6, 169n82, 270n125, n127, 271n172
Browning, Sandra Lee, 417n9
Brownstein, Henry, 199n121
Brucia, Carlie, 56
Brugman, Gerard, 198n76
Brummett, Patricia O'Donnell, 271n154
Bryant, Susan Leslie, 231n163
Buchanan, Christy Miller, 103n83, 197n53, 198n73
Buchbinder, Sharon, 360n30
Buck, Janeen, 356, 361n93, 385
Bucky, S. F., 331n38
Buerger, Michael, 414
Bugh, Henry, 212
Bukowski, William, 269n31, 303n111
Bulger, James, 519
Bullington, B., 454n44
Bumphus, Vic, 163n15

Burch, James, 266, 270n121, n129
Burgess, Robert, 231n135, n136
Burghardt, John, 361n81, n83
Burke, Jeffrey, 88
Burns, Jerald, 302n66, n67, 494n108
Burruss, George, Jr., 453n10
Bursik, Robert, Jr., 138n24, n29, n36, n54, 169n85, n93
Burt, Cyril, 179, 197n40
Burton, Velmer, 139n84, n86, 140n115, 163n7, n13, 197n30
Bushman, Brad, 38, 39, 91
Bushway, Shawn, 101n15, 231n180
Bushweller, Kevin, 302n72
Bussman, K., 230n113
Butterfield, Fox, 60n29, 269n44, 332n75, n95, 391n43, 414, 539n5
Butts, Jeffrey, 385, 391n42, 455n113, 493n34, 539n5
Bynum, Timothy, 270n79, 271n151, 303n108
Byrne, James, 138n47, 492n17, n18

C
Caeti, Tory, 26, 27, 102n36, 418n88
Cahalan, Margaret Werner, 493n51
Caldwell, Ami, 270n136
Calhoun, George, 198n101
Callahan, Charlene, 385
Callahan, Charles, 302n45
Callahan, S., 198n60
Calnon, Jennifer, 60n19
Campbell, Anne, 197n16, n39, n51
Campbell, Suzanne, 102n35
Cantor, David, 163n5, 320, 332n77
Capaldi, Deborah, 168n31, n32, 269n30, 331n30
Caplan, Arthur, 102n68
Capowich, George, 139n67, n71, n85
Carcach, Carlos, 522n23
Carr, Jackson, 201
Carrozza, Mark, 140n123, n126, 229n72
Carswell, Steven, 125
Carter, David, 27
Carter, Deborah Brown, 409, 418n84
Cartwright, Desmond, 239
Carver, Karen, 283
Caspi, Avshalom, 103n118, 168n39, 169n98, n99, 197n56, 229n38
Castellano, Thomas, 494n106
Catalano, Richard, 151, 168n44, n45, 269n33, 270n128, 301n7, 332n85, 361n51, n89, n90, n92, n94, 362n96
Cauce, Mari, 61n89
Cauffman, Elizabeth, 197n20, n77, 228n3
Cavanagh, Shannon, 361n91
Cernkovich, Stephen, 139n87, 140n128, n130, 167n2, 169n100, 188, 189, 269n38
Chaiken, Marcia, 332n60, n61, n66, n69
Challinger, D., 229n74, n75
Chamberlain, Patricia, 360n33, 493n42
Chamberlin, Robert, 360n24
Chambers, Jeff, 138n28
Chapman, Derek, 454n58
Chard-Wierschem, Deborah, 101n3, 139n99, 271n189, 539n3
Charles, Michael, 493n21
Chen, Fengling, 198n101
Chen, Yi Fu, 139n82

Chermak, Steven, 60n34, 408, 417n31
Chesney-Lind, Meda, 60n12, 186, 194, 195, 198n105, n106, 199n131, n140, n142, n143, n144, n148, n150, 269n4, 270n107, 408, 409, 418n76, n78, 494n83
Chien, I., 331n38
Chiesa, James, 360n28, n34
Chilton, Roland, 228n24
Chin, Ko-Lin, 258, 271n157
Chiricos, Ted, 38, 39, 138n49
Chong Yun, Steve, 271n158
Chow, Julian, 138n8
Christakis, Dimitri, 92
Christenson, R. L., 139n105, 283
Christiansen, Karl O., 103n120, 332n556
Christie, Nils, 141n181
Chung, He Len, 167n10
Chung, Ick-Joong, 167n12, 168n28
Cicchetti, Dante, 231n156
Cicourel, Aaron, 140n150, 418n61
Cimbolic, Peter, 103n77, n78
Clapp, Neale, 493n43
Clark-Daniels, Carolyn, 102n29
Clark, John, 198n118, 417n23
Clarke, Gregory, 88
Clarke, Ronald, 101n21, 102n55
Clayton, Richard, 302n50, 325
Cleckley, Hervey, 95
Clinard, Marshall, 522n33
Clingempeel, W. Glenn, 168n36, 333n104
Cloward, Richard, 122, 139n94, 243, 245, 260, 270n73, 331n33, 340
Coates, Robert, 492n7
Cobb, Michael, 199n122
Cochran, John, 102n22, 163n6
Coco (*Random Family* character), 123
Cohen, Albert, 122, 139n93, 260, 271n167, 279, 301n19
Cohen, Deborah, 229n69, 418n100, 419n105, n106
Cohen, Jacqueline, 61n49
Cohen, Lawrence, 61n51, 71, 102n23, n28
Cohen, Mark, 61n82, 359n1, n2, n3, n4
Cohen, Robert, 269n36
Colden, Cadwallader, 367
Cole, John, 237, 269n14, n15, n16, n29, n39
Cole, Kristin, 361n75, n76, n77
Coleman, John, 198n84, n85, 228n6
Coll, Xavier, 230n107
Collins-Hall, Lori, 283, 332n55
Colman, Adrian, 302n75
Colman, Robyn, 302n75
Conger, Rand, 139n100, 140n117, 167n14, 168n51, 229n35, n54, n66
Conklin, John, 103n75, 198n62
Conley, Dalton, 102n70
Conley, Darlene, 418n81
Connell, Patricia, 455n105
Conseur, Amy, 182
Conway, Allan, 494n83
Cook, Philip, 39, 101n21
Cook, William, 388, 391n71
Cooley, Charles H., 140n138
Coon, Dennis, 331n7
Cooper, Harris, 361n65
Cooper, Sara, 367
Coppa, Frank, 390n3
Corbett, Ronald, 484, 494n109

Corbitt, Elizabeth, 140n136, n143
Cordella, Peter, 103n105, 141n181
Cornell, Amy, 198n79
Cornell, Claire Pedrick, 230n95
Cornish, Derek, 101n21
Corrado, J., 331n36
Costa, Francis, 167n23
Costa, Joseph J., 228n8
Costanzo, Philip, 269n14
Cothern, Lynn, 455n96
Cottrell, Leonard, 140n153
Coulton, Claudia, 138n8
Cowie, J., 197n50, 198n87
Cowie, V., 197n50, 198n87
Cox, Louis, 131, 140n156, 458, 492n1
Cox, Stephen, 303n108
Craig, Rebecca, 493n65
Craig, Wendy, 197n32, 360n21, n22, n38
Cressey, Donald, 140n153
Crimmins, Susan, 30n3, 199n121
Cromwell, Paul, 492n3, n4
Crosby, L., 167n7
Crosby, Rick, 168n25
Cross, Tim, 361n86, n87
Crowder, Martin, 79
Crowell, Nancy, 360n22, 361n56, n65, n66, n80, 391n45, n67, n69, 418n55, n95, 494n127, 511, 522n36, 523n73
Cullen, Francis, 139n84, n86, n101, 140n115, n123, n126, 163n7, n13, 197n30, 229n52, n72, 237, 269n40, 301n20, 391n68
Cullen, Frank, 169n90
Cullen, Kevin, 271n147
Culliver, Concetta, 103n99
Culrose, Patti, 360n23
Cummings, E. Mark, 229n48
Cummings, Scott, 268n1
Cunningham, Phillippe, 332n103
Currie, Elliot, 454n84, 493n47
Curry, David G., 39, 239, 269n2, 270n102, n105, n108, n122, 271n185, n208
Curtis, Lynn, 271n146, 361n82
Cuzzola-Kern, 199n141

D
Daldin, Herman, 230n104
D'Alessio, Stewart, 60n26
Dalton, Katharina, 183, 198n65
Daly, Kathleen, 141n176, 197n7, 199n131
Daly, Martin, 61n53, 138n42, n51, 230n128, n129, n130
Dammer, Harry, 504, 523n46
Dane, Heather, 198n79
Daniele, Atonietta, 230n130
Daniels, R. Steven, 102n29
Dannefer, Dale, 60n14, 418n66, n70
Daro, Deborah, 230n132
Datesman, Susan, 31n56, n57
Davidson, Howard, 453n11
Davidson, William, 303n108
Davies, Mark, 140n131, 331n34
Davies-Netley, Sally, 231n163
Davies, Scott, 140n158
Davies, Susan, 168n25
Davis, Kenneth, 410, 417n47, 418n80
Davis, Nanette, 9, 30n2
Davis, Samuel, 417n33
Davison, Elizabeth, 102n26

Dawkins, Marvin, 332n74
Dawley, David, 269n43
Dawson, Robert, 385–86, 391n57
Day, L. Edward, 301n7
De Hann, Laura G., 138n7
De Li, Spencer, 102n48, 140n111
De Lisi, Matt, 418n84
De V. Peters, R., 361n53
De Witt, Cees A. M., 285
De Witt, Charles, 230n94
Dean, Charles, 163n2, 167n9, 197n6, 418n95
Deboutte, Dirk, 229n47
Decker, Scott, 39, 254–55, 270n79, n115, n122, n136, n137, 271n141, n151, 414
Dedel, Kelly, 453n1
DeFrances, Carol, 391n59
DeJong, Christina, 60n23, 102n49, 229n28
DeJong, Judith, 163n4, n4
DeKeseredy, Walter, 197n26
Delany-Shabazz, Robin V., 231n155
DeLone, Miriam, 60n17, n27, n33, 418n74
Demaray, Michelle Kilpatrick, 302n49
Dembitz, Nanette, 230n124
Dembo, Richard, 168n27
Demon, John, 31n43
Demuth, Stephen, 229n36
Deng, Xiaogang, 163n1, n11
Dengate, S., 79
Denno, Deborah, 182
Dentler, Robert, 60n44
Deptula, Daneen, 269n36
DeRios, M. D., 331n39
Derzon, James, 168n35
Deschenes, Elizabeth Piper, 454n67, 494n87
Devine, F. E., 101n9
Devlin, Daniel, 417n1
DeVoe, Jill, 302n48
Diaz, Rafael, 31n53, 197n54
DiClemente, Ralph, 168n25
Dignan, James, 517, 518, 523n88
DiLalla, Lisabeth Fisher, 103n108, n109
Dinitz, Simon, 493n52, 494n81
Dishion, Thomas, 140n108, 269n13, n30, 331n30, 360n12, n33, 361n59, 494n99
Ditchfield, John, 523n93
Dobbin, Shirley, 231n145
Dobkin, Patricia, 331n45, 332n51
Dodge, Douglas, 453n15
Dodge, Kenneth, 139n68, 168n40, 229n68, n71
Dodge, L. Mara, 381
Dolce, Philip, 390n3
Donaldson, Sam, 65
Donker, Andrea, 167n21
Donne, Ginette, 83
Donohue, J., III, 39
Donovan, John, 167n23
Donziger, Steven, 333n110, n114
Doob, Anthony, 512, 514, 518, 523n58, n59, n78, n84, n88, n95, 539n9
Dorn, Sherman, 282, 283
Dornfeld, Maude, 231n146, n147
Dougherty, Joyce, 454n47
Dowling, Elizabeth, 271n173
Down, William, 230n100
Downey, Douglas, 138n16, 229n73
Downs, William, 231n163
Draper, Patricia, 231n135, n136

Drevon, Christian, 102n71
Driver, Edwin, 102n63
Droegemueller, W., 230n97
DuBois, David, 361n65
Duffee, David, 523n38
Duggan, Anne, 360n30
Dulmus, Catherine, 285
Dumond, Doris, 418n95
Dunaway, R. Gregory, 60n45, 140n115, 163n7, n13, 197n30
Duncan, Greg, 138n12
D'Unger, Amy, 61n76, 167n19
Dunlap, Earl, 453n33
Dunn, Melissa, 198n102, 199n130, n145
Dunworth, Terence, 397, 417n15, n16
Dwiggins, Donna, 197n10

E
Earls, Felton, 139n63, n69, 181
Earnest, Terri, 139n65
Eccles, Jacquelynne, 103n83, 197n53, 198n73
Eck, John, 231n180, 400, 417n8, n20, n30, 539n6
Eckert, Penelope, 269n10
Edwards, Leonard, 231n177, 391n57, 453n19
Eftekhari-Sanjani, Hossain, 197n18
Eggebeen, David, 30n12, 229n76
Eggleston, Carolyn, 197n10
Eggleston, Elaine, 167n13
Egley, Arlen, Jr., 241, 270n64 n65, n66, n97, n122
Eisenberg, Marla, 285
Eisenberg, Terry, 414
Eisikovits, Z., 494n75
Eisner, Manuel, 522n33
Eitle, David, 60n26
Eldefonso, Edward, 493n54, n55
Elder, Glen, Jr., 168n51
Elder, Rob, 102n24
Elias, Albert, 493n43
Ellickson, Phyllis, 332n99
Elliott, Delbert, 60n14, n46, 169n88, 313, 321, 331n28, 332n82, n83, 357, 361n50, 493n41
Ellis, Lee, 102n73, 103n105, n120, 140n116, 168n69, 198n61, n70, n72
Ellison, Christopher, 229n58
Emanuel, Irvin, 182
Empey, LaMar, 493n43, n53
Engel, Robin Shepard, 60n19
Engen, Rodney, 60n20, n25, 493n74
English, Bella, 302n73
Ennett, Susan, 60n28, n36
Erickson, Maynard, 102n47, 493n43
Erikson, Erik, 4–5, 30n4, 87–88
Esbensen, Finn-Aage, 245, 270n100, n101, 271n152, n161, n185, 302n64, 417n10, 418n90, n91, n92
Espelage, Dorothy, 197n20, n77
Estes, Richard, 214
Evans, Gary, 30n13, 138n13, 139n86
Evans, Kristy, 270n124
Evans, T. David, 139n84, 140n115, 163n7, n13, 197n30
Eve, Raymond, 60n11, 198n118
Everingham, Susan, 360n28
Eves, Anita, 79
Ewing, Darlene, 454n49

Eye, Alexander von, 271n173
Eysenck, Hans, 94
Ezell, Mark, 454n46
Ezell, Michael, 61n76

F
Fagan, Abigail, 103n117, 230n90, 357, 493n41
Fagan, Jeffrey, 60n40, 61n78, 243–44, 270n72, n74, 418n70, 454n39, n67
Fairchild, Erika, 504, 523n46
Farley, Thomas, 229n69
Farnworth, Margaret, 60n46, 139n97, 155, 168n53, 301n8
Farr, Kathryn Ann, 333n118
Farrell, Graham, 332n87, n92
Farrington, David, 61n48, n61, n64, n67, 83, 102n56, n57, 103n112, n114, n116, 146, 151–53, 167n7, n11, 168n35, n42, 169n81, n84, n85, 210, 228n6, 230n80, n82, n83, n87, n88, 237, 269n15, n20, n22, n37, 270n130, 285, 332n101, 344, 348, 360n19, n20, n21, n22, n31, 361n52, n65, n90, n102, 362n104, 391n46, 400, 417n8, 472, 493n26, n27, n46, 494n91, n112, n113, 511, 514, 522n33, 523n93, 536, 539n4, n8
Farris, Elizabeth, 302n82
Fass, Simon, 391n72
Fastabend, Annemarie, 103n80
Faupel, Charles, 332n72, n81
Faust, Frederick, 360n17
Fein, Robert, 302n52
Feingold, Alan, 169n85
Fejes-Mendoza, Kathy, 197n10
Feld, Barry, 31n69, 385, 386, 391n55, n56, 454n57, n71, n77
Feldman, Marilyn, 103n92
Feldman, S. Shirley, 31n53, 197n54, 228n3
Fellerath, Veronica, 187
Felson, Marcus, 71, 102n23, n28, 102n53
Felson, Richard, 235, 269n25
Fendrich, Michael, 60n10, 229n30, 312, 331n5, n25, 332n59
Ferdinand, Theodore, 371, 391n24, n33, 418n53
Fergusson, David, 140n110, 168n40
Ferrero, William, 179, 197n2, n36, n37, n38
Ferri, Enrico, 76
Feucht, Thomas, 302n51
Feyerherm, William, 60n22, n39, 197n45
Figlio, Robert, 49–50, 60n15, 61n56, n65-66, n70, 101n2, 301n11, n11, n12, 539n2
Finckenauer, James, 523n48, n57
Findlay, Mark, 523n51
Finkelhor, David, 61n92, 174, 197n5, 215, 216, 230n109, n116, n119, n120
Finnegan, Terrence, 377, 427, 428, 436, 446, 461, 492n9, n10
Fischer, Craig, 494n76
Fischer, Mariellen, 81
Fishbein, Diana, 102n72, 103n75, n85, n86, 181, 183, 198n62, n63, n66, n67
Fisher, Deobrah, 359n4
Fisheret, Bonnie, 61n91
Fishman, G., 494n75
Fisk, Wendy, 231n157
Flannery, Daniel, 168n70, 197n24, 361n54
Flaving, Jeanne, 418n65

Fletcher, Kenneth, 81
Flewelling, Robert, 60n8, n28, n36
Flowers, Lucy, 367
Fogelson, Robert, 417n1
Foglia, Wanda, 102n43, n45, n46
Foley, Michael, 30n3
Fontana, Vincent, 230n124
Forde, David, 169n77
Forehand, Rex, 332n46, n47
Forero, Juan, 332n90
Formby, William, 102n29
Forst, Martin, 454n67
Fort, Jeff, 256
Fortas, Abe, 293, 372, 534
Foster, Holly, 167n3
Fowles, Richard, 138n40
Fox, James A., 36–37, 59n3
Fox, Robert J., 269n2
Fox, Sanford, 390n10, 391n18, n19, n26, n27, n29, 454n48, n82
Frank, James, 417n9
Fraser, Brian, 230n98
Fraser, Matthew, 293
Frazee, Sharon Glave, 102n26
Frazier, Charles, 60n24, 407, 409, 418n71, n77, 454n74
Frease, Dean, 301n19
Freeman-Gallant, Adrienne, 103n115, 168n52
Freeman, Taneekah, 492n8
Frehsee, D., 230n113
Freitag, Raelene, 231n160, n162
French, Howard, 501
Freng, Adrienne, 418n90, n92
Freud, Anna, 445, 455n89
Freud, Sigmund, 86–87, 180, 197n46
Frick, Paul, 198n79
Fritsch, Eric, 26, 27, 102n36, 418n88
Frodi, Ann, 198n74
Frydl, Kathleen, 417n30, 539n6
Fuddy, Loretta, 360n30
Fuentes, Angel Ilarraza, 453n27
Fuentes, Annette, 302n63
Fukurai, Hiroshi, 140n141
Fulkerson, Andrew, 102n54
Fyfe, James, 102n35, 418n65

G
Gaarder, Emily, 186, 198n107, n110, 454n61, 494n85
Gabor, Thomas, 362n100, 522n15
Gaffney, Michael, 139n63
Galant, Debra, 361n68
Gamble, Thomas J., 199n141
Gambrell, Marilyn K., 3
Ganousis, Jeanette, 455n105
Gant, Charles, 81
Garcia, Robert, 270n112
Gardner, William, 198n58
Garfinkel, Harold, 131, 140n137, n154
Garland, Ann, 198n78
Garnier, Helen, 140n122
Garofalo, Raffaele, 76
Garrison, Arthur, 385
Gary, Eileen, 361n60
Gates, Bill, 119
Gatowski, Sophia, 231n145
Gatti, Uberto, 523n60, n79

Gault, Gerald, 441–43
Geis, Gilbert, 27, 454n45
Gelles, Richard, 214–15, 230n95, n110, n111, n112, n133, 231n159
Gelsthorpe, Loraine, 516, 523n85, n57, n94
Gerard, D. L., 331n38
Gerber, Jurg, 333n116
Gerdes, D., 103n82
Gerstein, Dean, 229n31
Gerstein, Steven, 455n99
Gertz, Marc, 138n49
Gesch, C. Bernard, 79
Gesiriech, Sarah, 231n145
Giacobbe, George, 494n101
Giacomazzi, Andrew, 271n202
Gibbons, Don, 198n99, 454n44
Gibbs, Jack, 102n47
Gibbs, John, 163n7, n14, 197n30
Giblin, Matthew, 492n16
Gibson, Chris, 139n63, 302n76
Giddings, Martha, 408
Gies, Steve, 489
Giever, Dennis, 163n7, n9, n14, 197n12, 197n30
Giglio, Greg, 271n174, 331n41
Gilchrist, Lewayne, 167n12, 168n28
Gilligan, Carol, 176, 197n23
Gillis, A. R., 199n134, n135
Ginzberg, Eli, 167n24, 333n105, n107
Giordano, Peggy, 139n87, 140n128, n130, 167n2, 169n100, 188, 189, 269n8, n38
Giovino, G., 31n48
Giroux, Bruce, 168n33
Gitman, E., 494n75
Glad, Kathy, 230n103
Glaser, William, 301n21
Glasser, William, 481, 494n97
Glassner, Barry, 61n58
Glassoock, Bruce, 414
Glazerman, Steven, 361n81, n83, n85
Glazier, Mary, 249, 270n104, 271n159
Glever, Dennis, 169n80
Glueck, Eleanor, 94, 145–46, 158, 167n4, n5, n6, 185, 197n49, 198n93, n94, n95, n96, 228n23
Glueck, Sheldon, 94, 145–46, 158, 167n4, n5, n6, 185, 197n49, 198n93, n94, n95, n96, 228n23
Goddard, Henry, 96
Goede, Martijn de, 198n76
Goeke-Morey, Marcie C., 229n48
Gold, Martin, 198n118, 301n14, n15, n22, n23
Golden, Daniel, 453n11
Goldkamp, John, 102n35
Goldman, M. S., 332n56
Goldman, Nathan, 404, 418n52, n60
Goldstein, Herman, 417n6
Goldstein, Joseph, 417n48, 445, 455n89
Goldstein, Paul, 331n16, 332n59
Gomby, Deanna, 360n23
Gonzalez, E. J., 276
Goode, Erica, 455n97, n103
Goodman, Robert, 88
Goodwin, D. W., 331n43, n44
Gordon, Leslie, 139n100, 229n35, n66
Gordon, Linda, 231n140, 391n22
Gordon, Rachel, 254, 270n130
Gordon, Robert, 141n168

Gottesman, Irving, 103n108, n109
Gottfredson, Denise C., 138n30, 139n58, 231n180, 302n54, n79, 348, 351–52, 361n67, n69, n72, n73
Gottfredson, Gary, 138n30, 139n58, 302n54, n79, 361n72, n73
Gottfredson, Michael, 61n50-51, 138n30, 139n58, 160–65, 164, 165, 166, 169n71, n72, n74, n75, n79, n87, 301n16
Gough, Jaime, 421
Gould, Leroy, 60n13
Gould, Roger, 30n5
Gouvis, Caterina, 356, 361n93
Gove, Walter, 102n22
Gover, Angela, 494n111
Gowen, L. Kris, 31n53, 197n54
Graham, Marilyn, 343
Graham-Watson, Lorraine, 187
Granic, Isabela, 140n108, 269n13
Grant, Heath, 419n102, n103
Grasmick, Harold, 138n24, 138n29, n54, 169n82, n86, n89, n91, n93
Graves, Rick, 270n119, 332n67
Gray-Ray, Phyllis, 140n140, n146, n155
Green, Arthur H., 55
Green, Bruce, 454n49
Green, Donald, 39, 102n43
Green, Mary, 290
Greenberg, David, 138n17, n19
Greenberg, Stephanie, 138n47
Greene, Jack, 287, 302n57, n60
Greene, Michael, 139n61, n62
Greenhouse, Linda, 455n101
Greenwood, Peter, 31n71, 61n79, 331n2, 332n53, 344, 360n28, n34, n44, 391n50, n70, 414, 492n6, 493n40, 539n7
Gregorie, Trudy, 493n25
Griffen, Patrick, 454n54
Griffin, Yvette Tucker, 36
Griffith, William, 493n37
Grimes, Paul, 493n20
Grisso, T., 453n5
Grissom, Grant, 454n83
Griswold, Manzer, 198n99
Grossman, Jean, 361n60, n63, n64
Groves, W. Byron, 138n30, 139n57, 301n34
Grunbaum, Jo Anne, 9
Guarino-Ghezzi, Susan, 417n19
Guggenheim, Martin, 454n39
Gulley, Bill, 230n91
Gundry, Gwen, 230n87

H
Haack, D., 103n82
Haapanen, Rudy, 167n15, 169n95
Haefele, William, 269n20
Hagan, John, 102n22, 167n3, 168n59, 193–94, 195, 199n134, n135, 229n55, 522n13
Hagedorn, John, 247, 248, 269n58, 270n87, n96, 271n174, n207, 331n41, 332n68
Hahn, Andrew, 361n61, n62
Haight, Lois, 453n19
Halbfinger, David, 494n79
Hale, Donna, 391n23
Halemba, Gregory, 391n42
Halpern, Diane, 169n17
Haltigan, John, 199n141
Hamburg, Beatrix, 361n50

Hamilton, B.E., 30n20
Hammond, Rodney, 302n51
Hammond, Sean, 79
Hamparian, Donna, 61n67
Hampson, Sarah, 79
Hancock, Gareth, 523n93
Hanks, Carole,, 360n25
Hanlon, Thomas, 125
Hannor, Lance, 301n24
Hansell, Stephen, 301n28, 332n74
Hansen, David, 30n1, 31n85
Hansen, Diane, 357, 493n41
Hanson, Cindy, 269n20
Harachi, Tracy, 362n96
Harden, Hazel, 417n13
Harden, Philip, 103n95, 230n85
Harding, Karen, 81
Hardt, Robert, 607
Hareven, Tamara K., 31n38
Harhut, Chester, 453n12
Harlow, Caroline Wolf, 231n161
Harms, Paul, 453n25, n26, n28
Harrell, Adele, 361n91
Harrington, Kathy, 168n25
Harrington, Richard, 362n101
Harris, Gardiner, 332n94
Harris, Judith Rich, 211, 230n93, 234, 269n9, n11, n12, n17, n18
Harris, Mark, 138n31, 139n67
Harris, Monica, 140n136, n143
Harrison, Lana, 331n8
Harrison, Paige, 385
Harry, B., 198n68
Hartinger, Walter, 493n54, n55
Hartnagel, Timothy, 140n132
Hartstone, Eliot, 418n70, 454n67
Hartwig, Holly, 168n38, 199n146
Harvey, Holly, 44
Harwood, Henrick, 331n12
Haskett, Mary, 231n158
Hastie, Wendy, 209
Haurek, Edward, 198n118
Hawkins, Gordon, 523n41
Hawkins, J. David, 141n172, 151, 167n12, 168n28, n43, n44, n45, 269n33, 270n128, 301n7, 303n112, 332n85, 361n51, n89, n90, n92, n94, n95, 362n96
Hawton, Keith, 230n107
Hay, Carter, 139n102
Hay, Dale, 197n9, n13
Hayden, Tom, 261, 271n177
Haynes, Jack, 454n83
Haynie, Dana, 101n14, 197n55, 198n120, 235, 269n25
Healy, William, 96, 179, 197n41
Heaviside, Sheila, 302n66, n67
Heinzow, Birger, 103n80
Heitgerd, Janet, 138n36
Helfer, Ray, 230n121, n122
Helland, Ingrid, 102n71
Hellman, Daryl, 302n55, n80
Hellum, Frank, 31n82
Henderson, Charles, 360n24, n25
Henggeler, Scott, 168n36, 228n4, n21, 229n44, 269n20, 326, 332n103, 333n104, 472
Hennessy, James, 229n63
Herbert, Carey, 163n8

Herkner, Birgitta, 301n18
Herman, Judith, 230n108
Hernandez, Michael, 421
Hernandez, Ruth, 361n88
Herrenkohl, Todd, 168n43, 269n39
Herrera, Veronica, 198n103, n104, 229n43, 231n173
Herrnstein, Richard, 97, 101n11, 160, 168n67
Hershorn, Michael, 229n41
Hess, Taylor, 288
Hessing, Dick, 163n17
Hetherington, E. Mavis, 207
Hickman, Matthew, 417n14, 418n89
Higgins, James, 230n123
Hill, Karl G., 167n12, 168n28, 269n33, 361n51
Hindelang, Michael, 60n11, 97
Hinshaw, S. P., 81
Hippchen, Leonard, 103n76
Hirasing, Remy, 285
Hirschel, J. David, 418n95
Hirschi, Travis, 60n11, 61n50-51, 97, 101n20, 127–29, 140n121, 160–65, 164, 165, 166, 169n71, n72, n74, n75, n79, n87, 235, 236, 269n26, 301n16, 528
Hochhauser, Lois, 230n96
Hochstetler, Andy, 69
Hodges, Jill, 231n170
Hoffman, John, 229n31
Hoge, Robert, 168n63
Holden, Gwen A., 23
Holloway, Bruce, 361n65
Holmes, Malcolm, 140n125
Holsinger, Kristi, 198n102, 199n130, n145
Holtz, Larry, 417n46
Holzer, Charles, 271n183
Homes, Malcolm, 140n166, n167
Honig, Alice, 360n36
Hook, Edward, III, 168n25
Hoover, Daniel, 140n136, n143
Hope, Trina, 188, 189
Horn, W., 230n113
Horney, Julie, 39, 198n69
Horowitz, Ruth, 271n201, 321, 331n35, 332n57, n58, n62, n79
Horvath, John, 31n81
Horwood, L. John, 140n110, 168n40
Hoshi, Akemi, 332n101, 361n65
Hotaling, Gerald, 61n93
Houbé, Jill, 360n28
Hough, Richard, 198n78, 231n163
House, James, 168n55, n62
Houston, James, 271n206
Howard, Gregory, 503, 522n34, 523n38, n39
Howard, Philip, 523n93
Howell, James, 61n72, n80, 141n172, 269n45, 270n133, n134, n135, 333n106, 361n55, n95, 383, 391n49, 454n65, n67, 494n94
Howes, Paul, 18
Hoyt, Dan, 61n89
Hoza, Betsy, 269n30
Hsia, Heidi, 494n77
Huang, Bu, 168n44, n45, 332n85
Hubbard, Dana Jones, 198n81
Huff, C. Ronald, 39, 197n4, 244, 269n60, 270n75, n103, 271n153
Hughes, Thomas, 455n111
Huizinga, David, 57, 60n14, 61n80, 141n172, 228n13, 270n100, 271n185, 321, 331n28, 332n78, n82, n83

Hulsman, L., 141n181
Hunt, Geoffrey, 252, 270n124, 271n194
Hurlburt, Michael, 231n163
Hurst, Hunter, 388, 391n58, n66, 493n60
Hurst, Yolander, 417n9
Hurwitz, Emanuel, 302n81
Hussmann, Judith, 198n76
Husted, David, 168n26
Huston, H. Range, 271n142
Hutchings, Bernard, 84
Hutzler, John L., 31n54, n55

I

Immarigeon, Russ, 141n176
Inciardi, James, 318, 321, 331n8, n35, 332n57, n58, n62, n72, n79
Inglis, Ruth, 228n7, 230n99
Ingraham, James, 295
Ingram, A. Leigh, 139n98
Iovanni, Leeann, 140n157
Ireland, Timothy, 224, 231n176, 331n37
Irving, Mark, 511, 514
Irwin, John, 418n80
Irwin, Katherine, 357, 493n41
Isaacson, Lynne, 39

J

Jacklin, Carol, 198n57, n71
Jackson-Beck, Marilyn, 493n64
Jackson, Kenneth, 60n22, n23, 197n45, 229n28
Jackson, Lori, 103n92
Jackson, Pamela Irving, 242, 270n69
Jacobs, Bruce, 102n37, 302n68
Jacobs, Nancy, 419n102, n103
Jaffe, Peter, 229n42, 494n96
Jaffee, Sara, 103n118, 206, 229n38
James, Bernard, 302n104
James, Dominic, 231n142
James, William, 92
Jang, Sung Joon, 140n111, n112, 168n53, 229n50, n57, n70, 301n8
Janosz, Michel, 283
Jarjoura, Roger, 61n47, 139n105, 283
Jarvis, D., 493n50
Jeffrey, C. Ray, 102n69
Jenkins, Pamela, 27, 140n126
Jenkins, Patricia, 302n42
Jensen, Eric, 102n44, 333n116
Jensen, Gary, 60n11, 60n13, 198n118, 199n137, 270n98, 271n188
Jensen, Lene Arnett, 298n3
Jensen, Peter, 362n101
Jessica (Random Family character), 123
Jessor, Richard, 167n23, n24, 168n30
Joe, Karen, 270n107, 417n27
Joe-Laidler, Karen, 270n124
Johnsen, Matthew, 301n9, 302n43
Johnson, Brian, 454n59
Johnson, Bruce, 320, 332n60, n61, n66, n69, n78
Johnson, Byron, 140n111, n112
Johnson, Charlotte, 103n97
Johnson, Courtney, 269n14
Johnson, Dale, 360n37
Johnson, E. H., 303n112
Johnson, Jeffrey, 39
Johnson, Lyndon, 341, 375
Johnson, Mark, 286

Johnson, Robert, 140n145, 229n31
Johnston, Lloyd, 60n9, n16, 61n49, 101n12, 198n112, 310, 331n1, n9, n18, n19
Johnston, N., 229n29
Jolliffe, Darrick, 169n81, 523n93
Jones, Donald, 168n37, 211, 230n89, n92
Jones, Lisa, 216, 230n119, n120
Jones, Marshall, 168n37, 211, 230n89, n92, 361n78
Jones (of Breed v. Jones), 439
Jones, Peter, 61n69
Jones, Richard Lezin, 493n67
Jones, Sharon, 453n22
Jones, Shayne, 138n44
Jones-Walker, Cheryl, 495n132
Jorgensen, Jenel, 88
Jou, Susyan, 301n6, n25
Judah, Richard, 81
Jules, Darlyne, 440
Junger, Marianne, 163n17, 169n78
Junger-Tas, Josine, 503, 512, 523n42, n43, n58
Jurgens, Janelle, 198n101
Justice, Blair, 230n124
Justice, Rita, 230n124

K

Kaduce, Lonn, 454n74
Kahan, Dan, 418n68
Kaiser, G., 269n22
Kalb, Larry, 57, 169n81
Kandel, Denise, 140n131, 331n34
Kane, Candice, 266
Kangaspunta, Kristiina, 522n35
Kann, Laura, 9
Kantor, Glenda Kaufman, 230n112
Kaplan, Howard, 139n74, 140 n141, n142, n144, n145, 332n55
Kapler, Robert A., 23
Karoly, Lynn, 360n28
Kassebaum, Nancy, 341
Kassenbaum, G., 331n27
Katkin, D., 454n44
Katz, Jack, 70–71, 102n22, 103n104
Kaufman, Jeanne, 231n164
Kaufman, Joanne, 302n51
Kaufman, Leslie, 493n67
Kaufman, Robert, 418n67
Kawai, Eriko, 270n130
Kazdin, Allan, 362n101
Keane, Carl, 163n3
Keenan, Kate, 168n33, 269n28, n39
Keilitz, Ingo, 103n100
Keith, Bruce, 206, 228n1
Kelley, Thomas, 31n72
Kelling, George, 417n11
Kelly, Delos, 31n82, 102n47, 239, 301n30, n33, n34, n35
Kelly, John, 207
Kemp, Vicky, 516, 523n85, n87, n94
Kempe, C. Henry, 212–13, 225, 230n97, n101, n102, 230n121, n122
Kempe, Ruth, 230n101, n102
Kempf, Kimberly, 61n77, 140n124
Kempf-Leonard, Kimberly, 51, 61n71-72, 102n50, 199n141, 453n10
Kendall-Tackett, Kathleen, 230n109
Kennedy, A. M., 276
Kennedy, David, 414, 417n1, 418n101
Kennedy, Leslie, 169n77

Kennedy, Mike, 302n69, n70
Kennedy, Randall, 407, 418n69
Kent, Morris, 438
Kerner, Hans-Jurgen, 101n3, 139n99, 167n17, 269n22, 523n67, n75, n76, n77, n80, n82, n86, n89, n90, n91, n92, 539n3
Kerns, 167n16
Kerper, Hazel, 492n3, n4
Ketchum, Sandy, 44
Kider, Suzanne, 494n112, n113
Kierkus, Christopher, 229n37
Kiger, Gary, 168n46
Kilburn, M. Rebecca, 360n28
Killias, Martin, 503, 522n12, 522n33
Killinger, George, 492n3, n4
Kilpatrick, Dean, 55
Kim, Julia Yun Soo, 229n30, 312, 331n25
Kim, Kee Jeong, 168n51
King, Neville J., 25
King, Robert, 168n29
Kinkelhor, David, 61n93
Kinlock, Timothy, 61n60, 167n10
Kinsbourne, Marcel, 79
Kistner, Janet, 231n158
Kjelsberg, Ellen, 88
Kleck, Gary, 38, 39
Kleiman, Mark, 271n198
Klein, Dorie, 197n47
Klein, Helen, 494n98
Klein, Jody, 60n22, 197n45, 418n59
Klein, Malcolm, 31n59, 239, 251, 260, 261, 269n48, n50, n51, 270n78, n86, n114, 271n146, n169, n181, n182, 503, 523n42
Klepper, Steven, 102n41
Klinger, David, 418n63, n65
Klockars, Carl, 332n72, n81
Knox, George, 268n1, 269n2
Knupfer, Anne Meis, 390n6
Kobrin, Solomon, 31n59, n82, 138n33, n34
Kochanek, Kenneth, 30n22
Koebel, LaDonna, 301n7
Kohfeld, Carol, 102n40
Kohlberg, Lawrence, 92–93
Komiya, Nobuo, 501
Kong, Rebecca, 506, 523n54
Konopka, Gisela, 185, 198n88, n89, n90
Koons, Barbara, 138n35
Kopczynski, Mary, 356, 361n93
Kopie, Kathy, 230n120
Koposov, Roman, 168n29
Kosterman, Rick, 168n44, n45, 332n85, 361n51
Kovandzic, Tomislav, 102n34, 139n76
Kowalski, Kathiann, 385
Kraemer, Helena Chmura, 362n101
Krahn, Harvey, 140n132
Kramer, John, 60n26, n32
Krämer, Ursula, 103n80
Krauss, Clifford, 332n89
Krebs, Johnson, 386
Krisberg, Barry, 141n172, n173, 271n199, 360n6, 454n84, 472, 492n7, 493n47, 494n75
Kritz, Ariel, 351
Krivo, Lauren, 39, 138n15, 138n31, 139n67
Krohn, Marvin, 101n3, 102n27, n58, 103n115, 139n99, n106, 140n159, 153, 167n1, n24, 168n30, n50, n52, n53, 229n56, 269n30,

270n131, 271n189, 283, 301n8, n9, 302n43, 331n32, 332n55, 539n3
Kruttschnitt, Candace, 168n64, 231n146, n147
Krutz, Ellen, 138n35
Kubrin, Charis E., 138n37
Kumpfer, Karol, 139n102, 331n42, 360n15
Kurlychek, Megan, 454n59
Kurtz, David, 408
Kurz, Gwen, 50, 61n68

L
La Sala, Kala, 398
Laak, Jan ter, 198n76
Lab, Steven, 30n25, 494n92
Lafave, Debra Beasley, 273
Lafazia, Andrea, 362n96
LaFree, Gary, 138n2, 501, 523n40
LaGrange, Randy, 332n84
LaGrange, Teresa, 139n90
Lahey, Benjamin, 270n130
Laidler, Karen Joe, 271n194
Laird, Robert, 168n40, 229n68
Lally, J. Ronald, 360n36
LaMay, Mary, 197n17
Land, Kenneth, 61n51, 102n28, 138n45, 167n19
Lane, Jodi, 267, 269n3, 271n205
Lane, Roger, 417n1
Langan, Patrick, 522n33
Lange, James, 350, 361n58, 391n48
Langley, Sandra, 199n121
Lansing, Amy, 198n78
Lanyado, Monica, 231n170
Lanz, Teresa, 231n153
LaPrairie, Carol, 141n178
LaRosa, John, 61n52
Larson, David, 140n111
Larson, James, 361n70, n71
Latessa, Edward, 494n130
Lattimore, Pamela, 102n51, 271n139
Lau, Anna, 230n127
Laub, John, 61n75, 103n110, 156, 158, 159, 167n13, 168n54, n58, n60, n65, 229n29, 230n79, n86, 237
Laucht, M., 103n82
Laufer, Bill, 140n124
Laundra, Kenneth, 168n46
Lauritsen, Janet L., 61n86-87, 332n70, n71
Laursen, Erik, 333n113
Law, Fergus, 230n107
Law, Jacqueline, 231n175
Lawrence, Richard, 140n129, 301n3, 302n41, n59, 492n15
Lawson, Willow, 79
Lazoritz, Martin, 168n26
Le Blanc, Marc, 61n57, 271n180, 283
Le, Thao, 489
Lebel, Thomas, 140n160
LeBlanc, Adrian Nicole, 123
Lee, Leona, 102n38, 454n41
Lee, Matthew, 138n39, 139n65, n92, 140n114
Lee, Ruth, 198n97, 331n38
Leiber, Michael, 60n26, n32, 139n97
Leiter, Jeffrey, 301n9, 302n43
Lemert, Edwin, 131, 138n4, 140n134, n147, 454n43
Leone, Peter, 361n67
Lerner, Richard, 271n173

LeRoy, Martin, 270n117
Leschied, Alan, 168n63
Leukefeld, Carl, 325
Leuven, Miranda van, 198n76
Levine, Murray, 199n137
Levitt, Steven, 37, 594, 60n5, 70, 101n18, 318, 332n64, n65
Lewicka, S., 103n82
Lewin, Tamar, 228n9
Lewis, Dorothy Otnow, 103n92
Lewis, Julia, 207
Lewis, Oscar, 108, 138n6
Lhotzky, Stephan, 522n7
Li, Fuzhong, 269n30, 331n30
Liazos, Alexander, 303n107
Lichter, Daniel, 30n12, 229n76
Lieb, Roxanne, 361n52
Lillard, Lee, 168n55, 229n70
Lilly, J. Robert, 493n21
Limber, Susan, 285
Lin, Kuei-Hsiu, 139n100, 229n35, n66
Lin, Nan, 168n57
Lincoln, Alan, 228n5, 230n87
Lindsay, William, 231n175
Lindsey, Benjamin, 372–73
Lindstrom, Peter, 302n58
Linnoila, Marku, 163n4
Linster, Richard, 102n51, 271n139
Lipsey, Mark, 168n35, 493n46
Lishner, Denise, 303n112
Liska, Allen, 138n46
Liu, Jianhong, 138n46
Liu, Xiaoru, 139n74
Livingston, Mark, 523n93
Lizotte, Alan, 38, 39, 101n3, 103n115, 139n99, n106, 155, 167n1, n 24, 168n30, n52, n53, 229n56, 270n131, n132, n138, 271n140, n189, 283, 301n8, n9, 302n43, 332n55, 419n104, 539n3
Lochman, John, 269n29
Loeber, Rolf, 57, 61n61, n80, n90, 88, 141n172, 146, 149–50, 167n7, n11, 168n33, n35, n40, 169n81, 197n9, n13, 228n2, n5, n17, 229n49, n62, 237, 269n15, n20, n28, n37, n39, 270n130, 360n22, 361n90, 362n104, 493n46, 511, 536, 539n8
Loftin, Colin, 27n78
Logalbo, Anthony, 385
Logan, Charles, 454n44
Logan, T. K., 325
Lombroso, Cesare, 76, 100, 178–79, 197n1, n2, n36, n37, n38
Lombroso-Ferrero, Gina, 102n62
Long, David, 361n84
Long, John, 271n153, n166, n171
Longshore, Douglas, 163n10, 169n90
Lopez, D. A., 271n154
Lorenz, Frederick, 167n14, 168n51, 229n35
Lotke, Eric, 138n18
Loukas, Alexandra, 302n40
Lovrich, Nicholas, 139n63
Lowe-Webb, Roselyn, 231n153
Lubinskis, David, 197n18
Luchterhand, Elmer, 418n53
Ludwig, Jens, 39
Lundberg, Ingvar, 301n18
Lundman, Richard, 360n6, n10, 417n23, n28, n51, 418n64, n67, 454n44

Lyall, Sarah, 523n64
Lynam, Donald, 95, 168n40, 169n96, 197n56, 325
Lynch, James, 522n32
Lynch, Michael, 78, 103n79
Lynskey, Dana, 163n9
Lyon, Reid, 103n102
Lyons, Horace, 522n27

M
Macallair, Dan, 26, 493n45
Maccauley, J., 198n74
Maccoby, Eleanor, 177, 197n27, 198n57, n71
MacCoun, Robert, 318, 331n29, 332n63, n119
MacDermid, Shelley, 138n7
MacDonald, John, 194, 199n143, 271n139
Mace, David, 88
MacKenzie, Doris Layton, 102n48, 231n180, 332n101, 348, 360n31, 361n65, 391n53, 400, 417n8, 483, 494n91, n91, n105, n107, n111, n112, n113, n114
Macksey-Amiti, Mary Ellen, 331n5, 332n59
MacMillan, Ross, 159, 168n59, n64
Maguire, Edward, 417n8
Mahoney, Anne R., 140n133
Mahoney, Dennis, 493n28
Mai, Noemi, 333n108
Major, Aline, 241, 270n64, n65
Malecki, Christine Kerres, 302n49
Males, Mike, 26
Malinosky-Rummell, Robin, 30n1, 31n85
Malisova, L., 103n82
Mallar, Charles, 361n84
Mallory, W. A., 103n100
Malone, Patrick, 149, 269n16, 301n17
Mangione, Peter, 360n36
Mann, Emily, 360n46
Mannheim, Herman, 102n61
Mansfield, Wendy, 302n82
Maras, A., 103n82
Marcotte, Paul, 454n57
Marenin, Otwin, 169n92
Marini, Margaret Mooney, 197n19
Markle, Gerald, 228n24
Markman, Howard, 228n18
Markowitz, Fred, 138n46
Marshall, Chris, 31n84
Marshall, Donnie, 333n117
Marshall, Ineke, 31n84, 523n43
Marshall, Paul, 103n77, n78, n81
Martin, Catherine, 325
Martin, David, 229n69
Martin, Gregory, 432
Martin, Jamie, 163n14, 197n30
Martin, Joyce, 30n20, 30n22
Martin, Lawrence, 31n75, n77
Martin, M. O., 276
Martin, Randy, 102n60
Martinez, Ramiro, Jr., 117, 139n77
Maruna, Shadd, 140n160
Mason, Alex, 198n80
Mason, Craig, 454n58, n64
Mason, Robert, 230n123
Mâsse, Louise, 331n45, 332n51, 361n53
Massey, Charles, 301n28
Massey, James, 102n27, n58
Mathur, Anita K., 230n113

Matsueda, Ross, 140n139
Matthys, Walter, 88
Matza, David, 126, 140n119, n120, n133, n151, n152
Maughan, Barbara, 88, 168n33
Maume, Michael, 138n39, 139n92
Maupin, James, 385, 453n32, 495n136
Maxfield, Michael, 231n168
Maxim, Paul, 163n3
Maxson, Cheryl, 197n4, 245, 246, 270n77, n86, n103
Maxwell, Christopher, 150, 168n34
Maxwell, Sheila Royo, 150, 168n34
Mays, G. Larry, 271n193, 385
Mazerolle, Paul, 139n84, n85, n86, 163n2, 167n8, n9, n15, 169n95, 197n6, 198n77
McBride, Duane, 333n109
McCabe, Kristen, 198n78
McCall, Patricia, 167n19
McCarthy, Bill, 101n19, 102n22, 229n55
McCloskey, Laura Ann, 198n103
McConnell, Sheena, 361n85
McCord, Joan, 228n4, 301n7, 360n9, n11, n12, n22, 361n53, n56, n59, n65, n66, n80, 362n100, 391n45, n67, n69, 418n55, n95, 494n99, n127, 511, 522n36, 523n73
McCord, William, 360n9
McCorkle, Richard, 269n63
McCubbin, Michael, 486
McDermott, Joan, 302n61, n62
McDevitt, Jack, 414
McDill, E. L., 302n53
McDonald, Lance, 231n178
McDowall, David, 27, 31n78, 101n3, 139n99, 455n92, 539n3
Mcentire, Ranee, 138n49
McFarlane, Elizabeth, 360n30
McGahey, Richard, 138n11
McGarrell, Edmund, 417n31
McGlothlin, W., 332n72
McGrath, John, 138n48
McGuigan, K., 332n99
McGuire, James, 493n46
McHale, Rosalie, 494n77
McKay, Henry D., 112, 113, 138n22, n25, 229n27, 238–39, 339, 355, 360n7
McKinney, J. D., 278, 301n16
McLanahan, Sara, 205, 229n33
McMahon, R. J., 361n53
McManus, Terry, 302n92
McMillan, Dean, 231n170
McMillan, Richard, 138n26
McMorris, Barbara, 168n64
McNeal, Elizabeth, 103n77, n78
McNeil, Donald, 522n10
McNeill, Richard, 138n30, 139n58
McNulty, Betsie, 489
McNulty, Thomas, 60n37, 138n21, 139n70
McPartland, J. M., 302n53
McPherson, Susan, 231n178
Mear, Daniel, 197n29
Meares, Tracey, 418n68
Mears, Daniel, 494n129
Measelle, Jeffrey, 103n118
Medaris, Michael, 302n105, 303n106
Mednick, Brigitte, 103n90
Mednick, Sarnoff, 61n55, 84, 103n90, n106, n120, 229n51

Meeker, James, 267, 269n3, 271n205
Meesters, Cor, 81, 163n3, 169n82
Meier, Robert, 140n161
Meltzer, Howard, 88
Menacker, Julius, 302n81
Menard, Scott, 169n88, 321, 331n28, 332n83
Mendel, Richard, 362n99
Mennel, Robert M., 31n38, 390n1, n4, n9
Merkens, Hans, 522n13
Merlo, Alida, 388, 391n71
Mero, Richard, 168n55
Mertinko, Elizabeth, 350, 361n58, 391n48
Merton, Robert, 116, 117, 119, 136, 139n72
Merva, Mary, 138n40
Meseck-Bushey, Sylvia, 230n91
Messerschmidt, James, 191, 197n3, n31, 199n128, n133
Messner, Julie, 88
Messner, Steven, 60n42, 119, 120, 138n1, n26, 139n76, n91
Metsger, Linda, 102n44
Michel, Sonya, 360n35
Miethe, Terance, 269n63
Mihalic, Sharon, 357, 493n41
Milich, Richard, 140n136, n143, 325
Miller, Alden, 492n7
Miller, Brenda, 230n100, 231n163
Miller, Darcy, 197n10
Miller, J. Mitchell, 302n76
Miller, Jerome, 459, 492n5
Miller, Jody, 192, 250, 270n110, n111
Miller, Joshua, 95
Miller, Laurie, 360n22
Miller, Marc, 31n71
Miller, Ruddy, 302n48
Miller, Stuart, 493n52, 494n81
Miller, Ted, 61n82, 337–38, 359n1, n4
Miller, Walter, 239, 241, 269n46, n47, n53, n55, n56, n61, 270n64, n71, n83, 271n145, n191, n192, 340, 360n14
Miller-Johnson, Shari, 237, 269n14, n15, n16, n29
Minor, Kevin, 385
Minton, Sophia, 367
Mio, J.S., 331n39
Mirowsky, John, 138n50, 197n14, n15
Mischel, Walter, 90
Mitchell, Nick, 140n160
Mitchell, Ojmarrh, 391n53, 494n111
Mnacker, F., 30n20
Moak, Stacy, 391n64
Moch, Annie, 30n13, 138n13
Model, Karyn, 360n34
Modzeleski, William, 302n51, n52
Moffitt, Terrie, 81, 103n74, n88, n118, 147, 165, 167n17, 168n39, n40, 169n94, n96, n98, n99, 197n56, 229n38
Monahan, Thomas, 229n26
Monnet, Danette, 163n9
Monroe, Lawrence, 60n44
Monroe, R. R., 103n93
Monti, Daniel, 268n1
Moon, Melissa, 391n68
Moore, Eugene, 454n83
Moore, Joan, 186, 198n108, n109, 250–51, 269n62, 270n70, n96, n106, n112, 271n153
Moore, Kristin, 140n127

Moore, Mark, 271n198, 332n96, 361n95, 391n56, 413, 417n1, 418n97, n99
Moore, Melanie, 139n105, 283
Moore, Melinda, 60n40
Morash, Merry, 408, 418n75
Morenoff, Jeffrey, 138n38, 139n66, n69, n75
Morley, Elaine, 356, 361n93
Morris, Allison, 197n11
Morris, E., 168n69
Morris, Norval, 61n48, 101n21, 103n120, 228n5, 269n21, 417n1, 418n97
Morris, Ruth, 185, 198n86, n91, 228n24
Morrison, Diane, 301n7
Morse, Stephen J., 31n46
Morselli, Carlo, 101n6
Mosher, Clayton, 333n116
Mrug, Sylive, 269n31
Mueller, David, 271n202
Mukherjee, Satyanshu, 523n72
Mullis, I. V. S., 276
Mulvey, Edward, 61n52
Munson, M. L., 30n20
Muris, Peter, 81, 163n3, 169n82
Murph, Thomas, 494n104
Murphy, Fred, 60n7
Murphy, Patrick, 331n29, 333n119
Murray, Charles, 103n101, 131, 140n156, 458, 492n1
Mutchnick, Robert, 102n60
Muvihill, Donald, 271n146
Myers, David, 454n58, n64
Myers, Jane, 168n38, 199n146
Myers, Kristen, 301n9, 302n43
Myers, Stephanie, 405, 417n51, 418n56

N
Nader, P. R., 302n71
Nagin, Daniel, 102n29, n30, n33, n41, 140n110, 167n12, n19, 168n28, n40, n66
Najaka, Stacy Skroban, 348
Najman, Jake, 103n117, 230n90
Nalini, Ambady, 140n135
Nalla, Mahesh, 139n97
Nanjundappa, G., 331n39
Nansel, Tonja, 285
Napier, Susan, 230n134
Nation, Maury, 285
Ndiaye, Mademba, 522n30
Neaigus, Alan, 331n8
Neal, Stephen, 198n58
Needle, Jerome, 271n195
Neff, Matthew, 341
Nelson, Gordon K., 228n8
Ness, Arlin, 494n100
Neumark-Sztainer, Dianne, 285
New, Michelle, 231n170
Newcomb, Michael, 167n20
Newman, Graeme, 31n45, 332n87, 503, 512, 522n34, 523n38, n39, n47, n72
Nicewander, W. Alan, 160, 168n68
Nichols, Michael, 376
Niederhoffer, Arthur, 259, 271n162, n163
Nimer, Richard, 493n24
Nixon, Richard, 375
Nobiling, Tracy, 60n33
Noone, Diana, 331n23
Noriega, Manuel, 322
Norman, Michael, 495n135

Noronha, José Carvalho de, 522n20
Novak, Scott, 325
Novotney, Laurence, 350, 361n58, 391n48
Npales, Michelle, 140n160
Nugent, M. Elaine, 25
Nurco, David, 61n60, 167n10
Nurge, Dana, 414
Nye, F. Ivan, 60n11, n43, n44, 206, 229n40

O
Oakes, Jeannie, 301n31, n32, n36
O'Brien, Robert, 39
O'Connor, Sandra Day, 221
Odem, Mary, 194, 199n139, 391n28
O'Donnell, Julie, 301n7
Offord, David, 361n78, 362n101
O'Grady, Kevin, 125
Ohlin, Lloyd, 31n39, n40, 122, 139n94, 231n135, n136, 243, 245, 260, 270n73, 331n33, 340, 391n20, 492n7
Olds, David, 360n24, n25, n26, n27
O'Leary, Cecilia, 140n162
Olexa, Carol, 301n29
Olivares, Kathleen, 163n7
Olsen, Virgil, 60n44
Olson, Jeffrey, 361n90, n94
Olweus, Dan, 285
O'Malley, Patrick, 60n9, n16, 61n49, 101n12, 198n112, 310, 331n1, n18, n19
Onek, David, 454n84, 493n47
Onishi, Norimitsu, 501, 522n25
Orbuch, Terri, 168n55, n62
Orlandi, Mario, 361n75, n76, n77
Orme, Nicholas, 31n29
Ormrod, Richard, 61n92, 174, 197n5, 215, 230n116
Ornstein, Miriam, 60n8
Osborn, Denise, 102n24
Osborne, Lynn, 369, 391n14
Osgood, D. Wayne, 61n62, 101n12, 138n28, 160, 168n31, n68, 198n59, n112, 301n64, 332n74, 418n90, n91, n92
Ostresh, Erik, 140n125
Ostrow, Miriam, 333n105, n107
O'Sullivan, Kate, 494n104
O'Toole, Brian, 230n106
Ou, Suh-Ruu, 361n47
Ousey, Graham, 138n39
Overpeck, Mary, 285
Owen, Barbara, 494n87
Owuor, Otula, 522n31

P
Paasch, Kathleen, 283
Packer, Herbert, 417n50
Padilla, Felix, 242, 262, 270n68, 271n186
Padina, Robert, 332n84
Pagani-Kurtz, Linda, 361n53
Pagani, Linda, 163n12
Paige, Karen, 198n67
Painter, Kate, 523n93
Pajer, Kathleen, 198n58, n75
Pallone, Nathaniel, 229n63
Paolucci, Henry, 101n8
Papillo, Angela Romano, 140n127
Papp, Lauren M., 229n48
Papy, Joseph, 493n24
Paramore, Vickie, 194, 199n144

Parent, Dale, 494n115
Parent, Sophie, 163n12
Parker, Faith Lamb, 341
Parker, Karen, 138n41
Parkinson, Patrick, 230n106
Parks, Roger, 417n21
Parmelee, Arthur, 103n89
Parson, Jeffrey Lee, 525
Paschall, Mallie, 60n8, n28, n36
Pasternak, Robert, 103n102
Paternoster, Raymond, 101n15, 102n42, 140n157, 163n2, 167n9, 168n61, n66, 197n6
Paterson, Andrea, 493n65
Patterson, Gerald, 167n7, 168n31, 344–45, 348, 360n32, n33
Patterson, James, 140n116
Paulozzi, Len, 302n51
Paulson, Amanda, 432
Payne, Allison Ann, 302n79
Payne, Gary, 139n84, n86
Pear, Robert, 493n66
Peat, J. K., 472
Peay, Lenore, 341
Peel, Robert, 394
Pelham, Molina, Jr., 81
Pelham, William, 103n97
Peng, Samuel, 302n56
Pennell, Susan, 39, 270n136
Pepler, D. J., 197n32
Peralta, Robert, 332n74
Perel, James, 198n58
Perez, Cynthia, 167n1, n24, 168n30
Pérez, Deanna, 316, 317
Perkins, Craig A., 61n84
Perlera, Jasira, 156
Perone, Paul, 269n4
Perry, Cheryl, 285
Perry, T. B., 269n6
Petechuk, David, 269n39
Peter, Katharin, 302n48
Peters, Carolyn, 36
Petersen, Courtney, 60n21
Petersilia, Joan, 114, 138n43, 360n22, 391n50, 417n8, 484, 494n109, n131, 522n32, 539n7
Peterson, Dana, 418n90, n92
Peterson, John, 31n82
Peterson, Ruth, 39, 138n15, 138n31, 139n67
Petrocelli, Matthew, 140n165
Pettit, Gregory, 139n68, 168n40, 229n68, n71
Pfeiffer, Christian, 504, 506, 522n8, n37, 523n52, n53, n55, n56, n69
Phillips, Julie, 60n30, n38
Phillips, M., 454n44
Phipps, Polly, 361n52
Phleps, Charles, 360n25
Pi, Chung-Ron, 391n72
Piaget, Jean, 92
Pickering, Lloyd, 139n104, 163n17, 301n2
Pickett, Robert, 390n8
Pickrel, Susan, 333n104
Piehl, Anne Morrison, 414, 419n101
Pierce, Christine Schnyder, 453n6, n7
Piersma, Paul, 455n105
Pihl, Robert, 103n95, 230n85, 361n53
Piliavin, Irving, 418n53, n62
Pilla, Ramani, 285

Pilnick, Paul, 493n43
Pincus, Jonathan, 103n92
Pink, William, 301n30
Piorkowski, Chaya, 341
Piper, Elizabeth, 60n40
Piquero, Alex, 102n52, 103n84, 139n84, n85, 140n165, 163n2, 167n9, n10, n15, n18, 169n76, n95, n96, 197n6, 198n77
Planty, Mike, 302n48
Platt, Anthony, 31n37, n52, 133, 141n170, 368–69, 390n5, n12, n13, 455n88
Platt, Christina, 332n48
Platt, Jerome, 332n48
Platt, Tony, 140n162
Pleck, Elizabeth, 31n39, n40, n42, n44, 391n20, n21
Ploeger, Matthew, 101n16, 197n29
Podboy, J. W., 103n100
Poe-Yamagata, Eileen, 454n72
Pogarsky, Greg, 38, 39, 102n29, n30, n33, n52
Polk, Kenneth, 301n5, n19, n27, n29
Pollak, Otto, 179, 197n42, n43, n44
Pollock, Carl B., 230n121
Polsenberg, Christina, 60n22, 197n45
Pope, Carl, 60n22, n39, 197n45, 408
Porterfield, A.L., 607
Posey, Cody, 65
Post, Charles, 103n98
Potter, Lloyd, 302n51
Pottieger, Anne, 321, 331n35, 332n57, n58, n62, n79
Poulin, François, 360n12, 361n59, 494n99
Powell, D. R., 360n36
Powell, R. T., 454n81
Pranis, Kay, 141n177
Pratt, Travis, 169n90, 198n81
Pratts, Michale, 271n142
Pribesh, Shana, 138n50
Price, Dwight, 425, 453n17
Price, Joseph, 230n103
Pridemore, William, 523n38
Priest, Thomas, 409, 418n84
Prinz, Ronald, 167n16
Pruitt, Matthew, 138n41
Prysock, Randall, 403
Pugh, M. D., 140n130, 269n38
Puritz, Patricia, 494n126
Putka, Gary, 303n109
Puzzanchera, Charles, 377, 427, 428, 436, 446, 454n51, n53, n67, n68, n70, 455n86, 461, 492n9, n10
Pyatt, Jonathan, 302n104

Q
Qin, Ping, 103n111
Quinn, Kathleen, 231n175
Quinney, Richard, 141n169, n170
Quisenberry, Neil, 138n44

R
Rabiner, David, 149, 301n17
Rachin, Richard, 494n97
Raeder, Myrna, 231n150
Raffalovich, Lawrence, 138n26
Rafter, Nicole Hahn, 102n65
Rahav, G., 229n74, n75
Raine, Adrian, 103n76, n90, n94, n106, 229n51

Rainville, Gerard, 454n52, n69, n73, n75
Rand, Alicia, 61n56
Rand, Michael, 61n81, n83, 302n48
Range, Lillian, 231n163
Rankin, Joseph, 61n85
Rasmussen, Andrew, 9
Rathus, Spencer, 197n10, n22, 198n64, 269n7, 331n14, 332n49
Raudenbush, Stephen, 138n38, 139n64, n66, n75
Rausch, Sharla, 454n44
Ray, Melvin, 140n140, n146, n155
Reaves, Brian, 417n14, 418n89
Rebellon, Cesar, 139n81, 229n31, n34
Rechea-Alberola, Cristina, 523n43
Redding, Richard, 454n58, n60, n62
Reddy, Marisa, 302n52
Reed, Mark, 193, 199n136
Regnerus, Mark, 140n113
Regoeczi, Wendy C., 57
Regoli, Bob, 418n84
Rehnquist, William, 295
Reichel, Philip, 523n44, n72
Reid, John, 360n33, 493n42
Reiff, Michael, 285
Reisig, Michael, 139n60, 271n202, 417n21
Reiss, Albert, 138n11, n33, n34, n47, 181, 269n21, 417n23, n51
Rendleman, Douglas R., 31n31, n36
Rennison, Callie Marie, 61n81, n83
Reno, Janet, 417n6
Reppucci, N. Dickon, 453n8, n9
Resig, Michael, 169n92
Reuter, Peter, 231n180, 318, 331n29, 332n63, n119
Reynolds, Arthur, 360n46, 361n47
Reynolds, Mike, 27
Reynolds, Morgan, 101n10
Ribeaud, Denis, 523n43
Rich, William, 103n100
Richmond, F. Lynn, 301n19
Riddell, Steve, 453n13
Rijsdijk, Fruhling, 103n118
Riksheim, Eric, 408
Riley, K. Jack, 414
Rind, Bruce, 231n173
Rindlisbacher, Martin, 522n33
Ripple, Carol, 341
Rivara, Frederick, 182, 302n45
Rivera, Craig, 228n13
Roberts, Aki, 501
Roberts, Julian, 523n95
Roberts, Robert, 139n103
Robertson, Angela, 493n20
Robertson, Craig, 140n140, n146, n155
Robertson, Dylan, 360n46
Robey, Ames, 198n97
Robinson, Gail, 31n68
Robinson, Paul, 229n46
Robinson, Sheri, 302n40
Rodeheaver, Daniel, 523n81
Rodick, J. Douglas, 269n20
Rodriguez, Nancy, 391n54
Rodriguez, Xochitl, 277
Roehling, P. V., 332n56
Rogers, D. E., 167n24
Rogers, Joseph, 230n91
Rogers, Kevin, 493n20

Rogosch, Fred, 231n156
Rohde, Charles, 360n30
Rohde, Paul, 88
Rohsenow, D. J., 331n13
Rohter, Larry, 522n18
Romig, Dennis, 493n28
Root, Maria, 230n118
Rose, Mary, 269n14
Rose, Nancy, 494n104
Rosen, Lawrence, 229n29
Rosenbaum, Alan, 229n41
Rosenbaum, Jill Leslie, 199n148, 229n45, 494n87
Rosenfeld, Richard, 119, 120, 138n1, 139n91, 332n70, n71
Rosenfield, E., 331n38
Rosenthal, Lawrence, 247, 270n88
Rosenthal, Marguerite, 391n32, 493n56
Rosenthal, Robert, 140n135
Rosenwal, Richard, 198n97
Ross, Catherine, 138n50, n52, 197n14, n15
Rossman, Shelli, 356, 361n93
Roth, Byron, 85
Rothman, David, 31n50, 455n88
Rountree, Pamela Wilcox, 138n45
Rouse, Martin, 31n67
Roush, David, 453n33
Rowe, David, 103n107, n116, n119, 160, 168n68, n70, 197n24, 230n91
Rowe, Richard, 88
Rowe, Wendy, 419n102, n103
Rowland, Melisa, 332n103
Roy, Sudipto, 493n23
Ruben, A., 79
Ruben, Douglas, 230n125
Rubin, H. Ted, 417n47, 454n42, 469, 493n39
Rubin, K. H., 285
Rubin, Robert, 198n58
Ruchkin, Vladislav, 168n29, 229n47
Ruddy, Sally, 302n48
Rudolph, Jennifer, 139n87, 140n128, 167n2, 188, 189
Ruefle, William, 27
Ruotsala, Gloria, 351
Russell, Diana, 216, 230n108, n117
Rust, Roland, 359n2
Rutter, Michael, 168n39
Ryan, Barbara, 231n142
Ryan, George, 302n51
Ryan, James, 492n19
Ryan, Kimberly, 61n89
Rydell, C. Peter, 360n28, n34
Ryer, Charles, 231n178

S
Saarem, Kristin, 102n71
Sabel, Jennifer C., 9
Sack, William, 230n123
Sagatun, Inger, 231n177
Salerno, Anthony, 390n2, n11, 494n116
Saltmarsh, N. R., 9
Sample, Lisa, 199n141
Sampson, Robert, 61n75, 103n110, 138n30, n38, n47, 139n57, n64, n66, n69, n75, 156, 158, 159, 168n54, n58, n60, n65, 229n29, 230n79, n86, 237, 409, 418n82
Samuelson, Leslie, 140n132
Samuelsson, Stefan, 301n18

Sanborn, Joseph, 435, 454n50, n77
Sanchez-Jankowski, Martin, 262, 271n187
Sanders, Matthew, 360n28
Sanders, Wiley B., 31n34
Sansone, Lori, 231n163
Sansone, Randy, 231n163
Sao, Khon, 258
Sas, Lousie, 494n96
Saugstad, Ola, 102n71
Saunders, Benjamin, 55
Saunders, Frank, 198n98
Savage, Joan, 522n33
Savitz, L., 229n29
Savolainen, Jukka, 228n25
Scali, Mary Ann, 494n126
Scalia, Antonin, 534
Schafer, Joseph, 27
Schafer, Walter, 301n5, n27, n29
Schaffner, Laurie, 186, 188, 198n111
Schaste, Robert, 494n97
Scheider, Anne, 493n33
Scheurman, Leo, 138n33, n34
Schicor, David, 239
Schiff, Mara, 141n182
Schinke, Steven, 361n75, n76, n77
Schlossman, Steven, 194, 199n139, 391n28
Schmeidler, James, 168n27, 332n78
Schmidt, Annesley, 493n21, n24
Schmidt, Eberhard, 103n80
Schmidt, M. H., 103n82
Schmidt, Melinda, 453n8, n9
Schneider, Anne, 469, 493n35, n37, n38
Schneider, Hans Joachim, 501
Schneider, Peter, 469, 493n37
Schochet, Peter, 361n81, n83
Schoenthaler, Stephen, 79
Schoenwald, Sonja, 332n103
Scholssman, Steven, 360n8
Schreck, Christopher, 163n16, 302n76
Schrof, Joannie M., 27
Schulenberg, John, 310, 331n1, n8, n18, n19
Schumacher, Michael, 50, 61n68
Schuster, Mark, 229n69
Schutt, Russell, 60n14, 418n66, n70
Schwab-Stone, Mary, 168n29, 229n47
Schwarts, Hersey, 239
Schwartz, Ira, 26–27, 31n73, n74, n83,
    391n38, 451, 453n29, 454n46, 455n114,
    493n44, n64, 494n75
Schwartz, Joseph, 138n32
Schwartz, Martin, 197n26
Schweinhart, Lawrence, 360n40, n41, n42,
    n43, n45
Schwendinger, Herman, 199n125, n133
Schwendinger, Julia, 199n125, n133
Sealock, Miriam, 60n18, 197n45, 199n149
Sederstrom, John, 138n43
Sedlack, Michael, 360n8
Seeley, John, 88
Segady, Thomas, 27, 31n51
Segal, Nancy, 119
Seguin, Jean, 103n95
Selke, William, 141n174
Sellin, Thorsten, 3, 49–50, 61n65, 101n2,
    102n64, 301n11, n12, 539n2
Seng, Magnus, 230n105
Senna, Joseph, 391n41
Seydlitz, Ruth, 27

Seymour, Anne, 493n25
Shannon, Lyle, 61n67, 301n10
Shannon, Sarah, 522n2
Shantz, David, 102n59
Shapira, Nathan, 168n26
Shau, Chang, 454n58
Shaw, Clifford R., 112, 113, 138n22, n25,
    229n27, 238–39, 339, 355, 360n7
Shaw, Daniel, 230n78
Shea, Daniel, 197n18
Shelden, Randall, 31n81, 60n12, 195,
    199n142, n150, 369, 391n14, 409,
    418n78, 430, 494n83
Shelder, J., 332n52
Sheley, Joseph, 270n123
Shepard, Robert, 453n23, 454n75
Shepard, Robert, Jr., 418n87, 492n2, 494n94
Shepard, Robin, 418n64
Sheppard, David, 270n132, 271n140,
    419n102, n103, n104
Sherkat, Darren, 229n58
Sherman, Arloc, 110
Sherman, Lawrence W., 231n180, 332n101,
    344, 348, 360n28, n31, 361n52, n65, n79,
    362n104, 400, 417n7, n8, n30, 467,
    493n26, n27, 494n91, 539n4
Shichor, D., 31n82, 102n47
Shields, Margie, 231n153
Shifley, Rick, 141n180
Shine, James, 425, 453n17
Shirley, Mary, 60n7
Shope, Jean, 9
Short, James, 60n11, n43-44, 139n96, 239,
    269n27
Shortis, Jennifer, 176
Shover, Neal, 61n59
Sia, Calvin, 360n30
Sickmund, Melissa, 283, 332n97, n98, 376,
    387, 391n63, 418n72, 454n63, n72, 476,
    478, 493n61, n62, n63, n68, n69, n71,
    n72, n73, 494n78, n80, n84
Siegel, Jane, 231n169
Siegel, Larry, 103n105, 199n132, 391n41
Sieverdes, Christopher, 494n82
Sifaneck, Stephen, 244, 245
Sigmon, Jane Nady, 25
Silva, Phil, 81, 168n39, 169n98, n99, 197n56
Silver, H. K., 230n97
Silverman, F. N., 230n97
Silverman, Mitchell, 230n134
Silverman, Robert, 139n90
Simcha-Fagan, Ora, 138n32
Simon, Betsy, 125
Simon, Leonore, 230n84
Simon, Rita James, 190, 197n8, n47, 198n115,
    n116
Simon, Thomas, 302n51
Simons, Julie, 454n58
Simons, Leslie, 229n54
Simons, Ronald, 139n82, 139n100, 140n117,
    167n14, 209, 229n35, n54, n66
Simpson, John, 199n134, n135, n149
Simpson, Sally, 60n18, 197n45, 199n126,
    n127
Sims, Calvin, 501
Singer, Simon, 301n6, n25, 455n92
Skinner, B. F., 89, 90
Skogan, Wesley, 138n47, 417n21, n30, 539n6

Skuse, David, 231n170
Slade, Eric, 229n59, n60
Slater, E., 197n50, 198n87
Slaughter, Ellen, 418n70, 454n67
Slawson, John, 96
Sloan, John Henry, 522n33
Sloan, John J., 102n34
Small, John, 198n97
Smallish, Lori, 81
Smart, Carol, 199n124
Smart, Nicola, 231n175
Smeenk, Wilma, 167n21
Smetena, Judith, 229n39
Smith, Anne H. W., 231n175
Smith, Beverly, 391n17
Smith, Brian, 168n45, 362n96
Smith, Carolyn, 31n79, 103n115, 139n106,
    168n52, 197n52, 198n119, 228n13,
    229n50, n56, n57, n70, 230n83, n88,
    231n171, 231n176, 270n131, 301n9,
    302n43
Smith, Daniel, 55
Smith, Douglas, 60n22, n44, 197n45, 418n58,
    n59, n66, n79
Smith, G. T., 332n56
Smith, Lars, 102n71
Smith, Michael, 140n165
Smith, Steven, 454n52, n69, n73, n75
Smith, William, 102n26
Snoek, Heddeke, 88
Snyder, Howard, 8, 30n18, 31n80, 61n67, 283,
    377, 408, 418n72, 427, 428, 436, 446,
    454n63, n72, 461, 487, 492n9, n10,
    493n34, n72, n73, 495n133, n134,
    523n59, n62
Snyder, Phyllis, 31n75, n77
Snyder, Thomas, 302n48
Soderstrom, Irina, 385, 494n106
Soler, Mark, 454n37
Solnit, Albert, 445, 455n89
Somerville, Dora, 185, 198n92
Sonnenberg, Sherrie, 199n141
Sorenson, Ann Marie, 163n6, 169n82,
    270n125, n127, 271n172
South, Scott, 139n76
Sowers, Karen, 285
Sparrow, Malcolm, 417n1
Spatz Widom, Cathy, 223–24, 231n164, n166,
    n167, 331n37, 360n22, 361n56, n65, n66,
    391n45, n67, n69, 418n55, n95, 494n127,
    511, 522n36
    See also Widom, Cathy
Speckart, George, 332n72, n81
Spencer, Margaret Beale, 495n132
Spergel, Irving, 139n95, 239, 260, 261, 263,
    266, 269n41, n42, n52, 270n67, 271n175,
    n176, n185, n200, n208
Spielvogel, Jackson, 31n27
Spiess, Michele, 332n102
Spohn, Cassia, 60n17, n27, n33, 418n74
Spracklen, Kathleen, 269n30, 331n30
Sprague, John, 102n40
Springate, Margaret, 231n145
Sprott, Jane, 60n21, 514, 523n59, n78
Sprowls, J., 454n44
Spunt, Barry, 199n121
Sridharan, Sanjeev, 361n91
Stack, Susan, 61n55

Staff, Jeremy, 101n17, 140n109
Stahl, Anne, 332n97, n98, n115, 377, 427, 428, 436, 446, 453n2, n3, n24, 454n40, n68, n85, 455n87, 461, 492n9, n10
Stairs, Jayne, 60n26, n32
Stapleton, William Vaughan, 271n195
Stearns, Elizabeth, 301n37
Steele, Brandt, 230n97, n121, n122, n124
Steele, Patricia, 492n7
Steele, Ric, 332n46, n47
Steen, Sara, 60n20, n25, 359n2, 493n74
Steffensmeier, Darrell, 60n26, n32, 61n49, 138n3, 198n120, 199n122, n123
Steffensmeier, Renee Hoffman, 199n122
Steib, Victor, 455n95
Stein, Judith, 140n122, 163n10
Steiner, Hans, 198n77
Steingürber, Hans-J., 103n80
Steinhart, David, 453n36
Steinharthe, David J., 31n58, n63
Steinmentz, Suzanne, 214, 230n110
Stephens, Gene, 141n179
Stern, Susan, 155, 229n50
Stevenson, Jim, 231n170
Stewart, Eric, 139n82, 140n117
Stiles, Beverly, 139n74
Stockard, Jean, 39
Stokes, Robert, 287, 302n57, 60
Stolzenberg, Lisa, 60n26
Stone, Daryl, 269n2
Stone, Lawrence, 31n26, n32, n33
Stout, David, 455n104
Stouthamer-Loeber, Magda, 167n7, n23, 168n33, 169n81, 228n2, n5, n13, n17, 229n49, n62, 269n28, 270n130
Strain, Eric, 332n50
Strang, Heather, 467, 493n26, n27
Strasburg, Paul, 404, 418n54
Straus, Murray, 208, 214–15, 228n5, 229n61, n64, n65, 230n87, n110, n111, n112, n113, 231n159
Streib, Victor, 417n49, 448, 455n98, n102
Stretesky, Paul, 78, 103n79
Strodtbeck, Fred, 239, 269n27
Strolovitch, Dara, 39
Strom, Kevin, 391n59
Struck, Doug, 501
Styfco, Sally, 341, 361n49
Sullivan, Mercer, 262, 271n184
Sutherland, Edwin, 96, 126, 127, 140n118
Sutphen, Richard, 408
Sutton, John R., 31n41, 391n30, n31
Sutton, P. D., 30n20
Swahn, Monica H., 8, 30n18
Swanger, Harry, 455n105
Swanson, Christopher, 283
Swanston, Heather, 230n106
Sykes, Gini, 255, 271n143
Sykes, Gresham, 126, 140n119, n120, n163, n164
Sykes, Richard, 417n23
Szymanski, Linda, 391n62, n65, 417n32, 454n78, 455n112

T
Tabor, Mary, 331n15
Tagle, Robert, 253
Tagliabue, John, 522n9

Tanamly, Susie, 333n108
Tannenbaum, Frank, 131, 140n134, n149
Tanner, Julian, 140n158
Tappan, Paul, 373
Tatelbaum, Robert, 360n24
Taussig, Cara, 231n179, n181
Taylor, Alan, 103n118, 229n38
Taylor, Carl, 244, 249, 270n76, n99, 271n173
Taylor, Ralph, 138n35
Taylor, Robert, 26, 27, 102n36, 418n88, n92
Taylor, Stephanie, 229n69
Taylor, Terrance, 417n10, 418n90
Teachman, Jay, 283
Teevan, James, 163n3
Temple, Judy, 360n46, 361n47
Terlouw, Gert-Jan, 503, 523n42
Terrill, William, 139n60
Terry-McElrath, Yvonne, 333n109
Terry, Robert, 269n29, 418n54
Theriot, Matthew, 285
Thomas, Charles, 31n80, n84, 230n87
Thomas, Christopher, 271n183
Thomas, Melvin, 60n31, n35
Thomas, W. I., 184, 198n82, n83
Thompson, Carol, 61n59
Thompson, Kevin, 169n97, 199n137, 270n125, n127, 271n172
Thompson, Robert, 519
Thomse, P. R., 168n74
Thornberry, Terence, 38, 39, 60n15, 61n56, n70, n80, 101n3, 103n115, 139n99, n105, n106, 141n172, 153–55, 168n47, n48, n49, n50, n52, n53, n60, 228n13, n22, 229n56, 231n171, n176, 254, 262, 269n30, 270n121, n129, n131, 271n189, 283, 301n8, n9, 302n43, 331n32, 332n55, 418n70, 539n3
Thornton, Craig, 361n84
Thrasher, Frederick, 138n23, 238, 239, 248, 260, 269n49
Thurman, Quint, 271n202
Tibbetts, Stephen, 61n63, 103n91, 169n76
Tidd, Simon, 359n2
Tierney, Joseph, 361n63, n64, 377, 436
Tierney, Nancy, 427, 428, 446, 461, 492n9, n10
Tiny (female gang member), 255
Tita, George, 414
Titchener, Edward, 92
Tittle, Charles, 60n44, 169n82, n86, n89, n91, n93
Tobias, Aurelio, 230n107
Tobias, J. J., 417n1
Tobin, Kimberly, 270n131
Toby, Jackson, 228n24, 283
Tolan, Patrick, 360n22
Tomas, Josep, 230n107
Tomson, Barbara, 239
Tonry, Michael, 31n39, n40, n69, 61n48, 101n21, 103n114, n120, 138n11, n33, n34, 138n47, 159, 197n7, 228n5, 230n82, 231n, n136, 269n21, 360n16, n21, 361n95, 391n20, n56, 417n1, 418n97, 506, 511, 512, 514, 518, 522n11, 523n58, n59, n78, n84, n88, n95, 539n4, n9
Torbet, Paricia McFall, 391n62, n65, 492n14, 493n60
Torres, Jose, 271n174, 331n41

Tracy, Paul, 51, 60n15, 61n66, n71-72, 102n50
Tracy, Sharon, 31n81
Trapani, Catherine, 197n10
Trasler, Gordon, 61n55
Traver, Harold, 523n83
Travis, Jeremy, 494n129
Traynelis-Yurek, Elaine, 494n101
Tremblay, Pierre, 101n6
Tremblay, Richard, 61n73, 103n95, 168n40, 169n78, n12, 269n39, 283, 301n7, 331n45, 332n51, 348, 360n21, n22, n38, 361n53
Tremlow, Stuart, 302n77
Trickett, Alan, 102n24
Triplett, Ruth, 61n47
Trocki, Karen, 230n108
Trojanowicz, Robert, 417n13
Tromovitch, Philip, 231n173
Trostle, Lawrence, 271n160
Trueg, Gernot, 523n67, n75, n76, n77, n80, n82, n86, n89, n90, n91, n92
Trump, Donald, 119
Tuch, Steven, 418n66
Tucker, James, III, 36
Tumin, Melvin, 271n146
Turley, Alan, 250, 270n109
Turner, K. B., 417n10
Turner, Susan, 163n10
Tuthill, Richard, 367
Tyler, Jerry, 27, 31n51
Tyler, Kimberly, 31n70

U
Uggen, Christopher, 101n17, 140n109, 194, 199n138
Ulmer, Jeffrey, 60n26, n32
Umbreit, Mark, 468, 493n29

V
Vaillant, George, 159
Valdez, Avelardo, 244, 245
Valentine, Jeffrey, 361n65
Valier, Claire, 138n27
Vallant, G. E., 331n26
Van de Wiel, Nicolle, 88
Van den Haag, Ernest, 101n5
Van der Laan, Peter, 167n21
Van der Wal, Marcel, 285
Van Dijk, Jan, 522n35
Van Eenwyk, Juliet, 9
Van Engeland, Herman, 88
Van Goozen, Stephanie, 88
Van Kammen, Welmoet, 167n7, 168n33, 269n28
Van Kesteren, John, 522n33, 523n43
VanBuren, Holly, 333n109
Vander Ven, Thomas, 140n123, n126, 229n72
Vander Waal, Curtis, 333n109
Vanderschueren, Franz, 522n17
Vastag, Brian, 325
Vaughn, Joseph, 465–66, 493n22
Vazsonyi, Alexander, 139n104, 163n17, 168n70, 197n24, 301n2, 361n54
Vedder, Clyde, 185, 198n92
Vega, Angelo, 270n96
Velez, Maria, 39, 138n15, 139n56
Venables, Jon, 519
Venables, Peter, 103n106

Venkatesh, Sudhir Alladi, 70, 101n18, 318, 332n64, n65
Ventura, S. J., 30n20
Verde, Alfredo, 523n60, n79
Verhulst, Frank, 167n21
Verlur, D. E., 331n39
Vermeiren, Robert, 167n22, 168n29, 229n47
Veysey, Bonita, 60n42
Videon, Tami, 139n80, 229n32
Vides, Brian, 156
Vieraitis, Lynne, 139n76
Vieth, Victor, 231n155
Vigil, James Diego, 260, 270n82, n112, 271n153, n158, n165, n166, n170, n171
Vila, Bryan, 362n97, 522n33
Viles, D., 229n74, n75
Villemez, Wayne, 60n44
Vinovskis, Maris, 341
Virkkunen, Matti, 163n4
Visher, Christy, 102n51, 418n58, n66
Vitaro, Frank, 163n12, 168n40, 331n45, 332n51, 361n53
Vito, Gennaro, 494n108
Vivona, T. Scott, 454n67
Voeller, Kytja, 103n87
Volayka, Jan, 103n120
Volenik, Adrienne, 391n42, 455n105
Vollmer, August, 394, 417n4
Vollrath, Fred, 273
Voss, Harwin, 60n13
Vossefuil, Bryan, 302n52
Vuchinich, S., 167n7

W
Wagner, Carla, 335
Waite, Linda, 168n55, 229n70
Waitrowski, Michael, 301n28
Wakefield, M., 31n48
Walker, Emily, 492n18
Walker, Gary, 453n18
Walker, Lewis, 494n117
Walker, Samuel, 6017, n27, 417n1, n2, n26, 418n74
Walker, Sandra Gail, 522n14
Walker, Todd, 360n37
Walkowiak, Jens, 103n80
Wall, Julie, 271n183
Wallace, John, 332n54
Wallace, Lisa Hutchinson, 391n64
Wallace, Rodrick, 138n9
Wallach, Jo, 494n97
Waller, Irvin, 362n98, 512
Wallerstein, Judith, 206, 207
Walsh, Anthony, 102n73, 139n89
Walsleben, Marjorie, 285, 290, 302n65
Walters, Richard, 90
Walts, Brenda, 302n103
Walz, Liz, 141n175
Wang, Ching-Tung, 230n131
Wang, Zheng, 271n156
Ward, David, 140n153, 169n86, n91
Waring, Elin, 414, 419n101
Warner, Barbara, 138n55
Warner, Jean, 493n33
Warr, Mark, 168n56, 197n29, 269n23, n24, n32, n34, 270n90
Washington, Donovan, 343
Washington, Guy, 343

Wasserman, Gail, 51, 269n39, 360n22
Watson, Donnie, 333n108
Watson, John, 89, 90
Watt, Toni-Terling, 188, 189
Wattenberg, William, 198n98
Watts, Kareem, 440
Watts, W. David, 332n80
Webb, Barry, 102n55
Webb, Vincent, 391n54
Webster, Pamela, 168n55, n62
Webster-Stratton, Carolyn, 230n121, 361n48
Weeks, Ashley, 228n23
Wei, Evelyn, 167n23
Weikart, David, 360n40, n42, n43
Weiner, Neil Alan, 214
Weiner, Tim, 332n90, 522n19
Weis, Joseph, 60n11, 151, 168n43
Weisburd, David, 417n20, 539n6
Weisel, Deborah, 270n79, n115, 271n151
Weisheit, Ralph, 246, 247, 270n84, 332n81
Weishew, Nancy, 302n56
Weisman, Stephanie, 361n72, n73
Weiss, Alexander, 60n34, 417n31
Weisstub, David, 486
Weisz, John, 230n127
Weitekamp, E., 101n3, 139n99, 167n17, 523n67, n75, n76, n77, n80, n82, n86, n89, n90, n91, n92, 539n3
Weitzer, Ronald, 409, 418n66, n83
Weldon, Ward, 302n81
Wells, James, 385
Wells, L. Edward, 61n85, 246, 247, 270n84
Wells, Nancy, 30n13, 138n13
Wells, William, 39
Welsh, Brandon, 102n56, n57, 332n101, n101, 344, 348, 360n18, n28, n31, 361n52, n65, 362n98, n102, n104, 391n46, 400, 417n8, 472, 493n26, n27, 494n91, n112, n113, 511, 512, 514, 539n4
Welsh, Wayne, 287, 302n39, n57, n60
Welte, John W., 61n88
Wen, Patricia, 270n118
Werner, Norman, 418n60
West, Donald J., 61n67, 83, 103n112, n113, 230n80, n81, n87, 269n22
West, Valerie, 138n17, n19
Wheaton, Blair, 168n59
Wheeler, Etta, 212
Wheeler, Stanton, 140n153
Whitcomb, Debra, 231n143, n148
White, Helene Raskin, 332n74, n81, n84, n85
White, Jennifer, 61n74
White, Joseph, 454n55
White, Michael, 102n35
White, Norman, 192
Whitehead, Barbara Dafoe, 228n19
Whitehead, John, 30n25, 494n92
Whitlock, Monica, 197n4, 270n103
Whyte, William, 270n113
Widom, Cathy, 231n168, n172, 361n80
    See also Spatz Widom, Cathy
Wiebe, Richard, 169n84
Wiebush, Richard, 231n160, n162, 489, 492n17
Wieczorek, William F., 61n88
Wiederman, Michael, 231n163
Wiener, Jörg-A., 103n80

Wiersema, Brian, 61n82, 359n1
Wiesner, Margit, 168n32
Wig, Janet, 511
Wikström, Per-Olof, 522n33
Wilcox, Pamela, 138n44, 302n50
Wilder, Esther, 188, 189
Wilhelm, C., 103n82
Will, Jeffrey, 138n48
Williams, Bryn, 231n170
Williams, D., 103n96
Williams, James, 523n81
Williams, Kirk, 361n50, 472
Williams, Linda Meyer, 199n132, 230n109, 231n169
Williams, Nicolas, 301n20
Williams, Phil, 523n47, n49, n50
Williams, Stephanie, 140n127
Williamson, Deborah, 385
Willie, Charles, 418n60
Wilner, D., 331n27
Wilson, B., 332n72
Wilson, David, 301n28, 348, 384, 391n53, 493n46, 494n112, n113
Wilson, Edmond O., 102n66
Wilson, G. T., 331n40
Wilson, James, 97, 101n7, n11, 102n22, 160, 168n67, 302n53, 360n22, 391n50, 417n8, n11, 522n32, 539n7
Wilson, Janet, 101n12, 198n112
Wilson, Jeremy, 417n31
Wilson, John, 141n172
Wilson, Margo, 61n53, 138n42, n51, 230n128, n129, n130
Wilson, Mary Ellen, 212
Wilson, O. W., 417n5
Wilson, Susan, 229n42
Wilson, William Julius, 110, 111, 113, 138n14, n20, 248, 270n81, n92, n94
Windham, Amy, 360n30
Windle, Michael, 198n80
Wines, Enoch, 367
Winfree, Thomas, Jr., 245, 271n152, n193, 417n10
Wingood, Gina, 168n25
Winick, Charles, 331n27
Winneke, Gerhard, 103n80
Winner, Lawrence, 454n74
Winterdyk, John, 501, 512, 514, 516, 522n29, 523n60, n61, n70, n71, n74, n79, n83, n85
Wise, Nancy, 198n118
Wish, E., 332n78, n86
Wislar, Joseph, 60n10, 229n30, 312, 331n25
Wissow, Lawrence, 229n59, n60
Witmer, Helen, 60n7
Witty, Helen Marie, 335
Witty, John, 335
Wofford, Sharon, 169n88
Wolfe, David, 229n42
Wolfgang, Marvin, 49–50, 51, 60n15, 61n56, n65-66, n70, 101n2, 102n61, 229n29, 277–78, 301n11, n12, 539n2
Wolfinger, Nicholas, 206
Wolford, Bruce, 301n7
Wonders, Jerome, 270n96
Wong, Janelle, 39
Wood, Daniel, 271n204
Wood, Peter, 102n22, 163n6

Woods, Kristi, 270n86
Woolard, Jennifer, 453n8, n9
Woolfenden, Susan, 472
Wooton, Barbara, 103n110, 230n77
Worden, Robert, 405, 417n51, 418n56, n64
Wordes, Madeline, 453n22
Wright, Bradley, 140n111, n126, 165, 169n98, n99
Wright, Claudia, 31n62
Wright, Daryl, 361n86, 87
Wright, James, 270n123
Wright, John Paul, 139n101, 140n123, 229n52, n72, 237, 269n40, 301n20, 391n68
Wright, Lloyd, 332n80
Wright, Nat, 333n111, n112, n113
Wright, Richard, 332n70, n71
Wu, Bohsui, 408, 453n27

Wu, Chyi-In, 139n100, 167n14, 229n66
Wu, Lawrence, 139n88
Wundram, Sabine, 103n80
Wundt, Wilhelm, 92
Wung, Phen, 138n33

X
Xiang, Zongping, 360n445

Y
Yablonsky, Lewis, 261, 271n178, n179
Yates, Amy Michelle, 143
Yeisley, Mark, 139n76
Yisheng, Dai, 522n28
Yisrael, Donnovan Somera, 31n53, 197n54
Yokoyama, Minoru, 501, 523n71
Yue, Liling, 522n29
Yun Soo Kim, Julia, 60n10

Z
Zaff, Jonathan, 140n127
Zak, Lydia, 229n42
Zatz, Marjorie, 269n54
Zeeb, Linda, 228n20
Zernike, Kate, 325, 523n63, n66
Zhang, Joshua, 270n123
Zhang, Lening, 61n88, 140n148, 163n1, n11
Zhang, Quanwu, 269n28
Zhao, Jihong, 139n63
Zigler, Edward, 231n179, n181, 341, 361n49
Zimmerman, Joel, 103n100, n103
Zimmerman, Rick, 325
Zimring, Franklin, 391n60, 440, 454n74, 523n41
Zingraff, Matthew, 231n174, 301n9, 302n43

Subject Index

Note: Italic pages numbers refer to figures, exhibits, and tables.

A

ABA (American Bar Association)
    National Juvenile Justice Standards
        Project, 25
    on police discretion, 409
    recommendations, 480, 486, 535, 537
    studies by, 424, *425*
abandonment, 213
abortion, 39, 529–30
abuse. *See* child abuse and neglect;
        emotional abuse; sexual abuse
academic achievement, 9, 24, 273, 277–81
ACF (Administration for Children and
        Families), 341
active speech, 292–94
ACYF (Administration of Children, Youth,
        and Families), 341
ADAM (National Institute of Justice's
        Arrestee Drug Abuse Monitoring
        program), 320
ADD (attention deficit disorder), 81, 94
addict, 307, 314
addiction-prone personality, 314
ADHD (attention deficit/hyperactivity
        disorder), 81, 100, 210
adjudication, *377–79*, 381, 435–36, 451
adjudication hearing, 378–79, 440–42
Administration for Children and Families
        (ACF), 341
Administration on Children, Youth, and
        Families (ACYF), 341
Adolescent Girl in Conflict, The (Konopka), 185
adolescent-limited, 147
adoption studies, 84–85, 100
adult justice system. *See* criminal justice
adult offenders
    and gangs, 242, 245
    link to juvenile offenders, 51
    separation from juveniles, 513–15
    treatment of, 18, 19
    See also criminal justice
advisement hearing, 219
AFDC (Aid to Families with Dependant
        Children), 187
Africa, 500, 507
African Americans
    bias and, 44–47, 111, 406–7, 409
    crime rates for, 38–39, 45
    criminal court and, 386, 422
    and detention, 427–28
    drop out rate of, 282
    economic disparity and, 111, 113

family life of, 203
gang involvement by, 255, 256–57
GTC and, 164
incarceration rates for males, 477–78
victimization rates and, 53–55
views of police, 395–96
waiver and, 440
aftercare and reentry
    international programs for, 514, 515
    process of, *378*, 487–89
    revocation procedures, 490
    supervision, 488–89
    United Nations standards for, *509*
after-school programs, 352–54
age
    crime rates, 38, 47–48
    death penalty, 72, *374*, 381, 451, 537
    detention trends, *427–29*
    discretionary justice, 408
    gangs, 248
    international justice systems, 510, 514
    of responsibility, 510
    statistics, 34–*36*, 47–48
    victimization, 53, 54
    waiver, 437
age-graded theory, 156–59, 166, 237
age of onset, 49, 146–47
aggressive law enforcement, 410
aging-out process
    defined, 11
    latent trait theory and, 160, 164
    and problem solving, 69
    reasons for, 48, 153
    See also life-course theories
Aid to Families with Dependant Children
        (AFDC), 187
alcohol abuse
    Alcoholics Anonymous, 327
    and alcoholism, 307–8
    at-risk youths and, 5
    gateway drug theory and, 315, 321
    school prevention of, 290
    statistics on, 9, 307, *311*, 505
    and victimization, 56
    and violence, 320
alienation, 281
alternative courts, 383–85
American Bar Association. *See* ABA
American Bar Association's National
        Juvenile Justice Standards Project, 25
"American Dream," 112, 119, 120
American Indians, *45*, 55 135 396
American Judicature Society, *425*, 426
American Law Institute's Model Youth
        Correction Authority Act of 1940, 474

"Amy's Law," 143
anabolic steroids, 309
anesthetic drugs, 308
anger, 115, 116, 118
Anna Casey Foundation, 4
anomie/strain
    biological development and, 4, 5, 176–77
    differential opportunity, 122
    General Strain Theory, 117–19, 136, 223,
        279
    goals and, 116, 119, *121*, 122, 129
    institutional anomie theory, 119–20
    international delinquency and, 497–500,
        504, 507
    relative deprivation, 116–17
    strain theory, 116, 136, 279
    view of gangs, 260–61, *263*
anthropological view of gangs, 259–60, *263*
Anti-Gang Office, Houston (TX), 25
APD (antisocial personality disorder), 210
appellate process, 449
apprenticeships, 14–17, 28
Arizona, 387, 411, 443
arousal theory, 82, 95
Arrestee Drug Abuse Monitoring program
        (ADAM), 320
arrests
    and age, 47–48
    discrimination and, 47, 111, 406–7
    procedures for, 400–401
    rates of, *37*, 44–*45*
    and social class, 47
Asia, 135, 500
Asian youths, *45*, 255–56, 258–59, 396
ATF (Bureau of Alcohol, Tobacco, Firearms,
        and Explosives), 393, 414
at-risk youths
    defined, 5
    future outlook for, 8, 10
    influences on, 3, 6–7, 152–53
    statistics, 5–6
    substance abuse and, 316–17
attention deficit disorder (ADD), 81, 94
attention deficit/hyperactivity disorder
        (ADHD), 81, 100, 210
attention problems
    ADD, 81, 94
    ADHD, 81, 100, 210
    and school failure, 279, 299
attorneys, 381, 422–23, 451, 535
Australia, 467, 499–500, *511–15*
Austria, 504, *506*, 508–*11*, 513
authority conflict pathway, 149–50
AVCI (Department of Justice Anti-Violent
        Crime Initiative), *265*

B

Bad Kids (Feld), 386
bail, 431, 517
balanced and restorative justice programs (BARJ), 327
balanced probation, 467–68
balancing-of-the interest approach, 220
ballers, 245
Baltimore (MD), 396–97
BARJ (balanced and restorative justice) programs, 327
Barrio Gangs (Vigil), 260
barrios, 246, 257
battered child syndrome, 212, 225
BBBS (Big Brothers Big Sisters Program), 350–51, 357, 382
behavior modification, 344–45, 481
behavioral theory
    and control, 75–76
    and the media, 90–92
    overview of, *86*, 89–90, 100
    social learning theory, 90
behaviorism, 89
"Beijing Rules," 508
Belgium, 510, *511*, 513, 514
benefits of delinquency, 68–69, 74, 89
Berkeley (CA), 394
best interests of the child, 18, 442, 533
Bethesda Day Treatment Center Program, 472
beyond a reasonable doubt, 372, 441, 442
Beyond Probation (Murray and Cox), 131
Beyond the Best Interest of the Child (Goldstein et al.), 445
BGCs (Boys and Girls Clubs of America), 353
bias
    and gender, 173, 408–9
    See also racial discrimination
bifurcated process, 379, 441, 442, 451
Big Brothers Big Sisters Program, 350–51, 357, 382
Bill of Rights, 541
    See also U.S. Constitution
bindover. *See* waiver
biochemical factors, 77–78, *86*, 100
biological development. *See* developmental views
biosocial theories
    biochemical factors, 77–78, *86*, 100
    and biological development, 76–77, 146, 183
    Biosocial Study, 182
    contemporary, 77
    evolutionary, 85–*86*
    genetic influences, 82–85
    hormones, 181, 183
    neurological dysfunction, 78–82
    origins of, 76–77
    overview of, *86*, 100
    See also GTC
birth cohort study, 49–50, 51
birthrate statistics, 5, *10*
Black Gangster Disciples gang, 256
blacks. See African Americans
Blackstone Rangers gang, 256
blended families, 204
Bloods gang, *253*, 256, 257

Blueprints for Violence Prevention, 357
boot camps, 457, 458, 483–85, 519, 537
border control, 323
Boston (MA)
    gun control and, 393
    House of Reformation, 368
    IQ studies, 96
    juvenile courts, 371
    law enforcement prevention, 265, 394, 459
Boston's Mid-City Project, 340
Boston's Operation Ceasefire, 413–14
Boston's Youth Violence Strike Force (YVSF), 265
Boys and Girls Clubs of America (BGCs), 353
Brazil, 499
Bridge over the Racial Divide, The (Wilson), 111
broken home, 204
bullying
    causes of, 285
    and family deviance, 210
    intervention programs for, 285
    prevention of, 357
    and school shooters, 286
    seriousness of, 284, 285, 300
Bureau of Alcohol, Tobacco, Firearms, and Explosives (ATF), 393, 414
Bureau of Justice Statistics, 52

C

California, 26, 407, 473–74
    See also Los Angeles
California 8% Solution, 468
California Superior Court, 439
California Youth Authority, 483
callous-unemotional (CU) traits, 184
Cambridge Study in Delinquent Development (CSDD), 83, 152–53, 210–11
Cambridge-Somerville Youth Study, 339–40
Canada, 135, 499, 504–6, 509–11, 514
Canadian LEAP program, 187
capital punishment. *See* death penalty
capitalism, 132–33
Capitalism, Patriarchy, and Crime (Messerschmidt), 191
CAPTA (Child Abuse Prevention and Treatment Act) of 1974, 218
CAR (Children At Risk), 355–56
career. *See* employment
Carr siblicide, 201
CASA (Court Appointed Special Advocates), 424
case managers strategy, 430
case processing, *377*, 422
Caucasians. *See* whites
Causes of Delinquency (Hirschi), 127–28, 528
CCTV (closed-circuit television), 220, 221, 227
CD (conduct disorder), 88
CDC (Centers for Disease Control and Prevention), 9
Ceasefire Working Group, 414
Center for Research on Women, 191
Center for Restorative Justice & Peacemaking, 136

Center for the Study and Prevention of Violence (CSPV), 357
Center on Addiction and Substance Abuse, 305
Centers for Disease Control and Prevention (CDC), 9
Centuries of Childhood (Aries), 12
CFSRs (Child and Family Service Reviews) Act of 1994, 222
chancery court, 14, 16, 28
Charlotte (NC), 413
Chicago (IL)
    detached street workers program, 265–66
    gangs in, 238–39, 242, 246, 256, 261
    intervention programs in, 347
    law enforcement in, 264, 410
    social disorganization theory, 112
Chicago Area Project, 339, 355
Chicago Bar Association, 21
Chicago Intervention Network, 266
Chicago IQ studies, 96
child abuse and neglect
    authorities, 10–11
    causes of, 216–17, 227
    child protection system, 217–22
    cohort studies on, 223–24
    and court, 219–22
    defined, 213–14
    disposition and, 219, 220
    drug abuse and, 316
    effects of, 222–24, 227
    emotional abuse, 213
    extent of, 214–16, 227
    family counseling and, 225
    female socialization and, 186, 188–89
    FVPF, 226
    historical perspective, 17, 18, 212, 225
    link with delinquency, 224
    Poor Laws, 15
    prevention programs, 226, 382
    psychodynamic theories on, 88–89
    statistics, 214–16
    See also child savers; sexual abuse
Child Abuse Prevention and Treatment Act of 1974 (CAPTA), 218
Child and Family Service Reviews Act of 1994 (CFSRs), 222
Child-Parent Center (CPC), 347
child prostitution, 498, 499
child protection system
    abused children and court, 220–22, 227
    background on, 217–18
    processes, 26, 218–20
Child Protective Services (CPS), 215, 217
child savers
    critique of, 133, 368–69, 533
    House of Refuge, 367–68
    Illinois Juvenile Court Act of 1899, 371–73
    mission of, 18, 367
Child Savers, The (Platt), 133, 368–69
childcare/childrearing, 161–62, 202, 203, 343–46, 352–54
childhood
    in colonial America, 16–17, 28
    infant mortality, 4, 10, 12, 14
    and the media, 90–92
    in the Middle Ages, 12–14
    and psychodynamic theory, 86–89

trait theory and, 98–99
view of, 28
Children Act (England) of 1908, 515
Children At Risk (CAR), 355–56
Children's Aid Society, 369–70, *371*
Children's Bureau, U.S., 373, 474
Children's Defense Fund (CDF), 5–6
Children's Rights Council (CRC), 7
China, 500, 513, 515
CHINS (children in need of supervision), 22, 374, 375
chivalry hypothesis, 179–80, 408
choice theory
analysis of, 75, 76, 98
criminality and crime, 66–67, 70–71
GTC and, 160, 166
and prevention, 72–75
rational choice, 67, 262–63
routine activities, 71–72
social developments, 68–70
summarized, 99
cholization, 257
cholo, 257
chronic offender
age of onset, 49, 146–47
birth cohort study, 49–50, 152–53
chronic/nonchronic recidivists, 50, 165
as criminal, 51–52
defined, 1, 10
drug use and, 320–21
factors influencing, 50–52, 152–53, 165
future outlook, 527
cigarette smoking
age limit laws, 310
statistics on, 9, *311*, 505
as status offense, 20, 22
civil liberties. *See* schools and legal rights
civil rights, 27, 486–87
Civilian Conservation Corps, 473–74
classical criminology, 66–67
Cleveland (OH), 396–97
cliques, 234, 237
closed-circuit television (CCTV), 220, 221, 227
co-offending, 233, 235
cocaine, 37, 306, 316, 320, 322–23
cognitive behavioral theory
developmental stages, 92–93, 175–78
information processing, 93–94, 195
overview of, *86*, 100
cognitive transformation, 188–89
Cold War, 261, 497, 504, 538
collective efficacy, 115–16
college boy, 122
colonial America, 16–17, 28
Colorado, 489
Columbia (South America), 322–23
Columbia University study on television viewing, 92
Columbine High School massacre, 386, 499
Commonwealth Fund, 174
Communities That Care (CTC), 356
community
aftercare and, 488–89
BARJ programs and, 327
and chronic offending, *51*, 153
collective efficacy, 115–16
disposition and, 445

and fear, 114–15, 287
gangs and, 233, 247
gentrification, 113
instability, 114, 120, 136
juvenile court judges and, 426
and police, 394–97, 400, 405, *410*, 412–13
routine activities theory and, 71
and school crime, 287, 290, 291–92
and social control, 112, 115, 171
teen courts and, 385
and victimization risk, 54–55
community-based prevention programs
drug abuse control, *322*, 324, 326–28
examples of, 125, 355–56, 532
gang control and, 265–66
overview of, 355
community-based treatment programs
characteristics of successful, 472–73, 490
corrections and, *464*, 465–66
decarceration and, 465, 474
deinstitutionalization, 135
in England, 520
Massachusetts Experience, 459
nonresidential, 471–73
past and future of, 459, 536
residential, 470–71, 490
restitution, 468–70
restorative justice, 466–67
status offenders and, 23, 25
types of, 457
See also probation
Community Outreach Through Police in Schools Program, 411
community service, 467, 468
complaint, 434
Comprehensive Employment Training Act, 134
concept of delinquency, 18–20, 526–27, 538
conditions of probation, 461–64
conduct disorder (CD), 88
confidentiality, 218, 296–98, 449–51, 510
conflict theory, 132–33, 135–36
Connecticut, 16, 17
contagion effect, 211
contemporary life course concepts
adolescent-limited vs. life-course persisters, 147
age of onset, 146–47
continuity of crime, 150–51
multiple pathways, 148–50
overview, 146
problem behavior syndrome, 147–48
See also life-course theories
continuity of crime, 150–51
control. *See* prevention
control group, 339
control theory, 126–29, 136, 235
controversial status youth, 234
COPS (Office of Community Oriented Policing Services), 396–97, 415
corner boy, 122
corporal punishment, 208–9, 215, 295, 486
corrections
boot camps, 457, 458, 483–85, 519, 537
community based, *464*
educational/vocational/recreational programs, 482–83
overview of, 480–81

secure, 473–75
treatment techniques, 481–82
wilderness programs, 483
See also inmates; institutions
cortisol, 181
costs
of crime, 53
and intervention, 344–47
of juvenile violence, 336–38, 530
of prevention programs, 344–47, 355, 358
and teen courts, 384–85
cottage system, 473
Court Appointed Special Advocates (CASA), 424
covert pathway, 149–50
CPC (Child-Parent Center), 347
CPS (Child Protective Services), 215, 217
CPS (Crown Prosecution Service, England), 516, 518
crack, 37, 306
CRC (Children's Rights Council), 7
CREASAT (UCLA's Comprehensive Residential Education, Arts, and Substance Abuse Treatment) program, 327
Creating the Dropout (Dorn), 282–83
Crime and Disorder Act of 1998 (England), 519
Crime and Human Nature (Wilson and Herrnstein), 97
Crime and the American Dream (Messner and Rosenfeld), 119
Crime in the Making (Sampson and Laub), 156–57
crime rates
factors affecting, 38–39, 107
and gender, 174, 177–78, 190–91
international comparisons of, 502–8
racial differentials, 46
trends, 34–37, 526–27
validity, 37, 40
criminal atavism, 76
criminal justice
and adults, 19, 28
compared to juveniles, 22–23, 28
internationally, 508
juvenile courts and, 385–86, 441
juvenile justice values and, 365, 380–82, 388–89
racism and, 386
waiver and, 437–40
Criminal Justice and Public Order Act of 1994 (England), 219
criminality, 70, 97, 535
Criminality of Women, The (Pollak), 179
CRIPA (Civil Rights of Institutionalized Persons Act), 486–87
Crips gang, *253*, 256, 257
critical feminist views, 191–95
cross-national research, 502–4
crowds, 234
Crown Court (England), 519
Crown Prosecution Service (CPS, England), 518
CSDD (Cambridge Study in Delinquent Development), 83, 152–53, 210–11
CSPV (Center for the Study and Prevention of Violence), 357

CTC (Communities That Care), 356
cultural deviance theory, 120–22, 136
cultural transmission, 112, *113*
culture of poverty, 108
curfew laws, 26–27, 29, 410, 412–13
custodial interrogation, 402–3, 415

D

Dade County (FL) paddling incident, 295
Dakar (Senegal), 500
Dallas (TX), 26
D.A.R.E. (Drug Abuse Resistance
        Education) program, 324, 325, *398*
Dare to Be You (DTBY), 125
dark figures of crime, 34
data, 33, *34*, 45–46, *503*, 528
David and Lucile Packard Foundation, 202
daycare programs, 345–46
DBD (disruptive behavior disorder), 87, 88
DDAP (Detention Diversion Advocacy
        Program), 429, 430
DEA (Drug Enforcement Administration),
        414
death penalty
        age and, 72, *374*, 381, 451, 534
        "Amy's Law," 143
        juveniles and, 11, 21, *374*
        legal issues, 447–49
        statistics, 447, *448*
        U.S. Supreme Court and, 72, *374*, 381,
            447–48, 534
death squads, 499
defense attorney, 381, 422–23, 451, 535
"degradation ceremony," 131
deinstitutionalization
        decarceration, 465, 474
        future outlook of, 536
        in Massachusetts, 459, 471, 473
        and relabeling, 23
        theory of, 135, 383
        See also community-based treatment
            programs; institutions
Delinquency and Human Nature (Wilson and
        Herrnstein), 160
Delinquency and Opportunity (Cloward and
        Ohlin), 122
delinquency control. *See* prevention
Delinquency in a Birth Cohort (Wolfgang et
        al.), 49–51
delinquent boy, 122
Delinquent Boys (Cohen), 122
Delinquent Girl, The (Vedder and
        Somerville), 185
delinquent subcultures, 122
Denmark, 504–7, 510, *511*
Denver (CO), 372–73, 472
Denver Youth Survey, 57
Department of Health and Human Services
        (DHHS), 215, 341
Department of Justice, 34, 52, 320, 375, 486
Department of Justice Anti-Violent Crime
        Initiative (AVCI), 265
Department of Labor, 354
designer drugs, 309–10
desistance, 188–89
        See also aging-out process
detached street workers, 265, 340
detention

in adult jails, 429–30
alternatives for, 429
debate over, 427–29
facilities for, 380, 427, 440
hearing process, 378
home, 445
new approaches to, 429, 534–35
preventive, 431
trends in, 428
Detention Diversion Advocacy Program
        (DDAP), 429, 430
determinate sentence, 446
deterrence, 72–75
developing(ed) countries, 497, 501, 508, 520
developmental views
        contemporary life course theories, 146–51
        evaluating, 165
        and future outlook, 528
        latent trait, 144, 160–66
        prevention and, 342, 358
        stages of development, 92–93, 174–77
        and stress, 4, 5, 176–77
        theoretical model, 63, 143–44, 166
        See also life-course theories
DHHS (Department of Health and Human
        Services), 215, 341
Diamonds gang, 262
DID (dissociative identity disorder), 222
diet, 78, 79, 110
differential association theory, 126, *127*
disaggregated, 35
discipline
        and behavioral theory, 89–90
        effects of inconsistent, 152, 225
        parental, 152, 208–9
        "Stubborn child" laws, 17
        through history, 14, 15, 17
discretionary justice
        bias and, 406–9, 415
        criminal and juvenile justice and, 381
        environmental factors, 405, 415
        law enforcement and, 399, 403–6, 517
        limiting, 409–10, *411*
        situational factors and, 406
discrimination. *See* racial discrimination
disorders, 87
disposition
        child abuse and neglect cases, 219, 220
        in England, 519–20
        juvenile justice processes and, 379, 442,
            444–45
        options for, 444–45, 451
        predisposition report, 442, 444, 463
        purpose of, 445, 451
        residential community treatment, 470–71
        right to treatment and, 485
        sentencing, 445–47, 511, 513, 519–20
        statistics on juvenile, 404–5, *446*
        United Nations standards and, *509*
        See also probation
disruptive behavior disorder (DBD), 87, 88
dissociative identity disorder (DID), 222
District of Columbia, 107, 320, 409, 438, 536
diversion, *378*, 433–34, 451, 512, 517–18
divorce, 185, 204–7, 225
dower system, 13–14
drift, 126
dropping out

causes of, 282, 299–300
and race, 282–83
and school policy, 282, 283
statistics, 8, 10, 282
teen pregnancy and, 187
tracks and, 280
truancy, 24
drug abuse
        at-risk youths and, 5–6, *163*
        causes of, 312–14
        and child abuse, 217
        crime rates for, 38, 305
        delinquency link, 50, 320–21, 329
        and drug testing, 296, 297, *374*
        gangs members and, 242–45, 252
        international, 498, 505–7
        pathways to, 315–19
        and peers, 129
        prevention of, 125, 290, 321–28, 324–26
        and problem behavior syndrome, 147
        problem solving and, 68
        statistics on teenage, 9, 305, 310–12, 329,
            505–6
        surveys of, 310–12, 316–17
        treatment for, 326–28
        trends and future outlook, 305, 310–12,
            328–29, 530
        and truancy, 24
        and victimization, 56, 57
        See also cigarette smoking; drugs
Drug Abuse Resistance Education program
        (D.A.R.E.), 324, 325, *398*
drug control
        border control, 323
        community-based, 322, 324, 326
        and drug dealing, 322, 323
        education, *322*, 324
        future outlook, 328–29
        harm reduction, *322*, 327–28
        law enforcement efforts, 322–23
        needle exchange programs, 328
        overview of strategies for, 321–22, 329
        treatment as, *322*, 326–27, *445*
drug courts, 383–85
drug dealing
        drug abuse, 313, 315–19
        drug control, 322, 323
        gangs, 242–45, 252–54, 262
        losers and burnouts, 319, 329
        Mexican American gangs, 244–45
        teen violence, 38
        violence in Brazil, 499
Drug Enforcement Administration (DEA),
        414
drug testing, 296, 297, *374*
drug trafficking. *See* drug dealing
drug use. *See* drug abuse
drugs
        anesthetic, 308
        cocaine, 37, 306, 316, 320, 322–23
        crack, 37, 306
        designer, 309–10
        ecstasy, 309–10, 323, 328
        gateway, 307, 315, 321
        hallucinogens, 308–9
        heroin, 307, 310–11, 322–23
        inhalants, 308
        legalization of, 329

LSD, 308–9
marijuana and hashish, 9, 306, 316, 321
mescaline, 308
Methedrine, 309
PCP, 308
sedatives and barbiturates, 308
steroids, 309
stimulants, 309
tranquilizers, 308
See also alcohol abuse; cigarette smoking
DTBY (Dare to Be You), 125
due process rights
and detention, 432
juvenile court and, 425, 438, 441
juvenile justice history and, 374, 375, *380*, 451
and *parens patriae*, 441
right to treatment and, 486
school discipline and, 295
United Nations on, *509*

E
early prevention
daycare programs, 345–46
home-based programs, 343–44
improving parenting skills, 344–45
preschool, 346–47
school programs for primary grades, 347–49
Eastern Europe, 498, 506, 507
economics
at-risk youths, 5, 57, 153
benefits of crime, 75
consumerism, 9
costs of delinquency, 336–38
crime rates, 38, 190
drug dealing and, 318–19, 328–29
future outlook on, 527, 530
and gangs, 242, 248, 250, 262, 266
institutional anomie theory, 119–20
international delinquency and, 497, 498, 501, 508
Middle Ages, 12–15
racial disparity, 46, 111
social conflict theory and, 132–33
and social disorganization theory, 112
social problems and, 109–11
stress and health, 6, 203
truancy, 24
See also costs; employment; poverty
ecstasy, 309–10, 323, 328
education
crisis in, 10, 275–77, 299
drug control and, 324, 325
and economic success, 275
inadequate opportunity, 7–8
incarcerated juveniles and, 482–83
poverty and, *110*
preschool, 346–47
as prevention, 341
statistics on, *275*, *276*
teen pregnancy and, 187
as treatment, 379
EEG (electroencephalogram), 78, 80
egalitarian families, 193
ego identity, 4–5, 213
8% Early Intervention Program, 468
Eighth Amendment

corporal punishment and, 295
cruel and unusual punishment, 448
death penalty and, *374*, 381, 534
inmates right to treatment, 486
reasonable bail, 431
text of, 541
Eisenhower National Clearinghouse, 8
electronic monitoring, 465–66, 490
Elizabethan Poor Laws of 1601, 15
emotional abuse, 213, 216
emotional problems, 53, 55, *312*, 314, 317
employment
career as turning point, 156–57
and crime rates, 38
education and, 299
and gang membership, 248
inmate vocational training and, 483
job training, 354–55, 383
and parental efficacy, 209–10
risk taking, 9
social development and, 68–69
social structure theories and, 109
England
Children Act of 1908, 515
Crime and Disorder Act of 1998, 519
Criminal Justice and Public Order Act of 1994, 219
Crown Court, 519
Crown Prosecution Service (CPS) 518
delinquency in, 498, 504, *506*
drug use in, 505, *507*
history of policing in, 394, 415
juvenile justice process, 515–18
legal tradition in, 18, 28
moral discipline, 15–16
Poor Laws, 14, 15
probation history in, 458–59
punk and skinhead movement in, 259
sentencing in, 519–20
17th and 18th century, 14–16
social workers in, 516, 519
use of police cautions, 517–18
youth court in, 518–19
English Poor Laws, 14, 15
Enlightenment, 15
environment
arousal theory, 82
biosocial theory and, 77–78, 99
family deviance and, 211
and problem behavior syndrome, 147–48
versus genetics, 82–85
equipotentiality, 77
Essexfields Rehabilitation Project, 471
ethnicity. *See* race
Europe
and colonial America, 16
corporal punishment in, 209
delinquency in, 498
gangs in, 260–61
history of childhood in, 12–15
illegal drugs, 328, 505–6
restorative justice, 135, 468
European Sourcebook of Crime and Criminal Justice Statistics (Council of Europe), 502, *503*
evolutionary theory, 85, *86*, 179
experimental group, 339
extravert, 94–95

F
familicide, 217
family(ies)
abuse and violence within, 56–57, 216–17
breakup, 185, 204–7, 225
crime and genetics, 82–85
drug abuse and, *312–14*
dysfunctional, 201–4, 225, 260
economic concerns and, 5, *110*, 120, 203
efficacy, 208–10
egalitarian, 193
factors and at-risk youths, 50, *51*
future outlook on, 529–30
gangs as substitute for, 242, 260, 263
historical views of, 12–16
importance of, 73, 171, 185
intrafamily conflict, 206, 208
paternalistic, 12
and prevention, 134, 148–49, 343–45, 357
and problem behavior syndrome, 147
prosocial bonds, 152–54
psychological/biosocial theory and, 77, 78, 98–99, 182
risk factors and, 50, *51*, 152–53
role in combating truancy, 24, 25
siblicide, 201
sibling and twin similarities, 83–84, 87, 100, 211
and socialization, 122–24, 184
and treatment, 225, 470–71
See also child abuse and neglect; family structure; parents
Family Educational Rights and Privacy Act (FERPA), 298
family group homes, 470–71
family structure
and chronic offending, *51*
delinquency link, *206*
divorce, 185, 204–7, 225
non-traditional, 6, *7*, 14–15, 202–3, 225
power-control theory and, 193–94
and race, 46
routine activities theory and, 71
and victimization risk, 54
Fast Track, 148–49
Fathering After Violence Project (FVPF), 226
FBI (Federal Bureau of Investigation), 20, 34, 37, 40, 242
FBI Uniform Crime Report *See* UCR
FCCs (family group conferences, Australia), 512
FDA (Food & Drug Administration), 310
Federal Bureau of Investigation (FBI), 20, 34, 37, 40, 242
female gangs, 248–50, 252, 255, 267, 529
Female Offender, The (Lombroso and Ferrero), 179
feminist views, critical, 190–95
FERPA (Family Educational Rights and Privacy Act), 298
Fifth Amendment
double-jeopardy, *374*, 439
due process, 432, 437, 441
text of, 541
final order, 449
financial impact of crime. *See* costs
financial restitution, 27, *445*, 468
Finland, 505, *507*

First Amendment, 292–95, 450, 541
Five Hundred Delinquent Women (Glueck),
  185
Florida, 20, 24, 273, 295, 467
football players' hazing incident, 33
foster care, 222, 357, *445*, 470
Fourteenth Amendment
  and corporal punishment, 295
  double jeopardy, 439
  and due process, 432, 441, 443, 486
  text of, 541
  unreasonable search and seizure, 376
Fourth Amendment
  custodial interrogation and, 415
  drug testing and, 297
  text of, 541
  unreasonable search and seizure, 296,
    374, 376, 401–2
France, 489, 504–7, 510–13
free speech, 292–94
free will, 66
freedom of speech, 292–94
Freudian psychology, 86–87
friends. *See* peers
future outlook
  at-risk teens, 8, 10
  concept of delinquency, 526–27, 538
  drug abuse and control, 305, 310–12,
    328–29, 530
  economic impact of delinquency, 530
  family influences, 529–30
  gangs, 264–65, 529, 530
  incarceration, 536–37
  international, 538
  juvenile justice, 385–89, 531, 533–38
  prevention, 11, 356–58, 530–31, 537, 538
  restructuring society, 261, 298
  rise in female delinquency, 529
  school failure/crime and, 530
  seriousness of delinquency problem, 526
  statistically, 36–37
  theoretical models, 98, 528, 538
  See also reform
FVPF (Fathering After Violence Project), 226

G
Gang, The (Thrasher), 239
Gang Alternative Prevention Program
  (GAPP), 266
Gang Prevention and Intervention survey,
  260
Gang Resistance Education and Training
  (G.R.E.A.T.), 288, 410–12
gangs
  anomie/strain and, 260–61, 263
  anthropological view of, 259–60, 263
  characteristics of members, 186, 240, 248
  communication and, 244–45, 251–*53*
  controlling, 233, 263–67, 340, 410, 414
  criminality and, 243–44, 252–55, 257, 267
  and cultural transmission, 112
  definitions of, 238–39
  and economics, 242, 248, 250, 262, 266
  female, 248–50, 252, 255, 267, 529
  formation/structure of, 250–51, 267
  future outlook on, 264–65, 529, 530
  G.R.E.A.T., 288, 411–12
  historically, 237, 240–42, 267

illegal drugs and, 242–45, 252, 318–19
impact of, 233, 267
initiation into, 249, 257, 259
internationally, 237, 497, 499–501, 508–9
location of, 241, 246–48, 256
names of, 243
organized crime and, 242, 256
problem behavior syndrome and, 147
psychological view of, 261–62
race and, 255–59, 408
rational choice view of, 262–63
schools and, 288
social disorganization/sociocultural view
  of, 260–61
social factors and, 47, 69–70, 107
statistics on, 10, 241–42
study of, 239
theory of delinquent subcultures, 122
trends and, 238, 241, 246–48
types of, 243–46
victimization factors and, 56, 57
and violence, 254–55, 267
and weapons, 39, 242, *253*, 254, 414
GAPP (Gang Alternative Prevention
  Program), 266
gateway drugs, 307, 315, 321
gender
  and aggression, 183
  bias and, 173, 408–9
  biological/psychological differences in,
    78, 178–80
  chivalry hypotheses, 179–80
  contemporary socialization views, 186,
    188–89
  contemporary trait views and, 180–82
  continuity of crime and, 151
  and crime statistics, 174, 177–78
  critical feminist views, 191–94
  and cultural deviance theory, 121
  and delinquency statistics, 42–44
  detention and, 428
  differences, 174–77, 184–85, 195
  discretionary justice and, 408
  divorce and, 205
  drug abuse and, 320
  and English police cautions, *518*
  and evolutionary theory, 85, 179
  future outlook and, 529, 538
  and gangs, 248–50
  historical views of, 12–15, 184–85
  and individual-level theories, 98
  institutions and, 479–80, 491
  juvenile justice system and, 194–95, 422
  liberal feminist views, 190–91
  masculinity hypothesis, 173
  and peer relations, 234
  power-control theory, 193–94
  psychological disturbances and, 183–84
  and scripts, 177
  and self-control, 163, 164
  and victimization, 53, 55
  and violence, 44, 177–78, 192
gender-schema theory, 177
General Accountability Office (GAO), 325
general deterrence, 72–73, *75*, 99
General Strain Theory (GST), 117–19, 136,
  223, 279
General Theory of Crime. *See* GTC

genetic influences
  biosocial theory and, 82–*86*, 88
  and drug abuse, *312*, 314
  family deviance, 210, 211
  and gender, 178–80
gentrified, 113
Germany, 261, 498, 504–*6*, *511*, 515
get tough policies/programs
  boot camps, 457, 483, 485, 537
  and gangs, 267
  illegal drugs and, 323
  internationally, 514, 520
  juvenile justice system and, 363, 386–89,
    437, 440, 446–47
  prevention and, 335
GGI (guided group interaction), 482
globalization, 261, 504, 527
Glueck research, 94, 145–46, 156, 158–59
GRADS (Graduation, Reality, and Dual-
  Role Skills), 187
graffiti, 251–52, 258, 260, 499
G.R.E.A.T. (Gang Resistance Education and
  Training), 288, 410–12
Great Britain. *See* England
group homes, 470
group therapy, 326–27, 481–82
GST (General Strain Theory), 117–19, 136,
  223, 279
GTC (General Theory of Crime)
  the act and the offender, 160–61
  analysis of, 162–65
  choice theory and, 166
  self-control and, 161–62
guardian *ad litem*, 423
guns
  control of, 36, 393, 527
  crime rates and, 39
  and gangs, 39, *253*, 254, 414
  Partnerships to Reduce Juvenile Gun
    Violence Program, 413, 415
  and schools, 289, *374*, 499
  Youth Firearms Violence Initiative and,
    396–97

H
hallucinogens, 308–9
HALT (*Het Alternatief*), 512
harm reduction, 327–28
Head Start, 134, 340, 341, 347, 382
hearings, 220, 295–96, 437, 449–50
hearsay, 221
Henry J. Kaiser Family Foundation study, 90
heredity. *See* genetic influences
heroin, 307, 310–11, 322–23
high-risk lifestyle. *See* risk-taking
Hispanics
  arrest statistics and, *45*
  drop out rate of, 282
  gangs, 242, 250–51, *253*, 257–58
  in *Random Family*, 123
  self-report and gender, 42
  and victimization, 55
home visitation, 343–44, 357, 382
home-based prevention programs, 343–44
homeboys, 244, 245
Hong Kong (China), 515
Honolulu (HI), 24, 194
hormones, 78, 177, 181, 183

house arrest, *464*, 465, 490
House of Reformation, 367–69
House of Refuge, 21, 338, 531
Houston (TX), 25
Houston Parent-Child Development Center, 345–46
human development. *See* developmental views
human rights, 11, 15, 18, 27, 486
   See also civil rights
Hungary, *507*, 510, *511*
hustlers, 244–45

I

IAP (Intensive Aftercare Program) model, 488–89
identity crisis, 88
illegal drugs. *See* drugs
Illinois Juvenile Court Act of 1899, 371–73, 531
Improving America's Schools Act of 1994, 298
in loco parentis (Latin), 295, 401
incarceration. *See* corrections; inmates; institutions
indeterminate sentence, 445–46
index crimes, 34, 35, 37, 40, 44
individual counseling, 481
individual views, 63, 65–67, 98, 99
   See also choice theory; trait theory
individualized treatment model, 446
Industrial Revolution, 394, 415
Inglewood (CA), 396–97
inhalants, 308
inmates
   female, 479–80
   group therapy for, 481–82
   individual therapy for, 481
   life after release, 114
   male, 479
   profile of typical, 477–78
   training programs for, 482–83
   value system of, 479
   See also corrections; institutions
Institute for Social Research (ISR), 41, *42*, 54, 310
institutions
   aftercare and reentry, 487–90
   boot camps, 457, 458, 483–85, 519, 537
   civil rights and, 486–87
   development of juvenile, 369–71, 373
   educational/vocational/and recreational programs in, 482–83
   female inmates in, 479–80
   government treatment facilities, 457–58, 459
   history of, 14, 473–75, 490
   House of Reformation, 368
   House of Refuge, 367–68
   inmate counseling, 481–82, 491
   institutional racism, 46, 114
   international, 513–15
   legal right to treatment in, 485–86
   male inmates in, 479
   overview of treatment in, 480–81
   physical conditions in, 476–77
   Poor Laws, 15
   population trends, 475–76

resident profile, 477–78
and status offenders, 20–21
types of, 457–58
and urbanization, 367
and wilderness programs, 483
See also corrections;
   deinstitutionalization; social institutions
intake process, 219, 431–34, 462–63
intelligence
   behavioral theory, 96–97, 100
   and chronic offending, *51*, 152
   contemporary theories on, 97
   controversy over, 97
   IQ and, 85, 96–97, 100
   nature/nurture theories, 96–97
Intensive Aftercare Program (IAP) model, 488–89
intensive supervision, *464*, 465, 490
interactional theory, 154–56, 166
international, school security, 289
International Association of Chiefs of Police, 394, 508, 510
international delinquency
   Africa, 500, 507
   aftercare, 515
   age of responsibility and, 510, 514
   The Americas, 499
   anomie/strain, 497–500, 504, 507
   Asia, 135, 500
   Australia, 467, 499–500, *511*–15
   Austria, 504, *506*, 508–11, 513
   Belgium, 510, *511*, 513, 514
   Canada, 499, 504–6, 509–11, 514
   causes and statistics, 506–8, 520
   China, 500, 513, 515
   cross-national research, 502–8, 520
   data sources, *503*, 520
   Denmark, 50–57, 504–7, 510, *511*
   Eastern Europe, 498, 506, 507
   Finland, 505, *507*
   future outlook, 538
   gangs and, 237, 260–61, 497, 499–501, 508–9
   Germany, 261, 498, 504–6, *511*, 515
   get tough programs, 514, 520
   Hungary, *507*, 510, *511*
   incarceration, 513, 515
   Japan, 500, 501, 509–*11*, 513
   juvenile drug use, 505–6
   juvenile justice systems and, 508, 510–11
   New Zealand, 165, 499–500, 510–15
   policing, 510
   precourt diversion programs, 512
   property crime, 505
   Scandinavia, 285, 498
   sentencing policies, 511, 513
   sex trade, 498, 499
   South America, 499
   Switzerland, 504, *506*, 510, *511*, 513
   transnational/international crime and, 504
   trends in, 497–98, 504–6, 520
   violent crime, 504–5
   See also England; Europe; Russia; Sweden
international literacy scale scores, 276
International Self-Report Delinquency study (ISRD), 503

INTERPOL (International Criminal Police Organization), 502–3
interstitial group, 238
intervention
   in Canada, 514
   Chicago Intervention Network, 266
   child abuse and neglect cases, 222
   community policing model, 396–97
   daycare programs and, 345–46
   in English justice system, 517
   Fast Track, 148–49
   Fathering After Violence Program, 226
   future outlook and, 356–58
   home visitation, 343–44, 357
   improving parenting skills, 344–45
   and juvenile justice, 382–83, 388, 389
   mentoring as, 349–51
   Oregon Social Learning Center, 344–45
   root causes and, 342–43
   school programs, 285, 346–49
   trait theory and, 99
   See also community-based prevention programs; prevention programs; school-based prevention programs
intrafamily conflict, 206
IQ, 85, 96–97, 100
Islands in the Street (Sanchez-Jankowski), 262
ISR (Institute for Social Research), 41, *42*, 54, 310
ISRD (International Self-Report Delinquency) study, 503
Italy, 504–7, 510, *511*, 513

J

Jacksonville (FL), 24
Japan, 500, 501, 509–*11*, 513
JDA (Juvenile Delinquents Act, Canada), 514
JIPS (juvenile intensive probation supervision), 465
Job Corps, 354–55, 383
job training, 354–55, 383
jobs. *See* employment
Jonesboro killings, 281–82
judges
   bias by, 46
   in England, 519
   get-touch approach and, 323
   role of, 426, 445–46, 451
JUMP (Juvenile Mentoring Program), 349, *350*, 382–83
juvenile court
   abolishment of, 385–86
   and abused children, 220–22
   adjudication hearing, 378–79, 440–41
   appellate process, 449
   bias and, 46, 408–9
   case flow, 422
   confidentiality, 449–51
   defense attorneys, 381, 422–23, 451
   deterrence, 72
   disposition, 442, 444–*45*
   drug courts, 383–85
   due process, 422, 425, 438, 441, 442
   future outlook for, 533–34, 538
   international perspective on, 510–13
   jurisdiction of, 422

juvenile court (*continued*)
open vs. closed hearings, 449–50
players in, 422–26, 451
probation revocation by, 460–61
prosecutors, 381, 424–26, 451
the public defender, 424, *425*
purpose of, 21, 373
sentencing structures, 445–46
and status offenders, 21–22, 28–29
teen courts, 384–85
See also disposition; judges; juvenile
justice process; probation; waiver
Juvenile Court Act of 1889, 21, *380*
juvenile court trial, *See also* juvenile justice
process
Juvenile Delinquency Prevention and
Control (JDP) Act of 1968, 375, 531
Juvenile Delinquents Act (JDA, Canada),
514
Juvenile Dispositions Standards
Commission, 447
Juvenile Gangs in Context (Klein), 240
juvenile intensive probation supervision
(JIPS), 465
Juvenile Justice and Delinquency
Prevention Act of 1974, 375, 383, 429,
430, 537
Juvenile Justice and Delinquency
Prevention Act of 2002, 478
juvenile justice history
child savers, 18, 133, 367–69
Children's Aid Society, 369–70
England and, 14–16
House of Refuge, 367–69
ideology, *380*
Illinois Juvenile Court Act, 371–73
institutions, 369
leading cases in, *374*
overview, 363, 365–66
and reform, 373–75
urbanization, 366–67
juvenile justice in England, 515–18
juvenile justice process
adjudication, 378–79, 381
arrest, 400–401, 404
bail, 431
case flow/processing, *377*, 378, 388, 422
custodial interrogation, 402–3
disposition, 379
diversion, 433–34
intake, 431–33
petition, 380, 434–35
plea/plea bargaining, 435–36, 441
police and, 376, *399*
precourt diversion program, 512, 517–18
pretrial procedures, 219, 378
preventive detention, 431
purpose of, 381
search and seizure, 401–2
statutory exclusion, 436–37
transfer hearing, 437
treatment, 379–80
violent/property crime case processing,
377
See also detention; juvenile court; juvenile
justice system; waiver
Juvenile Justice Reform Act of 1977, 447
juvenile justice system

aftercare/reentry, 487–90
choice theory and, 99–100
civil rights and, 486–87
compared to British, 515, 517–19
costs and prevention, 336–38
crime rates and policy, 39
crisis in, 537–38
and cross-national research, *502*
and delinquency control, 336
and discretion, 404
discrimination, 44–47
due process rights, 374, 375, *380*
future outlook, 385–89, 531, 533–38
gender and, 194–95
get tough policies and, 363, 386–89, 437,
440, 446–47
goals of, 365, 372
graduated sanctions and, 383, 444
international view of, 508–13, 538
jurisdiction, 11, 26
and labeling, 129–30
legal status of offenders, 22–23, 28, 401
philosophy/values of the, 365, 380–82,
388–89, 424, 437
public protection philosophy and, 439
racial discrimination and, 328
sentencing reform, 446–47
and social class, 47
and social conflict theory, 132–33
specific deterrence, 74
strategy and reform, 380, 382–85, 388, 389
terminology, 19, 380, *382*
trait theory and, 99
treatment of LD youths by, 80, 82
urbanization and, 366–67
variations among states, 375–76
See also aftercare and reentry; criminal
justice; juvenile court; juvenile justice
history; juvenile justice process; law
enforcement; *parens patriae*; police
Juvenile Mentoring Program (JUMP), 349,
350, 382–83
juvenile officers, 398, 415
juvenile prosecutor, 424–26
Juvenile Residential Facility Census,
476–77

K
Kauai (HI) gender study, 181
Kentucky, 25, 486
"Kids at Risk," 265
King County Superior Court, Seattle (WA),
25
klikas, 250–51
knifing-off, 158, 159
Kohlberg's stages of development, 92–93

L
labeling
diversion and, 433, 434, 512
"dramatization of evil," 131
effect of, 130, 136
juvenile justice process and, 131, 438
learning disabled youths, 82
policy and, 134–35, 357
process of, 129–*30*
relabeling, 23
school tracks and, 279–80

self-labeling, 129
theory, 129–32
See also social stigma
Lafave incident, 273
latent delinquents, 89
latent trait theories
compared to life-course, 144, 165
General Theory of Crime, 160–65
overview of, 160, 166
Latino. *See* Hispanics
Latino Homicide (Martinez), 117
law enforcement
aggressive, 410
curfew laws and, 412–13
drug control by, 322–23
future outlook of, 534, 538
gang control and, 263–65, 267
international policing, 508–10
juvenile court and, 386
Law Enforcement Management and
Administrative Statistics survey, 396
organizational bias and, 409
parole guidelines and, 487–88
probation officers, 460, 462–64
and school security, 289, 290
specialized juvenile police programs and,
394
urban police department organization,
398
See also police
Law Enforcement Assistance
Administration (LEAA), 375, 394
Law on Regulation of Business Affecting
Public Morals of 1985 (Japan), 509–10
LD (learning disability), 80, 82
LEAA (Law Enforcement Assistance
Administration), 375, 394
LEAP (Learning, Earning and Parenting),
187
Learning Disabilities Association of
America, 80
learning disability (LD), 80, 82
learning theories, 90, 126, *127*, 136
least detrimental alternative, 445
least developed countries, 508
least restrictive alternative, 474
legal responsibility of youth, 19–20
legal rights
confidentiality, 218, 296–98, 449–51, 510
freedom of speech, 292–94
future outlook, 537
treatment, 485–87, 491
of youth, 19
See also schools and legal rights
legal status of delinquency, 18–19
legalization of drugs, 329
LEMAS (Law Enforcement Management
and Administrative Statistics) survey,
396
Lemert's Cycle of Secondary Deviance,
131
liberal feminist views, 190–91, 195
liberation view, 249–50
life-course persister, 147
life-course theories
age-graded, 156–59
and gang involvement, 262
Glueck Research, 145–46

interactional, 154–56
overview of, 144–45, 165, 166
social development model, 151–54
See also contemporary life course concepts
life transformations, 188–89
Lindesmith Center, 305
literacy scale scores, *276*
Loeber's Pathways to Crime, *150*
London Metropolitan Police, 394
Los Angeles Crips and Bloods, 243, 256, 257
Los Angeles/Los Angeles County (CA)
challenges of gang control in, 266–67, 410, 414
gangs in, 242, 246, 251, 256, 261
study of female arrestees in, 194
study of gang girls in, 186
Los Angeles Regional Gang Information Network, 267
Louisiana status offense laws, *21*
low-visibility decision making, 403, 415
lower classes
capitalism and the, 132–33
and child abuse, 217
cultural deviance theory, 120–21, *122*
and education, 279, 340, 341
and gangs, 239, 246, 259–61, 262
history of childhood in, 12
juvenile justice history and, 367–69
organizational bias and, 409
LSD, 308–9
Lydia E. Hoffman Family Residence, 109
Lyman School for Boys, 473

M
Maine Boys' training School, 473
Maine public defenders, *425*
Maisons de justice, 512
mandatory sentence, 446
marijuana
effects of, 306
as gateway drug, 321
hashish, 306
importation and, 323
physical abuse and, 316
use statistics, 9, 324, 505
marriage, 13–14, 156–59, 166
Marxist feminists, 191–95
Maryland, 16, *21*, *425*, 527
masculinity hypothesis, 173, 179
Massachusetts, 16, 17, 459, 473
Massachusetts Department of Youth Services, 459
Massachusetts Stubborn Child Law of 1646, 21
Maxson's Gang Typology, *246*
MBD (minimal brain dysfunction), 78, 80, 81
McMartin Day Care case, 220
MDMA (ecstasy), 309–10, 323, 328
media, 3, 38, 90–92
See also television
Memphis (TN), 369
mentoring, 349–51, 383
Mepham High School hazing incident, 33
Mercy Education Project, 298
mescaline, 308
meta-analysis, 384
Methedrine, 309

Mexican American gangs, 244–45, *253*
Mexican-American Drug Use and Dropout Survey, 316
Mexico, 499
Miami (FL), 320, 321
Miami middle school killing, 421
Michigan, 450
Middle Ages, 12–14
middle-class measuring rods, 122
milieu therapy, 482
military service, 158, 159, 166
"Million Mom March," 36
Milwaukee gang study, 247, 248
minimal brain dysfunction (MBD), 78, 80, 81
Minnesota Study of Twins Reared Apart, 84, 87
"minor child," 18–19
minorities. *See* race
Miranda rights, 381, 388, 402–3
Mississippi, 465
Missouri, 428, 448, 450, 472
MOBY (Mobilization for Youth), 340, 355
monetary restitution, 27, *445*, 468
Monitoring the Future. *See* MTF
Montana, 425, 467
Montreal Longitudinal-Experimental Study, 348
motivated offenders, 71, 72
MPD. *See* DID
MST (multisystemic therapy), 326, 357, 471, 472
MTF (Monitoring the Future)
Drug Use Survey, 310–11, 312, 329, 505
gender statistics, 178
race and statistics, 45
self-report survey, 41, 43–44
victimization data, 54
MTFC (multidimensional treatment foster care) program, 470
multiple pathways, 148–50, 166
multisystemic therapy (MST), 326, 357, 471, 472
murder, 11, 35–36, 65, 337

N
Nairobi (Kenya), 500
National Advisory Commission on Criminal Justice Standards and Goals, 24, 375
National Advisory Committee on Handicapped Children, 80
National Bar Association, 480
National Center for Educational Statistics, 279
National Center for Juvenile Justice, 388, 487
National Center for Prosecution of Child Abuse, 222
National Child Welfare Resource Center on Legal and Judicial Issues, 221
National Council for Research on Women, 177
National Council of Juvenile and Family Court Judges, 426, 537
National Council on Alcoholism and Drug Dependence (NCADD), 308
National Council on Crime and Delinquency, 24, 407, 479, 486

National Crime Victimization Survey (NCVS), 34, *42*, 52–54
National Gang Crime Research Center, 248
National Gang Survey, 247
National Incident-Based Reporting System (NIBRS), 37, 40
National Institute of Justice's Arrestee Drug Abuse Monitoring program (ADAM), 320
National Institute of Justice's International Center, 504
National Institute on Drug Abuse (NIDA), 311
National Parents' Resource Institute for Drug Education (PRIDE) survey, 311, 312, 329
National Research Council and Institute of Medicine's Panel on Juvenile Crime, 388
National School Safety and Security Services, 291
National Survey on Drug Use and Health, 311, 324, 329
National Youth Anti-Drug Media Campaign, 324
National Youth Gang Center, 242
National Youth Gang Survey (NYGS), *239*, 253–56
National Youth Survey (NYS), 312–13, 321
Native Americans, *45*, 55, 135, 396
Nature Assumption, The, (Harris), 211
nature/nurture theories, 77, 96–97
NCADD (National Council on Alcoholism and Drug Dependence), 308
NCLB (No Child Left Behind) Act of 2001, 277
NCVS (National Crime Victimization Survey), 34, *42*, 52–54
negative affective states, 117–19
neglect. *See* child abuse and neglect
neighborhoods. *See* community
Netherlands, 498, 504–7, 511–13
neurological dysfunction
ADHD, 81, 100
arousal theory, 82
biosocial theory and, 78–80, *86*, 182
learning disabilities, 80, 82
and psychopaths, 96
neuropsychology, 528
neuroticism, 87, 89, 94–95
Neutral Zone, 266
neutralization techniques, 126, *127*
Nevada, 489
New Jersey, 457, 475
New York (NY)
Children's Aid Society, 369–70
drugs and delinquency in, 320
gangs, 241, 246, 261
police department formation, 394
public schools study, 79
school climate improvement program, 289, 291
South Bronx, 123, 365
SPCC, 370–71
YouthBuild U.S.A., 355
New York House of Refuge, 367–68, 473
New York state, 96, 109, 374, 432

New Zealand, 165, 499–500, 510–15
NIBRS (National Incident-Based Reporting System), 37, 40
NIDA (National Institute on Drug Abuse), 311
NMV (No More Victims), 3, 107
No Child Left Behind (NCLB) Act of 2001, 277
No More Victims (NMV), 3, 107
nonresidential programs, *464*, 471–73
North Carolina, *425*
Northbrook incident, 173
Northern Reception Center and Clinic, 474
nuclear family, 202
nurture/nature theories, 77, 96–97
nutrition, 49, 78, 110
NYEC (National Youth Employment Coalition), 483
NYGS (National Youth Gang Survey), *239*, 253–56
NYS (National Youth Survey), 312–13, 321

O

ODD (oppositional defiant disorder), 88
Office of Community Oriented Policing Services (COPS), 396–97, 415
official delinquency, 34
Ohio, 187, 473
OJJDP (Office of Juvenile Justice and Delinquency Prevention)
  community-based prevention programs, 356
  deinstitutionalization and, 536
  detention restrictions, 429, 430, 535
  evaluation of corrections facilities, 475, 537
  Evaluation of Teen Courts Project, 385
  Partnerships to Reduce Juvenile Gun Violence Program, 413–14
  purpose of, 23, 222, 349, 375
  recommendations of, 537–38
  strategic planning and, 531
  surveys, 357
Oklahoma, 297
Oklahoma Secondary Schools Activities Association (OSSAA), 297
Olweus anti-bullying program, 285
Omnibus Safe Streets and Crime Control Act of 1968, 375
"once an adult, always an adult," 387
100 Black Men of Palm Beach County, Inc., 467
Operation Blue Orchid, 498
Operation Ceasefire, 413–14
Operation Gray Lord, 323
Operation Night Life, *265*
Operation Webslinger, 323
Operation Weed and Seed, 134
opportunity
  and criminality, 70, 99
  and latent trait theories, 160–61, 164
  liberal feminism and, 190
  and parental efficacy, 209
  situational crime prevention, 74
oppositional defiant disorder (ODD), 88
Orange County (CA), 50, 468
Oregon Social Learning Center (OSLC), 344–45, 470

organizational bias, 409
organized crime and gangs, 242, 256
orphan trains, 369, *371*
OSLC (Oregon Social Learning Center), 344–45, 470
OSSAA (Oklahoma Secondary Schools Activities Association), 297
Ottawa (Canada), 353
overt pathway, 149

P

Packard Foundation, 222
PALS (Participate and Learn Skills), 353
parens patriae
  child savers and, 369
  defined, 16
  and deterrence, 72
  divorce and, 204
  and due process rights, 441–442
  Illinois Juvenile Court Act and, 372
  international adherence to, 514, 515, 520
  juvenile justice processes and, 376, *380*, 426, 432, 438
  legal status, 19, 28, *371*
  and status offense, 21–22
  and waiver, 20
parental responsibility laws, 26–27
parents
  abused as abusers, 216, 225, 227
  and age of onset, 146
  behavioral theory and, 89–90
  criminal/deviant, 57, 83, 210–11
  custodial interrogation and, 402–3
  daycare programs and, 345–46
  deviant, 210–11
  domination by, 5, 15
  drug abuse prevention and, 305, 314
  dysfunctional divorced, 207
  future outlook and, 529–30
  Head Start program and, 341
  historical role of, 12–14, 17
  impact on children, 3, 28, 202, 211
  juvenile justice process and, 381
  parental efficacy, 122–24, 156, 208
  prevention programs for, 125, 343–45, 348
  psychodynamic theories involving, 89
  responsibility laws, 26–27
  rights of, 217–18
  risk factors and, 152–53
  and scripts, 93
  and sexual abuse, 186
  single, 202–3, 343
  social development model and, 152–53
  teenage, 156, 187, 188
  versus peer influence, 234–35
  See also child abuse and neglect; family; family structure
parole. *See* aftercare and reentry
Parson case, 525
Part I offenses, 34, 35, 37, 40, 44
Part II offenses, 34, 35, 40, 44
Participate and Learn Skills (PALS), 353
Partnerships to Reduce Juvenile Gun Violence Program, 413, 415
"party deviance," 180–81
paternalism hypothesis. *See* chivalry hypothesis
paternalistic family, 12

PATHE (Positive Action Through Holistic Education), 351
pathways to crime, 148–50, 166
pathways to drug abuse, 315–19
patriarchy, 191–93
PBS (problem behavior syndrome), 147–48, 152, *312*, 315–17
PCP (phencyclidine), 308
Peace-Builders, 349
peer pressure
  aging-out, 69
  chronic offending, *51*
  drug abuse, *312*, 313, 325
  legal responsibility, 19
  risk taking, 9
  teen courts and, 384
peer relations
  and delinquency, 235
  groups and influences, 234–35, *237*, 267
  intimacy and trust, 236
  rejection/acceptance, 237
  structure of, 235–36, 267
  See also gangs
peers
  and co-offending, 233
  deviant identity and, 130, 211
  group processes, 234–35, 243
  group therapy and, 481–82
  and PBS, 147
  relations amongst, 234–37
  risk factors and, 153
  school and socialization, 274–75
  and scripts, 93–94
  social bonds and, 128, 129, 153–54
  and socialization, 124, 177
  and victimization, 57
PEIP (Prenatal/Early Infancy Project), 343–44
"penis envy," 180
Pennsylvania, 337–38, 404, *425*, 438–39, 467
Perry Preschool, 346
persistence, 11, 49, 152, 158, 319
  See also chronic offender
personal privacy, 296–97
personality
  and antisocial behaviors, 94–96, 163
  delinquent, 94, 152
  and gender differences, 175–76, 178
  and psychodynamic theory, 86–87
petition, *380*, 434–35
Philadelphia (PA), 49–51, 277–78, *371*, 394
Philadelphia Collaborative Perinatal Project, 182
Philadelphia Family Court, 25
Phoenix diet study, 79
PINS (person in need of supervision), 22, 374, 375
Pittsburgh (PA), 467
Pittsburgh Youth Study, 57, 150
Planned Parenthood, 210
plea/plea bargaining, 378, 435–36, 441
Pledge of Allegiance, 295
pledge system, 394
PMS (premenstrual syndrome), 183
police
  chivalry hypothesis and, 179–80, 408
  community policing, 394–97, 412–13

as deterrent, 37, 72
discrimination and, 44–45, 47, 407
effectiveness of programs and, *400*
in England, 516–18
and gangs, 247, 255, 263–65, 267, 288
history of juvenile, 394
International Association of Chiefs of Police, 394, 508, 510
international juvenile, 508–10, 516–18
juvenile justice process and, 376, 378
methods employed by, 400–403
and prevention, 124, 325, 410–15
problem-oriented policing, 400, *410*, 413–15
reports and statistics, *34*, 37
role of, 394, 398–99, 415
saturation control by, 410
in schools, 410–12
search and seizure and, 296
social conflict theory and, 132–33
truancy, 25
and UCR reports, 34
and violent offenders, 399–400
widening the net, 434
See also discretionary justice; law enforcement
Police Executive Research Forum, 415
policy
age-graded theory and, 159
and chronic offenders, 52
community policing model and, 396–97
cross-national research and, 503–4, 508
and discretionary justice, 405–6
gang control and, 267
prevention programs and, 356–58
school delinquency control and, 298–99
sociological theories and, 133–36
See also get tough policies/programs
Poor Laws, 15, 16, 28
population, 5–6, 10, 36–37, 527
Posey family, 65
Positive Action Through Holistic Education (PATHE), 351
positive peer culture (PPC), 482
post-traumatic stress disorder (PSTD), 55, 213
poverty
at-risk youths, 5–7
as cause of crime, 525–26
cultural views and, 111, 119, 120–*21*
cycle of, *110*
and dropping out, 282
and school crime, 287
social structure theory and, 108–10, 113–14
and urbanization, 367
See also economics; lower classes
poverty concentration effect, 113
power, 132–33, 193–94
power-control theory, 193–95
PPC (positive peer culture), 482
predatory crime, 71
predisposition report, 442, 444, 463
pregnancy. *See* teen pregnancy
premenstrual syndrome (PMS), 183
Prenatal/Early Infancy Project (PEIP), 343–44
preschool, 346–47

President's Commission on Law Enforcement and the Administration of Justice, 374–75
prestige crimes, 255
pretrial conference, 219
prevention
classifying, 340, 342, 358, 389
community policing model, 396–97
and cross-national research, *502*
deterrence, 72–75
evaluating methods of, 11, 75, 382
family counseling, 225
future of, 11, 356–58, 530–31, 537, 538
history of, 338–40, 358
home-based programs, 343–44
juvenile justice strategy and, 382
life cycle research and, 52
nonjustice/alternative, 336
overview of, 335–36
police and, 37, 394
and public health, 340, 342
school crime, 287–89, 291
school delinquency, 298–99, 300, 410–12
situational, 74
trait theory and, 98–100
treatment as, 458
of truancy, 24–25
and victimization, 57
See also community-based prevention programs; intervention; prevention programs; school-based prevention programs
prevention programs
after-school, 352–54
Blueprints, 357
Boston's Mid-City Project, 340
Buddhism and Asian gang members, 258
Cambridge-Somerville Youth Study, 339–40
Chicago Area Project, 339
Comprehensive Employment Training Act, 134
costs and, 336–38, 344–47, 355, 358
D.A.R.E., 325
detached street worker, 265–66
DTBY, 125
Fast Track, 148–49
Fathering after Violence Project, 226
Gang Alternative Prevention Program, 266
Head Start, 134, 340, 341, 382
history of, 338–40, 342–48
Job Corps, 354–55
job training, 354–55, 383
"Kids at Risk," *265*
mentoring, 349–51
National Youth Gang Survey, 253
Neutral Zone, 266
No More Victims, 3, 107
Operation Weed and Seed, 134
police and, 410–15
Prenatal/Early Infancy Project, 343–44
preschool, 346–47
public support of, 388
Safe Harbor, 291
and social policy, 134–36
social structure-based programs, 124
Targeted Community Action Plan, 532

YouthBuild U.S.A., 355
See also community-based prevention programs; intervention; school-based prevention programs
preventive detention, 431
PRIDE (National Parents' Resource Institute for Drug Education) survey, 311, 312, 329
primogeniture, 13
Principles of Criminology (Sutherland), 126
privacy, 296–98, 466, 510
probable cause, 381, 403
probation
balanced approach to, 467–68
Boston's Operation Ceasefire and, 414
and case processing, *374*, 379
conditions of, 461–64
contemporary, 460
duties of officers, 462–64
electronic monitoring, 465–66
historical development of, 458–59
Illinois Juvenile Court Act and, 372
intensive supervision, *464*, 465, 490
juvenile court trials and, 442, 444, *445*
nature of, 460–61, 490
organization and administration, 462
restitution, 468–70
restorative justice, 466–67
as social control, 464
and treatment, 458, 463
trends, *461*, 535–36
problem behavior syndrome (PBS), 147–48, 152, *312*, 315–17
problem-oriented policing, 400, *410*, 413–15
Problem-Solving Partnerships (PSP) program, 415
Program of Research on the Causes and Correlates of Delinquency, 146
Project ALERT, 324
Project New Pride, 472
Project on Policing Neighborhoods, 404
Project Return, 114
Project Safe Neighborhoods, 397
property crime, 24, *377*, 388, 505, *506*
prosecutors, 424–26, 434, 436, 451, 518
prosocial bonds, 152–54
prostitution, 186, 214
protective factor, 342
Provo experiment, 471
pseudomaturity, 147
PSP (Problem-Solving Partnerships) program, 415
psychodynamic theory, 86–89, 100, 146, 180
psychological health, 7, 109–10, 207, 326
psychological theories
behavioral, 89–92, 180
cognitive, 92–94, 175
and drug abuse, 314–15
and gangs, 261–62, *263*
and gender, 183–84, 195
intelligence, 96–97
overview, 86, 100
personality, 94–96, 176
psychodynamic, 86–89
psychopathic personality, 95–96, 100, 148
psychoses, 87, 89
psychotherapy, 481

PTSD (post-traumatic stress disorder), 55, 213
public defender, 424, *425*
Puerto Rico, 486–87
punishment
    behavioral theory and, 89–90, 99
    chronic offenders and, 49, 50
    and classical criminology, 66–67
    corporal, 208–9
    effectiveness of, 11, 73, 74
    and general deterrence, 72–73
    General Theory of Crime and, 160
    legal versus social, 73
    in the Middle Ages, 14
    and paternalistic families, 12, 28
    social class and power, 261
    specific deterrence, 73–74
    See also death penalty
Pure Food and Drug Act of 1906, 306

Q
QOP (Quantum Opportunities Program), 349–50
Quantum Opportunities Program (QOP), 306

R
race
    corporal punishment and, 208
    detention and, 428, 491
    and dropping out, 282–83
    gangs and, 255–59
    inadequate educational opportunity, 7–8
    and individual-level theories, 98
    inequality and crime rates, 38–39, 46–47
    and police, 395–96
    racial disparity, 110–11
    and self-control, 164
    self-report and, 44–45
    statistics on, 34, 44, 422
    and victimization, 53, 54, 55
racial discrimination
    discretionary justice and, 407–8
    economic disparity and, 111
    institutional racism, 46, 114
    juvenile justice system, 44–46
    racial differentials and, 46–47
    racial profiling, 45, 406, 408, 409
    War on Drugs and, 328
racial disparity, 110–11
racism. *See* racial discrimination
Racketville, Slumtown, and Haulburg (Spergel), 260
Rand Corporation research, 313, 329, 344, 346
Randall's Island (NY), 368
Random Family (LeBlanc), 123
randomized experimental deign, 339
rational choice, 67, 262–63, *312*, 315
Reaching Out to Adolescent Dads (ROAD), 187
reaction formation, 122
reality therapy, 481
recidivism
    and age, 48–49
    boot camps and, 457, 484–85
    chronic/nonchronic, 50–52, 165
    foster care and, 470

inmate therapy and, 491
    restitution and, 469
    waiver and, 439
    wilderness programs and, 483
recreational programs, 483
reentry. *See* aftercare and reentry
reform
    Factory Act, 17
    Illinois Juvenile Court Act, 371–73
    juvenile corrections, 474
    juvenile institutions, 473
    juvenile justice, 373–75, 380, 386, 531, 534
    policing, 394
    restructuring society, 261, 298
    sentencing, 446–47
    status offense laws, 24–28, 29
reform schools, 15, 369, *371*, 471, 473
Regional Truancy Court (Philadelphia), 25
rehabilitation
    effectiveness of, 11, 327, 374–75, *380*
    juvenile justice and, 372, 432
    programs for, 99, 326–27
    secure corrections, 473–75
relative deprivation, 116–17
religion, 13, 14, 124–25
removal. *See* waiver
representing, 251
residential homes/placement, 20–21, *378*
residential programs, 327, 445, *464*, 470–71, 490
resource dilution, 210
restitution, 27, *445*, 468–70, 490, 512
restorative justice, 135–36, *464*, 466–67, 536, 538
restructuring society, 261, 298
retreatists, 122, 243
review hearing, 219
revocation procedures, 490
rewards of crime, 68–69, 74, 89, 262
right to privacy, 296–98, 466, 510
right to treatment, 485–86, 491, 537
Rio de Janeiro (Brazil), 499
Rise and Shine, 298
risk factor, *51*, 152–53, 342
risk taking
    arousal theory, 82, 99
    at-risk teens, 8
    causes of, 9
    and criminality, 70
    evolutionary theory and, 85
    General Theory of Crime and, 160, *163*
    and legal responsibility, 19
    and problem solving, 68
    and victimization, 56, 57
ROAD (Reaching Out to Adolescent Dads), 187
Rochester Youth Development Study (RYDS), 83, 254, 262
role conflicts, 398
role diffusion, defined, 4–5
Romania, 498, *507*, 510
routine activities theory, 71–72, 99
Roxbury Youthworks, 459
runaways
    dysfunctional home lives and, 186, 188–89, 201–2
    sexual abuse and, 214
    as status offenders, 1, 20–21, 28

rural programs, 471
Russia
    drug use in, *507*
    former Soviet Union, 261, 497, 504, 538
    gangs in, 261
    hardship and social change in, 497, 504
    international sex trade, 498
    juvenile justice system in, 510, *511*, 513
    juvenile violence in, 505
    Russian Revolution, 260–61
RYDS (Rochester Youth Development Study), 83, 254, 262

S
Safe Harbor, 291
safe school zone, 288
SafeFutures Initiative, 356
Salinas (CA), 396–97
Sampson and Laub's age-graded theory, 156–59, 166
San Antonio (TX), 396–97
Santa Fe High School and school prayer, 294
S.A.R.A. (Scanning, Analysis, Response, and Assessment), 413
Scandinavia, 285, 498
    See also Finland; Sweden
Scanning, Analysis, Response, and Assessment (S.A.R.A.), 413
Schaffer Library of Drug Policy, 307
school(s)
    alienation in, 281, 299
    bullying in, 285
    challenges facing, 275–77, 299
    chronic offenders and, 50, *51*, 153
    climate of, 280–81, 289, 291
    completion statistics, *274*
    compulsory attendance, 292, 299
    critical analysis of current system, 274
    delinquency link, 273–74
    discipline in, 295–96
    dropouts, 187, 282–83
    historical role of, 15
    importance of, 171
    performance in, 57, 81, 124, 152
    police in, 410–12
    prayer in, 294–95
    preschool, 346–47
    race and policy, 282–83
    retention statistics, 8
    role of, 274
    school failure rationale, 80
    security, 288–89, *290*, 300
    socialization and, 274–75, 299
    tracking in, 279–80
    truancy from, 24
    See also education; school-based prevention programs; school delinquency; school failure; schools and legal rights
school-based prevention programs
    after-school, 352–54
    bullying, 285
    combating truancy, 24–25
    Community Outreach Through Police in Schools Program, 411–12
    D.A.R.E., 324, *325*
    Dare to Be You, 125
    evaluating, 348–49

Fast Track, 148–49
G.R.E.A.T., 411–12
Positive Action Through Holistic
    Education, 351
prevalent strategies of, 299
Safe Harbor, 291
Seattle School Development Project,
    347–48
for teens, 351–52
violence prevention curricula, 351–52
school delinquency
    Canada shooting, 499
    Columbine High School, 386, 499
    and community, 287, 291–92
    German high-school killings, 498
    international security, 289
    Jonesboro killings, 281–82
    and juvenile authorities, 10–11
    location and, 284
    policy and, 288
    prevention, 298–99
    reducing, 287–89
    shootings, 284, 286–87
    violence/theft statistics, 283–84
    weapons and, 39, 281–82, 284, 374, 499
school failure
    and attention problems, 279, 299
    causes of, 278–81
    correlates of, 278
    and delinquency prevention, 299
    disadvantage-saturation thesis of, 279
    and drug abuse, 316–17
    economic consequences and, 275
    future outlook and, 530
    linked to delinquency, 182, 277–78
    psychological/behavioral dysfunction
        and, 278
    students writing achievement levels, 276
school failure rationale, 80
school prayer, 294–95
school shootings, 284, 286–87
School Survey on Crime and Safety, 283,
    284
schools and legal rights
    compulsory attendance, 292, 299
    confidentiality, 296–98, 449–51, 510
    discipline, 295–96
    free speech, 292–94
    prayer, 294–95
    privacy, 296, 298
scripts, 93–94, 177
SDM (social development model), 151–56
SDS (Students for a Democratic Society), 261
search and seizure, 401–2, 415
Seattle (WA), 25, 347
Seattle Social Development Project (SSDP),
    347–48
secure corrections, 473–75
sedatives and barbiturates, 308
self-control, 161–65, 177, 261
self-fulfilling prophecy, 130, 280
self-labeling, 129
Self-Management and Resistance Training
    Moves (SMART) program, 353
self-report
    data sources and uses of, 34, 41–42, 503
    gender and, 42, 43–44
    nature of, 40–41

racial patterns, 44–45
    victimization and, 54
sentencing, 445–47, 511, 513, 519–20, 535
Serious and Violent Offender Reentry
    Initiative, 488
sexual abuse
    defined, 213
    drug abuse and, 316
    exploitation of children, 214, 498, 499
    female socialization and, 186, 188–89,
        191
    gangs and, 250
    inmates and, 479–80
    international sex trade, 498, 499
    link to delinquency, 223–24
    prostitution as, 186, 214
    PSTD, 55
    statistics, 215–21
sexuality
    activity statistics, 9
    at-risk youths, 5
    and cultural deviance theory, 121
    evolutionary theory and, 85
    link to female delinquency, 180–81, 194
    and PBS, 147
    precocious, 180
    psychodynamic theory and, 87
    status offense, 22, 28
shelter care, 428, 429
siblings, 83–84, 211
single parents, 202–3, 343
Sisters in Crime (Adler), 190
situational crime prevention, 74, 75, 100
Sixth Amendment rights, 221, 441, 541
skinhead movement, 259, 261, 498
slangers, 245
SMART (Self-Management and Resistance
    Training) Moves program, 353
smoking. See cigarette smoking
social bond, 127–28, 154
social capital, 157–58, 166
social change, 14–16, 72, 108, 261, 298
social class
    child abuse and neglect, 217
    and delinquency link, 47
    drug abuse and, 312–13
    and gangs, 246, 259–60
    history of childhood and, 12–13, 15
    and individual-level theories, 98
    money and power, 132
    and peer acceptance, 234
    power-control theory and, 193–94, 261
    and relative deprivation, 116–17
    schools and, 279, 281, 299
    social conflict theory, 132–33
    and sociological views, 108, 110–11
    See also economics; social structure
        theories
social conflict theory, 132–33, 135–36
social control
    abuse and delinquency, 222
    as cause of delinquency, 127–29
    evaluating theories on, 129
    General Theory of Crime, 160–61
    risk taking and, 9
    social disorganization theory, 112–13, 115
social control agents. See social institutions
social development model (SDM), 151–56

social disorganization
    and drug abuse, 312–13
    poverty and, 287
    theory, 112–16, 120–22, 260–61, 263
social institutions
    gangs as, 69–70, 239, 240, 250
    institutional anomie theory, 119–20
    interactional theory and, 154–56
    intervention, 148–49
    labeling, 129–32
    liberal feminism, 190
    social control, 115
    social policy, 134–36
    socialization, 122–26
    sociological views, 108, 112–13
    See also school
social investigation report, 442, 444, 463
social learning theory, 90, 126, 127, 223, 348
social problems
    and chronic offenders, 50–52, 147–48, 166
    crime rates, 38–39, 46
    inner-city, 108–9
    substance abuse, 316–17
    and victimization, 57
social process theories
    control, 127–29
    influences, 121–26, 136
    learning, 126–27
social programs. See prevention programs
social services
    in Canada, 514
    child abuse and neglect, 218–20
    community-based policing, 412–13
    Detention Diversion Advocacy Program,
        430
    discretionary justice, 405
    juvenile corrections, 475
social stigma
    deterrence, 73
    diversion and, 433
    residential treatment programs and, 327
    secrecy, 19
    status offenders, 22, 23, 26–28, 380
    waiver and, 438
    See also labeling
social structure theories
    anomie/strain theory, 116–20
    critical feminists, 191–94
    cultural deviance, 120–21
    cultural values, 111–12
    gangs, 239
    overview, 108, 136
    and prevention, 124
    social disorganization, 112–16, 136
    and social policy, 134
    social problems, 108–11
    and sociological views, 107–8
socialization
    contemporary views on gender and, 186,
        188–89
    control theories, 127–29
    and crime, 121–26
    cultural deviance theory, 121, 122
    defined, 121, 274
    and desistance, 188
    female exploitation and, 191
    and gender differences, 174–75, 195
    and Head Start, 340, 341

socialization (*continued*)
  historical views of gender and, 184–85
  learning theories, 126
  peer acceptance and, 234
  and schools, 274–75, 299
  social development model, 151–54
  and social policy, 134
Society for the Prevention of Cruelty to
    Animals (SPCA), 212
Society for the Prevention of Cruelty to
    Children (SPCC), 370–71
Society for the Prevention of Pauperism,
    367
sociological views
  compared to individual views, 65–67
  cultural deviance theory, 120–21
  nurture theory, 96–97
  overview of, 107–8
  social conflict theory, 132–33
  and social policy, 134–36
  social process theories, 121–29
  social reaction theories, 129–32
  theoretical model, 63
  See also social structure theories
sociopathic personality, 95–96, 261
source control, 322–23
South America, 322, 499
South Bronx (NY), 123, 365
South Carolina, 351
Southeast European Cooperative Initiative,
    498
Soviet Union, former, 261, 497, 504, 538
SPCA (Society for the Prevention of Cruelty
    to Animals), 212
SPCC (Society for the Prevention of Cruelty
    to Children), 370–71
specific deterrence, 73–75, 99
Spectrum Wilderness Program, 483
Spergel's Community Gang-Control
    Program, *266*
spontaneous remission. *See* aging-out
    process
SSDP (Seattle Social Development Project),
    347–48
stable slum, 246
"Standard Minimum Rules for the
    Administration of Juvenile Justice"
    (United Nations)
  goals of, 508, 520, 538
  highlights of, *509*
  juveniles and the justice system, 513, 515
State Agricultural and Industrial School, 473
states
  child protection system and, 218–19
  confidentiality of court proceedings,
    450–51, 533
  DSO mandate and, 536
  juvenile court and, 425
  juvenile custody rate, 475–76, *478*
  juvenile executions, *448*, 451
  legal status of delinquency and, 18–19
  National Conference of State
    Legislatures, 535
  probation, 460–61, 462
  reform schools, 473
  sentencing efforts of, 445, 532–33
  treatment of offenders by, 375–76

waiver and, 436–37
status offender(s)
  categories, 22, 28
  compared to adult and delinquents,
    22–23, 375
  curfew laws, 26–27
  defined, 1, 20, 526
  detention and, 430–31
  gender and, 194
  history of, 20–22, 28
  social class and, 47
  state laws, *21*, 24–27, 29
  statutory concept of, 526, 527, 538
  treatment of, 23
steroids, 309
stimulants, 309
strain. *See* anomie/strain
strain theory, 116, 136, 279
strategic planning, 531
Street Wars (Hayden), 261
stress. *See* anomie/strain
student subculture, *280*
Students for a Democratic Society (SDS),
    261
studies
  Biosocial Study, 182
  bullying, 285
  Cambridge-Somerville Youth Study,
    339–40
  Cambridge Youth Survey, 83, 152–53,
    210–11
  of child abuse, 223–24
  Columbia University, 92
  costs of violence, 338
  Delinquency in a Birth Cohort, 49–51
  Denver Youth Survey, 57
  drug use and delinquency, 310–12,
    316–17, 321
  Glueck Research, 145–46
  Henry J. Kaiser Family Foundation, 90
  IQ, 96–97
  Milwaukee gangs, 247, 248
  Minnesota Study of Twins Reared Apart,
    84, 87
  National Crime Victimization Survey, 54
  Operation Night Life, *265*
  Philadelphia cohort study, 49–51, 277–78
  Pittsburgh Youth Study, 57
  Rochester Youth Development Study, 83,
    254, 262
  television violence, 91–92
  trait differences in male/female
    delinquents, *181*
study of delinquency, 10–12, 28
subcultures, *121*, 122
substance abuse. *See* drug abuse
Suffolk County Probation Department
    (Yaphank, NY) South County Truancy
    Reduction Program, 25
supervision, 488–89
suppression effect, 458
surveys. *See* studies
swaddling, 14
Sweden
  delinquency in, 285, 287, 504, *507*
  juvenile justice system in, 510, *511*
Switzerland, 504, *506*, 510, *511*, 513

Synar Amendment of 1992, 310
Syracuse University Family Development
    Research Program, 345
systematic review, 384

T
target-hardening technique, 74
TCAP (The Targeted Community Action
    Planning) initiative, 532
technology, 108, 323, 525, 528
Tecumseh, Oklahoma random drug testing,
    297
teen courts, 384–85
teen pregnancy
  and abortion, 39, 529–30
  crime rates, 38, 39
  and desistance, 188
  early sexuality and, 180
  preventing, 187, 298
  as risk factor, 152
  statistics, 4, 8, 10, 203
television
  behavioral theory and, 90–92
  and childrearing, 202
  Columbia University study on, 92
  sociological views and, 107–8
  and teen violence, 3
Texas, 316–17, 447
theoretical models
  background on, 63
  critiques of, 98
  and cross-national research, *502*
  and future outlook, 98, 528, 538
  See also developmental views; individual
    views; sociological views
therapy
  family, 225
  group, 326–27, 481–82
  individual, 481
  inmate, 481–82
  multisystemic, 326, 357, 471, 472
  psychotherapy, 481
  as treatment, 225, 481–82
tobacco. *See* cigarette smoking
tracking, 279–80
trait theory
  behavioral control, 76
  biosocial, 77–86
  critiquing, 98
  defined, 66, 100
  future outlook and, 528
  and gender, 180–83, 195
  origins of, 76–77
  psychological, 86–98
  See also biosocial theories; psychological
    theories
tranquilizers, 308
transfer. *See* waiver
transfer hearing, 437
transitional neighborhood, 112, 246
transnational crime, 504
treatment
  adults versus juveniles, 18, 19, 372
  boot camps and, 457, 483–85
  and cross-national research, *502*
  for drug abusers, 326–28
  education and, 379

individualized treatment model, 446
inmate counseling, 481–82
institutional, 11, 457–58, *464*, 480–81, 536
intensive supervision, *464*, 465, 490
juvenile justice processes and, 379–80,
    433–34
life cycle research and, 52
placement and, 424, *445*
probation as, 458, 463
programs for inmates, 482–83
right to, 485–86
secure corrections, 473–75
status offenders, 23, 26, 29
therapy as, 225, 481–82
United Nations standards for, *509*
See also community-based treatment
    programs; probation; rehabilitation
truancy
    burglary and, 24
    and compulsory school attendance, 292
    court-ordered school attendance, 445
    current approaches to, 24–25, 410
    defined, 273
    South County Truancy Reduction
        Program, 25
    as status offense, 1, 23
truly disadvantaged, 110
turning points, 156–57
Twenty-First Century Community Learning
    Centers, 352
twin studies, 83–84, 87, 100
Two Sexes, The (Maccoby), 177
typology of gangs, 243, 244, *246*

U
UCLA's Comprehensive Residential
    Education, Arts, and Substance Abuse
    Treatment (CREASAT) Program, 327
UCR (Uniform Crime Report)
    crime rate statistics, *35*
    liberal feminism and, 191
    methods/uses of, 34, 35–36, *42*
    and NIBRS, 40
    validity of data, 37, 40
Unadjusted Girl, The (Thomas), 184
UNCJS (United Nations Survey of Crime
    Trends and Operations of Criminal
    Justice Systems), 502, *503*
underachievers, 277
underclass, 110
unemployment. *See* employment
Unexpected Legacy of Divorce, The
    (Wallerstein et al.), 207
Uniform Crime Report. *See* UCR
Uniform Juvenile Court Act, 401
United Nations, 502, 503, 508, *509*
    See also "Standard Minimum Rules for
        the Administration of Juvenile Justice"
United Nations Survey of Crime Trends
    and Operations of Criminal Justice
    Systems (UNCJS), 502, *503*
University of Hawaii, 24
University of Michigan's Institute for Social
    Research (ISR), 41, *42*, 54, 310
University of New Hampshire's Crimes
    Against Children Research Center, 216
Urban Institute, 282

urbanization, 366–67, 388
U.S. Bureau of Justice Statistics, 52
U.S. Census Bureau, 6, 10, 52–53, 65, 525
U.S. Children's Bureau, 373, 474
U.S. Constitution
    Bill of Rights, 541
    First Amendment, 292–95, 450
    Sixth Amendment, 221, 441, 541
    See also Eighth Amendment; Fifth
        Amendment; Fourteenth Amendment;
        Fourth Amendment
U.S. Department of Health and Human
    Services, 215, 341
U.S. Department of Health and Human
    Services' NIDA, 311
U.S. Department of Justice, 34, 52, 320, 375,
    486
U.S. Department of Justice Anti-Violent
    Crime Initiative (AVCI), 265
U.S. Department of Labor, 354
U.S. Federal Bureau of Investigation (FBI),
    20, 34, 37, 40, 242
U.S. Food and Drug Administration (FDA),
    310
U.S. RDA (recommended daily allowance),
    79
U.S. Secret Service, 286
U.S. Supreme Court
    appellate process and, 449
    children in court, 217–18, 227
    corporal punishment, 295–96
    death penalty, 72, *374*, 381, 447–48, 534
    due process and, 374, 432, 441–43, 533–34
    free speech and schools, 292–94
    influence on juvenile court proceedings,
        388
    juvenile court and, 422
    juvenile justice process issues and, 431
    Miranda rights and, 403
    police control by, 394
    on privacy, 449–50
    random drug testing decision, 296, 297
    right to treatment and, 486, 537
    and school prayer, 294–95
    search and seizure, 296, 402
    waiver and, 437, 438–39
USA PATRIOT Act of 2001, 132
utilitarianism, 66

V
values of juvenile justice, 365, 380–82,
    388–89
Ventura School for Female Juvenile
    Offenders, 483
Vice Lord Nation, 243
victim service restitution, 468
victimization
    age and, 53, 56–58
    bullying and, 285
    and curfew laws, 26
    emotional/financial impact of, 53, 55
    homicide trends, *8*
    lifestyle and, 34, 54, 56
    and mental health problems, 53, 55
    and National Crime Victimization
        Survey, 52–54
    parents and, 3, 206

race and, 407
risk factors, 54–56
school crime and, 282, 287, 291
and self-control, 163
statistics, 55
victim data, 34, 37
victims and their criminals, 54
Victims of Child Abuse Act of 1990, 221
video games, 90–91
Vietnam objectors and free speech, 292–93,
    294
violence
    alcohol abuse and, 320
    Blueprints for Violence Prevention
        initiative, 357
    causes of, 3, 38
    Columbine massacre, 386, 499
    and gangs, 254–55, 261, 267
    and gender, 44, 177–78, 192
    hazing, 33
    international youth, 498–501, 504–8
    and the media, 90–92
    murder, 11, 35–36, 65, 337
    Northbrook incident, 173
    and PBS, 147
    and PMS, 183
    post-traumatic stress disorder and, 55
    poverty, 7
    prevention curricula, 351–52
    problem-oriented policing and, 413–15
    and problem solving, 68
    racial differentials and, 46
    school programs addressing, 411–12
    in schools, 283–84
    and scripts, 94
    statistics, 10, 35–36, 39
    and television, 3, 90–92
    violent crime case processing, *377*, 388,
        399–400
    See also child abuse and neglect; guns;
        sexual abuse
violence prevention curricula, 351–52
Violent Crime Control and Law
    Enforcement Act of 1994, 375
Violent Schools—Safe Schools (study), 282
Virginia, 16, 17, 489
Virginia schools "minute of silence", 294–95
vocational programs, 483

W
W. C. Mepham High School hazing
    incident, 33
waiver
    and case processing, *377*, 378
    debate over, 437–40, 451
    defined, 19
    due process and, 437
    future outlook on, 535
    and get tough policies, 387
    international practice of, 510–11
    and *parens patriae*, 20
    and plea bargaining, 435
    procedures, 436–37
    sentencing reform and, 446–47
    statistics on, 436
    transfer hearing, 437
War on Drugs, 310, 328

Washington D.C., 107, 320, 409, 438, 536
Washington public defenders, *425*
Washington's Juvenile Justice Reform Act of
    1977, 447
watch system, 394
wayward minors, 22
weapons, 57, 242, 257–58, 281–82, 290
    See also guns
West Milton (PA) day treatment program,
    472
Westinghouse Learning Corporation
    evaluation, 341
whites
    arrest statistics and, *44–45*
    bias and, 44–47, 406–7, 409
    detention rates and, 428
    economic disparity and, 111
    gang involvement of, 255, 259
    incarceration rates of, 477–88
    racial disparity and, 111
    victimization rates and, 53, 54

views of police by, 396
waiver and, 440
well-being and income, 4
WHO (World Health Organization), 79,
    502–3
Wickersham Commission of 1931, 394
widening the net, 434
wilderness programs, 483
Wisconsin, *21*
World Health Organization (WHO), 79,
    502–3
writ of habeas corpus, 439, 443, 449

Y
Yaphank (NY), 25
YCJA (Youth Criminal Justice Act, Canada)
    of 2003, 510–11, 514
YFVI (Youth Firearms Violence Initiative),
    396–97
YMCA (Young Men's Christian
    Association), 265

YOA (Young Offenders Act, Canada), 514
Young Men's Christian Association
    (YMCA), 265
Young Offenders Act (YOA), 514
Youth Criminal Justice Act (YCJA, Canada)
    of 2003, 510–11, 514
Youth Development and Delinquency
    Prevention Administration, 375
Youth Firearms Violence Initiative (YFVI),
    396–97
Youth Justice and Criminal Evidence Act of
    1999 (England), 519
YouthBuild U.S.A., 355, 383
Ypsilanti (MI), 346
YVSF (Boston's Youth Violence Strike
    Force), *265*

Z
Zero to Six (study), 90
zero tolerance policy, 287–88

Photograph Credits

Chapter Openers: 3, 33, 65, 107, 143, 173, 201, 233, 273, 305, 335, 365, 393, 421, 457, 497, and 525 © 2004 Turner Broadcasting System, Inc. CNN is a trademark of Turner Broadcasting System, Inc. Licensed by Turner Learning, Inc. All Rights Reserved.

5 © Mike Blake/Reuters/Corbis; **11** © AP/Wide World Photos; **13** The Pierpont Morgan Library/Art Resource, NY; **17** Christie's Images/Corbis; **22** © Stone/Getty Images; **36** © AP/Wide World Photos; **44** © AP/Wide World Photos; **48** © Richard Hutchings/PhotoEdit; **52** © Michael Newman/PhotoEdit; **56** Getty Images; **67** © Phil McCarten/PhotoEdit; **70** © Ariel Skelly/Corbis; **73** © AP/Wide World Photos; **82** © Frank Siteman/Stock Boston; **91** © D. Hurst/Alamy Images; **109** © Viviane Moos/Corbis; **111** © Joel Gordon; **118** © Michael Newman/PhotoEdit; **124** © AP/Wide World Photos; **135** © Felicia Martinez/PhotoEdit; **145** © Chuck Savage/Corbis; **154** © Michael Newman/PhotoEdit; **156** © AP/Wide World Photos; **164** © Spencer Grant/PhotoEdit; **175** © Dennis MacDonald/PhotoEdit; **176** © Ed Quinn/Corbis; **179** © Richard Lord/PhotoEdit; **185** © Cleo Photography/PhotoEdit. All rights reserved; **193** © Dwayne Newton/PhotoEdit; **202** © Joel Gordon; **205** © Viviane Moos/Corbis; **209** © AP/Wide World Photos; **212** American Humane Society; **225** © Michael Newman/PhotoEdit; **239** © Yang Liu/Corbis; **240** © Michael Abramson/Black Star; **249** © Nancy Siesel/Corbis-Saba; **258** © Spencer Platt/Getty Images; **264** © A. Ramey/PhotoEdit; **277** © AP/Wide World Photos; **286** © AP/Wide World Photos; **288** © AP/Wide World Photos; **293** © AP/Wide World Photos; **298** Ricardo Thomas/*The Detroit News*; **307** © Richard Hutchings/PhotoEdit; **309** © Amy Etra/PhotoEdit; **313** © Joel Gordon; **323** © AP/Wide World Photos; **324** © Michael Newman/PhotoEdit; **326** © AP/Wide World Photos; **338** © A. Ramey/PhotoEdit; **339** Courtesy of Chicago Area Project; **351** © AP/Wide World Photos; **354** Jeff Greenberg/Alamy; **366** Stock Montage; **370** Stock Montage; **376** © AP/Wide World Photos; **379** Courtesy of Juvenile Justice Alternative Education Program, Denton County, Texas; **387** © Michael Newman/PhotoEdit; **395** © Cleve Bryant/PhotoEdit; **398** © AP/Wide World Photos; **402** © Kelly Wilkinson/*Indianapolis Star*/Sipa; **404** © A. Ramey/PhotoEdit; **412** Bureau of Justice Assistance, U.S. Department of Justice; **423** © Shelly Gazin/Corbis; **433** © Rich Graulieh/*Palm Beach Post*; **440** *Bucks County Courier Times* © Jay Crawford; **444** © Joel Gordon; **447** © AP/Wide World Photos; **460** © A. Ramey/PhotoEdit; **466** © Joel Gordon; **474** From the Collection of the Rochester Public Library Local History Division; **477** © AP/Wide World Photos; **484** © A. Ramey/PhotoEdit; **500** Eric Miller/Africanpictures.net; **505** © AP/Wide World Photos; **513** AFP/AFP/Getty Images; **519** © AP/Wide World Photos; **527** © Mannie Garcia/Corbis; **529** © A. Ramey/PhotoEdit; **534** © Gabe Palmer/Corbis

1971
Mckeiver v. Pennsylvania establishes that a jury trial is not constitutionally required in a juvenile hearing but states can permit one if they wish.

The Twenty-Sixth Amendment to the Constitution is passed, granting the right to vote to 18-year-olds.

1972
Wisconsin v. Yoder gives parents the right to impose their religion on their children.

Wolfgang publishes *Delinquency in a Birth Cohort.*

1973
In re Snyder gives minors the right to bring proceedings against their parents.

San Antonio Independent School District v. Rodriguez establishes that differences in education based on wealth were not necessarily discriminatory.

1974
Federal Child Abuse Prevention Act.

Buckley Amendment to the Education Act of 1974, the Family Education Rights and Privacy Act. Students have the right to see their own files with parental consent.

Juvenile Justice and Delinquency Prevention Act.

1970
In re Winship establishes that proof beyond a reasonable doubt is necessary in the adjudicatory phase of a juvenile hearing. A juvenile can appeal on the ground of insufficiency of the evidence if the offense alleged is an act that would be a crime in an adult court.

White House Conference on Children.

1965

1970

1969
Tinker v. Des Moines School District establishes that the First Amendment applies to juveniles and protects their constitutional right to free speech.

1975
Goss v. Lopez establishes that a student facing suspension has the right to due process, prior notice, and an open hearing.

1968
Ginsberg v. New York establishes that it is unlawful to sell pornography to a minor.

1977
*Report of the Committee of the Judiciary, especially concerning the rights of the unborn and the right of 18-year-olds to vote.

Juvenile Justice Amendment of 1977.

Ingraham v. Wright establishes that corporal punishment is permissible in public schools and is not a violation of the Eighth Amendment.

American Bar Association, Standards on Juvenile Justice.

Washington State amends its sentencing policy.

1967
President's Commission on Law Enforcement recognizes the problems of the juvenile justice system.

In re Gault, a U.S. Supreme Court decision establishes juveniles have the right to counsel, notice, confrontation of witnesses, and the avoidance of self-incrimination. In general, the court holds that Fourteenth Amendment due process applies to the juvenile justice system, specifically in adjudicatory hearings.

1966
Kent v. United States—initial decision to establish due process protections for juvenile at transfer proceedings.

1979
International Year of the Child.

...continued from front endsheets

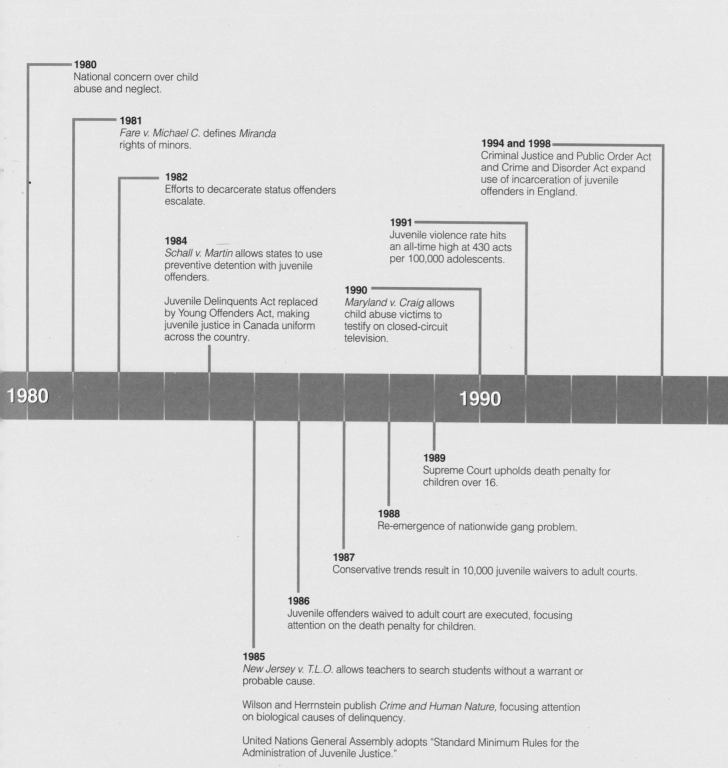

1980
National concern over child
abuse and neglect.

1981
Fare v. Michael C. defines *Miranda*
rights of minors.

1982
Efforts to decarcerate status offenders
escalate.

1984
Schall v. Martin allows states to use
preventive detention with juvenile
offenders.

Juvenile Delinquents Act replaced
by Young Offenders Act, making
juvenile justice in Canada uniform
across the country.

1994 and 1998
Criminal Justice and Public Order Act
and Crime and Disorder Act expand
use of incarceration of juvenile
offenders in England.

1991
Juvenile violence rate hits
an all-time high at 430 acts
per 100,000 adolescents.

1990
Maryland v. Craig allows
child abuse victims to
testify on closed-circuit
television.

1980

1990

1989
Supreme Court upholds death penalty for
children over 16.

1988
Re-emergence of nationwide gang problem.

1987
Conservative trends result in 10,000 juvenile waivers to adult courts.

1986
Juvenile offenders waived to adult court are executed, focusing
attention on the death penalty for children.

1985
New Jersey v. T.L.O. allows teachers to search students without a warrant or
probable cause.

Wilson and Herrnstein publish *Crime and Human Nature,* focusing attention
on biological causes of delinquency.

United Nations General Assembly adopts "Standard Minimum Rules for the
Administration of Juvenile Justice."